S0-BGU-436

Managing Organizational Behaviour in Canada

Managing Organizational Behaviour in Canada

PAT R. SNIDERMAN
Ryerson University

JULIE BULMASH
George Brown College

DEBRA L. NELSON
Oklahoma State University

JAMES CAMPBELL QUICK
University of Texas at Arlington

Australia Canada Mexico Singapore Spain United Kingdom United States

Managing Organizational Behaviour in Canada

by Pat R. Sniderman, Julie Bulmash, Debra L. Nelson, and James Campbell Quick

Associate Vice President, Editorial Director:
Evelyn Veitch

Executive Editor:
Anthony Rezek

Senior Marketing Manager:
Charmaine Sherlock

Senior Developmental Editor:
Karina Hope

Photo Researcher:
Kristiina Bowering

Permissions Coordinator:
Kristiina Bowering

Senior Production Editor:
Bob Kohlmeier

Copy Editor:
Lisa Berland

Proofreaders:
Karen Bennett,
Edie Franks

Indexer:
Dennis A. Mills

Production Coordinator:
Kathrine Pummell

Design Director:
Ken Phipps

Interior Design:
Liz Harasymczuk

Cover Design:
Liz Harasymczuk

Cover Images:
Nick Daly/Getty Images;
Holly Harris/Getty Images;
Stockbyte Gold/Alamy

Compositors:
Alicja Jamorski,
Brenda Prangley

Printer:
Quebecor World

Printed and bound in the United States
1 2 3 4 09 08 07 06

For more information contact Nelson, 1120 Birchmount Road, Toronto, Ontario, M1K 5G4. Or you can visit our Internet site at http://www.nelson.com

Library and Archives Canada Cataloguing in Publication

Managing organizational behaviour in Canada / Pat R. Sniderman ... [et al.].

Adaptation of: Organizational behavior.

Includes bibliographical references and indexes.
ISBN 0-17-616981-4

1. Organizational behavior—Textbooks. I. Sniderman, Pat. R. (Patricia Rosemary), 1952– II. Nelson, Debra L., 1956– Organizational behavior.

HD58.7.M364 2005 658
C2005-903336-3

Brief Contents

Part 5 Integrative Cases

Part 6 OBXtras

Contents

Chapter 13

Preface

Welcome to the first edition of *Managing Organizational Behaviour in Canada.* Our vision is to provide a distinctly Canadian text based on a solid foundation of up-to-date OB research and theory that encourages critical thinking and is relevant to the lives of our readers. Our commitment to sound learning and teaching pedagogy is reflected throughout the text.

As Canadian authors who have been teaching organizational behaviour to undergraduate university and college students for close to 20 years, we continue to love what we teach and are inspired by the ways in which organizational behaviour research has been able to contribute to improving both the bottom line of organizations as well as the working experience and satisfaction of their managers and employees. We continue to be amazed at how much difference a single enlightened leader can make to his or her organization, department, or team. We hope that this text helps inspire, educate, and develop more of these special individuals who want to make a difference by improving their organizations through effective and ethical management of people rather than at their expense. The heightened awareness of corporate social responsibility and the public consequences of unethical behaviour in recent years may also help nurture enlightened organizational leaders as we move forward. Our hope is that this book helps provide the scientific foundation for the claim that "Good ethics is good business."

The body of organizational behaviour knowledge has exploded over the past two decades, and OB textbooks have been getting both thicker *and* thinner. "Essentials" texts have emerged in response to the information overload from traditional texts. Instructors, and even textbook authors, explain that they do not teach or test all the information contained in the comprehensive texts, because there is just too much. Our goal in writing this text was to find the right middle ground between an "essentials" text and a "huge" text. Essentials texts usually eliminate applications, organizational realities, exercises, and cases. In our view, these are important pedagogical tools for learning and student engagement, so rather then reduce them, we expanded them. We kept the text to a manageable size by not including material (or in some cases included it on the website only) that we found we usually leave out in our teaching, or that is peripheral to the field.

Features That Encourage Critical Thinking and Student Engagement

The features in this book, designed to encourage critical thinking and student engagement, include the following:

- ***Experiential Exercises*** have been carefully selected and have been used successfully by the authors. We are fortunate to be able to include 12 of Dorothy Marcic's wonderful experiential exercises, which we have selected on the basis of being both engaging *and* useful for analyzing key theory points. For example, in Chapter 14, we include Marcic's wonderful organizational design exercise called "Words-in-Sentences Company." In Chapter 10 we include the best leadership exercise we have ever used, designed by Cook, called "Don't Topple the Tower." Experiential exercise instructions include the purpose, group size, time required, and materials needed to facilitate planning. As much as possible, we have tried to include both short and long exercises because many of us teach in three-hour blocks, so 50-minute exercises were considered to be ideal.

- *"Critical Thinking"* boxes have been written for each chapter. They consist of short questions, mini-cases, short exercises, and survey instruments that invite the students, after each subtopic of the chapter, to comprehend, apply, analyze, synthesize, or evaluate something they have just read about. This unique feature has been designed based on Bloom's Taxonomy and his six levels of learning,[1] as follows: **(1) knowledge**, the ability to recognize and recall facts, **(2) comprehension**, the ability to demonstrate understanding of the material, **(3) application**, the ability to apply comprehension to new situations, **(4) analysis**, the ability to critically analyze a theory or concept, **(5) synthesis**, the ability to analyze information from a wide variety of sources and meld the facts and theories into a coherent concept or position, and **(6) evaluation**, the ability to critique. These Critical Thinking boxes can be assigned either outside of class or during class, to break up a long lecture, using "buzz groups" to engage students in two-way communication. One example of a Critical Thinking box is "Can You Spot Defensive Communication?" in Chapter 6. Students are asked to read an interchange between a boss and employee and to label all the examples they can find of active listening, supportive and defensive communication, as previously explained in the text.

? CRITICAL THINKING

- *Self-assessments* have been included in each chapter. These are also represented as Critical Thinking boxes but they differ in that they focus on helping students increase their self-awareness. Knowledge of self is a key component in effective management of others, and we have carefully selected these self-assessments so that students begin to critically examine their own strengths and weaknesses in managing organizational behaviour. One example of a powerful self-assessment exercise is "What Is Your Conflict Management Style?" in Chapter 11. These self-assessments can also be assigned outside of or during class to engage students in the material and help them experience its relevance.
- *"Implications for Life"* boxes are a unique feature of this text. These boxes take an area of knowledge from the chapter and apply it to a real-life situation that an undergraduate would relate to. Their purpose is to increase the relevance of the OB research and concepts to young people who may not yet have had managerial experience. One example of *Implications for Life* is "Stages of Team Development Confessions: One student's reflections on a difficult team experience using the five-stage model of team development" in Chapter 7. This feature motivates student learning by demonstrating the value of the OB concepts in everyday life.
- *CTV Critical Thinking News Clips* offer students the opportunity to explore current OB issues and controversies through short CTV news clips. These video news clips are summarized at the end of each of the four main parts of the text and are followed by critical thinking questions for discussion. The videos are also available through the website.
- *Review Questions* have been included at the end of each chapter and we have also added higher levels of critical thinking in the ***Discussion and Communication*** and ***Ethics Questions.*** Our experience has convinced us that encouraging learners to frequently ask and answer questions about OB material greatly facilitates their learning and retention, especially when the questioning is made interesting and relevant to their lives. The discussion and communications questions help with application and the ethics questions further develop evaluation abilities. They provoke

1. Adapted from B. S. Bloom, ed. (1956), *Taxonomy of Educational Objectives: The Classification of Educational Goals: Handbook I: Cognitive Domain* (New York: Longmans, Green).

students to think about what is right and wrong as well as about the various ways to resolve ethical conflicts in organizations. An example of an ethical question included in Chapter 9 is, "Is it ever ethical to manipulate people for the good of the organization? Defend your point of view with examples. Use the guidelines for ethical decision making in Chapter 8."

Features That Help Students Learn about the Context

The features in this book designed to illustrate the context of OB include the following:

- ***"Learning about the Context"*** opening vignettes in each chapter use Canadian and global examples from companies such as Home Depot, Toyota Motor Manufacturing Company, Oticon SA, Intuit Canada, and the RCMP. These help the students understand the relevance of the material to practising managers, business leaders, communities, and countries and build their appreciation of how critical the effective management of OB is to Canada's economy and well-being. We make reference to the "learning about the context" companies throughout each chapter and used them to help exemplify key concepts.
- ***"Organizational Reality"*** boxes, interspersed throughout each chapter, offer additional insights into real-life organizational issues and practices.
- ***Website links*** offer students further opportunities to discover more information about the organizations, scholars, and business leaders discussed in the text.
- ***"Implications for Organizational Effectiveness"*** sections conclude each chapter to summarize the impact of the chapter concepts on the organization as a whole, its effectiveness, and long-term viability in the context of a turbulent and global business environment.
- An ***end-of-chapter case*** is included in each chapter. The cases are based on real-world Canadian and global situations that have been modified slightly for learning purposes. These cases and discussion questions have been selected or created to focus specifically on chapter concepts. Through these cases, students apply their knowledge, check their comprehension, and think more critically about organizational behaviour through analysis, synthesis, and evaluation.
- Seven ***Integrative Cases*** have been included in addition to the end-of-chapter cases because, as instructors ourselves, we find that we never have enough cases for teaching and for testing. All these cases have been selected because they lend themselves well to teaching and testing, and the questions have been geared to the key concepts discussed in related chapters.
- ***Additional cases*** have also been provided on the text's website so that instructors have a wide variety of rich cases to choose from. See www.sniderman.nelson.com.

Writing and Organization

We were determined to write a book that was both ***comprehensive and focused.*** With the explosion of research and scholarship in the organizational behaviour field worldwide, this meant eliminating those topics that we found ourselves ignoring in the classroom, adding topics that seemed to be missing and reorganizing so as to avoid chapters that were disjointed or which had subtopics that did not relate well to each other. To accomplish these goals we created ***OBXtras*** for five topics that (1) did not seem to logically fit with any of the chapters, (2) were relevant to more than one chapter, (3) made any one chapter far too long and cumbersome, or (4) seemed to lend themselves to a less formal treatment than the one taken in the chapters. These five topics are Stress and Well-Being at Work, Emotional Intelligence, Behaviour Modification, Self-Managed Work Teams (SMWTs), and Managing in a Virtual World.

A textbook is only as good as its ***writing and organization***. Chapters were reworked and reorganized so that they would flow well and so that subtopics would meaningfully relate to one another. The authors were careful to make the linkages between subtopics explicit so that the reader would understand the nature of the journey through each chapter. For example, we created the GHOST model to introduce students to organizational behaviour and the open systems framework. GHOST stands for goals, human resources, organizational structure, and technology. We tie this model to the case at the end of the first chapter as well as to the ideas in the organizational change and design chapters.

For a number of the more heterogeneous or complex chapters, we created figures that serve as ***visual chapter organizers,*** which depict not only the flow of the chapter but also the cause-and-effect relationships between the various subtopics, making them easier to understand and recall. Examples are "Elements of a Positive Workplace" in Chapter 2, "Conditions and Processes for Team Effectiveness" in Chapter 7, "An Organizing Framework for Understanding Power and Influence in Organizations" in Chapter 9, and the summary chart "Comparing Leadership Theories" in Chapter 10.

Use of the ***Integrated Learning System*** is featured in *Managing Organizational Behaviour in Canada* and its ancilliaries. This integrated structure creates a comprehensive teaching and testing system. ***Learning Objectives*** at the beginning of each chapter outline the goals for study. These objectives are reinforced throughout each chapter in the ***Chapter Summary*** and again throughout the ancilliaries. Each piece of the intgegrated learning system reinforces the other components to help students learn quickly and to ease lecture preparation.

Each chapter also has a list of ***key terms*** in alphabetical order with page references, and a ***glossary*** is provided at the end of the book listing all key terms with their definitions.

Research and Concepts are Current and Comprehensive

The book is based on ***extensive research of classic and contemporary literature***. With the assistance of our amazing research assistant Vicki Skelton and our peer reviewers from across the country, we were able to incorporate into each chapter the latest and most comprehensive research. New and emerging concepts such as chaos theory, complex adaptive systems, spaghetti organization designs, appreciative inquiry, knowledge management, employee engagement, the GLOBE study of national cultures, spirituality in the workplace, e-leadership, emotions in conflict, and process conflict were incorporated. In some cases, a more contemporary view was taken of traditional concepts. For example, the body of knowledge on "resistance" to change was reframed as "reactions" to change, and "cynicism" was added as a reaction.

Also included are a few traditional theories that the Canadian authors believe have continuing importance and usefulness for an undergraduate OB course. Examples of these theories are the punctuated equilibrium model, Theory X–Y, Mintzberg's management roles, work alienation, socio-technical systems, JCM implementation principles, supportive communication, the XYZ model for initiating a complaint, individual blocking behaviours in teams, organization-wide communication strategies, guidelines for ethical decision making, and power in the boss-employee relationship.

At the end of the textbook is a lengthy chapter-by-chapter ***reference list*** that students can refer to for in-depth treatments of the chapter topics.

Ancillary Package

- ***Instructor's Resource CD-ROM*** (ISBN 0-17-625257-6): Key instructors' ancillaries (Instructor's Manual, Test Bank, ExamView, PowerPoints) are provided on CD-ROM, giving instructors the ultimate tool for customizing lectures and presentations.

- ***Video*** (ISBN 0-17-625258-4): CTV video clips have been selected to support the themes of the book and broaden students' understanding of the organizational behaviour concepts presented throughout the text. Information on using the videos can be found on the Instructor's Manual.
- ***Turning Point: JoinIn™ on TurningPoint®:*** Now you can author, deliver, show, assess, and grade, all in PowerPoint ... with *no* toggling back and forth between screens! JoinIn on TurningPoint is the only classroom response software tool that gives you **true** PowerPoint integration. With JoinIn, you are no longer tied to your computer. You can walk about your classroom as you lecture, showing slides and collecting and displaying responses with ease. There is simply no easier or more effective way to turn your lecture hall into a personal, fully interactive experience for your students. If you can use PowerPoint, you can use JoinIn on TurningPoint!
- ***Website*** (www.sniderman.nelson.com): A rich website complements the text, providing many extras for students and for instructors. Resources include Test Yourself questions, PowerPoint slides, and supplementary cases.
- ***Our Feature Presentation: Organizational Behavior*** (Joseph E. Champoux, The University of New Mexico): "Our Feature Presentation: Organizational Behavior" adds excitement and relevance to organizational behaviour topics through selected film scenes from popular film releases. This unique product combines a workbook with actual film clips on CD and video, eliminating the need to purchase or rent costly videos. Film provides your students a visual portrayal of abstract management concepts and provides inexperienced students a greater feeling of reality and connection to the topic. Further, there are many unique aspects of film such as editing, sound, framing, and focusing techniques that make it a powerful communication device that often goes beyond what we can experience in reality. Equally powerful are the reactions of the varied responses of the viewer that can spark lively debate.

Our Reviewers Are Appreciated

We would like to thank our professional peers and colleagues who reviewed the manuscript to evaluate scholarly accuracy, writing style, and pedagogy and provided enormously valuable feedback and suggestions. Thank you all so much!

Louis Clarke, University of Saskatchewan
Joan Condie, Sheridan College
Claude Dupuis, Athabasca University
David R. Hannah, Simon Fraser University
Gerald Hunt, Ryerson University
Judith Hunter, Sheridan College
Joanne Leck, University of Ottawa
Stephen Lynch, University of Guelph
Louis Masson, SAIT
Rosemary McGowan, Brescia University College
Jennifer Percival, University of Ontario Institute of Technology
Shirley Richards, Humber College
Ron Shay, Kwantlen University College
Elizabeth Speers, George Brown College
Thea Vakil, University of Victoria
Frank Vuo, Lethbridge Community College
Gretchen Whetham, College of the Rockies
Diane White, Seneca College

We would also like to thank our Ryerson University colleagues who generously reviewed chapters of the text and made many helpful suggestions: Nina Cole, Sandra Kalb, Gerald Hunt, Maurice Mazerolle, Agnes Meinhard, Lou Pike, Shannon Reilly, Neil Rothenberg, Ian Sakinofsky, Claudette Smith, and Margaret Yap.

The following students provided support and valuable feedback and helped to make the text a more student-friendly resource: Ruzzle Co, Langara College; Mariam Hossain, Ryerson University; Karl Kotlarz, College of the Rockies; Martha Orr, George Brown College; Douglas A. Phelps, University of Calgary; Sandra Raymont, College of the Rockies; James Southgate, University of Guelph; Limor Markman, York University; and Ben Reitzes, University of Toronto.

Acknowledgments

Managing Organizational Behaviour in Canada represents a true team effort, and we are grateful to our team members who made the process run smoothly. We could not have managed without our research assistant, Victoria Skelton, from the University of Toronto. She is an amazing researcher and a wonderful person. We are indebted to our acquisitions editor, Anthony Rezek, for his leadership, patience, and determination. Karina Hope, our developmental editor, was a pleasure to work with by always being there for us when we had questions, by keeping us on track, by being so kind and friendly, and by remembering everything! Kristiina Bowering did a fabulous job of finding interesting photographs and getting permissions while staying on budget. Many thanks to Bob Kohlmeier, our production editor, and to Lisa Berland, our copy editor, who greatly improved the manuscript with her insights, expertise, and meticulous attention to detail.

We are indebted to Celeste Brotheridge, from the University of Regina, for allowing us to use three of her wonderful cases, and to Anwar Rashid and Maurice Archer, retired from Ryerson University, for allowing us to update and revise many of their rich cases from *Canadian Cases in Organizational Behaviour*. We also thank Shannon Reilly, from Ryerson University and George Brown College, for her three cases, which she adapted for the text, and for her contribution to the GHOST model in Chapter 1.

Pat would like to thank her wonderful husband Morley and her children Matt and Laura for their love, support, and inspiration. She would also like to thank her mother Judy, for teaching and modelling the values that guide her work and her life.

Julie would like to thank her wonderful husband Hank who encouraged her to write this text and inspired her to pursue her dreams, and her children Eric, Lorin, and Benjamin for their love and support.

This book has been a labour of love for both of us. It has made us better teachers and also better learners. We hope it does the same for you.

Pat Sniderman and Julie Bulmash

About the Authors

Pat R. Sniderman

Pat R. Sniderman (née Rosman) is currently a professor of organizational behaviour at Ryerson University in Toronto, where she has been teaching and learning since 1985. Prior to that she received her undergraduate and graduate degrees in psychology from Boston and York (Ontario) Universities, and her thesis, entitled "Job Satisfaction, Self-Esteem and the Fit between Perceived Self and Job on Valued Competencies," was published in the *Journal of Psychology*.

Pat's focus in her academic life has been on creating excellence in learning and teaching through research, program leadership, and curriculum design. She won the 2005 Ryerson University GREET award for teaching excellence in the Faculty of Business. She was nominated as the McConnell Fellow for the Faculty of Business, which involved stimulating and funding innovative, student-centred teaching projects that forged links between the classroom and the external community. She designed and wrote an organizational behaviour course for distance education, which was also broadcast on CJRT Radio (currently JazzFM). Her 12 docu-lectures were integrated with segments of her interviews with managers and scholars such as John Kotter, Richard Hackman, Peter Senge, and Chris Argyris.

She was appointed by the University to the Ontario Provincial Committee for university validation of the new high school curriculum and was invited by the Human Resources Professional Association to join the committee to review the certification of HR professionals. She has been a member of the Editorial Board of the Human Resources Professionals Association of Ontario, *HR Professional* magazine, and she has been Program Director, Human Resources Management and Chair of the external HR Advisory Committee.

Throughout Pat's career she has been committed to experiential learning and student engagement. To this end she has been actively involved in the university learning and teaching committee; the interpersonal skills teaching centre, which designs and runs teaching simulations for problem-based learning; and the University McConnell Group, which managed the McConnell Foundation gift to support innovative, experiential, and community-based learning and teaching.

She ran the Faculty of Business International Charrette, which is an intensive problem-solving teaching event that brings in international experts to mentor top students. Pat also chaired the Innovative Curriculum Committee for her school and continues to play an active role in revamping the school of business management curriculum so that it is more Integrative, based on core Competencies and Experiential (ICE). Pat continues to teach the introductory OB course as well as Managing Interpersonal Dynamics, Organization Development and Human Resources Management. She is always looking for new and better ways to engage students in critical thinking and self-reflection, and writing this book helped further this goal.

In addition to her academic work, Pat has worked as a Senior Human Resources Manager, Director of Organization Development and Management Trainer at Dylex Ltd and Manulife Financial. She has also served as a consultant in human resources and organization development to organizations such as Magellan Aerospace, McDonald Douglas Canada, the Ontario Ministry of Environment, Health and Labour, Eatons Canada, the Ontario Aids Foundation and the Ontario Aerospace Council. Her consulting work has specialized in the areas of facilitation, team building, strategic and business planning, organization diagnosis, restructuring, and change management.

Pat is originally from England with Hungarian parents. She has lived in Toronto since 1974, is happily married to Morley and has two wonderful children, Matt and Laura.

Julie Bulmash

Julie Bulmash is a professor at George Brown College in Toronto, where she teaches organizational behavior, human resource management, compensation, management of change, and organizational effectiveness.

Julie began her career in social services. She was a psycho-educational consultant in a large Toronto hospital, and later she provided therapeutic family services at community-based clinics. In the early 1990s Julie entered the private sector and held progressively senior human resources management positions at corporations in several industries, including chemicals, software development, and telecommunications.

Julie began her academic career several years ago. She has taught at Humber College, Ryerson University, the University of Toronto, and George Brown College, where she is currently a professor in the School of Business.

Julie has extensive experience in the design, development, and delivery of human resource strategies intended to assist organizations in achieving their objectives. She has developed compensation and benefit systems, redesigned performance management programs, implemented human resource information systems, and has worked to ensure the effective management of change in both profit and not-for-profit sectors.

Julie obtained her undergraduate degree with honours in psychology at Concordia University in Montreal. She did graduate work in assessment and counselling at the University of Toronto, and took her MBA from Heriot-Watt University in Edinburgh, Scotland.

With her extensive business background and her practical focus, Julie works hard to create a collaborative learning environment. She aims to provide her students with the opportunity to integrate academic theory with an understanding of real life business experiences. Her students are challenged to compare what they have learned in the classroom with the best practices of organizations.

Julie has a passion for teaching human resource management and organizational behaviour. She is an enthusiastic and creative educator, profoundly dedicated to helping students achieve their personal goals. Julie consistently receives high marks from her students. At George Brown, she has been nominated for the prestigious Crystal Apple Award, which recognizes an instructor's ability to motivate and inspire through quality teaching methods.

Julie is committed to community improvement; she has worked for many years in the area of mental health. Currently Julie is president of the Canadian Mental Health Association for York Region in Ontario. The CMHA is a national organization that helps people in need of support. It has developed important mental health initiatives and is a powerful advocate for mental health reform.

Julie lives in Toronto with her wonderful husband Hank, her three children, Eric, Lorin, and Benjamin, and her golden retriever named Riley.

Debra L. Nelson

Dr. Debra L. Nelson is the CBA Associates Professor of Business Administration and Professor of Management at Oklahoma State University. She received her Ph.D. from the University of Texas at Arlington, where she was the recipient of the R. D. Irwin Dissertation Fellowship Award. Dr. Nelson is the author of over 70 journal articles focusing on organizational stress management, newcomer socialization, and management of technology. Her research has been published in the *Academy of Management Executive, Academy of Management Journal, Academy of Management Review, MIS Quarterly, Organizational Dynamics, Journal of Organizational Behavior,* and other journals. In addition, she is coauthor/coeditor of several books, including *Organizational Behavior: Foundations, Realities, and Challenges,* 4th ed. (South-Western/Thomson Learning, 2003), *Gender, Work Stress and Health* (American Psychological Association, 2002), *Advancing Women in Management* (Blackwell, 2002) and *Preventive Stress Management in Organizations* (American Psychological Association, 1997).

Dr. Nelson has also served as a consultant to several organizations including AT&T, American Fidelity Assurance, Sonic, State Farm Insurance Companies, and Southwestern Bell. She has presented leadership and preventive stress management seminars in a host of organizations, including Blue Cross/Blue Shield, Conoco, Oklahoma Gas and Electric, Oklahoma Natural Gas, and Preview Network Systems. She was honoured with the Greiner Graduate Teaching Award in 2001, the Chandler-Frates and Reitz Graduate Teaching Award in 1997, the Regents' Distinguished Teaching Award in 1994, and the Burlington Northern Faculty Achievement Award at OSU in 1991. Dr. Nelson also serves on the editorial review board of *The Academy of Management Executive.*

James Campbell Quick

Dr. James (Jim) Campbell Quick is a professor of organizational behaviour at the University of Texas at Arlington, director of the doctoral program in business administration, and former associate editor of *The Academy of Management Executive.* He earned an A.B. with Honors from Colgate University, where he was awarded a Harvard Business School Association Internship. He earned an M.B.A. and a Ph.D. at the University of Houston. He completed postgraduate courses in behavioural medicine (Harvard Medical School) and combat stress (University of Texas Health Science Center at San Antonio).

Dr. Quick is a Fellow of the Society for Industrial and Organizational Psychology, the American Psychological Association, the American Psychological Society, and the American Institute of Stress.

Dr. Quick framed preventive stress management with his brother (Jonathan D. Quick, MD, MPH). He has received over $235 000 in funded support for research, scholarship and intellectual contributions from the Society for Human Resource Management, Hospital Corporation of America, the State of Texas, and the American Psychological Association. His articles have been published in leading journals such as the *Academy of Management's Journal, Review,* and *Executive, Journal of Organizational Behavior, Air University Review, Stress Medicine,* and the *Journal of Medical Education.* He received the 1990 Distinguished Professional Publication Award for *Corporate Warfare: Preventing Combat Stress and Battle Fatigue,* coauthored with Debra L. Nelson and his brother for the American Management Association's *Organizational Dynamics.*

He is coauthor of *Preventive Stress Management in Organizations* (American Psychological Association, 1997), originally published in 1984 and released as *Unternehmen ohne Stress* in German. He is coauthor of the *Organizational Behavior: Foundations, Realities, and Challenges,* 4th ed. (South-Western/Thomson Learning, 2003) and *Stress and Challenge at the Top: The Paradox of the Successful Executive* (John Wiley & Sons, 1990). He is coeditor of the *Handbook of Occupational Health Psychology* (APA, 2002), *The New Organizational Reality: Downsizing, Restructuring, and Revitalization* (APA, 1998), *Stress and Well-Being at Work* (APA, 1992), and *Work Stress: Health Care Systems in the Workplace* (Praeger Scientific, 1987), for which he has received the 1987 Distinguished Service Award from the UTA College of Business. He is a member of Beta Gamma Sigma and Phi Beta Delta honor societies and the Great Southwest Rotary Club, where he is a Paul Harris Fellow.

Dr. Quick was the American Psychological Association's stress expert to the National Academy of Sciences on National Health Objectives for the year 2000. Dr. Quick was a scientific exchange delegate to the People's Republic of China. He is an editorial board member of *Stress Medicine.*

Dr. Quick was recognized with the Texas Volunteer Recognition Award (American Heart Association, 1985), a listing in *Who's Who in the World,* 7th ed. (1984–85), The Maroon Citation (Colgate University Alumni Corporation, 1993), a Minnie Stevens Piper Professorship Award nomination (2001), and a Presidential Citation from the American Psychological Association (2001).

Colonel Quick, U.S. Air Force (Ret.), was the Senior Individual Mobilization Augmentee at the San Antonio Air Logistics Center (AFMC), Kelly AFB, Texas, in his last assignment. He was Distinguished Visiting Professor of Psychology, 59th Medical Wing (1999). His awards and decorations include the Legion of Merit, Meritorious Service Medal, and National Defense Service Medal with Bronze Star. He is married to the former Sheri Grimes Schember.

part one

An Introduction to Organizational Behaviour

chapter one

LEARNING OBJECTIVES

By the end of this chapter, you will be able to do the following:

1. Define *organizational behaviour* (OB) and explain its roots.
2. Explain the relationship of organizational behaviour to the study of management.
3. Explain some of the benefits of studying organizational behaviour.
4. Describe an open systems framework for understanding how an organization functions, including the GHOST model to describe the internal organization.
5. Give an overview of the formal/informal framework and new paradigms for understanding how an organization functions.
6. Discuss the demands for good corporate governance and ethical behaviour.
7. Explain the challenges and opportunities for effective OB management brought about by increased globalization and competition.
8. Explain the challenges and opportunities for effective OB management brought about by increased workforce diversity.
9. Explain the challenges and opportunities for effective knowledge management in organizations.

learning about the context

Telus Values Diversity and Ethical Behaviour

Telus is a Canadian firm with approximately 20 000 employees. It provides voice, wireless, and data/IP communications solutions to businesses and consumers and was created in 1999 with the merger of Telus Corporation and BC Telecom. Darren Entwistle, CEO of Telus, is fervent about harnessing the energy and talents of employees as a means to make the company prosper. To further his commitment to ongoing employee communication, Telus provides regular opportunities for individuals to give honest, confidential feedback about what it is like to work at Telus. Their semi-annual "Pulsecheck" online survey helps management evaluate and improve the quality of leadership, communication, and employee engagement.

Telus has also distinguished itself by valuing diversity and by focusing on creating a high-performance, ethical culture. Telus provides an inclusive, nondiscriminatory, and respectful workplace. In a recent survey, 85 percent of Telus employee participants agreed that the company "respects employees of different ages, race, colour, gender, sexual orientation, religions, ethnic origin, language, marital status, family status and disability." Telus is strongly committed to high ethical standards and they publish a 19-page ethics policy. The policy includes guidelines and case studies on topics such as confidentiality of customer information, personal and corporate integrity, company assets, and conflict of interest. Telus also has an "EthicsLine," which is a toll-free telephone number through which employees can request guidance or make a good-faith report, sometimes called "whistle-blowing," about misconduct or perceived violation of the policy.

Each Telus employee takes part in a learning process called "Growing for High Performance," which involves the following four steps:

STEP 1: Employees learn about the Telus values, which are to: embrace change and initiate opportunity, have a passion for growth, believe in spirited teamwork and have the courage to innovate. They also learn about corporate strategy, business expectations, and what the company expects of them personally. Information is provided through a variety of communication tools, such as monthly performance meetings, a weekly online video, an online magazine, the team Telus portal, an online reference database, weekly e-letters from the CEO, and company-wide e-mail and voice-mail messages.

STEP 2: Employees assess themselves against set expectations so that growth and developmental opportunities can be planned. Many tools are available for this task, such as a self-assessment tool, a 360-degree feedback survey tool, and discussions with a manager.

STEP 3: Using an online e-performance tool, employees work with their managers to create a customized career development plan and set personal objectives.

STEP 4: Employees pursue learning options such as e-courses, instructor-led courses, job shadowing, mentoring, and individual coaching.

SOURCES: J. J. Salopek, "Canada Calling," *Training and Development* 57 (November 2003): 11, 34–35, 46–47; Telus, "Corporate Social Responsibility Report, 2002," 21, http://about.telus.com/careers/index.html; G. Bellett, "Bottom Line and Staff Both Count," *Windsor Star,* January 21, 2002, C8; "A Canadian Leader; Telus Awarded for Development System," *Canadian HR Reporter* (March 8, 2004): 16; Telus, *Ethics,* http://about.telus.com/governance/ethics.html.

The opening vignette about Telus gives a good example of a company that is working hard to create an energized and spirited workforce while at the same time valuing diversity and ethics. That is what this book is all about. It is about how to create an organizational culture that drives performance and brings out the very best in people as they work interdependently toward a common goal.

As you read the material in this book, think about your own energy at work or at college/university, and think about what makes the difference in those times that you feel energized and committed to your task, versus the times that you feel bored, alienated, or even hostile. Think about the factors that are about your own interests, as well as those to do with the task itself, the working environment, your boss, and the reward system. Even though each one of us has our own unique preferences, talents, and styles, our behaviour *can* be influenced. The more you learn about organizational behaviour, the more mastery you will have over your own behaviour and the behaviour of others at work, and in life.

In this opening chapter, we first define organizational behaviour (also called OB), its roots, and its relationship to the discipline of management. Then we explore the many benefits of studying OB. We go on to describe in depth, the important "open systems" framework for understanding the organization itself, followed by a brief overview of the "formal/informal" model as well as a few of the newer organizational paradigms. Finally, we review three of the current challenges and opportunities for effective OB management. These challenges/opportunities are: (1) the demands for good corporate governance and ethical behaviour, (2) increased globalization and competition, (3) workforce diversity, and (4) knowledge management.

Define organizational behaviour (OB) and explain its roots.

WHAT IS ORGANIZATIONAL BEHAVIOUR (OB)?

Organizational behaviour (OB) is a field of study that seeks to understand, explain, predict and change human behaviour, both individual and collective, in the organizational context.[1]

organizational behaviour (OB)
A field of study that seeks to understand, explain, predict, and change human behaviour, both individual and collective, in the organizational context.

Today, we study organizational behaviour at three different levels: First, at the individual level we study issues such as employee motivation and perception. Second, at the group level we study issues such as teams, communication, job design, and leadership. Third, at the organization-wide level we study topics like change, culture, and organizational structure. Also, increasingly we are studying at the interorganizational (network) level with such issues as outsourcing, organizational networks, strategic alliances, and mergers, as discussed in Chapter 14.

OB scientists are observing a manager who is conducting a performance appraisal interview, so they can provide feedback and guidance.

Roots of Organizational Behaviour

The field of organization behaviour emerged as a distinct field in the mid-1940s and is a discipline that has grown out of contributions from numerous earlier fields of study, such as psychology, sociology, engineering, anthropology, and management. Each of these sciences (as well as others) have had their own important and unique influences on the discipline of organizational behaviour, and they are summarized in Exhibit 1.1.

EXHIBIT 1.1

Some of the Interdisciplinary Roots of OB

Discipline	Influences on OB Topics
Psychology	Work teams, work motivation, training and development, power and leadership, human resource planning, and workplace wellness
Sociology	Group and intergroup dynamics, roles, norms and standards of behaviour that emerge within groups, compliant and deviant behaviour, effects of codes of ethics in organizations
Engineering	Design of work, efficiency, performance standards, productivity, and goal-setting; includes scientific management
Anthropology	Organizational culture, origins of culture, patterns of behaviour
Administrative science (management)	Design, implementation, and management of various administrative and organizational systems

Psychology is the science of human behaviour, which traces its own origins to philosophy and the science of physiology. Since its origin, psychology has itself become differentiated into a number of specialized fields, such as clinical, experimental, organizational, and social psychology. The topics in organizational psychology, which include work teams, work motivation, training and development, power and leadership, human resource planning, and workplace wellness, are very similar to the topics covered by organizational behaviour.[2] The famous **Hawthorne studies,** which involved a series of research projects conducted by social psychologists at the Hawthorne plant of Western Electric in the 1920s and 1930s, demonstrated the impact of psychological processes and peer pressure on individual behaviour and performance. These studies marked the beginning of the Human Relations movement.[3]

psychology
The science of human behaviour.

Hawthorne studies
Studies conducted at the Hawthorne plant of Western Electric in the 1920s and 1930s that demonstrated the impact of psychological processes and peer pressure on individual behaviour and performance.

Sociology, the science of society, has made important contributions to knowledge about group and intergroup dynamics in the study of organizational behaviour. Because sociology takes the society rather than the individual as its point of departure, the sociologist is concerned with the variety of roles within a society or culture, the norms and standards of behaviour that emerge within societies and groups, and the consequences of compliant and deviant behaviour within social groups.[4]

sociology
The science of society.

Engineering is the applied science of energy and matter. Engineering has made important contributions to our understanding of the design of work. By taking basic engineering ideas and applying them to human behaviour in work organizations, Frederick Taylor had a profound influence on the early years of the study of organizational behaviour and coined the term **scientific management,** which is Frederick Taylor's system for using research to determine the optimum degree of specialization and standardization for a job task.[5] Taylor was ahead of his times in many ways, and his ideas were often controversial during his lifetime. Nevertheless, applications of his original ideas are embedded in organizational goal-setting programs, such as those at Black &

engineering
The applied science of energy and matter.

scientific management
Frederick Taylor's system for using research to determine the optimum degree of specialization and standardization for a job task.

Decker, IBM, and Weyerhaeuser.[6] You will learn more about how scientific management led to later studies of job design in Chapter 5.

anthropology
The science of the *learned* behaviour of human beings.

Anthropology is the science of the *learned* behaviour of human beings and is especially important to understanding organizational culture. Current research in this tradition has examined the effects of efficient cultures on organization performance[7] and how pathological personalities may lead to dysfunctional organizational cultures.[8]

management
The study of overseeing activities and supervising people in organizations.

Management, originally called administrative sciences, is a discipline concerned with the study of overseeing activities and supervising people in organizations. It emphasizes the design, implementation, and management of various administrative and organizational systems. March and Simon took the human organization as their point of departure and concerned themselves with the administrative practices that would enhance the effectiveness of the system.[9] Management is the first discipline to take the modern corporation as the unit of analysis, and this viewpoint distinguishes the discipline's contribution to the study of organizational behaviour.

Explain the relationship of organizational behaviour to the study of management.

Organizational Behaviour and Management

organizations
Groups of people who work interdependently toward some common purpose.

managers
People in organizations who perform jobs that involve the direct supervision of other people.

In organizational behaviour (OB), as in the discipline of management, we study **organizations.** These are defined as groups of people who work interdependently toward some common purpose. While this may be your first course in OB, you do already have quite a bit of knowledge and experience about the subject. All of you participate in organizations. Your family is an organization; so is your school, your sports team, your project teams, your student association, your religious institution, this class, etc. In some of these organizations you are a member and in others you are a leader or manager. **Managers** are defined as people in organizations who perform jobs that involve the direct supervision of other people. The nature of managerial work includes planning, organizing, leading, and controlling, as depicted in Exhibit 1.2. The study of organizational behaviour explores managerial roles and challenges as they relate to the management of an organization's human resources.

Planning involves defining goals that flow from the business strategy, setting performance objectives, and creating action plans. Organizing includes dividing up the tasks and establishing work roles or departments in order to carry out the plans. Leading involves communicating, motivating, and managing conflict. Finally, controlling includes monitoring financial and human performance.[10] Managers are concerned with financial, technological, and intellectual capital, in addition to human capital.[11]

EXHIBIT 1.2

Functions of a Manager

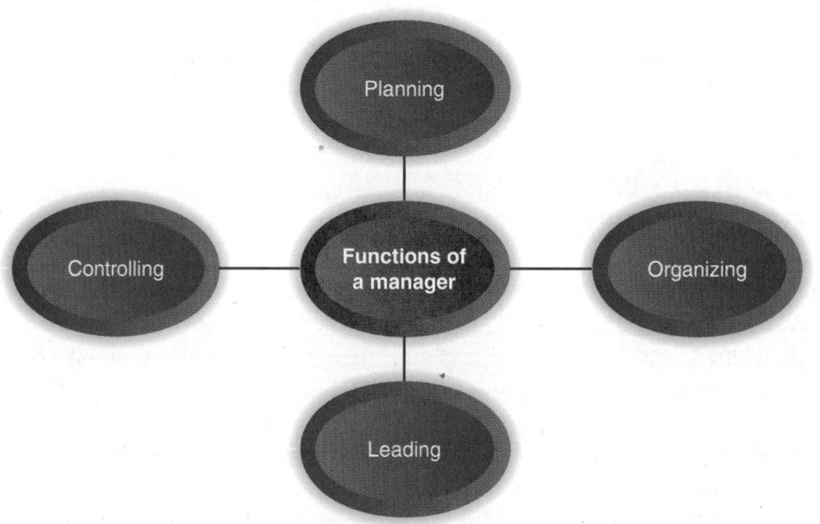

Human capital is defined as the knowledge that employees possess and generate, including their skills, experience, and creativity. The discipline of organizational behaviour focuses on developing human capital and strengthening the people side of the manager's responsibilities for planning, organizing, leading, and controlling. Leading-edge companies such as Corning Corporation in the U.S. work hard to determine the degree to which they are making the most of their people assets, i.e., human capital. Corning, for example, has built upon the "HC (human capital) bridge" framework developed by HR scholars. In this framework, key pools of talent are identified for investment. These are the talent pools in which a change in the skill level or availability of talent will have a dramatic impact on performance.[12] The companies invest heavily in attracting, training, developing and motivating employees and then they measure the efficiency, effectiveness, and impact of initiatives to strengthen their human capital.

human capital
The knowledge that employees possess and generate, including their skills, experience and creativity.

The job of a manager is a complex one and involves a number of diverse roles, as outlined by Henry Mintzberg's important work in the 1970s entitled *The Nature of Managerial Work.* Mintzberg discovered that managers are required to perform interpersonal, informational, and decisional functions that encompassed tasks related to the management of people as well as those related to the management of information, material, and financial resources.[13] The following 10 different kinds of roles have been identified: interpersonal roles include those of figurehead, leader, and liaison; informational roles include being a monitor, a disseminator of information, and a spokesperson; and decisional roles include being an entrepreneur, disturbance handler, resource allocator, and negotiator. Despite the wide acceptance of Mintzberg's work in the Western context, recent studies suggest that managerial roles vary in non-Western contexts such as Asia.[14]

Also, Mintzberg's model creates an impression of certainty and control that does not accurately reflect the day-to-day realities in the life of a busy manager. John Kotter's study in the late 1970s revealed that, at least at the most senior levels, managers face a high degree of uncertainty and have to get things done through a "large and diverse group of people despite having little direct control over most of them."[15] Complete Self-Assessment 1.1 to explore your own reactions to the uncertainty that is increasingly part of a manager's job. The study of organizational behaviour explores managerial roles and challenges as they relate to the management of an organization's human resources.

THE BENEFITS OF STUDYING ORGANIZATIONAL BEHAVIOUR

Explain some of the benefits of studying organizational behaviour.

As you can see from our earlier definition of organizational behaviour, it is an applied **behavioural science.** This means that it is based on research that improves one's ability to understand, predict, and influence the behaviour of others. Partially because of its strong foundation in science, there are many benefits to learning about organizational behaviour. Here we discuss three of them. First, OB concepts and skills help managers become more effective, thereby improving their companies' bottom lines. Second, mastering OB enables you to become more effective at influencing others, both as a formal manager and when you need to influence people over whom you have little or no control. While OB research has focused on behaviour in the workplace, many of the findings can be applied to managing behaviour outside of work as well. Third, the study of OB benefits you if you choose to major in the field of organizational behaviour or plan to work in the dynamic field of strategic human resources management.

behavioural science
Research that improves one's ability to understand, predict, and influence the behaviour of others.

Benefit: Improved Managerial Effectiveness and Bottom Line

In many of the chapters in this book, you will be learning about research that connects effective management of OB to various aspects of a company's bottom line, such as sustaining high performance over changing market conditions, improving individual and

CRITICAL THINKING: Application & Synthesis

SELF-ASSESSMENT 1.1: CHAOS AND THE MANAGER'S JOB

Managers' jobs are increasingly chaotic as a result of high rates of change, uncertainty, and turbulence. Some managers thrive on change and chaos, but others have a difficult time responding to high rates of change and uncertainty in a positive manner. This questionnaire gives you an opportunity to evaluate how you would react to a manager's job that is rather chaotic.

Listed below are some statements a 37-year-old manager made about his job at a large and successful corporation. If your job had these characteristics, how would you react to them? After each statement are five letters, A–E. Circle the letter that best describes how you would react according to the following scale:

A. I would enjoy this very much; it's completely acceptable.
B. This would be enjoyable and acceptable most of the time.
C. I'd have no reaction one way or another, or it would be about equally enjoyable and unpleasant.
D. This feature would be somewhat unpleasant for me.
E. This feature would be very unpleasant for me.

1. I regularly spend 30–40 percent of my time in meetings. A B C D E
2. A year and a half ago, my job did not exist, and I have been essentially inventing it as I go along. A B C D E
3. The responsibilities I either assume or am assigned consistently exceed the authority I have for discharging them. A B C D E
4. At any given moment in my job, I average about a dozen phone calls to be returned. A B C D E
5. There seems to be very little relation in my job between the quality of my performance and my actual pay and fringe benefits. A B C D E
6. I need about two weeks of management training a year to stay current in my job. A B C D E
7. Because we have very effective equal employment opportunity in my company and because it is thoroughly multinational, my job consistently brings me into close contact at a professional level with people of many races, ethnic groups, and nationalities and of both sexes. A B C D E
8. There is no objective way to measure my effectiveness. A B C D E
9. I report to three different bosses for different aspects of my job, and each has an equal say in my performance appraisal. A B C D E
10. On average, about a third of my time is spent dealing with unexpected emergencies that force all scheduled work to be postponed. A B C D E
11. When I need to meet with the people who report to me, it takes my secretary most of a day to find a time when we are all available, and even then I have yet to have a meeting where everyone is present for the entire meeting. A B C D E
12. The university degree I earned in preparation for this type of work is now obsolete, and I probably should return for another degree. A B C D E
13. My job requires that I absorb about 100–200 pages a week of technical material. A B C D E
14. I am out of town overnight at least one night a week. A B C D E
15. My department is so interdependent with several other departments in the company that all distinctions about which department is responsible for which tasks are quite arbitrary. A B C D E
16. I will probably get a promotion in about a year to a job in another division that has most of these same characteristics. A B C D E

SELF-ASSESSMENT 1.1: (CONT.)
CHAOS AND THE MANAGER'S JOB

17. During the period of my employment here, either the entire company or the division I worked in has been reorganized every year or so. A B C D E
18. While I face several possible promotions, I have no real career path. A B C D E
19. While there are several possible promotions I can see ahead of me, I think I have no realistic chance of getting to the top levels of the company. A B C D E
20. While I have many ideas about how to make things work better, I have no direct influence on either the business policies or the personnel policies that govern my division. A B C D E
21. My company has recently put in an "assessment centre" where I and other managers must go through an extensive battery of psychological tests to assess our potential. A B C D E
22. My company is a defendant in an antitrust suit, and if the case comes to trial, I will probably have to testify about some decisions that were made a few years ago. A B C D E
23. Advanced computer and other electronic office technology is continually being introduced into my division, necessitating constant learning on my part. A B C D E
24. The computer terminal and screen I have in my office can be monitored in my boss's office without my knowledge. A B C D E

For scoring instructions, please go to the end of the chapter, p. 33.

SOURCES: "Chaos and the Manager's Job," in *Organizational Behavior: Experiences and Cases,* 4th ed., ed. D. Marcic, 296–97 (Minneapolis/St. Paul: West Publishing, 1995); Peter B. Vaill, "A Manager's Job," in *Managing as a Performing Art: New Ideas for a World of Chaotic Change* (San Francisco: Jossey-Bass, 1989). Reprinted by permission of John Wiley & Sons, Inc.

group productivity, and increasing organizational adaptability.[16] There have been a large number of studies that speak to the strong connection between how firms manage their people and the economic results achieved. For example, effective management of OB improves the bottom line by reducing the costs of employee turnover, which can be huge. The cost of losing an employee is estimated to be as much as 200 percent of that employee's salary. In addition, a poor hiring decision can cost $66 000 for an employee with a university degree.[17] Also, studies from the automobile, apparel, semi-conductor, steel manufacturing, oil refining, and service industries show that "substantial gains, on the order of 40 per cent, can be obtained by implementing high performance management practices."[18] Recently published research has also shown a strong link between the effectiveness of human capital management and the degree of measurable shareholder value.[19] Management of OB has become increasingly important partly because traditional sources of competitive advantage, such as market share, proprietary technology, access to capital, and regulated markets, have become less powerful, so it is the effective management of OB and the creation and maintenance of a high-performing organization that becomes the crucial differentiating factor.[20]

Benefit: More Effective Influence

While many people assume that managing OB is just "common sense," this is, in fact, a misconception. Because the field of organizational behaviour is based on a vast body of international scholarly research and practice, as you gain mastery in the field, you will become able to better understand, and therefore predict and influence the behaviour of others.

For those of you who are or plan to be managers, having this improved mastery is essential, because you will not be able to achieve your work objectives unless you can influence the employees working under your supervision. Introductory organizational behaviour is a required course in most business programs at colleges and universities all over the world, and many business students also take advanced OB courses to help them become more capable managers.

IMPLICATIONS FOR LIFE

Improving Your Ability to Understand, Predict, and Influence

Learning about OB improves your ability to understand, predict, and influence the behaviour of others. For example, imagine for a moment that you are living in a house with five other university/college students you have just met. You each have your own bedroom but you share the common spaces. You have been living together for a month and things have been going smoothly. Everyone has been pretty polite but cautious. Suddenly, seemingly for no reason, people start arguing or ignoring each other. Cliques are forming and one of the students is getting very bossy. It is getting very unpleasant. What should you do?

Here is how the science of OB can help. OB improves your ability to:

1. *Understand:* The OB research and subsequent theories about team dynamics discussed in Chapter 7 will help you understand what is going on here. First, you will understand that you are a team because you share the goal of having a decent place to live and also have a high degree of interdependence in the common spaces of the house. Second, by learning about the typical stages of team development you will understand that for the first month, being strangers, your team was in the "forming" stage and after the first month you moved into the second stage, which is called "storming." This stage, you learn, is actually necessary, albeit difficult, if you are to become a high-performing team. It is characterized by interpersonal conflict, the formation of cliques, and power struggles.
2. *Predict and influence:* If you had learned more about teams and the stages of team development prior to moving in, you would have been able to predict what was likely to happen and you would have noticed early warning signs. Read ahead to Chapter 7 to learn more about the science in the stages of a team's development

Canadian Council of Human Resources Organizations (CCHRA)

The Canadian Council of Human Resources Associations (CCHRA) is the result of the collaborative efforts of 10 provincial and specialist human resources associations that currently represent the interests of more than 18 000 professionals across Canada. The mission of CCHRA is to establish national core standards for the human resources profession, promote communication among participating associations, serve as the recognized resource on equivalency for human resources qualifications across Canada, and provide a national and international collective voice on human resources issues. http://www.cchra-ccarh.ca/en/

For those of you who do not plan to be managers, this material will help you influence your co-workers and bosses, and even people in your lives outside of work. For example, the more you can anticipate when a boss or co-worker is willing to comply with a request, when a friend might get angry, or when a manager might respond favourably to a new idea, the more mastery you have over your life. Also, as organizations are becoming less hierarchical and more team-based, being able to accurately predict and influence behaviour is becoming a "must" in advancing one's career.

Benefit: A Career in Human Resources Management

Some of you may choose to become experts in the people side of the business (as opposed to the accounting, marketing, IT, or finance sides). If you do, the study of OB will not only help you influence others but it also might be the first step toward a major or minor in organizational behaviour or the related discipline of human resources management. Human resources professionals and managers help organizations and other managers maximize human performance, and improve the quality of work life and the bottom line. See Organizational Reality Box 1.1 for an example of an entry-level human resources management job at Home Depot.

Describe an open systems framework for understanding how an organization functions, including the GHOST model to describe the internal organization.

AN OPEN SYSTEMS FRAMEWORK FOR EXPLAINING HOW ORGANIZATIONS FUNCTION

Now that we defined the discipline or OB and explored some of the benefits of studying it, we move into a more in-depth look at the organization itself, assisted by a few theoretical frameworks that help us understand it. No discussion of OB can begin without first exploring the ways that organizations are viewed conceptually. Over the years, many

organizational reality 1.1

A Career in Human Resources and Organizational Behaviour at Home Depot

Home Depot is fast becoming an employer of choice and this is due, in part, to the fact that there is now an HR manager within each store in North America. There are currently 160 internal HR professionals in Home Depots across Canada, actively involved in all elements of organizational behaviour and human resources management. HR activities include attracting and recruiting hourly and salaried associates; designing jobs; designing motivational schemes and reward systems; training managers in leadership and in how to communicate with, motivate, and appraise staff; and executing processes to facilitate organizational change and renewal.

Josie Gullusci is a graduate of Ryerson University in Toronto and is enjoying the benefits of having studied OB as part of her Bachelor of Commerce degree and HRM major. Josie is the HR Assistant at Home Depot and reports to the Manager of Organizational Effectiveness.

Josie Gullusci graduated in 2003 from Ryerson University with a Bachelor of Commerce degree and a major in Human Resources Management. Soon after graduation, she got a job as a program assistant for the Organization Effectiveness (OE) and Store Leadership Programs within the Human Resources Division. One of Josie's roles has been to assist the OE manager with the Human Resources Review Program. As part of this review, managers solicit structured feedback from their superiors, employees, and peers, through Home Depot's web-based 360-degree feedback process. Josie has been the contact person for all inquiries regarding this process. In addition, she has delivered classroom training sessions for the online portion of the Performance Management Training program. She has also been responsible for organizing a written presentation for CEO Bob Nardelli's annual visit from Atlanta. As program assistant to the Store Leadership Program, Josie has been helping Home Depot keep up with its growing need for talented managers by identifying and developing high-potential management candidates. Through this program, the company brings people with 4 to 10 years of management experience into an accelerated 2-year management training program and grooms them to be store managers.

Josie says that she is learning a great deal by managing a large number of projects at one time and especially loves the classroom training part of her role. Josie really enjoys the field of human resources and the chance to learn about the business. It has also allowed her to understand how the human resources function supports the overall strategy of Home Depot and helps contribute to the overall success of the business.

SOURCE: Josie Gullusci (program assistant) and Steve Tyer (former manager, Organization Effectiveness), Home Depot, interview with the author, March 16, 2004.

different models and organizational frameworks have been proposed. Today, the corporation is the dominant organizational form for much of the Western world, but other organizational forms have dominated other times and societies. Some societies have been dominated by religious organizations, such as the temple corporations of ancient Mesopotamia and the churches in colonial North America.[21] Other societies have been dominated by military organizations, such as the clans of the Scottish Highlands and the regional armies of the People's Republic of China.[22]

During the past several decades, systems concepts have been used to help us understand the bigger picture of organizations rather than just the parts, and for exploring how the "various parts both affect and are affected by each other."[23] The open systems framework derives from the models of ecosystems in biology, so that organizations are viewed as living organisms, interacting with their environment and requiring balance to survive.

The open system view of organizations, derived from the models of ecosystems in biology, views systems as living organisms.

We will examine this model in detail by looking at its five main components: (1) the external task environment in which the organization operates; (2) the inputs to the organization; (3) the internal organization itself, referred to as the GHOST model (**g**oals, **h**uman resources, **o**rganizational **s**tructure, and **t**echnology); (4) the outputs created by the organization; and finally (5) the feedback processes.

External Task Environment

external task environment
Sectors with which the organization interacts directly and that have a direct impact on the organization's ability to achieve its goals.

An organization's **external task environment** includes those sectors with which the "organization interacts directly and that have a direct impact on the organization's ability to achieve its goals."[24] These sectors, as shown in Exhibit 1.3, include the industry to which the company belongs, the raw materials needed to produce the output, the human resources, the financial resources, the market in which the company operates, the technology, the economic conditions, legislative changes and government, and sociocultural and international forces. Organizations frequently have to cope with many of these sectors or with sectors that are highly volatile, create formal jobs and even entire departments, in order to keep track of or influence the forces that may present challenges or opportunities in the future. These jobs are called **boundary-spanning roles,** defined as those that link and coordinate an organization with key elements in the task environment.[25] Examples of boundary-spanning roles are market researchers, government lobbyists, and competitive intelligence departments.

boundary-spanning roles
Jobs that link and coordinate an organization with key elements in the task environment.

Although factors in the task environments of Canadian organizations vary greatly, we will address, in the second half of this chapter, three forces in the task environments that present challenges and opportunities for the management of OB in most Canadian companies today. These three forces are the demands for good corporate governance and ethical behaviour (sociocultural), increased globalization (global economic), diversity (sociocultural and demographic), and effective knowledge management (information technology and human resources.)

Organizational Inputs

organizational inputs
All the human, informational, material, and financial resources taken from the external task environment and used by the organization.

From the external task environment, organizations select the human, informational, material, and financial resources that they need to create their products or services. In the open systems model these are referred to as the **organizational inputs.** For example, the organizational inputs of a clothing store would include clothes, hangers, fixtures, job applicants, computers, pricing information, fashion information, and retail space.[26]

EXHIBIT 1.3

An Organization's External Task Environment

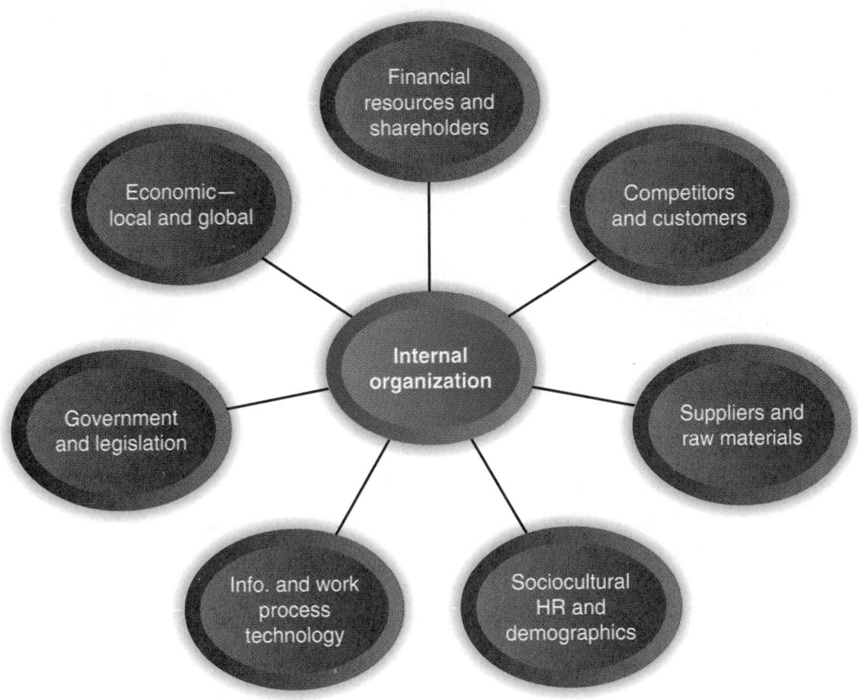

Knowledge & Application

APPLYING THE OPEN SYSTEMS MODEL TO ASSESS YOUR COLLEGE/UNIVERSITY

Which of the external environments from the following list do you think educational institutions like yours pay (and should pay) particular attention to, and why?

- Competitors, i.e., other educational institutions or programs
- Customers, i.e., graduate schools and employers
- Suppliers (high schools and other colleges/universities)
- Technology, i.e., learning and teaching, library sciences
- Economic conditions
- Legislation and/or government
- Sociocultural and demographic changes
- International forces

The GHOST Model for the Internal Organization

Inputs from the external task environment are taken into what we are calling the "internal organization." In the original "opens systems" model, created in the mid-1960s, it was called the "transformation process" because it is here that the inputs get transformed into outputs.[27] To make the complex workings of the internal organization more understandable in this introductory chapter, we have created the GHOST model. As you read the chapters that follow you will learn about each element of the internal organization in much more depth. The purpose of the GHOST model here is to give you the big picture of how organizations function so that you will have a roadmap of where we are going. All these functions are depicted in an open systems model in Exhibit 1.4.

goals (G)
The action strategies that leaders create and follow to accomplish the organization's purpose and vision.

Goals (G) are defined here as those action strategies that leaders create and follow to accomplish the organization's purpose and vision. Organizational leaders create goals based on the organization's reason for being, the threats and opportunities that are perceived to exist in the external task environment, and the business strategy. You will read more about the critical element of visioning in the leadership and change chapters, and you will also learn about effective goal-setting in the motivation chapter.

human resources (H)
The employees and managers in the organization, including the nature of their relationships, their values, and the impact of the reward system on their behaviour.

An organization's **human resources (H)** are the employees and managers in the organization, and we include in this category the nature of their relationships, the way they communicate, and the impact of the reward system on their behaviour. Many of the chapters in the book are devoted to these subjects.

organizational structure (OS)
The manner in which an organization's work is designed, as well as how departments, divisions, and the overall organization are designed.

Organizational structure (OS) is defined as the manner in which an organization's work is designed, as well as how departments, divisions, and the overall organization are designed. A key aspect of effective organizational behaviour is ensuring that these components complement rather than conflict with each other. Organization leaders assisted by OB experts attempt to design or adjust the organizational structure (OS) to fit the organization's goals, and then recruit, manage, and motivate the people toward effectively carrying out these goals. You will learn more about this complex and fascinating topic in

EXHIBIT 1.4

An Open Systems Framework of Organizational Functioning with the GHOST Model of the Internal Organization

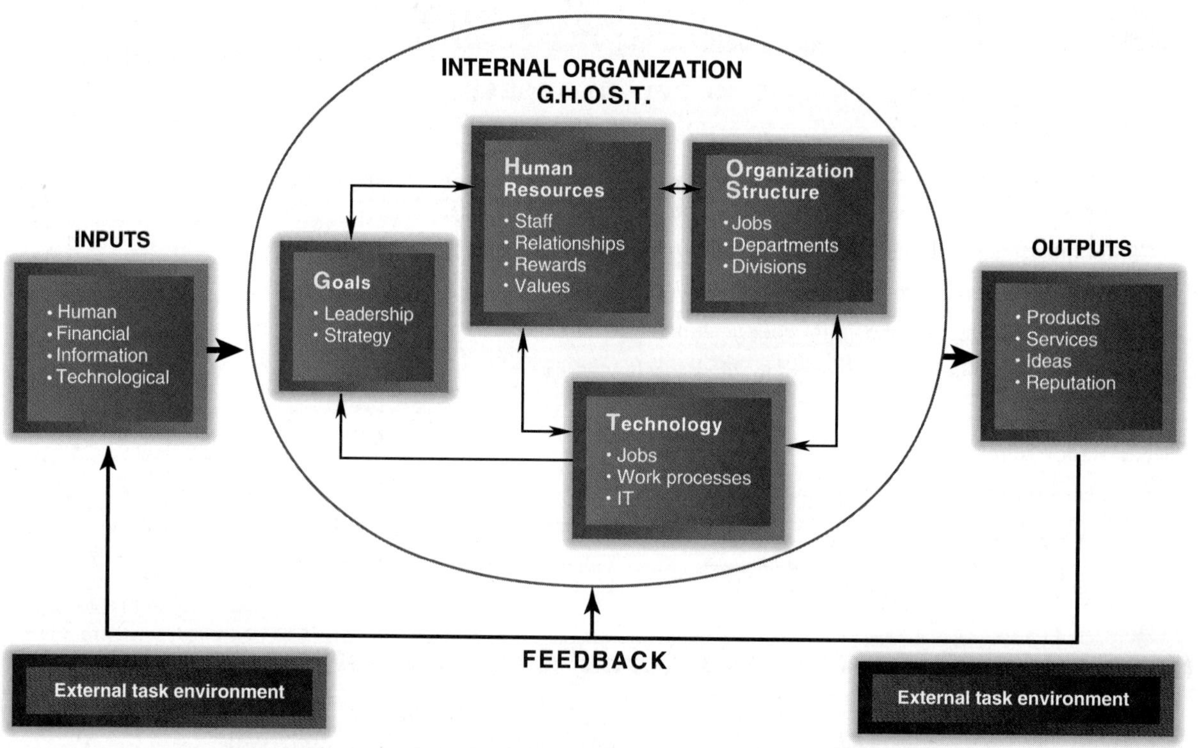

SOURCE: Adapted by P. Sniderman and S. Reilly from Harold Leavitt, "Applied Organizational Change in Industry: Structural, Technological, and Humanistic Approaches," in *Handbook of Organizations,* ed. J. G. March (Chicago: Rand McNally, 1965), 1145. Reprinted by permission of James G. March.

Chapter 14. **Technology (T)** is the wide range of tools, knowledge, information technology, work processes, and techniques used to transform the inputs into outputs.

technology (T)
The wide range of tools, knowledge, and/or techniques used to transform the inputs into outputs.

To clarify the open systems view of the GHOST elements in the internal organization we will continue to use the example of a clothing store. Organization leaders will develop the goals (G) based on the company's purpose as well as the business strategy—that is, the kind of clothing store the company wants to be (high or low end, target market, etc.)—in the current and expected task environment. For example, leaders would consider the nature of the competition, the prices of various types of fabrics, available talent, economic conditions, and any tax breaks or government restrictions that might be in place. The goals will then be carried out through the organization's internal organization in the following way: the human resources (H) are the managers and employees needed to convert the inputs, such as clothes, product knowledge, and information, into outputs. In assessing the human resources category we would also explore the nature of relationships as well as whether the reward systems support the goals and structure. The organization's structure (OS) is the management hierarchy and the design of the various store jobs. The technology (T) of the store would include the face-to-face selling, the visual merchandising, the promotions, the computers, the product knowledge training, etc. The organizational culture is seen in the assumptions that employees make about how they work together and their perceptions of what is ethical and appropriate.

Organizational Outputs

The outputs in the clothing store example would be things like sold clothes, satisfied customers, and reputation. The **organizational outputs** include the products and services as well as the more intangible outputs such as reputation, image, and ideas. Outputs can be identified at the organizational, team, and individual levels. For example, organization-level outputs are stakeholder satisfaction and profitability. Team-level outputs include team performance or team reject rates. Individual outputs include absenteeism and sales per month.[28]

organizational outputs
The products and services, as well as the more intangible outputs such as reputation, image, and ideas.

Feedback Processes

The feedback processes in the model, indicated by the heavy arrows in Exhibit 1.4, are critical to our understanding of what makes an organization effective. **Feedback** is any information that people or organizations receive about their behaviour or performance, its effect on others, or comparison to a standard or expectation. Feedback is discussed in depth in Chapter 6, on communication. In the example of the clothing store, an effective organization will not only measure sales or market share as an output but will also set up processes or employee roles to solicit ongoing formal feedback ("boundary spanning") from customers. The customer comment card, when taken seriously, is one example of a formal feedback, or boundary-spanning process. Essentially, when an organizational system is working well, like a living system, it is *open* to feedback from its external environment and adapts accordingly so as to prosper and survive. One of the most significant barriers to systems being open to feedback is resistance to change.

feedback
Any information that people or organizations receive about their behaviour or performance, its effect on others, or comparison to a standard or expectation.

THE FORMAL/INFORMAL FRAMEWORK AND NEW PARADIGMS FOR UNDERSTANDING HOW ORGANIZATIONS FUNCTION

Give an overview of the formal/informal framework and new paradigms for understanding how an organization functions.

The open systems view of the organization, just discussed, looks at the entire functioning of the organization, including its relationship to the external environment. As you can see from our exploration of the GHOST model of the internal organization, it tends to focus on the **formal organization,** which includes its official, legitimate, and most visible parts, such as its technology and structure. The conceptualization of the internal organization in the open systems framework has been criticized as limited, because it leads us to think that

formal organization
The official, legitimate, and most visible part of the system.

the internal workings of an organization are purely logical and rational and can be represented by a linear flow chart as we have done back in Exhibit 1.4.

informal organization The unofficial and less visible part of the system.

organizational culture A pattern of basic assumptions that are considered valid and that are taught to new members as the way to perceive, think, and feel in the organization.

The second model of organizations that we explore goes beyond the formal aspects of the internal organization to the **informal organization.** This includes the unofficial and less visible elements such as beliefs, assumptions, values, and unspoken norms of behaviour that emerge in the **organizational culture,** which is a pattern of basic assumptions that are considered valid and that are taught to new members as the way to perceive, think, and feel in the organization.[29] Organizational culture is addressed in depth in Chapter 12. The informal organization is more indefinite and lacks a clear structure, so it has been harder to study.[30] Wang and Ahmed call the informal organization the "hidden energy" that flows behind the organization chart and that facilitates the constant flow of knowledge within and outside the organization.[31]

The informal organization has lately become much more important in organization theory, and this is reflected in the contemporary study of learning and knowledge management, discussed at the end of this chapter. Current technology capabilities have led to a dramatic increase in the amount of informal organizational communication. We are now seeing a growth in new forms of association in which middle managers and even executives are becoming "ardent networkers, alumni group participants and professional association joiners ... filling roles once filled by employers: providing identity, community and support for their members."[32] The formal and informal elements of the organization are depicted in Exhibit 1.5.

New Organizational Paradigms

Increased understanding of the power of the informal internal organization has led to new paradigms, or frameworks, for thinking about how organizations behave and actually function. These paradigms tend to stress and elaborate on the internal organization's dynamic capacity for self-organization, learning, and complex adaptation. These newer frameworks are useful for managers because they draw our attention to the "softer" aspects of organizational life such as relationships, trust, and interconnections that, while less visible and easy to control directly, can be highly influential. We explore two of these newer frameworks: chaos theory and the theory of the organization as a complex adaptive system, or CAS.

Chaos Theory and OB

One example of a new organizational paradigm is Margaret Wheatley's application of quantum physics, chaos, and field theory to organizations. In her view, organizations are made up not of separate parts that can be controlled, but rather of "fields" that influence our interactions, directions, and decisions. These fields are both visible (such as the stated organizational values or culture) and invisible (such as informal norms and expectations), as suggested earlier by the model of the informal organization. In her groundbreaking

The informal organization is the "hidden energy" beneath the surface of the organization.

EXHIBIT 1.5

Formal and Informal Organization

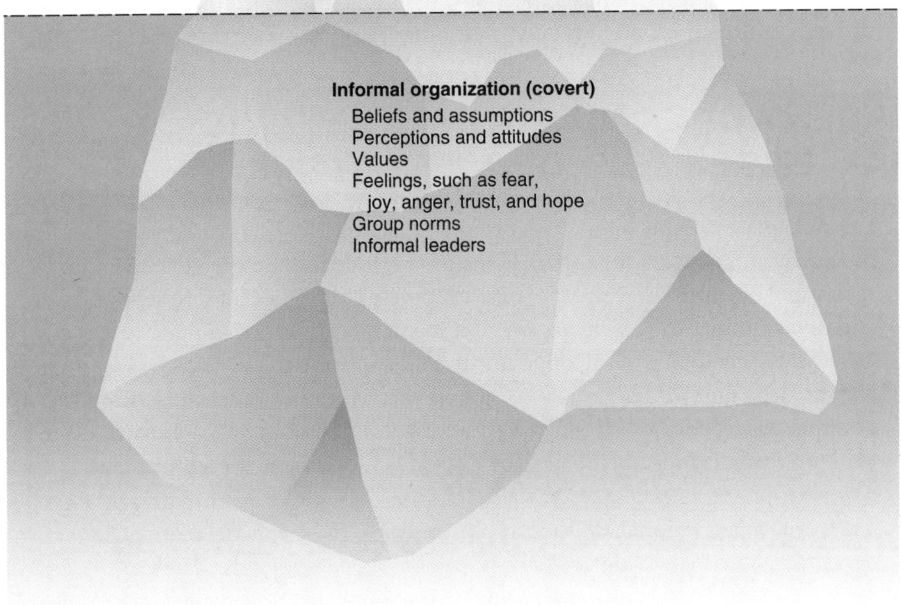

book entitled *Leadership and the New Science: Learning about Organization from an Orderly Universe,* she writes:

> We can imagine organizational space in terms of fields, with employees as waves of energy, spreading out in regions of the organization, growing in potential. How do we tap into that energy? How do we turn the employees' energy into behaviour for the organization, into something observable and probable?[33]

Another important aspect of her organizational model is the nature of the relationships, networks, and interconnections, both seen and unseen, that direct human behaviour. In her view, imposed organizational structures should not be permanent. Rather, they need to come and go so that a structure emerges that actually supports the relationships that are most necessary.[34] The job of leaders, therefore, is to create fields that influence, to disseminate information widely, to recognize fields that are not readily visible, and to encourage self-organization and learning through widespread participation.[35]

Human Systems Dynamics Institute

Human systems dynamics as a field of study began in 1990 with the first meeting of the Chaos Network. Though the field was not named until 2001, the work began when 40 practitioners and academics met in Washington, D.C., calling themselves the Chaos Network, to explore the theory and practice of applying chaos and complexity theory to the fields of human interactions.
http://www.hsdinstitute.org

Organizations as Complex Adaptive Systems (CAS)

Another example of a new paradigm is the work of Edwin Olson and Glenda Eoyang. They have applied ideas from complexity science to organizational change.[36] When an organization is viewed as a complex adaptive system (CAS), it is the informal organization that emerges and guides people's actions as they self-organize and form patterns of behaviour. A complex adaptive system can be defined as follows: *complex* means that organizations are composed of multiple and diverse pieces in differing relationships. *Adaptive* means that the organization is constantly "learning" new and effective means to fit with its environment in ways that enable a healthy, harmonious existence. *System* means that it all works together.[37] Complexity theory suggests that all organizations are complex, adaptive systems that continuously self-organize and co-evolve.[38] Like Wheatley's view, this view of organizations is an alternative to the machine model, and emphasizes the importance of self-organization, informal learning, and adaptation. For Olson and Eoyang, who are active in the Human Systems Dynamics Institute, three conditions exist for self-organization to occur: (1) a container, which sets the bounds for the self-organizing system and may be physical, organizational, or conceptual; (2) significant differences, which determine the patterns or fields that emerge based on differences in power, expertise, gender, educational background, etc.; and (3) transforming exchanges, which are the all-important connections, mentioned by Wheatley, that could be created through information, money, energy, or other resources.[39]

CURRENT ORGANIZATIONAL BEHAVIOUR CHALLENGES AND OPPORTUNITIES

Later chapters expand upon, and explore in depth, the elements of the transformation processes and organizational paradigms just introduced. Before we move into exploring each topic in depth, however, we turn to some of the issues that present both challenges and opportunities to OB management and are increasingly shaping changes at work.[40]

These challenges and opportunities flow from the external task environment and, as depicted in Exhibit 1.6, we group them into the four categories: (1) corporate governance and ethics, (2) globalization and competition, (3) workforce diversity, and (4) knowledge management. We now provide an overview of each of these.

6

Discuss the demands for good corporate governance and ethical behaviour.

Demands for Good Corporate Governance and Ethical Behaviour

Sociocultural and regulatory forces as well as the demands of shareholders have combined to exert forces on Canadian organizations to act in more responsible and ethical ways. In the wake of several accounting scandals and the introduction of the Sarbanes-Oxley Act (SOX) in the U.S. in 2002, Canada has been issuing guidelines for reforms in corporate governance such as the adoption of a code of business conduct for senior officers and whistle-blowing hotlines for employees.[41]

EXHIBIT 1.6

Current OB Challenges and Opportunities

OB Challenge/Opportunity	Examples
Corporate governance and ethical behaviour	Corporate governance, ethical practices, triple bottom line, and corporate social responsibility (CSR)
Globalization and competition	Hyper-change, global competition and restructuring, customer demands for quality
Workforce diversity	Culture, age, gender, mental and physical diversity, race, ethnicity, sexual orientation
Knowledge management	Knowledge acquisition, retention and sharing, tacit knowledge, and communities of practice (CoP)

SOURCE: M. W. McCall, Jr. and M. M. Lombardo, "What Makes a Top Executive?" *Psychology Today*, February 1983: 26–31.

Corporate governance is the system of control and performance monitoring of top management.[42] According to the Conference Board of Canada, corporate governance is about factors and institutions that control management's exercise of power, its accountability to shareholders, and the formal and informal processes by which stakeholders may influence management decisions.[43] The Bank of Montreal, for example, announced that they were separating the two roles of CEO and Chairman of the Board, setting up "reputational risk committees" and an anonymous employee hotline, and providing protection for "whistle blowers."[44] Intolerance of unethical practices in organizational and political life has increased dramatically, and leaders today are developing codes of ethics and statements of corporate values and are increasing their investments in the staff and infrastructure required to develop an ethical organizational culture. Read more about these trends in Chapter 2.

corporate governance
The system of control and performance monitoring of top management.

In addition to expanded efforts to improve corporate governance, many companies are expanding their definition of their expected outputs to include a so-called **triple bottom line.** This is defined as an organization's ability to generate environmental and societal benefits in addition to economic ones.[45]

triple bottom line
A company's ability to generate economic, environmental, and social benefits.

The environmental and societal bottom lines refer to another term that has become popular in recent years, which is **corporate social responsibility (CSR).** This refers to the obligation of a firm to use its economic, legal, ethical, and philanthropic resources to improve the welfare of society at large, independent of direct gains of the company.[46] The economic component of CSR is the fundamental responsibility to make a profit and grow, and the legal component is the duty to obey the law. In addition, during the past decade there has been an increasing emphasis on two additional components: the responsibility to be *ethical* and respect and ensure the rights of others, and the responsibility to be *philanthropic* in the broader community.[47] "Companies need to show that they're not just greedy institutions," says Debra Dunn, senior vice president of corporate affairs at Hewlett-Packard, a world leader in CSR.[48]

corporate social responsibility (CSR)
The obligation of a firm to use its economic, legal, ethical, and philanthropic resources in ways to benefit the society at large and to improve the welfare of society at large, independent of direct gains of the company.

It seems that more and more companies are now taking CSR more seriously, but critics of the CSR trend argue that "It's how you make your money that counts, not what you do with it."[49] To support this criticism of the current popularity of CSR, they cite the example of the collapsed energy giant Enron, which was a generous corporate donor while at the same time engaging in unethical and fraudulent practices.[50]

Ethical behaviour means acting in ways consistent with one's personal values and the commonly held values of the organization and society. Ethics and ethical decision making are explored in more depth in Chapters 2 and 8. In Chapter 8 you will find a set of detailed guidelines to help you make ethical decisions. Suffice it to say, for now, that the three ethical theories summarized below help organizational leaders govern as good corporate citizens who strive to behave ethically:

ethical behaviour
Acting in ways consistent with one's personal values and the commonly held values of the organization and society.

- Theories that help us explore the *consequences* of our behaviours. For example, it is ethical if it results in the greatest good for the most people.[51] This approach to ethics is called utilitarianism and was suggested by John Stuart Mill.
- Theories that provide us with *universal rules* to guide our decisions. For example, morality based on legality is based on this approach, as are morals in theology whereby moral rules are based on the Bible, the Talmud, and the Koran.[52] Kant worked toward the ultimate moral principle in formulating his categorical imperative,

The World Council for Corporate Governance
The World Council for Corporate Governance was established in 2001 as an independent, not-for-profit international network with the aim of galvanizing good governance practices worldwide.
http://www.wcfcg.net

Knowledge & Application

WHAT IS THE CSR OF A UNIVERSITY OR COLLEGE?

Using the definition and explanations given of CSR, describe the corporate social responsibilities of your university or college.

a universal standard of behaviour.[53] Kant argued that individuals should be treated with respect and dignity and that they should not be used as a means to an end. He argued that we should put ourselves in the other person's shoes and ask if we would make the same decision if we were them.

- Theories that emphasize the *character, personal virtues, and integrity* of the individual. These are based on an Aristotelian approach to character, and have been advocated most notably by Robert Solomon.[54] The centre of Aristotle's vision was on the inner character and virtuousness of the individual, not on the person's behaviour or actions. Thus, the "good" person who acted out of virtuous and "right" intentions was one with integrity and ultimately good ethical standards.

Explain the challenges and opportunities for effective OB management brought about by increased globalization and competition.

Increasing Globalization and Competition: Challenges and Opportunities

Competition

Most firms are encountering challenges brought about by unprecedented global competition in their external environments and must find creative ways to deal with rapidly changing task environments.[55] Competition in the world economies has increased significantly during the past couple of decades, especially in industries such as banking, finance, and air transportation. The competition may lead to downsizing and restructuring, yet it provides the opportunity for revitalization as well.[56] The challenge of competition has been further intensified by far-reaching global, economic, and organizational changes. For example, the collapse of the Soviet Union was followed quickly by the demise of the Berlin Wall. In the Soviet Union, "Perestroika" led to the liberation of the satellite countries and the breaking away of the Soviet Union's member nations. Canada, the U.S., and Mexico have dramatically reduced trade barriers in accordance with the North American Free Trade Agreement (NAFTA), which took effect in 1994. The formation of the European Union (EU) has provided many opportunities for Canadian organizations, including 350 million potential customers. All of these world events have brought about change, uncertainty, and the need to think globally.

The world has become a global macroeconomic village with a borderless market.

Globalization

The world has become a global macroeconomic village with a borderless market in which all firms, large and small, must compete.[57] Only a few years ago, business conducted across national borders was referred to as "international" activity. The word "international" carries with it a connotation that the individual's or the organization's nationality is held strongly in consciousness.[58] *Globalization*, in contrast, implies that the world is free from national boundaries and that it is really a borderless world.[59] What were once referred to as multinational organizations (organizations that did business in several countries) are now referred to as transnational organizations.

In **transnational organizations**, the global viewpoint supersedes national issues.[60] Transnational organizations operate over large global distances and are multicultural in terms of the people they employ. Nortel and Bombardier Aerospace are examples of Canadian transnational organizations that operate worldwide with diverse populations of employees. Bombardier, for example, generates nearly 60 percent of its annual revenues from the North American market and 31 percent from Europe. While the Asia-Pacific region currently accounts for only 9 percent of revenues, the company is trying to increase this to 15 percent by 2020 to reduce its dependence on the North American and European markets.[61] Read about another transnational organization, Napster, in Organizational Reality 1.2.

transnational organization
An organization in which the global viewpoint supersedes national issues.

Customer Demands for Quality

An increasingly borderless and competitive marketplace has forced organizations to become more customer-focused to meet customers' expectations of high-quality products and services. For example, Canadian Pacific Hotels discovered that its business travellers were looking for "beyond the call of duty" efforts to rectify problems, recognition of their individual preferences, and lots of flexibility regarding arrival and checkout times. In order to capture a greater share of this market, they changed the management structure and put systems and incentives in place to make sure that every property was in compliance with the new emphasis. After implementing these changes, CP Hotels' share of the Canadian business travel market jumped by 16 percent.[62]

Quality has the potential to give organizations a competitive edge in meeting international competition. Total quality has been defined in many ways.[63] We define **total quality management (TQM)** as the total dedication to continuous improvement and to customers so that the customers' needs are met and their expectations exceeded. TQM is a customer-oriented philosophy of management with important implications for virtually all aspects of organizational behaviour. One recent study explored the relationship between the adoption of total quality management practices and the corresponding

total quality management (TQM)
The total dedication to continuous improvement and to customers, so that the customers' needs are met and their expectations exceeded.

organizational reality 1.2

Global Corporations and Sovereign Nations

Napster is the revolutionary organization that engaged in music file sharing over the Internet and drew the wrath of the music industry. The music industry went after Napster under American copyright law. Although the conflict led to an impasse and an interesting legal scenario, consider a far more provocative and potent alternative scenario: What if Napster were based in the People's Republic of China rather than the United States? Within this scenario, Americans could exchange their own music under protection of the Chinese regime rather than being declared copyright criminals by their own country's courts. While the Recording Industry Association of America might be outraged, the Chinese national government would simply tell the trade association to stop meddling in its internal affairs.

Or, what if North American companies share information about their European customers and employees in defiance of European Community (EC) rules and regulations? While the EC has stricter standards for data protection and consumer privacy than those in the United States, American companies do violate EC rules with the explicit support of the U.S. government. Thus, a marketing plan in America may be a felony in Europe, and collaborative supply-chain management in China may lead to an arrest and a fine in New York or London. While it would be foolish to confuse legalistic behaviour with principled behaviour, current trends in globalization appear to pit global corporations against sovereign nations.

SOURCE: M. Schragy, "What If Napster Were Based in China?" *Fortune*, May 28, 2000, 194.

competitive advantages achieved by the TQM organizations. A strong relationship was found, suggesting that organizations that adopted TQM enjoyed a competitive advantage over organizations that did not.[64] The study also suggested that when companies tune their human capital management to focus the TQM initiatives on *both* employee commitment and customer satisfaction, rewards for shareholders are substantial. Quality leads to competitive advantage through customer responsiveness, results acceleration, and resource effectiveness.[65]

Explain the challenges and opportunities for effective OB management brought about by increased workforce diversity.

Managing Workforce Diversity: Challenges and Opportunities

diversity
All forms of individual differences, including race, ethnicity, culture, gender, age, marital status, religious beliefs, educational background, stage in one's career, physical and mental ability, personality, social status, and sexual orientation.

Globalization and sociocultural and demographic changes at home have resulted in contemporary work organizations that have tremendously diverse workforces. **Diversity** includes all forms of individual differences, including race, ethnicity, culture, gender, age, marital status, religious beliefs, educational background, career stage, physical and mental ability, personality, social status, and sexual orientation. A number of these elements and the related topics of stereotyping and prejudice are addressed in Chapters 2 and 3.

Diversity is an asset when it is well managed, but it can also pose management challenges in terms of conflict, stereotyping, lower organizational commitment, and high employee absenteeism or turnover.[66] While our definition of diversity includes over a dozen types, we explore briefly the following six elements, which often present OB challenges and opportunities, as shown in Exhibit 1.7. These six are culture, age, gender, physical/mental disabilities, race/ethnicity, and sexual orientation.

Cultural Diversity

Canadians are often viewed favourably for international assignments because of their experience with a two-language culture and a reputation as being culturally sensitive.[67] When Canadians are sent on international assignments they are usually given sensitivity training to help them better understand the cultural assumptions of the people they will be working with as well as learn about their own cultural assumptions and biases.[68] Another way organizations address the challenge of cultural diversity is to use cross-cultural task

EXHIBIT 1.7

Types of Workforce Diversity

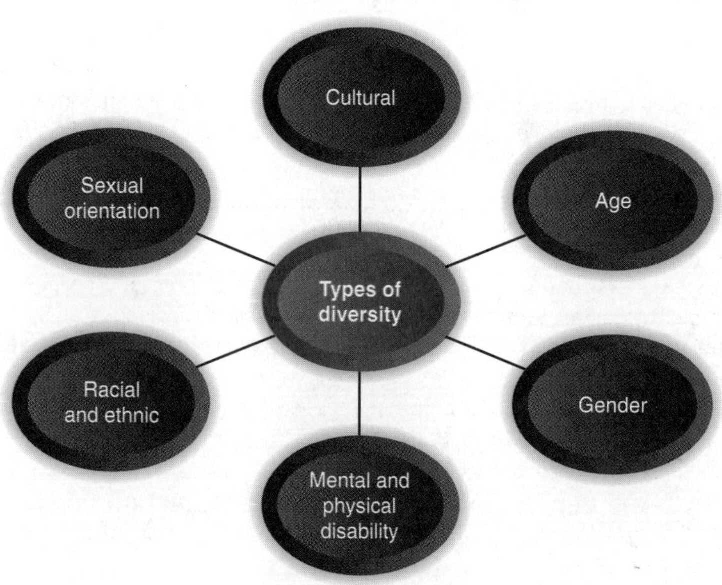

forces or teams. For example, GE Medical Systems Group (GEMS), which has almost half of its 15 000 employees working abroad, has developed a vehicle for bringing managers from each of its three regions (the Americas, Europe, and Asia) together to work on a variety of business projects. Under the Global Leadership Program, several work groups made up of managers from various regions of the world are formed. The teams work on important projects, such as worldwide employee integration, to increase the employees' sense of belonging throughout the GEMS international organization.[69] Read more about how organizations deal with cultural differences in Chapter 12.

Age Diversity

Organizations today, for the first time, consist of a mix of four generations, which have been called "Veterans, Boomers, Xers and Nexters."[70] Each generation has different needs, expectations, skills, and work styles.[71] Generational diversity in the workforce brings creative synergy but also can bring conflict based on values, views, thinking, and working styles.[72] In addition to the challenge of understanding and managing the different generations in the work place, the current and expected demographic shifts are posing challenges and opportunities to the recruitment and retention of employees.[73] Figures released by the Canadian census confirm that the country is aging rapidly. The median age of the working population (20 to 64) is approximately 41, which is 3 years older than it was a decade earlier and shows the biggest increase since 1921.[74]

Catalyst
Catalyst is the premier non-profit research and advisory organization working to advance women in business, with offices in New York, San Jose, and Toronto. The leading source of information on women in business for the past four decades, Catalyst has the knowledge and tools that help companies recruit, retain, and advance top talent and enable women to reach their potential.
http://www.catalystwomen.org

Gender Diversity

Another challenge and opportunity for effective OB management is capturing the human potential offered by the participation of increasing numbers of women in the workforce. In 2003 the Canadian labour force consisted of over nine million men and almost eight million women.[75] Statistics also show that more Canadian women are obtaining higher degrees: women hold 36 percent of all doctorates, 52 percent of master's degrees, and 55 percent of bachelor's degrees.[76] However, while women's participation in the workforce and in senior management is steadily increasing, 2002 salaries for women persist at a level of an average 64.2 percent of their male counterparts' earnings, and in 2003 women held only 11.2 percent of corporate director positions in Canada, up from 9.8 percent in 2001.[77]

The challenge faced by organizations as they attempt to develop the potential of, and rewards for, female employees and managers is referred to as the **glass ceiling.** This is defined as a transparent barrier that keeps women from rising above a certain level in organizations.

glass ceiling
Transparent barrier that keeps women from rising above a certain level in organizations.

Mental and Physical Ability Diversity

A **disability** is defined as an activity limitation or a participation restriction associated with a physical or mental condition or a health problem. Physical disabilities include the following types: hearing, seeing, speaking, agility, mobility, and learning. Mental disabilities include illnesses such as depression and anxiety, and companies face the challenge of increasing rates of mental disability. According to the Global Business and Economic Roundtable on Addiction and Mental Health, North American businesses alone lose about $60 billion annually as a result of depressed employees. These costs accrue from lost productivity, absenteeism, and problems related to diminished customer service.[78] Progressive companies have been able to develop their human capital by encouraging and nurturing the talents of people with disabilities. For example, the Rick Hansen Secondary School in Mississauga, Ontario, has doors, furniture, and push-button drinking fountains. Special pathways are marked on the floor for students with visual impairments. Another best-practice example is Granite Brewery in Toronto. It has menus in Braille, a carpeted area that provides a quiet area for people with hearing loss, complete access to the pub with wide front doors, and employees trained to provide customer service for people with disabilities.[79]

disability
An activity limitation or a participation restriction associated with a physical or mental condition or a health problem.

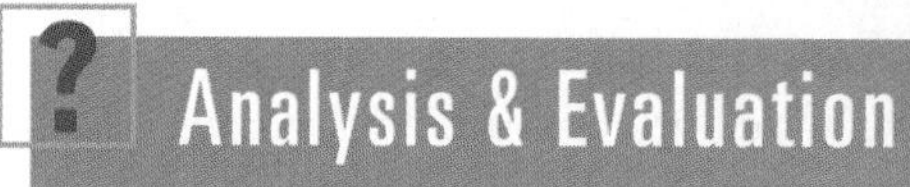

Analysis & Evaluation

THE COSTS AND BENEFITS OF EMBRACING DIVERSITY

How much money and time should organizations spend to accommodate diversity and strengthen their human capital? What are the potential benefits? Should there be a limit?

Racial and Ethnic Diversity

Demographic changes in Canada have led to immigrants representing approximately 20 percent of the Canadian workforce, while those who arrived in the 1990s represented almost 70 percent of the total growth in the labour force during the decade. Studies reveal that approximately 46 percent of Vancouver's population, 53 percent of Toronto's, and 23 percent of Montreal's were first-generation Canadians and that the majority of immigrants to Canada now come from Asia.[80] With an aging society and labour shortages forecast in nearly every sector, Canadian employers are starting to recognize the opportunity and potential in recruiting and retaining workers from all cultural, racial, and ethnic groups.[81]

Sexual Orientation

Sociocultural changes have resulted in greater attention being given to the issue of sexual orientation in the workplace. Thirty-four thousand same-sex common-law couples, were counted in Canada in the 2001 census. This represents 0.5 percent of all couples, compared to 0.3 percent in the U.S. and 0.4 percent in New Zealand.[82] Sexual orientation is an emotionally charged issue. Often, heterosexual resistance to accepting gay, lesbian, or bisexual workers is caused by moral beliefs. Although organizations must respect these beliefs, they must also send a message that all people are valued. The threat of job discrimination leads many gay men and lesbians to keep their sexual orientation secret at work. This secrecy has a cost, however. Closeted gay workers report lower job satisfaction and organizational commitment, and more role conflict and conflict between work and home life issues than do openly gay workers or heterosexual workers.[83] People who work in organizations full of fear, distrust, stigmatization, and harassment are not likely to be able to perform well. A tolerant atmosphere can improve the productivity of heterosexual and homosexual workers alike.

Diversity Management

Effective diversity management is advantageous in a multitude of ways; for example, a 2003 Catalyst study suggested that companies with a higher representation of women in senior management positions had a 35 percent higher return on investment (ROI) than companies with the lowest women's representation.[84] When organizations embrace diversity they also create more positive organizational environments, which you will learn about in Chapter 2.[85] Canadian leaders in diversity management are companies such as Pelmorex Inc., the Bank of Montreal, IBM Canada, and Oracle (discussed in Organizational Reality 1.3).[86] In these companies and others, managers are trained in nondiscriminatory interview techniques and rewarded financially for embracing diversity. In addition, these organizations create formal diversity management roles, set up communication networks, and use outreach programs to recruit employees from minority groups.[87]

organizational reality 1.3

Diversity Training at Oracle

Oracle Corporation is the world's second-largest software company and the largest independent provider of software for enterprise information management. Oracle provides software that powers the Internet. Its Canadian head office is located in Mississauga, Ontario, and its subsidiary, La Société d'Informatique Oracle du Québec Inc., is based in Montreal. Oracle Canada has an equal-opportunity program and is committed to fairness in hiring, recruiting, and accommodating potential employees.

Every Oracle employee attends an orientation session, which covers the concepts of workplace diversity and a harassment-free workplace. The managers are all required to take training in "Targeted Selection," which covers behaviour-based hiring techniques and minimizes interviewer bias by teaching them to ask questions that focus on meeting the requirements of the job. The company's managers are also responsible for ensuring that all efforts are being made to recruit and hire the best qualified people, reflecting the diversity of their regions. To make the broadest range of people aware of upcoming vacancies, Oracle has worked with outreach agencies from across the country. Many such agencies have links from their sites to Oracle's Career Opportunities website.

Oracle's main offices are accessible to persons with disabilities. These buildings are equipped with specially designed doorways, work spaces, hallways, washrooms, doors, elevators, drinking fountains, and fire-escape plans to accommodate the needs of persons with disabilities. The company has also implemented a very progressive telecommuting program, whereby qualified employees are able to perform their business duties from home. This program provides easier accessibility and increased productivity for many employees with disabilities. It also provides more flexibility to employees who might otherwise have to travel a great distance to and from work.

SOURCE: Adapted from Oracle Corporation Canada Limited. Ontario Ministry of Citizenship, *Creating a Diverse Workforce at Every Level,* February 15, 2001, http://www.equalopportunity.on.ca/eng_g/subject/index.asp?action=search_7&file_id=13099. © Queen's Printer for Ontario, 2001. Reproduced with permission.

Knowledge Management: Challenges and Opportunities

Explain the challenges from and opportunities for effective knowledge management in organizations.

Sociocultural expectations, economic pressures, and an explosion in information and information-processing technology have led to increasing demands for effective knowledge management within and between organizations. Organizations need to manage the accelerating demands for knowledge acquisition, transfer, and retention. Intellectual capital is a key driver of innovation and competitive advantage in today's knowledge-based economy, but organizations and managers have been finding it difficult to leverage the knowledge assets of their firms because of "misguided approaches and hurried excitement," as well as a recognition that improved information technology is not necessarily the solution and cannot replicate or replace the deep tacit knowledge held by humans.[88]

Knowledge management (KM) is defined as a conscious strategy of getting the right knowledge to the right people at the right time and helping people share and put information into action in ways that strive to improve organizational performance.[89] **Tacit knowledge** is knowledge that resides within an individual and is built through years of experience.[90] As baby boomers begin to retire, organizations face the challenge of capturing and transferring the wisdom that people with tacit knowledge have acquired over the years.[91] The OB elements that have been found to lead to effective KM include an organizational culture that promotes the free flow of information among employees and across department lines as well as the presence of several mediums through which employees can transfer their knowledge. In addition, effective KM requires that employees not be overloaded with information that does not affect them or is not relevant to what they do.[92] In recent years, progressive organizations have been experimenting with new ways to encourage the social construction of knowledge between their

knowledge management (KM)
A conscious strategy of getting the right knowledge to the right people at the right time and helping people share and put information into action in ways that strive to improve organizational performance.

tacit knowledge
Knowledge that resides within an individual.

members. Socially constructed models of knowledge management view knowledge as linked with social and learning processes through both explicit programs as well as informal social interaction.[93] Thus, the trend is to think not so much about who works for whom, but rather who *needs* to work with whom, so that the right knowledge gets shared with the right people at the right time.[94] This view of knowledge acquisition and transfer gives credence to the formal/informal model of organizations as well as the new paradigms that view organizations as chaotic, complex adaptive systems, as discussed earlier in the chapter.

communities of practice (CoP)
Groups of people informally bound together by shared expertise and passion for joint enterprise.

Recent innovations such as **communities of practice (CoP),** which are groups of people informally bound together by shared expertise and passion for joint enterprise, have been implemented.[95] These communities of practice help drive strategy, sometimes start new lines of business, and are ideal forums for sharing and spreading best practice across the company.[96] Also, information technology scholars are beginning to shift their attention from "individual" to "social" software, defined as programs that enable a group of people to accomplish common goals. Scholars at MIT have gone so far as to develop mobile phone applications that facilitate interactions among nearby previously unacquainted colleagues with similar interests![97]

IMPLICATIONS FOR ORGANIZATIONAL EFFECTIVENESS

Organizations face many challenges and opportunities that did not exist 50 years ago. Organization leaders therefore expect their managers at all levels to use OB knowledge and skills to develop their human capital. Today, leaders are responsible for generating environmental and societal benefits in addition to economic ones, and for governing responsibility and ethically in a global business climate that is highly competitive, turbulent, and diverse. Successful organizations gain and maintain competitive advantage by investing in, developing, and measuring the efficiency, effectiveness, and impact of initiatives that strengthen their human capital. They actively manage workforce diversity and capture the significant opportunities that can be exploited from valuing employees of different ages, gender, race, ethnicity, culture, ability, and sexual orientation.

Contemporary models of how organizations actually function, such as the open systems model, the formal/informal model, and the model of the organization as a complex adaptive system, have informed leaders about the importance of paying close and ongoing attention to the relevant sectors of the organization's task environment and to ensure that the subsystems are working well together. The exploding information demands on organizations and their members, combined with the expected loss of wisdom that will occur when the baby boom generation retires, has added further support for the need to better knowledge management (KM) vehicles. These KM vehicles include those required for formal knowledge acquisition, transfer, and retention as well as the creation of informal "spaces" or knowledge-sharing communities so that the right knowledge gets shared with the right people at the right time.

Chapter Summary

1. Organizational behaviour (OB) is a field of study that seeks to understand, explain, predict, and change human behaviour, both individual and collective, in the organizational context, and it is studied at four different levels. Organizational behaviour is an applied behavioural science and has grown out of contributions from numerous earlier fields of study such as psychology, sociology, engineering, anthropology, and management.
2. *Organizations* are defined as groups of people who work interdependently toward some common purpose. The job of a manager is a complex one and involves a number of diverse roles, which encompass tasks related to the management of people as well as those related to the management of information, material, and financial resources. Managerial work includes planning, organizing, leading, and controlling. *Planning* involves defining goals that flow from the business strategy, setting performance objectives, and creating action plans. *Organizing* includes dividing up the tasks and establishing work roles or departments in order to carry out the plans. *Leading* involves communicating, motivating, and managing conflict. Finally, *controlling* includes monitoring financial and human performance.
3. There are at least three benefits to studying OB. First, OB concepts and skills help managers improve their company's bottom line. Second, mastering OB enables managers to become more effective at influencing others, both as formal managers and when they need to influence people over whom they have little or no control. Third, OB knowledge can lead to a specialization in the field of human resources management in the workplace, as well as graduate studies in OB or human resources management.
4. The open systems framework and the GHOST model of the internal organization helps us understand the bigger picture of organizations, how the various parts both affect and are affected by each other, and how the organization interacts with its external task environment. The model is examined by exploring (1) the external task environment; (2) the organizational input; (3) the internal organization itself, which consists of the goals (G), human resources (H), organizational structure (OS), and technology (T); (4) the organizational outputs; and finally, (5) the feedback processes.
5. A second theoretical model of an organization stresses that it is what you do not see (below the surface) that is most influential. This model views the organization as consisting of two distinct dimensions: the formal organization, which is more observable, and the informal organization, which is less observable. New organizational paradigms build on the informal model of an organization, viewing it as a system of fields in "organized chaos" or as a complex adaptive system that is influenced by transforming exchanges.
6. Corporate governance is the system of control and performance monitoring of top management, and demands for more accountability in this area are increasing in the face of recent scandals. Organizations are now being evaluated on their corporate social responsibility (CSR), which is the obligation of a firm to use its economic, legal, ethical, and philanthropic resources in ways that benefit the society at large and to improve the welfare of society at large, independent of direct gains of the company. Firms are also being scrutinized more closely in terms of their ethical behaviour and triple bottom line.
7. Globalization and heightened competition present opportunities and challenges and have forced transnational and local organizations to think globally and to become more quality- and customer-focused.
8. Workplace diversity is an asset when it is managed, but it can also pose management challenges. Diversity in culture, age, gender, physical/mental disabilities, sexual orientation, and race/ethnicity are explored in the context of the challenges and opportunities.
9. Effective knowledge management (KM) is becoming increasingly important as the quantity of information explodes and more vehicles are needed for the acquisition, retention, and sharing of relevant and tacit knowledge.

Key Terms

anthropology (p. 6)
behavioural science (p. 7)
boundary-spanning roles (p. 12)
communities of practice (CoP) (p. 26)
corporate governance (p. 19)
corporate social responsibility (CSR) (p. 19)
disability (p. 23)
diversity (p. 22)
engineering (p. 5)
ethical behaviour (p. 19)
external task environment (p. 12)
feedback (p. 15)
formal organization (p. 15)
glass ceiling (p. 23)
goals (G) (p. 14)
Hawthorne studies (p. 5)
human capital (p. 7)
human resources (H) (p. 14)
informal organization (p. 16)
knowledge management (KM) (p. 25)
management (p. 6)
managers (p. 6)
organizational behaviour (p. 4)

organizational culture (p. 16)
organizational inputs (p. 12)
organizational outputs (p. 15)
organizational structure (OS) (p. 14)
organizations (p. 6)
psychology (p. 5)
scientific management (p. 5)
sociology (p. 5)
tacit knowledge (p. 25)
technology (T) (p. 15)
total quality management (TQM) (p. 21)
transnational organization (p. 21)
triple bottom line (p. 19)

Review Questions

1. What are some of the scientific disciplines from which organizational behaviour has emerged as a distinct field of study?
2. Argue that effectively managing organizational behaviour requires more than common sense.
3. What is the value of viewing an organization using an open systems framework?
4. What are the main functions of a manager and why is it said that the job of a contemporary manager is chaotic?
5. Explain all the elements of the GHOST model of the internal organization.
6. What types of diversity exist in the Canadian workforce and why is it important for managers to value and manage diversity effectively?
7. What is meant by knowledge management?

Discussion and Communication Questions

1. How do the formal aspects of your work environment affect you? What informal aspects of your work environment are important?
2. How can managers be encouraged to develop global thinking? How can managers dispel stereotypes about other cultures?
3. (*Communication question*) Create a CSR statement for this organizational behaviour class.

Ethics Questions

1. Is it ethical to use scientific knowledge to influence people toward achieving one's own objectives? Do you think that organizational behaviour could be considered to be a tool for manipulation and exploitation by people in positions of power?
2. Suppose you would be able to beat the competition if you presented a prospective customer with negative information about the competition's quality program. Should you provide the information? Assume that the information relates to safety. Would that make a difference in whether you told the customer?
3. What are some of the concerns that a person with AIDS would have about his or her job? What are some of the fears that co-workers would have? How can a manager balance these two sets of concerns?

Application & Analysis

EXPERIENTIAL EXERCISE 1.1: MY ABSOLUTE WORST JOB

Purpose: To explore the common characteristics of best versus worst jobs and their impact on morale and productivity

Group size: Dyads

Time required: 30–40 minutes

Materials needed: None

Instructions:

1. Write answers to the following questions:
   What was the worst job you ever had? Describe the following:
   a. The type of work you did
   b. Your boss
   c. What made the job so bad
   d. The organization and its policies
   e. Your co-workers

   What is your dream job?

2. Individuals share: Find someone you do not know, and share your responses.

3. Dyads share: Get together with another dyad (preferably new people). Partner "A" of one dyad introduces partner "B" to the other dyad, then "B" introduces "A." The same process is followed by the other dyad. The introduction should follow this format: "*This is Mary Cullen. Her very worst job was sewing buttons in a clothing factory, and she disliked it because.... She would rather be a financial analyst.*"

4. Quartets share: Each group of four meets with another quartet and is introduced, as before.

5. Number of people in categories: Your instructor asks for a show of hands on the number of people whose worst jobs fit into the following categories:
   a. Manufacturing
   b. Sales
   c. Service
   d. Unskilled labour
   e. Skilled trades
   f. Clerical
   g. Managerial/administrative
   h. Professional

6. Group responses: Your instructor gathers data on worst jobs from each group and asks the groups to answer the following questions:
   a. What are the common characteristics of the worst jobs in your group?
   b. How did your co-workers feel about their jobs?
   c. What happens to morale and productivity when a worker hates the job?
   d. What was the difference between your own morale and productivity in your worst job versus a job you really enjoyed?
   e. Why do organizations continue to allow unpleasant working conditions to exist?

7. Group discussion: Your instructor leads a group discussion on parts (a) through (e) of Question 6.

SOURCE: D. Marcic, J. Seltzer, and P. Vaill, "My Absolute Worst Job: An Icebreaker," *Organizational Behavior: Experiences and Cases*, 6th ed. (Mason, OH: South-Western College Publishing, 2001), 9–10.

Application & Analysis

EXPERIENTIAL EXERCISE 1.2: WHAT'S CHANGING AT WORK?

Purpose: This exercise provides an opportunity to discuss changes occurring in your workplace or university. These changes may be for the better or the worse. However, rather than evaluating whether they are good or bad changes, begin by simply identifying the changes that are occurring. Later you can evaluate whether they are good or bad.

Group size: 4–6

Time required: 30 minutes

Materials needed: None

Instructions:

Step 1. The class forms into groups of approximately six members each. Each group elects a spokesperson and answers the following questions. The group should spend at least five minutes on each question. Make sure that each member of the group makes a contribution to each question. The spokesperson for each group should be ready to share the group's collective responses to these questions:

a. *What are the changes occurring in your workplace and university?* Members should focus both on internal changes, such as reorganizations, and on external changes, such as new customers or competitors. Develop a list of the changes discussed in your group.

b. *What are the forces that are driving the changes?* To answer this question, look for the causes of the changes that members of the group are observing. For example, a reorganization may be caused by new business opportunities, by new technologies, or by a combination of factors.

c. *What signs of resistance to change do you see?* Change is not always easy for people or organizations. Do you see signs of resistance, such as frustration, anger, increased absences, or other forms of discomfort with the changes you observe?

Step 2. Once you have answered the three questions in Step 1, your group needs to spend some time evaluating whether these changes are good or bad. Decide whether each change on the list developed in Step 1(a) is a good or bad change. In addition, answer the question "Why?" That is, why is this change good? Why is that change bad?

Step 3. Each group shares the results of its answers to the questions in Step 1 and its evaluation of the changes completed in Step 2. Cross-team questions and discussion follow.

Step 4. Your instructor may allow a few minutes at the end of the class period to comment on his or her perceptions of changes occurring within the university or businesses with which he or she is familiar.

Application, Analysis & Synthesis

CASE: CANDYCO

CandyCo has been in business since 1950, producing a wide array of candy products. At any one time, CandyCo employs 1000–1100 people, three-quarters of whom work in manufacturing. Most of these employees work shifts, generally day or evening. In addition there is a roster of part-time employees who are called in to handle peak production requirements. The rest are employed in sales and marketing (100), building and site maintenance (20), quality control and food safety (20), human resources (15), and finance (20). Current production facilities are located in Greenville, Ontario, and a small neighbouring rural community. There are few other employers in the area, and many local family members have found both full- and part-time employment with the company. In some cases, extended families are working at CandyCo.

CandyCo's mission is to produce European-quality candy products that exceed other locally produced ones for taste and price. The growth of product lines, distribution channels, and international competition wins reflect a continued pattern of success over the long term. The last competition win was two years ago for its chocolate liqueur assortment.

The Crocker family has owned the company since the beginning. The majority shareholders are currently two members of the founder's family whose only roles are on the board of directors. The president, George Frank, is related to them by marriage and has spent his entire career with CandyCo, working his way up to the top job from his first summer job in the shipping and receiving department. Because of stock options he personally owns 5 percent of the company stock and is eligible to purchase another 5 percent before he retires.

The day-to-day running of the company is left to the executive team. As long as the company is making money and meets all legal requirements, the shareholders/Crocker family members are happy with things the way they are. They do not involve themselves in executive team decisions. At each quarterly meeting of the board of directors, they generally give the leadership team "pats on the back" and tell them to keep up the good work.

A year and a half ago, the board of directors approved the allocation of funds to build a new, state-of-the-art manufacturing facility on industrial land next to the current primary production plant and head office. The building is well underway, and employees have been speculating about what will happen to jobs in the new plant as well as the existing facilities. There is some concern that automation may mean fewer jobs.

CandyCo is regarded as a good corporate citizen in the community. They sponsor children's sports teams and support local charities. Pay is competitive with other candy manufacturers and health and dental benefits are provided for all full-time employees. Last year an incentive bonus plan was implemented for employees based on divisional results and meeting individual sales targets for those in sales. In addition, employees who have been with the company for five years are eligible to buy shares, but few have done so, except for those in senior roles who have a stock matching plan as part of their benefits.

There are four product divisions: chocolate, hard candy, chewy candy, and special occasion specialties (SOS). Each has its own manufacturing, marketing, and sales teams led by assistant vice presidents or directors reporting to the VPs. The salespeople are spread across the country and come to head office once a quarter to meet with their divisional counterparts, learn about new products, review sales goals and sales results, and share sales tips. These meetings are held at the local golf and country club. Most of the sales team members are only vaguely familiar with the sales representatives of the other divisions as they seldom interact, even though they visit the same group of customers. Employees in other departments view these meetings as parties for the "chosen few" and a waste of time and money: "If they can spend money on that, why can't they send some more our way?"

The executive team is made up of people who have advanced through the ranks within the company as well as two people who were recruited from outside: the VP of SOS, Stephane Dubois, and the VP of Finance, Veronica Chang. Both of the newcomers have been with the organization less than one year. They are considered industry "stars." The president is hoping for one of them to become president when he retires in two years and is having ongoing discussions with the VP of HR, Reena Patel, about how to make the transition a smooth one. All the other VPs are somewhat aware of the succession plan but there is a lack of clarity about the details. Reena has suggested that the details be shared at the next executive team meeting to eliminate the speculation and start to build consensus about the future.

In the past three months it has become increasingly obvious that there is conflict between the SOS division and the other product divisions. Stephane angrily walked out of the last executive team meeting. "I am not going to put up with all of the whining you are doing about my sales people stepping on your toes with the distributors as special occasions draw close. If your divisions can't stand the heat, you should get away from the fire. My team and I are winners and intend to stay that way, whether you like it or not. In my previous organization, I had the best results and that is why I was hired here: to make a big impact on the marketplace. We're doing that."

After Stephane left, the VP of chocolate, Sandra Lewis, continued to complain about reduced sales in her division and the negative effect this could have on her and her employees' quarterly bonuses. "It seems like the only division that gets any attention around here is SOS. My clients tell me they have no time for us. They've already talked to SOS." The hard candy and chewy candy VPs, Lorne and Vern, admitted they were concerned about their employees' bonuses as well as their own and that they were tired of playing second fiddle to SOS. George commented, "Don't worry about it. He's the new kid on the block and is just trying to prove himself. It will all settle down in time. He's a good guy with great skills and a wonderful network of contacts. As a matter of fact, he introduced me to some potential clients just last week. Because he speaks excellent French he is opening up new markets for us."

The VP finance confirmed that lately overall sales revenues have taken a serious drop, the cost of supplies and utilities have risen, and further noted that competitors are doing very well: "At the confectionery conference last week I spoke with the finance people from four other candy manufacturers. They said that that despite the intense competition and corporate mergers that have taken place, they're seeing increased sales, cash flow, and profits on their existing lines as well as their new sugar-free goods. All their market segments are growing. Louis from Bon-Bon Confectionary Products said they have had to put in extra production runs for some of their lines. The other finance folks seemed to think that, despite the interest in healthy snacks, people still want to have exceptional sweet treats and are willing to pay for them. My concern is that our overall numbers don't seem to be tracking upward the same way theirs are. As a matter of fact, ours are dropping, except for SOS, and we've got to do something about it." She also added that this drop is an even greater concern since there has been money invested in the construction of the new manufacturing plant. Revenues are not meeting budgeted levels and the amounts going into the construction project have seriously affected overall cash flow, as contractors are demanding regular installment payments for work done.

Veronica has spoken privately with Reena, VP of Human Resources, over lunch about some of her frustrations. In her previous organization, there was more discussion at the executive team level of overall concerns and trends. "I've got the current numbers to show the declines as well as some ideas to suggest how we could get back on track. I need some input from the whole executive team about how we should proceed." Reena said she needed some input also and that they should raise these concerns at the next executive team meeting. Reena confirmed that her department has been receiving questions and complaints about the way the company is now operating from employees in many departments. "People are worried about job security once the new plant is completed and are asking what will happen to their families if there is less work because of automation. People in shipping and receiving have complained about the number of packages of promotional items that keep arriving for the offsite meetings held for the sales teams. They want to know why the sales folks spend big bucks on golf shirts, gym bags, fancy jackets, and cases of wine."

Four long-service production line employees have complained about the stock option program, asking why only the senior members of staff get company matching. "We work harder than them, put in overtime when asked, and what do we get for it? Nothing! We suggest improvements and no one listens to us. No one asked for our ideas on the setup of the new plant, and we could make good suggestions. It's all about being a boss or in sales." They said they came to her as representatives of a larger group of employees. "We need to deal with these complaints sooner rather than later. If we don't address some of these issues fast, we will have bigger problems with staff morale and productivity." George commented: "I haven't had anybody complain to me. People tell me they liked the staff picnic your people organized. In fact, I think employees are pretty happy." There was no agreement to investigate further.

In brief private meetings with each of the executive team members you have learned that they dread the twice-monthly meetings. They don't think these meetings are productive or deal with the "real" issues, even though only one has specifically said what the "real" issues are from his or her perspective. The two newest members say that they have just been left to sink or swim so they are doing the best they can to try to fit in and be productive. Stephane said, "This is such a tiny town mentality here. It drives me nuts. They think they can keep doing things the old way. If I were running this company, we'd do some overall goal setting, restructure to capitalize on the sales teams, replace some of the executives, focus on important market segments, and listen to what our finance and human resources people have to say. They know the numbers, the people, and how to get the best results. I'm running full steam ahead and am beating my targets. It's been frustrating, not knowing who I can trust to actually help me out. Everyone is concerned about his or her own division."

The president has said he feels like he's refereeing a game in which he doesn't know the rules and cannot understand why the executives can't just get along and keep the company on track. "They are all grownups and I know they each know their stuff, so I don't see what the problem is."

1. What elements of CandyCo's task environment should they be paying attention to?
2. Use the GHOST model to describe CandyCo's internal organization.
3. What evidence is there to suggest that an informal organization exists at CandyCo?

EXHIBIT 1.8

CandyCo Organizational Chart

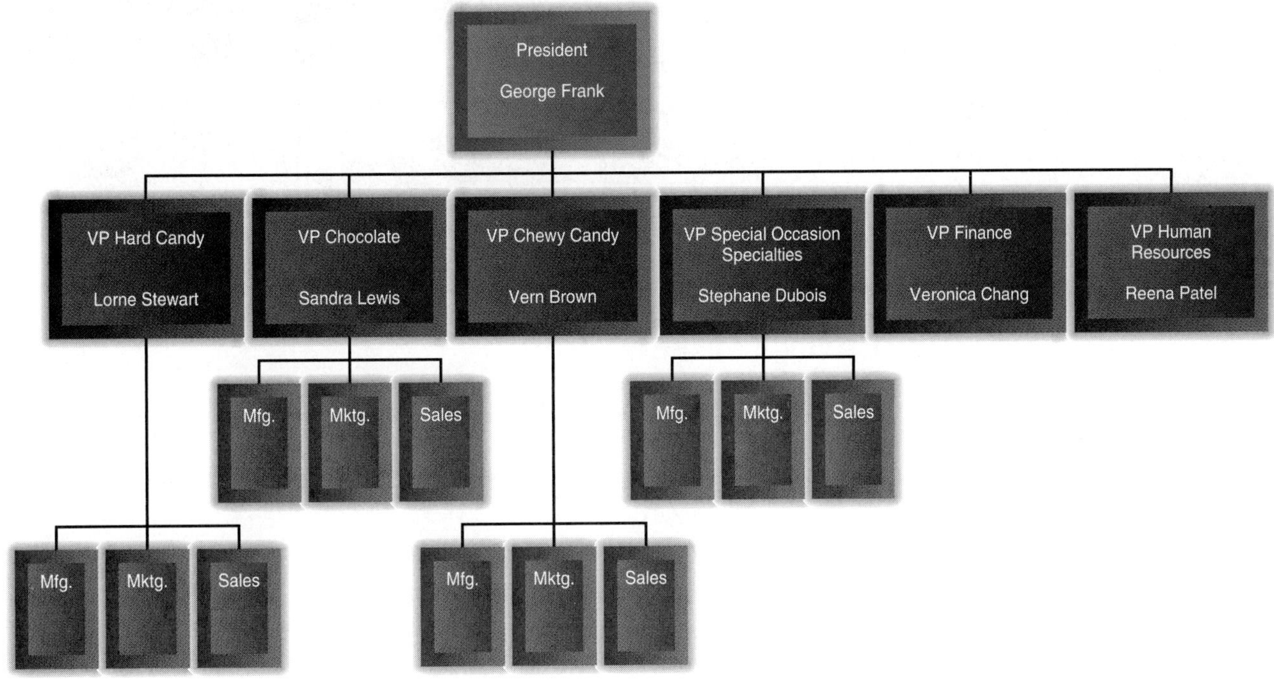

Scoring Instructions for Self-Assessments

Self-Assessment 1.1: Chaos and the Manager's Job

Give yourself

- 4 points for each A
- 3 points for each B
- 2 points for each C
- 1 point for each D
- 0 points for each E

Compute the total, divide by 24, and round to one decimal place.

Values, Ethics

chapter two

LEARNING OBJECTIVES

By the end of this chapter, you will be able to do the following:

1. Explain why it is important for organizations to create a positive workplace environment.
2. Explain what a positive work environment looks like and the various elements that organizations must consider.
3. Describe what attitudes are and discuss the factors that influence the relationship between attitudes and behaviour.
4. Define the work-related attitudes of job satisfaction, organizational commitment, and employee engagement.
5. Explain the individual and organizational outcomes that can result when organizations are not viewed as a positive place to work.
6. Distinguish between different types of values and describe the factors that influence these values.
7. Describe a model of the individual and organizational influences on ethical behaviour and how locus of control, Machiavellianism, and cognitive moral development and value systems affect ethical behaviour.

learning about the context

Dofasco Inc.—'Our Product Is Steel, Our Strength Is People'

"Our strength is people" is not just a slogan; it is a core value, a guiding principle that makes Dofasco a thriving business, a company that time and time again has been hailed as one of the best employers to work for in Canada.[1]

Dofasco Inc. is a Canadian steel producer that employs over 7200 people at its main steelmaking operations, located on 730 acres in Hamilton, Ontario. The non-organized company is North America's most successful steelmaker and a global steel industry leader. Since 1990, Dofasco has increased its productivity by 50 percent, about twice the rate of the Canadian manufacturing sector, and has less than 1 percent employee turnover.[2] For the third consecutive year Dofasco has been listed in the ***Report on Business Magazine*** as one of the 50 Best Employers in Canada. Furthermore, it has been recognized as one of Canada's top 100 employers by ***Maclean's*** magazine and was awarded the 2002 Healthy Workplace Award from the National Quality Institute for the company's commitment to the health, safety, and well-being of employees.[3]

In an industry that has been severely challenged by globalization, how does a company like Dofasco do it? What differentiates this company? Dofasco values its relationships with its stakeholders—shareholders, employees, community, suppliers, and customers—respecting the contributions these stakeholders make to its success. In a recent article in ***Fast Company,*** Dofasco was praised for its focus on the "triple bottom line"; an organization that not only shows concern for profits but also focuses on environmental and social issues.[4] In 2004, Dofasco was the only steelmaker in the world to be included on the Dow Jones Sustainability World Index. It marked the sixth consecutive year the company has been listed on the index. Taking the lead on environmental issues, Dofasco maintains an ongoing dialogue with its neighbouring community on company decisions that affect these communities and demonstrates an ongoing commitment to community leadership development, voluntarism, civic improvement, and corporate giving.

Dofasco's relationship with its employees is unique; employees feel they have a stake in the company and something to gain in preserving and expanding Dofasco. The entire company receives profit sharing based on 14 percent of the company's pretax profits. In addition to employees' base salary, Dofasco has added a variable compensation plan that is applicable to all employees. Decision making has been placed in the hands of the employees, and the organization has many cross-functional teams that take responsibility for cross-functional areas such as quality. The company offers progressive training programs and has invested more than $15 million a year to further develop and enhance the skills of Dofasco people. It provides a scholarship program and has onsite fitness facilities that are free to employees.[5]

What makes Dofasco a positive place to work? It is this unique relationship with employees; it is about building a relationship based on trust and respect, high expectations, shared responsibility, shared rewards, and treating individuals equitably and with dignity. Employees at Dofasco feel a sense of pride in working at this company; they understand how they can contribute and that they are appreciated and valued. It is about nurturing this relationship and consistently demonstrating that "our strength is people."[6] A quote from former CEO John Mayberry expressed these values so clearly: "How do you get happy shareholders? Start with satisfied customers. How do you get satisfied customers? Start with happy employees."[7]

SOURCES: Dofasco home page, accessed July 17, 2004, from http://www.dofasco.ca/bins/content_page.asp; C. Dahle, "A Steelmaker's Heart of Gold: Why a 'Triple Bottom Line' Is Good Business—in One of the World's Toughest Businesses," *Fast Company*, June 2003, 46; K. Macklem, "Top 100 Employers," *Maclean's*, October 20, 2003, 28; Dahle, "A Steelmaker's Heart of Gold," 46; *Ibid*.; Dofasco home page, accessed July 17, 2004, from http://www.dofasco.ca/bins/content_page.asp?cid=2347-2350-2508; Dahle, "A Steelmaker's Heart of Gold," 46.

This chapter focuses on the individual differences that have an impact on creating a positive work environment: attitudes, values, and ethics. The first part describes what a positive environment looks like and the various elements that organizations must pay attention to if they are going to create a positive place to work. The second part discusses several work-related attitudes and the effect these attitudes can have on individual and organizational performance. The third part explores the relationship between employee values and individual perception as it relates to a positive work environment. The fourth part discusses ethics in the workplace and those factors that influence individual ethical choices. To conclude, we identify the impact these attitudes and values can have on organizational effectiveness.

Explain why it is important for organizations to create a positive workplace environment.

WHY IS IT IMPORTANT TO CREATE A POSITIVE WORK ENVIRONMENT?

Have you ever been attracted to or wanted to work for an employer that treats its employees like they are commodities? Over the past two decades the world of work has changed significantly, and our values regarding work and what we want from our work experience has changed.[1] Employees today desire a greater balance and harmony between work and personal life and are willing to give up 21 percent of their work hours and salary to achieve more balance, nearly double the amount reported just seven years ago.[2] A recent study conducted by Towers Perrin cites factors such as opportunities for advancement, work-life balance, challenging work, and a competitive health care benefits package as being important to employees. Today's employees are informed about the opportunities in the marketplace, they are loyal to themselves, individualistic in defining their employment relationships, highly mobile, and are not as concerned with developing long-term relationships with any particular employer.[3]

However, as individuals we are all different, and, depending on where we are at in our careers, our age, and our values, we place different priorities on what is important to us at different times in our relationship to the organization. For example, if you are newly married and contemplating starting a family, financial rewards may be more important to you than retirement benefits. Or if you are just starting out in your career, training and development may be more important to you than extensive employee benefits.

What is it that sets a company like Dofasco apart from other organizations? Organizations such as Dofasco recognize that organizational sustainability is not just about profits, it is about the organization's responsibility to the community in which it operates and it is about how the organization transacts business from an ethical and moral perspective.[4] These organizations take the time to understand how the world of work has changed, who their employees are, what motivates their employees, what attitudes employees hold, and what they value.[5] They are **high-performing organizations,** producing extraordinary results that extend beyond customer service and shareholder gain. They improve faster than their competition and maintain that rate while satisfying all stakeholders. These organizations are open to new ideas, consistently challenging their assumptions, scrutinizing their performance.[6] They demonstrate corporate social responsibility (CSR) using their ethical, philanthropic, legal, and economic resources in ways to benefit others. Just think about the last charity event or community award your school or an organization proudly sponsored. These organizations have adopted a triple-bottom-line attitude, resolute in their belief that a responsible corporate "citizen" cares about the impact its operations have on the environment, the community, and its people.

high-performing organizations
Organizations that produce extraordinary results and sustain this performance over time and over changing market conditions. These organizations adapt industry best practices while preserving their unique processes. They view failures as opportunities for continuous learning.

As we will read about in this chapter, a common theme that is expressed by these organizations is that they all place a high value on employee "currency." They seek individuals who are energized and capable, and in return they nurture and develop their employees. They create work environments that are positive and productive and consistently strive to manage these elements, utilizing **best practice methods** to accomplish these goals. *Best practice* is defined as the processes, practices, and systems identified in an organization that are

best practice methods
The processes, practices, and systems that an organization does particularly well and that are widely recognized as improving the organization's performance and efficiency in specific areas.

performed exceptionally well and are widely recognized as improving an organization's performance and efficiency in specific areas.[7] Typically the task of management is to find and adapt industry best practices. These organizations bring the "outside in" while maintaining their "signature processes." Signature processes are those processes that have evolved from management's values and aspirations. They embody a company's history. They are unique to that organization.[8] Think about a company where you have worked. What is it that this organization did that made you feel happy to be at work and motivated you to go the extra mile? Was it the way the managers treated the employees, or perhaps the family-like atmosphere that you really enjoyed, or was it how the organization consistently recognized your contributions? What was it that this organization did differently from all others you have worked for? What would make you want to recommend this organization to others who are looking for work? Do you think other organizations should consider emulating these "best practices"?

WHAT DOES A POSITIVE WORK ENVIRONMENT LOOK LIKE?

Explain what a positive work environment looks like and the major elements that organizations must consider.

Ever heard the expression "whistle while you work"? What does an organization need to do to make you feel this way? In the fairytale "Snow White," can you recall what the dwarfs did to make Snow White feel happy? A positive work environment can mean different things in different organizations, and it can mean different things to different people.

Each organization is unique. How organizations choose to create their own environment will be different depending on what the organization values. For example, why would one organization offer free gym memberships and another not even consider it? Why does one company provide an annual bonus plan and make this plan eligible to all employees and

EXHIBIT 2.1

Elements of a Positive Workplace

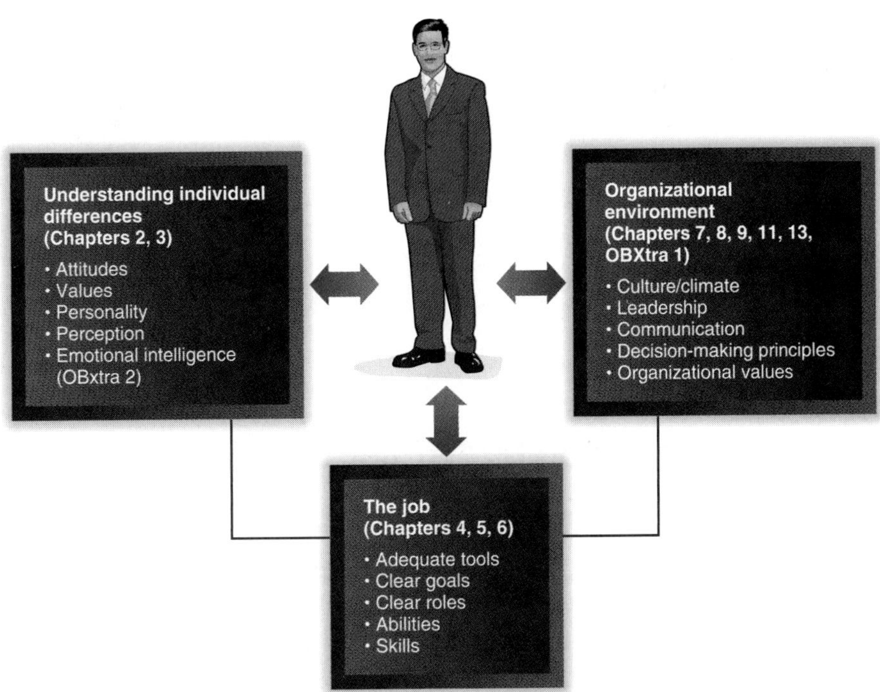

another not provide any form of recognition? But more importantly, do you even care about bonus plans or free gym memberships? Perhaps you are the kind of person who values a job with lots of variety and the ability to work on several different projects. How would you describe your ideal "positive" environment?

There are three critical elements that all organizations must consider if they are serious about creating and sustaining a positive place to work. Exhibit 2.1 provides a framework that characterizes these elements, which take into account the organizational environment, the components of the job, and individual characteristics. Successful organizations pay attention to these elements and take time to understand the influence that they can have on the individual employee, thus optimizing the synergy between these elements to create a positive work environment.

Organizational Environment

High-performing organizations articulate who they are, what they value, where they are going, and how employees can help them get there. The culture is strong, adaptive, and strategically appropriate; leaders influence, motivate, and enable others, they create a vision and mission and help people understand what they can do to contribute. Organizational values are clear and leaders express these values in a consistent fashion, acting as role models to ensure alignment across the organization. Self-serving political behaviours are minimized. Communication is open and supports knowledge management, problem solving, and effective coordination of work. Decision making is ethical; policies, procedures, and practices are carefully designed and align to achieve organizational goals.[9] For example, the philosophy of the company you just joined is to support its communities, and employees will receive paid time off to do so. However the first time you asked your manager for some time off you received a lukewarm response. Time and time again you experienced the same response to your request. How would you feel? Over time, this lack of congruency between what you thought the values were and what the actual values are negatively affect your level of enthusiasm. The response you received was incongruent with what you expected. Interestingly, research found that the attitudes that employees develop are independent of their predispositions.[10] In this case, you entered into the organization with a positive attitude but over time your attitude changed. In the chapters that follow you will learn more about how leaders create a positive work environment.

Components of a Job

All of us would like to do a "good job," but how often is it that we are placed in a job where the roles, responsibilities, and accountabilities are unclear? Or perhaps you have worked hard to upgrade your skills and although you have spoken to HR and your manager, you find yourself stuck in a job that is limited in scope and does not provide you with any opportunity to use your new skills and abilities. Organizations that create positive work environments clearly articulate the purpose of the job, how the job contributes to the success of the organization, and how an individual can contribute to that success, and they effectively design the jobs to optimize employee motivation. You will learn more about how organizations manage these components in the chapters that follow.

Understanding Individual Differences

Ever heard the expression "different strokes for different folks"? Organizations need to understand the differences that their employees bring and leverage these differences. High-performing organizations do this very well. These differences reflect the attitudes employees may hold and the values that employees possess, understanding an employee's personality traits and how employees respond to situations from an emotional and ethical perspective. Reflecting on future staffing challenges, Kevin Boyce, president of Unilever Canada, highlighted the importance that organizations need to give to these individual differences: "I think companies like ourselves [Unilever] are going to have to find a new way to attract people down the road. What motivates a 21-year-old coming out of any university today is significantly different than what motivated me coming out of university."[11] In the next section we explore these individual differences with a particular focus on employee attitudes and values, continuing our examination of an individual's personality and perceptual differences in Chapter 3 and concluding with a feature section on a topic that has been identified as being highly important to an individual's business and personal success called Emotional Intelligence.

EMPLOYEE ATTITUDES

Describe what attitudes are and discuss the factors that influence the relationship between attitudes and behaviour.

In the late 1990s, a sagging economy and a plethora of industry consolidations drove many employers to focus on organizational efficiencies. CEOs focused on managing costs and implementing several initiatives to ensure financial viability. Gone were the days when employees were awarded large cash bonuses as recognition for a job well done! Trimming the management ranks, freezing salaries, not replacing employees who left the organization, and increasing job responsibilities were common expectations. As a result, employees felt overworked, stressed, and underappreciated. It was often heard in the corridors that "this is not the same place it used to be." An **attitude** emerged: if an individual was going to "go the extra mile" they wanted some reward; "show me the money or give me some much needed time" became the order of the day.

attitude
A psychological tendency expressed by evaluating an entity with some degree of favour or disfavour. It is the basis of an evaluative response to a particular situation, event, or issue.

As we can see from this example, attitudes help form an evaluative response to a particular situation, event, or issue. They are a psychological tendency expressed by evaluating an entity with some degree of favour or disfavour. We respond favourably or unfavourably toward many things: animals, co-workers, our own appearance, and politics. A workplace can induce a good or bad attitude amongst employees, and a poor attitude can indeed affect economic outcomes. In a study that examined the attitudes of workers at different bank branches, researchers found that once employees were hired they adopted the favourable or unfavourable attitude exhibited by the branch before they arrived. Additionally, they found that those branches exhibiting less favourable attitudes showed a higher incidence of turnover, lower level of sales, and lower rate of sales growth. Researchers concluded that there are happy and unhappy workplaces as well as happy and unhappy workers.[12]

Attitudes are learned. Our responses to people and issues evolve over time. Two major influences on attitudes are direct experience and social learning. Direct experience with an object or person is a powerful influence on attitudes. How do you know that you like biology or dislike math? You have probably formed these attitudes from experience in studying the subjects. Research has shown that attitudes that are derived from direct experience are stronger, held more confidently, and more resistant to change than attitudes formed through indirect experience.[13] One reason attitudes derived from direct experience are so powerful is their availability. This means that the attitudes are easily accessed and are active in our cognitive processes.[14] When attitudes are available, we can call them quickly into consciousness. Attitudes that are not learned from direct experience are not as available, so we do not recall them as easily. In social learning, the family, peer groups, religious organizations, and culture shape an individual's attitudes in an indirect manner.[15] Children learn to adopt certain attitudes by the reinforcement they are given by their parents when they display behaviours that reflect an appropriate attitude. This is evident when very young children express political preferences similar to their parents'. Peer pressure moulds attitudes through group acceptance of individuals who express popular attitudes and through sanctions, such as exclusion from the group, placed on individuals who espouse unpopular attitudes. Substantial social learning occurs through modelling, in which individuals acquire attitudes by merely observing others. After overhearing other individuals expressing an opinion or watching them engaging in a behaviour that reflects an attitude, the observer adopts the attitude.

Culture also plays a definitive role in attitude development. Consider, for example, the contrast in the North American and European attitudes toward vacation and leisure. The typical vacation in North America is two weeks, and some workers do not use all of their vacation time. In Europe, the norm is longer vacations; and in some countries, a holiday means everyone taking a month off. Europeans value work-life balance. This attitude is expressed by providing longer vacations believed to be important to health and performance.

Factors That Influence the Relationship between Attitude and Behaviour

Several factors can influence the relationship between attitudes and behaviour. These factors are attitude relevance, timing of measurement, personality factors, and social constraints.

Attitudes that address an issue in which we have some self-interest are more relevant for us, and our subsequent behaviour is consistent with our expressed attitude.[16] Suppose there is a proposal to raise income taxes for those who earn $150 000 or more. If you are a student, you may not find the issue of great personal relevance. Individuals in that income bracket, however, might find it highly relevant; their attitude toward the issue would be strongly predictive of whether they would vote for the tax increase.

The timing of the measurement can also affect the relationship; the shorter the time between the attitude measurement and the observed behaviour, the stronger the relationship. For example, voter preference polls taken close to an election are more accurate than earlier polls.

Personality factors also influence the attitude–behaviour link. One personality disposition that affects the consistency between attitudes and behaviour is the extent to which people base their behaviour on cues from others and situations, called self-monitoring. Low self-monitors rely on their internal states when making decisions about behaviour, while high self-monitors are more responsive to situational cues. Low self-monitors therefore display greater correspondence between their attitudes and behaviours.[17] High self-monitors may display little correspondence between their attitudes and behaviours because they behave according to signals from others and from the environment. Another trait that is highly correlated to attitude is agreeableness. The more easy-going you are, the more positive an attitude you will have.[18]

Social constraints affect the relationship between attitudes and behaviour. The social context provides information about acceptable attitudes and behaviour. New employees in an organization, for example, are exposed to the attitudes of their work group. Suppose a newcomer from Afghanistan holds a negative attitude toward women in management because in his country the prevailing attitude is that women should not be in positions of power. He sees, however, that his work group members respond positively to their female supervisor. His own behaviour may therefore be compliant because of social constraints. This behaviour is inconsistent with his attitude and cultural belief system. So therefore, social constraints can in certain instances override cultural belief systems.

Take a look at Organizational Reality 2.1 to learn more about the attitudes expressed by Four Seasons Hotel and what makes this organization one of the top 100 best companies to work for.

Define the work-related attitudes of job satisfaction, organizational commitment, and employee engagement.

Work-Related Attitudes

Attitudes are an integral part of the world of work. Three work-related attitudes that are commonly used to describe an employee's level of positive feeling toward an organization are job satisfaction, organizational commitment, and employee engagement. See Exhibit 2.2.

organizational reality 2.1

"The People at Four Seasons Set the Experience Apart"

For the seventh year in a row, Four Seasons Hotels and Resorts has been named in *Fortune Magazine*'s list of 100 best companies to work for. Four Seasons, the world's most honoured hotel company, has won awards for employee satisfaction and repeatedly receives unprecedented recognition and accolades worldwide for its positive employee practices and exceptional customer service. It has the lowest employee turnover rate in the industry and ranks the highest in customer loyalty.

What is it about this company that makes it so successful? Christopher Hart, regional VP and general manager of Four Seasons Hotel Toronto, points to the quality of service that Four Seasons provides to its customers. "This service is delivered by our employees; it is the employees who set this experience apart! We can't have good service if we don't have happy, productive, and positive employees; employees who are dedicated, committed, and inspired to deliver exceptional guest service."

Creating a positive environment is ingrained in the culture of Four Seasons. The company has always focused on its employees. For Four Seasons, this means establishing a mission statement based on the Golden Rule: Do unto others as you would have them do unto you. "We treat our employees with the same level of respect that they in turn give to our guests' comments," says Isadore Sharp, chairman and CEO of Four Seasons Hotels and Resorts.

From the initial recruitment, where the company screens for the skills and values that are important to developing its employees through training and mentoring programs, the company is constantly nurturing its employees so that they can be the best they can be, so that they can deliver exceptional service.

Employees' opinions are valued, and Four Seasons listens to what is important to employees. Every 12 months each hotel/resort conducts an opinion survey worldwide with their managers and every 18 months they conduct employee opinion surveys. On a more personal level, the general managers of various hotels hold informal meetings every month with a representative from different departments to ask for their opinions. These meetings are a chance for employees to talk about basic problems and give the general managers a chance to address the issues right away. "It makes sure we are connected, it is a safety valve, a chance to respond quickly," says Hart.

Employees are recognized and rewarded for their work. There are ample career opportunities available worldwide. All positions are posted and the company offers numerous training programs in support of employee development. The company's benefit programs are competitive and, in addition to base salary, all managers are eligible to receive incentives based on a format that focuses on people, product, and profit; as well, most hotels offer an employee profit-sharing plan. One of the perks of working for Four Seasons is that employees get to stay free at Four Seasons Hotels worldwide after a period of service. In the employee corridor, one can see the pictures of employees of the month, a recognition ritual that is highly valued.

Social responsibility is also an important value. Four Seasons is a major supporter of the Terry Fox Run, which takes place in Canada and many countries around the world. The Run raises funds for cancer research, and the company has continuously demonstrated its support for the community.

What is it that makes Four Seasons a positive place to work? Hart sums it up by saying, "Our greatest asset is our people. They are the key to our success. We treat people with dignity and respect and this is reflected in their exceptional service delivery. It is this quality that is important to our guests and the degree to which we can provide and evolve it worldwide is also the degree to which we can differentiate ourselves and stay ahead of the rest. Employees stay because of the culture and a feeling if you do a good job here you can grow. But it is a never-ending process, and a continual quest to improve."

SOURCES: Christopher Hart (regional VP and general manager, Four Seasons Hotel), interview with Julie Bulmash, August 24, 2004; Four Seasons Hotels and Resorts, "About Us," accessed August 24, 2004, from http://www.fourseasons.com/about_us/company_information/about_us_10.html; E. A. Locke, "The Nature and Causes of Job Satisfaction," in *Handbook of Industrial and Organizational Psychology*, ed. M. Dunnette (Chicago: Rand McNally, 1976).

EXHIBIT 2.2

Work-Related Attitudes

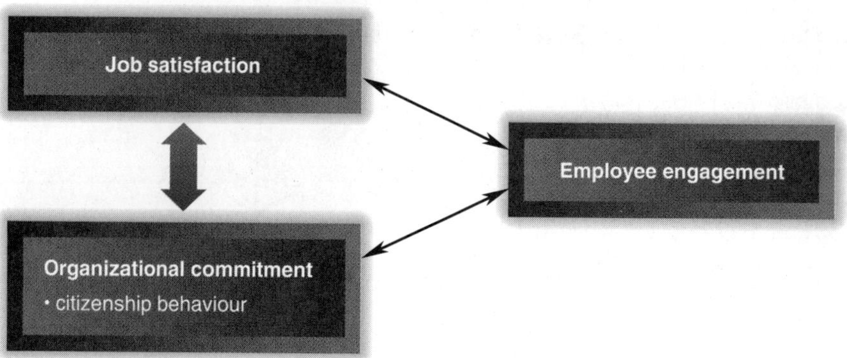

Job Satisfaction

job satisfaction
A pleasurable or positive emotional state resulting from the appraisal of one's job or job experiences.

Job satisfaction is a pleasurable or positive emotional state resulting from the appraisal of one's job or job experiences.[19] It has been treated both as a general attitude and as satisfaction with five specific dimensions of the job: pay, the work itself, promotion opportunities, supervision, and co-workers.[20]

An individual may hold different attitudes toward various aspects of the job. What makes employees want to stay at a company and what makes others want to leave?

In a recent World at Work survey on job satisfaction, 89 percent of those surveyed said they were satisfied or somewhat satisfied with their current job. The top five reasons for staying in a job are: like the work (78 percent), like the co-workers (68 percent), like the mission and activities of the company (61 percent), learning a lot (57 percent), and salary satisfaction (53 percent). So if these are the reasons why employees would want to stay, the absence of these opportunities contributes to an employee's level of dissatisfaction.

Dissatisfaction can also occur if employees' expectations when hired are not met. All employees develop a certain set of beliefs about the terms of the exchange agreement regarding what they will do and what the organization will provide. This is called a psychological contract. Unlike formal employment agreements, the psychological contract is inherently perceptual. How one person interprets the terms and conditions of the employment relationship may not be shared by the other.[21] Dissatisfaction can occur when an employee perceives that the organization has violated the contract by failing to fulfill one or more of its obligations.[22] For example, you expected to receive an annual increase based on your performance but to your surprise the company does not provide annual increases. How might this affect your level of satisfaction?

If you are dissatisfied, can a potential employer entice you to leave your current employment? A recent World at Work survey identified the five most appealing offers another employer can make to entice an employee: promotion, profit sharing or stock options, fewer work hours, opportunity to work from home one day a week, and different job responsibilities.[23] Do any of these options appeal to you?

Consider you own level of job satisfaction. Complete Self-Assessment 2.1 and assess your level.

The Impact of Culture on Job Satisfaction

Like all attitudes, job satisfaction is influenced by culture. Operating in a global environment necessitates that managers understand how these attitudes can influence an employee's behaviour.

Employees from different cultures may have differing expectations of their jobs. Intrinsic job characteristics and job satisfaction is stronger in rich countries, countries

Knowledge & Application

SELF-ASSESSMENT 2.1 ASSESS YOUR JOB SATISFACTION

Think of the job you have now or a job you've had in the past. Indicate how satisfied you are with each aspect of your job below, using the following scale:

1 = Extremely dissatisfied
2 = Dissatisfied
3 = Slightly dissatisfied
4 = Neutral
5 = Slightly satisfied
6 = Satisfied
7 = Extremely satisfied

1. The amount of job security I have.
2. The amount of pay and fringe benefits I receive.
3. The amount of personal growth and development I get in doing my job.
4. The people I talk to and work with on my job.
5. The degree of respect and fair treatment I receive from my boss.
6. The feeling of worthwhile accomplishment I get from doing my job.
7. The chance to get to know other people while on the job.
8. The amount of support and guidance I receive from my supervisor.
9. The degree to which I am fairly paid for what I contribute to this organization.
10. The amount of independent thought and action I can exercise in my job.
11. How secure things look for me in the future in this organization.
12. The chance to help other people while at work.
13. The amount of challenge in my job.
14. The overall quality of the supervision I receive on my work.

For scoring instructions, please go to the end of the chapter, p. 70.

SOURCE: R. Hackman and G. Oldham, *Work Redesign,* pp. 284, 317. Copyright © 1980. Reprinted by permission of Prentice-Hall, Inc., Upper Saddle River, N.J.

with better governmental social welfare programs, and more individualistic countries. By contrast, extrinsic job characteristics are stronger and positively related to job satisfaction in all countries. It is the value placed on these characteristics that differentiates the level of satisfaction.[24]

In a comparison of employees in the United States and India, the factors leading to job satisfaction differed substantially. Leadership style, pay, and security influenced job satisfaction for the Americans. For the employees in India, however, recognition, innovation, and the absence of conflict led to job satisfaction.[25]

A recent Ipsos-Reid global poll found major differences in employee satisfaction around the world. Workers in Denmark are by far the happiest employees on the planet—61 percent describe themselves as very satisfied with their job. Norwegians are close, with 54 percent very satisfied, followed by Americans at 50 percent satisfied, and Canada and most Western European countries almost as high with two out of five employees describing themselves as very satisfied. At the other end of the scale were Estonia, China, Czech Republic, Ukraine, and Hungary, ranging from 6 to 11 percent of workers very satisfied with their jobs. These results point to the importance of expectations and hope as well as current economic conditions.[26] It is important for managers to understand these influences.

Ipsos

Ipsos is a leading global survey-based market research group offering a full suite of research services, guided by industry experts and bolstered by advanced analytics and methodologies in advertising, marketing, public affairs, media and customer loyalty research, as well as forecasting and modelling.
www.ipsos-na.com

Organizational Commitment

organizational commitment
The strength of an individual's identification with an organization.

Another important work attitude for managers to understand is **organizational commitment** (OC). OC is the strength of an individual's identification with an organization. It is an emotional response to a positive appraisal of the work environment. The individual identifies with the organizational goals and values and feels strongly about maintaining his or her membership in that organization.[27]

affective commitment
The type of organizational commitment that is based on an individual's desire to remain in an organization.

There are three kinds of organizational commitment: affective, continuance, and normative. **Affective commitment** encompasses loyalty and is expressed by employees showing a deep concern for the organization's welfare. It is an employee's intention to remain in an organization because of a strong desire to do so. It consists of three factors:

- A belief in the goals and values of the organization
- A willingness to put forth effort on behalf of the organization
- A desire to remain a member of the organization[28]

continuance commitment
The type of organizational commitment that is based on the fact that an individual cannot afford to leave.

normative commitment
The type of organizational commitment that is based on an individual's perceived obligation to remain with an organization.

Continuance commitment is an employee's tendency to remain in an organization because the person cannot afford to leave.[29] Sometimes, employees believe that if they leave, they will lose a great deal of their investments in time, effort, and benefits and that they cannot replace these investments. **Normative commitment** is a perceived obligation to remain with the organization. Individuals who experience normative commitment stay with the organization because they feel that they should.[30]

Certain organizational conditions encourage commitment. Participation in decision making, job security, and certain job characteristics also positively affects commitment. These job characteristics include autonomy, responsibility, and interesting work.[31] A 2002 *Globe and Mail* poll found that 79 percent of people employed by a large company agreed with this statement: "The more socially responsible my company becomes the more motivated/loyal an employee I become." The pharmaceutical company GlaxoSmith Kline reported increased motivation, productivity, and loyalty after allowing employees to choose where a portion of the corporation's donations would go.[32]

Benefitscanada
Canadian Tire, Canada's largest hard goods retailer, has over 38 000 employees across Canada. Read about the "Canadian TireWay" and how Canadian Tire has promoted employee satisfaction and loyalty since its inception at www.benefitscanada.com. To learn more about Canadian Tire, go to **http://www2.canadiantire.ca/CTenglish/vision.html.**

Several researchers have examined organizational commitment in different countries. One study of workers in Saudi Arabia found that Asians working there were more committed to the organization than were Westerners and Arab workers.[33] Another study revealed that American workers displayed higher affective commitment than did Korean and Japanese workers.[34] The reasons for these differences need to be explored.

Managers can increase affective commitment by communicating that they value employees' contributions and that they care about employees' well-being. Affective commitment also increases when the organization and employees share the same values, and when the organization emphasizes values like moral integrity, fairness, creativity, and openness.[35]

Organizational Citizenship Behaviour

organizational citizenship behaviour
Behaviour that is above and beyond the call of duty.

When employees feel a sense of commitment to an organization they often exhibit **organizational citizenship behaviour**—behaviour that is above and beyond the call of duty. When was the last time you decided to stay late at work and pitch in, knowing full well that you would not receive extra remuneration? Or perhaps you demonstrated this behaviour by joining the company after-hours softball team and proudly representing your company at a tournament.

Citizenship behaviour is especially important in team-based organizations where the influence of the group can have an impact on individual citizenship behaviour. The more the behaviour is demonstrated by the group, the more the individual will engage in this behaviour.[36] Employees at companies that engage in creating a positive work environment frequently demonstrate this behaviour. At Dofasco, employees get the opportunity to work for local fundraising campaigns. The employees are seconded to these local campaigns, where they are able to provide needed resources to their local community and are enriched by this experience.[37]

Employee Engagement

So how would you describe an employee who feels satisfied with his or her job, demonstrates commitment, and exhibits organizational citizenship behaviour? A relatively recent term, **employee engagement,** is defined as the state of emotional and intellectual involvement that employees have in their organization. Engaged employees are those who stay with the organization, feel comfortable expressing their views, and strive to achieve their best. Engaged employees are fully involved and enthusiastic about their work. In an engaged workforce, leaders listen closely to employee's ideas and concerns. These leaders are held accountable for structuring the organization so that employees' voices are heard.[38]

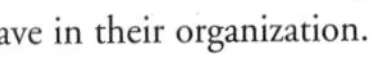

employee engagement
A state of emotional and intellectual involvement that employees have in their organization.

Engagement is closely linked to job involvement. Job involvement is defined as the degree to which the job situation is central to the person and his or her identity. However, engagement is an antecedent to job involvement in that individuals who experience deep engagement in their roles should come to identify with their jobs.

Employees who are engaged exhibit an intensive desire to be a member of the organization; they speak positively about their employer to all and perform work that contributes to business success.[39] Employee engagement can be viewed not only from an employee perspective but most importantly from an organizational perspective. It as an organizational attitude that values employees' contributions and believes that employees are an important component for ensuring organizational sustainability. It is expressed by the actions taken by these organizations. High-performing organizations are known for their engaged workforces. In fact, a recent survey on the best employers in Canada indicated that these companies all shared one major trend in common: high engagement scores. In another study, researchers found a 23 percent difference between the 50 best companies and the rest of the 128 organizations that participated in the 2003 study.[40] Take some time to read the opening vignette on Dofasco and Organizational Reality boxes 2.1 on Four Seasons Hotels and 2.3 on Blake, Cassels to see how some best-practice organizations express this attitude.

Job satisfaction, organizational commitment, and employee engagement are important work attitudes that managers can strive to improve among their employees. The majority of the evidence suggests that job satisfaction is an antecedent to organizational commitment. Increasing job satisfaction is likely to increase commitment as well. But some support exists for the role of job satisfaction as an outcome of commitment. Satisfied employees are more likely to help their co-workers, make positive comments about the company, and refrain from complaining when things at work do not go well.[41] Satisfied workers are more likely to want to give something back to the organization because they want to reciprocate their positive experiences.[42] Irrespective of which attitude comes first, the sum total of a satisfied workforce who is committed to the organization and demonstrates strong citizenship behaviour can be referred to as "engaged."(See Exhibit 2.3.)

Can we assume that a satisfied and engaged employee is also a productive employee? Next we turn our attention to the outcomes that may result from positive or negative work environment.

ATTITUDES, BEHAVIOUR, AND OUTCOMES

Explain the individual and organizational outcomes that can result when organizations are not viewed as a positive place to work.

Does this sound like an experience that you have ever had? The alarm clock rings and you pull yourself out of bed. Another day another dollar, you think to yourself. You go to work and encounter a colleague who is complaining about the extra overtime they have to put in. You take your coffee to the desk, you open your e-mail and you discover 35 messages from disgruntled customers, all of which need to be answered "as soon as possible." Your message light is flashing. You have 25 voice-mail messages, the first one from your CEO informing employees that the annual Christmas party, which you have been looking forward to, has been cancelled due to cost constraints. You sit back on your

organizational reality 2.3

Blake, Cassels and Graydon LLP

Blake, Cassels & Graydon LLP (Blakes) is a leading Canadian law firm with over 500 lawyers in nine offices located in Canada, the United States, Europe, and China. Over the years, Blakes has received prestigious international designations and rankings, including being named "Canadian Law Firm of the Year" by Chambers and Partners Legal Publishers in 2004 and the leading business law firm in Canada, according to *The International Who's Who of Business Lawyers 2003/2004*. Additionally, for two consecutive years (2003 and 2004), Blakes has been recognized in *Maclean's* magazine as one of "Canada's Top 100 Employers" and one of the Top 10 Companies for Promoting Women.

Blake, Cassels and Graydon is the only Canadian law firm to be listed in Maclean's *magazine as one of "Canada's Top 100 Employers."*

Jim Christie, the firm's chairman, says, "We work hard to make Blakes a great place to work and are pleased to be included in the list of 'Canada's Top 100 Employers.' At Blakes, our goal is to partner with our clients to provide them with all the legal services they require. We recognize that one of the best ways to achieve that goal is to invest in our lawyers and staff by providing training opportunities, recognizing achievement and creating a positive work environment."

Creating a positive work environment at Blakes involves helping lawyers and staff feel like they are part of the Blakes family. They work in teams and support each other to deliver optimum service to clients. Their views are respected, their contributions are valued, and their experience and expertise are shared with others.

Blakes lawyers teach courses at educational institutions, participate in the law school bar admission programs, write articles, and speak at seminars. Many lawyers serve as volunteer members of boards and are supporters of hospitals, educational institutions, and charitable foundations. Blakes lawyers and staff contribute to the well-being of local communities by providing support toward the annual United Way campaign, participating in Habitat for Humanity projects, and raising money for other charities through local office initiatives. The firm has a casual day one Friday each month when money raised is contributed to the charity of choice.

"Celebrations are an integral part of the Blakes culture," explains Julie Bean, chief administrative officer at Blakes. "The firm recognizes long-service employees, hosts an annual holiday Christmas staff and children's party, and organizes a family picnic in the summer. A favourite weekly ritual is Thursday's 'cookie day,' where Blakes lawyers and staff enjoy cookies and freshly brewed coffee and tea." When there is a celebration at Blakes, all office locations participate. To celebrate the opening of its Chicago and New York offices, the firm held a trivia contest, provided T-shirts to all staff, and hosted a special opening of the offices.

Open communication is a core value at Blakes. The opinions of its lawyers and staff are highly valued. From suggestions on topics they would like to learn more about at lunch-and-learn programs, to the introduction of any new programs, feedback from lawyers and staff is always solicited and new programs are piloted first before implementation.

A balance between work and life is important at Blakes. Human resources programs offered by the firm include the employee assistance program (EAP), a voluntary confidential counselling, information, and referral service; and a subsidized emergency children's daycare program to assist working parents. Blakes also plans a wellness week that will include seminars on handling stress and other health-related topics.

In 2006, Blakes will be celebrating its 150th anniversary. The firm's signature, "Blakes means business," is not just a catch phrase but a discipline that defines how the firm helps clients achieve their business objectives. To achieve this goal, Blakes invests in its lawyers and staff by creating a positive place to work. The firm develops the skills of its lawyers and staff, gives back to the community, shares its knowledge and expertise, and values a work and life balance. Blakes is a firm where lawyers and staff are "engaged" and feel proud to work there.

SOURCES: K. Macklem, "Top 100 Employers," *Maclean's,* October 11, 2004, 2; Julie Bean (chief administrative officer, Blake, Cassels and Graydon LLP), interview, October 6, 2004, Toronto, Ont.

EXHIBIT 2.3

The Influence of Attitudes on Individual and Organizational Outcomes

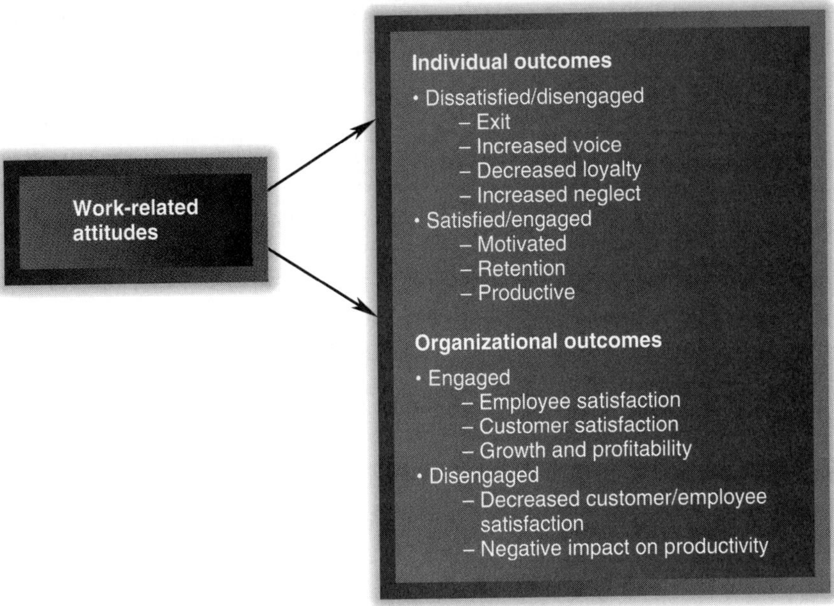

chair and put your hands behind your head; you can't concentrate on your job and you think to yourself, "What an unpleasant place to work." And all you can think about is the weekend. Here is something to consider: Are satisfied workers more productive? Or are productive workers more satisfied? What is the impact of a satisfied workforce on organizational performance?

Influence on Organizational Performance

A positive relationship exists between satisfied and engaged workers and organizational performance. Today's leaders recognize that organizational performance is optimized when employees feel a sense of connection to their teams, organization, and job, and that positive work attitudes lead to customer satisfaction. This sense of engagement results in higher levels of motivation, energy, and performance, which positively impact the bottom line.[43]

Harvard business professor James L. Heskett calls this effect "the value profit chain," citing statistical evidence of the relationship between employee satisfaction, customer satisfaction, and results. He identifies three tenets: (1) long-term growth and profitability start with employee satisfaction, loyalty, and productivity; (2) employee satisfaction today equals customer satisfaction tomorrow; and (3) customer satisfaction equals growth and profitability the day after tomorrow.[44]

Influence on Individual Behaviour

Whereas the relationship between organizational performance and a positive work attitude is clear, the relationship between job satisfaction and individual performance is not as clear. One view holds that satisfaction causes good performance. If this were true, then the manager's job would simply be to keep workers happy. Although this may be the case for certain individuals, job satisfaction for most people is one of several causes of good performance. Another view holds that good performance causes satisfaction. If this were true, managers would need to help employees perform well, and satisfaction would follow. However, some employees who are high performers are not satisfied with their jobs.

The research shows modest support for both views, but no simple, direct relationship between satisfaction and performance has been found.[45] One reason for these results may be the difficulty of demonstrating the attitude–behaviour links we described earlier in this chapter. Another reason for the lack of a clear relationship between satisfaction and performance is the intervening role of rewards. Employees who receive valued rewards are more satisfied. In addition, employees who receive rewards that are contingent on performance (the higher the performance, the larger the reward) tend to perform better. Rewards thus influence both satisfaction and performance. The key to influencing both satisfaction and performance through rewards is that the rewards are valued by employees and are tied directly to performance. Another reason may be that job satisfaction is too narrow an indicator. Researchers suggest that employee engagement may be a better predictor of performance. When employees feel connected to the organization and feel a special attachment with the organization and its mission, they will go the extra mile.[46] These employees demonstrate strong citizenship behaviour, enjoy working at their companies, and demonstrate a level of commitment that contributes positively to the company bottom line.

In-Touch Survey Systems
In-Touch Survey Systems provides location-specific employee satisfaction measurement and reporting solutions. View their website for details.
www.intouchsurvey.com

If employees are not satisfied, what behaviour can we expect to see? Researchers William Turney and Daniel Feldman have identified four different types of behavioural responses: exit, increased voice, decreased loyalty, and increased neglect. When dissatisfied some employees choose to leave a company, finding work elsewhere (**e**xit), others get very vocal and increase their voice by talking to superiors and peers about what can be done to improve conditions (increased **v**oice), while other employees reduce their involvement and withdraw from any additional organizational activities (decreased **l**oyalty) or perhaps choose to reduce their level of effort, evidenced by a decrease in work quality and increased absenteeism (increased **n**eglect).[47] Do any of these sound familiar? Which one of these behaviours do you engage in: exit, voice, loyalty, or neglect (EVLN)?

Changing Employee Attitudes: Employee Opinion Surveys

Finding out what employees think about an organization and engaging employees in dialogue on how to continuously improve the working environment are important components in creating a positive workplace. A common tool used by organizations to assess employee attitudes is the employee opinion survey. These surveys reveal employees' level of satisfaction or dissatisfaction with specific facets of their jobs and are useful indicators of employee turnover and productivity. They indicate not only how the employees feel but what is causing this feeling.[48]

Managers are important catalysts for encouraging attitude change. High-performing organizations use the results from the surveys as an opportunity to engage employees in active dialogue and utilize this input to create an action plan.[49] Maritime Life, a Halifax-based insurance firm, surveys employees each year to gauge employee satisfaction. This company believes that employee satisfaction is the root of customer satisfaction and uses the results of these surveys as a tool for operational improvement.[50]

There are several types of surveys that can be used to measure job satisfaction. One of the most widely used surveys is the Job Descriptive Index (JDI). This index measures the specific facets of satisfaction by asking employees to respond yes, no, or cannot decide to a series of statements describing their jobs. Another popular questionnaire is the Minnesota Satisfaction Questionnaire (MSQ),[51] which asks employees to respond to statements about their jobs using a five-point scale that ranges from very dissatisfied to very satisfied. Exhibit 2.4 presents some sample items from each questionnaire.

EXHIBIT 2.4

Sample Items from Satisfaction Questionnaire

Job Descriptive Index

Think of the work you do at present. How well does each of the following words or phrases describe your work? In the blank beside each word given below, write

Y for "Yes" if it describes your work

N for "No" if it does NOT describe it

? if you cannot decide

WORK ON YOUR PRESENT JOB

____ Routine

____ Satisfying

____ Good

Think of the majority of people that you work with now or the people you meet in connection with your work. How well does each of the following words or phrases describe these people? In the blank beside each word, write

Y for "Yes" if it describes the people you work with

N for "No" if it does NOT describe them

? if you cannot decide

CO-WORKERS (PEOPLE)

____ Boring

____ Responsible

____ Intelligent

Minnesota Satisfaction Questionnaire

1 = Very dissatisfied

2 = Dissatisfied

3 = I can't decide whether I am satisfied or not

4 = Satisfied

5 = Very Satisfied

On my present job, this is how I feel about:

____ The chance to work alone on the job (Independence)

____ My chances for advancement on this job (Advancement)

____ The chance to tell people what to do (Authority)

____ The praise I get for a good job (Recognition)

SOURCES: The Job Descriptive Index is copyrighted by Bowling Green State University. The complete forms, scoring key, instructions, and norms can be obtained from Dr. Patricia C. Smith, Department of Psychology, Bowling Green State University, Bowling Green, OH 43403. Minnesota Satisfaction Questionnaire from D. J. Weiss, R. V. Davis, G. W. England, and L. H. Lofquist, Manual for the Minnesota Satisfaction Questionnaire (University of Minnesota Vocational Psychology Research, 1967).

VALUES

Another source of individual difference is employee values. **Values** are enduring beliefs that a specific mode of conduct or end state of existence is personally or socially preferable to an opposite or converse mode of conduct or end state of existence.[52] (See Organizational Reality 2.2.) Unlike attitudes, values exist at a deep level. As individuals grow and mature, they learn values, which may change over the life span as an individual develops a sense of self. Values guide behaviour by providing criteria that an individual can use to evaluate and define actions and events in the work surrounding him or her. An individual, personal set of values determines which type of action and events are desirable or undesirable.[53] For example, as recognition for a job well done your company

values
Enduring beliefs that a specific mode of conduct or end state of existence is personally or socially preferable to an opposite or converse mode of conduct or end state of existence.

organizational reality 2.2

Employer-Supported Volunteerism

Today's employers are recognizing the value of corporate social responsibility and community involvement as they pursue goals that are not just focused on profits. Triple-bottom-line thinking is a characteristic shared by high-performing organizations. One way that employers demonstrate this commitment is through "employer-supported volunteering." These organizations encourage and support employees who perform work in the community.

Thousands of Canadian Red Cross volunteers serve communities around the world and across the street.

A majority of Canadian volunteers are employed in the paid labour force. In 2000, about one-half of all employee volunteers received at least one form of support from their employers and 22 percent of Canadian employee volunteers received recognition from their employers for their volunteer work, up from 14 percent from 1997. This recognition took the form of employers providing workplace facilities for volunteer activities, time off for volunteer activities, and work schedule flexibility to accommodate volunteering activities.

The benefits to all the stakeholders are numerous. Communities benefit from the employees' expertise and employee volunteers gain transferable job-related skills and competencies that the Conference Board of Canada has found to be "employability skills" of the business environment. Organizations benefit as employees who volunteer exhibit increased job satisfaction, motivation, and enhanced morale, and they tend to have a more positive attitude toward their employer, which translates directly to the bottom line. The connection to the bottom line was revealed by a study conducted at Sears in the U.S. that looked at the links between employee attitude, customer relations, and sales. An improvement of employee attitudes by five points resulted in a 1.3 point improvement in customer satisfaction, which resulted in a 0.5 percent improvement in revenue. When applied to Sears, 0.5 percent improvement in revenue meant additional sales of $65 million per year. What does your organization do to demonstrate its commitment?

SOURCES: Volunteerism Canada, http://www.volunteer.ca, accessed October 10, 2004; Conference Board of Canada, *Employability Skills 2000*; NQI, "The Business Case for Excellence," August 15, 2004, http://www.nqi.ca/articles/articles.

offers you four possible awards; an additional week of vacation, access to a Whistler cabin for $20.00 a night, credits toward a paid sabbatical program after three years with the company, an opportunity to be recognized at the companies annual meeting, free airline tickets and $3,000 in spending money or a cash bonus. Which one would you choose and why? Or perhaps none of these appeal to you.

Distinguish between different types of values and describe the factors that influence these values.

Instrumental and Terminal Values

instrumental values
Values that represent the acceptable behaviours to be used in achieving some end state.

terminal values
Values that represent the goals to be achieved or the end states of existence.

Rokeach distinguished between two types of values: instrumental and terminal. **Instrumental values** reflect the means to achieve goals; that is, they represent the acceptable behaviours to be used in achieving some end state. Instrumental values identified by Rokeach include ambition, honesty, self-sufficiency, responsibility, independence, and courage. **Terminal values,** in contrast, represent the goals to be achieved or the end states of existence. Rokeach identified achievement, happiness, love, pleasure, self-respect, social respect, equality, and freedom among the terminal values. Terminal and instrumental values work in concert to provide individuals with goals to strive for and acceptable ways to achieve the goals. The highest-ranked instrumental values were honesty, ambition, responsibility, a forgiving nature, open-mindedness, and courage. The highest-ranked terminal values were world peace, family security, freedom, happiness, self-respect, and wisdom.[54]

Factors That Influence Values

Individuals vary widely in their value systems. Why do some individuals value achievement and others don't? Why is it that certain individuals demonstrate an intense concern for other individuals and their welfare and others couldn't care less? What factors influence an individual's value system? This discussion wouldn't be complete without examining the influence of diversity on an individual's value system. The term **diversity** refers to all forms of differences among individuals. The core elements of diversity have a life-long impact on behaviour and attitudes. These include factors such as age, race, ethnicity, culture, gender, physical attributes, and sexual orientation. Secondary dimensions of diversity are those elements that people acquire, discard, or can change through their lives. These include such factors as educational background, stage in one's career, marital status, and religious beliefs.[55] (See Exhibit 2.5.)

diversity
All forms of individual differences, including race, ethnicity, culture, gender, age, marital status, religious beliefs, educational background, and stages in one's career.

Although we have identified several types of diversity, we have chosen to discuss three core characteristics (age, gender, and culture) and one secondary characteristic (stage in one's career).

Age

Different generations hold different values! It is very important for managers to understand the various differences so that they can manage more effectively. Four different age groups have been characterized as (1) traditionalists, born between 1922 and 1945; (2) baby boomers, born between 1946 and 1964; (3) Generation X, born between 1965 and 1980; and (4) Generation Y (also called baby busters or echo boomers, nexters, and/or millennials), born between 1981 and 2000.

Within each age group, certain generic characteristics can be identified. For example, traditionalists tend to be loyal to the organization, respect authority, get the job done, and have a "don't rock the boat" type of attitude. Baby boomers, on the other hand, are known for challenging authority, preferring to work in flat organizations

EXHIBIT 2.5

Factors That Influence Individual Values

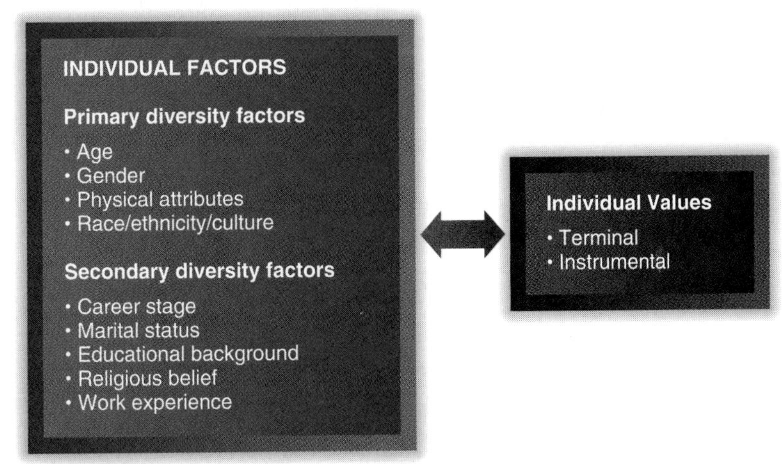

engaging in a lot of team work, have a "live to work" mentality, and typically bend the rules. Generation X places a premium on intellectually stimulating work, learning opportunities, and advancement, respecting competence and skills over seniority, and they tend to value work environments where there is an emphasis on education and continued learning. Generation Y demonstrates a "work to contribute" mentality, preferring to engage in very casual relationships with superiors. These employees think in the near term and want immediate payoff for a job well done.

Ever worked with someone who was much older than you? How were their values different from yours? The values of the different generations shape our attitudes to work and the way we interact with managers, colleagues, and subordinates.

Gender

"A woman's work is never done." Do you recall ever hearing this saying? What value were you brought up with about women's contribution to society?

The past several decades have witnessed dramatic growth in the number of women who are part of the paid workforce. In 2002, 56 percent of all women aged 15 and over had jobs, up from 42 percent in 1976. In 2003 the Canadian labour force consisted of over 9 million men and almost 8 million women. Women made up 46.4 percent of the labour force, up from 37 percent in 1976.[56] In 2002, 56.4 percent of Canadian women were employed.[57] Statistics also show that more Canadian women are obtaining higher degrees: Women hold 36 percent of all doctorates, 52 percent of master's degrees, and 55 percent of bachelor's degrees.[58] While women's participation in the workforce is increasing, their shares of the rewards of participation are not increasing commensurately. Women hold only 11.2 percent of corporate director positions in Canada (476 out of 4247 corporate directors), up from 9.8 percent in 2001.[59] As well, the proportion of companies with no women board directors has remained unchanged since 2001, at 51.4 percent. Only three publicly traded companies have women chairing their boards: Indigo Books and Music, Samuel Manu-Tech Inc., and Corus Entertainment.[60] Crown corporations continue to have the highest women's representation on boards, at 23.7 percent. Women like Linda Cook, CEO of Shell Canada, are still the exception, not the rule. In 2002, salaries for women persisted at a level of an average 64.2 percent of their male counterparts' earnings.[61]

glass ceiling
A transparent barrier that keeps women from rising above a certain level in organizations.

In addition to lower earnings, women face other obstacles at work. As mentioned in Chapter 1, the **glass ceiling** is a transparent barrier that keeps women from rising above a certain level in organizations. The glass ceiling is not based on women's lack of ability to handle upper-level management positions. Instead, the barrier keeps women from advancing higher in an organization because they are women. The Bank of Montreal, a leader in helping women break the glass ceiling, found that a number of myths existed in the workplace. For example, while respondents to a survey said: "We would love to promote women if they had the proper education," human resource information revealed that this myth did not fit the facts and that, in fact, the bank's women were as educated as the men.[62]

The glass ceiling is also turning out to be bad for business. A 2003 Catalyst study entitled "The Bottom Line: Connecting Corporate Performance and Gender Diversity" suggested that companies with a higher representation of women in senior management positions financially outperformed companies with proportionally fewer women at the top. These companies had a 35 percent higher return on equity (ROE) and a 34 percent higher total return to shareholders (TRS) than companies with the lowest women's representation.

Career Stage

The stage at which an employee is in terms of his or her career can also influence the employee's values. For example, a recent graduate would be more interested in obtaining a position that afforded opportunities for career development. In this stage individuals are typically starting out and require a steady salary and some stability. Base pay will be more important to this group than variable pay. In contrast, older individuals who are contemplating winding down their careers will place greater value on retirement benefits and may value the opportunity to share their knowledge and experience with others.

Cultural Differences in Values

As organizations face the challenges of operating in a global marketplace with an increasingly diverse workforce, it has become essential for managers and employees to understand the influence of culture on values. Value systems of other nations are different, and understanding these cultural differences enables employees to appreciate diversity, work effectively with diverse cultures, and effectively leverage the value that individuals can bring to the workplace.

What if your organization decided to open a branch plant in another country and you were sent there to work? How would the cultural differences affect you? For example, the culture in France tends to be hierarchical, rule bound, and structured, with very clear job roles. Compare this to Canada, where we are more accustomed to team-based structures and engaging in decision making at all levels. If you were used to working in a team-based open environment with very little structure and making your own decisions, and then you found yourself in a very structured, hierarchical environment, what effect might this have on your ability to work well with others? Would working in this type of structure compromise your level of job satisfaction?

The findings from the Global Leadership and Organizational Behavior Effectiveness (GLOBE) Research Project provide a framework in which to analyze differences across cultures. This project, conceived by Robert J. House, Wharton School of Business, University of Pennsylvania, in 1991, examined the inter-relationships between societal culture, organizational culture, and organizational leadership. It involved over 170 social scientists and management scholars from 61 countries. This team of researchers has identified nine critical cultural dimensions that will help us to understand cultural differences and similarities. It is important to note that this research updates the seminal research work of Geert Hofstede on cross-cultural values. Geert Hofstede identified five main dimensions that he used to analyze cross-cultural differences. These are (1) power distance, (2) individualism versus collectivism, (3) masculinity versus femininity, (4) uncertainty avoidance, and (5) long- versus short-term orientation.[63] For the purposes of presenting the reader with the most up-to-date research, we will focus on the

EXHIBIT 2.6

Cultural Dimensions—Comparison of GLOBE Study and Hofstede

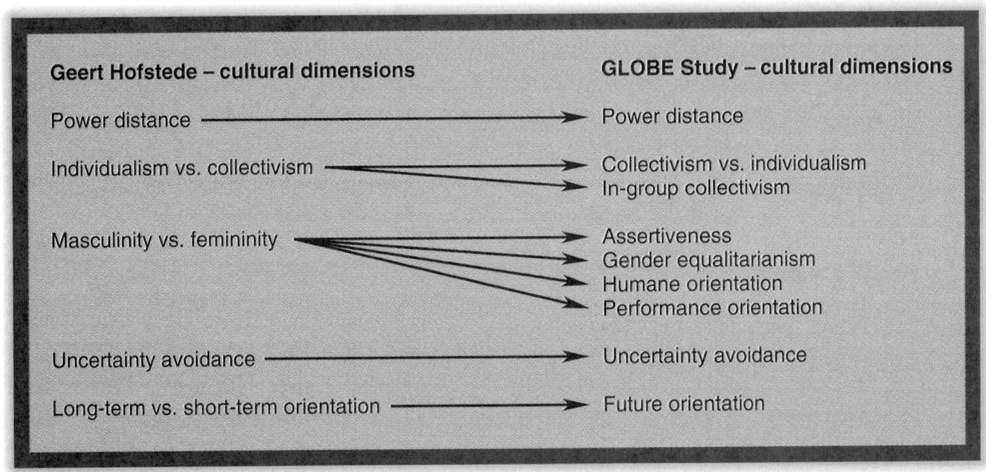

nine critical dimensions detailed in the GLOBE project and the research outcomes. The nine dimensions are (1) assertiveness, (2) future orientation, (3) gender equalitarianism, (4) uncertainty avoidance, (5) power distance, (6) institutional emphasis on collectivism versus individualism, (7) in-group collectivism, (8) performance orientation, and (9) humane orientation.[64] (See Exhibit 2.6.)

Power Distance

power distance
The degree of inequality among people that a culture considers normal.

Power distance refers to the differences expressed in a society with respect to status, authority, and wealth. It refers to the degree of inequality among people that the population considers normal, from relatively equal (that is, small power distance) to extremely unequal (large power distance). In high-power cultures employees are used to a hierarchical management approach where conflicts are resolved by going through specific levels of formal authority. Countries that ranked high were Russia, Spain, and Thailand. Low-ranking countries, such as Netherlands, Denmark, and Israel, value group inputs to decisions and expect their decisions to be challenged and discussed by employees.

Individualism versus Collectivism

individualism versus collectivism
The degree to which individuals are expected to be part of a group in their organization or in their society.

Individualism versus collectivism refers to the degree to which individuals are expected to be part of a group in their organization or in their society. This dimension focuses on whether society's institutions favour autonomy or collective behaviour. Countries that are high on this dimension, such as Denmark, Singapore, Japan, and Sweden, expect individuals to participate in group activities and they reward the group for its membership. An obligation to one's social group is considered important and the self is viewed as interdependent of the group. In contrast, low-ranking countries, such as Greece, Italy, and Argentina, value autonomy and individualism where individual goals are considered more important than the group goals. Collectivist cultures value a person's contributions to relationships in the work team, whereas individualist cultures value a person's contribution to task accomplishment.

In-Group Collectivism

in-group collectivism
The extent to which members of a society take pride in membership in their immediate social group.

In-group collectivism refers to the extent that members in a society consider membership within their immediate social group to be important. This group could be family, circle of friends, or the organization where they currently are employed. High scores obtained by countries such as the Philippines, China, India, and Iran indicate societies where family and close relationships are highly valued and highly regarded. Members of these groups would expect special treatment because they belong to the inner circle. Low scores were found in countries such as Denmark, New Zealand, and Sweden, where the weight of one's inner circle is not considered as important as other cultural considerations.

Assertiveness

assertiveness
The extent to which a society encourages people to be confrontational and assertive with respect to their views.

Assertiveness refers to the extent to which a society encourages people to be confrontational and assertive with respect to their views. Countries such as Spain, the U.S., and Germany rated the highest on this scale, while Sweden, New Zealand, and Switzerland rated the least assertive. Assertive countries are competitive and resolute in their ability to make things happen. They value expressiveness, emphasize results, and reward performance. For example, consider the political differences between Canada and the U.S. in their response to the war in Kuwait. The U.S. became actively involved in managing the political process whereas Canada decided to adopt a wait-and-see approach.

Gender Differentiation

gender differentiation
The extent to which a society views gender roles as different.

Gender differentiation refers to how a society views gender role differences. Countries such as Egypt, India, and Turkey scored high on this dimension as they accord men higher social status than women, whereas countries such as Canada, Denmark, Hungary, and Poland scored low. In these countries women were accorded a higher status in society, they played a stronger role in decision making, and they tended to hold positions of power and authority.

Humane Orientation

Humane orientation refers to the degree to which a society encourages and rewards individuals for being altruistic, caring, and generous. Malaysia, Ireland, and the Philippines are among the highest-ranking countries that demonstrate a sympathetic and kind approach to others. The values of kindness, love, and generosity are given a high priority. Germany, Spain, Greece, Hungary, and France rated the lowest. In low-ranking countries, power and material possessions are more important and individuals tend to focus more on their own development and self-enhancement.

humane orientation
The degree to which a society encourages and rewards individuals for being altruistic, caring and generous.

Performance Orientation

Performance orientation refers to how much a society values initiative, continuous improvement, and exceptional performance. Singapore, Switzerland, Hong Kong, Canada, and the U.S. have the highest scores, whereas Greece, Russia, Italy, and Venezuela scored the lowest. In the United States and in Canada, productivity and profitability are significant drivers of organizational performance. We frequently hear employees express how the long hours of work and extensive performance requirements have taken their toll on the quality of life. In Europe quality of life takes precedence over productivity. For example, in Spain, shops will close for several hours at midday so that people can enjoy their lunch at neighbouring cafés. Think about how your understanding of this value might influence your ability to work within a heterogeneous team where members come from different cultures. How prudent would it be for you to schedule a meeting at lunchtime if your counterparts valued time off at lunch as fundamental?

performance orientation
The degree to which a society values initiative, continuous improvement, and exceptional performance.

Uncertainty Avoidance

Uncertainty avoidance refers to how much a society relies on its social norms to explain unpredictable future events. It is the degree to which people in a country prefer to use formalized procedures, structure, or laws to deal with situations that occur. Countries with high scores, such as Germany, Denmark, and Switzerland, demonstrate a strong tendency toward applying a consistent set of rules and laws to manage situations. These countries are not as tolerant of rule breakers and are more formal in their interactions with others. These societies value consistency and orderliness and are fastidious in their approach to challenges. Countries with low scores, such as Russia, Greece, and Venezuela, are more tolerant of ambiguity and are not as structured in their approach.

uncertainty avoidance
The degree to which people in a country prefer structured over unstructured situations.

Future Orientation

Future orientation refers to the extent to which a society supports and rewards future-related behaviours. The countries that scored high on this factor—Canada, Netherlands, and Switzerland—demonstrated a propensity to save for the future, exhibited a significant ability to plan for the long term and make investments that yielded long-term gain and were able to delay gratification. The countries that ranked low on this dimension were Russia, Italy, and Poland.

future orientation
The extent to which a society supports and rewards future-related behaviours.

Interested in Where Canada Ranks on These Dimensions?

Canada ranked high on gender differentiation, performance, and future orientation, mid-level on power distance, assertiveness, individualism versus collectivism, uncertainty avoidance, and humane orientation, and low on in-group collectivism.[65]

What Managers and Employees Can Do to Manage Diversity in the Workplace

Values can affect how we view other people and groups, how we perceive various issues that can arise at work, how we may determine an individual's action, and how we can influence others. An important competency for managers and employees today is to develop a greater understanding and appreciation of different value systems. Managers must be able to understand the differences between cultures so that they can respond in a "culturally sensitive way." For example, if a manager is providing direction to an employee who is from a culture with high power distance, it would be prudent for the manager to ensure the employee has a specific understanding as to the chain of command when faced with a problem. Providing the employee with the hierarchy of command will alleviate undue stress. Go to Self-Assessment 2.2, "What Are Your Cultural Values?" to attain a greater understanding of your own values.

The following suggestions can help managers and employees understand and work with the diverse values that characterize the global environment:[66]

1. Learn more about and recognize the values of other peoples. They view their values and customs as moral, traditional, and practical.
2. Avoid prejudging the business customs of others as immoral or corrupt. Assume they are legitimate unless proved otherwise.
3. Find legitimate ways to operate within others' ethical points of view—do not demand that they operate within your value system.
4. Avoid rationalizing "borderline" actions with excuses such as the following:
   - "This isn't really illegal or immoral."
   - "This is in the organization's best interest."
   - "No one will find out about this."
   - "The organization will back me up on this."
5. Refuse to do business when stakeholder actions violate or compromise laws or fundamental organizational values.
6. Conduct relationships as openly and as aboveboard as possible.

Knowledge & Application

SELF-ASSESSMENT 2.2: WHAT ARE YOUR CULTURAL VALUES?

Instructions

In the following questionnaire, indicate the extent to which you agree or disagree with each statement. For example, if you strongly agree with a particular statement, you would circle the 5 next to that statement.

1 = Strongly disagree
2 = Disagree
3 = Neither agree nor disagree
4 = Agree
5 = Strongly agree

Questions	**Strongly Disagree**				**Strongly Agree**
1. It is important to have job requirements and instructions spelled out in detail so that employees always know what they are expected to do.	1	2	3	4	5
2. Managers expect employees to follow instructions and procedures closely.	1	2	3	4	5
3. Rules and regulations are important because they inform employees what the organization expects of them.	1	2	3	4	5
4. Standard operating procedures are helpful to employees on the job.	1	2	3	4	5
5. Instructions for operations are important for employees on the job.	1	2	3	4	5
6. Group welfare is more important than individual rewards.	1	2	3	4	5

SELF-ASSESSMENT 2.2: WHAT ARE YOUR CULTURAL VALUES? (CONT.)

Questions	Strongly Disagree				Strongly Agree
7. Group success is more important than individual success.	1	2	3	4	5
8. Being accepted by the members of the work group is very important.	1	2	3	4	5
9. Employees should only pursue their goals after considering the welfare of the group.	1	2	3	4	5
10. Managers should encourage group loyalty even if individual goals suffer.	1	2	3	4	5
11. Individuals may be expected to give up their goals in order to benefit group success.	1	2	3	4	5
12. Managers should make most decisions without consulting subordinates.	1	2	3	4	5
13. Managers must often use authority and power when dealing with subordinates.	1	2	3	4	5
14. Managers should seldom ask for the opinions of employees.	1	2	3	4	5
15. Managers should avoid off-the-job social contacts with employees.	1	2	3	4	5
16. Employees should not disagree with management decisions.	1	2	3	4	5
17. Managers should not delegate important tasks to employees.	1	2	3	4	5
18. Managers should help employees with their family problems.	1	2	3	4	5
19. Management should see to it that workers are adequately clothed and fed.	1	2	3	4	5
20. Managers should help employees solve their personal problems.	1	2	3	4	5
21. Management should see that health care is provided to all employees.	1	2	3	4	5
22. Management should see that children of employees have an adequate education.	1	2	3	4	5
23. Management should provide legal assistance for employees who get in trouble with the law.	1	2	3	4	5
24. Management should take care of employees as they would treat their children.	1	2	3	4	5
25. Meetings are usually run more effectively when they are chaired by a man.	1	2	3	4	5
26. It is more important for men to have professional careers than it is for women to have professional careers.	1	2	3	4	5
27. Men usually solve problems with logical analysis; women usually solve problems with intuition.	1	2	3	4	5
28. Solving organizational problems usually requires an active, forcible approach typical of men.	1	2	3	4	5
29. It is preferable to have a man in a high-level position rather than a woman.	1	2	3	4	5

For scoring instructions, please go to the end of the chapter, p. 70.

IMPLICATIONS FOR LIFE

What You Can Do to Help Employers Create a Positive Work Environment That Is Right for You

Seek a "values" fit between you and the company: Looking for a job can be daunting—even for someone with experience and work history. But working in a company that does not fit with who we are can only make our experience at work more unpleasant. Start with an assessment of your values as they relate to the workplace. What is most important to you? Is it the opportunity to get ahead or is work–life balance more important? Perhaps you value teamwork and public recognition. Investigate the companies where you think there will be opportunities and take some time to find out what it is like to work at that company. Check the web page, read articles about the company, and ask others about their experience.

Be open and honest when asked how to improve the organization: As we have seen, many companies conduct job satisfaction surveys to obtain a pulse on employee attitudes. These organizations use the feedback to improve operations. You can help! Be open and honest when asked for your opinion.

Know yourself: Explore the resources the organization offers. Many employers have policies and benefit programs that can help you. For example, some companies have a tuition reimbursement program, which enables you to pursue a course of study and receive reimbursement from your employer. Some employers have an employee assistance program, which provides you with services such as psychological, family, and financial counselling. Understanding your needs and the programs your company offers will help you create a more positive place to work.

Seek opportunities: Explore the opportunities that your company has to offer. Is there a job posting board or perhaps a career centre? Discuss your career development with your manager and seek opportunities for your development. Take control of your career!

ETHICAL BEHAVIOUR

If you were offered a free trip from a friend, is there any reason to think that you were doing something unethical? Well, what if you were a cabinet minister? Would your answer be any different? Recently, a Liberal cabinet minister came under attack and received negative press for not disclosing that she had accepted a free trip to a lodge—a lodge she says was run by a close personal friend. Typically, Cabinet guidelines require all ministers to disclose any gift they receive that exceeds $200 in value. The purpose of this rule is to avoid conflict of interest so that officeholders are not beholden to private interests. To clear this minister of any conflict, the ethics counsellor chose to invoke a clause under the guidelines that says officeholders are allowed gifts, hospitality, and other benefits if they are from "family members and close personal friends."[67] The public was outraged. What is your reaction? Do you think she did something unethical by not disclosing this "gift"?

ethical behaviour
Acting in ways consistent with one's personal values and the commonly held values of the organization and society.

As discussed in Chapter 1, ethics is the study of moral values and moral behaviour. **Ethical behaviour** is acting in ways consistent with one's personal values and the commonly held values of the organization and society.[68] Ethical issues are a major concern in organizations. Many large companies have adopted ethical codes and today more than ever companies demonstrating triple-bottom-line thinking is considered the norm. There is evidence that paying attention to ethical issues pays off for companies. In the early 1990s, James Burke, then the CEO of Johnson & Johnson, put together a list of companies that devoted a great deal of attention to ethics. The group included Johnson & Johnson, Coca-Cola, Gerber, Kodak, 3M, and Pitney Bowes. Over a 40-year period, the market value of these organizations grew at an annual rate of 11.3 percent, as compared to 6.2 percent for the Dow Jones industrials as a whole.[69] Doing the right thing can have a positive effect on an organization's performance.

Failure to handle situations in an ethical manner can cost companies. Employees who are laid off or terminated are very concerned about the quality of treatment they receive. Honestly explaining the reasons for the dismissal and preserving the dignity of the employee will reduce the likelihood that the employee will initiate a claim against the company. One study showed that less than 1 percent of employees who felt the company was being honest filed a claim; more than 17 percent of those who felt the company was being less than honest filed claims.[70]

Unethical behaviour by employees can affect individuals, work teams, and even the organization. Organizations thus depend on individuals to act ethically. One such company that has been in the news recently is Nortel Networks. Resulting from the recent scandal relating to financial irregularities, Nortel has appointed a corporate ethics and compliance officer to oversee the organization who will be responsible for training for staff in ethical issues, helping boards and management develop ethical codes, chairing an ethics committee, and establishing an ethics hot line.[71] Ethics hot lines have been introduced by many organizations. Recently, Inco and CIBC introduced hot lines and training for their employees. Go to the Experiential Exercise at the end of this chapter to get a better understanding of your own ethics.

Ethics Centre

The Canadian Centre for Ethics and Corporate Policy is a registered Canadian charity governed by volunteers and supported by organizations and individuals who share a commitment to ethical values. The centre offers a variety of resources on ethics and corporate responsibility to the business community and individuals.
http://www.ethicscentre.ca.

Today's high-intensity business environment makes it more important than ever to have a strong ethics program in place. In a survey of more than 4000 employees conducted by the Washington, D.C.–based Ethics Resource Center, one-third of the employees said that they had witnessed ethical misconduct in the past year. If that many employees actually saw unethical acts, imagine how many unethical behaviours occurred behind closed doors! The most common unethical deeds witnessed were lying to supervisors (56 percent), lying on reports or falsifying records (41 percent), stealing or theft (35 percent), sexual harassment (35 percent), drug or alcohol abuse (31 percent), and conflicts of interest (31 percent).[72] The ethical issues that individuals face at work are complex. A review of articles appearing in the *Wall Street Journal* during one week revealed more than 60 articles dealing with ethical issues in business. The themes appearing throughout the articles were distilled into 12 major ethical topics: stealing, lying, fraud and deceit, conflict of interest, cheating, personal decadence, interpersonal abuse, rule violations, accessory to unethical acts, ethical dilemmas, and hiding versus divulging information.[73]

Nortel promotes ethics by hiring a corporate ethics compliance officer.

7

Describe a model of the individual and organizational influences on ethical behaviour and how locus of control, Machiavellianism, and cognitive moral development and value systems affect ethical behaviour.

Influences on Organizational Behaviour

The model that guides our discussion of individual influences on ethical behaviour is presented in Exhibit 2.7. It shows both individual and organizational influences.

Individual Influences

It has been suggested that ethical decision making requires three qualities of individuals:[74]

1. The competence to identify ethical issues and evaluate the consequences of alternative courses of action.
2. The self-confidence to seek out different opinions about the issue and decide what is right in terms of a particular situation.
3. Tough-mindedness—the willingness to make decisions when all that needs to be known cannot be known and when the ethical issue has no established, unambiguous solution.

What are the individual characteristics that lead to these qualities? Our model presents four major individual differences that affect ethical behaviour: locus of control, Machiavellianism, cognitive moral development, and value systems.

Locus of Control

locus of control
An individual's generalized belief about internal control (self-control) versus external control (control by the situation or by others).

One individual influence on ethical behaviour is **locus of control.** Locus of control is a personality variable that affects individual behaviour. Individuals with an internal locus of control believe that they control events in their lives and that they are responsible for what happens to them. In contrast, individuals with an external locus of control believe that outside forces such as fate, chance, or other people control what happens to them.[75]

Machiavellianism

Machiavellianism
A personality characteristic indicating one's willingness to do whatever it takes to get one's own way.

Another individual difference that affects ethical behaviour is Machiavellianism. Niccolò Machiavelli was a sixteenth-century Italian statesman. He wrote *The Prince,* a guide for acquiring and using power.[76] The primary method for achieving power that he suggested was manipulation of others. **Machiavellianism,** then, is a personality characteristic indicating one's willingness to do whatever it takes to get one's own way. A high-Mach indi-

EXHIBIT 2.7

Individual/Organizational Model of Ethical Behaviour

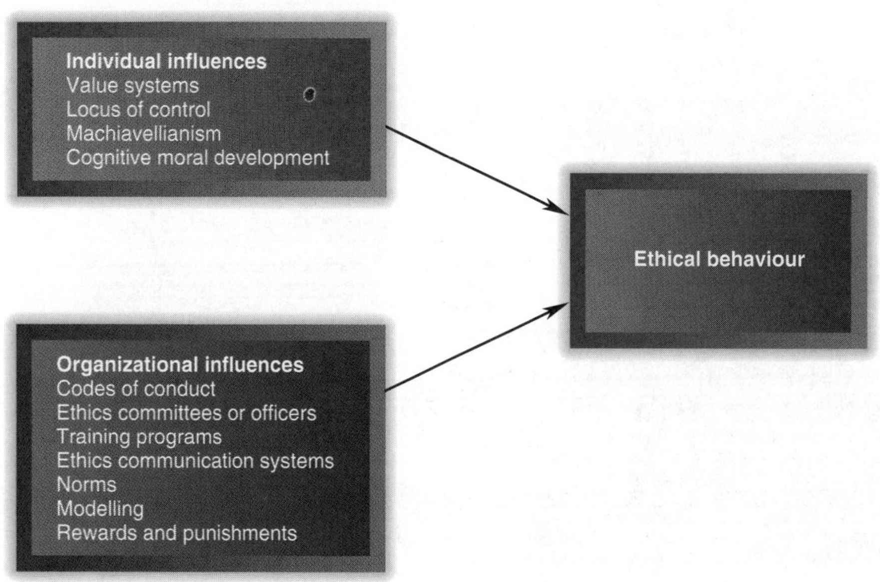

vidual behaves in accordance with Machiavelli's ideas, which include the notion that it is better to be feared than loved. Low-Machs, in contrast, value loyalty and relationships. They are less willing to manipulate others for personal gain and are concerned with others' opinions.

Cognitive Moral Development

An individual's level of **cognitive moral development** also affects ethical behaviour. Psychologist Lawrence Kohlberg proposed that as individuals mature, they move through a series of six stages of moral development.[77] With each successive stage, they become less dependent on other people's opinions of right and wrong and less self-centred (acting in one's own interest). At higher levels of moral development, individuals are concerned with broad principles of justice and with their self-chosen ethical principles. Individuals at higher stages of development are less likely to cheat,[78] more likely to engage in whistle-blowing,[79] and more likely to make ethical business decisions.[80]

cognitive moral development
The process of moving through stages of maturity in terms of making ethical decisions.

Value Systems

Have you seen the movie *The Insider*, with Russell Crowe? This is the true story of Jeffrey Wigand, a scientist who worked for a prominent tobacco company. Before joining the tobacco industry, Wigand worked in the pharmaceutical industry for a company that was well respected for its ethical practices. Wigand exhibited a strong sense of integrity, social responsibility, and honesty. He believed that a scientist's responsibility is to contribute in a positive way to society. In his research at the tobacco company he discovered that the company was producing a more addictive form of tobacco and this product would ultimately be detrimental to individual health. It became clear to him that the more addictive the product became, the more people would buy the product, thus increasing sales and company profitability. Jeffrey Wigand felt compelled to speak out on this issue. But when he did, he was ostracized, experienced alienation and harassment, and was ultimately fired from his job. Being a man of high integrity, Wigand felt compelled to warn society of this danger. He testified before Congress at an inquiry into the tobacco industry and spoke on *60 Minutes*. Wigand "blew the whistle" on his employers. He was an individual who demonstrated a strong ethical and moral sense and an unerring sense of social responsibility.

Values are systems of beliefs that affect what the individual defines as right, good, and fair. Ethics reflects the way the values are acted out. Ethical behaviour, as noted earlier, is acting in ways consistent with one's personal values and the commonly held values of the organization and society.

Employees are exposed to multiple value systems: their own, their supervisor's, the company's, the customers', and others'. In most cases, the individual's greatest allegiance will be to personal values. When a value system conflicts with the behaviour the person feels must be exhibited, the person experiences a value conflict. Suppose, for example, that an individual believes honesty is important in all endeavours. Yet this individual sees that those who get ahead in business fudge their numbers and deceive other people. Why should the individual be honest if honesty doesn't pay? It is the individual's values, a basic sense of what is right and wrong, that override the temptation to be dishonest.[81]

Individual differences in values, locus of control, Machiavellianism, and cognitive moral development are important influences on ethical behaviour in organizations. Given that these influences vary widely from person to person, how can organizations use this knowledge to increase ethical behaviour? One action would be to hire individuals who share the organization's values. Another would be to hire only internals, low-Machs, and individuals at higher stages of cognitive moral development. This strategy obviously presents practical and legal problems.

There is evidence that cognitive moral development can be increased through training.[82] Organizations could help individuals move to higher stages of moral development by providing educational seminars. However, values, locus of control, Machiavellianism, and cognitive moral development are fairly stable in adults.

The best way to use the knowledge of individual differences may be to recognize that they help explain why ethical behaviour differs among individuals and to focus managerial efforts on creating a work situation that supports ethical behaviour. Managers can offer such guidance by encouraging ethical behaviour through codes of conduct, ethics committees, ethics communication systems, training, norms, modelling, and rewards and punishments.

Organizational Influences

Organizations today are being held accountable for their actions. This means demonstrating good corporate citizenship through sound ethical practices. Raising awareness of ethical behaviour through the development of a corporate code of ethics/conduct, effectively communicating what is expected from employees in terms of behaviour, and rewarding this behaviour through sound employment policies and practices are critical components of effective management. Remember the tainted Tylenol scandal in 1982? Johnson & Johnson relied on their ethical codes to guide them. Go to http://www.jnj.com/community/policies/pharmaceutical_medicine.htm to view their code.

IMPLICATIONS FOR ORGANIZATIONAL EFFECTIVENESS

Why do organizations care about creating a positive work environment? Today's leaders recognize that optimal organizational performance is achieved when employees feel a sense of connection—connection to their organization, to the people they work with, to the groups they interact with. These leaders understand that it is the employees who truly make the difference and recognize that employees are their greatest competitive advantage. "The 100 Companies to Work For" all share a basic belief—they put people first and they create a positive work environment where employees can flourish and contribute optimally to organizational goals.[83]

"Putting people first" means that organizations must consider the organizational environment, the job characteristics, and those individual differences that contribute to organizational effectiveness. It means identifying differences and managing these differences to optimize the value that employees can bring and assessing how these differences influence work behaviour.

Employees' values can be influenced by several factors. Managers who recognize these influences will gain valuable insights into why an employee may respond in a certain way. We have seen how employee attitudes can be a powerful determinant of how satisfied, involved, and productive employees can be in the workplace. Harnessing these attitudes by engaging employees in active dialogue provides managers with a tool for effecting change, creating an environment where employees feel that they are being listened to and valued.

Organizations that take time to understand these differences are successful at creating a work environment that is positive, productive, and profitable. Recall the discussion on the value profit chain? Long-term growth and profitability start with employee satisfaction, which leads to customer satisfaction, which equals growth and profitability the day after tomorrow.[84]

Why do organizations care about creating a positive work environment? Simply said, it makes good business sense![85] So the next time you are asked by your human resources representative or your manager why you are leaving your company, give your answer a lot of thought and think about why you would choose to stay at a particular company. What is it about that company that makes it a great place to work? Chapter 3 will continue our examination of these individual factors.

Chapter Summary

1. To achieve optimum organizational performance, organizations need to understand individual differences and the influences these differences have on an individual's ability to perform effectively. High-performing organizations utilize best practice methods to achieve this state and are cognizant of triple-bottom-line thinking; considering not just profits as a sole indicator of performance but how the organization is viewed from a community and employee perspective. Creating a positive work environment impacts employee satisfaction, which in turn impacts customer satisfaction and ultimately positively influences organizational profitability.
2. Organizations that focus on creating a positive work environment take into account individual differences such as values, attitudes, and personality as well as understanding the interplay and influence that the job and organizational climate can have on an individual's experience. Some of the elements that contribute to an employee's positive experience at work are clear roles and goals, adequate tools to do the job, strong leadership, and the individual's having values that are congruent with organizational values.
3. Attitudes are an evaluative response to a particular situation. Factors that influence the relationship between attitudes and behaviour are attitude specificity, attitude relevance, timing of measurement, personality factors, and social constraints. Attitudes are formed through direct experience and social learning. Direct experience creates strong attitudes because the attitudes are easily accessed and active in cognitive processes.
4. Three important work attitudes are job satisfaction, organizational commitment, and employee engagement. Job satisfaction is a positive emotional state resulting from the appraisal of one's job or job experiences; organizational commitment focuses on an individual's identification with the organization and employee engagement is the state of emotional and intellectual involvement that employees have in an organization.
5. Attitudes have a direct influence on individual and organizational outcomes. Individuals who are satisfied and engaged demonstrate a high level of motivation, commitment, and citizenship behaviour. Individuals who are disengaged/dissatisfied typically demonstrate EVLN: exit, voice, decreased loyalty and increased neglect. Organizationally an engaged workforce demonstrates employee and customer satisfaction.
6. Values are enduring beliefs and are strongly influenced by cultures, societies, and organizations. Instrumental values reflect the means to achieving goals; terminal values represent the goals to be achieved. There are several factors that influence an individual's values. Understanding the influence of diversity on an employee's value system is an important element to consider. The nine main dimensions for analyzing cross-cultural values are assertiveness, power distance, individualism versus collectivism, in-group collectivism, performance orientation, humane orientation, uncertainty avoidance, gender differentiation, and future orientation.
7. Ethical behaviour is influenced by the individual's value system, locus of control, Machiavellianism, and cognitive moral development. It is important for organizations to recognize that these differences vary widely from person to person—and to use this knowledge to increase ethical behaviour in the workplace.

Key Terms

affective commitment (p. 44)
assertiveness (p. 54)
attitude (p. 39)
best practice methods (p. 36)
cognitive moral development (p. 61)
continuance commitment (p. 44)
diversity (p. 51)
employee engagement (p. 45)
ethical behaviour (p. 58)
future orientation (p. 55)
gender differentiation (p. 54)
glass ceiling (p. 52)
high-performing organizations (p. 36)
humane orientation (p. 55)
individualism versus collectivism (p. 54)
in-group collectivism (p. 54)
instrumental values (p. 50)
job satisfaction (p. 42)
locus of control (p. 60)
Machiavellianism (p. 60)
normative commitment (p. 44)
organizational citizenship behaviour (p. 44)
organizational commitment (p. 44)
performance orientation (p. 55)
power distance (p. 54)
terminal values (p. 50)
uncertainty avoidance (p. 55)
values (p. 49)

Review Questions

1. Describe what a positive environment looks like.
2. Define what an attitude is and list the factors that influence the relationship between attitudes and behaviour. Why do some individuals seem to exhibit behaviour that is inconsistent with their attitudes?
3. Discuss three work-related attitudes that are commonly used to describe an employee's level of positive feeling towards an organization.
4. Define values. Distinguish between instrumental values and terminal values. Are these values generally stable, or do they change over time?
5. What are the factors that can influence values?
6. What are the nine main dimensions used to describe cross-cultural differences?
7. What is the relationship between values and ethics?
8. How does locus of control affect ethical behaviour?
9. What is Machiavellianism, and how does it relate to ethical behaviour?
10. What are the outcomes associated with a positive workplace?

Discussion and Communication Questions

1. What jobs do you consider to be most satisfying? Why?
2. How can managers increase their employees' job satisfaction?
3. Suppose you have an employee whose lack of commitment is affecting others in the work group. How would you go about persuading the person to change this attitude?
4. In Rokeach's studies on values, the most recent data are from 1981. Do you think values have changed since then? If so, how?
5. What are the most important influences on an individual's perceptions of ethical behaviour? Can organizations change these perceptions? If so, how?
6. How can managers encourage organizational citizenship?
7. (*Communication question*) Suppose you are a manager in a customer service organization. Your group includes seven supervisors who report directly to you. Each supervisor manages a team of seven customer service representatives. One of your supervisors, Linda, has complained that Joe, one of her employees, has "an attitude problem." She has requested that Joe be transferred to another team. Write a memo to Linda explaining your position on this problem and what should be done.
8. (*Communication question*) Select a company that you admire for its values. Use the resources of your university library to answer two questions. First, what are the company's values? Second, how do employees enact these values? Prepare an oral presentation to present in class.
9. (*Communication question*) Think of a time when you have experienced conflict or anxiety resulting from an inconsistency between your beliefs and your actions. Analyze your experience in terms of the attitude and behaviour involved. What did you do to resolve your anxiety? What other actions could you have taken? Write a brief description of your experience and your responses to the questions.

Ethics Questions

1. Is it ethical for an organization to influence an individual's ethical behaviour? In other words, is ethics a personal issue that organizations should stay away from? Is it an invasion of privacy to enforce codes of conduct?
2. Suppose a co-worker is engaging in behaviour that you find personally unethical, but the behaviour is not prohibited by the company's ethical standards. How would you handle the issue?
3. Some people have argued that the biggest deficiency of business school graduates is that they have no sense of ethics. What do you think?
4. Is it possible to operate in a completely ethical manner and be successful in business when your competitors engage in unethical tactics?
5. How do Machiavellianism and locus of control affect an individual's cognitive moral development?

EXPERIENTIAL EXERCISE 2.1: IS THIS BEHAVIOUR ETHICAL?

Purpose: To explore your opinions about ethical issues faced in organizations
Group size: 4–5 per group
Time required: 30 minutes
Materials needed: Ethical issues assigned by instructor
Instructions:

Step One: Groups will be randomly assigned one of the following ethical issues. Once your group has been assigned, you will have two tasks:

1. First, formulate your group's answer to the ethical dilemmas.
2. After you have formulated your group's position, discuss the individual differences that may have contributed to your position. Consider the individual differences presented in this chapter as well as any others that you feel affected your position on the ethical dilemma.

Step Two: Your instructor will then lead the class in a discussion of how individual differences may have influenced your positions on these ethical dilemmas.

1. Is it ethical to take office supplies from work for home use? Make personal long-distance calls from the office? Use company time for personal business? Or do these behaviours constitute stealing?
2. If you exaggerate your credentials in an interview, is it lying? Is lying in order to protect a co-worker acceptable?
3. If you pretend to be more successful than you are in order to impress your boss, are you being deceitful?
4. How do you differentiate between a bribe and a gift?
5. If there are slight defects in a product you are selling, are you obligated to tell the buyer? If an advertised "sale" price is really the everyday price, should you divulge the information to the customer?
6. Suppose you have a friend who works at the ticket office for the convention centre where Garth Brooks will be appearing. Is it cheating if you ask the friend to get you tickets so that you won't have to fight the crowd to get them? Is buying merchandise for your family at your company's cost cheating?
7. Is it immoral to do less than your best in terms of work performance? Is it immoral to accept workers' compensation when you are fully capable of working?
8. What behaviours constitute emotional abuse at work? What would you consider an abuse of one's position power?
9. Are high-stress jobs a breach of ethics? What about transfers that break up families?
10. Are all rule violations equally important? Do employees have an ethical obligation to follow company rules?
11. To what extent are you responsible for the ethical behaviour of your co-workers? If you witness unethical behaviour and don't report it, are you an accessory?
12. Is it ethical to help one work group at the expense of another group? For instance, suppose one group has excellent performance and you want to reward its members with an afternoon off. The other work group will have to pick up the slack and work harder if you do this. Is this ethical?

SOURCE: Issues adapted from J. O. Cherrington and D. J. Cherrington, "A Menu of Moral Issues: One Week in the Life of The Wall Street Journal," *Journal of Business Ethics* 11 (1992), 255–65. Reprinted with kind permission of Springer Science and Business Media.

Application, Analysis & Synthesis

CASE: WORKING AT WAL-MART

This case is dedicated to Brent McLain, a beautiful young soul who lost his life early but left his mark on everyone he knew.

Brent had a problem. His father was celebrating a major birthday this Saturday and Brent was scheduled to work from 4:00 to 8:00 p.m. Brent came from a close-knit family where all family milestones were celebrated together over an extended meal. If Brent worked this shift, he would have to miss his father's birthday dinner. If he called in sick, he would feel like a liar since he was not actually ill; he did not even feel a cold coming on. He was sure that his manager would not give him the time off. When Brent first started this job, he had asked that he not be scheduled to work on his day of Sabbath. His manager simply said that the auto scheduler, a computer program designed to create employee work schedules, could not accommodate this, and then walked away. There was no room for discussion. "How much is this job worth to me, anyway" Brent asked himself.

Brent was a 22-year-old fourth-year engineering student living at home. Wanting to avoid student loans, Brent applied to work at Wal-Mart as an associate in the photo lab processing film. Since the store was new, all the associates had to undergo orientation before the store could be opened. Groups of 30 to 40 associates met in the basement meeting room of a hotel. Each associate received a copy of the Wal-Mart associate handbook. The store manager reviewed portions of the handbook related to codes of conduct and told the associates, "At Wal-Mart, you should never hear the phrase 'It's not my job,' since associates are empowered by Wal-Mart." He explained the profit-sharing program and the stock ownership plan along with the benefits. The associates then watched a video entitled "You've Picked a Great Place to Work" that described Wal-Mart's success as a business and how it had grown from a single store that Sam Walton had opened to become the world's largest retailer. Various quotations from Sam Walton, such as, "If you want a successful business, your people must feel that you are working for them— not that they are working for you" were sprinkled liberally throughout the videos. The manager also outlined Sam Walton's guiding principles:[1]

1. Be committed to your work. Your passion will be contagious to those around you.
2. Treat associates as partners and be a servant leader.
3. Make your work exciting and motivational by setting high goals, using job rotation, and encouraging competition.
4. Communicate as much information as you can to associates. Associates with information feel empowered and care about the organization.
5. Demonstrate appreciation on a regular basis. Praise is priceless.
6. Have fun at work, show enthusiasm, and celebrate successes.
7. Listen to your associates. They know what the customers are thinking and they have ideas about how to improve operations.
8. Go beyond meeting your customers' expectations.
9. Pay careful attention to expenses and keep them to a minimum.
10. Be open to trying things that haven't been tried before. Take risks.

The manager then taught the associates the infamous Wal-Mart cheer:
Manager: "Give me a W."
Associates: "W."
Manager: "Give me an A."
Associates: "A."
Manager: "Give me an L."
Associates: "L."
Manager: "Give me a squiggly."
Associates: "Squiggly" (while doing something that resembles the twist).
Manager: "Give me an M."
Associates: "M."
Manager: "Give me an A."
Associates: "A."
Manager: "Give me an R."
Associates: "R."
Manager: "Give me a T."

Associates:	"T."
Manager:	"What's that spell?"
Associates:	"Wal-Mart!"
Manager:	"Who's number one?"
Associates:	"The customer always."
Manager:	"What store is number one?"
Associates:	"[Store number] 999 customer service all the time."

The associates were required to sing this song at every morning meeting and after the store had closed for the evening. At these meetings, the associates would also be informed of how the store was doing in terms of sales levels. The orientation ended with a presentation in which each associate's name was called and the associate was presented a nametag that doubled as a swipe card to be used for the time clock. Brent left the orientation session feeling excited about being part of the Wal-Mart team. It was his first real job and he was impressed with the "family" approach that the managers talked about during the orientation. The managers had encouraged employees to become passionate about Wal-Mart, to share in Sam's vision, and to put Wal-Mart's needs first.

A few days after the orientation session, Brent began working in the photo lab. During his four-hour shift, he placed the film in one end of the developing machine and out the other end came the negatives. Next, he placed the negatives in a scanner, made adjustments for colour, and ordered prints. He then placed these prints and negatives in an envelope and started the process over again with another film. Although Brent sometimes enjoyed looking at the prints, he found his job to be rather routine. He looked forward to troubleshooting when a machine would break down. He tried to process the film as quickly and perfectly as possible so that the customers would be happy with the service that Wal-Mart provided. As did other employees, he learned his job within a few days. There were very few skills to master and the procedures were clearly laid out. Brent realized that employees could be easily replaced (and were) but having the right attitude, one of commitment and a sense of duty, seemed to be particularly important.

At first, having the right attitude was not a problem for Brent. Brent believed that it was better to light one candle than to curse the darkness.[2] Because he always thought the best of others and let any problems slide off like Jell-O nailed to a wall, he had simply dismissed any doubts that he had about his work as unimportant. After a few weeks, however, Brent began to notice that his co-workers were complaining about many things, such as shifts, management, procedures, and, especially, the song that they were taught as part of their orientation. Ever since his manager criticized him for suggesting some new procedures (or "complaining" as his manager called it), Brent thought that it was best to keep quiet. When he had an idea, he thought of a line from a poem that he had read in high school, "The Charge of the Light Brigade": "Theirs not to make reply, Theirs not to reason why, Theirs but to do and die." Whereas Brent used to "go the extra mile," now he did only as much as he needed to keep his job. He would tell himself that Wal-Mart was a means to an end, just as he was a means for Wal-Mart. He was glad that he was getting an education so that he wouldn't have to be a Wal-Mart "lifer." He almost felt bad for the lifers. In a year or two, he'd be a professional engineer, a prestigious occupation paying more than they could ever dream about. More importantly, he had choices; they did not.

Within a year, most of the people that had started at the same time as Brent had left. There seemed to be an increased focus on following rules. For example, although they brought water into the photo lab for the equipment, associates were not permitted to bring in water or other beverages for themselves. Also, although the photo lab employees were able to develop a workable holiday schedule for themselves, the manager refused to accept this schedule because the auto scheduler "would not permit it." Exceptions, negotiations, and relaxation of the rules were not possible.

There were four additional incidents along the same theme that stood out for Brent. After doing an inventory count for several hours, an associate named Roger stepped outside the store for his coffee break. Once back on the job, he noticed that he had left his electronic inventory scanner outside. So, Roger went outside and found his scanner where he left it. However, when he went back into the store, his manager confronted him, indicating that it was inappropriate for an associate to take two coffee breaks and that this formal warning would be placed on Roger's personnel record. Roger quit his job that afternoon. On her last day of work, another associate, Judy, came into the store wearing a pair of khaki shorts. Her manager rushed toward Judy, stopped her a few feet from the door, used his badge to measure her shorts, and told her to go home and change her clothes because her shorts were more than the length of a badge above her knees. Judy did go home but did not return to work.

Similarly, Colette, a cashier, had joined the army reserves and then informed Wal-Mart that she would require every third weekend off. Colette thought that this minor unavailability could be inputted into the auto scheduler and that all would be fine. Even during weeks in which she could not work weekends, she was available for 30 hours of work. However, as with Roger, Colette was informed by her manager that he would not be able to schedule her for the minimum 12 hours per week and that she would have to make a choice between the army and Wal-Mart. Colette then requested a leave of absence that was also denied by her manager. Although she was only one of a handful of employees to receive the four-star cashier award for excellent work and customer service, Colette was subsequently dismissed.

Brent thought about another incident in which Michel, a high school student, requested holidays during the first week of August so that he could participate in an annual family camping trip. Although Michel had submitted his request four months in advance, his manager waited until the middle of July to inform him that he could not find anyone to cover for Michel and, that, as a result, he would have to either work those days or lose his job. Michel decided to miss his family holiday. He didn't want to work at McDonald's or some other place that paid new employees about two dollars less per hour than Wal-Mart did.

On this day at work, Brent was especially apprehensive. Besides having to make a decision regarding his father's birthday dinner, Brent was also concerned about some material that he had come across while surfing the Net. Several websites reported that Wal-Mart is sued, on average, two to five times per day by customers, employees, and other parties.[3] The case that really stood out for Brent dealt with the issue of religious discrimination.[4] A store manager who was displeased with the unwillingness of a Seventh Day Adventist to work during her Sabbath made disparaging comments about the plaintiff's religion and provided an inaccurate account of the activities of the plaintiff and another employee who had both accessed the company's computer system using a management password. Although he fired the plaintiff, he did not fire the other employee who did not practise the plaintiff's religion.

Even though most of these sources contained actual court documents, Brent was skeptical. After all, it is reasonable to expect that any organization would experience these sorts of issues, especially one as visible and as large as Wal-Mart with its $244.5 billion in sales in the 2002–2003 fiscal year, more than 1.3 million associates worldwide, over 3200 facilities in the United States and 1100 units in other countries, and more than 100 million customers per week.[5] In fact, it may well be that Wal-Mart is the target of even fewer lawsuits than other companies its size. And, after all, Brent thought to himself, Wal-Mart has earned the title of top Corporate Citizen by the 2000 Cone/Roper Report of philanthropy and the third most admired company in America by *Fortune Magazine* in 2001.[6] However, after reflecting on what was happening in his own workplace, Brent did not know what to think.

As he walked into the store, Brent felt as though hundreds of eyes were watching him from every direction. He ducked into the washroom but this only reminded him of a case in which a Wal-Mart manager had secretly set up a camera in a unisex washroom in an attempt to catch potential shoplifters in the act.[7] Two employees, however, found this to be invasive and the courts agreed. Although the camera did not actually record anything, the jury considered this irrelevant. "Rightly so," Brent thought. "The washroom is the last sanctuary of mankind." After glancing at the ceiling, Brent slipped into the employee lunchroom.

The walls of the lunchroom were plastered with posters containing slogans such as "Our people make the difference" and "Associates are partners." On the table was an open can of cashews. Although Brent and the other associates normally enjoyed eating whatever food was on the lunchroom table, on this occasion, Brent muttered, "I'd have to be nuts to eat any of those!" He was reminded of another case[8] in which Wal-Mart was ordered to pay $20 million in damages to four employees for defamation, eavesdropping, and outrageous conduct. A manager who was concerned about theft in the store set up a video camera in the employee break room and placed several open packages of nuts and candy on the table as bait. After the manager viewed the tape, he fired four employees without notice. During the resulting trial, another Wal-Mart manager testified that opened packages of nuts and candy were regularly donated to charity or given to employees.

Brent normally has a friendly chat with Monique, a visible minority woman who worked in electronics, but "Not today," he thought. "Why take chances?" Brent was referring to a case[9] in which Wal-Mart was fined $40 000 for secretly recording employee conversations. Brent waved at Monique as he proceeded to the photo lab. He also thought about a case[10] in which a manager fired a white female employee, telling her that she "would never move up with the company being associated with a black man." Wal-Mart was subsequently ordered to pay her $94 000 in damages. "What's the deal here?" Brent thought. "Wal-Mart seems to concern itself with associates' choice of marital partners, elimination of bodily fluids, and religion. If this is how the world's largest retailer treats its employees, what do I have to look forward to in the rest of my career? Maybe I'm expecting too much. After all, this is just a job."

Having reached the photo lab, Brent started loading film into the processor, something he would do for his entire shift. He tried to block out all the questions that he had about his workplace. One question that he was unable to stop thinking about, however, was what he should do about his father's birthday dinner. "Should I not go to Dad's birthday party at all; should I try to ask my manager for time off (and, if so, how); should I pretend to have a cough and ask to go home early on Saturday?" Brent was contemplating his options when another possibility entered his mind, "Or . . . should I just leave for 20 minutes or so and get my co-workers to cover for me?"

Reflection Questions

1. Describe Brent's work-related attitudes and how they are influenced by management.
2. How do employees at Wal-Mart demonstrate organizational commitment?
3. Discuss the influence of these attitudes on organizational outcomes and suggest ways that management can increase commitment and engage employees more effectively. Reference Exhibit 2.3.
4. Describe Brent, Colette, and Michel's cultural values. Reference Exhibit 2.6 to decide which cultural factors are relevant.

Human Resources Extension

1. What are Brent's alternatives regarding attending his father's birthday party? What should he do? Why?
2. What are Brent's alternatives regarding his general employment situation? What should he do? Why?
3. What policies and procedures should Wal-Mart consider to manage diversity in the workplace?

Debating the Issues

Your instructor may assign you to one of the following groups:
Group 1: Argue in favour of the employment practices described in the case.
Group 2: Argue against the employment practices described in the case.

Notes

1. Sam Walton, *Made in America: My Story* (New York: Doubleday, 1992).
2. Christopher Leadership Course.
3. L. Laska, *99 Verdicts against Wal-Mart* (2000), Wal-Mart Litigation Project, www.wal-martlitigation.com/99verdic.htm, accessed November 8, 2001.
4. *Tincher v. Wal-Mart, 155 F.3d 1317,* cited in Laska.
5. Wal-Mart, *News,* www.walmartstores.com/wmstore/wmstores/Mainnews.jsp?BV, accessed November 10, 2003.
6. Wal-Mart, *News,* www.walmartstores.com/wmstores/Mainnews.jsp?BV, accessed November 8, 2001.
7. L. Pierce and B. Appell, *Jury Fed-Up with Employer* (2001), www.silver-freedman.com/library/mar_99_br5.html, accessed November 8, 2001.
8. *Stringer v. Wal-Mart,* Wayne Co. (KY Circ. Ct.), cited in Laska.
9. *Desilets v. Wal-Mart,* 171 F.3d 711 (1st Cir. 1999), cited in Laska.
10. *Deffenbaugh-Williams v. Wal-Mart,* 156 F.3d 581, cited in Laska.

Scoring Instructions for Self-Assessments

Self-Assessment 2.1: Assess your Job Satisfaction

Compute your scores for the facets of job satisfaction as follows.

Pay satisfaction:
Q2 + Q9 = Divided by 2:

Security satisfaction:
Q1 + Q11= Divided by 2:

Social satisfaction:
Q4 + Q7 + Q12 = Divided by 3:

Supervisory satisfaction:
Q5 + Q8 + Q14 = Divided by 3:

Growth satisfaction:
Q3 + Q6 + Q10 + Q13 = Divided by 4:

Scores on the facets range from 1 to 7. (Scores lower than 4 suggest that there is room for change.)

This questionnaire is an abbreviated version of the Job Diagnostic Survey, a widely used tool for assessing individuals' attitudes about their jobs. Compare your scores on each facet to the following norms for a large sample of managers.

Pay satisfaction: 4.6
Security satisfaction: 5.2
Social satisfaction: 5.6
Supervisory satisfaction: 5.2
Growth satisfaction: 5.3

How do your scores compare? Are there actions you can take to improve your job satisfaction?

Self-Assessment 2.2: What are Your Cultural Values?

The questionnaire measures each of the five basic culture dimensions. Your score can range from 5 to 35. The numbers in parentheses that follow are the question numbers. Add the scores for these questions to arrive at your total score for each cultural value. The higher your score, the more you demonstrate the cultural value.

Value 1: Uncertainty avoidance (1, 2, 3, 4, 5). Your score: _____.
A high score indicates a culture in which people often try to make the future predictable by closely following rules and regulations. Organizations try to avoid uncertainty by creating rules and rituals that give the illusion of stability.

Value 2: Individualism versus collectivism (6, 7, 8, 9, 10, 11). Your score: _____.
A high score indicates collectivism, or a culture in which people believe that group success is more important than individual achievement. Loyalty to the group comes before all else. Employees are loyal and emotionally dependent on their organization.

Value 3: Power distance (12, 13, 14, 15, 16, 17). Your score: _____.
A high score indicates a culture in which people believe in the unequal distribution of power among segments of the culture. Employees fear disagreeing with their bosses and are seldom asked for their opinions by their bosses.

Value 4: Long-term/short-term (18, 19, 20, 21, 22, 23, 24). Your score: _____.
A high score indicates a culture in which people value persistence, thrift, and respect for tradition. Young employees are expected to follow orders given to them by their elders and delay gratification of their maternal, social, and emotional needs.

Value 5: Masculinity/femininity (25, 26, 27, 28, 29). Your score: ____.
A high score indicates masculinity, or a culture in which people value the acquisition of money and other material things. Successful managers are viewed as aggressive, tough, and competitive. Earnings, recognition, and advancement are important; quality of life and cooperation are not as highly prized.

Part One: Introduction (28:57 minutes)

HENRY MINTZBERG AND THE EFFECTIVE EXECUTIVE *(9:40 MINUTES)*

This clip features management guru Henry Mintzberg explaining why he does not believe that an MBA qualifies someone to be an effective senior manager. Mintzberg argues that knowing one's business is more important than management education, and the example of the Provigo grocery chain in Montreal is used to make this point. Ric Irving from York University provides a counterargument.

Critical Thinking Questions

1. Provigo executives fired all the professional managers and experts when they took over. What do you think of this?
2. What is the role of a general management education today, given current OB challenges and opportunities?
3. Which is more important for a senior manager today, general or specialized knowledge? Why?
4. Are the concepts expressed by the Provigo executives applicable outside of the retail industry?

IMPACT OF GLOBALIZATION ON CANADIAN INDUSTRY *(2:04 MINUTES)*

This clip highlights the impact on the Canadian textile industry of the rising Canadian dollar, improved quality of products made overseas, and the lifting of quotas limiting the amount of foreign textiles sold in Canada. Competition from China is getting tougher and quality is improving. One result is that Texturon Inc., a textile manufacturer, went from 1200 employees to 9.

Critical Thinking Question

1. Should Canada be maintaining duties and quotas on foreign goods and/or services to protect Canadian industry and jobs?

ETHICS OF DOING BUSINESS ACROSS BORDERS *(2:04 MINUTES)*

This clip investigates a southern Chinese toy factory that uses child labour to make toys.

Critical Thinking Questions

1. Should Canadian companies do business with overseas firms that use child labour or other unethical practices?
2. Should consumers buy their products?

ETHICS COURSE AT NEXEN *(1:29 MINUTES)*

This clip looks at the Canadian energy company Nexen's commitment to ethics. The company requires all its employees to take an ethics course, and each unit has an "integrity leader." An investment in Sudan was turned down based on ethical concerns. The clip also raises the issue of corporate hypocrisy, such as the fact that Enron had an ethics video.

Critical Thinking Questions

1. To what extent do companies "walk the talk" when they say they value ethical practices?
2. Does the culture of a company influence an individual's ethics at work, or are our ethical values stable and resistant to the type of corporate culture and ethical norms?

ETHICS AND VALUES: "VIRTUES PROJECT" BROUGHT TO WALKERTON *(2:06 MINUTES)*

This clip features Linda Kavelin-Popov of B.C. and her "Virtues Project," which she used to helped residents of Walkerton Ont. heal after the tainted water tragedy. The Virtues Project is based on 52 values derived from all the major world religions, and participants in the project explore their own values and how to live in accordance with them.

Critical Thinking Questions

1. Which values from your spiritual beliefs or religion guide you in your personal life? Work life? Is there a difference?
2. How might learning about organizational behaviour contribute to avoiding a crisis like Walkerton?

UNIONS AT WAL-MART *(1:53 MINUTES)*

This clip features the recent attempt to unionize Wal-Mart employees in Quebec.

Critical Thinking Questions

1. Should companies as successful as Wal-Mart be paying their employees higher wages?
2. Do you think that unions can sometimes be a good thing for an organization?

SHOULD ONTARIO ELIMINATE MANDATORY RETIREMENT? *(1:55 MINUTES)*

This clip explores the pros and cons of mandatory retirement at age 65.

Critical Thinking Questions

1. Does age discrimination exist in the workplace?
2. Should mandatory retirement at 65 be retained? Why or why not?

CHANGING IMMIGRATION POLICIES TO HELP MEET SKILLS GAPS *(2:14 MINUTES)*

This clip explores projected skills shortages in Canada and how immigration policies need to change so that immigrants can help mitigate the impact of a declining and aging population and fuel economic growth.

Critical Thinking Questions

1. What impact will increased immigration have on managing workforce diversity?
2. Should the credentials of immigrants be less scrutinized than they currently are so as to permit quicker access to their skill sets?

BREAKING THROUGH THE GLASS CEILING: MICHELINE BOUCHARD, CEO *(1:52 MINUTES)*

This clip features Micheline Bouchard, CEO of Advanced Research Technologies Inc. and formerly Motorola, as an example of a woman who has broken through the glass ceiling.

Critical Thinking Questions

1. What are the factors that sustain the glass ceiling?
2. What are the keys to eliminating the glass ceiling in the workplace?

JOB SATISFACTION HIGHER IN SOME PROVINCES THAN OTHERS *(1:49 MINUTES)*

This clip explores variations in job satisfaction by province and why workers in Quebec and Halifax are the most satisfied.

Critical Thinking Questions

1. How important is a balanced lifestyle to you now? How do you think that will change five years from now?
2. What family-friendly policies are most important to you?
3. Is it possible for men and women to have both a satisfying job and a satisfying family life?

ENABLING A HEALTHY WORKFORCE AT DOFASCO *(1:51 MINUTES)*

This clip features Dofasco and its numerous programs, such as a worker ice rink, gym, health assessment, and fitness classes, which support employee health and wellness. It highlights the relationship between a healthy and fit workforce and productivity.

Critical Thinking Questions

1. Do you agree that a healthy and fit employee is always more productive?
2. What other factors contribute to employee productivity

Individual Processes and Behaviour

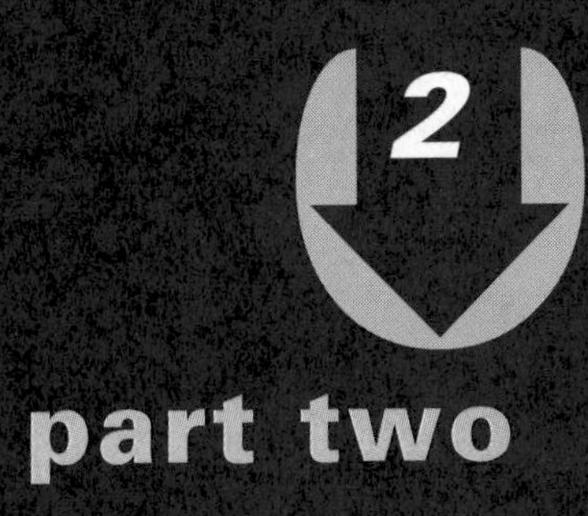

part two

Perception and Personality

chapter three

LEARNING OBJECTIVES

By the end of this chapter, you will be able to do the following:

1. Define *social perception* and explain how characteristics of the perceiver, the target, and the situation affect it.
2. Identify the six common barriers to social perception.
3. Explain the attribution process and how attributions affect managerial and employee behaviour.
4. Explain why it is important to manage our impression on others.
5. Define *personality* and explain four theories of personality.
6. Identify several personality characteristics and their influences on behaviour in organizations.
7. Explain how personality is measured.
8. Discuss Carl Jung's contribution to our understanding of individual differences and explain how his theory is used in the Myers-Briggs Type Indicator.

learning about the context

Jim Carrey: The Man of Many Personalities and Master of Perception

The Mask; Ace Ventura: Pet Detective; Me, Myself & Irene. Do you recognize these movie titles? Perhaps you associate these movies with the actor who portrayed the lead character. In the movie *The Mask,* the character Stanley Ipkiss jumps into a river to save a drowning man and finds a mask floating in the water. He picks it up and suddenly without warning the mask clings to his face. The events that follow are hilarious. Stanley's face turns green, his body twists and turns in usual ways, and his personality undergoes a radical shift. Stanley is suddenly transformed from a weak, ineffective, introverted person into a wacky superhero. Insecurity is replaced by flamboyance, and his body takes on superhuman powers.

Jim Carrey is the actor, and he is famous for his zaniness, portrayals of split personality, epic face-pulling, a head full of lunatic voices, and a natural drive to do anything for a laugh. Born in Newmarket, Ontario, Carrey found his calling at an early age. He knew he was destined to become a comedian. "I started in second grade. I was in music class and we were practising for the Christmas assembly. One day I started fooling around by mocking the musicians on a record. The teacher thought she'd embarrass me by making me get up and do what I was doing in front of the whole class. So I went up and did it. She laughed and the whole class went nuts. My teacher asked me to do my routine for the Christmas assembly and I did. That was the beginning of the end," says Carrey. From that day on Jim Carrey did not look back. At age 15, he preformed at Yuk Yuk's, a Toronto comedy club, and by age 19 he had moved to L.A. and was a regular at a famous comedy club, The Comedy Store.

The critics have said that Jim Carrey is one of the funniest comedian/actors to enter the Hollywood scene in a long time. He has been nominated for and won numerous awards, receiving a Golden Globe Award for his performance in *The Truman Show* and for his portrayal of Andy Kaufman in the film *Man on the Moon.* He has been hailed as one the great comics of his generation and the finest physical comedian since the silent era of movies. He demonstrates natural gifts of slapstick, parody, and absurdism and in his recent movies he has shown great depth, being able to demonstrate a more serious side. His performance in the movie *The Eternal Sunshine of the Spotless Mind* has been cited as his best work yet, showing a poignant, toned-down, and serious side of his nature. In a recent *New York Times* article, Carrey has been quoted as saying that "he has put more of himself into this film [*Eternal Sunshine*] and he promised that the next one will be 100% me."

So how would you describe the personality of this actor? What are some of the core traits that we can infer from watching Jim Carrey perform and by examining his career history? A glimpse into his personality tells us he is extraverted, people-oriented, flexible, adaptable, and highly driven, to say the least. What is your perception? How does Jim's portrayal of the characters influence your perception? When Jim Carrey says that the next film will be "100% me," what do you think that character would look like?

SOURCES: AskMen.com, *Jim Carrey,* http://www.askmen.com/men/january00/7c_jim_carrey.html, accessed August 3, 2004; A. O'Hehir, "The Jim Carrey Show," *The Well,* December 7, 1999, http://www.salon.com/ent/movies/feature/1999/12/07/carrey/ accessed August 4, 2004; C. James, "Captain Video Prepares for Takeoff," *The New York Times,* March 7, 2004 (Late Edition East Coast), 2.1.

In Chapter 2 we discussed how values and work attitudes influence an individual's behaviour. In this chapter we will continue to explore how our individual characteristics influence behaviour with a focus on individual perception and personality. This chapter is divided into two sections. In the first section we examine the factors that influence perception and how to manage our perceptions in the workplace. In the second section we look at those characteristics that shape our personality and the influence that these characteristics have on our interpretation of workplace situations. At the end of the chapter, we will learn about a famous personality test called the Myers-Briggs and the "Big Five" personality traits.

INTRODUCTION TO PERCEPTION AND PERSONALITY IN THE WORKPLACE

Consider how you might interpret this situation. You are on your way to lunch when you run into a colleague who asks you if you are going to the monthly departmental meeting. You are new to the company, just one week into the job, and you are surprised to find that there is a meeting and you were not informed. You look for your boss but he is nowhere to be found. You are not sure what to do but ultimately you decide to attend. When you enter the room, everyone is talking and you don't know anyone and people ignore you. Your first impression—that these fellow colleagues are unfriendly and aloof! You decide not to stay at the meeting. After all, you are a shy person and you have never been very comfortable in new situations. As you leave the room you think to yourself that maybe, just maybe, you made a mistake joining this company.

Just then, the elevator door opens and out walks your boss. He is frazzled and preoccupied. He apologizes for not telling you about the meeting and he informs you that he has been preoccupied because of a major problem with a key customer. You find out that this problem has taken the collective efforts of your entire department to resolve. Everyone had been working around the clock to fix the situation and this meeting was the first time your team had an opportunity to discuss their issues and the impact on the company. Suddenly it makes sense why everyone in the room appeared preoccupied and did not pay much attention to you! You think to yourself perhaps your initial reaction may have been a bit hasty. Perhaps your perceptions were incorrect.

How we view a situation and how we respond to that situation can be shaped by our personality, perceptions, emotions, and experience. In this scenario the new hire was unaware of the situation. He had three choices: he could have approached a colleague and started talking, stayed at the meeting accepting the situation, or withdrawn. This person chose to leave, filling himself with negative thoughts about his colleagues and thinking that joining this firm was a mistake. He viewed the situation from a pessimistic perspective: "glass half empty" as opposed to "glass half full." Were his perceptions accurate? What personality traits did this individual possess that contributed to his response? What should he have done?

Studies have shown that there exists a direct relationship between the personality traits we possess, our perceptions, and our emotional response. Martin Seligman's book *Learned Optimism* suggests that how we perceive a situation can influence our behavioural response to situations. He distinguishes between the traits exhibited by an optimistic person and those exhibited by a pessimistic person, suggesting that anyone can learn how to be more positive in their interactions by identifying and using many of the strengths and personality traits we already possess, such as humour, kindness, and generosity—a concept he calls "learned optimism."[1]

Optimists are more successful at work and in school. In his research, Seligman found that newly hired salesmen who were optimists sold 37 percent more insurance in their first two years than did pessimists. In another study he tested 500 members of a first-year class. He found that their scores on a test of optimism were a better predictor of actual grades during the first year than SAT score or high school grades.[2]

So the next time you are faced with a situation, think about how your perceptions influence your response to the particular situation and what influence your personality had on the outcome. Was your response appropriate for the situation? How did you respond and, most importantly, how should you have responded? Understanding how we view and interpret situations and manage these interactions will influence our success at work.

INTRODUCTION TO SOCIAL PERCEPTION

Define *social perception* and explain how characteristics of the perceiver, the target, and the situation affect it.

Perception involves the way we view the world around us. It adds meaning to information gathered via the five senses of touch, smell, hearing, vision, and taste. Perception is the primary vehicle through which we come to understand ourselves and our surroundings. **Social perception** is the process of interpreting information about another person. Consider the first time you went to a new school. When you went to register, how you were greeted? Did you feel welcome? What were the surroundings like? Did they feel warm and inviting? Did you think that the people were friendly and that you were going to feel comfortable in this new environment?

social perception
The process of interpreting information about another person.

Virtually all management activities rely on perception. In appraising performance, managers use their perceptions of an employee's behaviour as a basis for the evaluation. One work situation that highlights the importance of perception is the selection interview. The consequences of a bad match between an individual and the organization are devastating for both parties, so it is essential that the data gathered be accurate. Typical first interviews are brief, and the candidate is usually one of many seen by an interviewer during a day. How long does it take for the interviewer to reach a decision about a candidate? In the first four to five minutes, the interviewer often makes an "accept" or "reject" decision based on his or her perception of the candidate.[3]

Perception is also culturally determined. Based on our cultural backgrounds, we tend to perceive things in certain ways. Read the following sentence:

> Finished files are the result of years of scientific study combined with the experience of years.

Now quickly count the number of *f*'s in the sentence. Individuals for whom English is their second language see all six *f*'s. Most native English speakers report that there are three *f*'s. Because of cultural conditioning, *of* is not considered an important word and is ignored.[4] Culture affects our interpretation of the data we gather, as well as the way we add meaning to it. Valuing diversity, including cultural diversity, has been recognized as the key to international competitiveness.[5] This challenge and others make social perception skills essential to managerial success.

In a typical job selection interview, the interviewer often makes the decision whether to hire in the first four or five minutes of the interview—simply based on his or her perception of the candidate.

Factors That Influence Our Perception of Others

Three major categories of factors influence our perception of another person: (1) characteristics of ourselves as perceivers, (2) characteristics of the target person we are perceiving, and (3) characteristics of the situation in which the interaction takes place. See Exhibit 3.1.

Characteristics of the Perceiver

Several characteristics of the perceiver can affect social perception. One such characteristic is familiarity with the target (the person being perceived). When we are familiar with a person, we have multiple observations on which to base our impression of him or her. If the information we have gathered during these observations is accurate, we may have an accurate perception of the other person. However, familiarity does not always mean accuracy. Sometimes, when we know a person well, we tend to screen out information that is inconsistent with what we believe the person is like.

The perceiver's attitudes also affect social perception. Suppose you are interviewing candidates for a very important position in your organization—a position that requires negotiating contracts with suppliers, most of whom are male. You may feel that women are not capable of holding their own in tough negotiations. This attitude will doubtless affect your perceptions of the female candidates you interview. To better understand how Canada's employment legislation has influenced the perception of attitudes, see Organizational Reality 3.1.

EXHIBIT 3.1

A Model for Social Perception

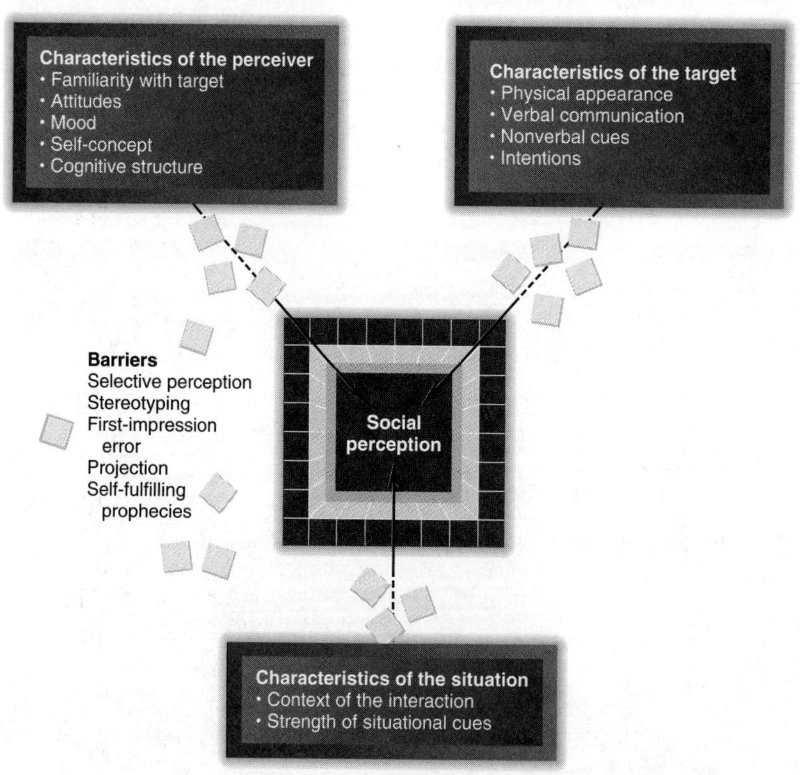

organizational reality 3.1

How Canada's Employment Legislation Has Influenced Our Perception of Attitudes

Ever heard the expression "It's women's work"? This attitude toward women in the workplace has prevailed in North American culture for decades. With the introduction of Canada's Employment and Pay Equity Acts, these challenges are being met head on. From a recent speech by the chief commissioner of the Human Rights Commission entitled "Creating a Level Playing Field," the commissioner refers to the effectiveness of Ontario's employment legislation. She states that this legislation has gone a long way toward managing these perceptions. "Over the past 17 years women have made considerable progress in the public and private sectors under federal jurisdiction. In 1987 they made up 40% of the private sector workforce. This representation now stands at 45%. Most importantly, their share of management positions is 20%, which is in line with the Canadian average of 21%, and there now exist a qualified pool of women to facilitate succession planning."

SOURCE: Mary M. Gusella (chief commissioner, Canadian Human Rights Commission), *Creating a Level Playing Field for Women.* Presented at the Global Colloquium on Creating a Level Playing Field for Women, March 5, 2004, in Washington D.C., http://www.chrc-ccdp.ca/media_room/speeches-en.asp?id=265&content_type=2&pm=1, accessed July 26, 2004.

Mood can have a strong influence on the way we perceive someone.[6] We think differently when we are happy than we do when we are depressed. In addition, we remember information that is consistent with our mood state better than information that is inconsistent with our mood state. When in a positive mood, we form more positive impressions of others. When in a negative mood, we tend to evaluate others unfavourably. Think about the last time you were in a bad mood. How did this state affect your perceptions of others?

Cognitive structure, an individual's pattern of thinking, also affects social perception. Some people have a tendency to perceive physical traits, such as height, weight, and appearance, more readily. Others tend to focus more on central traits, or personality dispositions. Cognitive complexity allows a person to perceive multiple characteristics of another person rather than attending to just a few traits.

Another factor that can affect social perception is the perceiver's self-concept. An individual with a positive self-concept tends to notice positive attributes in another person. In contrast, a negative self-concept can lead a perceiver to pick out negative traits in another person. Greater understanding of self allows us to have more accurate perceptions of others.

Characteristics of the Target

Characteristics of the target, the person being perceived, influence social perception. Physical appearance plays a big role in our perception of others. The perceiver will notice the target's physical features, such as height, weight, estimated age, race, and gender. Clothing says a great deal about a person. Blue pinstriped suits, for example, are decoded to mean banking or Bay Street. Perceivers tend to notice physical appearance characteristics that contrast with the norm, that are intense, or that are new or unusual.[7] A loud person, one who dresses outlandishly, or a very tall person will be noticed because he or she provides a contrast to what is commonly encountered. In addition, people who are novel can attract attention. Cintas, a company that specializes in manufacturing uniforms, bases its business on helping companies project the right image for their customers by providing them with appropriate uniforms. For more details, see Organizational Reality 3.2.

organizational reality 3.2

Cintas: The Uniform Company

Cintas helps companies to create a positive corporate image.

A police officer, a firefighter, or a dental assistant.... What do you associate these occupations with? How about the customer service person at Tim Hortons, the hospital volunteer at your local hospital or the person who serves you at the local McDonalds?

All these occupations require the jobholder to wear a uniform. These uniforms establish a set of preconceived expectations related to that individual's role and responsibilities, framing our perceptions.

Cintas is the industry expert in helping companies project the right image to their customers. It is the largest uniform supplier in North America, with more than 500 000 clients. More than five million people wear Cintas clothing each day. Cintas operates 365 facilities in the U.S. and Canada, including 14 manufacturing plants and seven distribution centres that employ more than 27 000 people. Some of its customers are Marriott Hotels, Delta Air Lines, McDonald's, and Starbucks.

The company has been recognized by *Fortune* magazine as one of the most admired companies three years in a row, it was named in *Business Week*'s Global 1000 as one of the world's most valuable companies, and was awarded two of the "Top Ten Image of the Year" designs, the highest honour bestowed for uniform designs in the uniform industry. Go to the website to learn more about how this company helps organizations manage perception.

SOURCE: Cintas, "Corporate Profile," http://www.cintas-corp.com/company/corporate_profile, accessed July 26, 2004.

Physical attractiveness can often influence our impression of others. Job interviewers typically rate attractive candidates more favourably, and these candidates are awarded higher starting salaries. People who are perceived as physically attractive face stereotypes as well. We will discuss these and other stereotypes later in this chapter.

Verbal communication from targets also affects our perception of them. We listen to the topics they speak about, their voice tone, and their accent and make judgments based on this input. Consider the last time you were at a group meeting with individuals whom you had just met for the first time. Think about your perceptions of these people. Perhaps someone did not speak at all and you thought they might be shy, or perhaps someone took total control of the meeting and you thought he was a control freak. Now think about the next few times you met. Did you still have the same perception?

Nonverbal communication conveys a great deal of information about the target. Eye contact, facial expressions, body movements, and posture all are deciphered by the perceiver in an attempt to form an impression of the target. The *intentions* of the target are inferred by the perceiver, who observes the target's behaviour. We may see our boss appear in our office doorway and think, "Oh no! She's going to give me more work to do." Or we may perceive that her intention is to congratulate us on a recent success. In any case, the perceiver's interpretation of the target's intentions affects the way the perceiver views the target.

Characteristics of the Situation

The situation in which the interaction between the perceiver and the target takes place also influences the perceiver's impression of the target. The social context of the interaction is a major influence. Meeting a professor in his or her office affects your impression in a certain way that may contrast with the impression you would form had you met the professor in a local restaurant. It is interesting to note that social context plays a different role in varying cultures. In Japan, social context is very important. Business conversations after working hours or at lunch are taboo. If you try to talk business during these times, you may be perceived as rude.[8]

The *strength of situational cues* also affects social perception. As we discussed earlier in the chapter, some situations provide strong cues as to appropriate behaviour. In these situations, we assume that the individual's behaviour can be accounted for by the situation, and that it may not reflect the individual's disposition. This is the **discounting principle** in social perception.[9] For example, you may encounter an automobile salesperson who has a warm and personable manner, asks about your work and hobbies, and seems genuinely interested in your taste in cars. Can you assume that this behaviour reflects the salesperson's personality? You probably cannot, because of the influence of the situation. This person is trying to sell you a car, and when dealing with potential customers, the car salesperson is likely trying to win the customers' business by taking an interest in their personal life.

discounting principle
The assumption that an individual's behaviour is accounted for by the situation.

You can see that characteristics of the perceiver, the target, and the situation all affect social perception. It would be wonderful if all of us had accurate social perception skills. Unfortunately, barriers often prevent us from perceiving another person accurately.

Barriers to Social Perception

Identify six common barriers to social perception.

We would all like to think that our perceptions are objective and accurate. However, researchers have suggested that there are several barriers that can lead us to form inaccurate impressions of others. Six barriers to social perception (also referred to as "perceptual screens" in Chapter 6) are selective perception, stereotyping, first-impression error, projection, self-fulfilling prophecies, and attribution theory (attributing causes to behaviour).

Selective Perception

To sort through the vast amount of information we receive, people automatically employ the first barrier to social perception: selective perception. **Selective perception** is our tendency to choose information that supports our viewpoints. Individuals often ignore information that makes them feel uncomfortable or threatens their viewpoints. Suppose, for example, that a sales manager is evaluating the performance of his or her employees. One employee does not get along well with colleagues and rarely completes sales reports on time. This employee, however, generates the most new sales contracts in the office. The sales manager may ignore the negative information, choosing to evaluate the salesperson only on contracts generated. The manager is exercising selective perception.

selective perception
The process of selecting information that supports our individual viewpoints while discounting information that threatens our viewpoints.

Stereotyping

stereotype
A generalization about a group of people.

The second barrier to social perception is stereotyping. A **stereotype** is a generalization about a group of people. Stereotypes reduce information about other people to a workable level, and they are efficient for compiling and using information. Stereotypes become even stronger when they are shared with and validated by others.[10] Stereotypes can be accurate, and when they are accurate they can be useful perceptual guidelines. Most of the time, however, stereotypes are inaccurate. They harm individuals when inaccurate impressions of them are inferred and are never tested or changed.[11] Information technology careers, for example, have been stereotyped such that fewer young people are entering the field. The stereotype of these careers is outdated and inaccurate. Test your own knowledge of gender stereotypes with Self-Assessment 3.1: Sex Role Stereotypes.

Globally, people form stereotypes of people they live and work with. Researchers surveying a group of transnational employees about their stereotypes resulted in the following caricature-based descriptions; "Japanese managers are clever and cunning. They are reserved, express no emotions, and communicate indirectly." American managers are "arrogant, confident, and loud."[12] Clearly, these stereotypes can influence how we interact with others. Have you met an American or Japanese manager who does not fit this stereotype?

First-Impression Error

first-impression error
The tendency to form lasting opinions about an individual based on initial perceptions.

The third barrier to social perception is formed by first impressions. First impressions are lasting impressions, so the saying goes. Individuals place a good deal of importance on first impressions, and for good reason. We tend to remember what we perceive first about a person, and sometimes we are quite reluctant to change our initial impressions.[13] **First-impression error** occurs when we observe a very brief bit of a person's behaviour in our

Knowledge & Application

SELF ASSESSMENT 3.1: SEX ROLE STEREOTYPES

Below is a list of characteristics that are often used to indicate gender differences. If you believe that a characteristic is more like a typical male, mark an *M* in the space provided. Mark an *F* if you believe a characteristic is more like a typical female. Mark an *N* if you believe there is no difference.

1. M Aggressive
2. M Dominant
3. F Excitable in a major crisis
4. F Home-oriented
5. M High mechanical aptitude
6. F Feelings easily hurt
7. M Never cries
8. M Strong need for security
9. N Indifferent to others' approval
10. N Likes math and science
11. F Emotional
12. N Has difficulty making decisions

For scoring instructions, please go to the end of the chapter, p. 105.

SOURCE: J. T. Spence, R. Helmreich, and J. Stapp, "The Personal Attributes Questionnaire: A Measure of Sex Role Stereotypes and Masculinity–Femininity," *JSAS Catalog of Selected Documents in Psychology* (1974): 4, 43.

first encounter and infer that this behaviour reflects what the person is really like. Primacy effects can be particularly dangerous in interviews, given that we form first impressions quickly and that these impressions may be the basis for long-term employment relationships.

Projection

Projection, also known as the false-consensus effect, is a cause of inaccurate perceptions of others. It is the misperception of the commonness of our own beliefs, values, and behaviours such that we overestimate the number of others who share these things. We assume that others are similar to us, and that our own values and beliefs are appropriate. People who are different are viewed as unusual and even deviant. Projection occurs most often when you surround yourself with others similar to you. You may overlook important information about others when you assume we are all alike and in agreement.[14]

projection
Overestimating the number of people who share our own beliefs, values, and behaviours.

Self-Fulfilling Prophecies

Self-fulfilling prophecies are the fifth barrier to social perception. Ever had someone say to you, "Be careful what you wish for"? Sometimes our expectations affect the way we interact with others such that we get what we wish for. Early studies of self-fulfilling prophecies were conducted in elementary school classrooms. Teachers were given bogus information that some of their pupils had high intellectual potential. These pupils were chosen randomly; there were really no differences among the students. Eight months later, the "gifted" pupils scored significantly higher on an IQ test. The teachers' expectations had elicited growth from these students, and the teachers had given them tougher assignments and more feedback on their performance.[15]

self-fulfilling prophecy
The situation in which our expectations about people affect our interaction with them in such a way that our expectations are fulfilled.

Self-fulfilling prophecies has been observed in work organizations as well.[16] A manager's expectations of an individual affect both the manager's behaviour toward the individual and the individual's response. For example, suppose your initial impression is that an employee has the potential to move up within the organization. Chances are you will spend a great deal of time coaching and counselling the employee, providing challenging assignments, and grooming the individual for success.

Managers can harness the power of the self-fulfilling prophecy to improve productivity in the organization. It appears that high expectations of individuals come true. Can a manager extend these high expectations to an entire group and have similar positive results? The answer is yes. When a manager expects positive things from a group, the group delivers.[17]

Attribution in Organizations

Explain the attribution process and how attributions affect managerial and employee behaviour.

Another possible barrier to perception is the way in which we attribute the cause for someone's behaviour. For example, when someone is late for work do we attribute this behaviour to something the person did or something outside a person's control? For example, your staff meeting is called for 9:00 a.m. and one of your colleagues walks in at 9:30 a.m. Do you think to yourself that the reason this individual is late is due to an external event like major traffic or do you think that this person is undisciplined and does not care? The attributions, or inferred causes, we provide for behaviour have important implications in organizations.

Attribution theory explains how we pinpoint the causes of our own behaviour and that of other people.[18] Attributions can be made to an internal source of responsibility (something within the individual's control) or an external source (something outside the individual's control). Suppose you perform well on an exam in this course. You might say you aced the test because you are smart or because you studied hard. If you attribute your success to ability or effort, you are making an internal attribution.

attribution theory
A theory that explains how individuals pinpoint the causes of their own behaviour and that of others.

Alternatively, you might make an external attribution for your performance. You might say it was an easy test (you would attribute your success to degree of task difficulty) or that you had good luck. In this case, you are attributing your performance to sources beyond your control, or external sources. You can see that internal attributions include such causes as ability and effort, whereas external attributions include causes like task difficulty or luck.

Attribution patterns differ among individuals.[19] Achievement-oriented individuals attribute their success to ability and their failures to lack of effort, both internal causes. Failure-oriented individuals attribute their failures to lack of ability, and they may develop feelings of incompetence as a result of their attributional pattern. Evidence indicates that this attributional pattern also leads to depression.[20] Women managers, in contrast to men managers, are less likely to attribute their success to their own ability. This may be because they are adhering to social norms that compel women to be more modest about their accomplishments, or because they believe that success has less to do with ability than with hard work.[21]

Attributional Biases

fundamental attribution error
The tendency to make attributions to internal causes when focusing on someone else's behaviour.

self-serving bias
The tendency to attribute one's own successes to internal causes and one's failures to external causes.

The attribution process may be affected by two very common errors: the fundamental attribution error and the self-serving bias. The tendency to make attributions to internal causes when focusing on someone else's behaviour is known as the **fundamental attribution error.**[22] The other error, **self-serving bias,** occurs when focusing on one's own behaviour. Individuals tend to make internal attributions for their own successes and external attributions for their own failures.[23] In other words, when we succeed, we take credit for it; when we fail, we blame the situation on other people.

Both of these biases were illustrated in a study of health care managers who were asked to cite the causes of their employees' poor performance.[24] The managers claimed that internal causes (their employees' lack of effort or lack of ability) were the basis for their employees' poor performance. This is an example of the fundamental attribution error. When the employees were asked to pinpoint the cause of their own performance problems, they blamed a lack of support from the managers (an external cause), which illustrates self-serving bias.

There are cultural differences in these two attribution errors. As described above, these biases apply to people from Canada and the United States. In more fatalistic cultures, such as India's, people tend to believe that fate is responsible for much that happens. People in such cultures tend to emphasize external causes of behaviour.[25] In China, people are taught that hard work is the route to accomplishment. When faced with either a success or a failure, Chinese individuals first introspect about whether they tried hard enough or whether their attitude was correct. In a study of attributions for performance in sports, Chinese athletes attributed both their successes and failures to internal causes. Even when the cause of poor athletic performance was clearly external, such as bad weather, the Chinese participants made internal attributions. In terms of the Chinese culture, this attributional pattern is a reflection of moral values that are used to evaluate behaviour. The socialistic value of selfless morality dictates that individual striving must serve collective interests. Mao Zedong stressed that external causes function only through internal causes; therefore, the main cause of results lies within oneself. Chinese are taught this from childhood and form a corresponding attributional tendency. In analyzing a cause, they first look to their own effort.[26]

Implications of Attribution Theory in the Workplace

Attribution theory has many applications in the workplace. Managers use attributions in all aspects of their jobs. Determining the causes of job performance is a major task for the manager, and attribution theory can be used to explain how managers go about determining causality. In addition, knowledge of the fundamental attribution error and self-serving bias can help a manager guard against these biases in the processes of looking for causes of behaviour on the job. Consider the situation where an employee is unable to meet a project deadline. The employee has identified the source of the problem as a lack of resources and communicates this to the manager. The manager, on the other hand, has assumed that the reason the project was not finished on time was due to the employee's poor abilities and skills. Which attribution is correct? It is important for managers to investigate and check out the facts before making an assumption. This information will help the manager be more realistic about their employee's performance contributions.

Attributions can affect an individual's behaviour as well, and can affect motivation. For example, suppose you must give an important presentation to your executive management group. You believe you have performed well, and your boss tells you that you've done a good job. To what do you attribute your success? If you believe careful preparation and rehearsal led to your success, you're likely to take credit for the performance and to have a sense of self-efficacy about future presentations. If, however, you believe that you were just lucky, you may not be motivated to repeat the performance because you believe you had little influence on the outcome.

One situation in which a lot of attributions are made is the employment interview. Candidates are often asked to explain the causes of previous performance (Why did you perform poorly in math classes?) to interviewers. In addition, candidates often feel they should justify why they should be hired (I work well with people, so I'm looking for a managerial job). Research shows that successful and unsuccessful candidates differ in the way they make attributions for negative outcomes. Successful candidates are less defensive and make internal attributions for negative events. Unsuccessful candidates attribute negative outcomes to things beyond their control (external attributions), which gives interviewers the impression that the candidate failed to learn from the event. In addition, interviewers fear that the individuals would be likely to blame others when something goes wrong in the workplace.[27]

MindData

MindData offers insightful articles and quantitative tests to help explore employee diversity, behaviour, and motivation. How can employers benefit from MindData's resources? Can the site help job seekers learn more about how personality, perception, and attribution related to on-the-job situations? Check out the website and see for yourself.
http://www.minddata.com

The Importance of Managing Perception

Explain why it is important to manage our impression on others.

Most people want to make favourable impressions on others. This is particularly true in organizations, where individuals compete for jobs, favourable performance evaluations, and salary increases. The process by which individuals try to control the impressions others have of them is called **impression management.** Individuals use several techniques to control others' impressions of them.[28] See Organizational Reality 3.3 to see how Second City has turned impression management into a business.

impression management
The process by which individuals try to control the impressions others have of them.

Some impression management techniques are self-enhancing. These techniques focus on enhancing others' impressions of the person using the technique. Name-dropping, which involves mentioning an association with important people in the hopes of improving one's image, is often used. Managing one's appearance is another technique for impression management. Individuals dress carefully for interviews because they want to "look the part" in order to get the job. Self-descriptions, or statements about one's characteristics, are used to manage impressions as well.

Another group of impression management techniques are other-enhancing. The aim of these techniques is to focus on the individual whose impression is to be managed. Flattery is a common other-enhancing technique whereby compliments are given to an individual in order to win his or her approval. Favours are also used to gain the approval of others. Agreement with someone's opinion is a technique often used to gain a positive impression. People with disabilities, for example, often use other-enhancing techniques. They may feel that they must take it upon themselves to make others comfortable interacting with them. Impression management techniques are used by individuals with disabilities as a way of dealing with potential avoidance by others.[29]

Are impression management techniques effective? Most of the research has focused on employment interviews. Those candidates who worked on creating a positive impression performed better in interviews, were more likely to obtain additional site visits with potential employers, and were hired more often.[30] In addition, employees who engage in impression management are rated more favourably in performance appraisals than those who do not.[31]

organizational reality 3.3

Second City: Training Employees to Manage Perceptions

Mike Myers, Gilda Radner, John Candy, Rick Moranis, Catherine O'Hara, and Eugene Levy all began their careers at Second City. Second City was a cabaret theatre that has turned into a North American comedy institution. It is a theatre company showcasing internationally famous comedy troupes known for improvisation, creating comedy sketches satirizing aspects of everyday life. In addition to its live theatre, Second City provides top-quality training skills to individuals and corporations. Its corporate training program provides professionals with the skills to communicate more effectively in the workplace, teaching key improvisational techniques to help people think better on their feet, create new ideas quickly to serve customers better and manage workplace conflict. This training helps employees interact more effectively with others and engage customers and clients; providing them with the tools they need to make a "positive impression" on others.

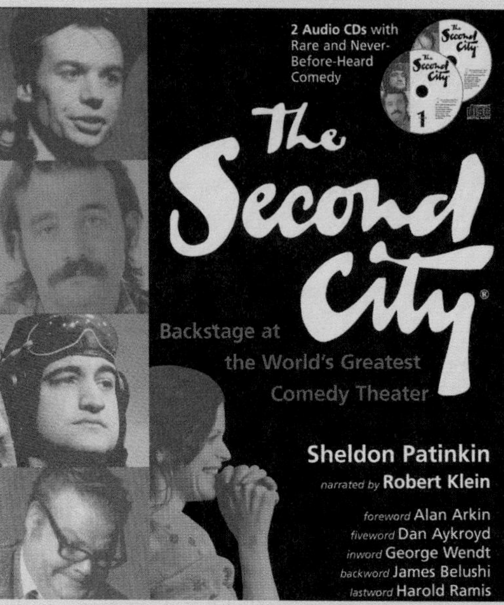

Many students at the Second City Training Centre use the training to improve their business skills.

SOURCE: The Second City, "Corporate Services" and "Training & Education," http://secondcity.com, accessed July 26, 2004.

iLogos
iLogos Research analyzes the economics of staffing management for large corporations worldwide. Recently a report on "Perception vs. Reality" was released, which revealed information about online jobseeker behaviour and their preferences and expectations regarding large corporations conducting online recruiting.
http://www.ilogos.com/en/ilogosreports/

Impression management seems to have an impact on others' impressions. As long as the impressions conveyed are accurate, this process can be a beneficial one in organizations. If the impressions are found to be false, however, a strongly negative overall impression may result. Furthermore, excessive impression management can lead to the perception that the user is manipulative or insincere.[32]

How do you manage your impressions at work? Look at Implications for Life to consider what your desk says about you.

IMPLICATIONS FOR LIFE

What Does Your Desk Say about You?

If your desk lies under a mountain of paperwork and polystyrene cups, it could be sending out a negative message about you to your colleagues. According to a study in the *Journal of Personality and Social Psychology,* the state of your desk speaks volumes about your personality. Sam Gosling, who led the study, said managers will often look around a room and form an impression of the person working or living there. We sometimes make very important decisions about people. And we may be partially basing those opinions on a person's workspace.

Think about what type of impression you make at work. Is your desk cluttered or neat? What does your workspace say about you?

SOURCE: A. Banks, "What Your Desk Can Say about Your Personality," *Computer Weekly,* July 2003, 32.

INTRODUCTION TO PERSONALITY

5

Define *personality* and explain the four theories of personality.

In the previous section we discussed how employee perceptions can influence behaviour in the workplace. In this section we discuss the influence of personality on perceptions and how our personality can affects our behaviour.

We have all had to work with people who are difficult to get along with. For example, have you ever worked with someone who continuously made promises to deliver some work but procrastinated to the point that your team's product quality was compromised? Or perhaps you have worked with someone who constantly watched the clock and left no matter how close you were to completion. Or maybe you have had to work with someone who you felt was very judgmental. To many individuals, the worst type of personality is the "the dreaded power freak." Does anyone you know come to mind?

In David Weiner's book *Power Freaks,* he describes the personality characteristics of a power freak as an individual driven by a need to dominate situations, someone who strives to enhance their status, showing little or no regard for others. Power freaks tend to focus on themselves, and demonstrate personality traits such as superficial charm, an inflated sense of self-worth, and a tendency to be cunning; as well, they're often callous and manipulative. Typically these individuals do not take responsibility for their actions, nor do they show any empathy, remorse, or guilt.[33] Does this description remind you of anybody you know? What strategies have you used that have been effective in dealing with an individual like this? What makes these individuals behave in consistent ways in a variety of situations? Understanding our own natural traits and those traits of others will help us manage how we interact with others more effectively and enable us to develop strategies to deal with people in our work environment.

personality
A relatively stable set of characteristics that influence an individual's behaviour.

Personality is an individual difference that lends consistency to a person's behaviour. It is defined as a relatively stable set of characteristics that influence an individual's behaviour. It is an individual's characteristic patterns of thought, emotion, and behaviour, together with the psychological mechanisms—hidden or not—behind those patterns.[34] These characteristics are stable over time, ascribed to the individual, and psychological in nature.[35]

Although there is debate about the determinants of personality, heredity and environment are cited as having a significant influence on personality. Some interesting studies have supported the position that heredity is a determinant of personality. Identical twins who are separated at birth and raised apart in very different situations have been found to share personality traits and job preferences. For example, about half of the variation in traits like extraversion, impulsiveness, and flexibility was found to be genetically determined; that is, identical twins who grew up in different environments shared these traits.[36] In addition, the twins held similar jobs.[37] Thus, there does appear to be a genetic influence on personality.

Another determinant of personality is the environment a person is exposed to. Family influences, cultural influences, educational influences, and other environmental forces shape personality. Examining personality in a cross-cultural context has received considerable attention. Researchers suggest that there are basic personality differences between social and cultural groups, and we can compare different personality types using national characteristics. Consider the cross-cultural dimensions defined by Hofstede, discussed in Chapter 2. Each cultural group establishes its own norms, and these norms and rules are connected with behaviour and personality of members within a culture.[38] For example, *amae* is a common Japanese verb meaning to presume upon other people's benevolence. Is this a personality dynamic that is waiting to be discovered in North America? Does it have any explanatory value outside of Japan?[39] CPI/Hazell & Associates, an international consulting company that specializes in talent management and organizational development, helps its clients manage these cultural components. Some of the services they provide are cross-cultural training, coaching, and consulting services to thousands of employees across the globe, helping employees learn how to work with culturally diverse populations and preparing employees for expatriate assignments so that they "hit the ground running." Learn more about CPI/Hazell & Associates by going to www.hazell.com.

Personality Theories

Four major theories of personality are trait theory, psychodynamic theory, humanistic theory, and integrative approach theory. Each theory has influenced the study of personality in organizations.

Trait Theory

trait theory
The personality theory that states that in order to understand individuals, we must break down behaviour patterns into a series of observable traits.

Some early personality researchers believed that to understand individuals, we must break down behaviour patterns into a series of observable traits. According to **trait theory,** combining these traits into a group forms an individual's personality. Gordon Allport, a leading trait theorist, saw traits as broad, general guides that lend consistency to behaviour.[40] Thousands of traits have been identified over the years. More recently, researchers have argued that all traits can be reduced to five basic factors. The "Big Five" traits include extraversion, agreeableness, conscientiousness, emotional stability, and openness to experience.[41] Descriptions of the "Big Five" are shown in Exhibit 3.2. The "Big Five" are broad, global traits that are associated with behaviours at work.

From preliminary research, we know that introverted and conscientious employees are less likely to be absent from work.[42] In making peer evaluations, individuals with high agreeableness tend to rate others more leniently, while individuals with high conscientiousness tend to be tougher as raters.[43] Extraverts tend to have higher salaries, receive more promotions, and are more satisfied with their careers.[44] Across lots of occupations, people who are conscientious are high performers. When you view more specific occupations, however, different patterns of the "Big Five" factors are related to high performance. For customer service jobs, individuals high in emotional stability, agreeableness, and openness to experience perform best. For managers, emotional stability and extraversion are traits of top performers.[45] To test your understanding, turn to the Application & Analysis box.

The trait approach has been the subject of considerable criticism. Early trait theorists tended to ignore the influence of situations and cultural differences. A survey of 500 Chinese students showed that they saw themselves as substantially different from Americans on many traits, in particular on agreeableness, assertiveness, and conscientiousness. Americans are seen as more assertive but only somewhat less extraverted and conscientious than Chinese.[46]

EXHIBIT 3.2

The "Big Five" Personality Traits

Extraversion	The person is gregarious, assertive, and sociable.
Agreeableness	The person is cooperative, warm, generous, and agreeable.
Conscientiousness	The person is hardworking, organized, decisive, and dependable.
Emotional stability	The person is calm, self-confident, and cool.
Openness to experience	The person is creative, curious, perceptive, and cultured.

SOURCES: P. T. Costa and R. R. McCrae, *The NEO-PI Personality Inventory* (Odessa, FL: Psychological Assessment Resources, 1992); J. F. Salgado, "The Five Factor Model of Personality and Job Performance in the European Community," *Journal of Applied Psychology* 82 (1997): 30–43.

Application & Analysis

PERSONALITY TRAITS

Some of the key personality traits essential for heath care jobs have been identified as a nurturing and stable disposition, ability to manage stress, service orientation, and flexibility. Think about the last time you or someone you cared for was in the hospital or had to deal with a major medical problem. What was your impression of the health care staff? What personality traits did they exhibit? What traits do you think are essential?

SOURCE: E. Heubeck, "Key Personality Traits Essential for Health Care Jobs," *USAToday.com,* November 19, 2002, http://www.usatoday.com/money/jobcenter/workplace/healthcare/2002-11-19-personality_x.htm.

Psychodynamic Theory

Based on the work of Sigmund Freud, **psychodynamic theory** emphasizes the unconscious determinants of behaviour.[47] Freud saw personality as the interaction among three elements of personality: the id, ego, and superego. The id is the most primitive element, the source of drives and impulses that operate in an uncensored manner. The superego, similar to what we know as conscience, contains values and the "shoulds and should nots" of the personality. The contribution of psychodynamic theory to our understanding of personality is its focus on unconscious influences on behaviour.

psychodynamic theory
The personality theory that emphasizes the unconscious determinants of behaviour.

Humanistic Theory

Carl Rogers believed that all people have a basic drive toward self-actualization, which is the quest to be all you can be.[48] The **humanistic theory** focuses on individual growth and improvement. It is distinctly people-centred and also emphasizes the individual's view of the world. The humanistic approach contributes an understanding of the self to personality theory and contends that the self-concept is the most important part of an individual's personality.

humanistic theory
The personality theory that emphasizes individual growth and improvement.

Integrative Approach

Recently, researchers have taken a broader, more integrative approach to the study of personality.[49] To capture its influence on behaviour, personality is described as a composite of the individual's psychological processes. Personality dispositions include emotions, cognitions, attitudes, expectancies, and fantasies.[50] Dispositions, in this approach, simply mean the tendencies of individuals to respond to situations in consistent ways. Influenced by both genetics and experiences, dispositions can be modified. The **integrative approach** focuses on both dispositions and situational variables as combined predictors of behaviour.

Managers should learn as much as possible about personality in order to understand their employees. Hundreds of personality characteristics have been identified. In the next section we discuss five main characteristics.

integrative approach
The broad theory that describes personality as a composite of an individual's psychological processes.

Personality Characteristics in Organizations

Identify several personality characteristics and their influences on behaviour in organizations.

The five main characteristics we have selected are locus of control, self-efficacy, self-esteem, self-monitoring, and positive/negative affect (see Exhibit 3.3).

Locus of Control

What is the difference between someone saying "I was late because of the traffic" and "I was late because I should have planned for a delay in traffic because, when the weather is bad, traffic always is slower"? An individual's generalized belief about internal (self)

EXHIBIT 3.3

Personality Characteristics in Organizations

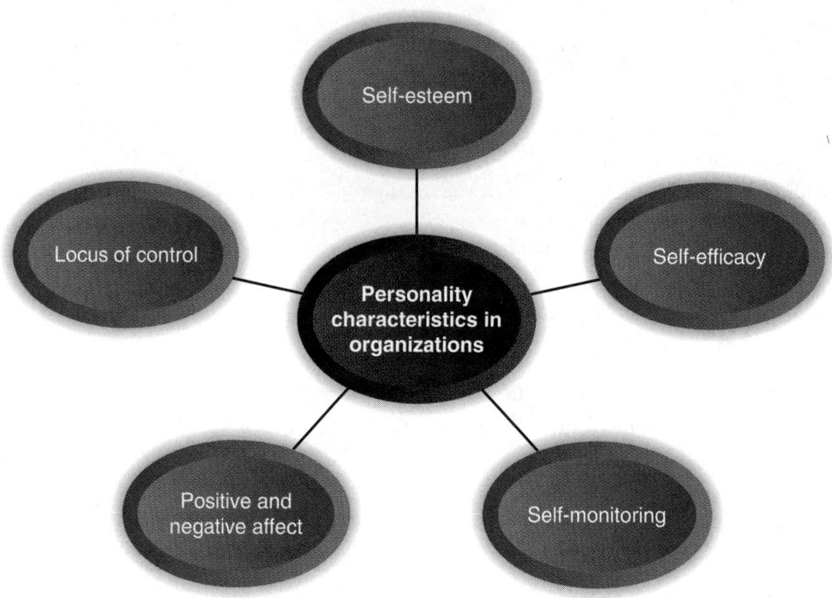

versus external (situation or others) control is called locus of control (see Chapter 2). People who believe they control what happens to them are said to have an internal locus of control, whereas people who believe that circumstances or other people control their fate have an external locus of control.[51] Research on locus of control has strong implications for organizations. Internals (those with an internal locus of control) have been found to have higher job satisfaction and performance, to be more likely to assume managerial positions, and to prefer participative management styles.[52]

Individuals who are internally or externally driven have similar positive reactions to being promoted, which include high job satisfaction, job involvement, and organizational commitment. The difference between the two is that internals continue to be happy long after the promotion, whereas externals' joy over the promotion is short lived. This might occur because externals do not believe their own performance led to the promotion.[53]

Knowing about locus of control can prove valuable to managers. Because internals believe they control what happens to them, they will want to exercise control in their work environment. Allowing internals considerable voice in how work is performed is important. Internals will not react well to being closely supervised. Externals, in contrast, may prefer a more structured work setting, and they may be more reluctant to participate in decision making.

Self-Efficacy

generalized self-efficacy
An individual's beliefs and expectations about his or her ability to accomplish a specific task effectively.

When you hear someone say "I can't do that task," what do you think? **Generalized self-efficacy** is a general belief about one's own capabilities to deal with the events and challenges that make life demanding. Employees with high generalized self-efficacy have more confidence in their job-related abilities and other personal resources (e.g., energy, influence over others, etc.) that help them function effectively on the job. People with low generalized self-efficacy often feel ineffective at work and may express doubts about performing a new task well. Previous success or performance is one of the most important determinants of self-efficacy. People who have positive beliefs about their efficacy for performance are more likely to attempt difficult tasks, to persist in overcoming obstacles, and to experience less anxiety when faced with adversity.[54]

Generalized self-efficacy is often confused with locus of control; however, they are distinctly different. Self-efficacy means possessing the skills required to execute courses of action that will result in a desired outcome. Locus of control refers to whether or not a person believes that the consequences of his or her efforts are controlled by others. For example, a salesman with high self-efficacy may have confidence in his ability to meet customer expectations, but does not necessarily blame himself for all lost sales.[55] There is another form of self-efficacy, called task-specific self-efficacy, which we will cover in Chapter 8.

Self-Esteem

When someone criticizes you, how do you feel? Are you crushed, or do you put context around the comment? **Self-esteem** is an individual's general feeling of self-worth. Individuals with high self-esteem have positive feelings about themselves, perceive themselves to have strengths as well as weaknesses, and believe their strengths are more important than their weaknesses.[56] Individuals with low self-esteem view themselves negatively. They are more strongly affected by what other people think of them, and they compliment individuals who give them positive feedback while cutting down people who give them negative feedback.[57]

self-esteem
An individual's general feeling of self-worth.

Evaluations from other people affect our self-esteem. For example, you might be liked for who you are or you might be liked for your achievements. Being liked for who you are is more stable, and people who have this type of self-esteem are less defensive and more honest with themselves. Being liked for your achievement is more unstable; it waxes and wanes depending on how high your achievements are.[58]

A person's self-esteem affects a host of other attitudes and has important implications for behaviour in organizations. People with high self-esteem perform better and are more satisfied with their jobs.[59] When they are involved in a job search, they seek out higher-status jobs.[60] A work team made up of individuals with high self-esteem is more likely to be successful than a team with lower average self-esteem.[61]

Very high self-esteem may be too much of a good thing. When people with high self-esteem find themselves in stressful situations, they may brag inappropriately.[62] This may be viewed negatively by others, who see spontaneous boasting as egotistical. Very high self-esteem may also lead to overconfidence, and to relationship conflicts with others who may not evaluate this behaviour favourably.[63] Individuals with high self-esteem may shift their social identities to protect themselves when they do not live up to some standard. Take two students, Denise and Teresa, for example. If Denise outperforms Teresa on a statistics exam, Teresa may convince herself that Denise is not really a good person to compare against because Denise is an engineering major and Teresa is a physical education major. Teresa's high self-esteem is protecting her from this unfavourable comparison.[64]

Self-esteem may be strongly affected by situations. Success tends to raise self-esteem, whereas failure tends to lower it. Given that high self-esteem is generally a positive characteristic, managers should encourage employees to raise their self-esteem by giving them appropriate challenges and opportunities for success.

Self-Monitoring

A characteristic with great potential for affecting behaviour in organizations is **self-monitoring**—the extent to which people base their behaviour on cues from other people and situations.[65] High self-monitors pay attention to what is appropriate in particular situations and to the behaviour of other people, and they behave accordingly. Low self-monitors, in contrast, are not as vigilant to situational cues and act from internal states rather than paying attention to the situation. As a result, the behaviour of low self-monitors is consistent across situations. High self-monitors, because their behaviour varies with the situation, appear to be more unpredictable and less consistent.

self-monitoring
The extent to which people base their behaviour on cues from other people and situations.

Research is currently focusing on the effects of self-monitoring in organizations. In one study, the authors tracked the careers of 139 MBAs for five years to see whether high self-monitors were more likely to be promoted, change employers, or make a job-related geographic move. The results were yes to each question. High self-monitors get promoted because they accomplish tasks through meeting the expectations of others and because they seek out central positions in social networks.[66] They are also more likely to use self-promotion to make others aware of their skills and accomplishments.[67] However, the high self-monitor's flexibility may not be suited for every job, and the tendency to move may not fit every organization.[68] Because high self-monitors base their behaviour on cues from others and from the situation, they demonstrate higher levels of managerial self-awareness. This means that, as managers, they assess their own workplace behaviour accurately.[69] Read about a Li Yifei, a high self-monitor, in Organizational Reality 3.4.

organizational reality 3.4

A Tai Chi Champion Heads MTV China

Running MTV China has to rank as one of the world's great jobs. Li Yifei has that job. Growing up in Beijing, she was a national tai chi champion and graduated from Beijing's most elite foreign language university. From there, she went to Baylor University and studied political science. In 1999, MTV named her head of its new China operation. With China's economic growth, limitless potential, and young people who are children of the Cultural Revolution, it is an exciting place to be.

Li's job, however, is not without its challenges. Viewers in China are an older and conservative group who are not used to belly-baring VJs, and MTV is limited to between one and four hours of programming a day. Li's high self-monitoring personality has helped her deal with the mostly male authorities because she has had to adopt something other than her natural style, which is straightforward, confident, and smart. "Particularly as a woman in China, you have to be a little bit softer, and humble," Li said.

Last year she persuaded CCTV, the national television network, to produce China's version of the MTV awards. The program got a 7.9 percent rating. An American interviewer noted that 7.9 percent was not a very good rating. In return, Li mentioned that in China this means that 150 million viewers were watching, which is well over half the U.S. population. This response shows that Li is not afraid to be assertive when the situation calls for it. In reading the situation and behaving accordingly, Li appears to be a high self-monitor. Training in tai chi helped her develop this trait. Tai chi participants learn to be both soft and pliable, and tough and strong. Tai chi emphasizes changing stances in a dynamic manner.

SOURCES: B. Powell et al., "25 Rising Stars: What Will the World Look Like a Decade or Two from Now?" *Fortune,* May 14, 2000, 140; W. Liao, *The Essence of T'ai Chi* (Boston: Shambhala, 1995).

You can use Self-Assessment 3.2 to assess your own self-monitoring tendencies.

Positive/Negative Affect

positive affect
An individual's tendency to accentuate the positive aspects of himself or herself, other people, and the world in general.

negative affect
An individual's tendency to accentuate the negative aspects of himself or herself, other people, and the world in general.

As discussed earlier in the chapter, researchers have explored the effects of persistent mood dispositions at work. Individuals who focus on the positive aspects of themselves, other people, and the world in general are said to have **positive affect**.[70] In contrast, those who accentuate the negative in themselves, others, and the world are said to possess **negative affect** (also referred to as negative affectivity).[71] These individuals demonstrate a level of pessimism that can influence their behaviour at work.

Interviewers who exhibit positive affect evaluate job candidates more favourably than do interviewers whose affect is neutral.[72] Employees with positive affect are absent from work less often.[73] Individuals with negative affect report more work stress.[74] Individual affect also influences the work group. Positive individual affect produces positive team affect, and this leads to more cooperation and less conflict within the team.[75]

Positive affect is a definite asset in work settings. Managers can do several things to promote positive affect, including allowing participative decision making and providing

Analysis & Evaluation

SELF ASSESSMENT 3.2: ARE YOU A HIGH OR LOW SELF-MONITOR?

For the following items, circle T (true) if the statement is characteristic of your behaviour. Circle F (false) if the statement does not reflect your behaviour.

1.	I find it hard to imitate the behaviour of other people.	T	F
2.	At parties and social gatherings, I do not attempt to do or say things that others will like.	T	F
3.	I can only argue for ideas that I already believe.	T	F
4.	I can make impromptu speeches even on topics about which I have almost no information.	T	F
5.	I guess I put on a show to impress or entertain others.	T	F
6.	I would probably make a good actor.	T	F
7.	In a group of people, I am rarely the centre of attention.	T	F
8.	In different situations and with different people, I often act like very different persons.	T	F
9.	I am not particularly good at making other people like me.	T	F
10.	I am not always the person I appear to be.	T	F
11.	I would not change my opinions (or the way I do things) in order to please others or win their favour.	T	F
12.	I have considered being an entertainer.	T	F
13.	I have never been good at games like charades or at improvisational acting.	T	F
14.	I have trouble changing my behaviour to suit different people and different situations.	T	F
15.	At a party, I let others keep the jokes and stories going.	T	F
16.	I feel a bit awkward in company and do not show up quite as well as I should.	T	F
17.	I can look anyone in the eye and tell a lie with a straight face (if it is for a good cause).	T	F
18.	I may deceive people by being friendly when I really dislike them.	T	F

For scoring instructions, please go to the end of the chapter, p. 105.

SOURCE: M. Snyder, *Public Appearances, Private Realities: The Psychology of Self-Monitoring.* Copyright © 1987 by W. H. Freeman and Company. Used with permission.

Psychtests
Managers must learn as much as possible about personality in order to understand employees. Visit psychtests.com to discover the various online tests and applications that help organizations assess the personality of workers. How are these tests likely to help increase productivity in the workplace? What real-world applications does the site list for its online tests?
http://www.psychtests.com

pleasant working conditions, rewarding employees for appropriate behaviour, and coaching employees so that they can learn to manage the challenges in the workplace in a more effective way. We need to know more about inducing positive affect in the workplace and managing our emotions in the workplace.

Measuring Personality

Explain how personality is measured.

Measuring personality traits can provide the employer with valuable information about their interactions with others and how best to respond to them. It can help the employee more effectively work with others. Several methods can be used to assess personality. These include projective tests, behavioural measures, and self-report questionnaires.

The **projective test** is one method used to measure personality. In these tests, individuals are shown a picture, abstract image, or photo and are asked to describe what they

projective test
A personality test that elicits an individual's response to abstract stimuli.

see or to tell a story about what they see. The rationale behind projective tests is that each individual responds to the stimulus in a way that reflects his or her unique personality. The Rorschach ink blot test is a projective test commonly used to assess personality.[76]

behavioural measures
Personality assessments that involve observing an individual's behaviour in a controlled situation.

There are **behavioural measures** of personality as well. Measuring behaviour involves observing an individual's behaviour in a controlled situation. We might assess a person's sociability, for example, by counting the number of times he or she approaches strangers at a party. The behaviour is scored in some manner to produce an index of personality. Some potential problems with behavioural measures include the observer's ability to stay focused and the way the observer interprets the behaviour. In addition, some people behave differently when they know they are being observed.

The most common method of assessing personality is the *self-report questionnaire.* Individuals respond to a series of questions, usually in an agree/disagree or true/false format. A popular self-report questionnaire is the Myers-Briggs Type Indicator (MBTI). The Myers-Briggs Type Indicator is a personality inventory that has been developed to measure individual differences in human behaviour. Many organizations use the MBTI, and we will focus on it as an example of how some organizations use personality concepts to help employees appreciate diversity.

Discuss Carl Jung's contribution to our understanding of individual differences and explain how his theory is used in the Myers-Briggs Type Indicator.

A Popular Application of Personality Theory in Organizations: The Myers-Briggs Type Indicator (MBTI)

Myers-Briggs Type Indicator (MBTI)
An instrument developed to measure Carl Jung's theory of individual differences.

Temperament Research Institute
The Temperament Research Institute has designed its online service to facilitate the exploration of its unique method for understanding personality and individual differences in the workplace. What is the TRI Methodology, and how does it relate to the Myers-Briggs Type Indicator? What benefit does this enhanced application of the MBTI offer to organizations? Go to Temperament Research Institute's website to learn more.
http://www.tri-network.com

The **Myers-Briggs Type Indicator (MBTI)** questionnaire is based on the work of Swiss psychiatrist Carl Jung. Carl Jung built his work on the notion that people are fundamentally different, but also fundamentally alike. His classic treatise, *Psychological Types,* proposed that the population was made up of two basic types—extraverted and introverted.[77] He went on to identify two types of perception (sensing and intuiting) and two types of judgment (thinking and feeling). Perception (how we gather information) and judgment (how we make decisions) represent the basic mental functions that everyone uses.

Jung suggested that human similarities and differences could be understood by combining preferences. We prefer and choose one way of doing things over another. We are not exclusively one way or another; rather, we have a preference for extraversion or introversion, just as we have a preference for right-handedness or left-handedness. We may use each hand equally well, but when a ball is thrown at us by surprise, we will reach to catch it with our preferred hand. Jung's type theory argues that no preferences are better than others. Differences are to be understood, celebrated, and appreciated.

During the 1940s, a mother–daughter team became fascinated with individual differences among people and with the work of Carl Jung. Katharine Briggs and her daughter, Isabel Briggs Myers, developed the Myers-Briggs Type Indicator to put Jung's type theory into practical use. The MBTI is used extensively in organizations as a basis for understanding individual differences.[78] The MBTI has been used in career counselling, team building, conflict management, and understanding management styles.[79] Companies like Allstream use the MBTI in their management development programs to help employees understand the different viewpoints of others in the organization and to help teams realize that diversity and differences lead to successful performance. The MBTI has been found to have good reliability and validity as a measurement instrument for identifying a type.

The Preferences

There are four basic preferences in type theory and two possible choices for each of the four preferences. The combination of these preferences makes up an individual's psychological type. The basic preferences are: extraversion versus introversion, sensing versus intuiting, thinking versus feeling, and judging versus perceiving. Exhibit 3.4 shows these preferences.

EXHIBIT 3.4

Type Theory Preferences and Descriptions

Extraversion	Introversion	Thinking	Feeling
Outgoing	Quiet	Analytical	Subjective
Publicly expressive	Reserved	Clarity	Harmony
Interacting	Concentrating	Head	Heart
Speaks, then thinks	Thinks, then speaks	Justice	Mercy
Gregarious	Reflective	Rules	Circumstances
Sensing	**Intuiting**	**Judging**	**Perceiving**
Practical	General	Structured	Flexible
Specific	Abstract	Time-oriented	Open-ended
Feet on the ground	Head in the clouds	Decisive	Exploring
Details	Possibilities	Makes lists/uses them	Makes lists/loses them
Concrete	Theoretical	Organized	Spontaneous

Extraversion/Introversion

The **extraversion/introversion** preference represents where you get your energy. The extravert (E) is energized by interaction with other people. The introvert (I) is energized by time alone. Extraverts represent approximately 70 percent of the U.S. population.[80] Jung contended that the extraversion/introversion preference reflects the most important distinction between individuals. In work settings, extraverts prefer variety, and they do not mind the interruptions of the phone or visits from co-workers. They communicate freely but may say things that they regret later. Introverts prefer quiet for concentration, and they like to think things through in private. They do not mind working on a project for a long time and are careful with details. Introverts dislike telephone interruptions, and they may have trouble recalling names and faces.

extraversion
A preference indicating that an individual is energized by interaction with other people.

introversion
A preference indicating that an individual is energized by time alone.

Sensing/Intuiting

The **sensing/intuiting** preference represents perception, or how we prefer to gather information. In essence this preference reflects what we pay attention to. The sensor (S) pays attention to information gathered through the five senses and to what actually exists. The intuitor (N) pays attention to a "sixth sense" and to what could be rather than to what actually exists.[81] Approximately 70 percent of people in the United States are sensors.[82]

At work, sensors prefer specific answers to questions and can become frustrated with vague instructions. They like jobs that yield tangible results, and they enjoy using established skills more than learning new ones. Intuitors like solving new problems and are impatient with routine details. They enjoy learning new skills more than actually using them. Intuitors tend to think about several things at once, and they may be seen by others as absentminded. They like figuring out how things work just for the fun of it.

sensing
Gathering information through the five senses.

intuiting
Gathering information through the "sixth sense" and focusing on what could be rather than what actually exists.

Thinking/Feeling

The **thinking/feeling** preference represents the way we prefer to make decisions. The thinker (T) makes decisions in a logical, objective fashion, whereas the feeler (F) makes decisions in a personal, value-oriented way. Thinkers tend to analyze decisions, whereas feelers sympathize. Thinkers try to be impersonal, whereas feelers base their decisions on how the outcome will affect the people involved.

thinking
Making decisions in a logical, objective fashion.

feeling
Making decisions in a personal, value-oriented way.

In work settings, thinkers do not show much emotion, and they may become uncomfortable with people who do. They respond more readily to other people's thoughts. They are firm-minded and like putting things into a logical framework. Feelers, in contrast, are more comfortable with emotion in the workplace. They enjoy pleasing people and need a lot of praise and encouragement.

judging preference
Preferring closure and completion in making decisions.

perceiving preference
Preferring to explore many alternatives and flexibility.

Judging/Perceiving

The **judging/perceiving preference** reflects one's orientation to the outer world. The judger (J) loves closure. Judgers prefer to lead a planned, organized life and like making decisions. The perceiver (P), in contrast, prefers a more flexible and spontaneous life and wants to keep options open. For judgers in all arenas of life, and especially at work, there is a right and a wrong way to do everything. They love getting things accomplished and delight in marking off the completed items on their calendars. Perceivers tend to adopt a wait-and-see attitude and to collect new information rather than draw conclusions. Perceivers are curious and welcome new information. They may start too many projects and not finish them.

To learn more about your preferences, take the test in Experiential Exercise 3.1 at the end of the chapter.

The Sixteen Types

The preferences combine to form 16 different psychological types. The MBTI establishes criteria for types. There are no right or wrong types; each type has its own strengths and weaknesses. Type has been found to be related to learning style, teaching style, and choice of occupation. Type has also been used to determine an individual's decision-making style and management style. Recent studies have begun to focus on the relationship between type and specific managerial behaviours. The introvert (I) and the feeler (F), for example, have been shown to be more effective at participative management than their counterparts, the extravert and the thinker.[83]

IMPLICATIONS FOR ORGANIZATIONAL EFFECTIVENESS

In Chapter 2, we discussed how organizations that create a positive work environment take the time to understand what their employees value and how employees' attitudes affect their performance.

An integral part of successfully sustaining a positive place to work is understanding employee perceptions. In a recent study on why organizations failed to achieve their desired results, researchers reviewed the perceptions of 359 front-line management personnel. Managers from 30 different organizations were asked to rate the effect that 25 different performance factors had on their ability to achieve business outcomes. To the researchers' surprise, the study concluded that the managers felt their views were not going to be heard regardless of survey outcomes. The managers perceived that whatever they said would not be acted upon nor make a difference.[84] Once management understood these concerns they were able to develop a program whereby these views were identified, validated, and acted upon.

In addition to managing perceptions, effective organizations hire the right people with the right skills and personality traits that best suit the job and provide development opportunities to enhance employee contributions. Ever work with someone who was introverted, individualistic, and preferred to work alone but they were stuck in a job that demanded customer service and building strong customer relationships, qualities that more appropriately fit an extravert? How effective were they at their job?

But what if the person was effective at his or her job but was very difficult to work with? Ever heard the expression, "He is a good person but I wouldn't want to work with him"? What is it that the person is doing that makes others perceive this individual in this way? High-performing organizations provide feedback to their employees as to how to effectively interact with their peers, and provide developmental opportunities in a number of areas to enhance employee performance. Research suggests that how well we, as individuals, can develop our social and personal competencies is a key determinant of how satisfied we are at work and how successful we will be within an organization.[85] Turn to OBXtra 2 to learn more about the important topic of emotional intelligence.

Chapter Summary

1. Individual differences are factors that make individuals unique. These differences include personality, perception, skills and abilities, attitudes, values, and ethics. Social perception is the process of interpreting information about another person. It is influenced by characteristics of the perceiver, the target, and the situation.
2. Barriers to social perception include selective perception, stereotyping, first-impression error, projection, and self-fulfilling prophecies.
3. Attribution is the process of determining the cause of behaviour. It is used extensively by managers, especially in evaluating performance.
4. Impression management techniques, such as name-dropping, managing one's appearance, self-descriptions, flattery, favours, and agreement, are used by individuals to control others' impressions of them.
5. Personality is a relatively stable set of characteristics that influence an individual's behaviour. The trait theory, psychodynamic theory, humanistic theory, and integrative approach are all personality theories.
6. Managers should understand personality because of its effect on behaviour. Several characteristics affect behaviour in organizations, including locus of control, self-esteem, self-monitoring, and positive/negative affect. Personality has a stronger influence in weak situations, where there are few cues to guide behaviour.
7. Measuring personality traits can provide the employer with valuable information about how an employee interacts with others. Several methods can be used to assess personality. These include projective tests, behavioural measures, and self-report questionnaires.
8. One useful framework for understanding individual differences is type theory, developed by Carl Jung and measured by the Myers-Briggs Type Indicator (MBTI). Companies use the MBTI in their management development programs to help employees understand more about themselves and how they can effectively work well with others.

Key Terms

attribution theory (p. 85)
behavioural measures (p. 96)
discounting principle (p. 83)
extraversion (p. 97)
feeling (p. 97)
first-impression error (p. 84)
fundamental attribution error (p. 86)
generalized self-efficacy (p. 92)
humanistic theory (p. 91)
impression management (p. 87)
integrative approach (p. 91)
introversion (p. 97)
intuiting (p. 97)
judging preference (p. 98)
Myers-Briggs Type Indicator (MBTI) (p. 96)
negative affect (p. 94)
perceiving preference (p. 98)
personality (p. 89)
positive affect (p. 94)
projection (p. 85)
projective test (p. 95)
psychodynamic theory (p. 91)
selective perception (p. 83)
self-esteem (p. 93)
self-fulfilling prophecy (p. 85)
self-monitoring (p. 93)
self-serving bias (p. 86)
sensing (p. 97)
social perception (p. 79)
stereotype (p. 84)
thinking (p. 97)
trait theory (p. 90)

Review Questions

1. What are individual differences, and why should managers understand them?
2. Define personality, and describe its origins.
3. Describe four theories of personality and explain what each contributes to our knowledge of personality.

4. Describe the eight preferences of the Myers-Briggs Type Indicator. How does this instrument measure Carl Jung's ideas?
5. What factors influence social perception? What are the barriers to social perception?
6. Describe the errors that affect the attribution process.

Discussion and Communication Questions

1. What contributions can high self-monitors make in organizations? Low self-monitors?
2. How can managers improve their perceptual skills?
3. Which has the stronger impact on personality: heredity or environment?
4. How can managers make more accurate attributions?
5. How can managers encourage self-efficacy in employees?
6. How can self-serving bias and the fundamental attribution error be avoided?
7. *(Communication question)* You have been asked to develop a training program for interviewers. An integral part of this training program focuses on helping interviewers develop better social perception skills. Write an outline for this section of the training program. Be sure to address barriers to social perception and ways to avoid these barriers.
8. *(Communication question)* Form groups of four to six, then split each group in half. Debate the origins of personality, with one half taking the position that personality is inherited, and the other half taking the position that personality is formed by the environment. Each half should also discuss the implications of its position for managers.

Ethics Questions

1. What are the ethical uses of personality tests? What are the unethical uses?
2. Suppose a manager makes an incorrect attribution for an employee's poor performance (for instance, the manager cites equipment failure), and peers know the employee is at fault. Should they blow the whistle on their colleague?
3. Suppose one of your colleagues wants to eliminate all biases and stereotypes from the hiring process. He suggests that only résumés be used, with no names or other identifying data—only experience and education. What are the ethical consequences of this approach? Would any group be unfairly disadvantaged by this approach?
4. Suppose a manager makes a misattribution of an employee's poor performance. What are the ethical consequences of this?

Analysis & Evaluation

EXPERIENTIAL EXERCISE 3.1: PERSONALITY TYPES AND MANAGEMENT STYLES

Purpose: To determine personality according to Jung's personality typology

Group size: Individual

Time required: 15–20 minutes to complete and score inventory

Materials needed: None

Instructions: For each item circle either "a" or "b." If you feel both "a" and "b" are true, decide which one is more like you, even if it is only slightly more true.

Part I. This questionnaire will help you determine your preferences.

1. I would rather
   a. Solve a new and complicated problem.
   b. Work on something I have done before.
2. I like to
   a. Work alone in a quiet place.
   b. Be where the action is.

3. I want a boss who
   a. Establishes and applies criteria in decisions.
   b. Considers individual needs and makes exceptions.

4. When I work on a project, I
   a. Like to finish it and get some closure.
   b. Often leave it open for possible changes.

5. When making a decision, the most important considerations are
   a. Rational thoughts, ideas, and data.
   b. People's feelings and values.

6. On a project, I tend to
   a. Think it over and over before deciding how to proceed.
   b. Start working on it right away, thinking about it as I go along.

7. When working on a project, I prefer to
   a. Maintain as much control as possible.
   b. Explore various options.

8. In my work, I prefer to
   a. Work on several projects at a time, and learn as much as possible about each one.
   b. Have one project that is challenging and keeps me busy.

9. I often
   a. Make lists and plans whenever I start something and may have to seriously alter my plans.
   b. Avoid plans and just let things progress as I work on them.

10. When discussing a problem with colleagues, it is easy for me to
    a. See "the big picture."
    b. Grasp the specifics of the situation.

11. When the phone rings in my office or at home, I usually
    a. Consider it an interruption.
    b. Do not mind answering it.

12. Which word describes you better?
    a. Analytical.
    b. Empathetic.

13. When I am working on an assignment, I tend to
    a. Work steadily and consistently.
    b. Work in bursts of energy with "down time" in between.

14. When I listen to someone talk on a subject, I usually try to
    a. Relate it to my own experience and see if it fits.
    b. Assess and analyze the message.

15. When I come up with new ideas, I generally
    a. "Go for it."
    b. Like to contemplate the ideas some more.

16. When working on a project, I prefer to
    a. Narrow the scope so it is clearly defined.
    b. Broaden the scope to include related aspects.

17. When I read something, I usually
    a. Confine my thoughts to what is written there.
    b. Read between the lines and relate the words to other ideas.

18. When I have to make a decision in a hurry, I often
    a. Feel uncomfortable and wish I had more information.
    b. Am able to do so with available data.

19. In a meeting, I tend to
    a. Continue formulating my ideas as I talk about them.
    b. Only speak out after I have carefully thought the issue through.

20. In work, I prefer spending a great deal of time on issues of
    a. Ideas.
    b. People.

21. In meetings, I am most often annoyed with people who
    a. Come up with many sketchy ideas.
    b. Lengthen meetings with many practical details.

22. I am a
    a. Morning person.
    b. Night owl.

23. What is your style in preparing for a meeting?
    a. I am willing to go in and be responsive.
    b. I like to be fully prepared and usually sketch an outline of the meeting.

24. In a meeting, I would prefer for people to
    a. Display a fuller range of emotions.
    b. Be more task oriented.

25. I would rather work for an organization where
    a. My job was intellectually stimulating.
    b. I was committed to its goals and mission.

26. On weekends, I tend to
    a. Plan what I will do.
    b. Just see what happens and decide as I go along.

27. I am more
    a. Outgoing.
    b. Contemplative.

28. I would rather work for a boss who is
    a. Full of new ideas.
    b. Practical.

In the following, choose the word in each pair that *appeals* to you more:

29. a. Social.
    b. Theoretical.

30. a. Ingenuity.
    b. Practicality.

31. a. Organized.
    b. Adaptable.

32. a. Active.
    b. Concentration.

Scoring Key

Count one point for each item listed below that you have circled in the inventory.

Score for I	Score for E	Score for S	Score for N
2a	2b	1b	1a
6a	6b	10b	10a
11a	11b	13a	13b
15b	15a	16a	16b
19b	19a	17a	17b
22a	22b	21a	21b
27b	27a	28b	28a
32b	32a	30b	30a
Total 5	3	4	4

Circle the one with more points—I or E. (If tied on I/E, don't count #11.)

Circle the one with more points—S or N. (If tied on I/E, don't count #16.)

Score for T	Score for F	Score for J	Score for P
3a	3b	4a	4b
5a	5b	7a	7b
12a	12b	8b	8a
14b	14a	9a	9b
20a	20b	18b	18a
24b	24a	23b	23a
25a	25b	26a	26b
29b	29a	31a	31b
Total 7		7	

Circle the one with more points—T or F.

Circle the one with more points—J or P. (If tied on J/P, don't count #23.)

Your score is

I or E 5 S or N 4. T or F 7 J or P 7

Part 2. Once you have added up your scores and have determined your preference, learn more about what characteristics are frequently associated with your type by going to http://www.teamtechnology.co.uk/mb-types/mb-types.htm and http://en.wikipedia.org/wiki/Myers-Briggs.

SOURCE: D. Marcic and P. Nutt, "MBTI Types and Management Styles" and "Personality Inventory," in D. Marcic, ed., *Organizational Behavior: Experiences and Cases* (St. Paul: West, 1989), 9–16. Used with permission.

Application, Analysis & Synthesis

CASE: TRILOGY SOFTWARE, INC.

As a student at Stanford University, Joe Liemandt did part-time consulting jobs for various Palo Alto computer companies. On these consulting jobs, he noticed that computer companies were very inefficient in selling and delivering their products. "He was surprised at how primitive the process was. Much of it was handwritten, using cumbersome inventory manuals and often requiring lengthy consultation between the company's salespeople and its engineers." Intrigued by this order-processing (or sales configuration) problem, Liemandt began to work on a software idea that would become the foundation of his software development company.

Liemandt saw opportunity stamped all over the sales configuration problem. His research on the problem revealed that other companies like IBM and Hewlett-Packard were working on it as well. With this kind of competition he worried that his window of opportunity was closing. So a few months before graduation in 1990, 21-year-old Joe Liemandt dropped out of Stanford to start Trilogy Software. He convinced four classmates to join him, three of whom juggled classes and work until they graduated.

Liemandt says, "Starting Trilogy was the easy part. Keeping it going in the early years wasn't." Venture capitalists were not interested in investing in Trilogy. To keep the firm financially afloat, Liemandt took consulting jobs and leveraged one credit card against another, having 22 credit cards outstanding at one point. After Trilogy moved to Austin, Texas, in 1991, Hewlett-Packard signed a $3.5-million contract with Trilogy for sales configuration software and support services. Hewlett-Packard in effect abandoned its own effort to develop sales configuration software.

Soon other big customers purchased Trilogy's software. Called Selling Chain, the software enabled companies to "use computers to configure orders for a range of products from airplanes to shoes to telephone switches, and to perform other complex tasks." Boeing, for instance, used Selling Chain to cut the cost of processing aircraft orders. A Boeing 747 contains more than six million parts, and customers can select from hundred of options. Without Trilogy's software, the sales configuration process required a salesperson to make numerous customer visits. The salesperson also had to spend considerable time working with Boeing engineers "to make sure all the chosen pieces fit together, renegotiating the price at every step." However, use of the Selling Chain software enabled the salesperson to make a single visit to a customer and, using a laptop computer, to configure the 747 complete with a price quote. This was possible because Selling Chain knew "which parts go together and how much they cost."

Trilogy's business grew rapidly. For more than 10 years now, the company has provided sales configuration technology and tools to the largest companies in the computer equipment manufacturing industry, including enterprise server and storage manufacturers such as Hewlett-Packard, NCR, Motorola, and SGI. Trilogy also provides guided selling applications to the computer industry. These applications help manufacturers "market and sell products and services online and across all sales channels, with solution discovery and customization, customer-specific pricing, order management, and more."

Trilogy has become one of the largest privately owned enterprise software companies. It specializes in developing e-business solutions for other companies in the computer, automotive, communications, and financial services industries. Trilogy provides industry-specific solutions that "help large enterprises increase the effectiveness, efficiency, and profitability of customer-facing activities like sales, marketing, and service."

What is the secret to Trilogy's astounding growth and success? Liemandt credits Trilogy's success to the types of people the company hires and how they are treated. Most of Trilogy's new employees come from computer science departments at top-flight schools such as MIT, Harvard, Carnegie-Mellon, Rice, Stanford, and Berkeley. Trilogy attracts top talent by giving employees a lot of responsibility right away. One 22-year-old, in describing the attraction of working for Trilogy, says the company gives people more responsibility than they think they can possibly handle and then lets them go do the job. According to Liemandt, "What matters is the ability to learn, adapt, and figure out what the answer is. You've got to be willing to get in over your head and struggle to make things happen." Trilogy expects "everyone in the company to demonstrate leadership capability, regardless of their role."

Liemandt also looks for risk takers. He says, "You've got to be willing to jump off a cliff for your idea." Indeed, a significant element of Trilogy's training for new recruits focuses on developing their risk-taking propensity. Liemandt asserts that "he learned the hard way that taking risks and suffering the consequences are a crucial part of business. And he wants new hires to understand the experience firsthand."

Liemandt puts Trilogy's college recruits through a rigorous three-month-long corporate boot camp known as Trilogy University. During the first month, training sessions last from 8:00 a.m. until midnight. In the second week, new hires are divided into teams and given three weeks to complete difficult projects. Teams that do well win a two-day trip to Las Vegas, where Liemandt also encourages the recruits to take risks. The objective of Trilogy University is "to develop creative people who work well in teams, adapt to swift changes in customer demands—and take chances." Liemandt maintains that nothing "brings a group of people together like risk."

"By hiring great people and giving them mission-critical responsibilities from the first day on the job," Trilogy is better able to respond to competitive challenges and achieve its goals.

Discussion Questions

1. Using the various personality characteristics discussed in this chapter, how would you describe Joe Liemandt's personality?
2. What perceptions have you formed of Joe Liemandt? How do you think your perceptions are affected by characteristics of you as the perceiver and Liemandt as the perceptual target? To what extent have the barriers to social perception influenced your view of Liemandt?
3. Which barriers to social perception seem to influence Joe Liemandt's attitudes and behaviour? Explain your answer.
4. Suppose that you were offered a job at Trilogy. Given the information contained in the case, would you be inclined to accept the job offer? Explain your answer.

Source: This case was written by Michael K. McCuddy, The Louis S. and Mary L. Morgal Professor of Christian Business Ethics and Professor of Management, College of Business Administration, Valparaiso University. This case was developed from material contained on Trilogy's website at http://www.trilogy.com and in the following articles: J. Maloney and E. Brown, "So You Want to Be a Software Superstar," *Fortune,* June 10, 1996, 104–11; J. McHugh, "Holy Cow, No One's Done This!" *Forbes,* June 3, 1996, 122–28; E. Ramstad, "High Rollers: How Trilogy Software Trains Its Recruits to Be Risk Takers," *Wall Street Journal,* September 21, 1998, A11, A10.

Scoring Instructions for Self-Assessments

Self-Assessment 3.1 Sex Role Stereotypes

Scoring: For 1, 2, 5, 7, 9, and 10, give yourself 1 point for each M rating and 0 for F or N.

For 3, 4, 6, 8, 11, and 12, give yourself 1 point for each F rating and 0 for M or N.

Maximum points = 12; a high score indicates a strong belief in traditional gender roles and a tendency to stereotype sex roles.

Self-Assessment 3.2 Are You a High or Low Self-Monitor?

Scoring: To score this questionnaire, give yourself 1 point for each of the following items that you answered T (true): 4, 5, 6, 8, 10, 12, 17, and 18. Now give yourself 1 point for each of the following items that you answered F (false): 1, 2, 3, 7, 9, 11, 13, 14, 15, and 16. Add both subtotals to find your overall score. If you scored 11 or above, you are probably a high self-monitor. If you scored 10 or under, you are probably a low self-monitor.

LEARNING OBJECTIVES

By the end of this chapter, you will be able to do the following:

1. Define *motivation* and explain why it matters.
2. Describe Maslow's hierarchy of needs and its applications and limitations.
3. Describe how Theory X and Theory Y assumptions about people may influence a manager's attempt to motivate an employee.
4. Compare and contrast ERG theory with Maslow's hierarchy of needs.
5. Explain the needs for achievement, power, and affiliation and how understanding these needs can help a manager motivate employees.
6. Describe the Herzberg's two-factor theory of motivation and compare it to ERG and Maslow's hierarchy.
7. Describe the expectancy theory of motivation and illustrate, using examples, how it can be applied.
8. Explain Adam's equity theory of motivation, equity sensitivity, and the various ways that employees respond to perceived inequities.
9. Explain how individuals are motivated by perceptions of distributive, procedural, and interactional justice.
10. Explain the purposes of goal setting, the characteristics that make goal setting effective, its limitations, and applications to management by objectives (MBO).
11. Describe a few cultural differences in motivation.

learning about the context

Home Depot Canada Recognizes The Importance of Motivating Employees

Home Depot Canada attributes much of its tremendous success to having motivated and passionate store-level employees. Annette Verschuren, the president, said in an interview: "I can tell you within two seconds of entering a store whether morale is good. With an unhappy workforce you have nothing and you will never be great."[1] Ms. Verschuren was hired in 1996, and her qualities have contributed to the motivational climate that has been created across the over 100 stores in Canada. She describes herself as being "fascinated by human behaviour and fascinated by how you can influence people to do things in support of your organization."[2]

Home Depot Canada's goal is to show its associates that it cares about their personal well-being, and the company tries to meet employee needs for financial security. Its unique benefits programs includes support for nutrition and physical fitness, Home Depot Canada even offers part-time associates health care benefits and a bonus program, whereby a cashier can receive an annual bonus of between $400 and $800 in charitable donations and an employee stock purchase plan. Home Depot in the U.S. recently also offered big incentives to store managers who met sales targets in the last quarter of 2003. Their prizes were Chevrolet Silverado pickup trucks painted orange to match the company logo!

One of eight basic values at Home Depot is "Taking Care of Their People." This core value is described as follows: "The key to success is treating people well. We do this by encouraging associates to speak up and take risks, by recognizing and rewarding good performance and by leading and developing people so they may grow."[3] The *Financial Post* describes Home Depot's educational facility in Toronto as the "Harvard of hardware." Every associate is expected to undergo at least four hours of training a month. Home Depot won the 2002 Retail Council of Canada Award for employee development, in recognition of the ongoing training offered to employees to help them learn and grow. Home Depot Canada has grown very quickly, which enables employees to grow and self-actualize as well. Ms. Verschuren explains that her company invests a lot in its people both through technical and leadership training. In addition, each store has a human resources manager to help the leaders attract people, motivate people and invest in people. The hothouse environment fuelled by training and growth means that almost all employees can be upwardly mobile if they choose to be. Emily Vincent, a training administrator in Toronto, says she started at a Home Depot outlet in Ottawa three years ago, working in their seasonal department. "I was slugging bricks," says Ms. Vincent. "I just applied because I was looking for a job. I didn't want to work retail and I had no interest in hardware. But people were just so enthusiastic about their work. I never got around to looking for another job. For me, it's all about passion."[4]

SOURCES: M. Troy, "Motivating Your Workforce: A Home Depot Case Study," *Discount Store News* (June 10, 2002): 29; G. Crone, "Home Schooling: Before They Sell Their First Can of Paint, Home Depot Wants Its 'Associates' to Spend a Lot of Time at Its Harvard of Hardware," *Financial Post,* January 31, 2000, C01; Home Depot, "Benefits Info," www.recruitingsite.com/corpfiles/homedepot/benefits.htm; Home Depot, "Living Our Values," www.recruitingsite.com/corpfiles/homedepot/livingourvalues.htm.

Define *motivation* and explain why it matters.

WHAT IS MOTIVATION AND WHY DOES IT MATTER?

motivation
The set of forces, internal (individual needs and motives) and external (environmental forces), that initiate work-related behaviour and determine its form, direction, intensity, and duration.

intrinsic motivation
A person's internal drive to do something because of such things as interest, challenge, and personal satisfaction.

extrinsic motivation
Motivation that comes from outside the person, such as pay, tangible rewards, or a promotion.

Motivation plays an important role in moving an organization toward excellence, as you saw in the Home Depot example. **Motivation** is defined as the set of forces, internal (individual needs and motives) and external (environmental forces), that initiate work-related behaviour and determine its form, direction, intensity and duration"[1] The term *motivation* comes from the Latin root word *movere,* which means "to move," and motivation is one of the more complex topics in organizational behaviour.

Internal forces are often referred to as intrinsic motivation and external forces as extrinsic motivation. **Intrinsic motivation** is defined as a person's internal drive to do something due to such things as interest, challenge, and personal satisfaction. **Extrinsic motivation** is defined as motivation that comes from outside the person, such as pay, tangible rewards, or a promotion.[2]

In a 2001 Gallup poll it was discovered that 16 percent of Canadian employees are "actively disengaged" from their work, which is estimated to cost the Canadian economy more than $27.7 billion a year in lost productivity. Only 24 percent of Canadian employees reported that they were fully engaged in their work.[3] Poor employee motivation reduces the return on employee investment through lowered productivity, absenteeism costs, and the costs of employee turnover. Every time an employee leaves an organization, she or he takes away know-how as well as the time and money it costs to train him or her. Employee turnover may also mean a loss of relationships with important customers and suppliers, and of course it means additional recruiting, hiring, and training costs.[4] In addition to all the financial costs associated with an unmotivated employee, there are also the more subtle costs to the work climate. It is very unpleasant to work with an unmotivated employee or teammate, or live with an unmotivated family member or friend. On the other hand, companies ranked as Canada's top employers, like Janssen-Ortho and Flight Centre Ltd., are those that put time and money into their motivation and recognition programs.[5]

Despite the agreement about the significance of work motivation for organization effectiveness, there is considerable controversy over which of the many factors contributes most to actually motivating an individual in a particular situation.[6] Many theories have been proposed, over time, to help us better understand and influence motivation; however, no single motivation theory has been able to explain all of the variance in human behaviour. All the theories discussed in this chapter have historic significance and provide insights and clues to the nature of human motivation. However, each theory has its limitations and will be critiqued accordingly. Some companies, such as Manitoba Lotteries Corporation (MLC), have taken the OB theories discussed in this chapter and have developed their own simplified model of motivation and performance. As depicted in Exhibit 4.1, MLC recognizes that in order for employees to perform effectively, they must first understand what is expected of them; but in addition, they need both ability and willingness (motivation).[7]

This chapter is divided into two main sections. First, we explore five *need* theories of motivation. All these theories address the question, "*What* motivates someone?" The five need theories are Maslow's need hierarchy, McGregor's X-Y theory, Alderfer's ERG

EXHIBIT 4.1

Manitoba Lotteries "Performance Equation"

PERFORMANCE = (Role clarity + Goal clarity) + Ability + Willingness (Motivation)

SOURCE: Manitoba Lotteries Corporation, Performance and Development Program, 2003. Courtesy of the Manitoba Lotteries Corporation.

theory, McClelland's theory of learned needs, and Herzberg's two-factor theory. Then we explore the so-called *process* theories of motivation. These theories all explore the question, "*How* is a person motivated?" The first process theory we explore is Victor Vroom's expectancy theory. Then we review theories relating to perceptions of justice and equity, and finally we explore goal-setting theory. See Exhibit 4.2 for an overview of the models to be reviewed in the chapter. Behaviour modification is also considered to be a process motivation theory by some scholars, and it is addressed in OBXtra3.

NEED THEORIES OF MOTIVATION

Need theories give primary consideration to variables *within* the individual that give rise to motivation and behaviour, and they all try to answer the question, "What motivates you at work?" Philosophers and scholars have theorized for centuries about human needs and motives. During the past century, attention narrowed to understanding motivation in businesses and other organizations.[8]

In this section we explore five need theories of motivation, as shown in the first column of Exhibit 4.2: Maslow's need hierarchy, McGregor's X-Y theory, Alderfer's ERG theory, McClelland's theory of learned needs, and Herzberg's two-factor theory.

Maslow's Hierarchy of Needs

Describe Maslow's hierarchy of needs and its applications and limitations.

Abraham Maslow proposed a need theory of motivation emphasizing psychological and interpersonal needs, in addition to physical needs and economic necessity. The core of Maslow's theory of human motivation is a **need hierarchy** of five categories.[9] Maslow labelled the five hierarchical categories as physiological needs, safety needs, belongingness needs, esteem needs, and the need for self-actualization. Physiological needs include the need for food and shelter. Safety needs include the need for security and predictability. Belongingness includes the need for love, friendship and community. Esteem includes the need for recognition and status and self-actualization means the need to fulfill one's potential and to be all that one can be.

need hierarchy
Maslow's theory that people are motivated by five sets of needs, and that as a lower need is gratified, the person becomes motivated by the next need in the hierarchy.

One distinguishing feature of Maslow's need hierarchy is the **progression hypothesis,** which states that the lowest level of ungratified need motivates behaviour.[10] This implies that as one level of need is met—for example, the physiological need for food—a person progresses to the next higher level of need—which would be for safety—and so forth.

progression hypothesis
The lowest level of ungratified need motivates behaviour.

This progression hypothesis has been criticized as faulty by many who argue that many an artist or passionate entrepreneur continues to self-actualize in spite of having not met his or her need for financial security. However, if Maslow's theory is accurate, a 2003 Statistics Canada finding revealing that one-third of all part-time Canadian workers lack the benefits to feel safe and secure implies they would have difficulty fulfilling their social, esteem, and self-actualization needs.[11] In spite of the lack of empirical support for Maslow's theory, his ideas have had an impact on North American human resources management and legislation, which ensures minimum wages and standards

EXHIBIT 4.2

Content and Process Theories of Motivation

Content Theories of Motivation	Process Theories of Motivation
Maslow's hierarchy of needs	Vroom's expectancy theory
McGregor's X-Y theory	Organizational justice & equity theory
Alderfer's ERG theory	Goal-setting theory
McClelland's theory of learned needs	Behaviour modification (see OBXtra3)
Herzberg's two-factor theory	

that are deemed to be necessary for productivity and retention. It seems that for the first time job security has been rated as more important than salary, at least by Canadian IT professionals.[12] Perhaps this is because salaries have reached an acceptable level in the industry, so the need for safety is emerging as most important.

Social needs are targeted through activities such as team retreats, company golf days, picnics, and parties. Companies attempt to fulfill employees' esteem needs through praise, recognition, and reward programs, like that at WestJet, described in Organizational Reality 4.1, and Marriott International, which encourages a number of so-called pride-builders down the line.[13] As discussed, self-actualization is the realization of one's full potential. Companies try to help employees self-actualize by supporting their career development, assigning challenging assignments, and by giving them promotions and lateral developmental moves. Increasingly, organizations are realizing that formally nurturing and cultivating an employee's career in-house isn't only an effective morale booster, it also makes good business sense.[14] A study of what motivates salespeople in different countries revealed that "opportunity to use abilities" was rated highest by Canadians, while money was ranked fourth.[15] Companies such as Pratt and Whitney Canada, Dun and Bradstreet, and Delta Hotels spend a great deal of time and money on helping their employees grow and self-actualize. For example, at Delta Hotels, all managers go through a day-long career planning workshop where they can discuss advancement and skills development with their staff. Individuals can self-actualize at any age. For example, Nic Fiore is a ski instructor at Badger Pass in Yosemite National Park. He tells a journalist at Workforce that he has not yet "reached the pinnacle of the type of person he wants to be." He is 82 years old.[16]

Maslow's *need hierarchy* is depicted in Exhibit 4.3, which also shows how the needs relate to Douglas McGregor's assumptions about people, which will be discussed next.

organizational reality 4.1

WestJet Recognition Programs

WestJet Airlines is well known for its culture of empowerment. Clive Beddoe, the airline's founder, chairman, and CEO, says his company tries to fuel employee energy and passion by giving power to individuals. WestJet offers employees profit sharing, personal days, flexible benefits, bonus programs, and health spending accounts. As well, WestJet puts great emphasis on internal recognition through its "Smile" program. Guests and employees can nominate people for a "Smile" award in recognition of the "many ways our people wow and amaze travellers with the caring, fun way they go about doing their jobs." In the fall of 2003, the company received 2571 stories and sent 4665 recognition letters to their "WestJetters." Letters were judged and winners received prizes such as a two-night stay at the Fairmont Empress in Victoria.

WestJet guests and employees can nominate people for a "Smile" award in recognition of the "many ways our people wow and amaze travellers with the caring, fun way they go about doing their jobs."

SOURCES: C. Howes and C. Cattaneo, "No Perk Too Rich if You're in Demand," *National Post*, September 30, 2000, D03; www.westjet.com.

EXHIBIT 4.3

Maslow's Hierarchy, Theory X, and Theory Y

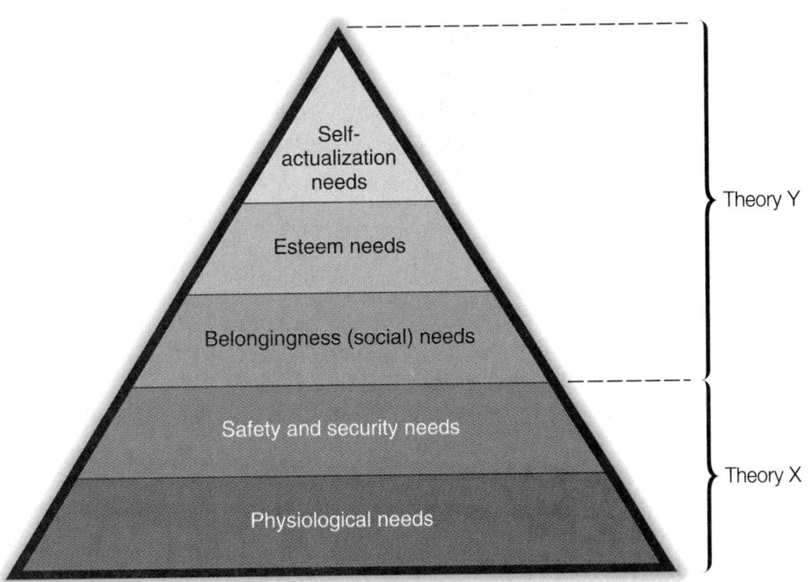

Theory X and Theory Y

Describe how Theory X and Theory Y assumptions about people may influence a manager's attempt to motivate an employee.

In the early 1950s, Douglas McGregor proposed Theory X and Y and built upon Maslow's notion of lower- and higher-order needs. However, rather than using the distinction between higher- and lower-order needs to explain the motivation of employees, he used them to explain managerial bias and behaviour toward their employees.

McGregor argued that when managers held a certain set of assumptions about their followers, which he labelled **Theory X,** they tended to try to motivate employees by meeting their lower-level physiological and safety needs. Today, in Canada, over five decades later, some managers continue to have Theory X assumptions, particularly about employees in low-paying jobs, when in fact employees are motivated by higher-order needs. For example, supervisors who closely monitor their employees and organizations that install monitoring devices can be viewed as having Theory X assumptions. A recent article argues that "Theory X involves regarding workers as oversized children; Theory Y means treating them as adults."[17] The author cites a few examples of Theory X assumptions in practice, such as HSBC, the London-based bank, announcing that it was going to charge employees for personal telephone calls made from the office.

Theory X
A set of assumptions of how to manage individuals who are motivated by lower-order needs.

By contrast, when managers held a different set of assumptions about their followers, which McGregor labelled **Theory Y,** they tended to try to motivate employees by meeting their higher-order needs for belongingness, esteem, and self-actualization.[18] McGregor's Theory X–Y combined with a number of studies on leadership styles, discussed in Chapter 10, resulted in recognition that, in general (although not always), when employees are trusted, they tend to be more effective. Employee participation programs are one consequence of McGregor's Theory Y assumptions. Ford Motor Company's first step in revitalizing its workforce through an employee involvement (EI) program was based on Theory Y assumptions about human nature.[19]

Theory Y
A set of assumptions of how to manage individuals who are motivated by higher-order needs.

The Theory X and Y assumptions are listed in Exhibit 4.4.

EXHIBIT 4.4

McGregor's Assumptions about People

Theory X

- People are by nature indolent. That is, they work as little as possible.
- People lack ambition, dislike responsibility, and prefer to be led.
- People are inherently self-centred and indifferent to organizational needs.
- People are by nature resistant to change.
- People are gullible and not very bright, the ready dupes of the charlatan and the demagogue.

Theory Y

- People are not by nature passive or resistant to organizational needs. They have become so as a result of experience in organizations.
- The motivation, the potential for development, the capacity for assuming responsibility, and the readiness to direct behaviour toward organizational goals are all present in people; management does not put them there. It is a responsibility of management to make it possible for people to recognize and develop these human characteristics for themselves.
- The essential task of management is to arrange conditions and methods of operation so that people can achieve their own goals best by directing their own efforts toward organizational objectives.

SOURCE: From "The Human Side of Enterprise" by Douglas M. McGregor; reprinted from *Management Review*, November 1957. Copyright 1957 American Management Association International. This work is protected by copyright and the making of this copy was with the permission of Access Copyright. Any alteration of its content or further copying in any form whatsoever is strictly prohibited.

Knowledge, Application, & Evaluation

DO YOU HOLD X OR Y ASSUMPTIONS ABOUT PEOPLE?

Review McGregor's Theory X–Y in Exhibit 4.4 and think about people doing low-level jobs to examine your own assumptions about their motivation. Decide whether you naturally tend to hold Theory X or Theory Y assumptions about people.

Compare and contrast ERG theory with Maslow's hierarchy of needs.

ERG theory
Alderfer's theory that people are motivated by three sets of needs and that as a lower need is gratified, the person becomes motivated by the next need in the hierarchy, but when unable to fulfill a higher need, they will regress to a lower one.

frustration regression hypothesis
Theory that when people are frustrated in their ability to satisfy a higher-order need they regress to the next lower category of needs and intensify their desire to gratify these needs.

ERG Theory

Clayton Alderfer, while agreeing with McGregor's notion of higher- and lower-order needs and recognizing the value of Maslow's contribution to understanding motivation, believed that the original need hierarchy was not quite accurate.[20] Alderfer simplified Maslow's hierarchy from five to three need categories. He called these three sets of needs **e**xistence (E), **r**elatedness, (R), and **g**rowth (G). In this **ERG theory,** the existence need addressed Maslow's physiological and physical safety needs; relatedness addressed the needs for interpersonal safety, belongingness, and interpersonal esteem; and growth referred to self-esteem and self-actualization.

ERG theory also addressed the criticism of Maslow, mentioned earlier, that lower-order needs always had to be met before higher-order needs by proposing the **frustration regression hypothesis,** which suggested that when people are frustrated in their ability to satisfy a higher-order need they regress to the next lower category of needs and intensify their desire to gratify these needs. For example, an employee may begin to focus on friendships and socializing at work when he or she becomes stuck in a dead-end job but can't leave due to a poor economy. ERG theory has not received much empirical support and it has been subject to a great deal of criticism; however, it and Maslow's hierarchy remain intuitively interesting and historically important.

McClelland's Theory of Learned Needs

Explain the needs for achievement, power, and affiliation and how understanding these needs can help a manager motivate employees.

While the three preceding theories assume that all human beings have basically the same need structure and alternatives, David McClelland's theory suggested that secondary needs were operating as well. These secondary needs (1) did not progress in a hierarchical manner, (2) were learned, and (3) varied based on an individual's personality. McClelland discovered that some individuals were more motivated by a need for achievement, whereas others had a strong need for power and others a strong need for affiliation. He also discovered that each need had quite different implications for managerial behaviour.

Need for Achievement

The **need for achievement** is a learned need that concerns issues of excellence, competition, challenging goals, persistence, and overcoming difficulties.[21] A person with a high need for achievement seeks excellence in performance, enjoys difficult and challenging goals, and is persevering and competitive in work activities. Questions that address the need for achievement are ones like these: Do you enjoy difficult, challenging work activities? Do you strive to exceed your performance objectives? Do you seek out new ways to overcome difficulties?

need for achievement
A learned need that concerns an individual's issues of excellence, competition, challenging goals, persistence, and overcoming difficulties.

Individuals with a high need for achievement have three unique characteristics. First, they set goals that are moderately difficult yet achievable, because they want both challenge and a good chance for success. Second, they like to receive feedback on their progress toward these goals. Because success is important to them, they like to know how they are doing. Third, they do not like having external events or other people interfere with their progress toward the goals. They are most comfortable working on individual tasks and activities that they control. Successful entrepreneurs tend to score high on their need for achievement.[22]

Need for Power

The **need for power** is a learned need that is concerned with making an impact on others, the desire to influence others, the urge to change people or events, and the desire to make a difference in life. The need for power is interpersonal, because it involves influence attempts directed at other people. People with a high need for power like to be in control of people and events. McClelland makes an important distinction between socialized power, which is used for the social benefit of many, and personalized power, which is used for the personal gain of the individual. The former is a constructive force in organizations, whereas the latter may be a very disruptive, destructive force in organizations. Read more about these in Chapter 9, on power and influence.

need for power
A learned need that concerns an individual's need to make an impact on others, influence others, change people or events, and make a difference in life.

A high need for power was one distinguishing characteristic of managers rated the "best" in McClelland's research. Specifically, the best managers had a very high need for socialized power, used for the collective well-being of the group, as opposed to personalized power.[23] These managers were concerned for others; had an interest in the organization's larger goals; and had a desire to be useful to the larger group, organization, and society. Also, the more effective managers had lower needs for affiliation.[24] Status is an important consideration for people with a high need for power. The more they are able to rise to the top of their organizations, the greater is their ability to exercise power, influence, and control so as to make an impact. Successful managers have the greatest upward velocity in an organization; they rise to higher managerial levels more quickly than their contemporaries.[25] These successful managers benefit their organizations most if they have a high socialized power need.

Need for Affiliation

The **need for affiliation** is a learned need concerned with establishing and maintaining warm, close, intimate relationships with other people.[26] People with a high need for affiliation are motivated to express their emotions and feelings to others while expecting

need for affiliation
A learned need that concerns an individual's need to establish and maintain warm, close, intimate relationships with other people.

Local Rotary clubs are a great way for business-people to fulfill their need for affiliation.

other people to do the same in return. They find conflicts and complications in their relationships disturbing and are strongly motivated to work through any such barriers to closeness. The relationships they have with others are therefore close and personal, emphasizing friendship and companionship.

People who have moderate to low needs for affiliation are more likely to feel comfortable working alone for extended periods of time. Modest or low levels of interaction with others are likely to satisfy these people's affiliation needs, allowing them to focus their attention on other needs and activities. People with a high need for affiliation, in contrast, always hope to be included in a range of interpersonal activities, in or away from work. They may play important integrative roles in group or intergroup activities because they work to achieve harmony and closeness in all relationships.

Understanding which of the three needs dominates in any one individual can help you motivate him or her. For someone motivated by a need for achievement, you can

EXHIBIT 4.5

Comparing Maslow, Alderfer and McClelland's Need Theories of Motivation

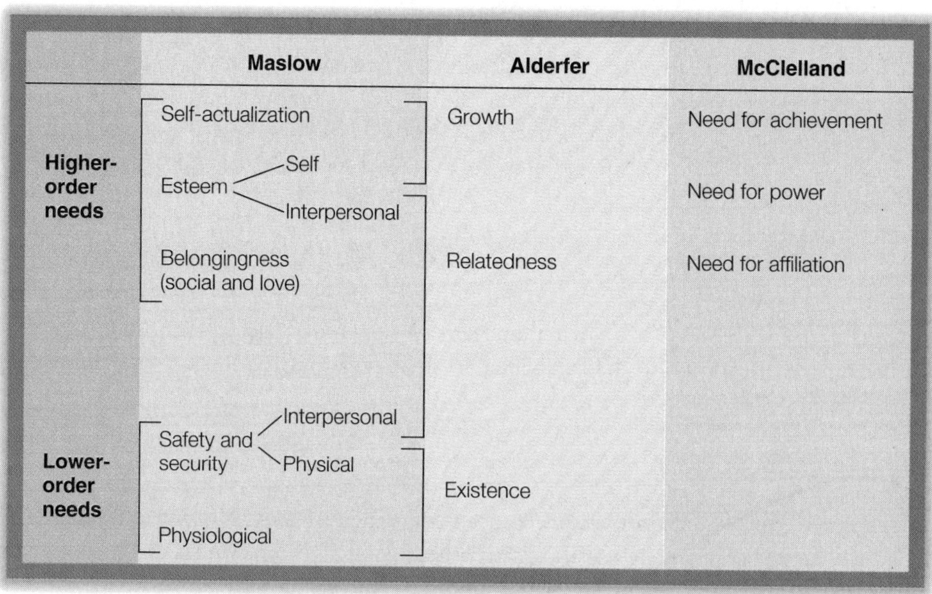

	Maslow	Alderfer	McClelland
Higher-order needs	Self-actualization	Growth	Need for achievement
	Esteem — Self; Interpersonal		Need for power
	Belongingness (social and love)	Relatedness	Need for affiliation
Lower-order needs	Safety and security — Interpersonal; Physical		
	Physiological	Existence	

explain how the task offers an opportunity to take on a challenging but achievable goal.[27] For someone motivated by a need for power, you can show how the project can make a difference or influence the direction of a unit. For someone motivated by a need for affiliation, you can point to the relationships he or she will build as a result, and perhaps create a team environment for the person.

Exhibit 4.5 is a summary chart of the three need theories of motivation just discussed; it shows the parallel relationships between the needs in each of the theories. While Maslow and Alderfer would refer to higher- and lower-order needs, McClelland does not make a similar distinction.

Knowledge, Application, & Evaluation

USING MCCLELLAND'S THEORY OF LEARNED NEEDS TO EXAMINE YOUR OWN MOTIVATION

Review the descriptions of McClelland's three learned needs and pick the one that seems to capture your main source of motivation. Are you mainly motivated by the need for achievement, affiliation, or personalized or socialized power?

Herzberg's Two-Factor Theory of Motivation

Describe the Herzberg's two-factor theory of motivation and compare it to ERG and Maslow's hierarchy.

Frederick Herzberg took a different approach to understanding motivational needs than did Maslow, McGregor, Alderfer, or McClelland. Rather than seeking to define universal or individual motives, he examined the differences between satisfaction and dissatisfaction at work. His theory became known as the two-factor theory of motivation.[28] Herzberg asked people to describe two important incidents at their jobs: one that was very satisfying and made them feel exceptionally good at work, and another that was very dissatisfying and made them feel exceptionally bad at work. As depicted in Exhibit 4.6, Herzberg defined **motivators** as intrinsic factors in the job that lead to satisfaction, such as achievement and the challenge of work itself, and **hygiene factors** as extrinsic factors surrounding the job that lead to dissatisfaction, such as company policies and pay.[29] Take a few minutes to complete Self-Assessment 4.1 to explore the different situations in which you experience work *satisfaction* and/or work *motivation.*

motivators
Intrinsic factors in the job that lead to satisfaction, such as achievement and the work itself.

hygiene factors
Extrinsic factors surrounding the job that lead to dissatisfaction, such as company policies and pay.

Motivators

Motivators in Herzberg's original research were identified as responsibility, achievement, recognition, advancement, and the work itself. Motivators are more important than hygiene factors, because they directly affect a person's motivational drive to do a good job. When they are absent, the person will be unmotivated to perform well and achieve excellence. According to Herzberg, job satisfaction and motivation are facilitated by designing motivators into a job. This process is known as **job enrichment,** which is defined as designing or redesigning jobs by incorporating motivational factors into them. Job enrichment and the later "Job Characteristics Model" are explored in depth in Chapter 5. Companies can strengthen the motivators in a job by assigning challenging tasks. For example, iSTARK in Concord, Ontario, an e-business company providing web-based productivity tools for the international cement and concrete industry, gives people special projects to keep them excited. They find that because of the enthusiasm generated by the work itself, workloads are seldom an issue and target dates are never a problem.[30] Exhibit 4.6 shows that salary can be a motivator in some situations. Many organizational reward systems now include other financial benefits, such as stock options, as part of an employee's compensation package.

job enrichment
Designing or redesigning jobs by incorporating motivational factors into them.

SELF-ASSESSMENT 4.1: WHAT'S IMPORTANT TO EMPLOYEES?

A. Read through the list below and put one or two check marks beside each item that would be particularly satisfying and/or motivating for you.

1. Which of the things would make you like working at this company (i.e., which would satisfy you)?
2. Which of the things would make you want to work harder for this company (i.e., which would motivate you)? (Note: There may be overlap—some things that satisfy you may also motivate you.)

Satisfying	Motivating	
____	____	1. The company is loyal to its employees, and rarely fires or lays anyone off.
____	____	2. Entry-level employees get four weeks' vacation time.
____	____	3. Every Friday afternoon, the company sponsors a "beer blast" social hour.
____	____	4. When you do your job well, you can expect your boss to compliment you and express appreciation.
____	____	5. Your boss allows you to set your own hours.
____	____	6. Many days you can work at home on your computer, as long as you call in periodically to check for messages.
____	____	7. The work environment is nice—comfortable chairs and pleasant music.
____	____	8. If you sell a lot, you get good bonus money.
____	____	9. The employees who get promoted always seem to be the ones who deserve it the most.
____	____	10. The company has a softball team—and it's your favourite sport!
____	____	11. You feel that if you do your job well, it really has a positive impact on your customers' lives.
____	____	12. The people who do good work generally get the most interesting work assignments.
____	____	13. Your company's salaries are 20 percent higher than salaries for similar positions at other companies.
____	____	14. Your co-workers are a lot of fun—they have good senses of humour.
____	____	15. The company offers an "employee of the month" award.

B. Review the list of things that motivate you. What do they seem to have in common?

SOURCE: D. Marcic and J. Seltzer, *Organizational Behaviour; Experiences and Cases,* 5th ed. (1998), Instructor's Manual, p. 117. Reprinted by permission of South-Western, a division of Thomson Learning, www.thomsonrights.com. Fax 800-730-2215.

Hygiene Factors

In two-factor theory, job dissatisfaction occurs when the hygiene factors are either not present or not sufficient. In the original research, the hygiene factors were company policy and administration, technical supervision, salary, interpersonal relations with one's supervisor, working conditions, and status. When these hygiene factors are poor or absent, the person complains about "poor supervision," "poor medical benefits," or whatever hygiene factor is poor. Employees experience a deficit and are dissatisfied when the hygiene factors are not present. However, even in the absence of good hygiene factors, employees may still be very motivated to perform their jobs well. For example, if one

EXHIBIT 4.6

The Motivation–Hygiene Theory of Motivation

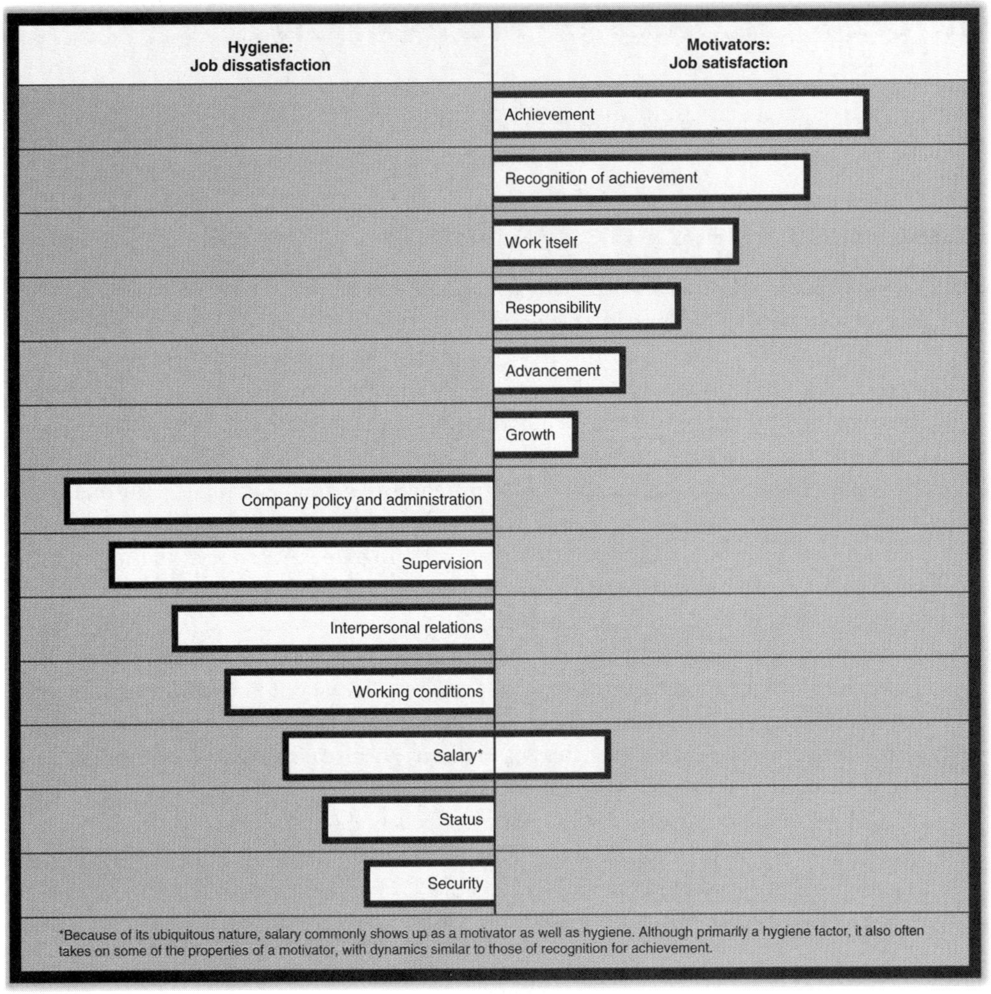

Hygiene: Job dissatisfaction	Motivators: Job satisfaction
	Achievement
	Recognition of achievement
	Work itself
	Responsibility
	Advancement
	Growth
Company policy and administration	
Supervision	
Interpersonal relations	
Working conditions	
Salary*	Salary*
Status	
Security	

*Because of its ubiquitous nature, salary commonly shows up as a motivator as well as hygiene. Although primarily a hygiene factor, it also often takes on some of the properties of a motivator, with dynamics similar to those of recognition for achievement.

SOURCE: Reprinted from Frederick Herzberg, *The Managerial Choice: To Be Efficient or to Be Human* (Salt Lake City: Olympus, 1982). Reprinted by permission.

enjoys a particular job, one can be highly motivated, even if one's supervisor is weak. Although this may appear to be a paradox, it is not, because the motivation and hygiene factors are independent of each other.

Two conclusions can be drawn at this point. First, hygiene factors are of some importance up to a threshold level, but beyond the threshold there is little value in improving the hygiene factors. Second, the presence of motivators is essential to enhancing employee motivation to excel at work. The extensive benefits programs at Home Depot can be considered hygiene factors, and while they do not directly motivate or create enthusiasm, they prevent dissatisfaction. Hygiene factors cannot stimulate psychological growth or human development and may be thought of as maintenance factors, because they contribute to an individual's basic needs such as physiological and safety needs.

Herzberg's two-factor theory has been criticized because research results have not shown a clear dichotomization of incidents into hygiene and motivator factors. For example, employees almost equally classify pay as a hygiene factor and as a motivation factor. A second criticism is the absence of individual differences in the theory. Specifically, individual differences such as age, sex, social status, education, and occupational level may influence the classification of factors as motivation or hygiene. Finally, almost all of the supporting data for the theory come from Herzberg and his students using his peculiar type of critical-incident storytelling technique. These criticisms challenge and qualify, yet do not invalidate, the theory.

PROCESS THEORIES OF MOTIVATION

Now that we have reviewed the five content theories of motivation, we move on to the more contemporary process theories of motivation. These are Vroom's expectancy theory, equity theory, organizational justice theory, and goal-setting theory.

7

Describe the expectancy theory of motivation and illustrate, using examples, how it can be applied.

expectancy theory
The theory that people exert effort if they expect that their effort will result in good performance, and that this performance will be instrumental in getting them valued outcomes.

expectancy
The belief that effort leads to performance (E–P).

instrumentality
The belief that performance is related to rewards/outcomes (P–O).

valence
The importance, attractiveness, desirability, or anticipated satisfaction one places on a particular outcome.

Expectancy Theory of Motivation

Victor Vroom, a Canadian OB scholar, created expectancy theory in the mid-1960s. **Expectancy theory** is founded on the notion that people believe there are relationships between the effort they put forth, the performance they achieve, and the outcomes they receive. The key constructs in the expectancy theory of motivation are "expectancy," "instrumentality," and the "valence" or value of an outcome.[31] **Expectancy** is the belief that effort (E) leads to performance (P). For example, "If I spend more hours studying, I will get a better grade on the test." **Instrumentality** is the belief that performance (P) is related to outcomes (O) or rewards; for example, "If I get good grades, these will be instrumental in helping me get into a graduate program." **Valence** is the importance, attractiveness, desirability, or anticipated satisfaction with outcomes.[32] A model of expectancy theory is depicted in Exhibit 4.7.

Expectancy, instrumentality, and valence are all important to a person's motivation. Expectancy and instrumentality concern a person's beliefs about how effort, performance, and rewards are related. For example, a person may firmly believe that an increase in effort, such as spending more hours studying, has a direct, positive effect on test performance and that a reduced amount of effort results in an equivalent reduction in performance. Another person may have a very different set of beliefs about the effort–performance link. The person might believe that regardless of the amount of additional studying, no improvement in test performance is possible. Therefore, the perceived relationship between effort and performance varies from person to person and from activity to activity.

EXHIBIT 4.7

An Expectancy Model for Motivation

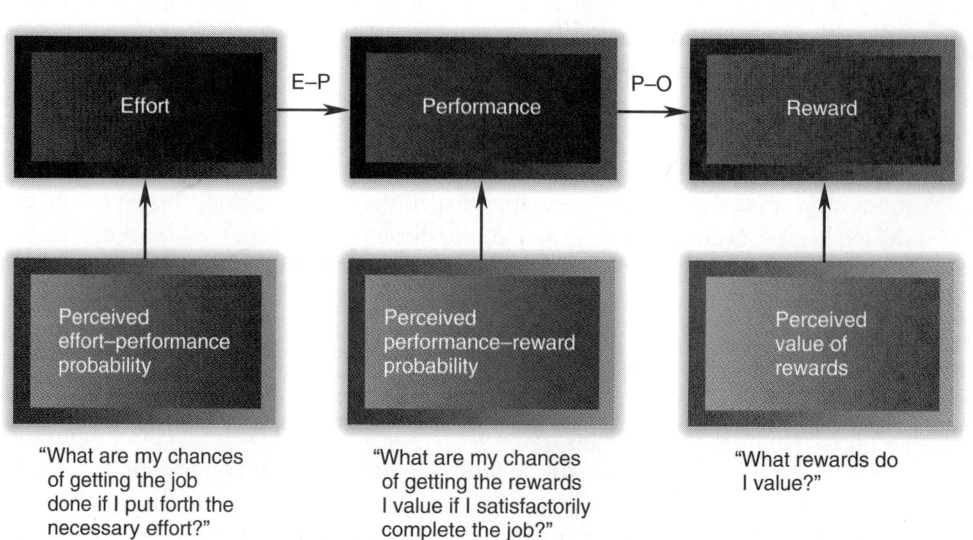

Individual perceptions are also influenced by a person's feelings of self-efficacy, his or her past experiences, as well as situational variables such as organizational or classroom climate.[33] For example, a recent study revealed that all students, particularly test-anxious students, performed poorly and were less motivated when they experienced their teachers as very evaluative and critical.[34] Applying expectancy theory, we would say that in a highly evaluative classroom climate, affected primarily the E–P expectancy of test-anxious students. In spite of having high valence for passing the course with a good grade and believing that good test grades would lead to passing the course (P–O) they had low expectation (instrumentality) that their efforts (E) would lead to good test performance (P). They therefore became less motivated and subsequently reduced their effort.

In a similar fashion, people vary in their beliefs about the link between performance and rewards in various situations. One person may believe that an improvement in performance (e.g., getting better grades at college or university) has a direct, positive effect on the outcomes/rewards (e.g., job prospects or admittance to graduate school), whereas another person may believe that an improvement in grades has no effect on these outcomes/rewards. From the perspective of expectancy theory, *it is the person's belief about the relationships between these constructs that is important,* not the actual nature of the relationship. A person's motivation increases along with his or her belief that effort leads to performance and that performance leads to rewards, assuming the person wants the rewards. During volatile times in business, the performance–reward linkage may be confusing. According to research in 2002, only one-third of employees in a survey of 335

NCEO

The National Center for Employee Ownership (NCEO) is a leading publisher of information concerning employee ownership programs. Visit the site to learn more about employee stock-ownership plans (ESOPs) and how they motivate employees. How does employee ownership relate to the expectancy theory of motivation? How do employee stock-ownership plans create a strong relationship between human efforts and rewards?

http://www.nceo.org

organizational reality 4.2

Managing Expectations at Human Genome Sciences

It is not hard to manage employees in boom times when companies realize big profits and gains, which are shared with employees through handsome salary increases and stock options. Those are among the rewards employees seek for strenuous efforts and high performance on the job. However, motivating employees in volatile times is much more challenging because rewards are not always available for high performance.

William Haseltine founded Human Genome Sciences (HGS) as a pioneer in the race to develop gene-based drugs. Haseltine met the challenge of motivating employees in volatile times. He communicated clearly with employees to keep their expectations realistic, and persuaded them to take the long view to rewards and payoffs for high performance by giving them stock options. Stock options are one way of rewarding employees in small, new start-ups such as HGS. However, it can be challenging to know when to exercise one's stock options. Dr. Haseltine urged employees to be cautious in their financial commitments and judicious in the exercise of their vested options, though he never discouraged them from the exercise of their options.

William Haseltine, founder and former CEO of Human Genome

The cash that comes with rising stock markets can help motivate employees and boost morale, but ever-rising expectations of reward and payoff can be illusory. Therefore, employees should be cautious about financial over-commitment and should manage their own expectations about rewards and payoffs for performance.

SOURCE: C. Hymowitz, "In the Lead: Motivating Employees in Volatile Era Means Managing Expectations," *The Wall Street Journal,* May 2, 2001, B1.

companies worldwide said they believed that they would earn more if they improved their performance. This suggests that companies need to create stronger links between performance and desired outcomes such as pay, in order to keep motivation strong.[35] Another important idea within the expectancy theory of motivation is the idea that the *valence*, or value, that people place on various rewards varies. One person prefers salary to benefits, whereas another person prefers just the reverse.

Valence and expectancy are particularly important in establishing priorities for people pursuing multiple goals during times of change or stress.[36] As discussed in Organizational Reality 4.2, some CEOs work to manage expectations during volatile times in order to help and to motivate employees,

Diagnosing Motivational Problems and Taking Corrective Action Using Expectancy Theory

Within the expectancy theory framework, motivational problems stem from three possible causes. These causes are (1) a lack of belief that increased effort will lead to improved performance (low expectancy), (2) a lack of belief that improved performance will lead to a greater likelihood of achieving desired outcomes/rewards (low instrumentality), and/or (3) a lack of desire for the outcome/rewards offered (low valence). After diagnosing the cause of the motivational problem, managers can take corrective action using expectancy theory, in the following ways:

- If the motivational problem is related to the person's belief that effort will not result in performance, the person can be shown how additional training or an alteration in the kind of effort put forth can be converted into improved performance. For example, the student who does not believe that spending more hours studying the course notes and textbook will result in improved marks on tests might be trained in time management or note-taking, or shown how to distinguish important from less important text material. Alternatively, the performance measures (i.e., the test itself) may be poor and may need to be revised to reflect the curriculum expectations.
- If the motivational problem is related to the person's belief that performance will not result in rewards, one has to diagnose whether the belief is unfounded or not. For example, in some organizations good performers do not get the promotions or other types of recognition because of discrimination or ineffective performance measurement. In other cases, the person may not be aware of the less obvious performance requirements for obtaining a certain outcome or reward. For example, a top salesperson may become unmotivated (lowered instrumentality) when a colleague with a lower sales record gets a promotion instead of him or her. Perhaps there were performance criteria other than sales that were important, which the top salesperson was unaware of. In this case, instrumentality could be strengthened by clarifying what performance is required to achieve the desired promotion.
- If the motivational problem is related to the value the person places on, or the preference the person has for, certain rewards or outcomes, the solution lies in influencing the value placed on the rewards or altering the rewards themselves.

Equity Theory and Organizational Justice

While expectancy theory helps us understand an individual's motivation in terms of th perception of the links between effort and performance and between performance anc outcome, equity and justice theories add another important dimension, and that is th concept of perceived equity.

Application, Analysis & Synthesis

USING EXPECTANCY THEORY TO DIAGNOSE A MOTIVATION BREAKDOWN

Adam was 19 years old and a very hard-working and confident data entry clerk. He wanted to make a lot of money so that he could get a place of his own. His production was the highest in his group but, being on an hourly rate, he did not benefit financially from his excellent performance. He believed, however, that his hard work and demonstrated results would eventually pay off, and that soon he would be promoted to supervisor at $8 per hour more. After Adam had been a year in the job, with consistently high performance, Serge, a 28-year-old co-worker, with a poorer production record, got the promotion to the supervisory role. Adam was very upset, particularly since Serge always seemed to be "goofing off" and talking to people. No one told Adam why he had been overlooked. In time, Adam's production dropped to the level of his co-workers. Six months after Serge's promotion, Adam quit for a job paying $1.00 an hour more.

1. Use expectancy theory to analyze Adam's motivation before and after Serge's promotion.
2. Based on your analysis, recommend what could have been done differently by management to motivate and retain Adam after promoting Serge.

Equity Theory

Explain Adams's equity theory of motivation and the various ways that employees respond to perceived inequities.

Stacy Adam's equity theory was the first to suggest that individuals are motivated by perceptions of fairness and justice. According to **equity theory,** people determine whether they have been treated fairly by first examining the ratio of their inputs relevant to their outcomes, and then comparing this ratio to the input-to-outcome ratio of a comparison other.[37] Inputs include their effort, time, and cognitive resources. Outcomes include the rewards or privileges received from the job, such as pay, promotions, and opportunities for professional development or enjoyable work.[38]

equity theory
People determine whether they have been treated fairly by first examining the ratio of their inputs relevant to their outcomes and then comparing this ratio to the input-to-outcome ratio of a comparison other.

Inequity occurs when a person perceives that he or she has received more, or less, than is deserved, based on the perceived input/outcome ratio of a *referent (comparison) other.* Perceptions of equity or inequity depend heavily on the person or role one chooses to compare oneself to. Possible comparisons are oneself (in the present compared to the past or expected future), other individuals, groups, organizations, or systems. Which comparison other one chooses is influenced by a number of factors, such as the information one has about each one, their credentials, as well how much the person respects and looks up to the person or role.[39]

Exhibit 4.8 shows one equity situation and two inequity situations, one of which is negative, called perceived under-reward, and the other positive, called perceived over-reward. For example, under-reward inequity in (b) could be perceived if the comparison other earned a higher salary, and over-reward inequity in (c) could occur if the person (the perceiver) had more vacation time, in both cases all else being equal. Although not illustrated in the example, nontangible inputs, like emotional investment, and nontangible outcomes, like job satisfaction, may well enter into a person's perceived equity equation.

Possible Responses to Perceived Inequity

Regardless of personality, once inequity is experienced as tension, this tension motivates a person to act in a manner to resolve the inequity. The various actions a person might take when he or she perceives that a situation is inequitable or unjust are as follows:

- Try to change his or her outcomes
- Change his or her inputs
- Try to alter the comparison other's outcomes
- Alter the comparison other's inputs

EXHIBIT 4.8

Equity and Inequity at Work

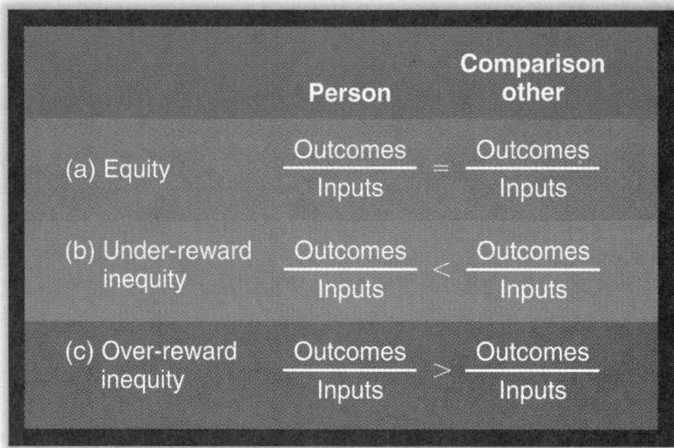

- Change who is used as a comparison other
- Rationalize the inequity
- Leave the situation

Limitations of Equity Theory

A few limitations of equity theory are as follows: While some research has shown that people tend to select comparison others who are similar to them, confusion still exists around the basis for selecting the comparison other.[40] Also problematic is equity theory's heavy emphasis on pay as an outcome, as well as the difficulty the theory has had in explaining the overpayment condition. Although most studies of equity theory take a

IMPLICATIONS FOR LIFE

Applying Equity Theory to Getting an Unfair Test Mark

Equity theory can be applied to a situation you might find yourself in. For example, what actions might you take if you receive a test mark that you feel is unfair relative to another student?

Well, you might try to change your outcomes by talking to the instructor to try to get him to raise your mark or let you take the test again, or do an additional assignment. Or, you might change your inputs by putting in more or less study time for the next test or by changing your study habits. Another thing you might try is to alter the comparison other's outcomes by trying to get the instructor to lower the mark of the fellow student whom you compared yourself to. Or you might try to alter the comparison other's inputs by trying to get the fellow student to spend less time studying for the next test. Then again, you might decide to pick a different comparison other or rationalize the inequity by saying to yourself that the comparison other is smarter, or that the teacher is showing favouritism! Finally you might choose to leave the situation by dropping the course.

Given all these options in the face of perceived inequity, which option do you think you would choose and why? What factors will affect your choice? Might it depend partly on the process by which the instructor assessed your test or perhaps on the way your instructor treats you when you complain? Read more about procedural and interactional justice in the next section.

short-term perspective, equity comparisons over the long term should be considered as well, since increasing, decreasing, or constant experiences of inequity over time may have very different consequences for people.[41]

Organizational Justice Theory

Explain how individuals are motivated by perceptions of distributive, procedural and interactional justice.

More recent research into perceptions of equity at work has been conducted by organizational justice scholars, who have identified three types of organizational events that are evaluated in terms of equity or justice. These types of events are outcomes, organizational processes, and interpersonal interactions at work. **Distributive justice** is the term given to judgments regarding the fairness of outcomes or allocations, as discussed in equity theory. **Procedural justice** is the term given to judgments regarding the fairness of elements in organizational processes, and **interactional justice** is the term given to judgments regarding the fairness of interpersonal interactions.[42]

distributive justice
The term given to judgments regarding the fairness of outcomes or allocations, as discussed in equity theory.

procedural justice
The term given to judgments regarding the fairness of elements in organizational processes.

interactional justice
The term given to judgments regarding the fairness of interpersonal interactions.

Current organizational justice research is seeking to better understand how we make fairness judgments, why workers are concerned with organizational justice, and the nature of organizational justice.[43] While equity theory gives the impression that people make judgments about input-to-outcome ratios in a controlled or systematic way, this may be true only when we have the time and cognitive resources to commit to the process. Recent research suggests that in other situations, we make equity judgments automatically, using shortcuts (heuristics) and our instincts, and that these fairness judgments, once formed, are resistant to change.[44]

Procedural and Interactional Justice

Even if an employee perceives inequity because someone else got a better raise (distributive justice), that same employee may believe that the procedure by which the raises were decided was in fact fair and unbiased (procedural justice). Perceptions that procedures used were fair can, therefore, mitigate perceptions of inequity in distribution of outcomes. In one study of procedural justice during performance appraisals, it was discovered that employees make two different types of justice process judgments: one regarding the fairness of appraisal forms and procedures themselves and one regarding the rater's fairness in giving performance feedback and allowing a fair hearing.[45] The interaction behaviour of the rater is sometimes called interactional justice and can be viewed as a subset of procedural justice. Research shows that if a supervisor or coach treats employees or team members with dignity and respect and shows concern for their well-being, perceptions of interactional justice will be high, and the employees and team members will be more likely to accept feedback and outcomes, both positive and negative.[46]

GoalManager
GoalManager.com is one of the leading online resources for developing employee incentives.
http://www.goalmanager.com

Goal Setting and Management by Objectives (MBO)

Explain the purposes of goal setting, the characteristics that make goal-setting effective, its limitations, and applications to management by objectives (MBO).

Need theories, expectancy theory, and equity and justice theories all contribute to our understanding and help us influence a person's motivation. A final, powerful, and well-researched motivation theory is goal-setting theory. **Goal setting** is the process of establishing desired results that guide and direct behaviour. Goal-setting theory is based on laboratory studies, field research experiments, and comparative investigations by Edwin Locke, Gary Latham, John M. Ivancevich, Ruth Kanfer, Gerard Seijts, and others.[47] Locke and Latham's groundbreaking original research drew the following conclusions: (1) Setting specific high goals leads to higher performance than setting no goals, or setting abstract goals such as doing one's best. (2) As long as the goals are perceived to be attainable, the higher the goal difficulty, the higher the performance. (3) Feedback, participation, and competition affect performance only to the extent that they lead to commitment to specific *high* goals. (4) The relationship between goal setting and performance is mediated by direction, effort, persistence (all motivational), and task strategies (cognitive.)[48]

goal setting
The process of establishing desired results that guide and direct behaviour.

Goals help crystallize the sense of purpose and mission that is essential to success at work, and it has been found that effective goal setting is a more powerful predictor of

EXHIBIT 4.9

The Four Mechanisms by Which Goals Affect Performance

1. Goals direct attention and effort toward goal-relevant activities.
2. Goals energize, so that high goals lead to greater effort than low goals.
3. Goals affect persistence.
4. Goals affect action indirectly by leading to the arousal, discovery, and/or use of task-relevant knowledge and strategies.

SOURCE: E. A. Locke and G. P. Latham, "Building a Practically Useful Theory of Goal Setting and Task Motivation: A 35-Year Odyssey," *American Psychologist* 57, no. 9 (September 2002): 706–07. Copyright © 2002 by the American Psychological Association. Adapted with permission.

performance than a person's goal orientation or personality.[49] As shown in Exhibit 4.9, goals affect performance by directing employees' attention, energizing employees, affecting persistence, and leading to arousal and discovery of task-relevant knowledge and strategies.[50]

The finding that the setting of specific, challenging goals was more effective than setting "do your best goals" was called into question by Kanfer and Ackerman's studies published in 1989. These studies showed that air cadets, performing a complex air traffic control task, performed worse when they were assigned a specific, challenging goal compared to when they were instructed to do their best. It was concluded that when a task is complex or novel and the person is in the process of learning, a specific, difficult goal distracts from developing the required learning strategies needed to master the task.[51]

Locke, Latham, and Seijts have replicated the findings of Kanfer and Ackerman and developed goal-setting theory further to include the development of learning goals as well as outcome goals. **Learning goals** provide clear markers of progress and reduce the risk of self-demoralization that can occur when current accomplishments are gauged against an outcome goal, while **outcome goals** provide clear direction as to a desired end or outcome in the long term. While specific outcome goals should be set when the only issue is motivation and the person has the abilities and knowledge to perform the task, specific and challenging learning goals should be set when individuals initially lack the knowledge or skill to perform the task.[52]

learning goals
Goals that provide clear markers of progress and reduce the risk of self-demoralization that can occur when current accomplishments are gauged against an outcome goal.

outcome goals
Goals that provide clear direction as to a desired end or outcome in the long term.

Terry Fox epitomizes effective goal setting. In spite of his spreading cancer, he was able to run halfway across Canada and has left a legacy that continues to raise millions for cancer treatment.

Also, while setting specific, challenging goals has been found to motivate constructive effort, recent research has demonstrated that it also motivates intentional *unethical* behaviour when people fall short of their goals, with or without economic incentives.[53] In these studies, research participants were asked to create words from anagrams and also to check their work. One group was given a specific number of words to create and the other was told to "do your best to create as many words as you can." Ethical behaviour was measured by coding the congruence between participants' actual productivity and the claims they made about their productivity.

Characteristics of Effective Goal Setting

When setting goals for yourself or with others, it is helpful to keep the following guidelines in mind:[54]

- *SMART goals:* To cue or focus the person's attention on exactly what is to be accomplished and to arouse the person to peak performance, goals should be specific (S), measurable (M), attainable (A), relevant (R), and have a time frame (T).[55]
- *Challenging goals*: Research shows that people exert more effort when they perceive the goal as challenging them.
- *Goal commitment:* The goal–performance relationship is strongest when people are committed to their goals. Commitment increases when people view attaining the goal as important and when they believe they are capable of attaining the goal.
- *Goal feedback:* For goals to be effective, people need summary feedback that reveals progress in relation to their goals.
- *Learning goals for complex or new tasks:* The power of goals to influence performance depends in part on the complexity of the task and whether the person has the skills and task strategies for accomplishment. Thus, for complex or new tasks, set specific and challenge learning goals as well as outcome goals.
- *Participation:* Encourage participation in goal setting but provide information so that challenging goals are set or the benefits of participation do not result.

Companies set both quantitative and qualitative goals with employees. The Western Company of North America (now part of BJ Services Corporation) allowed about 15 percent of a manager's goals to be of a qualitative nature.[56] A qualitative goal might be to improve relationships with customers. Further work might convert the qualitative goal into quantitative measures such as number of complaints or frequency of complimentary letters. In this case, however, the qualitative goal may well be sufficient and most meaningful.

In Self-Assessment 4.2 you are asked to evaluate your goal setting at school or work for the five dimensions of goal difficulty, goal specificity, peer competition, goal feedback, and participation in goal setting. Which of these factors, or the additional ones just mentioned, affect your motivation in working toward goals? Do you tend to set learning goals or just outcome goals?

Management by Objectives

Management by objectives (MBO), a term coined by Peter Drucker, is a participative goal-setting process in which organizational objectives are cascaded down the organization and integrated with unit and individual goals and objectives. MBO programs have been pervasive in organizations for nearly 50 years.[57] This does not mean that goal setting begins at the bottom of the organization. It means that goal setting is applicable to all employees, with lower-level organizational members and professional staff having a clear influence over the goal-setting process.[58]

management by objectives (MBO)
A participative goal-setting process in which organizational objectives are cascaded down the organization and integrated with unit and individual goals and objectives.

Organizational goal setting is an essential prerequisite to individual goal setting; the two must be closely linked for the success of both.[59] At FedEx, all individual objectives must be tied to the overall corporate objectives of people, service, and profit. In planning, discretionary control is usually given to individuals and departments to develop operational and tactical plans to support the corporate objectives. The emphasis is on formulating a clear, consistent, measurable, and ordered set of goals to articulate *what* to do. The evaluation component consists of interim reviews of goal progress, conducted by managers and employees, and formal performance evaluation. The reviews are mid-term assessments designed to help employees take self-corrective action. NexInnovations, based in Calgary, designed a modified MBO performance management system and started by rewriting over 200 job descriptions. They started with their six key corporate objectives and identified business unit objectives, individual objectives, and action plans.

Knowledge & Application

SELF-ASSESSMENT 4.2: TASK–GOAL ATTRIBUTE QUESTIONNAIRE

Listed below is a set of statements that may or may not describe the job or school objectives toward which you are presently working. **Read each statement carefully and rate each on a scale from 1 (agree completely) to 7 (disagree completely)** to describe your level of agreement or disagreement with the statement. *Please answer all questions.*

1. I am allowed a high degree of influence in the determination of my work/school objectives.

2. I should not have too much difficulty in reaching my work/school objectives; they appear to be fairly easy.
3. I receive a considerable amount of feedback concerning my quantity of output on the job/in school.

4. Most of my coworkers and peers try to outperform one another on their assigned work/school goals.
5. My work/school objectives are very clear and specific; I know exactly what my job/assignment is.

6. My work/school objectives will require a great deal of effort from me to complete them.

7. I really have little voice in the formulation of my work/school objectives.
8. I am provided with a great deal of feedback and guidance on the quality of my work.
9. I think my work/school objectives are ambiguous and unclear.

10. It will take a high degree of skill and know-how on my part to attain fully my work/school objectives.

11. The setting of my work/school goals is pretty much under my own control.
12. My boss/instructors seldom let(s) me know how well I am doing on my work toward my work/school objectives.
13. A very competitive atmosphere exists among my peers and me with regard to attaining our respective work/school goals; we all want to do better than anyone else in attaining our goals.

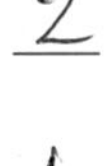

14. I understand fully which of my work/school objectives are more important than others; I have a clear sense of priorities on these goals.

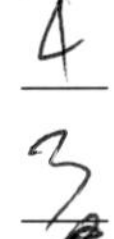

15. My work/school objectives are quite difficult to attain.
16. My supervisor/instructors usually ask(s) for my opinions and thoughts when determining my work/school objectives.

For scoring instructions please go to the end of the chapter, p. 133.

SOURCE: Adapted from R. M. Steers, "Factors Affecting Job Attitudes in a Goal-Setting Environment," *Academy of Management Journal* 19 (1976): 9.

"Anybody the President walks up to, wherever he is in the country, should be able to say not only what the corporate objectives are, but what they are doing right now, and how it supports it."[60]

Because goal-setting programs are somewhat mechanical by nature, they are most easily implemented in stable, predictable settings, which hardly exist anymore in the current, turbulent business environment. Harry Levinson, a gifted psychologist, published a critique of MBO in 1970 that has been re-published in the *Harvard Business Review* and still bears consideration more than 30 years later. Essentially, he argues that the failing of MBO systems are that they force unit managers to commit to goals they don't believe are realistic, that an obsession with objectivity means that quality is neglected, and that individuals' needs and desires are not taken into account.[61]

CROSS-CULTURAL DIFFERENCES IN MOTIVATION

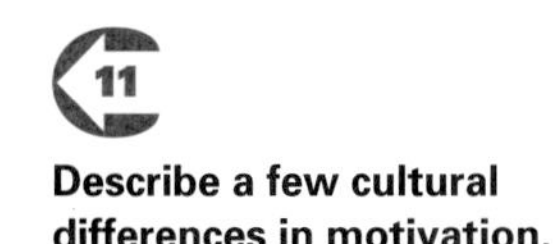

Describe a few cultural differences in motivation.

Most motivation theories in use today have been developed by Americans about Americans.[62] When researchers have examined the universality of these theories, they have found cultural differences, at least with regard to Maslow's, McClelland's, Herzberg's, and Vroom's theories. For example, while self-actualization may be the pinnacle need for Americans in Maslow's need hierarchy, security may be the most important need for people in cultures such as Greece and Japan who have a high need to avoid uncertainty.[63] Although individual achievement is an important need for North Americans, research noted earlier in the chapter suggested that other cultures do not value achievement as much as Americans do. In Asian countries with collectivist cultures, belongingness rather than self-actualization was viewed as the highest need on the hierarchy in early studies. Recent research, however, is suggesting that there has been some movement from a more collectivist orientation toward more self-orientation.[64] The two-factor theory has been tested in other countries as well. Results in New Zealand did not replicate the results found in the United States; supervision and interpersonal relationships were important motivators in New Zealand rather than hygienic factors as in the U.S.[65]

Application of expectancy theory, especially when applied in pay-for performance schemes (discussed in the next chapter), may also vary by country. While most Canadians expect a positive correlation between performance and pay, or some other desired outcome, this expectation may not be so obvious in several other parts of the world, according to Lionel Laroche, president of ITAP Canada, a cross-cultural training and consulting organization located in Toronto. He writes that "In countries like France and Greece, where the best graduates often choose government positions with secure paychecks for life, it is quite difficult to attract good employees with pay schemes that included bonuses for achieving specific objectives."[66] He also says that in Hong Kong, where people value risk and are motivated by financial gains, people expect to receive financial rewards within a matter of weeks, and if they have to wait until their next annual performance review they are likely to look for another employer.

Knowledge, Application, & Evaluation

CULTURAL DIFFERENCES IN MOTIVATION IN CANADA

In your project team, discuss the ethnic backgrounds of each team member to discover possible cultural differences in motivation. Rank the following in order of preference at this stage of your life.

Motivator	Rank
Individual achievement and growth (North America)	1
Performance-based rewards (U.S.A.)	5
Secure paycheques for life (France and Greece)	2
Belongingness and community (Asia)	3
Receiving financial rewards immediately (Hong Kong)	
Good supervision and interpersonal relationships (New Zealand)	4

Discuss the differences. How important is ethnic background? Did any themes emerge that define our Canadian culture? How important is age or stage of life in these rankings?

IMPLICATIONS FOR ORGANIZATIONAL EFFECTIVENESS

Effectively managed companies recognize that unmotivated or disengaged employees cost huge amounts in terms of lost productivity and employee turnover. In addition, a lack of motivation creates a negative work climate that can be felt by customers and co-workers. Enthusiastic and motivated employees create an infectious and passionate work environment. Home Depot, for example, accomplishes this by providing intensive training and retraining, by meeting the security needs of part-timers through a comprehensive benefits program, and by offering recognition and reward. Another example discussed, WestJet, sent 4655 recognition letters to their employees in 2002.

In this chapter you learned about a number of theories of motivation, all of which teach us lessons about how to help people become motivated to fulfill their needs and work toward organizational and personal goals. The later motivation theories, such as the justice, expectancy, and goal-setting theories, may be more scientifically sound than earlier theories, such as the two-factor theory and Maslow's hierarchy; nevertheless, the older theories of motivation have conceptual value, show us the importance of human needs, and provide a basis for the later theories.

Managers cannot assume they understand employees' needs. They should recognize the variety of needs that motivate employee behaviour. Individual employees differ in their needs, and managers should be sensitive to ethnic, national, gender, and age differences in this regard. Employees with high needs for power must be given opportunities to exercise influence, employees with high needs for achievement must be allowed to excel at work, and employees with high needs for affiliation need interaction opportunities and recognition. Managers can increase employee motivation by training (increased perceptions of success because of increased ability), coaching (increased confidence), and task assignments (increased perceptions of success because of more experience). Managers should ensure that rewards are contingent on good performance and that valued rewards, such as time off or flexible work schedules, are available. Managers must attempt to understand what their employees want, and organizations need to train their managers in the various motivational techniques discussed.

Chapter Summary

1. Learning about how to motivate an employee is critical to the job of a manager. Organizations with unmotivated employees pay a huge price in lost productivity and the cost involved in continually replacing and training staff.
2. Need theories of motivation answer the question "What motivates you at work?" Maslow suggests five needs, from lower to higher as follows: physiological, safety, belongingness, esteem, and self-actualization. His theory includes a progression hypothesis.
3. Theory X and Y, developed by McGregor, suggests that managers hold one of two sets of assumptions about their employees. X assumptions are mistrusting while Y assumptions are trusting of employees.
4. Alderfer proposed his ERG theory as a way of simplifying Maslow's five needs down to three. His theory also assumes a frustration regression hypothesis.
5. According to McClelland, the needs for achievement, power, and affiliation are learned needs, and individuals differ as to which of the three is a dominant motivator for them. Managers need to understand which of the three needs dominates for each employee and motivate them accordingly.
6. Herzberg's two-factor theory suggests that motivators such as the work itself lead to job satisfaction, while hygiene factors, such as working conditions, prevent job dissatisfaction but do not necessarily motivate.
7. Expectancy theory states that people exert effort if they expect that their effort will result in good performance and that this performance will be instrumental in getting them valued outcomes. Managers can influence employee motivation by strengthening E–P and P–O perceptions and by ensuring that rewards are valued.
8. Equity theory (distributive justice) states that individuals are motivated by the perception of inequity or injustice, as measured by "input" and "outcome" ratios in comparison to a comparison other. Choice of a comparison other is important to equity theory, and a number of responses to perceived inequity can result.

9. Procedural justice relates to judgments regarding the fairness of elements in organizational processes, and interactional justice is the term given to judgments regarding the fairness of interpersonal interactions.

10. Goals direct attention and effort toward desired outcomes and, if set properly, motivate higher levels of performance. In order for goal setting to be effective, goals need to be specific and challenging. Commitment to goals is increased when people view the goal as important and they believe that they can attain it, and employee participation in goal setting helps if a more difficult goal results; ongoing feedback on progress is key. Management by objectives (MBO) is a participative goal-setting process that is implemented through the organization by integrating individual, unit, and organization objectives.

11. Theories of motivation are culturally bound, and differences occur between nations.

Key Terms

distributive justice (p. 123)
equity theory (p. 121)
ERG theory (p. 112)
expectancy (p. 118)
expectancy theory (p. 118)
extrinsic motivation (p. 108)
frustration regression hypothesis (p. 112)
goal setting (p. 123)
hygiene factors (p. 115)
instrumentality (p. 118)
interactional justice (p. 123)
intrinsic motivation (p. 108)
job enrichment (p. 115)
learning goals (p. 124)
management by objectives (MBO) (p. 125)
motivation (p. 108)
motivators (p. 115)
need for achievement (p. 113)
need for affiliation (p. 113)
need for power (p. 113)
need hierarchy (p. 109)
outcome goals (p. 124)
procedural justice (p. 123)
progression hypothesis (p. 109)
Theory X (p. 111)
Theory Y (p. 111)
valence (p. 118)

Review Questions

1. How can knowledge of motivation theories help managers?
2. What are the five categories of motivational needs described by Maslow? Give an example of how each can be satisfied.
3. What are the Theory X and Theory Y assumptions about people at work? Describe how a college or university instructor might behave in the classroom if he or she had Theory X assumptions about students.
4. What three learned needs does McClelland identify?
5. How do hygiene and motivational factors differ? What are the implications of the two-factor theory for managers?
6. How is inequity determined by a person in an organization? How can inequity be resolved if it exists?
7. What are the key concepts in the expectancy theory of motivation?

Discussion and Communication Questions

1. What do you think are the most important motivational needs for the majority of people? Do you think your needs differ from those of most people?
2. How would expectancy theory help a teacher motivate a student who is hard-working but continues to do poorly on tests?
3. Assume you are leaving your current job to look for employment elsewhere. What will you look for that you do not have now? If you do not have a job, assume you will be looking for one soon. What are the most important factors that you will seek?
4. If you were being inequitably paid in your job, which strategy do you think would be the most helpful to you in resolving the inequity? What tactics would you consider using?
5. What important experiences have contributed to your moral and ethical development? Are you working to further your own moral maturity at this time?
6. (*Communication question*) Develop an oral presentation about the most current management practices in employee motivation. Find out what at least four different companies are doing in this area. Be prepared to compare these practices with the theory and research in the chapter.
7. What goals do you set for yourself at work? In your personal life? Will you know if you achieve them?

Ethics Questions

1. Suppose your company knew what employees wanted at work and was unwilling to spend the money to meet their needs. Do you think this would be unethical?
2. Suppose your company has an employee who has been with the company for a long time and now has health problems that will prevent him or her from being fully productive for at least a year. Should the company attempt to carry this person for that period of time, even though the person will not be able to perform? Should the person's pay and benefits be reduced according to performance?
3. Assume you know an employee who is being underpaid because the company believes it can save money and the employee will not complain. Is this unethical? Should you tell the employee about the underpayment condition?
4. Suppose the organization you work for simply assigns employees their task goals without consulting them. Is this an ethical problem? Should the organization consult its employees? What are the consequences of not consulting them?

Knowledge & Application

EXPERIENTIAL EXERCISE 4.1: MOTIVATING THE SIMPSONS

Purpose: To use expectancy theory to diagnose motivation problems

Group size: 4–6

Time required: 20 minutes

Materials needed: None

Instructions:

1. Form groups and discuss the best answer to why the five Simpsons were not motivated.
2. Class reconvenes and goes over solutions to the five situations.

None of the Simpsons is feeling very motivated. For each of the following scenarios, indicate whether the motivation problem concerns low E–P expectancies, low P–O expectancies, or low valences by circling the response.

E–P Expectancy: Does the person perceive that if he or she exerts effort, he/she will be able to perform the work successfully?
P–O Expectancy: Does the person perceive that outcomes are likely to be obtained if he or she performs successfully?
Valence: Does the person desire the outcomes that would result from successful performance?

1. Bart works as a $6.75-per-hour stock clerk. If he does his job well, he could very possibly get his picture and name posted in the store as the Employee of the Month. Bart's a high school student and his hunch is that if his friends see his picture on the wall of the store, he'll get razzed about it mercilessly.

   E–P Expectancy **P–O Expectancy** **Valence**

2. Homer became a social worker because he wanted to change the world. He works with kids from dysfunctional families and knows that he could make a big difference in their lives if only he could spend enough time with them. But it's hard to do a good job—government funds have been cut and staffing at the human services department is minimal. Homer's case load is so large that he can only deal with crises that come up, and maybe spend 5 minutes per week checking in by phone with some of the kids who are assigned to him.

   E–P Expectancy **P–O Expectancy** **Valence**

3. Lisa accepted a job with a large software development firm in part because the company offered plenty of opportunity for promotion. Lisa's feeling bitter, though. She's noticed that the best workers aren't getting promoted—it's the "networkers" who are.

   E–P Expectancy **P–O Expectancy** **Valence**

4. Marge is 61 years old and looking forward to retirement in a few years. Her company has recently reorganized and she is now a member of a self-managed work team. Because the team has little supervision, the members are responsible for all decisions related to production processes, quality control, budgeting, inventory control, hiring and firing, etc., for the specialty item that they produce. After all of her years in the company, Marge certainly knows how to do these things. But her view is that these activities mostly benefit younger employees who appreciate being given more responsibility and a chance to make a name for themselves. Marge would rather not be bothered with the extra work; she just wants to ride out her time until retirement.

   E–P Expectancy **P–O Expectancy** **Valence**

5. Maggie is new to her company and is hoping to get the respect of her boss, Mr. Burns. She knows that he compliments other people for a job well done, but all he ever seems to do is criticize her. She feels like she doesn't even know what he is looking for.

   E–P Expectancy **P–O Expectancy** **Valence**

SOURCE: D. Marcic, J. Seltzer, and P. Vail, *Organizational Behavior: Experiences and Cases,* 6th ed. (Mason, OH: South-Western College Publishing, 2001), 45–47. Lynn E. Miller, La Salle Univeristy, and Richard M. Weiss, University of Delaware. Used with permission.

Knowledge & Application

EXPERIENTIAL EXERCISE 4.2: WHAT TO DO?

Purpose: This exercise provides you and your group with a brief scenario of an inequity at work. Your task is to consider feasible actions for redress of this inequity.

Group size: 4–6

Time required: 20 minutes

Materials needed: None

Instructions:

Step 1. Read the following scenario.

John and Mary are full professors in the same medical school department of a large private university. As a private institution, neither the school nor the university makes the salaries and benefits of its faculty a matter of public record. Mary has pursued a long-term (14-year) career in the medical school, rising through the academic ranks while married to a successful businessman with whom she has raised three children. Her research and teaching contributions have been broad ranging and award winning. John joined the medical school within the last three years and was recruited for his leading-edge contribution to a novel line of research on a new procedure. Mary thought he was probably attracted with a comprehensive compensation package, yet she had no details until an administrative assistant gave her some information about salary and benefits a month ago. Mary learned that John's base contract salary is 16 percent higher than hers ($250 000 versus $215 000), that he was awarded an incentive pay component for the commercialization of his new procedure, and that he was given an annual discretionary travel budget of $35 000 and a membership in an exclusive private club. Mary is in a quandary about what to do. Given pressures from the board of trustees to hold down costs associated with public and private pressure to keep tuition increases low, Mary wonders how to begin to close this $70 000+ inequity gap.

Step 2. Discuss the equity issues in the above situation using the text material on organizational justice and equity theory. Do the outcome differences here appear to be gender-based, age-based, performance-based, or marital status-based? Do you need more information? If so, what additional information do you need?

Step 3. Consider each of the seven strategies for the resolution of inequity as portrayed in this situation. Which ones are feasible to pursue based on what you know? Which ones are not feasible? Why? What are the likely consequences of each strategy or course of action? What would you advise Mary to do?

Step 4. Once your group has identified feasible resolution strategies, choose the best strategy. Next, develop a specific plan of action for Mary to follow in attempting to resolve the inequity so that she can achieve the experience and the reality of fair treatment at work.

Step 5 (Optional). Your group may be asked to share its preferred strategy for this situation and your rationale for the strategy.

Application, Analysis & Synthesis

CASE: SOUTHWOOD'S DAIRY

This case depicts the story of a small Canadian dairy products company that was established many years ago. Although the company has been able to maintain its profitability since then, it has not under gone any expansion or organizational changes. The case focuses on the operation by which the firm's products are distributed to various stores and restaurants located within a radius of about 80 kilometres of the dairy.

The distribution unit is run by a manager who has below him one supervisor, one shipper, and ten driver-deliverers. The unit is responsible for supplying various outlets with dairy products, from milk to ice cream. Each driver has a specific route and customers (retail outlets), and their satisfaction is his or her responsibility. The shipper is responsible for the stock in the refrigerators and is the one who supplies the milk and other dairy products to the local drivers. The drivers and the shipper report to the supervisor, who is responsible for the daily local operations. He also fills in on a route if one of the drivers is absent.

Each driver is responsible for maintaining his or her own vehicle as well as for giving an account of the dairy products received each day. Although the driver does not have to perform repairs upon the trucks, he or she arranges for all maintenance work, which is performed by a local garage. On the route some customers have credit arrangements with the company, while others are on a cash basis. The driver must provide invoices and/or cash to cover the depletion of the stocks in the truck.

Al Brown, the shipper, has been with the firm for 35 years. He arrives at work early to load the dairy products onto the trucks. He is supposed to keep track of what has come from the production department and what has been shipped out through the drivers. He keeps track of the requirement patterns of the drivers and he loads enough milk and other dairy products on each truck for that truck's rounds, without too much left over. He remains on the premises throughout the day to distribute additional stock should the driver require it. He is also responsible for the maintenance of the building.

Jerry Jones is the dairy manager. The last seven of his twenty years' service have been in this position. It is Jerry who oversees production, marketing, and finance. It was Jerry who designed the present delivery routes and the local internal control system. At a recent meeting with the company president, Jerry made the following general comments about the problems now facing the company with regard to the motivation of the drivers.

"I find this a difficult area, as we pay our drivers by the week. At one time we did have them on a commission basis but there was a problem in that some drivers' routes always had higher sales than others. If a driver's sales are down and it is due to poor performance, I'll tell them straight out what the problem is. I feel this is a much more effective way to motivate than to beat around the bush. By using this method, I let the driver knows exactly where he or she stands. If this proves to be ineffective, then I'll come down harder than is actually needed. This is a good motivating technique as they now know they are being watched very closely.

"To make sure they are doing what is expected, I constantly check up on them. This means going around at night after they have gone and making sure the truck is gassed up and the oil level is fine. If one of these particular things has not been done, I'll either phone that particular person to come in and do it right away or I'll keep it in mind and if something comes up I'll reinforce the criticism of their poor performance with one of those instances.

"As regards priorities, the customer is number one in this business and if they have any complaints I'll go directly to their store and find out what the problem is. I'll then go back to the driver to discuss the problem and try and clear up any static that has been created. I'll warn the driver that if we lose that customer I'll give him or her three more accounts in place of the one that might be lost. I control inventories by charging the drivers for everything that goes on their truck. They add up their bills on a cash-in sheet every night. At the end of every week they take an inventory count of their truck and I compare that with the cash-in sheets. If they are short, I may decide that the shortage is to be made up from their paycheques. So far I haven't found it necessary to do this, as I feel that I'm able to trust my drivers. It would be very hard for them to try and beat our inventory control system."

One of Jerry's former drivers recently expressed his feelings about his old job in the following words:

"You couldn't do anything around there without Jerry breathing down your neck. No matter what you did, it was always wrong. Whenever there was a customer complaint, Jerry always assumed that the driver was at fault and never gave us the opportunity to tell our side of the story. He also assumed that no one could do anything without having him tell us what and how to do it. Some of the drivers had been around for 15 years and Jerry was still telling them what to do. As a result, there was no incentive to do better. When he was telling someone that they were not doing something right, he would always like to have some of the other drivers around so he could give the tough guy image. I once asked him about this and the lack of praise, and he responded, 'If you've done something wrong, you'll hear about it; do a good job and you won't hear from me.'

"The inventory system is very lax. The coolers are never locked so whenever I could, I used to get extra stock in order to make sure I was never short. Al used to give us credit or replacement stock if we told him that something went bad and had to be disposed of. It was never recorded. One common practice was to deliver short to a customer, make up the bill, and receive payment. Then the driver would go get the few missing items for the customer and get paid for them without making up another bill. The driver would pocket this money and would be able to replenish the stock whenever Al wasn't around, like at lunch time."

Questions

1. Use Theory X and Y to explain the way Jerry tries to motivate his drivers.
2. Use expectancy theory to explain the behaviour of the drivers.
3. If you were to replace Jerry as the dairy manager, what changes would you recommend to more effectively meet the needs of the drivers and improve their motivation?

SOURCE: Written by Anwar Rashid, from *Canadian Cases in Organizational Behaviour*, 3rd ed., by S. Anwar Rashid, Maurice Archer, and Randy Hoffman.

Scoring Instructions for Self-Assessments

Self-Assessment 4.2: Task–Goal Attribute Questionnaire

Place your response (1 through 7) in the space provided. For questions 2, 7, 9, and 12, subtract your response from 8 to determine your adjusted score. For each scale (e.g., participation in goal setting), add the responses and divide by the number of questions in the scale.

Participation in Goal Setting:

Question 1 4

Question 7 (8– 2) = 6

Question 11 6

Question 16 6

Total divided by 4 22/4 5.5

Feedback on Goal Effort:

Question 3 5

Question 8 4

Question 12 (8– 5) = 3

Total divided by 3 = 12/3 = 4

Peer Competition:

Question 4 5

Question 13 2

Total divided by 2 = 7/2 = 3.5

Goal Specificity:

Question 5 2

Question 9 (8 – 4) = 4

Question 14 4

Total divided by 3 = 10/3 = 3.3

Goal Difficulty:

Question 2 (8 – 6) = 2

Question 6 3

Question 10 4

Question 15 3

Total divided by 4 = 12/4 = 3

Interpreting your average scores for each task-goal attribute:

A score of 6 or 7 is very high.
A score of 4 is a moderate level.
A score of 1 or 2 is very low.

chapter five

LEARNING OBJECTIVES

By the end of this chapter, you will be able to do the following:

1. Explain what is meant by job design and why it is important.
2. Explain the work simplification roots of job design and contrast them to the contemporary search for meaning, engagement, and spirituality at work.
3. Compare and contrast job enlargement, job rotation, and job enrichment.
4. Describe the Job Characteristics Model (JCM) and how it is used to improve the design of jobs.
5. Briefly describe the social information-processing (SIP) and interdisciplinary models of job design.
6. Apply the individual job design concepts to the design of teams.
7. Explore cross-cultural aspects of work design.
8. Describe four alternative work arrangements that impact the work–family balance: job sharing, reduced workload and the four-day work week, flextime, and telecommuting.

learning about the context

Toyota Motor Manufacturing Canada: Leaders in Work Design

At Toyota Motor Manufacturing Canada (TMMC) in Cambridge, Ontario, job design is taken very seriously. Every team, which, on average, consists of five or six members, has a leader, and each group in the plant has from one to six teams. Toyota's goal is to keep the groups small so that that each team member is able to see the work process from beginning to end. You will learn in this chapter that this is called building "task identity" into the design of the job. Ray Tanguay, president of TMMC, explains that a big part of creating meaningful jobs is, even when expanding, to design the work and facilities in ways that are conducive to teamwork: short lines, teams that are not too large, and jobs in which people can do a whole piece of work.

In addition, Toyota gives employees the power to control the quality of their own work. They call this principle *Jidoka*, which is a system that indicates problems with a process or with equipment. If team members spot a problem, they are responsible for correcting the problem. If they cannot, they can call attention to the problem by either pushing an emergency stop (E-Stop) button, which stops the line immediately, or by pulling on the "andon" cord above their workstation. Pulling on the andon cord lights up the andon board, thereby calling the team leader. The team leader would then go to the station and help fix the problem or help the employee catch up on his or her process so the line can go back to its normal operation. If the team leader is unable to solve the problem, the line can be stopped using the E-Stop button. The production line warning can be given as often as necessary during a shift if team members are uncertain about the quality of the part they have received, the performance of a piece of equipment, poor fitting, or the member cannot keep up with the cycle time of the job. This power to plan or control one's own work is called *autonomy*, and when employees have autonomy designed into their jobs, they experience higher degrees of responsibility for the outcomes of their work, which leads to better performance and higher satisfaction.

Toyota also tries to use people for the more complex jobs and automate wherever a task is ergonomically difficult, where safety is a concern, or if it is highly repetitive. For these jobs, robots are used; however, Toyota restricts the use of machines to only those things that make life easier for the workers. In addition, work spaces, such as floor racks, are designed to be as flexible as possible so that employees can easily take them apart and put them back together in a way that works more effectively. Toyota's "lean production system" has become a standard in work design since it uses committed employees with ever-expanding responsibilities to achieve zero waste, 100 percent good product, delivered on time, every time.

In addition to creating jobs in which employees have autonomy and task identity, Toyota uses job rotation extensively, to add variety to the jobs and reduce ergonomic burden. Team members get hired into a team, initially learning one or two jobs and eventually more as they gain experience and skills. Then, every two hours, they get a chance to rotate.

SOURCES: "The Kindergarten That Will Change the World," *The Economist* (London), March 4, 1995 (vol. 334, issue 7904), 63–65; Ray Tanguay (president, Toyota Motor Manufacturing, Canada), interview, November 1995; J. O'Brien, "Manufacturing: Toyota Members Stop at Nothing for Build Quality," *Birmingham Post* (Birmingham, U.K.), February 20, 2003, 26; Toyota Motor Manufacturing Canada, http://www.toyota.ca/tmmc.html.

The purpose of this chapter is to help you better understand various concepts and approaches to job design that have been developed over the years. This understanding will allow you to distinguish a well-designed job from one that is poorly designed and also gives you ideas on how to create or redesign meaningful jobs for individuals and teams. Job design theories and concepts apply many of the motivation theories discussed in Chapter 4. Specifically, they explore how the design of a job, rather than a reward system, can meet an employee's needs and strengthen his or her intrinsic motivation. The example in the chapter opener from Toyota Motor Manufacturing Canada exemplifies some of the ways that good work design, like giving employees the power to control the quality of their own work, giving them a chance to see a work process from beginning to end, and rotating employees to increase skill variety, can improve employee motivation and performance.

We begin the chapter by defining job design and explaining why it is important. Then we provide a brief overview of the "scientific management" roots of job design and the limitations of this approach. We go on to contrast scientific management with the contemporary search for meaning, engagement, and spirituality at work. Next, we address three approaches to job design developed between the late 1800s and the 1970s: job enlargement, job rotation, and job enrichment. The third section examines, in depth, the Job Characteristics Model, which is the most popular current perspective on how to design individual jobs. Fourth, we touch on two alternative approaches to job design, the social information processing and interdisciplinary approach. Next we apply the job design principles to designing work for teams using the socio-technical systems approach, followed by an exploration of some cross-cultural aspects of work design. Finally, we examine four alternative work arrangements that impact the work–family balance.

Explain what is meant by job design and why it is important.

WHAT IS JOB DESIGN AND WHY IS IT IMPORTANT?

job design
The process of assigning tasks to a job, including the interdependency of those tasks with other jobs.

Whether an organization is large or small, usually it is not possible for everyone to do everything, so managers and organizational designers have to decide who is going to do what job and how the jobs will relate to each other. This is **job design,** the process of assigning tasks to a job, including the interdependency of those tasks with other jobs. These decisions have an impact on what employees will be doing on a day-to day basis, on the contacts they will have with other people, on the kinds of competencies that will be required, and on how they feel about their jobs.

For example, if an entrepreneur is adding a bakery/café with three employees to an existing store, he or she has to decide how to assign tasks and design the individual jobs in that café. Should it have servers who take orders, clean tables, make the coffee, serve it, and take cash, or should it have a separate cashier, separate coffee maker, and separate server/cleaner? If the roles will be separate, in what ways would they need to interact and be dependent upon each other? If the roles are combined, would the employees be more or less efficient? Would the jobs be more or less meaningful? What would be the impact on customer satisfaction? Each design would have different advantages and disadvantages, and the approaches to job design discussed in this chapter will help you explore what these are.

Application

DESIGN YOUR 'IDEAL' JOB

Spend a few minutes and design the ideal job for yourself. This is a "blue sky" exercise. Let your imagination run wild. Think about past jobs you have had and what you liked or didn't like about them. Think about other jobs and then create an ideal for yourself. Write out some specifics that make it an ideal job for you.

WORK SIMPLIFICATION VERSUS THE CONTEMPORARY SEARCH FOR MEANING AT WORK

Explain the work simplification roots of job design and contrast them to the contemporary search for meaning, engagement, and spirituality at work.

Work Simplification and Job Design

Early attempts to improve the design of jobs focused on improving organizational performance by increasing efficiency and reducing costs. **Scientific management**, Frederick Taylor's system for using research to determine the optimum degree of specialization and standardization for a job task, discussed in Chapter 1, emphasized **work simplification.** This is the standardization and the narrow, explicit specification of task activities for workers.[1] In the example of the café, work simplification would lead to three (or more) separate jobs, so that one worker would serve the coffee, one would make it, and one would do the cash. Jobs designed through scientific management have a limited number of tasks, and each task is scientifically specified so that the worker is not required to think or deliberate. According to Taylor, the role of management and the industrial engineer was to calibrate and define each task carefully. The role of the worker was to execute the task. The elements of scientific management, such as time and motion studies, pay for individual pieces of work, and the scientific selection of workers, all focused on the efficient use of labour to the economic benefit of the corporation.

scientific management
Frederick Taylor's system for using research to determine the optimum degree of specialization and standardization for a job task.

work simplification
Standardization and the narrow, explicit specification of task activities for workers.

Two arguments supported the efficient and standardized job design approach of scientific management. The first argument was that Taylor's unique approach to work standardization helped create a functional workforce because work simplification allowed workers of diverse ethnic and skill backgrounds to work together in a systematic way. The second argument was that work simplification led to production efficiency in the organization and, therefore, to higher profits. This economic argument for work simplification tended to dehumanize employees and treat them as a means of production or a machine part. This is still a problem in some modern service jobs, such as those that involve flipping hamburgers.

A fundamental limitation of scientific management and work simplification is that it undervalues the human capacity for thought and ingenuity and leads to alienation. **Work alienation** represents the extent to which a person is disengaged from the world of work and holds a generalized unenthusiastic outlook toward it.[2] Jobs designed through work simplification use only a portion of a person's capabilities. This underutilization makes work boring, monotonous, and under-stimulating. Failure to fully utilize workers' capacities in a constructive fashion may cause a variety of work problems and lead to high turnover. Contemporary approaches to job design have been able to overcome many of these problems, thereby creating meaningfulness, helping to retain talent and reducing employee turnover.[3]

work alienation
The extent to which a person is disengaged from the world of work and holds a generalized unenthusiastic outlook toward it.

The Contemporary Search for Meaning in Job Design

While the goal to design jobs for efficiency still remains important, as indicated by the Toyota example and their extensive use of robotics, contemporary job redesign efforts go beyond the goal of efficiency and also try to design jobs that are meaningful so that incumbents do not become alienated and unmotivated.[4] Increasingly, people want more from work than what organizations traditionally provide. People desire work that is more meaningful and more fully in accord with their lives.[5] **Meaningfulness** is defined as the value of a work goal or purpose, judged in relation to an individual's own ideals or standards.[6] Meaningfulness has been viewed in OB research in at least two different ways: (1) the degree to which a job is experienced as meaningful, and (2) the way in which one views work and its degree of centrality in one's life.

meaningfulness
The value of a work goal or purpose, judged in relation to an individual's own ideals or standards.

When Margot Franssen started the Body Shop in Canada, she wanted to help employees find meaning in their work, so employees are encouraged to work on community projects on company time.

Better Workplace Now
Better Workplace Now is a leading Web portal for information related to rethinking the definition and purposes of work. The site explores every facet of the "meaningful workplace," from job enrichment and motivation to cross-training and work simplification. Visit the site to learn more about theories and case studies of work and job design.
http://www.betterworkplacenow.com

The Meaningfulness of Work

Viktor Frankl, in his book *Man's Search for Meaning*, published in 1959, stated that a person's search for meaning is the "primary motivation in his life and not a secondary rationalisation of instinctual drives."[7] Others have gone even further and suggested that meaning and purpose are primary contributors to a person's mental health and well-being, and most researchers agree that meaningful work improves organizational commitment at all levels.[8] Organizational behaviour researchers in the last decade have also broadened the concept of meaningfulness with an exploration of the concept of **employee engagement,** discussed in Chapter 2, defined as a state of emotional and intellectual involvement that employees have in their organization.

employee engagement
The state of emotional and intellectual involvement that employees have in their organization.

workplace spirituality
That which grounds people through the meaningfulness of their work, enabling them to transcend the tedious aspects of their work and to connect to others.

In engagement, people employ and express themselves physically, cognitively, and emotionally during role performances.[9] The concept of engagement entails active use of emotions and behaviours as well as thoughts. This concept is also related to a large body of research on the "human spirit" called spirituality at work.[10] **Workplace spirituality** has been defined in numerous ways; we define it here as that which grounds people through the meaningfulness of their work, enabling them to transcend the tedious aspects of their work and to connect to others.[11] Thus, to meet current employees' needs, jobs should be designed in ways that, to the extent possible, they can offer meaning, engagement, and an opportunity for connectedness.

Centre for Spirituality at Work
The Centre for Spirituality at Work is for people who want to deepen the connection between who they are and the work they do, for those who want to release, nurture, and claim the sacred in their work and in their workplaces. One of their many offerings is a certificate in corporate social responsibility, offered in collaboration with the Conference Board of Canada.
www.spiritualityatwork.org

Work Definition and Centrality

While work is found to play a central role in the life of individuals in most industrialized countries, studies such as those conducted by Meaning of Work (MOW) International Research Team and others have revealed that perceived meaningfulness also depends in part upon the centrality of work in a culture. **Work centrality** is defined as a person's beliefs regarding the degree of importance that work plays in their lives, and it has been found to vary in different cultural settings.[12] Also, research has suggested at least five different profiles, by country, in the way that work in general is perceived and defined. Definitions vary from work as providing positive personal identity (e.g., the Netherlands) to work as primarily a physical activity a person must do that is usually devoid of positive affect (e.g., Japan).[13] Although the meaning of work differs among countries, new theorizing about job design also suggests that individual employees can alter work meaning and work identity by changing task and relationship configurations in their work.[14]

work centrality
A person's beliefs regarding the degree of importance that work plays in his or her life.

Knowledge & Application

HOW CENTRAL IS WORK TO YOUR LIFE?

1. Review the definitions of work centrality and work alienation.
2. Jot down all the various roles you play in your life at the moment: student, son or daughter, husband or wife, grandchild, relative, sibling, partner, friend, employee, etc.
3. Try to rank these roles in terms of the importance that each one plays in your life.
4. Think about the criteria you used to decide on your rankings.
5. How much time do you spend in each role? How fully can you be yourself in the role? How engaged are you in the role? What you think other people expect of you? How much you enjoy the role?

APPROACHES TO JOB DESIGN: JOB ENLARGEMENT, JOB ROTATION, AND JOB ENRICHMENT

Three approaches to job design that were developed during the early twentieth century are job enlargement, job rotation, and job enrichment (see Exhibit 5.1).

Job Enlargement and Job Rotation

Compare and contrast job enlargement, job rotation, and job enrichment.

Job enlargement and job rotation were developed to overcome the boredom and alienation that resulted from work simplification.[15] **Job enlargement** is a method of job design that increases the number of tasks in a job. For example, in the café example, job enlargement might result in a server both making coffee and cleaning tables. **Job rotation,** a variation of job enlargement, exposes a worker to a variety of specialized job tasks

job enlargement
A method of job design that increases the number of activities in a job to overcome the boredom of overspecialized work.

EXHIBIT 5.1

Three Approaches to Job Design

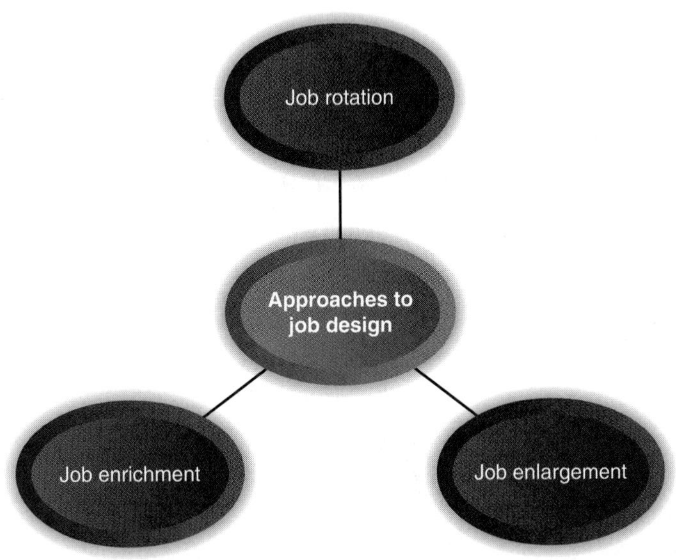

job rotation
A variation of job enlargement in which workers are exposed to a variety of specialized jobs over time through rotation.

over time through rotation. In this case, instead of having servers both making coffee and cleaning tables at the same time, the workers would be cross-trained and would rotate between coffee makers and cleaners. In the chapter opener, you learned about the extensive use of job rotation at the Toyota plant in Cambridge, Ontario, where job rotation is used not only to increase variety but also to reduce ergonomic burdens such as repetitive strain injuries.

The reasoning behind these approaches to the problems of overspecialization is as follows. First, the core problem with overspecialized work was believed to be lack of variety. That is, jobs designed by scientific management were too narrow and limited in the number of tasks and activities assigned to each worker. Second, a lack of variety led to understimulation and underutilization of the worker. Third, the worker would be more stimulated and better utilized by increasing the variety in the job, which could be accomplished by increasing the number of activities or by rotating the worker through different jobs. For example, job enlargement for a lathe operator in a steel plant might include selecting the steel pieces to be turned and performing all of the maintenance work on the lathe. As an example of job rotation, an employee at a small bank might take new accounts one day, serve as a cashier another day, and process loan applications on a third day.

One of the first studies of the problem of repetitive work was conducted at IBM after World War II. The company implemented a job enlargement program during the war and evaluated the effort after six years.[16] The two most important results were a significant increase in product quality and a reduction in idle time, both for people and for machines. Less obvious and measurable are the benefits of job enlargement to IBM through enhanced worker status and improved manager–worker communication. Thus, job enlargement does counter some of the problems of work simplification.

cross-training
A variation of job enlargement in which workers are trained in different specialized tasks or activities.

Like job enlargement, in **cross-training** workers are trained in different specialized tasks or activities. Job rotation assumes cross-training, but not all cross-trained employees actually rotate through jobs. Rather, they may move to a new permanent assignment or act as a backup for an absent employee. Job enlargement, job rotation, and cross-training all include horizontally enlarging jobs; that is, the number and variety of an employee's tasks and activities are increased. Pharmaceutical company Eli Lilly has found that job rotation can be a proactive means for enhancing work experiences for career development and can have tangible benefits for employees in the form of salary increases and promotions.[17] The Canadian Department of Foreign Affairs and International Trade, Gap Inc.,

Team members at Toyota rotate through different jobs, thereby experiencing more variety and reducing ergonomic burden.

Ford Canada, and the Bank of Canada all use job rotation for similar benefits.[18] In cross-training, workers are trained in different specialized tasks or activities. Canadian Tire uses cross-training to enable its customer service agents to handle a wide range of customer requests. Through cross-training, the company has improved efficiency, responsiveness, and customer satisfaction.[19]

However, while job enlargement, cross-training, and job rotation do increase the variety of work, thereby reducing boredom, they may not increase motivation or the meaningfulness experienced by the worker. A third approach to job design, called job enrichment, addresses these limitations.

Job Enrichment

Whereas job enlargement increases the number of job activities at the same level of responsibility, job enrichment increases the amount of job responsibility and employee control. **Job enrichment** is a job design or redesign method aimed at increasing the degree to which workers control the planning, execution, and evaluation of their work. Job enrichment builds on Herzberg's two-factor theory of motivation (discussed in Chapter 4), which distinguished between motivators and hygiene factors for people at work. Whereas job enlargement recommends increasing and varying the number of activities a person does, job enrichment recommends increasing the recognition, autonomy, and opportunity for advancement. For example, adding maintenance activities enlarges the lathe operator's job, while having the operator meet directly with customers

job enrichment
A method of job design that increases the degree to which workers control the planning, execution, and evaluation of their work.

IMPLICATIONS FOR LIFE

Job Design at Home

Traditional job design theories are not just useful for managers in the workplace; they can also be useful when designing jobs at home. Think about a situation where you might be living in a student house while attending college or university. A number of jobs need to be designed to ensure that the house runs smoothly. For example, common areas in the house need to be kept clean, students need to buy food and cook their evening meal, laundry has to be done, money has to be collected, and bills have to be paid. Here is what the jobs would look like if designed according to each of the three traditional approaches just discussed:

- *Scientific management:* If using a scientific management approach, one of the students would conduct time and motion studies to determine how long each task would take and what kinds of skills were needed. Then the housemates would be matched to each task based on each of their particular strengths and weaknesses. Work simplification would be the guiding principle, so the jobs would be highly specialized. Probably one student would be assigned to wash the laundry, one to folding it, one to food shopping, one to cooking, one to clean-up, etc. Each would become a specialist in their own particular task and would carry it out with skill and efficiency.
- *Job enlargement/job rotation:* If using a job enlargement/job rotation approach, students would either take on two or more of the above tasks, to add variety, or would rotate by week or month to different jobs.
- *Job enrichment:* If using a job enrichment approach, students would design the jobs to increase the amount of control they have over the work. This would mean that they would probably each do their own shopping, cooking, cleaning of common areas and laundry, and payment of bills.

Question: Which job design approach or combination of approaches would work best for the house as a whole and for each individual, do you think? Why?

(something that the operator's boss used to do) enriches the job. In the café example, adding serving customers as a job task would be an example of job enrichment.

Herzberg believed that only certain jobs should be enriched and that the first step is to select the jobs appropriate for job enrichment.[20] A classic seven-year implementation study of job enrichment at AT&T found the approach beneficial.[21] Job enrichment required a big change in management style, and AT&T found that it could not ignore hygiene factors like pay and working conditions in the work environment just because it was enriching existing jobs. Although the AT&T experience with job enrichment was positive, a critical review of job enrichment did not find that to be the case generally.[22] One problem with job enrichment as a strategy for work design is the lack of consideration for individual differences among employees. Some of these limitations have been addressed by the Job Characteristics Model, which is discussed next. Before you read about it, diagnose the motivating potential of your own job using Self-Assessment 5.1.[23]

Application & Analysis

SELF-ASSESSMENT 5.1: DIAGNOSING YOUR JOB

This questionnaire challenges you to examine the motivating potential in your job. If you are not currently working, complete the questionnaire with a view to assessing your "job" as a student at college or university. For each of the following five questions, circle the number that most accurately describes the characteristics of your job.

1. How much **autonomy** is there in the job? That is, to what extent does the job permit a person to decide on his or her own how to go about doing the work?

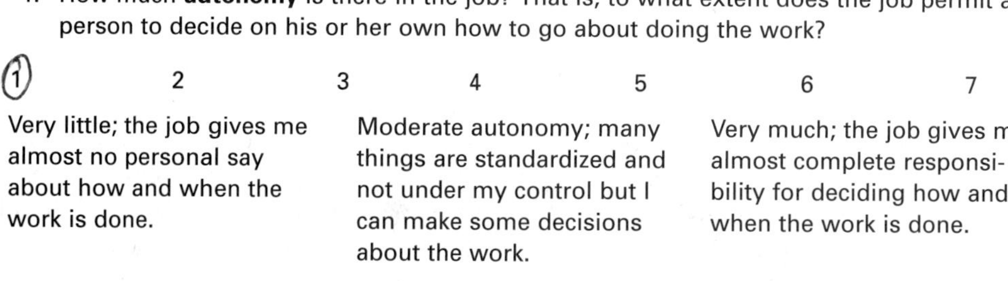

1	2	3	4	5	6	7
Very little; the job gives me almost no personal say about how and when the work is done.			Moderate autonomy; many things are standardized and not under my control but I can make some decisions about the work.			Very much; the job gives me almost complete responsibility for deciding how and when the work is done.

2. To what extent does the job involve doing **a "whole" and identifiable piece of work?** That is, is the job a complete piece of work that has an obvious beginning and end? Or is it a small part of the overall piece of work, which is finished by other people or by automatic machines?

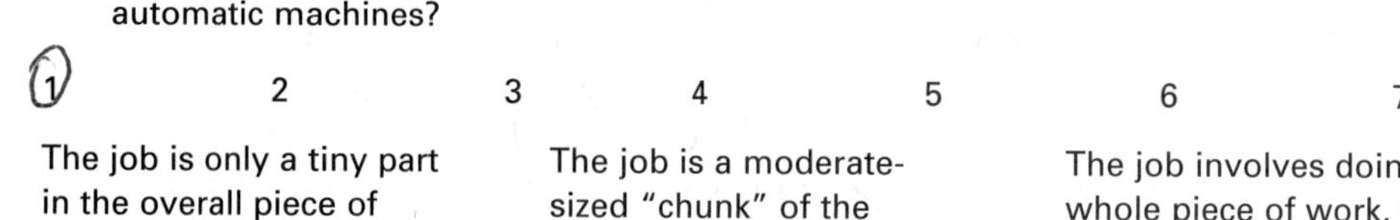

1	2	3	4	5	6	7
The job is only a tiny part in the overall piece of work; the results of my activities cannot be seen in the final product or service.			The job is a moderate-sized "chunk" of the overall piece of work; my own contribution can be seen in the final outcome.			The job involves doing the whole piece of work, from start to finish; the results of my activities are easily seen in the final product or service.

3. How much variety is there in the job? That is, to what extent does the job require you to do many different things at work, using a variety of your skills and talents?

1	2	3	4	5	6	7
Very little; the job requires the person to do the same routine things over and over again.			Moderate variety.			Very much; the job requires the person to do many different things, using a number of different skills and talents.

4. In general, **how significant or important is the job?** That is, are the results of your work likely to affect significantly the lives or well-being of other people?

1	2	3	4	5	6	7
Not at all significant; the outcome of the work is not likely to affect anyone in any important way.			Moderately significant.		Highly significant; the outcome of the work can affect other people in very important ways.	

5. To what extent does doing the **job itself provide you with information about your work performance**? That is, does the actual work itself provide clues about how well you are doing—aside from any feedback your co-workers or supervisor may provide?

1	2	3	4	5	6	7
Very little; the job itself is set up I could work forever without finding out how well I was doing.			Moderately; sometimes doing the job provides me with feedback, sometimes it does not.		Very much; the job is set up so that I get almost constant feedback as I work about how well I am doing.	

For scoring instructions, please go to the end of the chapter, p. 161.

SOURCE: J. R. Hackman and G. R. Oldham, "The Job Diagnostic Survey: An Instrument for the Diagnosis of Jobs and the Evaluation of Job Redesign Projects," Technical Report No. 4, 1974, 2–3 of the Short Form. Reprinted by permission of Greg R. Oldham.

THE JOB CHARACTERISTICS MODEL OF JOB DESIGN

Describe the Job Characteristics Model (JCM) and how it is used to improve the design of jobs.

Partly in response to the limitations of job enrichment, just discussed, the Job Characteristics Model was initiated during the mid-1960s. This model is an approach to the design of work that makes a significant departure from the earlier approaches by recognizing that while some universal principles of a well-designed job do exist, their effects are *moderated* by individual differences and preferences. The JCM originated with Richard Hackman, Greg Oldham, and their colleagues, who conducted a large study of workers in 11 different industries.[24] The study measured and classified relevant task characteristics for 47 jobs and found certain characteristics that seemed to lead to increased motivation and performance, but they did not affect all workers in the same way. Hackman and Oldham went on to design the Job Characteristics Model,[25] which is useful to managers in two significant ways: First, it helps us diagnose the degree to which a job has motivation potential, and second, it helps us redesign jobs to increase the likelihood that employees will find them motivating. The **Job Characteristics Model (JCM)** states that workers who perform jobs that contain five core job characteristics will be more likely to achieve favourable work outcomes. In addition, workers who have high growth need strengths (GNS) are more likely to achieve these outcomes than those with low growth need strength. The JCM, shown in Exhibit 5.2, is among the most "well known and complete theories for explaining job design characteristics and their relationships to work motivation."[26] The JCM remains the most popular current perspective on job design and has been extensively studied since its creation in 1980.[27]

Job Characteristics Model (JCM)
States that workers who perform jobs that contain five core job characteristics will be more likely to achieve favourable work outcomes. In addition, workers who have high growth need strengths (GNS) are more likely to achieve these outcomes than those with low growth need strength.

The Job Characteristics Model has been tested in many countries around the world. In one study in Hong Kong, incumbents and their supervisors both completed questionnaires about the incumbents' jobs.[28] The study generally supported the JCM; however, task significance was not a reliable core job characteristic. This result suggests either national differences in the measurement of important job dimensions or cultural biases about work.[29] It also reinforces the idea that value differences may exist between different cultures with regard to jobs.

EXHIBIT 5.2

The Job Characteristics Model (JCM)

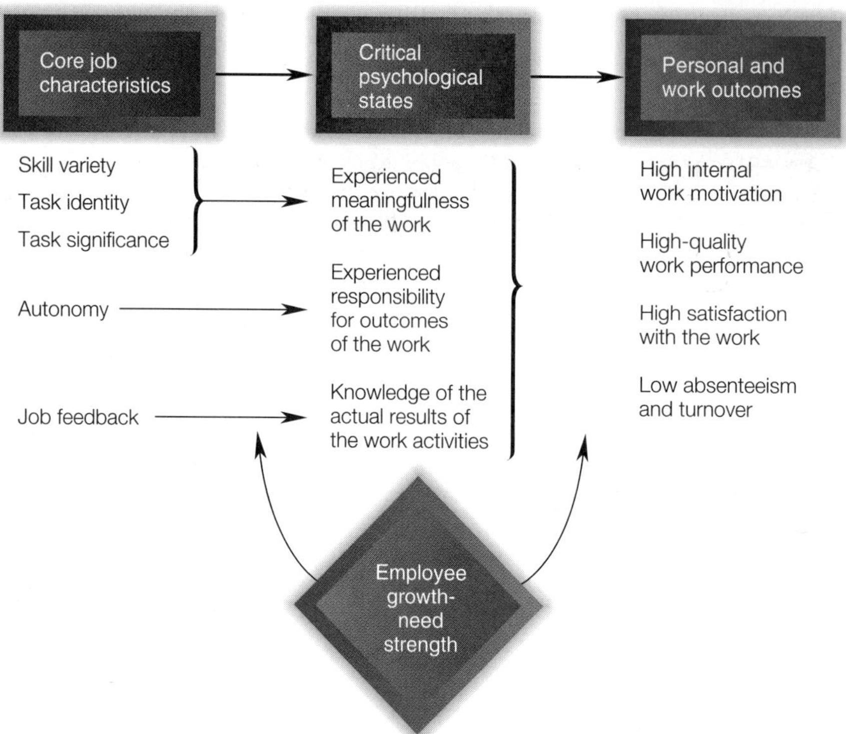

Source: J. R. Hackman and G. R. Oldham, "The Relationship among Core Job Dimensions, the Critical Psychological States, and On-the-Job Outcomes," *The Job Diagnostic Survey: An Instrument for the Diagnosis of Jobs and the Evaluation of Job Redesign Projects*, 1974. Reprinted by permission of Greg R. Oldham.

The model is made up of the following key concepts: five core job characteristics, a motivating potential score, critical psychological states, individual growth need strength, and implementing principles. We now discuss each of these.

The Five Core Job Characteristics

Central to the JCM are the five so-called *core job characteristics*. The model assumes that if the five core characteristics are perceived to be present in a job, the job holder is more likely to experience meaningfulness, responsibility, and knowledge of results. Examples of each of the five core characteristics are given in Exhibit 5.3, and they are defined as follows:

skill variety
The degree to which a job includes different activities and involves the use of multiple skills and talents of the employee.

task identity
The degree to which the job requires completion of a whole and identifiable piece of work—that is, doing a job from beginning to end—or being able to see how one's work fits in.

1. **Skill variety:** The degree to which a job includes different activities and involves the use of multiple skills and talents of the employee. This characteristic is very similar to the concept of job enlargement.
2. **Task identity:** The degree to which the job requires completion of a whole and identifiable piece of work—that is, doing a job from beginning to end—or being able to see how one's work fits in. This characteristic is built in to the design of the various groups at Toyota Motor Manufacturing, as discussed earlier, so that team members can see the work process from beginning to end. While high task identity, also called job scope, has typically been viewed as beneficial for organizations and their members, some research has suggested that it leads to organizational commitment only up to an optimal point and only during the early career stages.[30]

3. **Task significance:** The degree to which the job has a substantial impact on the lives or work of other people, whether in the immediate organization or in the external environment. Task significance along with task identity and skill variety relate to the concepts of meaningfulness and engagement, discussed earlier.
4. **Autonomy:** The degree to which the job provides the employee with substantial freedom, independence, and discretion in scheduling the work and in determining the procedures to be used in carrying it out. This characteristic is very similar to the concept of job enrichment and is reflected in Toyota's concept of *Jidoka*. Recent research has identified three different facets of work autonomy, which are "work method" autonomy (the degree of discretion/choice individuals have regarding work methods), "work schedule" autonomy (the extent to which workers feel they can control the scheduling, sequencing, or timing of their work), and "work criteria" autonomy (the degree to which workers have the ability to modify or choose the criteria for evaluating their performance).[31]
5. **Feedback from the job itself:** The degree to which carrying out the work activities results in the employee's obtaining direct and clear information about the effectiveness of his or her performance. This characteristic describes feedback that comes, not from one's supervisor, employees or co-workers, but directly from job performance. It is related to the critical psychological state of knowledge of the results of ones work.

task significance
The degree to which the job has a substantial impact on the lives or work of other people, whether in the immediate organization or in the external environment.

autonomy
The degree to which the job provides the employee with substantial freedom, independence, and discretion in scheduling the work and in determining the procedures to be used in carrying it out.

feedback from the job itself
The degree to which carrying out the work activities results in the employee's obtaining direct and clear information about the effectiveness of his or her performance.

EXHIBIT 5.3

Examples of Core Job Characteristics

Skill Variety

High:	The owner-operator of a garage who does electrical repair, rebuilds engines, does body work, and interacts with customers
Low:	A body shop worker who sprays paint eight hours a day

Task Identity

High:	A cabinetmaker who designs a piece of furniture, selects the wood, builds the object, and finishes it to perfection
Low:	A worker at a furniture factory who operates a lathe solely to make table legs

Task Significance

High:	A caretaker who is one of two, responsible for a small elementary school
Low:	A caretaker who is one of twenty, responsible for a large office building

Autonomy

High:	A telephone installer who schedules his or her own work for the day, makes visits without supervision, and decides on the most effective techniques for a particular installation
Low:	A telephone operator who must handle calls as they come according to a routine, highly specified procedure

Job Feedback

High:	An electronics factory worker who assembles a radio and then tests it to determine if it operates properly
Low:	An electronics factory worker who assembles a radio and then routes it to a quality control inspector who tests it for proper operation and makes needed adjustments.

SOURCE: Gary Johns and Alan M. Saks, *Organizational Behaviour: Understanding and Managing Life at Work*, 5th ed. Copyright © 2000. Adapted by permission of Pearson Education, Inc., Upper Saddle River, N.J.

The Overall Motivating Potential Score of a Job

Hackman and his colleagues also proposed that the five core job characteristics interact to determine an overall Motivating Potential Score (MPS) for a specific job. The MPS indicates a job's potential for motivating incumbents. The MPS formula is as follows:

$$\text{MPS} = \frac{\begin{bmatrix}\text{Skill}\\ \text{variety}\end{bmatrix} + \begin{bmatrix}\text{Task}\\ \text{identity}\end{bmatrix} + \begin{bmatrix}\text{Task}\\ \text{significance}\end{bmatrix}}{3} \times [\text{Autonomy}] \times [\text{Feedback}].$$

An owner-operator of a garage has skill variety, task identity, task significance, autonomy, and job feedback.

If you completed Self-Assessment 5.1, you analyzed the motivating potential of your present job or some other job that you have held. If you look at the scoring instructions at the end of the chapter you will notice that MPS scores, based on those jobs studied, range from 0 to 343. Take a moment now to reflect on your responses to that assessment in light of what you have read about the Job Characteristics Model. Do you think your score accurately reflects the motivation potential of the job you assessed?

Employee Growth-Need Strength

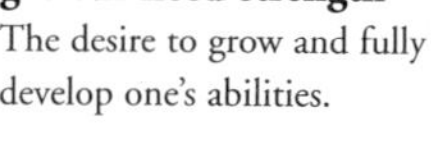

growth-need strength
The desire to grow and fully develop one's abilities.

If the MPS score you calculated in Self-Assessment 5.1 seemed high or low in comparison to your own personal experience of the job you assessed, it may be because you have high or low growth-need strength. **Growth-need strength** is the desire to grow and fully develop one's abilities. This concept is related to Maslow's need for self-actualization and Alderfer's need for growth, discussed in Chapter 4. The JCM, while on the one hand suggesting a universal set of core job characteristics, also recognizes that individuals respond in unique ways, depending upon their need for growth at the time. People with high growth-need strengths respond favourably to jobs with a high MPS and those with low growth-need strengths respond less favourably to such jobs.

Critical Psychological States

Finally, the JCM goes on to suggest that the five core job characteristics stimulate three critical psychological states according to the relationships specified in the model. These critical psychological states are defined as follows:

Analysis & Evaluation

EVALUATING CORE JOB CHARACTERISTICS

Use the definitions of the five core characteristics and the examples in Exhibit 5.3 to evaluate the following jobs in terms of whether each of the five core characteristics is high, average, or low.

- Server at Tim Hortons
- University/college professor
- Salesperson at the Gap
- Student painter

Note: Further develop your skills by completing Experiential Exercise 5.1 at the end of the chapter.

1. *Experienced meaningfulness of the work:* The degree to which the employee experiences the job as one that is generally meaningful, valuable, and worthwhile.
2. *Experienced responsibility for work outcomes:* The degree to which the employee feels personally accountable and responsible for the results of the work he or she does.
3. *Knowledge of results:* The degree to which the employee knows and understands, on a continuous basis, how effectively he or she is performing the job.

Principles for Implementing Improved Job Design

The JCM researchers discovered five useful concepts for implementing job design and redesign: (1) combining tasks into larger jobs, (2) forming natural work teams to increase task identity and task significance, (3) establishing relationships with customers, (4) loading jobs vertically with more responsibility, and/or (5) opening feedback channels for the job incumbent. The relationship between these five implementing principles and the core job characteristics is outlined in Exhibit 5.4. For example, if an automotive mechanic received little feedback on the quality of repair work performed, one redesign strategy would be to solicit customer feedback one month after each repair.

As shown in Exhibit 5.4, tasks can be combined. This involves assigning tasks that are performed by different workers and assigning them to a single individual. An even better way to create task identity is to form natural work teams, as Toyota does, because this also increases task significance. Often this is accomplished by establishing client relationships and putting employees in charge of a customer group or region. Jobs can also be improved by what is called "vertical loading," which simply means that responsibility is brought down from above (vertically); that is, from the supervisor. This is the same as giving more autonomy or job enrichment. Finally, jobs can be improved by opening feedback channels which means that information that used to go to a boss is routed directly to the employee to strengthen job feedback.

A number of problems can arise in the implementation of job redesign. First, an initial drop in performance can be expected as workers accommodate to the change. Second, first-line supervisors may experience some anxiety or hostility because they perceive an erosion of their power or control. Third, unless workers received adequate training, they may not be able to handle the increased autonomy or additional tasks. Fourth, when jobs are redesigned through "vertical loading," employees are given more responsibilities that used to be carried by their bosses. Often pay rates are not adjusted accordingly and employees feel exploited. For this reason, unions have often objected to job redesign efforts.

The International Quality & Productivity Center (IQPC)

The International Quality & Productivity Center (IQPC) is dedicated to providing practical information on business trends to help organizations remain competitive and profitable. The group's research reveals the richness and diversity of approaches to the design of work across various economic regions.
http://www.iqpc.com

EXHIBIT 5.4

Implementing Principles for Improving Core Job Characteristics

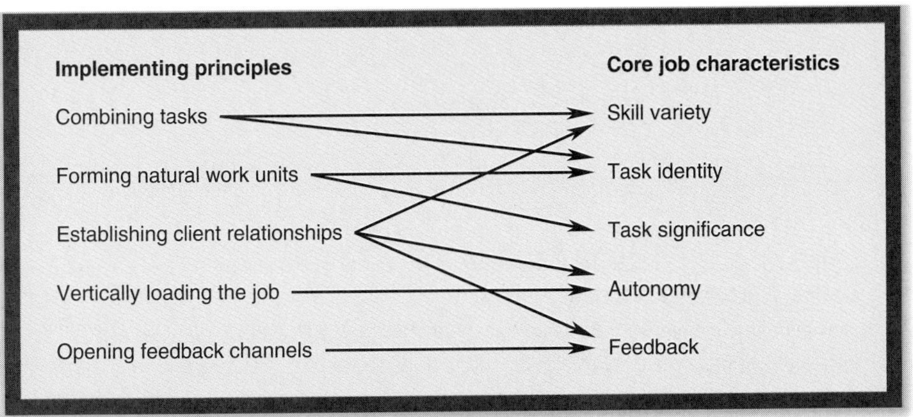

SOURCE: J. Richard Hackman and Greg R. Oldham, *Work Redesign*, 1st ed. (Reading, MA: Addison-Wesley, 1980), 135. Copyright © 1980 Addison-Wesley. Reprinted by permission of Pearson Education, Inc., Upper Saddle River, N.J.

5

Briefly describe the social information-processing and interdisciplinary approaches to job design.

ALTERNATIVE APPROACHES TO JOB DESIGN

In addition to job enlargement, job rotation, job enrichment, and the Job Characteristics Model, other approaches to job design have been proposed. We discuss two of these alternative approaches: the social information-processing model (SIP) and the interdisciplinary model.

Social Information Processing

social information-processing model
A model that suggests that the important job factors depend in part on what others tell a person about the job.

The traditional approaches to the design of work emphasize *objective* characteristics of jobs, such as variety and the ability to plan and control one's own work. In contrast, the **social information-processing (SIP) model** emphasizes the *interpersonal* aspects of work design. Specifically, the SIP model says that what others tell us about our jobs is important.[32] The SIP model has four basic premises about the work environment.[33] First, other people provide cues we use to understand the work environment. Second, other people help us judge what is important in our jobs. Third, other people tell us how they see our jobs. Fourth, other people's positive and negative feedback helps us understand our feelings about our jobs. People's perceptions and reactions to their jobs are shaped by information from other people in the work environment.[34] In other words, what others believe about a person's job may be important to understanding the person's perceptions of, and reactions to, the job.

This does not mean that objective job characteristics are unimportant; rather, it means that others can modify the way these characteristics affect us.[35] While objective task complexity may be a motivator, the presence of others in the work environment, social interaction, or even daydreaming may be important additional sources of motivation.

The Interdisciplinary Approach

The interdisciplinary approach to job design offers a different perspective again, by suggesting that no one approach can solve all job design problems. Rather, four approaches—the mechanistic, motivational, biological, and perceptual/motor approaches—are necessary in order to design jobs for optimum effectiveness. This approach allows the job designer or manager to consider trade-offs and alternatives among the approaches based on desired outcomes.[36] One study using the interdisciplinary approach to improve jobs evaluated 377 clerical, 80 managerial, and 90 analytical positions.[37] The jobs were improved by combining tasks and adding ancillary duties. The improved jobs provided greater motivation for the incumbents and were better from a perceptual/motor standpoint. The jobs were poorly designed from a mechanical engineering standpoint, however, and they were unaffected from a biological standpoint. See Exhibit 5.5 for an overview of the positive and negative outcomes that one could expect when taking each of the four distinct approaches to job design.

6

Apply the individual job design concepts to the design of teams.

WORK DESIGN FOR TEAMS

socio-technical systems theory
Theory proposing that work design should jointly optimize the social and technical systems of an organization.

Up to this point we have been discussing job design for individual jobs, and many of the concepts regarding the need to increase job feedback, autonomy, variety, and meaningfulness apply as well to the work of teams. You will be exploring the impact of a team's design on its effectiveness in Chapter 7, but we introduce the ideas here with what is called **socio-technical systems theory (STS)**. Socio-technical systems theory, originally developed in the early 1950s, takes many of the ideas just discussed at the individual level and applies them to the team level. Essentially, STS views the team, not the individual job, as the basic building block of an organization and argues that a well-designed team creates meaningfulness and engagement (*socio-*) as well as the greatest technical efficiency (*technical*).[38]

EXHIBIT 5.5

Summary of Outcomes from the Interdisciplinary Approach to Job Design

(Discipline)	Positive Outcomes	Negative Outcomes
Mechanistic Approach (mechanical engineering)	Decreased training time Higher personnel utilization levels Lower likelihood of error Less chance of mental overload Lower stress levels	Lower job satisfaction Lower motivation Higher absenteeism
Motivational Approach (industrial psychology)	Higher job satisfaction Higher motivation Greater job involvement Higher job performance Lower absenteeism	Increased training time Lower personnel utilization levels Greater chance of errors Greater chance of mental overload and stress
Biological Approach (biology)	Less physical effort Less physical fatigue Fewer health complaints Fewer medical incidents Lower absenteeism Higher job satisfaction	Higher financial costs of changes in equipment or job environment
Perceptual Motor Approach (experimental psychology)	Lower likelihood of error Lower likelihood of accidents Less chance of mental stress Decreased training time Higher personnel utilization levels	Lower job satisfaction Lower motivation

SOURCE: Reprinted from *Organizational Dynamics,* Winter 1987, copyright © 1987, with permission from Elsevier Science.

As summarized in Exhibit 5.6, internal self-regulation is central in STS theory, and this mirrors the job design principles of autonomy and job enrichment by providing the employee with substantial freedom, independence, and discretion in scheduling the work and in determining the procedures to be used in carrying it out. In STS it is the work group that makes these decisions. The principle of redundancy of skills is reflected in the individual models through the concepts of cross-training, job rotation, and job enlargement. Finally the principle of viewing the individual as complementary to the machine rather than an extension of it is reflected in the increased attention paid to meaningfulness and not just to task efficiency. Socio-technical system design is integral to the design of self-managed work teams (SMWTs), discussed in OBXtra 4."

Toyota Motor Manufacturing, highlighted in the chapter opener, exemplifies a number of the STS principles, as work teams are central to the plant's design, team members are all cross-trained, they self-regulate through the practice of *Jidoka,* and through a high degree of standardization, the focus is on the team members' discretionary roles rather than the prescribed ones. The main coordination mechanism at Toyota and in STS systems is standardization of skills.[39]

EXHIBIT 5.6

STS Principles of Design

1. The work system, comprising a set of activities that make up a functioning whole, is the basic unit (rather than the individual job)
2. The work group is central
3. The work group should regulate the system internally (rather than be externally controlled by supervisors)
4. Create redundancy of functions rather than redundancy of parts, thus focusing on the development of multiple skills in the individual (and therefore increasing the "response repertoire" and flexibility of the group)
5. Focus on the discretionary rather than the prescribed character of work roles
6. The individual is seen as complementary to the machine rather than an extension to it
7. Increase variety for both the individual and the organization (rather than decreasing variety)

SOURCE: G. Farias and A. Varma, "Integrating Job Characteristics, Socio-technical Systems and Reengineering: Presenting a Unified Approach to Work and Organization Design," *Organization Development Journal* 18, no. 3 (Fall 2000): 13. Reprinted by permission.

Explore cross-cultural aspects of work design.

CROSS-CULTURAL ASPECTS OF WORK DESIGN

While cross-cultural commonalities do exist, nations and ethnic groups have unique ways of understanding and designing work.[40] As organizations become more global and international, an appreciation of the perspectives of other nations is increasingly important. In an international study, 5550 people in 20 different countries completed the Work Value Scales (WVS).[41] The WVS is composed of 13 items measuring various aspects of the work environment, such as responsibility and job security. The study found two common basic work dimensions across cultures: work content (measured by items such as "the amount of responsibility on the job") and job context (measured by items such as "the policies of my company"). This finding suggests that people in many cultures distinguish between the nature of the work itself and elements of the context in which work is done. This supports Herzberg's two-factor theory of motivation (see Chapter 4) and the concepts of job enrichment discussed earlier in this chapter. Although the meaning of work differs among countries, new theorizing about job design also suggests that individual employees can alter work meaning and work identity by changing task and relationship configurations in their work.[42]

The Japanese, Germans, and Scandinavians in particular have distinctive perspectives on the design and organization of work.[43] Each country's perspective is forged within its unique cultural and economic system, and each is distinct from the approaches used in Canada and the United States.

The Japanese Approach

The Japanese began harnessing their productive energies during the 1950s by drawing on the product quality ideas of W. Edwards Deming.[44] In addition, the central government became actively involved in the economic resurgence of Japan, and it encouraged companies to conquer industries rather than to maximize profits.[45]

Whereas Frederick Taylor and his successors in North America emphasized the job of an individual worker, the Japanese work system emphasized the strategic level and encouraged collective and cooperative working arrangements.[46] The Japanese emphasize performance, accountability, and self-directedness in defining work, as seen in their success with what is called lean production methods.

Lean production methods use committed employees with ever-expanding responsibilities to achieve zero waste, 100 percent quality product, delivered on time, every time. This concept is similar to the concept of socio-technical systems (STS), although there are some differences.[47] In particular, STS gives greater emphasis to teamwork and self-managed and autonomous work groups, to the ongoing nature of the design process, and to human values in the work process. The approaches are similar, however, in that both differ from Taylor's scientific management and both emphasize job variety, feedback to work groups and teams, support of human resources, and control of production variance close to the point of origin. Hence, the Japanese emphasis on lean production has led to a renewed consideration of the STS concept.

lean production
Using committed employees with ever-expanding responsibilities to achieve zero waste, 100 percent quality product, delivered on time, every time.

The German Approach

The German approach to work has been shaped by Germany's unique educational system, cultural values, and economic system. The Germans are a highly educated and well-organized people. For example, their educational system has a multi-track design with technical and university alternatives. The German economic system puts a strong emphasis on free enterprise, private property rights, and management–labour cooperation. A comparison of voluntary and mandated management–labour cooperation in Germany found that productivity was superior under voluntary cooperation.[48] Germany's workers are highly unionized, and their discipline and efficiency have enabled Germany to be highly productive while its workers labour substantially fewer hours than do most Canadians (see Organizational Reality 5.1).

The traditional German approach to work design was **technocentric**, an approach that placed technology and engineering at the centre of job design decisions. Recently, German industrial engineers have moved to a more **anthropocentric** approach, which places human considerations at the centre of job design decisions. The technocentric approach uses a natural scientific process in the design of work, whereas the anthropocentric approach relies on a more humanistic process. In the anthropocentric

technocentric
Placing technology and engineering at the centre of job design decisions.

anthropocentric
Placing human considerations at the centre of job design decisions.

organizational reality 5.1

Hours of Work and Flextime Outside of Canada

According to one survey, Canadian workers have it relatively easy. While the average Korean employee is on the job a staggering 55.1 hours every week, a typical Canadian's workweek is a more moderate 42.2 hours. That is lower than 28 other nations, including the U.S. at 42.4 hours a week. The United Kingdom has the longest working hours in the European Union, and nearly half of all employees there have no flexible working arrangements in their jobs at all. While the Germans average 40 hours per week at work, the French 39, and the Belgians 38, the British are averaging nearly 44 hours per week at work. These working conditions in Britain have led several groups representing working employees to urge companies to develop alternative working arrangements for employees. These groups cite evidence that there is strong demand for part-time work, for reduced hours, and for teleworking.

Fewer than 33 percent of British employees are able to work in any kind of flextime arrangement, only about 25 percent are allowed to take parental leave, and just 16 percent have access to job sharing. There is evidence that stress has increased for employees throughout the British economy, divorce rates are now the highest in the European Union, and productivity is suffering. The inflexible job approach makes it very difficult for employees to balance work–life demands and thus has a dampening effect on both employee motivation and on results. Several large British companies, including BP, British Telecommunications, and Lloyds TSB, are now beginning to offer employees alternative work arrangements, including part-time and school term-time jobs, job shares, and self-rostering.

SOURCES: C. Adams, "Employers Urged to Be Flexible Friends," *Financial Times*, August 22, 2001, 3; E. Schuster, "Big Government Will Lead the Way," *Newsmagazine*, July 9, 2001, 28:4.

approach, work is evaluated using the criteria of practicability and worker satisfaction at the individual level and the criteria of endurance and acceptability at the group level.

The Scandinavian Approach

The Scandinavian cultural values and economic system stand in contrast to the German system. The social democratic tradition in Scandinavia has emphasized social concern rather than industrial efficiency. Scandinavians place great emphasis on a work design model that encourages a high degree of worker control and good social support systems for workers.[49] The Scandinavian variant of STS, which they call "democratic dialogue," goes beyond the work team level and emphasizes the formation of company partnerships. Local knowledge is developed in sharing information from other companies.[50] Circumstantial and inferential scientific evidence provides a sufficiently strong basis for legislative and policy actions for redesigns aimed at enhancing worker well-being. An example of such an action for promoting good working environments and occupational health was Swedish Government Bill 1976/77:149, which stated, "Work should be safe both physically and mentally, but also provide opportunities for involvement, job satisfaction, and personal development."[51] In 1991, the Swedish Parliament set up the Swedish Working Life Fund to fund research, intervention programs, and demonstration projects in work design. For example, a study of Stockholm police on shift schedules found that going from a daily, counter-clockwise rotation to a clockwise rotation was more compatible with human biology and resulted in improved sleep, less fatigue, lower systolic blood pressure, and lower blood levels of triglycerides and glucose.[52] Hence, the work redesign improved the police officers' health.

Describe four alternative work arrangements that impact the work–family balance: job sharing, reduced workload and the four-day work week, flextime, and telecommuting.

ALTERNATIVE WORK ARRANGEMENTS THAT IMPACT THE WORK–FAMILY BALANCE

Organizations attempt to improve employee motivation in ways that go beyond the design of actual jobs for individuals and teams. Creating nontraditional work arrangements that facilitate a healthier balance between work and family life, while not strictly job design strategies, have been found to increase employee satisfaction and retention. While a variety of alternative work arrangements exist, we briefly explore the following five.

Worker councils in Scandinavia advise management on many company issues.

Job Sharing

Increasingly, Canadian workers have become more vocal about their wishes for a greater balance between their work and non-work lives and are willing to change employers or give up pay to get it. For this reason, flexible, customized and alternative work arrangements have been growing in popularity, and it is predicted that they will continue to do so.

Job sharing is an alternative work pattern in which more than one person occupies a single job. Job sharing may be an alternative to teleworking for addressing demographic and labour pool concerns. Job sharing is found throughout a wide range of managerial and professional jobs, as well as in production and service jobs. It is not common among senior executives. B.C. Biomedical Laboratory, ranked as the number one company to work for in Canada in 2002, makes extensive use of the work pattern of job sharing. Ninety percent of the workforce at B.C. Biomedical Lab is female, contributing to the high need for work flexibility to accommodate family responsibilities. Many of the women job share with other women in order to juggle shifts to take days off for school plays or if their children are sick. The employees can switch days off with little notice, going through only one person.[53]

job sharing
An alternative work pattern in which more than one person occupies a single job.

Reduced Workload and the Four-Day Work Week

Studies as to the relative success of reduced workload arrangements have reported overall positive findings, with all stakeholders being supportive except for co-workers, who had the most reservations.[54] Employees opting for a four-day workweek work four ten-hour days and enjoy a three-day weekend. This arrangement provides the benefit of more time for those who want to balance work and family life through weekend travel. However, the longer workdays may be a drawback for employees with many family or social activities on weekday evenings. Hence, the four-day workweek has both benefits and limitations.

Flexibility Online
Advances in technology are transforming the workplace in new ways that require a high level of skill among members of the workforce. Visit Flexibility Online to read the latest news and research concerning the virtual office and flexible working. What are some of the top stories and issues listed at the site?
http://www.flexibility.co.uk

Flextime

Flextime is a third alternative work pattern in which employees can set their own daily work schedules. This arrangement is often used to ease traffic and commuting pressures. It is also somewhat responsive to individual biorhythms, allowing early risers to go to work early and nighthawks to work late. Flextime options take many forms in organizations depending on the nature of the work and the coordination requirements in various jobs. Typically 9:00 a.m. to 3:00 p.m. is the required core working time for everyone in the company. Even in companies without formal flextime programs, flextime may be an individual option arranged between supervisor and subordinate. For example, a first-line supervisor who wants to complete a university degree may negotiate a work schedule accommodating both job requirements and course schedules at the university. Flextime options may be more likely for high performers who assure their bosses that work quality and productivity will not suffer.[55]

flextime
An alternative work pattern that enables employees to set their own daily work schedules.

Telecommuting

Telecommuting, also called "telework," is when an employee works from the home, a satellite office, or mobile office with a computer connection to the main office. New technologies and electronic commerce are changing the face of work environments, dramatically in some cases. Organizational

Eighty-seven percent of telecommuters believe they are more productive working at home.

telecommuting
When an employee works from the home, a satellite office, or mobile office with a computer connection to the main office.

Reality 5.2 discusses how the government of New Brunswick has used technology to transform the way it provides services to the people of New Brunswick. With the advent of e-government, many jobs have changed. New technologies are a double-edged sword that can be used to improve job performance, or to create stress. On the positive side, modern technologies are helping to revolutionize the way jobs are designed and the way work gets done. Read all about this trend in job design in OBXtra 5, "Managing in a "Virtual World."

IMPLICATIONS FOR ORGANIZATIONAL EFFECTIVENESS

Jobs in organizations are interdependent and are usually designed to complement and support other jobs in the organization and to make a contribution to the organization's overall mission and goals. Jobs and teams are the building blocks of the organization and the way they are designed has a critical impact on individual, group, and organizational effectiveness.

Individual jobs are created as a result of differentiation, which is necessary because no one can do it all. Even small organizations must divide work so that each person is able to accomplish a manageable piece of the whole. The decisions an organization makes about how it will divide up the work has a huge impact both on the efficiency of the organization as well as on the resulting engagement of employees. In Canada, where labour costs are very high relative to most other countries, organizations need engaged and committed employees in order to effectively compete. The joint optimization of both the social and the technical systems at work continues to be a goal worth striving for.

Work means different things to different national groups; therefore, job design efforts at multinational organizations must be sensitive to local cultural values and beliefs. In crafting work tasks and assignments, managers should make an effort to fit the jobs to the people who are doing them. There are no universally accepted ways to design

organizational reality 5.2

New Brunswick Making Waves with e-Government

The development of e-government is transforming how Canadians obtain services and information, interact with government representatives, and become involved in political and business processes. The province of New Brunswick has made waves by becoming one of the first agencies in the world to deliver government services electronically. With the vision of becoming a global leader in the digital economy of the twenty-first century, the province of New Brunswick recognizes that, over time, e-government has the potential to revolutionize the relationship between New Brunswickers and government. According to one survey, 61 percent of small and medium-sized enterprises in Canada are connected to the Internet. Atlantic Canada compares favourably with the rest of Canada, with New Brunswick at 61 percent, Nova Scotia at 66 percent, Prince Edward Island at 66 percent, and Newfoundland and Labrador at 61 percent.

To date, the province of New Brunswick offers 35 government transactional services, 172 forms, and hundreds of information items online. There are currently 24 500 people employed in 687 companies in the knowledge industry in New Brunswick—almost the same number of workers as in the forest industry. New Brunswick Premier Bernard Lord states, "The eNB strategy is designed to create opportunities for all New Brunswickers to participate and prosper in the 21st century economy and the information revolution by harnessing together the resources of the public, private, and academic sectors."

SOURCES: New Brunswick, *eNB Strategy,* www.enb.ca/pages/strategy-e.asp; New Brunswick, *eNB e-Government,* www.enb.ca/pages/gov-e.asp; New Brunswick, *eNB e-Business,* www.enb.ca/pages/bus-e.asp; New Brunswick, "Release of eNB Action Plan (02/08/08)," www.gnb.ca/cnb/news/pre/2002e0800pr.htm; Jacques Bensimon, "Canada's e-government Conference" (speech given at the Canada's e-Government Conference for the Public Sector & Business, October 28, 2002, Fredericton, NB), National Film Board of Canada, http://www.nfb.ca/publications/en/speeches/02-10-28.html.

work, and early efforts to find them have been replaced by a number of alternatives. Early approaches to job design were valuable for manufacturing and administrative jobs of the mid-1900s. Now, however, with the changing nature of work in Canada; employees' demand for more meaningful work; time to balance work, family, and life; and a legislative framework that emphasizes employees' rights, managers are being challenged to find new ways to define work and design jobs. Toyota Motor Manufacturing of Canada, discussed at the beginning of this chapter, is a good example of a nontraditional approach to job design. The distinguishing feature of job design in the foreseeable future is flexibility. Dramatic global, economic, and organizational changes dictate that managers be flexible in the design of work in their organizations. Jobs must be designed to fit the larger organizational structure.

Chapter Summary

1. Job design is the process of assigning tasks to a job, including the interdependency of those tasks with other jobs. What this means is that managers and organizational designers have to decide how to group tasks into separate jobs and job descriptions. Effective job design is important because the decisions will impact employee activities as well as their motivation and performance.
2. The earliest approach to job design was scientific management. This approach, advocated by Frederick Taylor, emphasized work simplification, which is the standardization and the narrow, explicit specification of task activities for workers. Work simplification, while resulting in increased efficiencies, also had the unintended effect of creating worker alienation and increased absenteeism and turnover. In addition to the limitations of work simplification, increasingly, people want more from work than what organizations traditionally provide. People desire work that is more meaningful and more fully in accord with their lives. *Meaningfulness* is defined as the value of a work goal or purpose, judged in relation to an individual's own ideals or standards. Citizens of different countries vary in their degree of work centrality or work alienation. The concept of meaningfulness has been advanced with explorations of two more recent concepts: job engagement and workplace spirituality.
3. Job enlargement, job rotation, cross-training, and job enrichment are all approaches to job design that were created to help overcome work alienation. Job enlargement increases the number of tasks in a job. Job rotation rotates a worker through a variety of specialized job tasks over time. Cross-training is a variation of job enlargement in which workers are trained in different specialized tasks or activities but may not rotate regularly. Job enrichment is a job design method aimed at increasing the degree to which workers control the planning, execution and evaluation of their work. Whereas job enlargement involves increasing and varying the number of activities a person does, job enrichment involves increasing the recognition, responsibility, and opportunity for achievement.
4. The Job Characteristics Model (JCM) of job design is a framework for understanding person–job fit through the interaction of core job dimensions with a person's critical psychological states. The five core characteristics are skill variety, task identity, task significance, autonomy, and feedback from the job itself. The three critical psychological states that result from high levels of these five core characteristics are experienced meaningfulness of the work, experienced responsibility for work outcomes, and knowledge of results. Guidelines for improving the design of jobs are combining tasks, forming natural work units, establishing client relationships, vertically loading the job, and opening up feedback channels.
5. Two other approaches to job design are social information processing (SIP) and the interdisciplinary approach. The SIP model emphasizes the interpersonal aspects of work design and says that what others tell us about our jobs is important. The interdisciplinary approach proposes that no one approach can solve all the performance problems, and four approaches are necessary. These are the mechanistic, motivational, biological, and perceptual/motor approaches.
6. The socio-technical systems theory (STS) applies the notion of job enrichment at the group level. STS theory proposes that work design should jointly optimize the social and technical system of an organization, which is another way of saying that a well-designed job or work group creates meaningfulness and engagement (*socio-*) as well as the greatest technical efficiency (*technical*).
7. The cultural values and social organizations in Japan, Germany, and Scandinavia lead to unique approaches to the design of work.
8. Four alternative work arrangements impact work–family balance. These are job sharing, reduced workload and the four-day workweek, flextime, and telecommuting.

Key Terms

anthropocentric (p. 151)
autonomy (p. 145)
cross-training (p. 140)
employee engagement (p. 138)
feedback from the job itself (p. 145)
flextime (p. 153)
growth-need strength (p. 146)
Job Characteristics Model (JCM) (p. 143)
job design (p. 136)
job enlargement (p. 139)
job enrichment (p. 141)
job rotation (pp. 139–40)
job sharing (p. 153)
lean production (p. 151)
meaningfulness (p. 137)
scientific management (p. 137)
skill variety (p. 144)
social information-processing model (p. 148)
socio-technical systems theory (p. 148)
task identity (p. 144)
task significance (p. 145)
technocentric (p. 151)
telecommuting (p. 153)
work alienation (p. 137)
work centrality (p. 138)
work simplification (p. 137)
workplace spirituality (p. 138)

Review Questions

1. Explain what is meant by job design and why it is important for managers to understand.
2. Compare and contrast job enlargement, job rotation, and job enrichment.
3. Explain the increasing importance of meaningful work, engagement, and spirituality at work.
4. Identify and define the five core job dimensions and the three critical psychological states in the Job Characteristics Model.
5. What are the main implementing principles that guide the redesign of individual jobs, and how do they relate to the JCM?

Discussion and Communication Questions

1. Is there ever one best way to design a particular job?
2. What is the most important emerging issue in the design of work?
3. (*Communication question*) Read about new approaches to jobs, such as job sharing. Prepare a memo comparing what you have learned from your reading with one or more approaches to job design discussed in the chapter. What changes in approaches to jobs and job design do you notice from this comparison?
4. (*Communication question*) Interview an employee in your organization or another organization and develop an oral presentation about how the job the employee is doing could be enriched. Make sure you ask questions about all aspects of the employee's work (e.g., what specific tasks are done and with whom the employee interacts on the job).

Ethics Questions

1. Assume that a company is planning to redesign all of the jobs in one department based on the advice of a major consulting firm. Should the company discuss the job redesign plans with employees before implementing them? Should the employees have been consulted prior to hiring the consulting firm?
2. Assume that a company is aware of certain psychological or physical risks associated with a job, such as respiratory problems and cancer risk associated with the installation of asbestos. Assume also that the medical costs for workers will not be too great. Is it ethical not to warn employees about the possible health risks? Would it make a difference if the risks were less permanent, such as lower back tension or temporarily altered vision?

3. Suppose that the design of a particular job exposes employees to a health or safety risk and that redesigning the job would cost the company more than paying the medical claims if an employee is injured or hurt. Should the company tell employees doing the job about its decision not to redesign the job to make it safer? Is it ethical for the company not to redesign the job?

4. Assume that a company has many older, mature workers. Rather than retrain them in new technologies, the company wants to replace the older workers with younger ones. Should this be allowed?

Evaluation & Synthesis

EXPERIENTIAL EXERCISE 5.1: USE THE JCM TO ANALYZE AND REDESIGN JOBS

Purpose: To explore the job characteristics model (JCM) and consider how jobs can be redesigned

Group size: 4–6

Time required: 30 minutes

Materials needed: None

Instructions:

1. **Preparation:** Read the job design cases and consider how the jobs might be changed (5 min.).
2. **Group discussion:** Groups discuss each case and develop suggestions for redesign based on the models in the text (15 min.).
3. **Class discussion:** The instructor leads the class in discussion of the suggestions (10 min.).

Job Design Cases

You go to a party at your oldest brother's apartment and spend a nice evening talking to several of his friends. All are in their late 20s and do not seem very happy with the jobs they have. Your task is to think about how these jobs might be re-engineered or enriched.

1. Mary works as a receptionist at a large law firm. Her primary job is answering the telephone and switching the call to the correct lawyer. As most of the lawyers have their own secretaries and voice mail, she doesn't take messages. After installing the voice-mail system, for several months the law firm didn't have a receptionist. The managing partner received complaints from some elderly clients who didn't like the complex instructions and wanted a human receptionist. So the managing partner hired Mary and gave her written instructions for what to do if a caller doesn't ask to speak to a particular lawyer (e.g., if the client says, "I had an accident," the call should be forwarded to Ms. Johnson or Mr. Harman; if the client says, "I am in jail," the call is forwarded to Mr. Wilson, Ms. Inchira, or Mr. Wu). Mary also greets clients when they come to the office and asks which lawyer they want to see. Then she calls the office, and the lawyer of his/her secretary comes to the reception area and meets the client. Again, Mary has written instructions about whom to call if the client doesn't give a specific name.

2. John works as an intake counsellor for a citywide drug and alcohol treatment program. He interviews people who need treatment (often referred to the program by the courts) and determines a treatment plan for them. This could range from assigning the person to a local clinic for an hour a week of group or individual counselling with a drug and alcohol counsellor to admission for 28 days to a residential program ("drying out"). Because of the number of people who need drug or alcohol treatment and the city's human service budget limitations, John sees a large number of clients each day. He rarely finds out what happened for any individuals (unless they are referred again for treatment), although he gets summary statistics every three months on all the persons who are being treated.

3. Kanisha works as a technical services specialist. If there are problems with a computer, the network, or the printers, she is called. In a typical day, she gets 20 to 30 calls. Some require a minute or two to solve the problem, some require a short conversation to diagnose and solve the problem, and a few are more complex or unique and call for careful problem solving, sometimes involving the other technical services specialists and occasionally the information systems manager. Once or twice a month, a problem is so critical or urgent that Kanisha must work overtime until it is solved. Part of her job is servicing the printers (beyond putting in paper and toner, which others do) if they break. Although she is quite busy, Kanisha also has responsibility for implementing several new computer programs.

4. Jose works for a large insurance company in the dental reimbursements office. Each morning his supervisor gives him a long list of claims to be processed. He spends his whole day in front of a computer entering data and responding to questions preprogrammed into the system. When claims cannot be processed in that way (called "an exception"), he takes the exception to his manager, who directs Jose what to do. Several years of experience have taught Jose what the manager's action will be in each case, but the manager insists that all exceptions be brought to her. A problem for Jose is that each exception takes much longer to process than a regular claim; he often gets behind and the supervisor puts a lot of pressure on him to finish the day's work.

Source: Dorothy Marcic, Joseph Seltzer, and Peter Vaill, *Organizational Behaviour: Experiences and Cases*, 6th ed. (Mason, OH: South-Western College Publishing, 2001), 187.

Application, Analysis & Synthesis

CASE: MARITIME AIRLINES

Maritime Airlines, founded in 1938, employed just over 15 000 persons and operated a large, modern fleet of 107 aircraft. Finding itself in a highly competitive and turbulent business climate since 9/11, it decided that to retain and improve its market share it needed to undertake an aggressive $4-billion program to upgrade facilities and equipment over the next 10 years. It also felt that it needed to take action to improve the morale of its front-line employees.

One of the programs that management decided to undertake was a new Work Improvement Program (WIP) recommended by Dr. Arthur Spears, a highly respected management consultant. During Dr. Spears' previous employment with the New Brunswick Telephone Company, he had been able to increase labour productivity and morale and decrease absenteeism and employee turnover.

The company announced that they had retained Dr. Spears to introduce the WIP in the Reservations department. It proclaimed that this program would result in them becoming an "Employer of Choice" and that the job enrichment program would strip away the daily drudgery and routine associated with the job. Agents were to become human beings once more and not mindless attachments to computers. Newspapers and TV crews suddenly appeared on the reservation floor, shooting thousands of feet of film, snapping pictures and interviewing managers, supervisors, and agents.

The Problem

The Reservations Department employed over 300 agents along with 16 supervisors, 3 duty managers, 1 support manager and staff, and the reservations manager. Results of the annual employee survey indicated that morale in the Reservations Department was at an extremely low level in all areas except for in the Group and Tours (G & T) section. Overall, absenteeism and turnover were high, and productivity, measured in terms of promptness of service (POS), was low.

All employees in the Reservations Department had Promptness of Service (POS) goals for both telephone and e-mail inquiries, The POS target for telephone calls was 80 percent as an average over any one month. This factor would be achieved by answering 80 percent of all calls on average, within 20 seconds of the first ring. The average team had 20 agents, with an agent taking approximately 115 calls per shift. Over a period of two months the Reservations Department received over $1^1/_4$ million calls. The POS target for e-mail inquiries was 80 percent of inquiries to be responded to within 30 minutes. Telephone POS was holding fast at 65 percent and e-mail POS was at 50 percent.

EXHIBIT 5.4

Organization Chart of Reservations Department of Maritime Airlines during WIP Implementation

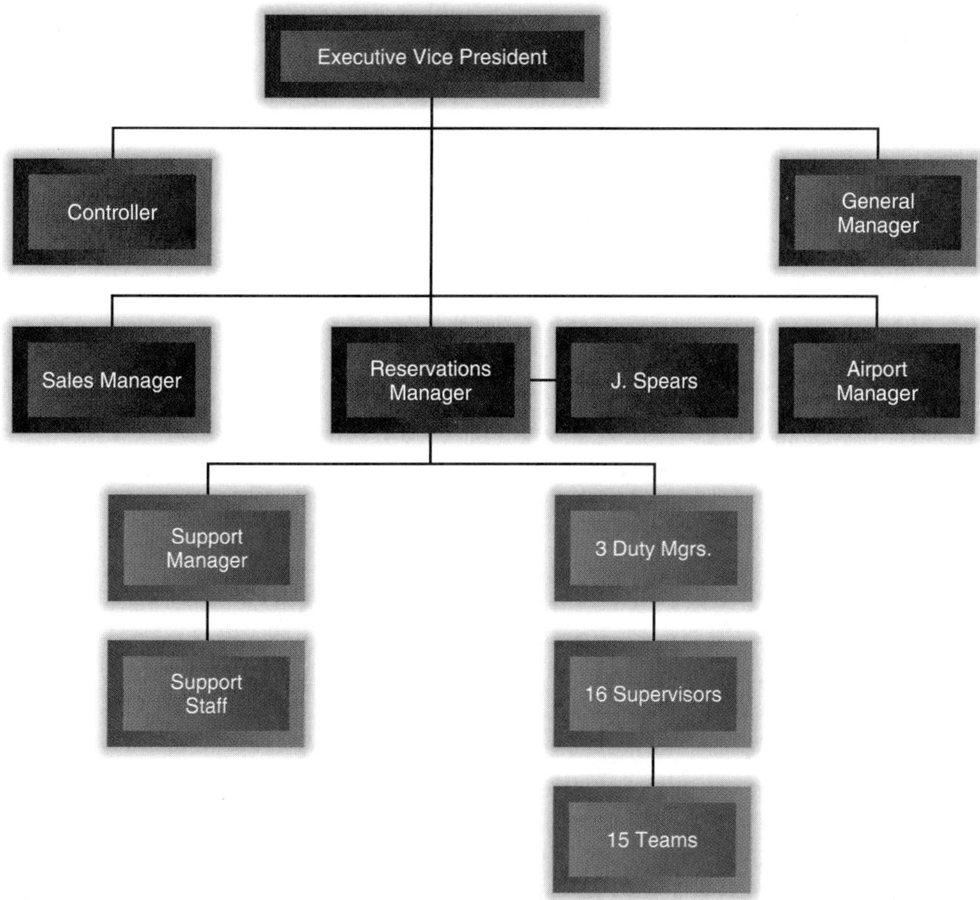

Microscopic View of a Team during Work Improvement Program

Total 20 Agents*
- 1 supervisory replacement — 1 Backup
- Fare expert — 1 Backup
- Equipment expert — 1 Backup
- Tours expert — 1 Backup
- Committee representative

* Prior to WIP, each team had 20 agents answering the phones.

Only the [G & T] section reported high morale and was achieving their POS targets. This section differed from the rest of the Reservations Department in a number of ways: G & T agents were located on a different floor, they were not monitored, and individuals were able to prioritize their own work. When calls or e-mails came in requesting information on group bookings or tours, they were immediately routed to G & T. Agents took the inquiries and were then responsible for serving that customer from beginning to end. G & T had also developed a system whereby the agent would send the customer a follow-up survey one week after trip completion. Surveys that indicated satisfied customers were displayed on the "Wall of Fame." If an individual wanted to be transferred to this section, he or she had to have been recognized as a high-potential candidate.

By contrast, general reservation agents replied to phone and e-mail inquiries to the main reservation site and then booked flights, cars, and hotels, and quoted fares. Their service times and e-mail activity were monitored by supervisors who received bonuses based on achievement of their POS targets. Any agent who achieved his or her POS targets for three months in a row received a letter or recognition from his or her supervisor and a commendation on the "Wall of Fame."

The Work Improvement Project (WIP)

After hiring Dr. Spears, Maritime Airlines set up a work improvement committee that came to be referred to as the WIP committee. The committee consisted of Spears; Elford, a senior training instructor; and Smith, one of the 16 reservations supervisors. The first step taken by the WIP committee was to take the job performed by the reservation agents (including groups and tours) and break it down into its many different aspects and then organize the agents into teams of "experts." Spears felt that each team should be a self-reliant entity; therefore, each team would have (a) an expert responsible for answering questions regarding planes and equipment, (b) a tours expert, (c) a rates expert who could read the complicated and often confusing tariffs, (d) an individual who would take over the team in the absence of the supervisor and (e) the right to elect a member to represent the team when new policies and procedures were being studied.

Problems with the WIP Project

However, once WIP was introduced, problems soon started to be noticed. Teams were carrying WIP one step further by electing backups to the experts. Experts were being pulled out of line for long periods of time helping fellow agents. And if the expert on the team was busy, agents would go to the backup agent and pull that agent out of line. Every expert on the team belonged to a committee which met at least once a month. The POS factors dropped dramatically to below 50 percent. Supervisors had been assigned the role of observers with little authority to eradicate abuses by agents. Prior to WIP it was unusual to see three or four agents standing or walking through the office unless on a break. During WIP it was the exception to see just four agents out of line. Everyone seemed to be standing and talking to each other or walking through the office. Everyone seemed to be on a coffee break.

Eight months after the official start of WIP, a corporate directive was sent notifying employees of the termination of the project. Within weeks, the team experts were once again either general or G & T agents. Supervisors were given carte blanche to discipline any individual not meeting the office standards. New information systems were purchased to compile reservation statistics on agents as they worked. The system kept track of the number of calls and e-mails taken, time agents spent at their terminals, fatigue factors, duration of average call and average time taken to respond to e-mails. Employee morale continued to decline, employee turnover increased and the company was again looking for a way to increase the productivity of the Reservations Department, but it looked as if no vague concepts such as core job characteristics, job enrichment or critical psychological states would ever be seriously considered again.

Questions

1. Using job design concepts and theories, explain why the reservation agents in the G & T section were more motivated and productive than the general reservation agents. Use the motivation theories from Chapter 4 to broaden your understanding of these differences.

2. Using job design concepts and theories, explain why the WIP was a failure within the Reservations Department.

3. If you had been hired instead of Dr. Spears, based on your current knowledge of how to design jobs to maximize their motivation potential, what recommendations for change would you have made and how would you have gone about implementing the redesign?

SOURCE: Written by Anwar Rashid, from *Canadian Cases in Organizational Behaviour*, 3rd ed., by S. Anwar Rashid, Maurice Archer, and Randy Hoffman. Copyright © 1985 by L & S Management. Reprinted with permission.

Scoring Instructions for Self-Assessments

Self-Assessment 5.1: Diagnosing Your Job

To score your questionnaire, place your responses to Questions 3, 2, 4, 1, and 5, respectively, in the blank spaces in the following equation:

$$\text{Motivating Potential Score (MPS)} = \frac{\overset{Q\#3}{[\ \ ]} + \overset{Q\#2}{[\ \ ]} + \overset{Q\#4}{[\ \ ]}}{3} \times \overset{Q\#1}{[\ \ ]} \times \overset{Q\#5}{[\ \ ]} = \underline{\qquad}.$$

If the MPS for the job you rated is between

- 200 and 343, it is high in motivating potential.
- 120 and 199, it is moderate in motivating potential.
- 0 and 119, it is low in motivating potential.

Part Two: Individual Processes and Behaviour (20:07 minutes)

THE BUSINESS OF MOTIVATIONAL SPEAKING *(8:34 MINUTES)*

This clip features the business of motivational speakers such as Allan Simmons, Anthony Robbins, and Brian Tracy. Speakers attend a convention learning how to improve their motivational speaking. Also features Gary Latham from the U of T.

Critical Thinking Questions

1. Is it possible to motivate someone to change?
2. What are the factors that make motivational speakers influential?
3. Do motivational speakers rely on any of the motivation theories discussed in the text?

TERRY FOX *(1:12 MINUTES)*

This clip celebrates the 20th anniversary of Terry Fox's Marathon of Hope for cancer research.

Critical Thinking Questions

1. Are extraordinary achievements accomplished only in the face of extreme adversity?
2. Do accomplishments like Terry Fox's depend on a certain kind of personality or could anyone have done what he did, given the same circumstances and physique?

JOB SATISFACTION AND JOB DESIGN *(1:42 MINUTES)*

This clip highlights the fact that close to 43 percent of Canadian workers report that they hate their jobs. Towers Perrin and Daniel Ondrack from the U of T are featured.

Critical Thinking Questions

1. Do four out of every ten people you know say they hate their jobs, as the Towers Perrin study indicates?
2. What are the reasons people you know give, most often, for being unhappy at work?
3. To what extent are you given autonomy, freedom, and challenge in your current job?

MEANINGFULNESS AND ENGAGEMENT AT WORK *(8:39 MINUTES)*

This clip features an interview with John Izzo, author of *Awakening the Corporate Soul.* Izzo explains how new graduates today seek balance, growth, and development more than just a paycheque. A study of new MBAs found that compensation was number six on their list of priorities. He cites research demonstrating the relationship between employee turnover and success and shows that engaged employees are great predictors of a firm's long-term success. He also mentions that an employee's relationship with his or her immediate supervisor is the best predictor of engagement. Companies have to recognize that employees are their only real asset in a knowledge economy.

Critical Thinking Questions

1. John Izzo's book is entitled *Awakening the Corporate Soul.* Is there such a thing as a "soul" of a company?
2. How high does pay rank on your list of priorities for a full-time job when you graduate? What else is important?

Behaviour

part three

6. **INTERPERSONAL AND ORGANIZATION-WIDE COMMUNICATION**

7. **TEAM DYNAMICS AND EFFECTIVENESS**

Interpersonal and Organization-Wide Communication

chapter six

6

LEARNING OBJECTIVES

By the end of this chapter, you will be able to do the following:

1. Using the communication process model, define *communication* and explain why effective communication is important at work.
2. Describe and give examples of the following four types of nonverbal communication: kinesics, speech variations (paralanguage), facial and eye behaviour, and use of interpersonal space (proxemics).
3. Describe the following barriers to communication: perceptual screens, language and jargon, status differences, filtering, and gender and cultural differences.
4. Describe the six characteristics of a defensive communication climate and illustrate how they create communication barriers.
5. Describe in detail three strategies for improving interpersonal communication: active listening, supportive communication, and effective feedback.
6. Explain the importance of effective organization-wide communication and give contemporary examples of downward and upward communication strategies.
7. Discuss the varying degrees of media richness in different communication vehicles and the current issues in electronic communication.

Janssen-Ortho Puts a Focus on Employee Communication

In 2002, the *Report on Business Magazine* survey of the "Fifty Best Companies to Work For in Canada" rated Janssen-Ortho, the Toronto-based pharmaceutical company, as the second-best place to work in Canada, so it's no wonder that Jim Mitchell, former president of Janssen-Ortho, said that lack of communication was his "mortal enemy."[1]

Greg Anderson, the vice president of Human Resources, oversees a number of processes at Janssen-Ortho to ensure that employee communications, both between managers and their employees and company-wide, are effective. To ensure that employee's voices are heard company-wide, the company conducts their full "Credo" survey every two years. The survey is based on Janssen-Ortho's Credo, which outlines the company's responsibilities to doctors, nurses, patients, employees, communities, and stockholders, in that order. The 160-item questionnaire is completed voluntarily and anonymously by employees, on company time. In the most recent survey, participation was 98 percent. Department leaders run feedback sessions, supported by their HR partners, and follow-up actions are developed to address the major concerns.

Another key to the communications strategy is the importance of effective communication between line managers and their employees. All managers and higher are assessed annually using Johnson & Johnson's (Janssen-Ortho's parent company) six "Global Standards of Leadership." These are as follows: Credo values/business results, customer/marketplace focus, innovation, collaboration, mastering complexity and change, and organizational and people development. These standards include behavioural descriptors that are used to develop and assess leadership skills, including those related to effective interpersonal communication. A few examples of the communications standards are as follows: "providing timely and honest feedback," "actively seeking constructive feedback to understand and address one's personal leadership effectiveness," and "communicates openly and frequently with partners."[2] Managers are required to hold department meetings at least once a month, and are held responsible for listening to their employees as well as communicating important information to them. An intranet site and a quarterly newsletter are also available with information and updates. All new managers are trained in communication skills, and ongoing training is provided through the Learning Calendar. In addition, the company holds monthly all-employee meetings in the dining room, which can hold up to 400 people. This dining room is in the centre of the Janssen-Ortho head office, and serves as a communication centre for employees. The dining room also houses a large TV screen, which provides up-to-date information on critical business drivers and financial measures using the "Balanced Scorecard" approach. Red, yellow, and green arrows indicate how the company is doing on each of the measures, so that employees stay well informed about the business.

SOURCES: S. Brearton and J. Daly, "The 50 Best Companies to Work for in Canada," *The Globe and Mail Report on Business Magazine,* December 27, 2002, 60; Janssen-Ortho, http://www.janssen-ortho.com; Greg Anderson (VP-HR Janssen-Ortho), interview, January 13, 2003; Johnson & Johnson, *Johnson & Johnson Global Standards of Leadership Reference Guide,* Johnson & Johnson Management Education Department, 2003.

Janssen-Ortho is an example of a company that takes interpersonal and organization-wide communication very seriously. Managers are held accountable for keeping their employees informed as well as listening to what they have to say. Also, senior management invests in company-wide communication by conducting regular surveys, all-employee meetings, and newsletters to keep communication flowing.

The first section of this chapter explains why effective interpersonal and organization-wide communication is so critical for organizational effectiveness. The second section presents a model of the overall communication process and sets the context for the chapter. The third section expands on the topic of nonverbal communication and its role in the overall communication process model. Fourth, we explore various types of communication barriers: perceptual screens, language and jargon, status differences, filtering, gender and cultural differences in communication, and defensiveness. The fifth section describes three broad strategies for improving interpersonal communication, which are active listening, effective feedback, and supportive communication. The final section explores organization-wide communication, including communicating through new technologies.

Using the communication process model, define communication and explain why effective communication is important at work.

THE IMPORTANCE OF EFFECTIVE INTERPERSONAL AND ORGANIZATION-WIDE COMMUNICATION

communication
The process by which information is exchanged between a sender and a receiver with the goal of reaching mutual understanding.

Communication is the process by which information is exchanged between a sender and a receiver with the goal of reaching mutual understanding.[3] This broad definition of communication includes verbal, nonverbal (e.g., facial expressions), and written communication. Current organizational trends present huge communication challenges. For example, there has been a dramatic increase in organizational alliances and cross-departmental teamwork. Employees are increasingly autonomous, and communication overload is rampant. While it seems obvious to most of us that effective communication, especially between managers and employees, is a critical foundation for effective performance in organizations as well as health and well-being,[4] only the best companies, such as Janssen-Ortho, discussed in the opening vignette, actually invest time and energy in their organization-wide communication.[5] Also, most of us are "amazingly blind to our own communication inadequacies,"[6] so effective management of organizational behaviour requires that companies help their managers and supervisors to become more effective communicators.

One large study of managers in a variety of jobs and industries found that managers with the most effective work units engaged in frequent communication with their employees, whereas the managers with the highest promotion rates engaged in networking activities with superiors.[7] Another study of male and female banking managers suggested that higher-performing managers are better and less apprehensive communicators than lower-performing managers.[8] Better supervisors keep those who work for them well informed and are skilled at appropriately screening information before distributing it. They also favour giving advance notice of organizational changes and explaining the rationale for organizational policies. Further, when supervisors and employees communicate and plan, they have a greater number of agreements about the employee's performance and behaviour.[9] Overall, effective communication is a key foundation for human relationships both at work and outside of work.

A COMMUNICATION PROCESS MODEL

Exhibit 6.1 presents a model of the communication process. The main components of the model are a sender, a receiver, a channel for transmission, barriers, and a feedback loop. The *sender* is the person originating the message. The sender has to *form* the message in his

EXHIBIT 6.1

A Communication Process Model

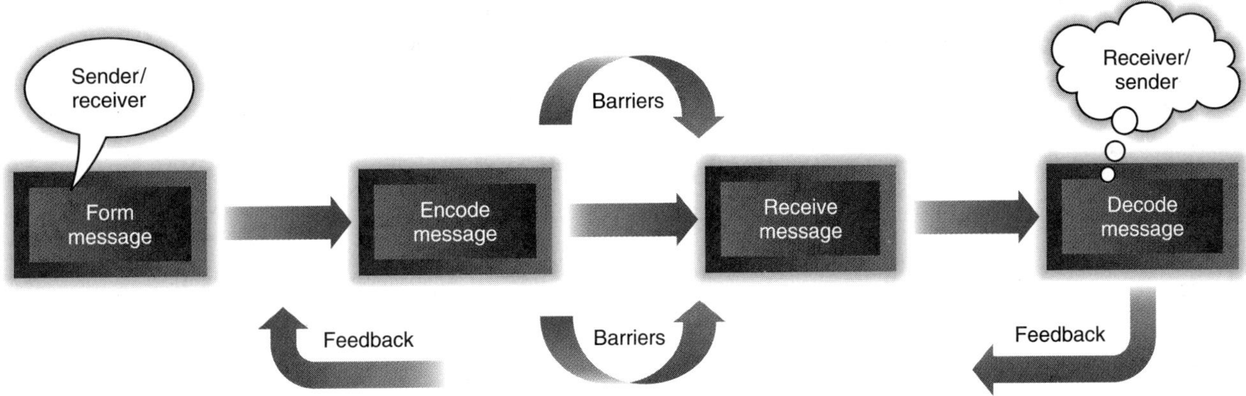

or her mind and then *encode* it into a message that can be transmitted. Messages can be encoded in words, gestures, pictures, sounds, etc. The *receiver* is the person receiving the message. The receiver must *receive* the message (i.e., be awake, not have a pillar blocking his or her view) and must then *decode* or understand the message, trying not to let barriers such as perceptual filters or the status of the sender distort the decoding.[10] These *barriers* and others are sometimes called *noise* and are discussed in detail in the section that follows.

The **message** contains the thoughts and feelings that the communicator intends to evoke in the receiver. The message has two primary components. The thought or conceptual component of the message (its content) is contained in the words, ideas, symbols, and concepts chosen to relay the message. The feeling or emotional component of the message (its affect) is contained in the intensity, force, and sometimes the gestures (in a face-to-face situation) of the communicator. The feeling component gives the message its full meaning. **Feedback** is any information that people receive about their behaviour or performance, its effect on others, or comparison to a standard or expectation. Feedback occurs when the receiver provides the communicator with a verbal and/or nonverbal response to the message, resulting in the original sender becoming the receiver and the original receiver becoming the sender. So, while visually the model depicts a one-way flow of information from sender to receiver, in fact, the communication is a transaction. This means that each person communicating is both a sender and a receiver simultaneously, not merely a sender or a receiver. As you speak, you receive mostly nonverbal feedback from listeners and this, in turn, influences the messages you continue to send.[11] Nonverbal communication is now discussed in more depth.

message
The thoughts and feelings that the communicator is attempting to elicit in the receiver.

feedback
Any information that people receive about their behaviour or performance, its effect on others, or comparison to a standard or expectation.

Knowledge & Application

THE CONSEQUENCES OF INEFFECTIVE VERBAL COMMUNICATION

Think about a time that you had a manager, teacher, or coach who was an expert in his or her field but was an ineffective verbal communicator. What were the consequences to you and the other senders and receivers he or she had to deal with?

NONVERBAL COMMUNICATION

Describe and give examples of the following four types of nonverbal communication: kinesics, speech variations (paralanguage), facial and eye behaviour, and use of interpersonal space (proxemics).

nonverbal communication
All elements of communication that do not involve words.

Nonverbal communication includes all elements of communication that do not involve words. Studies reveal that most of the meaning in a message is conveyed through nonverbal communication rather than through the words themselves.[12] As shown in Exhibit 6.2, words only communicate approximately 7 percent of the meaning that a receiver decodes from a message. About 38 percent comes from the tone of voice and 55 percent comes from other nonverbal cues. Also, research has shown that we tend to trust nonverbal communication more than we trust words. Do you think the man in Exhibit 6.2 is telling the truth?

Nonverbal communication includes tone of voice, pitch, loudness, body language, gestures, and laughs. As shown in Exhibit 6.3, researchers have divided these behaviours into four dimensions, which are kinesics (body movements,) facial and eye behaviour, variations in speech (paralanguage), and a person's use of interpersonal space (proxemics).

EXHIBIT 6.2

The Importance of Nonverbal Communication

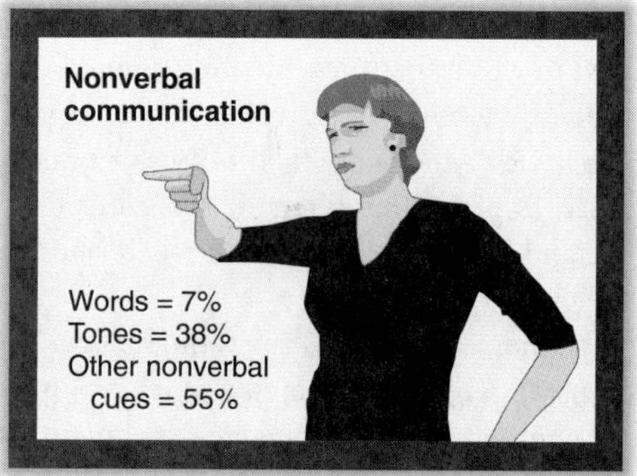

EXHIBIT 6.3

Four Dimensions of Nonverbal Communication

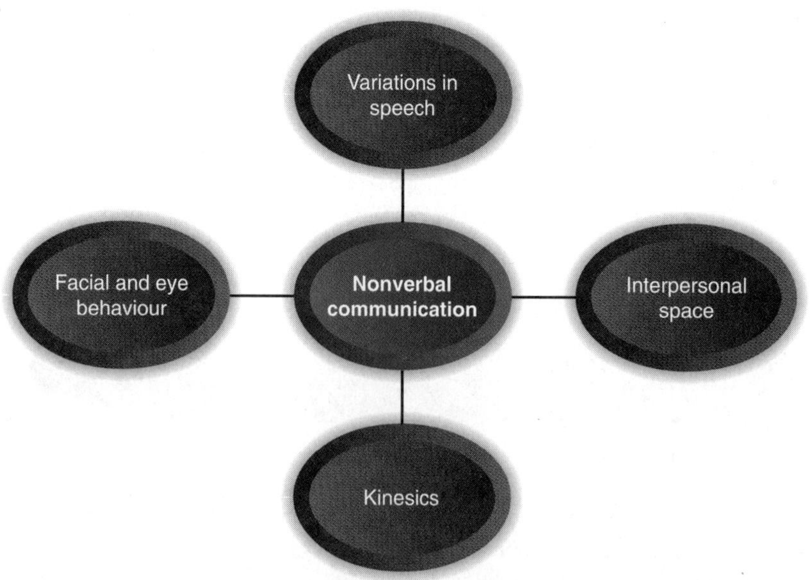

Kinesics

Kinesics is the study of body movements, including posture.[13] Kinesics is culturally bound and there are no gestures that are interpreted in the same way in all cultures. For example, the Canadian hand signal for "okay" is an insult in other countries. With this in mind, we can interpret some common Canadian gestures. Rubbing one's hands together or exhibiting a sharp intake of breath indicates anticipation. Stress is indicated by a closed hand position (that is, tight fists), hand wringing, or rubbing the temples. Nervousness may be exhibited through drumming fingers, pacing, or jingling coins in the pocket.

kinesics
The study of body movements, including posture.

Facial and Eye Behaviour

The face is a rich source of nonverbal communication. Facial expression and eye behaviour are used to sense others' emotional states. This is a skill that is central to effective interpersonal communication and also forms part of what is described as **emotional intelligence (EQ),** which is the ability to recognize and manage emotion in oneself and in others.[14] EQ is discussed in more depth in OBXtra 2, entitled "Emotional Intelligence." Even though six facial expressions seem to be universal across cultures (happiness, fear, sadness, surprise, anger, and disgust), eye contact and other facial expressions, such as frowns, raised eyebrows, and wrinkled foreheads, must all be interpreted in conjunction with the actors, the situation, and the culture. For example, while in Canada eye contact indicates honesty and forthrightness, this may not be true in other cultures. In Libya, for example, it is a serious offence to look directly at a woman.[15] See Exhibit 6.4 for some typical Canadian interpretations of nonverbal cues.

emotional intelligence (EQ)
The ability to recognize and manage emotion in one's self and in others.

Speech Variations (Paralanguage)

Speech variations (also called paralanguage) include pitch, loudness, tempo, tone, duration, laughing, and crying.[16] People often make inaccurate attributions about the sender when deciphering voice cues. For example, a high-pitched, breathy voice in a female may contribute to the stereotype of the "dumb blonde." Rapid, loud speech may be taken as a sign of nervousness or anger. Interruptions such as "Mmm" and "Ah-hah" may be used to speed up the speaker so that the receiver can get in a few words. Clucking of the tongue or the "Tsk-tsk" sound is used to shame someone. All these are used by the receiver to decipher meaning.

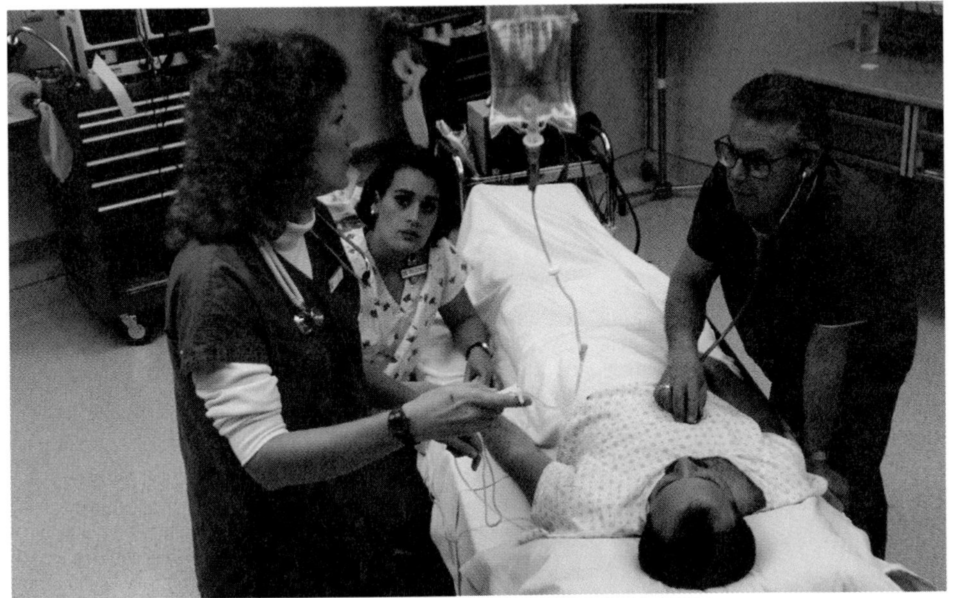

Direct eye contact helps improve communication, especially in hospital settings where miscommunication can have disastrous results.

EXHIBIT 6.4

Common Reactions to Nonverbal Cues in North America

Nonverbal Communication	Signal Received	Reaction from Receiver
Manager looks away when talking to the employee.	Divided attention.	My supervisor is too busy to listen to my problem or simply does not care.
Manager fails to acknowledge greeting from fellow employee.	Unfriendliness.	This person is unapproachable.
Manager glares ominously (i.e., gives the evil eye).	Anger.	Reciprocal anger, fear, or avoidance, depending on who is sending the signal in the organization.
Manager rolls the eyes.	Not taking person seriously.	This person thinks he or she is smarter or better than I am.
Manager sighs deeply.	Disgust or displeasure.	My opinions do not count. I must be stupid or boring to this person.
Manager uses heavy breathing (sometimes accompanied by hand waving).	Anger or heavy stress.	Avoid this person at all costs.
Manager does not maintain eye contact when communicating.	Suspicion or uncertainty.	What does this person have to hide?
Manager crosses arms and leans away.	Apathy or closed-mindedness.	This person already has made up his or her mind; my opinions are not important.
Manager continues to read a report when employee is speaking.	Lack of interest.	My opinions are not important enough to get the supervisor's undivided attention.

SOURCE: C. Hamilton and B. H. Kleiner, "Steps to Better Listening," *Personnel Journal*. Copyright © February 1987. Reprinted with permission, Personnel Journal. All rights reserved.

Use of Interpersonal Space (Proxemics)

Another key aspect of nonverbal communication is a person's individual's perception and use of interpersonal space, including territorial space.[17] The study of interpersonal space across cultures is called proxemics. People often become uncomfortable when operating in territorial spaces different from those in which they are familiar. Personal space tends to be larger in cultures with cool climates, such as Canada, Great Britain, and Northern Europe, and smaller in cultures with warm climates, such as southern Europe, the Caribbean, India, or South America.[18]

Application & Analysis

DISTANCE MAKES A DIFFERENCE

1. Choose a partner, go to opposite sides of the room, and face each other.
2. Very slowly begin walking toward each other while carrying on a conversation. You might simply talk about how you feel as you follow the activity. As you move closer, try to be aware of any change in your feelings. Continue moving slowly toward each other until you are only a few centimetres apart. Remember how you feel at this point.
3. Now, while still facing each other, back up until you're at a comfortable distance for carrying on the conversation.
4. Share your feelings with each other and/or the whole class.

SOURCE: R. Adler, N. Towne, and J. A. Rolls, *Looking Out/Looking In,* 1st Can. ed. Copyright © 2001. Reprinted by permission of Nelson, a division of Thomson Learning, www.thomsonrights.com. Fax 800-730-2215.

BARRIERS TO COMMUNICATION

Describe the following barriers to communication: perceptual screens, language and jargon, status differences, filtering, and gender and cultural differences.

As the old saying goes, "What *can* be misunderstood *will* be misunderstood!" What this implies is that, all too often, barriers get in the way of successful transmission of a message. **Barriers to communication** are factors that block or significantly distort successful communication. Some of the potential communication barriers are interpersonal and some are organizational. Barriers can occur at transmission (as shown in Exhibit 6.5) but can also exist at the forming, encoding, and decoding phases of the process. There are a great number of potential interpersonal and organizational barriers, and we focus on

barriers to communication
Factors that block or significantly distort successful communication.

EXHIBIT 6.5

Barriers to Communication

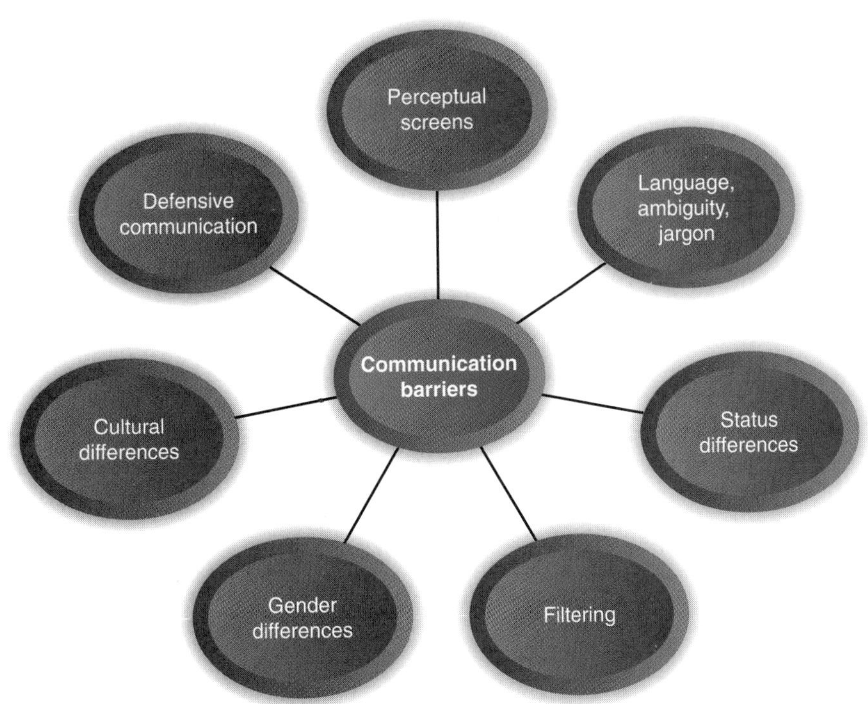

some of the most common, as outlined in Exhibit 6.5. These communication barriers are perceptual screens, language and jargon, status differences and filtering, gender and cultural differences, and defensiveness.

Barrier: Perceptual Screens

perceptual screens
The windows through which we interact with people in the world.

Trados
Trados (formerly Uniscape) is one of the pioneers of e-business globalization services, enabling international companies to launch successful enterprises in markets around the world. Visit the company's website to learn more about the challenges businesses face in communicating their messages and brands effectively across cultural and language barriers. How do Trados's products and services help businesses overcome communication challenges?
http://www.trados.com

Barriers to social perception were discussed in depth in Chapter 3. These barriers (stereotyping, selective perception, first impression error, projection, self-fulfilling prophecies and attributions) are also barriers to communication, and we refer to them as perceptual screens. **Perceptual screens** are the windows through which we interact with people in the world and are composed of the individual factors each person brings, such as age, gender, values, beliefs, past experiences, cultural influences, and individual needs. The communicator's and the receiver's perceptual screens influence the quality, accuracy, and clarity of the message. The screens influence whether the message sent and the message received are the same or whether distortion occurs in the process. For example, if a manager has a perceptual screen whereby he or she believes that older workers tend to resist change more than younger workers, the manager may make erroneous selection or promotion decisions. The effects of these screens are minimized when one is aware of one's needs, beliefs and biases and is therefore able to take actions that minimize their impact on one's judgments.

Barriers: Language, Ambiguity, and Jargon

Language is a central element in communication. It may pose a barrier if its use obscures meaning and distorts intent. When the native languages of supervisors and employees differ, the risk of barriers to communication exists. Less obvious are subtle distinctions in dialects within the same language, which may cause confusion and miscommunication. In a different vein, language barriers are created across disciplines and professional boundaries by technical terminology, and use of jargon may only serve to confuse, obscure, and derail any attempt at clear understanding for people unfamiliar with their meaning and usage. Use of jargon in the medical profession, for example, is being recognized as increasingly problematic. For example, younger doctors sometimes use terms they learned in medical school, like "reactive airways" instead of "asthma." Interestingly, recent statistics revealed that just over 67 percent of complaints heard by the Canadian College of Physicians and Surgeons dealt with communication problems, not medical competency.[19]

Barriers: Status Differences and Filtering

filtering
Deleting, delaying, or softening negative information as it moves up the hierarchy, so that it sounds more favourable.

Status differences related to the organizational hierarchy create another barrier to communication among people at work, especially within manager–employee pairs.[20] David Morand's research suggests that employees and their supervisors tend to modify their language based on the perceived status of the other person.[21] **Filtering** is deleting, delaying, or softening negative information as it moves up the hierarchy, so that it sounds more favourable. Because the employee is dependent on the manager as the primary link to the organization, the employee is more likely to distort, soften, or filter upward communication than either horizontal or downward communication.

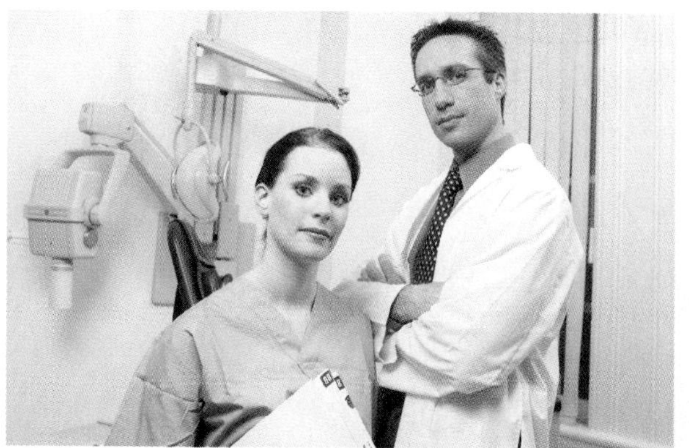

Effective communication skills between a physician and a nurse can help minimize the potential barriers of status differences and filtering.

When people at lower organizational levels fear sending bad news up to higher levels, information that is sensitive and critical to organizational performance may be lost. Deborah Tannen, a sociolinguist who has done extensive research on linguistic styles, refers to an incident in which a more junior co-pilot filtered his concern to the more senior pilot regarding ice buildup on the plane. Because of status difference between them, the co-pilot filtered his concern and did not express it as clearly or assertively as he might have with someone of equal status. As a result, the plane crashed.[22] Since that incident, some airlines now offer training programs for co-pilots to express themselves in more assertive ways. In addition to communications training to overcome the status barriers, effective supervisory skills can make the supervisor more approachable and help reduce the risk of problems related to status differences. New information technologies also provide another way to overcome status-difference barriers, because they make information more widely accessible to lower-level employees.[23]

Barrier: Gender Differences in Communication

Research into linguistic styles suggests a few interesting differences in the way males and females communicate, even though some researchers have been criticizing the validity of this research and argue, for example, that it is often status rather than gender that may account for the differences observed.[24] Some of the observed gender differences are as follows: First, in studies with children it was found that girls tend to focus more on the rapport-building dimensions of relationships, while boys tend to focus on the status dimensions.[25] Second, men and women have different conversational styles,[26] and women at work are more likely to downplay their certainty, while men at work are more likely to minimize their doubts. Third, women are less likely than men to be direct when telling others what to do.[27] Finally, it seems that individuals prefer to self-disclose and seek support from same—rather than opposite—gender friends.[28] Recognizing these gender differences in communication, some organizations send high-potential female managers for communications training. For example, since 1992 Carleton University's Centre for Research and Education on Women at Work, in Ottawa, has been offering a program that teaches management and communications skills to women.[29]

Barrier: Cultural Differences in Communication

When people of different cultural backgrounds communicate with one another, what the receiver understands may not be the same as what the speaker means, and there is quite a variation in polite behaviour.[30] Interestingly though, there do seem to be six facial expressions that are universal across cultures. These are the expressions for happiness, fear, sadness, surprise, anger, and disgust.[31] Important international differences in work-related values do, however, exist between people in Canada and other nations.[32] Cultural differences such as individualism versus collectivism and power distance have implications for cross-cultural communication, and these were discussed in depth in Chapter 2.[33] Bernard Isautier is the former president and CEO of Calgary-based Hurricane Hydrocarbons Inc. They produce crude oil in Kazakhstan and he, like other international executives, has stated that effective cross-cultural communication is an essential ingredient for success in international markets.[34] Effective cross-cultural communication is particularly important when managers interview job applicants from other cultures, mainly due to the differing assumptions that the two people might have. Adam Kaminsky shares a typical example:

> "One job candidate is an outgoing engineer from Germany. In his interview he uses a formal tone and exhibits a very academic demeanour, because that is common courtesy in his native country. The manager who is conducting the interview immediately assumes that the candidate is too formal and inflexible to be right for the job and decides to hire the previous interview candidate, who opened the interview with a joke about the local hockey team."[35]

Cross-cultural communicators also need to understand the difference between high-context and low context cultures as outlined in Exhibit 6.6. **Low-context cultures** use

low-context cultures
Cultures that use language primarily to express thoughts, feelings, and ideas as clearly and logically as possible.

high-context cultures
Cultures that value language as a way to maintain social harmony.

language primarily to express thoughts, feelings, and ideas as clearly and logically as possible while **high-context cultures** value language as a way to maintain social harmony. Rather than upset others by speaking clearly, communicators in high-context cultures, like Asia and the Middle East, learn to discover meaning from the context in which a message is delivered. By contrast, communicators in low-context cultures, like Canada and Europe, tend to be more direct.[36] Cross-cultural sensitivity training, also discussed in Chapter 2, usually includes training in cross-cultural communication with particular attention to the differences in nonverbal communication, discussed earlier.

Describe the six characteristics of a defensive communication climate and illustrate how they create communication barriers.

Barrier: Defensive Communication Climate

A defensive communication climate at work creates huge barriers to effective communication. Jack Gibb's classic 1961 article on defensive communication is still useful and relevant. Defensive communicators tend to point the finger and come across as *evaluative* rather than descriptive.[37] They also tend to use language that is *controlling*, saying, "Do this. Do that!" rather than defining problems and then discussing them, saying, "Let's talk about how to fix this." In general, honest and spontaneous communication creates less defensiveness than communication that is *strategic or manipulative*, although clearly it is often beneficial, before speaking, to determine whether it will help or hinder the relationship. Defensive communicators tend to be *neutral and indifferent* rather than being empathic, and they often talk in ways that appear *superior* by putting other people down and make them feel inferior. Finally, defensive communicators come across as *overly certain* and dogmatic and have trouble saying "I don't know." See Exhibit 6.7 for an overview of the six characteristics of a defensive communication climate.

Defensive communication in organizations can lead to a wide range of problems, including injured feelings, communication breakdowns, alienation in working relationships, destructive and retaliatory behaviours, nonproductive efforts, and problem-solving failures. When such problems arise in organizations, everyone is prone to blame everyone else for what is not working.[38]

Defensive communication climates are not limited to the workplace. Unfortunately, many families and classrooms are characterized by defensive communication climates in which those with higher status, like parents or older siblings, exhibit one or more of the characteristics. These defensive communication climates are especially damaging to young children and inexperienced or insecure employees.

EXHIBIT 6.6

Low- and High-Context Communication Styles

Low Context	High Context
Majority of information carried in explicit verbal messages, with less focus on the situational context.	Important information carried in contextual cues (time, place, relationship, and situation). Less reliance on explicit verbal messages.
Self-expression valued. Communicators state opinions and desires directly and strive to persuade others to accept their own viewpoint.	Relational harmony valued and maintained by indirect expression of opinions. Communicators abstain from saying "no" directly.
Clear, eloquent speech considered praiseworthy. Verbal fluency admired.	Communicators talk "around" the point, allowing the other to fill in the missing pieces. Ambiguity and use of silence admired.

SOURCE: R. B. Adler and N. Towne, *Looking Out/Looking In,* 10th ed. (New York: Harcourt Brace, 1999), 221. Copyright © 2002. Reprinted by permission of Wadsworth, a division of Thomson Learning, www.thomsonrights.com. Fax 800-730-2215.

EXHIBIT 6.7

Characteristics of a Defensive Communication Climate

Evaluation	The supervisor is critical and judgmental and will not accept explanations from subordinates.
Control	The supervisor constantly directs in an authoritarian manner, and attempts to change other people.
Strategy	The supervisor manipulates subordinates and often misrepresents or twists and distorts what is said.
Neutrality	The supervisor offers minimal personal support for and remains indifferent to employees' personal problems and conflicts.
Superiority	The supervisor reminds employees who are in charge, closely oversees the work, and makes employees feel inadequate.
Certainty	The supervisor is dogmatic and unwilling to admit making mistakes.

SOURCE: J. R. Gibb, "Defensive Communication," *Journal of Communication* 11 (1961): 143. Reprinted by permission of Oxford University Press.

Defensive communicators tend to point the finger and come across as evaluative rather than descriptive.

IMPLICATIONS FOR LIFE

Communication in a Student House

The material in this chapter has implications for life at work, at home, and at school. Imagine, for example, that you recently had a falling out with a housemate about keeping the house clean and the dishes washed.

Barriers to Communication

- *Perceptual screen:* This barrier reflects the windows through which we interact with people in the world. This may be a barrier if one of your housemates has had a previous experience in which a roommate did not do his or her fair share of cleanup. This may cause him to want to implement a very rigid cleanup schedule, which may be resisted by the other housemates.
- *Status differences:* Might cause a barrier if the messy housemate was the one who signed the lease with the landlord and decided who was going to live there.
- *Filtering:* Because of the perceived higher status of the messy housemate, you and the others might filter your concerns at first, not wanting to make her mad, and not tell her how much her failure to do her share of the cleanup bothers you,
- *Cultural differences:* Or, some of you might be from a high-context culture in which explicit verbal confrontation is discouraged and opinions are expressed indirectly.
- *Defensiveness:* Finally, one of you might express your concern to her openly but in a way that is evaluative and causing her to become defensive and aggressive.

Describe in detail three strategies for improving interpersonal communication: active listening, supportive communication, and effective feedback.

STRATEGIES FOR EFFECTIVE INTERPERSONAL COMMUNICATION

Now that we have explored some of the possible barriers to communication, we review a few of the strategies that have been found to help individuals significantly improve the effectiveness of their interpersonal communication. The good news is that effective interpersonal communication requires a set of skills, and these skills can be mastered over time, at home and at work. The bad news is that in order to improve one's interpersonal communication skills, it takes time, practice, feedback, and a genuine interest in becoming a better communicator and more self-aware. All of the approaches work better when you take the time to first explore and admit to yourself your assumptions and biases, so that you can open yourself up to hearing what the other person has to communicate. There are three general approaches to improving interpersonal communication. These are active listening, supportive communication, and effective feedback

Active Listening

active listening
A process that goes beyond passively absorbing a speaker's words. It consists of hearing, attending, understanding, responding, and remembering.

One of the key skills for effective interpersonal communication is active listening. **Active listening** is a process that goes beyond passively absorbing a speaker's words. It consists of hearing, attending, understanding, responding, and remembering.[39] Active listeners are able to hear the feelings and emotional dimensions of the messages people send them, as well as the content of the ideas and issues. "Listening involves not only the ears, but also mind, eyes and body."[40] This kind of listening emphasizes two-way rather than one-way communication, putting emphasis on the feedback loop of the communication process model. This means that active listeners do not do all the talking, they take turns speaking, and they avoid interrupting.[41] Active listening can be accomplished through a number of different strategies. We discuss four of them here, as outlined in Exhibit 6.8.

Take a few minutes to evaluate your own active listening skills using Self-Assessment 6.1. Studies indicate that all employees spend as much as one-third of their working hours involved in listening. For top executives, that proportion escalates to almost two-thirds of the work day.[42] Derek Burney, president and CEO of the Canadian company Corel Corporation, says he looks for active listening skills when he hires people: "I look for someone who can listen and take part in a conversation and not have judgments rolling into it."[43]

EXHIBIT 6.8

Active Listening Strategies

Active Listening	
You show interest	You show interest as a listener by maintaining eye contact and affirming the talker. You use simple statements like "I see" and "Uh-huh" and "Yes, I understand."
You paraphrase	You actively listen by paraphrasing what you hear. For example, "So what you're saying is ...?"
You reflect back the speaker's implicit thoughts or feelings	You actively listen for the deeper feelings being expressed by the speaker. You reflect these back as you understand them. For example, "It sounds as if you are really fed up with school."
You ask sincere, open-ended questions	You ask questions like, "Can you tell me more about that?" to help you better understand.

SOURCES: R. B. Adler, N. Towne, and J. A. Rolls, *Looking Out/Looking In,* 1st Can. ed. (Toronto: Harcourt, 2001), 290; D. A. Whetten and K. S. Cameron, *Developing Management Skills,* 5th ed. (Upper Saddle River, NJ: Prentice Hall, 2002), 232.

Application & Analysis

SELF-ASSESSMENT 6.1: ARE YOU AN ACTIVE LISTENER?

Think of the last time you had a difficult communication with someone at work, home or school and jot down a few notes about that incident. Then use the rating scale below to evaluate your active listening in that situation.

Rating Scale

6 = Strongly agree; 5 = Agree; 4 = Slightly agree; 3 = Slightly disagree; 2 = Disagree; 1 = Strongly disagree

1. I **showed interest** by keeping eye contact and saying things like "Uh-huh" and "I see."	6 5 4 3 2 1
2. I **paraphrased** often. This means that when I wasn't sure, I repeated back what I thought I heard to check for accuracy and to show that I was listening.	6 5 4 3 2 1
3. I went beyond paraphrasing and also empathized by **reflecting back the core feelings** that I was sensing in the message.	6 5 4 3 2 1
4. I encouraged two-way communication by **asking sincere questions,** by **not interrupting,** and by **giving the person time to talk.**	6 5 4 3 2 1

For scoring instructions, please go to the end of the chapter, p. 195.

SOURCE: Adapted from model in David A. Whetten and Kim S. Cameron, *Developing Management Skills*, 6th ed. (Upper Saddle River, NJ: Prentice Hall, 2005), 216. Adapted by permission of Pearson Education, Inc., Upper Saddle River, NJ.

Showing Interest

Active listeners show interest use verbal and nonverbal affirmations. The purpose of an affirmation is to communicate attentiveness, not necessarily agreement. Verbal affirmations include simple statements such as "I see," "Uh-huh," and "Yes, I understand." As discussed earlier in the chapter, eye contact is a nonverbal affirmation that may help open up a relationship and improve communication between two people.

Paraphrasing

After an appropriate time, active listeners paraphrase the speaker's message to check for understanding and show the receiver that he or she was listening. Paraphrasing is also useful because it serves as feedback to the speaker and reflects back the speaker's expressed message the way the receiver heard it. Paraphrasing usually starts with the statement, "So what you're saying is ..." or "It sounds like ..." or "What I'm hearing you say is ..."

Reflecting with Empathy

People often communicate subtle or implied thoughts and feelings in addition to what they express out loud. A good active listener has **empathy,** which is the ability to understand and be sensitive to someone else's feelings and thoughts. He or she can pick up on the deeper message and reflect it back to the speaker, thereby helping the speaker to clarify his or her thoughts and become more aware. This is called reflective listening.[44] For example, an employee may be anxious about how to talk with a difficult customer concerning a problem. This may be implicit in his discussion with his supervisor because of the previous discussions about this customer. If his feelings of anxiety are not expressed, the supervisor may want to clarify them using reflection. For example, the supervisor might say, "It sounds as if you may be worried about the customer's reaction when you inform him." This might help the employee shift the focus of his attention

empathy
Understanding and being sensitive to someone else's feelings and thoughts.

from the main problem, which is in the software, to the issue of discussing the matter with the customer. It may also give the listener a better perspective on the situation. However, if a secure, empathetic relationship with the speaker does not already exist, the listener runs a risk of overreaching or creating defensiveness. Even if the listener is correct, the speaker may not want those feelings brought to awareness. Therefore, it is important to exercise caution and care in reflecting core feelings to a speaker.[45]

Asking Sincere Open-Ended Questions

counterfeit questions
Disguised attempts to send a message, not receive one.

Sincere and open-ended questioning is a key component of active listening. Despite their apparent benefits, not all questions are equally helpful. Examples of sincere open-ended questions are: "Can you explain what you mean by…?" and "How did you feel when he said that?" The opposite of sincere questions are called **counterfeit questions,** which are really disguised attempts to *send* a message, not receive one.[46] Examples of counterfeit questions are questions that trap a speaker, like "You didn't like that movie, did you?" and negative questions that make statements, like "Did you forget to mail the package I gave you?" Here is another example of a counterfeit question, set in a context (in italics) that leads to a defensive response on the part of the responder:

> For example, Elizabeth, in her late 20s, is happy to be making Thanksgiving dinner for her extended family in her own home. Her mother, who is visiting, is helping out in the kitchen. As Elizabeth prepares the homemade stuffing for the turkey, her mother remarks, *"Oh, you put onions in the stuffing?"* Feeling suddenly as if she were 16 again, Elizabeth turns on her mother and says, "I'm making the stuffing, Mom. Why do you have to criticize everything I do?" "I didn't criticize," her mother says, "I asked a question. What's got into you? I can't even open my mouth."[47]

Supportive Communication

supportive communication
Communication that addresses the problem at hand while seeking to preserve a positive relationship between the communicators.

Supportive communication (also referred to as nondefensive communication) is communication that addresses the problem at hand while seeking to preserve a positive relationship between the communicators.[48] When communicators are supportive, people are

EXHIBIT 6.9

Four Attributes of Supportive Communication

Supportive Communication	Example
You focus on the problem, not on personal traits.	You say, "Our relationship is deteriorating" rather than "You are insensitive."
Your communication is specific, not global.	Instead of saying, "You are always late," you would tend to say, "You have been late for the last three meetings."
You own your statements and feelings about someone else's actions.	You use "I" statements rather than "we" or "they." For example, instead of saying, "The group feels you are not contributing," you would say, "It makes me angry when you remain silent at our meetings."
Congruence: Your words and body language match your thoughts and feelings.	For example, if something is bothering you and you are asked, "What's wrong?" you will express what is wrong, rather than saying, "Nothing, I'm fine!"

SOURCE: Adapted from David A. Whetten and Kim S. Cameron, *Developing Management Skills,* 6th ed. (Upper Saddle River, NJ: Prentice Hall, 2005), 216. Adapted by permission of Pearson Education, Inc., Upper Saddle River, NJ.

less likely to have adverse responses, such as blame and anger.[49] As described earlier and shown in Exhibit 6.7, communicators create defensiveness in receivers when they are evaluative, controlling, strategic, neutral, superior, or overly certain. Drawn from this model are a number of attributes of supportive communication, four of which are shown in Exhibit 6.9 and discussed here. These are: (1) focusing on the problem rather than the person, (2) using specific rather than global language, (3) taking responsibility for (owning) your communications, and (4) matching your words and your body language to what you are thinking and feeling (congruence).

Focusing on the Problem Rather Than the Person

In supportive communication it is important not to point the finger or attack personal traits, which often cannot be changed. For example, instead of saying, "You have a bad attitude," it is better to refer to the other person's observable behaviour or verbatim statements in clean, neutral words and sentences like: "When you failed to reprimand employees…," "I get confused when you do not speak up in meetings," "It was embarrassing when you told Joe he was an idiot yesterday in front of his employees." Avoid mentioning intrinsic or personality-based attributes like "lazy" or "rude." For example, you might say: "The dishes were left unwashed in the sink last night and I had to clean up," instead of "You are lazy and messy!" To be a supportive communicator, when in a conflict, it helps enormously to shift our perception from thinking there is something wrong with the other person, to observing that we do not like something they are doing or saying.[50] Converting a person focus to a problem or behaviour focus allows us to disengage emotionally and become more objective.[51]

Using Specific, Not Global, Language

Global language—language that is general, extreme, absolute, or vague—is more likely to create defensiveness in the other person than is specific language. Here are a few examples comparing specific with global language: (1) A supervisor might say, "I liked the way you asked the customer what she was looking for" (specific), rather than "Good job!" (global). (2) If you say, 'Last night you left your dishes in the sink and I had to clean up" (specific), it would be better than if you said, "You always leave your dishes in the sink and I had to clean up" (global). Even if the latter is true, the person is more likely to listen to you when you use the more specific statement because it avoids extremes and absolutes.[52]

Taking Responsibility for (Owning) One's Communication

owning communication
Taking responsibility for one's statements and acknowledging that the source of the ideas is oneself and not the other person or group.

Owning communication is taking responsibility for one's statements and acknowledging that the source of the ideas is oneself and not another person or group.[53] Own your feelings by making "I" statements and describe your own emotional response to the person's behaviour with words for actual feelings ("angry," "worried," "disappointed"). For example, perhaps you are upset with a teammate for continually being late for group meetings. Owning your communication, you would say, "It really bothers me when you show up late for our meetings after I have made an effort to be on time." Even if all group members are equally bothered by the behaviour, saying "*We* are upset when you show up late for meetings," is disowned communication and is more likely to make the teammate defensive.

Supportive communicators actively listen and address the problem at hand while seeking to preserve a positive relationship with the other person.

Application & Analysis

SELF-ASSESSMENT 6.2: ARE YOU A SUPPORTIVE COMMUNICATOR?

Think about the last time you had a difficult communication with someone at work, home, or school and, if you wish, use the same example that you used in Self-Assessment 6.1. Use the rating scale below to evaluate four attributes of your supportive communication in that situation.

Rating Scale

6 = Strongly agree; 5 = Agree; 4 = Slightly agree; 3 = Slightly disagree; 2 = Disagree; 1 = Strongly disagree

1. My communication **focused on the problem at hand** and not on the person's traits or characteristics. For example, I would have tended to say "Our relationship is deteriorating" rather than "You are insensitive." 6 5 4 3 2 1
2. I was **congruent**. My words and body language tended to match what I was thinking and feeling. For example, if something was bothering me and I was asked "What's wrong?" I would express what was wrong, rather than saying, "Nothing, I'm fine!" 6 5 4 3 2 1
3. My communications tended to be **specific** rather than global. For example, instead of saying, "You are always late," I would tend to say, "You have been late for the last three meetings." 6 5 4 3 2 1
4. I **owned** my communications rather than disowned them. I used "I" statements rather than "we" or "they." For example, instead of saying, "The group feels you are not contributing," I would say "I feel angry when you remain silent at our meetings." 6 5 4 3 2 1

For scoring instructions, please go to the end of the chapter, p. 195.

SOURCE: Adapted from model in David A. Whetten and Kim S. Cameron, *Developing Management Skills,* 6th ed. (Upper Saddle River, N.J.: Prentice Hall, 2005), 216. Adapted by permission of Pearson Education, Inc., Upper Saddle River, N.J.

Matching Verbal and Nonverbal Communication with One's Thoughts and Feelings (Congruence)

congruent communication
Communicating verbally and nonverbally exactly what a person is thinking and feeling.

Most researchers and observers agree that the best interpersonal communications, and the best relationships, are based on congruence.[54] **Congruent communication** is when a person communicates verbally and nonverbally exactly what he or she is thinking and feeling.[55] As you learned in the section about nonverbal communication, only 7 percent of the meaning of the message actually comes from the words themselves. We trust the nonverbal message more than we do the verbal so when there is a mismatch, misunderstanding and defensiveness can result. This mismatch is referred to as "incongruence." An example of incongruent communication is if a friend seems angry and you ask, "Hey, what's wrong?" and he says, "Nothing, I'm fine," but he is clenching his fists or his tone of voice is angry. Here, there is an obvious mismatch between his words and body language. Sometimes this type of incongruence is called "masking emotions."[56] While it may, at times, be appropriate to mask emotions or to choose to be incongruent, more often incongruence is unintentional and one is unaware of the mixed messages one is giving. This then becomes a barrier to interpersonal communication, especially in relationships that are important.

CAN YOU SPOT DEFENSIVE COMMUNICATION?

Read the following interchange between a boss and subordinate and evaluate and label all the examples you can find of active listening and supportive and defensive communication.

Boss: "You idiot! Now you've ruined our chances at getting Xantex's business. We all told you your idea would never work, but you had to go and do it anyway. You're always trying to do things your own way instead of following company policy."

Subordinate: "I'm really sorry, I would be just as mad if I were ..."

Boss: "It's too late now. We've just lost a potential $500 000 sale."

Subordinate: "I feel terrible about what I did but I still think I can save the deal if you give me a chance."

Boss: "You think you can save it?"

Subordinate: "Yes. Let's sit down with Barry and brainstorm all our options."

Effective Feedback

Thus far we have explored active listening and supportive communication as two of the important strategies for effective interpersonal communication. A third key strategy is effective feedback.[57] While giving someone positive feedback usually is not a problem, people often get defensive when getting negative feedback if it is not done properly. As shown in Exhibit 6.10, some of the characteristics of effective feedback (problem, not person oriented, specific, not global) relate to the attributes of supportive communication just discussed, but there are also a few additional characteristics that are important to remember when giving feedback to someone at work.

For example, it is important to make feedback constructive and balance the positive with the negative. Feedback should include active listening and be interactive with the person receiving it rather than one way. Also feedback needs to be timely, frequent, and given in an appropriate (private) setting. Finally, it is important to be clear on the purpose of the feedback. Use Self-Assessment 15.1 in Web Chapter 15 (Performance Management, Feedback, and Rewards) to assess your skills in giving someone feedback.

EXHIBIT 6.10

Characteristics of Effective Feedback

- Specific
- Timely
- Focus on problem, not person
- Frequent
- Constructive and balanced
- Purposeful
- Interactive
- In the appropriate setting

SOURCE: Adapted from S. de Janasz, K. O. Dowd, and B. Z. Schneider, *Interpersonal Skills in Organizations* (New York: McGraw-Hill Irwin, 2002), 126. Reproduced with permission of the McGraw-Hill Companies.

Explain the importance of effective organization-wide communication and give contemporary examples of downward and upward communication strategies.

EFFECTIVE ORGANIZATION-WIDE COMMUNICATION

Up to this point, we have discussed barriers to interpersonal communication and how to increase its effectiveness. While companies have to develop the interpersonal communication skills of their managers, to be successful they must also ensure effective and timely organization-wide communication up and down the hierarchy. About 20 percent of communication problems that harm the organization and drain profitability can be prevented or solved by communication policy guidelines.[59] In fact, a 2003 Watson Wyatt study suggested that companies with the most effective employee communication programs provided a 26 percent total return to shareholders (TRS) from 1998–2002 compared to a 15 percent TRS experienced by firms that communicate least effectively. The researchers also propose that a significant improvement in communication effectiveness is associated with a nearly 30 percent increase in market value, as well as a positive impact on reducing employee turnover.[60] According to the study, effective organization-wide communication drives superior performance for at least four reasons:[61] (1) Employees feel connected to the business and understand their role. (2) New employees connect more quickly to the company culture. (3) Communication quickly connects employees to changing business challenges. (4) Management connects with employees during organizational change.

Communicating Up and Down the Hierarchy

In order for organizations to achieve their current and future business objectives, they need to deliver consistent and clear messages to all parts and levels of the organization, be able to hear the voices of their employees, and encourage dialogue across the organization.[62] Recent developments in organizational design also have had a big impact in improving organization-wide and interdepartmental communication. Read more about these developments in Chapter 14.

Downward Communication

downward communication
Communication that flows from one level of a group or organization to a lower level.

Downward communication is communication that flows from one level of a group or organization to a lower level. Research and experience have shown that employees want to be kept informed. Traditional methods for downward communication are newsletters (written and electronic), memos, meetings, video broadcasts, company magazines, and manuals. Janssen-Ortho, Sears, Scotiabank, Manitoba Lotteries, Coast Capital Savings Credit Union, Canfor Corporation, FedEx, the Royal Canadian Mint, and the City of Waterloo are just a few of the many examples of Canadian companies that have invested heavily in organization-wide employee communication processes, and have reaped the benefits.

At Manitoba Lotteries Corporation, downward communication strategies are multifaceted. For example, key messages are delivered through an intranet employee website and "Food for Thought" lunch-and-learn sessions.[63] As well, interpersonal communication is included as one of the core competencies of supervisors and is assessed as part of the annual performance appraisal process.[64]

The Royal Canadian Mint has also introduced some innovative downward communication tools. They are using new technology to keep employees up to date with the latest HR news and issues. They also have an internal video system showing PowerPoint presentations in their company cafeteria.[65] Canfor Corporation, an integrated forest-products company based in Vancouver, British Columbia, has transformed its internal communications with the introduction of news-based iiDirect. Employees regularly check iiDirect to see what is happening in their industry.[66] Finally, Ontario Power Generation develops and shows quarterly "Report on Performance" videos that teach employees the language of finance while following the performance of the company.[67]

learning maps
A communication tool that uses pictures and other visuals to deliver key messages in a consistent manner while at the same time engaging employees.

A relatively new downward communication approach uses a tool called "learning maps." **Learning maps** use pictures and other images and facilitated group discussions to deliver key messages in a consistent manner while at the same time engaging employees.[68] Bank of Montreal, Scotiabank, and Inco are a few examples of companies using learning maps to improve downward communication. See Organizational Reality 6.1 for more information about Inco's use of learning maps.

Another recent development in employee communications is the emergence of communication champions through the organization. **Communication champions** are employees who take on communication responsibilities in addition to their regular responsibilities. In 2000, when a South African financial services organization was decentralized, the internal communication function was redesigned. Each division assigned a qualified employee to be the internal communications consultant, and each cost centre also democratically elected a person to act as the communications champion. As a result, an organization of about 34 000 employees had 680 communication champions in place to help improve trust and communication between employees and superiors.[69]

communication champions
Employees who take on communication responsibilities in addition to their regular responsibilities.

organizational reality 6.1

Learning Maps Improve Downward Communications at Inco

The tradition of the mining industry used to be called "mushroom management" by labour: *"Keep 'em in the dark and cover 'em with manure to keep 'em happy."* The less the employee knew about company operations—particularly financially—the better. How far the mining industry has progressed in overcoming this tradition can be seen in a downward communication initiative introduced at Inco in 2000. The initiative, called "Understanding our Business," uses "learning maps" to open the books to the rank and file and informs every employee in some detail about how the company is making its money.

The series of three learning maps, combined with workshops, cover everything from the history of the nickel business and the threats facing the industry to where Inco gets its money, what expenses are, and where potential snags and losses are. Although the learning maps resemble a board game designed to make learning interesting and fun, the figures are cold, hard, and real. "We use actual numbers that are updated on a quarterly basis," says Dorothy Cayen, the Ontario division's accounting manager. Asked why Inco decided to emphasize employee communication, Cayen said: "To remain a viable operation in the long term, we have to engage all our employees. It's the only way we will ever achieve our objectives."

SOURCE: J. Gast, "Management Opens Up in a New Program: Better Communications Resulting from Sessions," *Sudbury Star,* Sudbury, Ont., October 24, 2000, A11. Used by permission.

Many companies ensure that company-wide communication is effective by holding frequent all-staff meetings or town halls.

Upward Communication

upward communication Communication that flows to a higher level in the group or organization.

Upward communication is communication that flows to a higher level in the group or organization. As discussed in the earlier section on communication barriers, status differences often lead to filtering. If employees engage in silence or filtering and withhold their ideas and opinions, management loses critical feedback and the communication process breaks down. Unionized organizations have had formal upward communication processes called "grievance processes" for decades. As shown in Exhibit 6.11, organizations now use processes like employee surveys, suggestion boxes, employee hotlines, meetings/town halls, and multi-source feedback to improve upward communications.

Employee Surveys

In the 1980s many companies began to use anonymous employee attitude surveys to improve upward communications. Universities also utilize these upward communication tools when they ask students to complete course evaluation surveys. As you read in the opening vignette, Janssen-Ortho conducts their "Credo" survey regularly, to ensure that employee voices are heard. You can learn more about this organization development tool in Chapter 13.

Suggestion Boxes and Hotlines

Suggestion boxes have also become popular. The Toyota plant in Cambridge, Ontario, for example, has had huge successes with its suggestion program.[70] As well, telephone and electronic hotlines are used as suggestion boxes. For example, at Scotiabank, a toll-free telephone line called "Team Voice" provides employees with a direct feedback channel for upward communication.[71]

Meetings and Town Halls

Also popular in recent years are "town hall" meetings and workplace forums such as Manitoba Lotteries Corporation's TalK2us program, where employees have an opportunity to voice their concerns with management.[72] Another approach to upward communication is the "search conference." The search conference, which is also a large group organization development intervention, is discussed in Chapter 13. The City of Waterloo in Ontario conducts a search conference every year with 60 randomly selected employees, to hear employee voices.[73]

EXHIBIT 6.11

Upward Communication Strategies

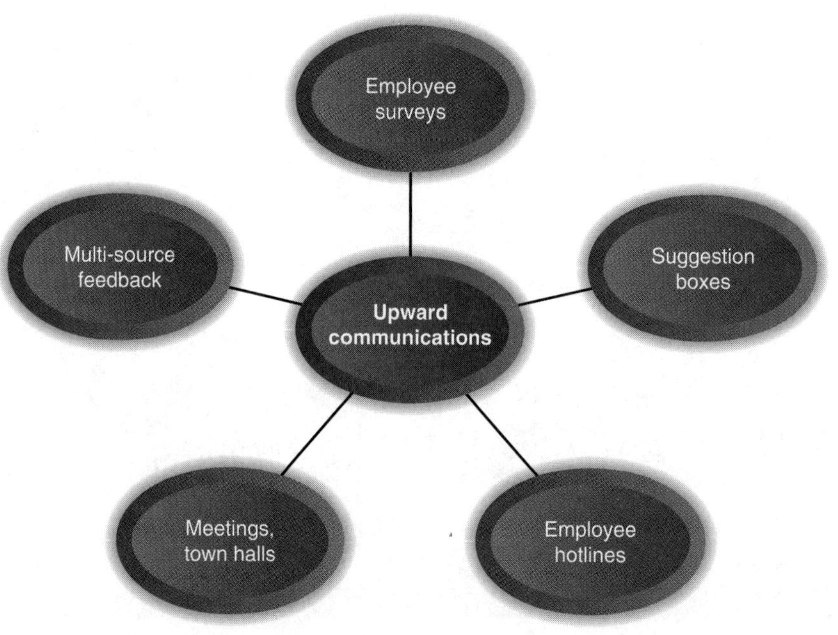

? Synthesis & Evaluation

DEVELOP A COMMUNICATION STRATEGY FOR THE STUDENT HOUSE

Using the information given in the "Implications for Life" feature about communication barriers in a student house, and the material in the chapter, make recommendations for improving both interpersonal and house-wide communications.

Multi-Source (360-degree) Feedback

Multi-source or **360-degree feedback**, whereby structured feedback is received from one's supervisor, subordinates, peers, and customers, is an effective and popular strategy for upward communication and performance management. Companies such as Rogers Communication, the Toronto-based University Health Network (UHN), FedEx, the Toronto Community Housing Corporation, and most major banks use multi-source feedback.[74]

multi-source (360-degree) feedback
Structured feedback received from supervisor, subordinates, peers, and customers.

Media Richness and Current Issues in Electronic Communication

Discuss the varying degrees of media richness in different communication vehicles and the current issues in electronic communication.

When trying to improve organization-wide communication, it is helpful to think about what channel is best suited to a message you want a receiver to understand. Communication channels, also called communication media, vary in the degree to which they can provide information richness. **Media richness** is defined as the amount and variety of information that a communication medium can carry.[75] Exhibit 6.12 compares different media with regard to data capacity and information richness.

media richness
The amount and variety of information that a communication medium can carry.

Electronic communication and especially e-mail has increased the amount of lateral and cross-functional communication. Research comparing e-mail to face-to-face communication found that the effects vary with the nature of the decisions, and may depend on the complexity and content of what needs to be communicated.[76] Thus, e-mail has strengths and advantages in communication as well as limitations with which to exercise caution. While new communication technologies obviously provide faster, more immediate

EXHIBIT 6.12

Communication Media: Information Richness and Data Capacity

Medium	Information Richness	Data Capacity
Face-to-face discussion	Highest	Lowest
Telephone	High	Low
Electronic mail	Moderate	Moderate
Individualized letter	Moderate	Moderate
Personalized note or memo	Moderate	Moderate
Formal written report	Low	High
Flyer or bulletin	Low	High
Formal numeric report	Lowest	Highest

SOURCE: Created by E. A. Gerloff from "Information Richness: A New Approach to Managerial Behavior and Organizational Design" by Richard L. Daft and R. H. Lengel in *Research in Organizational Behavior* 6 (1984): 191–233. Reprinted by permission of JAI Press Inc.

access to information than was available in the past, one negative aspect of electronic communication is its impersonal nature. Because of this, some people feel much less inhibited when using e-mail, and end up sending caustic messages they would never consider saying in person. This behaviour has come to be known as "flaming." MoodWatch, the software system described in Organizational Reality 6.2, helps guard against "flaming" e-mails.

Another effect of the new technologies is that because the important nonverbal cues we rely on to decipher messages are missing, the emotional element of the message is more difficult to access. In spite of this fact, according to a U.S. Accountemps survey in 2002, it was found that 92 percent of executives said managers often sent an e-mail message rather than meeting one-on-one, and 76 percent said they themselves used it as a substitute for face-to-face conversation.[77] Communication via e-mail also changes group interaction because group members participate more equally, and charismatic or higher-status members may have less power.[78] In addition, clues to power, such as organizational position and departmental membership, may not be available, so the social context of the exchange is altered. This problem is already being overcome in a number of companies through the use of videoconferencing technology, which allows face-to-face communication with people at distant locations. For example, Mercer Human Resource Consulting in the U.K. has installed 512 group videoconferencing systems in 15 of its offices across the country. Their Polycom system permits integrated voice, video, data, and web communications.[79]

Virtual teams are becoming more and more common, and at present, most do not have the enabling technology of videoconferencing. Issues specific to virtual teams are addressed in OBXtra 5, entitled "Managing in a Virtual World." Suffice it to say here that while communication and team dynamics are challenging when team members are all in one location, they are even more challenging when the team is a virtual one. Communicating in virtual teams requires extra efforts for a number of items, including the following: (1) ensuring the appropriate technology and computer skills are in place, (2) keeping databases current, (3) defining operating principles, (4) defining when a communication should be sent up the hierarchy, and (5) using the phone to clarify issues when necessary.[80]

organizational reality 6.2

MoodWatch Looks for "Flames" in E-Mail

While the new technology of e-mail has enhanced dramatically the ability to communicate volumes of information electronically, it has also opened the door for some employees to act in uninhibited ways, sending scorching missives called "flames" through the wires. David Kaufer, head of the English Department at Carnegie Mellon University, has worked to codify what constitutes a "flame." Vitriolic, hostile, abusive, and bullying e-mails are not common across the Internet, yet they do occur and may have devastating emotional impact on the receiver. Even if unintended, these missives can do psychological harm and damage. Hence, Kaufer has made an effort to develop a system that is essentially an emotional spell-checker and has been built into a popular e-mail program as a feature called MoodWatch.

MoodWatch is an interesting feature that is used while you write e-mails. While writing the e-mail, a tiny icon of an ice cube remains in the window as long as the language is good and positive. If you move toward "flame" territory, the ice cube turns into a chili pepper. If you keep going, you may get a second or third chili pepper in the window. Finally, if you try to send the message in that form, you get a warning: "Your message ... is the sort of thing that might get your keyboard washed out with soap." MoodWatch is an excellent assistant and complement for self-control.

SOURCES: T. E. Weber, "Worried Your E-Mail May Offend the Boss? Just Check It for Chilis," *The Wall Street Journal,* September 25, 2000, B1; *MoodWatch,* Computing at Cornell, http://www.cit.cornell.edu/computer/email/eudora/moodwatch.html.

Application & Evaluation

IS ELECTRONIC MONITORING ETHICAL?

Should employees be able to use company communication technologies for non-work communications? Should employers have access to employee e-mails and text messages? Is it ethical for them to have this access? Under what (if any) conditions would you support the practice of monitoring employee communications?

IMPLICATIONS FOR ORGANIZATIONAL EFFECTIVENESS

Effective communication is the glue that holds a company and its many stakeholders together. Not only must information be transmitted clearly, but these days it must also be done quickly and efficiently. While vehicles for information transmission have become more sophisticated and complex, when people need to work together to get things done it takes effective interpersonal communication and the ability to actively listen and minimize defensiveness. Enlightened organizations invest heavily in both the soft and hard elements of communication and believe that you can never communicate too often. They set up a number of company-wide communication technologies and processes for upward, downward, and lateral communication to make sure that employee voices can be heard. In this way, critical information is not lost and employees feel connected and empowered. They also train their managers to be supportive communicators and active listeners so that they can coach, counsel, and mentor their employees, as discussed in Chapter 4, and mediate and facilitate conflict, as will be discussed in Chapter 11.

Chapter Summary

1. Communication is critical to organizational effectiveness, and the main components of the communication process model are: a sender, a receiver, a channel, barriers, and a feedback loop, which makes the original sender also a receiver and the original receiver also a sender.
2. Nonverbal communication includes all elements of communication that do not involve words, such as kinesics, facial and eye behaviour, paralanguage, and proxemics.
3. A number of barriers to communication can interfere with its effectiveness. Five of these barriers are perceptual screens, language/jargon, gender and cultural differences in communication, and a defensive communication climate.
4. Defensive communication climates are characterized by communication that includes evaluation, control, strategy, neutrality, superiority, and certainty.
5. Three strategies for effective interpersonal communication are active listening, supportive communication, and effective feedback. Active listening includes showing interest, paraphrasing, reflecting back the speaker's implicit thoughts and feelings, and asking sincere open-ended questions. Supportive communication includes focusing on the problem rather than the personal traits of the other person, using specific rather than general language, taking responsibility for (owning) one's statements and feelings, and matching one's words to one's thoughts and feelings (congruence.) Effective feedback includes supportive communication as well as being balanced, timely, frequent, interactive, and given in an appropriate setting.
6. Organizations need to train their managers to be effective interpersonal communicators but also need to invest in organization-wide communication strategies. Downward

communication strategies include newsletters, memos, meetings, and manuals. Contemporary approaches include learning maps, communication champions, employee websites, internal video systems, and employee news sites. Upward communication strategies include suggestions boxes, open-door policies, attitude surveys, telephone and electronic hot lines, town hall meetings, workplace forums, search conferences, and multi-source (360-degree) feedback processes.

7. Communication channels such as face-to-face, telephone, and electronic mail have very different data capacities and potential for rich information. Lateral communication has been increased by the electronic communication, but e-mail can be impersonal and is weakened by the absence of nonverbal information.

Key Terms

active listening (p. 178)
barriers to communication (p. 173)
communication (p. 168)
communication champions (p. 185)
congruent communication (p. 182)
counterfeit questions (p. 180)
downward communication (p. 184)
emotional intelligence (EQ) (p. 171)
empathy (p. 179)
feedback (p. 169)
filtering (p. 174)
high-context cultures (p. 176)
kinesics (p. 171)
learning maps (p. 184)
low-context cultures (p. 175)
media richness (p. 187)
message (p. 169)
multi-source (360-degree) feedback (p. 187)
nonverbal communication (p. 170)
owning communication (p. 181)
perceptual screens (p. 174)
supportive communication (p. 180)
upward communication (p. 186)

Review Questions

1. What are the four components of active listening?
2. Compare and contrast supportive and defensive communication climates.
3. Give examples of effective downward and upward strategies for organization-wide communication.
4. Describe how gender and culture can lead to communication barriers.
5. Illustrate how a high-context communication style might make communication difficult for you in a new relationship.
6. Describe the six characteristics of a defensive communications climate.

Discussion and Communication Questions

1. With whom are you the most comfortable and nondefensive in conversation? What does the person do that makes you so comfortable or nondefensive?
2. What nonverbal behaviours do you find most helpful in others when you are attempting to talk with them? When you try to listen to them?
3. *(Communication question)* Identify a person at work or at the university who is difficult to talk to and arrange an interview in which you practise good reflective listening skills. Ask the person questions about a topic in which you think he or she is interested. Pay particular attention to being patient, calm, and nonreactive. After the interview, summarize what you learned.

Ethics Questions

1. Suppose that you have heard informally that one of your best friends at work is going to be fired. Should you tell your friend or not? If yes, how would you communicate it?
2. Assume you are a good, empathetic listener. Someone at work confides in you concerning wrongdoing, yet does not ask your advice about what to do. Should you tell the person what to do? Encourage the person to confess? Report the person?
3. If you had access to a competitor's internal communication system, would you use that information to achieve competitive advantage?
4. Is it unethical to be incongruent with another person?

Application & Analysis

EXPERIENTIAL EXERCISE 6.1: IMPROVING YOUR SUPPORTIVE COMMUNICATION AND ACTIVE LISTENING SKILLS

Purpose: To both assess one's self as well as observe someone else with regard to his or her supportive communication and active listening skills.

Group size: Three-person teams

Time required: 45–60 minutes

Materials needed: None

Instructions:

1. Transfer your scores from Self-Assessments 6.1 and 6.2 to the Self-Assessment Chart provided below. Calculate your total and average supportive communication (SC) and active listening (AL) scores. Jot down a real-life example from a prior experience to support the way you scored yourself. Try to write down exactly what you said and did. Be prepared to discuss this in your small group. (5–10 min.)
2. Form groups of three as follows:
   - Self-assessor
   - Active listener
   - Observer
3. For the first round, self-assessor tells active listener about his or her eight self-assessment scores and examples. Observer takes notes on active listening skills of active listener, using the eight-item Observer Checklist provided below. (5 min.)
4. When self-assessor and active listener have finished their discussion, observer gives active listener feedback using Observer Checklist below. (5 min.)
5. Repeat, switching roles so that each person has a turn in each of the three roles. (20 min.)
6. After the third round, help each other develop improvement plans using the strategies described in the text. (10 min.)
7. Discuss what you learned from this exercise as a class. (10–15 min.)

   Total SC Score = _____/24

   Average SC Score = _____/6

   Total AL Score = _____/24

   Average AL Score = _____/6

Observer Checklist

Circle the appropriate number based on the following rating scale

6 = Strongly agree; 5 = Agree; 4 = Slightly agree; 3 = Slightly disagree; 3 = Disagree; 1 = Strongly disagree

1. The listener **showed interest** by keeping eye contact and saying things like "Uh-huh" and "I see." 6 5 4 3 2 1
2. The listener was a good active listener in that s/he **paraphrased** often. This means that when not sure, the listener repeated back what s/he thought s/he heard to check for accuracy and to show that s/he was listening. 6 5 4 3 2 1
3. The listener sometimes went beyond paraphrasing and **reflected the core feelings** that s/he was sensing in the message. 6 5 4 3 2 1
4. The listener encouraged two-way communication by asking sincere questions, by not interrupting, and by giving time to talk. 6 5 4 3 2 1

Application & Analysis

EXPERIENTIAL EXERCISE 6.2: PREPARING FOR AN EMPLOYMENT-SELECTION INTERVIEW

Purpose: Employment-selection interviews are one of the more important settings in which supervisors and job candidates use communication skills. There is always the potential for defensiveness and confusion as well as lack of complete information exchange in this interview. This exercise allows you to think through ways to maximize the value of an employment-selection interview, whether you are the supervisor or the candidate, so that it is a productive experience based on effective applied communication.

Group size: 4–6

Time required: 30–45 minutes

Materials needed: None

Instructions:

1. Form groups.
2. Develop a set of guidelines for the supervisor to prepare for and then conduct an employment-selection interview. Consider the following questions in developing your guidelines.
   a. What should the supervisor do before the interview?
   b. How should the supervisor act and behave during the interview?
   c. What should the supervisor do after the interview?
3. Develop another set of guidelines for the employee to prepare for and then be involved in an employment-selection interview. Consider the following questions in developing your guidelines.
   a. What should the employee do before the interview?
   b. How should the employee act and behave during the interview?
   c. What should the employee do after the interview?
4. Once each group has developed the two sets of guidelines, the instructor will lead the class in a general discussion in which groups share and compare their guidelines. Consider the following questions during this discussion.
   a. What similarities are there among the groups for each set of guidelines?
   b. What unique or different guidelines have some of the groups developed?
   c. What are essential guidelines for conducting an employment-selection interview?

Analysis Evaluation, & Synthesis

CASE: THE FAMILY STORE

Your small consulting company has been working with the senior executives of the Family Store, a regional convenience store chain with 10 local stores. Garrett, George, and Gavin VanDoer jointly founded the business over 25 years ago. Garrett, the president and majority shareholder, has brought you in to help them improve organizational effectiveness. The senior executives and all other members of management, including store managers, are family members.

As well as the three brothers, there are two younger members of the executive team. The senior VP of finance is Garrett's daughter, Marielle, and the senior VP of marketing and retail sales is Gavin's son, Frankie. Marielle and Frankie have each been with the company for five years. As family members graduate from college, they are expected to come into the business immediately as managers. A job is either created or found for them and they are expected to be up to full speed within a week. Most of them start out as store managers although some do start work in head office and are later transferred to a store so they know the "nuts and bolts" of the business.

The business plan for this year includes further expansion of the number of stores to 20 but there has been some concern raised recently with this plan. Sales have been dropping over the past year and a half in all stores. Employee turnover in the stores is higher than they experienced previously. Of the four new stores opened in the past two years, sales results are satisfactory in only two stores.

You met Garrett through a mutual business acquaintance who has used your services in the past. During your initial meeting, Garrett impressed you with his overall business knowledge and openness to new ideas. Just over a month ago, you met with the full executive team to discuss how to improve the overall operation of the business. Garrett provided the team members with an outline of why he has asked for your help prior to the meeting.

Marielle provided some good insights about possible causes of reduced sales and employee turnover she had heard in the staff cafeteria: grumbling about performance reviews and backlashes from customer complaints that seemed to take too long to address. She also reminded them that the financials were going to get worse if something was not done quickly. "We can't afford to expand when we're not even meeting targets in our existing stores. It's too much of a strain on our resources." Gavin, George and Frankie rolled their eyes as she spoke and started shuffling papers. Marielle sighed and sat back as if to say, "Why don't they ever seem to want to listen to me?"

During the meeting, Gavin appeared to be uninterested in the discussion of the possible reasons for the loss in sales and employee turnover. He sat near the door, arms crossed, making side comments to George and Frankie, whose chairs were pulled close to his, that you were unable to hear and which he declined to repeat for the benefit of the whole group. During the discussion of how best to obtain information, he provided input only when asked a direct question. As the chief operating officer, Gavin is responsible for purchasing and service innovation. You were unable to speak with him privately to determine if he was truly on board with the work that Garrett wanted to do. Frankie's response when asked about his reaction to the tentative plan was, "Yeah. Yeah. OK." You hoped you could get him on board during the second meeting when the plan was finalized.

Subsequently, you met with them again to confirm the approach that would be taken to determine what was happening from both a customer and employee perspective. Once again, Gavin seemed uninvolved and did not contribute much to the discussion, although he did say that he thought the employee survey questions about management were a waste of time since, "Our kids are all bright and know how to work with others. They've been involved in team sports since they were old enough to run and skate." Frankie sat up straighter and smiled as Gavin said this.

Marielle once again was very animated during the discussion, asking many perceptive questions, such as, "What happens if we find out that some of the managers are part of the problem? After all, they are our brothers and sisters. How will we deal with them?" Frankie just shrugged, laughed and said, "Just fire them all. What's the matter, are you worried you're part of the problem?" Garrett shook his head and rolled his eyes at this comment, before saying, "If that is the case we will have to deal with them appropriately, depending on what we find out." Marielle smiled gratefully at him before sitting back in her chair and shuffling her papers.

George chipped in with, "Marielle, you are just imagining problems where there are none. My kids love this company and everything we stand for. They wouldn't do anything to jeopardize business success. It's what helped them get the fancy cars and terrific vacations. They love being store managers and developing relationships with the employees and clients." Gavin mumbled, "Waste of time and money. Don't see the point. Let's get this over with. I want to go to the golf club for lunch."

You shared your concerns about commitment to the plan with Garrett after the meeting and he assured you, "They will come around. George thinks his kids are perfect. He's already had to deal with some behaviour he'd rather forget from them when they were in school. Gavin hates change and doesn't much care for work. He'd rather play golf, but when the rubber hits the road, he usually gets on board. It may take some persuasion but I can get him there. Frankie likes to appear disinterested and flippant, but he's got a sharp mind for business. The information he's provided us on competitor strategies is brilliant. Marielle and I see eye to eye on business. She's the one I'd like to take over as president one day."

You recently completed both the customer and employee surveys that provided room for written comments to help determine what steps to take to improve business results and employee retention. Through your research you have learned the following:

Customer feedback—100 customers (10 from each store):

- Satisfaction with the goods available in the stores is high.
- Satisfaction with prices is high.
- Satisfaction with the shopping experience is low.
- Satisfaction with the physical store decor and product layout is high.
- Satisfaction with the personal service received from cashiers and clerks is high.

- Over 70 percent of the customers wrote written comments on the poor working relationships seen between the employees and store managers, with many commenting on the authoritarian, "drill-sergeant" style of the store managers.

Several customers, in one store surveyed, commented that they didn't like how the store manager berated employees in front of customers—"That belongs out of the public eye," and "When I come in to buy milk, I don't need to see someone standing there with arms crossed watching the employees like a hawk. I only shop here when there is no alternative." "While your prices are reasonable, I find the atmosphere in the store tense and unfriendly. The clerks are nice but they seem to jump whenever the manager comes into view. Almost like they are afraid."

Employee feedback—230 (20 from each store and 30 from head office):

- Satisfaction with the work is high.
- Satisfaction with pay and benefits is high.
- Satisfaction with career opportunities is low.
- Satisfaction with the quality and timeliness of feedback is low.
- Satisfaction with quantity and quality of communications from company managers and leaders is low.
- 80 percent of employees said they would take another job elsewhere if the opportunity came up.
- 65 percent of employees disagreed that constructive work-related feedback was given in a private location.

Here are some sample statements that were included in the comments section of the survey:

- "My manager's behaviour is embarrassing to me. I know these customers. They are my neighbours. They should not be included in what I consider to be private discussions."
- "My store manager is loud and unpleasant and treats me like I know nothing about this business. He's always right. He needs some people skills if he wants to succeed in a retail store. It was better when Tina was the manager. The customers have told me that they only come here when the other stores are closed. It's too bad. We sell high-quality products at reasonable prices compared to other small stores."
- "All my manager does is complain about what I do wrong. He never praises me for going the extra mile for a customer or when I help another clerk who is really busy. I feel like I can't win."
- "My manager is self-centred and uncaring. When I was in the hospital, she never called to see how I was or asked how I was doing when I came back to work. She expected me to be at full speed the first day back."
- "My manager continually makes mistakes when working cash and then tries to shrug off the mistakes with the customers. She never knows prices or what's on sale. Then I'm ordered around like a child to get the correct price for the customer."
- "My manager is always giving me negative feedback. I wish someone could give her some about how she works. She's a joke. I'd give her feedback but she'd fire me like she did Joe, and I need this job."
- "I've been a buyer for eight years. I know what I'm doing and I don't need some new manager telling me to do things that don't make sense and would cost more in the end. I should be managing him!"
- "In the marketing department we have to be on top of what our competitors are doing. We get this information by networking. Frankie likes to think he's the only one who can do this right. He has an ego the size of Toronto and always questions the information we bring back. Then, to make matters worse, he presents it as his own. He never gives us credit for the great scoops we get."

Questions:

1. What barriers to effective communication are evident in the case?
2. Given the nature of the feedback you have received from the customers and employees, what are your major concerns about presenting this information back to the senior executives to avoid defensiveness? Which attributes of supportive communications will be most important and why?

3. Develop a communication strategy for the executive team to use when communicating the results of the survey to the rest of the company.

SOURCE: Copyright S. Reilly 2005. Used with permission.

Scoring Instructions for Self-Assessments

Self-Assessment 6.1: Are You an Active Listener?

Transfer your scores out of 6 to the following chart. The closer your total score is to 24, the more you are an active listener:

Showing interest	___/6
Paraphrasing	___/6
Reflecting back the core feelings	___/6
Encouraged two-way communication	___/6
Total score	___/24

Self-Assessment 6.2: Are you a Supportive Communicator?

Transfer your scores out of 6 to the following chart. The closer your total score is to 24, the more you are a supportive communicator:

I focus on the problem, not the person	___/6
I am congruent	___/6
I am specific, not global	___/6
I own my communications and use "I" language	___/6
Total score	___/24

Team Dynamics and Effectiveness

chapter seven

LEARNING OBJECTIVES

By the end of this chapter, you will be able to do the following:

1. Define what is meant by a team and distinguish it from a group.
2. Describe different types of task interdependence.
3. Provide examples of different types of work teams.
4. Describe the five-stage model of team development.
5. Describe the punctuated equilibrium model of team development.
6. Define *team effectiveness*.
7. Describe the organizational influences on team effectiveness.
8. Describe how team design influences team effectiveness.
9. Explain the important internal process influences on team effectiveness.
10. Describe individual blocking behaviours (social loafing, loss of individuality, co-dependency and other blocking roles) that reduce team effectiveness.
11. Describe special issues in managing diverse and multicultural teams.
12. Describe strategies for addressing common operating problems and improving team effectiveness.

learning about the context

Problem-Solving Circles at Honda Canada

At a time when most automakers are cutting production in Canada, Honda Canada Manufacturing (HCM) has increased its production levels and has even added a new model to its line. Its approach to innovation and employee management, including employee problem-solving circles, continues to encourage change in the firm.

Honda only opened its doors in Canada in 1986 when it began production of the Accord for the North American market. But HCM has pushed its way to the top of the industry by encouraging innovation within its plants, using cutting-edge technology, and creating an atmosphere in which employees are urged to contribute to the continuous improvement of the Honda brand. HCM has two plants in Alliston, Ontario, where it builds the Civic sedan, the Acura 1.7, the Odyssey minivan, the Acura MDX, and the Honda Pilot SUV. What you notice when you first enter the facility are all the white coats. This is part of HCM's *single citizen concept.* "Everyone is on the same team with the same uniform. There are no private offices and everyone is an associate of the company," explains Vaughn Hibbits, Honda's vice-president of administration.

An interesting adaptation of the single citizen concept at HCM are the NH (New Honda) Circles, which are problem-solving teams of employees attempting to find cost-cutting or efficiency improvement opportunities. Anyone from any part of the company can join a circle that is exploring an idea that interests him or her. Thus, associates from various areas of the company, from the production floor to the accounting department, can bring their own unique perspectives to a particular problem.

NH Circle awards are given to recognize the efforts of teams. "The NH Circle awards are not judged strictly on how the improvements cut costs. We are interested in the process as much as the final result in this particular program," says Hibbits. Two NH Circle conferences are held every year, during which teams can present their ideas to senior management. Any associate is allowed to attend the sessions. Various improvements have arisen from the approximately 90 NH circles. For instance, the rags used to wipe down dashboards prior to painting were previously registered as waste. The NH Circles found a washable rag that could be used for this purpose. This reduced registered waste by 200 kilos a year. Another NH Circle found that 35 000 cubic metres of water could be saved per year by relocating water sprays and rinse tanks in the paint pre-treating process. Through the efforts of its NH Circles, HCM has won awards for reducing greenhouse emissions and for recycling as much as 98 percent of its waste.

NH Circles allow employees to interact with people from different areas of the company both inside and outside work hours. The 18-hectare HCM site includes a recreation centre, an NHL-sized rink, physical fitness areas, a baseball diamond, and volleyball and tennis courts. There are currently 50 hockey teams made up of HCM associates.

Sources: R. Colman, "Shifting into High Gear: Honda Canada Drives Process Innovation with Its Employees," *CMA Management* 76, no. 7 (October 1, 2002); G. S. Vasilash, "A New Spin on Quality Circles," *Automotive Production,* Cincinnati, OH, vol. 108, no. 10 (October 1996), 56.

The problem-solving circles at Honda Canada provide an example of how teams can be used to increase efficiency and stay ahead of the competition. In many organizations today, work teams play a vital role.[1] You may have had the experience of working on a project in a team, either at school or at your workplace. What was that experience like? Did you enjoy working in the team? What role did you play? Was your team effective? What factors contributed to its success or failure? What could the team have done differently? These are some of the questions that we will consider in this chapter as we explore the OB theory, practice, and research on work teams, and the characteristics that make them effective.

We begin by distinguishing a team from a group and then elaborate on the definition of a team by examining different types of interdependence. We then provide examples of a number of different temporary and permanent work teams. Next, we examine two models that explore the stages of development that teams naturally go through before they become productive and effective. We define team effectiveness and introduce the following four general areas that influence how effective teams are likely to become: First, we explore the *organizational influences,* which include the clarity of the team's mission, the degree to which the organization provides the team with sponsorship and support, the team's access to resources, and methods by which teams are measured and rewarded. Second we explore the *team design influences,* which include the composition of its members, its size, and the nature of the task itself. Third, we describe the various *internal process influences* on team effectiveness. These include the importance of building goal clarity and agreement, the fulfillment of critical task-oriented and maintenance-oriented roles, the development of productive team norms and cohesion, and the implementation of effective team decision-making procedures. Fourth, we review some of the *individual blocking behaviours* that reduce team effectiveness, such as social loafing, loss of individuality, co-dependency, and a number of destructive team roles. We end the chapter by highlighting some of the special issues in managing multicultural teams and by providing some strategies for improving team effectiveness. Topics related to team decision making, such as groupthink and polarization, are addressed in the chapter on decision making, Chapter 8.

Define what is meant by a team and distinguish it from a group.

WHAT IS A TEAM?

group
Two or more people with common interests, objectives, and continuing interaction.

A **group** is two or more people having common interests, objectives, and continuing interaction. Formal and informal groups form in organizations for different reasons. Informal groups evolve in the work setting to satisfy a variety of member needs not met

Now boarding ... WestJetters kick into high gear at 2002's Ride for Life.

by formal groups. For example, organizational members' needs for affiliation or belongingness, as discussed in Chapter 4 on motivation, might be satisfied through informal athletic or interest groups. Often, informal athletic teams or interest groups representing a department, unit, or company may achieve semi-official status, such as the various CARE (Create A Remarkable Experience) teams of WestJet Airlines employees who participate in a wide range of charitable fundraisers such as the Heart and Stroke Foundation's "Ride for Life" and Big Brothers and Big Sisters' "Bowling for the Bigs" competitions.[2]

A **team** is defined as two or more people with a common objective who are interdependent upon each other to achieve a particular task and who hold themselves accountable to each other.[3] All work teams are groups, but not all groups are work teams. While groups do not necessarily work interdependently to achieve an organizational objective, teams do. The latter also emphasize goals and roles that are understood and agreed to by all, open dialogue, and team-driven behaviour.[4] Work teams are task-oriented groups that are supported by their organization and are very useful in performing work that is complicated, complex, interrelated, or much greater than one person can handle. Obviously, individuals working in organizations cannot do everything themselves because of the limitations of time, expertise, knowledge, and other resources. Individual limitations are often overcome and problems are solved through teamwork and collaboration. Many companies credit teamwork for their successful turnarounds. For example, John Rogers, CEO of MDS Inc., credits teamwork for the quiet transformation of the company from a small, traditional medical test lab into Canada's most profitable scientific research and biotech company.[5]

team
Two or more people with a common objective who are interdependent upon each other to achieve a particular task and who hold themselves accountable to each other.

HOW TEAMS DIFFER

While teams differ from groups, teams themselves also differ from each other in a few significant ways. First, teams differ in the degree and nature of the task-driven interaction required to get the work done (task interdependence). Second, teams differ in terms of whether they are permanent or temporary.

Task Interdependence

Describe different types of task interdependence.

One of the key features that distinguish a team from a group is the fact that in a team, members are interdependent upon each other to accomplish their tasks. **Task interdependence** is the degree of task-driven interaction among work team members.[6] While all teams contain some task interdependence, the nature of this interdependence can be reciprocal, sequential, or pooled, as outlined in Exhibit 7.1. We can use a sports analogy to convey the differences in these three types of task interdependence.

task interdependence
The degree of task-driven interaction among work team members.

Pooled Interdependence

Some teams work like baseball teams, with individual members having set responsibilities and the performance of the team resulting from the sum of (pooling of) the performance of the individual members. Such teams are said to have pooled interdependence. When

Application & Analysis

IS IT A GROUP OR A TEAM?

1. Think about the various groups to which you belong or have belonged in the past. Decide which of them you would classify as groups and which of them you would qualify as teams, according to our definition.
2. If you found yourself stuck in a snowstorm with many other drivers, would you consider yourselves to be a team or a group? Explain.

EXHIBIT 7.1

Three Types of Interdependence in Teams

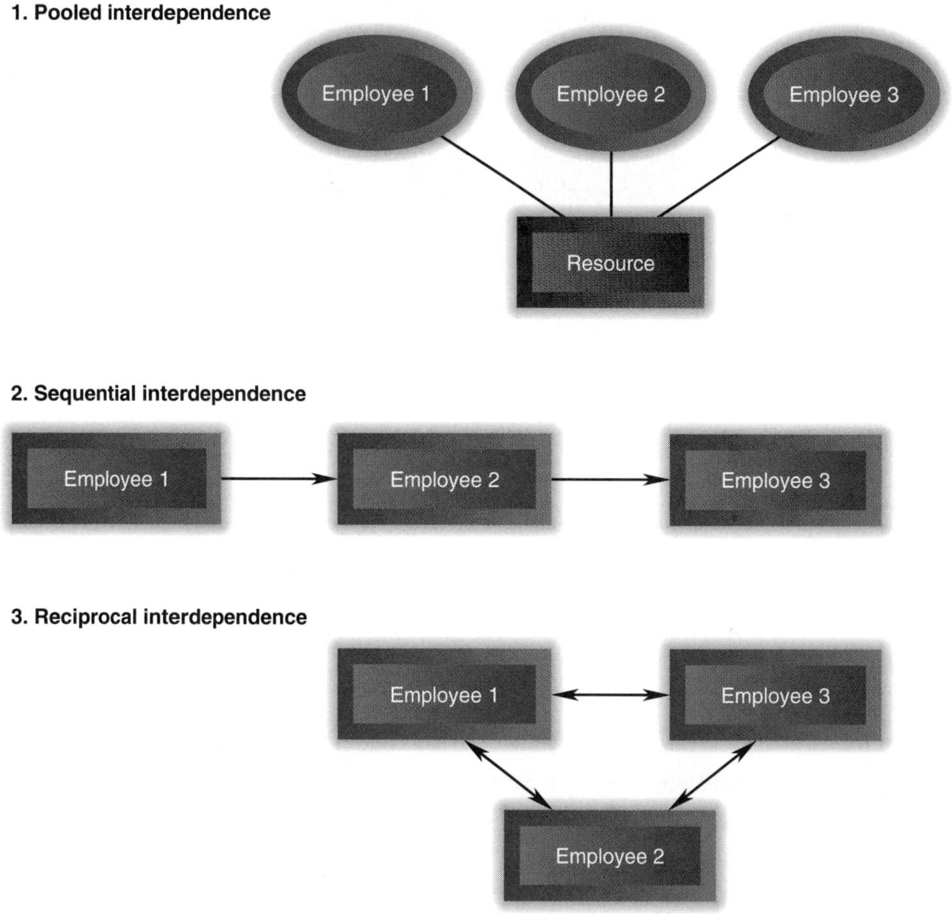

1. Pooled interdependence

Employee 1 | Employee 2 | Employee 3 → Resource

2. Sequential interdependence

Employee 1 → Employee 2 → Employee 3

3. Reciprocal interdependence

Employee 1 ↔ Employee 3; Employee 1 ↔ Employee 2; Employee 3 ↔ Employee 2

task interdependence is pooled, it means that team members work individually but either draw from a pool of common inputs or pool their outputs. For example, part of the success of the renowned Orpheus Chamber Orchestra that has been performing without a conductor for over 30 years lies in members' recognition that they have individual as well as collective responsibility for the orchestra's performance. Members work as individual specialists with their respective instruments but they contribute to interpretation debates and decisions about phrasing and other musical aspects. Their pooled efforts have resulted in outstanding performances that have earned the orchestra four Grammy awards.[7]

Sequential Interdependence

Other work teams function like football teams through coordinated action or sequential interdependence. Such teams rely on each other for resources with the output of one member becoming the input of another. For example, Ironlink, a Canadian company with the motto "making transportation simple," uses teams with sequential interdependence to transport over-sized construction materials from central Ontario to Northern Alberta. On one occasion, to meet a very tight deadline, an Ironlink team was put together in the following manner: The 3770-kilometre journey began with a rig driver in Montreal, who picked up the load in Barrie and took it as far as Winnipeg. There, the load was transferred to another carrier and hauled to Edmonton. A third carrier completed the haul, taking the equipment to Fort Mackay.[8] The three-day journey required coordinated sequential action, with team member three being highly dependent on the outputs of team member two, who was in turn dependent on the outputs of team member one.

Reciprocal Interdependence

Still other teams work like doubles tennis teams, with individuals having primary yet flexible responsibilities. In such teams, members have reciprocal interdependence, with work being exchanged back and forth among them. The Trillium Health Centre is a good example of reciprocal interdependence in teams.[9] As one of the leading community hospitals in Ontario, it is committed to the development of innovative, collaborative, and cutting-edge patient care services. Trillium is home to the busiest emergency department in Canada and the largest free-standing day surgery facility in North America. It provides services under the umbrella of eight health systems: cardiac care, diagnostics and pharmaceuticals, emergency services, medicine, mental health, neurosciences/musculoskeletal services, surgery, and women's and children's health. Community advisory panels, family physicians, and community agencies work hand in hand with staff, physicians, and volunteers to create a consultative, cooperative framework for the delivery of health care services in Mississauga and Etobicoke. Recognized as one of Canada's top 100 employers, Trillium Centre was awarded the prestigious Canadian College of Health Service Executives and 3M Health Care Quality Team Award in 2002. This award recognizes quality and innovation as well as exemplary teamwork. As patients move through the various medical examinations, treatments, or procedures, team members from different health systems exchange information about their separate responsibilities in a reciprocal manner.

Different Types of Work Teams

Provide examples of different types of work teams.

In addition to varying in the nature of their task interdependence, some teams come together to work temporarily on specific projects and disband when the projects are completed, while others are permanent and ongoing. Also, increasingly, teams can either be housed together or be virtual. Read more about virtual teams in OBXtra 5, entitled "Managing in a Virtual World."

Temporary teams include task forces, ad hoc committees, project teams, and commissions of inquiry. For example, governments at all three levels in Canada have established commissions of inquiry with expert members drawn from various disciplines or geographic locations to investigate such matters as the treatment and status of Aboriginal peoples, the tainted blood supply of the Canadian Red Cross in the 1990s, or barriers to new immigrants' access to employment in trades and professions in Canada.

Permanent work teams remain together and have ongoing responsibility for specific functions in the organization. For example, **self-managed work teams (SMWTs)** are teams whose members have autonomy to carry out interdependent tasks and make decisions that were once reserved for managers. Also called *self-directed teams* or *autonomous work groups,* these teams are made up of natural work groups, such as the members of the production and marketing departments of a manufacturing organization who are respectively responsible for producing the company's goods and getting them to the market. Such teams become knowledgeable in all the skills necessary to complete the task. They

self-managed work team (SMWT)
A team whose members have autonomy to carry out interdependent tasks and make decisions that were once reserved for managers.

Knowledge & Application

TASK INTERDEPENDENCE IN YOUR OB TEAM

If you have been assigned to do a team project for this class, review the expectations, inputs, outputs, goals, and required interdependencies for it. Decide which of the three types of task interdependence will be required.

are empowered to plan, implement and control all work processes, and may assume responsibilities for hiring, team performance reviews, and training. Read more about SMWTs in OBXtra 4.

Work teams may also be differentiated on the basis of their objectives. Some work teams are established to solve specific problems, such as improving quality, improving work processes, increasing efficiency, or enhancing the work environment. Such work teams go by a number of different names, such as problem-solving teams, process improvement teams, and quality circles. Their purpose is to make recommendations about the specific problem, but they are not necessarily responsible for implementing the suggested solutions.

quality circle
A small group of employees who work voluntarily on company time, typically one hour per week, to address work-related problems such as quality control, cost reduction, production planning and techniques, and even product design.

One of the most widely used types of problem-solving work teams in organizations is the quality circle. **Quality circles** are small groups of employees who work voluntarily on company time—typically one hour per week—to address work-related problems such as quality control, cost reduction, production planning and techniques, and even product design. As you read in the chapter opener, Honda Canada Manufacturing is one of the many Canadian companies that have used quality circles, which they call NH (New Honda) circles, for successful productivity improvements. Membership in a quality circle is typically voluntary and is fixed once a circle is formed, although some changes may occur as appropriate. Quality circle members are trained in various problem-solving techniques that they use to address the work-related problems. Quality circles were popularized as a Japanese management method when an American, W. Edward Deming, exported his thinking about quality circles to Japan following World War II.[10] Quality circles became popular in North America in the 1980s and led to TQM (discussed in

organizational reality 7.1

Teamwork Day at Xerox Corporation

Xerox Corporation has major operations in Rochester, New York, and hosts its annual Teamwork Day in the city's convention centre. The theme for Teamwork Day 2000 was knowledge sharing. Knowledge is power and people have a tendency to hoard it rather than share it. Xerox pioneered total quality management (TQM) in America and initiated Teamwork Day as an annual event. TQM can help a team solve a specific problem, which is good. What is even better is when the team shares the solution with other teams that have the same problem. Hence, knowledge sharing between teams can leverage problem-solving power throughout a company.

Two key questions in knowledge sharing are "Who needs our new solution?" and "Where do we go to ask about a solution to our problem?"

Recognizing the importance of teamwork, Xerox CEO Anne M. Mulcahy was a driving force behind Teamwork Day 2000.

Participating Xerox teams came from manufacturing, purchasing, sales, engineering, and customer service. The organizers of Teamwork Day 2000 arranged these diverse teams into *knowledge zones* on the convention centre floor so that they would begin to talk with their neighbours. Grassroots knowledge grows slowly through close contact. A key lesson from Teamwork Day 2000 was the need for lightning bolts to get knowledge sharing really moving fast. Lightning bolts are the urgent, energizing demands of leadership that get good ideas travelling quickly through bright people. Teamwork works best when creative ideas move from team to team, energizing an entire company.

Source: T. A. Stewart, "Water the Grass, Don't Mow, and Wait for Lightning to Strike," *Fortune (Asia)*, July 24, 2000, 212–13.

Chapter 1), which was pioneered by Xerox in North America. Read about "Teamwork Day" at Xerox in Organizational Reality 7.1.

Quality teams and quality circles must deal with substantive issues if they are to be effective; otherwise, employees begin to believe the quality effort is simply a management ploy. Quality circles do not necessarily require final decision authority to be effective if their recommendations are always considered seriously and implemented when appropriate. The effectiveness of quality circles has been disputed by some studies while others have found them to be effective for a period of time, and then their contributions begin to diminish.[11] This may suggest that quality teams and quality circles must be reinforced and periodically re-energized to maintain their effectiveness over long periods of time.

HOW TEAMS DEVELOP

Researchers have extensively studied how the dynamics of teams change over the course of the team's life. Understanding these stages of a team's development is important because it helps team members and team leaders more effectively address the issues raised by each stage. Two models of team development have stood the test of time. They are Tuckman and Jensen's five-stage model, and Gersick's punctuated equilibrium model.

The Five-Stage Model of Team Development

Describe the five-stage model of team development.

According to the five-stage model of team development, teams pass through five stages of development, each of which must be successfully negotiated before the team can become mature, productive, and effective.[12] The five stages are referred to as *forming, storming, norming, performing,* and *adjourning*. As depicted in Exhibit 7.2, teams do not necessarily progress through these stages in a linear fashion. Instead, they often regress to earlier stages when team membership changes, either through the loss of an established member or the inclusion of a newcomer. Teams may then engage in some activities common in earlier stages of development as they adjust to their loss or accommodate the newcomer. Development through these stages may therefore not always be smooth because of demographic diversity, persistent conflict, and the formation of sub-teams.[13] However, recent research does continue to support the model's proposal that members of teams that have been meeting longer make significantly fewer statements characteristic

EXHIBIT 7.2

The Five-Stage Model of Team Development

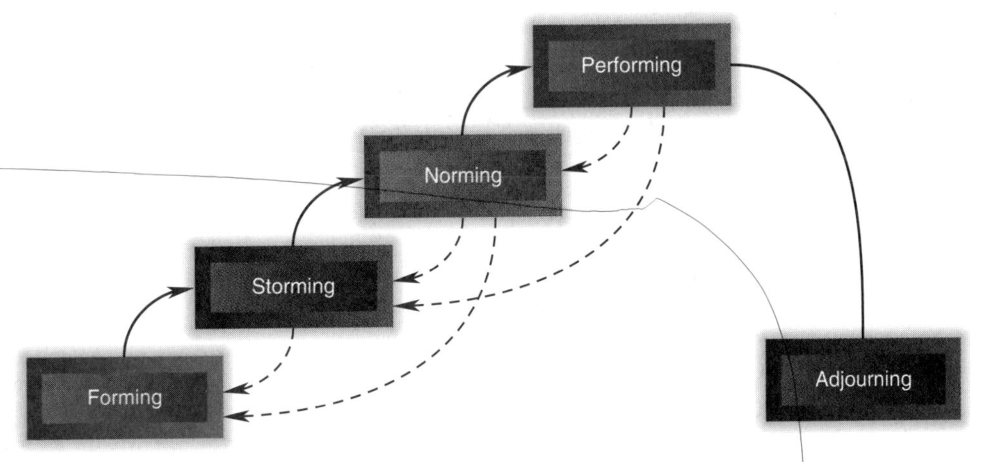

SOURCE: B. W. Tuckman and M. A. C. Jensen, "Stages in Small Group Development Revisited," *Group and Organizational Studies* 2 (1977): 419–27. Reprinted by permission.

of the forming or dependency stage of development and significantly more statements indicative of the performing or work stage.[14]

Stage 1: Forming (Dependency and Inclusion)

forming
The first stage in team development, characterized by politeness, superficiality, and uncertainty.

When team members meet for the first time, they often experience discomfort and uneasiness because they do not yet know each other and the team's purpose may still be unclear. This first stage of group development, called **forming**, is characterized by politeness, superficiality, and uncertainty. Questions that are on team members' minds in this stage include: Who are these other people? What is expected of me? Who is going to lead? Team members try to determine what the rules of engagement are and what behaviours are expected of them. They depend on the designated leader or whoever assumes a leadership role to provide direction. Members remain polite and superficial and often engage in "pseudo-work," such as discussions about activities unrelated to the team's goals. Symptoms of the forming stage are silence, self-consciousness, and superficiality.[15]

Stage 2: Storming (Counterdependency and Fighting)

storming
The second stage of team development, characterized by conflict, confusion, power struggles, and the emergence of cliques.

Storming is one of the natural stages of team development and is characterized by the emergence of different opinions and conflict.

The second stage of team development is called **storming**. This stage is characterized by conflict, confusion, and the emergence of cliques as team members struggle over issues of leadership and control. At this stage, typical questions that arise in team members' minds are: How will we handle differences of opinion? How will we communicate negative information? Do I want to stay in this team?[16] Disagreements occur over goals, procedures, and various roles, and tensions arise between members' conflicting needs for individuality and conformity to the emerging rules of the team. In order for a team to resolve the interpersonal conflicts of this stage, team members need to refocus on their goals, use supportive communication strategies to gain better understanding, identify their sources of conflict, and use conflict management strategies as discussed in Chapter 11.

Stage 3: Norming (Trust and Structure)

norming
The third stage of team development, characterized by cohesion, trust, and clarification of group roles and norms.

Norming, the third stage of team development, is characterized by cohesion, trust, and clarification of group roles and norms. Typical questions in team members' minds during this stage are: What are the norms and values of this team? How can I best get along with everyone else? How can I show my support to others?[17] In this stage, the team experiences its first sense of trust and cohesiveness. Team members have overcome the interpersonal conflicts of the storming stage, have resolved the leadership struggles, and have developed a stronger sense of team identity. This leads to more structure within the team as well as consensus about team objectives, member roles, and behavioural norms.

Stage 4: Performing

Performing is the fourth stage in team development when the team has achieved synergy and is reaching its full potential. Not all teams reach this stage, and simply finishing a job does not mean that the team has actually reached the performing stage in terms of its development. When a team does reach the fourth stage, team members make significant progress in reaching a high level of performance. Questions at this stage include: How can we continuously improve? How can we become more creative? How can we maintain a high level of energy?[18] By this time, team members have gotten to know each other well, have resolved interpersonal conflicts, and have developed cooperation and commitment to the team's goals. These high-performance teams focus their energy on task accomplishment and are characterized by shared purpose, high levels of trust, a blurring of formal distinctions, and clarity around core competencies.

performing
The fourth stage in team development, when the team has achieved synergy and is reaching its full potential.

IMPLICATIONS FOR LIFE

Stages of Team Development Confessions

One student's reflections on a difficult team experience using the five-stage model of team development:

Forming: It is the second class and the professor has assigned me to a four-person team. I am angry that I wasn't given the choice of who to work with. One of my teammates is reading the newspaper, another is playing on his laptop, and another is asking the teacher questions about expectations. A real keener, that one! We all have to fill out a biography and share it with the team. What a waste of time! Everyone is pretty polite but oh so superficial! I tell them the usual, and nothing more. I am not going to take any chances. I'll wait and see what happens.

Storming: It is week five, and the 20-page research report is due in three weeks! I have been trying to set up a meeting but no-one returns my e-mails, except for "Keener" of course, who right away took over as leader and wanted to do the whole project single-handed. I know that I would make a better leader since I'm an assistant store manager part-time and I have had some leadership training. The team finally meets and starts telling it like it is. There is a lot of arguing and fighting about project goals and who should have done what. Two cliques seemed to form, one headed up by me and one by "Keener." I encourage people to put all their ideas on the table. After three hours, we're exhausted, but it feels as if we at least moved beyond the forming stage! We plan to meet on the weekend.

Norming: We finally start to get a feel for who is good at what. I tell them about my background. "Keener" tells us that he is on probation and has to do well in this course. "Newspaper Reader" admits that he hasn't read any of the textbook yet because his parents were in a car accident and he has had to take care of his younger siblings. "Laptop" wants to be a software developer and is uninterested in the people side of management. Wow, if only I had known all these things about them earlier. We start to get our first sense of being a team. The atmosphere shifts. We focus on our goals and honestly express what each of us is willing to put into the project for the next two weeks. We begin to clarify who will do what and what we expect from each other.

Performing: Wow, the report is due in one week and instead of finishing early, we all try to make our parts even better. We are actually enjoying our team meetings, and are learning from each other. It's nice to be in a team where one can be so honest with one another. Who would have thought?

Adjourning: It's weird; even though these are not people I would choose to be friends with, I'm actually a bit sad that the project is finished because in the end we worked so well together. It seems that sometime differences do make things better. If I ever have a chance to work on a project with Keener, Newspaper Reader, and Laptop again, I would say yes.

Stage 5: Adjourning

adjourning
The final stage of team development for temporary teams, characterized by concern with wrapping up.

Adjourning is the final stage of team development for temporary teams, characterized by concern with wrapping up. This final stage is typical of informal and temporary work teams such as ad hoc committees and task forces. Once their objective has been accomplished such teams no longer have a reason to stay together. Attention is focused on wrapping up activities. In some groups, anticipation of their disbandment may cause disruption and conflict. In other groups, members express appreciation of each other and regret at the pending separation.

Describe the punctuated equilibrium model of team development.

The Punctuated Equilibrium Model of Team Development

Team development in temporary task teams seems to be somewhat different from the five-stage model just discussed. This difference has been captured by the punctuated equilibrium model of team development. This model (depicted in Exhibit 7.3), developed originally by C. J. Gersick, proposes that project teams, rather than developing gradually over time, progressed through "an alternation of stasis and sudden change."[19] These phases appear to be task-deadline driven, with evidence that a transition occurs around the midpoint of the time assigned to the team.[20] According to this model, temporary teams experience an initial phase of inertia, punctuated by a transition phase around the midpoint when team members realize that more work or better quality work needs to get accomplished. Researchers compare this midpoint transition to a "midlife crisis" for the team. This phase of disequilibrium can be identified by bursts of activity, changes in leadership, and expressions of concern. This is followed by phase two, which is a new period of equilibrium and inertia.[21] Researchers have recently compared the punctuated equilibrium and five-stage models of team development and have found that both patterns can be observed simultaneously in project teams.[22]

As discussed in the next section, one of the key influences on team effectiveness is the degree to which team members and leaders successfully manage their internal processes, including their storming and transition stages of development.

EXHIBIT 7.3

Punctuated Equilibrium Model

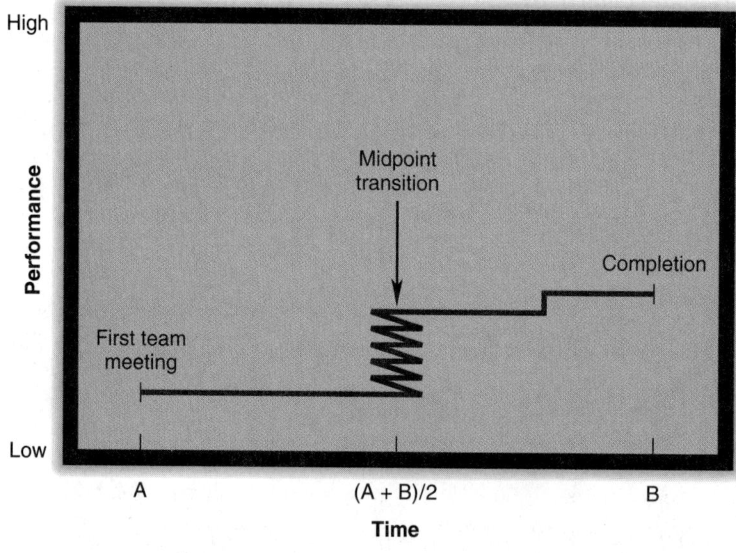

SOURCE: Based on A. Chang, P. Bordia, and J. Duck, "Punctuated Equilibrium and Linear Progression: Toward a New Understanding of Group Development," *Academy of Management Journal* 46, no. 1 (2003): 106–17.

EXHIBIT 7.4

Conditions and Processes for Team Effectiveness

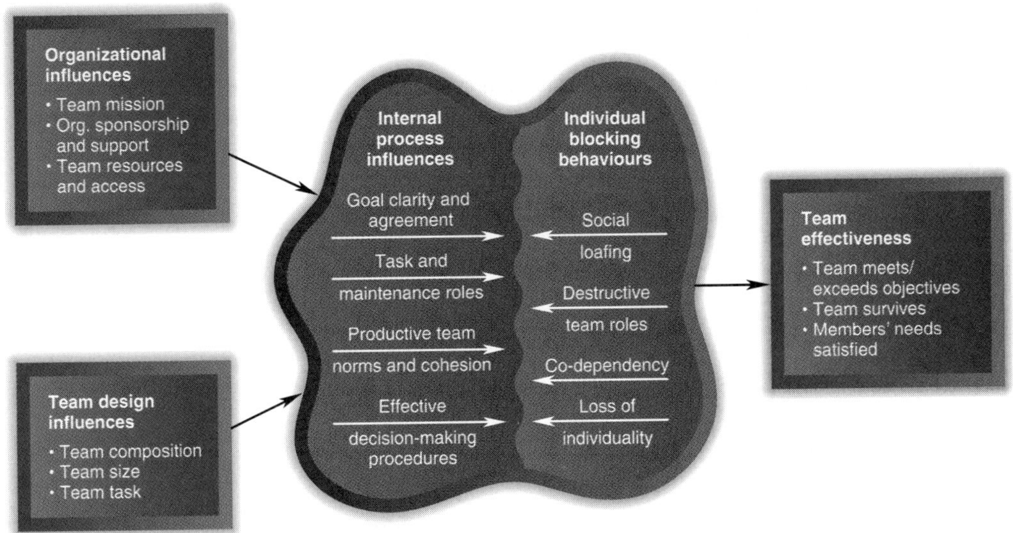

TEAM EFFECTIVENESS

Define team effectiveness.

team effectiveness
Achieved when the team survives, meets its objectives, and the needs of its members are satisfied to the extent that they would be willing to work together again.

Team effectiveness is considered to have been achieved when the following three criteria have been met: the team survives, it meets its objectives, and the needs of team members have been satisfied to the extent that they would be willing to work together again. Note that this definition goes beyond the mere achievement of objectives. Team survival is an effectiveness criterion because at times, during the storming stage of team development, teams splinter, sometimes losing key players along the way. Also, the reason that meeting members' needs is important is that in most work teams, after adjourning, members are more than likely to have to work together again, so it is important that members have developed mutual respect.

Organizational behaviour research has revealed a number of conditions that affect the chances that a team will be effective. As shown in Exhibit 7.4, team effectiveness depends upon (1) the organizational influences, (2) the team design influences, (3) the way team members manage important internal process, including their stages of development, and (4) the individual behaviours that reduce team effectiveness. Each of these sets of influences is now discussed in depth.

Organizational Influences on Team Effectiveness

Describe the organizational influences on team effectiveness.

Teams do not operate in isolation from the rest of the organization. Teams are most effective when certain organizational conditions and sponsorship behaviours are present. We distinguish here between the organizational sponsor (the person who has decided that a team is needed) and the team leader (the person assigned to lead the team). Teams are more effective when (1) the organizational sponsor is supportive and engaged, (2) when the team's mission has been made clear, (3) when appropriate resources have been made available to the team, (4) when the team's performance can be clearly measured, and (5) when team rewards are available and well managed.

Organizational Sponsorship and Support

The organizational sponsor who has set up the team needs to achieve a balance between setting limits (so that individuals and teams do not stray far from their mission) and removing barriers (so that individuals can accomplish their work). The organizational sponsor must also continue to be available to coach the team or team leader when required and pay attention to both internal team processes as well as outputs.[23] Read about the executive team at Southwest Airlines in Organizational Reality 7.2.

Clear Team Mission

mission
The overall purpose of a team.

According to Richard Hackman of Harvard, and others, the most significant barrier to team effectiveness is the existence of unclear or meaningless goals.[24] A **mission** is the overall purpose of a team, the raison d'être for its existence. Whether assigned by the organizational sponsor or self-determined, it is an indication that all members of the team agree to go in the same direction. The importance of mission is exemplified in IBM's Process Quality Management, which requires that a process team of not more than 12 people develop a clear understanding of mission as the first step in the process.[25] The nature of a team's mission presents different kinds of challenges. For example, teams that primarily "recommend things" are usually temporary teams, as discussed in the earlier section of the chapter. Their special challenges are to get off to a quick start and to plan well for the ultimate handoff. On the other hand, permanent teams whose missions are "to make or do things" face challenges in what Katzenbach calls "critical delivery points," such as where accounts get managed or where products get designed. In these types of teams, organizational sponsors need to ensure effective performance management and reward systems.[26]

Resources and Access

Teams also must be given access to required resources, such as budget, work space, key stakeholders, and especially information. They need to be empowered to make their own decisions within the context of their mission.[27] Recent research indicates that for certain teams to be effective, they also need to be given the power to network externally. In these teams, called "X-teams," members need to be free to lobby for resources, connect to new change initiatives, obtain up-to-date information, and link to other groups inside and outside the company.[28]

organizational reality 7.2

Southwest's Top Management Team

Legendary CEO and founder Herb Kelleher oversaw a major leadership transition at Southwest Airlines on June 19, 2001, when two key executives took on new challenges running the airline. While Kelleher remained as chairman of the board, Jim Parker became vice chairman and CEO, and Colleen Barrett became president and COO of the airline. In addition to these top two executives, Southwest has three executive vice presidents. Few airlines, if any, have replicated the sustained success Southwest enjoys in growth, customer satisfaction, and profitability.

One key to the company's success is the top team's emphasis on people and relationships. Southwest spends more money recruiting and training people than any other airline. Another key to the company's success is leadership continuity. Herb Kelleher led the company for 30 years, from 1971 through 2001. The new top executives at Southwest have been on the team for nearly as long. So, the new top team is likely to build on the airline's historical strength and success rather than take it in a new direction. The new top team reinforces the unique culture of the airline, which values civility, openness, candour, and positive relationships. They were tested by the terrorist attacks of September 11, 2001, and, while more than 100 000 people in the airline industry lost jobs following the attack, Southwest's top team announced no layoffs. A hallmark of the airline has been the positive relationship the top team nurtures with operating employees and unions alike.

SOURCE: J. H. Gittell, "Investing in Relationships," *Harvard Business Review* (June 2001): 28–29. Used with permission.

Team Performance Measures and Rewards

Work teams need to know what performance measures are being used to assess their effectiveness. For example, a medical emergency team's performance measures might include the success rate in saving critically injured patients or the average number of hours a patient is in the emergency room before being transferred to a hospital bed. In one study, individuals who were actively involved in teams in different organizations were interviewed about what performance dimensions they thought should be included in an ideal performance evaluation of teams.[29] The five evaluation criteria most commonly identified were problem solving, quality of work, workload allocation, meeting of objectives, and team attitude. Prior knowledge of these performance evaluation criteria can be useful in promoting team effectiveness.

Most organizations have reward systems that are geared to individual performance, so investments have to be made in designing, implementing, and evaluating effective team rewards. In some sales teams, for example, people are all supposed to work together but in fact they are competing for good clients and commissions. Chapter 5 provides an overview of various options for managing team performance and rewards such as team bonuses and gain sharing programs.

Team Design Influences on Team Effectiveness

Describe how team design influences team effectiveness.

While the aforementioned organizational conditions must be in place to facilitate team effectiveness, the way a team is *designed* also influences its chances of success. A number of design factors have been found to be important, and we discuss three of these here: the nature of the team task itself, the size of the team, and its composition.

Team Task

The nature of the task assigned to the team must be taken into account both when selecting members and when deciding upon the optimal size for the team. A team with reciprocal task interdependence is going to be more complex to coordinate, so the optimal size will be smaller than if the interdependence is sequential or pooled. Also, the nature of the task will guide the team sponsor or leader in terms of who should be on the team. Another factor that needs to be considered is whether the task is structured or unstructured, and this will influence the type of leadership required.

Team Size

The size of a team has been found to influence team effectiveness. Researchers have agreed that the more team members interact, the greater the likelihood that they will develop shared understandings and interpretations. According to Jon Katzenbach, effective teams range in size between 2 and 25 people, and the majority have fewer than 10.[30] Therefore, smaller teams tend to be more effective because large numbers of people have trouble interacting constructively as a group and doing real work together.[31]

As mentioned earlier, optimum size also depends, in part, on the type of task interdependence. When the team task involves primarily pooled interdependence, adding skilled team members will probably increase productivity. For example, if a team is assigned to complete a crossword puzzle together, members can divide up the clues and work independently before pooling their answers. In this case, a larger team would probably finish before a smaller team. However, the composition of the team members would also influence outcome because one of the smaller teams may have a member with significantly more knowledge about the subject than others. When task interdependence is sequential or reciprocal, however, a team that gets too large begins to experience "process losses" as communicating and coordinating become more difficult.[32]

Composition of Teams

team composition
The collection of the team members' characteristics.

Team composition refers to the collection of the team members' characteristics in terms of the skill mix, as well as the degree of homogeneity and heterogeneity or diversity. For teams to be effective, they must have the right mix of skills in three areas: technical or functional skills related to the specific team task, problem-solving and decision-making skills, and interpersonal skills.[33] In addition to a complementary skill mix, a great deal of research has explored optimum degrees of diversity for team effectiveness. Teams whose compositions are diverse have been found to experience, in general, more conflict, power struggles, and tension. This has been observed in mixed sex and age groupings as well as in groups with ethnic diversity.[34] However, research on the relative effectiveness of heterogeneous versus homogeneous teams has been mixed. Some research has indicated that even though team members in diverse teams have to work harder to understand and accept each other, they tend to more effective in finding creative solutions to complex problems.[35] For example, when team composition was explored in terms of the mix of extraverts and introverts (in the discussion of personality in Chapter 3), those teams having 20–40 percent members with high extraversion outperformed all other team compositions, including teams composed of all extraverts.[36] On the other hand, research exploring the impact of ethnic differences found no significant differences in creative performance.[37] Currently scholars are taking the view that building demographic diversity into a team will not necessarily ensure a high level of team performance. The relationship between diversity and performance seems to vary depending on the nature of the individual traits being measured, the degree to which diverse information is shared,[38] the stage in the team's life, and the differences that are *perceived,* often influenced by stereotypes, whether or not they are real.[39]

Explain the important internal process influences on team effectiveness.

Internal Process Influences on Team Effectiveness

It is not enough for organizational leaders to set up the organizational conditions and design teams appropriately. The manner in which a team handles its internal processes also has a big influence on its subsequent effectiveness. High-performance teams work hard at clarifying their goal priorities and ensure that critical team roles, including leadership roles, are carried out. Teams need to be cohesive, develop productive norms, and discuss and agree upon appropriate decision-making procedures. Lastly, teams have to manage their own stages of development and the interpersonal conflicts that inevitably arise.[40] Complete Self-Assessment 7.1 to explore how effective your OB project team is at the moment.

Goal Clarity and Agreement

Teams must convert the mission set out by the organization into specific goals and priorities.[41] If teams fail to establish specific goals, or if these goals do not relate directly to the team's overall purpose, "team members become confused, pull apart, and revert to mediocre performance." [42] Goal clarity and agreement helps team members pull in the same direction at the same time.[43] Once a strong foundation of **g**oal clarity and agreement has been established, teams can build on this foundation to clarify **r**oles, **p**rocedures for decision making, and **i**nterpersonal issues. This model, called the GRPI model, is useful as an approach to diagnosing team effectiveness and planning for improvement, as shown in the analysis and synthesis exercise later on in the chapter.[44]

Fulfillment of Task and Maintenance-Oriented Roles

role
A set of behaviours that are expected of a person occupying a particular position in a social unit.

A **role** is a set of behaviours that are expected of a person occupying a particular position in a social unit. Some roles in teams, like the roles in most student organizations, are formal or official, but formal, written job descriptions can only help partially with role definition. For example, to use a sports analogy, they can only tell you whether you are

Knowledge & Application

SELF-ASSESSMENT 7.1: HOW EFFECTIVE IS YOUR OB PROJECT TEAM?

The following 20 items serve as a checklist for you to use in describing the effectiveness of a team you belong to. The larger the number of statements answered yes, the more likely the team is productive and members are satisfied.

	Mostly Yes	Mostly No
1. The atmosphere is relaxed and comfortable.		
2. Team discussion is frequent, and it is usually pertinent to the task at hand.		
3. Team goals are clear and agreed to.		
4. People listen to each others' suggestions and ideas.		
5. Disagreements are tolerated and an attempt is made to resolve them.		
6. There is general agreement on most courses of action taken.		
7. The team welcomes frank criticism from inside and outside sources.		
8. When the team takes action, clear assignments are made and accepted.		
9. There is a well-established, relaxed working relationship among the members.		
10. There is no evidence of social loafing in the team.		
11. Members strive hard to help the team reach its goals.		
12. The norms of the behaviour seem to support goal attainment.		
13. When the team gets together, people take on the roles needed to get the tasks done.		
14. When we get together, people take on roles to mediate conflict and encourage others to contribute their ideas.		
15. None of the team members seem to be trying to block the team's progress.		

SOURCE: Adapted from A. J. DuBrin, *Contemporary Applied Management*, Plano, TX, Business Publications Inc., 1985, pp.169–70. Used by permission.

a centre or a forward but they cannot specify how you should behave on a day-to-day basis.[45] Role definition needs to go further and clarify the behaviours that are associated with the formal roles.

An effective team carries out various "task" functions to perform its work successfully and various "maintenance" functions to ensure member satisfaction and a sense of team spirit. An effective team also tries to minimize the emergence of individual "blocking" roles, and these are discussed later on in the chapter. To achieve the task and maintenance functions of a team, individual members must contribute to the collective effort by playing various roles.[46] Team roles that *block* effectiveness are discussed in the next section on individual influences on team effectiveness.

Task-Oriented Roles

Task-oriented roles are those activities directly related to the effective completion of the team's work. For example, the initiator suggests ideas, defines problems, and proposes approaches and/or solutions to problems. The information seeker asks for ideas, suggestions, information, or facts. The challenger plays devil's advocate to prevent groupthink and complacency. In addition, an effective team must have a coordinator, someone who can act as a liaison between the different units represented on the team in order to achieve unity of effort. This is especially important in cross-functional teams, where different perspectives have the potential to arouse conflict. Having effective integrators on

task-oriented roles
Activities directly related to the effective completion of a team's work.

its cross-functional teams of artists, designers, printers, and financial experts enabled Hallmark Cards to cut its new-product development time in half.[47]

The effective use of task-oriented roles leads to the success of the group, and the failure to use them may lead to disaster. For example, the successful fulfillment of the two task-oriented roles of "initiator" and "coordinator" by a senior resident in an emergency room (ER) saved the life of a knife wound victim.[48] The victim was stabbed half a centimetre below the heart, and the senior resident acted quickly to stem the bleeding, begin intravenous fluids, and monitor the victim's vital signs.

Maintenance-Oriented Roles

maintenance-oriented roles Activities essential to effective, satisfying interpersonal relationships within a team.

Maintenance-oriented roles are those activities essential to effective, satisfying interpersonal relationships within a team. For example, following another team member's lead may be as important as leading others. Communication gatekeepers within a team ensure balanced contributions from all members. Because task activities often create tension in teams as they work together, tension-reduction activities are important to decrease negative or destructive feelings. For example, in a study of 25 work teams over a five-year period, humour and joking behaviour were found to enhance the social relationships.[49] The researchers concluded that performance improvements in the 25 teams indirectly resulted from improved relationships attributable to the humour and joking behaviours. Maintenance-oriented roles enhance togetherness, cooperation, and teamwork, enabling members to achieve psychological intimacy while furthering the success of the team. For example, in-flight crews on WestJet Airlines have gained an excellent reputation for friendly and cheerful service, which reduces some of the anxiety and stress passengers often experience when flying. By telling jokes, singing, and even playing musical instruments, they not only help passengers to relax and enjoy the flight but they also enhance interpersonal relationships and psychological intimacy among team members.[50]

Exhibit 7.5 presents a sample of other task-oriented and maintenance-oriented roles found in effective, well-functioning teams.

Team Leadership Roles

The task and maintenance-oriented roles shown in Exhibit 7.5 are often carried out by formal team leaders. However, in many teams, formal leaders are not assigned, and the leadership roles (both task and maintenance) are shared among team members or rotated. From the leadership perspective, what is important is not that one individual necessarily

Performing maintenance-oriented roles, such as that of gatekeeper, ensures balanced contributions from all members.

EXHIBIT 7.5

Task-Oriented and Maintenance-Oriented Roles in Effective Teams

Roles	Description	Example
Task-Oriented Roles		
Initiator	Stating the goal or problem, making proposals about how to work on it, setting time limits.	"Let's set up an agenda for discussing each of the problems we have to consider."
Information seeker	Asking team members for specific factual information related to the task or problem, or for their opinions about it.	"What do you think would be the best approach to this, Jack?"
Information provider	Sharing information or opinions related to the task or problems.	"I worked on a similar problem last year and found ..."
Coordinator	Coordinates sub-groups and pulls together ideas.	"If you each give me your ideas, I'll pull them together so that next time we meet we can identify common themes."
Elaborator	Building on one another's ideas and suggestions.	"Building on Don's idea, I think we could ..."
Summarizer	Reviewing the points covered by the team and the different ideas stated so that decisions can be based on full information.	Taking notes and summarizing the discussion when requested.
Consensus tester	Periodic testing about whether the team is nearing a decision or needs to continue discussion.	"Let us go around one more time and each give our suggestions on this to see if we really do agree."
Challenger	Plays devil's advocate to ensure that all ideas are challenged and groupthink doesn't set in.	"Wait a minute! If we all immediately agree, we must be missing something. Let's look at it from another angle."
Maintenance-Oriented Roles		
Harmonizer	Mediating conflict among other members, reconciling disagreements, relieving tensions.	"Don, I don't think you and Sue really see the issue that differently."
Compromiser	Admitting error at times of team conflict.	"Well, I'd be willing to change if you provided some help on ..."
Gatekeeper	Making sure all members have a chance to express their ideas and feelings and preventing members from being interrupted.	"Sue, we haven't heard from you on this issue."
Encourager	Helping a team member make his or her point. Establishing a climate of acceptance in the team.	"I think what you started to say is important, Jack. Please continue."

SOURCE: Adapted from "Team Processes" in D. Ancona, T. Kochan, M. Scully, J. Van Maanen, and D. E. Westney, *Managing for the Future: Organizational Behavior and Processes,* 1st ed. (Cincinnati, OH: South-Western College Publishing, 1996), 9. Reprinted by permission of South-Western, a division of Thomson Learning, www.thomsonrights.com. Fax 800-730-2215.

carries out all these roles, but rather that the team ensures that both task and maintenance roles are adequately carried out. Where leadership problems arise, it is important to find solutions and build team leader effectiveness.[51] Effective teams tend to share leadership. For example, one person may be the team's task leader, who sets the agenda, initiates much of the work activity, and ensures that the team meets its deadlines. Another team member may take a leadership role in maintaining effective interpersonal relationships in the group. Hence, shared leadership provides an effective status structure that results in a well-functioning team.

Norms, Team Cohesion, and Productivity

norms of behaviour
The standards that a work team uses to evaluate the behaviour of its members.

Teams are more effective when their **norms of behaviour** are the standards that a work team uses to evaluate the behaviour of its members. They may be written or unwritten,

CRITICAL THINKING: Application & Synthesis

ANALYZING THE INTERNAL PROCESSES OF YOUR OB PROJECT TEAM

Goals: What is your team's mission? What are your shared goal priorities for the project in terms of hours to be spent, minimum grade expectations, and completion time frames? Are your goals SMART? (See Chapter 4.) Are the goals you have set for yourself challenging? Have you set up feedback mechanisms by which to keep track of how you are doing?

Roles: How will the task-oriented roles such as initiating, coordinating, and consensus-testing be handled? What about the maintenance-oriented roles such as encouraging and gatekeeping? Are there people in your team who play these roles naturally or do you need to consciously assign people to play them each time you interact?

Procedures for Decision Making: Have you discussed how information will be shared and how you will make decisions as a team? Will you settle for a majority vote or will you try for consensus? What kinds of meetings will you have and how often? What are your expectations regarding missed meetings? Will notes be taken? How will absent members be kept informed?

Interpersonal Relationships: Have you discussed how you will address conflicts during your storming stage? Have you explored each of your preferred styles of interpersonal conflict management (Chapter 11)? Have you discussed the steps you will take once you find yourselves in a conflict, such as taking time to explore your sources of conflict? Have you reviewed communication strategies which minimize defensiveness such as "I" statements and paraphrasing (Chapter 6)?

---

verbalized or not verbalized, implicit or explicit. As long as individual members of the team understand them, the norms can be effective in influencing behaviour. Norms may specify what members of a team should do (such as a specified dress code), or they may specify what members of a team should not do (such as executives not behaving arrogantly with employees). Behavioural norms evolve over a period of time and may exist in any aspect of a team's life.[52] They may evolve informally or unconsciously, or they may arise in response to challenges, such as the norm of disciplined behaviour by firefighters in responding to a three-alarm fire.[53] Some behavioural norms become written rules, such as a team's attendance policy or an ethical code of conduct. Other norms remain informal, although they are no less well understood by team members. Dress codes and norms about after-hours socializing may fall into this category. Norms that create awareness of emotions and help regulate emotions are critical to team effectiveness.[54]

Behavioural norms also evolve around performance and productivity.[55] Such norms are among the most important from the organization's perspective. Performance and productivity norms even influence the performance of sports teams.[56] The team's productivity norm may or may not be consistent with, and supportive of, the organization's productivity standards. A high-performance team sets productivity standards above organizational expectations with the intent to excel. Noncompliant or counterproductive teams may set productivity standards below organizational expectations due to having lower standards or with the intent of damaging the organization.

team cohesion
The interpersonal attraction binding team members together,

Team cohesion is defined as the interpersonal attraction binding team members together. When a team has positive norms around performance and productivity, team cohesion can enhance job satisfaction for members and improve organizational productivity.[57] Highly cohesive teams at work may not have many interpersonal exchanges away from the workplace. Nevertheless, they are able to control and manage their membership better than work teams low in cohesion. This is due to the strong motivation in highly cohesive teams to maintain good, close relationships among the members. Team cohesion enables a team to exercise effective control over its members in relation to its behavioural norms and standards. Complete Self-Assessment 7.2 to explore the degree of cohesion in a team to which you belong.

Application & Analysis

SELF-ASSESSMENT 7.2: HOW COHESIVE IS YOUR TEAM?

Think about a team of which you are a member. Answer each of the following questions in relation to this team by circling the number next to the alternative that most reflects your feelings.

Do you feel that you are really a part of your team?

5 — Really a part of the team.

4 — Included in most ways.

3 — Included in some ways, but not in others.

2 — Do not feel I really belong.

1 — Do not work with any one team of people.

If you had a chance to do the same activities in another team, for the same pay, how would you feel about moving?

1 — Would want very much to move.

2 — Would rather move than stay where I am.

3 — Would make no difference to me.

4 — Would rather stay where I am than move.

5 — Would want very much to stay where I am.

How does your team compare with other teams that you are familiar with on each of the following points?

The way people get along together.

5 — Better than most.

3 — About the same as most.

1 — Not as good as most.

The way people stick together.

5 — Better than most.

3 — About the same as most.

1 — Not as good as most.

The way people help one another on the job.

5 — Better than most.

3 — About the same as most.

1 — Not as good as most.

For scoring instructions, please go to the end of the chapter, p. 231.

SOURCE: From S. E. Seashore, *Group Cohesiveness in the Industrial Work Group* (University of Michigan, 1954). Reprinted by permission.

A classic study of cohesiveness in 238 industrial work teams found cohesion to be an important factor influencing anxiety, tension, and productivity within the groups.[58] Specifically, work-related tension and anxiety were lower in teams high in cohesion, and they were higher in teams low in cohesion. This suggests that cohesion has a calming effect, reducing work-related tension and anxiety. Member satisfaction, commitment, and communication are better in highly cohesive teams, while goal conflict, unpleasant experiences, and domination of a subgroup occur more often in teams that are low in cohesion. Team cohesion is influenced by a number of factors, most notably time, size, the prestige of the team, external pressure, and internal competition. Team cohesion evolves gradually over time through a team's normal development. Prestige or social status also influences a team's cohesion, with more prestigious teams, such as the Canadian Forces, being highly cohesive. Finally, external pressure and internal competition influence team cohesion. High team cohesion can, however, also lead to lowered productivity, if the team's norms do not support the organizational objectives. Highly cohesive teams can also suffer from groupthink, which is a deterioration of mental efficiency, reality testing, and moral judgment resulting from pressures within the group. Groupthink is discussed in detail in Chapter 8. See Exhibit 7.6 for an overview of the relationship between team cohesion and productivity.

Effective Team Decision-Making Procedures

Teams are more effective when procedures have been agreed to about issues such as how decisions will be made, how information will be shared, what kinds of meetings the team will have, and the norms the team needs to reinforce or distinguish.[59] Agreements on these procedural issues establish the operating guidelines and set the organizational boundaries and decision-making limits within which the team must function. For example, teams need to decide whether all decisions will be made as a team or not, whether teams will make decisions using consensus or majority vote, and how any conflicts between team members or ethical dilemmas will be handled. We will be exploring team decision-making in more depth in Chapter 8.

Describe individual blocking behaviours (social loafing, loss of individuality, co-dependency and other blocking roles) that reduce team effectiveness.

Individual Behaviours That Reduce Team Effectiveness

As we have seen, the success of a work team depends a great deal on the organizational conditions, the team's initial design, and the manner in which team members handle their internal process issues as they move through the various stages of development. Finally, there are some individual blocking behaviours that can severely hamper the team's efforts. These blocking behaviours include social loafing, loss of individuality, co-dependency, and individual blocking roles.

Social Loafing

social loafing
The failure of a team member to contribute personal time, effort, thoughts, or other resources to the team.

Social loafing occurs when individual team members rely on the efforts of other team members and fail to contribute their own time, effort, thoughts, or other resources to a team.[60] This may create a real drag on the team's efforts and achievements. Some scholars argue that, from the individual's standpoint, social loafing, or free riding, is rational behaviour in response to an experience of inequity or when individual efforts are hard to observe. However, it becomes a problem for the team, which loses potentially valuable resources possessed by individual members.[61] Research has uncovered a number of antecedents of social loafing. These include a failure to clearly identify individual contributions, situations where individual contributions either lack challenge or uniqueness, low intrinsic involvement, individualistic orientation, low group cohesion, and lack of peer appraisal.[62] Recent research also suggests that social loafing is more prevalent when task interdependence is high.[63]

EXHIBIT 7.6

The Relationship between Team Cohesion and Productivity

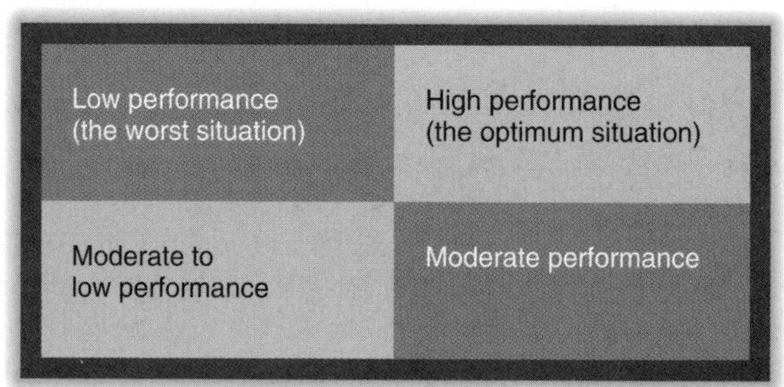

Social loafing can be minimized by having identifiable individual contributions to the team product as well as member peer evaluation systems.[64] For example, if each team member is responsible for a specific input, a member's failure to contribute will be noticed by everyone. If members must formally evaluate their contributions to the team they are also less likely to loaf. In studying a sample of 330 undergraduate students enrolled in an introductory cross-disciplinary business course, some researchers found that the use of an evaluation system with early implementation at multiple points and specific evaluation criteria reduced the negative effects of social loafing and led students to view team experiences in a more positive light.[65] Experiential Exercise 7.3, at the end of the chapter, gives you an opportunity to create a team evaluation system that will clarify mutual expectations up front, minimize the likelihood that your team will experience social loafing, and likely improve your team experience and effectiveness.

Loss of Individuality

Social loafing may be detrimental to group achievement, but it does not have the potentially explosive effects of **loss of individuality**. This is a social process in which individual team members lose self-awareness and its accompanying sense of accountability, inhibition, and responsibility for individual behaviour.[66] When individuality is lost, people may engage in morally reprehensible acts and even violent behaviour as committed members of their team or organization. For example, loss of individuality accounts for the looting, rioting, and wanton destruction that has occasionally occurred after sports events, such as when the Vancouver Canucks lost the final in the Stanley Cup in 1995. A crowd estimated at 70 000 jammed a couple of streets, and booze-fuelled hooligans led looting and vandalism attacks. More than 100 people were arrested.[67] It was also one of several contributing factors that led to a hockey crowd exploding in Montreal four days after Rocket Richard's suspension, on St. Patrick's Day, 1955. Fans went on a rampage, smashing windows and battling with police on Ste. Catherine Street, causing half a million dollars in damage.[68]

loss of individuality
A social process in which individual team members lose self-awareness and its accompanying sense of accountability, inhibition, and responsibility for individual behaviour.

Co-dependency

Co-dependency occurs when one person tries to control another and to be responsible for the consequences of the behaviour of that other person. When individuals with co-dependent behaviours become team members, they can destroy the team's efficiency, productivity, and harmony.[69] Team members who are co-dependent demonstrate characteristics that conflict with the characteristics of a well-functioning team as well as blocking roles. Co-dependents do not commit to the team's mission and may constantly argue about it. They do not trust their team members and therefore hoard information, seeing it as something to be controlled rather than shared. They experience boundary distortion, which is an inability to recognize the personal boundaries between themselves and others, resulting in anxiety and tension for everyone. They tend to over-personalize everything, always perceiving unintended slights or insults and thinking that others are either for them or against them. Their unpredictable behaviour creates tension in the team as members try to avoid making any comments that might be misinterpreted. As a result, interpersonal relationships become strained. Finally, co-dependents cannot separate accountability from blame, and therefore instead of taking responsibility for their actions, they shift responsibility to others. Exhibit 7.7 summarizes the differences between the characteristics of successful members of self-managed work teams compared to those of co-dependents.

co-dependency
When one person tries to control another and to be responsible for the consequences of the behaviour of that other person.

The characteristics of a co-dependent individual are detrimental to group cohesion, which is so important to team effectiveness. Yet these characteristics are difficult to identify in an interview, and managers or team leaders may unwittingly select co-dependent

EXHIBIT 7.7

Characteristics of Successful Team Members and Co-Dependents

Successful Members of Self-Managed Teams	Problems Created by Co-Dependent Individuals
Open-mindedness	Tend to operate in a dualistic world where everything is seen as black or white.
Emotional stability	Described as individuals with constant anxiety and boundary issues, constantly inhibited in relationships by lack of self-esteem and fear of rejection.
Accountability	Have not learned the distinction between accountability and blame, and because of their own insecurities always try to shift responsibility to others.
Problem-solving abilities	Unable to make decisions and implement actions to carry them out.
Good communication skills	Tend to hoard information, seeing it as a valuable commodity in short supply.
Good at conflict resolution	Caught in a web of self-defeating behaviours that create conflict.
Trust	Learn very early in life that it is dangerous to trust anyone, and carry that into adulthood.

SOURCE: R. A. Cook and J. L. Goff, "Coming of Age with Self-Managed Teams: Dealing with a Problem Employee," *Journal of Business and Psychology* 16, no. 3 (2002): 490. With kind permission from Springer Science and Business Media.

individuals for team membership. When this occurs, the team faces the problem of dealing with the conflict inevitably caused by the presence of a co-dependent member. Dealing with conflict at work is discussed in detail in Chapter 11.

Blocking Roles

blocking roles
Roles that inhibit the team or its members from achieving what they could have achieved and destroy morale and cohesion.

In addition to the abovementioned destructive behaviours of co-dependents, other individual team members can be observed to engage in roles that block the team's progress. **Blocking roles** are defined as those roles that inhibit the team or its members from achieving what they could have achieved and destroy morale and cohesion. Often these roles are observed by team members engaged in political behaviour, as discussed in Chapter 9. Common blocking roles are described in Exhibit 7.8 and include dominating, overanalyzing, stalling, remaining passive, overgeneralizing, fault-finding, premature decision making, presenting opinions as facts, rejecting, pulling rank, resisting, and deflecting.[70] Use the Application & Analysis box to explore examples of blocking roles that you have engaged in or observed in others.

EXHIBIT 7.8

Individual Blocking Roles That Reduce Team Effectiveness

Activities	Description
Dominating	Excessive talking, interrupting, or cutting others off
Overanalyzing	Splitting hairs and examining every detail excessively
Stalling	Not allowing the group to reach a decision or finalize a task by sidetracking the discussion, being unwilling to agree, repeating old arguments, and so on
Remaining passive	Not being willing to engage in the team's task; staying on the fringe or refusing to interact with other team members; expecting others to do the team's work
Overgeneralizing	Blowing something out of proportion and drawing unfounded conclusions
Faultfinding	Being unwilling to see the merits of others' ideas or criticizing others excessively
Premature decision making	Making decisions before goals are stated, information is shared, alternatives are discussed, or problems are defined
Presenting opinions as facts	Failing to examine the legitimacy of proposals and labelling personal opinions as truth
Rejecting	Rejecting ideas based on the person who stated them rather than on their merits
Pulling rank	Using status, expertise, or title to get ideas accepted rather than discussing and examining their value
Resisting	Blocking all attempts to change, to improve, or to make progress; being disagreeable and negative about virtually all suggestions from other team members
Deflecting	Not staying focused on the topic of the team's discussion; changing the subject or deflecting attention away from the main points

SOURCE: David A. Whetten and Kim S. Cameron, *Developing Management Skills,* 6th ed. (Upper Saddle River, NJ: Prentice Hall, 2005), 459–60. Copyright © 2005. Reprinted by permission of Pearson Education, Inc., Upper Saddle River, NJ.

Application & Analysis

OBSERVING BLOCKING BEHAVIOUR

Check off (✓) any possible blocking roles you have either engaged in yourself or observed in others in a team to which you belong. If any of these roles are evident, try to think of an example that illustrates their use of the blocking behaviour.

	No	Yes	Example
1. Dominating	___	✓	___
2. Overanalyzing	___	✓	___
3. Stalling	___	✓	___
4. Remaining passive	___	___	___
5. Overgeneralizing	___	✓	___
6. Faultfinding	___	___	___
7. Premature decision making	___	✓	___
8. Presenting opinions as facts	___	___	___
9. Rejecting	___	___	___
10. Pulling rank	___	___	___
11. Resisting	___	___	___
12. Deflecting	___	___	___

Describe special issues in managing diverse and multicultural teams.

MANAGING DIVERSE AND MULTICULTURAL TEAMS

Internal work team processes have become more complex in the global workplace, with teams composed of members from many cultures and backgrounds. Homogeneous teams in which all members share similar backgrounds are giving way to teams with token diversity in which all but one member come from the same background, bicultural teams in which two or more members represent each of two distinct cultures, and multicultural teams in which members represent three or more ethnic, linguistic, or national backgrounds, with different values and priorities.[71]

Cultural Diversity in Teams

Our discussion of diversity earlier in the text has particular relevance to multicultural work teams. Diversity in a team may increase the uncertainty, complexity, and inherent confusion in team processes, making it more difficult for the team to achieve its full potential. The complexity of diversity may also make it difficult to implement empowerment processes, unless the impacts of cultural differences are taken into account.[72] One study that examined the effects of diversity on transnational teams found that initially diversity had a detrimental impact on team functioning. However, as highly heterogeneous teams found ways to interact and communicate, they created a common identity and functioned better.[73] Diversity in a team enhances the team's ability to be more creative and innovative and to deal more sensitively with other multicultural customers and teams.[74]

Another study, conducted by a team of Canadian, American, and an Australian researchers, identified three key influences in multicultural teams, as follows: (1) Team members bring their cultural norms to work, and different cultures regard teamwork differently. (2) Perception of cultural difference influences team performance, and different cultural groups regard "difference" differently. (3) Very diverse teams may have communication problems or may be more effective.[75] The researchers learned the following important lessons from their study of multicultural teams.

- Recognize that the effect of cultural diversity depends on how the team is structured and the nature of the task. Bringing tacit knowledge to the surface and making it explicit may be difficult, but may also be the key to team success.
- Evaluate teams in terms of team processes and individual outcomes as well as task accomplishment. Multicultural teams may take longer to achieve their potential, but may be considerably more effective than monocultural teams when they do.
- Create a climate of support for teams and for diversity. Walk the talk; showing support is much more important than just talking about it.
- Design team-level rewards to be consistent with cultural norms. Rewarding team success is important, but one-size-fits-all approaches may be risky. Managers need to get to know what's important to all team cultures, and act appropriately.
- Provide ongoing training in cultural diversity and team skills as well as task-related skills. Untrained teams will struggle. Recognizing and respecting cultural difference is the key, but it must be continually reinforced to be effective.

Fastcompany.com

What makes teams work? Fastcompany.com interviewed more than a dozen leaders from a wide range of industries to learn secrets and insights about effective team building. What general principles are given at the following link for the development of productive teams? **http://www.fastcompany.com/magazine/40/one.html**

Gender Diversity in Teams

In addition to national and cultural diversity, teams often have gender diversity. One study of gender diversity found that men and women in gender-balanced teams had higher job satisfaction than those in homogeneous teams.[76] Gender-based differences in behaviour pose additional challenges to effective team performance. For example, an important influence on a team's performance is its ability to respond effectively to available feedback on its actions. Responding effectively may mean changing its course of actions midstream or making adaptations to plans based on negative feedback. However, since men and women respond differently to negative feedback, mixed-gender teams may find it difficult to make an appropriate group-level response to such feedback. Compared to their male counterparts, women tend to be more responsive to negative feedback. Men, on the other hand, tend to view feedback as information that can be ignored. Such differences in responses can create gender-based interpersonal conflicts that can ultimately reduce team effectiveness.[77]

Canada's first female prime minister, Kim Campbell, identified attitudes to hierarchical structures as another gender-based difference that can impact teams. According to Campbell, women tend to be less enthusiastic than men about hierarchies. Thus, when women join leadership teams, hierarchies become less rigid and ultimately change the way teams function.[78] Finally, gender stereotypes may play a role in determining who emerges as leader in a team where no leader has been assigned. In a study of emergent leadership among 62 men and 60 women, groups performed "sex-neutral" tasks; that is, tasks not classified as either masculine or feminine. Men and women both emerged as leaders, and neither gender had significantly more emergent leaders. However, group members who described themselves in masculine terms were significantly more likely to emerge as leaders than group members who described themselves in feminine, androgynous (both masculine and feminine), or undifferentiated (neither masculine nor feminine) terms.[79]

STRATEGIES FOR IMPROVING TEAM EFFECTIVENESS

Describe strategies for addressing common operating problems and improving team effectiveness.

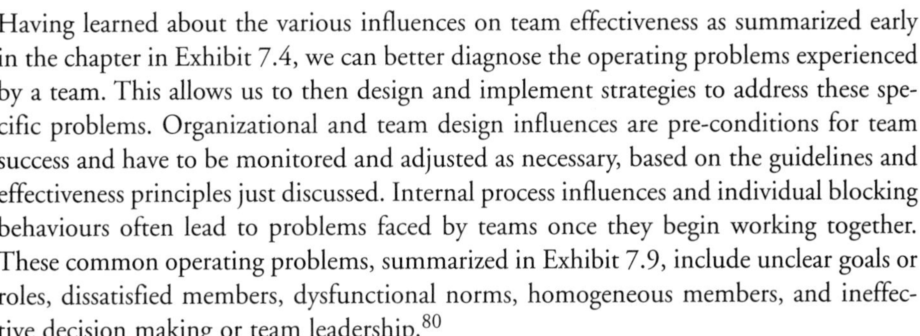

Having learned about the various influences on team effectiveness as summarized early in the chapter in Exhibit 7.4, we can better diagnose the operating problems experienced by a team. This allows us to then design and implement strategies to address these specific problems. Organizational and team design influences are pre-conditions for team success and have to be monitored and adjusted as necessary, based on the guidelines and effectiveness principles just discussed. Internal process influences and individual blocking behaviours often lead to problems faced by teams once they begin working together. These common operating problems, summarized in Exhibit 7.9, include unclear goals or roles, dissatisfied members, dysfunctional norms, homogeneous members, and ineffective decision making or team leadership.[80]

Team building refers to a broad range of planned activities that help teams improve the way they accomplish tasks and help team members enhance their interpersonal and problem-solving skills.[81] A number of team-building interventions to address specific operating problems have already been, or will be, addressed in this text. For example, the goal-setting and supportive communication strategies already discussed in Chapters 4 and 7 are used to help teams with operating problems in these areas. Also, team decision-making techniques and conflict management that will be discussed in Chapters 8 and 11 are frequently used to help improve team effectiveness.

team building
A broad range of planned activities that help teams improve the way they accomplish tasks and help team members enhance their interpersonal and problem-solving skills.

EXHIBIT 7.9

Influences on Team Operating Problems

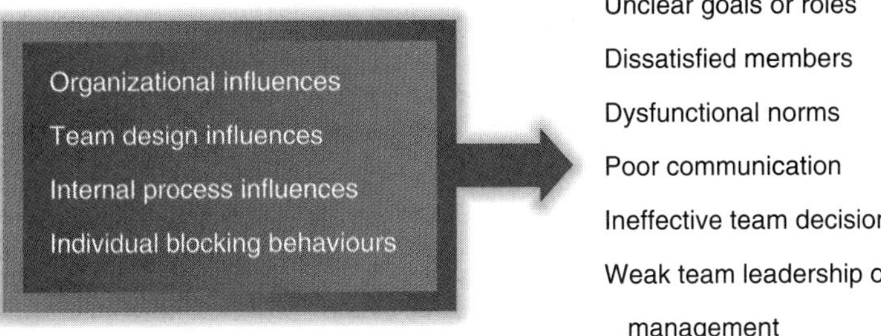

Unclear goals or roles
Dissatisfied members
Dysfunctional norms
Poor communication
Ineffective team decision making
Weak team leadership or conflict management

SOURCE: Adapted from Don Harvey and Donald R. Brown, *An Experiential Approach to Organization Development,* 6th ed. (Upper Saddle River, NJ: Prentice Hall, 2001), 284. Copyright © 2001. Adapted by permission of Pearson Education, Inc., Upper Saddle River, NJ.

One approach to team building that has become popular in recent years is the use of outdoor challenges. Participants go through a series of outdoor activities, such as climbing a 4-metre wall. Physical challenges usually require the participants to work as a team and focus on trust, communication, decision making, and leadership. For example, a team of financial advisors from Burlington's CIBC Wood Gundy went mountain climbing up Mount Howard in the Canadian Rockies for their team building.[82] Employees from CIBC, TD Canada Trust, Levi Strauss, Canadian Tire, the Toronto Stock Exchange, Microsoft, and GlaxoSmithKline have all tried building their teams by learning to play in a rock band.[83] Playing Lego in Toronto, cooking classes in Stratford—you name it, someone has tried to use a creative vehicle to build a team somewhere![84]

While activities like these do improve team communication, build trust, and strengthen bonds, the full benefits of the team building will not be realized unless the activity is preceded by a diagnosis, followed up with a dialogue about the experience, and concluded with some action planning to improve team functioning back on the job. It is for this reason that many companies use a more comprehensive approach to team building, called **team development**. This is an educational process of continually reviewing and evaluating team functioning and identifying and establishing new and more effective ways of operating.[85] Team development is also a central intervention in the professional practice of organization development (OD), which is discussed in depth in Chapter 13. The strength of team development is that it begins with a systematic diagnosis of the internal team processes and individual behaviours, assisted by a third-party facilitator, then the information collected is summarized and fed back to the team in a two- to three-day retreat, after which the team addresses priority issues and then creates an action plan for improvement.

team development
An educational process of continually reviewing and evaluating team functioning and identifying and establishing new and more effective ways of operating.

IMPLICATIONS FOR ORGANIZATIONAL EFFECTIVENESS

Several scholars have explored the advantages that organizations gain from using team structures. They suggest that teams tend to result in increased productivity, more creative solutions to problems, better product or service quality, fewer hierarchical levels,

Application, Analysis & Synthesis

DIAGNOSING TEAM TROUBLE AND DECIDING WHAT THE LEADER SHOULD DO

You are the committee chair for the graduation party. Your committee has been working on the party for two months now and you are behind schedule. You have just left the last meeting and are reflecting on the group dynamics. You have five committee members, four who have been on the committee since the beginning and one "rookie" recently asked to join the team to bring "fresh ideas." What follows is a sample of the dialogue that just took place:

Jen: How can we not have a band? The grad dance always has a band and it's my job to book one.

Lee: DJs are way better and bands are expensive and take long breaks.

Don: Forget the music; we were meant to decide on the location today.

Pete: Yes, if I don't book the hall today, we might lose it.

You: Look, people, we aren't getting anywhere. Let's get back to our agenda.

Rookie: I quit; this is a complete waste of time.

1. What are some of the operating problems evident in this team?
2. Using the five-stage model of team development, identify which stage(s) the committee is at, defending your choice with facts from the dialogue above.
3. What should you do, as the leader, to develop your team and improve its effectiveness?

reduced absenteeism and turnover, more harmonious labour-management relations, and increased profitability.[86]

As competition and change continue to accelerate, organizations are pushing decision making down to lower levels of the organization, so that decisions can be made closer to the customer. Often, this results in team-based organizations as discussed in Chapter 14, but even if the whole structure is not redesigned, teams are being used more and more frequently and in more diverse situations than ever before because many decisions are too complex for any one individual to handle. Organizations also use teams because, as they have become very large, teams provide employees with a community and a number of social benefits.

Organizations have to provide the proper conditions for teams to prosper. They need to ensure the active involvement of an organizational sponsor who is supportive and engaged. The team needs to be given a clear mandate and mission with appropriate physical, financial, technological, and human resources. Clear team-based performance measures as well as team-based rewards and recognition programs must be established for the team. When organizational sponsors design teams, they need to take into account both the desired mix in terms of technical, problem-solving, and interpersonal skills, but also design for optimum levels of diversity, based on the nature of the task itself and the type of interdependence that will be required. The organizational sponsor needs to monitor the team's development, with an understanding that teams inevitably go through stages of storming and disequilibrium. When teams are multicultural or diverse, organization sponsors need to pay particular attention to the emergence of operating problems and need to invest in coaching or team development.

Chapter Summary

1. A *group* consists of two or more people who interact to meet common interests and objectives, while a *team* consists of two or more people with a common objective who are interdependent around a particular task and who hold themselves accountable to each other.
2. Task interdependence is the degree of task-driven interaction among work team members. It can be pooled, sequential, or reciprocal. When task interdependence is pooled, it means that team members work individually but either draw from a pool of inputs or pool their outputs. When task interdependence is sequential, team members rely on each other for resources, with the output of one member becoming the input of another. In teams with reciprocal task interdependence, work is being exchanged back and forth among them.
3. There are many types of temporary and permanent work teams such as task forces, self-managed work teams, and quality circles.
4. In the five-stage model of team development, a team goes through the stages of forming, storming, norming, and performing in a non-linear manner and then adjourns. Each stage has to be managed well in order for the team to reach the performing stage.
5. In the punctuated equilibrium model of team development (which applies to temporary teams), rather than developing gradually over time, teams progress through an alternation of stasis and sudden change, with the midpoint of the team's life being the transitional phase.
6. Team effectiveness is achieved when the team survives, meets its objectives, and the needs of team members have been satisfied to the extent that they would be willing to work together again. Team effectiveness depends upon (1) the organizational influences; (2) the team design influences; (3) the way team members manage important internal process, including their stages of development; and (4) the individual blocking behaviours that reduce team effectiveness.
7. Organizational influences on team effectiveness include an organizational sponsor who is supportive and engaged, a clear team mission, appropriate resources, clear performance measures, and effective and well-managed team rewards.
8. Team design influences on team effectiveness are team size, composition, and the nature of the task itself, including the type of task interdependence.
9. Internal team process influences on team effectiveness include the following: Goals that flow from the organizational mission and are clear and agreed upon. The fulfillment of critical task-oriented and maintenance oriented roles, cohesion, productive norms, and appropriate decision-making procedures. Also, teams have to manage their stages of development and the interpersonal conflicts that inevitably arise.
10. Individual blocking behaviours that can reduce team effectiveness include social loafing, loss of individuality, co-dependency, and individual blocking roles.

11. Cultural and gender diversity, while initially creating additional challenges to team effectiveness, often lead to teams that are more creative and effective than homogeneous teams.
12. Teams often experience operating problems such as unclear goals or roles, dissatisfied team members, dysfunctional norms, poor communication, ineffective decision-making processes, and weak team leadership or conflict management. Two general approaches to improving team effectiveness are team building and team development. Strategies for improving team effectiveness can be found in a number of the chapters of the text.

Key Terms

adjourning (p. 206)
blocking roles (p. 218)
co-dependency (p. 217)
forming (p. 204)
group (p. 198)
loss of individuality (p. 217)
maintenance-oriented roles (p. 212)
mission (p. 208)
norming (p. 204)
norms of behaviour (p. 213)
performing (p. 205)
quality circle (p. 202)
role (p. 210)
self-managed work team (SMWT) (p. 201)
social loafing (p. 216)
storming (p. 204)
task interdependence (p. 199)
task-oriented roles (p. 211)
team (p. 199)
team building (p. 221)
team cohesion (p. 214)
team composition (p. 210)
team development (p. 222)
team effectiveness (p. 207)

Review Questions

1. What are the different types of task interdependence and why is it important to understand these differences?
2. How do we measure team effectiveness and what are the four categories of influences on how effective a team is likely to be?
3. Compare and contrast the five-stage model with the punctuated equilibrium model of team development.
4. Describe at least five task and five maintenance functions that effective work teams must perform, and explain five of the individual blocking behaviours that reduce team effectiveness.
5. When designing a team, what are the various considerations one must take into account to minimize operating problems and maximize the chances that the team will be effective?

Discussion and Communication Questions

1. Which was the most effective team of which you have been a member? What made that team so effective?
2. Have you ever experienced peer pressure to act more in accordance with the behavioural norms of a team? What happened?
3. (*Communication question*) Draft a memo to your supervisor or student association, describing your observations about work teams and groups in your workplace or your university. Where have you observed teams or groups to be most effective? Why? What changes might be made at work or in the university to make teams more effective?
4. (*Communication question*) Interview an employee or manager about what he or she believes contributes to cohesiveness in work groups and teams. Ask the person what the conclusions are based on. Be prepared to discuss what you have learned in class.

Ethics Questions

1. Assume that someone is engaged in social loafing in a team of which you are a member. What should you do? Is this person acting in an unethical manner?
2. Does a moral dilemma arise when an individual is expected to subordinate his or her individuality and autonomy to the will of the work team? Suppose you are a member of a work team that is getting ready to act in a way you believe is unethical or immoral. What should you do? Will you be responsible for the actions of the entire team?
3. If an organization does not set up the proper conditions for team effectiveness as outlined in the chapter, and a team fails, who should take responsibility for the failure and why? Organizational sponsor? Team leader? Team members?

Application & Analysis

EXPERIENTIAL EXERCISE 7.1: ARE WE HAVING FUN YET?

Goals: To give you an opportunity to demonstrate your understanding of the five stages in the development of teams.

Time required: 35 minutes

Materials needed: 5 overhead transparencies and five markers

Instructions:

1. Your instructor will divide the class into five groups. Each group will be assigned one of the stages in the five-stage model of team development: forming, storming, norming, performing, or adjourning.
2. Brainstorm the list of characteristics, including feelings, actions, etc., that you think would typically be part of the make-up of your assigned stage. Plan a nonverbal presentation for the class in which your small group will demonstrate these various characteristics. List the characteristics (using words and phrases) on the overhead transparency.
3. After each group makes its presentation (in the same order as the model), one member of the group will display his or her group's transparency and will answer any questions or challenges from other groups.

Debriefing:

1. How useful is this model
   a. To you as a student looking back over your many experiences with group assignments in school?
   b. To a manager who is in the process of creating a team that will be assigned to a complex task?
2. What strategies would be help a team get through the "storming" stage?
3. How well does this model fit your experience compared to the punctuated equilibrium model?

SOURCE: C. A. Sales, F. A. Owen, and M. A. Lesperance, *Experiential Exercises in Organizational Behaviour* (Toronto: Prentice Hall, 2000), 165–67. Reprinted with permission by Pearson Education Canada Inc.

Application

EXPERIENTIAL EXERCISE 7.2: MERGER AT MOTHER HUBBARD SHOES: EXPLORING TEAM ROLES

Purpose: To explore group processes and study group decision making.

Group size: Divide the class into an even number of groups consisting of 6–8 people. Groups should be of equal size and will be paired up.

Time required: 50 minutes

Materials needed: Merger Information and Observer Checklist

Instructions:

1. **Form groups and read case (5 minutes)**
   Groups will be paired. Paired groups will consist of a problem-solving group (A) with an observer group (B). A's are instructed to read the case "Merger at Mother Hubbard Shoes-Pat Johnson." B's review the task-oriented, maintenance-oriented and blocking roles in the text as well as the observer checklist below. Each person in B can be assigned to observe an individual team member in A.

2. **Group decisions in "fishbowl" format (20 minutes)**
   Group A discusses the case and develops a group ranking while group B members are silent observers. "Fishbowls" (inner circle of Group A with outer circle of group B) should be set up for each pairing.

3. **Observations (15 minutes)**
   Group B shares their observations of team roles with Group A. Then group A can comment.

4. **Class Discussion (10 minutes)**

   - To what extent were goals clear and agreed to?
   - Which team roles helped or hindered the team's effectiveness?
   - Where any behavioural norms evident?
   - Was the team cohesive?
   - How effective were the team decision-making procedures?
   - What could have been done differently to improve team effectiveness?

Observer Checklist

	Name	Name	Name	Name	Name	Name	Name	Name
Initiator								
Information seeker								
Information provider								
Coordinator								
Elaborator								
Summarizer								
Harmonizer								
Compromiser								
Encourager								
Dominator								
Overanalyzer								
Remains passive								
Rejecting								
Deflecting								

Merger at Mother Hubbard Shoes

Mother Hubbard Shoes manufactures and imports children's shoes and sells them in its own chain of retail stores. It has 60 stores spread over nine regions throughout the northeast. Chris Peters and Pat Johnson are two of the regional managers, each responsible for six stores. Each store has a store manager, an assistant manager, and 8 to 12 salespeople who are mostly part-time employees.

Pat has been with Mother Hubbard Shoes since 1988. Joining the company after getting an MBA from LaSalle University, Pat was promoted to regional manager eight months ago. The store managers in Pat's region have between 1 and 30 years of service with Mother Hubbard, Pat has a good relationship with the store managers but does not feel completely knowledgeable about all of them yet. The store managers are:

- Marlene—Age 31; 10 years of service. Satisfactory performer. This has been her only employer. She is single and in three months is planning a five-week trip to Europe made possible by using several years of accumulated vacation time and savings.

- William—Age 62; 30 years of service. Satisfactory performer. Heavily involved in the Rotary. Looking forward to retiring to Florida in three years with his wife, a full-time homemaker.
- Roger—Age 53; 18 years of service. Good performer. Worked in manufacturing with another shoe company before joining Mother Hubbard. Shifted to retail sales when that manufacturing plant was closed. His wife was recently laid off after her company merged and then downsized its staff.
- Natalie—Age 57; 17 years of service. Outstanding performer. Started with the company after raising her children. Does not have her degree but is attending college part-time.
- Charles—Age 38; 1 year of service. Good performer and also a LaSalle graduate. This is his third employer. The last two companies he worked for each merged and then downsized staff. Charles had the least seniority and was laid off. Is caring for two young children from his former marriage.
- Arnold—Age 29; 3 years of service. Outstanding performer. Married to a young architect who is just starting her own business, Arnold has had some financial problems the last few years.

Last Friday at the quarterly corporate sales meeting, Pat Johnson's boss announced that the rumours they had been hearing were true. Mother Hubbard would merge with a large, competing shoe manufacturer/retailer. Pat's boss did not have any further information but was certain that it would mean at least a 10 percent cut in stores and staff at all levels of the organization (i.e., one store totally closed, others possibly reduced). The regional managers were advised to develop a ranking of store managers that would be used to prepare a layoff listing.

SOURCE: Adapted from D. Marcic, J. Seltzer, and P. Vaill, *Organizational Behavior: Experiences and Cases*, 6th ed. (Mason, OH: South-Western College Publishing, 2001), 93, 377. (Original source cited in Marcic is D. Finn and J. Seltzer, 2000.) Reprinted by permission of South-Western, a division of Thomson Learning, www.thomsonrights.com. Fax 800-730-2215.

Application

EXPERIENTIAL EXERCISE 7.3: USING PEER EVALUATION AND GRADE REDISTRIBUTION TO MINIMIZE SOCIAL LOAFING AND IMPROVE EFFECTIVENESS IN TEMPORARY TEAMS

Purpose: To use an objective peer evaluation process combined with possible grade redistribution to minimize social loafing and improve the effectiveness of student teams.

Group size: Use existing class project teams.

Time required: 30–60 minutes to define and agree on peer evaluation criteria (60 minutes at the end of term to evaluate each other and agree on contribution percentage).

Materials needed: Writing materials

Instructions:

Part 1: Early in the Team's Development

1. In your OB project team, in one of your early meetings, brainstorm and agree on five to ten criteria that you will use to evaluate each other. Examples of criteria could be high-quality work, punctuality at meetings, open communications, etc.
2. Define these criteria (your expectations of each other) using *action verb sentences.* For example, to define "high-quality work," one action verb sentence could be: "Proofreads work to ensure absence of spelling and grammatical errors." See the examples of action verbs that follow.

3. Insert your criteria into the team evaluation template provided, adding as many columns as necessary. In the example given, it is assumed that there are four members in the team. Adjust the template so that there is one column per team member plus one extra column for the assessor on the left. The four lines under each team member's name (in each category) are for each person's rating of that individual, including his or her self-rating. For example, the four ratings in the column called "John" contain three ratings given by John's team mates (Sue, Chris, and Sam) and one given by John, evaluating himself.

Examples of Action Verbs to Define Peer Evaluation Criteria

Abides	Brings	Discusses	Keeps	Proofreads
Advises	Checks	Displays	Leads	Plans
Agrees	Clarifies	Ensures	Listens	Researches
Analyzes	Communicates	Follows	Meets	Responds
Argues	Coordinates	Gives	Notifies	Stays
Arrives	Demonstrates	Helps	Participates	Suggests
Asks	Develops	Initiates	Prepares	Treats

Part 2: Half-Life Check-In and Mock Grade Redistribution

1. About halfway through the project, conduct a mock peer evaluation using the criteria developed.
2. Follow the grade redistribution steps provided in the example to calculate each person's individual contribution percentage (ICP). Use the ICP to calculate what each team member's grade would be if the instructor had given you a 75% on your team project.
3. Use this check-in to improve your peer evaluation document and your team's effectiveness

Part 3: Upon Project Completion

1. Upon completion of your project, complete your peer evaluations of each other using the team evaluation template and calculate each team member's ICP according to the step-by-step instructions below.

Example Team Peer Evaluation Template for Four-Person Team

Criteria *5 = Excellent* *4 = Very good* *3 = Good* *2 = Fair* *1 = Very poor*	Assessor	John	Sue	Chris	Sam
Criterion 1: High Quality of work • **Proofreads** work to ensure absence of spelling and grammatical errors • **Includes** full references for all research • **Follows** guidelines on the course outline • **Explains** underlying OB concepts	*John*	5	5	4	2
	Sue	4	5	5	2
	Chris	4	5	4	2
	Sam	4	5	5	4
AVERAGE INDIVIDUAL SCORE–1		**4.25**	**5**	**4.5**	**2.5**
Criterion 2: Good Attendance	John	4	4	4	3
Action Verb _______	Sue	3	5	4	3
Etc.	Chris	3	4	4	4
	Sam	3	4	5	5
AVERAGE INDIVIDUAL SCORE–2		**3.25**	**4.25**	**4.25**	**3.75**
Criterion 3: Participates in Meetings	John	5	4	4	3
Action Verb _______	Sue	4	5	3	4
Etc.	Chris	4	4	4	4
	Sam	4	4	4	4
AVERAGE INDIVIDUAL SCORE–3		**4.25**	**4.25**	**3.75**	**3.75**
INDIVIDUAL TOTAL SCORE	Step 1	11.75*	13.5*	12.5*	11.25*
TEAM TOTAL SCORE	Step 2	49**	49**	49**	49**
INDIVIDUAL CONTRIBUTION PERCENTAGE (ICP)	Step 3	0.24	0.27	0.26	0.23

Steps to Translate Peer Evaluation Score into Individual Contribution Percentages

1. Add up the individual average scores for each person on your Peer Evaluation Form. This total is **the individual total score** (indicated by * above).

   Example above: John: 4.25 + 3.25 + 4.25 = 11.75

2. Now add up all the individual total scores to get a **TEAM total score** (indicated by ** above).

   In this team it's 11.75 + 13.5 + 12.5 + 11.25 = 49

3. Then divide the individual total score * by the TEAM total score ** to get the person's **individual contribution percentage (ICP):**

   Example: John: $\frac{11.75}{49} = 0.24$

4. Check that all the **ICPs add up to 100%** (i.e., John 0.24 + Sue 0.27 + Chris 0.26 + Sam 0.23 = 1.00).

5. If the grade received for the team project is, for example **73%,** the total grade allotment for the team will be 73 × 4 (number of team members) = 292. Then, each student will get the following grade based on his or her **ICP**:

   John gets 0.24 × 292 = 70%

   Sue gets 0.27 × 292 = 79%

   Chris gets 0.26 × 292 = 76%

   Sam gets 0.23 × 292 = 67%

   292

SOURCE: © P. Sniderman and G. Bingham with the assistance of students K. Rattray, J. Yau, J. Bastiampillai, H. Phillips, N. Lucas-Richardson, and E. Chan. Ryerson University, 2005.

Application, Analysis & Synthesis

CASE: CHILI SAUCE TECHNICIANS AND TEAM DYNAMICS

Many university students work during the summer, some attend summer school, and a few do both. John Hartman, Bill Todman, and Robert Drake fell into the latter category. They attended a six-week early summer session that ended the second week of July. As they approached final exams, they discussed what they would do in the last half of the summer. Their finances were next to nothing, so they couldn't travel. Job prospects were not good, but they decided to find jobs. Even minimum-wage jobs could generate enough income for rent, food, and gasoline if each could work at least 40 hours a week.

John, Bill, and Robert attended the University of Guelph in Guelph, Ontario, a pleasant community but one with few summer job opportunities in July. A friend of Robert's suggested they drive to Toronto about 100 kilometres away and apply at the food-processing plant owned by H. J. Heinz. On July 11, they completed their last exams and left for Toronto at 2:00 p.m. Shortly after 3:00 p.m., they found the plant and were directed to the employment office. The three were interviewed individually by a recruiter who was in his 50s. By 4:30 p.m., he had decided to hire them. They were instructed to report for work at 6:00 a.m. the next day in the kitchen area of the main facility.

As they drove back to Guelph, the reality of their job situation suddenly hit them. While all three had grown up in small Ontario towns, none of them had worked directly, or even indirectly, in a food commodity or agricultural situation. The food processing plant, really a complex of facilities, was operating "in season," which meant that there were three nine-hour shifts and they were needed from 6:00 a.m. to 4 p.m. with an hour for lunch. This meant that they would have to drive back to Guelph in rush hour. The three would be working 44-hour weeks for minimum wage with no opportunity for overtime pay. They also realized they would have to leave Guelph no later than 4:45 a.m. each day in order to arrive at the plant prior to the 6:00 a.m. start time. While this type of daily schedule seemed formidable, they decided they didn't have much choice, as they didn't have enough money to pay the next month's rent.

The next morning they arrived at the plant a few minutes before 6:00 a.m., punched their time cards, and went to the kitchen. The kitchen was a large room with four huge ovens. As they entered the room, they were caustically greeted by the lead oven operator (cook). He immediately told them that he never graduated from high school and that he thought college students were rich brats. The morning went downhill from there. Robert was assigned to operate two valves located above a raised narrow walkway between the ovens and a row of large mixing bowls. Each oven had a mixing bowl; they were connected by eight-centimetre pipes with pumps that moved a prepared mixture of ingredients from the bowl to the oven. John and Bill were assigned to the mixing bowls, where they were instructed to prepare various seasoning ingredients (sugar, salt, garlic, and others) in two of the bowls for mixing. The ingredients were mixed for several minutes and then pumped into an oven along with of tomato pulp for cooking chili sauce. The valves operated by Robert, when opened, filled two large vats. Each container held 500 gallons of tomato pulp. A 15-centimetre pipe connected the vats to a huge, fully enclosed storage container in which tomato pulp was prepared. This storage container held thousands of gallons of pulp.

The first day on the job was very exhausting, somewhat confusing, and at times humiliating for Robert, Bill, and John. A kitchen supervisor provided job instructions early in the work shift. Then he left and wasn't seen again until early in the afternoon. After working several days in the kitchen, the three found out that the supervisor had management responsibilities in three other departments of the plant. During periods when the supervisor was elsewhere, the lead cook exercised supervision. His supervision consisted of yelling obscenities and finding fault with the performance of Robert, Bill, and John.

After the first day in the kitchen, they were ready to quit. But on the way home, they decided to go back the next day. In fact, they worked in the kitchen for nearly four weeks. By the end of the first week, they had even come to the conclusion that the kitchen was probably the best place to work. It was extremely clean and air conditioned, but it was nearly unbearable when the lead cook became particularly abusive toward them.

On Thursday afternoon of the fourth week, chili sauce production ended and John, Robert, and Bill were reassigned to other departments. John reported to the quality control lab, where ketchup, chili sauce, and other products were tested. He functioned as a lab assistant. Robert and Bill were sent to the bottling lines, where ketchup was bottled and filled bottles were capped, labelled, and placed into cases. The cases were picked up from conveyor belts and hand-stacked on pallets for movement by forklift to a large warehouse. Robert and Bill were stationed at the end of the line, where the cases were taken off the conveyor and stacked. Depending upon the size of the bottle, a case of ketchup could weigh nearly 23 kilograms.

The work of stacking cases was strenuous and at times so exhausting that Robert and Bill couldn't work as fast as the line moved. Line speed was controlled by a machine operator. A machine collected bottles from the line, turned them over, and deposited them in cases. Each case was then sealed by another machine as it moved along the conveyor. There were five conveyor lines, three of which were working at any given time.

Each machine operator was a long-service female employee. Even though these women were within eight metres of Robert and Bill, the noise of the production line prevented any conversation. Very quickly, however, the two realized that these women had a relatively low opinion of seasonal workers and they apparently experienced considerable delight in varying the speed of the line. They could increase line speed sufficiently to make it almost impossible for Robert and Bill to remove and stack every case of ketchup. Robert and Bill would yell at them to slow down. When the women heard them, they responded only with laughter.

After several hours of back-breaking work, Robert slipped and fell as he tried to stack a case. The women applauded while three cases fell off the end of the conveyor. Bottles broke and the line had to stop for glass and ketchup to be removed from the floor. As soon as the mess was cleared, the line resumed. Three more times during the work shift, boxes fell off the end of the conveyor.

As the three travelled home that day, they discussed the day's work experiences. Robert and Bill decided that the next day, when the women increased the line speed, one of them would throw a case against the wall so that bottles would break and force the line to stop. They realized their behaviour might get them fired.

At 10:30 the next morning, the first opportunity arose where they could take the drastic action that had been contemplated. Bill threw a case against the wall; glass and ketchup flew as far as six metres. The line stopped. Two more times that day, he and Robert threw cases against the wall. The women, of course, saw them do this but did nothing about it except to stop the line for cleanup.

Discussion Questions

1. What kind of task interdependence is evident in the kitchen and the bottling lines?
2. Explain why the team on the bottling line is ineffective.
3. What team design influences could be held partially accountable for the problems that emerged between the three seasonal employees and the long-service machine operators?
4. Describe the internal process weaknesses on the bottling line team which contributed to the eventual violent outbursts and displays of individual blocking behaviours.

SOURCE: Adapted with permission from "Chili Sauce Technicians and Job Performance," D. L. Nelson and J. C. Quick, *Organizational Behavior: Foundations, Realities and Challenges* (Mason, OH: South-Western, 1994), 196–97. Reprinted by permission of South-Western, a division of Thomson Learning, www.thomsonrights.com. Fax 800-730-2215.

Scoring Instructions for Self-Assessments

Self-Assessment 7.2: How Cohesive Is Your Team?

Scoring Key: Add up your circled responses. If you have a number of 20 or above, you view your team as highly cohesive. If you have a number between 10 and 19, you view your team's cohesion as average. If you have a number of 7 or less, you view your team as very low in cohesion.

Creativity and Decision Making

chapter eight

8

LEARNING OBJECTIVES

By the end of this chapter, you will be able to do the following:

1. Define *creativity* and describe the four stages of the creative process.
2. Explain how creativity is influenced by individual factors, organizational factors, and the degree of fit between the individual and the organization.
3. Define *decision making* and explain what is meant by an effective decision and an ethical decision.
4. Explain the rational decision-making model and its underlying assumptions.
5. Compare the rational model with the "bounded rationality" and "garbage can" models of decision making as well as the "intuitive decision-making" models.
6. Explain how risk aversion, escalation of commitment to a losing course of action, and cognitive style influence individual decision making.
7. Explore the various levels of group participation in decision making and their effects.
8. Summarize the advantages and disadvantages of group versus individual decision making.
9. Explain the specific disadvantages of groupthink and group polarization.
10. Describe four methods to improve group decision making: brainstorming, nominal group technique (NGT), the Delphi technique, and devil's advocacy.

learning about the context

Fostering Creativity at Intuit Using Napping Rooms

Intuit Canada is a rapidly expanding software developer which has more than 300 employees and produces the products QuickTax and Quicken. Since the year 2000, Intuit's Edmonton headquarters has fostered employee creativity by providing three napping rooms (dubbed "Hotel Intuit"), each equipped with a single bed, a night table with an alarm clock, and replacement linens so that each napper has fresh sheets.

Napping rooms have proved to be effective, not only because short afternoon naps reduce fatigue thereby enhancing performance, but they also support the "incubation" stage in the creative process. Research has shown that making time for reflection and relaxation supports the creative process. This is why people often get their best ideas at night or upon awakening. Experts target fatigue as one of the main impediments to creativity, which is a problem because 65 percent of people polled report not getting enough sleep. Sleep experts argue that naps, or "siestas," common in most of the world outside of North America offer significant benefits which, though appreciated by students, pilots, and shift workers, are still viewed with skepticism by the average 9–5 Canadian worker.

Sleep experts suggest that the optimum length of time for a "power" nap so as not to feel lethargic afterward is 10–20 minutes.

SOURCES: L. Anthony, "Some Companies Come around to the Value of Naps: They Are Finding That Having a Little On-the-Job Rest Can Actually Be Better in the Long Run for Business," *Guardian,* Charlottetown, P.E.I., February 17, 2003, C1; J. Sinnema, "Perking Things Up: Some Employers Find Interesting Ways to Boost Creativity," *Times-Colonist,* Victoria, B.C., May 21, 2003, D1; T. Poze, "Analogical Connections—The Essence of Creativity," *Journal of Creative Behavior* 17 (1983): 240–41; "Staying at Hotel Intuit," *Maclean's,* October 28, 2002 (vol. 115, no. 43), 27.

Synectics

Synectics Inc. is an established global consulting firm that helps organizations dramatically increase the creativity of their people to formulate powerful ideas that accelerate performance and generate new wealth. The pioneer in the field of corporate creativity, Synectics has improved the performance of hundreds of organizations such as Nestlé, Unilever, Coca-Cola, Universal Studios, and Citigroup.
http://www.synecticsworld.com

This chapter is divided into three overall parts. Part one examines creativity, part two explores individual decision making, and part three explores group decision making.

We begin in part one by exploring the stages of *the creative process* and how it is influenced by individual and organizational factors, including right brain versus left brain preferences and the fit between the individual and the organization. In part two, we define decision making and explain what is meant by an effective and ethical decision.

Then we review the traditional, rational model of *individual decision making* and compare it to three other models that attempt to explain how individuals identify problems and make decisions *in reality.* These alternatives to the rational model are called the "bounded rationality" model, the "garbage can" model, and the "intuitive decision making" model. We continue with a review of the various factors that influence how individuals make decisions. These factors include differences in risk aversion, varying tendencies to escalate one's commitment to a losing course of action, and differences in cognitive style preferences for gathering information and making judgments.

We then move on to part three of the chapter, which explores aspects of *group decision making.* We explore the effects of group participation in decision making and the advantages and disadvantages of making decisions in groups versus as individuals. We then expand on two important disadvantages of group decision making, which are "groupthink" and "group polarization." We then provide a brief overview of effective techniques for improving group decision making.

CREATIVITY AT WORK

1

Define *creativity* and describe the four stages of the creative process.

creativity
A process influenced by individual and organizational factors that results in the production of novel and useful ideas, products, or both.

Creativity is a process influenced by individual and organizational factors that results in the production of novel and useful ideas, products, or both.[1] As you saw in the chapter opening, companies such as Intuit Canada are actively seeking ways to foster and encourage employees to be more creative in their decision making. Creativity is an especially important competency in today's turbulent business environment.[2] Creativity is often considered to be unique to artists, writers, and musicians, but this is not the case at all. Creativity can be found, and indeed is required, in all aspects of business and management.[3]

Creativity is important in today's turbulent business environment. Creativity is often considered to be unique to artists but this is not the case at all. Creativity is required in all aspects of business and management.

Synectics Inc., a company that specializes in fostering business innovation, distinguishes between what they call "big C" and "little C" creativity.[4] "Big C" creativity is the "big breakthrough," and often people feel that if they have not created something huge, they are not creative and they lose heart. Instead, Synectics argues, managers need to promote and recognize "little C" creativity, which is the "small stuff" of everyday life when employees are "making up each day as they go along, as the market shifts, as the office environment shifts, as the politics in the office shifts."[5] Creativity is a process that is, at least in part, unconscious. This is why the sleep experts mentioned in the chapter opener emphasize the importance of being well rested at work, and offering employees a place to take "power" naps.

The Four Stages of the Creative Process

The four stages of the creative process, summarized in Exhibit 8.1, are preparation, incubation, illumination, and verification.[6]

- *Preparation:* Preparation means seeking out new experiences and opportunities to learn, because creativity grows from a base of knowledge. Travel and educational opportunities of all kinds open the individual's mind.
- *Incubation:* During incubation, the individual engages in other pursuits while the mind considers the problem and works on it. Incubation is a process of reflective thought and is often conducted subconsciously. Research has shown that making time for reflection and relaxation supports the creative process, which is why often people get their best ideas at night or upon awakening.[7]
- *Illumination*: Illumination occurs when the individual senses an insight for solving the problem. This stage is also called the "aha" experience. Scott Abbot and Chris Haney, the two Canadian journalists from Montreal who co-founded the hugely successful board game Trivial Pursuit, had this kind of "illumination" experience. The two men were getting ready to do war in a best-of-seven Scrabble series when they had the stroke of genius to create a trivia game.[8]
- *Verification:* Finally, verification is conducted to determine whether the solution or idea is valid. This is accomplished by thinking through the implications of the decision, presenting the idea to another person, or trying out the decision.

Individual Influences in Creative Problem Solving

Explain how creativity is influenced by individual factors, organizational factors, and the degree of fit between the individual and the organization.

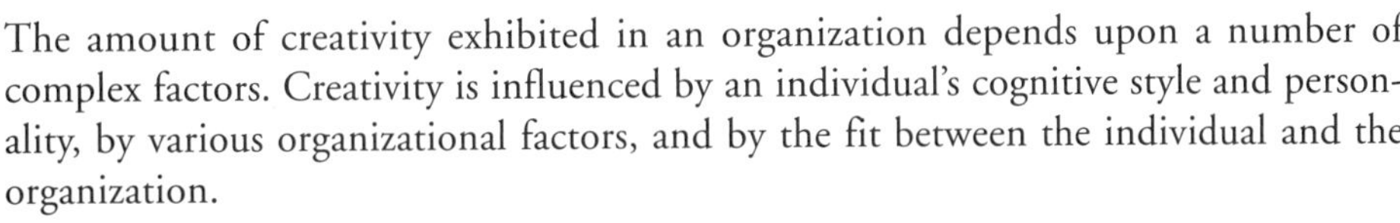

The amount of creativity exhibited in an organization depends upon a number of complex factors. Creativity is influenced by an individual's cognitive style and personality, by various organizational factors, and by the fit between the individual and the organization.

Cognitive Processes, Personality Factors, and Mental Blocks

Several individual variables are related to creative problem solving. Try out the brain teasers in Self-Assessment 8.1 to see if you prefer logical or creative problem solving.

EXHIBIT 8.1

The Four Stages of the Creative Process

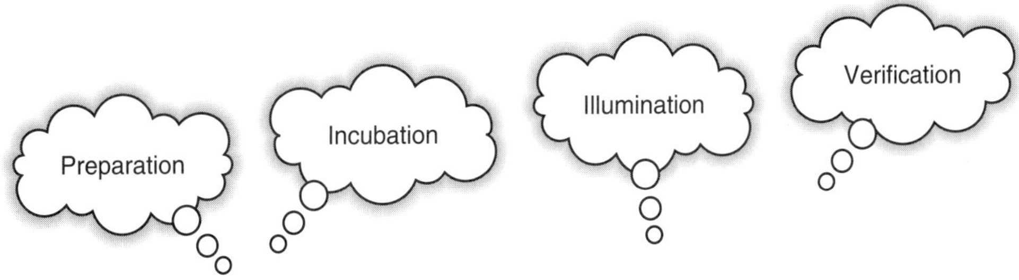

? Application & Analysis

SELF-ASSESSMENT 8.1: PRACTISE CREATIVE PROBLEM SOLVING

Try the following creative problem-solving challenge. Each of the following problems is an equation that can be solved by substituting the appropriate words for the letters. Have fun with them!

Examples: 3F = 1Y (3 feet = 1 yard.)
4LC = GL (4 leaf clover = Good luck.)

1. M + M + NH + V + C + RI = NE.
2. "1B in the H = 2 in the B."
3. 8D – 24H = 1W.
4. 3P = 6.
5. HH & MH at 12 = N or M.
6. 4J + 4Q+ 4K = All the FC.
7. S & M & T & W & T & F & S are D of W.
8. A + N + AF + MC + CG = AF.
9. T = LS State.
10. 23Y – 3Y = 2D.
11. E – 8 = Z.
12. Y + 2D = T.
13. C + 6D = NYE.
14. Y – S – S – A = W.
15. A & E were in the G of E.
16. My FL and South P are both MC.
17. "NN = GN."
18. N + P + SM = S of C.
19. 1 + 6Z = 1M.
20. "R = R = R."
21. AL & JG & WM & JK were all A.
22. N + V + P + A + A + C + P + I = P of S.
23. S = H of R = USC.

SOURCE: *A Whack on the Side of the Head* by Roger Von Oech. Copyright © 1983, 1990, 1998 by Roger Von Oech. By permission of Warner Books.

Try the following logical problem-solving exercise, entitled "Who Owns the Fish?" which is attributed to Albert Einstein:

There are five houses in a row, in five different colours. In each house lives a person from a different country. Each person drinks a certain drink, plays a certain game, and keeps a certain pet. No two people drink the same drink, play the same game, or keep the same pet.

- The Brit lives in a red house.
- The Swede keeps dogs.
- The Dane drinks tea.
- The green house is on the left of the white house.
- The green house owner drinks coffee.
- The person who plays tennis rears birds.
- The owner of the yellow house plays chess.
- The man living in the house right in the centre drinks milk.
- The Norwegian lives in the first house.
- The man who plays poker lives next to the man who keeps cats.
- The man who keeps horses lives next to the one who plays chess.
- The man who plays billiards drinks beer.
- The German plays golf.
- The Norwegian lives next to the blue house.
- The man who plays poker has a neighbour who drinks water.

Question: Who owns the fish?
Answer: Your instructor can provide the solutions to this challenge.

SOURCE: Adapted from E. O. Welles, "The Billionaire Next Door," *Inc.* 23, no. 6 (May 2001): 80–85. Used with permission.

One group of factors involves the cognitive processes that creative individuals tend to use, such as **divergent thinking**,which refers to the individual's ability to generate several potential solutions to a problem.[9] In addition, associational abilities and the use of imagery are associated with creativity.[10] Unconscious processes such as dreams are also essential cognitive processes related to creative thinking.[11] Personality factors have also been related to creativity in studies of individuals from several different occupations. These characteristics include intellectual and artistic values, breadth of interests, high energy, need for achievement, independence of judgment, intuition, self-confidence, and a creative self-image.[12] Tolerance of ambiguity, intrinsic motivation, risk taking, and a desire for recognition are also associated with creativity.[13] There is also evidence that people who are in a good mood are more creative. One study found that individuals who were in a good mood were more successful at creative problem solving than people whose mood was neutral.[14]

divergent thinking
An individual's ability to generate several potential solutions to a problem.

Mental blocks can diminish creativity. Examples of mental blocks include searching for the "right" answer and being afraid to look foolish.[15] Part of creativity training involves learning to open up mental blocks that keep us from generating creative alternatives to a decision or problem. See Exhibit 8.2 for a full list of mental blocks to creativity, and ask yourself whether you experience any of these blocks to your own creativity.

Most of us are more comfortable using either logic or creativity, and we show that preference in everyday decision making. Self-Assessment 8.2 is an activity that helps you determine which process, logic or creativity, is your preferred one. Complete the self-assessment now, and then read on to interpret your score.

Right Brain versus Left Brain Preferences

As shown in Exhibit 8.3, our brains have two lateral halves. The right side is the centre for creative functions and intuition, while the left side is the centre for logic, detail, and planning. Individuals predisposed to a right-brain preference tend to be more creative. There are advantages to both kinds of thinking, so the ideal situation is to be "brain-lateralized" or to be able to use either logic or creativity or both, depending on the situation. There are ways to develop the side of the brain you may not be accustomed to using. To develop your right side, or creative side, you can ask "what if" questions, engage in play, and follow your intuition. To develop the left side, you can set goals for completing tasks and work to attain these goals. For managers, it is important to see the big picture, craft a vision, and plan strategically—all of which require right-brain skills. It is equally important to be able to understand day-to-day operations and flow chart work processes, which are left-hemisphere brain skills.

EXHIBIT 8.2

Mental Blocks to Creativity

Searching for the "right" answer.	Following the rules.
Trying to be logical.	Avoiding ambiguity.
Striving for practicality.	Being afraid to look foolish.
Avoiding problems outside our own expertise.	Fearing failure.
Believing we are not really creative.	Not making play a part of work.

SOURCE: R. Von Oech, *A Whack on the Side of the Head* (New York: Warner, 1983).

SELF-ASSESSMENT 8.2: WHICH SIDE OF YOUR BRAIN DO YOU FAVOUR?

There are no "right" or "wrong" answers to this questionnaire. It is more of a self-assessment than a test. Do not read the questions more than once. Don't overanalyze. Merely circle "a" or "b" to indicate which answer is more typical of you.

1. Typically, when I have a problem to solve,
   (a) I make a list of possible solutions, prioritize them, and then select the best answer.
   (b) I "let it sit" for a while or talk it over with someone before I attempt to reach a solution.
2. When I sit with my hands clasped in my lap (*fold your hands that way right now before going on, then look at your hands*), the thumb that is on top is:
   (a) My right thumb.
   (b) My left thumb.
3. I have hunches
   (a) Sometimes, but do not place much faith in them.
   (b) Frequently, and I usually follow them.
4. If I am at a meeting or lecture, I tend to take extensive notes.
   (a) True
   (b) False
5. I am well-organized, have a system for doing things, have a place for everything and everything in its place, and can assimilate information quickly and logically.
   (a) True
   (b) False
6. I am good with numbers.
   (a) True
   (b) False
7. Finding words in a dictionary or looking up names in a telephone book is something I can do easily and quickly.
   (a) True
   (b) False
8. If I want to remember directions or other information,
   (a) I make notes.
   (b) I visualize the information.
9. I express myself well verbally.
   (a) True
   (b) False
10. To learn dance steps or athletic moves,
    (a) I try to understand the sequence of the steps and repeat them mentally.
    (b) I don't think about it; I just try to get the feel of the game or the music.

For scoring instructions, please go to the end of the chapter, p. 269.

EXHIBIT 8.3

Functions of the Left and Right Brain Hemispheres

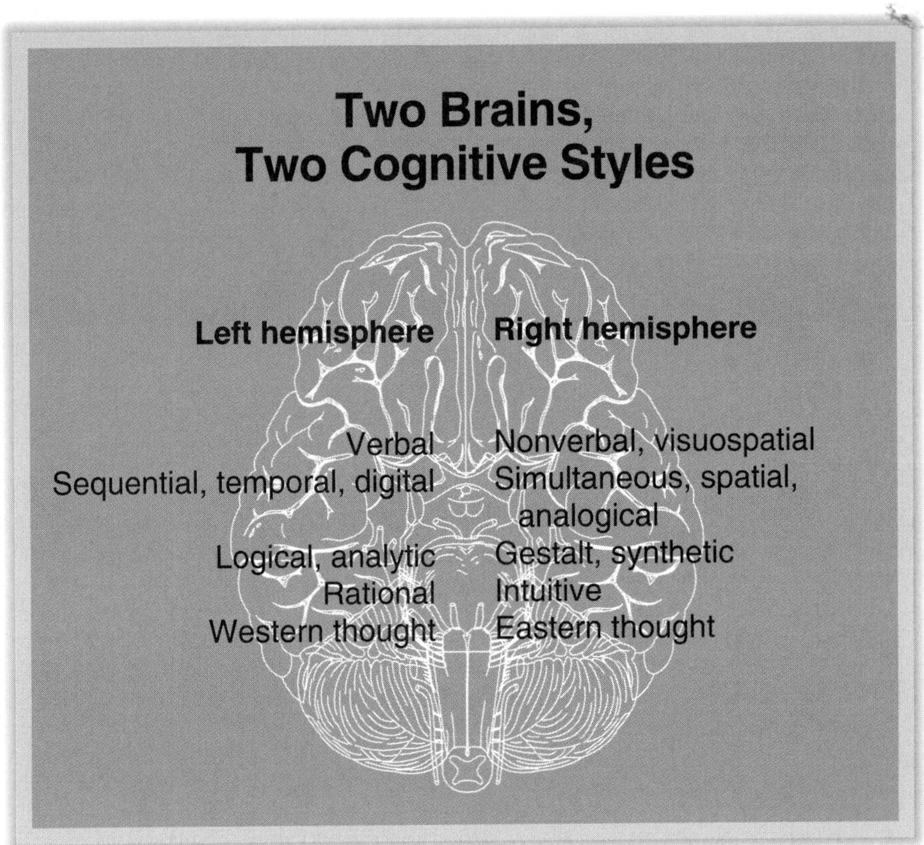

SOURCE: Based on an idea from *Left Brain, Right Brain* by Springer and Deutsch, p. 272. © 1993 by Sally P. Springer and Georg Deutsch (New York: W. H. Freeman and Company, 1993).

Organizational Influences on Creativity

We explore the organizational influences on creativity by looking first at the organizational factors that facilitate creativity, and then at the organizational factors that create barriers to creativity.

Organizational Facilitators of Creativity

Following are factors within the organization that facilitate creativity:

- *Leadership:* Leaders can encourage norms that are associated with increased group innovation, such as support for risk taking, tolerance of mistakes, teamwork, and speed of action.[16] Leaders can encourage and facilitate creativity by taking risks themselves, by serving as creative role models, and by listening to employee ideas, regardless of where they come from. Richard Branson, founder and chairman of U.K.-based Virgin Atlantic, believes that if you do not use your employees' creative potential, you are doomed to failure. At Virgin Atlantic, the culture encourages risk taking and rewards innovation. Rules and regulations are minimized as is analyzing ideas to death. Branson says an employee can have an idea in the morning and implement it in the afternoon.[17] 3M is well-known for fostering innovation and creativity. It has developed a model of 12 leadership competencies, one of

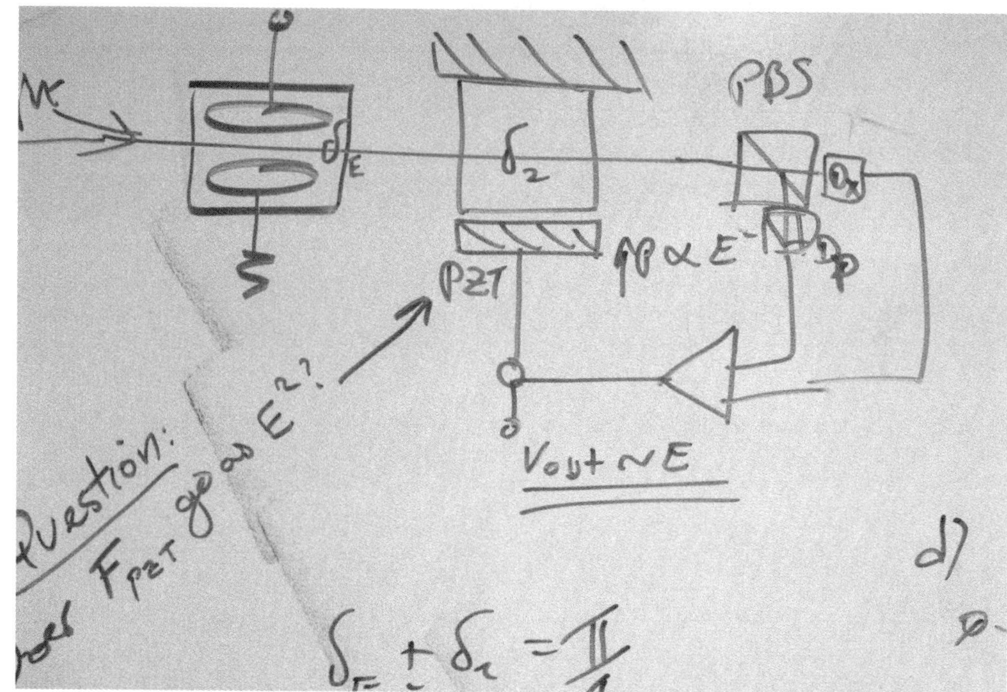

"Displayed thinking" on whiteboards at the Steelcase offices encourages people to talk about their ideas with others.

which is called "nurturing innovation" and is defined as follows: "A leader must create an environment that supports new ideas and takes risks."[18] 3M also has a policy that all employees can use 15 percent of their time to a project of their choosing.

- *Organizational structure:* The structure of an organization can also facilitate innovation and creativity. During the "Evergreen" project at Harvard University, 160 companies were studied over a 10-year period to discover which management practices truly produced results. One of the many findings was that when the chain of command was minimized and the structure kept simple, employees were freer to create and innovate.[19] Lucent Technologies has an operating business group whose sole focus is to incubate internal technologies and opportunities. The value of creativity and innovation is given visibility through this group, and its president reports to Lucent's chief operating officer.[20]
- *Physical environment and communication:* Information flow and the physical environment in a company are important so that ideas can surface and be heard.[21] Companies like Oticon, a Danish hearing-aid manufacturer also discussed in Chapter 14, use open-plan offices that eliminate office walls and cubicles so that employees interact more frequently.[22] Steelcase went even further and introduced what they called "displayed thinking" to one floor of their office building. This involved providing everyone with whiteboards on which they wrote down the ideas they were wrestling with. People would pass the whiteboards on the way to the coffee area and would stop to talk to people about their ideas.[23]
- *Recognition:* Recognition for creativity is also important. At NetGenesis, an e-commerce company in the U.S., risk takers are rewarded and recognized through their "heroes" program, called the NetGenesis Rocks Award.[24] Studies of the role of organizational rewards in encouraging creativity have mixed results. Some studies have shown that monetary incentives improve creative performance, whereas others have found that material rewards do not influence innovation activity.[25]
- *Culture:* Allowing employees to fail, making work more fun, and providing creativity training also facilitate creativity. Google's culture, for example, encourages experimentation and supports failure.[26] Google allows all employees 20 percent of their time to work on personal interests (upping 3M's famous 15 percent).[27] Also, it offers

employees visual symbols of its culture by providing 30 different kinds of cereal in the office, as well as ever-changing cubicle configurations.[28] Another way companies can encourage creativity is exposing employees to new ideas. This can be done in several ways, including job rotation, which moves employees through different jobs and gives them exposure to different information, projects, and teams. Employees can also be assigned to work with groups outside the company, such as suppliers or consultants. Finally, managers can encourage employees to surround themselves with stimuli that they have found to enhance their creative processes. These may be music, artwork, books, or anything else that encourages creative thinking.[29]

Organizational Barriers to Creativity

Creativity killers include focusing on how work is going to be evaluated, being watched while you are working, and competing with other people in win–lose situations. These barriers include internal political problems, harsh criticism of new ideas, destructive internal competition, and avoidance of risk.[30] A 2003 study of barriers to creativity in a Hong Kong hotel revealed four factors that were perceived by supervisors and managers to be significant. These factors were low commitment to the organization and system, fear of change and criticism, time and work pressure, and rigid rules and company style.[31]

Creativity is a global concern. Poland, for example, is undergoing a major shift from a centrally planned economy and single-party rule to a market economy and Western-style democracy. One of the major concerns for Polish managers is creativity. Finding ingenious solutions and having the ability to think creatively can be a question of sink or swim for Polish organizations, which are making the transition to a faster pace of learning and change.[32]

Organizational–Individual Fit

Research has indicated that creative performance is highest when there is a match, or fit, between the individual and organizational influences on creativity. For example, when individuals who desire to be creative are matched with an organization that values creative ideas, the result is more creative performance.[33] Research suggests that when leader-employee relationships are positive, employees with moderately innovative individual characteristics will be more creative and innovative than if relationships with the leader are less positive.[34] A common mistaken assumption regarding creativity is that either you have it or you do not. Research refutes this myth and has shown that individuals can be trained to be more creative.[35]

Application & Analysis

ANY BARRIERS TO CREATIVITY AT YOUR COLLEGE OR UNIVERSITY?

Explore any barriers to creativity in the educational institution you are currently attending and/or in the courses you are taking.

- Do you ever experience harsh criticism of your suggestions or ideas in class?
- Do you experience any destructive competition with other students?
- Do you feel encouraged to take risks with your ideas and work?
- Are there rigid rules and regulations regarding your work outcomes or expected style?

Define *decision making* and explain what is meant by an effective decision and an ethical decision.

INDIVIDUAL DECISION MAKING AT WORK

decision making
A conscious process of making choices among one or more alternatives and developing a commitment to a course of action.

programmed decision
A simple, routine matter for which a manager has an established decision rule.

nonprogrammed decision
A new, complex decision that requires a creative solution.

Decision making is a conscious process of making choices among one or more alternatives and developing a commitment to a course of action. All of us are required to make decisions at work and at home. The decisions we face can range from very simple, routine matters for which we have established decision rules (**programmed decisions**) to new and complex decisions that require creative solutions (**nonprogrammed decisions**).[36] Scheduling lunch hours for one's work group is a programmed decision. The manager performs the decision activity on a daily basis, using an established procedure with the same clear goal in mind. In contrast, decisions like buying out another company are nonprogrammed. The decision to acquire a company is unique and unstructured, and requires considerable judgment. Regardless of the type of decision made, it is helpful to understand as much as possible about how individuals and groups make decisions.

Making Effective Individual Decisions

effective decision
A timely decision that meets a desired objective and is accepted by the individuals affected by it.

Regardless of the type of decision made, it is helpful to understand as much as possible about how individuals and groups can make more **effective decisions**, which are those that are timely, meet desired objectives, and are accepted by the individuals affected by them.[37] Decision making is also a critical activity in the lives of managers. Sometimes the decisions are painful and involve closing businesses, firing people, and admitting wrong. Former AT&T CEO Bob Allen announced a layoff of 30 000 people in the wake of the company's losses from its purchase of NCR, which was a bad decision.[38]

Ethical Issues in Individual Decision Making

ethical decision
A decision that is made after exploring alternatives and their consequences so that actions are consistent with one's personal values and commonly held values of the organization and society.

Another criterion that is increasingly being used to decide whether a decision is effective is the ethical implications of the decision. Ethical decision making in organizations is influenced by many factors, including individual differences and organizational rewards and punishments.[39] Ethical behaviour has been explored in Chapters 1 and 2, and here we apply ethical behaviour to decision making. An **ethical decision** is not easily defined but we define it as a decision that is made after exploring alternatives and their consequences so that actions are consistent with one's personal values and commonly held values of the organization and society. While many individuals draw their ethical guidelines and values from their religion or culture, we have offered a set of eight guidelines that can be helpful in evaluating a set of alternatives when making a decision. They are summarized in Exhibit 8.4.

Models of Decision Making

Defining what we mean by an effective and ethical decision does not go far enough in helping us to understand, predict, and influence decision-making behaviour. OB scholars have developed a number of decision-making models over the years, to accomplish this understanding. We will now explore four of the models, the first of which is the traditional rational model of decision making.

Explain the rational decision-making model and its underlying assumptions.

The Rational Model of Decision Making

rationality
A logical, step-by-step approach to decision making, with a thorough analysis of alternatives and their consequences.

Rationality refers to a logical, step-by-step approach to decision making, with a thorough analysis of alternatives and their consequences as shown in Exhibit 8.5. The eight-step rational model of decision making comes from classic economic theory and contends that the decision maker is completely rational in his or her approach. The rational model has the following important assumptions:

1. The outcome will be completely rational.
2. The decision maker has a consistent system of preferences, which is used to choose the best alternative.

EXHIBIT 8.4

Guidelines for Ethical Decision Making

- **Front page test**: Would I be embarrassed if my decision became a headline in the local newspaper?
- **Golden rule test**: Would I be willing to be treated in the same manner?
- **Dignity and liberty test**: Are the dignity and liberty of others preserved by this decision?
- **Equal treatment test**: Are the rights and welfare of lower-status people given full consideration?
- **Personal gain test**: Is an opportunity for personal gain clouding my judgment?
- **Congruence test**: Is this decision or action consistent with my espoused principles?
- **Procedural justice test**: Can the procedures used to make this decision stand up to scrutiny by those affected?
- **Cost-benefit test**: Does a benefit for some cause unacceptable harm to others? How critical is the benefit? Can the harmful effects be mitigated?
- **Good night's sleep test**: Whether or not anyone else knows about my action, will it produce a good night's sleep?

SOURCE: David A. Whetten and Kim S. Cameron, *Developing Management Skills,* 5th ed. (Upper Saddle River, NJ: Prentice Hall, 2002), 59. Reprinted by permission of Pearson Education, Inc., Upper Saddle River, NJ.

3. The decision maker is aware of all the possible alternatives.
4. The decision maker can calculate the probability of success for each alternative.[40]

The above assumptions of the rational model have been called into question by more contemporary models, which recognize that there are time constraints and limits to human knowledge and information-processing capabilities. In addition, a manager's preferences and needs change often. Thus the rational model is a good starting point, which captures the way a decision should be made but does not reflect the true complexities and imperfections involved in managerial decision making.[41]

As outlined in Exhibit 8.5, the rational model of decision making consists of eight steps:

- *Recognizing the problem and identifying the objective:* The first two steps are recognition of the problem and clarifying the objective of the decision. As discussed in Chapter 3, often our perceptions are distorted and we may fail to perceive that a problem exists, or we may be reacting to a symptom rather than dealing with the root cause of the problem. Problem identification is probably the most important and difficult step in decision making.
- *Gathering and evaluating data and diagnosis:* The third step in the decision-making process is gathering information relevant to the problem. The person must pull together sufficient information about why the problem occurred. This involves conducting a thorough diagnosis of the situation and going on a fact-finding mission. Information overload can be overwhelming at this stage.
- *Listing and evaluating alternatives and selecting the best course of action:* The fourth and fifth steps involve listing and evaluating alternatives and selecting the alternative that best meets the decision objective. During these steps, a thorough "what if" analysis should also be conducted to determine the various factors that could influence the outcome. It is important to generate a wide range of options and creative solutions, and as you will see in the "bounded rationality" model, in reality we rarely explore all alternatives in full, but rather we select the first alternative that is "good enough."
- *Implementing the decision, gathering feedback and following up:* Finally, the decision is implemented, feedback is gathered, and a follow-up is conducted to see whether the decision met its objective.

EXHIBIT 8.5

The Rational Decision-Making Process

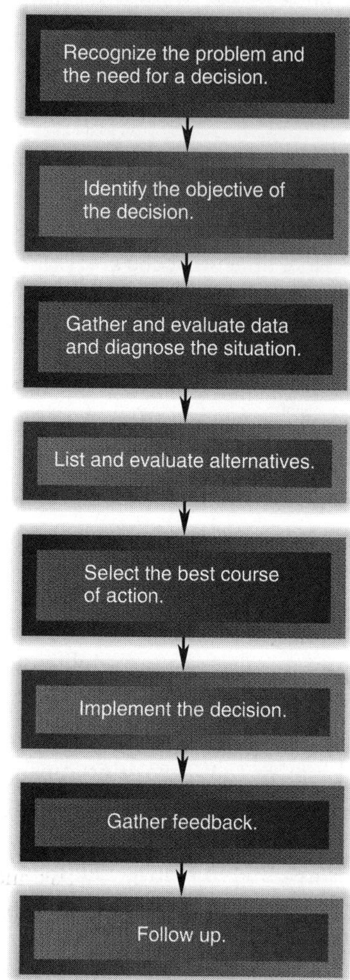

Given the limitations of the rational model, at least three alternative models of decision making have been proposed, as shown in Exhibit 8.6. These models are the bounded rationality model, the garbage can model, and the intuitive decision-making model.

Compare the rational model with the "bounded rationality" and "garbage can" models of decision making as well as the "intuitive decision-making" models.

bounded rationality
A theory that suggests that there are limits to how rational a decision maker can actually be.

satisfice
To select the first alternative that is "good enough," because the costs in time and effort are too great to optimize.

The Bounded Rationality Model of Decision Making

Recognizing the deficiencies of the rational model, Herbert Simon suggested that there are limits on how rational a decision maker can actually be. His decision theory, the bounded rationality model, earned him a Nobel Prize in 1978. Simon's model, also referred to as the "administrative man" theory, rests on the idea that there are constraints that force a decision maker to be less than completely rational. The bounded rationality model has four assumptions:

1. Managers select the first alternative that is satisfactory.
2. Managers recognize that their conception of the world is simple.
3. Managers are comfortable making decisions without determining all the alternatives.
4. Managers make decisions by rule of thumb or heuristics.

Bounded rationality assumes that managers **satisfice**; that is, they select the first alternative that is "good enough," because the costs of optimizing in terms of time and effort are too great.[42] Further, the theory assumes that managers develop shortcuts, called

EXHIBIT 8.6

Models of Decision Making

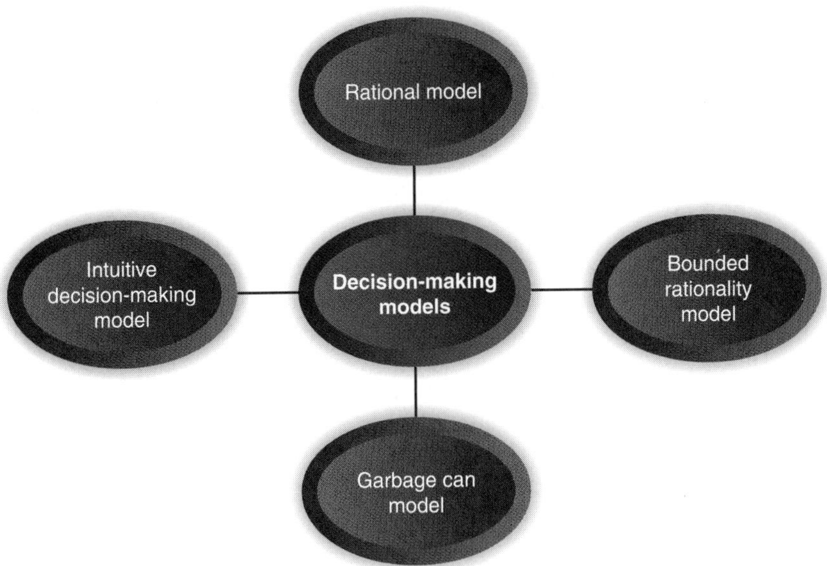

heuristics, to make decisions in order to save mental activity. Heuristics "reduce the complex tasks of assessing probabilities and predicting values to simpler judgmental operations."[43] Heuristics are rules of thumb that allow managers to make decisions based on what has worked in past experiences.

heuristics
Shortcuts in decision making that save mental activity.

Does the bounded rationality model more realistically portray the managerial decision process? Research indicates that it does.[44] One of the reasons managers face limits to their rationality is that they must make decisions under risk and time pressure. The situation they find themselves in is highly uncertain, and the probability of success is not known.

IMPLICATIONS FOR LIFE

How Realistic Is the Rational Model of Decision Making in Your Experience?

Think about the decision you made to attend the university/college/program you are currently attending and answer each of the following questions honestly:

1. Was the choice completely rational? Yes ____ No ____
2. When you thought about your preferences, did they remain fairly consistent over time? Yes ____ No ____
3. Were you aware of all the possible alternatives? Yes ____ No ____
4. Were you able to calculate the probability of success for each alternative? Yes ____ No ____

You probably did *not* answer "Yes" to all of the above questions. There are time constraints and limits to human knowledge and information-processing capabilities. In addition, our preferences and needs often change. Now think about how you actually made your decision:

- Did you maybe select the first alternative that was "good enough" *(satisfice)* because of the costs in time and effort? Did you maybe find yourself making any shortcuts, to save your mental energy *(heuristics)*?

- Did you perhaps feel that the way you made your decision appeared to happen out of sheer luck (or bad luck)? On the high-speed playing field of today's world, we sometimes make critical decisions quickly, with incomplete information (*the position taken by the garbage can model of decision making*).
- Finally, did you perhaps make your decision using your gut feel, your intuition? This is your internal reservoir of cumulative experience, from which you distilled, at a level below your consciousness, a direction, or an urge to do or not do something.

The Garbage Can Model of Decision Making

garbage can model
A theory that contends that decisions in organizations are random and unsystematic.

The idea of taking shortcuts when making decisions in uncertain times as well as the notion of "satisficing" are taken further in the garbage can model. Because of increasing evidence that the decision-making process in organizations appears to be haphazard and unpredictable, the **garbage can model** (depicted in Exhibit 8.7) proposes that while decisions seem to be random and unsystematic, in fact they are influenced by four independent streams.[45] These streams are:

- Problems or concerns
- Solutions or methods
- Participants more or less ready to be active in the decision-making matter
- Choice opportunities.

The interaction between these four streams determines whether a decision will be made and what the outcomes will be.[46] The quality of the decision depends on timing. The right participants must find the right solution to the right problem at the right time. The garbage can model goes even further than the bounded rationality model in illustrating the idea that not all organizational decisions are made in a step-by-step, systematic fashion. Especially under conditions of high uncertainty, the decision process may be chaotic. Some decisions appear to happen out of sheer luck. On the high-speed playing field of today's businesses, managers must make critical decisions quickly, with incomplete information, and must also involve employees in the process.

EXHIBIT 8.7

The Garbage Can Model

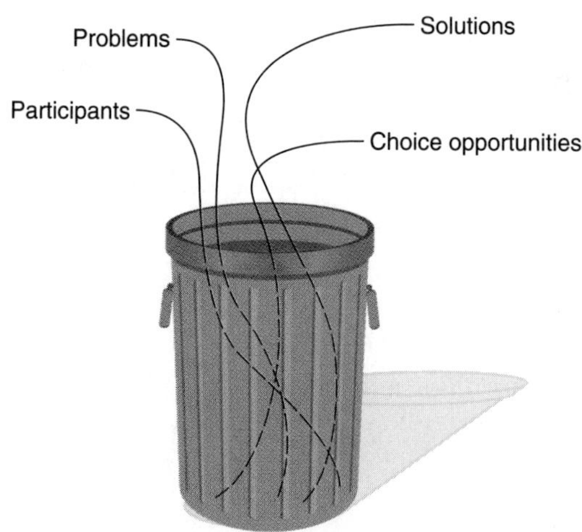

SOURCE: From M. D. Cohen, J. G. March, and J. P. Olsen in *Administrative Science Quarterly* 17 (March 1972): 1–25. Reprinted by permission of the Administrative Science Quarterly. © Johnson Graduate School of Management, Cornell University.

The Intuitive Decision-Making Models

Henry Mintzberg, in his work on managerial roles, found that in many cases managers do not appear to use a systematic, step-by-step approach to decision making. Rather, Mintzberg argued, managers make judgments based on "hunches" or gut feel.[47] Bob Lutz, Chrysler's company president at the time, decided to create a sexy, expensive, two-seater sports car (later to become the Dodge Viper) while on a weekend drive. Now CEO of Exide Technologies, Bob has trouble describing exactly how he made the most critical decision of his career. "It was this subconscious, visceral feeling. And it just felt right," he said.[48] Organizational Reality 8.1 highlights how companies like Intrawest use "what if" scenarios to help them tap into their intuition about possible directions for developing a new site.

Daniel Isenberg studied the way senior managers make decisions and found that intuition was used extensively, especially as a mechanism to evaluate decisions made more rationally.[49] While intuition used to have a bad reputation as a method of decision making, recent research is suggesting that today's fast-paced business environment makes intuition a viable approach.[50] Khatri and Ng confirmed this when they surveyed senior managers from the computer, banking, and utilities industries and found that intuition was positively associated with organizational performance in unstable environments while negatively associated with organizational performance in stable environments.[51]

Just what is intuition? **Intuition** is defined here as the internal reservoir of cumulative experience, from which one distills, at a level below consciousness, a direction, or an urge to do or not do something. There are many definitions of *intuition* in the managerial literature. Chester Barnard, one of the early influential management researchers, argued that intuition's main attributes were speed and the inability of the decision maker to determine how the decision was made.[52] Other researchers have contended that intuition occurs at an unconscious level and that this is why the decision maker cannot verbalize how the decision was made.[53] Increasing numbers of researchers have recognized, as Barnard did, the pivotal role of nonlogical and intuitive decision making in management contexts.[54] Intuition has been variously described as follows:

intuition
The internal reservoir of cumulative experience, from which one distills, at a level below consciousness, a direction or an urge to do or not do something.

- A sophisticated form of reasoning based on "chunking" that an expert hones after years of job-specific experience.[55]
- Being able to bring to bear on a situation everything you've seen, felt, tasted, and experienced in an industry.[56]
- The ability to know or recognize quickly and readily the possibilities of a situation.[57]

organizational reality 8.1

Visioneers at Intrawest

Intrawest is a world leader in destination resorts and adventure travel. The Canadian company is based in Vancouver, British Columbia, and is a public company listed on the New York and Toronto stock exchanges. Founded in 1976 by Joe Houssein, today Intrawest owns or is involved with 14 mountain resorts in North America and Europe along with two warm-weather resorts in the U.S. Executives at Intrawest use a process they called "envisioning" to make key decisions on how to develop a new property. Their process begins with gathering a couple of dozen community members, outside experts, and Intrawest "visioneers" to get the lay of the land. The visioneers work in small groups and create "what if" scenarios about the possibilities for development. This helps them tap into their intuition about development possibilities. Also, they allow themselves the freedom to be creative and to initially come up with wild ideas without censoring them. Then they regroup and put together a draft document summarizing their decisions. This document eventually becomes the blueprint for development.

SOURCES: J. Sutherland, "It Takes a Village," *The Globe and Mail ROB Magazine,* April 2005, 26–34; www.intrawest.com.

- Accessing the internal reservoir of cumulative experience and expertise developed over a period of years, and distilling out of that response, or an urge to do or not do something, or choose from some alternatives—again without being able to understand consciously how we get the answers.[58]

These definitions share some common assumptions. First, there seems to be a notion that intuition is fast. Second, intuition is utilized at a level below consciousness. Third, there seems to be agreement that intuition involves learned patterns of information. Fourth, intuition appears to be a positive force in decision making. Dan Jarvis, CEO of the leisure and travel group for Intrawest, remembers when he and company president Joe Houssain were struggling with how to attract investors to its initial public offering in 1990. The two of them were in the Vancouver head office when "a solution to the problem crystallized."[59] The solution, which was to sell off the company's urban assets and focus on perfecting its resort formula, resulted in a wide assortment of buyers. It was only later, they write, that they "realized how distracting it (*their various urban assets*) had been."[60] This exemplifies the power of intuition as we have defined it.

As well, the use of intuition may lead to more ethical decisions. One study found a strong link between cognitive moral development and intuition. The development of new perspectives through intuition leads to higher moral growth, and thus to more ethical decisions.[61] Finally, while intuition can be very helpful in decision making, especially when problems get more complex and ambiguous, executives are the first to admit that their instincts are often plain wrong.[62] Self-checking, self-awareness—recognizing your own moods, emotions, and drives—and ongoing feedback seem to be crucial to making sound, intuitive decisions.[63]

Comprehension & Application

WHICH DO YOU TRUST MORE, YOUR INTUITIVE OR RATIONAL DECISIONS?

Think about a decision that you made using your intuition (defined as the internal reservoir of cumulative experience, from which one distills at a level below consciousness, a direction, or an urge to do or not do something). Using this memory, compare it to a decision you made more consciously and rationally. Which type of decision making do you have more confidence in?

Explain how risk aversion, escalation of commitment to a losing course of action, and cognitive style influence individual decision making.

Individual Influences on Decision Making

We have now explored a number of different models that help us better understand the complexities of individual decision making. We have explored the rational model, the bounded rationality model, the "garbage can" model, and the intuitive model. While all of these models give us unique insights into the processes by which individuals make decisions, OB researchers have also discovered a number of key individual differences that affect a person's decision-making behaviour. Three individual characteristics that have been found to influence decision making are the degree to which a person is risk-averse, varying tendencies toward a phenomenon called "escalation of commitment to a losing course of action," and a person's cognitive style. We now discuss each of these.

Risk Aversion

risk aversion
The tendency to choose options that entail fewer risks and less uncertainty.

Many decisions involve some element of risk. For managers, hiring decisions, promotions, delegation, acquisitions and mergers, overseas expansions, new product development, and other decisions make risk a part of the job. Individuals differ in terms of their willingness to take risks. Some people experience **risk aversion,** which is the tendency to choose options that entail fewer risks and less uncertainty. Other individuals are risk takers; that is, they accept greater potential for loss in decisions, tolerate greater uncertainty, and in general are more likely to make risky decisions. Risk takers are also more likely to take the lead in group discussions.[64] Upper-level managers face a tough task in managing risk-taking behaviour because by discouraging lower-level managers from taking risks, they may stifle creativity and innovation. At the same time, if they encourage risk taking, they must allow employees to fail without fear of punishment. One way to accomplish this is to consider failure "enlightened trial and error."[65]

Escalation of Commitment to a Losing Course of Action

While some individuals tend to be risk averse, others have a tendency toward a phenomenon that is called **escalation of commitment to a losing course of action.**[66] This phenomenon has been referred to in various ways, including the "gambler's fallacy," being "knee deep in the big muddy," the sunk cost effect, and "having too much invested to quit."[67] In situations characterized by escalation of commitment, individuals who make decisions that turn out to be poor choices tend to hold fast to those choices, even when substantial costs are incurred.[68]

escalation of commitment to a losing course of action The tendency to continue to support a failing course of action.

Here is an example of this phenomenon in action: Suppose an oil producer thinks there is an opportunity to uncover oil by drilling at an old site. He gathers a group of investors and shows them the data, which suggest that oil can be found there, and they chip in to finance the venture. They drill to a certain depth, but nothing is found. Convinced they did not drill deep enough, the producer goes back to the investors and requests additional financial backing to continue drilling. The investors consent, and he drills deeper, only to find nothing again. He approaches the investors, and after lengthy discussion, they agree to provide more money to drill deeper. Another example is Motorola, which lost billions of dollars on Iridium, a constellation of 66 satellites that would allow subscribers to make phone calls globally. Despite known problems, managers continued to invest in the project, and Iridium eventually had to declare bankruptcy.[69] This phenomenon also occurs in daily life, for example in interpersonal relations, when waiting for someone who is late, and in gambling behaviour.[70]

Why do decision makers sometimes throw good money after bad? Why do they continue to provide resources to what looks like a losing venture? Recent research findings provide the following explanations: First, it depends, in part, upon the person's **self-efficacy**. This is defined as an individual's beliefs and expectancies about his or her ability to perform a specific task effectively. In a Canadian study on the role of self-efficacy in escalating commitment to a losing course of action, it was found that individuals who were high on self-efficacy were significantly more inclined to engage in escalating commitment than low self-efficacy subjects.[71] Perceived self-efficacy and early success may also be a factor in gambling behaviour. Research into gambling behaviour has shown that players who experience early wins tend to bet more than their less successful counterparts. By the same token, managers with successful track records are more likely to persist in the face of failure because "their self confidence tells them they will win through in the end."[72] A second reason people may hang on to a losing course of action is *optimism and control.* Some people are overly optimistic and overestimate the likelihood that positive things will happen to them. Other people operate under an illusion of control—that they have special skills to control the future that other people don't have.[73] Finally, a tendency to escalate commitment can be explained by *cognitive dissonance theory.* This theory assumes that humans dislike inconsistency, and that when there is inconsistency among their attitudes or inconsistency between their attitudes and behaviour, they strive to reduce the dissonance.[74]

self-efficacy An individual's beliefs and expectancies about his or her ability to perform a specific task effectively.

Organizations can deal with escalation of commitment in several ways. One is to split the responsibility for decisions about projects so that one individual can make the initial decision on a project while someone else can make subsequent decisions. Another suggestion is to provide individuals with a graceful exit from poor decisions so that their images are not threatened. Another suggestion is to have groups, rather than individuals, make an initial decision because in a group, individuals may experience a diffusion of responsibility for the failed decision rather than feeling personally responsible.[75] Finally, it has been suggested that individuals be encouraged to begin with doubts rather than certainty, insist on facts not optimism, tell the truth, even if it hurts, and try to subtract ego from the equation![76]

Comprehension & Application

HAVE YOU EVER BEEN KNEE DEEP IN THE BIG MUDDY? THINK ABOUT THE REASONS WHY.

Sometimes we continue to do things even though we see that we are in a losing course of action. Often, when we invest a lot of time, money, or energy into something, we feel we have "too much invested to quit" so we put even more into it to help justify our original decision.

Think of a situation where you have seen this happen, or been there yourself. Write down *all* the possible reasons why the person engaged in a losing course of action might escalate his or her commitment to it by putting even more time, energy, or money into it.

Cognitive Style Preference

cognitive style
An individual's preference for gathering information and evaluating alternatives.

A third individual influence on decision-making behaviour is that of personality and **cognitive style.** In Chapter 3 we introduced Jungian theory and the Myers-Briggs Type Indicator (MBTI) as a way of understanding and appreciating personality differences among individuals. This theory is also useful in pointing out that individuals have different styles of making decisions. Carl Jung's original theory identified four decision-making styles, which he called sensing with thinking (ST), sensing with feeling (SF), intuition with thinking (NT), and intuition with feeling (NF).[77] Research with managers and MBA students has supported the relationship between type of cognitive style and decision making-behaviour.[78] See Exhibit 8.8 for an overview of these differences.

EXHIBIT 8.8

Impact of Cognitive Style on Individual Decision Making

Sensing with Thinking (ST)	• Make decisions based on logic and facts • May avoid risk • May alienate by ignoring impact of decision on others
Sensing with Feeling (SF)	• Seek data but make decisions based on values and perceived impact of decision on others • Able to take calculated risks • Handle interpersonal problems well • May have trouble accepting new ideas that break the rules
Intuition with Thinking (NT)	• Focus on possibilities and then evaluate them objectively and impersonally • Love to initiate ideas • Focus decisions on the long term • Tend to ignore arguments based on facts • Tend to ignore feelings of others • Innovate and take risks
Intuition with Feeling (NF)	• Focus on possibilities and then evaluate them in terms of affect on people involved • Tend to be participative decision makers • Make decisions based on values and personal preferences rather than on more objective data • May become too responsive to the needs of others

GROUP DECISION MAKING AT WORK

Explore various levels of group participation in decision making and their effects.

Now that we have explored the various models of individual decision making and the way that risk aversion, escalation of commitment, and cognitive style influence it, we turn to another important OB issue for managers. This is the question of when, if, and how to use groups to make decisions at work.

What Is Participative Decision Making?

participative decision making
Decision making in which individuals who are affected by decisions influence those decisions.

Participative decision making occurs when individuals who are affected by decisions influence those decisions. Often referred to as empowerment, and discussed in depth in Chapter 9 on power and influence, participative decision making has been found to increase employee creativity, job satisfaction, and productivity.[79] Also, it has been found to buffer employees from the negative experiences of organizational politics.[80] As our economy becomes increasingly based on knowledge work, and as new technologies make it easier for decentralized decision makers to connect, participative decision making will undoubtedly increase.[81] At Cisco Systems, instantaneous information access has made participative decision making easy, as you can see in Organizational Reality 8.2.

What Level of Group Participation in Decision Making?

The Vroom-Yetton-Jago normative decision model helps managers decide when and how to use participative decision making.[82] The theory describes five different forms of managerial decision making on a continuum that ranges from the manager making a decision alone, all the way to the manager permitting a group to make a decision within prescribed limits.[83] For example, employees could be variously involved in identifying problems, generating alternatives, selecting solutions, planning implementations, or evaluating results. Research shows that if employees cannot be provided with full participation, the highest payoffs seem to come with involvement in generating alternatives, planning implementations, and evaluating results.[84] There are five forms of decision making described in the model, as follows:

- *Decide.* The manager makes the decision alone and either announces it or "sells" it to the group.

organizational reality

organizational reality 8.2

At Cisco, Decisions Are Made in Real Time

Cisco Systems makes decisions differently than do most companies, and much faster. It uses live, hot information, disseminated throughout the company, to empower people throughout the organization to make decisions. The quicker that people get information, the quicker they can solve problems. When the quarter ends and financial reports are needed, Cisco executives are not stressed: They are finished by 3 or 4 p.m. Closing the books used to take 14 days; now it is done instantaneously. Revenues, margins, earnings per share, and other stats are tracked each day, and the information is actually available hourly. Real-time books are like sashimi: You can slice and dice them, but not cook them. The information has to be fast and perfect.

It took four years for Cisco to convert to real-time management accounting. This makes Cisco agile enough to take advantage of opportunities like expansions in Japan. It also lets Cisco managers participate in decisions. Every supervisor can see everything about the company's operations. They can look at margins and products, and see the effects of their decisions. Managing in real time means that every decision takes time and money, and every decision maker must have the information he or she needs. Driving decision making deep into the organization is powerful stuff at Cisco.

SOURCE: T. A. Stewart, "Making Decisions in Real Time," *Fortune* (June 26, 2000): 332–34.

- *Consult individually.* The manager presents the problem to the group members individually, gets their input, and then makes the decision.
- *Consult group.* The manager presents the problem to the group members in a meeting, gets their inputs, and then makes the decision.
- *Facilitate.* The manager presents the problem to the group in a meeting and acts as a facilitator, defining the problem and the boundaries that surround the decision. The manager's ideas are not given more weight than any other group member's ideas. The objective is to get concurrence.
- *Delegate.* The manager permits the group to make the decision within the prescribed limits, providing needed resources and encouragement.[85] You can read more about teams that are fully empowered to make their own decisions in the OBXtra entitled Self-Managed Work Teams.

The key to the normative decision model is that a manager should use the decision method most appropriate for a given decision situation. The leader works through decision trees like the one in Exhibit 8.9, which shows five contingencies to consider when making decisions under time pressure. Vroom has also developed a Windows-based computer program called Expert System that can be used by managers to determine which style to use.[86] There is also a body of research that informs us as to the advantages and disadvantages of team versus individual decision making. We discuss these aspects now.

Summarize the advantages and disadvantages of group versus individual decision making.

Advantages of Group Decision Making

synergy
A positive force that occurs in groups when group members stimulate new or better solutions through the process of mutual influence and encouragement.

The advantages of group decision making tend to include (1) more knowledge and information through the pooling of group member resources; (2) increased acceptance of, and commitment to, the decision, because the members had a voice in it; (3) greater understanding of the decision, because members were involved in the various stages of the decision process; and (4) **synergy**, which is a positive force that occurs in groups when group members stimulate new or better solutions through the process of mutual influence and encouragement. For judgment tasks requiring an estimate or a prediction, groups are usually superior to individuals because of the breadth of experience that multiple individuals bring to the problem.[87] On tasks that have a correct solution, other studies have indicated that the most competent individual outperforms the group.[88] This finding has been called into question, however. Much of the previous research on groups was conducted in the laboratory, where group members interacted only for short periods of time. Researchers wanted to know how a longer experience in the group would affect decisions. Their study showed that groups who worked together for longer periods of time outperformed the most competent member 70 percent of the time. As groups gained experience, the best members became less important to the group's success.[89] This study demonstrated that experience in the group is an important variable to consider when evaluating the individual versus group decision-making question. Given the emphasis on teams in the workplace, many managers believe that groups produce better decisions than do individuals, yet the evidence is mixed. It is evident that the conditions for team effectiveness discussed in Chapter 7 have an influence on the results obtained, and more research needs to be conducted in organizational settings to help answer this question. Exhibit 8.10 provides a brief overview of the advantages and disadvantages of group decision making.

EXHIBIT 8.9

Time-Driven Model

TIME-DRIVEN MODEL

Instructions: The matrix operates like a funnel. You start at the left with a specific decision problem in mind. The column headings denote situational factors that may or may not be present in that problem. You progress by selecting High or Low (H or L) for each relevant situational factor. Proceed down from the funnel, judging only those situational factors for which a judgment is called for, until you reach the recommended process.

<table>
<tr><th></th><th>Decision Significance</th><th>Importance of Commitment</th><th>Leader Expertise</th><th>Likelihood of Commitment</th><th>Group Support</th><th>Group Expertise</th><th>Team Competence</th><th></th></tr>
<tr><td rowspan="22">PROBLEM STATEMENT</td><td rowspan="18">H</td><td rowspan="13">H</td><td rowspan="5">H</td><td>H</td><td>–</td><td>–</td><td>–</td><td>Decide</td></tr>
<tr><td rowspan="4">L</td><td rowspan="3">H</td><td rowspan="2">H</td><td>H</td><td>Delegate</td></tr>
<tr><td>L</td><td rowspan="3">Consult (Group)</td></tr>
<tr><td>L</td><td>–</td></tr>
<tr><td>L</td><td>–</td><td>–</td></tr>
<tr><td rowspan="8">L</td><td rowspan="4">H</td><td rowspan="3">H</td><td rowspan="2">H</td><td>H</td><td>Facilitate</td></tr>
<tr><td>L</td><td rowspan="3">Consult (Individually)</td></tr>
<tr><td>L</td><td>–</td></tr>
<tr><td>L</td><td>–</td><td>–</td></tr>
<tr><td rowspan="4">L</td><td rowspan="3">H</td><td rowspan="2">H</td><td>H</td><td>Facilitate</td></tr>
<tr><td>L</td><td rowspan="3">Consult (Group)</td></tr>
<tr><td>L</td><td>–</td></tr>
<tr><td>L</td><td>–</td><td>–</td></tr>
<tr><td rowspan="5">L</td><td>H</td><td>–</td><td>–</td><td>–</td><td>–</td><td>Decide</td></tr>
<tr><td rowspan="4">L</td><td rowspan="4">–</td><td rowspan="3">H</td><td rowspan="2">H</td><td>H</td><td>Facilitate</td></tr>
<tr><td>L</td><td rowspan="3">Consult (Individually)</td></tr>
<tr><td>L</td><td>–</td></tr>
<tr><td>L</td><td>–</td><td>–</td></tr>
<tr><td rowspan="4">L</td><td rowspan="3">H</td><td rowspan="3">–</td><td>H</td><td>–</td><td>–</td><td>–</td><td>Decide</td></tr>
<tr><td rowspan="2">L</td><td rowspan="2">–</td><td rowspan="2">–</td><td>H</td><td>Delegate</td></tr>
<tr><td>L</td><td>Facilitate</td></tr>
<tr><td>L</td><td>–</td><td>–</td><td>–</td><td>–</td><td>–</td><td>Decide</td></tr>
</table>

SOURCE: V. H. Vroom, "Leadership and the Decision-Making Process," *Organizational Dynamics* 28 (2000): 82–94. Copyright © 2000, with permission from Elsevier.

EXHIBIT 8.10

Advantages and Disadvantages of Group Decision Making

Advantages	Disadvantages
Synergy—improved performance	Pressure to conform: groupthink
More knowledge and information	Domination of a forceful members
Greater understanding of decision	Time required
Increased commitment to decision	Group polarization

Disadvantages of Group Decision Making

The disadvantages of group decision making include (1) pressure within the group to conform and fit in; (2) domination of the group by one forceful member or a dominant clique, who may ramrod the group into a decision; and (3) the amount of time required, because a group makes decisions more slowly than an individual.[90]

Explain the specific disadvantages of groupthink and group polarization.

The Problems of Groupthink and Group Polarization

Two potential liabilities found in group decision making that have been extensively researched are groupthink and group polarization, and we elaborate on these now.

Groupthink and Its Symptoms

groupthink
A deterioration of mental efficiency, reality testing, and moral judgment resulting from pressures within the group.

Pressure on a group to conform increases as the group becomes more cohesive. As discussed in Chapter 7, highly cohesive teams have a tendency to make ineffective group decisions caused by a phenomenon called "groupthink." **Groupthink** was defined by its founder, Irving Janis, as a deterioration of mental efficiency, reality testing, and moral judgment resulting from pressures within the group.[91] Cohesive groups tend to favour solidarity because members identify strongly with the group.[92] High-ranking teams that make decisions without outside help are especially prone to groupthink, because they are more likely to think alike.[93] Two other conditions that encourage groupthink are time constraints and having to make a decision that will have a great impact on the group members and on outside parties.[94]

A group suffering from groupthink shows recognizable symptoms. Exhibit 8.11 presents these symptoms and makes suggestions on how to avoid groupthink. An incident that has been examined for these symptoms of groupthink is the space shuttle *Challenger* disaster. On January 28, 1986, 73 seconds into its flight, the *Challenger* exploded, killing all seven members of its crew. The evidence pointed toward an O-ring seal that was still cold from nighttime temperatures and failed to do its job. A presidential commission was convened, and its investigation cited flawed decision making as a primary cause of the accident. An analysis of the *Challenger* incident indicated that the negative symptoms of groupthink increased during the 24 hours prior to the decision to launch the spacecraft.[95] National Aeronautics and Space Administration (NASA) management officials were warned by engineers that the launch should be cancelled because the O-rings would not withstand the colder temperatures. The engineers were pressured by their bosses to stifle their dissent, and their opinions were devalued. Further, the decision to launch was made by polling managers—engineers were not polled. The decision makers were overconfident because of the success of the previous shuttle and NASA's record of success. Some managers knew that a redesign of the rocket casings had been ordered, but this information was withheld from other decision makers. Consequences of groupthink include an incomplete survey of alternatives, failure to evaluate the risks of the

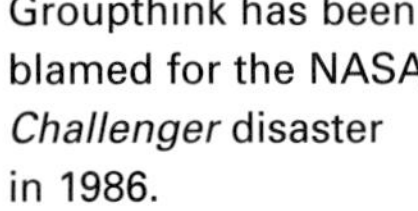

Groupthink has been blamed for the NASA *Challenger* disaster in 1986.

EXHIBIT 8.11

Symptoms of Groupthink and How to Prevent It

Symptoms of Groupthink

- *Illusions of invulnerability.* Group members feel they are above criticism. This symptom leads to excessive optimism and risk taking.
- *Illusions of group morality.* Group members feel they are moral in their actions and therefore above reproach. This symptom leads the group to ignore the ethical implications of their decisions.
- *Illusions of unanimity.* Group members believe there is unanimous agreement on the decisions. Silence is misconstrued as consent.
- *Rationalization.* Group members concoct explanations for their decisions to make them appear rational and correct. The results are that other alternatives are not considered, and there is an unwillingness to reconsider the group's assumptions.
- *Stereotyping the enemy.* Competitors are stereotyped as evil or stupid. This leads the group to underestimate its opposition.
- *Self-censorship.* Members do not express their doubts or concerns about the course of action. This prevents critical analysis of the decisions.
- *Peer pressure.* Any members who express doubts or concerns are pressured by other group members, who question their loyalty.
- *Mindguards.* Some members take it upon themselves to protect the group from negative feedback. Group members are thus dominated by the leaders or other group members who are hiding information that might lead them to question their actions.

Guidelines for Preventing Groupthink

- Ask each group member to assume the role of the critical evaluator who actively voices objections or doubts.
- Have the leader avoid stating his or her position on the issue prior to the group decision.
- Create several groups that work on the decision simultaneously.
- Bring in outside experts to evaluate the group process.
- Appoint a devil's advocate to question the group's course of action consistently.
- Evaluate the competition carefully, posing as many different motivations and intentions as possible.
- Once consensus is reached, encourage the group to rethink its position by reexamining the alternatives.

SOURCE: Irving L. Janis, *Groupthink: Psychological Studies of Policy Decisions and Fiascoes*, 2nd ed. Copyright © 1982 by Houghton Mifflin Company. Used with permission.

preferred course of action, biased information processing, and a failure to work out contingency plans. The overall result of groupthink is defective decision making. This was evident in the *Challenger* situation. The group considered only two alternatives: launch or no launch. They failed to consider the risks of their decision to launch the shuttle, and they did not develop any contingency plans.

Groups can also make decisions that are unethical. Beech-Nut, for example, admitted selling millions of jars of "phony" apple juice that contained cheap, adulterated concentrate. Groupthink may have been responsible for this unethical decision. Beech-Nut was losing money, and its managers believed that other companies were selling fake juice. They were convinced that their fake juice was safe for consumers and that no laboratory test could conclusively distinguish real juice from artificial ingredients. Normally a reputable company, Beech-Nut ignored caution and conscience in favour of bottom-line mentality, ignored dissent, and thus suffered damage to its reputation because of unethical practices.[96] Unethical group decisions like the one at Beech-Nut can be prevented by using the techniques for overcoming groupthink. Appointing a devil's advocate who constantly questions the group's course of action can help bring ethical issues to the surface. Exhibit 8.11 presents Janis's guidelines for preventing groupthink.

Many of these suggestions focus on the notion of ensuring that decisions are evaluated completely, with opportunities for discussion from all group members. This strategy helps encourage members to evaluate one another's ideas critically. One review of the decision-making processes in the *Challenger* incident proposed that two variables, time and leadership style, are also important to include.[97] When a decision must be made quickly, there is more potential for groupthink. Leadership style can either promote groupthink (if the leader makes his or her opinion known up front) or avoid groupthink (if the leader encourages open and frank discussion). Other techniques for improving group decision making are reviewed in the next section.

Analysis & Evaluation

SPOTTING SYMPTOMS OF GROUPTHINK IN A TEAM

Select a cohesive group in which you are currently a member or have been in the recent past. Use Exhibit 8.11 to evaluate whether the group exhibits or has exhibited any of the eight symptoms of groupthink that are described. The more cohesive the group, and the longer the group has been together, the more likely that you will find one or more of these symptoms.

group polarization
The tendency for group discussion to produce shifts toward more extreme attitudes among members.

Mindjet
Mindjet is a company that specializes in producing visual-thinking software tools that enhance the group decision-making process. What do you think are some of the potential limitations to using technological aids in decision making?
http://www.mindjet.com

Group Polarization

Another disadvantage that has been observed in studies is that individuals tend to make more extreme decisions when they are in groups, compared to when they make decisions alone.[98] Individuals who were initially against an issue became more strongly opposed, and individuals who were in favour of the issue became more strongly supportive following discussion. These shifts came to be known as **group polarization**, defined as the tendency for group discussion to produce shifts toward more extreme attitudes among members.[99] The tendency toward polarization has important implications for group decision making.

Several ideas have been proposed to explain why group polarization occurs. One explanation is the social comparison approach. Prior to group discussion, individuals believe they hold better views than the other members. During group discussion, they see that their views are not so far from average, so they shift to more extreme positions.[100] A second explanation is the persuasive arguments view. It contends that group discussion reinforces the initial views of the members, so they take a more extreme position.[101]

Describe four methods to improve group decision making: brainstorming, nominal group technique (NGT), the Delphi technique, and devil's advocacy.

Techniques to Improve Group Decision Making

The key to stimulating innovation, and overcoming the disadvantages of group decision making just discussed, is to structure the opportunity for constructive dissent among members.[102] Using one of the following group decision-making techniques can help accomplish this. Once a manager has determined that a group decision-making approach should be used, he or she can determine the technique that is best suited to the decision situation. Four techniques will be summarized: brainstorming, nominal group technique, Delphi technique, and devil's advocacy.

Brainstorming

brainstorming
A technique for generating as many ideas as possible on a given subject, while suspending evaluation until all the ideas have been generated.

Brainstorming is a technique for generating as many ideas as possible on a given subject, while suspending evaluation until all the ideas have been generated. Brainstorming is a good technique for generating alternatives. Participants are then encouraged to build upon the suggestions of others, and imagination is emphasized. One example of an organization that benefited from brainstorming is the Alberta Children's Hospital. See how

Brainstorming is a good technique for developing a large number of alternatives when trying to make a decision or solve a problem. Participants are encouraged to suspend judgment and be outlandish.

it does brainstorming the right way in Organizational Reality 8.3. Evidence suggests, however, that group brainstorming is less effective than a comparable number of individuals working alone. In groups, participants engage in discussions that can make them lose their focus.[103]

One recent trend is the use of electronic brainstorming instead of face-to-face brainstorming in groups. Electronic brainstorming overcomes two common problems that can produce group brainstorming failure: production blocking and evaluation apprehension. In face-to-face brainstorming, individuals are exposed to the inputs of others. While listening to others, individuals are distracted from their own ideas. This is referred to as production blocking. When ideas are recorded electronically, participants are free from

organizational reality 8.3

Brainstorming Works

Brainstorming has become a very common method by which to generate creative ideas in Canadian organizations. For example, a nursing education team at the Alberta Children's Hospital (ACH) had several brainstorming sessions before they came up with the idea of having an annual nursing skills fair, which they called "Spring Carnival Days." Brainstorming sessions are successful because they follow a few simple rules:

1. *Stress quantity over quality.* The purpose of brainstorming is to make lists, not choices. Encouraging quantity of ideas forces people with their own agendas to think beyond their own opinions.
2. *Suspend judgment.* No one is allowed to criticize an idea or say that it is not feasible. Failure to enforce this rule results in a discussion about what is not going to work, which is a worthless activity.
3. *Do not set limits.* The way to get really useful unexpected ideas is to encourage participants to be outlandish. Creativity comes easily when participants are willing to play. Suppose you are looking for ways to design a unique staff celebration. You might ask the group, "How would Steven Spielberg design this party?" He might film staff at work and then use the film in the celebration. Taking a detour can revive a stalled brainstorming session.
4. *Forget about seniority.* Individuals will be inhibited in the meetings where their bosses are present. For the purposes of the brainstorming sessions, everyone has to have the same rank. There should not be anyone in the room who has veto power over the ideas.

SOURCES: "Spring Carnival Days," *The Canadian Nurse* 100, no. 3 (March 2004): 15; C. Caggiano, "The Right Way to Brainstorm," *Inc.* (July 1999): 94–96.

hearing the interruptions of others; thus, production blocking is reduced. Some individuals suffer from evaluation apprehension in brainstorming groups. They fear that others might respond negatively to their ideas. In electronic brainstorming, input is anonymous, so evaluation apprehension is reduced. While electronic brainstorming is more costly than the face-to-face version, studies indicate that anonymous electronic brainstorming groups outperform face-to-face brainstorming groups in the number of ideas generated.[104]

Knowledge & Application

TRY BRAINSTORMING IN YOUR NEXT MEETING

Use the four rules of brainstorming from Organizational Reality 8.3 in your next team meeting to experience the difference they make at the idea generation stage of group decision making.

Nominal Group Technique

nominal group technique (NGT)
A structured approach to group decision making that focuses on generating alternatives and choosing one.

Another technique that helps improve group decision making is called the **nominal group technique (NGT)**. This is a structured approach to decision making that focuses on generating alternatives and choosing one but, in doing so, minimizes the influence of peer pressure, face saving, or domination by a forceful team member. NGT is also a good technique to use in a situation where group members fear criticism from others.[105] NGT involves the following discrete steps:

1. Individuals silently list their ideas.
2. Ideas are written on a chart one at a time until all ideas are listed.
3. Discussion is permitted, but only to clarify the ideas. No criticism is allowed.
4. A written vote is taken.

The reason that the method is called the "nominal" group technique is because the group is a group in name (nominal) only. While there is a common goal, the interdependence has been significantly reduced.

Delphi Technique

Delphi technique
A structured approach to decision making which gathers the judgments of experts.

A third technique, called the **Delphi technique**, requires no face-to-face communication, and possible contamination, by gathering the judgments of experts for use in decision making. Experts at remote locations respond to a questionnaire. A coordinator summarizes the responses to the questionnaire, and the summary is sent back to the experts. The experts then rate the various alternatives generated, and the coordinator tabulates the results. The Delphi technique is valuable in its ability to generate a number of independent judgments without the requirement of a face-to-face meeting.[106]

Devil's Advocacy

devil's advocacy
A technique for preventing groupthink in which a group or individual is given the role of critic during decision making.

The fourth method, called **devil's advocacy**, is a technique for preventing groupthink in which a group or individual is given the explicit role of critic during decision making. The person assigned to be the "devil's advocate" has the task of coming up with the potential problems of a proposed decision. This helps organizations avoid costly mistakes in decision making by identifying potential pitfalls in advance.[107] Usually, this role is rotated among group members so that it is played by different people at each meeting. The conscious use of a "devil's advocate" during student team meetings can greatly improve the quality of decisions that are made.

Choosing a Group Decision-Making Technique

Before choosing a group decision-making technique, the manager should carefully evaluate the group members and the decision situation. Then the best method for accomplishing the objectives of the group decision-making process can be selected. If the goal is generating a large number of alternatives, for example, brainstorming would be a good choice. If group members are reluctant to contribute ideas, the nominal group technique would be appropriate. The need for expert input would be best facilitated by the Delphi technique. To guard against groupthink, devil's advocacy or dialectical inquiry would be effective. Decisions that concern quality or production would benefit from the advice of quality circles or the empowered decisions of quality teams. Finally, a manager who wants to provide total empowerment to a group should consider self-managed work teams, discussed in OBXtra4.

IMPLICATIONS FOR ORGANIZATIONAL EFFECTIVENESS

Canadian organizations need to encourage creativity and innovation in order to effectively compete. Leaders can remove barriers to creativity and facilitate innovation by both hiring individuals with creative potential and removing organizational barriers to creativity. Individuals differ in their preferences for risk, as well as in their styles of gathering information and making judgments. Understanding individual differences can help managers maximize strengths in employee decision styles and build teams that capitalize on strengths. Creativity can be encouraged by providing employees with a supportive environment and training to nourish innovative ideas. Also, by creating lean organizational structures and cultures that foster and recognize creative decision making, organizational leaders can encourage risk taking and create policies that are conducive to the four stages of the creative process.

Decision making is important at all levels of every organization. At times managers may have the luxury of following a purely rational model of decision making and optimizing (selecting the best alternative), but more often they are forced to satisfice (select the alternative that is good enough). And, at times, the decision process can even seem unpredictable and random, relying more on intuition than facts.

When decisions are complex and the need for acceptance is high, leaders should encourage group decision making and guide the groups toward productive norms. Teams must learn about the risks of groupthink and polarization and must be trained to watch for the negative symptoms of groupthink. Also, organizations need to provide groups with resources and training in the various methods that have been found to improve group decision making.

Chapter Summary

1. The four stages of the creative process are preparation, incubation, illumination, and verification.
2. Creativity is influenced by individual factors such as cognitive processes, personality, mental blocks, and right versus left brain preferences. Creativity is also influenced by organizational factors and the degree of fit between the individual and the organization. Facilitators of creativity include leadership, organizational structure, physical environment and communication, recognition, and culture.
3. Decision making is defined as a conscious process of making choices among one or more alternatives and developing a commitment to a course of action. There are two types of decisions that managers need to make. These are programmed decisions, which are simple, routine matters for which a manager has an established decision rule, and there are nonprogrammed decisions, which are new and complex decisions that require creative solutions. Effective decisions are defined as those that are timely, meet desired objectives, and are accepted by the individuals

affected by them, and ethical decisions are those that are made having explored alternatives and their consequences so that actions are consistent with one's personal values and commonly held values of the organization and society.

4. The rational model of decision making is a logical, step-by-step approach that includes a thorough analysis of alternatives and their consequences. The model assumes that the outcome will be completely rational, that the decision maker has a consistent set of preferences that he or she is aware of all the possible alternatives and that he or she is able to calculate each alternative's probability of success.
5. Three models are proposed in contrast to the rational model. These are (1) The bounded rationality model of decision making, which suggests that there are limits to how rational a decision maker can actually be and argues that they "satisfice" and use heuristics; (2) the "garbage can" model of decision making, which proposes that decisions in organizations are, in fact, random and unsystematic; and (3) the intuitive decision-making model, which argues that intuition, at a level below consciousness, gives the decision maker a direction, or an urge to do or not do something.
6. Three types of individual differences influence decision making. These are the degree to which the decision maker is risk averse, the degree to which he or she has a tendency to escalate commitment to a losing course of action, and his or her cognitive style (using Jung's typology).
7. Managers sometimes use different degrees of participative decision making to make decisions, rather than deciding on their own. Participative decision making occurs when individuals who are affected by decisions influence those decisions.
8. Some advantages of group decision making are that (1) groups can pool resources and therefore have more knowledge and information than individuals; (2) members are more likely to accept and commit to a decision because they have had a voice in it; (3) members will have a better understanding of the decision because they have been involved in the various stages; and (4) groups can achieve synergy, which is the positive force that occurs when group members stimulate new or better solutions through the process of mutual influence and encouragement.
9. Two important disadvantages of group decision making are groupthink and group polarization. Groupthink is a deterioration of mental efficiency, reality testing, and moral judgment resulting from pressures within the group, and group polarization is the tendency for group discussion to produce shifts toward more extreme attitudes among members. The symptoms of groupthink are illusions of invulnerability, illusions of group morality, illusions of unanimity, rationalization, stereotyping the enemy, self-censorship, peer pressure, and mindguarding.
10. Four methods that help improve group decision making are brainstorming, nominal group technique (NGT), the Delphi technique, and devil's advocacy.

Key Terms

bounded rationality (p. 244)
brainstorming (p. 256)
cognitive style (p. 250)
creativity (p. 234)
decision making (p. 242)
Delphi technique (p. 258)
devil's advocacy (p. 258)
divergent thinking (p. 237)
effective decision (p. 242)
escalation of commitment to a losing course of action (p. 249)
ethical decision (p. 242)
garbage can model (p. 246)
group polarization (p. 256)
groupthink (p. 254)
heuristics (p. 245)
intuition (p. 247)
nominal group technique (NGT) (p. 258)
nonprogrammed decision (p. 242)
participative decision making (p. 251)
programmed decision (p. 242)
rationality (p. 242)
risk aversion (p. 248)
satisfice (p. 244)
self-efficacy (p. 249)
synergy (p. 252)

Review Questions

1. Compare the garbage can model with the bounded rationality model. Compare the usefulness of these models in today's organizations.
2. Define effective and ethical decision making.
3. What are the four stages of the creative process?
4. Describe the advantages and disadvantages of group decision making.
5. Describe the symptoms of groupthink and identify actions that can be taken to prevent it.
6. Explain the limitations of the rational model of decision making.
7. How is decision making affected by an individual's personality?

Discussion and Communication Questions

1. Why is identification of the real problem the first and most important step in the decision-making process? How does attribution theory explain mistakes that can be made as managers and employees work together to explain why the problem occurred?
2. How can organizations effectively manage both risk taking and escalation of commitment in the decision-making behaviour of employees?
3. How will you most likely make decisions based on your cognitive style? Do you think that your cognitive style might influence your approach to ethical decision making?
4. How can you develop your creativity as a decision maker?
5. (*Communication question*) Form a team of four persons. Find two examples of recent decisions made in organizations: one that you consider a good decision, and one that you consider a bad decision. Two members should work on the good decision, and two on the bad decision. Each pair should write a brief description of the decision. Then write a summary of what went right, what went wrong, and what could be done to improve the decision process. Compare and contrast your two examples in a presentation to the class.

Ethics Questions

1. Think of a decision made by a group that you feel was an unethical one. What factors led to the unethical decision?
2. How can organizations encourage ethical decision making?
3. How do cultural differences affect ethical decision making?
4. Describe groupthink as an ethical problem.

Application & Analysis

EXPERIENTIAL EXERCISE 8.1: WILDERNESS SURVIVAL

Purpose: To understand team dynamics and team decision-making processes

Group size: Any number of groups from 6 to 9 members

Time required: 50 minutes

Materials needed: None

Background

Sometimes group decision making is more effective than individual decision making. Research shows that if the decision is simple, it is better to have one person responsible; however, if the problem is more complex, group decision making is more effective. In this exercise, you'll get a chance to compare the results of individual and group decision making.

The Situation

You have gone on a Boundary Waters canoe trip with five friends to upper Minnesota and southern Ontario in the Quetico Provincial Park. Your group has been traveling Saganagons Lake to Kawnipi Lake, following through Canyon Falls and Kennebas Falls and Kenny Lake.

Fifteen to 18 miles away is the closest road, which is arrived at by paddling through lakes and rivers and usually portaging (taking the land path) around numerous falls. Saganagons Lake is impossible to cross in bad weather, generally because of heavy rain. The nearest town is Grand Marais, Minnesota, 60 miles away. That town has plenty of camping outfitters, but limited medical help, so residents rely on hospitals farther to the south.

The terrain is about 70 percent land and 30 percent water, with small patches of land here and there in between the lakes and rivers. Bears are not uncommon in this region. It is now mid-May, when the temperature (daytime) ranges from about 25° to 70°, often in the same day. Nighttime temperatures can be in the 20s.

Rain is frequent during the day (nights, too) and can be life-threatening if the temperature is cold. It is unusual for the weather to stay the same for more than a day or two. Generally, it will rain one day and be warm and clear the next, with a third day windy—and it is not easy to predict what type of weather will come next. In fact, it may be clear and warm, rainy and windy, all in the same day.

Your group of six was in two canoes going down the river and came to some rapids. Rather than taking the cottage route on land, the group foolishly decided to shoot the rapids by canoe.

Unfortunately, everyone fell out of the canoes and some were banged against the rocks. Luckily no one was killed, but one person suffered a broken leg and several others had cuts and bruises.

Both canoes were damaged severely. Both were bent clear in half, one with an open tear of 18", while the other had two tears 12" and 15" long. Both had broken gunwales (upper edges on both sides). You lost the packs that held the tent, most clothing, nearly all the food, cooking equipment, fuel, first aid kit, and flashlight. Your combined possessions include one jackknife, four canoe paddles, a pocketful of hard candies, five dollar bills, and 65 cents in change.

You had permits to take this trip, but no one knows for sure where you are and the closest phone is in Grand Marais. You were scheduled back four days from now, so it is likely a search party would be sent out in about five days (since you may have been delayed a day or so in getting back). Just now it has started to drizzle and it looks like rain will follow.

Your task now is to figure out how to survive in these unpredictable and possibly harsh conditions until you can get help.

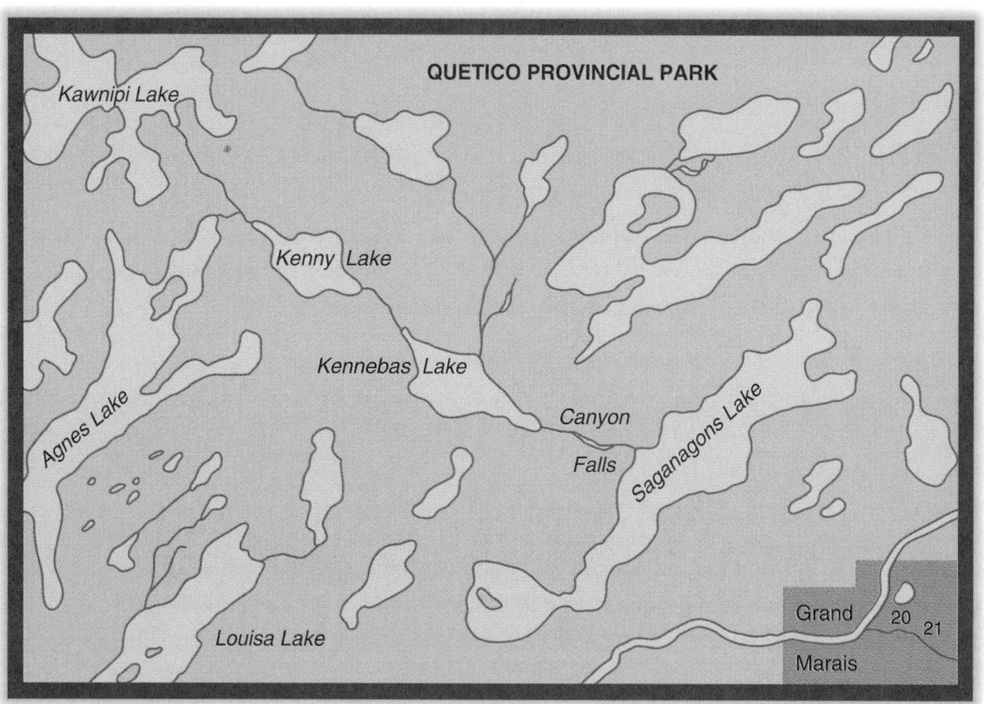

Instructions:

	Unit Time	Total Time
1. Introduction and individual ranking	**5 min.**	**5 min.**

Read the background on case and rank-order the 14 items on the list in terms of survival value. The item considered most valuable should be ranked "1" and the least valuable should be ranked "14." Individuals should place their rankings on Table 1, column B.

2. Group discussion	**20 min.**	**25 min.**

In groups of six to nine members (with one or two optional observers who are asked to refer to the appendix "Observing and Understanding Group Processes" at the end of this exercise and to take notes and later give feedback), come to a consensus on the ranking of the items. Use Table 1, column C. Members should not vote or "horse trade," but rather should try to have everyone more or less agree on the ranking. When someone disagrees, members should try to listen carefully. When someone feels strongly, that person should attempt to use persuasive techniques.

3. Correct answers given	**5 min.**	**30 min.**

Instructor posts the correct answers and gives the reasons for those rankings, according to the experts. Students put correct rankings in column D of Table 1.

4. Computation of Table 1	**5 min.**	**35 min.**

a. Compare your answer, listed under column B, with the correct answer, listed under column D. Subtract D from B in each row, taking the absolute value (do not count minus signs). That will be the individual error, which is then listed under column A. For example:

if you answered . . .	if correct answer was . . .	difference is:
2	11	9
10	5	5
12	1	11

b. Total the numbers in column A (none of which should be negative numbers) to get your individual score.
c. Subtract column D from column C in each row, again using absolute values, to get the group error, which should be listed under column E.
d. Total the numbers in column E (none of which should be negative numbers) to get your group score.
e. Subtract column C from column B in each row and put the results (absolute value) in column F. This is your persuasion score, which measures how much you are able to influence other group members to your thinking. Spend a few minutes during your group discussion talking about the persuasion score. Who had the lowest (this person was the most persuasive) and who had the highest (this person was the least persuasive) scores? Table 1 should now be complete.

5. Computation of Table 2 **5 min.** **50 min.**

a. Average member score: Add the individual scores (step b, column A) of all group members and divide by the number of members in the group. Put this number in the indicated column.
b. Group score (step d, column E): Put this number in the indicated column.
c. Synergy: If your group score is lower than your average member score, then put "yes" in the column for Synergy. If your group score is higher than your average member score, then put "no" in the column for Synergy.
d. Best member score: This is the number of the member who has the lowest individual score. Put this score in the indicated column.

Table 1

Rank-order the following in terms of survival assistance, putting the most valuable as "1"

Items	**A (B – D) Individual Error**	**B Your Ranking**	**C Group Ranking**	**D Expert Ranking**	**E (C – D) Group Error**	**F (B – C) Persuasion**
Fanny pack of food—cheese, salami, gorp						
Plastic-covered map of Boundary Waters						
Six PFDs (personal flotation devices)						
Two fishing poles, broken						
Set of clothes for three (wet)						
One yellow Frisbee						
Water purification tablets						
Duct tape, one 30′ roll						
Whiskey, one pint, 180 proof						
Insect repellent, one bottle						
Matches, 30, dry						
Parachute cord, 35′						
Compass						
Six sleeping bags, synthetic, medium weight						

Individual Score (Total of A) ________

Group Score (Total of E) ________

Persuasion Score (Total of F) ________

6. **Group feedback (optional)** **10+ min.**
   Observers give feedback to group and group talks about how it did in terms of decision making, who was most persuasive, and so on.

7. **Class discussion** **10+ min.** **50 min.**
   Instructor leads discussion on group decision making and how each group did in this exercise, answering the following questions.

8. **Group discussion**
   As a class, discuss the following questions:
   a. To what extent did group discussion change the accuracy of the answers?
   b. Which behaviours helped/hindered the decision-making process?
   c. What happened if a person had a very accurate individual score, but was not very persuasive in the group; conversely, what happened if a person had a poor individual score and was very persuasive in the group?

Table 2

	Groups					
Items	**1**	**2**	**3**	**4**	**5**	**6**
Average Member Score						
Group Score						
Synergy						
Best Member Score						

APPENDIX: OBSERVING AND UNDERSTANDING GROUP PROCESSES

Individuals learn, in part, by reflecting on their own experiences and trying to build on strengths and improve weaknesses. On the other hand, groups have difficulty being similarly reflective. When participating in a group, there is a tendency for individuals to be actively involved in whatever task the group is doing, and to ignore the way in which the group is operating (what might be called the *group process*). Over time, for groups or teams to become more effective, an important factor for groups to learn from their own experiences is to pay some attention to their processes. A conversation about group process can be as simple as asking the questions, "what did we do well; what could we improve?" or could be more complete by having the group talk about some of the elements of group process from a guide, such as the following:

1. **Interactions**

Names of group members	**Frequency of participation**	**Influence (low 1–10 high)**	**Reasons for influence rating (events, influence styles)**	**Shifts and patterns in participation and/or influence (note events)**

First, in the Frequency column, simply make a mark each time an individual participates in the group interaction. A second dimension of group process to assess is the impact of what people say. One can have influence without extensive participation if the group members listen carefully to what one says and change decision or the directions of the conversation as a result. In a general sense, however, greater participation is often linked to greater influence. In the next two columns on the matrix, identify on a scale of 1–10 how much influence you felt each member had and note why and/or what events were related to your rating.

Third, consider shifts and patterns in participation (e.g., someone became more talkative or became silent) or influence. Did you see any changes? What events preceded the shift? Were these patterns you noticed in participation (e.g., if Person A talked, Person B immediately followed, or Person C seemed to speak only to Person A)? Record your observations in the final column of the matrix.

2. **Observing nonverbals**
   In addition to listening to the verbal comments, many things may be learned from the nonverbal behavior of the group. Interactions may generate feelings in group members that are unspoken but observable in nonverbal behaviours. For example, does someone seem to have stopped listening? Do you see inconsistencies between verbal and nonverbal messages (i.e., does someone say that she is "fine" but have a frown on her face)? What do nonverbal cues tell you about how group members are feeling? What is the general climate of the group?

SOURCE: D. Marcic, J. Seltzer, and P. Vaill, *Organizational Behavior: Experiences and Cases*, 6th ed. (Mason, OH: South-Western College Publishing, 2001), 87–92. Appendix adapted by Joseph Seltzer.

Application & Analysis

CASE: CASUAL TOGS, INC.

Casual Togs is a 30-year-old firm producing moderately priced women's apparel, headquartered in Western Canada. About 80 percent of production is sold to department stores in cities throughout the country. The remaining 20 percent is sold to small women's specialty shops. All clothes carry the firm's well-known brand label. Products are principally shirts and blouses, with some knit dresses making up the balance.

The owner and principal stockholder, Cy Geldmark, is an entrepreneur. Cy served a long apprenticeship in the New York garment district and saved part of his wages until he could open his own firm, staffed primarily with relatives and friends. An innovator, Cy pioneered in the "mix and/or match" coordinate idea of fashion ensembles whereby a customer of moderate means could build a complete wardrobe of work and casual clothes. Designers with trend-setting styles and above-average quality (considering the semi-mass-production methods employed) helped propel Casual Togs to a prominent position in the industry. However, the mix-and-match coordinate idea was not patented, and intense competition has now developed from larger firms as well as from new, smaller companies with fresh fashion ideas. In Cy's words, price competition is "deadly."

The company has rapidly expanded in the last 10 years, setting up production plants in five provinces where all facilities are leased. Notwithstanding the use of the latest in large-capacity cutters and high-speed sewing machines, production hinges on a great expenditure of personal effort by the individual worker. Many quality checks are necessary before a garment is finished.

In an attempt to coordinate production and delivery, Casual Togs is constructing a new multi-million-dollar central distribution plant at the present home office location, where all administrative and some production functions are performed. All production runs will be shipped to this new facility and then dispatched by a computer-programmed delivery-inventory scheduling method. The facility is planned to help cope with an increasingly serious problem of merchandise being returned from customers who refuse acceptance because delivery is later than promised.

The fashion industry is characterized by five distinct selling "seasons" so garments must be ordered, produced, and delivered within a relatively short time period. The five-season cycle produces unusual production and forecasting problems. On the basis of pilot sales during the first two weeks of each season, forecasts are developed about the quantity and styles to be produced for the entire season. Once the bolts of cloth are cut into a particular season's patterns, there is no turning back. If pilot sales are not indicative of the rest of the season or if the sales forecast is in error, the company is saddled with stock that can be disposed of only through discount outlets, usually at a loss.

In an effort to increase the accuracy of sales forecasting and to pinpoint specific reasons for late deliveries, Cy instituted a computer printout of each day's sales, as reported by e-mail by field sales staff. This printout was initially distributed to the president, the vice president of sales, the sales forecast manager, the treasurer, the production manager, and the eight regional sales managers. All of those people were located at the firm's headquarters offices. The printout was voluminous, often running 100 or more pages.

Cy relied greatly on his "feel of the situation" for making decisions. Although he made all final important operating and policy decisions, he said that all department heads should feel free to act as "you see fit." He said that he would back any decisions made without consultation with him. Despite Cy's exhortations that he need *not* be consulted, almost all vice presidents and departmental managers conferred daily with him, usually about the progress of the current fashion season's products. During each fashion season, many style modifications and quantity level changes were made. With rare exceptions, Cy made all important daily decisions in those matters.

The daily decision sessions were marked by emotional outbursts by various management personnel. The meetings were informal and nonscheduled and different groups would meet at different times with Cy. The groups were not even based on functional lines. If one individual felt that a daily printout indicated change "X," regardless of whether or not it affected his department, he would go to the president asking that the change be effected. If another department manager or even a vice president were present and disagreed, inevitably a shouting match developed in the president's office. Usually Cy remained impassive during such interchanges, giving his decision after all participants had finished.

Some management personnel said that Cy was "too lenient" and should curb the emotionally charged sessions because they were disruptive and led to erroneous decisions. These same critics pointed to Cy's reputation as an easy mark for suppliers; if a supplier had some previous tie from the old days or was remotely related to someone in Cy's family, he would be assured of at least some orders, despite the fact that his prices were higher than those of competing suppliers.

Often the president's sister, Judy, who was vice president in charge of administration, would wander into the daily decision sessions. She would often object to proposed changes on the grounds that they had been proposed by "imbeciles" or were "too damned expensive." Judy was everywhere, initiating changes herself in every department. Her decisions affected everything from copier paper to salesmen's commissions to rest period schedules for the clerical help. She often countermanded a department manager's instructions and would hire and fire personnel without the manager's knowledge. Judy's personality was judged abrasive by all who had contact with her. She was given to using profanity publicly at a "longshoreman's quality level." When speaking "normally," she could be heard for some distance. Cy always backed Judy's decisions once they were made. Although the formal organizational chart depicted Judy and the treasurer as being on the same level, the treasurer, Stan Seeburg (Cy's nephew), was not allowed to approve any expenditure over $1000 without Judy's informal approval. Judy was one of the original founders and owned 12 percent of the firm's stock. From time to time Cy tried, by his own admission, to calm her down, with a notable lack of success. But several sources reported that if Judy and her brother had an argument in private, Judy always deferred to her brother's decisions.

For many years Cy's chief source of sales data and forecast was Andy Johnson, sales forecast/budget manager. Andy prepared daily handwritten recaps from telephone reports in the earlier years and from the printout in more recent years. Using intuition and a very thorough knowledge of the garment industry, Andy would prepare the season's forecasts and modify them as the actual sales started coming in. He had a rapport with Cy and was quite proud of the clearly evident esteem the president had for him.

That rapport was important to Andy for more than reasons of self-esteem. Andy had been with the firm for 15 years, but despite his knowledge had never been promoted. He resented this keenly and attributed his lack of success to the fact that he was not a relative or of the same nationality as the other managers. "At least," said Andy once, "Cy listens to me more than to these shirt-tail relatives." Andy was one of the very few people who called the president by his first name in public.

In a recent change in office location, Andy and his former co-worker, Sol Green, were moved from one large, shared office, which housed subordinates as well, to individual glass-partitioned offices. The subordinates were now located adjacent to Andy's and Sol's offices. After this move, Sol was promoted to manager/internal accounting and sales, and was given control over all subordinates who previously had worked collectively for Andy and Sol.

Andy was given one new man to help with sales forecasts and budgets; the new man had an MBA and was trained in statistical analysis. Andy held a bachelor's degree in business. Bill Smith, the new man, suggested several new methods of collating and analyzing the daily printout to Andy, who abruptly rejected the ideas, saying, "Cy isn't used to getting data in that form; he would be confused by a change."

As the daily printouts began to be more detailed and more widely distributed, Andy became more critical of them than usual. He said that they didn't "really" show what styles were leading, and that there were many errors. Andy quoted personal conversations with field salespeople to prove his points. When Bill cited several new styles in what had previously been one category, Andy replied that he was using horse sense to report data in a way that Cy and others would best understand. Andy was away from his desk for long periods during this time, attending numerous management meetings that the president called. The pattern of the meetings was as before, or worse; there were loud, emotional arguments punctuated by fist-pounding and door-slamming.

The problem of returns was now most acute; on average, 40 percent of all shipments were being returned. Although all management personnel agreed that the reason for returns was late deliveries, some managers argued that forecasting by style lines was inaccurate and resulted in erroneous production scheduling, and others said that there was no coordination between the nine production centres and the shipping department, which was located at the home office site. Still others said that shipping and/or production methods were not efficient. The production manager said that there was a disparity between the delivery dates given by customers and those in the salespeople's orders, which served as the basis of a production run. The sales manager maintained that poor quality was the real reason for returns; customers did not want to become embroiled in arguments with home office personnel over quality questions and therefore they wrote "late delivery" on sub-standard merchandise because it was simpler.

In an effort to solve the dilemma, Cy hired an experienced market analyst, Stan Levine, who had a strong computer-oriented background. Stan was given a private office and the authority to effect any changes he deemed necessary. Several events happened immediately; a supplemental recap of the printout was published every day by Stan in addition to Andy's handwritten recap, and the printout format was changed. Sol objected violently to the new format, saying that it did not provide accounting with the categorizations necessary for their work. Andy began a "war" with Stan, "to show up this egotistical, snot-nosed kid."

At the same time, several new designers were hired, salespeople's commission schedules were changed, many regional vice presidents were put on the road "temporarily," and Andy, backed by Cy, cut all departments' budgets by 15 percent (the company was in the middle of a 12-month budget period).

Approximately four weeks after all those changes had occurred, the following events transpired: returns had increased to an even higher level; many old customers had stopped ordering, saying that poor quality and late deliveries made Casual Togs too undependable; the distribution centre construction was halted at midpoint "because the company could not find a qualified individual to fill the job of supervisor"; the five plant centres fell, on average, 15 percent under previously established production goals; two of the new designers resigned; Judy fired the new vice president of industrial relations after he had been on the job four weeks (he held a three-year management contract for $60 000 a year); Andy Johnson, Sol Green, and Stan Levine weren't speaking to each other; Andy began distributing two daily sales recap reports to a select, small group of top managers; and the computer service department complained directly to Cy that their new workload was too great because Stan now required them to produce a daily selling forecast, by week, month, and season.

Casual Togs Inc. Organization Chart

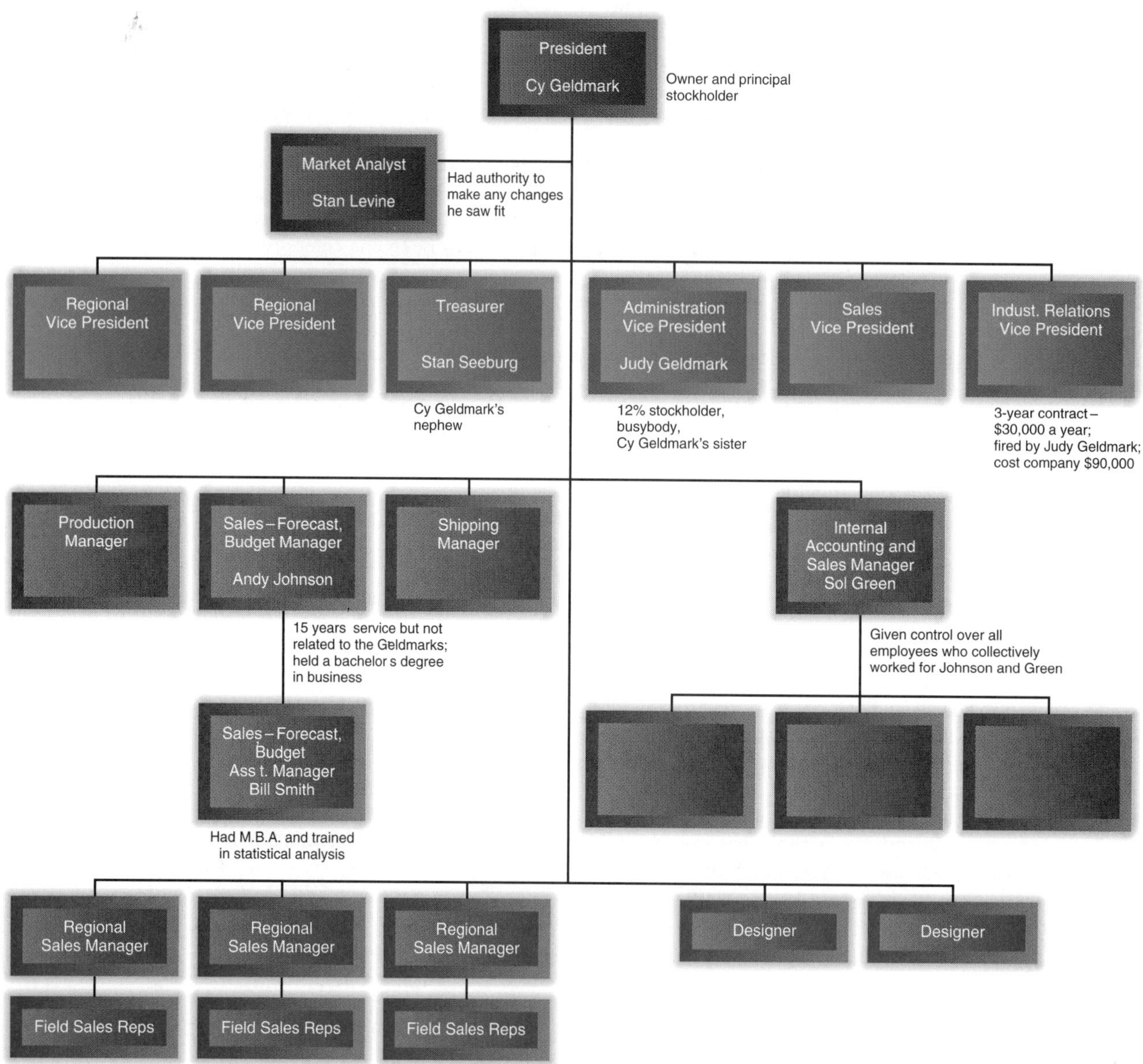

Discussion Questions:

1. Use the rational decision-making model to diagnose some of the causes of this ineffective decision making.
2. What are some of the individual characteristics that seem to be influencing the decision-making effectiveness of Cy and Andy?
3. What are some of the causes of the group decision-making weaknesses at Casual Togs?
4. What are your recommendations for improving individual and group decision making at this company?

Scoring Instructions for Self-Assessments

Self-Assessment 8.2: Which Side of Your Brain Do You Favour?

Interpretation

- Four, five, or six "A" answers indicate lateralization—an ability to use either hemisphere easily and to solve problems according to their nature rather than according to a favoured manner.
- One, two, or three "A" answers indicate right-hemisphere dominance; corresponding traits include inventiveness, creativity, innovation, risk taking, whimsy, and an ability to see the "big picture."
- Seven, eight, or nine "A" answers indicate a left-hemisphere dominance—a tendency toward attention to detail, the use of logic, and traits of thoroughness and accuracy.

Power and Influence

chapter nine

9

LEARNING OBJECTIVES

By the end of this chapter, you will be able to do the following:

1. Define *power, influence,* and *political behaviour*; explain why they are important to study; and describe how they can be observed in organizations.
2. Describe in detail six individual sources of power.
3. Describe empowerment and explain how it can increase the power of both the boss and the employee.
4. Describe the steps an employee can take to become influential with his or her boss.
5. Describe four organizational conditions that enable individuals and subunits to gain power.
6. Describe influence tactics and their outcomes.
7. Describe some of the nonsanctioned influence tactics (political behaviour).
8. Explain the organizational and individual conditions that foster political behaviour in organizations.
9. Explain strategies for minimizing political behaviour in organizations.

learning about the context

Empowerment at Aquila Networks Canada (Fortis Inc.)

Aquila Networks Canada (bought by Fortis Inc. in June of 2004) is an electric utility with more than 525 000 customers in British Columbia and Alberta. Aquila's power linemen are empowered to take ownership of the distribution system, and they drive all service and maintenance work.

This was made possible by the introduction of laptops that are linked to a global positioning system (GPS), which centres on their trucks to allow them to identify nearby power lines and their voltages. The linemen are empowered through their access to information, which is one of six sources of power discussed in the chapter. They have access to information through an AM/FM system that models Aquila's entire electrical network, linking transmission and distribution facilities (including 185 000 transformers, 900 000 conductor segments, and more than one million poles) to actual geographical and customer information. Thus, field employees are provided with critical information that they need to fulfill customer service expectations. This allows them to instantly update information into the Aquila software application called "Field View" that has been continuously enhanced since 1995 with ideas and suggestions from over 300 Aquila employees.

The empowerment initiative has created cost savings by reducing the need and time for printing, plotting, data translation, and facility checking because the field staff record all required information on the distribution facilities right at the field site. Employees have a real sense of pride, enthusiasm, and ownership, and the 200 linemen and 100 contractors "now feel that this tool is theirs, and will tell you that the data is their new lifeline."[1]

SOURCES: P. Drinnan, "A New Lifeline for the Field," *Transmission and Distribution World* 55, no. 7 (July 1, 2003); "Canadian Utility Honoured in Seattle for Technological Innovation," *Canada Newswire*, April 26, 2004; "HD Fortis Inc. Closes Deal to Acquire Alberta and BC Utilities," *Market News Publishing*, June 10, 2004.

Effective management of organizational behaviour requires that you be able to influence the people around you, whether or not you are officially in a position of power. Also, as you learned in the chapter opener about Aquila Networks Canada, empowering employees is becoming increasingly viable with the help of new technologies, and empowerment is a strategy that builds power and influence for both management and employees, leading to improved organizational performance.

This chapter begins with an introduction to the topic of power and influence and explains why it is so important to study. Then an organizing framework is provided to help you navigate the chapter and understand the dynamics of power and influence in organizations. The chapter is then divided into three main parts: Part one explores six individual sources of power and the degree of follower commitment or compliance usually associated with using each of them. Part two explores power in the boss–subordinate relationship, and this includes both how a bosses can increase power through employee empowerment as well as how subordinates can increase power through managing their relationships with their bosses. Part three is a review of the influence tactics that are used and generally sanctioned in the workplace. Part four takes a look at those influence tactics that are often observed in the workplace but are not sanctioned by the organization, hence being labelled as "political" rather than "influence" tactics. Part five looks at power and influence from a more macro perspective and explores which organizational conditions enable subunits to (1) gain power and influence and (2) encourage political (nonsanctioned) tactics. Strategies are then suggested for leaders who wish to try to minimize and discourage the extensive use of political (nonsanctioned) tactics.

Define *power, influence,* and *political behaviour*; explain why they are important to study; and describe how they can be observed in organizations.

INTRODUCTION TO POWER AND INFLUENCE IN ORGANIZATIONS

In the late 1970s power was still regarded as a "dirty word" in organization studies. Since then, however, attitudes and perspectives have been steadily changing. Now, instead of trying to stop people from seeking and using power, we recognize that it is a natural part of organizational life and we want people to learn how to use their power in more effective and positive ways.[2]

What Are the Differences between Power, Influence, and Political Behaviour?

power
The ability of one party to change or control the behaviour, attitudes, opinions, objectives, needs, or values of another party.

influence
The process of affecting the thoughts, behaviour, and feelings of others.

political behaviour
Influence attempts that are for personal gain and are not officially sanctioned by an organization.

Power is the ability of one party to change or control the behaviour, attitudes, opinions, objectives, needs, or values of another party.[3] **Influence** is the process of actually exercising this power by affecting the thoughts, behaviour, and feelings of others. **Political behaviour** is defined as influence attempts that are for personal gain and are not officially sanctioned by an organization.[4] The use of power, politics, and influence in the workplace, which may be one of the most common workplace issues, can be defined as "those activities taken within organizations to acquire, develop, and use power and other resources to obtain one's preferred outcomes in a situation in which there is uncertainty or disagreement about choices."[5]

Why Are Power, Influence, and Political Behaviour Important to Study?

Because of increasing uncertainty and change in both the internal and external environments of organizations, there is also increasing uncertainty and disagreement about choices. Thus power and influence have become central elements in effective leadership. Failures to understand power and politics can be costly to nonsupervisory employees as well. They need to learn about power and organizational politics, so that they successfully manage the inevitable political behaviour in organizations, rather than being at its mercy!

Organizational charts and job titles indicate formal leadership roles, but they do not necessarily reveal much about who has the real power and influence in the organization. Rosabeth Moss Kanter has developed a scholarly approach to determining who has power and who feels powerless. This is important to understand for both supervisory and nonsupervisory employees.[6] Some of the common symptoms of supervisory **powerlessness** are as follows: bossiness, overly close supervision, inflexible adherence to the rules, a tendency to do the job oneself rather than training employees to do it, focusing on budget cutting, and punishing others.[7]

powerlessness
A lack of power.

What Are the Symbols of Power?

By contrast to symptoms of powerlessnes, actions such as the ability to intercede on someone's behalf or to get early access to important information indicate that the supervisor is powerful and has influence. Also, recognizing symbols of power can be particularly useful in finding a mentor. Rosabeth Kanter observed a number of distinct symbols of power and wrote about them over 20 years ago, but they are still relevant today. They are summarized in Exhibit 9.1.

An Organizing Framework for Understanding Power and Influence in Organizations

Exhibit 9.2 provides you with a framework for understanding the many complex issues involved in understanding power and influence in organizations. It also offers a roadmap for the organization of this chapter. As you can see, power can come from at least six sources (or antecedents) such as the power to reward and punish (coercive power) and it can also come from being empowered by a boss. Both of these antecedents require the use of influence tactics in order to create outcomes such as compliance, commitment or active/passive rejection of the influence attempt.

Dilbert
Scott Adams is the creator of "Dilbert," the wildly popular comic strip that pokes fun at corporate culture and political behaviour in the workplace. Visit the Dilbert website and read through recent strips. How does the underlying humour in Dilbert relate to symbols of power and powerlessness?
http://www.dilbert.com

EXHIBIT 9.1

Rosabeth Moss Kanter's Symbols of Power

1. *Ability to intercede for someone in trouble:* An individual who can pull someone out of a jam has power.
2. *Ability to get placements for favoured employees:* Getting a key promotion for an employee is a sign of power.
3. *Exceeding budget limitation:* A manager who can go above budget limits without being reprimanded has power.
4. *Procuring above-average raises for employees:* One faculty member reported that her department head distributed 10 percent raises to the most productive faculty members although the budget allowed for only 4 percent increases. "I don't know how he did it; he must have pull," she said.
5. *Getting items on the agenda at meetings:* If a manager can raise issues for action at meetings, it's a sign of power.
6. *Access to early information:* Having information before anyone else does is a signal that a manager is plugged in to key sources.
7. *Having top managers seek out their opinion:* When top managers have a problem, they may ask for advice from lower-level managers. The managers they turn to have power.

SOURCE: R. Kanter, "Power Failure in Management Circuits," *Harvard Business Review* (July–August 1979): 31–54.

INDIVIDUAL SOURCES OF POWER AND THEIR EFFECTS

Describe in detail six individual sources of power.

One of the earliest classifications of social power was suggested years ago by French and Raven. They originally identified five sources of power and called them legitimate, reward, coercive, referent, and expert power.[8] Contemporary OB scholars have added "information access" as a sixth source of power and we now explore each of these six sources of power, as depicted in the top-left side of Exhibit 9.2.

Legitimate Power

legitimate power
Power that is based on a person holding a formal position. Others comply because they accept the legitimacy of the position of the power holder.

Legitimate power, which is similar to authority, is power that is based on a person holding a formal position. Others comply because they accept the legitimacy of the position of the power holder.[9] Conceptually, the authority bestowed upon an individual by the organization is legitimate power. For example, if you find yourself thinking: "My supervisor has a right to expect me to carry out his/her instructions," you are responding to a perception that he or she possesses legitimate power.[10] When someone gets promoted to a position of "manager" he or she has been given a potential source of legitimate power. However, legitimate power is not enough to guarantee influence. It doesn't matter that a manager thinks he or she has the right to influence his or her employees. What matters is that the employees must themselves believe that the manager has the right to tell them what to do.

Reward Power

reward power
Power based on a person's access to rewards. Others comply because they want the rewards the power holder can offer.

Reward power is power based on a person's access to rewards. Others comply because they want the rewards the power holder can offer.[11] For example, managers control the rewards of salary increases, bonuses, praise, and promotions. Reward power can lead to better performance, but only as long as the employee sees a clear and strong link between performance and rewards. Researchers have found that the higher the perceived reward power of a supervisor, the more effort expended by the subordinate.[12] Reward power

EXHIBIT 9.2

Organizing Framework for Understanding Power and Influence in Organizations

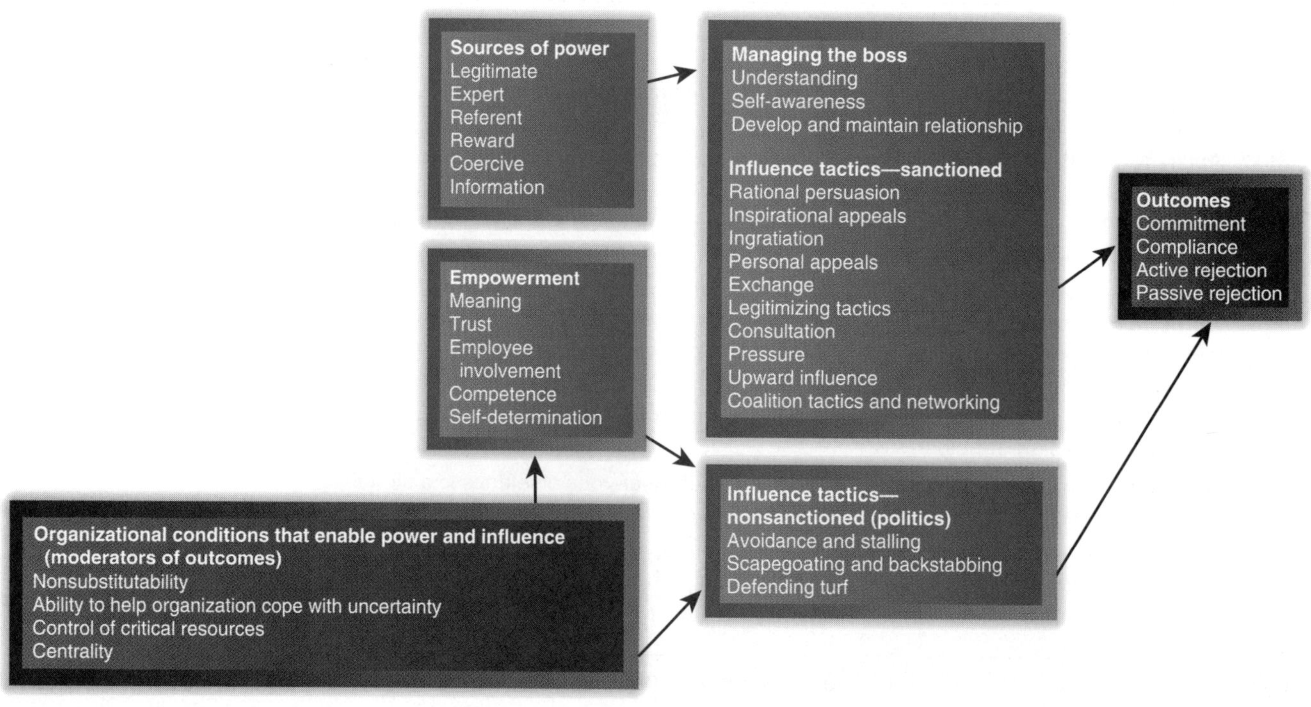

Reward power comes in many forms including praise, bonuses, prizes and promotions.

works only if the person values the reward being offered (valence) and perceives high performance-reward probability, in expectancy theory terms.

Coercive Power

coercive power
Power that is based on a person's ability to punish. Others comply because they fear punishment or some negative consequence.

Coercive power is power that is based on a person's ability to punish. Others comply because they fear punishment or some negative consequence. If you find yourself acting in a certain way because you are thinking: "My supervisor can fire me if I neglect my duties" or "My supervisor can make things unpleasant here," then you believe that your supervisor holds coercive power over you.[13] Coercive power can be used in a number of different ways, and some are more effective than others. Threatening to put a university student on probation or suspension if a certain GPA is not met, is an example of using coercive power. Verbal abuse and physical punishment are other, less effective examples of using coercive power to influence. For example, when specially trained stand-in bosses adopted a bullying style, drawing on coercive power, over 60 percent of the subordinates told researchers they wished to leave their jobs.[14]

Research has shown that both coercive power and legitimate power tend to increase employee perceptions of stress.[15] However, in the case of supervisory power, using coercive power, through consequences such as warnings, reprimands, and disciplinary actions, is a necessary component for effectively influencing the negative behaviour of some employees. See Exhibit 9.3 for examples of how the various sources of power are communicated.

EXHIBIT 9.3

Communicating Individual Sources of Power

Legitimate Power	"Do it because I'm the boss."
Reward	"Do it because there is something in it for you."
Coercive	"Do it or else."
Referent	"Do it because you respect, like or identify with me."
Expert	"Do it because you value my expertise on the matter."
Information	"Do it because you want access to the information I have."

Referent Power

referent power
A power that is based on a person's attractiveness to and friendship with others. Others comply because they respect and like the power holder.

Referent power is a power that is based on a person's attractiveness to and friendship with others. Others comply because they respect and like the power holder. Sentiments such as: "My supervisor makes me feel personally accepted" are indicative that the supervisor has referent power.[16] Charismatic individuals are often thought to have referent power, and this is discussed in more depth in Chapter 10 where we explore leadership. Researchers have found that referent power is a strong predictor of employees' satisfaction with their supervisors and that it is more effective than other power bases, in influencing employee behaviour.[17] Do you agree that a charismatic manager or professor whom you like and respect is more likely to influence you?

Expert Power

expert power
Power based on a person's expertise, competence, and information in a certain area. Others comply because they believe in the power holder's knowledge and competence.

Expert power is power based on a person's expertise, competence, and information in a certain area. Others comply because they believe in the power holder's knowledge and competence. Like referent power, expert power does not come with the position, it has to be earned. When expert power has been established, it can be very effective in influencing others. The following sentiments are a reflection of perceived expert power: "My supervisor has considerable professional experience to draw from in helping me do my work." "My supervisor can provide me with needed technical knowledge."[18] Newly appointed employees are often too modest about their areas of expertise and do not capitalize on this power source, or make it explicit, as much as they could.[19] It is also worth mentioning however, that supervisors, when first promoted from a technical position, sometimes rely *too much* on their expert power, and don't develop their other power sources with employees. In Organizational Reality 9.1, you can see that the CEO of CHUM, Jay Switzer, relies on expert power.

organizational reality 9.1

From Referent to Expert Power at CHUM

Allen Waters purchased CHUM in 1954 and bought Citytv, founded by Moses Znaimer and Phyllis Switzer in 1978. Over five decades CHUM has grown from a tiny Toronto radio station into a $500 million coast-to-coast multimedia enterprise, with 28 radio stations, 8 local TV stations, and 17 digital and specialty channels. In 2002, CHUM licensed 1600 hours of programming to 150 countries and has exported its Citytv format to such places as Finland, Colombia, and Spain.

Jay Switzer was a TV programmer before becoming CEO at CHUM.

Jay Switzer worked as Citytv's chief programmer for 10 years and was president of CHUM television for three years prior to getting the top job at CHUM in May of 2003. Switzer replaced the "mercurial visionary" Moses Znaimer, who was reported to have a "Jupiter-sized ego" and a great deal of referent power. By contrast, Switzer relies on his expert power. Both leaders have build follower commitment but with very different styles and power sources. Switzer is well known for his regulatory expertise and was Znaimer's number-crunching right-hand man. Switzer stands out as disarmingly low-key, congenial, and accessible, and he claims that he was not seeking the powerful job of CEO. "It wasn't my dream or my plan to run CHUM.... Presidents are supposed to be Type A personalities with large ambitions. That's not me. When I go home at night, I'm still a TV programmer."

SOURCES: A. Holloway, A. Mlynek, and R. Starr, "The Countdown Continues; Skates, Radio and Vaccines Join Our List of Canada's Top 75 companies," *Canadian Business* 76, no. 4 (March 3, 2003); "Following Moses," *Marketing Magazine* 108, no. 19 (May 19, 2003), 19; D. Hayes, "TV Brat," *National Post Business,* May 2003, 64–69; M. Fraser, "CHUM Set to Move in a New Direction?" *National Post,* December 2, 2002.

Information Power

In today's knowledge economy, access to information is particularly important. **Information power** is power based on a person's access to important information. Others comply because they want the information the power holder has. Information power is not only held by people with legitimate power. It may also flow upward from subordinates to managers, as well as laterally to peers and co-workers. Key to the idea of information power is the person's central position in the communication networks of the organization, both formal and informal. As is the case in many progressive organizations, technology and information access is enabling much higher levels of empowerment than ever before. For example, at Aquila Networks Canada in Alberta, linemen are empowered to take ownership of the distribution system and they drive all service and maintenance work, as described at the beginning of the chapter.

information power
Power based on a person's access to important information. Others comply because they want the information the power holder has.

POWER IN THE BOSS–EMPLOYEE RELATIONSHIP

In this section we take a more in-depth look at the power issues and opportunities in the relationship between boss and employee. Contemporary research demonstrates that, contrary to traditional beliefs about the finite nature of power, power is in fact, "unlimited when accrued through partnering and learning."[20] This means that bosses can share power with subordinates by empowering them, and that when this is done well, the boss' power can also increase. Also, employees can increase their own power by learning to manage their bosses. We now look at both of these aspects of power in the boss–employee relationship: expanding power through empowerment and managing the boss. As depicted in the organizing framework in Exhibit 9.2. empowerment acts as an additional source of power while "managing the boss" is considered to be an influence tactic.

Expanding Power through Empowerment

Describe empowerment and explain how it can increase the power of both the boss and the employee.

Empowerment is defined as "creating conditions for heightened motivation through the development of a strong sense of personal self-efficacy."[21] Empowerment involves sharing power with employees so that they learn to believe in their ability to do the job.

empowerment
Creating conditions for heightened motivation through the development of a strong sense of personal self-efficacy.

IMPLICATIONS FOR LIFE

Sources of Power and Birth Order

The sources of power can be used to understand some dynamics between siblings, particularly the impact of birth order.

- *Expert power:* Usually the oldest sibling has expert power because they have been around longer and therefore know more.
- *Referent power:* Often the youngest sibling has referent power because he or she is sweet and charming and knows how to work a room full of adults.
- *Legitimate power:* Parents have the most of this, being at the top of the familial hierarchy, but the older the sibling, usually the more legitimate power they have.
- *Coercive power:* Usually the biggest, not necessarily the oldest, sibling has this, and uses it to bully smaller ones.
- *Information power:* Less powerful siblings can often use their access to negative information about more powerful siblings, to their advantage. By divulging this information to people higher up (i.e., parents or older siblings) they can gain power.
- *Reward power:* Having this depends upon resources availability but usually older siblings have more access to resources. However, younger siblings, through their referent power with parents, can sometimes access resources and gain power with older siblings.

organizational reality 9.2

Empowerment at Whole Foods Market

The Whole Foods Market in Toronto opened in May of 2002 and it follows the U.S. parent company's practice of employee empowerment. Whole Foods strives to build positive and healthy relationships among team members, and "us versus them" thinking has no place in their company. They believe that the best way to do this is to encourage participation and involvement at all levels of their business. Some of the ways Whole Foods does this is through the use of self-directed teams that meet regularly to discuss issues, solve problems, and appreciate each other's contributions. Another way is through team member forums and advisory groups.

Whole Foods empowers employees to make decisions that are usually reserved for upper-level management.

Information is power, and Whole Foods Market also uses open-book management, which allows every employee complete access to the company's financial information, including salaries. Reports are distributed monthly that include sales, product costs, and profits for all stores. This information is sensitive, but because individual teams make decisions about spending, ordering, and pricing, the information is essential. Teams must have full operating and financial information to be truly empowered. Although Whole Foods caters to an elite market, its philosophy isn't elitism; it's empowerment.

SOURCES: G. Dess and J. Picken, "Changing Roles: Leadership in the 21st Century," *Organizational Dynamics* (Winter 2000): 18–33; E. Kelly, "Health-Food Chains Spar for Baby-Boomers," *Fortune* (April 3, 2000): 56–60; C. Joinson, "The Cost of Doing Business?" *HR Magazine* (December 1999): 86–92; M. Mazzetti, "Managing Texas-Style," *Texas Monthly* (December 2000): 64–78; Whole Foods Market, *Welcome to Whole Foods Market Toronto,* http://www.wholefoodsmarket.com/stores/toronto/index.html.

One example of a high degree of empowerment is the use of self-managed teams (SMWTs), which are discussed in OBXtra 4. Another, less extreme example of empowerment is the Whole Foods Market in Toronto. Employees there love their jobs, and empowerment is the reason. Read about the specifics in Organizational Reality 9.2.

The driving idea of empowerment is that the individuals closest to the work and to the customers should make the decisions. This not only makes the best use of employees' skills and talents but also results in increased power and effectiveness for the bosses of empowered employees.

For example, on January 13, 1982, Washington D.C. was hit by one of the worst blizzards in years, closing the airport for much of the day.[22] When Air Florida Flight 90 was finally given clearance to take off, the captain elected not to follow standard de-icing procedures. During take-off, the first officer noticed something strange, "That doesn't seem right—it can't be right," he said. When the captain asserted, "Yes it is!" the first officer began to question his own judgment. Less than one minute later, the plane slammed into the 14th Street Bridge, killing five people before crashing into the Potomac River, then killing 69 passengers and crew. As illustrated by this example, when employees feel powerless, their effectiveness is reduced, sometimes with devastating consequences.

Application & Analysis

SELF-ASSESSMENT 9.1: ARE YOU AN EMPOWERED EMPLOYEE?

Read each of the following statements carefully. Then, using the rating scale below, circle the number that best expresses your level of agreement. Mark only one answer for each item, and respond to all items. (If you are not employed, discuss these questions with a friend who is employed. Is your friend an empowered employee?)

Rating scale:

5 = strongly agree, 4 = agree, 3 = sometimes agree/sometimes disagree,
2 = disagree, 1 = strongly disagree, and 0 = undecided/do not know

1.	I feel free to tell my manager what I think.	5 4 3 2 1 0
2.	My manager is willing to listen to my concerns.	5 4 3 2 1 0
3.	My manager asks for my ideas about things affecting our work.	5 4 3 2 1 0
4.	My manager treats me with respect and dignity.	5 4 3 2 1 0
5.	My manager keeps me informed about things I need to know.	5 4 3 2 1 0
6.	My manager lets me do my job without interfering.	5 4 3 2 1 0
7.	My manager's boss gives us the support we need.	5 4 3 2 1 0
8.	Upper management (directors and above) pays attention to ideas and suggestions from people at my level.	5 4 3 2 1 0

For scoring instructions, please go to the end of the chapter, p. 297.

SOURCE: *Survey-Feedback-Action (SFA)*, FedEx Corporation, Memphis, TN.

Because the complexity and speed of change is more than most high-level executives can manage on their own, increasingly, corporate leaders are relying on the skills, education and competences of their employee's at all organizational levels.[23] Take a look at Self-Assessment 9.1 to assess the degree to which you feel self-empowered.

A number of dimensions comprise the essence of empowerment. For example, employees feel empowered when they feel their work has meaning, when they feel competent, and when they feel they have the power of self-determination.[24] Meaning was discussed in Chapter 5 in the context of designing meaningfulness into the job itself. It is also possible to empower through meaning by articulating a clear and meaningful vision and goals. When individuals feel they "own" a goal, they are more willing to take personal responsibility for it.[25] According to Gleick, "When meaning is in place in an organization, employees can be trusted to move freely, drawn in many directions by their energy and creativity."[26]

About Management

About.com provides excellent resources for managers looking to keep up with the latest trends related to empowerment. Visit the site to find articles, tips, and resources that help managers effectively empower workers. **http://management.about.com/**

Another dimension of empowerment is the belief that one has the ability to do the job well, called *competence*. Without competence, employees will feel inadequate and lack a sense of empowerment. Bosses build competence by providing adequate support, information, and resources, and this may include helping employees to develop important relationships and networks. Also, ongoing support must be offered to newly empowered employees as they build confidence and skills.[27]

A third empowerment dimension is called *self-determination*. This is a feeling of having control and reflects a sense of freedom about how individuals do their own work. Employees who feel they're just following orders from the boss cannot feel empowered. Self-determination is similar to the concept of autonomy discussed in Chapter 5, and it is strongly related to job satisfaction.[28] Self-determination is influenced by bosses who create opportunities for employees to participate in decision making. This means participation in the forms of both voice and choice.[29]

Barriers to Empowerment

While empowerment is easy to advocate, it remains difficult to put into practice for a number of reasons. First, even when employees have the information and skills to be empowered, such as in the case of the first officer on Air Florida Flight 90, the boss still has to trust the employee. Second, empowerment means that "today's executive must bargain, negotiate and sell ideas like any other politician."[30] You will be reading about power struggles in Chapter 11, on conflict management. Empowered employees are less likely to say "How high?" when a boss says "Jump!" Bosses, especially middle managers, may find it hard to give up control, and their needs for achievement, recognition, and security have to be addressed if empowerment efforts are to succeed.[31] Third, sometimes empowerment fails because empowered employees lack the necessary skills, authority, or information to do the job well. Empowerment must be deployed selectively and managers must differentiate those employees who are ready to handle and want the extra responsibilities.[32] Fourth, even is the employee is ready and able to be empowered, self-efficacy may not be an important enough intrinsic motivator for any one individual who may be more motivated by social interaction, or money, or competition, for example.[33]

Describe the steps an employee can take to become influential with his or her boss.

Managing the Boss

In addition to the sources of power already discussed, and empowerment, employees can also have access to the legitimate power of their bosses. Because of status differences, and the communication barriers that may arise from these differences (discussed in more detail in Chapter 6), employees often feel intimidated and fail to perceive the potential power source available to them when they build a positive relationship with the boss. An employee's relationship to his or her boss is a crucial one, because the boss is an employee's most important link with the rest of the organization.[34] Building a relationship with the boss can mean the difference between a successful career and "a life of misery."[35]

The employee–boss relationship is one of mutual dependence even though the boss has more legitimate power. Because it is a mutual relationship, employees need to take an active role in managing it and, as outlined in Exhibit 9.2, managing the boss is considered to be an influence tactic that involves three basic steps, as shown in Exhibit 9.4.

EXHIBIT 9.4

Managing One's Boss

Make sure you understand your boss and the context, including:

- Your boss's goals and objectives.
- The pressures on him or her.
- Your boss's strengths, weaknesses, blind spots.
- His or her preferred work style.

Assess yourself and your needs, including:

- Your own strengths and weaknesses.
- Your personal style.
- Your predisposition toward dependence on authority figures.

Develop and maintain a relationship that:

- Fits both your needs and styles.
- Is characterized by mutual expectations.
- Keeps your boss informed.
- Is based on dependability and honesty.
- Selectively uses your boss's time and resources.

SOURCES: Adapted and reprinted by permission of *Harvard Business Review.* From J. J. Gabarro and J. P. Kotter, "Managing Your Boss," *Harvard Business Review* (May–June 1993): 165. Copyright © 1993 by the Harvard Business School Publishing Corporation; all rights reserved.

These steps are as follows: (1) making sure one understands one's boss and his or her context, (2) assessing oneself and one's needs, and (3) developing and maintaining a relationship that is mutually rewarding and respectful. We expand on influence tactics later on in the chapter.

ORGANIZATIONAL CONDITIONS THAT ENABLE POWER AND INFLUENCE

Describe four organizational conditions that enable individuals and subunits to gain power.

While individuals at work can tap into their sources of individual power and build a stronger power base through empowerment and by having a good relationship with their bosses, certain organizational conditions either enable or constrain their power potential. In the organizing framework shown in Exhibit 9.2, these conditions are depicted as moderators of the cause-and-effect relationship between the sources, the influence tactics, and the outcomes.

In organizations, the nature of the unit within which a person works, the person's access to critical resources, and the organization's structure also impact the degree to which he or she can access sources of power. These conditions are summarized in Exhibit 9.5. Access to power is enabled when an individual or subunit (1) controls critical resources, (2) can reduce uncertainty, (3) is central to the organization's success, and/or (4) is difficult to replace.[36] The key to all four of these power enablers is dependency. When a group controls something that another group needs, it creates a dependent relationship and gives one group power over the other, or at least moderates the relationship between capacity for power and actual influence.[37]

Control of Critical Resources (Including Information) or Activities

One enabler of individual and subunit power is the degree of control over critical resources.[38] When a subunit or individual controls an important resource, which another person or group desires, that subunit or individual holds power. Also, groups seen as powerful tend to be given more resources from top management.[39] Examples of important

EXHIBIT 9.5

Conditions That Enable Power and Influence

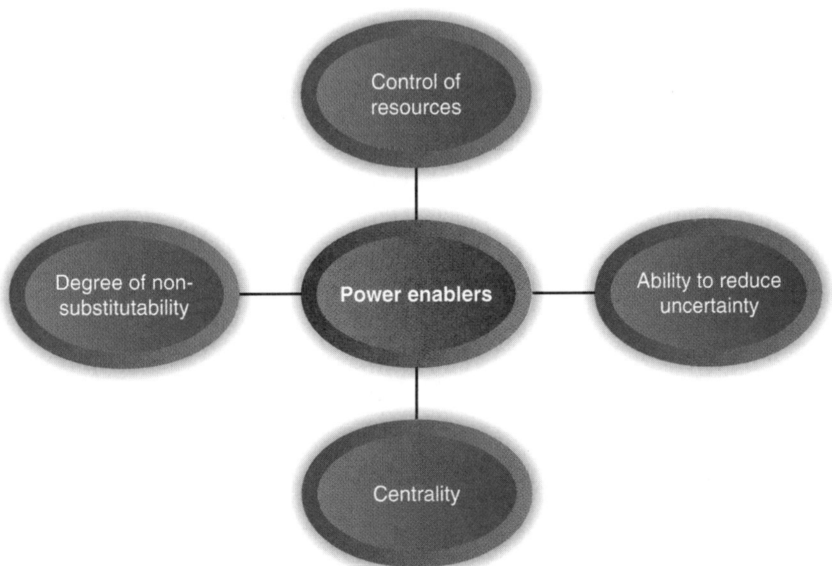

resources in organizations are staff, budget dollars, office space, equipment, labs, and access to information. Organizational power can also be obtained to the extent that an individual or group controls activities or work processes that other groups depend on in order to complete their tasks.[40]

Centrality

Another factor that can give a group control power is a high degree of centrality within the organization. If a group's functioning is important to the organization's success, it has high centrality. For example, if no unit can plan a business trip without getting approval from the accounting unit, accounting becomes power enabled as a result of its centrality.

Nonsubstitutability

nonsubstitutability
The extent to which a group performs a function that is indispensable to an organization and for which there is no alternative provider.

Another condition that can enable individual and subunit power is **nonsubstitutability**. This is the extent to which a group performs a function that is indispensable to an organization and for which there is no alternative provider. For example, if only one person in an organization has the expertise to start up a system after a shutdown, everyone becomes dependent on that person, who then becomes power enabled through his or her degree of nonsubstitutability.

Ability to Help Organization Cope with Uncertainty

Changing or uncertain conditions in an organization's internal and external environments have an impact on which individuals and subunits can gain power. If a subunit or individual has the ability help deal with uncertainty, it has power.[41] Researchers conducting a study of power in 27 subunits of 9 health care clinics in Israel found that coping with uncertainty was more of a predictor of subunit power than either centrality or nonsubstitutability.[42] External drivers such as social, political, legal, economic, and technological changes create uncertainty and results in power being gained and lost as the organization's environment changes.[43] For example, when SARS entered Canada, the infection control departments of Canadian hospitals gained power since their knowledge and expertise became critical to helping their organizations cope with the uncertainty of the disease.

Describe influence tactics and their outcomes.

CONVERTING POWER TO INFLUENCE

While individual power sources, empowerment, a good relationship with one's boss, and certain organizational conditions create power potential, this does not automatically translate into influence. We can all think of individuals who are officially in positions of power but hold little actual influence. It is important to remember that the definition of influence is that it is the process of actually *affecting* the thoughts, behaviour, and feelings of others. We now turn to the question of how to convert power into actual influence.[44]

What Are the Influence Tactics?

People use a wide variety of influence tactics in organizations. Some of the more common ones are use of expertise, inspirational appeal, ingratiation, personal appeal, coalition tactics, pressure, exchange, legitimizing tactics, and upward appeal.[45] See Exhibit 9.6 for definitions and examples of each of these influence tactics.

EXHIBIT 9.6

Organizationally Sanctioned Influence Tactics

Tactic	Definition	Example
Rational persuasion	The person uses logical arguments and factual evidence to persuade you that a proposal or request is viable and likely to result in the attainment of task objectives.	This new procedure will save us $150 000 in overhead. It makes sense to hire John; he has the most experience.
Consultation	The person seeks your participation in making a decision or planning how to implement a proposed policy, strategy, or change. The person is willing to modify his proposal based on your input.	This new attendance plan is controversial. How can we make it more acceptable? What do you think we can do to make our workers less fearful of the new robots on the production line?
Inspirational appeals	The person makes a request or proposal that arouses enthusiasm by appealing to your values and ideals, or by increasing your confidence that you can do it.	Being environmentally conscious is the right thing. Getting that account will be tough, but I know you can do it.
Ingratiation	The person seeks to get you in a good mood or to think favourably of him or her before asking you to do something.	You are amazing; I can always count on you. So do I have your support on this?
Personal appeals	The person appeals to your feelings of loyalty and friendship towards him or her when asking you to do something.	Hey, we've been friends for a long time and I've helped you out before. Do this for me.
Coalition tactics	The person seeks the aid of others to persuade you to do something or uses the support of others as an argument for you to agree also.	All the other supervisors agree with me. I'll ask you in front of the whole committee.
Pressure	The person uses demands, threats, frequent checking, or persistent reminders to influence the other person.	If you don't do this, you're fired. You have until 5:00 to change your mind, or I'm going without you.
Exchange	The person offers an exchange of favours, indicates a willingness to reciprocate a favour at a later time, or promises the person a share of the benefits.	You owe me a favour. I'll take you to lunch if you'll support me on this.
Legitimizing tactics	The person seeks to establish the legitimacy of a request by claiming the authority or right to make it, or by verifying that it is consistent with organizational rules.	Listen, I'm only asking you to do what is outlined in our strategic plan.
Upward appeal	The person gains support from someone with higher authority or expertise.	The president supports my proposal.

SOURCES: First two columns adapted from G. Yukl and C. M. Falbe, "Influence Tactics and Objectives in Upward, Downward, and Lateral Influence Attempts," *Journal of Applied Psychology* 75 (1990): 132–40. Copyright © 1990 by the American Psychological Association. Reprinted with permission; G. Yukl, P. J. Guinan, and D. Sottolano, "Influence Tactics Used for Different Objectives with Subordinates, Peers and Superiors," *Group and Organization Management* 20 (September 1995): 272. Copyright © 1990 by the American Psychological Association. Adapted with permission.

What Are the Reactions to Use of Power and Influence?

Reactions to using different kinds of power and influence vary on a continuum from follower rejection to compliance to commitment, and the tactics have been found to affect a number of employee variables, such as performance, productivity, satisfaction with supervision, job satisfaction, turnover and absenteeism,[46] increased stress, and reduced organizational commitment.[47] We now explore two common reactions to power and influence attempts: follower compliance and follower commitment.

Follower Compliance

When leaders use reward (exchange), coercive (pressure), or legitimate (legitimizing and upward appeal) power and influence, followers tend to comply.[48] That is, employees will do what the manager asks them to, at least temporarily. Reliance on these sources of power is dangerous, however, because it may require the manager to be physically present and watchful in order to apply rewards or punishment when the behaviour occurs. Constant surveillance creates an uncomfortable situation for managers and employees and eventually results in a dependency relationship. Employees will not work unless the manager is present. When told: "Do this because I'm your boss" (legitimate power), most employees will comply. However, the use of legitimate power has not been linked to organizational effectiveness or to employee satisfaction, and where managers rely heavily on legitimate power alone, organizational goals are not necessarily met. In fact, pressure has been found to be the least effective influence tactic.[49] Unfortunately, the legitimate, reward, and coercive power bases, while least effective, are the ones most likely to be used by managers.[50]

Follower Commitment

Expert (use of expertise) and referent power (inspirational and personal appeals) have strong relationships with satisfaction and follower commitment.[51] It is through expert power that vital skills, abilities, and knowledge are passed on within the organization. Employees internalize what they observe and learn from managers they perceive to be experts. Use of expertise (rational persuasion) and coalition tactics are used most often to get support from peers and superiors to change company policy. Overall, the most effective tactic in terms of achieving objectives is use of expertise. Referent power also tends to lead to follower commitment; Michael J. Fox's referent power, for example, has made him influential in encouraging people to give financial support to research on Parkinson's disease.

Consultation and inspirational appeals are particularly effective for gaining support and resources for a new project.[52] When investors form coalitions and put pressure on firms to increase their research and development efforts, it works.[53] In another example, researchers surveyed 132 environmental champions from a variety of industries, including manufacturing, electric utilities, retail, financial services, and others. The results showed that the two most successful tactics were coalition building and inspirational appeal. Successful champions enlisted the endorsement of others, and this gave them added credibility when selling their environmental issue to decision makers. They also appealed to the decision makers' values and ideals. Interestingly, they hesitated to credit inspirational appeal as a key factor in their success, perhaps out of modesty.[54]

Influencing the Boss

Use of expertise (rational persuasion) has been found to have a positive effect on supervisors' assessments of promotability, while ingratiation may have a negative effect since supervisors see their employees' ingratiation attempts as self-serving attempts to get ahead.[55] When supervisors believe an employee's motive for doing favours for the boss is simply to be a good citizen, they are likely to reward that employee. However, when the

Knowledge & Application

WHAT INFLUENCE TACTICS ARE BEING USED IN YOUR TEAM?

Using Exhibit 9.6, try to identify examples of influence attempts observed within your OB project team. Jotting down your own personal examples will help you remember them.

motive is seen as brownnosing (ingratiation), supervisors respond negatively.[56] Ingratiation can take many forms, including flattery, opinion conformity, and subservient behaviour. Most people have a difficult time rejecting the positive advances of others and ingratiation often works as an influence tactic because the target feels positive toward the source, even if the ingratiation attempt is fairly blatant.[57] It seems that a well-disguised ingratiation is hard to resist; however, as it becomes more obvious that the employee has something to gain by impressing the boss, the likelihood that ingratiation will succeed decreases.[58]

How can a manager use influence tactics well? First, a manager can develop and maintain open lines of communication in all directions: upward, downward, and lateral. Then, the manager can treat the people he or she is trying to influence with basic respect. Finally, the manager can understand that influence relationships are reciprocal—they are two-way relationships. As long as the influence attempts are directed toward organizational goals, the process of influence can be advantageous to all involved.

CONVERTING POWER TO NONSANCTIONED INFLUENCE TACTICS (POLITICAL BEHAVIOUR)

Describe some of the nonsanctioned influence tactics (political behaviour).

Unfortunately, not all influence attempts are directed toward organizational goals. Some are for personal gain and in fact are counterproductive for the organization. The distinction between whether an influence attempt is viewed as productive or counterproductive has received much attention in the OB literature. No consensus has yet been reached but our view is that the distinction depends on (1) the perceived *motive* of the power holder and (2) whether the power holder's behaviour is *sanctioned* (approved) by the organization. Thus **sanctioned influence tactics** are those that are approved of and that people consider acceptable because they are part of the organization's norms. The 10 influence tactics discussed in the previous section are generally (although not always) viewed as sanctioned influence attempts.

sanctioned influence tactics
Those tactics that are approved of and that people consider acceptable because they are part of the organization's norms.

By contrast, **nonsanctioned influence tactics** are those influence attempts that are for personal gain and are not officially sanctioned by an organization.[59] Engaging in these influence tactics is also referred to as *political behaviour,* as defined in the beginning of the chapter. Usually, people are secretive when they engage in political behaviour and would be embarrassed if it were widely publicized since it is seen as devious and immoral.[60] The "front page test" discussed as a guideline for ethical decision making in Chapter 8 is a useful complement to this definition. We explore nonsanctioned influence tactics not to encourage their use, but rather to deter you from using them as well as to help you spot them in others. Heightened awareness will increase your ability to neutralize attempts to influence you using these nonsanctioned and often unethical tactics.[61]

nonsanctioned influence tactics
Those influence attempts that are for personal gain and are not officially sanctioned by an organization. They are also referred to as *political tactics.*

Unfortunately, as organizations become increasingly competitive, as resources become scarcer, and as there are fewer and fewer opportunities for vertical advancement, political behaviour has become more prevalent. Political tactics are often referred to as the "dark" side of power; examples include attacking or blaming others (scapegoating), avoiding or stalling (e.g., failing to return e-mails, memos, or phone calls), intimidation, deceit, taking credit for other people's work, manipulation, and control of information.[62] Complete Self-Assessment 9.2 to assess the amount of political behaviour in an organization

Application & Analysis

SELF-ASSESSMENT 9.2: PERCEPTIONS OF POLITICAL BEHAVIOUR

Think about an organization you are familiar with and rate your perceptions based on the eight questions that follow using the following rating scale.

Rating Scale:
1 = Strongly Disagree
2 = Disagree
3 = Neutral
4 = Agree
5 = Strongly Agree

1. Agreeing with powerful others is the best alternative in this organization. 1 2 3 4 5
2. Promotions around here are not valued much because how they are determined is so political. 1 2 3 4 5
3. I have seen changes made here that only serve the purposes of a few individuals, not the whole unit or department. 1 2 3 4 5
4. Sometimes it is easier to remain quiet than to fight the system. 1 2 3 4 5
5. Favouritism, rather than merit, determines who gets good raises and promotions around here. 1 2 3 4 5
6. Telling others what they want to hear is sometimes better than telling the truth. 1 2 3 4 5
7. It is safer to think what you are told than to make up your own mind. 1 2 3 4 5
8. Inconsistent with organizational policies, promotions in this organizations generally do not go to top performers. 1 2 3 4 5

To score this exercise, please go to the end of the chapter, p. 297.

SOURCE: Adapted from K. M. Kacmar and D. S. Carlson, "Further Validation of the Perceptions of Politics Scale (POPS): A Multiple Sample Investigation," *Journal of Management* 23, no. 5 (1997): 656. Reprinted by permission of Sage Publications, Inc.

you are familiar with. It is important to note that while most of the organizational politics studies have been conducted in North America, OB researchers are beginning to examine cross-cultural differences in this topic. For example, one recent study recently found that perceptions of organizational politics affected British employees more strongly than Israeli employees.[63]

FORCES FOR AND AGAINST POLITICAL BEHAVIOUR IN ORGANIZATIONS

Organizational leaders behave in ways that either encourage or discourage political behaviour in their organizations. It is important for leaders and managers to avoid or prevent conditions that encourage political behaviour and to implement strategies to minimize it. We now discuss the forces for and against political behaviour in organizations.

Explain the organizational and individual conditions that foster political behaviour in organizations.

Conditions That Encourage Political Behaviour in Organizations

While power and influence are necessary for managerial effectiveness, most types of non-sanctioned influence tactics (political behaviour), with a few exceptions, tend to drain energy from an organization and reduce an organization's overall health and effectiveness. Research suggests that a large majority of workers spend at least 25 percent of their time on "cover-your-back" communication, conflicts with other people and departments, and hidden agendas. One-quarter of workers said that these activities took up more than half of their time.[64] Recent research at MedLink Ltd., one of Canada's leading companies in the medical field, revealed that the use of power and politics was one of the most common workplace issues. Negative outcomes of political behaviour include lowered performance, increased absenteeism and intention to quit, stress, anxiety, and reduced job satisfaction.[65] When employees perceive that there are dominant interest groups or cliques at work, they are less satisfied with pay and promotions. When they believe that the organization's reward practices are influenced by who you know rather than how well you perform, they are less satisfied.[66] In addition, when employees believe that their co-workers are exhibiting increased political behaviour, they are less satisfied with them.

Niccolò Machiavelli wrote a book called *The Prince* in 1513 that promotes cynical beliefs about human nature and the acceptability of using manipulative tactics to satisfy one's personal goals.

While competitive pressures and flatter organizations mean that political behaviour is on the rise, some organizations are still more political than others. This is due to a number of organizational and individual conditions or forces that tend to either encourage or discourage political behaviour. Because political behaviour is so counterproductive, it is important to understand what these conditions are, so that they can be minimized.

Downsizing and the trend toward flatter organizations have created conditions that foster political activity due to fewer opportunities and more competition for vertical advancement. A recent study found that 63 percent of respondents agreed that fear and insecurity was stimulating competitive behaviour.[67] The weakening of the traditional authority structure has also made political behaviour more prevalent.[68] Other organizational conditions that also tend to encourage political activity are unclear goals, autocratic decision making, ambiguous lines of authority, scarce resources, and uncertainty.[69]

In addition to organizational conditions that foster more political behaviour, certain individuals are more likely to engage in political behaviour than others. Individuals with a personality characteristic called "Machiavellianism" tend to be more willing to engage in unsanctioned political behaviours and believe that the "end justifies the means." **Machiavellianism** is defined as a personality characteristic indicating one's willingness to do whatever it takes to get one's own way.[70] This characteristic is named after Niccolò Machiavelli, who wrote a book called *The Prince* back in 1513. In this book, Machiavelli advised ambitious royalty on the rise how to be ruthlessly cruel, and when to hide their intentions. See the left-hand column of Exhibit 9.7 for a summary of the forces that support political behaviour in organizations.

Machiavellianism
A personality characteristic indicating one's willingness to do whatever it takes to get one's own way.

Strategies to Minimize Political Behaviour in Organizations

Explain strategies for minimizing political behaviour in organizations.

While it cannot be completely eliminated from organizations, leaders can take a proactive stance to minimize and manage the political behaviour that inevitably occurs.[71] Instruments like the "Perception of Politics Scale" (POPS) have been developed to measure perceptions of dysfunctional politics; Self-Assessment 9.2 illustrates a modified version of this.[72] There are a number of ways that organizations and leaders can discourage

EXHIBIT 9.7

Forces for and against Political Behaviour

Conditions That Support Political Behaviour	Strategies for Minimizing Political Behaviour
Fewer advancement opportunities	Transparent promotion and reward policies
Unclear goals	Avoid hiring high Machs
Autocratic decision making	Open communication
Ambiguous authority	Clear resource allocation policies
Scarce resources	Punish organizational politicians
Uncertainty	
Leaders high on Machiavellianism (high Machs)	

and minimize the incidence of political, self-serving influence tactics. We discuss three such strategies as summarized in Exhibit 9.7. These strategies are (1) implementing transparent promotion and reward policies, (2) ensuring open communications and a supportive organizational climate, and (3) clarifying the resource allocation processes.

Transparent Promotion and Reward Policies

One way to kill office politics is through effective and transparent human resources policies. Performance appraisals that are fact-based and as objective as possible help create less political behaviour, because compensation and promotion decisions are more likely to be viewed as clear and fair. The Bank of Montreal, for example, uses a multilevel performance review system "... making it harder to get a promotion through manipulation and schmoozing. The process is a safeguard so that a single person can't make a unilateral decision."[73] Another key is to clarify expectations regarding performance. This can be accomplished through the use of clear, quantifiable goals and through the establishment of a clear connection between goal accomplishment and rewards.[74]

Open Communications and Supportive Organizational Climate

Open communication is another strategy for managing political behaviour. Uncertainty tends to increase political behaviour, and communication that reduces the uncertainty is important. Following the guidelines for organization-wide communication, discussed in Chapter 6, minimizes the likelihood of destructive political behaviour. A supportive climate allows employees to discuss controversial issues promptly and openly. This prevents the issue from festering and potentially causing friction among employees.[75]

Clarify the Resource Allocation Process

Managing scarce resources well is also important. An obvious solution to the problem of scarce resources is to increase the resource pool, but few managers have this luxury. Clarifying the resource allocation process and making explicit the connection between performance and resources can also help discourage dysfunctional political behaviour.

Punish Organizational Politicians

Finally, since some political behaviour is inevitable, it is important that when observed, these organizational politicians are punished rather than rewarded for their behaviour. This sends a message to the rest of the organization and minimizes the likelihood that other organizational members will follow suit.

Application & Evaluation

THINK ABOUT THE ETHICAL IMPLICATIONS OF INFLUENCE

Is it ever ethical to manipulate people for the good of the organization? Defend your point of view giving examples. Use the guidelines for ethical decision making in Chapter 8.

IMPLICATIONS FOR ORGANIZATIONAL EFFECTIVENESS

Organizational leaders need to train their managers at all levels in the effective and constructive use of power and influence. Power and influence are critical to effectively getting work done through other people and managers often need to influence people over whom they do not have direct authority. Also, as employees become more empowered to manage complex tasks and multiple stakeholders, their managers need to be given enough power so that that they can neutralize any influence attempts of their employees, which may be self-serving rather than for the good of the unit.

Organizational leaders also need to pay attention to the organizational conditions that either enable or limit the power of their managers and subunits. No units should become overly nonsubstitutable and checks and balances need to be put in place in cases where managers or subunits have an inordinate degree of control over resources. Leaders should ensure that managers or units exist which can reduce uncertainty for the organization and recognize that these units will gain power, just by virtue of their capacity to do so. Finally, leaders need to recognize that managers and subunits that by their nature are central to the main purpose of the business will inevitably hold more power, so steps should be taken to build up the power bases of subunits that support these functions with high centrality

Lastly, increased competition and flatter organizations have resulted in organizations that have become highly political. To minimize the amount of political behaviour, company boards and organizational leaders need to pay ongoing attention to a few key conditions: First, members of company boards and hiring managers should be careful not hire leaders who have Machiavellian (high Mach) personalities. Second, organizational leaders need to ensure that promotion and reward policies are transparent and based on performance. Third, leaders need to ensure that there are good organization-wide communication processes and that communications between managers and their employees is open and frequent. Fourth, leaders need to create and communicate clear resource allocation processes. Finally, when political behaviour does manifest itself and is clearly self-serving and nonsanctioned, leaders must take appropriate action to punish the organizational politicians and send a message to the rest of the organization that this behaviour is not tolerated.

Chapter Summary

1. Power is the ability of one party to change or control the behaviour, attitudes, opinions, objectives, needs, or values of another party. Influence is the process of affecting the thoughts, behaviour, and feelings of others, and political behaviour involves influence attempts that are for personal gain and are not officially sanctioned by an organization. Power, its symbols, influence, and political behaviour are important to study because power to influence are central elements in leadership and because both supervisory and nonsupervisory employees need to understand power and politics so as they successfully manage the inevitable political behaviour in organizations, rather than being at its mercy and becoming powerless.

2. Six individual sources of power are legitimate, reward, coercive, referent, expert, and information power. Legitimate power is based on a person holding a formal position. Reward power is power based on a person's access to rewards. Others comply because they want the rewards the power holder can offer. Coercive power is based on a person's ability to punish. Others comply because they fear punishment or some negative consequence. Referent power is based on a person's attractiveness to and friendship with others. Others comply because they respect and like the power holder. Expert power is power based on a person's expertise, competence, and information in a certain area. Others comply because they believe in the power holder's knowledge and competence. Information power is power based on a person's access to important information. Others comply because they want the information the power holder has.

3. Bosses can share power with subordinates by empowering them; when this is done well, the boss' power can also increase. Empowerment means creating conditions so that employees will be more motivated by a strong sense of personal self-efficacy, meaningful work, and self-determination. Barriers to empowerment include the following: (1) bosses failing to trust their employees; (2) resistance on the part of bosses to have to bargain, negotiate, and sell ideas their ideas to employees; (3) empowered employees lack the necessary skills, authority, or information to do the job well; and (4) self-efficacy may not be an important enough intrinsic motivator for an employee to want to take on the added responsibilities that go along with empowerment.

4. Employees can increase their own power by learning to manage their bosses. This involves making sure one understands one's boss and his or her context, assessing oneself and one's needs, and developing and maintaining a relationship that is mutually rewarding and respectful.

5. Subunits and individuals have the potential to gain power when four conditions exist: when they control critical resources or activities; when they have the ability to help the organization cope with uncertainty, either within the organization or externally; when they have a high degree of centrality within the organization; or when they are nonsubstitutable.

6. Power is converted to influence through the use of many influence tactics. A few of these are these are use of expertise (rational persuasion), inspirational appeals, consultation, pressure, personal appeals, exchange, coalition tactics, ingratiation, legitimizing, and upward appeal. When leaders use expert (use of expertise) and referent power (inspirational and personal appeals) they are likely to produce follower commitment. However, when leaders use reward (exchange), coercive (pressure), or legitimate (legitimizing and upward appeal) power and influence, the result tends to be only compliance.

   Also, in terms of managing one's boss, use of expertise (rational persuasion) has been found to have a positive effect on supervisors' assessments of promotability, while ingratiation may have a negative effect.

7. The 10 influence tactics just discussed are generally viewed as sanctioned influence attempts, which are those that people consider acceptable because they are part of the organization's norms. By contrast, nonsanctioned influence tactics are those influence attempts that are for personal gain and are not officially sanctioned by an organization. Engaging in these influence tactics is also referred to as political behaviour. Examples of political behaviour include attacking or blaming others, avoiding or stalling, intimidation, deceit, taking credit for other people's work, manipulation, and control of information.

8. Conditions that foster political behaviour in organizations include unclear goals, autocratic decision making, ambiguous lines of authority, scarce resources, and uncertainty. The personality characteristic of Machiavellianism also increases the likelihood of political behaviour.

9. Political behaviour can be minimized by having transparent promotion and reward policies, by having open communication, and by clarifying resources allocation processes.

Key Terms

coercive power (p. 275)
empowerment (p. 277)
expert power (p. 276)
influence (p. 272)
information power (p. 277)
legitimate power (p. 274)
Machiavellianism (p. 287)
nonsanctioned influence tactics (p. 285)
nonsubstitutability (p. 282)
political behaviour (p. 272)
power (p. 272)
powerlessness (p. 273)
referent power (p. 276)
reward power (p. 274)
sanctioned influence tactics (p. 285)

Review Questions

1. What are the differences between power, influence, and political behaviour?
2. What are the six sources of power? Give an example of each source being used to influence someone.
3. What are the four organizational conditions that enable individuals to gain power? Do any of these conditions ever exist when you work in project teams at university or college? Explain.
4. Describe five sanctioned influence tactics and give an example of each one in use.
5. Why is the relationship between boss and employee so important and what are the steps recommended for building a good relationship with one's boss?
6. What are some ways to empower people at work?

Discussion and Communication Questions

1. Describe the main challenges in working for a boss who lacks power.
2. As a student, do you experience yourself as powerful, powerless, or both? What are your sources of power with fellow students and with your teachers?
3. What are the most common forms of political behaviour that you see in your work or school environment?
4. Are people in your work environment empowered? How could they become more empowered?
5. Do you think that political behaviour is inevitable in work organizations? Why or why not?

Ethics Questions

1. Which of the sources of power has the most potential for abuse? How can the abuse be prevented?
2. Is it possible to have an organization where all power is equally shared, or is the unequal distribution of power a necessary evil in organizations? Explain.
3. Is it ever ethical to manipulate people for the good of the organization? Defend your point of view with examples. Use the guidelines for ethical decision making in Chapter 8.

Application & Analysis

EXPERIENTIAL EXERCISE 9.1: SOCIAL POWER ROLE PLAYS

Purpose: To learn about each of French and Ravens' five sources of power and explore reactions to influence attempts using these sources

Group size: Five groups of equal size

Time required: 45 minutes

Materials needed: None

Instructions:

A. Assign one of the French and Raven types of power to each group.

B. Read the following paragraph and prepare an influence plan using the type of power that has been assigned to your group. When you have finished your planning, select one member to play the role of instructor, then choose from your own or another group a "student" who is to be the recipient of the "instructor's" efforts.

You are an instructor in a college class and have become aware that a potentially good student has been repeatedly absent from class and sometimes is unprepared when he is there. He seems to be satisfied with the grade he is getting, but you would like to see him attend regularly, be better prepared, and thus do better in the class. You even feel that the student might get really turned on to pursuing a career in this field, which is an exciting one for you. You are respected and liked by your students, and it irritates you that this person treats your dedicated teaching with such a cavalier attitude. You want to influence the student to start attending regularly.

1. Role-playing: Each group role-plays its influence plan. During the role-playing, members in other groups should think of themselves as the student being influenced.
2. After each role play, the class discusses the scenario based on the following issues:
   a. The power source used was ...
   b. If I were the student, as a result of this influence attempt I would likely comply or not comply.
   c. Any change that would come about would be temporary or long lasting.
   d. My own personal reaction is resistant or accepting.
   e. As a result of the influence attempt, my relationship with the instructor would probably be worse or better.

SOURCE: Adapted from Gib Akin, *Exchange* 3, no. 4 (1978): 38–39. Reprinted by permission of Gib Akin, McIntire School of Commerce, University of Virginia.

Application & Evaluation

EXPERIENTIAL EXERCISE 9.2: EMPOWERMENT IN THE CLASSROOM

Purpose: To explore empowerment strategies in the classroom

Group size: 6–8

Time required: 30–45 minutes

Materials needed: None

Instructions:

1. Each group is to brainstorm ways in which students might be more empowered in the classroom. The ideas do not have to be either feasible or reasonable. They can be as imaginative as possible.
2. Each group should now analyze each of the empowerment ideas for feasibility, paying attention to administrative or other constraints that may hamper implementation. This feasibility discussion might include ideas about how the college or university could be altered.
3. Each group should present its empowerment ideas along with its feasibility analysis. Questions of clarification for each group should follow each presentation.
4. Discuss the following questions as a class:
   a. Who is threatened by the power changes caused by empowerment?
   b. Are there unintended or adverse consequences of empowerment? Explain.

Application, Analysis & Synthesis

CASE: CONSOLIDATED LIFE

Part I

It all started so positively. Three days after graduating with his degree in business administration, Mike Wilson started his first day at a prestigious insurance company, Consolidated Life. He worked in the Policy Issue Department. The work of the department was mostly clerical and did not require a high degree of technical knowledge. Given the repetitive and mundane nature of the work, the successful worker had to be consistent and willing to grind out paperwork.

Rick Belkner was the division's vice president, "the man in charge" at the time. Rick was an actuary by training, a technical professional whose leadership style was laissez-faire. He was described in the division as "the mirror of whoever was the strongest personality around him." It was also common knowledge that Rick made $125 000 a year while he spent his time doing crossword puzzles.

Mike was hired as a management trainee and promised a supervisory assignment within a year. However, because of a reorganization, it was only six weeks before he was placed in charge of an eight-person unit. The reorganization was intended to streamline workflow, upgrade and combine the clerical jobs, and implement and upgrade the computer system. It was a drastic departure from the old way of doing things and created a great deal of animosity and anxiety among the clerical staff.

Management realized that a flexible supervisory style was necessary to pull off the reorganization without immense turnover, so they gave their supervisors a free hand to run their units as they saw fit. Mike used this latitude to implement group meetings and training classes in his unit. In addition, he assured all members raises if they worked hard to attain them. By working long hours, participating in the mundane tasks with his unit, and being flexible in his management style, he was able to increase productivity, reduce errors, and reduce lost time. Things improved so dramatically that he was noticed by upper management and earned a reputation as a "superstar," despite being viewed as free-spirited and unorthodox. The feeling was that his loose, people-oriented management style could be tolerated because his results were excellent.

A Chance for Advancement. After a year, Mike received an offer from a different Consolidated Life division located across town. Mike was asked to manage an office in the marketing area. The pay was excellent and it offered an opportunity to turn around an office in disarray. The reorganization in his present division at Consolidated was almost complete, and most of his mentors and friends in management had moved on to other jobs. Mike decided to accept the offer.

In his exit interview he was assured that if he ever wanted to return, a position would be made for him. It was clear that he was held in high regard by management and staff alike. A huge party was thrown to send him off. The new job was satisfying for a short time, but it became apparent to Mike that it did not have the long-term potential he was promised. After bringing on a new staff, computerizing the office, and auditing the books, he began looking for a position that would both challenge him and give him the autonomy he needed to be successful.

Eventually word got back to his former vice president at Consolidated Life, Rick Belkner, that Mike was looking for another job. Rick offered Mike a position with the same pay he was now receiving and control over a 14-person unit in his old division. After considering other options, Mike decided to return to his old division, feeling that he would be able to progress steadily over the next several years.

Enter Jack Greely. Upon his return to Consolidated Life, Mike became aware of several changes that had taken place in the six months since his departure. The most important change was the hiring of a new divisional senior vice president, Jack Greely. Jack had been given total authority to run the division. Rick Belkner now reported to Jack. Jack's reputation was that he was tough but fair. It was necessary for people in Jack's division to do things his way and "get the work out."

After a week Mike realized the extent of the changes that had occurred. Gone was the loose, casual atmosphere that had marked his first tour in the division. Now, a stricter, task-oriented management doctrine was practised. Morale of the supervisory staff had decreased to an alarming level. Jack Greely was the major topic of conversation in and around the division. People joked that MBO now meant "management by oppression."

Mike as greeted back with comments like "Welcome to prison!" and "Why would you come back here? You must be desperate!" It seemed like everyone was looking for new jobs or transfers. Their lack of desire was reflected in the poor quality of work being done.

Mike's Idea: Supervisor's Forum. Mike felt that a change in Jack's management style was necessary in order to improve a frustrating situation. Realizing that it would be difficult to affect his style directly, Mike requested permission from Rick Belkner to form a Supervisor's Forum for all the supervisors on Mike's level in the division. Mike explained that the purpose would be to enhance the existing management-training program. The forum would include weekly meetings, guest speakers, and discussions of topics relevant to the division and the industry. Mike thought the forum would show Greely that he was serious about both his job and improving morale in the division. Rick gave the okay for an initial meeting.

The meeting took place and 10 supervisors who were Mike's peers in the company eagerly took the opportunity to "blue sky" it. There was a euphoric attitude about the group as they drafted their statement of intent. It read as follows:

To: Rick Belkner

From: New Issues Services Supervisors

Subject: **Supervisor's Forum**

On Thursday, June 11, the Supervisor's Forum held its first meeting. The objective of the meeting was to identify common areas of concern among us and to determine topics that we might be interested in pursuing.

The first area addressed was the void that we perceive exists in the management-training program. As a result of conditions beyond anyone's control, many of us over the past year have held supervisory duties without the benefit of formal training or proper experience. Therefore, what we propose is that we utilize the Supervisor's Forum as a vehicle by which to enhance the existing management-training program. The areas that we hope to affect with this supplemental training are: (a) morale/job satisfaction; (b) quality of work and service; (c) productivity; and (d) management expertise as it relates to the life insurance industry. With these objectives in mind, we have outlined below a list of possible activities that we would like to pursue.

1. Further utilization of the existing "in-house" training programs provided for manager trainees and supervisors, i.e., Introduction to Supervision, E.E.O., and Coaching and Counselling.
2. A series of speakers from various sections in the company. This would help expose us to the technical aspects of their departments and their managerial style.
3. Invitations to outside speakers to address the Forum on management topics such as managerial development, organizational structure and behaviour, business policy, and the insurance industry. Suggested speakers could be area university professors, consultants, and provincial insurance officials.
4. Outside training and visits to the field. This could include attendance at seminars concerning management theory and development relative to the insurance industry. Attached is a representative sample of a program we would like to have considered in the future.

In conclusion, we hope that this memo clearly illustrates what we are attempting to accomplish with this program. It is our hope that the above outline will be able to give the Forum credibility and establish it as an effective tool for all levels of management within New Issue. By supplementing our on-the-job training with a series of speakers and classes, we aim to develop prospective management personnel with a broad perspective of both the life insurance industry and management's role in it. Also, we would like to extend an invitation to the underwriters to attend any programs at which the topic of the speaker might be of interest to them.

cc: J. Greely
Supervisors

The group felt the memo accurately and diplomatically stated the dissatisfaction with the current situation. However, they pondered what the results of their actions would be and what else they could have done.

Part II

An emergency management meeting was called by Rick Belkner at Jack Greely's request to address the "union" being formed by the supervisors. Four general managers, Rick Belkner, and Jack Greely were at that meeting. During the meeting it was suggested that the Forum be disbanded to "put them in their place." However, Rick Belkner felt that if "guided" in the proper direction, the Forum could die from lack of interest. His stance was adopted but it was common knowledge that Jack Greely was strongly opposed to the group and wanted its founders dealt with. His comment was: "It's not a democracy and they're not a union. If they don't like it here, then they can leave." A campaign was directed by the supervisors to determine who the main authors of the memo were so they could be dealt with.

About this time, Mike's unit had made a mistake on a case, which Jack Greely was embarrassed to admit to his boss. This embarrassment was more than Jack Greely cared to take from Mike Wilson. At the managers' staff meeting that day, Jack stormed in and declared that the next supervisor to "screw up" was out the door. He would permit no more embarrassments of his division and repeated his earlier statement about "people leaving if they didn't like it here." It was clear to Mike and everyone else present that Mike Wilson was a marked man.

Mike had always been a loose, amiable supervisor. The major reason his units had been successful was the attention he paid to each individual and how they interacted with the group. He had a reputation for fairness, was seen as an excellent judge of personnel for new positions, and was noted for his ability to turn around people who had been in trouble. He motivated people through a dynamic, personable style and was noted for his general lack of regard for rules. He treated rules as obstacles to management and usually used his own discretion as to what was important. His office had a sign saying: "Any fool can manage by rules. It takes an uncommon man to manage without any." It was an approach that flew in the face of company policy, but it had been overlooked in the past because of his results. However, because of Mike's actions with the Supervisor's Forum, he was now regarded as a thorn in the side, not a superstar, and his oddball style only made things worse.

Faced with the fact that he was rumoured to be out the door, Mike appraised the situation.

Part III

Mike decided on the following course of action:

1. Keep the Forum alive but moderate its tone so it didn't step on Jack Greely's toes.
2. Don't panic. Simply outwork and outsmart the rest of the division. This plan included a massive retraining and re-motivation of his staff. He implemented weekly meetings, cross-training with other divisions, and a lot of interpersonal "stroking" to motivate the group.
3. Evoke praise from vendors and customers through excellent service and direct that praise to Jack Greely.

The results after eight months were impressive. Mike's unit improved the speed of processing 60 percent and lowered errors 75 percent. His staff became the most highly trained in the division. Mike had a file of several letters to Jack Greely that praised the unit's excellent service. In addition, the Supervisor's Forum had grudgingly attained credibility, although the scope of activity was restricted. Mike had even improved to the point of submitting reports on time as a concession to management.

Mike was confident that the results would speak for themselves. However, one month before his scheduled promotion and one month after an excellent merit raise in recognition of his exceptional work record, he was called into Rick's office. Rick informed him that after long and careful consideration the decision had been made to deny his promotion because of his lack of attention to detail. This did not mean he was not a good supervisor, just that he needed to follow more instead of taking the lead. Mike was stunned and said so. But before he said anything else, he asked to see Jack Greely the next day.

The Showdown. Sitting with Rick and Jack, Mike asked Jack if he agreed with the appraisal Rick had discussed with him. He said that he did. When asked if any other supervisor surpassed his ability and results, both Rick and Jack stated that Mike was one of the best—if not the best—

they had. Then why, Mike asked, would they deny him a promotion when others of less ability were approved? The answer came from Jack: "It's nothing personal, but we just don't like you. We don't like your management style. You're an oddball. We can't run a division with 10 supervisors all doing different things. What kind of business do you think we're running here? We need people who conform to our style and methods so we can measure their results objectively. There is no room for subjective interpretation. It's our feeling that if you really put your mind to it, you can be an excellent manager. It's just that you now create trouble and rock the boat. We don't need that. It doesn't matter if you're the best now; sooner or later as you go up the ladder, you will be forced to pay more attention to administrative duties and you won't handle them well. If we correct your bad habits now, we think you can go far."

Mike was shocked. He turned to face Rick and blurted out nervously, "You mean it doesn't matter what my results are? All that matters is how I do things?" Rick leaned back in his chair and said in a casual tone, "In so many words, yes."

Mike left the office knowing that his career at Consolidated was over, and immediately started looking for a new job.

Discussion Questions

1. Identify Mike's individual sources of power with his boss, Rick, his staff, and the other supervisors.
2. In what way did Mike's creation of the Supervisor's Forum set up organizational conditions that enabled him to increase his power?
3. How effectively did Mike manage his relationship with his boss, Rick?
4. Identify all the different types of influence tactics and political behaviours evident in the case.
5. Was it ethical for Mike to start the Supervisor's Forum as a strategy to try to change Jack's management style? Was it ethical for Rick and Jack to threaten Mike? Who was most responsible for Mike's lack of success at Consolidated: Mike himself, Rick, or Jack?

SOURCE: Adapted from Terrence E. Deal and Allen A. Kennedy, *Corporate Cultures: The Rites and Rituals of Corporate Life* (adapted from pages 107–27). Copyright © 1982 by Addison-Wesley Publishing Company, Inc. Reprinted by permission of Perseus Books PLC, a member of Perseus Books, L.L.C.

Scoring Instructions for Self-Assessments

Self-Assessment 9.1 Are You an Empowered Employee?

To determine if you are an empowered employee, add your scores.

32–40: You are empowered! Managers listen when you speak, respect your ideas, and allow you to do your work.

24–31: You have *some* power! Your ideas are considered sometimes, and you have some freedom of action.

16–23: You must exercise caution. You cannot speak or act too boldly, and your managers appear to exercise close supervision.

8–15: Your wings are clipped! You work in a powerless, restrictive work environment.

Self Assessment 9.2: Perceptions of Political Behaviour

Interpretation: The higher the score out of 40, the more you perceive dysfunctional political behaviour in this organization.

LEARNING OBJECTIVES

By the end of this chapter, you will be able to do the following:

1. Define leadership.
2. Explain the trait perspective of leadership.
3. Describe the behavioural perspective of leadership, including task and people-oriented leadership styles and the Managerial (Leadership) Grid.
4. Explain the contingency perspective of leadership.
5. Describe the path–goal leadership theory and how it can be used to decide how to lead in particular situations.
6. Explain Fiedler's contingency theory of leadership.
7. Explain the leadership substitutes theory.
8. Explain the key elements of transformational leadership and contrast it with transactional leadership.
9. Outline six additional issues in leadership research: LMX theory, e-leadership, gender issues, cross-cultural issues, servant leadership, and ethics in leadership.

learning about the context

Participative Leadership at Manitoba Lotteries Corporation

When Winston Hodgins took over Manitoba Lotteries Corporation (MLC) in early 2000, the organization was in turmoil with public confidence at an all time low. Winston and his vice president of human resources, Marilyn Robinson, led an amazing turnaround in two and a half years, building an organization that is proud, engage, and profitable.

Winston Hodgins had a career of over 30 years in the Manitoba provincial civil service and in public finance. His background was in economic development, not in gaming. He is described as having strong business acumen and he is respected for his ethics and integrity. Winston is not described as flashy, but rather as a down-to-earth leader who is compassionate and respects each individual employee. Winston has a participative leadership style, is very inclusive when making decisions, and seldom invokes an ultimate veto. He takes care not to put his ideas forward before he has heard from his followers. He doesn't want to prevent people from expressing different opinions but encourages employees in coming up with new ideas. Winston Hodgins led the transformation, but the development of a vision, mission, mandate, and set of core values was accomplished through the collective efforts of a guiding team and continual communication and feedback with other employees.

Winston's leadership is empowering. At the outset, the human resources team, lead by Marilyn Robinson, was given the necessary financial and human resources with which to help him lead the transformation. After a significant restructuring and downsizing in casino operations, managers and supervisors were empowered and given leadership training and career development.

All middle managers and supervisors at MLC now work towards 11 key competencies, which serve as a "glue" to all human resources policies and practices. Ongoing organization development initiatives, led by Judith Hayes, director of Organizational Development and Training Services, help employees develop their own careers and understand how their own competency development supports the overall strategic plan and the betterment of the province's programs in health, education, community and social services, and economic development.

SOURCES: B. J. Bowes, "People Power Saves Day. Remarkable Turnaround for Manitoba Lotteries," *Winnipeg Free Press,* April 12, 2003, Metro, F1; Marilyn Robinson (Vice President, Human Resources, Manitoba Lotteries Corporation) and Judith Hayes (Director of OD & Training, MLC), interview with the author, August 26, 2003; http://www.mlc.mb.ca/MLC/info_strategic.htm.

Winston Hodgins led the Manitoba Lotteries Corporation in an extraordinary turnaround. In the chapter opener you read about his people-oriented leadership style as well as about some of his defining traits. For years, researchers have been trying to understand, predict and control effective leadership behaviour ... for obvious reasons. If we can understand what it takes to be an effective leader, then we can nurture more leaders in our organizations.

To begin this chapter, we define leadership. Then, we explore a number of leadership theories classified into four different perspectives. First, we explore the trait or competency perspective, which tries to identify a set of traits that leaders have in common. Second, we examine the behavioural perspective, which proposes that it is the leader's behaviours, not traits, that determine effectiveness. Third, we look at the contingency perspective, which argues that there is no one best way to lead, but rather that the appropriate leadership behaviour depends on the situation and the followers. Fourth, we explore the transformational perspective of leadership, central to which is the notion of vision and charisma. After reviewing theories according to these four perspectives, we explore a few additional issues in leadership research, including leader–member exchange (LMX) theory, e-leadership, gender and cross-cultural issues in leadership, ethical leadership, and servant leadership.

Define leadership.

DEFINING LEADERSHIP

leadership
The ability of an individual to influence, motivate, and enable others to contribute toward the effectiveness and success of organizations of which they are members.

Our working definition of leadership is taken from the Global Leadership and Organizational Behavior Effectiveness (GLOBE) study of 62 societies: **Leadership** is the ability of an individual to influence, motivate, and enable others to contribute toward the effectiveness and success of organizations of which they are members.[1] The large volume of leadership theories over the decades have been classified into at least four different perspectives. This chapter has been organized accordingly. The four perspectives are represented in Exhibit 10.1 and are as follows: the trait (or competency) perspective, the behavioural perspective, the contingency perspective, and the transformational leadership perspective.

EXHIBIT 10.1

Four Perspectives on Leadership

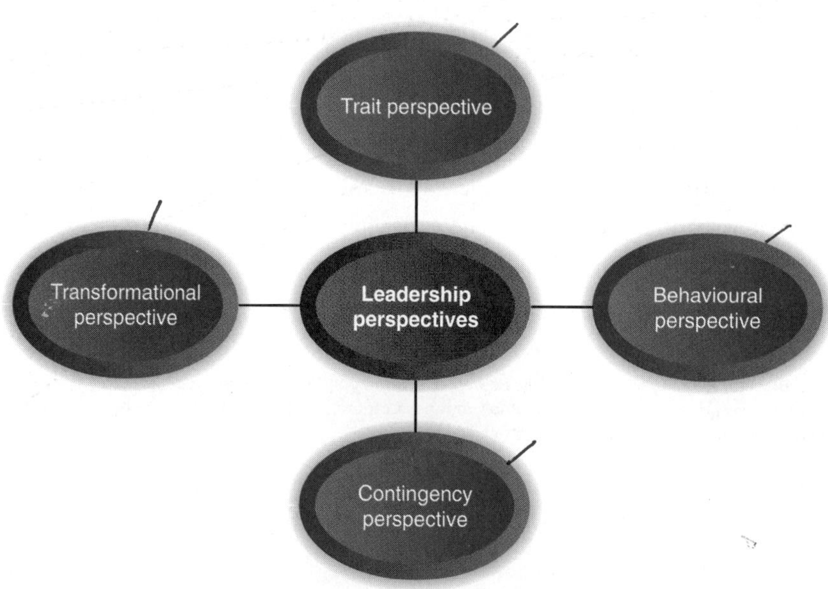

Leadership has a long, rich history in organizational behaviour. One recent article estimates that there have been more than 5000 studies of leadership in the past 70 years.[2] In this chapter, we explore many of the theories and ideas that have emerged along the way in that history. Given the large amount of research on this subject, one might expect agreement on its definition, but this is not the case. The definition itself tends to vary depending upon the perspective taken because, "There are almost as many definitions of leadership as there are persons who have attempted to define the concept."[3] Canadian Major-General Lewis MacKenzie, who is considered one of the most experienced peacekeepers in the world, defines leadership as "Getting people to do things they don't necessarily want to do and have them enjoy the experience."[4]

Canadian Major-General Lewis MacKenzie, now retired, is considered to be one of the most experienced peacekeepers in the world.

Application & Analysis

DOES LEADERSHIP MATTER?

Take a position on the following statement and prepare to defend your point of view:

> In most workplaces leadership doesn't really matter. As long as people know what needs to be done, they will do it and they will do it well. Just train them, give them the goals, and leave them alone.

THE TRAIT PERSPECTIVE

Explain the trait perspective of leadership.

Historically, the first of the four perspectives taken by leadership scholars was the trait perspective. **The trait perspective of leadership** proposes that leaders are more likely to have certain personality, social, physical, or intellectual traits, than nonleaders.[5] This line of research has yielded insufficient evidence to conclude that leaders can be distinguished from followers on the basis of physical attributes. In the second half of the 20th century a number of personality traits were explored but again, it was difficult to prove a universal set of traits that defined leaders in every situation.

trait perspective of leadership
A perspective that proposes that leaders are more likely to have certain personality, social, physical, or intellectual traits, than nonleaders.

In the early 1990s, trait perspective research re-emerged with more emphasis on so-called leadership competencies. In contrast to traits, which tend to be viewed as inborn, **competencies** are learned behaviours such as skills, abilities, and values. A few key competencies that do appear to be associated with successful leaders include *drive* (a broad term that includes achievement, motivation, ambition, energy, tenacity, and initiative); *leadership motivation* (the desire to lead but not to seek power as an end in itself); *honesty and integrity; self-confidence* (which is associated with emotional stability); *cognitive ability*; and *knowledge of the business.*[6] Emotional intelligence has also been associated with effective leadership; this is discussed in depth in OBXtra2. John Kotter, although

competencies
Learned behaviours such as skills, abilities, and values.

The Niagara Institute

The Niagara Institute is a private, not-for-profit foundation established in 1971 to enhance the quality of Canadian leadership in business, government, and non–governmental organizations.
http://www.niagarainstitute.com

not a trait theorist, recently wrote that he saw four competencies of good leaders: drive and energy, intelligence, mental and emotional health, and integrity.[7] Drive and energy do seem to come up in most descriptions of successful leaders. For example, Linda Cook, the CEO of Shell Canada, is described as fiercely competitive with a steely will. In oil circles she is known for her high energy and business judgment. She is quoted as saying, "There's no substitute for hard work and delivering on promises. I always think of the Chinese proverb that says, 'I got where I am because of luck and the harder I work the luckier I get.'"[8]

Even though the trait (competency) theories have had very limited success in identifying the universal, distinguishing attributes of leaders, certain traits may increase the likelihood of an individual being a better leader, but they do not guarantee it. This is why many companies try to articulate and train core leadership competencies. See Organizational Reality 10.1 for an overview of 3M's leadership competency model and how it is used.

Describe the behavioural perspective of leadership, including task and people-oriented leadership styles and the Managerial (Leadership) Grid.

THE BEHAVIOURAL PERSPECTIVE

behavioural perspective of leadership
A perspective that proposes that effective leaders behave in certain desirable ways.

Theories subscribing to the behavioural perspective of leadership emerged in the 1940s and 1950s as a response to the deficiencies of the trait perspective theories. **The behavioural perspective of leadership** proposed that effective leaders behave in certain desirable ways. Researchers from Ohio State University and the University of Michigan asked followers to rate their supervisors on a large number of behaviours and discovered that leaders varied in the degree to which they were perceived as task-oriented, people-oriented, neither, or both. Task- and people-oriented leader behaviours are independent of each other. That is, a leader may be high on both, low on both, or high on one while low on the other. Complete Self-Assessment 10.1, entitled "Are You an Effective Leader?" to assess your own leadership style in terms of task, people, and laissez-faire orientation. To learn even more about yourself, ask someone who knows you to complete the assessment on how he or she views your behavioural leadership style.

organizational reality 10.1

3M's Leadership Competency Model

In the mid-1980s, 3M began work on trying to identify competencies necessary for success in general manager positions. This work continued for nine years and was used for succession planning and development. By 1995, management was increasingly concerned about the lack of depth in leadership bench strength for the top executive positions, and a global HR team was formed from within the company to further develop the competency framework. The competency list was developed by reviewing the organizational behaviour literature and the changes in 3M's leadership philosophy and by addressing the hypersensitive global business environment. Key executives and managers were actively involved in the process and the global HR team involved internal HR practitioners from Europe, Asia, Latin America, Canada, and the United States.

3M's resulting leadership competencies form three clusters. The first cluster is called "Fundamental." This cluster includes ethics and integrity, intellectual capacity and maturity, and judgment. They call the second cluster "Essential." Essential competencies are customer orientation, developing people, inspiring others, and business health and results. The third cluster is called "Visionary." Visionary competencies include global perspective, vision and strategy, nurturing innovation, building alliances, and organizational agility. All competencies have behavioural definitions. For example, "global perspective" has four behaviours associated with it, one of which is "Actively stays current on world economics, trade issues, international market trends, and opportunities."

3M uses its leadership competency model during performance appraisals, in leadership development, and in succession planning.

SOURCE: Margaret E. Alldredge and Kevin J. Nilan, "3M's Leadership Competency Model: An Internally Developed Solution," *Human Resources Management* 39, no. 2/3 (Summer/Fall 2000): 133–45. Reprinted with permission of John Wiley & Sons, Inc.

Application & Analysis

SELF-ASSESSMENT 10.1: ARE YOU AN EFFECTIVE LEADER?

To get a better idea of what your leadership style is and how productive it would be, fill out the questionnaire below. In addition, if you have time, ask someone who knows you to complete the questionnaire on how *they* see your leadership style. If you are currently a manager or have been a manager, answer the questions considering "members" to be your employees. If you have never been a manager, think of situations when you were a leader and consider "members" to be the people you were trying to influence toward a certain goal you cared about. Your answers should reflect your attitudes and behaviours as they are now, not as you would like them to be. Be honest.

Circle the response that fits. The response choices for each item are as follows:

A = always B = often C = occasionally D = seldom E = never

1. I would act as the spokesperson of the group. A B C D E
2. I would allow the members complete freedom in their work. A B C D E
3. I would encourage overtime work. A B C D E
4. I would permit the members to use their own judgment in solving problems. A B C D E
5. I would encourage the use of uniform procedures. A B C D E
6. I would pressure members for greater effort. A B C D E
7. I would stress being ahead of competing groups. A B C D E
8. I would let the members do their work the way they think best. A B C D E
9. I would speak as the representative of the group. A B C D E
10. I would be able to tolerate postponement and uncertainty. A B C D E
11. I would try out my ideas in the group. A B C D E
12. I would turn the members loose on a job, and let them go on it. A B C D E
13. I would work hard for a promotion. A B C D E
14. I would get swamped by details. A B C D E
15. I would speak for the group when visitors are present. A B C D E
16. I would be reluctant to allow the members any freedom of action. A B C D E
17. I would keep the work moving at a rapid pace. A B C D E
18. I would let some members have authority that I should keep. A B C D E
19. I would settle conflicts when they occur in the group. A B C D E
20. I would allow the group a high degree of initiative. A B C D E
21. I would represent the group at outside meetings. A B C D E
22. I would be willing to make changes. A B C D E
23. I would decide what will be done and how it will be done. A B C D E
24. I would trust the members to exercise good judgment. A B C D E
25. I would push for increased production. A B C D E
26. I would refuse to explain my actions. A B C D E
27. Things usually turn out as I predict. A B C D E
28. I would permit the group to set its own pace. A B C D E
29. I would assign group members to particular tasks. A B C D E
30. I would act without consulting the group. A B C D E
31. I would ask the members of the group to work harder. A B C D E
32. I would schedule the work to be done. A B C D E
33. I would persuade others that my ideas are to their advantage. A B C D E
34. I would urge the group to beat its previous record. A B C D E
35. I would ask that group members follow standard rules and regulations. A B C D E

For scoring instructions, please go to the end of the chapter, p. 328.

task-oriented style
A style of leadership in which the leader spells out duties and specific tasks, tells people what to do and how to do it, ensures employees follow rules, and encourages employees to reach peak performance. Also called *production* or *autocratic style,* and referred to in early studies as *initiating structure.*

The leader with a **task-oriented style** (also referred to as production-oriented and autocratic) spells out duties and specific tasks, tells people what to do and how to do it, ensures employees follow rules, and encourages employees to reach peak performance. This style was also referred to in early studies as *initiating structure* because leaders with this style tended to initiate a lot of structure, so that people would have very clear directions.[9] For example, Brenda Hoffman, a native of Guelph, Ontario, was given six months to do what the Toronto Stock Exchange had not accomplished in four years: install a new multimillion-dollar trading engine to replace the crash-prone CATS (Computer Assisted Trading System). Brenda is known to have a task-oriented leadership style. She had to set the tone for aggressive targets so that people understood clearly what the expectations and delivery schedules were. She is a strong advocate of giving clear direction so that everyone understands their part on the team. She is quoted as saying, "You don't want to follow around like a bunch of tadpoles!"[10]

employee, people-oriented, or democratic style
A style of leadership in which the leader shows trust and respect, engages in two-way communication, listens, encourages, gives recognition and provides socio-emotional support. Also referred to as *consideration.*

The leader with an **employee, people-oriented,** or **democratic style** shows trust and respect, engages in two-way communication, listens, encourages, gives recognition, and provides socio-emotional support to followers. This style was initially called *consideration* in the Ohio leadership studies because when leaders used this style, followers viewed them as considerate and respectful.[11] Winston Hodgins, described in the chapter opener, is an example of a leader with a people-oriented style.

Leadership.Com
Leadership.com strengthens business by helping leaders take full advantage of the most valuable assets of any company: its people and their knowledge. The site provides the tools every leader needs to create successful organizations and inspires individuals to hone their leadership skills and vision.
http://www.leadership.com

Many senior managers today believe that the old "command and control" approach to leadership is a recipe for failure. Philip Hughes, president and CEO of Newfoundland Power, states that "if senior management is telling people what to do instead of asking them what they want, your organization is in trouble."[12] Hughes believes, like Winston Hodgins, that senior management has to be genuinely people-oriented and care about employee development. "I don't think faking it cuts it anymore," he states. John Mayberry, CEO of Dofasco Inc., believes that the two-way communication that is an integral part of a people-oriented leadership style helps managers find out what the real problems are. "And, it shouldn't be a big deal for one of the senior management team to do a crew visit and be on the front line, because people are more comfortable and they will tell you a little bit about what is going wrong."[13] Mary Jo Haddad, appointed to the job of president and CEO of the Hospital for Sick Children in Toronto in 2004, is another example of a people-oriented leader. She is described as having a leadership style that is "warm and generous, yet firm when required."[14]

John Mayberry (left), former president and CEO of Dofasco Inc., and board chairman Chuck Hantho examine car parts for the automobile industry made with steel produced by the company.

A third style that emerged in the early studies of leadership behaviour was called the **laissez-faire style** or uninvolved. This is an employee-centred leadership style in which the manager permits his or her employees to function within prescribed limits.[15] This is similar to the "delegating" style discussed in the next section under the heading of situational leadership.

laissez-faire style (uninvolved)
An employee-centred leadership style in which the manager permits his or her employees to function within prescribed limits.

Knowledge & Application

TAKING A BEHAVIOURAL PERSPECTIVE OF LEADERSHIP IN THE CLASSROOM

Determine whether the following instructor behaviours are task- or people-oriented:

Instructor:	Task-Oriented	People-Oriented
Provides a detailed course outline to students	___	___
Asks students for their opinions	___	___
Sets up student debates	___	___
Starts each class by going over the class agenda	___	___
Offers bonus marks for early completion of research papers	___	___
Assigns students to teams rather than letting students choose their own	___	___
Checks up on whether students have completed pre-class readings	___	___
Encourages students to visit him/her during office hours	___	___
Offers praise to students who offer constructive comments during class	___	___

The Leadership (Managerial) Grid

Leadership (Managerial) Grid
A model that proposes that the best way to lead is to show high concern for results (task) and high concern for people.

Robert Blake and Jane Mouton developed their **Leadership Grid** (originally called the Managerial Grid) based on the behavioural perspective of leadership just discussed. They took the two attitudinal dimensions of concern for task and concern for people and developed a model based on various combinations of these styles. The Leadership Grid includes five styles and proposes that the best way to lead is to show high concern for results (task) *and* high concern for people. The *organization man manager* (5,5) is a middle-of-the-road leader who has a medium concern for people and production. This leader attempts to balance a concern for both people and production without a commitment to either. The *authority-compliance manager* (9,1) has great concern for production and little concern for people. This leader desires tight control in order to get tasks done efficiently and considers creativity and human relations unnecessary. The *country club manager* (1,9) has great concern for people and little concern for production, attempts to avoid conflict, and seeks to be well liked. This leader's goal is to keep people happy through good interpersonal relations, which are more important to him or her than the task. The *team manager* (9,9) is considered ideal and has great concern for both people and production. This leader works to motivate employees to reach their highest levels of accomplishment, is flexible, responsive to change, and understands the need for change. The *impoverished manager* (1,1) is often referred to as a laissez-faire leader. This leader has little concern for people or production, avoids taking sides, and stays out of conflicts; he or she does just enough to get by. See Exhibit 10.2 for an overview.

Fundamental to the Leadership Grid model was the implicit assumption that there was "one best way" to lead, called the "team manager" style, showing high concern for results *and* high concern for people (9,9). This is the basis on which the Grid was formerly used for team building and leadership development in many companies around the world. Kingston Technology Company's cofounders exemplify this team style, as you can see in Organizational Reality 10.2.

EXHIBIT 10.2

The Leadership Grid

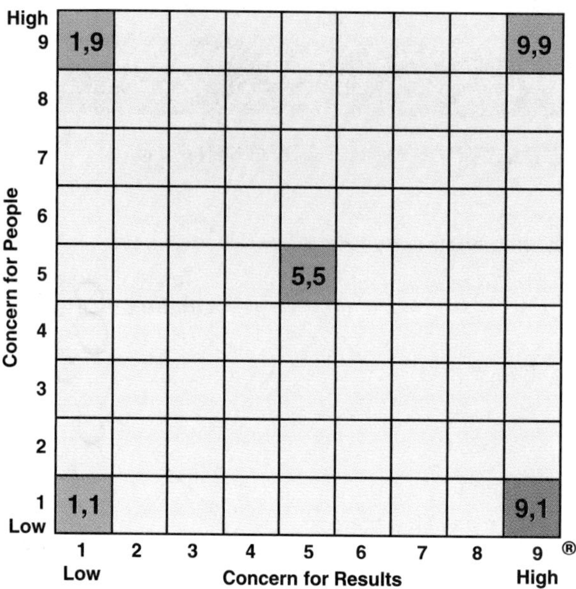

1,9 Country Club Management: Thoughtful attention to the needs of the people for satisfying relationships leads to a comfortable, friendly organization atmosphere and work tempo.

9,9 Team Management: Work accomplishment is from committed people; interdependence through a "common stake" in organization purpose leads to relationships of trust and respect.

5,5 Middle-of-the-Road Management: Adequate organization performance is possible through balancing the necessity to get work out while maintaining morale of people at a satisfactory level.

1,1 Impoverished Management: Exertion of minimum effort to get required work done is appropriate to sustain organization membership.

9,1 Authority-Compliance Management: Efficiency in operations results from arranging conditions of work in such a way that human elements interfere to a minimum degree.

SOURCE: The Leadership Grid® figure from *Leadership Dilemmas—Grid Solutions,* by Robert R. Blake and Anne Adams McCanse (formerly the Managerial Grid by Robert R. Blake and Jane S. Mouton). Houston: Gulf Publishing Company (grid figure: p. 29). Copyright 1991 by Blake and Mouton and Scientific Methods, Inc. Reproduced by permission of the owners.

Explain the contingency perspective of leadership.

contingency perspective of leadership
A perspective that proposes that effective leadership depends upon the degree of fit between the leader's style and various factors in the particular situation.

THE CONTINGENCY PERSPECTIVE

The third perspective of leadership is called the "contingency" perspective. Theories that take a contingency perspective disagree with the implied "one best way to lead" assumption just discussed. The **contingency perspective of leadership** suggests that effective leadership depends upon the degree of *fit* between the leader's style and various factors in the particular situation. By their nature, contingency theories are "if–then" theories: *If* the situation is ____, *then* the appropriate leadership behaviour is ____. Leadership theories that take a contingency perspective differ from each other mainly in terms of *which* employee and situational factors must be considered when deciding how best to lead. The term "contingency" comes from the notion that the best leadership style is "contingent upon" certain factors in the situation. We examine three leadership theories that take a contingency perspective. They are the path–goal theory of leadership, Fiedler's contingency theory, and leadership substitutes theory (see Exhibit 10.3).

Describe the path–goal leadership theory and how it can be used to decide how to lead in particular situations.

Path–Goal Contingency Theory

The most widely accepted contingency theory is path–goal theory. It was originally developed by Martin Evans, a distinguished professor of organizational behaviour at the University of Toronto. Later expanded upon by Robert House, path–goal theory proposes that leader effectiveness is based on an expectancy theory of motivation.[16] From the perspective of path–goal theory, the basic role of the leader is to clear the follower's path to the goal. Evans's and House's research suggests that leaders *can* and should change their style to fit follower and workplace characteristics (contingencies). They argue that

organizational reality 10.2

People and Results at Kingston Technology

When David Sun and John Tu founded Kingston Technology Inc. in 1987, Tu bet Sun a new car that they would not last a year in the business. Who won? Sun did—and got a new Jaguar. Kingston designs and manufactures memory products, with sales of more than $1.6 billion in 2000.

One key to Kingston's success is its founders' abilities to focus on both people and on results. The focus on people stems from a belief that the company is really more family than business. Employees receive gargantuan bonuses when the company is successful. Just in case the company fails, Sun and Tu have established a number of programs to care for employees. "Even if nobody ever buys a PC again and the whole industry is out of business, if I can take care of my employees, then I have no shame on myself," says Sun.

David Sun and John Tu of Kingston Technology—taking time to smell the roses.

Kingston's focus on results is equally important. The sales force was reorganized three times in two years to take advantage of quick openings in the market. If a customer needs an important piece of technology, Kingston has been known to fly it in and hand-deliver it the same day. Managers never renege on deals, even if a sudden swing in the chip market diminishes Kingston's profit margin.

Along with a focus on both people and results, the philosophy that guides Kingston contributes to its success. "You've got to take the approach that every day is a rose garden," says Sun. "It's an easy-going philosophy. Other companies are so intense. We are not."

SOURCE: E. O. Welles, "Flexible Flyers," *Inc.* (October 17, 2000): 172–75.

the leader should use the most appropriate of four leader behaviour styles to help followers clarify the paths that lead them to work and personal goals.[17] The key concepts in the theory are shown in Exhibit 10.4.

The Centre for Leadership Excellence

The Saint Mary's University Centre for Leadership Excellence (CLE) was created to foster leadership research partnerships and deliver leadership assessment and development services to public and private sector organizations in the Atlantic Provinces.
http://www.cleleadership.ca

EXHIBIT 10.3

Three Theories of Leadership That Take a Contingency Perspective

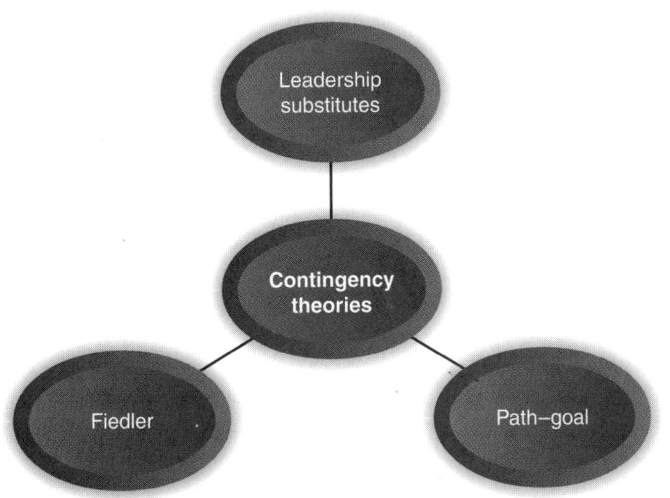

EXHIBIT 10.4

The Path–Goal Theory of Leadership

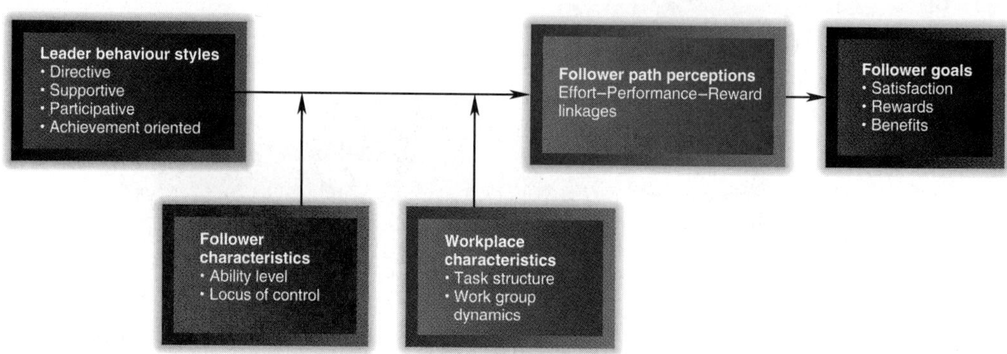

A leader selects from the four leader behaviour styles, shown in Exhibit 10.4, the one that is most helpful to followers at a given time. The directive style is used when the leader must give specific guidance about work tasks, schedule work, and let followers know what is expected. The supportive style is used when the leader needs to express concern for a follower's well-being and social status. The participative style is used when the leader must engage in joint decision-making activities with followers. The achievement-oriented style is used when the leader must set challenging goals for followers and show strong confidence in those followers. When selecting the appropriate leader behaviour style, the leader must consider both the followers and the work environment. The contingencies to consider are as follows:

- Follower characteristics: ability level and whether locus of control is external or internal
- Workplace characteristics: task structure and work group dynamics

These characteristics are included in Exhibit 10.4. Let us look at two examples. In Example 1, the followers are inexperienced and working on an ambiguous, unstructured task. The leader in this situation might best use a directive style. In Example 2, the followers are highly trained professionals, and the task is a difficult, yet achievable one. According to path–goal theory, the leader is advised to use an achievement-oriented style in this situation.

The path–goal theory assumes that leaders adapt their behaviour and style to fit the characteristics of the followers and the environment in which they work. Actual tests of the path–goal theory and its propositions provide conflicting evidence.[18] The path–goal theory does have intuitive appeal and offers a number of constructive ideas for leaders who lead a variety of followers in a variety of work environments.[19]

Application & Evaluation

USING PATH–GOAL THEORY TO DECIDE HOW TO LEAD

You have been hired as a senior tennis coach and unit head for a large group of eight-year-olds at a four-week summer day camp. Reporting to you will be four junior tennis coaches, one who has done the job before and three who are new. Their jobs are to teach five 45-minute coaching sessions throughout the day as well as swim with the children and supervise playground activities. Using path–goal theory, what leadership styles would you use in this situation and why? How would you change your style over the course of the four-week session?

Fiedler's Contingency Theory

Explain Fiedler's contingency theory of leadership.

Fiedler's theory of leadership proposed in the late 1960s was the first to take a contingency perspective. Fiedler's research suggested that high task and high people orientation was not best in all situations. Rather, effective leadership depends upon the match between the leader's style (task or relationship oriented) and the degree of control he or she has in the situation. When a leader has high control, the situation is considered to be "favourable"; when control is low the situation is "unfavourable." As shown in Exhibit 10.5, the favourableness of the leader's situation depends upon three key factors or contingencies:

- **Position power** is the authority associated with the leader's formal position in the organization. It denotes the amount of power and influence a leader has over followers to hire, fire, discipline, and reward.
- **Leader–member relations** describe the quality of interpersonal relationships between a leader and the group members. It is the degree to which followers trust and respect the leader.
- **Task structure** describes the degree of clarity, or ambiguity, in the work activities assigned to the group. It is the degree to which the jobs are clear, well defined, and structured.

position power
The authority associated with the leader's formal position in the organization.

leader–member relations
The quality of interpersonal relationships between a leader and the group members.

task structure
The degree of clarity, or ambiguity, in the work activities assigned to the group.

Fiedler developed the "least preferred co-worker" (LPC) questionnaire to measure leadership styles. Fieldler defined the **least preferred co-worker (LPC)** as the person a leader has least preferred to work with over his or her career. A low LPC score means the leader is task-oriented while a high LPC score means the leader is relationship-oriented. The LPC score is a controversial element in contingency theory.[20] It has been critiqued conceptually and methodologically because it has low measurement reliability. Fiedler's leadership theory is the only one to consider the leader's power as one of the factors in deciding how to lead. The contingency theory suggests that low- and high-LPC leaders are each effective if placed in the right situation.[21] Specifically, low-LPC (task-oriented) leaders are most effective in either very favourable or very unfavourable leadership situations. In contrast, high-LPC (relationship-oriented) leaders are most effective in situations of intermediate favourableness. Exhibit 10.5 shows the nature of these relationships and suggests that leadership effectiveness is determined by the degree of fit between the leader and the situation. What, then, is to be done if there is a misfit? That is, what happens when a low-LPC leader is in a moderately favourable situation or when a high-LPC leader is in a highly favourable or highly unfavourable situation? According to Fiedler, it is unlikely that the leader can alter his or her style, as a result of personality. Fiedler recommends, therefore, in contrast to path–goal theorists, that the leader's situation be changed to fit the leader's style.[22] An example of this is when Steve Smith, CEO of WestJet Airlines, was let go in October 2000 because his autocratic leadership style did not fit the corporate culture of employee-oriented leadership and empowerment.[23] Siobhan Vinish, director of public relations and communications for WestJet, said that "Smith's way of leading and managing would work very well in a different organization."

least preferred co-worker (LPC)
The person a leader has least preferred to work with over his or her career.

The two contingency theories just discussed share common features in that they both recommend that leadership style be adapted to various contingencies in the leader's situation. They differ, however, in two important ways: First, each theory has a slightly different approach to classifying the types of leadership styles, and second, each theory has a somewhat different approach to defining which contingencies (variables) in the situation, the leader should attend to when deciding how to lead. Because no *one* theory of leadership can explain all situations, we use the insights from both theories to help us better understand the dynamics of effective leadership in different situations. Fiedler's theory and path–goal theory, along with other leadership theories, are compared in Exhibit 10.6, later in the chapter.

EXHIBIT 10.5

Using Fiedler's Contingency Theory

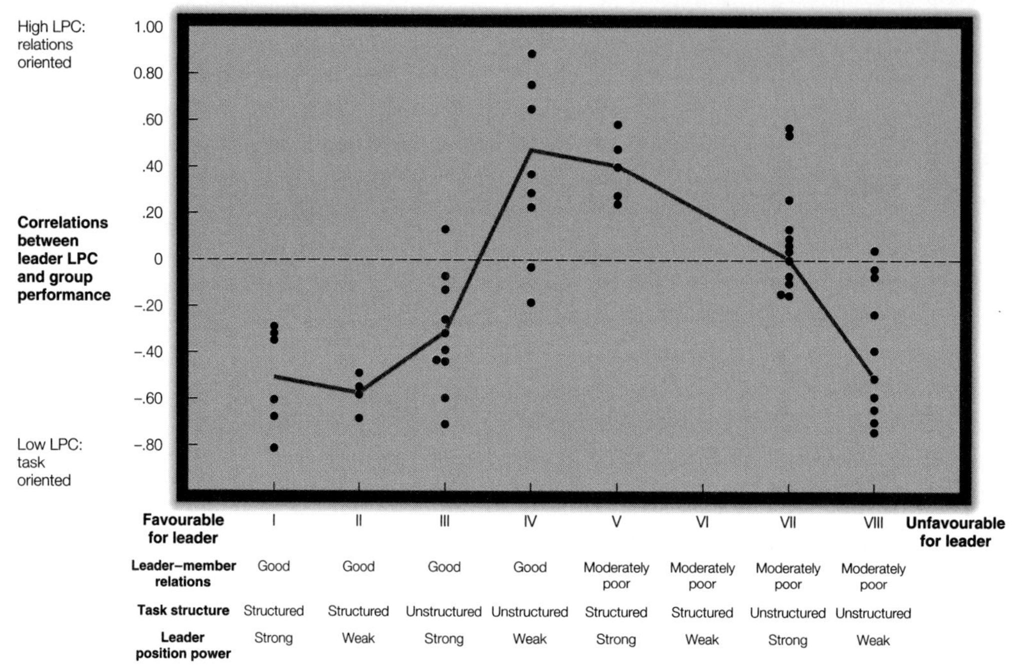

SOURCE: F. E. Fiedler, *A Theory of Leader Effectiveness* (New York: McGraw-Hill, 1964). Reprinted with permission of the author.

Explain the leadership substitutes theory.

leadership substitutes theory
The theory that in some situations leaders can reduce the amount of leadership they exercise because it becomes unnecessary due to existing substitutes or "neutralizers."

transactional leadership
A process of social exchange between followers and leaders that involves a number of reward-based transactions. The transactional leader clarifies performance expectations, goals, and a path that will link achievement of the goals to rewards.

Leadership Substitutes Theory

The fifth leadership theory taking a contingency perspective is called the **leadership substitutes theory.** The central idea behind this theory is that in some situations leaders can reduce the amount of leadership they exercise because existing substitutes or "neutralizers" make it unnecessary.[24] For example, when a task is very satisfying to an individual or when an employee gets direct feedback about performance from the work itself (sales commissions for example), the behaviour of his or her supervisor (leader) becomes much less important to or influential on the follower. Other things that can substitute for leadership include high skill on the part of the employee, team cohesiveness, and formal controls on the part of the organization. Research on this idea is generally supportive, and other factors that act as substitutes are being identified. The reason that this theory is classified as a contingency theory is because it suggests that when these contingencies (high job feedback, team cohesiveness, etc.) are present, the leadership style can become very laissez-faire or "delegating," similar to the fourth quadrant in the situational leadership model.[25]

See Exhibit 10.6 for a summary of the leadership models discussed thus far.

Explain the key elements of transformational leadership and contrast it with transactional leadership.

THE TRANSFORMATIONAL PERSPECTIVE

The trait, behavioural, and contingency theories discussed thus far are classified as primarily transactional theories of leadership. **Transactional leadership** is a process of social exchange between followers and leaders that involves a number of reward-based transactions. The transactional leader clarifies performance expectations, goals, and a path that will link achievement of the goals to rewards.[26] The theories discussed thus far have

EXHIBIT 10.6

Comparing Leadership Theories

Theory	Leadership Styles	Contingencies Used in Leadership Theory
Behavioural perspective	• High task • High people • Laissez-faire	N/A
Leadership grid theory	• Authority compliance (9,1) • Country club (1,9) • Team • Middle-of-the road • Impoverished	N/A
Path–goal theory	• Directive • Supportive • Participative • Achievement-oriented	• Locus of control • Ability of followers • Task structure • Work-group dynamics
Fiedler's theory	• Low LPC • High LPC • Task structure	• Leader position power • Leader–member relations
Leadership substitutes theory	• Delegating • Direct job feedback • Cohesive group • Skilled employees	• Satisfying task

varied by describing which type of exchanges (people or task oriented) work best, and in what situations (nature of the task, follower characteristics, leader power, etc.). By contrast, **transformational leadership** occurs when a leader inspires followers to share a vision, empowers them to achieve the vision, and provides the resources necessary for developing their personal potential. Transformational leaders serve as role models, support optimism, and mobilize commitment as well as focus on the followers' needs for growth.[27]

transformational leadership
Leadership that inspires followers to share a vision, empowers them to achieve the vision, and provides the resources necessary for developing their personal potential. Transformational leaders serve as role models, support optimism, and mobilize commitment as well as focus on the followers' needs for growth.

Characteristics and Behaviours of Transformational Leaders

According to Bernard Bass there are four key characteristics of transformational leaders. These are charisma, the ability to inspire loyalty, individualized consideration, and the ability to stimulate followers to think about old problems in new ways. **Charisma** is defined as a personal trait that gives a leader referent power over followers. Referent power was discussed in Chapter 9; *charisma* is a Greek word meaning "gift." The charismatic leader's unique and powerful gifts are the source of the leader's great influence with followers. In charismatic leadership, the leader uses the force of personal abilities and talents to have profound and extraordinary effects on followers,[28] and charismatic leadership is especially effective in times of uncertainty.[29] Several researchers have attempted to demystify charismatic leadership and distinguish its two faces, since it carries with it not only great potential for high levels of achievement but also shadowy risks of destructive courses of action that might harm followers or other people.[30] The ugly face of charisma is revealed in the personalized power motivations of Adolf Hitler in Nazi Germany and David Koresh of the Branch Davidian cult in Waco, Texas. Both men led their followers into struggle, conflict, and death. Recently, researchers have been expressing concern over

charisma
A personal trait that gives a leader referent power over followers.

IMPLICATIONS FOR LIFE

Using the Contingency Leadership Theories to Coach Winning Teams

While most of the contingency leadership research has been conducted in organizational settings, many of the theories apply to life outside of work as well. Consider the following examples:

Fiedler: When coaching a sports team, Fiedler's theory would suggest that when each person's role is well defined; when the coach has the power to hire, fire, and discipline; and when followers trust and respect him or her, the best coach will use a task-oriented leadership style. However, in a less favourable situation, for example if the coach has to get approvals to change players or discipline them, a coach with a more relationship-oriented leadership style would be best. Do you agree?

Path–goal: According to path–goal theory, the coach is also advised to pay more attention to the ability levels of the players. For both the high- and low-power situations described above, if players are rookies, a directive style is recommended, but with pros, the coach is advised to take a more achievement-oriented style. Do you agree?

Leadership substitutes: Leadership substitutes in this situation might be a highly experienced group of players who have played together for a long time. In that case, leadership substitutes theory would advise that the coach use minimal leadership, also called a delegating style.

the "cult" of charisma and the folly of relying on this personal attribute when hiring CEOs. Writers are concerned that charismatic authority, by its very nature, discourages criticism and creates a "yes man" culture including symptoms of groupthink, discussed in Chapter 8.[31]

The brighter face of charisma is revealed in the socialized power motivations of leaders like Isadore Sharpe of Four Seasons Hotels, Frank Stronach of Magna International in Canada, and Richard Branson of Virgin Atlantic Airways in the U.K.[32] Whereas charismatic leaders with socialized power motivation (see Chapter 4) are concerned about the collective well-being of their followers, charismatic leaders with a personalized power motivation, like Hitler and Koresh, are driven by the need for personal gain and glorification.[33]

While charisma (according to Bass's research) was the characteristic that best predicted transformational leadership, four other behaviours were significant as well. These behaviours are the ability to articulate a vision or mission, model the vision, build commitment to it, and demonstrate personal integrity. While charisma is important, it is not enough to bring about transformational change. Bill Fulton, who replaced the charismatic Scott Paterson as CEO of Yorkton Securities, stated: "A charismatic leader is nice, but for things to work in the long term you need consistency and follow-up. The vision may excite people but it doesn't stick on its own."[34]

Central to effective transformational leadership are certain key leadership behaviours such as a well-thought-out, well-articulated vision and mission, which are modelled by the leaders so that followers understand and are committed to it.[35] (See Exhibit 10.7.)

vision
A picture of the future with some implicit or explicit commentary on why people should strive to create that future.

Vision refers to a picture of the future with some implicit or explicit commentary on why people should strive to create that future. Transformational leadership assumes that the leader is leading some kind of change rather than conducting business as usual, so you will be reading more about vision in Chapter 13, on managing change. John Kotter explains that a good vision "serves three important purposes. First, by clarifying the general direction of the change ... it simplifies hundreds of thousands of more detailed decisions. Second, it motivates people to take action in the right direction, even if the steps are personally painful. Third, it helps coordinate the actions of different people ... in a remarkably fast and efficient way."[36]

EXHIBIT 10.7

Characteristics and Behaviours of Transformational Leaders

Characteristics (Bass)	Behaviours (Kanungo)
Charisma (idealized influence): followers have complete faith in him/her	Articulates vision, mission
Inspirational motivation: inspires loyalty in the organization	Models the vision
Individualized consideration: gives personal attention to all members	Builds commitment to mission
Intellectual stimulation: enables followers to think about old problems in new ways	Demonstrates personal integrity

SOURCES: B. M. Bass and P. Steidlmeier, "Ethics, Character and Authentic Transformational Leadership Behaviour," *Leadership Quarterly* 10, no. 2 (1999): 184; R. Kanungo, "Leadership in Organizations: Looking Ahead to the 21st Century," *Canadian Psychology* 39, no. 1–2 (1998): 78.

When Martha Piper took over as president of the University of British Columbia in the latter part of 1997, her main priority was to shed light on an exciting, long-term future. The resulting strategic vision and plan came to be known as Trek 2000. The "visioning" process began with a bold statement that she wanted to make UBC "the pre-eminent university in Canada." Dr. Piper stated in an interview: "The vision is so helpful because you can get buried in the detail of running this place—and every two or three months, I can bring it out and see where we are."[37] Peter Housley, who garnered a reputation as a visionary change artist at Zellers, also stresses the importance of focusing on the vision, the big picture, to lead change.[38] Another example of successful visioning and transformation is the turnaround at Manitoba Lotteries Corporation (MLC), described in the chapter opener, which began with a collective visioning and strategic planning process. See Exhibit 10.8 for MLC's mission statement.

John Kotter
This website includes a biography of Dr. John Kotter, distinguished leadership scholar at the Harvard Business School, as well as information on his books, speeches, videos, and new ideas.
http://www.johnkotter.com

Contemporary research into transformational leadership has explored more focused subdimensions of transformational leadership. Rafferty and Griffin's model proposes the five dimensions of vision, inspirational communication, intellectual stimulation, supportive leadership, and personal recognition.[39] Kouzes and Posner propose a model that includes

Peter Housley garnered a reputation as a visionary change artist at Zellers.

EXHIBIT 10.8

Manitoba Lotteries Corporation (MLC) Mission and Vision

The MLC's **mission** is to provide a fun and entertaining gaming experience in a socially responsible manner to generate benefits for all Manitobans.

Our Vision is

- To be a world-class gaming organization that provides products and services that meet or exceed our customers' and guests' expectations in a socially responsible manner.
- To be a flexible, innovative and learning-focused organization.
- To have an excellent work environment, characterized by respectful relationships and a well-trained and productive staff.
- To be a stable organization with strong management, predictable results, and measurable goals.
- To be operating on sound business principles and practices.
- To have a presence and image that demonstrates that MLC contributes to the province.
- To mitigate the potential adverse consequences of gaming.
- To have successful First Nations Casinos that contributes to the economic development of First Nations communities.

SOURCE: Manitoba Lotteries Corporation, "Our Vision and Our Goals," http://www.mlc.mb.ca/MLC/info/info_strategic.htm. Courtesy of the Manitoba Lotteries Corporation.

modelling the way, inspiring a shared vision, challenging the process, enabling others to act, and encouraging the heart.[40] There is also evidence that some of the behaviours associated with transformational leadership can be learned.[41] As companies increasingly operate in a global economy, there is a greater demand for leaders who can practise transformational leadership by converting their visions into reality,[42] and by inspiring followers to perform "above and beyond the call of duty."[43]

While transactional qualities have tended to be associated with managers, transformational qualities have tended to be associated with leaders. However, Bernard Bass's recent work suggests that transformational leaders also demonstrate three transactional factors in addition to transformational ones. These three transactional factors are as follows: First, they reward their followers for carrying out their assignments; second, they actively manage by exception; and third, they demonstrate "passive" leadership, waiting for problems to emerge before correcting them.[44] Bass's research with over 100 leaders suggests that transformational leadership adds to the effects of transactional leadership, but exceptional transactional leadership cannot substitute for transformational leadership.[45]

Outline six additional issues in leadership research: LMX theory, e-leadership, gender issues, cross-cultural issues, servant leadership, and ethics in leadership.

ADDITIONAL ISSUES IN LEADERSHIP RESEARCH

Additional leadership research that does not fit into one of the four perspectives just discussed (trait, behavioural, contingency, or transformational) includes the following: LMX theory, e-leadership, gender differences, cross-cultural differences, ethics in leadership, and "servant" leadership.

Application & Analysis

CAN YOU SPOT A TRANSFORMATIONAL LEADER?

Using the characteristics of transformational leaders summarized in Exhibit 10.7, select two or three people who have supervised or directed you in some way (at home, work, or school) and analyze whether they display the characteristics of a transformational leader.

Leader–Member Exchange (LMX) Theory

Leader–member exchange theory, or LMX, proposes that leaders may form different relationships with followers. The LMX scale assesses the degree to which leaders and followers trust, depend upon, and have mutual respect for each other's capabilities. These dimensions determine whether the followers will be part of the leader's "in-group" or "out group." In-group members tend to be similar to the leader and given greater responsibilities, more rewards, and more attention. They work within the leader's inner circle of communication. As a result, in-group members are more satisfied, have lower turnover, and have higher organizational commitment. In contrast, out-group members are outside the circle and receive less attention and fewer rewards.[46] Research on LMX suggests that in-group members are more likely to engage in organizational citizenship behaviour, while out-group members are more likely to retaliate against the organization.[47] Also, the type of stress varies by the group to which a subordinate belongs. In-group members' stress comes from the additional responsibilities placed on them by the leader, whereas out-group members' stress comes from being left out of the communication network.[48]

e-Leadership

Today, leaders typically lead teams in which members are located, not in the same office or building, but in different places around the country, and often in different places around the world. Many leaders and team members stay in contact with each other by interacting through telephone, overnight express mail, fax machines, and groupware tools such as e-mail, bulletin boards, chat, and video-conferencing. In response to these changes, organizational scientists have begun to talk about **e-leadership** to refer to leaders who conduct many of the processes of leadership largely though electronic channels. Indeed, given the rapidity of technology growth in organizations and their global reach, researchers now suggest that in the near future, e-leadership will be the routine rather than the exception in our thinking about what constitutes organizational leadership.[49] Some of the challenges involved in leading e-teams differ from those of traditional teams.[50] For example, one study suggests that when leading multi-manager remote teams it is important to have a face-to-face kick-off meeting with all involved to resolve the following issues: "Define explicit roles, responsibilities, deliverables, and communication mechanisms with the other managers and team members who work for them.... any manager who knows that he or she will be unavailable should appoint a designate.... each manager should know the escalation path, that is the path for transmission of issues and concerns to progressively higher levels of management." The authors also stress the need for sensitivity to cultural norms, especially where virtual teams span multiple regions of the world.[51]

e-leadership
Leadership processes conducted largely through electronic channels.

Boeing-Rocketdyne, which is the major U.S. manufacturer of liquid-fuelled rocket engines, put together a virtual team to drive the costs of rocket engines down by 100 times, get the engine to market 10 times faster, and increase the life of a rocket engine by three times—and they did so successfully. What Boeing-Rocketdyne learned was that the leader of such teams needed to be the "spoke in the centre of the wheel" in terms of coordination. The leader also needed to help the team create a common language as well as document results for the entire team.[52] Leading virtual teams requires creativity, because face-to-face interaction that is the hallmark of leadership is not possible. Organizational Reality 10.3 shows how STMicroelectronics mastered the challenge of leading virtual teams. Learn more about e-leadership in OBXtra5, entitled "Managing in a Virtual World."

organizational reality 10.3

Virtual Teaming at STMicroelectronics

STMicroelectronics (STM) got good news! They won a coveted order to design and build microchips for new navigational mapping systems to be installed in Fiat and Peugeot cars. Now the bad news: The customers needed the chips fast, and STM's specialists were scattered all over the globe. Key players lived in France, England, Italy, India, California, and Arizona, spanned fourteen time zones, and spoke six different languages. Time and costs meant they couldn't meet in one location. Virtual teaming was the only way to get it done.

Being a member of a virtual team is both a blessing and a curse. The blessing is that you can design something in the morning, e-mail it out, and by the afternoon have everyone's input from everywhere. The curse is that when a team member's cell phone is turned on, he or she can forget about eight-hour days or uninterrupted meals and relaxing weekends.

The old command-and-control style of leadership does not work with virtual teams. The team leader's job is not to make decisions but to build mutual commitment and confidence. Multiple leaders were used at STM, and leader roles shifted as tasks shifted. And virtual teaming was not always the answer. Groupware or no groupware, sometimes there was no substitute for face-to-face collaboration. At one point, an engineer from India temporarily moved to San Jose, California, to deal with technical problems that were slowing the project down. Leading virtual teams requires a new form of leadership, one that revolves around adaptability.

SOURCE: J. Katzenbach and D. Smith, "Virtual Teaming," *Forbes,* May 21, 2001, 48–51. Reprinted by permission of Forbes Magazine.

Gender and Leadership

A great deal of research has been conducted in recent years into the question "Do women and men lead differently?" Historical stereotypes persist, and a good manager is still perceived as predominantly masculine.[53] Research however, suggests that women are more effective, and tend to use a more people-oriented style, more contingent rewards, and more individualized consideration than men.[54] Some researchers even go so far as to argue that under contemporary conditions, hiring a female boosts the odds of getting a great executive![55] Female leaders seem to have an advantage in transformational leadership because it encompasses "some behaviours that are consistent with the female gender role demand for supportive, considerate behaviours."[56] However, researchers have also found that female leaders are at a disadvantage arising from the incongruity between the traditional female role and many leader roles.

Although legitimate gender differences may exist, the same leadership traits may be interpreted differently in a man and a woman because of stereotypes, or, according to Jennifer Cliff at the University of Alberta and others, because of the way male and female leaders talk about their leadership styles rather than how they actually run their companies. After interviewing 229 small business owners, the interviews revealed that "owners of each sex, talk as if they lead according to gender stereotypes. But then go out and act in less gender-specific ways."[57]

Cultural Differences in Leadership

The situational approaches to leadership would lead to the conclusion that a leader must factor in culture as an important situational variable when exercising influence and authority. Thus, global leaders should expect to be flexible enough to alter their approaches when crossing national boundaries and working with people from foreign cultures.[58] For example, the massive GLOBE study led by Robert House at the Wharton School identified 22 leadership attributes that were universally desirable and eight that were undesirable (e.g., irritable, ruthless.) They also found that many leadership attributes

? Knowledge & Application

SELF-ASSESSMENT 10.2: NATIONAL CULTURE AND LEADERSHIP

Effective leadership often varies by national culture, as the GLOBE study and Hofstede's research has shown. This exercise gives you the opportunity to examine your own leadership orientation compared to norms from 10 countries. In the questionnaire below, indicate the extent to which you agree or disagree with each statement. For example, if you strongly agree with a particular statement, circle the 5 next to the statement.

1 = strongly disagree 2 = disagree 3 = neither agree nor disagree
4 = agree 5 = strongly agree

Questionnaire	Strongly Disagree Strongly Agree
1. It is important to have job instructions spelled out in detail so that employees always know what they are expected to do.	1 2 3 4 5
2. Managers expect employees to closely follow instructions and procedures.	1 2 3 4 5
3. Rules and regulations are important because they inform employees what the organization expects of them.	1 2 3 4 5
4. Standard operating procedures are helpful to employees on the job.	1 2 3 4 5
5. Instructions for operations are important for employees on the job.	1 2 3 4 5
6. Group welfare is more important than individual rewards.	1 2 3 4 5
7. Group success is more important than individual success.	1 2 3 4 5
8. Being accepted by the members of your work group is very important.	1 2 3 4 5
9. Employees should pursue their own goals only after considering the welfare of the group.	1 2 3 4 5
10. Managers should encourage group loyalty even if individual goals suffer.	1 2 3 4 5
11. Individuals may be expected to give up their goals in order to benefit group success.	1 2 3 4 5
12. Managers should make most decisions without consulting subordinates.	1 2 3 4 5
13. Managers should frequently use authority and power when dealing with subordinates.	1 2 3 4 5
14. Managers should seldom ask for the opinions of employees.	1 2 3 4 5
15. Managers should avoid off-the-job social contacts with employees.	1 2 3 4 5
16. Employees should not disagree with management decisions.	1 2 3 4 5
17. Managers should not delegate important tasks to employees.	1 2 3 4 5
18. Managers should help employees with their family problems.	1 2 3 4 5
19. Managers should see to it that employees are adequately clothed and fed.	1 2 3 4 5
20. A manager should help employees solve their personal problems.	1 2 3 4 5
21. Management should see that all employees receive health care.	1 2 3 4 5
22. Management should see that children of employees have an adequate education.	1 2 3 4 5
23. Management should provide legal assistance for employees who get into trouble with the law.	1 2 3 4 5
24. Managers should take care of their employees as they would their children.	1 2 3 4 5

25. Meetings are usually run more effectively when they are chaired by a man. 1 2 3 4 5
26. It is more important for men to have a professional career than it is for women to have a professional career. 1 2 3 4 5
27. Men usually solve problems with logical analysis; women usually solve problems with intuition. 1 2 3 4 5
28. Solving organizational problems usually requires an active, forcible approach, which is typical of men. 1 2 3 4 5
29. It is preferable to have a man, rather than a woman, in a high-level position. 1 2 3 4 5

For scoring instructions, please go to the end of the chapter, p. 329.

SOURCES: Peter Dorfman, *Advances in International Comparative Management* 3 (1988), 127–50. Reprinted by permission of JAI Press Inc.; D. Marcic and S. M. Puffer, "Dimensions of National Culture and Effective Leadership Patterns: Hofstede Revisited," *Management International* (Minneapolis/St. Paul: West Publishing, 1994), 10–15.

were desirable in some cultures and undesirable in others (e.g., ambitious, elitist).[59] The study also revealed that societies high on power distance, like Russia, Thailand, and Spain, tended to expect obedience toward superiors while countries low on power distance favoured stronger participation in decision making.[60] Also, leaders who gave subordinates autonomy were viewed more positively in Germany and Austria than in the Czech Republic and Portugal.[61] Even when U.S. managers are transferred to Canada, they often have to adapt their leadership styles. For example, when Tom Healy headed up the Best Buy expansion into Canada, he was coached by psychologists to help him better understand how his leadership style was likely to come across in a Canadian context. Guy Beaudin, Healy's personal coach, stated that his job was to "Ensure that Tom doesn't come across as a stereotypical American manager, expecting his Canadian staff to follow the 'American way or no way.' " He was there, he said, to provide a brief of Canadian culture and bridge the communication gap.[62] There are also differences between the American view of transformational leadership and that found in the United Kingdom. The U.K. approach to transformational leadership is much closer to what we refer to as servant leadership in the next section.

Complete Self-Assessment 10.2 to learn more about your own cultural orientation to leadership.

Servant Leadership

servant leadership
The view that the leader is the servant of his or her followers. It places the interest of the followers before the self-interest of the leader and emphasizes personal development and empowerment of followers.

Robert Greenleaf was director of management research at AT&T for many years. He believed that leaders should serve employees, customers, and the community, and his essays are the basis for today's view called "servant leadership." **Servant leadership** views the leader as the servant of his or her followers. It places the interest of the followers before the self-interest of the leader and emphasizes personal development and empowerment of followers. Greenleaf's personal and professional philosophy was that leaders lead by serving others. Other tenets of servant leadership are that work exists for the person as much as the person exists for work, and that servant leaders try to find out the will of the group and lead based on that. Servant leaders are also stewards who consider leadership a trust and desire to leave the organization in better shape for future generations.[63] Although Greenleaf's writings were completed 30 years ago, it is only recently that they have been published and are becoming more popular.[64] Recent research suggests that servant leadership is very similar to transformational leadership but that they differ in terms of the leader's focus. The transformational leader's focus is directed towards the organization while the servant leader's focus is on the followers.[65] Also it seems to involve more connectedness between leaders and followers, and more vulnerability on the part of the leader.[66]

The Sheldon Chumir Foundation for Ethics in Leadership

The Chumir Foundation of Calgary was created from a bequest by Sheldon M. Chumir, Rhodes Scholar, lawyer, businessman, civil libertarian, and Alberta MLA (1986 to 1992). Mr. Chumir believed that ethical values are fundamental to a healthy society, and wished this foundation to operate so as to influence ethical actions in the practical world of politics, business, and government, as well as community structures and processes. Mr. Chumir has been described as a "challenging man" in that he challenged his friends and society to be all they could be. He chose to dedicate the bulk of his assets to the creation of a foundation to continue his challenge to us—to ensure leadership motivated by ethical resolve and purpose. **http://www.chumirethicsfoundation.ca**

Ethics in Leadership

With the recent highly publicized scandals regarding unethical behaviour, such as the collapse of Enron and the lawsuit against Martha Stewart, more attention has been devoted to questions of morality and ethics in leadership. Corporate leaders play a central role in setting the ethical tone and moral values for their organizations. For example, as chairman and CEO of Johnson & Johnson, James Burke played a pivotal role in modelling ethical leadership at the company in the 1970s and 1980s. Further, Johnson & Johnson ranked number 1 in the *Fortune* list of most admired corporations in corporate leadership, in part due to the ethical and moral values reflected in the J&J culture and credo.[67] Prominent leadership researchers, such as Bass and Kanungo, have turned their attention to the ethical values of leaders and the potential dark side of charismatic leadership as mentioned earlier.[68] Essentially, they present theoretical arguments to show that in order to be truly transformational, leadership must be grounded in moral foundation. Corporate social responsibility has gained renewed popularity and companies are now ranked annually in terms of their performance as corporate citizens in Canada.[69] For 2004, the top five corporate citizens for employee relations were Zenon Environmental, MDS, Alcan, Dofasco, and Tembec.[70]

IMPLICATIONS FOR ORGANIZATIONAL EFFECTIVENESS

Findings from the many OB studies of leadership suggest a number of important implications for organizations. First, transactional managers need to be trained to understand the different leadership styles and their impact on followers. Second, leaders need to learn how to recognize employee and environmental contingencies, as well as gender and cultural differences, so that they can adapt their styles accordingly. Third, according to Fiedler, managers should be assessed and selected carefully, so that their natural styles can be matched to the demands of the situation. Fiedler's research also implies that organizations need to ensure that managers have sufficient power to lead. Fourth, organizations are well advised to design jobs in such a way as to minimize the need for hands-on leadership, building leadership substitutes into the job wherever possible. Fifth, leaders need to try to build trust in their exchanges with followers and avoid creating in-groups and out-groups. Finally, as organizations become increasingly virtual, the additional challenges of e-leadership will need to receive greater attention.

Organizations needing transformational leaders have to carefully select managers who possess charisma and who have the ability to articulate and model a vision for large-scale change. Research cautions organizations as to the limitations of transformational leadership alone and suggests that transactional qualities are also needed, in order to institutionalize any changes. Also, increasingly corporate leaders play a central role in setting the ethical tone and moral values for their organizations. While effective leadership has been found to be a critical determinant of an organization's performance, it is important to recognize the influence of other factors also. These include environmental factors (such as general economic conditions), technological factors (such as efficiency), and the degree of investment in human resources processes and support, such as the training programs and coaches employed by MLC to help managers implement their action plans.

Chapter Summary

1. Leadership is the ability of an individual to influence, motivate, and enable others to contribute toward the effectiveness and success of organizations of which they are members. Over the years, a great deal of research has been conducted to try to understand, predict, and control leadership behaviour; however, there is no one theory that can explain all of the complexities of what makes an effective leader. The research findings can be classified into at least four different perspectives: the trait, behavioural, contingency, and transformational perspectives.

2. The *trait* or competency perspective of leadership proposes that leaders possess certain personality, social, physical, or intellectual traits that are not possessed by nonleaders. Theories taking the trait perspective have had limited success in identifying the universal, distinguishing attributes of leaders. However, much current research and company practice focuses on learned leadership competencies, (rather than inborn traits) that are required to lead successfully in a particular company.

3. Leadership theories that take a behavioural perspective propose that, rather than possessing traits, leaders *behave* in certain ways that distinguish them from nonleaders. All of the behavioural theories explore both the task- and people-oriented behaviours (styles) of leaders but vary as to the number and names of the leadership styles as well as their prescription for the "one best way" to lead. In the production, task-oriented, or autocratic style of leadership the leader spells out duties and specific tasks, tells people what to do and how to do it, ensures employees follow rules, and encourages employees to reach peak performance. This style was also referred to in early studies as initiating structure. The leader with an employee-centred, people-oriented, or democratic style shows mutual trust and respect, engages in two-way communication, listens, encourages, gives recognition, and provides socio-emotional support to followers. This style was initially called consideration. The laissez-faire style or uninvolved style is an employee-centred leadership style in which the manager permits employees to function within prescribed limits. The Managerial (Leadership) Grid is a behavioural model which proposes that the best way to lead is to show high concern for results (task) and high concern for people.

4. Leadership theories that take a contingency perspective propose that effective leadership is not so much determined by the leader's traits or characteristic behaviours (style) but rather by the degree of fit between the leader's style and the factors in a particular situation.

5. Path–goal theory suggests that the leader should use the most appropriate of four leader behavioural styles to help followers clarify the paths that lead them to work and personal goals. The four styles in path–goal theory are (1) the directive style, which is used when the leader must give specific guidance about work tasks, schedule work, and let followers know what is expected; (2) the supportive style, which is used when the leader needs to express concern for a follower's well-being and social status; (3) the participative style, which is used when the leader must engage in joint decision-making activities with followers; and (4) the achievement-oriented style, which is used when the leader must set challenging goals for followers and show strong confidence in those followers. The contingencies to consider when selecting the best style to lead are the skill and abilities of employees, their locus of control, the structure of the task, and the dynamics of the work group.

6. According to Fiedler's contingency theory, task-oriented leaders are most effective in highly favourable or highly unfavourable leadership situations, and relationship-oriented leaders are most effective in moderately favourable leadership situations. Favourable situations are defined as those in which the leader has a high degree of power, the group task is structured, and leader–member relations are positive.

7. Leadership substitutes theory states that certain factors in a situation act as substitutes for leadership and need to be considered as one of the contingencies when deciding how to lead and what is affecting follower behaviour. Substitutes include direct job feedback, satisfying tasks, cohesive groups, and skilled employees.

8. Leadership theories that take a transformational perspective explore the degree to which leaders can transform, or bring about changes in organization. The characteristics of transformational leaders include charisma, the ability to inspire loyalty, individualized consideration, and the ability to stimulate followers to think about old problems in new ways. While transactional leadership is a process of social exchange between followers and leaders that involves a number of reward-based transactions, transformational leadership occurs when a leader inspires followers to share a vision, empowers them to achieve the vision, and provides the resources necessary for developing their personal potential. Transformational leaders serve as role models, support optimism, and mobilize commitment as well as focus on the followers' needs for growth. Central to the notion of transformational leadership are the concepts of charisma and vision.

9. Contemporary issues in leadership research include explorations of leader–member exchange (LMX), e-leadership, gender differences, cross-cultural differences, "servant" leadership, and ethics in leadership.

Key Terms

behavioural perspective of leadership (p. 302)
charisma (p. 311)
competencies (p. 301)
contingency perspective of leadership (p. 306)
e-leadership (p. 315)
employee, people-oriented, or democratic style (p. 304)
laissez-faire style (uninvolved) (p. 305)
leader–member relations (p. 309)
leadership (p. 300)
Leadership (Managerial) Grid (p. 305)
leadership substitutes theory (p. 310)
least preferred co-worker (LPC) (p. 309)
position power (p. 309)
servant leadership (p. 318)
task-oriented style (p. 304)
task structure (p. 309)
trait perspective of leadership (p. 301)
transactional leadership (p. 310)
transformational leadership (p. 311)
vision (p. 312)

Review Questions

1. Define *leadership* and distinguish between transformational and transactional leadership.
2. Compare House's path–goal theory of leadership with the situational leadership model.
3. Explain a few leadership challenges that are unique to e-leadership.
4. If you found yourself in a situation where you had to lead a group of willing but inexperienced students to run an orientation session, what information would you seek and how would the leadership theories help you decide what style to use?
5. What are the key variables in Fiedler's leadership theory that would help you select the right kind of leader for a situation?
6. How might an understanding of leadership substitutes help you design a job?

Discussion and Communication Questions

1. Do you (or would you want to) work in a task-oriented, people-oriented, or laissez-faire work environment? What might be the advantages of each work environment? The disadvantages?
2. Is your supervisor or professor someone who is high in concern for task? High in concern for people? Both? Neither?
3. (*Communication question*) Who is the leader you admire the most? Write a description of this person including his or her characteristics and attributes that you admire. Note any aspects of this leader or his or her behaviour that you find less than wholly admirable.

Ethics Questions

1. Is it ethical for leaders to tell followers unilaterally what to do without asking their opinions or getting any input from them?
2. Is it acceptable for a leader to take credit for the work of followers for whom he or she has responsibility?
3. If a leader is using a delegating leadership style and big problems develop in the team's work, is the leader still responsible for what happens?
4. What should you do if your supervisor acts in an unethical or illegal manner? Talk with the supervisor? Immediately report the action to the company's ethics committee?

Knowledge & Application

EXPERIENTIAL EXERCISE 10.1: DISCUSSION OF SELF ASSESSMENT 10.1: ARE YOU AN EFFECTIVE LEADER?

Purpose: To self-diagnose individual leadership styles and apply the behavioural perspective of leadership

Group size: 5–8

Time required: 20 minutes

Materials needed: None

Instructions:

1. Complete and score Self-Assessment 10.1.
2. Instructor asks each student to go to a corner of the room that represents his or her style:
   - Uninvolved (low task, low people)
   - Task-oriented (high task, low people)
   - People-oriented (high people, low task)
   - Balanced (high people, high task)
3. Form small groups of five to eight people with a mix of styles, if possible.
4. Groups discuss the following:
   - Which style would you prefer your boss to have? Why?
   - Is one's leadership style fixed or do you tend to lead differently in different situations?

Knowledge & Application

EXPERIENTIAL EXERCISE 10.2: DON'T TOPPLE THE TOWER

Purpose: This action exercise helps to examine leader-member relationships that affect team performance on a tangible production project. Primary attention is on the thoughts and interaction behaviours of the leader. During the postproduction briefing, other situational factors are examined, such as skill differences among workers, worker needs, expectations, perceptions, physical factors, and so on.

Group size: 3 people

Time required: 35–65 minutes

Materials needed: Large index cards (5 × 7 recommended), 20 per team, strips of cloth or head scarves suitable for blindfolds (two per team), and a watch or clock for timing production periods.

Instructions:

1. The objective is to see how many folded index cards can be stacked two cards per tier, with each tier at a 90-degree angle to the tier below, to form a multi-tiered tower of up to 20 cards. You say it sounds easy? Wait until you are a worker and try to do it blindfolded.
2. Participants are assigned to three-person teams (random is best) and each team is given a number corresponding to the number on the summary chart (drawn on the board as shown on the following page.
3. The production exercise will be repeated (in five-minute intervals timed by your instructor) three times. Roles are to be rotated following each action cycle. The roles are:
   - Leader (one person)
   - Subordinates, builders (two people)

Team	Leader's name	Goal (# of cards)	Actual (# of cards)	T-P Leadership Style?
1	I. II. III.			
2	I. II. III.			
etc.				

Note: If any teams have to have four people, one person can take the role of observer, but this is not recommended.

4. Each team receives 20 index cards and two blindfolds. Fold cards lengthwise in the middle to form "tents." If 5 × 7 cards are used, each tent will be 2 1/2 × 7, flared about an inch at the bottom.
5. After teams and materials are assembled, decide who will be the first leader, and what the team output goal will be for a five-minute production round. *It is the leader's responsibility to establish a team output goal.* Post the name of leader I and the output goal (expressed as the number of cards to be stacked without toppling the tower) on the board. Establish whatever procedures you need to ensure good performance, so long as they are consistent with the instructions that follow. Blindfold the two initial builders, and designate them as worker A and worker B. If you have time, *practise* until the instructor is ready to start all teams on the first five-minute production period. After practising, replace all cards to the pile.
6. After each of the three production periods, count the number of cards stacked without toppling the tower, then post the score in the "*Actual*" column.
7. Workers should give feedback to the leader regarding their perceptions of his or her *leadership style in terms of task and people orientation,* and leader should post this as well.

Production Rules

1. Workers use *non-dominant hand* for stacking cards. They are not permitted to use their dominant hand at all.
2. Worker A and B *take turns stacking the cards.* Worker A will place the first card, then worker B will place the second card parallel to the first, as close or far apart as directed by the leader. This forms the base tier. Worker A then places the third card at right angles to the base; worker B places the fourth card parallel to the third. Work continues in this manner, with workers alternating the stacking of each card, with two parallel cards per tier.
3. *The leader is not permitted to touch the workers or the cards at any time during the production period.* Since workers are blindfolded, the leader must guide the work verbally through instructions to the work team.
4. The round is terminated for a team when either (a) the goal is achieved, i.e., 10 cards have been stacked as predicted; (b) that a card that was previously stacked on the tower is knocked off, or the entire tower topples; or (c) the instructor calls time at the end of five minutes. If a worker is placing a card and that card slips off without knocking off another card, the leader may direct the worker to retrieve the card and resume building.

Exercise Debrief

1. At the end of all production rounds, participants jot down their answers to the following question, which is posted on the board:
   "What are all the things we can learn about effective leadership from this exercise?"
2. All team members should jot down a few thoughts about their experience as a leader or worker in that round. Did you feel anxiety, frustration, and satisfaction? Any suggestions for improvement?
3. Instructor takes up ideas and relates to concepts of leadership learned in the chapter, such as task versus people orientation, leadership traits, characteristics of the followers and the task, individual differences, goal-setting, reward systems, needs, and expectancies.

SOURCE: Curtis W. Cook, "Debriefing with Serialized Theory Development for Task-Team Development," *Exploring Experiential Learning: Simulations and Experiential Exercises* (Tempe, AZ: Bureau of Business and Economic Research, Arizona State University, 1978): 7–8. Cited in P. L. Hunsaker and C. W. Cook, *Managing Organizational Behaviour* (Boston: Addison- Wesley, 1987). Reprinted by permission.

Application, Analysis & Synthesis

CASE: HILL ENTERPRISES

When Hill Enterprises was founded 10 years ago, its total assets consisted of one automatic lathe, one contract worth $2200, and one employee. That employee was Robert Hill, president and sole owner, then 29 years old. He had one objective in forming Hill Enterprises—that of retiring with $10 million in his personal bank account at the age of 45.

According to Robert Hill, the reasons Hill Enterprises was able to survive the first difficult years were his considerable abilities as a machinist, which he had developed during the nine years he was employed in the machine shop of a large manufacturing company, his willingness to work long and hard hours, and his knack for raising money for working capital. During the early years, he would customarily spend his evenings working at the plant and his days visiting banks, insurance companies, and personal friends in an attempt to acquire sufficient funds to continue operations. For the most part he was successful, and though he often had the feeling he was a bit overextended financially, his business continued to grow and show profits.

Robert Hill felt another reason for his success was his ability to inspire the work force to work toward his personal goal of $10 million. His typical comment in interviewing a prospective employee was: "If you work for me you will have to work hard, for I intend to retire with ten million dollars by the time I am 45. This means overtime, long hard hours, and unswerving loyalty to Hill Enterprises. If you are willing to do this, I'll make sure that you will get your share of the profits."

Potential employees who were willing to accept these conditions found that Robert Hill meant what he said. Loyalty to the common cause was based on the number of hours of overtime an employee put in. This high amount of overtime had two effects. First, Hill Enterprises was able to give its employees approximately double the take-home pay they could receive from other companies, thus reinforcing the promises Mr. Hill had made concerning financial rewards to individual employees. Second, even though the company was constantly growing and the work force was increasing in size, the large amount of overtime kept the number of employees to a minimum so that Mr. Hill had continuing face-to-face contact with them and could maintain a personal relationship with each.

As Hill Enterprises grew and progressed, Robert Hill continued his earlier pattern of operations. He set a gruelling pace, continuing to work long hours late into the night and spending a large share of his time during the day attempting to raise additional working capital and financial support. He often held important conferences at 5:00 a.m. in order that supervisory personnel would be free to handle their regular work during the "normal" working hours. Mr. Hill seemed to enjoy the pace and pressure and seemed especially to like his frequent contact with the employees. His office consisted of a single beat-up desk in one corner of the production area. Thus he was immediately available to all to help with any problem, whether it was a production problem or a personal one. Many employees availed themselves of his accessibility, and while he was in the plant he seemed to be constantly talking with one employee or another, either in his "office" or on the production floor. Often he would report on the progress of his personal bank account to the staff, a practice which they enjoyed tremendously, as Mr. Hill would very vividly recount his financial manipulations.

The employees of Hill Enterprises responded to the situation by working long hours in poor environmental surroundings and under the constant pressure of schedules and production deadlines. Hill Enterprises at this stage had set up operations in a deserted store building, and physical working conditions were considerably less attractive than those of competing organizations.

Under the constant pressures to meet schedules, tempers were often short. The accepted way to reduce individual tension was to "fly off the handle." It was the privilege of the president as well as of any employee, and it was a privilege that was often used. Robert Hill had the reputation of being able to deliver the best "dressing-down" of anyone in the organization, and it was not unusual for an employee to comment on the skill with which Mr. Hill had "chewed him or her out." This give-and-take was not all one sided and employees, regardless of their position, felt free to talk back to Mr. Hill or the other supervisors and often did. And because this was the accepted way to decrease tension and to achieve action, the incident over which an outburst occurred was immediately forgotten. The employees seemed to enjoy their existence with Hill Enterprises, and underneath the tension and pressure each employee felt that he or she was capable and was contributing to the goals of the company. But some nine years after the start of Hill Enterprises, as Robert Hill had often feared, his intricate financial dealings caught up with him. His considerably expanded enterprises were without adequate working capital and he was forced to bring in a new partner, Daniella Robbins, who was willing to invest sufficient funds to keep the company going.

One faction of the work force thought that the arrival of Robbins was just another of Mr. Hill's seemingly endless manipulations for capital. The other faction believed that her arrival was the harbinger of the end of Hill Enterprises as they had known it. They sensed that it would be only a matter of time until Mr. Hill would lose control of the internal workings of his organization and that the high wages and overtime pay would be cut.

The immediate influence of the arrival of Robbins upon the operations of Hill Enterprises was negligible. Operations continued at the same hectic pace, and Mr. Hill's personal activities did not appear to be appreciably different. He maintained his old "office" and was still available to help out on any particular problems that arose. However, as time passed, it became more and more obvious to the employees that Robbins demanded a great deal of Mr. Hill's time. Although he retained his desk in the corner of the shop for awhile, Mr. Hill soon set up new headquarters in the more plush surroundings of a new building that had been constructed adjacent to the shop facilities to house the sales and office activities of Hill Enterprises. Because of his new location and the demands made upon him by his new partner, Mr. Hill was unable to spend as much time with the employees in the shop as before. In addition, Robbins's apparent aloofness to the workings and problems of the production shop and its employees created resentment.

The employees noticed that shortly after Mr. Hill had moved his office, the time-honoured method of "blowing off steam" as a prelude to constructive effort on a problem became more and more ineffectual. Mr. Hill was no longer around to arbitrate really serious disagreements and his customary "O.K., now that we've got that out of our system, let's get to work," was absent. While blowing off steam was still an accepted practice, an element of bitterness seemed to be apparent in such outbursts that occurred. This bitterness and a sense of resentment toward Robbins permeated the atmosphere of the shop, with the result that many employees adopted a fatalistic attitude toward both the future of Hill Enterprises and their own personal futures.

In this atmosphere a second major organizational change occurred. A new man with the title of "Works Manager" arrived to fill the vacuum created by Mr. Hill's forced attention to matters other than production. This man, Phil Bellows, was the son-in-law of Daniella Robbins, the new partner. He was 35 years old, a graduate of McGill University, and had had 10 years' experience as an industrial engineer with a large chemical company. He was hired by Hill Enterprises on the insistence of Daniella Robbins, who felt that the production activities were inefficient and excessively costly. His appearance on the scene came as a surprise to the shop and production employees.

During the first few days with the company, employees often saw Bellows and Robbins in the production area. They appeared to be conversing in earnest, and often pointed and gestured toward machines or individuals. Bellows continually took notes on a large clipboard which he carried with him. During this period, none of the employees was spoken to by either Bellows or Robbins. The employees in the shop had not had official indication of Bellows' duties, responsibilities, or position in the company. They knew only by rumour that he was the new works manager.

Bellows made the following comments about his responsibilities at Hill Enterprises shortly after his arrival:

> This company has a tremendous potential and an unlimited future. Robert Hill is a dynamic individual with great skills. He has certainly been successful to date. Ms. Robbins and I, I think, will complement these skills and make the company even more successful. Ms. Robbins has the ability and experience to do some long-range planning and get our financial affairs in order and I have the responsibility and ability to make our production activities more effective. A major part of the problem as I see it is that we use our time inefficiently in production. We don't have any effective scheduling procedures or channels or responsibility or authority, with the result that the employees spend a lot of time bickering with each other and conversing about things with which they should not really be concerned. Their job is to get out the production. Our job is to organize the production activities in such a way that this can be done at least cost. The whole basis for the situation is that in the past Hill Enterprises has been small enough to be controlled effectively by one man. Now, however, we are no longer really a small firm and we cannot continue to operate like one. I have some ideas and some techniques which I plan to initiate that I think will increase the effectiveness and efficiency of our production operations by 50 percent in very short order.

At the beginning of his third week as works manager, Bellows issued a series of changes in procedures to the production employees. Without exception these changes were made without consulting any of the employees in the shop. All of them were issued in by e-mail, a new practice which many of the employees felt was unnecessary and undesirable because of the effectiveness with which they felt the existing informal channels of communication had been used. The extent of the changes requested by Bellows was significant, ranging from changes in production scheduling techniques to changes in working conditions for individual employees. One employee estimated that to carry out those e-mail orders, hundreds of additional hours "which were just not available" would be required.

Bellows' personal contacts with individual employees were limited and consisted mostly of quick and forceful answers to any questions or problems that might be brought to his attention. Many of his decisions seemed to indicate a lack of awareness of the capacity of the tools used in the production processes. For example, because of his insistence on machine speedups for certain operations, several expensive tools were ruined and valuable production time was lost. After having received several e-mails from Bellows which they considered unreasonable, one small group of employees had christened him with the nickname "The Fool." As the number of e-mails coming from Bellows' office increased, the resentment toward these e-mails became more apparent, and a strong adverse reaction to his presence was evident on the part of the production employees.

Some four months after Bellows' arrival, cooperation between the "old-timers"—both the supervisors and the workers—hit a new high. Unfortunately, this "cooperation" was used to undermine any and all changes that the new works manager attempted to put into effect. As new orders and procedures originated from Bellows' office, the employees carried out the orders to the letter of the law because, in many cases, they afforded a justified means of wasting time and reducing production. Bellows gave no indication that he was aware of this situation.

Bellows also attempted to establish formal channels of communication within the production operations, for he felt that much needless discussion and confusion was in existence under the present system. He issued several organizational charts that described the "approved" way in which communication was to be handled within the organization. These charts were uniformly ignored by the employees, who continued to rely on the previously accepted informal channels of action. It even became an unwritten policy that all information channelled to Bellows under the new system was censored and reviewed by the person or persons to be affected before it was sent to Bellows.

Yet in this new atmosphere the old loyalties to Robert Hill did not fade entirely. The office manager, the plant superintendent, and several supervisors attempted to get his ear from time to time to inform him that things were not running smoothly. Mr. Hill was always surprised by such comments, and he attempted to reassure them by making remarks such as, "It will take some time for us to get to know each other well, but I'm sure that everything will be straightened out in a little while." In addition, he made several trips to the production area, talking with the employees individually and asking them to give Bellows a chance, as it was important for the success of Hill Enterprises.

Morale seemed to improve for a short while until Bellows issued a statement stating that no one in the plant was to bother the president with plant problems without consulting him first. Shortly after this statement was issued by Bellows, Robert Hill again made several trips to the production area, talking to individual workers and attempting to explain that other problems prevented his spending as much time in the shop as he previously had. In several instances, he started to report on the status of his personal bank account. Noting that this was not too well received, however, he discontinued this practice.

As time passed, the situation continued to deteriorate. Many of Bellows' acts and orders seemed to be in direct contradiction to Mr. Hill's former policies and procedures. The individuals affected were confused as to which procedure to follow. Attempts to have Bellows clarify his orders either left the questioner more confused than before or were greeted with a curt, "We don't have time to discuss that. It is perfectly clear. Just read the e-mail." Within a few months, many of the employees talked of leaving to look for other employment and a few did. Nine months after Bellows had taken the position of works manager approximately 25 percent of the production force had taken new jobs. The morale among those remaining was poor and a significant increase in product rejects was experienced. But during the same period both Robbins and Bellows felt that important advances had been made in "cleaning up" production activities and that the company was "looking better all the time."

Discussion Questions:

1. What is your assessment of the strengths and weaknesses of Hill Enterprises nine months after Phil Bellows became works manager?
2. Using the leadership theories from the chapter, compare and contrast the leadership practices of Robert Hill and Phil Bellows and assess their appropriateness given what you know about the employees at Hill Enterprises.
3. What other problems in the areas of motivation, communication or team dynamics became evident under the leadership of Phil Bellows?
4. If you could go back in time and advise Robert Hill how to handle the situation when he brought in a partner and was required to spend more time away from the shop floor, what would you have suggested?

SOURCE: Harry R. Knudson, *Understanding Organizational Behavior: A Casebook*, 1st ed. Copyright © 1991. Adapted by permission of Pearson Education, Inc., Upper Saddle River, NJ.

Scoring Instructions for Self-Assessments

Self-Assessment 10.1: Are You an Effective Leader?

People-oriented:

Place a check mark by the number if you answered either A or B to any of these questions:
2 ___ 4 ___ 6 ___ 8 ___ 10 ___ 12 ___ 18 ___ 20 ___ 22 ___ 24 ___ 28 ___

Place a check mark by the number if you answered either **D or E** to any of these questions:
14 ___ 16 ___ 26 ___ 30 ___

Count your check marks to get your **total people-oriented score.** ___

Task-oriented:

Place a check mark by the number if you answered either **A or B** to any of these questions:
3 ___ 7 ___ 11 ___ 13 ___ 17 ___ 25 ___ 29 ___ 31 ___ 34 ___

Place a check mark by the number if you answered **C or D** to any of these questions:
1 ___ 5 ___ 9 ___ 15 ___ 19 ___ 21 ___ 23 ___ 27 ___ 32 ___ 33 ___ 35 ___

Count your check marks to get your **total task-oriented score.** ___

Interpretation of scores:

Range	Range		
People 0–7	Task 0–10	You are not involved enough in either the task or the people.	Uninvolved
People 0–7	Task 10–20	You tend to be autocratic, a whip-snapper. You get the job done, but at high emotional cost to your followers.	Task-oriented
People 8–15	Task 0–10	People are happy in their work, but sometimes at the expense of productivity.	People-oriented
People 8–15	Task 10–20	People enjoy working for you and are productive. They naturally expend energy because they get positive reinforcement for doing a good job.	Balanced

As a leader, most people tend to be more task-oriented or more people-oriented. Task orientation is concerned with getting the job done, while people orientation focuses on group interactions and the needs of individual workers. Effective leaders, however, are able to use both styles, depending on the situation. There may be times when a rush job demands great attention placed on task completion. During a time of low morale, though, sensitivity to workers' problems would be more appropriate. The best managers are able to balance both task and people concerns. Therefore a high score on both would show this balance. Ultimately, you will gain respect, admiration, and productivity from your workers.

Suggestions:
Uninvolved: Devise strategies for developing task-oriented and people-oriented styles.
Task-oriented: How can you develop a more people-oriented style? What problems might occur if you do not do so?
People-oriented: How can you develop a more task-oriented style? What problems might occur if you do not do so?
Balanced: Do you see any potential problems with your style? Are you a fully developed leader?

Self-Assessment 10.2: National Culture and Leadership

This instrument measures four of Hofstede's traditional dimensions of national culture-uncertainty avoidance, individualism, power distance, and masculinity. It also measures a fifth dimension, paternalism. Transfer your scores from the survey to the following chart to determine your own leadership orientation on each of these dimensions. Refer back to Chapter 2 for the definitions of each dimension.

- The closer your score to the maximum score, the higher you are on that dimension.
- Explore, relative to you, how the dimensions vary in strength.

Uncertainty Avoidance	Individualism	Power Distance	Paternalism	Masculinity
1 5	6 4	12 4	18 3	25 2
2 5	7 4	13 3	19 3	26 1
3 5	8 4	14 3	20 3	27 1
4 4	9 3	15 2	21 3	28 1
5 4	10 3	16 2	22 2	29 2
11 3	17 3	23 2		
		24 1		
Total 24/25	Total 21/30	Total 17/30	Total 14/35	Total 7/25
%Score ____	%Score ____	%Score ____	%Score ____	%Score ____

chapter eleven

LEARNING OBJECTIVES

By the end of this chapter, you will be able to do the following:

1. Define *conflict* and explain its underlying emotional components.
2. Distinguish between task, relationship, and process conflicts.
3. Differentiate between four different forms of conflict in organizational interactions.
4. Describe the various structural and personal sources of conflict in organizations.
5. Compare and contrast functional and dysfunctional conflict.
6. Describe three approaches that prevent dysfunctional organizational conflict.
7. Describe five different styles of conflict management using the dual-concerns model.
8. Explain six conflict management strategies that can be used to help disputants resolve their conflicts.
9. Define *negotiation* (bargaining), distinguish between distributive and integrative bargaining, and explain the bargaining zone model.

learning about the context

Alternative Dispute Resolution Helps the RCMP Address Internal Conflicts

Alternative dispute resolution (ADR) was introduced in January 1997 in the Ontario civil justice system. The Royal Canadian Mounted Police (RCMP) also adopted ADR in 1997 and was one of the first organizations in North America to see the "link between their approaches to conflict management, cultural transformation and service delivery." As the ADR system took hold, in addition to improving morale and relationships, it resulted in significant dollar savings. The RCMP has set up a National ADR Steering Committee and has created a permanent Office of the ADR Advisor. About 150 employees from across the force have received training in mediation and act as third parties to people in conflict. ADR coordinators participate in a cross-country video conference every month, which allows them to share experiences and ideas across divisions. In addition, three-day interest-based negotiation courses are offered throughout the year.

In the internal guide entitled "Let's Talk," ADR is defined as "the informal methods used to resolve disputes, such as simple negotiation and mediation, which are outside the formal grievance and discipline process." The objective of ADR at the RCMP is to offer a fair, friendly, flexible, and fast way for people to jointly work out a resolution to a dispute that leaves everyone happier with the outcome. The ADR system at the RCMP tries to resolve conflicts at the lowest possible level, create incentives to communicate, and include an explicit right for either party to withdraw.

If employees have conflicts with other employees that they cannot resolve on their own, they are encouraged to contact their ADR coordinator or their union rep to begin the mediation process. A simple mediation contract (that is destroyed at the conclusion of the mediation) is signed by the parties. The mediator does not take sides, but helps people develop their own creative solutions to problems. Upon resolution, a memorandum of understanding is drafted by the mediator using the language of the disputants.

In addition to training ADR mediators for each region of the force, conflict management has been included as one of the core functional competencies for management. The ADR process at the RCMP has been very successful. Employees have praise for the process as shown in the following quotation:

> The mediator was empathetic, non-judgmental and neutral to both parties involved. I walked away feeling I had been fairly treated by all concerned. What was most interesting was to be able to view this matter from the perspective of the employer.... I congratulate and fully support those responsible for initiating this method to resolve disputes.

SOURCES: J. F. Lynch, "Beyond ADR: A Systems Approach to Conflict Management," *Negotiation Journal* 17, no. 3 (July 2001): 212; B. Zanin, "The Evolution of ADR: Our System Of Conflict Resolution Has Come To A Turning Point," *Pony Express* (RCMP), July 5, 2000, http://www.rcmp-learning.org/adr/adr0007.htm; RCMP, *Let's Talk ADR: A Guide,* May 26, 1999, http://www.rcmp-learning.org/docs/ecdd1224.htm; RCMP, "ADR Initiative," *Pony Express,* http://www.rcmp-learning.org/adr/adr0001.htm; RCMP, *Alternative Dispute Resolution in Six Easy Steps,* March 18, 1998, http://www.rcmp-learning.org/docs/ecdd1127.htm.

Conflict is an inevitable part of life in any organization that includes a hierarchy, unequal distribution of power, and limited resources. Increasing competition and globalization exacerbate the conflict by magnifying differences among people in terms of personality, values, attitudes, perceptions, languages, cultures, and national backgrounds.[1] These differences bring with them greater potential for incompatibility and conflict. In addition, as organizations become flatter and more team-based, workers become more interdependent and are responsible for more decision making.[2] The frequency and severity of work-related conflict and harassment is increasing, as is the demand for mediators in Canada.[3] Conflict in organizations can take many forms ranging from "... informal arguments over office space to formal lawsuits over employment issues that can cost organizations thousands of dollars and person hours."[4] Estimates show that managers spend about 25 percent of their time dealing with conflict, which is the equivalent of one day every week.[5] Many employees and managers lack the self-confidence to deal with workplace conflict and "simply hope it'll magically disappear."[6]

The RCMP's implementation of an alternative dispute resolution (ADR) system is one example of how Canadian organizations are responding to the increasing amounts of interpersonal, group, and organizational conflict. In addition to introducing organization-wide ADR processes, some companies are turning to in-house conflict coaches and are creating special conflict management jobs, such as facilitators and ombudsmen.[7]

In the first part of this chapter, we define conflict and explain its underlying emotional components. Then we distinguish task, relationship, and process conflict and describe the various forms of inter-organizational, inter-group, intra-group, and interpersonal conflict. We then explore the various sources of conflict that emerge from the *structure* of the organization itself as well as *personal* sources of conflict, such as personality differences and ineffective communication. We end the first part of the chapter by exploring conflict outcomes and whether conflict is functional (healthy) or dysfunctional (unhealthy) for the organization.

The second half of the chapter explores the variety of conflict-management strategies because the most critical determinant of whether conflict outcomes are functional or dysfunctional is the manner in which the conflict is handled. First, we review three *preventative* conflict-management strategies. Then we describe the dual-concerns model of conflict management, followed by an overview of six methods for managing conflict effectively. We conclude the chapter with a brief look at issues in negotiations and bargaining.

Define *conflict* and explain its underlying emotional components.

THE NATURE OF CONFLICT IN ORGANIZATIONS

conflict
The perception, in an interdependent relationship, of incompatible wishes, goals, attitudes, emotions, or behaviours.

Conflict is the perception, in an interdependent relationship, of incompatible wishes, goals, attitudes, emotions, or behaviours.[8] Contemporary definitions of conflict assume that "to be in conflict is to be emotionally activated."[9] Many people feel uncomfortable with conflict because of the accompanying emotion, and in the Western world, conflict at work is more often viewed to be negative than positive.

Conflict and Emotion

behavioural component of emotion
The verbal and nonverbal messages we express when we communicate.

physiological component of emotion
The bodily experience of emotion.

It is important to understand the behavioural, physiological, and cognitive components of the emotional experience.[10] The **behavioural component of emotion** includes the verbal and nonverbal messages we express when we communicate. Most emotional expression occurs nonverbally through facial expressions, voice, and gestures; often, a mismatch between our verbal and nonverbal messages (incongruence, discussed in Chapter 6) can be a conflict trigger. It is because of this behavioural component of emotion that you will see many parallels between effective conflict management and supportive communication. The **physiological component of emotion** is "the bodily experience of emotion; it is the way emotion makes us feel and thus what makes emotional experience so compelling,"[11] The **cognitive component of emotion** involves the way we experience an emotion, which depends, in part, upon the way our mind appraises or interprets it. For example, the same joke might upset me while it makes you laugh. The way one's mind interprets a situation is key to understanding organizational conflict.[12]

cognitive component of emotion
The way our mind appraises or interprets emotion.

Task, Relationship, and Process Conflict

Distinguish between task, relationship, and process conflicts.

Traditional definitions of conflict have identified two distinct types of conflict, which have been called task and relationship (or socio-emotional) conflict. **Relationship (affective) conflict** is defined as interpersonal incompatibilities and typically includes feelings of anger, tension, and friction.[13] In contrast, **task (cognitive) conflict** is defined as differences in viewpoints and opinions that pertain to group tasks. Task conflict is evident when there are disagreements over different ideas, differences of opinions, and differences about the content of decisions. Task conflict may coincide with animated discussions but, by definition, have less of the intense negative emotions that are more commonly associated with relationship conflict.[14] Research suggests that people behave differently when involved in task and relationship conflicts.[15] While relationship conflicts tend to hinder group functioning, task conflict can actually promote group functioning and creativity.[16] Certain types of task conflicts, such as values conflicts, do, however, become more intense than others. Values conflicts are those that arise out of opposing principles or ideals involved in carrying out a task, and are often resolved with the help of a mediator or facilitator.[17]

relationship (affective) conflict
Interpersonal incompatibilities, typically including feelings of tension and friction.

task (cognitive) conflict
Differences in viewpoints and opinions pertaining to group task.

Contemporary OB researchers have also suggested a third type of conflict, called "process conflict." **Process conflict** is defined as controversies about aspects of *how* task accomplishment will proceed.[18] One recent study of MBA student teams showed that high-performing teams had low but increasing levels of process conflict, low levels of relationship conflict that rose slightly as deadlines got closer, and moderate levels of task conflict at the midpoint of group interaction. This relates to the punctuated equilibrium model of team development that was discussed in Chapter 7. Low-performing teams actually had a dip in process conflict during the midpoint of group interaction. The researchers wanted to know what factors led to this ideal conflict pattern in high-performing teams. They found that shared value systems, high levels of trust, and open discussions produced the ideal pattern.[19] Using Self-Assessment 11.1, explore task, relationship, and process conflict within a team that you are currently a member.

process conflict
Controversies about aspects of *how* task accomplishment will proceed.

? Application & Analysis

SELF-ASSESSMENT 11.1: ASSESS YOUR TEAM'S CONFLICT

Think of a team you are a member of, or one you were part of in the past. Answer the following eight questions regarding that team:

1. How much emotional tension was there in your team?

   No tension — Lots of tension

   1 2 3 4 5

2. How much conflict of ideas was there in your team?

   No idea conflict — Lots of idea conflict

   1 2 3 4 5

3. How often did people get angry while working in your team?

   Never — Often

   1 2 3 4 5

4. How different were your views on the content of your project?

   Very similar views — Very different views

   1 2 3 4 5

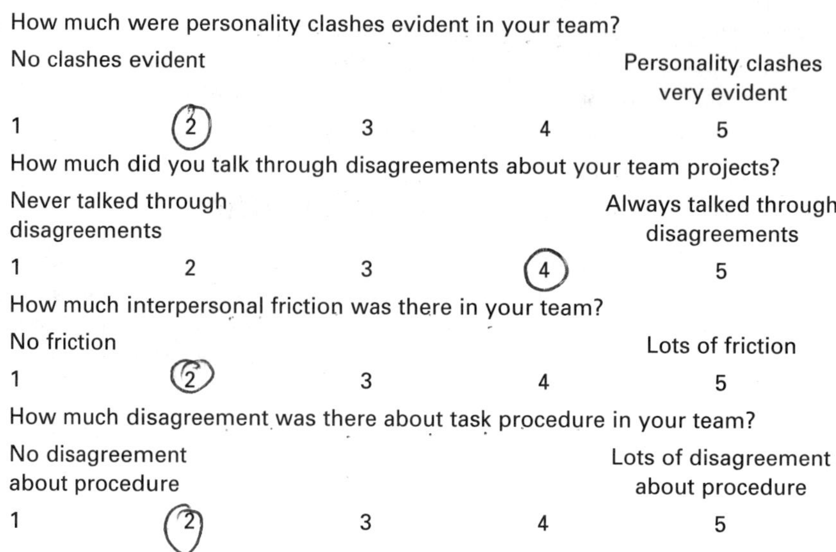
5. How much were personality clashes evident in your team?

No clashes evident				Personality clashes very evident
1	2	3	4	5

6. How much did you talk through disagreements about your team projects?

Never talked through disagreements				Always talked through disagreements
1	2	3	4	5

7. How much interpersonal friction was there in your team?

No friction				Lots of friction
1	2	3	4	5

8. How much disagreement was there about task procedure in your team?

No disagreement about procedure				Lots of disagreement about procedure
1	2	3	4	5

For scoring instructions, please go to the end of the chapter, p. 360.

SOURCE: Adapted from K. Jehn, "A Multimethod Examination of the Benefits and Detriments of Intragroup Conflict," *Administrative Science Quarterly* 40 (1995): 256–82. Reprinted by permission of the Administrative Science Quarterly.

3

Differentiate between four different forms of conflict in organizational interactions.

Forms of Conflict

Conflict is manifested in many different forms within and between organizations. These forms are interorganizational, intergroup, intragroup, and interpersonal conflict. We now briefly discuss each of these forms of conflict.

Interorganizational Conflict

interorganizational conflict Conflict that occurs between two or more organizations.

Conflict that occurs between two or more organizations is called **interorganizational conflict.** Competition, corporate takeovers, mergers and acquisitions, and new organizational arrangements such as strategic alliances often heighten interorganizational conflict. The conflict between Napster, the Internet music service company, and several record companies is an example of interorganizational conflict. Conflicts between organizations abound. Some of these conflicts can be functional, as when firms improve the quality of their products and services in the spirit of healthy competition, while others can be dysfunctional and destructive, such as the serious safety violations at Jetsgo during their price war with Air Canada, prior to Jetsgo going bankrupt.

Copyright infringement and antitrust laws are typical sources of interorganizational conflict in today's corporate environment. Here, Microsoft CEO Bill Gates testifies before a U.S. Senate panel, backing his company's case at an antitrust trial.

Intergroup Conflict

intergroup conflict Conflict that occurs between different groups or teams within an organization.

When conflict occurs between groups or departments, it is known as **intergroup conflict.** Intergroup conflict is becoming more and more prevalent and is manifested in the frequent "turf wars" between managers.[20] Groups in conflict tend to develop an "us against them" mentality whereby each sees the other team as the enemy, becomes more hostile, and decreases its communication with the other group.[21] These conflicts can lead to win–lose outcomes and negative consequences like territoriality, aggression, and prejudice toward the other group can result.[22] On the other hand, intergroup conflict can lead to functional outcomes such as re-evaluation and introspection within each group.

Intragroup (Team) Conflict

Conflict that occurs within a single group or team is called **intragroup conflict.** As discussed in Chapter 7, team conflict is a natural part of a team's development and can cause very negative outcomes for a team, if it is not confronted and managed during the storming or transition stage. We discuss strategies for managing conflict within a team in the next section of the chapter.

intragroup conflict
Conflict that occurs within a single group or team.

Interpersonal Conflict

Conflict between two or more people is called **interpersonal conflict.** As mentioned when we explored personal sources of conflict, one source is the different conflict styles that the two or more people bring to the dispute. We discuss interpersonal conflict management styles in depth later on in this chapter.

interpersonal conflict
Conflict that occurs between two or more individuals.

SOURCES OF CONFLICT IN ORGANIZATIONS

4

Describe the various structural and personal sources of conflict in organizations.

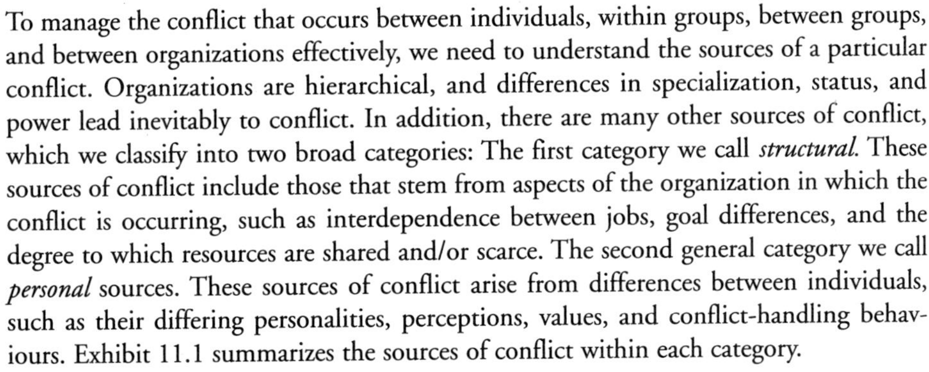

To manage the conflict that occurs between individuals, within groups, between groups, and between organizations effectively, we need to understand the sources of a particular conflict. Organizations are hierarchical, and differences in specialization, status, and power lead inevitably to conflict. In addition, there are many other sources of conflict, which we classify into two broad categories: The first category we call *structural.* These sources of conflict include those that stem from aspects of the organization in which the conflict is occurring, such as interdependence between jobs, goal differences, and the degree to which resources are shared and/or scarce. The second general category we call *personal* sources. These sources of conflict arise from differences between individuals, such as their differing personalities, perceptions, values, and conflict-handling behaviours. Exhibit 11.1 summarizes the sources of conflict within each category.

Structural Sources of Conflict

The causes of conflict related to the organization's structure include specialization, interdependence, common resources, goal differences, authority relationships, status and power differences, and jurisdictional ambiguities.

- *Specialization and goal differences:* When jobs are highly specialized, employees become experts at certain tasks and often have different goals. A classic conflict of specialization may occur between salespeople and engineers. Engineers are technical specialists responsible for product design and quality. Salespeople are marketing

EXHIBIT 11.1

Causes of Conflict in Organizations

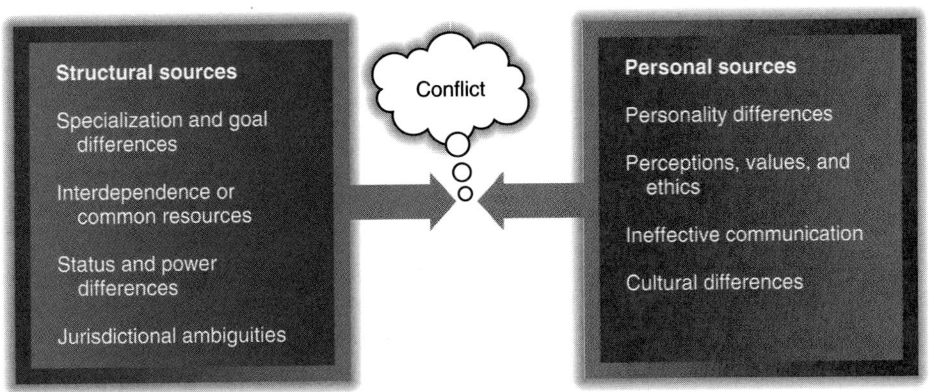

experts and liaisons with customers. Salespeople are often accused of making delivery promises to customers that engineers cannot keep because the sales force lacks the technical knowledge necessary to develop realistic delivery deadlines.

- *Interdependence or common resources:* Work that is interdependent requires groups or individuals to depend on one another to accomplish goals.[23] Depending on other people to get work done is fine when the process works smoothly. When there is a problem, however, it becomes very easy to blame the other party, and conflict escalates. Any time multiple parties must share resources, there is potential for conflict.[24] This potential is enhanced when the shared resources become scarce.
- *Status and power differences:* Most organizations are hierarchical and have status and power differences between management and nonmanagement workers. Managers may enjoy privileges—such as flexible schedules, personal telephone calls at work, and longer lunch hours—that are not available to nonmanagement employees. Also, individuals higher up in the hierarchy tend to have greater decision-making responsibility. This may result in resentment and conflict if lower level employees do not feel they have a voice.
- *Jurisdictional ambiguity:* The presence of unclear lines of responsibility within an organization, called **jurisdictional ambiguity,** can be a source of conflict.[25] When there is no definite source of responsibility for a problem, workers tend to "pass the buck," or avoid dealing with the problem. Conflicts emerge over responsibility for the problem.

jurisdictional ambiguity
The presence of unclear lines of responsibility within an organization.

Personal Sources of Conflict

The causes of conflict that arise from individual differences include skills and abilities, personalities, perceptions, values and ethics, emotions, communication barriers, and cultural differences.

- *Personality differences:* Individuals do not leave their personalities at the doorstep when they enter the workplace. Personality conflicts are realities in organizations. One personality trait that many people find difficult to deal with is abrasiveness or bullying.[26] Organizational Reality 11.1 shows how bosses perceived to be bullies have been coached to change their behaviour.
- *Perceptions, values, and ethics:* Differences in perception can also lead to conflict. For example, bosses and their employees may have differing perceptions about an organizational change, or team members may have differing perceptions about what is required in a group project. Also, students in a project team may have different work ethics or standards. When conflicts about values or ethics do arise, heated disagreement is common because of the personal nature of the differences.
- *Ineffective communication:* Nonsupportive communication and the many communication barriers discussed in Chapter 6, such as status differences, ambiguity, and information overload, are often the causes of conflict. Sometimes the cause is misunderstanding or mixed messages. At other times the cause relates to emotions and the fact that the communication causes defensiveness on the part of the listener.
- *Cultural differences:* Although cultural differences are assets in organizations, sometimes they can be seen as sources of conflict. Often, these conflicts stem from a lack of understanding of another culture. In one MBA class, for example, Indian students were horrified when Canadian students challenged the professor. Meanwhile, the Canadian students thought the students from India were too passive. Subsequent discussions revealed that professors in India expected to be treated deferentially and with great respect. While students might challenge an idea vigorously, they would rarely challenge the professor.

organizational reality 11.1

Bully Bosses

Abrasive managers often race up the corporate ladder and then run into a wall because of "red ink behaviours": destructive behaviours that cost their companies money. In the past, these individuals were encouraged to leave or, more often, fired. Now, consultants are offering programs to rehabilitate these "bully bosses" to resuscitate their stalled careers. Companies like Cisco, Hewlett-Packard, and Sun Microsystems are sending their bullies to training in order to save their talent but lose their abrasive behaviour.

At the Growth & Leadership Center in Silicon Valley, bullies go through a three-month coaching program aimed at improving their people skills. Executive coach Jean Hollands, leading one training session, pointed out one woman, saying "Look at her, she's so adorable. Do you know everyone around her thinks she's one piece of horror?" Both men and women exhibit bullying behaviours, including tantrum throwing and silently withholding support from subordinates. In the coaching program, bullies are taught behavior modification techniques. They learn to soften their voice and eyes, show vulnerability and patience, and communicate empathy. They're taught to pick up the pieces of "shattered glass" (all the damaged relationships they created) by apologizing for mistakes and repairing relationships. They learn better conflict management skills, and that they don't have to confront people at every provocation.

Do these programs work? Only time will tell. Initially, the "bullies" report satisfaction with their new and improved skills, and their companies seem pleased—they continue to send bullies through the program. The real test will be determining whether these kinder and gentler behaviours are a permanent part of the trainee's behaviour, or whether they will relapse into bullying mode when faced with conflicts on the job.

SOURCE: M. Conlin, "Tough Love for Techie Souls," *Business Week Online,* November 29, 1999.

Application & Analysis

IDENTIFY ALL THE SOURCES OF THIS TEAM'S CONFLICT—PART 1

The OB team consisted of five university students (two males and three females) who had been working on their case analysis for the past four weeks. The team will be getting a group grade. Three of the five students wanted to get an A on the project and two just wanted to pass. One of the students was a mature student who was also working full time and another student had failed the course last term and was retaking it because it was a required course. The team was having trouble scheduling meetings at times that were suitable to all concerned and there was a lot of anger and frustration expressed in the e-mails that went back and forth.

Using the examples of structural and personal sources of conflict just reviewed, identify and label all the sources of conflict in this team.

IS ORGANIZATIONAL CONFLICT HEALTHY OR UNHEALTHY?

Compare and contrast functional and dysfunctional conflict.

There have been a number of approaches to exploring the question of whether conflict is healthy or unhealthy. Early approaches assumed that conflict was detrimental to organizational performance and therefore should be eliminated. The later interactionist viewpoint proposed that task conflict had a curvilinear relationship to organizational performance, as shown in Exhibit 11.2.[27] This means that too little conflict lowers performance because it leads to complacency while too much conflict lowers performance because stimulation levels are too high and energy is diverted away from the task at hand.

Another approach to determining whether conflict is healthy or unhealthy is to observe whether its consequences or outcomes are positive (functional) or negative (dysfunctional). When conflict leads to positive outcomes it is called **functional conflict**,

functional conflict
A healthy, constructive disagreement between two or more people. Functional conflict can produce new ideas, learning, and growth among individuals.

EXHIBIT 11.2

The Curvilinear Relationship between Task Conflict and Performance

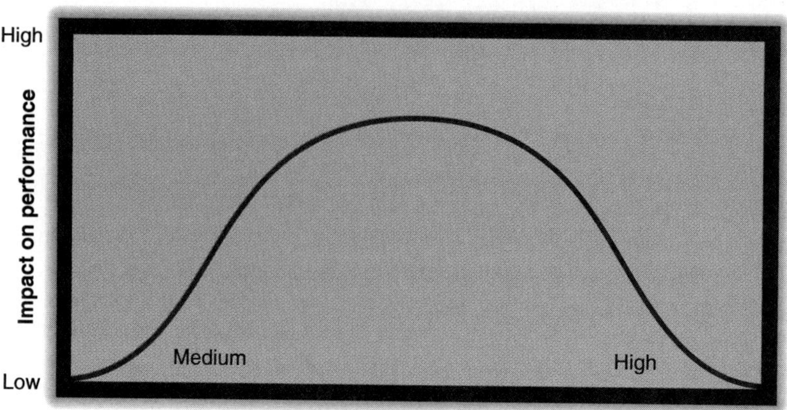

which is defined as a healthy, constructive disagreement between two or more people. Functional conflict can produce new ideas, learning, positive change, and growth among individuals.[28] When conflict is functional, individuals develop a better awareness of themselves and others. In addition, functional conflict can improve working relationships: when two parties work through their disagreements, they feel they have accomplished something together. By releasing tensions and solving problems in working together, morale is improved.[29] William Wrigley, Jr., the chewing gum magnate, is quoted as having said: "When two people in business always agree, one of them is unnecessary."[30] The positive and negative consequences of conflict are summarized in Exhibit 11.3.

Today's enlightened managers do not view conflict as problem; rather, they view it as a signal that something needs their attention and they are grateful for the early warning sign.[31] Because it tends to encourage creativity among individuals, this positive form of conflict can translate into increased productivity and organizational effectiveness if managed properly.[32] Also, managers sometimes actively stimulate conflict by appointing a "devil's advocate" when they suspect their group is suffering from "groupthink."[33] This was discussed in the context of decision making in Chapter 8.

EXHIBIT 11.3

Consequences of Conflict

Positive Consequences (Functional)	Negative Consequences (Dysfunctional)
• Leads to new ideas	• Diverts energy from work
• Stimulates creativity	• Threatens psychological well-being
• Motivates change	• Wastes resources
• Promotes organizational vitality	• Creates a negative climate
• Helps individuals and groups establish identities	• Breaks down group cohesion
• Serves as a safety valve to indicate problems	• Can increase hostility and aggressive behaviours

Recently a hockey dad engaged in dysfunctional conflict with his 9-year-old son's coach. He was charged with assault and was banned from attending games for five years.

When conflict leads to negative outcomes it is called **dysfunctional conflict**. This is defined as an unhealthy, destructive disagreement between two or more people. Its danger is that it takes the focus away from the work to be done and places the focus on the conflict itself and the parties involved. Excessive conflict drains energy that could be used more productively. Disagreements that involve anger and resentment directed at specific individuals rather than specific ideas are dysfunctional.[34] Individuals involved in dysfunctional conflict often rely on threats, deception, and verbal abuse to communicate. In dysfunctional conflict, the losses to both parties may exceed any potential gain from the conflict. In most cases, whether conflict becomes functional or dysfunctional depends on the extent to which one's emotions are involved, and the way that the parties attempt to manage the conflict.

dysfunctional conflict
An unhealthy, destructive disagreement between two or more people. Its danger is that it takes the focus away from the work to be done and places the focus on the conflict itself and the parties involved.

Application & Evaluation

EVALUATE THIS TEAM CONFLICT—PART 2

Is the conflict described in "Evaluate This Team Conflict—Part 1" an example of a task or relationship conflict? Is it functional or dysfunctional?

PREVENTING AND MANAGING CONFLICT

Organizational behaviour research has discovered many factors that prevent dysfunctional conflict and factors that either contribute or detract from effectively managing conflict when it occurs. A **conflict management strategy** is any action taken by a disputant or a third party to try to manage or resolve a conflict. In this second part of the chapter we explore a number of approaches to managing conflict.

conflict management strategy
Any action taken by a disputant or a third party to try to manage or resolve a conflict.

We begin with a brief overview of how organizations can create conflict-positive cultures and structures, thereby preventing dysfunctional conflict in the first place. Then we explore how disputants can manage their conflicts directly, using appropriate conflict management styles to fit their situation. This is followed by an overview of six conflict management strategies that organizations can use to help disputants resolve their conflicts. Next we provide an overview of third-party conflict management strategies and finally we explore the conflict management strategies involved in negotiation and bargaining.

Describe three approaches that prevent dysfunctional organizational conflict.

PREVENTATIVE CONFLICT MANAGEMENT STRATEGIES

A number of approaches have been found to prevent dysfunctional conflict in the first place: (1) creating a conflict positive organization, (2) including conflict resolution roles in an organization's structure, and (3) rotating employees through different jobs or departments.

Association for Conflict Resolution (ACR)

The Association for Conflict Resolution (ACR) is a professional organization dedicated to enhancing the practice and public understanding of conflict resolution. ACR represents and serves a diverse national and international audience that includes more than 6000 mediators, arbitrators, facilitators, educators, and others involved in the field of conflict resolution and collaborative decision making.
http://www.acrnet.org

Creating a Conflict-Positive Organization

Dean Tjosvold argues that well-managed conflict adds to an organization's innovation and productivity.[35] He discusses procedures for making conflict positive. Too many organizations take a win-lose, competitive approach to conflict or avoid conflict altogether. These two approaches view conflict as negative. A positive view of conflict, in contrast, leads to win-win solutions. See Exhibit 11.4 for a visual representation of these three organizational views of conflict.

According to Tjosvold, four interrelated steps are involved in creating a conflict-positive organization:[36]

1. *Value diversity and confront differences.* Differences should be seen as opportunities for innovation, and diversity should be celebrated. Open and honest confrontations bring out differences, and they are essential for positive conflict.
2. *Seek mutual benefits, and unite behind cooperative goals.* Conflicts have to be managed together. Through conflict, individuals learn how much they depend on one another. Even when employees share goals, they may differ on how to accomplish the goals. The important point is that they are moving toward the same objectives. Joint rewards should be given to the whole team for cooperative behaviour.
3. *Empower employees to feel confident and skillful.* People must be made to feel that they control their conflicts and that they can deal with their differences productively. When they do so, they should be recognized.
4. *Take stock to reward success and learn from mistakes.* Employees should be encouraged to appreciate one another's strengths and weaknesses and to talk directly about them. They should celebrate their conflict management successes and work out plans for ways they can improve in the future.

EXHIBIT 11.4

Three Organizational Views of Conflict

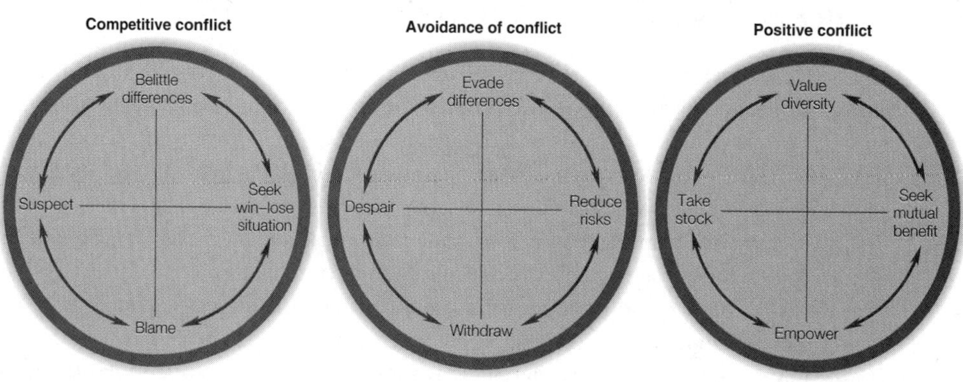

SOURCE: *The Conflict Positive Organization*, by Tjosvold, © 1991. Reprinted by permission of Prentice-Hall, Inc., Upper Saddle River, N.J.

Build Conflict Management Roles into the Organizational Structure

Another way to prevent dysfunctional conflict is to build conflict management roles into the structure of the organization, as the RCMP did with their Office of the ADR Advisor, discussed in the chapter opener. The office of the employee ombudsman and the formal complaints process at the Royal Bank of Canada is another example of building a conflict management role into the structure.[37] Nayaree Sunnasy is the employee ombudsman and it is her job to field employee complaints and referee finding a solution. Each year, her mediators handle more than 1000 work conflicts, at least one-third of which tend to be complaints by managers.[38] Roles such as these are often referred to as "integrator" roles, which are filled by those who act as a liaison between groups with very different interests.[39] Creating the integrator role is a way of opening dialogue between groups that have difficulty communicating.

Using cross-functional teams is another way of designing the organization's structure to prevent and manage conflict. In the old methods of designing new products in organizations, many departments had to contribute, and delays resulted from difficulties in coordinating the activities of the various departments. Using a cross-functional team made up of members from different departments improves coordination and reduces delays by allowing many activities to be performed at the same time rather than sequentially.[40] Read more about the increasing use of integrator roles and cross-functional teams in Chapter 14.

Rotate Employees

Many companies use a job rotation strategy to minimize the likelihood of conflict between people in diverse roles. For example, Toyota minimizes this source of conflict by rotating its senior people to areas outside their expertise.[41] The job rotation gives each executive insight into the other functions, thereby improving communication and understanding. The job rotation strategy minimizes sources of dysfunctional conflict based upon diverse skills, abilities, and specialization.[42]

INTERPERSONAL CONFLICT MANAGEMENT STYLES

Describe five different styles of conflict management using the dual-concerns model.

Even when an organization has been designed to minimize dysfunctional conflict, it will still occur. Most often it is the disputants themselves who try to manage conflicts that they have with each other. Each of us approaches an interpersonal conflict in a different way. Our style for managing conflict depends in part upon our personality, our past experiences with conflict (good and bad), and the role models we have had in our life. Our style may also vary depending upon who is involved or whether the conflict is a task or relationship conflict. The main factor that distinguishes functional from dysfunctional conflict is not the source itself, or the parties involved, but rather, *the way the parties address the conflict.* Conflict management skills have been found to be a major predictor of managerial success.[43] At Intel, for example, all full-time employees are required to take a half-day class on "constructive confrontation," where they learn how to fight about ideas in an atmosphere of mutual respect.[44] Be sure to complete Self-Assessment 11.2 to assess *your own* conflict management style, prior to reading this section.

Research has identified five general approaches to handling conflict, and each of them is classified based upon a dual-concerns model.[45] The two concerns are (1) the degree of assertiveness (the extent to which the person wants his or her goals met, also called "concern for self"), and (2) the degree of cooperativeness (the extent to which the person wants to see the other party's concerns met, also called "concern for other.")[46] Exhibit 11.5 graphs these two dimensions with the five conflict management styles, which are called avoiding, accommodating (or obliging), competing (or dominating, forcing), compromising, and collaborating (or integrating, problem solving). We now

SELF-ASSESSMENT 11.2: WHAT IS YOUR CONFLICT MANAGEMENT STYLE?

For each of the 15 items, indicate how often you rely on that tactic by circling the appropriate number.

	Rarely				Always
1. I argue my case with my co-workers to show the merits of my position.	1	2	3	4	5
2. I negotiate with my co-workers so that a compromise can be reached.	1	2	3	4	5
3. I try to satisfy the expectations of my co-workers.	1	2	3	4	5
4. I try to investigate an issue with my co-workers to find a solution that is acceptable to us.	1	2	3	4	5
5. I am firm in pursuing my side of the issue.	1	2	3	4	5
6. I attempt to avoid being "put on the spot" and try to keep my conflict with my co-workers to myself.	1	2	3	4	5
7. I hold on to my solution to a problem.	1	2	3	4	5
8. I use "give and take" so that a compromise can be made.	1	2	3	4	5
9. I exchange accurate information with my co-workers to solve a problem together.	1	2	3	4	5
10. I avoid open discussion of my differences with my co-workers.	1	2	3	4	5
11. I accommodate the wishes of my co-workers.	1	2	3	4	5
12. I try to bring all our concerns out in the open so that the issues can be resolved in the best possible way.	1	2	3	4	5
13. I propose a middle ground for breaking deadlocks.	1	2	3	4	5
14. I go along with the suggestions of my co-workers.	1	2	3	4	5
15. I try to keep my disagreements with my co-workers to myself in order to avoid hard feelings.	1	2	3	4	5

For scoring instructions, please go to the end of the chapter, p. 361.

describe each style in more detail and add a cautionary note that the degree a person shows "concern for self" and "concern for other" in a conflict is very much "in the eye of the beholder." For this reason, it is helpful to obtain feedback from the "other" as to how one's conflict management style is perceived. Ask someone to fill out Self-Assessment 11.2 to determine their perception of your conflict management style and compare it to your own.

Avoiding Style

avoiding
Style of conflict management that is a deliberate decision to take no action on a conflict or to stay out of a conflict situation. It indicates low concern for self and low concern for other.

The **avoiding** style of conflict management indicates low concern for others and for self. It reflects indifference to the concerns of either party.[47] It is low on both assertiveness and cooperativeness. Avoiding is a deliberate decision to take no action on a conflict or to stay out of a conflict situation. Avoiding has been associated with withdrawal, buck-passing, or sidestepping situations.[48] When the issue is trivial, or parties are angry and need time to cool down, it may be best to use avoidance. There is a potential danger in using an avoiding style too often, however. Research shows that overuse of this style results in negative evaluations from others in the workplace.[49]

EXHIBIT 11.5

Conflict Management Styles

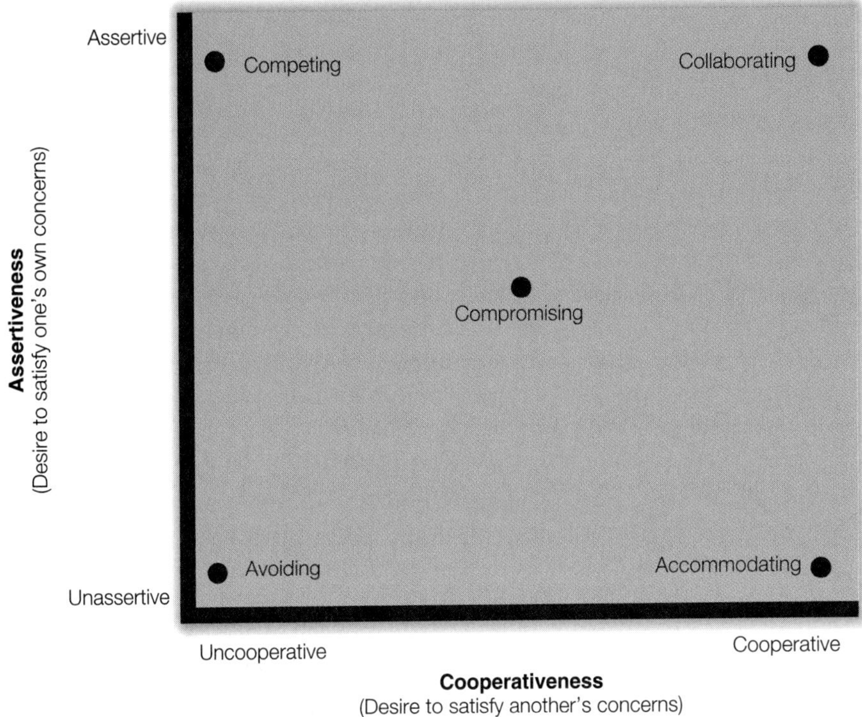

SOURCE: K. W. Thomas, "Conflict and Conflict Management," in *Handbook of Industrial and Organizational Psychology,* ed. M. D. Dunnette (Chicago: Rand McNally, 1976), 900. Used with permission of M. D. Dunnette.

Accommodating Style

The **accommodating** style (also known as obliging) indicates low concern for self and high concern for others. It means giving in to the other's wishes without attending to one's own.[50] This style is associated with attempting to play down differences and emphasize commonalities to satisfy the other person.[51] Accommodating is cooperative but unassertive. There is an element of self-sacrifice in this style that may take the form of "Selfless generosity, charity, or obedience to the other person's orders."[52] Appropriate situations for accommodating include times when you find you are wrong, when you want to let the other party have his or her way so that that individual will owe you similar treatment later. Over-reliance on accommodating has its dangers. Managers who constantly defer to others may find that others lose respect for them. In addition, accommodating managers may become frustrated because their own needs are never met, and they may lose self-esteem.[53]

accommodating
The style of conflict management (also known as obliging) that involves giving in to the other's wishes without attending to one's own. It indicates low concern for self and high concern for others.

Competing Style

Competing indicates high concern for self and low concern for others. It means the individual's pursuing his or her wishes at the other's expense. It is also known as dominating and forcing.[54] Competing is a style that is very assertive and uncooperative and has been identified with a win–lose orientation and bullying.[55] This style relies on the use of position power, aggression, verbal dominance, and perseverance. Often, this style is associated with bullying, confrontational remarks, accusations, personal criticism, threats, antagonistic jokes, or denial of responsibility at the expense of the other person.[56]

competing
The style of conflict management in which the individual pursues his or her wishes at the other's expense (also know as dominating and forcing). It indicates high concern for self and low concern for others.

However, in an emergency or in situations where you know you are right, it may be appropriate to put your foot down. Relying solely on competing strategies is dangerous, though, because people in authority who do so may become reluctant to admit when they are wrong, and may find themselves surrounded by people who are afraid to disagree with them.

Collaborating Style

collaborating
The style of conflict management (also known as integrating or problem solving) in which an attempt is made to fully satisfy the wishes of both parties. It indicates high concern for self and high concern for others.

Teambonding
Teambonding.com is a creative consulting firm that uses situational role-playing games and scenarios to help facilitate effective teamwork and cooperation. Visit the site to learn more about how its services help organizations manage intragroup conflict.
http://www.teambonding.com

The **collaborating** style (also known as integrating or problem solving) indicates high concern for self and high concern for others. It represents a desire to fully satisfy the wishes of both parties. Collaborating is an ideal win–win style that is high on both assertiveness and cooperativeness.[57] High degrees of collaboration involve openness, exchange of information, and examination of differences to reach an effective solution that is acceptable to both parties.[58] Conflicting parties tend to be more collaborative when an issue is complex and mutual commitment is indispensable or when it is clear that one party alone does not possess a solution to the problem. A collaborative approach is more likely to be taken when adequate time is available. Also, when the conflict involves a significant long term relationship, collaborating is recommended because it leads to improved relationships and effective performance.[59]

In a study involving 100 randomly paired dyads of business students, the collaborative conflict style was "generally perceived as the most appropriate (in terms of being both a polite, pro-social strategy and an adaptive, situationally appropriate strategy) and most effective style."[60] Collaboration may be effective in times when both parties need to be committed to a final solution or when a combination of different perspectives can be formed into a solution. Collaborating takes time and requires open, trusting behaviour and sharing information for the benefit of both parties.

Compromising Style

compromising
The style of conflict management that involves seeking an outcome midway between the preferred outcomes of both parties. It indicates intermediate concern for self and others.

The **compromising** style indicates intermediate concern for self and others. It means seeking an outcome that is midway between the preferred outcomes of both parties. Compromising is intermediate in both assertiveness and cooperativeness, because each party must give up something to reach a solution to the conflict. Compromises are often made in the final hours of union-management negotiations, when time is of the essence. Compromise may be an effective backup style when efforts toward collaboration are not successful.[61] Compromise means partially surrendering one's position for the sake of coming to terms. The solutions reached may be only temporary, and often compromises do nothing to improve relationships between the parties in the conflict. While it is

Knowledge & Application

CLASSIFYING CONFLICT MANAGEMENT STYLES

You are visiting a friend and his/her partner and you overhear the following dialogue:

Partner: You are such a slob. If you don't clean up those dishes from now on, I'm leaving!

Friend: But it was your turn to do dishes this week.

Partner: No way. You know I'm studying for the CA exam.

Friend: But I'm studying for the GMATs.

Partner: Yeah, but your exam isn't for another two weeks.

Friend: Fine, I'll do them.

Based on this short dialogue, use Exhibit 11.5 to classify: (1) your friend and (2) his or her partner's conflict management styles in this situation. Was the friend's style appropriate in the situation?

important to recognize that, by definition, compromises are not optimal solutions, in reality, many conflicts that are approached with collaborative styles do in fact involve some compromising along the way. Research on the five styles of conflict management indicates that although most managers favour a certain style, they do have the capacity to change styles as the situation demands.[62] A study of project managers found that managers who used a combination of competing and avoiding styles were seen as ineffective by the engineers who worked on their project teams.[63]

In another study of conflicts between R&D project managers and technical staff, competing and avoiding styles resulted in more frequent conflict and lower performance, whereas the collaborating style resulted in less frequent conflict and better performance.[64] Dean Tjosvold's suggestions for situations in which each conflict management style is most appropriate are summarized in Exhibit 11.6.

EXHIBIT 11.6

Uses of Five Styles of Conflict Management

Competing

1. When quick, decisive action is vital (e.g., emergencies).
2. On important issues where unpopular actions need implementing (e.g., cost cutting, enforcing unpopular rules, discipline).
3. On issues vital to company welfare when you know you are right.
4. Against people who take advantage of noncompetitive behaviour.

Collaborating

1. When the issue is complex and mutual commitment is indispensable.
2. When one party alone does not possess a solution to the problem.
3. When time is available.
4. When your objective is to learn.
5. To merge insights from people with different perspectives.
6. To work through feelings that have interfered with a relationship.

Compromising

1. When goals are important, but not worth the effort or potential disruption of more assertive modes.
2. When opponents with equal power are committed to mutually exclusive goals.
3. To achieve temporary settlements to complex issues.
4. To arrive at expedient solutions under time pressure.
5. As a backup when a win–win is not available as an option.

Avoiding

1. When an issue is trivial, or more important issues are pressing.
2. When you perceive no chance of satisfying your concerns.
3. When potential disruption outweighs the benefits of resolution.
4. To let people cool down and regain perspective.
5. When gathering information supersedes immediate decision.
6. When others can resolve the conflict more effectively.
7. When issues seem tangential or symptomatic of other issues.

Accommodating

1. When you find you are wrong—to allow a better position to be heard, to learn, and to show your reasonableness.
2. When issues are more important to others than to you. To satisfy others and maintain cooperation.
3. To build social credits for later issue, and build reciprocity.
4. To minimize loss when you are outmatched and losing.
5. When harmony and stability are especially important.
6. To allow employees to develop by learning from mistakes.

SOURCE: Adapted from *The Conflict Positive Organization* by Tjosvold, © 1991. Reprinted by permission of Prentice-Hall, Inc., Upper Saddle River, N.J.

Studies that compare conflict style preferences internationally suggest some interesting differences. See Organizational Reality 11.2 to read more about cultural differences between Turkish, Jordanian, and U.S. managers in one study and between U.S. and Canadian expatriates and Singaporeans in another. Differences in conflict management style preferences between cultures may lead to misinterpretation such that a person's conflict management style, in itself, can become a source of conflict.

Explain six conflict management strategies that can be used to help disputants resolve their conflicts.

METHODS FOR MANAGING CONFLICT

When disputants themselves are unable to manage their conflicts using their conflict management styles, managers can use a variety of conflict management methods to assist in successful conflict resolution. We discuss a few of these methods in this chapter: helping disputants to improve their communication, appealing to their superordinate goals, using a form of alternate dispute resolution, bringing in a third party, reducing their degree of task interdependence, expanding their resources, or, if all else fails, moving or rotating them. These conflict management strategies are summarized in Exhibit 11.7.

The XYZ model for initiating a complaint, summarized in Exhibit 11.8, builds on the ideas of owning one's communication and is particularly useful for teams that are in the throws of their storming stage, discussed in Chapter 7. The XYZ model has three essential components: a description of the troublesome behaviour, the disclosure of your feelings about the behaviour, and a statement about the effect that the person's behaviour had on you.[65] Additional strategies to improve intergroup communication are included in the overview of organizational development in Chapter 13.

organizational reality 11.2

International Conflict Style Preferences

Cultural differences influence the use of different styles of conflict management. For example, one study compared Turkish, Jordanian, and U.S. managers. All three groups preferred the "collaborating" style. Turkish managers also reported frequent use of the "competing" style, whereas Jordanian and U.S. managers reported that it was one of their least used styles.

The human resources manager of one U.S. telecommunications company's office in Singapore engaged a consultant to investigate the conflict in the office. Twenty-two expatriates from the United States and Canada and 38 Singaporeans worked in the office. The consultant used the Thomas model (Exhibit 11.5) and distributed questionnaires to all managers to determine their conflict management styles. The results were not surprising: The expatriate North American managers preferred the competing, collaborating, and compromising styles, while the Asians preferred the avoiding and accommodating styles.

Workshops were conducted within the firm to develop an understanding of the differences and how they negatively affected the firm. The Asians interpreted the results as reflecting the tendency of North Americans to "shout first and ask questions later." They felt that the North Americans had an arrogant attitude and could not handle having their ideas rejected. The Asians attributed their own styles to their cultural background. The North Americans attributed the results to the stereotypical view of Asians as unassertive and timid, and they viewed their own results as reflecting their desire to "get things out in the open."

The process opened a dialogue between the two groups, who began to work on the idea of harmony through conflict. They began to discard the traditional stereotypes in favour of shared meanings and mutual understanding.

SOURCES: M. K. Kozan, "Cultural Influences on Styles of Handling Interpersonal Conflicts: Comparisons among Jordanian, Turkish, and U.S. Managers," *Human Relations* 42 (1989): 787–99; S. McKenna, "The Business Impact of Management Attitudes towards Dealing with Conflict: A Cross-Cultural Assessment," *Journal of Managerial Psychology* 10 (1995): 22–27.

EXHIBIT 11.7

Conflict Management Strategies

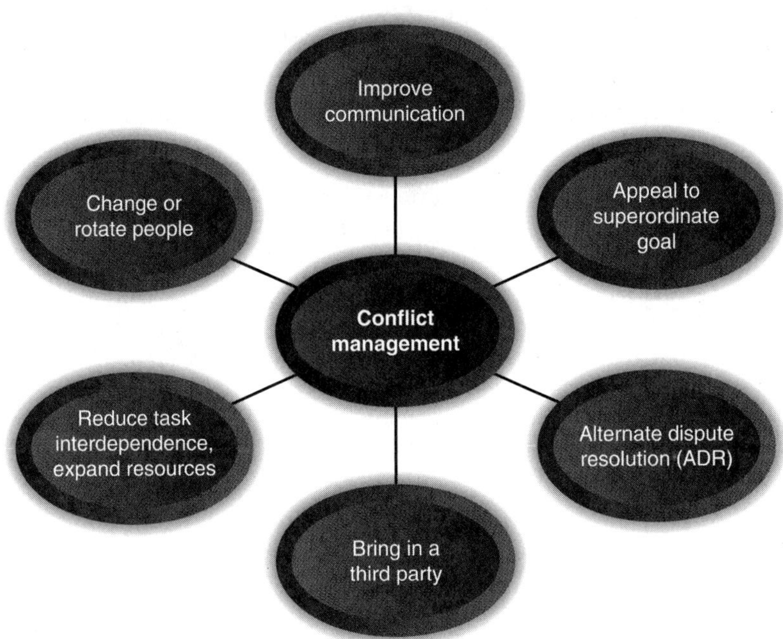

Appeal to Disputants' Superordinate Goal

Sometimes, improved communication is not enough to get disputing parties to cooperate. Another effective technique for resolving conflict is to appeal to a **superordinate goal**, which is an organizational goal that captures the imagination, and hence galvanizes people to take action that is more important to both parties in a conflict than their individual or group goals.[66] Superordinate goals cannot be achieved by an individual or by one group alone. The achievement of these goals requires cooperation by both (all) parties. This helps them realize their similarities rather than their differences. Indeed, much of the work on visioning, over the last two decades, has been driven by the need to articulate superordinate goals, or visions that can bring people together. One author puts it this way: "the creation of what is dreamed and imagined of a group."[67]

superordinate goal
An organizational goal that captures the imagination, and hence galvanizes people to take action that is more important to both parties in a conflict than their individual or group goals.

EXHIBIT 11.8

XYZ Approach to Initiating a Complaint

Step 1: Describe your complaint in terms of the behaviour that presented a problem for you **(X)**

"When you arrived 30 minutes late for our meeting ..."

Step 2: Outline the specific, observable consequences of this behaviour **(Y)**

"It meant that I had to wait at the corner in the pouring rain ..."

Step 3: Describe the feelings you experienced as a result of the person's behaviour or actions **(Z)**

"and it really made me angry and not want to count on you anymore."

Note: **X**, **Y**, and **Z** can be said in any order that feels right.

SOURCE: Adapted from David A. Whetten and Kim S. Cameron, *Developing Management Skills,* 6th ed. (Upper Saddle River, NJ: Prentice Hall, 2005), 368. Adapted by permission of Pearson Education, Upper Saddle River, NJ.

For a more mundane example, let us take a conflict between a Xerox sales representative and a Xerox service representative. Perhaps the customer is complaining to the sales rep that the machine is not working and it takes too long to get service. By appealing to a superordinate goal, such as the desire not to lose the customer, both employees can agree that keeping the customer happy is a goal worthy of pursuit and that this goal cannot be achieved unless the photocopiers are installed properly and serviced in a timely manner, and customer complaints are handled effectively by the sales rep. Keeping the customer requires that both departments cooperate to achieve the goal.

CRITICAL THINKING: Application & Synthesis

CREATING AN EFFECTIVE SCRIPT TO INITIATE A COMPLAINT

Imagine that you are having a conflict with a group member over the fact that he has been arriving late for team meetings for the past three weeks and he has been missing deadlines. Write out what you might say at the very beginning of the discussion, following the XYZ model described in Exhibit 11.8. Which of the supportive communication guidelines from Chapter 6 would you keep in mind during the discussion?

Alternate Dispute Resolution (ADR)

alternative dispute resolution (ADR)
Informal methods used to resolve disputes, such as simple negotiation and mediation, which are outside the formal grievance and discipline process.

One definition of **alternative dispute resolution (ADR)** is the informal methods used to resolve disputes, such as simple negotiation and mediation, which are outside the formal grievance and discipline process. Another definition is that it is any other approach to the one that is not working! While not always a third-party approach, it is also sometimes referred to as "assisted" dispute resolution. Essentially, the term ADR implies a nonadversarial approach to conflict resolution. ADR procedures are structured according to the wishes of the conflicting parties, as you saw in the RCMP example at the start of the chapter. The procedures range from unassisted negotiation at one end of the spectrum, to binding arbitration at the other. The most common nonadjudicative processes are negotiation and mediation, although there are others, such as the executive mini-trial, judicial mini-trial and early neutral evaluation.[68] The objective of ADR is to keep disputes out of the court system in an effort to cut down the costs of time, money, productivity, and emotional wear and tear.[69] These complaint-handling procedures provide ways for these companies to "minimize lawsuits and possibly avoid unionization."[70]

Using a Third Party

third party
Any individual who is not part of the initial conflict, but becomes involved in order to help manage or resolve it.

When the aforementioned strategies do not work, sometimes managers need to act as or bring in a third party. A **third party** is any individual who is not part of the initial conflict, but becomes involved in order to help manage or resolve it.[71] Increasingly, managers are being trained to act as third parties to help employees resolve personality conflicts, so it is now viewed as a core management competency in performance measurements.[72] Also, human resources professionals frequently act as third parties, and some organizations employ full-time facilitators within their HR department. Conflict management training has also become widespread in Canadian schools. For example, in the Toronto District School Board, students learn about conflict management using "art, drama, puppet shows, workshops and guest speakers."[73] In 2002/2003, seven district school boards in Alberta adopted a training program called "Healthy Interactions: Resolving Interpersonal Conflicts." The focus of this program is to help teachers and parents resolve conflicts in collaborative ways.[74] Many school boards throughout Canada have trained groups of students as peer mediators who help other students resolve conflicts in nonviolent ways.[75] Individuals who act as a third parties do so in one of three different ways: They can act as facilitators, coaches, or mediators, as summarized in Exhibit 11.9.

EXHIBIT 11.9

Types of Third-Party Interventions

Intervention	Definition
Facilitation	An informal process in which a neutral third party attempts to facilitate communication and the development of a solution.
Coaching	Managers pass along advice and information or set standards to help subordinates improve their work skills.
Mediation	A formal process in which a neutral third party, with no decision-making power, helps the disputing parties voluntarily settle the dispute by establishing ground rules for negotiation, opening channels of communication, articulating the needs of each, identifying the issues, and, if requested, making recommendations on disputed issues.
Arbitration	A formal process in which a third party who has been chosen by the disputing parties, after hearing evidence and oral argument, renders a decision that is binding on all parties.

More and more managers are using mediation as a conflict management technique both inside and outside the workplace.[76] **Mediation** is a formal process in which neutral third party, with no decision-making power, helps the disputing parties voluntarily settle the dispute by establishing ground rules for negotiation, opening channels of communication, articulating the needs of each, identifying the issues, and, if requested, making recommendations on disputed issues. Recently in Quebec, notaries, chartered accountants, chartered appraisers, and engineers have entrusted the IMAQ (Institut de médiation et d'arbitrage du Québec) with managing this free multidisciplinary civil and commercial mediation service. Pierrre Brochu, the president and CEO of BCE subsidiary Telebec, is a strong advocate of mediation and the IMAQ, which enabled Telebec and Hydro-Québec to resolve a dispute that had gone on for more than 20 years, in less than two months!

mediation
A formal process in which a neutral third party, with no decision-making power, helps the disputing parties voluntarily settle the dispute by establishing ground rules for negotiation, opening channels of communication, articulating the needs of each, identifying the issues, and, if requested, making recommendations on disputed issues.

Arbitration is a formal process in which a third party who has been chosen by the disputing parties, after hearing evidence and oral argument, renders a decision that is binding on all parties. Arbitration often follows unsuccessful mediation and puts the decision, known as the "award," in the hands of a neutral third party. The hearing is similar to a trial.[77]

arbitration
A formal process in which a third party who has been chosen by the disputing parties, after hearing evidence and oral argument, renders a decision that is binding on all parties.

Reducing Task Interdependence and/or Expanding Resources

Another indirect approach to helping disputants manage their conflicts is to reduce their task interdependence. This was discussed as a structural source of conflict and also as a team design factor in Chapter 7. When individuals are highly interdependent on each other for getting a job done, the likelihood of conflict is great. When direct conflict management, communications training, or appeals to a superordinate goal are unsuccessful, sometimes managers

Two managers and a mediator who is trying to get the conflicting parties to listen to each other.

IMPLICATIONS FOR LIFE

Office Conflicts

Cal and Joan, who work in the same office doing similar jobs, report to Barbara, who works in another building. Joan has sporadically complained to Barbara about Cal's bullying behaviour. For example, Cal bullied Joan into filling out all of the department's required monthly reporting forms, rather than sharing some of the task as is usually the case. Barbara had previously dismissed these complaints as just routine grumbling. Now she is spending a month working in the office with Cal and Joan while the other building is being renovated. Within a few days, she can see firsthand what Cal does and the effect it has on everyone else, not just Joan. During a routine exit interview, another employee complains about Cal and his "competing" style of handling conflict. Barbara realizes that the conflict is creating stress for everyone in the office. She values both Cal and Joan as good workers. Here is her assessment of the situation using the material you have just studied:

- *What kind of conflict is this and what are the sources of this conflict?* This is a task conflict and its sources seem to be both structural and personal. It has structural sources because there is interdependence between Cal and Joan, and personal sources because Cal seems to have a competing style of handling conflict and Joan does not. Also perhaps there are personality differences, and perhaps differences in perceptions, values, and ethics.

- *What are the possible consequences if this situation continues, and is the conflict functional or dysfunctional?* The conflict is dysfunctional and may lead to reduced departmental morale and performance; Joan and other employees who have been bullied may quit, like the other employee did; and Barbara will cease to be perceived as an effective leader.

- *Should Barbara intervene in this conflict? If so, how?* Barbara must intervene to prevent the conflict from escalating and threatening the department's productivity—as well as to keep Joan and other employees from quitting because of the stress. The overall issue is important, the relationship is important for smooth departmental functioning, the participants have equal power, and there is little immediate time pressure. Therefore, Barbara should serve as mediator or facilitator in this situation to help Cal and Joan collaborate on a mutually agreeable solution

SOURCE: Adapted from Carol F. Moore, Instructor's Manual for David A. Whetten and Kim S. Cameron, *Developing Management Skills,* 6th ed. (Upper Saddle River, NJ: Prentice Hall, 2005), 269. Adapted by permission of Pearson Education Inc., Upper Saddle River, NJ.

have to intervene by reducing the amount of interdependence in the task. For example, two employees who work at a ticket counter have sequential interdependence regarding their shifts. One cannot leave until the other one arrives, and often one or the other is late, causing conflict between them. One way to reduce their task interdependence is to create a buffer between them so that there is a 10-minute overlap between their shifts. This would also provide an opportunity for improved communication since on most days they will be working together for 10 minutes. This solution, does however, involve expanding resources. Sometimes, the source of a conflict is the fact that resources are scarce or have to be shared. Sometimes, providing more resources may be a solution; however, managers working with tight budgets may not have the luxury of obtaining additional resources.

Changing or Moving Disputants

Sometimes a conflict is prolonged and severe, and efforts at resolution fail. In such cases, it may be appropriate to change personnel. Transferring or firing an individual may be the best solution, but only after following due process.

Negotiation and Bargaining

Define *negotiation* (bargaining), distinguish between distributive and integrative bargaining, and explain the bargaining zone model.

While understanding conflict management styles and adapting them to the situation is often enough to understand and resolve a conflict, some conflicts require negotiation, (also called bargaining) between the parties. **Negotiation (bargaining)** is any interaction between two or more parties aimed at reaching an agreement based on both common and dividing interests.[78] People can negotiate directly, or can be assisted by third-party negotiators. The process of negotiating involves an open discussion of problem solutions, and the outcome often is an exchange in which both parties work toward a mutually beneficial solution. Negotiation is a joint process of finding a mutually acceptable solution to a complex conflict.

negotiation (bargaining)
Any interaction between two or more parties aimed at reaching an agreement based on both common and dividing interests.

Negotiating is needed when:

- Two or more parties must make a decision about interdependent goals and objectives and there is a conflict of interest between the parties such that what one party wants is not what the other party wants.
- The parties are committed to peaceful means for resolving the dispute.
- There is no clear or established method or procedure for making the decision.[79]

Distributive Bargaining

There are two major negotiating approaches often viewed as being on a continuum: distributive bargaining and integrative bargaining.[80] **Distributive bargaining** is a win-lose negotiating strategy, such that one party gains at the expense of the other. Resources are limited, and each party wants to maximize its share of the resources (get its part of the pie). It is at the end of the continuum and takes a competitive or win–lose approach to negotiations. In distributive negotiations, strategies and tactics typically include matters such as opening offers, the pattern of concessions, and the use of threats and commitments.[81]

distributive bargaining
A win–lose negotiating strategy, such that one party gains at the expense of the other.

In distributive bargaining, it is assumed that negotiators start bargaining with a gap between their positions and that the task is to locate a compromise between their *target points* (most favourable outcome) and their *resistance points* (least favourable acceptable outcome). This assumption, reflected in the so-called **bargaining zone** model, is depicted in Exhibit 11.10.[82] If there is an overlap between the two parties' resistance points, then there is potential for an agreement.

bargaining zone
The area identified by the bargaining limits (resistance points) of each side, in which compromise is possible, as is the attainment of a settlement satisfactory to both parties.

One factor that has been found to affect negotiator performance is the amount of power held by the negotiator. In particular, negotiation studies have relied on "the degree of nonsubstitutability," one of four organizational conditions of power, discussed in Chapter 9, to explore negotiator performance. Researchers have explored ways that negotiators increase their bargaining power and have defined the "availability of an outcome through alternative means" as the negotiator's **b**est **a**lternative **t**o the **n**egotiated **a**greement, referred to as the negotiator's BATNA.[83] The **BATNA** represents the best alternative if the negotiation fails, so negotiators often obtain attractive alternatives prior to entering a negotiation, to make them less dependent on the outcome and to create a more demanding resistance point. This model explains why job applicants are able to negotiate higher starting salaries when they possess another job offer.

BATNA
The best alternative to a negotiated agreement and also the resistance point.

Integrative Bargaining

At the other end of the negotiating continuum is **integrative bargaining**, which is a negotiating strategy in which there is acknowledgement that achieving a win–win outcome will depend on mutual trust and problem solving. In this approach the parties' goals are *not* seen as mutually exclusive and the focus is on making it possible for both sides to achieve their objectives. Integrative negotiation focuses on the merits of the issues and is a win–win approach. Strategies and tactics that are usually involved are learning about the other party's interests and needs, looking for opportunities for trades, and developing creative options.[84] For integrative negotiation to be successful, certain preconditions

integrative bargaining
A negotiating strategy in which there is acknowledgement that achieving a win–win outcome will depend on mutual trust and problem solving.

EXHIBIT 11.10

Bargaining Zone Model

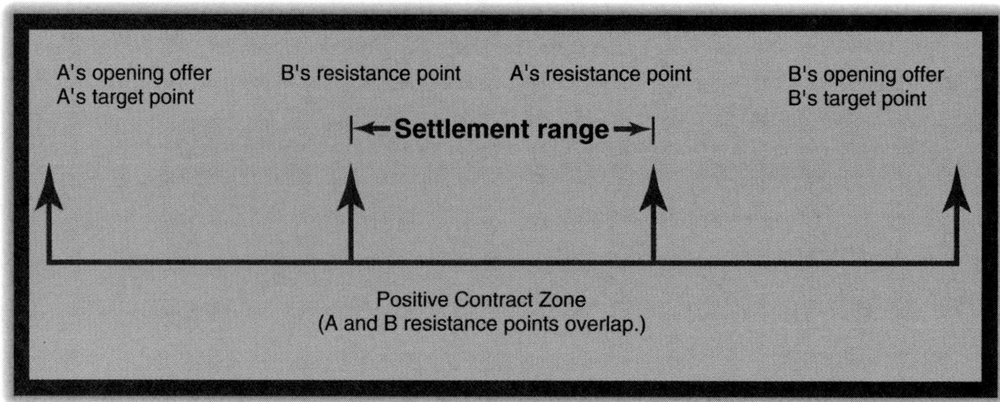

must be present. These include having a common goal, faith in one's own problem-solving abilities, a belief in the validity of the other party's position, motivation to work together, mutual trust, and clear communication.[85]

Alternative Dispute Resolution Institute of Canada

The ADR Institute of Canada (ADR Canada) provides national leadership in the development and promotion of dispute resolution services in Canada. They represent and support professionals who provide dispute resolution services and the individuals and organizations that use those services.
http://www.adrcanada.ca

In the integrative approach to bargaining, the mind-sets of negotiators are geared to how to "create" rather than "take" value.[86] Recent research is emphasizing the importance of negotiator mind-sets in determining whether a negotiation is perceived as integrative or distributive. Bazerman reports on studies in which simply changing the name of a negotiation from the "Wall Street" game to the "Community" game, changed the mental models of the parties involved and resulted in more integrative bargaining.[87] Often, negotiators initially take an integrative approach and then, if it does not work, they cut their losses and move to a more distributive approach.

IMPLICATIONS FOR ORGANIZATIONAL EFFECTIVENESS

Conflict is inevitable in organizational hierarchies, and increasing competition for scarce resources, rapid change, and greater interdependence leads to even more conflict. Organizational conflict manifests itself at all levels: between individual employees, within teams, between departments, and also between organizations during mergers or acquisitions. While conflict can be constructive, it can also get in the way of organizational performance and prevent organizations from achieving their strategic objectives.

The key factor that determines whether conflict will be functional or dysfunctional for an organization is the way in which it is managed. Enlightened leaders are facing conflict rather than avoiding it and are formalizing processes for preventing dysfunctional conflict in the first place by creating conflict-positive organizations, by building conflict management roles into the structure, and by rotating employees to build increased appreciating for diverse roles. Organizations are also managing dysfunctional conflict by communicating the superordinate goals more widely, and by clarifying roles and responsibilities, thereby reducing ambiguities and the potential for conflict and political behaviour. Managers are being trained to better understand their own conflict management styles, to learn how to initiate complaints in effective manners and to be able to act as third parties.

Chapter Summary

1. Conflict is the awareness, in an interdependent relationship, of discrepancies, incompatible wishes, or irreconcilable desires. It is important to understand the behavioural, physiological, and cognitive components of the emotional experience.
2. Traditional definitions of conflict have identified two distinct types of conflict, which have been called task and relationship conflict. Relationship conflict is defined as the awareness of interpersonal incompatibilities and typically includes feelings of anger, tension, and friction. Task conflict is defined as the awareness of differences in viewpoints and opinions that pertain to group tasks.
3. Conflict is manifested in many different forms within and between organizations. These forms are interorganizational, intergroup, intragroup, and interpersonal conflict.
4. Structural sources of conflict include specialization and goal differences, interdependence or common resources, status and power differences, and jurisdictional ambiguities. Personal sources of conflict include personality differences, perceptions, values and ethics, ineffective communication, and cultural differences.
5. The manager's task is to stimulate functional conflict and prevent or resolve dysfunctional conflict. Functional conflict is a healthy, constructive disagreement between two or more people and it can produce new ideas, learning, and growth among individuals. By contrast, dysfunctional conflict is an unhealthy, destructive disagreement between two or more people. Its danger is that it takes the focus away from the work to be done and places the focus on the conflict itself and the parties involved.
6. Three approaches that help prevent dysfunctional conflict are (1) creating a conflict positive organization, one that values diversity, empowers employees, and seeks win-win solutions to conflicts; (2) including conflict resolution roles in an organization's structure; and (3) rotating employees through different jobs or departments.
7. Success in managing conflict depends in part on the style of conflict management used. Individuals prefer one of five interpersonal conflict management styles, which differ depending on the degree (high–medium–low) of concern for others and concern for self. These styles are avoiding (low concern for self and low concern for other), accommodating (low concern for self and high concern for other), competing (high concern for self and low concern for other), compromising (medium concern for both), and collaborating (high concern for both).
8. Approaches managers can use to help others manage their conflicts include helping them improve their communication using the XYZ model, appealing to the disputants' superordinate goal, acting as or bringing in a third party, reducing task interdependence and/or expanding resources, and changing or moving the disputants.
9. Negotiation, also called bargaining, is any interaction between two or more parties aimed at reaching an agreement based on both common and dividing interests. Distributive bargaining is a win–lose negotiating strategy, such that one party gains at the expense of the other. The bargaining zone is the area identified by the bargaining limits (resistance points) of each side, in which compromise is possible, as is the attainment of a settlement satisfactory to both parties. By contrast, integrative bargaining is a negotiating strategy in which there is acknowledgement that achieving a win–win outcome is possible and will depend on mutual trust and problem solving.

Key Terms

accommodating (p. 343)
alternative dispute resolution (ADR) (p. 348)
arbitration (p. 349)
avoiding (p. 342)
bargaining zone (p. 351)
BATNA (p. 351)
behavioural component of emotion (p. 332)
cognitive component of emotion (p. 333)
collaborating (p. 344)
competing (p. 343)
compromising (p. 344)
conflict (p. 332)
conflict management strategy (p. 339)
distributive bargaining (p. 351)
dysfunctional conflict (p. 339)
functional conflict (p. 337)
integrative bargaining (p. 351)
intergroup conflict (p. 334)
interorganizational conflict (p. 334)
interpersonal conflict (p. 335)
intragroup conflict (p. 335)
jurisdictional ambiguity (p. 336)
mediation (p. 349)
negotiation (bargaining) (p. 351)
physiological component of emotion (p. 332)
process conflict (p. 333)
relationship (affective) conflict (p. 333)
superordinate goal (p. 347)
task (cognitive) conflict (p. 333)
third party (p. 348)

Review Questions

1. Describe the various emotional components in conflict.
2. Identify the structural and personal factors that contribute to conflict.
3. Discuss the four major forms of conflict in organizations and give an example of each.
4. Describe ways in which organizations can minimize or prevent dysfunctional conflict from erupting.
5. Identify and discuss five styles of conflict management, explaining the dual-concerns implications.
6. What are the most effective techniques for managing conflict at work?

Discussion and Communication Questions

1. What causes you the most conflict at work or school?
2. Are you comfortable with your preferred conflict management style? Would you consider modifying it?
3. (*Communication question*) Think of a person with whom you have had a recent conflict. Write a letter to this person, attempting to resolve the conflict. Use the concepts from the chapter to accomplish your objective. Be sure to address whether the conflict is functional or dysfunctional, what styles each party has used, effective strategies for resolving the conflict, and ineffective strategies that should be avoided.

Ethics Questions

1. What kind of ethical conflicts have you experienced at school or work? At home?
2. In what situations is the competing style of conflict management appropriate? What unethical behaviours might be associated with this style? How can these behaviours be avoided?
3. How can you stimulate conflict in an ethical manner?
4. In what situations is the competing style of conflict management appropriate? What unethical behaviours might be associated with this style? How can these behaviours be avoided?

Application & Analysis

EXPERIENTIAL EXERCISE 11.1: CONFLICTS OVER UNETHICAL BEHAVIOUR

Purpose: To explore conflicts caused by different values or ethics and to determine management's role in these conflicts

Group size: 5–8

Time required: 20 minutes

Materials needed: None

Instructions:
Many conflicts in work organizations arise over differences in beliefs concerning what constitutes ethical versus unethical behaviour. The following questionnaire provides a list of behaviours that you or your co-workers might engage in when working for a company.

Step 1: Individually go over each item, and circle the number that best indicates the frequency with which you personally would (or do, if you work now) engage in that behaviour. Then put an *X* over the number you think represents how often your co-workers would (or do) engage in that behaviour. Finally, put a check mark beside the item (in the "Needs Control" column) if you believe that management should control that behaviour.

	Never	Seldom	About half the time	Often	At every opportunity
1. Passing blame for errors to an innocent co-worker.	5	4	3	2	1
2. Divulging confidential information.	5	4	3	2	1
3. Falsifying time/quality/quantity reports.	5	4	3	2	1
4. Claiming credit for someone else's work.	5	4	3	2	1
5. Padding an expense account by over 10 percent.	5	4	3	2	1
6. Pilfering company materials and supplies.	5	4	3	2	1
7. Accepting gifts/favours in exchange for preferential treatment.	5	4	3	2	1
8. Giving gifts/favours in exchange for preferential treatment.	5	4	3	2	1
9. Padding an expense account by up to 10 percent.	5	4	3	2	1
10. Authorizing a subordinate to violate company rules.	5	4	3	2	1
11. Calling in sick to take a day off.	5	4	3	2	1
12. Concealing one's errors.	5	4	3	2	1
13. Taking longer than necessary to do a job.	5	4	3	2	1
14. Using company services for personal use.	5	4	3	2	1
15. Doing personal business on company time.	5	4	3	2	1
16. Taking extra personal time (lunch hour, breaks, early departure etc.).	5	4	3	2	1
17. Not reporting others' violations of company policies and rules.	5	4	3	2	1
18. Overlooking a superior's violation of policy to prove loyalty to the boss.	5	4	3	2	1

Step 2: Form groups of 6–8 people.

Step 3: Discuss the following questions:

1. Would (do) your co-workers seem to engage in these behaviours more often than you would (do)? Why do you have this perception?
2. Which behaviours tend to be most frequent?
3. How are the most frequent behaviours different from the behaviours engaged in less frequently?
4. What are the most important items for managers to control? How should managers control these behaviours?
6. What types of conflicts could emerge if the behaviours in the list occurred frequently?

Step 4: Class take-up.

Step 5 (optional): Select a particular behaviour from the list. Have two people debate whether the behaviour is ethical or not.

SOURCE: From *The Managerial Experience: Cases, Exercises, and Readings*, 3rd ed., by Sally Coltrin and Lawrence R. Jauch. Copyright © 1983 by The Dryden Press. Reprinted with permission of South-Western, a division of Thomson Learning, www.thomsonrights.com. Fax 800-730-2215.

Application & Analysis

EXPERIENTIAL EXERCISE 11.2: THE WORLD BANK GAME: AN INTERGROUP NEGOTIATION

Purpose: The purposes of this exercise are to learn about conflict and trust between groups and to practise negotiation skills. In the course of the exercise, money will be won or lost. Your team's objective is to win as much money as it can.

Group size: 6–12 (teams should be of equal size and there should be an equal number of teams)

Time required: 60 minutes

Materials needed: 20 cards per team with an *X* on one side

Instructions:

1. Your team will be paired with another team, and both teams will receive identical instructions. After reading these instructions, each team will have 10 minutes to plan its strategy. Each team is assumed to have contributed $50 million to the World Bank. Teams may have to pay more or may receive money from the World Bank, depending on the outcome.
2. Each team will receive 20 cards. These cards are the weapons. Each card has a marked side (*X*) and an unmarked side. The marked side signifies that the weapon is armed; the unmarked side signifies that the weapon is unarmed.
3. At the beginning, each team will place 10 of its 20 weapons in their armed position (marked side up) and the remaining 10 in their unarmed position (marked side down). The weapons will remain in the team's possession and out of sight of the other team at all times.
4. The game will consist of *rounds* and *moves*. Each round will be composed of seven moves by each team. There will be two or more rounds in the game, depending on the time available. Payoffs will be determined and recorded after each round.

Rules:

- A move consists of turning two, one, or none of the team's weapons from armed to unarmed status, or vice versa.
- Each team has one-and-a-half minutes for each move. There is a 30-second period between each move. At the end of the one-and-a-half minutes, the team must have turned two, one, or none of its weapons from armed to unarmed status or from unarmed to armed status. If the team fails to move in the allotted time, no change can be made in weapon status until the next move.
- The two-minute length of the period between the beginning of one move and the beginning of the next is unalterable.

Finances:

The funds each team has contributed to the World Bank are to be allocated in the following manner: $30 million will be returned to each team to be used as the team's treasury during the course of the game, and $20 million will be retained for the operation of the World Bank.

Payoffs:

- **If there is an attack:**
  - (a) Each team may announce an attack on the other team by notifying the banker during the 30 seconds following any minute-and-a-half period used to decide upon the move (including the seventh, or final, decision period in any round). The choice of each team during the decision period just ended counts as a move. An attack may not be made during negotiations.
  - (b) If there is an attack by one or both teams, two things happen: (1) the round ends, and (2) the World Bank assesses a penalty of $2.5 million on each team.
  - (c) The team with the greater number of armed weapons wins $1.5 million for each armed weapon it has over and above the number of armed weapons of the other team. These funds are paid directly from the treasury of the losing team to the treasury of the winning team. The banker will manage the transfer of funds.
- **If there is no attack:**

  At the end of each round (seven moves), each team's treasury will receive from the World Bank $1 million for each of its weapons that is at that point unarmed; and each team's treasury will pay to the World Bank $1 million for each of its weapons remaining armed.

Negotiations:

- Between moves, each team will have the opportunity to communicate with the other team through its negotiations. Either team may call for negotiations by notifying the banker during any of the 30-second periods between decisions. A team is free to accept or reject any invitation to negotiate.
- Negotiators from both teams are required to meet after the third and sixth moves (after the 30-second period following the move, if there is no attack).

- Negotiations can last no longer than three minutes. When the two negotiators return to their teams, the minute-and-a-half decision period for the next move will begin once again.
- Negotiators are bound only by (a) the three-minute time limit for negotiations and (b) their required appearance after the third and sixth moves.
- They are always free to say whatever is necessary to benefit themselves or their teams.
- The teams are not bound by agreements made by their negotiators, even when those agreements are made in good faith.

Special Roles:
Each team has 10 minutes to organize itself and plan team strategy. During this period, before the first round begins, each team must choose persons to fill the following roles:

- A *negotiator*—activities stated above.
- A *representative*—to communicate the team's decisions to the banker.
- A *recorder*—to record the moves of the team and to keep a running balance of the team's treasury.
- A *treasurer*—to execute all financial transactions with the banker.

The instructor will serve as the **banker** for the World Bank and will signal the beginning of each of the rounds. At the end of the game, each participant should complete the following questionnaire, which assesses reactions to the World Bank Game.

World Bank Questionnaire

1. To what extent are you satisfied with your team's strategy?

   Highly satisfied — Highly Dissatisfied

   1 2 3 4 5 6 7

2. To what extent do you believe the other team is trustworthy?

   Highly untrustworthy — Highly Trustworthy

   1 2 3 4 5 6 7

3. To what extent are you satisfied with the performance of your negotiator?

   Highly Dissatisfied — Highly Satisfied

   1 2 3 4 5 6 7

4. To what extent was there a consensus on your team regarding its moves?

   Very little — A great deal

   1 2 3 4 5 6 7

5. To what extent do you trust the other members of your team?

   Very little — A great deal

   1 2 3 4 5 6 7

6. Select one word that describes how you feel about your team:

   ____

7. Select one word that describes how you feel about the other team:

   ____

Negotiators only:

How did you see the other team's negotiator?

Phony and Insincere — Authentic and sincere

1 2 3 4 5 6 7

Discussion:
At the end of the game, the class will reconvene and discuss team members' responses to the World Bank Questionnaire. In addition, the following questions are to be addressed:

1. What was each team's strategy for winning? What strategy was most effective?
2. Contrast the outcomes in terms of win–win solutions to conflict versus win–lose solutions.

WORLD BANK RECORD SHEET

		Round One		Round Two		Round Three		Round Four	
		Armed	Unarmed	Armed	Unarmed	Armed	Unarmed	Armed	Unarmed
	Move	10	10	10	10	10	10	10	10
	1								
	2								
Required Negotiation	3								
	4								
	5								
Required Negotiation	6								
	7								

Funds in Team Treasury	$30 million				
Funds of Other Treasury	$30 million				
Funds in World Bank	$40 million				

SOURCE: Adapted by permission from N. H. Berkowitz and H. A. Hornstein, "World Bank: An Intergroup Negotiation," in J. W. Pfeiffer and J. E. Jones, eds., *The 1975 Handbook for Group Facilitators* (San Diego: Pfeiffer), 58–62. Copyright © 1975 Pfeiffer/Jossey-Bass. Reprinted with permission of John Wiley & Sons, Inc.

Application & Analysis

CASE: ALL-STAR CITY TOURS

Francine Jordache is the president and founder of All-Star City Tours, a company that provides a variety of tours of great Canadian and American cities. She started the company in 1993 to respond to the need for tours for spouses and partners attending conferences in Canada. Organizations were looking for comprehensive packages that would entertain the partners while the conferences were in session.

Calgary is the home base for the company that has expanded its operations with satellite offices in Halifax, Quebec City, Montreal, Toronto, and Vancouver. There are 520 Canadian employees, including 375 part-time regional staff. In 2002 Francine developed a partnership with an American, Ronnie Brice, to create a subsidiary to run tours in U.S. cities, American All-Star City Tours. So far, operations have been established in Seattle, New Orleans, Miami, and New York. Offices in Boston, Los Angeles, and Houston are in the planning stages. The American employees total 150, with 90 percent of them being part-time regional staff who work on specific events. The rest are permanent Seattle employees reporting to the VP, Tour Planning.

The primary focus of the company is to provide customers with a unique customized tour experience. Tours not only showcase the general tourist attractions and exclusive shopping in each city but also cover such things as garden tours showcasing spectacular private and public gardens, unusual public and private art collections, and gourmet food tours in which participants travel from one superior restaurant to another enjoying different dinner courses as well as local wines where available. All-Star arranges custom tours to suit the wishes of customers. Recently when a medical convention was in Toronto, a tour of a state-of-the-art research facility was arranged and both conference participants and their partners enjoyed a musical concert and fine dining as well as scientific information forums. Everyone raved about the high quality and uniqueness of the event, especially the merger of scientific and artistic elements. This is a typical reaction to the tours provided. A key attribute of all employees is "out of the box" creative thinking.

Shares in the Canadian company are held by Francine, her husband, and three "silent partners" who invested in the company in 1997 when she expanded in Canada. The parent company and Ronnie have equal ownership of the U.S. subsidiary. Ronnie is the president and Francine is the chairman of the board of the U.S. subsidiary. Canadian head office employees provide administrative support to the U.S. operations. Francine and Ronnie expect to establish a full U.S. head office once business growth makes it necessary. Ronnie's hope is to have this in place within the next year. Francine is not so sure it will happen this fast. Ronnie is continually on the go, rarely seeming to slow down, leaving voice and e-mail messages at two or three in morning with ideas for new business and expansion. Even Francine is amazed by her "go-go" approach to work, "Does she ever take a break or sleep?"

Francine's direct reports for the overall operation of the company are:

George Freewell, VP Financial Services – Calgary (25 people)

Penelope (Penny) Kidder, VP Human Resources – Calgary

Janet Browne, VP Marketing and Sales – Calgary (35 people)

William (Bill) Tremaine, VP Tour Planning – Calgary (60 people located in Calgary and Seattle)

Ronnie Brice, President US Operations – Seattle (attends meeting by teleconference or videoconference)

Francine has received a call from a contact in France asking her to consider expanding operations into Europe. She had already been thinking of expanding into the Caribbean and has made some preliminary enquiries with existing contacts. Francine has some concerns and reservations about expansion at this time. The head office employees have increased by 50 percent since the U.S. operation began. People are working overtime and she's sensing some burnout particularly in Janet's marketing and sales teams.

People in Janet's team are not interacting well with each other and other departments. Sales and marketing employees are frequently on the road and communicate mainly by e-mail and voice mail. Janet spoke to Penny last week; she doesn't know what to do about the constant friction between her sales and marketing team of 35 and Bill's tour planning team of 60. Lately they all seem to sniping at each other over who has overall responsibility to design, price, and plan tours. Janet and Bill's relationship has become more and more strained as the volume of contracts for service has grown. "It's at the point that I cringe when I see him coming my way. It seems all we ever talk about is problems between our teams. It has me wondering if I even like him any more."

Bill is frustrated with the processes for bringing in new business and coordinating service delivery. When everyone was in Calgary, things flowed smoothly with his direct involvement in all projects. He has 60 people in his department located in two cities, three-quarters of them in Calgary and the rest in Seattle. He confided in Penny that he is feeling stretched to the limit and is getting tired of the travel his job requires:

"I haven't had time to get my team together to talk about our internal working relationships and processes. We make things up as we go along. This is not the best way to get things done. The most recent blow up occurred over a tour that included visits to both Vancouver and Seattle. Both the Canadian and U.S. team members thought they should have sole responsibility for the project and it took weeks to get agreement on how to proceed. While it didn't directly affect the client in this case, negative feelings continue to hurt my department's working relationships. To add to everything else, we also have to consider Janet's folks and what they may have promised the client. This is not always clear in the documents we get. I need your help to get things back on track. Janet doesn't seem to want to talk to me about this stuff. I just want to work together to get the jobs done."

Yesterday Francine met with Penny who has been trying to influence the other VPs to implement a new reward system that will include bonuses based on customer satisfaction measures and teamwork efforts. The current bonus system is based on overall company results. This system is well understood and accepted by head office employees. Regional office employees have complained that since they only deal with local initiatives, their bonuses don't reflect what they actually do.

Penny also believes the senior team needs to meet more than once a month. In her previous role, the executive team met every two weeks, created and communicated company goals and objectives, as well as set clear performance expectations. Francine thinks Penny has good ideas and wants to discuss them with the whole leadership team. The problem is the executive meetings are already jam packed with agenda items. Given her recent conversations with the other VPs, Penny suggested that the leadership team have an off-site team building and planning retreat. Francine's response was, "We don't have time right now." Penny said, "We need to find time. Leave it with me so I can come up with some concrete ideas on how we might be able to do this."

George and his finance team of 25 people provide weekly reports on the company finances, balance sheet, and other data that are shared with Francine and, if U.S. numbers are involved, with Ronnie. Sometimes the leadership team discusses monthly financial information, but often, because of the length of the discussion of other agenda items, this gets minimal attention. George gets two minutes to say, "We're doing OK, we've made a bigger profit," or some other high-level statement.

"Ronnie always seems to want the numbers faster than we can produce them. Why can't she slow down and let me get the job done? No one else besides my team even seems to care much about the numbers, anyway. The silent partners pay more attention to the numbers than the executive team because they are concerned about overall return on investment." George and his team take pride in their accuracy and attention to detail. Ronnie's phone calls asking for U.S. numbers "Drive me around the bend. Ronnie seems to believe that pushing me will get things done faster. I just ignore her and get on with things at my own pace."

Near the end of the last leadership team meeting, Janet blew up at Bill and accused him of not supporting the marketing and sales team to creatively fulfill all client requests. "Some of your guys are slackers. They wait until the last minute to do things. Customers want to know progress." Bill countered with, "If you folks would just get your noses out of our business we could get more work done. Every time I try to bring this subject up with you, you have something more important to do."

Francine is at a loss. Penny has suggested an off-site leadership team meeting. This might be a good idea but everyone seems too busy. People aren't talking to each other. "What's happened? We used to be so cohesive. We can't expand when we're barely coping with what's on our plates and everyone is fighting."

Questions:

1. Identify the structural and personal sources of conflict between the leadership team members and between the departments. What role does emotion play in these conflicts?
2. Identify the forms of conflict that are evident in this case and the impact these forms of conflict have on the effectiveness of All-Star City Tours.
3. Identify and discuss the effectiveness of the conflict management styles used by each of the leadership team members.
4. Identify steps that the leadership team should take to avoid or minimize dysfunctional conflict.

SOURCE: Copyright S. Reilly, Ryerson University 2005. Used with permission.

Scoring for Self-Assessments

Self-Assessment 11.1: Assess Your Team's Conflict

Total for items 2, 4, and 6 = ____9____ indicating task conflict.

Total for items 1, 3, 5, and 7 = ____8____ indicating relationship conflict.

Total for item 8 = ____2____ indicating process conflict.

- Did your team experience higher relationship or task conflict?
- Did your team experience process conflict?
- What actions can you take to better manage task conflict? Relationship conflict? Process conflict?

- Was there an absence of both, or either, types of conflict in your team? What does this indicate?

Self-Assessment 11.2: What Is Your Conflict-Handling Style?

Scoring:

Collaborating		**Accommodating**		**Competing**		**Avoiding**		**Compromising**	
Item	**Score**	**Item**	**Score**	**Item**	**Score**	**Item**	**Score**	**Item**	**Score**
4.	3	3.	3	1.	3	6.	2	2.	4
9.	3	11.	3	5.	3	10.	2	8.	3
12.	4	14.	3	7.	2	15.	2	13.	4
Total =	10	**Total =**	9	**Total =**	8	**Total =**	6	**Total =**	10

Your primary conflict-handling style is: __________ (the category with the highest total).

Your backup conflict-handling style is: __________ (the category with the second-highest total).

Part Three: Interpersonal Processes and Behaviour (14:16 minutes)

HOCKEY PARENT RINK RAGE *(1.58 AND 1:41 MINUTES)*

These two clips feature incidents of rage and violence by parents of minor-league hockey players. The 2005 incident of Bradley Desrocher, a parent of a junior hockey player who is accused of attacking a coach, is discussed. In addition, the clip features controversial scenarios in which children pressure their parents to fight back and not be "chickens." Wayne Gretzky's dad is also featured.

Critical Thinking Questions

1. Are there certain conflicts when it is appropriate to fight back using force?
2. To what extent is the culture of "not being a chicken" still prevalent today?
3. Why has bullying and the use of physical force remained so prevalent in Canadian society?

NEGATIVE BOSS-EMPLOYEE RELATIONSHIPS AND NASTY E-MAILS ARE BAD FOR YOUR HEALTH *(1:58 AND 1:49 MINUTES)*

These clips explore British studies which found that a negative relationship between a boss and employee, and nasty e-mails from bosses, can negatively affect the health of employees.

Critical Thinking Questions

1. Can negative relationships with a teacher affect the health of his or her students?
2. What are the most typical factors that create negative relationships between a boss and his or her employees?
3. Have you ever received a nasty e-mail from someone in authority? How did you react?

BULLYING IN THE WORKPLACE *(6:50 MINUTES)*

This clip shows an interview of a victim of workplace bullying and an expert in workplace violence. The victim had been in her job for three years when a new employee who was a family member was hired. He verbally abused her and others, was aggressive, and on one occasion kicked her door in. Participants discuss how to deal with workplace bullying and abuse.

Critical Thinking Questions

1. Have any of you experienced workplace bullying or violence?
2. What are the main causes of bullying in the workplace?
3. If you were a supervisor and an employee complained to you about being bullied, what would you do?

Organizational Processes and Structure

part four

12. ORGANIZATIONAL CULTURE
13. ORGANIZATIONAL CHANGE AND DEVELOPMENT
14. ORGANIZATION STRUCTURE AND DESIGN
15. PERFORMANCE MANAGEMENT, FEEDBACK, AND REWARDS (WEBSITE ONLY: WWW.SNIDERMAN.NELSON.COM)

chapter twelve

LEARNING OBJECTIVES

By the end of this chapter, you will be able to do the following:

1. Define *organizational culture* and explain why it is important in today's business environment.
2. Identify the elements of culture and the various ways we can recognize culture.
3. Explain several ways that cultures can be described.
4. Explain the relationship between organizational culture and performance.
5. Explain why cultural fit is important to organizations and employees today.
6. Describe the role of the leader in shaping and sustaining culture.
7. Explain the relationship between organization–person fit and culture.
8. Identify cultural challenges facing leaders today.

A Canadian Cultural Icon

The employees at BCE were in shock! Their revered leader Jean Monty had quit. The news reverberated throughout the community and the stock market responded with a 17 percent decrease in BCE's share price.

Jean Monty had been at the helm for four years and his successes were noteworthy. But recently his strategy was met with failure. BCE's investment in Teleglobe was considered his most serious mistake, but critics also found fault with other parts of his strategy. They said he paid too much for CTV, and the company's investment in BCE Emerges Inc., the electronic commerce subsidiary, was yet another error in judgment. Because the culture of BCE is one that values integrity, honesty, and delivering on performance expectations, it does not tolerate failure and expects someone to take ownership for their actions. Jean Monty is a man of extremely high integrity and dignity. He expressed these values through his actions. He did what was expected of him—the only thing he could do: Quit!

What drove this behaviour? Why did Jean Monty feel he needed to quit? To understand these actions we need to understand the core values that drive this organization. What are BCE's guiding principles?

BCE is Canada's largest telecommunications company. It owns CTV, Canada's number one broadcaster; runs our leading national newspaper, the *Globe and Mail*; and provides telephony, Internet, and satellite TV through its principle subsidiary, Bell Canada. Bell Canada is a name that Canadians feel is synonymous with culture, part of the fabric of our society. Bell is 124 years old; its history dates back to the 19th century, beginning with one of the most significant innovations of our time—the telephone—the achievement of its inventor, Canadian Alexander Graham Bell.

BCE believes in sustainability through innovation, excellence, open communication, and social responsibility. These values are articulated through its numerous programs, practices, and initiatives. For example, in support of innovation, Bell University Laboratories draws together Bell Canada professionals with the Canadian university research community in key strategic areas of emerging wire line and wireless communications, e-business, new media, human–computer interaction, and e-health applications. To enhance the quality of life in communities, Bell contributes significantly to charities supporting community economic development funds designed to help build community capacity and sustain the economic and social fabric of our communities. Bell's "Walk for Kids" and its youth program "Be Web Aware" are just a few examples of how Bell articulates its values.

Tenets that guide Bell's decisions are figured prominently on their web page: "Good is never good enough, the customer drives everything, simpler is better and it's all about performance, results matter. Customer and shareholders want action, they do not want words, and they want to see more than progress—We know we must deliver. And delivery means that all employees demonstrate through their performance a commitment to these values."

Today, BCE operates in a highly competitive market facing significant competition from local and global players. The sluggish economic climate has impacted its sales as many organizations are limiting their corporate spending on IT and telecom infrastructure. Despite these challenges, the company managed to post a modest operating profit during 2003. Their strategy to deliver integrated communications has been a challenge for its leadership but it is no accident that revenue has grown. It is the culture of the organization, the core values that BCE has espoused that drive these actions.

Jean Monty did what he needed to do, and BCE continues to learn from its successes and failures.

SOURCES: "Jean Monty Quits as Head of BCE," *CBC Online*, accessed July 28, 2004 from http://www.cbc.ca/stories/2002/04/24/monty_020424; Hoover's Company Profiles, *Profile – BCE Inc.* (Austin, TX: Hoover's Inc., 2003); Datamonitor Company Profiles, *BCE Inc. – SWOT Analysis* (Datamonitor plc., 2004); Bell Canada Enterprises website, accessed July 20, 2004 from http://www.bce.ca.

This chapter is divided into three parts: part one is devoted to discussing the basics—what culture is, how we can recognize it and how we can describe it. In part two, we explore the topic of organizational performance as it relates to culture. We discuss various approaches to understanding effective cultures and look at the concept of organizational fit from the individual and organizational perspective. Next we discuss the role of the leader in shaping and sustaining culture. In part three, we identify the future challenges facing organizations today and the impact of these challenges on organizational sustainability.

LEARNING ABOUT CULTURE

Fortune
Each year *Fortune* magazine releases its list of the top employers in the U.S. Visit the site and do a keyword search on "best companies to work for."
http://www.fortune.com

Maclean's
Each year *Maclean's* publishes an article on the top 100 employers in Canada. Visit the website to learn more about this survey.
www.macleans.ca

Why are we attracted to one company and not another? Why do we choose to stay at one company and are proud of where we work? What makes us want to work for one company versus another?

In a famous study by McKinsey and Company titled "The War of Talent," 200 executives from various companies were asked why they joined, stayed, or left a company. They found that 58 percent of its respondents cited values and culture as being absolutely essential.[1]

Every year several high-profile business magazines publish surveys on the top companies to work for. In the 2004 article in *Fortune* magazine, J.M. Smucker and Company, a family-controlled business headquartered in Orrville, Ohio, was rated number one, its culture and management style noted as being highly impressive.[2] In the *Maclean's* magazine top 100 employers in Canada, the lead story in the 2004 issue is about how Yamaha Motors Canada enriches the lives of its community by partnering with the Canadian Mental Health Association to offer jobs for people recovering from severe mental illness.[3]

High-performing companies express who they are, what they value, and the type of behaviours they expect their employees to demonstrate. Leaders model these behaviours and align the organization programs and practices. These companies are unique and special; it is in this uniqueness that their culture is expressed. It has often been said that culture is the way we do things around here.

Define *organizational culture* and explain why it is important in today's business environment.

INTRODUCTION TO ORGANIZATIONAL CULTURE

organizational (corporate) culture
A pattern of basic assumptions that are considered valid and that are taught to new members as the way to perceive, think, and feel in the organization.

Organizational (corporate) culture has been defined as a pattern of shared values and beliefs that help individuals understand how the organization functions.[4] It defines the appropriate attitudes and behaviours that guide employee's actions.[5] It has been described as a pattern of shared basic assumptions learned by the group while solving problems of external adaptation and internal integration. These assumptions have worked well enough to be considered valid and therefore to be taught to new members as the correct way to perceive, think, and feel in relations to these problems.[6] A more contemporary definition views culture as a collective belief system that people within a company have about their ability to compete in the marketplace and how they act on those belief systems to bring value-added services and products to customers and profits to the company.[7]

Schneider simply identified culture as "the way we do things around here."[8]

Culture is about

1. Establishing patterns of belief or shared meaning and about shared understanding. This shared understanding originates from the common learning experiences that members of an organization share as they respond to external challenges. Members of organizations engage in problem solving and decision making in response to these challenges.
2. Organizations developing a pattern of basic assumptions as a result of learning what works and what does not. It is about sharing these experiences with organizational members and teaching members how to perceive, feel, and act when faced with similar challenges. Eventually these assumptions become part of the fabric of that organization and are embedded in the history of that organization.

3. Leaders translating this learning to organizational members by clearly articulating and expressing these values in words and actions.[9]
4. A sense of an organization's uniqueness. Because all organizations have different experiences, organizational culture becomes a unique characteristic of any organization.

Why Is Learning about Organizational Culture Important?

In order to survive, organizations have to achieve a level of performance. This performance can be defined in several ways but from a financial perspective, profitability is a key determinant of success. Extraordinary financial results are a visible outcome of a successful company. But how organizations actually align their strategy and people to achieve this result has been a hot topic of discussion among organizational behaviourists and researchers for decades.

As early as 1992, John Kotter and James Haskett explored the power of culture on financial performance. Their studies indicated that corporate culture can have a significant impact on a firm's long-term economic performance. They found that firms with a culture that emphasized the stakeholders—customers, suppliers, employees, stockholders—and leadership from managers at all levels outperformed firms that did not have these traits. However, some cultures inhibit strong long-term performance because they typically reinforce nonproductive behaviour. Although tough to change, corporate cultures could be made to focus on organizational performance. This change was considered complex, requiring time, leadership versus management, and guidance by a realistic vision of what kinds of cultures enhance performance—a vision they felt was hard to find in either the business community or the literature on culture at that time.[10]

Research on mergers and acquisitions additionally supports the claim that culture is tied to organizational performance. McKinsey and Company found that 61 percent of all acquisition programs fail. They defined failure as not earning a sufficient return on the funds invested—translating to poor financial performance. A key reason for this failure—"lack of cultural fit"![11]

A recent study by Right Management of 156 companies in North America, Europe, and Asia-Pacific found that differences in organizational culture, not national or cultural issues, were more likely to trip up a successful integration.[12]

Could this merger work? The largest merger in the hardware sector recently took place between Hewlett Packard (HP) and Compaq.[13] Early on, the analysts expressed significant concerns about the cultural synergy between the two organizations. Although it was felt that there was significant synergy between the product and customer markets and a new leader who wanted to change the HP business model, there were significant concerns regarding the "cultural fit." Compaq was known for its sales culture. It was hard driving and results focused. People were considered secondary to profits and through its turbulent years it downsized and upsized showing minimal allegiance to its employees. The HP culture, known as the HP Way, was legendary. It focused on engineering excellence and pride in producing high-quality products and in its research and development (R&D). Decision making was consensual and employees were treated like family with relatively few layoffs. Could this merger work? The markets were not sure. When the merger plans were announced HP's stock price tumbled 18 percent.[14]

Right Management
Right Management is a global leader in career transition and organizational consulting. Visit the website to learn more about their programs.
www.right.com

Organizations are like mini-societies: they have their own distinctive patterns of culture and subculture but these cultures can be fragmented and ineffective. They are not always uniform, strong, or high performing.[15] It takes a strong leadership, focused strategy, and aligned systems to make it work. High-performing organizations take culture seriously—they articulate to employees what the organization values; consistently demonstrate these values though integrated policies, procedures, and practices; and exhibit strong leadership.[16]

CIBC
CIBC is a leading North American financial institution that provides financial services to more than nine million customers. Learn more about its programs and practices.
www.cibc.com

Why is learning about culture so important? If we can understand organizational culture, leaders can directly influence organizational effectiveness, which translates ultimately into a sustainable, thriving entity.

Functions of Culture

Culture serves several functions. It provides a sense of identity to members and a way for employees to interpret the meaning of organizational events. It also coordinates members' efforts and clarifies what is important and what performance is expected in order to achieve organizational goals, operating as a control mechanism for shaping behaviour. Culture provides guidance to employees on how to adapt their behaviour to meet external and internal challenges, and identifies distinctive competencies of an organization to external stakeholders.[17] How well an organization does this depends on leadership and the ability of leaders to articulate and demonstrate consistently "what is important around here."[18]

At Indigo Books and Music, the number one priority is customer service. What this behaviour looks like is clearly articulated in the company manual. Some of the behaviours expected are acknowledging and greeting customers when they walk in the door, a willingness to go the extra mile and do what it takes to respond to a customer's request, and the ability to quickly provide the specific item requested by a customer.[19]

An important part of CIBC culture is the belief that organizations should "giving back" to the communities in which they do business. The CIBC "Spirit of Leadership" Community Award program recognizes and celebrates their commercial banking clients for these efforts. Each year five awards are presented to those clients who demonstrate unique giving and community spirit initiatives.[20]

Identify the elements of culture and the various ways we can recognize culture.

OBSERVING CULTURAL DIFFERENCES

Think about walking into a Tim Hortons. What do you think of? Coffee, donuts, or perhaps purchasing some Timbits? The smell of the coffee and the taste of the donuts is a familiar feeling. The employees are dressed in uniforms and each Tim's location no matter where you are in the country is the same in terms of design and feel. You are greeted in the same way and you have grown to expect that familiar service. There are people who will drive for kilometres just to have a Tim's coffee. Many of us on our coffee breaks ritually go to "Timmy's" for a coffee. Now, think about the language you use to order a Tim's coffee: double-double, large, regular, or small? How many people do you know who cannot wait for the "Roll up the Rim" contest?

Ever notice the coin box on the counter at a store? Tim Hortons also supports its local communities. Through a nonprofit charitable organization called the Children's Foundation they provide a camp experience for children who are economically disadvantaged in the local communities in which they serve. Tim Hortons is part of the fabric of our Canadian culture, aimed at providing good value to everyone.

As consumers' tastes grew, so did the choices at Tim Hortons. In addition to its coffee and donuts, Tim's also serves its popular soup and sandwich deals.

Now compare this experience to another coffee chain. Perhaps you frequent Starbucks. Here you are likely to hear jazz or blues playing in the background and you will be asked whether you want a tall, short, or grande coffee. Frappacinos and lattes are commonly ordered and paying a dear amount for a coffee is typical. Specialty coffees are abundant, as are specialty pastries and muffins, and you may even decide to bring home a pound of Gold Coast coffee. Starbucks also supports charitable causes. Its foundation is dedicated to enriching the lives of youth in underserved communities, providing funding for programs in literacy. The culture of Starbucks is one of novelty, it is about choice, it is for someone who is a "coffee aficionado." Go to the Application & Analysis feature to learn more.

Starbucks' company objective is to be the most recognized, most respected brand in the world.

Application & Analysis

HOW WOULD YOU DESCRIBE THE CULTURE OF YOUR FAVOURITE COFFEE SHOP?

The next time you feel like a coffee, a tea, or hot chocolate, enter your favourite place and look around. What do you see? What is the language you use to order your beverage? How do the employees respond to you? Is there a particular way in which you stand in line? Now compare this to another coffee/tea chain? How does this experience differ from Tim Hortons or Starbucks? What is it that is different between these experiences?

CULTURAL ELEMENTS: THE THREE LEVELS OF CULTURE

Edgar Schein, in his comprehensive book on organizational culture and leadership, suggests that organizational culture can be viewed at several levels. These levels range from being apparent and visible to tacit and invisible. His view of culture is presented in Exhibit 12.1. To achieve a complete understanding of an organization's culture, all three levels must be studied.

Artifacts

Symbols of culture in the physical and social work environment are called **artifacts.** They are the most visible and accessible level of culture. The key to understanding culture through artifacts lies in figuring out what they mean. These artifacts can be viewed at the surface level. Culture is what we hear, see, and feel when we encounter a "group." It is the language one hears as we interact with the group; it is the physical setting of the environment one encounters when we enter a building or an office. It is the ceremonies and rites, stories, rituals, and symbols we encounter.[21]

artifacts
Symbols of culture in the physical and social work environment.

EXHIBIT 12.1

Levels of Organizational Culture

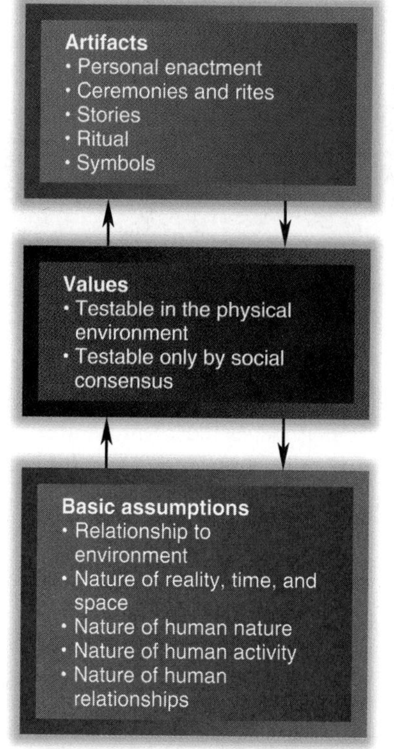

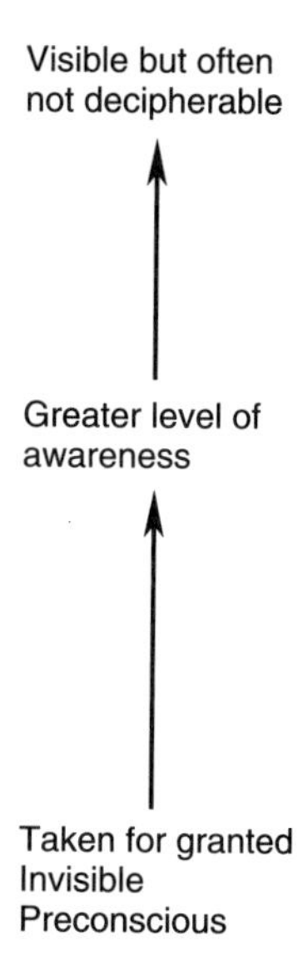

SOURCE: From Edgar H. Schein, *Organizational Culture and Leadership: A Dynamic View.* Copyright © 1985 Jossey-Bass, Inc. Reprinted by permission of John Wiley & Sons, Inc.

organizational reality 12.1

Roots—A Company of Tradition

Roots Canada has influenced Canadian culture—its logo and its name symbolize Canadian cultural heritage. Its symbol is a source of pride worn by our national heroes and athletes at the Olympic Games. Its name, Roots, means "ties"—ties to Canada. Roots manufactures many of its products in Canada. Its logo is a beaver sitting on some twigs. This beaver is a Canadian symbol of industriousness and productivity that reminds Canadians of the richness of its lands, its forests, trees, and wildlife. Roots opened its first store on Yonge Street in Toronto in 1973, and through its words and actions it pursues its vision. More recently, it was chosen to be the official outfitter for the 2004 Summer Olympics. This potent combination of athletics, glamour, and national pride is at the heart of what Roots is all about. So the next time you see a Roots logo, think about culture and how these artifacts contribute to Canadians' understanding of who we are and what we stand for.

Roots co-founders Michael Budman and Don Green.

SOURCE: Roots Canada website, accessed July 20, 2004, from http://www.roots.ca.

Ceremonies and Rites

Relatively elaborate sets of activities that are enacted time and time again on important occasions are known as organizational ceremonies and rites.[22] These occasions provide opportunities to reward and recognize employees whose behaviour is congruent with the values of the company. Ceremonies and rites send a message that individuals who both espouse and exhibit corporate values are heroes to be admired. Ceremonies also bond organization members together. Every year Bacardi & Company Limited celebrates its birthday worldwide. Across the globe everyone raises a glass and toasts the founder, Don Facundo Bacardi Masso. Employees' birthdays are celebrated as well. At the site in Toronto, employees are asked to join all the staff in the cafeteria to celebrate. Everyone receives a cake and they get to blow out the candles. It is a valued ritual at Bacardi, a family-oriented company.[23]

Six kinds of rites in organizations have been identified:[24]

1. *Rites of passage* show that an individual's status has changed. Academic graduation and retirement dinners are an example.
2. *Rites of enhancement* reinforce the achievement of individuals. An example is the awarding of certificates to sales contest winners.
3. *Rites of renewal* emphasize change in the organization and commitment to learning and growth. An example is the opening of a new corporate training centre.
4. *Rites of integration* unite diverse groups or teams within the organization and renew commitment to the larger organization. Company functions such as annual picnics fall into this category.
5. *Rites of conflict reduction* focus on dealing with conflicts or disagreements that arise naturally in organizations. Examples are grievance hearings and the negotiation of union contracts.
6. *Rites of degradation* are used by some organizations to visibly punish persons who fail to adhere to values and norms of behaviour. Some CEOs, for example, are replaced quite publicly for unethical conduct or for failure to achieve organizational goals. In some Japanese organizations, employees who perform poorly are given ribbons of shame as punishment.

Stories

Some researchers have argued that the most effective way to reinforce organizational values is through stories.[25] As they are told and retold, stories give meaning and identity to organizations and are especially helpful in orienting new employees. Part of the strength of organizational stories is that the listeners are left to draw their own conclusions—a powerful communication tool.[26]

Sometimes stories are about organizational heroes and their quests. Steve Jobs—the founder of Apple computers—is one such hero. Soon after Jobs left Apple in 1985, increased competition due to the emergence of the personal computer (PC) cost Apple market share. Microsoft's Windows operating system, which was compatible with any PC, was the catalyst for Apple's multi-billion dollar losses in the early 1990s. Apple suffered from a lack of quality senior leadership and innovation. After being away for over 11 years, Steve Jobs returned. His charisma and his ability to focus Apple's strategic goals allowed Apple to return to profitability within one year.[27] New products such as the iPod have fuelled Apple's resurgence under his leadership.[28] He managed to re-energize the company and return it to the black.

Research by Joanne Martin and her colleagues has indicated that certain themes appear in stories across different types of organizations:[29]

1. *Stories about the boss.* These stories may reflect whether the boss is "human" or how the boss reacts to mistakes.
2. *Stories about getting fired.* Events leading to employee firings are recounted.

Wal-Mart
Learn more about the Wal-Mart story and how Sam Walton, founder of Wal-Mart, created a sustainable corporate culture.
http://www.walmart.ca

3. *Stories about how the company deals with employees who have to relocate.* These stories relate to the company's actions toward employees who have to move—whether the company is helpful and takes family and other personal concerns into account.
4. *Stories about whether lower-level employees can rise to the top.* Often, these stories describe a person who started out at the bottom and eventually became the CEO.
5. *Stories about how the company deals with crisis situations.* The example of how RBC dealt with a computer crisis shows how a company overcomes obstacles.
6. *Stories about how status considerations work when rules are broken.* When Tom Watson, Sr., was CEO of IBM, a security guard once confronted him because he was not wearing an ID badge.

These are the themes that can emerge when stories are passed down. The information from these stories serves to guide the behaviour of organization members.

To be effective cultural tools, stories must be credible. You cannot tell a story about your flat corporate hierarchy and then have reserved parking spaces for managers. Stories that are not backed by reality can lead to cynicism and mistrust.

Rituals

Everyday organizational practices that are repeated over and over are rituals. They are usually unwritten, but they send a clear message about "the way we do things around here." While some companies insist that people address each other by their titles (Mr., Mrs., Ms., Miss) and surnames to reinforce a professional image, others prefer that employees operate on a first-name basis—from the top manager on down. Hewlett-Packard values open communication, so its employees address one another by first names only.

As everyday practices, rituals reinforce the organizational culture. Insiders who commonly practise the rituals may be unaware of their subtle influence, but outsiders recognize it easily. Consider the ritual practised at Wal-Marts across the country. Every morning before each store opens all employees recite the Wal-Mart cheer.

Symbols

Symbols communicate organizational culture by unspoken messages. Symbols are used to build solidarity in the organizational culture.[30] Symbols are representative of organizational identity and membership to employees. Have you ever noticed the Shopper's Drug Mart symbol? It is a mortar and pestle, which is the old-fashioned way to mix drugs. Nike's trademark "swoosh" is proudly tattooed above the ankles of some Nike employees. Apple Computer employees readily identify themselves as "Apple People." Bacardi & Company Limited's symbol is a bat. The story goes that during the time that Bacardi rums were first made, many of the people in the town were illiterate. To make the product marketable the company felt it needed a highly recognizable and attractive symbol—the symbol of the bat. Because the bat represented the old world virtues of faithfulness, loyalty, good fortune, and longevity, it was the perfect fit.[31]

At the level of artifacts, culture is clear. But in order to understand why some organizations choose to celebrate birthdays and others not, or perhaps why some organizations ritualistically honour their founders, we need to understand what the values of that organization.

Values

What does the organization value? Do they walk the talk? Values are the second, and deeper, level of culture. They reflect a person's underlying beliefs of what should be or should not be. Values are often consciously articulated, both in conversation and in a company's mission statement or annual report. At Indigo Books and Music their mission is "to provide booklovers, culture makers, entertainment seekers with the most inspiring richly stocked and inviting retail environment and to provide shareholders and employees with a meaningful return on investment."[32]

Values give rise to behavioural norms. They provide employees with a sense of direction and guidelines for day-to-day behaviour. However, there may be a difference between a company's **espoused values** (what the members say they value) and its **enacted values** (values reflected in the way the members actually behave).[33] This is very powerful if an organization is effective. Is there congruency between espoused and enacted values? Incongruent values gives employees mixed messages about what is important in an organization.

espoused values
What members of an organization say they value.

enacted values
Values reflected in the way individuals actually behave.

Values provide a useful anchor when an organization is in a state of flux. Consider the example of the Ontario Liberal Party before and after the provincial election of 2004. Throughout the election campaign Ontario Liberal leader, Dalton McGuinty, promised voters that his party would balance the budget and improve healthcare and education, while at the same time not raising taxes. However, less then eight months after having won the election the Liberals raised taxes and acknowledged that they could not maintain a balanced budget. This is a clear case of enacted values contradicting espoused values.[34]

In the corporate world, Samsung is an excellent example of a firm whose values underlie the adaptability and innovativeness of its culture. The CEO of Samsung sees the goal of the company as "freeing people from time and space" through better access to technology and easier-to-use products. Creativity and innovation are the soul of the company; they are core values and it is expected that all employees demonstrate these values in their jobs. Samsung is continually striving to create the next must-have electronics product aimed at hip young consumers worldwide. Samsung not only wants to be a leader in cutting-edge digital technology, but also wants to use that same technology to digitally integrate its divisions into one cohesive unit. This integration is going to be accomplished through the use of what it calls "?-Processes," which will connect R&D, production, and marketing to customers and partners.[35]

High-performing organizations articulate their values and reinforce behaviour by aligning their policies, procedures, and practices. For example, a company's recruitment practices can reflect this alignment. At Indigo books, CEO Heather Reisman has identified the values of passion, low ego, high achievement, and creativity as core values. The organization identified key behavioural indicators which reflect these values, hiring individuals who demonstrate a passion for their products and services, individuals who constantly strive to achieve more.[36]

Assumptions: 'The Essence of Culture'

Assumptions are the deeply held beliefs that guide behaviour and tell members of an organization how to perceive and think about things. These assumptions refer to the collective learning process experienced by members of an organization in response to adapting successfully to organizational challenges. They are shared mental models that members of an organization hold, beliefs that have developed over time. These beliefs about how to solve problems have become taken for granted, as they work repeatedly and reliably. They are the collective wisdom of an organization. Assumptions are not visible and need to be uncovered so that we can understand what truly is important to members of an organization.

assumptions
Deeply held beliefs that guide behaviour and tell members of an organization how to perceive and think about things.

For example, some basic assumptions that develop in organizations are in relation to how it should effectively respond to an environmental threat. Should it submit, dominate, or find a safe niche? If the organization was successful in the past when responding in a particular way then its members will often engage in that same behaviour when faced with a similar situation. Operating under the assumption that past behaviour is a good predictor of future performance, members of the organization develop an assumption about the best way to respond to this particular threat. In essence they develop a mental model based on their perceptions.

Members of the organization learn what works and what doesn't. They develop assumptions based on their experience. These assumptions or beliefs in turn give rise to values. These values give rise to behavioural norms—the way we should do things around here. This is evidenced in overt behaviour and artifacts.[37]

Application & Analysis

ANALYZING THE THREE LEVELS OF CULTURE

Select an organization you respect. Analyze its culture using the following dimensions.

The artifacts of ____________'s culture are as follows:

Rites and ceremonies:

Stories:

Rituals:

Symbols:

The values embedded in ____________'s culture are as follows:

The assumptions of ____________'s culture are as follows:

1. On what information did you base your analysis?
2. How complete is your view of this organization's culture?

Explain several ways that cultures can be described.

DESCRIBING CULTURAL DIFFERENCES

Why did you choose to study at a particular university? Perhaps it was the academic reputation of that university or maybe it was the size and personal attention you expected to receive. How would you describe the type of company environment that would work for you? Is it the organization's commitment to charitable work? Maybe it is the family activities or the focus on career development that attracts you? Think about what these environments should look like.

In the previous section, we discussed the levels of culture and its various elements. How can we best describe culture? This descriptions can be simplistically represented by terms such as "family friendly," "innovative," "risk taking," "customer focused," "people focused," "creative," and "adaptable," or more formally expressed through cultural models. In this section we will be examining three models; the risk and feedback model proposed by Deal and Kennedy,[38] the interpersonal interaction model described by Harrison and Stokes,[39] and the recent work of Dr. Jerry Want,[40] who describes culture on a continuum based on responsiveness to the customer and financial success, which he calls a hierarchy of cultures. See Exhibit 12.2.

Risk and Feedback Model

Deal and Kennedy's model of culture characterizes four types of organizations based on two factors in the marketplace: the degree of risk associated with the company's activities and the speed at which companies and employees get feedback on whether decisions or strategies are successful. Once the employee understands the culture, the employee will be able to accomplish things in a more effective way. A company may have a mix of these types in various departments. The four types of cultures described are: tough-guy macho; work-hard, play-hard; bet-the-company; and process. See Exhibit 12.3.

- *Tough-guy macho culture:* This type of organization operates in a high-risk, quick-feedback environment. Heroes of these organizations are tough and individualistic. It is common for these organizations to make large capital investments upfront, but results are known quickly. The focus is more on the present and on short-term planning. Typical industries include advertising, entertainment industries, and stock brokers.
- *Work-hard, play-hard culture:* This type of organization operates in a low-risk, quick-feedback environment and is successful through a high level of relatively low-risk activity. Here the individual identifies a need and fills it. Think about a salesperson.

EXHIBIT 12.2

Cultural Models

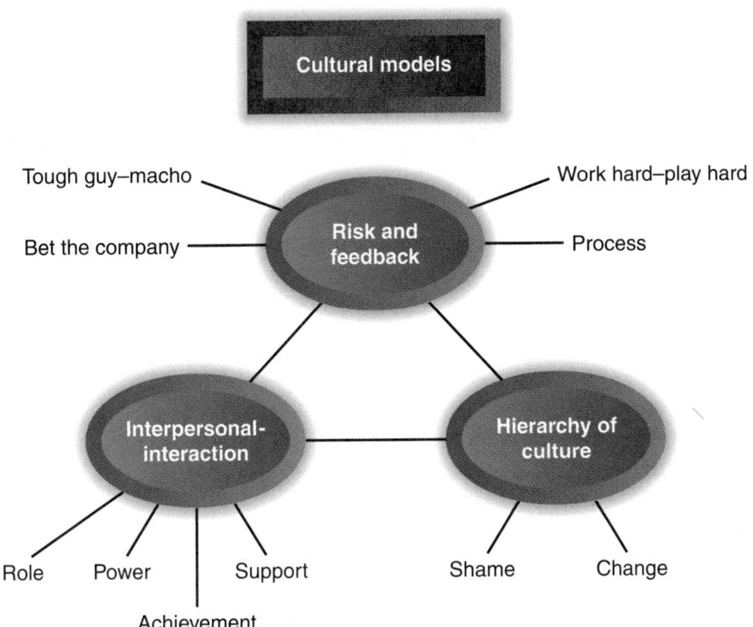

Typical industries where we may encounter this type of behaviour is in the retail or sales environments, real estate firms, and car dealers.

- *Bet-the-company culture:* This type of organization operates in a high-risk, slow-feedback environment. Large capital investments are typically required but the results of these investments are not known for a long time. Typical industries include aerospace and drug companies.
- *Process culture:* This type of organization operates in a low-risk, slow-feedback space. Here we see little or no feedback and the concentration is on how work is done and

EXHIBIT 12.3

Risk and Feedback Model

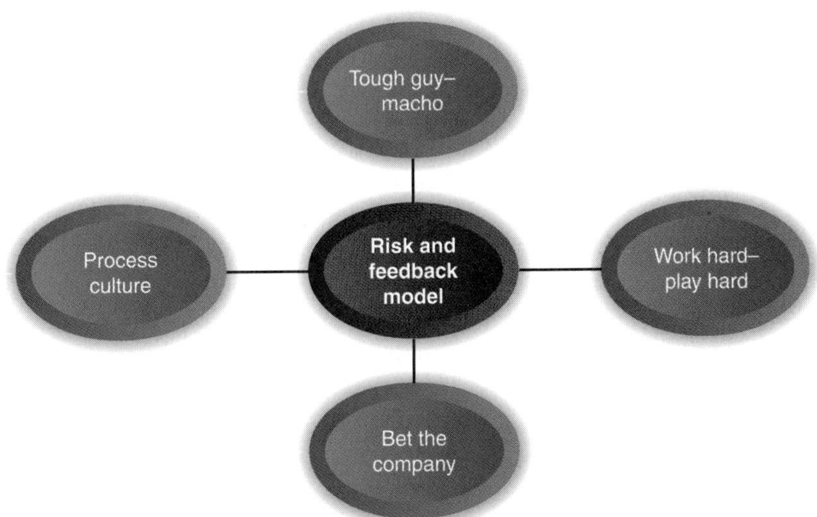

not what is done. People are cautious and procedures are followed. The heroes of these companies tend to be very orderly with a strong attention to detail. This type of culture can be found in accounting departments, regulated industries, and government.[41]

Interpersonal Interaction Model

Harrison and Stokes described a model of culture called the interpersonal interaction model. They suggested that organizations can be regarded as having one of four orientations: power, role, achievement, and support (see Exhibit 12.4).

- *The power orientation:* This type of organization places most of the decision-making responsibilities at the top of the organization. In power organizations leadership is based on paternalistic benevolence. Leaders are firm, fair, and generous with loyal subordinates. They have a sense of obligation to their followers and they exercise power according to their understanding of what is good for the organization and all employees. Employees are expected to be loyal followers. The people in power use resources to satisfy or frustrate the needs of others and thus to control others' behaviour. Leadership resides in the person of the leader(s) and rests on the leader's ability and willingness to administer rewards and punishments. The organizational structure is based on a hierarchy, communication is formal and guarded, and the reward structure tends to be external. Organizations that are excessively "power oriented" may tend toward ruling by fear, with an abuse of power.
- *The role orientation:* Unlike the power type culture, the emphasis here is placed on rules and regulations to make sure that things are done "right." The work that you do, the role that you play are carefully defined, with the expectation that employees will do what is required by the formal system. It is subject to explicit or implicit contracts between the organization and the individual. This type of culture values order, dependability, rationality, and consistency. Change can be difficult for such cultures because of the strict adherence to roles, as flexibility is not always easy. This type orientation may be best suited to a stable environment. In highly unionized environments we tend to find this type of culture. Collective agreements provide for an explicit classification of jobs and clearly define the type of work that is required.

EXHIBIT 12.4

Interpersonal Interaction Model

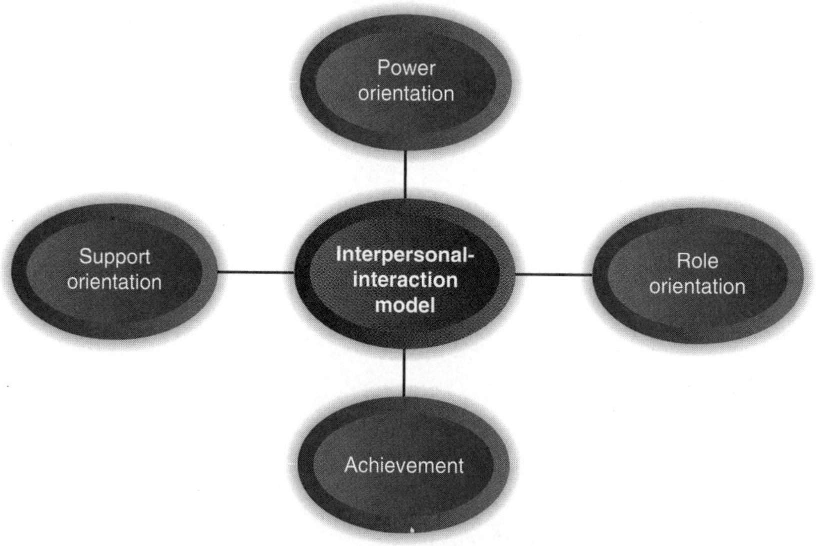

- *The achievement orientation:* This culture is egalitarian, and all employees are seen as being able to influence those decisions that concern getting the job done. Individuals use their authority to obtain the resources needed to complete the task. Here the work situation engages the total person—people give their all. Teamwork is common and people exhibit high morale. Here employees demonstrate a sense of urgency. However, due to this constant atmosphere people may feel some burnout.
- *The support orientation:* The support culture can be defined as an organization based on trust between the individual and the organization. Here people believe they are valued as human beings. This culture focuses on warmth and perpetuates a feeling of being cared for. People come to work not just because they like the work but also because they like the people. People in these organization celebrate together and spend time together, they communicate a lot. They value harmony. Organizations with a support orientation have as their goal the development of individuals, helping employees reach their potential. This culture assumes people want to contribute. On a negative note, in this environment there can be very little conflict as individuals like to avoid any strife and consensus is overvalued. Have you ever worked in this type of environment?

The Hierarchy of Corporate Cultures

This model, developed by Dr. Jenny Wart, identifies types of corporate environments that range from a lack of cultural integrity to highly successful cultures. Success is defined in terms of outcomes such as productivity, customer satisfaction, and investor confidence. Corporate cultures are classified into two basic categories: cultures of shame (failed and failing cultures) and cultures of change. See Exhibit 12.5.

Cultures of Shame

There are five different types of cultures of shame: predatory, frozen, chaotic, political, and bureaucratic cultures.

Predatory Cultures

Think about the word *predatory.* What does it mean within an organization? These cultures are viewed as punitive, alienating, and exploitive. In this type of culture we see lots of internal strife, warring factions, excessive conflicts between various groups. These organizations are so focused on internal, petty issues that employee productivity,

EXHIBIT 12.5

Hierarchy of Corporate Cultures

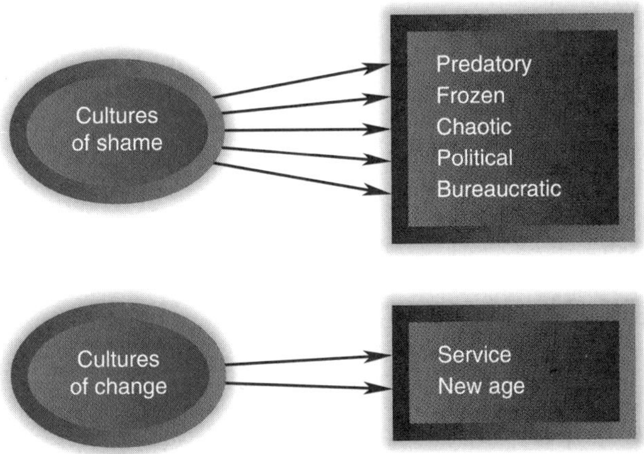

customer satisfaction, and marketplace and investor confidence are all compromised. There are warring factions and lots of internal conflicts between the various groups. Predatory cultures rarely change internally and appear to respond only when faced with extreme shareholder pressure, external pressure through the media, increased regulatory scrutiny, and punishment (legal action).

Frozen Cultures

Frozen cultures are not effective at long-term planning. They are paralyzed by gridlock and denial. These cultures have an aversion to risk taking. This aversion starts at the top and is imposed on the entire organization by uncertain management that fears mistakes. These organizations demonstrate a limited capacity for innovation and discourage new ideas. The management hierarchy must be maintained at all costs and going around the boss is considered a lethal career move. As a result, senior management is never really informed about growing problems better seen at lower levels of the organization. A current example is Stelco, Canada's second biggest steel producer, which is struggling to maintain its existence. The increasing competition facing the steel market over the past decade has forced this industry to cut costs, focus on efficiencies, and develop innovative facilities. But Stelco began to lag the trends as it continued to equate size and diversity of product with success even as the industry began to punish old-style integrated, unionized firms like Stelco and reward nonunion mini-mills and makers of niche products. Additionally, Stelco's internal challenges continue to plague its ability to stay alive as its unions have resisted overtures for significant wage cuts.[42]

Chaotic Cultures

Chaotic cultures are debilitating like frozen cultures but they are more fragmented and unfocused. Their mission and vision are unclear to all constituents. They have incongruent policies and practices, with one department following a different corporate strategy from another. It is not atypical to see this type of environment when an organization starts up or when there is a merger of companies. Creating a common culture amidst turf warfare can be challenging at best. Many software and Internet companies exhibit qualities of a chaotic culture as they seem to focus only on the technology at the expense of sound management and planning practices.

Political Cultures

We have all worked within political cultures, and even the most positive cultures have an element of politics. Political cultures transcend organizational size and industry. The internal jockeying for influence, resources, position, and career advancement dominates the agendas of companies with political cultures. The organization, as a whole, never equals the sum of its parts as turf warfare, hero building, and retaliation are common behaviours. Political cultures differ from predatory cultures in that they do have rules on how the politics are played while setting some implicit limits on the chaos created by the politics. Universities and large partnerships are examples of organizations that are dominated by political cultures.

In 1995, Motorola was the world leader in pagers and cell phones but by 1999 it was struggling as it failed to anticipate the industry's switch to digital cell phones from analogue. A major contributor to this failure was the way the organization was structured. This structure was based on a team model where divisions within Motorola would compete for the same funding and support from headquarters. This tribal approach meant that if a customer could not get the product it wanted from one Motorola division, another could develop the product. In the early 1980s and '90s, this structure worked, but when the competitive environment changed the structure no longer worked. Within each division at Motorola the managers became focused on the political infighting to obtain resources against each other, arguing over the merits of the switch from analogue to digital technology. The competition, led by Ericsson and Nokia, already made the switch to digital technology in the early 1990s, eroding Motorola's lead in the wireless industry.

Bureaucratic cultures

A bureaucratic culture is one that is characterized by highly routine tasks achieved through specialization and formalized rules. Decisions follow a specific chain of command. These types of cultures typically place the needs of customers below the needs of the bureaucracy. Bureaucratic cultures are associated with large organizations—typically phone companies, utilities, insurance companies, banks, associations, and government agencies, where checking and monitoring and complying with regulations are central to operations.

Cultures of Change

The hierarchy of corporate cultures includes two cultures of change, the service culture and new age cultures.

The Service Culture

Companies with service cultures focus on making sure that the customers' needs are first. Mission, strategy, structure, systems, policies, and operations all start and end with the customer. Service cultures recognize that their business or product is service. In true service cultures, the motto is "If you are not serving the customer, you better be serving someone who is."[43] Employees can make decisions and are empowered to solve problems. The employee is considered the link between the company and its customers. Business strategy is customer-centred. Have you ever flown WestJet? WestJet is the most successful low-cost carrier in Canadian history. The company knows what its customers want—low cost, good value, friendly and on-time service—and it delivers. It won an award for Canada's most respected company in 2003—coming in second overall and up from seventh in 2002, it came in first in customer service, second in HR management, second in top of mind, fifth in innovation and product/service development, and sixth in financial performance.[44]

organizational reality 12.2

Research In Motion: An Innovative "New Age" Company

Imagine you are on your way home from a meeting and you just remembered that you promised to e-mail an important client about a price change, or perhaps you are in a strange town and need to check on when your flight is leaving. In 1999, Research In Motion (RIM) developed the wireless handheld, which revolutionized the marketplace. RIM created a wireless handheld product called the BlackBerry. This product is an electronic organizer that can send and receive e-mails, help you find directions, book flights, and get stock quotes, to name a few of its functions. It became so popular that people were addicted to carrying these devices, saying that they could not live without their BlackBerry. Illustrative of a "new age" culture, RIM has created an environment where creativity and innovation are encouraged, fostering the independence to learn. It is casual and energy driven, inspiring individuals to expand their horizons and rewarding individual for their contributions.

The RIM 7780 Wireless Handheld™—The BlackBerry.

RIM Ltd. is a leading designer, manufacturer, and marketer of innovative wireless solutions for the worldwide mobile communications market. RIM is truly an example of a "new age" company.

SOURCE: Research In Motion website, accessed July 15, 2004, http://www.rim.com.

New Age Cultures

The new age corporate culture is the top performing culture as it combines innovation with strong commitment to the customer and its employees. It fosters an egalitarian work environment that encourages bottom up feedback from the workforce while employees share fully in wealth generated by the company. New age cultures are able to take advantage of opportunities within the marketplace or they create entirely new markets around new products and services—they create change and manage change effectively. They understand future customer needs and create new markets around these needs.

New age cultures are not about restrictive rules or rigid organization structure. Typically this type of organization has "guidelines" as opposed to rules. They operate with a more informal structure that promotes sharing and championing new ideas, talent, and resources. Policies and practices are aligned to support the values of the organization and employees have the opportunity to share in the long-term success of these organizations through their rewards and compensation programs.

Dominant Culture or Subculture

core or dominant culture
The primary values that are accepted throughout the organization.

subculture
Mini-cultures within an organization, typically defined by specific departments, teams, or divisions.

Edward Schein in his work on culture noted that typically in larger organizations we can find a dominant or core culture and numerous sets of subcultures. **The dominant culture** refers to a certain set of assumptions that are shared across all the units. The **core culture** is central to the functioning of the organization, forming the nuclear centre for how that organization operates in order to succeed.[45]

Schein believes that with time we find a number of discrete **subcultures** that have their own integrity. These subcultures develop as a result of the numerous interactions of various groups and the common challenges these groups face. Some of the subcultures will be in conflict with one another, as is the case with higher management and union groups.[46]

So the next time you attempt to describe culture, think about whether various subcultures exist and what they look like? How would you describe them?

Explain the difference between organizational culture and performance.

ORGANIZATIONAL CULTURE AND PERFORMANCE

In the previous section, we explored various forms of culture. But what differentiates the culture of a high-performing company from another? What are these defining characteristics? Can these characteristic be measured?

In the past decade several books have been written on the practices of highly successful companies. As early as 1982, the book *In Search of Excellence* by Peters and Waterman articulated traits of highly successful companies. Most recently books such as *Good to Great* and *Built to Last* have provided valuable insights about the internal workings of such famous companies as 3M, Sony, and Hewlett-Packard.

What makes these companies great? What makes them noteworthy? What is special about these cultures that makes us want to study and understand them? What common traits do these companies possess? In *Built to Last,* James Collins and Jerry Porras note that "the cultures in a visionary company are not soft or undisciplined" because visionary companies have such clarity about who they are, what they are about, and what they are trying to achieve. These companies tend not to have much room for people unwilling or unsuited to their demanding standards.[47]

John Kotter and James Heskett, in their book *Corporate Culture and Performance,* suggest that highly successful companies exhibit three main characteristics. First, these companies all exhibit a strong culture. Second, they anticipate and adapt effectively to change and they are all cognizant of the context in which they operate and align their internal resources accordingly. Third, they are clear on what internal resources they need to meet these challenges and ensure they align these resources to the situation to ensure an optimum "fit." Their extensive studies have led them to identify three theories, which we will examine in the following section: strong cultures; strategically appropriate cultures, the fit perspective; and adaptive cultures.

The Strong Culture Perspective

strong culture
An organizational culture with a consensus on the values that drive the company and with an intensity that is recognizable even to outsiders.

The strong culture perspective states that organizations with "strong" cultures perform better than other organizations.[48] A **strong culture** is an organizational culture with a consensus on the values that drive the company and with an intensity that is recognizable even to outsiders. Thus, a strong culture is deeply held and widely shared. It also is highly resistant to change. One example of a strong culture is IBM's. Its culture is one we are all familiar with: conservative, with a loyal workforce and an emphasis on customer service.

Strong cultures are thought to facilitate performance for three reasons. First, these cultures are characterized by goal alignment; that is, all employees share common goals. Second, strong cultures create a high level of motivation because of the values shared by the members. Third, strong cultures provide control without the oppressive effects of a bureaucracy.

Strong cultures improve organizational performance by energizing employees—appealing to their ideals and values and rallying them around a set of meaningful and unified goals. Strong cultures boost performance by sharing and coordinating employee behaviour. Stated values and norms focus employee's attention on organizational priorities that then guide their behaviour and decision making. They do so without impinging, as formal control systems do, on the autonomy necessary for excellent performance under changing conditions.[49]

But do strong cultures drive strong economic performance? Can the reverse be true? Evidence suggests we consider causality. What if the strong culture leads the firm down the wrong path? The Bay, for example, is an organization with a strong culture, but in the early 1990s, it focused inward, ignoring competition and changing consumer preferences and as a result suffered weak financial performance. Changing the Bay's strong but traditional culture has been a tough task. In an article entitled "Reinventing the Bay: CEO George Heller Is Returning Canada's Oldest Corporation to Its Roots," Heller says, "Retail is a blood sport and if you aren't prepared for that you get washed out.... We are now in a position to step on the gas because we can and we should. We can finally move forward with a very consumer centric business plan. Department stores went off the rails when they stopped being true department stores and started being very selective and self-serving with their array of goods and services. We are returning to those roots."[50]

Strategically Appropriate Culture

Explain why cultural fit is important to organizations and employees today.

The **strategically appropriate culture** perspective argues that a culture is good only if it "fits" its context. The context can refer to the objective conditions of the industry or perhaps the firm's strategy. This perspective suggests that a culture characterized by rapid decision making and no bureaucratic behaviour will enhance performance in a highly competitive deal-making environment of an mergers and acquisitions advisory firm but might hurt performance in a traditional fire insurance company. Likewise, a culture in which managers place a high value on excellent technology would help a computer manufacturer but would be inappropriate for a symphony orchestra. Sometimes there is a wide range of cultures within the same industry, with big differences in performance.[51] Nokia, the Finnish maker of wireless phones, has a young, sophisticated, hip culture, and it controls 27 percent of the market. Ericsson's culture is austere and conservative, more like a middle-aged Swedish engineer, and it has 10 percent of the market.[52] Both companies are tying their future success to the mobile Internet market, but the fit perspective predicts that the more agile Nokia will perform better in the future.

strategically appropriate culture
The perspective that a culture is good only if it fits its context. The context can refer to the objective conditions of the industry or perhaps the firm's strategy.

This theory has major implications for an organization's policies and practices related to attraction, socialization, and retention of employees. For example, if an organization requires quick decision making and a sense of urgency, hiring the right employees with the right skills and competencies, socializing those employees so that they understand these core values, and reinforcing these values through targeted compensation and reward programs will ensure that the organization can more effectively operate within its context. The concept of "fit" is a major challenge facing leaders today and will be discussed in more detail later on in the chapter.

The Adaptation Perspective

adaptive culture
An organizational culture that encourages confidence and risk taking among employees, has leadership that produces change, and focuses on the changing needs of customers.

The third theory about culture and performance is the adaptation perspective. Its theme is that only cultures that help organizations adapt to environmental change are associated with excellent performance. An **adaptive culture** is a culture that encourages confidence and risk taking among employees,[53] has leadership that produces change,[54] and focuses on the changing needs of customers.[55] 3M is a company with an adaptive culture, in that it encourages new product ideas from all levels within the company.

To test the adaptation perspective, Kotter and Heskett interviewed industry analysts about the cultures of 22 firms. The contrast between adaptive cultures and non-adaptive cultures was striking. The results of the study are summarized in Exhibit 12.6.

Adaptive cultures facilitate change to meet the needs of three groups of constituents: stockholders, customers, and employees. Nonadaptive cultures are characterized by cautious management that tries to protect its own interests. Adaptive firms showed significantly better long-term economic performance in Kotter and Heskett's study. One contrast that can be made is between Hewlett-Packard (HP), a high performer, and Xerox, a lower performer. The industry analysts viewed HP as valuing excellent leadership more than Xerox. Economic performance from 1977 through 1988 supported this difference: HP's index of annual net income growth was 40.2, as compared to Xerox's 13.1. Kotter and Heskett concluded that the cultures that promote long-term performance are those that are most adaptive.

Given that high-performing cultures are typically strong and adaptive and ensure strategic fit, it is important to know how managers can develop adaptive cultures.[56] In the next section, we will examine the leader's role in managing organizational culture.

Measuring Organizational Effectiveness Using Cultural Traits

Can cultural characteristics be measured? Recently the research of Daniel Dennison has examined the relationship between culture and organizational effectiveness. He found a compelling relationship between organizational culture and bottom-line business performance defined as return on assets, sales and revenue growth, market share, and profitability.

EXHIBIT 12.6

Adaptive versus Nonadaptive Organizational Cultures

	Adaptive Organizational Cultures	Nonadaptive Organizational Cultures
Core values	Most managers care deeply about customers, stockholders, and employees. They also strongly value people and processes that can create useful change (e.g., leadership up and down the management hierarchy).	Most managers care mainly about themselves, their immediate work group, or some product (or technology) associated with that work group. They value the orderly and risk-reducing management process much more highly than leadership initiatives.
Common behaviour	Managers pay close attention to all their constituencies, especially customers, and initiate change when needed to serve their legitimate interests, even if that entails taking some risks.	Managers tend to behave somewhat insularly, politically, and bureaucratically. As a result, they do not change their strategies quickly to adjust to or take advantage of changes in their business environments.

SOURCE: Adapted with the permission of The Free Press, a Division of Simon & Schuster Adult Publishing Group, from *Corporate Culture and Performance* by John P. Kotter and James L. Heskett.

He has identified several core cultural traits that impact performance, proposing that these traits can indeed be measured. The cultural traits are involvement, consistency, adaptability, and mission.

- *Involvement:* Dennison found that effective organizations empower people, build the organization around teams, and develop human capability at all levels.
- *Consistency:* Organizations are effective when they are consistent and well integrated. In a consistent organization, people's behaviour is rooted in a set of core values, leaders and followers are skilled at reaching agreement, and the organization's activities are well coordinated and integrated.
- *Adaptability:* This trait relates to an organization's capacity to adapt to change. Adaptable organizations are continuously improving their ability to add value for the customer. They understand and react to their customers and anticipate future needs. Organizational learning is significant.
- *Mission:* This trait refers to a clear sense of where an organization wants to go and how to get there.[57]

THE INFLUENCE OF LEADERSHIP ON CULTURE

Describe the role of the leader in shaping and sustaining culture.

How do effective the leaders shape and sustain culture? According to Edgar Schein, in his book *Organizational Culture and Leadership,* leaders play crucial roles in shaping and reinforcing culture.[58] The six most important elements in managing culture are (1) what leaders pay attention to, (2) how leaders react to crises, (3) how leaders behave, (4) how leaders allocate rewards, (5) how leaders hire and socialize employees, and (6) how leaders fire individuals.

Leaders in an organization communicate their priorities, values, and beliefs. Effective leaders focus the organization on business strategy, first and foremost. They communicate where the organization is going and engage employees in the methods of achieving those goals. They ensure that members of the organization understand what behaviour is required and how best to achieve a desired result. If these leaders are consistent in what they pay attention to, measure, and control, employees receive clear signals about what is important in the organization. If, however, leaders are inconsistent, employees spend a lot of time trying to decipher and find meaning in the inconsistent signals.

How Leaders Behave

Successful leaders model what behaviour is important to organizational success. They reinforce the values that support organizational culture. Robbins suggests that it is a leader's responsibility to identify the most important aspects of corporate culture and ensure that those desires are expressed in words and actions.[59] In a recent study on management activity, Philip Selznick concludes that the effective leader "is primarily an expert in the promotion and protection of values."[60] These leaders demonstrate what these words mean through their actions, thus making culture real and tangible; something that can be described.

How Leaders React to Crises

The way leaders manage a crisis communicates a powerful message about the corporate culture. Emotions are heightened during a crisis, and learning is intense. Consider the recent crisis faced by the customers of the Royal Bank of Canada. It was the first week in June, 2004, when RBC experienced a major computer problem; millions of RBC's retail customers across the country were locked out of their bank accounts; unable to withdraw cash except by electronic fund transfers, people were unable to make house or car payments.

Gordon Nixon, CEO of RBC.

The company rallied its forces to address this situation. The first and most critical act was to calm the fears of its customers and fix the problem. They did this by notifying all customers and reassuring them as to what this problem meant to them. The company web page had numerous processing updates on the reasons this problem occurred, when it was expected to be fixed, and whom to contact to get more information. Executives went on local radio stations to calm fears, hours at the banks were extended, and the CEO wrote a formal letter to all stakeholders to express an apology for the inconvenience and disruption with a promise to resolve any negative consequences experienced by the customers.[61]

How Leaders Allocate Rewards and Status

To ensure that values are accepted, leaders should reward behaviour that is consistent with their organization's values. Some companies, for example, may claim that they use a pay-for-performance system that distributes rewards on the basis of performance. However, when the time comes for raises, the increases are awarded according to length of service with the company. Imagine the feelings of a high-performing newcomer who has heard leaders espouse the value of rewarding individual performance and then receives only a tiny raise.

How Leaders Hire Individuals and Socialize Employees

A powerful way that leaders reinforce culture is through the selection of newcomers to the organization. Selection starts with identifying what skills and competencies the organization requires. If an organization is going to operate effectively in its environment, it needs to ensure that it gets the right people with the right skills at the right time and that it communicates to those employees what the organization values and what behavioural norms are expected to be followed.

Socialization is a powerful cultural communication tool. Newcomers learn the culture through organizational socialization—the process by which newcomers are transformed from outsiders to participating, effective members of the organization.[62]

Explain the relationship between organization–person fit and culture.

The Relationship between Organization–Person Fit and Culture

Organizations that hire individuals who fit the culture and socialize these individuals as to cultural norms are more effective at sustaining organizational culture. Evidence suggests that the definition of "perfect fit" is being expanded beyond a range of attributes listed on the résumé. It is the soft characteristics that are most important to how likely the candidate is to fit in the culture of the organization. Former GE CEO Jack Welch refers to these soft skills as the values that the organization holds. "We would not knowingly hire anyone in our company that wasn't boundaryless, that wasn't open to an idea from anywhere, that was not excited about a learning environment."[63] And GE is quite willing to toss out managers who do not sign on to the culture, even if they produce good results. "We take people with good results and ask them to move on to other companies because they do not have the values." It is this insistence on a values match over and above a talent and responsibility match that is gaining prominence.

Microsoft is another organization that sustains culture by ensuring the right fit. In a recent book written called *The Microsoft Way,* author Randall Stross claims that

IMPLICATIONS FOR LIFE

Do Your Skills and Abilities Match the Organizational Requirements?

We have discussed fit from the organizational perspective, but what about from your perspective?

So which environment is right for you? Are you a person who is very goal directed and performance driven but find yourself in an environment that is focused on process? Or perhaps you are a very creative person who needs a lot of thinking time but you find yourself in a company that requires approvals for every action and written documentation for every idea? Or are you a person who likes to work with others but you are in a company that values individual achievement and the jobs are more solitary. Or maybe change is not something you really enjoy and you prefer a straightforward, structured job with well-defined roles and responsibilities but you are in a company where change is the only constant and the flavour of the month is a common theme.

The culture of the organization, its values, and expectations in terms of performance will have an influence on how well you fit in—how comfortable you are in that organization. It is not just about the organization being clear about the skills and abilities it needs; it is also about you. What are your special competencies? What are your natural strengths? Finding the best fit is difficult but once you do the value that you will bring to that organization and the contributions you will make, will ensure the "right fit."

Microsoft "has pursued the best more successfully than other company, and has visibly reaped the rewards more dramatically than others too." A key component of Microsoft recruiting strategy is preferring an open slot to a "near fit."[64]

How Leaders Fire Individuals

A final element in how leaders influence culture relates to the approach that leaders take when they are faced with the decision to terminate employees. Some companies deal with poor performers by trying to find a place within the organization where they can perform better and make a contribution. Other companies seem to operate under the philosophy that those who cannot perform are out quickly. The reasons for terminations may not be directly communicated to other employees, but curiosity leads to speculation. An employee who displays unethical behaviour, and is caught, may simply be reprimanded even though such behaviour is clearly against the organization's values. Other employees may view this as a failure to reinforce the values within the organization.

CHALLENGES FACING LEADERS TODAY

Identify cultural challenges facing leaders today.

There are several cultural challenges facing leaders today. We will focus on three topical areas: maintaining an ethical and socially responsible culture, managing change, and developing a global culture. See Exhibit 12.7.

Developing and Sustaining an Ethical Organizational Culture

The recent plethora of ethical scandals, such as Conrad Black's alleged improprieties at Hollinger International,[65] current investigations into Nortel's financial accounting,[66] conflicts of interest at Yorkton Securities (now Orion Securities),[67] and of course the collapse of Enron has eroded public trust in corporations.[68] A recent report by the Toronto-based Centre for Ethical Orientation suggests that more than three-quarters of consumers stop buying the products or services of a mistrusted company and nearly two-thirds will not recommend its products to others. The centre also found that the corporation decays

EXHIBIT 12.7

Cultural Challenges Facing Leaders Today

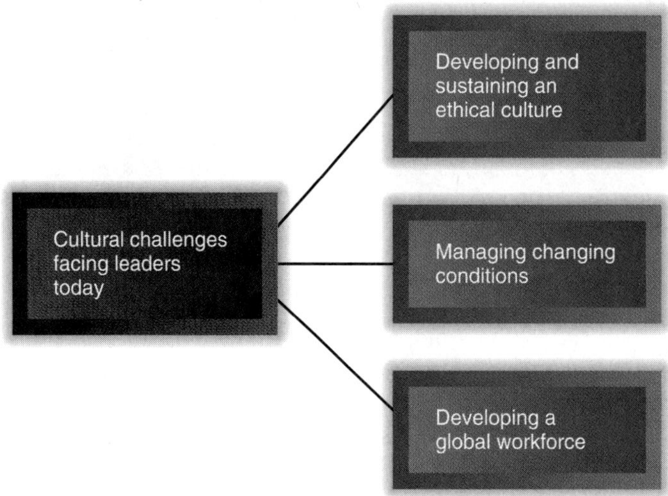

from within as employees who do not trust their employers tend to share less information with colleagues, produce less, and are more likely to quit their job. This loss of confidence is a critical issue for corporations today.

Recent reports have pointed to the lack of governance and poor enforcement of rules and regulations, citing corporate culture as a source of poor corporate behaviour.

organizational reality 12.3

Nestlé Canada: A Company That Values People over Profits

Nestlé is an example of an organization with a socially responsible culture. In an increasingly difficult climate in 2001, Nestlé Canada was faced with a decision on how to optimize production at its plant in Toronto, Ontario. In the past, this plant had always produced nut-free products but with increasing pressure to contain costs, Nestlé decided to alter its manufacturing policy to allow the production of chocolates with nuts; a production process that would be instituted eight months hence. As a result, Nestlé said that it would no longer be able to guarantee that Smarties, Kit Kat, Mirage, and Coffee Krisp would be free of nut contamination.

In Nestlé's corporate logo, there is a picture of a mother bird feeding her young. These birds are symbolic of Nestlé's corporate culture.

What happened next was astounding. This decision sparked a reaction from the community that was not anticipated by the executives at Nestlé. This reaction was one of outrage that people in the community with nut allergies could no longer buy nut-free chocolates. In an article entitled "How We Saved the Smarties," Jerry Nolfi, a parent of a child with major nut allergies, explained how people in the community reacted by setting up a website, www.savethesmarties.com. This website was flooded with e-mails from people across the country with personal stories of anguish; others were pleas to Nestlé Canada written by young children. Each e-mail was forwarded to Nestlé.

On May 14, almost three weeks to day after the website was posted, Nestlé Canada decided to reverse their original decision.

Nestlé's business principles of making a long-term commitment to the health and well-being of people in every country, its global commitment, an attempt to confidence, and search for trust clearly guided this decision. The company demonstrated through its actions that what it values is truly what it believes—"Putting People over Profits!" Go to www.nestle.com to learn more about Nestlé's culture.

SOURCE: Nestlé Canada website, accessed July 24, 2004, http://www.nestle.com.

These arguments suggest that the source of this behaviour lies deep in a business culture that has come to tolerate an excessive focus on corporate profits and individual rewards at the expense of all else.[69] The reasons most often cited for unethical corporate conduct are interesting. They include the belief that a behaviour is not really unethical, that it is in the organization's best interest, that it will not be discovered, and that the organization will support it because it offers a good outcome for the organization.[70]

In order to maintain an ethical culture a company must promote ethical norms and place expectations on individuals to behave accordingly. Leaders must examine their own mindsets and behaviours and then tackle culture head-on within their organizations by shifting the mindsets and beliefs that produce the real rules of behaviour that people follow. Organizations must ensure that managers and employees know how to deal with ethical issues in their everyday work lives.

Managers can encourage ethical behaviour by being good role models for employees, consistently modelling high standards of behaviour and norms expected of everyone. They can institute the philosophy that ethical behaviour makes good business sense and puts the company in congruence with the larger values of the society.[71]

Trust is another key to effectively managing ethical behaviour, especially in cultures that encourage whistle blowing. Employees must trust that whistle-blowers will be protected, that procedures used to investigate ethical problems will be fair, and that management will take action to solve problems that are uncovered.

An ethical corporate culture must clearly communicate the boundaries of ethical conduct and reinforce these boundaries utilizing the formal mechanisms structured within an organization. Many companies today have a code of conduct that guides their actions. One such organization is Johnson & Johnson. This organization has a code of conduct that guides its actions in fulfilling its responsibilities to its customers, employees, shareholders, and community. Its credo is shared by its family of companies worldwide.[72] Go to www.jnj.com to view their credo.

Reinforcing ethical behaviour means selecting employees who support the ethical culture, rewarding organization members who exhibit ethical behaviour, and conspicuously punishing members who engage in unethical behaviour. For example, some salespersons justify padding their expense accounts because everyone else does it. Declaring these justifications illegitimate and applying some form of punishment sends a clear message about the lack of tolerance for such behaviour.

Organizations that seek to encourage ethical behaviour can do so by using their organizational culture. By completing the questionnaire below, you can assess the ethical culture of an organization you are familiar with.

Application & Evaluation

SELF-ASSESSMENT 12.1: ORGANIZATIONAL CULTURE AND ETHICS

Think about the organization you currently work for or one you know something about and complete the following Ethical Climate Questionnaire.

Use the scale below and write the number that best represents your answer in the space next to each item.

To what extent are the following statements true about your company?

Completely false	Mostly false	Somewhat false	Somewhat true	Mostly true	Completely true
0	1	2	3	4	5

___ 1. In this company, people are expected to follow their own personal and moral beliefs.

___ 2. People are expected to do anything to further the company's interests.

___ 3. In this company, people look out for each other's good.

___ 4. It is very important here to follow the company's rules and procedures strictly.

___ 5. In this company, people protect their own interests above other considerations.

____ 6. The first consideration is whether a decision violates any law.

____ 7. Everyone is expected to stick by company rules and procedures.

____ 8. The most efficient way is always the right way in this company.

____ 9. Our major consideration is what is best for everyone in the company.

____10. In this company, the law or ethical code of the profession is the major consideration.

____11. It is expected at this company that employees will always do what is right for the customer and the public.

For scoring instructions, please go to the end of the chapter, p. 395.

Source: J. B. Cullen, B. Victor, and C. Stephens, "An Ethical Weather Report: Assessing the Organization's Ethical Climate," *Organizational Dynamics*, Autumn 1989.

Changing Organizational Culture

Changing situations may require changes in the existing culture of an organization. With rapid environmental changes such as globalization, workforce diversity, and technological innovation, the fundamental assumptions and basic values that drive the organization may need to be altered.

Marriott Hotels is one such company that faced this challenge. It is no surprise to those who work in hospitality that the industry expects long hours, variable schedules, and some very busy times throughout the year. In the late 1990s Marriot was finding it increasingly difficult to recruit talented people, as people wanted more time with their families. A company that prides itself on customer service, the company had to find a way to resolve this problem. In 2000 Marriott implemented a test program called management flexibility. The goal was to help managers achieve a better balance between their home and professional work while maintaining high-quality services. The company implemented several quick fixes right away. They reviewed the content of meetings, identifying nonessential and redundant content, and reduced the number of meetings that employees needed to attend. But the real problem that needed to be addressed was how the employees worked. The vice president said, "Transforming a company's culture can be harder than changing anything else. People's natural inclination is to hold on to whatever feels familiar even when there are alternatives."[73] Management focused on eliminating the assumption that you had to work at the hotel for a certain number of hours. "We are no longer looking for face time but for people to be at the hotel when they needed to be and go home when they didn't."[74] It meant rethinking the way they approached work. The company's leaders modelled this behavior and encouraged employees not to do things that did not make sense for their jobs and to find the best most efficient ways of doing things.[75]

One particular situation that often requires cultural change is a merger or acquisition. The blending of two distinct organizational cultures may prove difficult. Despite good-faith efforts, combining cultures is difficult, especially if organizational culture differences are supplemented by national culture differences.

Alterations in culture may also be required when an organization employs people from different countries. Research indicates that some organizational cultures actually enhance differences in national cultures.[76] One study compared foreign employees working in a multinational organization with employees working in different organizations within their own countries. The assumption was that the employees from various countries working for the same multinational organization would be more similar than employees working in diverse organizations in their native countries. The results were surprising, in that the differences between the employees of the multinational were significantly greater than the differences between managers working for different companies within their native countries. In the multinational, Swedes became more Swedish,

Canadians became more Canadian, and so forth. It appears that employees enhance their national cultural traditions even when working within a single organizational culture.[77] This is more likely to occur when diversity is moderate. When diversity is very high, employees are more likely to develop a shared identity in the organization's culture instead of relying on their own national culture.[78]

Changing an organization's culture is feasible but difficult.[79] One reason for the difficulty is that assumptions—the deepest level of culture—are often unconscious. As such, they are often nonconfrontable and nondebatable. Another reason for the difficulty is that culture is deeply ingrained and behavioural norms and rewards are well learned.[80] In a sense, employees must unlearn the old norms before they can learn new ones. Managers who want to change the culture should look first to the ways culture is maintained.

A model for cultural change that summarizes the interventions managers can use is presented in Exhibit 12.8. In this model, the numbers represent the actions managers can take. There are two basic approaches to changing the existing culture: (1) helping current members buy into a new set of values (actions 1, 2, and 3); or (2) adding newcomers and socializing them into the organization, and removing current members as appropriate (actions 4 and 5).[81]

The first action is to change behaviour in the organization. Even if behaviour does change, however, this change is not sufficient for cultural change to occur. Behaviour is an artifact (level 1) of culture. Individuals may change their behaviour but not the values that drive it. They may rationalize, "I'm only doing this because my manager wants me to."

Therefore, managers must use action 2, which is to examine the justifications for the changed behaviour. Are employees buying into the new set of values, or are they just complying?

EXHIBIT 12.8

Interventions for Changing Organizational Culture

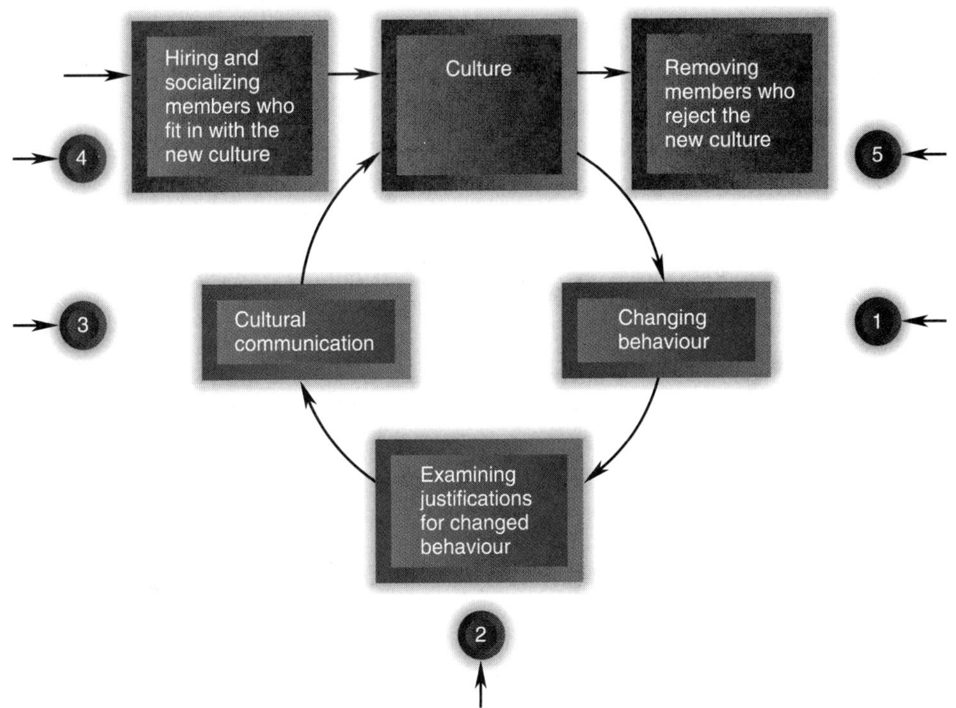

Source: From Vijay Sathe, "How to Decipher and Change Corporate Culture," Ch. 13 in *Gaining Control of the Corporate Culture* (R. H. Kilmann et al., eds.), Fig. 1, p. 245. Copyright © 1985 Jossey-Bass, Inc. Reprinted with permission of John Wiley & Sons, Inc.

The third action, cultural communication, is extremely important. All of the artifacts (personal enactment, stories, rites and ceremonies, rituals, and symbols) must send a consistent message about the new values and beliefs. It is crucial that the communication is credible; that is, managers must live the new values and not just talk about them. The communication must also be persuasive. Individuals may resist cultural change and may have to be persuaded to try the new behaviour by someone they respect and can identify with.

The two remaining actions (4 and 5) involve shaping the workforce to fit the intended culture. First, the organization can revise its selection strategies to more accurately reflect the new culture. Second, the organization can identify individuals who resist the cultural change or who are no longer comfortable with the values in the organization. Reshaping the workforce should not involve a ruthless pursuit of nonconforming employees; it should be a gradual and subtle change that takes considerable time. Changing personnel in the organization is a lengthy process; it cannot be done effectively in a short period of time without considerable problems.

Evaluating the success of cultural change may be best done by looking at behaviour. Cultural change can be assumed to be successful if the behaviour is intrinsically motivated—on "automatic pilot." If the new behaviour would persist even if rewards were not present, and if the employees have internalized the new value system, then the behaviour is probably intrinsically motivated. If employees automatically respond to a crisis in ways consistent with the corporate culture, then the cultural change effort can be deemed successful.

Given the current business environment, managers may want to focus on three particular cultural modifications: (1) support for a global view of business, (2) reinforcement of ethical behaviour, and (3) empowerment of employees to excel in product and service quality.

Developing a Global Organizational Culture

Diversity at Work

To meet the needs of managers and practitioners struggling with the demands of a non-homogeneous workforce, this online virtual diversity community called Global Diversity @ Work focuses on diversity and equity issues, providing valuable information and data on any diversity issue.
http://www.diversityatwork.com

With its corporate head office in Montreal, CGI is one of the many Canadian companies operating in a global environment. Founded in 1976, CGI is the largest Canadian independent IT services firm and the fifth largest in North America, with offices spread across North America, Europe, and Asia. Fostering partnerships, intrapreneurship and sharing, CGI recognizes the richness that different cultures bring to the company. The organization's members respect and honour each other and welcome this diversity while embracing the overall culture.

Global corporations suffer from the conflicting pressures of centralization and decentralization. Understanding the cultural differences that exist globally is fast becoming a core competency of multinational corporations. These organizations demonstrate values that support a global view of the company and its efforts. To do so, the values should be clear to everyone involved so that everyone understands them, and they must be strongly supported at the top. Management should embody the shared values and reward employees who support the global view. Finally, the values should be consistent over time. Consistent values give an organization a unifying theme that competitors may be unable to emulate.[82]

A major barrier facing managers who operate globally is "ethnocentrism." This is a belief that one's native country, culture, language, customs, mores, and way of conducting an operation are superior to any other nation. It is often attributable to lack of knowledge of foreign persons and situations. Being cognizant of one's ethnocentric tendencies is important in managing across cultures, but this is only part of what managers can do.[83] In Chapter 2 we discussed the GLOBE study, the work of Geert Hofstede and the five main dimensions that can be used to differentiate cultural differences: power distance, individualism versus collectivism, masculinity versus femininity, uncertainty avoidance, and long- versus short-term orientation. Being aware of these differences, respecting and valuing these differences, will enable organizations to operate more effectively in the global space.

Following are six specific guidelines for managers who want to create a global culture:[84]

1. Create a clear and simple mission statement. A shared mission can unite individuals from diverse cultural backgrounds.
2. Create systems that ensure an effective flow of information. Coordination councils and global task forces can be used to ensure that information flows throughout the geographically dispersed organization are consistent.
3. Create "matrix minds" among managers; that is, broaden managers' minds to allow them to think globally. IBM does this through temporary overseas assignments. Managers with international experience share that experience when they return to the home organization.
4. Develop global career paths. This means ensuring not only that home country executives go overseas but also that executives from other countries rotate into service in the home office.
5. Use cultural differences as a major asset. Think about the influence of the nine cultural dimensions identified in the Globe study discussed in Chapter 2. The former Digital Equipment Corporation (now part of Compaq Computer), for example, transferred its research and development functions to Italy to take advantage of the free-flowing Italian management style that encouraged creativity. Its manufacturing operations went to Germany, which offered a more systematic management style.
6. Implement worldwide management education and team development programs. Unified training efforts that emphasize corporate values can help establish a shared identity among employees.

These guidelines are specifically aimed at multinational organizations that want to create a global corporate culture, but other organizations can also benefit from them. Companies that want to broaden employees' views or to use the diversity of their workforce as a resource will find several of these recommendations advantageous.

IMPLICATIONS FOR ORGANIZATIONAL EFFECTIVENESS

Managing organizational culture is a key challenge for leaders in today's organizations. With the trend toward downsizing and restructuring, maintaining an organizational culture in the face of change is difficult. Effective organizations leverage culture. They define where they are going and how they are going to get there, they articulate the business strategy that will enable the organization to achieve these goals, and they define what behaviour is expected. Strong, cohesive, service-driven, high-achievement organizations build cultures that are strategically appropriate, adapt to the environment, and align their internal processes accordingly. They know what competencies they need and set out to attract and retain those employees who will fit the best in this culture. These organizations are clear on what behavior should look like and they reinforce this behavior by ensuring that its policies and practices are aligned. The socialization process and reward structures are particularly powerful tools. Leaders walk the talk and use culture as a communication tool to express what is important in that organization, modeling the behavior which sets the norms for the other employees to follow. Their leadership is essential for developing a culture that values diversity, supports empowerment, fosters innovations in product and service quality, and promotes ethical behavior.

Organizations that exhibit these qualities achieve a higher level of customer satisfaction, employee satisfaction, and ultimately can leverage their collective knowledge to ensure organizational sustainability. You can read more about the culture of these Canadian companies in a feature article published by *Maclean's* magazine called "Canada's Top 10 Employers" (http://www.macleans.ca/topstories/business).

Chapter Summary

1. Organizational (corporate) culture is a pattern of basic assumptions that are considered valid and that are taught to new members as the way to perceive, think, and feel in the organization. Organizational culture has several functions. It gives members a sense of identity and increases their commitment, reinforces their values, coordinates their efforts, and clarifies what is important, serving as a sense-making device for members, and serving as a control mechanism for shaping behaviour. Studies have found that corporate culture can have a significant impact on a firm's long-term economic performance.
2. The elements of culture can be viewed from three levels. The most visible and accessible level can be seen in the form of artifacts, symbols, rituals, and stories. Values are a second and deeper level, reflecting a person's underlying beliefs of what should and should not be. Values give rise to behavioural norms, providing employees with a sense of direction and guideline for day-to-day behaviour. Assumptions are the most hidden. They are deeply held beliefs, arising from the collective learning process experienced by an organization's members in response to adapting successfully to organizational challenges.
3. Culture can be described in many ways. Three models of culture which describe culture are the risk and feedback model proposed by Deal and Kennedy, the interpersonal interaction model described by Harrison and Stokes, and the hierarchy of cultures model developed by Dr. Jerry Want.
4. The relationship between culture and performance can be viewed from three perspectives: strong, adaptable, and strategically appropriate. Highly successful companies have a strong culture, one that exhibits a consensus on values; they are highly adaptive, being able to effectively anticipate and adapt to change; and they exhibit strategically appropriate behaviours, cognizant of the context in which they operate.
5. Cultural fit is important because if an organization is going to be able to anticipate, adapt, and exhibit strategically appropriate behaviours it will need to ensure that its policies and practices related to attraction, socialization, and retention of employees are aligned accordingly.
6. Leaders shape and reinforce culture by what they pay attention to, how they react to crises, how they behave, how they allocate rewards, and how they hire, socialize, and fire individuals.
7. Organization–person fit is important. Organizations that hire individuals who fit the culture and socialize these individuals as to cultural norms are more effective at sustaining their culture.
8. Challenges facing leaders today are ensuring that these leaders develop and sustain an ethical culture, manage changing conditions, and develop a global workforce.

Key Terms

adaptive culture (p. 382)
artifacts (p. 369)
assumptions (p. 373)
core/dominant culture (p. 380)
enacted values (p. 373)
espoused values (p. 373)
organizational (corporate) culture (p. 366)
strategically appropriate culture (p. 381)
strong culture (p. 381)
subculture (p. 380)

Review Questions

1. Explain the three levels of organizational culture. How can each level of culture be measured?
2. Describe five artifacts of culture and give an example of each.
3. Describe what a "culture of change" looks like.
4. Compare and contrast the differences between a power, role, support, and achievement orientation.
3. Explain three theories about the relationship between organizational culture and performance. What does the research evidence say about each one?
4. Contrast adaptive and nonadaptive cultures.
5. Explain the relationship between organization–person fit and culture.
6. How can managers assess the organizational culture? What actions can they take to change the organizational culture?
7. How does a manager know that cultural change has been successful?
8. What can managers do to develop a global organizational culture?

Discussion and Communication Questions

1. Name a company with a visible organizational culture. What do you think are the company's values? Has the culture contributed to the organization's performance? Explain.
2. Name a leader you think manages organizational culture well. How does the leader do this? Use Schein's description of how leaders reinforce culture to analyze the leader's behaviour.
3. Suppose you want to change your organization's culture. What sort of resistance would you expect from employees? How would you deal with this resistance?
4. Given Schein's three levels, can we ever truly understand an organization's culture? Explain.
5. To what extent is culture manageable? Changeable?
6. (*Communication question*) Select an organization that you might like to work for. Learn as much as you can about that company's culture, using library resources, online sources, contacts within the company, and as many creative means as you can. Prepare a brief presentation to the class summarizing the culture.

Ethics Questions

1. Are rites of degradation ethical?
2. Is it ethical to influence an individual's values through the organizational culture? If culture shapes behaviour, is managing culture a manipulative tactic? Explain.
3. How can leaders use organizational culture as a vehicle for encouraging ethical behaviour?
4. Korean *chaebols* hire individuals to fit their cultures. To what extent might this practice be considered unethical in Canada?
5. One way of changing culture is to remove members who do not change with the culture. How can this be done ethically?

Knowledge & Application

EXPERIENTIAL EXERCISE 12.1: COMPARING ORGANIZATIONAL CULTURES

Purpose: To explore the differences of culture

Group size: 4 or 5 students

Time required: 45 minutes

Materials needed: Internet access

Instructions:

1. **Students form small groups.** Each group should select from one of the following pairs of organizations (similar companies in similar industries) and gather information about the company culture.
   - WestJet Airlines and Air Canada
   - Stelco and Dofasco
   - Timothy's and Second Cup
   - Loblaws and Dominion
   - Bell Canada and Allstream
   - Sears and The Bay
2. Students are to describe these cultures using one or more of the following models:
   - Harrison and Stokes—Interpersonal Interaction Model
   - Deal and Kennedy—Risk and Feedback Model
   - Jerry Want—Hierarchy of Cultures

SOURCE: Adapted with the permission of The Free Press, a Division of Simon & Schuster Adult Publishing Group, from *Corporate Culture and Performance*, by John P. Kotter and James L. Heskett: Copyright © 1992 by Kotter Associates, Inc., and James L. Heskett. All rights reserved.

Application, Analysis & Synthesis

CASE: PATAGONIA'S CULTURE

Patagonia designs and manufactures clothing for use in a variety of sporting activities. Founded in the 1960s to make gear for mountain climbing, Patagonia has grown into a company that focuses on producing clothing for alpine climbing, skiing/snowboarding, rock climbing, surfing, fishing, paddling, mountain biking, and trail running. Patagonia makes all of its clothing to enable its users "to move more freely through the natural world." Patagonia markets its products via the Internet, through catalogues, and in stores located in the North America, Europe, Asia/Oceana, and South America.

Patagonia views its clothing products as tools—tools that are used by various sports enthusiasts to enable them to fully engage in their activities while minimizing intrusiveness on the natural environment. In designing its products, Patagonia seeks to develop the "best tool" for the specific activity. Patagonia defines the "best tool" as the one that is "most functional, with the least material, with the smoothest lines, with strength and lasting qualities."

The company describes itself as "environmentally conscious makers of quality outdoor clothing." In developing and manufacturing the "best tools" in selected lines of sports clothing, Patagonia is very environmentally conscious. The company works vigorously to lessen the negative environmental impact of the materials and processes used in producing its products. This environmental consciousness and activism pervades the company's culture.

Another important value that permeates Patagonia's culture is the expectation for and appreciation of people. Patagonia places a high value on its employees, expecting significant contributions from them while encouraging them to follow their individual passions. Patagonia says, "We prefer the human scale to the corporate, vagabonding to tourism, the quirky and lively to the toned down and flattened out." Clearly, Patagonia places a high value on people and their interests and passions. In describing the types of employees it wants, Patagonia's website says, "We're especially interested in people who share our love of the outdoors, our passion for quality, and our desire to make a difference."

Members of the Patagonia "organizational family" are known as *Patagoniacs*. Ron Hunter, for example, is a Patagoniac who works in the company's Environmental Programs Department. His job involves encouraging environmental activism among colleagues in the retail stores and in the Reno Service Center. He works to raise awareness and promote activism on a variety of environmental issues that are important to Patagonia. Ron uses climbing, skiing, hiking, and paddling to go to the outdoor places he loves. He "understands the importance of getting to know and love a place, while working for its protection."

Another Patagoniac is Chipper Bro Bell, formerly an itinerant freestyle Frisbee world champion. Initially employed as a switchboard operator even though he had no experience, Chipper started Patagonia's organic cotton T-shirt division in 1998. He disliked the paperwork associated with leading this division, however, and subsequently returned to the front desk. In this position "he has elevated the role of gatekeeper to high art, providing the same level of care and attention to the teenage job applicant as he does the visiting dignitary." Chipper also teaches surfing to Patagonia employees and continues his winning ways with a Frisbee, having won the World Beach Frisbee Championship a total of 11 times.

Still another Patagoniac is Kim Stroud, who manages the sample room. She invests a great deal of time and personal resources in caring for sick and injured birds. Kim runs an aviary at Patagonia that houses mostly owls and hawks. A few years ago Kim left the sample room to manage Patagonia's fledgling product development operation. Later she returned to the sample room to manage a team of 16 members, all of whom she treats like family.

Each Patagoniac is different but all share some common characteristics. Being a Patagoniac means loving the outdoors; being passionately committed to quality, to people, and to the environment; and desiring to make a difference.

Discussion Questions:

1. Explain Patagonia's culture using the levels of organizational culture model that is presented in Exhibit 12.1.
2. Using the concept of a strong culture, explain the nature of Patagonia's culture.
3. Can Patagonia's culture be described as an ethical organizational culture? Explain your answer.

SOURCE: This case was written by Michael K. McCuddy, The Louis S. and Mary L. Morgal Professor of Christian Business Ethics and Professor of Management, College of Business Administration, Valparaiso University. This case was developed from material contained on the Patagonia website at http://www.patagonia.com.

Scoring for Self-Assessment

Self-Assessment 12.1 Organizational Culture and Ethics

To score the questionnaire, first add up your responses to questions 1, 3, 6, 9, 10, and 11. This is subtotal number 1. Next, reverse the scores on questions 2, 4, 5, 7, and 8 (5 = 0, 4 = 1, 3 = 2, 2 = 3, 1 = 4, 0 = 5). Add the reverse scores to form subtotal number 2. Add subtotal number 1 to subtotal number 2 for an overall score.

Subtotal 1 ______ + Subtotal 2 ______ = Overall Score ______.

Overall scores can range from 0 to 55. The higher the score, the more the organization's culture encourages ethical behaviour.

Organizational Change and Development

chapter thirteen

LEARNING OBJECTIVES

By the end of this chapter, you will be able to do the following:

1. Define three different types of organizational change: developmental, transitional, and transformational.
2. Describe four targets of organizational change.
3. Explain six common individual reactions to change.
4. Explain three causes of organizational resistance to change.
5. Explain how Lewin's force field analysis model can be used to help manage change.
6. Discuss five strategies for managing individual reactions to change.
7. Explain Kotter's top-down approach to large-scale change.
8. Explain the distinguishing characteristics of the organization development (OD) approach to change management.
9. Give an overview of five OD interventions: survey feedback, process consultation, team development, appreciative inquiry, and open systems technology.

learning about the context

Indigo Books and Music: The Post-Merger Integration Challenge

When Heather Reisman, founding CEO of Indigo Books, merged her company with Chapters, she envisioned that out of the two companies would emerge a third, "better and stronger" entity. However, one of the reasons why mergers often fail to reach their potential is that there can be serious fallout when the two workforces are combined. Reisman knew that Chapter's former CEO, Larry Stevenson, had a very different philosophy and operating style from her. For these reasons, it was crucial for the new organization to deal with not only the immediate and very practical HR issues, but the cultural aspect as well. As Sue Croft, senior vice president of Human Resources and Organization Development at Indigo explained, the company faced the challenge of blending two companies into one cohesive culture.

An immediate issue HR had to deal with was the growth to 6000 employees, from 1000, as well as the conversion of everyone to the same payroll, benefits, and pension systems. Before Indigo could foster the right new culture, the cultural differences between the two merged organizations had to be identified. This was done through employee surveys, focus groups, and frequent interaction with employees.

The company also initiated the redesign of HR processes, as well as the design of an Indigo intranet and an Indigo training and development program. Sue Croft said that Indigo's leadership team strove to make the company the "Employer of Choice" in the Canadian retail industry. She added, "We believe that it is our accountability to provide people with the opportunity to do and be their best in a positive, energetic and successful workplace."

SOURCES: Sue Croft (Senior VP of Human Resources & Organization Development, Indigo Books & Music), interview with the author; K. Macklem, "The Book Lady," *Maclean's,* February 26, 2001, 40–45; www.cbc.ca; www.indigo.ca, accessed May 2003. Written by S. Moon.

All the major challenges facing organizations, discussed in Chapter 1, create forces for individual or organizational change. To recap, the challenges leading to change are increased globalization, hyper-competition and demanding customers, the increasing diversity of the workforce, continuing technological innovation, and demands for higher levels of moral and ethical behaviour. For the last decade, organizations have been in a state of tremendous turmoil and transition, and this trend is expected to continue into the far distant future. Consensus has been reached on two fronts: First, that massive organizational change is inevitable given the volatile nature of our competitive environment, and second, that adaptive, flexible organizations will have a competitive advantage over rigid, inflexible ones.[1]

planned change
Change that is an intentional and goal-oriented activity.

While change can be both planned and unplanned, this chapter explores strategies for effectively planning and managing various types of changes. **Planned change** is defined as change that is an intentional and goal-oriented activity. The primary focus of the chapter is organizational change, but some of the discussions and exercises ask you to apply the concepts to personal change. We begin with an exploration of the various types of organizational change and an examination of the four targets of change: structure (including downsizing and mergers and acquisitions), technology, tasks/work processes, and people and culture. Next, the chapter explores the varied causes of individual reactions and organizational resistance to change. The last section of the chapter examines the various strategies for overcoming resistance, managing change, and developing adaptive organizations, using ethical practices.

Define three different types of organizational change: planned, unplanned, and transformational.

TYPES OF ORGANIZATIONAL CHANGE

Research and practice have taught us that organizational (and individual) survival and effectiveness require that organizations (and people) change well before a crisis hits them. For example, sometimes it takes a heart attack for a person to start exercising, but in this case some damage has already been done and it is much harder to get fit after a heart attack than if one started exercising when healthy. John Chambers, CEO of Cisco Systems, talks about the need to "Change during good times while maintaining a steady course when times get tough."[2] Lynda Cranston, former CEO of Canadian Blood Services, captured the current business climate well by stating that "We are now being guided by diligent prudence in the face of the unforeseen."[3] Diligent prudence in the face of the unforeseen requires that leaders view their organizations as open systems (discussed in Chapter 1) and continually scan and monitor their internal and external environments for potential challenges and opportunities. This means that individuals with the organization are required to keep track of trends and plan contingencies for all critical environments such as legislators, competitors, technology, and customers,

developmental change
The improvement of a skill, method, or condition that for some reason does not measure up.

This chapter focuses on planned, rather than unplanned, change, and planned changes vary in timing, scope, and depth. Linda Ackerman identifies three types of change. The first type she calls **developmental change,** which she defines as the improvement of a skill, method, or condition that for some reason does not measure up.[4] Such changes, in essence, are a fine-tuning of the organization, or the making of small improvements, or the establishment of a "continuous motion" strategy for keeping pace with the operating environment.[5] Developmental change may not involve the entire system. Gregg Hanson, CEO of Wawanesa Mutual Insurance, feels that to be competitive, "the status quo is never an option, you're either moving forward or you're being left behind." Wawanesa undertakes major alterations as a matter of course, as their strategic group sees change on the horizon. This is a good example of developmental change.[6]

transitional change
Change that is introduced to have an organization evolve slowly: current ways of doing things are replaced by something new.

The second type of change Ackerman calls **transitional change,** defined as change that is introduced to have an organization evolve slowly: current ways of doing things are replaced by something new.[7] Transitional changes are system-wide and examples of transitional change are mergers, reorganizations, and the introduction of new services, processes, systems or technologies.

The most radical change Ackerman calls **transformational change,** which is when an organization moves to a radically different, and sometimes unknown, future state.[8] Transformational change is revolutionary rather than evolutionary. Transformational change requires a leap of faith for the organization and is the most difficult type of change to manage.[9] For example, at one point, Corning was a purveyor of cookware. Nowadays, it is a fibre optics powerhouse. Kimberly-Clark, originally a producer of commodity paper, transformed itself into the paper diaper business, successfully competing with Procter & Gamble through its Huggies line.[10] In transformational change, the organization's mission, culture, goals, structure, and leadership may all change dramatically.[11] Judith Chapman calls this "gamma" change, defined as a transition from one state to another or a quantum shift in the way that work and purpose is understood.[12]

transformational change
Change in which the organization moves to a radically different, and sometimes unknown, future state.

Knowledge & Application

CLASSIFY THESE CHANGES

Decide whether the following changes are developmental, transitional, or transformational:

1. Introducing a veggie burger at McDonald's
2. Adding automated teller machines to a bank nation-wide
3. Moving from selling copiers to providing document-processing solutions

TARGETS OF CHANGE

Describe four targets of organizational change.

While organizational change can be developmental, transitional, and transformational, it can also be directed internally toward a wide variety of organizational components, as summarized in Exhibit 13.1. Four common targets of change are (1) an organization's structure, (2) its technology, (3) its tasks or work processes, and (4) its people and culture. We begin by discussing the organization's structure as a target of change. Learn more about redesigning an organization's structure in Chapter 14.

EXHIBIT 13.1

Targets of Change

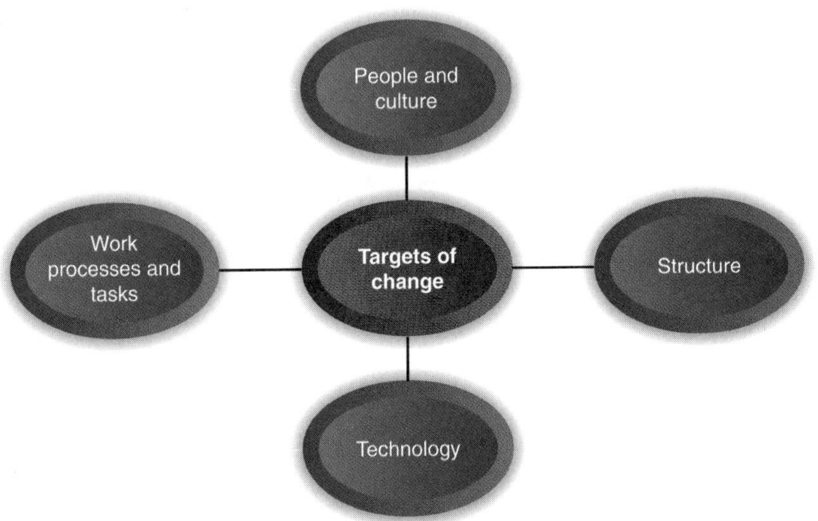

Changing the Organizational Structure

When companies restructure, downsize, merge with another company, form strategic alliances, or outsource part of their operations, these are all examples of changing the organization's structure.

Many companies restructured in the last two decades by reducing their layers of management, trying to improve vertical communication and the speed of decision making. Many times, this also included downsizing, motivated by the spread of economic competition and shareholder activism.[13]

downsizing
Intended reductions in the number of employees.

Downsizing, defined as intended reductions in the number of employees, while still popular as a way to quickly reduce labour costs, has been widely criticized as having adverse impacts on service quality,[14] and on the emotional and behavioural commitment and responses of survivors.[15] Those doing the downsizing also experience negative consequences such as huge increases in workload, a search for meaning, social and organizational isolation, and decreased family functioning.[16] Organizational restructuring often reveals inherent paradoxes such as cutting staff without reorganizing work, resulting in increased workloads for survivors. Often, organizations appear to have made the decision to downsize through across-the-board cutbacks without considering the consequences.[17] Recent studies even suggest that the victims of downsizing fare better than survivors.[18]

A seminal study of white-collar downsizing in 30 U.S. automobile firms identified six best practices that were all present in the firms that were downsizing most effectively.[19] These six best practices for the most successful downsizing were as follows:

1. Was implemented by command from the top down, but it was also initiated from the bottom up.
2. Was short-term and across-the-board, but it was also long-term and selective in emphasis.
3. Involved paying special attention to those employees who lost their jobs. It also involved paying special attention to those who didn't.
4. Was surgical and targeted inside the firm, but it was also generalized and included the firm's external network.
5. Resulted in small, semi-autonomous organizations, but it also resulted in large, integrated organizations.
6. Was emphasized as a means to an end as well as an end in itself.

Changing an organization's structure does not always include downsizing. As you will see in Chapter 14, an organization's structure is defined by how tasks are formally divided (also called differentiation) and coordinated (also called integration.) Often, restructuring includes delayering, also discussed in Chapter 14. For example, at the Canadian National Railway, Paul Tellier, former president and CEO, successfully reduced the layers of management from 10 (between president and line employees) to five.[20] In 2003, Bell Canada reorganized its structure into three self-contained areas: a division to serve individual consumers, a division to serve small and medium-sized businesses and a division to serve large corporations. The goal for the change in organization structure, in CEO Michael Sabia's words, was to "better serve customers and make decisions more quickly."[21]

Changing Technology

Many of the early studies in managing organizational change dealt with efforts aimed at technological change. Today, competitive factors often require organizations to introduce new equipment, tools, or automation. Bombardier recently implemented enterprise resource planning software and wrote that "the number one challenge with the implementation of Bombardier's ERP solution was managing change."[22]

Changing the Work Processes and Tasks

In addition to redesigning individual jobs, as discussed in Chapter 5, in the last decade, organizations have been trying to change entire work processes. Techniques such as total quality management (TQM), business process re-engineering, and flexible manufacturing have become common targets of change, in response to increasing competition and demands for cost reduction and quality. Standard Aero started a process in the mid-1990s to re-engineer their production processes. They moved to a cellular design, which involved relocating people and machines, acquiring new equipment, and reshaping some employees' job descriptions and measures of performance.[23]

Changing People's Attitudes and the Organizational Culture

As you saw in Chapter 12, an organization's culture is defined as "a pattern of basic assumptions that are considered valid and that are taught to new members as the way to perceive, think, and feel in the organization." At Indigo, as you just read about in the chapter opener, the targets of change were primarily the people and the blending of the two different cultures. Often, changing just the structure, or the technology, or the work processes, may not be enough to achieve a transformational change in the company. In addition, the actual culture of the company must also be targeted directly and values need to be articulated, as they were when Manulife merged with North American Life, as discussed in Organizational Reality 13.1. For example, when Newfoundland Power embarked upon a major change, management ensured that every employee was given the tools, training, and information to perform at optimal levels. In August 2002, the utility won an Atlantic Canada Human Resources Award for the culture change initiative.[24] Typically, cultural change takes much longer than structural change partly because it often requires re-examination of corporate values. Key strategies required to bring about cultural change are found later on in this chapter under the sections on overcoming resistance to change and the organization development approach to change.

organizational reality 13.1

Manulife Financial Articulates Its Core Values during Merger and Acquisition

Manulife Financial strives to instill values in the organization, and as a result, it is consistently ranked among Canada's top employers. Integrating values is particularly important during a merger and acquisition, as emotions among employees typically run high. But Lynne Alex, VP of HR at Manulife, observes that the rapid pace in which merger talks often progress makes detailed planning difficult. For example, when Manulife merged with North American Life, the new organization became the largest insurance company in Canada. However, the time between the original merger proposal and the formal announcement was less than two months.

Nonetheless, HR took a vital initiative by creating a statement outlining the values under which the company functioned, and promising to continue to abide by them. When the news of the merger became public, so too did the statement of principles. Alex maintains that it is important for a company to consistently live by clear corporate values and to restate them during a merger. This will reassure stakeholders that values will endure and that both new and old employees will be treated fairly. As Alex states, "The cultural stuff takes longer than structural change. It takes a while to create an affiliation with the new organization. That's why values are so important going in. You will have people's minds and hands before you have their hearts."

SOURCE: "Mergers and Acquisitions: Nearly 40% of Canadian Mergers Fail. Three Companies Are Taking a Values-Based Approach to Boost Their Odds of Success," *The Training Report,* October 1998, 13–14.

Analysis & Evaluation

CLASSIFY THE TARGET OF CHANGE

If your college or university decided that the library was inadequate and they developed a change strategy to acquire funding, train librarians, and upgrade their holdings, what type of change would this be? Defend your choice.

CHALLENGES TO EFFECTIVE CHANGE MANAGEMENT

The people aspects of change are the most critically important for successful transformations.[25] Even Michael Hammer, who launched the re-engineering movement, admits, "I was reflecting on my engineering background and was insufficiently appreciative of the human dimension. I've learned that it's critical."[26] If people are not taken into account, a change process will be negatively affected or may even fail. In fact, a recent article reported that only three out of ten change initiatives gave the return on investment that the leadership forecast.[27] Like organizations, people tend to cling to what has worked in the past, especially if they have been successful and they see no need for change.[28] As well, at times, what leaders perceive as "resistance" to change might in fact be the most logical reactions to it.

Most authors, change practitioners, and CEOs agree that the hardest part of any change project is managing the human side of change. Experience teaches us that there are many types of individual reactions to change and that the structure of groups and organizations may also create a form of resistance to change. The more you understand the reactions and causes of resistance to change, the better able you will be to address the concerns and barriers and be able to work with them, even turn them into positive forces n the change process.[29] First, we explore the challenges posed by individual reactions to change, then we explore the organizational processes that may act as forces against the change.

Explain six common individual reactions to change.

Individual Reactions to Change

People often react to change as a rational response that is based on self-interest. However, there are countless other ways that people react to change. Many of these centre around the notion of reactance—that is, a negative reaction that occurs when individuals feel that their personal freedom is threatened.[30] Some individuals are also more tolerant of ambiguity than others. Annual surveys done jointly by Environics and CROP Inc. in Montreal suggest that in recent years, the number of Canadians who feel confident in their ability to cope with change has declined.[31] Assess your own attitude toward ambiguity in Self-Assessment 13.1 and think about your results as you read the following material.

Newfoundland Power wins the Atlantic Canada Human Resources Award for their culture change initiative.

Knowledge & Application

SELF-ASSESSMENT 13.1: TOLERANCE FOR AMBIGUITY

Read each of the following statements carefully. Then rate each of them in terms of the extent to which you either agree or disagree with the statement using the following scale:

Completely Disagree			Neither Agree nor Disagree			Completely Agree
1	2	3	4	5	6	7

Place the number that best describes your degree of agreement or disagreement in the blank to the left of each statement.

____ 1. An expert who doesn't come up with a definite answer probably doesn't know much.

____ 2. I would like to live in a foreign country for a while.

____ 3. The sooner we all acquire similar values and ideals the better.

____ 4. A good teacher is one who makes you wonder about your way of looking at things.

____ 5. I like parties where I know most of the people more than ones where all or most of the people are complete strangers.

____ 6. Teachers or supervisors who hand out vague assignments give a chance for one to show initiative and originality.

____ 7. A person who leads an even, regular life in which few surprises or unexpected happenings arise, really has a lot to be grateful for.

____ 8. Many of our most important decisions are based upon insufficient information.

____ 9. There is really no such thing as a problem that can't be solved.

____ 10. People who fit their lives to a schedule probably miss most of the joy of living.

____ 11. A good job is one where what is to be done and how it is to be done are always clear.

____ 12. It is more fun to tackle a complicated problem than to solve a simple one.

____ 13. In the long run, it is possible to get more done by tackling small, simple problems rather than large and complicated ones.

____ 14. Often the most interesting and stimulating people are those who don't mind being different and original.

____ 15. What we are used to is always preferable to what is unfamiliar.

For scoring instructions, please go to the end of the chapter, p. 425.

Source: "Tolerance for Ambiguity" from D. Marcic and J. Seltzer, *Organizational Behavior: Experiences and Cases*, 5th ed. (Mason, OH: South-Western College Publishing, 1998), 281–83. Used with permission.

Traditional OB literature tended to refer to employee reactions to change as "resistance." This implied that the employees were somehow negative or in the wrong. By contrast, contemporary OB theorists view employee reactions to change as possible red flags regarding areas for improvement in the change process as well as potential sources of important information. Therefore, while we refer to some early OB research in this area, we use the term employee "reactions" to change rather than employee "resistance" to change.

The most common types of individual reactions to change are fear of the unknown, fear of loss, fear of failure, reluctance to break routines, cynicism, and selective perception. These are summarized in Exhibit 13.2 and are discussed below.

Fear of the Unknown

Change often brings with it substantial uncertainty. Employees facing a technological change, such as the introduction of a new computer system, may resist the change simply because it introduces ambiguity into what was once a comfortable situation for them. This is especially a problem when there has been little communication about the change.

EXHIBIT 13.2

Six Individual Reactions to Change

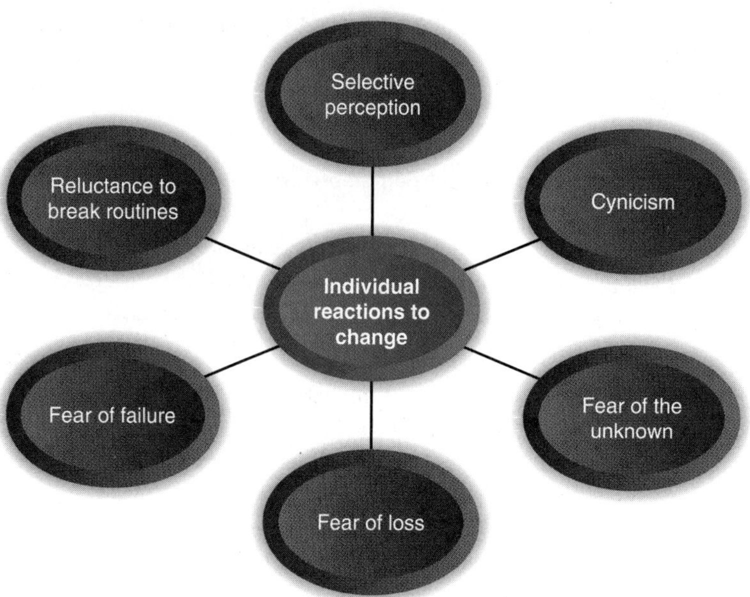

Fear of Loss

When a change is impending, employees may fear that they will lose something of value, either material or psychological. This reaction is also referred to as "direct cost." Some employees may fear job loss, particularly when an advanced technology like robotics is introduced. Employees may also fear reduction in their status because of a change.[32] Computer systems experts, for example, may fear being perceived as having less expertise when a more user-friendly networked information system is installed. Employees may also fear the departure of meaningful interpersonal relationships on the job. Organizational change may also shift the existing balance of power in the organization. Individuals or groups who hold power under the current arrangement may be threatened with losing these political advantages with the implementation of the change.

Fear of Failure

Employees may fear that changes will result in increased workloads or increased task difficulty, and they may question their own competencies for handling these. They may also fear that performance expectations will be elevated following the change, and that they may not measure up.[33] Reactions can also stem from a fear that the change itself will actually fail. In one large library that was undergoing a major automation effort, employees were doubtful that the vendor could really deliver the state-of-the-art system that was promised. In this case, the implementation never became a reality—the employees' fears were well founded.[34]

Reluctance to Break Routines

active inertia
A tendency to respond to the most disruptive changes by accelerating activities that succeeded in the past.

Through learning, people naturally form routines and develop habits. Organizational change often requires that these habits or routines be broken and that we move outside of our comfort zones and into ambiguous territory. Another way of viewing reluctance to break routines is what Donald Sull calls **active inertia.** Active inertia is when managers get trapped by success and respond in disruptive ways by accelerating activities that succeeded in the past.[35]

Selective Perception

In Chapter 3, you learned about perception and how we attend selectively to the huge amount of information bombarding our senses. One common reaction to change is that when we receive information that does not fit with the mental model we have created we either filter it out or ignore it.

Cynicism

After more than a decade of intense organizational change and many failures, it is no wonder that many employees become cynical about planned organizational change. Research shows that cynicism does not result from self-interest, misunderstanding, or low tolerance for change. Rather, **cynicism** is a "loss of faith in the leaders of the change based on a history of change attempts that have not been entirely successful."[36] This is sometimes referred to as "change fatigue." Cynical people affect other peoples' reactions to change as well. As discussed in Chapter 5, the social information-processing model teaches us that people's perceptions and reactions to their jobs (and changes) are shaped by information from other people in the work environment.[37]

cynicism
A loss of faith in the leaders of change based on a history of change attempts that have not been entirely successful.

Darlene Carter, a human resources business manager with Maritime Forces Atlantic in Halifax, discusses the frustration of dealing with what she calls "apathetic and atrophied" managers when trying to bring about change.[38] She describes cynical managers as troublesome because "They portray an ambience of not caring. They tune out to new ideas, and their staffs often suffer or become mirror images of them." Atrophied managers, she argues, are those who have become eroded and emotionally emaciated. They often speak of having been misused by the organization, and in fact, they may well have been. Cynicism is a particularly worrisome form of resistance because of the history associated with it. In overcoming this type of resistance, managers have to acknowledge past mistakes, legitimize the causes of concern, and invest time and energy to rebuild trust and keep their promises.

Knowledge & Application

DETERMINE CAUSES OF REACTIONS TO CHANGE

Consider how some students you know had difficulty coping with the changes in going from high school to postsecondary education. Using the concepts just discussed, identify the individual causes of their reactions to the change. How could the high school have better prepared the students? How can the postsecondary institution help them adjust?

Organizational Resistance to Change

Explain three causes of organizational resistance to change.

Various factors in the organizational environment may also create forces against change. In a Canadian survey exploring the barriers to successful change management, 82 percent of respondents indicated that organizational resistance to change was the number one barrier.[39]

More specifically, as shown in Exhibit 13.3, there are three common causes of organizational resistance to change: (1) the focus of the change may be too limited, (2) team norms may cause people to resist, or (3) formal organizational systems and processes may inadvertently act as barriers to change.

EXHIBIT 13.3

Causes of Organizational Resistance to Change

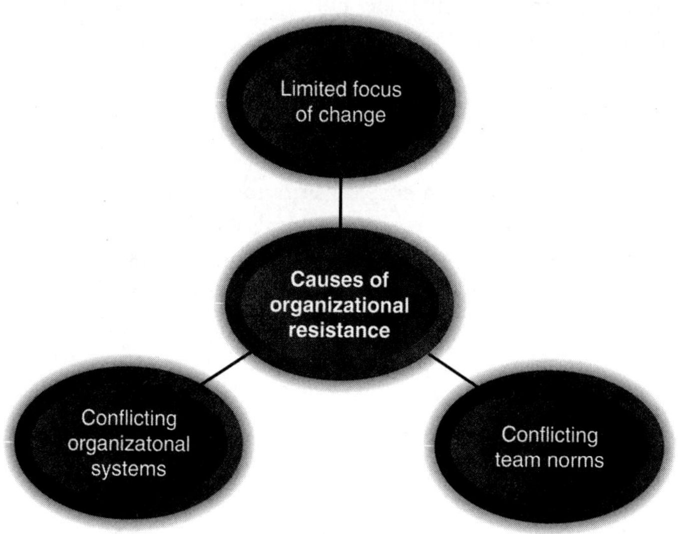

Limited Focus of Change

Organizations are made up of many interdependent subsystems and departments. Sometimes change initiatives fail because the change targets are too limited and the related departments, people, or processes are not aligned, making it difficult for implementation to succeed.

Conflicting Team Norms

In Chapter 7, you learned about how teams develop norms and often are pressured to conform to group expectations. If the desired organizational change is seen to conflict with any of these norms or expectations, resistance will become evident.

Conflicting Organizational Systems

Organization-wide systems and processes that shape employee behaviour are embedded in the company's policies, selection, training, and reward systems. Unless these structures and processes are altered, people will continue to behave in the "old" way. For example, when the University of Calgary moved to a competency-based performance management system, they initially faced resistance because, while performance expectations had changed, the existing training, support, and reward systems had not been adjusted to support the change. In order to overcome the resistance, the university made a number of changes to the organizational systems: It gave department heads the ability to reward performance through the use of "growth increments," it redesigned staff development and tuition support programs to address competency gaps, and it created a web-based learning link to support competency development.[40]

MANAGING ORGANIZATIONAL CHANGE AND DEVELOPMENT

Now that you have learned about many of the causes of individual reactions and organizational resistance to change, the question becomes what can organizational leaders do to recognize these barriers, address them, and successfully manage change in spite of them?

In this section, we begin by reviewing Lewin's force field analysis, a classic model for examining the forces for and against change. Then we explore two important models for managing change, first the classic *Harvard Business Review* article "Choosing Strategies for Change," by Kotter and Schlesinger, and then John Kotter's recent work on leading strategic change. We conclude the chapter by examining the "organization development" approach to managing change.

Lewin's Force Field Analysis Model

Explain how Lewin's force field analysis model can be used to help manage change.

In addition to learning about potential individual reactions and types of organizational resistance in any change situation, it also helps to explore the potentially positive forces for change as well. Kurt Lewin's force field analysis model, illustrated in Exhibit 13.4, does just this. The model has stood the test of time and continues to influence the way organizations manage planned change. Lewin's model is based on the idea of force field analysis,[41] which contends that a person's behaviour is the product of two opposing forces; one force pushes toward preserving the status quo, and the other force pushes for change. When the two opposing forces are approximately equal, current behaviour is maintained. For behavioural change to occur, the forces maintaining the status quo must be overcome. This can be accomplished by increasing the forces for change, by weakening the forces for the status quo, or by a combination of these actions. Practise applying force field analysis to a problem in your life by completing Self-Assessment 13.2.

Lewin's force field analysis model was the earliest model of organizational change, and provided the foundation for later models. According to Lewin, the crucial first hurdle in the change process is that of "unfreezing" the status quo. **Unfreezing** involves encouraging individuals to discard old behaviours by shaking up the equilibrium state that maintains the status quo. This is the first of three steps in Lewin's change model as shown in Exhibit 13.4.

unfreezing
The first step in Lewin's change model, in which individuals are encouraged to discard old behaviours by shaking up the equilibrium state that maintains the status quo.

In the example of making the decision to start exercising, described in Exhibit 13.5, unfreezing may occur if a person becomes ill or begins to have less energy. By unfreezing, individuals accept that change needs to occur. Organizations often accomplish unfreezing by eliminating the rewards for current behaviour and showing that current behaviour is not valued.[42] In the unfreezing stage, it helps to understand that people may need to go through "endings" before they can embrace "new beginnings."[43] You will learn about more recent terminology for unfreezing, such as "creating a sense of urgency" and "creating readiness for change," later on in the chapter.

The second step in the change process, according to Lewin, is **moving.** In the moving stage, new attitudes, values, and behaviours are substituted for old ones. An individual trying to move to a regular exercise routine may set an exercise goal, join a gym, or find a jogging partner in this stage. Organizations accomplish moving by initiating new options and explaining the rationale for the change, as well as by providing training to help employees develop the new skills they need. Employees should be given the overarching vision for the change so that they can establish their roles within the new organizational structure and processes.[44]

moving
The second step in Lewin's change model, in which new attitudes, values, and behaviours are substituted for old ones.

EXHIBIT 13.4

Lewin's Change Model

Unfreezing	Moving	Refreezing
Reducing forces for status quo	Developing new attitudes, values, and behaviours	Reinforcing new attitudes, values, and behaviours

CRITICAL THINKING: Application & Synthesis

SELF-ASSESSMENT 13.2: APPLYING FORCE FIELD ANALYSIS

This exercise uses Lewin's force field analysis, which is explained in Exhibit 13.4. Use it as outlined below to help you think through a problem you are currently facing.

1. Describe the problem, as specifically as possible.

   ____

   ____

2. List the forces driving change (as shown on the left side of the diagram).
3. List the forces restraining change (as shown on the right side of the diagram).

Forces driving change	Forces restraining change
____________	____________
____________	____________
____________	____________
____________	____________

4. What can you do, specifically, to remove the obstacles to change?

   ____

   ____

5. What can you do to increase the forces driving change?

   ____

   ____

6. What do you think are the benefits of breaking a problem down in this way, into forces driving change and forces restraining change?

   ____

refreezing
The final step in Lewin's change model, in which new attitudes, values, and behaviours are established as the new status quo.

Refreezing is Lewin's conception of the final step in the change process. In this step, the new ways of operating are reinforced. Exercising becomes a habit and a routine and the person feels rewarded for the new behaviour. At work, changes in the reward structure are often needed to ensure that the organization is not rewarding the old behaviours

EXHIBIT 13.5

Force Field Analysis of a Decision to Engage in Exercising

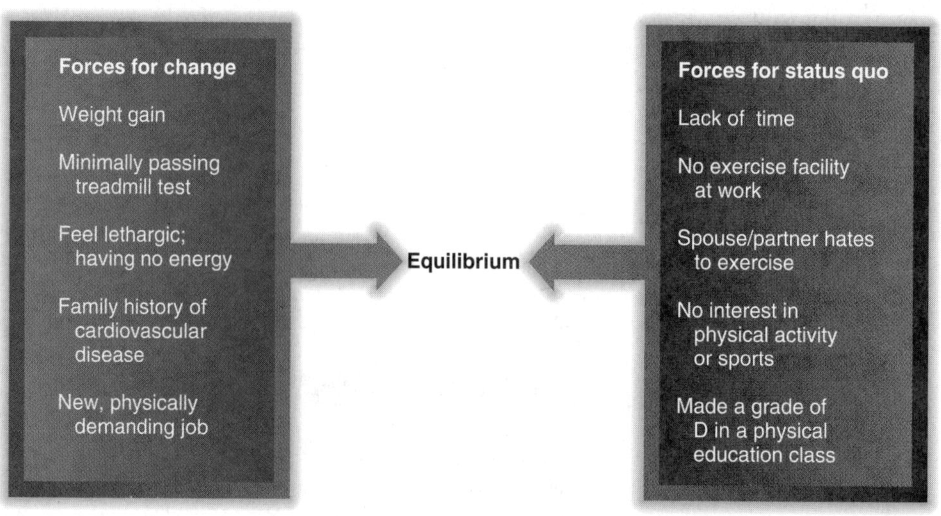

and merely hoping for the new behaviours. The term "refreezing" creates an image of something immovable, and is probably outdated in most of our current organizations where things never really stop changing. In fact, recent research does suggest that the term is perhaps misleading. A recent study of resistance to change demonstrated that success required constant vigilance over the forces working in the opposite direction of the change, and required that the plan be constantly adjusted and adapted to assure that genuine concerns were addressed.[45] What this means is that after a change is introduced, a great deal of work and listening needs to continue to ensure both that old habits do not begin to creep in again and that the changes fit the new and changing realities. More recent terminology for Lewin's refreezing stage includes "institutionalizing the changes" and "making the changes stick."

Managing Individual Reactions to Change

Discuss five strategies for managing individual reactions to change.

Traditionally, negative reactions to change were viewed as resistance that management had to overcome. The contemporary view holds that rather than viewing the reactions as resistance, it is better to view them as forms of feedback that can be used very productively to manage the change process. Even so, managing negative employee reactions to change is never easy, and it is always preferable to plan and manage the change carefully so as to prevent or minimize these reactions emerging in the first place. However, a certain amount of negative reaction is to be expected since change management is so complex and it will never go as smoothly as one would like. It is advisable to make strategies that address negative reactions a central part of the implementation plan itself.[46]

Kotter and Schlesinger, in a classic *Harvard Business Review* article, proposed a number of strategies for managing negative reactions to change. We compare and contrast five of these strategies, which are summarized in Exhibit 13.6.

Communication

In Chapter 6 you learned about the importance of effective interpersonal and organization-wide communication. You also learned about the various barriers to communication and ways to overcome them. During organizational changes, communication is critical to

EXHIBIT 13.6

Managing Individual Reactions to Change

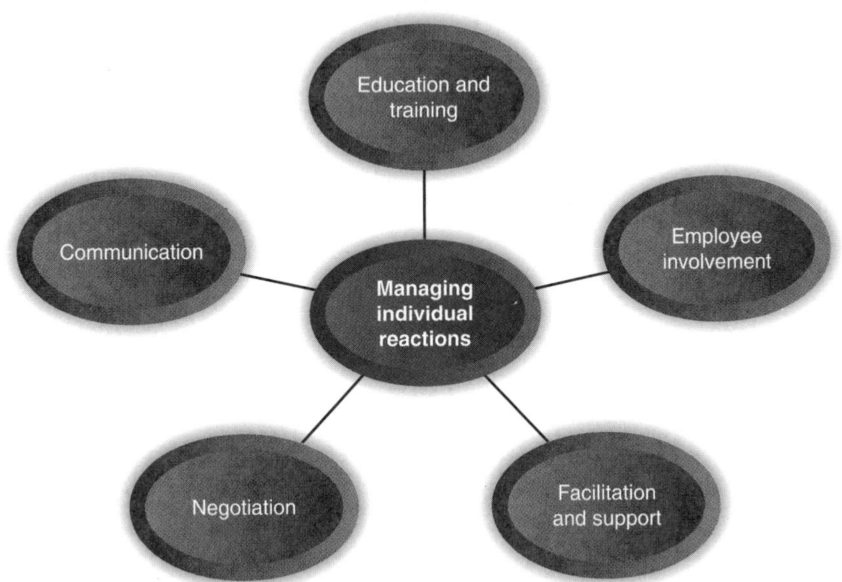

success because resistance to change can be caused by fear of the unknown. Recent research on employee reactions to large-scale changes have revealed that, on average, companies were perceived to have "under-communicated" by a factor of 10![47] Early communication about impending change is essential if employees are to buy in to it.

For example, Fred MacGillvray, president and CEO of the Halifax World Trade and Convention Centre, makes a concerted effort to keep workers updated on the business activities. "We have a promise to our employees that they won't hear anything in the media before they hear about it from us first."[48] It is important to communicate both the details of the change and the rationale behind it. Each employee must clearly understand the business rationale for the change as well as their role in making the new organization successful. If not, they will feel they are working in the dark. It is not uncommon for employees to say, "Don't know why we did this, who I'm working for, or what I'm supposed to do."[49] Providing accurate and timely information about the change can help prevent unfounded fears and potentially damaging rumours from developing.

Training and Education

Early and specific training helps people gain mastery and overcome a fear of failure. Manitoba Lotteries invested heavily in employee training, as well as communication, to accomplish their successful turnaround. They set up an intranet website, quarterly employee feedback and progress meetings, lunch and learn sessions, and a company-wide human resources advisory committee. Training was targeted toward overcoming employment barriers such as ESL, English, math, and computer skills. A management development program was also initiated in conjunction with the universities of Winnipeg and Manitoba.[50] Bombardier invested in a training program called Transitions to help managers learn change management skills.[51] See Organizational Reality 13.2 for more details.

Employee Involvement

There is substantial research support underscoring the importance of participation in the change process. Employees must be engaged and involved in order for change to work—as supported by the notion "That which we create, we support." Participation helps

organizational reality 13.2

Bombardier Executives Learn Change Management Skills Using a Computer Simulation

The history of Bombardier is marked with many radical changes. The company started off manufacturing vehicles for transportation on snow-covered terrain. Six decades later, it is a manufacturing powerhouse and a world leader in the railway, recreational vehicle, and aircraft industries. In order to help senior HR executives manage the many changes that occur at Bombardier, the company was among the first to invest in "Transitions." Designed by a trio of Canadian entrepreneurs, Transitions is essentially a computer game designed to immerse managers in change management concepts through emotionally engaging business simulations.

The change simulation is a business case regarding a fictitious company that manufactures equipment for use with global positioning satellites. The company is experiencing a business downturn in its traditional military market and is seeking a turnaround strategy. Hired as change consultants, trainees work in small teams to tackle a series of interactive modules. The modules involve interviewing imaginary employees and doing other research to determine the range of the company's difficulties, and then creating a strategy for change. A final three-hour module tests the team's ability to execute their plan.

To ensure the software encompasses current change management theories, a partnership was formed with Carol Beatty, director of the School of Industrial Relations at Queen's University. "It's complex—a real intellectual challenge" Beatty affirms. "It requires a lot of sophisticated knowledge to nail it down."

SOURCE: "Young Entrepreneurs Take On the Market with Simulations Software," *The Training Report*, July 1998, 5.

employees become involved in the change and establish a feeling of ownership in the process. When Eric Smith, newly appointed CEO of Vita Health Products, searched for a way to build employee morale during a time of major corporate change and aggressive growth, he decided to set up the employee initiative committee. The committee ensures effective employee representation and ongoing continuity and gives the employees within the company involvement and voice.[52]

Facilitation and Support

It is important to provide support to employees who are having trouble dealing with a change. Active listening is an excellent tool for identifying the reasons for the specific reactions and for uncovering fears. Setting up stress management workshops to encourage expression of concerns about the change can provide important feedback to improve the change process. Emotional support and encouragement can help an employee deal with the anxiety that is a natural response to change. Employees who experience severe reactions to change can benefit from talking with a counsellor. Peter Frost, author of *Toxic Emotions at Work,* published by Harvard Business School Press, writes about the unrecognized work of "toxin handlers," people who step into toxic situations and identify, contain, neutralize, or disperse the emotional poison often created by organizational change. Frost's research identifies five major themes in how these individuals provide facilitation and support: by listening, providing breathing room for healing, buffering pain, removing others from painful situations, and by reframing a person's view of a painful situation.[53]

Negotiation

As you learned in Chapter 11, there are numerous ways to manage conflict, and negotiation is one of them. Change initiatives can be supported by negotiating desired outcomes for employees who continue to react negatively to an important change. For example, during mergers and acquisitions, managers and employees may be offered retention bonuses to gain their commitment to stay with the company until a certain time. Another example is negotiating with an employee to give up a rigid job description in exchange for employee ownership options.[54]

Kotter and Schlesinger's original work also suggested a sixth strategy, which they called "coercion." You learned about the use of coercive power and the influence tactic called "pressure" in Chapter 9, so you know that coercion relies on threats of punishment. An example of using coercion to deal with resistance to change would be a manager telling an employee to accept a change or be fired. Since this strategy raises a host of ethical and moral issues in addition to creating all the negative effects of coercive power discussed, this strategy is not recommended unless absolutely necessary.

The reality of large-scale organizational change is that it can be difficult and complex, especially for middle managers who are often required to deal with a variety of employee reactions while they themselves are unsure about their future with the company. At times, employee reactions can be fiercely negative, and dealing with them can be a long and often arduous process. For example, Verizon Communications faced substantial resistance to change when it implemented its "customer connection" initiative, with the goal of building a cellular-phone network that ranked first in customer service. The change agent, Ben Powell, and his teammates tried to persuade the service employees to send new cellular phones out the door with fully charged batteries in them. The employees balked at the idea because they had to install the batteries, which took extra time. As Powell said, "When you meet this kind of resistance, the only thing you can do is keep plugging away.... Finally, in the last six months or so we have been getting to the point where we're really changing how we do business. But it's taken years. Not weeks. Not months. On a day-to-day basis, it feels like bowling in sand."[55]

IMPLICATIONS FOR LIFE

Applying the Change Models to Trying to Break a Bad Habit

While the theories discussed are very useful when managing organizational change, you can also apply many of them to managing changes in your own life. For example, let us apply the theories to a situation you may find yourself in. Perhaps you have been told by your doctor that unless you break a bad habit, your health will be at risk. We will use the example of trying to quit smoking here but you can apply it to any other change.

- *Individual reactions to change:* You may react positively to the change or, more than likely, you will react in one of the five ways discussed. Perhaps you *fear the unknown* because you have never tried to quit before and you don't know how you are going to feel or how your body will react. Perhaps you *fear the loss* of comfort that smoking brings, or loss of a group of smoking friends. Perhaps you have a *fear of failure* and don't trust in your ability to quit for good. Perhaps smoking has become a habit and a conditioned response to having a cup of coffee or taking a break. Perhaps you *selectively perceive* the information from your doctor about the health risks and you ignore it. Finally, perhaps you have listened to your doctors many times before and tried all their approaches and you are *cynical* about wasting your time even trying.
- *Organizational resistance to change:* If you look at your smoking peer group, you will better understand some of the organizational causes of resistance to change.
- *Limited focus of change:* In this example, perhaps a barrier is that the focus on quitting smoking is too limited. Perhaps to be successful, the focus needs to be broadened to include changing how you use your leisure time, or eating patterns, etc.
- *Conflicting team norms/organizational systems:* If the smoking is one of the norms or rewards in a social group, it will be very hard to quit while at the same time remaining active and comfortable in the team.
- *Managing individual reactions to change:* Depending upon the nature of your individual reactions and organizational resistance to quitting smoking, one or more of the following strategies may help:
  - Identify all of the forces that are for and against your quitting. Also explore what it would take for you to "unfreeze."
  - Do you have enough information about the effects of smoking and quitting (communication)?
  - Do you need any training on breaking the habit and replacing old behaviours or routines with new ones?
  - Do you need to get more involved in defining the problem and change strategy rather than accepting the edict from your doctor (employee involvement)?
  - Do you need to set up support systems to help you make the change, i.e., a smoking withdrawal group or hotline or a counselor or a patch (facilitation and support)?
  - Finally, do you need to motivate yourself by setting up some kind of win–win for quitting (negotiation)?

Explain Kotter's top-down approach to large-scale change.

The Top-Down Approach to Large-Scale Change

While the five strategies just discussed offer useful guidelines for dealing with individual reactions to change, OB scholars in the last two decades have taken more system-wide and strategic approaches to managing large-scale change. The large-scale change approaches fall into two general categories: the top-down approach and the organization development approach. We begin by reviewing John Kotter's top-down approach.

John Kotter's most recent book, *The Heart of Change,* follows his earlier bestseller entitled *Leading Change.* Both books prescribe an eight-step approach to leading change based on extensive research and company interviews.[56]

As shown in Exhibit 13.7, the first step in the eight-step model highlights the critical importance of *increasing urgency and creating readiness for change.* This step relates to Lewin's concept of "unfreezing," and research has shown that without high readiness, all of the following steps are likely to fail. Companies increase urgency by sharing competitive information lower down in the organization to create dissatisfaction, and by showing a gap between a desired future and the current reality.[57] Successful transformational change also requires the commitment of a *guiding change team,* which commits time to the change process itself. This team needs broad representation as well as the power to influence. The strategies for overcoming individual and organizational resistance to change should be implemented in the context of a *vision* that paints an engaging, clear, and realistic picture of the desired future. In addition, recent research suggests that the vision also should be adaptable. According to Todd Jick, "A guiding philosophy from which members of the organization can make local decisions on how to respond to challenges and opportunities is more important than a shared picture of what the organization wishes to become."[58] Strategies for *communicating and empowering action* have already been discussed in the previous section on overcoming resistance to change. *Creating short-term wins* can help overcome resistance and motivate staff. For example a CEO of a Canadian computer company saw the need to introduce a new computer operating system in his company. At the end of the training period a barbeque was held to celebrate the accomplishments and award prizes. These activities helped make the company's adjustment to the change a success.[59]

John Kotter, a professor of management at Harvard University, has developed an eight-stage process for successfully managing large-scale change.

The final two stages in Kotter's model relate to Lewin's "refreezing" stage. These steps are *don't let up* and *make the change stick.* Key concepts in these stages revolve around

EXHIBIT 13.7

The Eight Steps for Successful Large-Scale Change

Step	Description
1. Increase urgency	Raise a feeling of urgency so that people say "let's go," making a change effort well positioned for launch.
2. Build the guiding team	Help form a group that has the capability—in membership and method of operating—to guide a very difficult change process.
3. Get the vision right	Create the right vision and strategies to guide action in all of the remaining stages of change.
4. Communicate for buy-in	Communicate for change visions and strategies effectively so as to create both understanding and gut-level buy-in.
5. Empower action	Deal effectively with obstacles that block action, especially disempowering bosses, lack of information, the wrong performance measurement and reward systems, and lack of self-confidence.
6. Create short-term wins	Produce sufficient short-term wins, sufficiently fast, to energize the change helpers, enlighten the pessimists, defuse the cynics, and build momentum for the effort.
7. Don't let up	Continue with wave after wave of change, not stopping until the vision is reality, despite seemingly intractable problems.
8. Make change stick	Be sure the changes are embedded in the very culture of the enterprise so that the new way of operating will stick.

SOURCE: J. P. Kotter and D. S. Cohen, *The Heart of Change* (Boston: HBR Press, 2002). Reprinted with permission.

organizational resistance and building the recruitment, training, and reward systems that will support the desired behaviour in the long term.

Kotter's top-down model is often used as a guide to change initiatives.[60] The following actions provide an example of how Kotter's steps were followed in a recent organizational change initiative: A workshop was conducted to determine the organization's vision and mission. Strategic appointments were made and leaders were expected to act as the guiding team. Formal presentations, meetings, and a quarterly web survey ensured ongoing communication for buy-in. Employee empowerment was increased by setting up a core team of seven appointed people, reflecting all levels and jobs, who were selected and charged with identifying and addressing the issues that would transform the organization into a "great place to work." An additional seven "volunteer" members rotated through the team each quarter to increase involvement. This employee team also tracked the impact of changes throughout the life of the project and became integral to its eventual success.

It is important to mention that while the model suggests that change management is a logical, step-by-step process, this could not be farther from the reality. For example, John Mayberry, who recently retired as CEO of Dofasco, told the *Hamilton Spectator* that while Dofasco's rebirth by fire looks today like a logical, step-by-step evolution, in truth there was much confusion along the way and a lot or arguing.[61]

Analysis & Evaluation

IS IT EVER UNETHICAL TO IMPOSE ORGANIZATIONAL CHANGE?

Under what circumstances would it be unethical to apply the change management practices described thus far? Use the ethical guidelines from Chapter 8 (Exhibit 8.4) to develop these possible scenarios.

Explain the distinguishing characteristics of the organization development (OD) approach to change management.

The Organization Development Approach to Change

The organization development approach to change differs from the top-down approach, just described, in a number of significant ways. **Organization development (OD)** is defined as a system-wide application of behavioural science knowledge to the planned development and reinforcement of the strategies, structures, and processes that lead to organization effectiveness and adaptability.[62]

organization development (OD)
Organization development is a system-wide application of behavioural science knowledge to the planned development and reinforcement of the strategies, structures, and processes that lead to organization effectiveness and adaptability.

Organization development has a rich history. Some of the early work in OD was conducted by Kurt Lewin, Rensis Likert, and Eric Trist and his colleagues at the Tavistock Institute.[63] Organization development has been used extensively worldwide, and the approach is similar to the top-down approach in that they are both system-wide and address the strategy, structure, and processes of either the whole organization or one of its subunits. However, the OD approach has a number of distinctive characteristics and we explore five of them.

Change Based on Diagnosis: Action Research

The OD process starts early with a heavy emphasis on diagnosing the forces for and against change, determining the targets and scope of change, and identifying, ahead of time, possible negative individual reactions and areas of organizational resistance to change. The OD approach to change management is also referred to as action research, and it has a rich history in the organizational behaviour literature. **Action research** is an approach in which initial research about an organization provides information to guide subsequent action.[64] The steps of this approach are shown in Exhibit 13.8. The GHOST model of an organization, described in Chapter 1, is an example of a diagnostic model that is used by OD practitioners to diagnose an organization's strengths, weaknesses, and change goals during step three of the action research approach shown in Exhibit 13.8.

action research
An approach to change management in which initial research about an organization provides information to guide subsequent action.

EXHIBIT 13.8

The Action Research Approach in OD

Step	Explanation
1. Problem identification	A leader in the organization recognizes a problem or need for change
2. Consultation with behavioural science expert	Leader brings in a change agent to assist and relationships are built with client team(s)
3. Data gathering and preliminary diagnosis	Change agent and organization members conduct interviews, complete surveys, and gather organizational data using an organizational model
4. Feedback to client team(s)	Change agent feeds back data collected to client team and collects more if required
5. Joint diagnosis of problem	Change agent and client team(s) discuss the feedback and jointly determine the strengths weaknesses and change goals
6. Joint action planning	Change agent works with client team(s) to plan change strategies and OD interventions
7. Action	Actual changes are made from one organizational state to another. This may include installing new methods and procedures, reorganizing work designs, and training for new behaviours
8. Data gathering after action	Because action research is a cyclical process, data is gathered after the actions are taken to measure progress.

Source: T. G. Cummings and C. G. Worley, *Organization Development and Change,* 7th ed. (Mason, OH: South-Western, 2001), 24–25. Reprinted by permission of South-Western, a division of Thomson Learning, www.thomsonrights.com. Fax 800-730-2215.

The Organization Development Network (ODN) and the Association for Creative Change in Organization Renewal and Development (ACCORD)
These are both learning communities that develop, support, and inspire change practitioners and enhance the body of knowledge in human organization and systems development.
http://www.odnetwork.org
http://www.accord.org

OD is a Socio-Technical Approach to Change

The second distinctive characteristic of the OD approach is that it always gives as much attention to the human aspects as well as to the technical aspects of any organizational change. This is why it is referred to in the OB literature as a "socio-technical" approach to change. In a socio-technical approach, all decisions about what and how to change are made with stakeholder involvement in order to minimize ahead of time, to the extent possible, the negative individual reactions to the change discussed in the earlier section of the chapter. OD change practitioners seek to develop human potential while at the same time improving organizational efficiency and effectiveness.

Synthesis & Evaluation

USING THE GHOST MODEL TO DEVELOP A SET OF ACTION RESEARCH QUESTIONS

Suppose you have been called in as a change agent to help an organization reduce employee turnover in a hotel. Use the GHOST model described in Chapter 1 to create some diagnostic questions that will help determine the reasons that so many people are leaving after a short time.

OD Builds Improved Capacity for Self-Management

change agent
An individual who is assigned to guide and facilitate a change effort and who is able to influence organizational members while at the same time teaching them how to solve their own problems in the future.

Third, the OD approach to change has a learning component. By including a change agent in the process, usually from outside the organization, whose role is to collaborate, guide, and teach, organization members become more self-reliant. A **change agent** is an individual who is assigned to guide and facilitate a change effort and who is able to influence organizational members while at the same time teaching them how to solve their own problems in the future. Stephen Armstrong, an OD change consultant in Toronto, says that his job is to "convert organizations away from a dependence on a handful of key people and toward the creation of effective, cross-functional teams."[65] Another way of putting this is, "It is better to teach someone how to fish, than to fish for them."

OD Builds Change for the Long Term

The fourth feature of the OD approach to managing change is that it views organizational resistance as a natural outcome of opposing forces and that, therefore, change involves up-front modification of all relevant team, organizational, and HR systems as well as subsequent monitoring and reinforcement. While it might sound like a straightforward task to align hiring, reward, training, and promotion policies and processes with the desired changes, it is a complex process that can really derail a change if not done well. Exhibit 13.9 below provides a schematic overview of the relationships between organization development, the top-down approach, individual reactions to change, and organizational resistance to change.

EXHIBIT 13.9

Overview of Organizational Change and Development

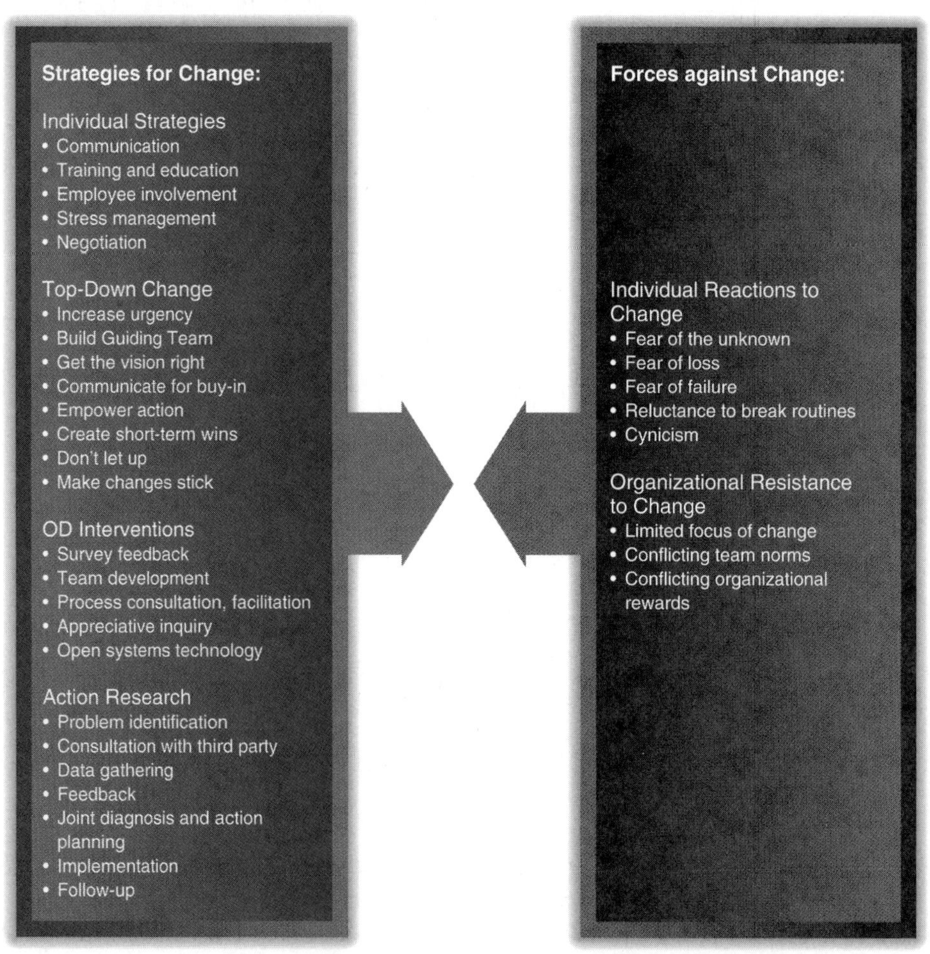

Organization Development Interventions

Give an overview of five OD interventions: survey feedback, process consultation, team development, appreciative inquiry and open systems technology.

Finally, the OD approach to change is distinctive in having produced a large number of practical change tools called "OD interventions." An **OD intervention** is any diagnostic or problem-solving activity that members of an organization participate in during an OD program which is designed to help them change.[66] OD interventions must be chosen and customized carefully and be based on the diagnosis of strengths, weaknesses, and change goals for the organization. We conclude this chapter with a brief overview of five OD interventions, which are survey feedback, team development, process consultation, appreciative inquiry, and open space technology.

OD intervention
Any diagnostic or problem-solving activity that members of an organization participate in during an OD program that is designed to help them change.

Survey Feedback

Survey feedback is a process of collecting from an organization or department through the use of a questionnaire or survey and feeding the data back. A large body of research indicates that these surveys have good reliability and validity, and they are useful tools for gathering employees' perceptions of their work environments. For survey feedback to be an effective method, however, employees must be assured that their responses to the questionnaire will be confidential and anonymous, and management must be prepared to follow up on the survey results.[67]

survey feedback
A process of collecting data from an organization or department through the use of a questionnaire or survey and feeding the data back.

Team Development

Team building and team development were discussed in Chapter 7, so we only mention them again here very briefly, because they are probably the most commonly used OD interventions. **Team development** is an educational process of continually reviewing and evaluating team functioning and identifying and establishing new and more effective ways of operating.[68] Following the action research model, team development begins with a diagnostic process in which team members identify problems, and it continues with the team planning actions to take in order to resolve those problems. The OD practitioner in team building serves as a facilitator, and the work itself is completed by team members.[69]

team development
An educational process of continually reviewing and evaluating team functioning and identifying and establishing new and more effective ways of operating.

Process Consultation and Facilitation

Process consultation and facilitation, pioneered by Edgar Schein, is an OD intervention that helps a group focus on its internal processes such as norms, communication, and group roles. It has a more specific focus than team building and involves a process facilitator/consultant.[70] The internal processes most often targeted are communication, conflict resolution, decision making, group interaction, and leadership. The role of the consultant, also called the facilitator, is to help employees help themselves. In this way, the ownership of a successful outcome rests with the employees.[71] The consultant guides the organization members in examining the processes in the organization and in refining them.

process consultation and facilitation
An OD intervention that helps a group focus on its internal processes, such as norms, communication, and group roles. It has a more specific focus than team building and involves a process facilitator/consultant.

Team development often involves taking teams on wilderness adventures where they learn to identify and establish new and more effective ways of operating.

Among the newer techniques on the horizon for managing change are **large group interventions,** which bring all of the key members of a group together in one room for an extended period of time to diagnose and plan organizational change. The advantage of large group interventions is that they can quickly have an impact because

large group interventions
An OD intervention that brings all the key members of an organization together in one room for an extended period of time to diagnose and plan organizational change.

organizational reality 13.3

Appreciative Inquiry at World Vision

In Chicago, World Vision used appreciative inquiry to solve problems of the inner city. The following four questions were used to interview a wide range of people:

1. What is it that gives "life" to your community? What do you love most about your community and what has contributed most to its vitality over the years?
2. What are your hopes for your community? What are its positive possibilities and how can they be most powerfully translated into reality?
3. Think of the best, most productive, most energizing partnership in which you've ever been involved. What were the forces and factors that made it possible?
4. What are your highest hopes and deepest aspirations for our partnership as we attempt to have a transformative presence in the City of Chicago?

Source: M. J. Mantel and J. D. Ludema, "From Local Conversations to Global Change: Experiencing the Worldwide Web Effect of Appreciative Inquiry," *Organization Development Journal* 18, no. 2 (Summer 2000). Reprinted by permission.

they involve many people at once. Large group interventions are intended to create a critical mass of people within an organization to support a change. These individuals then become internal change agents who implement the changes that are designed by the large group. There are a number of different types of large group OD interventions, including search conferences, whole-scale change, appreciative inquiry and open space technology. We briefly explore the latter two.

Appreciative inquiry

appreciative inquiry (AI)
A tool for connecting organizations to their positive change potential by opening every strength, innovation, achievement, imaginative story, hope, positive tradition, passion, and dream to systematic inquiry.

The action research model and the three OD interventions discussed thus far, survey feedback, team building, and process consultation, all tend to find what is wrong and forge solutions to fix the problems.[72] By contrast, appreciative inquiry (AI), developed in the last decade by David Cooperrider and his colleagues at the Case Western Reserve School of OB, focuses participants instead on future possibilities and all that is positive. **Appreciative inquiry (AI)** is a tool for connecting organizations to their positive change potential by opening every strength, innovation, achievement, imaginative story, hope, positive tradition, passion, and dream to systematic inquiry.[73] By focusing on that image of health and wholeness, the organization's energy moves to make that image real.[74] The five "D" cycle of: **d**efinition, **d**iscovery (appreciate the best of what is), **d**ream (envision what could be), **d**esign (co-construct what could be), and **d**estiny (sustain what will be) has been used by many organizations in the last decade to generate collective positive images of new and better futures.[75] Appreciative inquiry was used by World Vision to address the problems of the inner city in Chicago as outlined in Organizational Reality 13.3. Appreciative inquiry works because it gives way to "imagination and innovation; instead of negation, criticism."[76]

Open Space Technology

open space technology (OST)
A way to catalyze effective working conversations and problem solving in groups of up to 2000 people. Open space technology encourages individuals to self-organize and take responsibility for their own learning and actions.

Another large group intervention is open space technology (OST), created by Harrison Owen. **Open space technology (OST)** is a way to catalyze effective working conversations and problem solving in groups of up to 2000 people. Open space technology encourages individuals to self-organize and take responsibility for their own learning and actions.[77] Unique aspects of OST include the emphasis on self-organization and the philosophy that things will only get done well if individuals feel passionate about a particular topic. OST is guided by the following simple, but powerful rules: Whoever comes to the meeting are the right people. Whatever happens is the only thing that could have happened. Whenever it starts is the right time. When it's over, it's over. The "Law of Two Feet" means to leave when you are no longer contributing or learning.[78] Significant organizational improvements have been reported as a result of using OST in organizations all over the world.[79]

Educators at Ryerson University in Toronto explore collaborative research possibilities using open space technology.

IMPLICATIONS FOR ORGANIZATIONAL EFFECTIVENESS

Managing the human side of change is always challenging for organizations and if it is not well done, the organization will pay a price. The company must ensure that there are adequate resources for carrying out the change and ethical practices should be followed, such as maintaining employee confidentiality and providing employees with clarity regarding how information will be used and what the future holds in store for them.

Second, the targets of change need to be determined and attention needs to be given to the causes of individual and organizational resistance. Readiness for change needs to be created by raising the sense of urgency for all involved and a shared vision of the change should be developed and communicated, involving and engaging as many key players as possible.

Top management must be committed to the change and a guiding change team should visibly demonstrate support, because employees look to these leaders to model appropriate behaviour. Change strategies should include ongoing communication and feedback, education, employee involvement, facilitation, and support.

The experience of Indigo Music and Books, highlighted in the chapter opening, suggests that in addition to redesigning several HR processes, post-merger there is a need to continue to develop its corporate intranet and employee-training program. As well, the reward system within the organization must be adapted to ensure that new behaviours, rather than old ones, are being reinforced. Participation in the change process should also be recognized and rewarded, and small wins should be formally celebrated. When required, OD interventions such as team building, survey feedback, large group interventions, and process consultation should be used to facilitate and/or consolidate behavioural change.

Chapter Summary

1. Change can be developmental, transitional, or transformational in nature. Developmental change is the improvement of a skill, method, or condition that for some reason does not measure up. Transitional change is introduced to have an organization evolve slowly: current ways of doing things are replaced by something new, and in transformational change the organization moves to a radically different, and sometimes unknown, future state.
2. Four common targets of change are structure, technology, work processes and tasks, and people's attitudes and organizational culture. Many companies restructured in the last two decades by reducing their layers of management, trying to improve vertical communication and the speed of decision making. This approach often includes downsizing to reduce the number of employees in a company, often with limited success.
3. The human aspects of organizational changes have been found to be the most challenging. This is due to the many types of individual reactions and organizational resistance that emerge. Individuals have many different types of reactions to change, brought about by at least six causes: fear of the unknown, fear of loss, fear of failure, habit, selective perception, and cynicism.
4. Resistance also comes from the organization itself. Organizational resistance may emerge as the result of a limited focus of change, conflicting team norms, and organizational systems such as rewards, selection, and training that may conflict with the changed expectations.
5. Strategies for managing organizational change and development are founded on Lewin's classic change model, which proposed three stages of change: unfreezing, moving, and refreezing.
6. Change leaders can help manage change by reducing forces for the status quo and reinforcing new behaviours. They can increase communication about the change, educate and train, encourage employee involvement in the change efforts, provide facilitation and support to those who have difficulty dealing with change, and negotiate where necessary.
7. Kotter proposes a top-down approach to leading change. His eight stages include increasing urgency, building the guiding team, getting the vision right, communicating for buy-in, empowering employees to act, creating short-term wins, not letting up, and making the change stick.
8. Organization development is a system-wide application of behavioural science knowledge to the planned development and reinforcement of the strategies, structures, and processes that lead to organization effectiveness and adaptability. Its distinguishing characteristics are as follows: (1) Changes are based on diagnosis and action research. (2) Second, the OD approach gives as much attention to the human aspects as well as to the technical aspects of any organizational change. (3) Through the involvement of a change agent, organization members learn how to solve their own problems and build capacity for the future. (4) OD involves up-front modification of all relevant team, organizational, and HR systems as well as subsequent monitoring and reinforcement.
9. Five of the many OD interventions are survey feedback, team development, process consultation, appreciative inquiry, and open space technology.

Key Terms

action research (p. 414)
active inertia (p. 404)
appreciative inquiry (AI) (p. 418)
change agent (p. 416)
cynicism (p. 405)
developmental change (p. 398)
downsizing (p. 400)
large group interventions (p. 417)
moving (p. 407)
OD intervention (p. 417)
open space technology (OST) (p. 418)
organization development (OD) (p. 414)
planned change (p. 398)
process consultation and facilitation (p. 417)
refreezing (p. 408)
survey feedback (p. 417)
team development (p. 417)
transformational change (p. 399)
transitional change (p. 398)
unfreezing (p. 407)

Review Questions

1. Contrast developmental, transitional, and transformational change.
2. What are some typical individual reactions to organizational change and why do they occur? What strategies can leaders use to address these reactions?
3. Describe force field analysis and its relationship to Lewin's change model.
4. Explain each of Kotter's eight steps for successful change.
5. What is organization development and what are its distinguishing characteristics?
6. How does appreciative inquiry (AI) differ from more traditional OD interventions and what are its strength and weaknesses?

Discussion and Communication Questions

1. Can organizations prevent negative employee reactions to change? If so, how?

   If you were in charge of designing the ideal management development program, what topics would you include? Why?
2. (*communication question*) Find an article that describes an organization that has gone through change and managed it well. Develop an "Organizational Reality" feature of your own about the example you find using the format in this book. Prepare a brief oral presentation of your Organizational Reality for your class.
3. Apply what you learned by completing Self-Assessment 13.1 to an ambiguous situation that you have encountered in real life. Identify any causes of resistance that you experienced.

Ethics Questions

1. What constitutes abuse of a change agent's power? How can organizations prevent this?
2. Is it ethical for an organization to coerce individuals to change?
3. You are leading a management development seminar, and the supervisor of one of the participants asks how his employee is performing in the seminar. Should you reveal this information?
4. Suppose you are a consultant, and an organization asks you to deliver a team-building intervention. You know a little about team building, but not a lot. You do know that a competitor will probably get the job if you do not do it. What should you do?
5. Suppose you are a consultant, and a company asks you to assist in rewriting its policies and procedures manual to help eliminate the company's excessive absenteeism. From your limited knowledge about the company, you suspect that the problem lies elsewhere, and that changing the manual will not solve the problem. What should you do?
6. How might you apply the action research model to a change you want to make in your own life?

? Application & Evaluation

EXPERIENTIAL EXERCISE 13.1: ORGANIZATIONAL ASSESSMENT OF CAMPUS

Purpose: To give you experience in diagnosing and organization and recommending OD interventions.

Group size: 4–6

Time required: 30–60 minutes

Materials needed: University/College Profile Sheet, University/College Diagnosis Form

Instructions:

1. Work in your permanent teams or form teams of 4–6 people.
2. Assume that your team has been hired to conduct a diagnosis of problem areas in your university and to make preliminary recommendations for organization development interventions.
3. Individually complete the following "University/College Profile."
4. As a team, evaluate the strengths and weaknesses within each area (academics, teaching, social, cultural, and administrative) using the accompanying "University/College Diagnosis" form.
5. Make recommendations concerning organization development interventions for each area. Be as specific as possible in both your diagnosis and your recommendations.
6. Teams present its diagnosis and recommendations to the class.

University/College Profile

Not True 1 2 3 4 5 Very True

I. Academics and Scholarly Environment

1 2 3 4 5 1. There is a wide range of courses to choose from.

1 2 3 4 5 2. Classroom standards are too easy.

1 2 3 4 5 3. The library is adequate.

1 2 3 4 5 4. Textbooks are helpful.

II. Quality of Teaching on Campus

1 2 3 4 5 1. Teachers here are committed to quality instruction.

1 2 3 4 5 2. We have a high-quality faculty.

III. Campus Social Life

1 2 3 4 5 1. Students are friendly to one another.

1 2 3 4 5 2. It is difficult to make friends.

1 2 3 4 5 3. Faculty get involved in student activities.

1 2 3 4 5 4. Too much energy goes into drinking and goofing off.

IV. Cultural Events on Campus

1 2 3 4 5 1. There are ample activities on campus.

1 2 3 4 5 2. Student activities are boring.

1 2 3 4 5 3. The administration places a high value on student activities.

1 2 3 4 5 4. Too much emphasis is placed on sports.

1 2 3 4 5 5. We need more "cultural" activities.

V. Management by the University/College Administration

1 2 3 4 5 1. Decision making is shared at all levels of the organization.

1 2 3 4 5 2. There is unity and cohesiveness among departments and units.

1 2 3 4 5 3. Too many dept. clashes hamper the organization's effectiveness.

1 2 3 4 5 4. Students have a say in many decisions.

1 2 3 4 5 5. The budgeting process seems fair.

1 2 3 4 5 6. Recruiting and staffing are handled thoughtfully, with student needs in mind.

University Diagnosis

	Strength	Weakness	Intervention
1. Academic			
2. Teaching			
3. Social			
4. Cultural			
5. Administration			

SOURCE: "Organizational Assessment of Campus" by D. Marcic, *Organizational Behavior: Experiences and Cases,* 5th ed. (Mason, OH: South-Western, 1998), 278–279. Reprinted by of South-Western, a division of Thomson Learning, www.thomsonrights.com. Fax 800-730-2215.

Application & Evaluation

EXPERIENTIAL EXERCISE 13.2: TEAM BUILDING FOR TEAM EFFECTIVENESS

Purpose: This exercise will allow you and your team to experience an OD intervention called "Team Development"

Group size: Your OB Team

Time required: 60 minutes

Materials needed: None

Instructions: Part 1: Diagnosis
Working as a team, complete the following four steps:

1. Describe how you have worked together this semester as a team.
2. What has your team done especially well? What has enabled this?
3. What problems or conflicts have you had as a team? (Be specific.) What was the cause of the problems your team experienced? Have the conflicts been over ideas, methods, or people?
4. Would you assess the overall effectiveness of your team as excellent, good, fair, poor, or a disaster? Explain your effectiveness rating.

Instructions: Part 2: Intervention
A diagnosis provides the basis for intervention and action in organization development. Team development is a way to improve the relationships and effectiveness of teams at work. It is concerned with the results of work activities and the relationships among the members of the team. Complete the following three steps as a team.

Step 1: Discuss the following with regard to the relationships within your team:

a. How could conflicts have been handled better?
b. How could specific relationships have been improved?
c. How could the interpersonal atmosphere of the team have been improved?

Step 2: Answer the following questions with regard to the results of the team's work:

a. How could the team have been more effective?
b. Are there any team process changes that would have improved the team's effectiveness?
c. Are there any team structure changes that would have improved the team's effectiveness?

Step 3: Answer the following questions with regard to the place where you work

a. What have you learned about team building that you can apply there?
b. What have you learned about team building that would not be applicable there?

For more practice exercises, consult *Organizational Behavior: Experiences and Cases,* 5th ed., by Dorothy Marcic and Joseph Seltzer (Mason, OH: South-Western, 1998).

Analysis & Evaluation

CASE: GRIEG'S SUPERMARKET

Grieg's Supermarkets is small supermarket chain, located in a number of cities in Western Canada, and has been in operation for over 50 years. The store in question employs approximately 150 employees, of whom about 40 percent work on a part-time basis. The store is run by a store manager, an assistant store manager, followed by six department managers of equal authority: the Head Cashier, Grocery Manager, Meat Manager, Produce Manager, General Merchandise and Snack Bar Manager, and the Bakery Manager.

The Head Cashier is responsible for approximately 40 cashiers (20 part-time students working nights, and 10 part-time and 10 full-time older women working the day shifts). She was also responsible for 2 full-time and 10 part-time "Front Boys" who run the parcel pick-up and assist cashiers and customers at the checkouts. The leadership style of the current store manager is highly task oriented and employees are expected to comply without questioning. Employee turnover at the store is very high except among cashiers, where it is unusually low for this industry, mainly because of the Head Cashier. She has worked at the store for 10 years, and is a charismatic and dedicated leader who has been able to create a very positive working environment in her area. Customers often comment on how enthusiastic and pleasant the cashiers are and attribute their positive attitude to their loyalty to the store.

For some time, there had been rumours that the store was going to upgrade their inventory tracking systems and cash registers to improve productivity and inventory control. No one, not even the six department managers seemed to know if the rumour was true and suddenly, near the end of August, employees were formally informed of the imminent change. Cashiers were approached individually by the Head Cashier, and told that a schedule for training on the new systems was being set up. The training would take place at another Greig's store several kilometres away. Each cashier was required to attend training at this store far a period of 16 hours, spread over four sessions, each of 4 hours. The cashiers would be paid their regular hourly wages for the time spent in training. However, no transportation would be provided or paid for. Nor would the time spent in travel to and from the training site (well over half an hour in each direction) be compensated for by the company.

One week after the training of all the cashiers was completed, the new systems and product codes were installed. This was accomplished outside of store hours, in only one weekend. As of the following Monday morning, all cashiers were required to operate the new systems in actual, real transactions. No further training was allowed for anyone. The complete changeover, including product coding, training, and installation, took place in a period of only three to four weeks.

Fourteen new registers were installed. All were hooked up to a main terminal located in the office that overlooked the store. Cashiers would ring in groceries using an improved coding system that would identify the various product categories more accurately (e.g., a cashier punches in Σ728, and the register tape shows 1 bag, 2% Natrel milk, the price and date). The old codes were abandoned and a new set, consisting of over 700 codes, was implemented.

Each register was equipped with an electronic reference file containing all the codes as well as the procedure for ringing in transactions to each register. The split screen permitted looking up a code while checking out groceries; however, it was impossible for a cashier to maintain any type of speed and efficiency with out memorizing approximately 80 percent of the new codes. Also, the design of the new, accompanying checkout counter was such that the cashiers were now required to key in groceries with their right hand while simultaneously packing the groceries with the other. Previously, this was a two-step process, whereby the cashier rang groceries in first (with their left hand if they were left handed) before packing the bags with both hands. The old method also provided for the assistance of a runner, who packed the groceries into bags while the cashier rang the items in. The new system was specifically designed to eliminate the need for a "front boys."

The new system was also capable of recording the level of performance achieved by each cashier. Several aspects of individual performance, in fact, were analyzed and recorded by management, and a comparison of cashiers constantly took place. This had not been possible before the introduction of the new registers. Standards of performance were arbitrarily set by the store and assistant store manager, and the Head Cashier was expected to give feedback to the individual cashiers. When the Head Cashier expressed her concerns about the approach being taken, the assistant store manager would intervene and urge certain employees to "try harder."

Curiosity and excitement were the first reactions to the rumours of the impending change. However, when faced with the actuality of training and adjustment, the cashiers were in general both fearful and angry. They resented the fact that the training schedule had been arranged without first consulting them. They also resented the fact that the training took place at a very distant location, which had to be reached by their own means. The older women resented being trained by unfamiliar girls who were younger than themselves. In addition, some cashiers felt that the training time was insufficient, whereas others complained it was too long and repetitive. The Head Cashier made numerous suggestions to the store manager that she thought would help but repeatedly she was told that change is good and she should not be so "negative."

Once the new system was implemented, the cashiers were eager to receive feedback on their performance. The assessment of performance revealed that the older women who worked the day shift performed at a much lower rate than did the younger cashiers. Many of these older women had been employed at the store for over 10 years, and it was generally felt that, due to their resentment at being required to change after such a long period of time, they intentionally kept their speed down. These women appeared to be very set in their ways and determined to hold things up. They spoke of being confused about the necessity of the change, as well as voicing annoyance at having to memorize all the new codes and procedures.

The young cashiers, on the other hand, seemed to enjoy the challenge and often spoke of the new registers initially as being similar to "new toys." All the cashiers felt, however, that they could not pack the bags as well with only one hand as they used to do with two. It was harder to grasp and manipulate products, and more difficult to arrange things so that more goods would fit into one bag, and fit snugly. They complained that the atmosphere at the front had changed and they also missed the opportunity of socializing with the "front boys," who used to help pack the bags.

Six months after the implementation of new system, the store manager met with the assistant manager and seven department managers to review some puzzling statistics. On the one hand, check-out efficiency had improved, head count had been reduced, and inventory costs had decreased, but cashier turnover had doubled and year-over-year sales had declined by 5 percent.

Questions

1. What were the various individual employee reactions to the changes at Grieg's Supermarket?
2. What were some of the causes of organizational resistance to change?
3. In your view, what were the most significant mistakes made by the company in planning and implementing this change?
4. If you had been hired as an OD or change consultant by Grieg's Supermarket when they had first thought about implementing the new system, what steps, strategies, and/or OD interventions would you have recommended to them?

SOURCE: From *Canadian Cases in Organizational Behaviour,* 3rd ed., by S. Anwar Rashid, Maurice Archer, and Randy Hoffman.

Scoring Instructions for Self-Assessment

Self-Assessment 13.1 Tolerance for Ambiguity

Scoring: For even-numbered questions, add the total points. For odd-numbered questions, use reverse-scoring and add the total points. Your score is the total of the even- and odd-numbered questions.

Norms Using the Tolerance for Ambiguity Scale

Basis: The survey asks 15 questions about personal and work-oriented situations with ambiguity. You were asked to rate each situation on a scale from 1 (tolerant) to 7 (intolerant). (Alternating questions have the response scale reversed.) The index scores the items. A perfectly tolerant person would score 15 and a perfectly intolerant person 105. Scores between 20 and 80 are reported, with means of 45. The responses to the even-numbered questions with 7 minus the score are added to the response for the odd-numbered questions.

Perfectly Tolerant | **Perfectly Intolerant**

| | | | | | | | | | | |
15 24 32 40 48 56 64 72 80 88 96 105

Norms:
Public-sector managers: 43 ± 20
Private-sector managers: 44.6 ± 8.5

Organizational Structure and Design

chapter fourteen

14

LEARNING OBJECTIVES

By the end of this chapter, you will be able to do the following:

1. Define organizational structure and explain three reasons for learning about how to design an organization.
2. Explain what is meant by the terms *differentiation* and *integration.*
3. Explain the terms *hierarchy of authority, vertical differentiation,* and *span of control.*
4. Explain what is meant by *specialization* and *horizontal differentiation.*
5. Describe three types of departmental grouping: functional, divisional, and hybrid.
6. Define *centralization* and *decentralization.*
7. Explain various mechanisms for achieving vertical integration, including standardization and formalization.
8. Explain various mechanisms for achieving horizontal integration, including liaison roles, task forces, integrator roles, permanent cross-functional teams, and matrix structures.
9. Compare and contrast mechanistic and organic organizational structures.
10. Explain how understanding the four contextual variables, strategy, environmental uncertainty, size, and technology, can help leaders design the best structure for their organization.
11. Discuss the need for more nimble organizations, and describe three types of contemporary organizational structures: horizontal, front-back, and network structures.

learning about the context

Organization Design at e-Roleplay

Amy Marcus, a Canadian entrepreneur and a very creative person, had an idea: Train actors to play realistic customers so that salespeople and customer service reps could develop key skills. *And* train the actors to give feedback to the employees so that they could learn from their mistakes and improve, *and* do this all over the phone so that the role plays and feedback could be delivered individually without huge costs to the company. In 2000, Marcus and her business partner Gerry Troy started the company "e-Roleplay" which now employs 9 full-time and 120 part-time staff. Companies rave about the courses and the impact of the practice on their results. The company's organizational structure is shown in Exhibit 14.1.

e-Roleplay's technology (the tools, techniques, and actions used by an organization to transform inputs to outputs) is made to order, especially in the initial stage, when the project team works with the client to design the required role plays. For this work, the organization structure of e-Roleplay is very *organic*. The work is done in teams; communication is informal, open, and frequent; decision making is decentralized; and employees fulfill multiple roles. For example, the role players can be part of the demonstration sales team, they can be course writers, they can train other role players, and they can be pilot or test role players. Once a project has been secured, the course has been written, and the role players have been trained, the technology changes. At this stage the technology is mass production. The job is to deliver standardized, on-time, one-on-one practice to the employees of the client company, who number sometimes as many as 5000. For this reason, the organization structure becomes more *mechanistic*, emphasizing certain attendance rules, adherence to course parameters, predefined role play scenarios, and centralized decision making through the VP of Learning and shift supervisors.

In a larger organization, the service delivery organization would be a separate department, probably in a different space, called "Production" or "The Call Centre," but for a company in the early stages of growth, such as e-Roleplay, organic and mechanistic structures coexist in the same space.

SOURCES: A. Marcus (president, e-Roleplay), interview with the author, December 29, 2003; e-Roleplay, http://www.e-roleplay.com/public/index.htm. Reprinted by permission.

EXHIBIT 14.1

e-Roleplay's Organization Chart

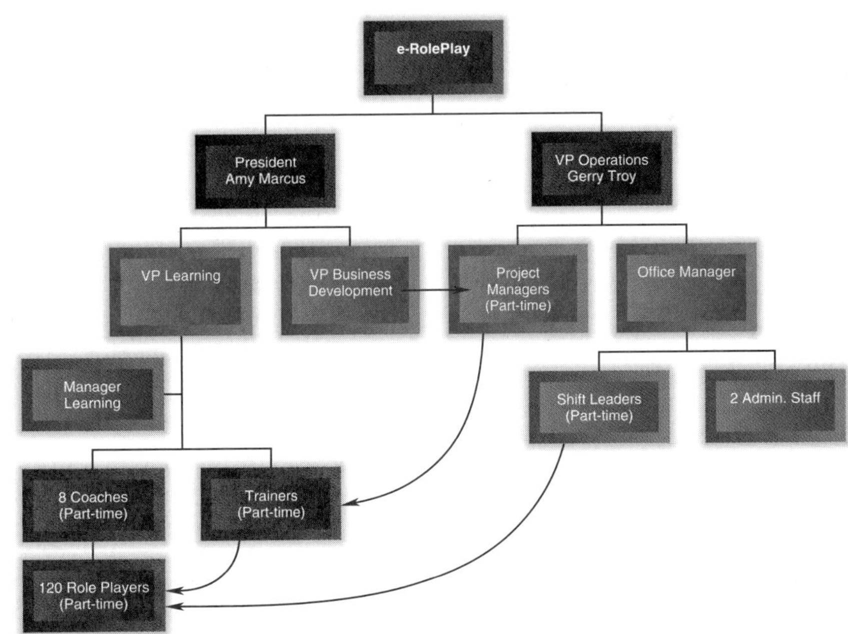

Note: The arrows indicate that the role players report to both the trainers and the shift leaders, and the trainers report to both the project managers and the VP Learning.

At e-Roleplay, described in the opening vignette, business partners Amy Marcus and Gerry Troy did it all at first. As the company grew, they decided to divide up the work and differentiate the structure into the three functions of sales, learning, and office management. Each function would be headed by a manager, who would report to one of them. With the start of the hierarchy, Marcus and Troy then became formal "integrators" with the added responsibility of ensuring that the three functions remained coordinated or "integrated" toward a common purpose. Then, as the business became more complex, more integrators were needed at lower levels, so project managers, coaches, trainers, and team leaders were added to the structure. As companies grow through their natural life cycles, an organizational structure will emerge one way or the other. Differentiation and integration will happen, simply because the founders can no longer do it all themselves.

We begin this chapter by defining organizational structure and explaining why it is important to understand the way organizations are divided up (differentiated) and integrated. In the first part of the chapter we explore five concepts that are used to *describe* an organization's structure. These key concepts are (1) the height of organizational hierarchy, (2) the degree of specialization and horizontal differentiation in the jobs, (3) the type of departmental grouping, (4) the degree to which decision making is centralized or decentralized, and (5) the types of vertical and horizontal integrating mechanisms in organizations. We conclude part one with the mechanistic-organic model, which summarizes these concepts in a useful organizing framework.

In part two of the chapter, we shift gears and explore how to best *design* an organization's structure. This involves understanding the organization's *context,* which includes the following four variables: (1) the degree of uncertainty in the organization's external task environment, (2) the organization's strategy, (3) the size of the organization, and (4) the nature of its work technology. To conclude, we look at contemporary organizational structures.

Define organizational structure and explain three reasons for learning about how to design an organization.

WHAT IS ORGANIZATIONAL STRUCTURE AND WHY IS IT IMPORTANT?

organizational design
The process of constructing and adjusting an organization's structure to match its environment and achieve its goals.

organizational structure (OS)
The manner in which an organization's work is designed, as well as how departments, divisions, and the overall organization are designed.

Organizational design is the process of constructing and adjusting an organization's structure to match its environment and achieve its goals. As discussed in the GHOST model in Chapter 1, **organizational structure (OS)** is the manner in which an organization's work is designed, as well as how departments, divisions, and the overall organization are designed. The literature is unified in that it perceives the central challenge of organization design as "to divide the tasks of a firm into manageable, specialized jobs, yet coordinate the tasks so that the firm reaps the benefit of harmonious action."[1] The purposes of this chapter and the benefits of learning how to design an organization's structure are threefold:

- First, if you want to start or grow a business, this material can help you decide how best to divide up the work and coordinate it in the most effective way.
- Second, if you work for a company, this material can help you recognize the sort of organizational structure that you are part of, and in recognizing certain dimensions of structure, you will gain valuable insights into why people behave the way they do, in this particular organizational design. The material can also help you choose a type of organizational structure that you prefer to work in since different structures lead to very different types of challenges and opportunities.
- Third and last, if you are in charge of running a mature company, this material will give you an introduction to how to assess the effectiveness of your current organizational structure and some clues as to how to redesign it if necessary.

Explain what is meant by the terms *differentiation* and *integration*.

Differentiation and Integration

The definition of organizational structure was refined when Paul Lawrence and Jay Lorsch wrote a groundbreaking article in the late 1960s in which they came up with the terms *differentiation* and *integration.* These two terms captured the notions of the dividing, grouping, and linking that form the essence of all organizational design processes.[2] **Differentiation** is defined as the process of deciding how to divide the work in an organization, and is also referred to as division of labour. Differentiation ensures that all essential organizational tasks are assigned to one or more jobs and that the tasks receive the attention they need. The more structurally differentiated the organization is, the more complex it is.[3] **Integration** is the process of coordinating the different parts of an organization.

differentiation
The process of deciding how to divide the work in an organization.

integration
The process of coordinating the different parts of an organization.

The dual tasks of differentiation and integration remain central to our understanding of organizational structure and design for organizations large and small. For example, all departments at Roots, previously the official outfitter for the Canadian Olympic Team, had to communicate and coordinate their efforts in order to outfit all members of the Olympic team. The designers had to pass their clothing plans on to a team that placed the orders for the proper amount of fabric. When the fabric arrived, the clothing had to be produced according to the designs and the sizes required, followed by placing the logos on the clothes. When the production was finished, the job was not yet complete. The clothes had to be packaged and delivered to the right people. This massive project required a great deal of coordination within the organization.

While differentiation and integration together define organization structure in its broadest sense, *differentiation* is further defined in terms of whether it is vertical or horizontal and *integration* is further defined (later on in the chapter) in terms of whether integrators are horizontal or vertical.

? Knowledge & Application

WHAT ORGANIZATIONAL STRUCTURE IS NOT

Many individuals who have never studied OB think that "organizational structure" is a term that describes everything about the way things are done in an organization. Write an explanation to teach such an individual that this in fact is not true but that, rather, the term "organizational structure" has a much more narrow meaning in OB. Explain both what organizational structure is and is not.

THE ORGANIZATIONAL HIERARCHY

3 **Explain the terms hierarchy of authority, vertical differentiation, and span of control.**

The organizational hierarchy is what is typically represented in an organizational chart and depicts how jobs and roles are divided up both vertically (up and down the hierarchy) and then horizontally by department. In addition to defining what is meant by the hierarchy of authority, we also explain the two related concepts of vertical differentiation and span of control.

Vertical Differentiation and the Hierarchy of Authority

The organizational hierarchy, or **hierarchy of authority,** is defined as the degree of vertical differentiation through reporting relationships and the span of control within the structure of the organization. The organizational chart is the most visible representation of vertical differentiation and the hierarchy of authority.[4]

hierarchy of authority
The degree of vertical differentiation through reporting relationships and the span of control within the structure of the organization.

vertical differentiation
The difference in authority and responsibility in the organizational hierarchy.

Vertical differentiation is the difference in authority and responsibility in the organizational hierarchy. Vertical differentiation can range in degree from very large to very small. For example, at e-Roleplay (see Exhibit 14.1), the degree of vertical differentiation is quite small, as there are only three levels of management between the president and the role players. In larger companies, such as banks, vertical differentiation tends to be much higher, and one can find as many as 15 levels of management!

Span of Control and Tall and Flat Structures

span of control
The number of people directly reporting to a manager.

tall organizational structure
A structure with many layers of management and narrow spans of control.

flat organizational structure
A structure with few layers of management and wide spans of control.

de-layering
The planned vertical compression of managerial levels of the hierarchy.

Span of control is defined as the number of people directly reporting to a manager. The spans of control of managers influence the nature of the hierarchy. Spans of control are referred to as either "wide," meaning a manager has a relatively large number of people directly reporting to him or her, or "small," meaning that the manager has relatively fewer people reporting to him or her. See Exhibit 14.2.

Tall organizational structures have many layers of management and narrow spans of control. As a result, they tend to be characterized by closer supervision and tighter controls. In addition, the communication becomes more burdensome, since directives and information must be passed through more layers. **Flat organizational structures** have fewer layers of management and wider spans of control. The trend over the last two decades has been for organizations to flatten their hierarchies and decentralize decision making so as to be able to adapt more quickly to customer demands. See Exhibit 14.3 for examples of flat and tall organizational structures.

Flat structures result in simpler communication chains and people are supervised less closely. This trend has been referred to as **de-layering,** which is the planned vertical compression of managerial levels of the hierarchy.[5] Harley-Davidson is an example of a company that *used* to be organized as a traditional tall hierarchy, often referred to as a "pyramid." By the early 1990s Harley's leaders realized that the tall organization with many management layers was creating problems for them. Read about how they de-layered and created a flatter, team-based structure, in Organizational Reality 14.1. You will learn more about "horizontal" organizational structures like the one at Harley-Davidson, in the section called "Contemporary Organizational Structures" at the end of this chapter.

EXHIBIT 14.2

Wide and Narrow Spans of Control

Example A: Wide Span of Control

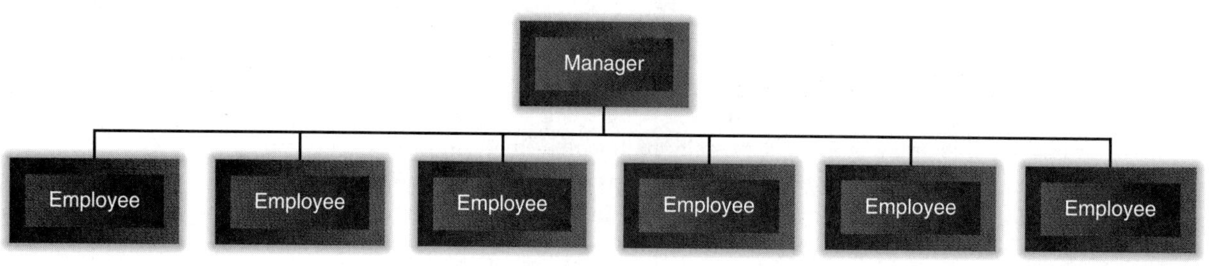

Example B: Narrow Span of Control

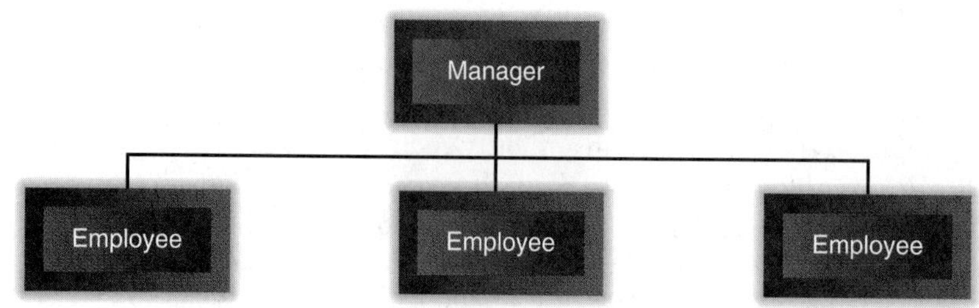

EXHIBIT 14.3

Tall and Flat Organizational Structures

Example 1: Tall organizational structure, narrow spans of control

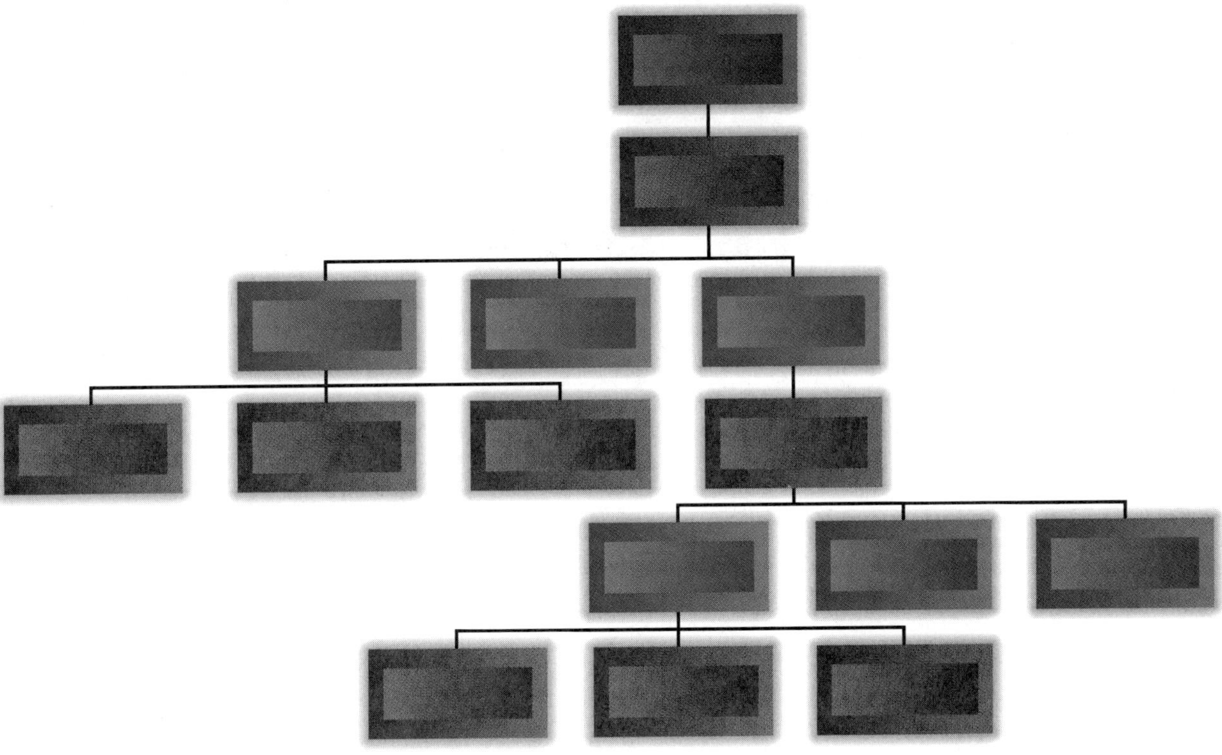

Example 2: Flat organizational structure, wide spans of control

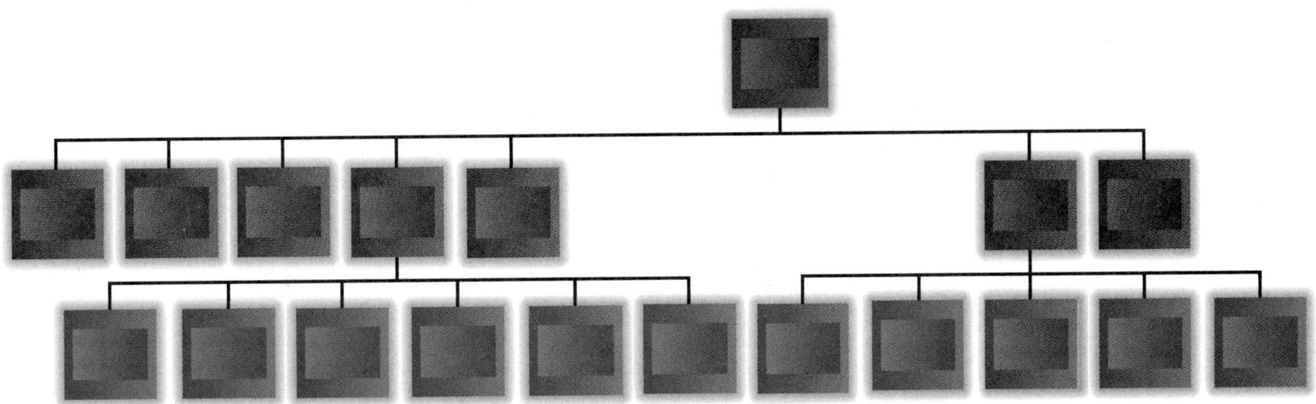

organizational reality 14.1

Upending the Pyramid Structure at Harley-Davidson

Harley-Davidson was organized in a traditional hierarchy or pyramid in 1987. At the top of the pyramid was the CEO and at the bottom were the operational employees, in various departments and functions that produced the motor bikes. By the early 1990s, Harley's senior team was convinced that the pyramid needed to be upended. They believed that with the right combination of shared leadership and individual responsibility, *any* form of organization might work. The senior team found several problems resulting from the current pyramid structure, including failure to meet customer needs, "process" problems, slow project start-ups, and the failure to vest responsibility and authority in the individual. In addition, too much independence and competition existed within the company, and not enough interdependence and collaboration.

At Harley-Davidson, the organizational structure is based on teamwork and relationships that are partnerships. The company moved away from a tall pyramid structure based on competition to a flatter one based on interdependence, collaboration, and cooperation.

As the senior team looked for alternative ways of organizing the company, one popular choice at the time was based on teams. Would a team-based organization suit Harley? Most of the company's employees were represented by labour unions, and *team* is a term loaded with hidden meaning for many union employees. Many Harley workers were represented by two international unions, and their previous experiences with the team concept had led them to hold strongly negative opinions about it. Hence, a team-based structure was likely to put Harley's labour relations at risk. In addition, many teams develop very tightly knit, cohesive bonds that are resistant to change and defend the status quo, even when change in the business environment calls for change in the company. Finally, aside from top teams in organizations, it was hard to find managers or senior managers in teams. So, a team-based organization was not right for Harley-Davidson.

Harley-Davidson wanted something really unusual—teamwork without teams. To achieve this, Harley began with what they dubbed a "customer-flow" organization, which was the sequence of supplier–worker–customer relationships throughout the company that resulted in the delivery of products and services. These chains of relationships were anchored in Harley's concept of partnering, which means that the relationship is interdependent, the interests of all parties in the relationship are valid, neither party can succeed alone, and the parties to the relationship are responsible both for each party's achievements and for the relationship. At Harley-Davidson, teamwork is based on relationships that are partnerships rather than on some form of team-based structure. The company was moving away from an independence and competition model of work relationships to one of interdependence, collaboration, and cooperation.

The definition of natural work teams at Harley-Davidson has three parts. First, a natural work team is a group of employees, both salaried and hourly, who produce products and services. This is called the "Produce Products Circle" or PPC. Second, a natural work team has the authority, within predetermined boundaries, to make decisions that support its activities, and it is accountable for the results. This is called the "Provide Support Circle" or PSC. Third, a natural work team is expected to transform itself quickly and smoothly in response to its customers' changing needs. This is called the "Create Demand Circle" or CDC. The company found that the three natural work groupings that emerged from its customer-flow organization were those that created demand, those that produced products or services, and those that supported the others, including all traditional staff functions such as finance, accounting, and human resource management. These three core processes in the organization were joined by the fourth core process of coordinating these activities, both internally and in relationships with external stakeholders.

The core process of coordinating would be the responsibility of the president of the company along with representatives from each of the other three natural work groups in creating demand, producing product, and providing support. This completed the upending of the traditional management pyramid at Harley and began the ushering in of what the company came to call the circle organization, which became official on July 1, 1993. The circle organization is Harley's way of organizing through a series of interdependent, interlocking, and collaborative natural work groups based on shared leadership and individual responsibility. Through natural work groups and the circle organization, Harley-Davidson was able to achieve teamwork without teams.

SOURCES: R. Terlink and L. Ozley, *More Than a Motorcycle: The Leadership Journey at Harley-Davidson* (Boston: Harvard Business School Press, 2000); C. Fessler, "Rotating Leadership at Harley-Davidson: From Hierarchy to Interdependence," *Strategy and Leadership* 25 (July/August 1997): 4.

Critics of de-layering suggest that it leads to diminished sources for internal management talent as well as burn-out for those managers who are left with extra workloads. However, some research also indicates that flatter structures encourage innovation.[6] Grant Gisel, founder and president of Sierra Systems Group Inc., believes that hierarchies stifle initiative and innovation so his company has a very flat structure in spite of having 900 employees worldwide and annual sales exceeding $120 million.[7] Established in 1966, Sierra Systems is Canada's oldest information technology consulting firm. When Gisel took the company public in 1998, he named a CEO, a chief financial officer, and several vice presidents to satisfy securities regulators. Beyond that there are only two management levels and three job categories: partners, who manage branches across the country; principals, who are in charge of projects; and the consultants, who work under them.

Application & Analysis

EXPLORING E-ROLEPLAY'S SPAN OF CONTROL

Are the spans of control wide or narrow at e-Roleplay? Is it a flat or tall organization? From the perspective of an individual who has a boss but no employees, compare and contrast the advantages and disadvantages of working in a tall versus flat organization structure.

SPECIALIZATION AND HORIZONTAL DIFFERENTIATION

Explain what is meant by specialization and horizontal differentiation.

Now that we have explored differentiation up and down the hierarchy (vertical differentiation), we take a closer look at differentiation *between* jobs at the same level and between departments *across* the organization. Differentiation between jobs is referred to as **specialization,** the degree to which individual jobs are narrowly defined and depend on unique expertise. If specialization is high, each employee performs only a narrow range of tasks. If specialization is low, employees perform a wide range of tasks and their jobs are seen as enriched.[8] We discussed this concept briefly in Chapter 1 and then again in Chapter 5. Specialization is part of scientific management, Frederick Taylor's system for using research to determine the optimum degree of specialization and standardization for a job task, at the opposite end of the spectrum from job enrichment and wholeness, or task identity. The degree of differentiation between organizational subunits is called **horizontal differentiation,** which is defined as the degree of differentiation between organizational subunits and is based on employees' specialized knowledge, education, or training.

specialization
The degree to which jobs are narrowly defined and depend on unique expertise.

horizontal differentiation
The degree of differentiation between organizational subunits, based on employees' specialized knowledge, education, or training.

Departmental Grouping (Departmentation)

Describe three types of departmental grouping: functional, divisional, and hybrid.

Horizontal differentiation leads to what is called **departmental grouping,** also called *departmentation.* This is the way that differentiated jobs are grouped together into departments. There are a number of ways to group departments, and each has different implications for organizational behaviour. Let us explore, for example, the hypothetical situation of a company that provides computer consulting services to a number of different retail clients such as the Gap, the Bay and Future Shop, as well as numerous smaller retailers. The company has the traditional functions of accounting, marketing, software design, human resources, and so on, and has to decide how to group them. They may choose to group all the accountants together, all the software designers together, and so on. On the other hand, the consulting firm may decide to group all those accounting, marketing, IT, and human resources jobs, which serve a particular customer, such as the Gap chain, together. The decision on how to group the various jobs will depend on a number of different variables, such as the company's strategy, the nature of the work, and

departmental grouping
The way that differentiated jobs are grouped together into departments. Also called *departmentation.*

the size of the company; these are discussed in depth in a later section of the chapter. What we explore now are the descriptions of these various approaches to departmental grouping as well as their advantages and disadvantages in terms of the *impact* each has on the ways that people working in those units behave. We now discuss three types of departmental grouping: functional, divisional, and hybrid.

Functional Grouping

functional grouping
Departmentation that groups together those employees who perform similar functions or who have similar expertise.

The most traditional way to group jobs into departments is by function. In the example of the consulting firm, deciding to group all the accountants into the accounting department, all the marketing people in the marketing department, etc., is an example of **functional grouping,** which is defined as grouping together those employees who perform similar functions or who have similar expertise.[9] Exhibit 14.4 shows an example of a company with a functional grouping. Another example is e-Roleplay, the company in our chapter opener. As the company grew, the founders decided to create the functional groupings of business development (sales), learning, and operations. This meant that all the sales jobs were grouped together, all the learning and training jobs were grouped together, and all the operations jobs were grouped together.

Advantages and Disadvantages

As mentioned, the way subunits are grouped together impacts the behaviour of those working in the subunits. An advantage of functional grouping is that it promotes in-depth skill development and career paths for specialists who can benefit from close contact with other people who have similar interests and areas of specialization. Functional groupings are most effective when in-depth expertise is critical to meeting organizational goals, when the organization needs to be centrally controlled, and when efficiency and consistency are important. Functional structures promote economies of scale because central functions are not duplicated.

However, the main disadvantages of functional groupings are that they create "silo" mentalities where employees focus on their specialty rather than the customers or the business as a whole. For example, more intergroup conflict is likely to occur, perhaps between the sales and finance groups, as discussed in Chapter 11, caused by specialization and goal differences. Also, since each functional group concentrates on its particular specialty, integration and coordination can become very difficult as they often depend solely upon the person managing the groups. Another negative impact of this type of grouping is that client response times tend to be slower since employees are focused on their specialties rather than their customers' needs. As a result, as the business environment has become more competitive and fast moving, contemporary organizations today are tending to move away from pure functional structures.[10] More and more organizations, as they grow, are combining functional groupings with those that enable faster, cross-functional responses, like the ones described next.

EXHIBIT 14.4

Functional Grouping

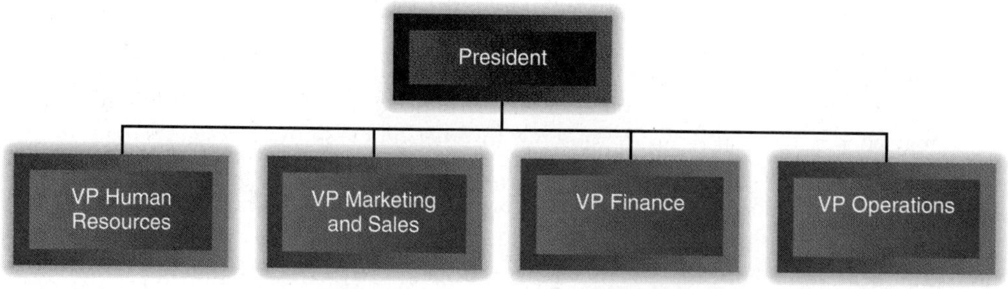

President

VP Human Resources | VP Marketing and Sales | VP Finance | VP Operations

Analysis & Evaluation

GROUPING BUSINESS SCHOOLS BY FUNCTION: IS THIS A GOOD THING?

Many of the large business schools within universities and colleges are divided into departments based on a particular business function or major, such as Accounting, Finance, Marketing, and Human Resources. What do you think are the advantages and disadvantages of structuring a business school by function, from the perspective of the customers, that is, business students and prospective employers of the students?

Divisional Grouping

Divisional grouping brings together employees based upon the organization's main outputs or geography, or both. This means that different functions, such as marketing, accounting, human resources, and production, would be grouped together to produce a certain type of product or to service a particular region, market, or large customer, as shown in Exhibit 14.5.

divisional grouping Departmentation that groups together employees based upon the organization's main outputs or geography.

For example, in November 2004, the Royal Bank of Canada restructured into four business units, based upon both geography (Canadian and U.S.) and product lines

EXHIBIT 14.5

Types of Divisional Groupings

Divisional Grouping by Client: Sierra Systems Group Inc.

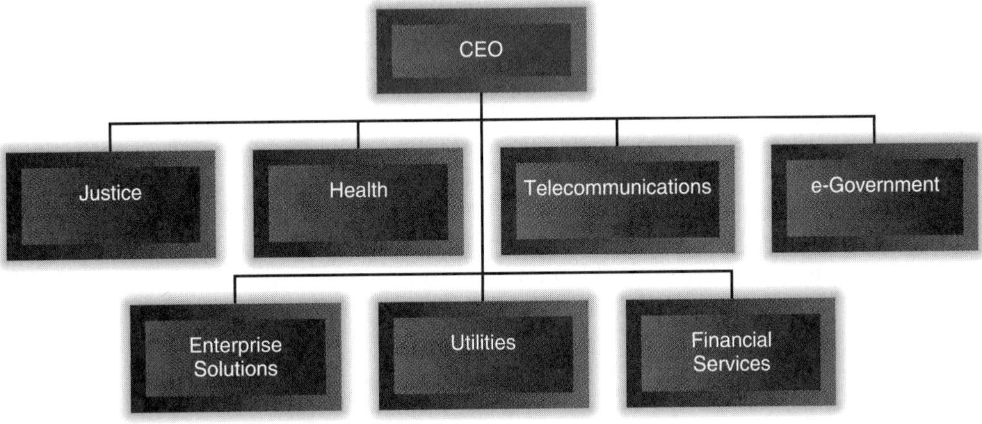

Divisional Grouping by a Mix of Product and Geography: Royal Bank of Canada

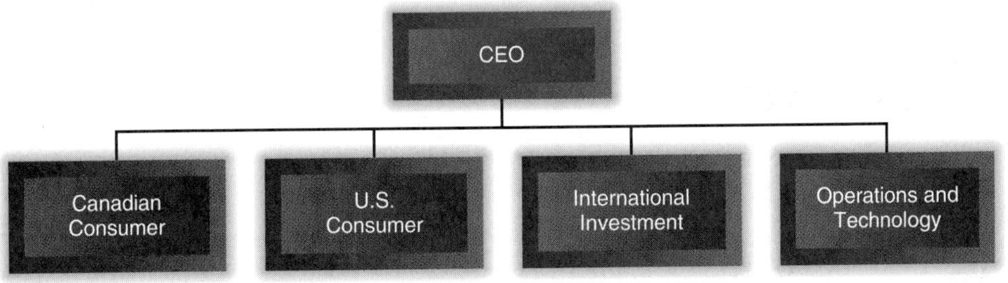

SOURCES: Sierra Systems Group Inc., *Annual Report 2002,* 15; S. Stewart, "RBC's Nixon Overhauls Bank, Poaches Stymiest from TSX," *The Globe and Mail ROB,* September 10, 2004, B13.

(consumer banking and investment banking), while retaining one functional grouping (operations and technology).[11] Sierra Systems Group Inc. has geographic groupings as well as seven divisional groupings based on the company's clients. These specialty groupings are justice, health, e-government, enterprise solutions, telecommunications, utilities, and financial services.[12]

Advantages and Disadvantages

The main advantage of divisional grouping is that it focuses the subunit employees on a critical output, customer, or geographic client group or industry. Because everyone's focus is on the output not their particular specialization, client responsiveness is improved. The main disadvantage of divisional grouping is higher cost due to duplication of resources (for example, three marketing departments, one for each product line) and weak integration across product lines.

Using the example of the computer consulting firm again, if, instead of putting all accountants in one department, marketing people in another, etc. (functional grouping), the company decided to group divisionally, by major client group, how might behaviour change? If all the functions related to consulting to the Gap organization were placed together, for example, then everyone involved in accounting, marketing, software design, human resources, etc., would be housed in the "Gap" department, division or team. This would mean that there would be much more cross-functional communication and focus towards the needs of the Gap customer. However, the company would be facing quite a bit of duplication of resources and expense because each client grouping would probably need these same types of expertise.

Hybrid Grouping

hybrid grouping
Departmentation that combines characteristics of each of the other types of grouping, tailored to specific strategic needs.

Today, the most common form of grouping is neither of the preceding but rather a mix (or hybrid) of them both. The **hybrid grouping** combines characteristics of each of the other types of grouping tailored to specific strategic needs. Often, as a company grows, it decentralizes into divisional groupings by product or geography but retains certain centralized functional groups to capitalize on economies of scale or required in-depth specialization.[13] Complex organizations must often redesign their organizational structures when they make acquisitions or when they merge with another company. Often they may create a hybrid structure by combining flat, decentralized operating units with centralized shared functions. In hybrid organizations, the challenge is to manage the interface between these very different organizational designs so that some units encourage creativity while others foster adherence to strict tolerances and specifications.[14]

Magellan Aerospace, a Canadian multinational, has a hybrid organizational structure.

In addition to the hybrid grouping, the matrix or multifocus structure is also used by some companies to capitalize on the benefits of both functional and divisional grouping. The matrix structure is discussed later on in the chapter in the section on horizontal integration. As shown in Exhibit 14.6, Magellan Aerospace, a Canadian multinational that designs,

EXHIBIT 14.6

Hybrid Grouping: Magellan Aerospace Corporation

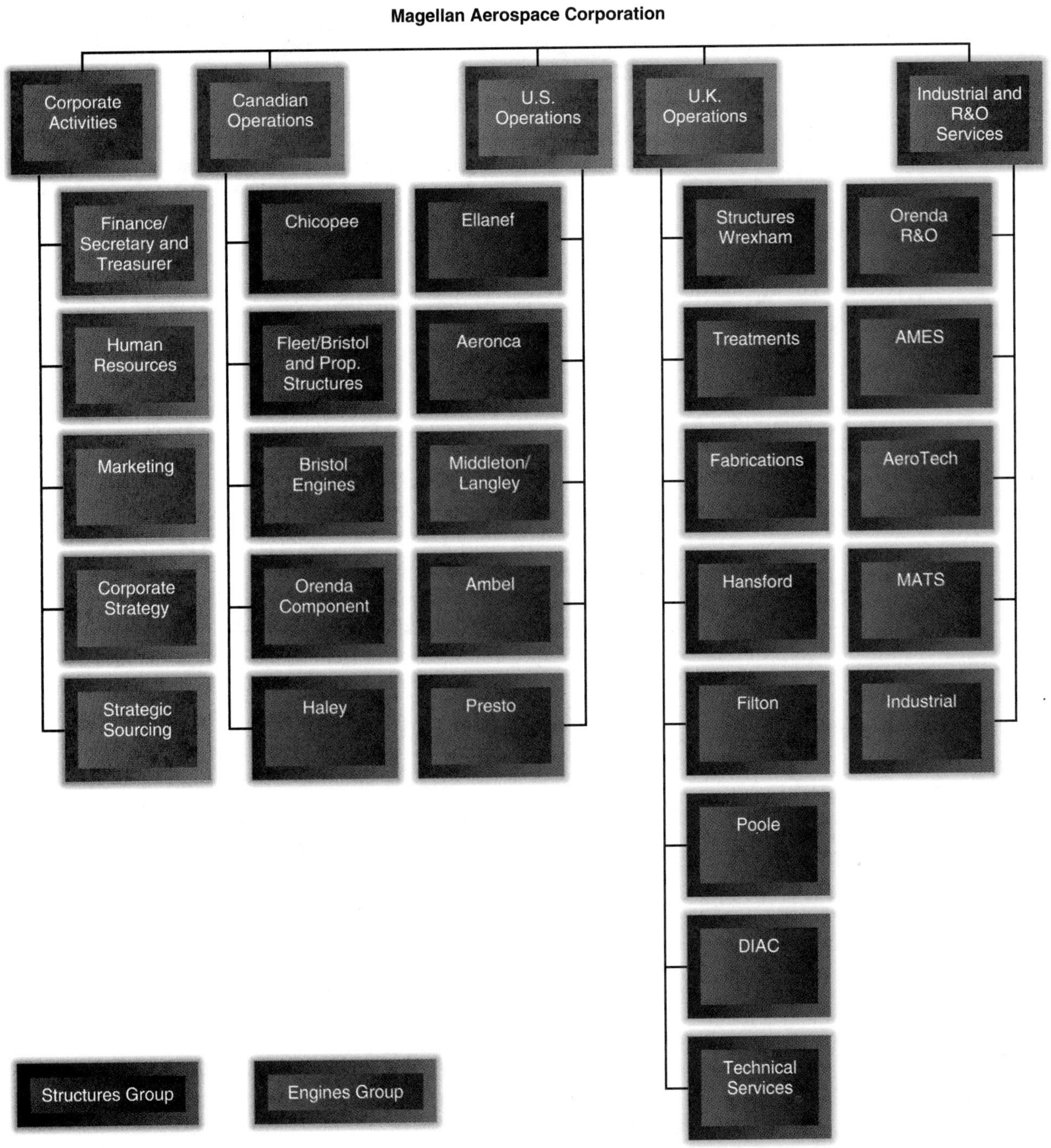

SOURCE: Reprinted by permission of Magellan Aerospace Corporation.

engineers, manufactures, and repairs a wide range of aerospace components and engines worldwide, uses a hybrid structure that combines divisional grouping (geographic and product) with functional groupings in its corporate services division.[15]

IMPLICATIONS FOR LIFE

Organizational Design and the Job Interview

When you go for a job interview, the material in this chapter can help you decide if you want to work in a particular organizational structure.

- *Span of control:* Find out how many other people would be reporting to your boss. If the answer is "many" you can predict that you will be less closely supervised, and receive less one-on-one training, than if the answer is "few."
- *Hierarchy:* Ask to see an organization chart to show how the unit you would be working in fits in the larger organization. Count the levels of management to determine if the structure is tall or flat. The taller the hierarchy, the longer time it takes to make decisions and the less autonomy you are likely to have.
- *Grouping of jobs and departmentation:* Check the organization chart to determine the way departments are grouped at the top of the organization. If it is mainly by function, then you can predict that functional expertise will be important. If it is by product, then the organization is likely to be product driven.

Define centralization and decentralization.

CENTRALIZATION AND DECENTRALIZATION

centralization
The degree to which decisions are made at the top of the organization.

decentralization
The extent to which decision-making authority has been delegated to lower levels of an organization.

Decentralization is the extent to which decision-making authority has been delegated to lower levels of an organization. An organization is **centralized** if the decisions are made at the top of the organization and **decentralized** if decision making is pushed down to lower levels in the organization.[16] Self-Assessment 14.1 gives you an opportunity to assess the degree of decentralization in an organization you are familiar with. Typically, organization structures with functional groupings and tall structures (narrow spans of control) tend to be more centralized than those with divisional groupings and flat structures.

Key to the success of decentralization of responsibility is that the appropriate authority be decentralized as well. The recent restructuring of the RCMP in Alberta has been criticized for its failure in this regard, in that "Reform initiatives were not perceived

Application & Analysis

SELF-ASSESSMENT 14.1: HOW DECENTRALIZED IS YOUR COMPANY?

Decentralization is one of the key design dimensions in an organization. It is closely related to several behavioural dimensions of an organization, such as leadership style, degree of participative decision making, and the nature of power and politics within the organization. The following questionnaire asks you to think about how decentralized your organization is. (If you do not have a job, have a friend who does work complete the questionnaire to see how decentralized his or her organization is.) Which level in your organization has the authority to make each of the following 11 decisions? Answer the questionnaire by circling one of the following:

1 = The CEO makes the decision.

2 = The division/functional head makes the decision.

3 = A sub-department head makes the decision.

4 = The first-level supervisor makes the decision.

5 = The employees themselves.

Decision Concerning:	**Circle Appropriate Level**				
a. The number of employees required.	1	2	3	4	5
b. Whether to employ a worker.	1	2	3	4	5
c. Internal labour disputes.	1	2	3	4	5

d. Employee overtime.	1	2	3	4	5
e. Delivery dates and order priority.	1	2	3	4	5
f. Employee scheduling.	1	2	3	4	5
g. Dismissal of an employee.	1	2	3	4	5
h. Methods of employee selection.	1	2	3	4	5
i. Method of work to be used.	1	2	3	4	5
j. Equipment/tools to be used.	1	2	3	4	5
k. Work allocation.	1	2	3	4	5

For scoring instructions, please go to the end of the chapter, p. 462.

SOURCE: Adapted from D. Miller and C. Droge, "Psychological and Traditional Determinants of Structure," *Administrative Science Quarterly* 31 (1986): 558. Reprinted by permission of the Administrative Science Quarterly.

as means for altering operations or behaviour. Rather they were perceived as means of coping with budget reductions.... In large part this was achieved through a wholesale downloading of fiscal responsibility onto the detachment with very little true managerial or structural realignment of its centralized bureaucracy."[17]

VERTICAL AND HORIZONTAL INTEGRATION IN THE ORGANIZATION

Explain various mechanisms for achieving vertical integration, including standardization and formalization.

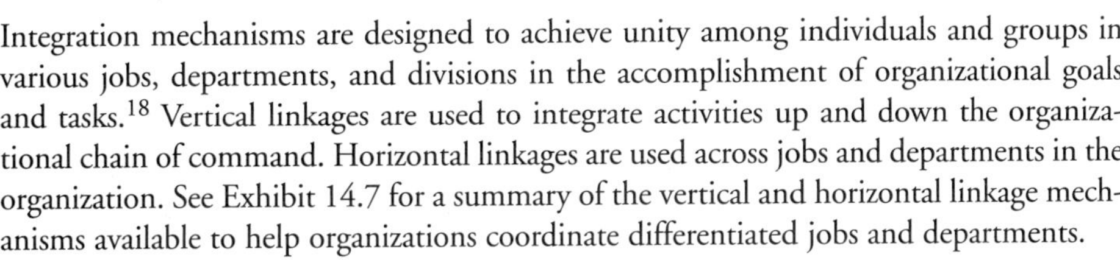

Integration mechanisms are designed to achieve unity among individuals and groups in various jobs, departments, and divisions in the accomplishment of organizational goals and tasks.[18] Vertical linkages are used to integrate activities up and down the organizational chain of command. Horizontal linkages are used across jobs and departments in the organization. See Exhibit 14.7 for a summary of the vertical and horizontal linkage mechanisms available to help organizations coordinate differentiated jobs and departments.

Vertical Integration

In addition to grouping jobs into departments and subunits, jobs within these subunits are differentiated in terms of how much power and authority each job will hold in the hierarchy. As organizations build a hierarchy of authority from top to bottom, so, too, organization designers need to ensure that there is communication and integration top down and bottom up. This is called vertical integration or vertical linkage**.** There are a number of mechanisms by which to achieve vertical integration, including hierarchical referral, rules and plans (standardization), and management information systems.[19] We now briefly discuss each of these.

EXHIBIT 14.7

Vertical and Horizontal Integration

Vertical Linkages	Horizontal Linkages
Hierarchical referral	Liaison roles
Rules and plans (standardization and formalization)	Temporary task forces
Management information systems and knowledge management	Integrator positions
	Permanent cross-functional teams and matrix organizations

Hierarchical Referral

The vertical lines on an organization chart indicate the lines of *hierarchical referral* up and down the organization. When employees do not know how to solve a problem, they can refer it up the organization for consideration and resolution. Work that needs to be assigned is usually delegated down the chain of command as indicated by the vertical lines. Hierarchical referral is the most traditional of the vertical linkage mechanisms and can be time-consuming.

Rules and Plans: Standardization and Formalization

standardization
The extent to which work activities are described and performed routinely in the same way.

Rules and procedures, as well as plans, employee handbooks, and schedules, provide standardized information for employees without requiring direct communication. **Standardization** is the extent to which work activities are described and performed routinely in the same way. Highly standardized organizations have little variation in the defining of jobs. This type of vertical integrator allows managers to manage by exception and to manage more people because they do not have to inform each employee of what is expected. Companies like McDonald's are well known for their use of high levels of standardization. For example, procedures are laid down in manuals to the smallest detail, such as cooking times for the French fries and the exact temperature of the cooking oil.

formalization
The degree to which an employee's role is defined by formal documentation (procedures, job descriptions, manuals, and regulations).

Formalization is the degree to which an employee's role is defined by formal documentation (procedures, job descriptions, manuals, and regulations). Military organizations depend heavily on formalization. The armed forces, for example, have a well-defined chain of command. Certain duties are expected to be carried out, and proper paperwork is to be in place. Standardization and formalization can also act as a leadership substitutes, as discussed in Chapter 10.

Management Information Systems and Knowledge Management (KM)

knowledge management (KM)
A conscious strategy of getting the right knowledge to the right people at the right time and helping people share and put information into action in ways that strive to improve organizational performance.

Management information systems and other knowledge management processes also serve as a vertical linkage mechanism. As discussed in Chapter 1, **knowledge management (KM)** is defined as a conscious strategy of getting the right knowledge to the right people at the right time and helping people share and put information into action in ways that strive to improve organizational performance. Also, increasingly sophisticated electronic mail and information systems allow managers and employees greater access to one another without having to be in the same place at the same time or even attached by telephone. These types of systems make information processing both vertically and horizontally more efficient and also enable innovation.

Explain various mechanisms for achieving horizontal integration, including liaison roles, task forces, integrator roles, permanent cross-functional teams, and matrix structures.

Horizontal Integration

In addition to the need for integration up and down the hierarchy (vertical integration), organizations need strong communication and coordination across jobs and between departments in the organization. The need for horizontal integration mechanisms increases as the complexity of the organization increases. There are a number of ways to build horizontal linkages into the design of the organization and these include liaison roles, task forces, integrator positions, permanent cross-functional teams, and matrix structures.

Liaison Roles

A liaison role is created when a person in one department or area of the organization has the responsibility for coordinating with another department. For example, in our hypothetical consulting company in which all accounting jobs and all marketing jobs are grouped together, perhaps one individual in accounting might be assigned as the marketing liaison. It would be his job to keep marketing informed of major developments, and also perhaps attend their weekly meetings so as to be kept informed. It would be his job to pass on important information to the rest of the accounting group.

Temporary Task Forces and Project Teams

Task forces are temporary committees composed of representatives from multiple departments who assemble to address a specific problem or opportunity affecting these departments.[20] In order to solve integration problems and break down the silos that come with functional groupings, organizations often create these temporary cross-functional task forces or project teams to come up with new ideas or solve problems. This approach is stronger than assigning a liaison role. In the functionally grouped consulting company, for example, a temporary Gap task force might be created so that all accounting, marketing, HR, and IT employees who are working on accounts for the Gap would meet regularly to share and coordinate their efforts during a major project or to solve a particular issue.

Integrator Roles

An even stronger device for horizontal integration is to designate a person or department as a full-time integrator. Such an individual must have the ability to get people together to resolve differences within the perspective of organizational goals.[21] In the consulting company example, the creation of a Gap Project Manager would be a way of creating an integrator role. This person's job would be to work with the different functions on all elements relating to the Gap accounts.

A real-life example of an integrator role is that of John Carrington at Barrick Gold Corp. In January 2004, he moved from his role as Chief Operating Officer (COO) to that of full-time integrator, in charge of championing the implementation of the new organization design, to ensure integration of development, operating, and closure activities.[22]

Permanent Cross-Functional Teams

Permanent cross-functional teams go even further than the creation of a formal integrator role. They cut across the existing lines of an organizational structure to create new entities that make organizational decisions. Ford used such a cross-functional team to develop the Taurus automobile, which was designed to regain market share in the United States. An example of a cross-functional team in our hypothetical consulting company would be the formation of a permanent Gap team that included marketing, accounting, human resources, and IT employees. The information exchanged by such a team should lead to a product or service that is acceptable to a wider range of organizational groups, as well as to customers.[23] These permanent cross-functional teams are discussed in more depth in the final section of the chapter, which explores the horizontal structure as an example of a contemporary organization.

Matrix Structures

matrix structure
Structures in which individuals simultaneously report to both a functional and a product or project manager.

Matrix structures build on the concept of cross-functional teams and fuse interdisciplinary experts into smoothly functioning ad hoc project teams. In matrix structures, individuals report to both a project manager (integrator role) and a functional head, such as the VP Accounting. This type of horizontal integration is used in large-scale consulting projects and other knowledge-related work where individuals need to be dedicated to projects for a period of time or where professionals can report to more than more project manager at one time.[24] Matrix structures capitalize on the benefits of both functional and divisional grouping as discussed in the previous section. See Exhibit 14.8 for an example of a matrix structure in our hypothetical consulting company.

This multiple focus ensures that the employees will pay equal attention to their specialization, such as audit standards, and to customer requirements, such as client needs, deadlines, etc. The matrix is used when both technical expertise and product or project

Ford used cross-functional teams to develop the Taurus automobile.

innovation and change are equally important and when human resources need to be shared across projects. Matrix structures became popular in the 1970s and 1980s; however, often the structure created convoluted roles and relationships, decreasing both performance and learning.[25] The matrix structure demands a high degree of openness and collaboration. Unless the multiple bosses communicate well, however, employees in this type of structure find it very difficult to manage.[26]

EXHIBIT 14.8

Matrix Structure

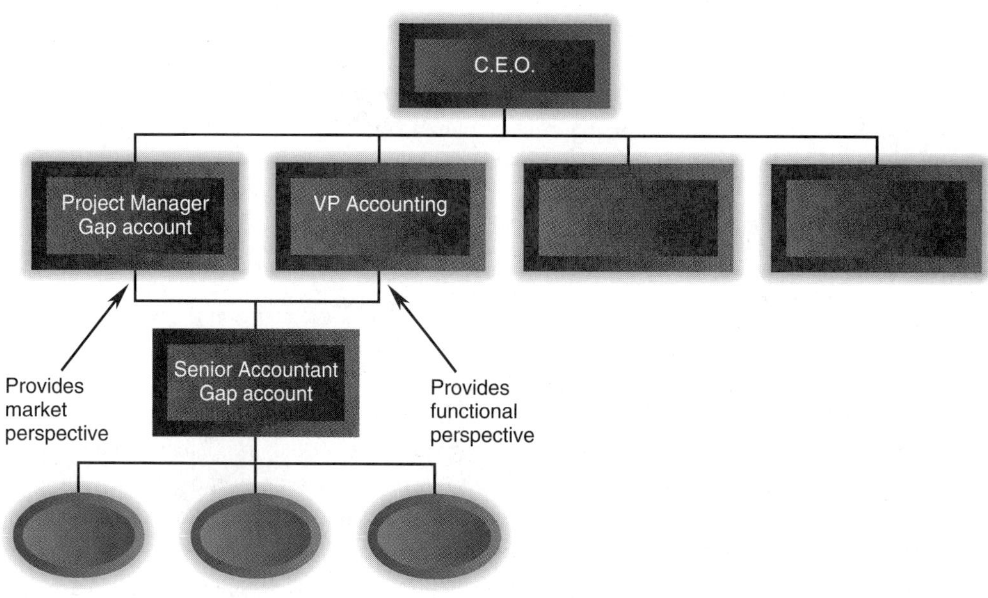

? Knowledge & Application

SELF-ASSESSMENT 14.2: USING ORGANIZATION DESIGN PRINCIPLES TO SELECT A PREFERRED STRUCTURE

1. a. I would prefer to work for a boss who has less than five other people reporting to him/her so that he/she would have time to guide and train me.

or

b. I would prefer to work for a boss who has 5–10 other people reporting to him/her, so that I would be less closely supervised.

a. _____

b. _____

2. a. I would prefer to work for a company with many levels of management so that there would be promotion potential.

or

b. I would prefer to work for a company with few levels of management so that decisions would be faster and I would have easier access to higher levels of management.

a. _____

b. _____

3. a. I would prefer to work with people who have the same specialization as I do so that I can learn from them.

or

b. I would prefer to work with people who have different areas of specialization so that as a team we can bring different perspectives, and the others would rely on me for my area of expertise.

a. _____

b. _____

4. a. I would prefer my work to focus on the company as a whole, rather than a particular product, market, or customer group, because then I would really understand the bigger picture and the company as a whole and I would work with different people across the company.

or

b. I would prefer my work to focus on a particular product, market, or customer group, rather than on the company as a whole, because then I would really understand my stakeholders and could provide a high quality service or product.

a. _____

b. _____

5. Do I think my preferences might change in the future? What factors might change them?

____

____

For scoring instructions, please go to the end of the chapter, p. 462.

AN ORGANIZING FRAMEWORK FOR UNDERSTANDING STRUCTURE: IS IT MECHANISTIC OR ORGANIC?

Compare and contrast mechanistic and organic organizational structures.

You have now explored five complex concepts that describe organization structure: the organizational hierarchy, specialization and horizontal differentiation, departmental grouping (also called departmentation), centralization and decentralization, and vertical and horizontal integration. In 1961, Burns and Stalker created a useful organizing framework that captures many of the preceding concepts in a more simplified way. This framework describes a continuum with two types of organization structures at either extreme. They labelled the two structural extremes as mechanistic structure and organic structure.[27] Their characteristics are summarized in Exhibit 14.9.

mechanistic structure
An organizational design that emphasizes structured activities, specialized tasks, and centralized decision making.

A **mechanistic structure** utilizes functional groupings, tends to be tall, and emphasizes clear lines of hierarchy. There is rigid departmental separation, work specialization and standardization and there is strong management control and centralization of power. Top management controls planning, problem solving, decision making, and directing.[28] Mechanistic organizations rely on design principles based on what is called a "redundancy of parts" perspective, meaning that people are viewed as substitutable and jobs are determined by the technology.[29]

organic structure
An organizational design that emphasizes teamwork, open communication, and decentralized decision making.

Organic structures by contrast, adopt a perspective called "redundancy of function" because they are based on the assumption that individuals are multiskilled. Organic structures utilize divisional or multifocused grouping, and tend to be flatter and team-based. There is a shift from vertical decision making to horizontal collaboration, communication is more informal and open, work is less standardized and specialized, and decision making is decentralized. New and emerging organization structures tend to be more organic, as you will see later on in the chapter.

Explain how understanding the four contextual variables, strategy, environmental uncertainty, size, and technology, can help leaders design the best structure for their organization.

HOW TO DESIGN THE BEST STRUCTURE FOR AN ORGANIZATION

Now that we have described the various elements of structure and their impacts on human behaviour, we ask the following question that is critical to organizational effectiveness: What is the *best* structure for a particular organization at a particular time? The answer to this question is, as we find so often in the study of OB, "It depends." Perhaps you recall when choosing a leadership style that we first had to examine certain "contingencies." Here too, in order to decide how best to design an organization's structure we have to examine certain contingencies, called contextual variables when referring to organization design. Some of these variables reside in the organization's external task environment and some are in the internal environment, discussed in Chapter 1 as part of the GHOST model.

contextual variables
The set of internal and external elements that influence the organization's design processes.

Contextual variables are the set of internal and external variables that influence the organization's design processes. Four important contextual variables that have been discovered to be important when deciding the most suitable organizational structure are:

1. The degree of environmental uncertainty that the organization is facing
2. The organization's strategy

EXHIBIT 14.9

Mechanistic and Organic Organizational Forms

Basic Design Dimensions	Mechanistic	Organic
Formalization	High	Low
Centralization	High	Low
Specialization	High	Low
Standardization	High	Low
Complexity	Low	High
Hierarchy of authority	Strong, tall	Weak, flat

3. The size of the organization
4. The nature of the work technology

Research and experience has shown that as these variables change, so *should* the organization structure. Unfortunately though, research has found that there appears to be little match between current organizational structures and their environmental contexts.[30] Although you may not be in a position to design or redesign an organization's structure in the near future, the material that follows will help you structure a small business as it grows and will help you spot when a structure is perhaps out of alignment with its context, thereby better understanding the behaviour that results.

Environmental Uncertainty and Structure

The first contextual variable to consider when designing an organization's structure is the degree of **environmental uncertainty** that is present. This is defined as the amount of instability and complexity in the organization's task environment, which, as you may recall from Chapter 1, comprises those elements of the organization's *external* environment that are directly relevant to the organization. These elements, which were summarized back in Exhibit 1.3, include, among others, globalization, competition, suppliers, economic conditions, and the legislative climate. According to Burns and Stalker, Lawler, and others, if the organization's environment is relatively certain, such as in a monopoly or regulated company, a more *mechanistic* structure, discussed earlier, is appropriate. However, the more uncertain the environment, the more *organic* the structure should be (see Exhibit 14.10).[31] When external environments are highly uncertain, top management has to support continuous change instead of relying on supervision and control. Decisions often have to be made on the basis of weak signals so fast, rich, and often chaotic information flows via internal and external networks are critical to the organization's success.[32]

environmental uncertainty The amount of instability and complexity in the organization's task environment.

There are two dimensions of environmental uncertainty in an organization's task environment, called complexity–simplicity and stability–instability. **Complexity** refers to the amount of *knowledge* needed to understand the elements of the external environment, such as the organization's markets, clients, competitors, and suppliers. When many dissimilar elements in an organization's task environment need to be considered, the environment is seen to be *complex.*[33] When few, similar elements are relevant, the environment is seen to be *simple.*

complexity The number of elements and amount of knowledge needed to understand the various stakeholders.

Stability is the extent to which unpredictable changes affect the organization's work and make it uncertain. Although the number of organizations operating in highly *stable* environments is decreasing, a few still exist as monopolies; federal, provincial, and local government services; or regulated industries.[34] More often, environments of organizations are unstable, and a few are so *dynamic* that no one is sure what tomorrow may bring.

stability The extent to which *unpredictable changes* affect the organization's work and make it uncertain.

For example, Ontario Hydro used to be a government-owned monopoly and as a result it was grouped functionally and had a mechanistic organizational design. When its environment became more uncertain, it was forced to become a more nimble, private-sector player in a competitive market; the company structure changed to a divisional

EXHIBIT 14.10

Structure and Environmental Uncertainty

External Environment	Organization Structure
High uncertainty	More organic structure
Low uncertainty	More mechanistic structure

SOURCE: J. Courtright, G. Fairhurst, and L. Rogers, "Interaction Patterns in Organic and Mechanistic Systems," *Academy of Management Journal* 32 (1989): 773–802.

? Application & Analysis

CLASSIFY THE ENVIRONMENTAL UNCERTAINTY OF YOUR COLLEGE OR UNIVERSITY

Think about the relevant elements in the *external task environment* of your college or university, for example, prospective employers, students, high schools, competitive educational institutions, technology, demographics, economy, political climate, government regulators, professional associations, etc. Using the definitions of "simple-complex" and "stable-unstable" how uncertain do you think the task environment of your college or university is at the moment? Given your classification, should your institution have a more organic or more mechanistic organization structure?

---

grouping and became more organic.[35] As well, over the last two decades and in particular since 9/11, organizations in the airline industry have encountered high complexity and instability, including deregulation, mergers, and changes in demands for better safety and security.

Strategy and Organization Structure

Centre for Effective Organizations

The Center for Effective Organization's pioneering research in the areas of organizational design and effectiveness has earned it an international reputation for research that bridges the gap between academic theory and management practice. The centre works with companies to research and develop new knowledge on cutting-edge issues of organization design and effectiveness.

http://www.marshall.usc.edu/web/CEO.cfm?doc_id=611

A second contextual variable that influences how organizational structure should be designed is the organization's strategy and goals. Strategies provide employee direction, decision guidelines, and criteria for performance.[36] Ed Lawler, director of the Centre for Effective Organizations (CEO), writes that "structure is the building block, and must be closely articulated with strategy ... because it determines how the organization will behave, what people are needed, and what reward system will work."[37] See the CEO's website for more information on their groundbreaking research in organization design.

Research has discovered that a *mismatch* between strategy and structure often occurs when an organization adopts a more innovative strategy but retains its mechanistic structure.[38] For example, in the U.S. airline industry, several carriers failed to adjust quickly enough to deregulation and the highly competitive marketplace. Only those airlines that were generally viewed as relatively flat structures with good information-processing systems have flourished in the turbulent years since deregulation.

One framework to help match an organization's strategy with its organizational structure is that of Danny Miller.[39] Miller suggests that companies tend to follow one of three different types of strategic profiles, which he categorizes as: (1) innovation, (2) market differentiation, and (3) cost control.

Innovation Strategy

Miller's framework recommends that if the strategy is to *innovate* then the structure needs to be highly organic with low formalization, a flat hierarchy, and high decentralization. This structure permits more speed and market responsiveness. Organic structures enable continuous innovation because they support effective knowledge management and vertical integration, making the company less dependent upon a hierarchy. For example, some of the new product lines introduced during the 1990s by Oticon A/S, a Danish hearing aid manufacturer, were based on incremental innovations developed spontaneously by a cross-functional product team made up of engineers and marketers. OB researchers call this capacity "knowledge integration."[40] Organic structures are suited to innovation strategies also because they enable knowledge "reconfiguration," which means the ability to continuously *recombine* resources. At Oticon, for example, roles are loosely defined, technical experts have only loose affiliations with their professional areas, employees have "multi-jobs," workstations are mobile, and interaction and dialogue are encouraged.[41] Read more about Oticon and its so-called spaghetti structure in Organizational Reality 14.2.

organizational reality 14.2

The Spaghetti Organization at Oticon A/S Denmark

Oticon A/S is a multinational Danish manufacturer of high-quality hearing aids, known for the considerable number of new products it introduced during the 1990s. The company has been studied in great depth so as to better understand its strong capabilities in developing and launching new products. One of the keys to its success has been its organic organizational structure.

When Lars Kolind took over as CEO of Oticon he had a vision for a completely different kind of organizational structure. His vision was to have just one team of 150 employees, all at headquarters.

Oticon A/S has a very flat organizational structure and is called a "spaghetti" organization.

To fulfill his vision, he made a number of structural changes: The formal hierarchy was replaced by a project-based organization where each employee was involved in a number of projects at the same time, and where each project was considered a "business unit" with its own resources. The structure was very flat and supported only three "managerial" roles: project managers, senior specialists, and coaches. To clearly symbolize the new culture, Lars Kolind himself had no office, but moved around with his trolley as appropriate, like any other employee! In general, the new structure led to the successful integration of the audiology, neuropsychology, and technology divisions that were previously in functional groupings. The top management team of the "old" organization was eventually replaced or redeployed internally; however, nearly all the staff of the "old" structure were brought into the new one. More than a decade after the restructuring, the horizontal structure remains very much the same, except that it has moved to a hybrid, a mix of horizontal and functional groupings, in that a few functions are now grouped centrally. Some critics argue that in fact, it is now a traditional matrix organization.

SOURCES: G. Verona and D. Ravasi, "Unbundling Dynamic Capabilities: An Exploratory Study of Continuous Product Innovation," *Industrial and Corporate Change* 12, no. 3 (2003): 577–606; T. D. Jick and M. A. Pierperl, *Managing Change: Cases and Concepts,* 2nd ed. (New York: Irwin, McGraw-Hill, 2003), 277; H. H. Larsen, "Oticon: Unorthodox Project-Based Management and Career in a Spaghetti Organization," *Human Resource Planning* 25, no. 4 (December 2002): 30–37; N. J. Foss, "Selective Intervention and Internal Hybrids: Interpreting and Learning from the Rise and Decline of the Oticon Spaghetti Organization," *Organization Science* 14, no. 3 (May/June 2003): 331.

Market Differentiation Strategy

However, if the company wants to be a niche marketer, a strategy Miller calls *market differentiation,* then the structure should be moderately organic but with some formalization and centralization. An example of this type of market differentiation strategy is the Mayekawa Company in Japan. Mayekawa's major product lines are custom-engineered heavy refrigeration systems for commercial and industrial use. Mayekawa does not sell hardware or compete on price but forms long-term partnerships with customers to custom design their refrigeration systems so that they can distinguish themselves with their *own* customers. Mayekawa's organization structure is made up of over 100 small, highly organic, legally dependent companies called *Doppos.* These *Doppos* belong to one or more forums called blocks, which link to the overall company called the *Zensha.* The *Zenshas* provide some centralization for making decisions, such as the overall strategic direction, marketing, and R and D, but the *Zensha* system is called a heterarchy rather than a hierarchy because centralization comes through a shared culture and effective communication, rather than through command and control.[42] Read more about network structures like that of Mayekawa, in the section on contemporary organizational structures at the end of this chapter.

Low Cost and Consistency Strategy

Lastly, if the main strategy is to compete based on *low cost and consistency*, then a mechanistic structure is best. A good example of a company with this strategy is McDonald's. Their strategy involves consistency, i.e., delivering exactly the same product in Toronto as in Moscow, as well as low cost. This is why the McDonald's restaurants have a high degree of standardization and formalization, delivered through thick manuals, inspections, and careful employee training.

Organization Size and Structure

A third contextual variable to consider when restructuring is the size of the company. For decades, organizational behaviour literature has argued that "small is beautiful," and firms have been trying to break down large hierarchies into smaller, more manageable business units or divisions. However, size can create a number of advantages in areas such as marketing, finance, product development, purchasing, and technology.[43] An unprecedented $3.4 billion in corporate mergers around the world during 1999 is powerful testimony to the benefits of scale and scope.[44] Companies are increasingly unwilling to sacrifice size and breadth for market responsiveness, or vice versa, and many of the new and emerging organization forms, discussed in the next section, are attempts to create new organizational designs that can mirror the responsiveness of a small firm without losing the advantages that can be associated with size.[45]

Pixar Animation Studios
Pixar Animation Studios is an award-winning computer-animation studio famous for the production of films such as *Toy Story*, *Monsters, Inc.*, and *The Incredibles*. Analyze Pixar's role within the larger Disney Corporation using the contextual variables of size, technology, environment, and strategy and goals. How does Disney benefit from Pixar's specialization and relationship to the Walt Disney Studios division?
http://www.pixar.com

What should the manager know about designing structures for large and small organizations? Exhibit 14.11 illustrates the relationships among many of the elements of structure and organizational size. Formalization, specialization, and standardization all tend to be greater in larger organizations, because they are necessary to control activities within the organization. For example, larger organizations are more likely to use documentation, rules, written policies and procedures, and detailed job descriptions than to rely on personal observation by the manager. The more relationships that have to be managed, the more formalized and standardized the processes need to be. For example, McDonald's has several volumes that describe how to make all its products, how to greet customers, how to maintain the facilities, and so on. This level of standardization, formalization, and specialization helps McDonald's maintain the same quality of product no matter where a restaurant is located. In contrast, at a small, locally owned café, your hamburger and French fries may taste a little different every time you visit. This is evidence of a lack of standardization

The Nature of Work Technology and Structure

technology (T)
The range of tools, knowledge, and/or techniques used to transform the inputs into outputs.

Finally, an organization's technology is also an important variable to consider when determining the organization's structure.[46] As described in the discussion of the organization as an open system in Chapter 1, **technology** is defined as the tools, techniques, and

EXHIBIT 14.11

Relationship between Organizational Size and Dimensions of Structure

Dimensions of Structure	Small Organizations	Large Organizations
Formalization	Less	More
Centralization	High	Low
Specialization	Low	High
Standardization	Low	High
Hierarchy of authority	Flat	Tall

actions used by an organization to transform inputs into outputs.[47] Research on the influence of technology on organizational design by three classic scholars (Joan Woodward, Charles Perrow, and James Thomson) has resulted in an important integrating concept called the **degree of routineness,** which has a very strong relationship with organizational structure.[48] This term refers to how repetitive and routine the organization's technology needs to be to transform inputs into outputs. Research suggests, in simple terms, that the higher the degree of routineness, the more mechanistic the structure should be, and the lower the degree of routineness, the more organic the structure should be.

degree of routineness
The extent of repetitiveness and routine required in an organization's technology to transform inputs into outputs.

This idea has received more recent support in the work of Harvey Kolodny, at the University of Toronto, and an international team of researchers. They examined twelve organizations in Canada, Sweden, and France to explore how they were being redesigned within the context of flexible new technology and an emerging paradigm of work. The companies studied were in the banking, food processing (confectionary), and electronics assembly industries, and for all companies, the environmental uncertainty was high.[49] The team found that the introduction of technology with a low routineness, such as computer-integrated networks, CAD/CAM systems, and computer-integrated manufacturing, led to more organic organizational structures with wider spans of control, flatter organizational hierarchies, more decentralized decision making, and lowered amounts of specialization and standardization.[50]

CONTEMPORARY ORGANIZATIONAL STRUCTURES

Discuss the need for more nimble organizations, and describe three types of contemporary organizational structures: horizontal, front-back, and network structures.

The forces reshaping organizations have both created the need for, and enabled, new, more nimble organizational structures. See Exhibit 14.12 for an overview of how increasing environmental uncertainty and the evolution of information processing since the 1950s have led to the evolution of contemporary organizational structures such as the network and virtual organizations.

Organizational behaviour theorists agree that "The question companies now face is not whether they need to be nimble, but how."[51] Some argue that the organization of the future will be a "chameleon-like" organism, self-restructuring, self-reshaping, and responding to a large variety of environmental forces.[52] Traditional studies of organizational structure have primarily explained its formal and tangible dimensions. However,

EXHIBIT 14.12

Environmental Conditions and the Evolution of More Nimble Structures

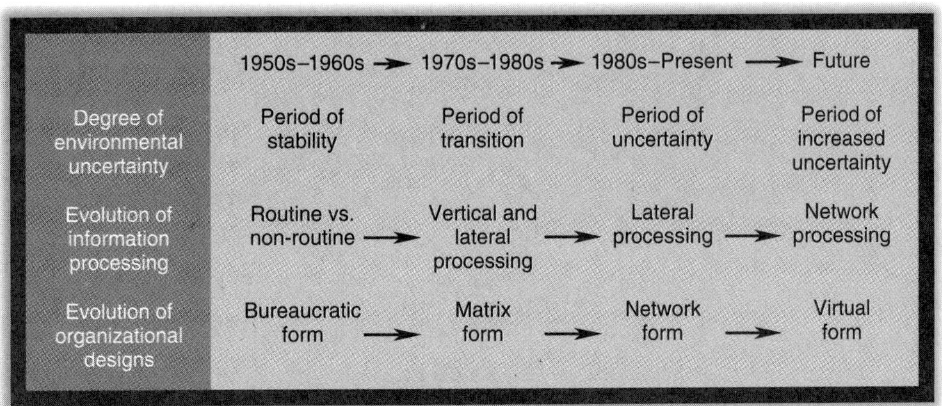

SOURCE: C. C. Dibrell and T. R. Miller, "Organization Design: The Continuing Influence of Information Technology," *Management Decision* (London) 40, no. 5/6 (2002): 620. Reprinted by permission of the Emerald Group Publishing Limited.

this does not reveal the "subtle energy" that flows behind the organizational chart. This "hidden energy" is commonly referred to as "informal structure" or "informal relationship," discussed in Chapter 1, and this energy plays a conspicuous role in many of the new and emerging organization designs such as network or knowledge-based organizations."[53] There is general agreement in the literature that traditional organizational structures with tall hierarchies and clear boundaries are giving way to more egalitarian structures with more fluid and complex boundaries.[54] There is also agreement that most organizations' structures will be a hybrid of different structures, customized to fit the differing needs of different parts of the organization.

In the past decade, many new organizational structures have been created. We review three of them: the horizontal structure (includes the lateral, spaghetti, cellular, and process-based structures), the front-back structure (also known as the customer-product structure), and the network structure (including virtual organizations, opportunity organizations, strategic alliances, value-added partnerships, and outsourced partners).

Horizontal Structure

horizontal structure
An organizational structure based on core processes where work focuses on the customer and on the entire sequence of activities (end-to-end) rather than on one activity.

The **horizontal structure** is an organizational structure based on core processes where work focuses on the customer and on the entire sequence of activities (end-to-end) rather than on one activity. As shown in Exhibit 14.13, horizontal structures rely on self-managed work teams (SMWTs), discussed in OBXtra4, as well as so-called process owners who have responsibility for each core process in its entirety. All the people who work on

EXHIBIT 14.13

Horizontal Structure

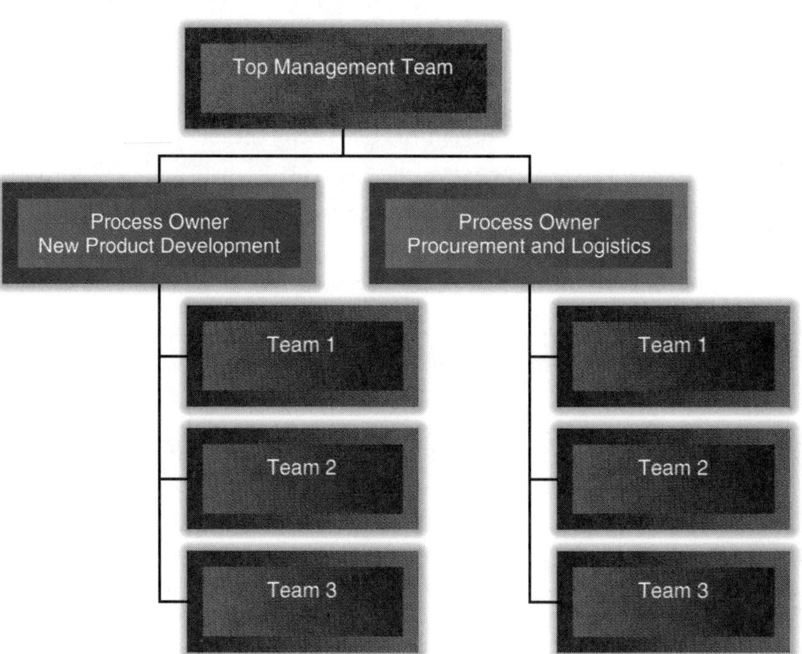

Notes:

1. New product development process includes market analysis, research, product planning, and testing.
2. Procurement and logistics process includes analysis, purchasing, material flow, and distribution.

SOURCE: Adapted from R. Daft, *Organization Theory and Design,* 7th ed. (Mason, OH: South-Western, 2000), 109. Reprinted by permission of South-Western, a division of Thomson Learning, www.thomsonrights.com. Fax 800-730-2215.

a particular process are brought together so they can easily communicate and coordinate their activities. This structure builds on the horizontal integration concepts summarized earlier in the chapter in Exhibit 14.7, which included horizontal integrators such as liaison roles, temporary task forces, integrator roles, permanent cross-functional teams, and matrix organizations. Horizontal organizations virtually eliminate both the vertical hierarchy and the old departmental boundaries.[55]

The circle organization, made up of interdependent natural work groups at Harley-Davidson, described back in Organizational Reality 14.1, is another good example of a horizontal organizational structure. People on the teams are given the skills, tools, and authority to make decisions central to the team's performance.[56] An early example of this type of structure was at Oticon A/S, a medium-size hearing aid manufacturer in Denmark. In 1990–1991 they introduced a horizontal structure, an open office plan with new mobile workstations, and a new paperless information system. The new organization had no formal hierarchy or traditional management positions and came to be known as a "spaghetti' organization, as described in Organizational Reality 14.2.[57]

A new version of this parallel structure in global organizations is the "opportunity-based" design mentioned earlier in the chapter. McKinsey Consulting reported in 2001 that they had studied two dozen companies that had adopted this kind of structure. Rather than "process owners," as shown in Exhibit 14.14, internal entrepreneurs who identify cross-functional or cross-geography opportunities can become "opportunity owners" who are authorized to mobilize whatever resources they need, to serve a key global account.[58] Like parallel structures these structures typically exist alongside the more traditional business unit (divisional) structures; however, in opportunity-based structures a number of fluid "opportunity units" exist that pull together elements of different businesses in order to tackle a particular project.

Front-Back Structure

The **front-back structure** (also called the customer/product structure) consists of front-end units that focus on customer segments and back-end units that focus on products and technologies. Accounting systems are designed so that revenues and costs can be assigned to both customer and product units, making them both profit-measurable.[59] The "back" part of the company is responsible for creating and producing the organization's products and services. The "front' part of the organization buys products from the back end and is charged with integrating and delivering them to customer segments.[60] See Exhibit 14.14 for an example of a front-back structure. A front-back structure differs from a strategic business unit (divisional grouping) structure because all products can go to *all the markets* served by the company's front end. Jay Galbraith gives an example of IBM, which formed customer-segment profit centres by gathering all relationship managers into industry groups.[61] The strength of this structure, according to Galbraith, is that it allows a firm to be simultaneously profit centre–driven and coordinated. Customers can buy all the products while at the same time the organization preserves business unit accountability and focus.[62]

front-back structure
An organizational structure that consists of front-end units focused on customer segments and back-end units focused on products and technologies. All units are profit-measurable.

In 2000, Hewlett-Packard CEO Carly Fiorina made the front-back structure the centrepiece of her restructuring effort. The highly decentralized company then had 83 units, each responsible for its own product development and sales and for hitting profit goals. This meant that customers had to deal with many different HP salespeople and it left the company so focused on small niches that it missed big opportunities like the Internet. The new organization was restructured into two back-end structures to develop the products, one for computers and one for printers. These would feed two front-end structures targeted to selling a full suite of products to consumers and companies. While some critics have argued that the front-back structure has been unsuccessful, recent reports indicate that it is being adapted to make it simpler. The responsibility for meeting financial goals will return to the back-end units, but each will still have a front-end sales unit that can sell all of HP's products.[63] Galbraith and Lawler agree that it is a challenge to make this type of structure to work.

EXHIBIT 14.14

The Front-Back Structure

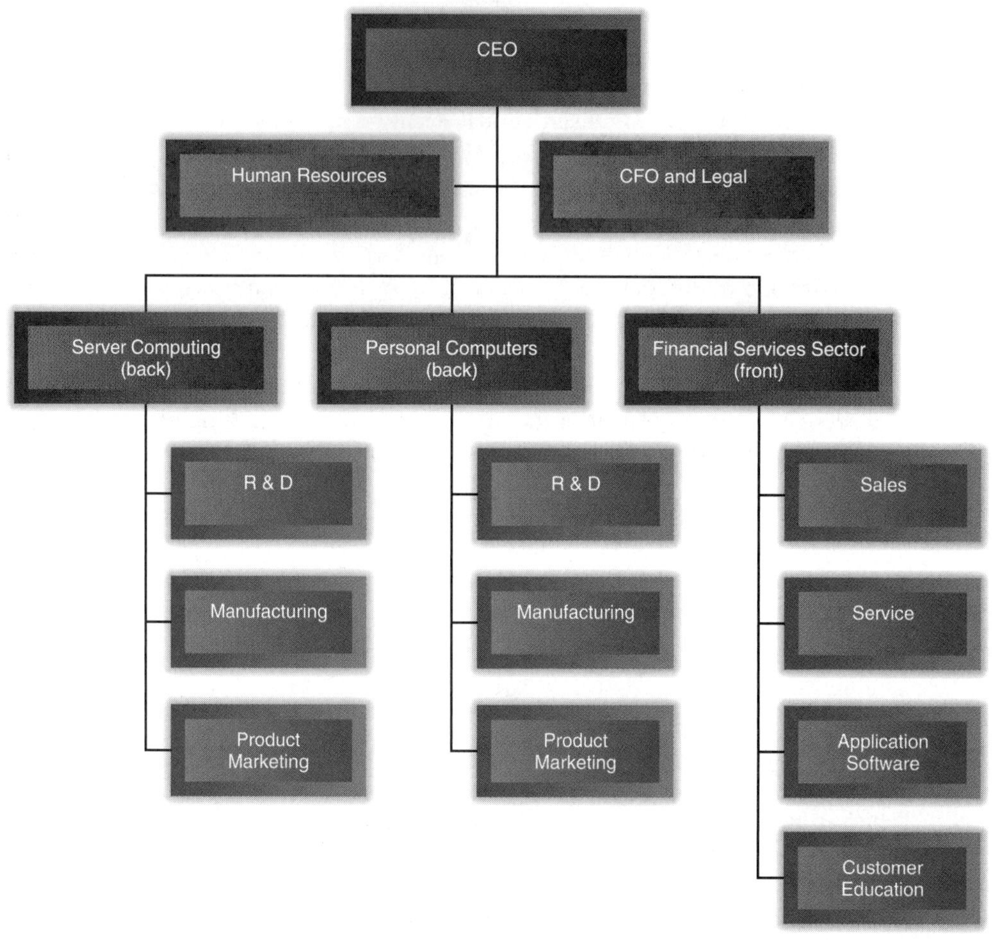

SOURCE: Adapted from J. Galbraith, *Tomorrow's Organizations: Crafting Winning Capabilities in a Dynamic World* (San Francisco: Jossey-Bass, 1998), 52. This material is used by permission of John Wiley & Sons, Inc.

Network Structure

network structure
An organizational structure in which the organization subcontracts most of its functions to separate companies and coordinates their activities from a small headquarters.

In the current competitive environment, many companies have realized that they cannot innovate and commercialize new products on their own. As result, more and more organizations are forming networks or value-added partnerships with suppliers, customers, and/or competitors. A **network structure** is an organizational structure in which the organization subcontracts most of its functions to separate companies and coordinates their activities from a small headquarters, as depicted in Exhibit 14.15.

These networks increase each firm's degree of freedom to manouevre and adjust to their environments, and they can be global in scope.[64] Network structures have brought outsourcing, downloading, interorganizational collaborations, and strategic alliances into common practice. Advances in information technology have been the basis for building the web-like structure of the network organization. However, while network structures create advantages of flexibility and risk reduction, they can also create additional problems of ethical responsibility. For example, when Nike was accused of producing shoes with child labour, the fact that Nike did not produce the shoes directly but networked with another organization, created ambiguity as to who was responsible.[65]

EXHIBIT 14.15

Network Structure

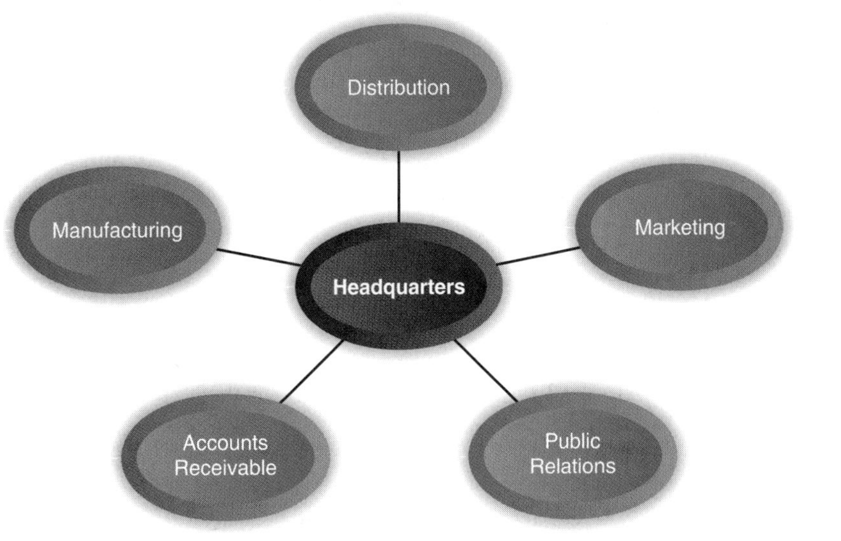

SOURCE: R. Daft, *Organization Theory and Design*, 7th ed. (Mason, OH: South-Western, 2000). Reprinted by permission of South-Western, a division of Thomson Learning, www.thomsonrights.com. Fax 800-730-2215.

Virtual organizations are temporary network organizations consisting of independent enterprises. Many dot.coms were virtual organizations designed to come together swiftly to exploit an apparent market opportunity. They may function much like a theatrical troupe that comes together for a "performance."[66] Trust can be a challenge for virtual organizations because it is a complex phenomenon involving ethics, morals, emotions, values, and natural attitudes. However, trust and trustworthiness are important connective issues in virtual environments. Researchers are suggesting that checkpoints and control systems over employees in the virtual organization are having negative effects and argue in favour of nurturing ethical behaviour through a new type of trust.[67] Read more about virtual organizations in OBXtra5, entitled "Managing in a Virtual World."

virtual organizations
Temporary network organizations consisting of independent enterprises.

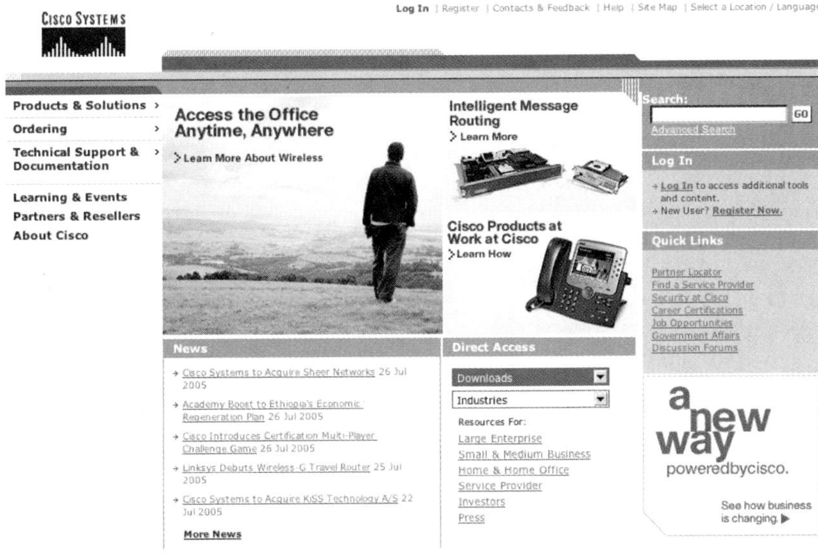

Cisco Systems is an example of a virtual organization.

Application, Analysis & Synthesis

CHALLENGE YOURSELF: DESIGN AN ORGANIZATIONAL STRUCTURE FOR CANDYCO

Go back and take a look at the CandyCo case at the end of Chapter 1 and explore the following questions related to organizational structure and design:

1. Based on its degree of environmental uncertainty, strategy, size, and technology, should CandyCo's organizational structure be more organic or mechanistic?
2. Which traditional or contemporary organizational structure, or combination of structures, discussed in this chapter do you think would work the best for CandyCo, and why?

IMPLICATIONS FOR ORGANIZATIONAL EFFECTIVENESS

An organization's structure describes how jobs and departments are formally divided, grouped, and linked. Organizational design and redesign is the process of constructing and adjusting an organization's structure to match key contextual variables, and it is critical to organization effectiveness. Elements of structure such as the hierarchy, the managers' spans of control, the degree of standardization, the extent to which decision making is centralized, and the basis upon which departments are grouped have enormous impacts on human behaviour. Organization leaders have the difficult task of ensuring that the structures of their organizations remain aligned with their strategies, the degree of uncertainty in their task environments, the sizes of their organizations, and their technology. This is no easy job. Not only does the outside world keep changing, but internal systems and processes are also in flux. Senior managers may have their own particular preferences for more mechanistic or organic designs, and their preferences may not be best for the organizational context. Also, power-hungry managers may seek to build hierarchies where a flatter, more responsive unit is required to compete. Employees and managers being brought in to the company need to understand the kind of structure required to compete and should be screened for fit. Organizational leaders need to be vigilant in monitoring both the elements of structure within their organizations as well as the fit between these elements and their external environments. Of all the impacts on organizational behaviour, decisions about organizational structure are the most influential and significant, and doing a good job in this area can create huge competitive advantage.

Chapter Summary

1. Organizational design is the process of constructing and adjusting an organization's structure to match its environment and achieve its goals, and organizational structure is the manner in which an organization's work is designed, as well as how departments, divisions, and the overall organization are designed. Three reasons for studying organizational structure and design are to help entrepreneurs start and grow their businesses, to help employees recognize the different dimensions of structure and their impact on behaviour, and to help managers assess the effectiveness of their current organizational designs and restructure based on the contextual variable.

2. Differentiation is defined as the process of deciding how to divide the work in an organization and is also referred to as division of labour. Differentiation ensures that all essential organizational tasks are assigned to one or more jobs and that the tasks receive the attention they need. The more structurally differentiated the organization is, the more complex it is. Integration is the process of coordinating the different parts of an organization. The dual tasks of differentiation and integration remain central to our understanding of organization structure and design.

3. Vertical differentiation is the difference in authority and responsibility in the organizational hierarchy. Vertical differentiation can range from a very large degree to a very small degree, and this is also captured by the term *hierarchy of authority*, which is defined as the degree of vertical differentiation through reporting relationships and the span of control within the structure of the organization. Span of control is defined as the number of people directly reporting to a manager. Some organizations are tall, with narrow spans of control and many levels, while others are flatter, with wide spans of control and few management levels. Flat and tall structures tend to encourage different types of behaviour.
4. Division of labour includes specialization, which is the degree to which individual jobs are narrowly defined and depend on unique expertise, and horizontal differentiation, which is defined as the degree of differentiation between organizational subunits and is based on employees' specialized knowledge, education, or training.
5. The way jobs are grouped together is called departmental grouping or departmentation. Three methods are functional grouping, which groups together those employees who perform similar functions or have similar expertise; divisional grouping, which groups together employees based upon the organization's outputs such as client or product; or by geography and hybrid grouping. Each type of grouping has associated advantages and disadvantages.
6. Another element of structure is the degree of centralization and decentralization in decision making throughout the organization.
7. Mechanisms that achieve vertical integration include hierarchical referral, rules and plans, and management information systems. Standardization is the extent to which work activities are described and performed routinely in the same way. Formalization is the degree to which an employee's role is defined by formal documentation such as procedures, job descriptions, manuals, and regulations.
8. Horizontal integration is accomplished through the use of liaison roles, temporary task forces, integrator positions, permanent cross-functional teams, and matrix structures.
9. Many of the elements of structure are summarized and simplified by the two structural extremes labelled mechanistic and organic. Mechanistic structures utilize functional grouping, tend to be tall, formal, with rigid specialization, standardization, and central control. At the other extreme, organic structures utilize divisional groupings, tend to be flatter and team-based and with more decentralized informal decision making.
10. Four contextual variables to consider when designing or redesigning an organization's structure are environmental uncertainty, strategy, size, and technology.
11. Forces reshaping organizations have created a need for and enabled contemporary structures that are more nimble and adaptive. Also, most structures are not of one pure type but are hybrids. Three contemporary types of structures that are becoming popular are the horizontal, front-back, and network structures.

Key Terms

centralization (p. 438)
complexity (p. 445)
contextual variables (p. 444)
decentralization (p. 438)
degree of routineness (p. 449)
de-layering (p. 430)
departmental grouping (p. 433)
differentiation (p. 429)
divisional grouping (p. 435)
environmental uncertainty (p. 445)
flat organizational structure (p. 430)
formalization (p. 440)
front-back structure (p. 451)
functional grouping (p. 434)
hierarchy of authority (p. 429)
horizontal differentiation (p. 433)
horizontal structure (p. 450)
hybrid grouping (p. 436)
integration (p. 429)
knowledge management (KM) (p. 440)
matrix structure (p. 441)
mechanistic structure (p. 444)
network structure (p. 452)
organic structure (p. 444)
organizational design (p. 428)
organizational structure (OS) (p. 428)
span of control (p. 430)
specialization (p. 433)
stability (p. 445)
standardization (p. 440)
tall organizational structure (p. 430)
technology (T) (p. 448)
vertical differentiation (p. 429)
virtual organizations (p. 453)

Review Questions

1. Explain how the terms *differentiation* and *integration* define organizational structure and the process of organizational design.
2. Describe the main concepts involved in understanding the nature of an organization's hierarchy.
3. Compare and contrast functional and divisional departmental grouping and give an example of each type of organizational chart.
4. Describe two examples of vertical and two horizontal integration mechanisms.

5. Compare and contrast organic and mechanistic organizational structures.
6. Explain the importance of environmental uncertainty in determining what structure would be best for an organization.

Discussion and Communication Questions

1. How would you describe the organization you work for or your college or university in terms of whether it is a very formal organization or an informal organization? Is it a tall organization? Is it grouped by function or division?
2. Give examples of differentiation and integration in a sports team or volunteer organization that you are familiar with.
3. (*Communication question*) Interview an administrator in your college or university about possible changes in size (Will the college or university get bigger? smaller?) and technology (Is the college or university making a significant investment in information technology?). What effects does the administrator anticipate from these changes? Be prepared to present your results orally to the class.

Ethics Questions

1. Is it ethical, in a highly decentralized company, to pay an employee in one province more than an employee in another province doing the same job?
2. Should legal limits be set to prevent large companies from engaging in very competitive behaviour to drive small companies out of business?
3. As an organization changes its structure over time, how much commitment should it show to employees who need to be retrained to fit into the new system? Or is it acceptable for the organization to hire new people to fit the new structure?
4. Suppose an employee complains about organizational design problems and suggests a solution. The organization is redesigned accordingly, but that employee's department is eliminated. Is it ethical for the company to terminate the employee? Should the company always make room for a person who has a beneficial idea for the organization?

Application, Analysis & Synthesis

EXPERIENTIAL EXERCISE 14.1: WORDS-IN-SENTENCES COMPANY

Purpose: To understand issues of organizational design
Group size: 6–8 (includes 1 observer)
Time required: 50–90 minutes
Materials needed: Words on index cards

EXERCISE SCHEDULE	**Unit Time**	**Total Time**
1. **Form groups, organizations, and assign workplaces**	2–5 min	2–5 min
Groups should have between six and eight members.		
(Assign 1 observer and 1 quality review board member to each group.) Each group is a company.		
2. **Read "Instructions," below**	5 min	7–10 min
Ask the instructor about any points that need clarification.		
3. **Design organizations**	7–15 min	14–25 min
Design your organizations using as many members as you see fit to produce your "words-in-sentences." You may want to consider the following.		
a. What is your objective?		
b. What type of task and environmental uncertainty do you have?		

EXERCISE SCHEDULE (continued)	Unit Time	Total Time
c. What is your objective?		
d. What technology would work here? What type of division of labour is effective?		
Assign one member of your group to serve on the Quality Review Board. This person may also take part in production runs.		
4. **Production Run 1**	7 min	21–32 min
The instructor will hand each WIS company sheet with a raw material word or phrase. When the instructor announces "Begin production," you are to manufacture as many words as possible and package them in sentences for delivery to the Quality Control Review Board. You will have 7 minutes. When the instructor announces "Stop production," you will have 30 seconds to deliver your output to the Quality Control Review Board. Output received after 30 seconds does not meet the delivery schedule and will not be counted.		
5. **Quality Review Board meets, evaluates output**	5–10 min	26–42 min
While that is going on, groups discuss what happened during the previous production run.		
6. **Companies evaluate performance and type of organization**	5–10 min	31–52 min
Groups may choose to restructure and reorganize for the next production run.		
7. **Production run 2 (same as Production Run 1)**	7 min	38–59 min
8. **Quality Review Board meets**	5–10 min	43–69 min
Quality Review Board evaluates output while groups draw their organization charts (for Runs 1 and 2) on the board.		
9. **Class discussion**	7–21 min	50–90 min
Instructor leads discussion of exercise as a whole. Discuss the following questions: a. What were the companies' scores for Runs 1 and 2? b. What type of structure did the "winning" company have? Did it reorganize for Run 2? c. What type of task was there? Technology? Environmental uncertainty?		

INSTRUCTIONS

Background

You are working in a small company that manufactures words and then packages them in meaningful English-language sentences. Market research has established that sentences of at least three words but not more than six words are in demand. Therefore, packaging, distribution, and sales should be set up for three- to six-word sentences.

The "words-in-sentences" (WIS) industry is highly competitive; several new firms have recently entered what appears to be an expanding market. Since raw materials, technology, and pricing are all standard for the industry, your ability to compete depends on two factors: (1) volume and (2) quality.

Your Task

Your group must design and participate in running a WIS company. You should design your organization to be as efficient as possible during each 10-minute production run. After the first production run, you will have an opportunity to reorganize your company if you want.

Raw Materials

For each production you will be given a "raw material word or phrase." The letters found in the word or phrase serve as raw materials available to produce new words in sentences. For example, if the raw material word is "organization," you could produce the words and sentence: "Nat ran to a zoo."

Production Standards
Several rules must be followed in producing "words-in-sentences." If these rules are not followed, your output will not meet production specifications and will not pass quality-control inspection.

1. The same letter may appear only as often in a manufactured word as it appears in the raw material word or phrase; for example, "organization" has two o's. Thus, "zoo" is legitimate, but not "zoonosis." It has too many o's and s's.
2. Raw material letters can be used again in different manufactured words.
3. A manufactured word may be used only once in a sentence and in only one sentence during a production run; if a word—for example, "a"—is used once in a sentence, it is out of stock.
4. A new word may not be made by adding "s" to form the plural of an already manufactured word.
5. A word is defined by its spelling, not its meaning.
6. Nonsense words or nonsense sentences are unacceptable.
7. All words must be in the English language.
8. Names of people and places are acceptable.
9. Slang is not acceptable.

Measuring Performance
The output of your WIS Company is measured by the total number of acceptable words that are packaged in sentences. The sentences must be legible, listed on no more than two sheets of paper, and handed to the Quality Control Review Board at the completion of each production run.

Delivery
Delivery must be made to the Quality Control Review Board 30 seconds after the end of each production run, or else all points are lost.

Quality Control
If any word in a sentence does not meet the standards set forth above, all the words in the sentence will be rejected. The Quality Control Review Board (composed of one member from each company) is the final arbiter of acceptability. In the event of a tie on the Review Board, a coin toss will determine the outcome.

SOURCE: "Words-in-Sentences Company" in D. Marcic, J. Seltzer, and P. Vaill, *Organizational Behavior: Experiences and Cases*, 6th ed. (Mason, OH: South-Western College Publishing, 2001), 207–209. Reprinted by permission of South-Western, a division of Thomson Learning, www.thomsonrights.com. Fax 800-730-2215.

Application, Analysis & Synthesis

EXPERIENTIAL EXERCISE 14.2: DESIGN AN ORGANIZATION TO BUILD A CASTLE

Purpose: To explore the relationship between organizational strategy and structure

Group size: Any size. Class is divided into three groups

Time required: Part 1: 20 minutes, Part 2: 45 minutes. The exercise has been divided into two parts so that if a full 60 minutes is not available, part 1 can stand alone.

Materials needed: Newsprint, markers and masking tape

Instructions:
Your group is one of three product-development teams working within the research and development division of the GTM (General Turret and Moat) Corporation. GTM has decided to enter new markets by expanding the product line to include fully designed and produced castles, rather than selling components to other companies, as it has in the past. Each of the three teams has been asked to design an organization that will design and produce a castle to sell. Given its limited resources, the company cannot put more than one design on the market. Therefore, the company will have to decide which of the three designs it will use and will discard the other two designs.

Part One: Design the Organization Structure ***(20 minutes)***

Step 1: Form three groups. Each group is designated as 1, 2, or 3. The instructor will give each group a memo from their CEO which clarifies the company direction for new product development.

Step 2. Your first task is to design an organization, guided by the memo you received, which will design, build, and sell a castle.

Step 3. Groups meet and write up their central goal statement on the newsprint.

Step 4. Groups design their organization's structure in order to complete their goal and draw their organization chart on the newsprint beneath the goal statement. These are posted around the room.

Step 5. Instructor leads a class discussion on how the different goals affected organization design. *(Skip this step and go directly to Step 6 if Part 2 will be completed.)*

Part 2: Design the Castle ***(45 minutes)***

Step 6. One to three people are selected from each group to act as first observers, and then consumers (judges). The instructor gives them the Observer's Guide.

Step 7. Each group is given 30 minutes to design its own castle and draws it on newsprint.

Step 8. Each group is given one to two minutes to make a sales presentation.

Step 9. Consumers (observers) tour building locations and hear sales pitches.

Step 10: Judges meet to determine the winner while others view competing designs. Judges announce the winning design.

Step 11. Instructor leads a class discussion on how the different goals affected organization and which design seemed most effective for this task.

SOURCE: Adapted from "Design and Build a Castle" from Dorothy Marcic and Richard C. Housley, *Organizational Behavior: Experiences and Cases*, 2nd ed. (St. Paul: West, 1989), 221–25. Reprinted by permission of South-Western, a division of Thomson Learning, www.thomsonrights.com. Fax 800-730-2215. For more practice exercises, consult the sixth edition of *Organizational Behavior: Experiences and Cases* by Dorothy Marcic, Joseph Seltzer, and Peter Vaill (Thomson, 2001).

Application & Synthesis

CASE: CERJUGO SA

Background

Cerjugo SA is the largest manufacturer and distributor of beer in a country in Latin America.* Started in 1960, Cerjugo currently sells 360 million bottles of beer annually with revenues last year in excess of $200 million. Cerjugo employs 2500 employees and its four beer brands account for 98 percent of the market share. The beer manufacturer has been growing steadily with the GDP of the country thanks to little competition and no new entrants in the market. Cerjugo has its own distribution fleet and manufacturing facility, its entire customer base is local, and customers are loyal to the flagship brand.

Per capita beer consumption in the country had been stable for many years. In order to find new opportunities for growth, Cerjugo management decided to expand their product lines into juices. They recognized early on that the juice business was very different from that of beer. In beer, there was little competition and profit margins were high, close to 40 percent. The profit margins for juice would be much lower and there were a number of competitors but they felt they could create a competitive advantage by (1) focusing on "freshness," i.e., all natural ingredients; (2) by leveraging their deep knowledge of their consumers; and (3) by capitalizing on an already strong retail customer base, which would triple as a result of adding juice products.

The Organizational Structure

The president of Cerjugo is Manuel Perreria. He currently has three key executives reporting to him: Jose Guzman, Feliz Arroz, and Maria Santiago. Jose is the director of Production; Feliz is the vice president of Sales, Marketing and Distribution; and Maria is the director of Finance and Administration. Each executive worked closely with Manuel and are involved in all major company decisions.

At the time of the expansion into juice, a new $50 million production facility was built across the street from the current juice plant. Organizationally, management assumed that the manufacturing, sales, and distribution of the new product lines could be fitted into the existing structure by adding new positions and employees. They added a production manager of juice manufacturing, juice production supervisors and employees, additional sales supervisors, and over 900 salespeople. Existing salespeople were trained to sell the new juice products in addition to the beer products that they were used to, and the sales compensation plan was modified so that a higher percentage of the pay would be variable based on total beer and juice revenues.

We focus on Cerjugo's two main divisions: the production division and the sales, marketing, and distribution division. Until a few years ago, the executive team had worked very well together with few major difficulties.

The Production Division: Jose Guzman

Jose Guzman, the director of production, has four senior managers reporting to him: Carlos Menga, manager, beer manufacturing; Dolores Bebida, quality control manager; Antonio Ben, the production planning manager; and George Novedad, manager, juice manufacturing. Carlos, Dolores, and Antonio have all been with Cerjugo for the past 15 years. George was hired two years ago when Cerjugo moved into the juice business. George is Harvard educated and had extensive experience in the juice business in North America before accepting Manuel's offer to join Cerjugo.

The production division has a strict hierarchy with many layers of management. Front-line employees such as assemblers and maintenance staff report to team leaders, who report to plant supervisors. Plant supervisors report to either Carlos or George. The jobs in the production division are highly specialized. Formal procedures have been documented and all new employees go through extensive training so that quality standards, safety standards, and efficiencies are maintained.

The Sales, Marketing and Distribution Division: Feliz Arroz

Feliz Arroz, the vice president of Sales, Marketing and Distribution, has been Manuel's second-in-command for many years. He is in charge of four departments, each headed up by a senior manager. These departments are distribution, trade marketing, market research, and sales. The sales department, which has 1400 employees, is further divided into urban sales and rural sales, and there are 13 rural sales managers reporting to the head of rural sales. Each sales representative serves a territory that usually consists of both licensed and non-licensed establishments. They supply retailers with product information and storefront displays. They also offer discounts and promotions, where appropriate, in an attempt to win limited retailer shelf space. A partial organization chart is shown in Exhibit A.

The Current Situation

Manuel is very concerned since the forecasted sales and profit targets for the juice business have not been met for the second year in a row. Perceptions in the market are that Cerjugo juice is not of a high quality, and consumers do not appear to be aware of the degree of "freshness" in the products. In addition, the sales force does not seem to fully understand the juice product attributes and tends to focus on selling beer rather than juice products. Turnover in the sales force has increased dramatically and there has been a great deal of in-fighting between Jose, Feliz, and Maria. They always seem to be at opposing ends of an issue and Manuel has to make decisions that inevitably angers one or other of them. The last straw came yesterday when Manuel heard rumours that George Novedad, his Harvard-educated manager of juice manufacturing, had received another job offer and was planning to resign. Last week, Manuel individually asked Feliz and Jose to give him their suggestions for how to improve the juice business.

Jose's response was as follows: "We need to continue to improve efficiencies, keep production and inventory costs to a minimum, and maintain a consistent and high-quality product. I have been doing this successfully for a very long time and I know that the most important success factors are to reduce changeover times on the bottling lines, keep my line capacities to a maximum, my inventory and storage costs down, and the shelf-life of my ingredients up. On the people side, the key to my success has been to have clear rules and work procedures so that we can keep errors and waste to a minimum. What we need to do now is the following: (1) Replace the natural vitamin C extract with artificial ascorbic acid. This will increase the shelf-life of the juices, which will increase its profitability. (2) Eliminate the 250mL packaging size. This will reduce the changeover times on the line and reduce our costs of production."

Feliz's response was as follows: "We need to create more customer demand and strengthen our competitive advantage. I have been doing this for a very long time and I haven't let you down yet. We do not have enough variety in either our flavours or our bottle sizes. Juice retailers

*The country is not named to protect the anonymity of the company on which this case is based.

and consumers are different from our beer customers. Our competitive advantage in this market is 'freshness.' That is our niche. What we need to do now is the following: (1) We currently have only two bottle sizes (250mL and 350mL). We need to introduce 900mL and 1.75L bottle sizes in order to be able to compete with the other players in the market. While these are unique sizes and packaging formats, they are essential to building the unique image of our brand. (2) We currently have only 12 juice flavours. Our market research shows that there is demand for at least another six flavours and that this would substantially improve both our sales and brand image as a full-scale juice company. Additionally, we should be aggressively going into the non-juice market like iced-tea, as this is a growing segment and would allow us to introduce an additional six concepts into the market. (3) We need to add elements of freshness and use all-natural ingredients in our juice. This will mean shorter shelf-life of our products but it will greatly increase our value proposition to customers and allow us to command the premium price in the market."

Manuel does not know where to go from here. He is thinking that maybe he needs to look at his organization's structure more closely. Perhaps, when the juice business was introduced, not enough attention was paid to how the organization should be designed to support this business strategy.

EXHIBIT A

Partial Organization Chart for Cerjugo SA

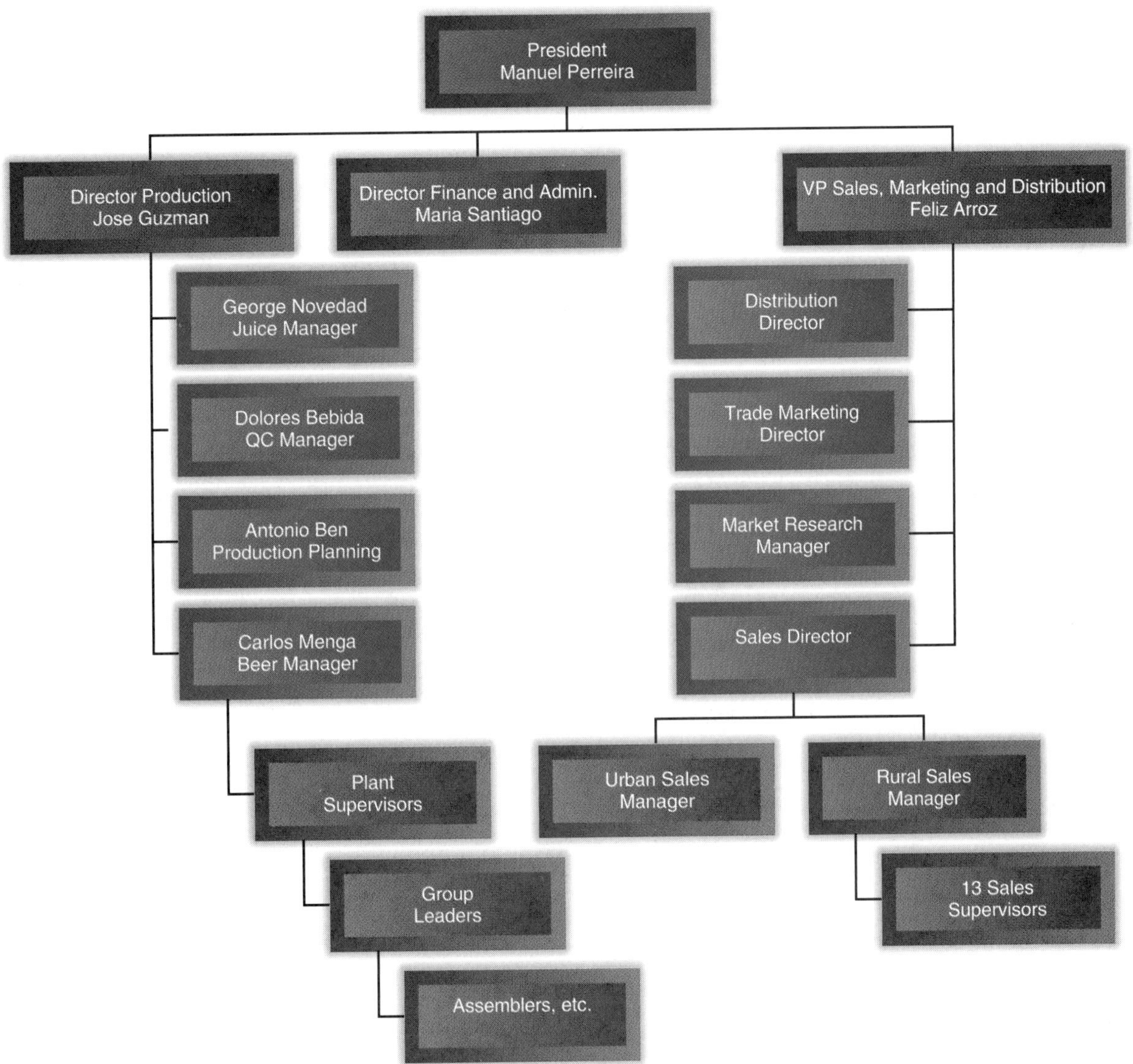

* Levels in the hierarchy are shown reporting to the Beer Manager only. All other management positions have people reporting to them directly, but these are not shown on this partial organization chart.

Discussion Questions

1. Describe Cerjugo's organizational structure in terms of the following organizational design concepts: span of control, centralization, specialization, and departmental grouping. Use facts from the case to defend your classifications.
2. Discuss the problems with Cerjugo's current structure.
3. Compare the degree of environmental uncertainty for the beer and juice businesses.
4. Use Miller's strategy framework to distinguish the organization's juice strategy from its beer strategy.
5. Based on this analysis, what organizational structure do you recommend for Cerjugo?

SOURCE: © P. Sniderman and D. Rethazy, 2005. Used with permission. Some of the information included has been added and changed from the actual facts of the case to offer students the opportunity to analyze more organization design concepts.

Scoring Instructions for Self-Assessments

Self-Assessment 14.1: How Decentralized Is Your Company?

Add up all your circled numbers. Total = ____.

The higher your number (for example, 45 or more), the more decentralized your organization. The lower your number (for example, 25 or less), the more centralized your organization

Self-Assessment 14.2: Using Organization Design Principles to Select a Preferred Structure

Scoring:

Transfer your check marks to the following chart

1. a. ____ You prefer to work for a manager with a narrow span of control
   b. ____ You prefer to work for a manager with a wide span of control
2. a. ____ You prefer to work for a company with a large degree of vertical differentiation and a hierarchy of authority
   b. ____ You prefer to work for a company with a small degree of vertical differentiation and hierarchy of authority
3. a. ____ You prefer a functional grouping
   b. ____ You prefer a divisional grouping
4. a. ____ You prefer working in a centralized unit
   b. ____ You prefer working in a decentralized unit

Total # a____ Total # b____

Interpretation

- If your total for **a** is greater than your total for **b** you prefer to work within a mechanistic organization structure.
- If your total for **b** is greater than your total for **a** you prefer to work within an organic organization structure.

Part Four: Organizational Processes and Structure (7:16 minutes)

CHAPTERS TAKEOVER OF INDIGO *(1:57 MINUTES)*

This clip features the 2001 hostile takeover of Chapters by Heather Reisman, CEO of Indigo.

Critical Thinking Questions

1. Is it possible to merge cultures effectively under conditions of a hostile takeover?
2. In your view, what are the key factors in merging two organizational cultures effectively?
3. What type of change (developmental, transitional, or transformational) is represented by this merger for former Chapters and Indigo employees?

COMPAQ MERGES WITH HEWLETT-PACKARD *(1:58 MINUTES)*

This clip features Carly Fiorina, former CEO of Hewlett-Packard, and the impending merger between Compaq and HP as well as expectations of possible job cuts that may come with it.

Critical Thinking Questions

1. How should companies address employee fears of job loss during a merger or acquisition?
2. When companies merge and develop new strategies to improve their bottom line, as Compaq and HP did, how should they approach the redesign of their organizational structure?

HARLEY-DAVIDSON *(1:42 MINUTES)*

This clip features the 100-year anniversary, in 2003, of the Harley-Davidson motorcycle company. It highlights the loyalty of Harley-Davidson customers and the "big family" culture of the company.

Critical Thinking Questions

1. Can you think of any other companies that inspire customer loyalty in the way that Harley-Davidson does?
2. What does it take to build this kind of brand loyalty?

MOLSON-COORS *(1:39 MINUTES)*

This clip discussed the recent merger of Molson's with the U.S.-based Coors.

Critical Thinking Question

1. Does the increase in U.S. control over Canadian businesses matter in the global economy of today?

Integrative Cases

part five

CASE 1: BRADLEY METALS

CASE 2: THE BREWSTER-SEAVIEW LANDSCAPING CO.

CASE 3: COLUMBIA PAPER COMPANY

CASE 4: FOX BUSINESS EQUIPMENT

CASE 5: THE CASE OF THE AMALGAMATED LABORATORY

CASE 6: METROPOLITAN GENERAL INSURANCE

CASE 7: RIDGWAY FURNITURE LIMITED

CASE 8: STRUCTURING WORK AT THE LIVING SKIES LONG-TERM CARE HOME

integrative case 1

Bradley Metals

The company about which this case is written has a casting shop in which the various metals are melted down and three mills in which final production takes place. There is a rod mill for brass and copper rods, a rolling and sheet mill for sheets of brass and copper used in cars etc., and a tube mill for tubes of copper and brass. One of the machines used in the rod mill, to which we shall refer later, is called a commutator roll. This machine sizes coils of copper to the customer's specifications. Then after the coils have passed through the machine they go either to inspection, packaging and shipping, or through other machines in the mill to be cut up into different lengths, segments, etc.

Bradley Metals was formed only six months ago, but the location has been the same since before World War II. Before Bradley Metals, a company called American Brass, a U.S. subsidiary company, used to be at this location. American was going to fold up its Canadian operations and concentrate their operations in the U.S. This meant that about 800 Canadian employees would be out of jobs. So the government did finally get a buyer. A company called Adams Machine Tools Ltd. bought the plant and there were some changes which the employees did not like but agreed to in order to keep their jobs.

Before the new owner took over, the plant employees were getting special premiums or bonuses according to the amount of their production. This was a substantial amount for most employees. In fact the operators on the commutator roll machine were getting, on an average, $50 to $100 a week in bonuses. But when the new owner took over, these bonuses were cut out completely. This made the employees very disgruntled toward management but they were still thankful they had their jobs because unemployment was very high in the small town where the plant was located.

Before the takeover, the employees worked fast because of the motivation provided by the bonuses. The employees felt that time wasted was money lost. And since making more money was their main concern, they rarely wasted time. They always took short breaks, never wasted time talking to each other, and were very careful and precise in their work, because if they had a jam-up in their machines, they would have to spend precious time trying to un-jam it.

The reason that most employees stayed after the firm was sold was that they could make up the loss of the bonuses by working overtime. Since they were not working as hard as before, production would slow down and get behind. In order to catch up, the mills had to work overtime. This overtime made up for the loss in pay, but now they would be working more hours for about the same pay. They were not working any harder, just longer.

As the employees were not getting bonuses any more, they no longer cared how many pieces they produced each day. All they had to do was meet a certain timed quota. In other words, there was a standard time limit for each operation performed and the workers were sure to use the time right up to the limit. For example, on the commutator roll machine, one of the operators called Jack would work at a fast pace and this way he could build up time so that he could "slack off" for a while. Jack would have to fill in a production sheet like all the other workers and he was always booked ahead. In fact sometimes he was booked ahead as much as 45 minutes. He would also sometimes report that a jam-up had occurred even when it had not. This was done because the operators were allowed so many minutes for un-jamming a machine, and this would give him even more leisure time. These extra minutes often came in handy, especially when working the midnight shift. An extra 45 minutes plus the half-hour lunch break meant that the workers could get over an hour's sleep. This was easy to do because there weren't any foremen around on the "midnights." On one midnight shift the foreman from the south rod-mill would come up about 12:15 a.m. to make sure everyone was in, then he would go back down to the south mill and sleep himself for about five or six hours. This was a common practice on midnight shift. The maintenance mechanics would usually get at least four to five hours' sleep a shift. Sometimes they got more, and sometimes less, if problems came up and they had work to do. They were lucky, because most maintenance work was done during the day shift. However, they still worked midnights to be on hand in case something did go wrong.

The crane operators were also lucky when they worked the midnight shift. The only reason a crane operator was needed on midnights was because the commutator roll machine was working, and it would need a crane to lift in and out the coils of copper required for each order. Usually, the operator would get most of the orders needed for the shift done right at the beginning of the shift. This way the crane driver could park his crane at the far end of the mill and catch a few hours' sleep himself.

This type of abuse also occurred on the day shift. The operators of the "straightener" who always worked on the day shift had so much time allotted for each length of copper rod that they ran through the straightener. They, along with the rest of the employees, had to fill out production sheets. One operator was always booked 15 to 20 minutes ahead of schedule, which would give him or her time to go to the washroom and talk to other workers. This operator also used the trick of writing down jam-ups when in fact they didn't happen, so as to gain an extra 5 or 10 minutes.

The extra minutes gained were also used to make allowance for breaks. Theoretically the employees were only allowed 10 minutes for a coffee break. However, if they wrote the breakdown on the production sheet, the break would have to be timed and the whistle blown to start the break and let workers know when the break was over. So instead of doing this, breaks were treated in an informal way and sometimes the workers would sneak in a 20- or even 25-minute coffee break.

You'd think it would be easy for the foremen to catch the workers who acted in this way. But, although some supervisors have an idea what's going on, they don't do anything about it because they don't want to cause any trouble with the employees. All an operator did was to keep his or her machine running—because the supervisor's office was far enough away that they couldn't see but could hear the machine running because it was so loud. In this way they would think the employees were working when in fact they weren't. And even if the foreman did come down for one reason or another, the employees could see him in time to make it look as if they were working. A coded message was passed to the workers involved and thus they were quickly alerted.

One or two of the employees didn't approve of what was going on but there wasn't much they could do about it without getting themselves into trouble. If they had told someone in authority they would have gotten themselves into trouble with the other workers. They would probably have been beaten up or had their cars damaged. You couldn't put anything past these employees because a lot of them acted crazy and childishly at times. One thing that went on for a long time was someone going around scratching parked cars with a nail. There were about 40 cars scratched over a six-month period. Then the security was increased and this seemed to stop it because there haven't been any cars scratched since. But they never did find out who was responsible.

Unlike the pay system, the basic organizational structure at this company did not change after the takeover. Each mill still had its own superintendent who had a number of supervisors under him each looking after one of the various departments. The individuals occupying these positions before the takeover continued to hold them after the takeover. About the only thing that changed was the company name. There were a few employees who quit, but the number was very small.

The employees had many fringe benefits like overtime pay, a dental plan, life insurance policy, pension plan, and seniority rights in lay-offs and dismissals. They had all these benefits thanks to their union, the United Auto Workers. However, the employees tended to take these fringe benefits for granted. So just because they had these benefits did not mean that they were happy. In fact most employees considered working for Bradley Metals a job and nothing more. Perhaps one reason for this was the employment there meant working shifts. One week an employee would work the midnight shift; the next week it would be the afternoon shift; and the following week it would be the day shift. Many employees rotated on this schedule throughout the year—year after year. However, some workers only worked days and afternoons and the lucky ones with considerable seniority just worked days. In fact there was one guy named Dave who was 62 years old, 3 years away from retirement, whose job was a "go-for." All he did was get what the others wanted to eat and drink on their breaks, help anyone who needed help, and just wander around trying to look busy. He was a real nice guy and all that, but a lot of the employees envied him his job. They wondered why the firm thought fit to pay him for really just passing the time.

Discussion Questions

1. List all the symptoms in the case that suggest that organizational behaviour at Bradley Metals is not being managed effectively.
2. Use motivation and job design theories to explore the causes of the negative employee behaviour mentioned in the case.
3. Use the model that outlines the conditions and processes for team effectiveness to explain the developments in this case.
4. Use the guidelines for ethical decision making to explore the ethics of the decisions made by the new owners and the employees since the takeover.
5. If you were to manage this company, what steps would you take to improve the situation?

SOURCE: S. Anwar Rashid, Maurice Archer, and Randy Hoffman, *Canadian Cases in Organizational Behaviour*, 3rd ed.

integrative case 2

The Brewster-Seaview Landscaping Co.

Part 1

During the summer of my freshman year in college, I worked for a small private landscaping company planting shrubs, seeding new lawns, cutting grass, and tending flower gardens. The company was located in my hometown of Seaview, N.J., which is a rural community on the coast about 80 miles from Philadelphia. The company was owned and run by Joe Brewster, a 45-year-old man who had lived in Seaview all his life. He had started the company some years ago and not only handled the paperwork (payroll, bills, estimates, and so on), but also worked along with the crew six days a week.

The crew consisted of five guys ranging in age from 17 to 20 years. We all lived in towns around Seaview and had gone to the regional high school, which was located in Seaview. Only two of us were attending college, but all had been hired personally by Joe following a short, informal interview. I can't be completely certain about the others, but I think all of us and several others sought the job because we needed work, enjoyed the outdoors, and had heard that Joe paid well and was an OK guy to work for. Working hours were from 8 a.m. to 4:30 p.m. with an hour off for lunch, Monday through Saturday. Once in a while we'd work overtime to help out some customer who had an urgent need. Each worker began at the same wage with the understanding that hard workers would be rehired the next summer at a higher wage. Several of the crew I was part of had been rehired under this policy.

Most of the customers we serviced lived in Seaview, knew Joe personally, and seemed to respect him. Joe owned one truck which he used to transport all of us and necessary supplies and equipment from job to job. Each morning he would read off a list of houses that had to be completed that day. He would then leave it up to us to decide among ourselves who would do what task while at a particular house. We also were the ones who determined by our work pace how long we would spend at each house. In doing the work itself, we were able to use our own ideas and methods. If we did a good job, Joe would always compliment us. If we lacked the necessary know-how or did a poor job, Joe was right there willing to help us. At each house, Joe worked along with us doing basically the same work we did. He dressed the same as we did and was always very open and friendly toward us. He seldom "showed his authority," and treated us as equals. Although our workday was scheduled to begin at 8, Joe never became upset or penalized us if we were 10 or 15 minutes late. Our lunch hour was usually an hour long starting anytime between 11:30 and 12:30 depending on what time we, the crew, felt like eating. Each member brought his own lunch to work and anytime during the day could take time off to go to the truck for a snack.

The crew itself became very well acquainted, and we were always free to talk and joke with each other at any time and did so. We enjoyed each other's company, although we did not socialize after hours. We also became very friendly with the customers. They were always eager to talk to us as we worked, and Joe never objected. All in all, the job had a very relaxed, easygoing atmosphere. I for one felt little pressure to hurry and, like the others, respected and liked Joe very much.

Part II

The attitude we had toward the job was very high. We sometimes talked among ourselves about how we felt a sense of responsibility toward the job. While we talked and joked a lot while working, little horseplay occurred; and the talking and joking did not interfere with the work. We were always working steadily and efficiently, seeking to keep ahead of schedule. The days seemed to go fairly quickly and a lot seemed to get done. I know Joe said that our output was 15 percent above that which other landscaping companies experienced with summer crews. We also took a lot of pride in our work. Feeling responsible for the job we did, we were constantly checking and rechecking every job to be sure it was perfect. We were always willing to work overtime for Joe when he needed us to do so.

Part III

I returned the following summer to work for Joe because of the strong satisfaction I had with the job the summer before. So did the others. However, we were in for a surprise. Many things had changed. Joe had increased the number of workers to 10, bought another truck, and hired two young college graduates from Philadelphia as crew supervisors. His plan was to concentrate on the paperwork and on lining up new customers, leaving the direct guidance of the two work crews to the new supervisors.

Joe had hired the two supervisors during the early spring after interviewing a number of applicants. Both were young (23 and 24), from the city, and had degrees in agricultural management from Penn State, but had not known each other previously.

We "oldtimers" were assigned to one crew and five new workers were hired for the other crew. These new workers had little experience in landscaping. Except for the working hours, which were the same as during the previous summer, the two supervisors were told that they could run their crew in any manner they wished as long as they kept to the schedule prepared by Joe. No one on the crew had known the supervisors before. Joe had found them through ads in the paper. The supervisors didn't dress quite as informally as Joe did, perhaps because they didn't do as much actual physical work, but they did dress casually in dungarees and shirts, the same as the crew. Though we called the supervisors by their first names, they did some nit-picky things. For example, Joe never cared who drove the truck or who did what job; sometimes a crew member would drive and Joe would talk with the rest of us. But the supervisors always drove the truck and decided when we would eat. Nor did the supervisors help us unload the tools as Joe had done. They stood around and watched us.

Both supervisors refused to tolerate tardiness in the morning and immediately set up a scheduled lunch hour which would remain the same throughout the summer. We were no longer allowed to go to the truck for a snack during the day and were constantly being watched over by our supervisor. The supervisors assigned us to specific tasks to be done at each job and told us how "they" wanted them to be completed. They also told us how much time we were to spend doing each job. They refused to let us talk to each other or to the customers (except about business) saying that it "only wasted time and interfered with our work." It was a more structured, more formal atmosphere than the summer before.

Part IV

I was disappointed at the new setup and a little bit surprised that Joe hadn't hired one of the more experienced members of the old crew as supervisor. But I figured it was necessary because of the increased volume of business so I tried to make the best of it. However, very soon my attitude and that of the rest of the old crew fell significantly. We began to hate the new supervisors and soon lost interest in the work itself. While I'm a person who usually is very conscientious and responsible, I have to admit that before long I, along with the others began, to put little care or concern into my work. The supervisors soon found it very difficult to get anyone to work overtime.

The new employees didn't react as strongly as we did, but I could tell that they weren't working with much enthusiasm, either.

I thought about talking to the supervisors but didn't because I'd only worked there the one year and figured that it was not my place to. The others were older than I and had worked there longer so I figured that they should, but no one did. Instead, we talked among ourselves and individually griped to Joe. Joe didn't seem to know how to deal with our complaints. He passed them off by saying, "Oh ... I'll talk to the supervisors and straighten it out with them." But nothing changed, and in fact they seemed to clamp down more and push even harder. This only made us madder. Our work rate continued to fall.

Incidentally, throughout this period we had little social interaction with the supervisors, but I noticed that they became more and more friendly with each other.

Meanwhile the new crew's difficulties increased. Being new and inexperienced, they couldn't do the work as easily as we could. Also the supervisors didn't, or couldn't, give them any adequate training. Their productivity went lower and lower. The supervisors were very upset and yelled at them, pushing them to get out their quota. We felt sorry for them and tried to help them; but we concentrated on reluctantly meeting our own quota.

I don't think Joe realized that the supervisors were not teaching the new crewmen. He was very busy and not around much, and I think he assumed that they were training the new men. I think he began to put pressure on the supervisors as the work rate fell, because things continued to get worse. We couldn't talk to customers, which surprised them. We couldn't even accept drinks. Production lagged greatly as compared to the previous summer, and the two supervisors struggled to meet the schedule and deal with customer complaints about quality. By July 15th, the overall productivity of the company was 5 percent below "normal" and way below the previous summer.

As Joe became aware of this huge decrease in production, he became very concerned and wondered what to do about it.

SOURCE: Adapted from Allan R. Cohen, Stephen L. Fink, Herman Gadon, and Robin D. Willits, *Effective Behavior in Organizations*, 5th ed. Copyright © 1992. Reproduced with permission of the McGraw-Hill Companies.

Discussion Questions

(Your instructor will assign one or more of the following questions.)

1. Use motivation theories to explain why the "old-timers" were less motivated and productive during their second summer at Brewster-Seaview than they were during the first.
2. Using concepts from the text, which of the path–goal leadership style(s) best describe(s) Joe's leadership style? And that of the new supervisors? Given the contingencies in each situation, whose style(s) were more effective and why?
3. Compare Joe's sources of power as well as the influence tactics he used to those of the two new supervisors.
4. Using the concepts from the text, list and describe the sources of power and the influence tactics used by Joe and the new supervisors
5. What are all the sources of conflict currently evident at Brewster-Seaview? Identify and evaluate the conflict management styles used by each party identified in the case. What approaches to conflict management would you recommend?
6. Identify and classify all the narrator's reactions to change during the second summer.
7. Recommend an action plan for Joe to help him improve the effectiveness of Brewster-Seaview Landscaping in the short term (the rest of this summer) and for the long term (next summer.)

integrative case 3

Columbia Paper Company

Directly and through subsidiaries, the company that we are concerned with in this case is engaged in the manufacture, sale, and distribution of fine uncoated printing and specialty papers. The company makes some 100 grades of fine paper, with the majority of its market being Canadian. In addition, the firm produces a full line of coated printing, fancy, and gloss paper. This paper is used in producing labels, brochures, greeting cards, and textbooks.

The company has two major manufacturing operations, one in Quebec and the other in Ontario. The latter location is responsible for the specialty coated papers. Over the last three years, the firm has modernized its Quebec mills to increase productivity and reduce costs through the application of newly developed technologies. The Ontario plant has also undergone modernization, but not to the extent that the Quebec plant has. Sales last year topped $129 million, with a net income of $4.5 million. The company employs a total of 1412 workers in its manufacturing and marketing operations.

The flow of authority, communication, and responsibility within the firm is as indicated on the organizational chart in Exhibit IC3.1. The plant consists of four departments with a supervisor in charge of each. All of the supervisors report directly to the superintendent of plant operations. Basically, his function is to ensure that the whole plant is operating efficiently day by day. This involves getting the materials and employees necessary to fill that day's customer orders. His decisions are mostly of a technical nature. He reports directly to both the assistant manager and manager of plant operations, depending on the type of plant production problems. The manager of plant operations is really the key person in the manufacturing organization. He reports to the vice president of the Ontario plant who in turn reports to the president of the company in Quebec. The vice president's decisions are on a strategic level but most of her authority has been delegated to the manager of plant operations. The vice president is rarely at the plant due to meetings both in Toronto and at the head office in Quebec.

The organization of the firm is hierarchical in nature with all decisions coming from the top and flowing down through each level of management. All employees are informed of changes by only one person—his or her immediate supervisor. Authority and responsibility has a clear and direct path from the top of the firm to the bottom.

Now we focus our attention on the Ontario plant's finishing department. The style of management practised by the day shift supervisor of this department is extremely autocratic. All tasks are briefly explained to new employees with no verbal or written communication of expected outputs. Only through questioning of fellow employees does a new employee find out what level of production per shift is demanded of him or her.

Supervision is very close on the day shift with the supervisor constantly inquiring as to where employees have gone if it is discovered that they are away from their posts. Tension is usually very high during this shift as opposed to the two others (evening and night shifts), when few of the "top brass" are around. The day supervisor's style of leadership is based on the use of fear. He often acts aggressively by yelling at employees and threatening to dock pay, demote, or fire the offending employee. He has unilateral power and uses his authority to motivate the workers in his charge. Communication is only one-way, that being downward from supervisor to worker.

EXHIBIT IC3.1

Organization Chart of the Ontario Subsidiary of the Columbia Paper Company

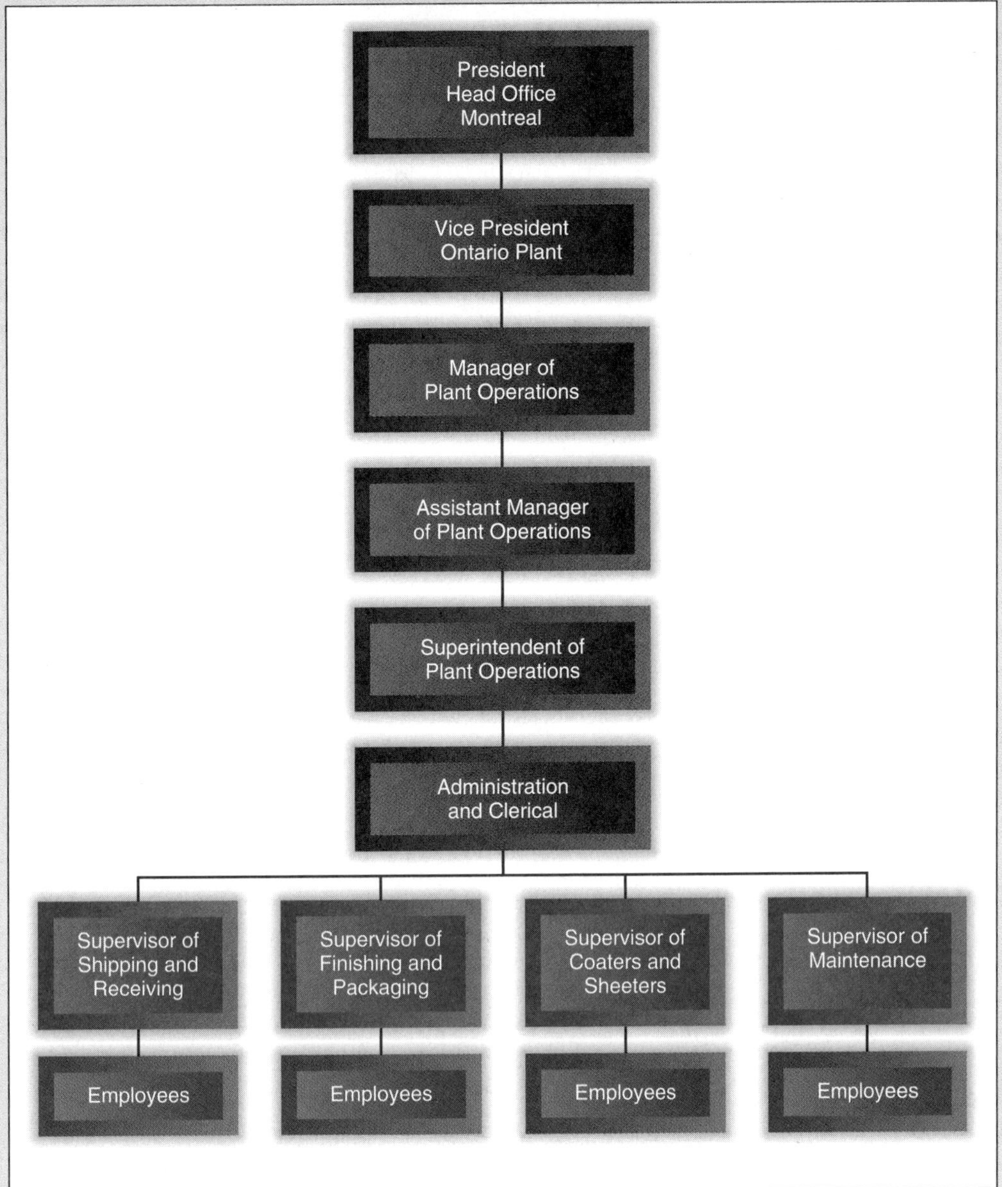

The manager of plant operations is, however, remarkably different. While he gives clear task direction and sets challenging production goals, he also has an "open-door" policy. He can be approached at any time regarding a problem and does take a genuine interest in his employees. When he notices good-quality work, or when production targets are exceeded, he makes a point of praising those responsible. He actively listens to an employee's opinion and if valid, he accepts it.

While the plant manager is liked very much by employees, he is disliked and resented by the supervisors. They see him as being too considerate or "soft." Once a month, the manager holds departmental meetings with all the supervisors and other employees in attendance. Any problem can be discussed, with priority being given to safety. Very clearly, there is some tension and conflict between the manager and his supervisors because of the different styles of leadership practised. In fact the only thing that suppresses this conflict is the hierarchical organizational structure, with its different levels of authority.

Teams play a very important role in this company. The monotony and repetition of the work demands group formation as one means of psychological release. Each department of the firm has its own groups or cliques and there is a slight interdepartmental rivalry present. This is evidenced by certain type of activities such as equipment (forklifts) being taken by one department from another or being deliberately misplaced just to frustrate the other departments.

In the finishing department, there are, to a degree, barriers to be overcome before a team accepts a new member. Such barriers include: (a) How much can he or she produce? (b) How fast can he or she acquire the necessary skills? (c) How willing is he or she to be accepted by the team? Acceptance is generally not difficult. However, one person was not so fortunate last summer. She was hired to do the final skid wrapping at the end of the finishing line. The team did not accept her from her very first day and they therefore increased production drastically to a rate which even an experienced wrapper could not keep up. As a result, the new employee did not last beyond her third day on the job.

The finishing department has an informal team leader of whom all members are to some extent afraid. Because of his quick sarcastic wit, he can take reprisal on an offending employee by causing him or her embarrassment in front of co-workers. The team leader sometimes breaks company policies to upset management and usually gets away with it. He consistently takes group member complaints to the union and occasionally to management. He is always filing grievances.

The team does give its members some release by making a "game of work." Many practical jokes are carried out, which do much to reduce the boredom of the job. Team pressures are prevalent when one deviates or begins to deviate from the so-called output levels. For example, one day a worker found himself with a full day's run of good paper that could be run quickly. After a while the other workers on the line sensed the increased pace of production and seriously suggested that the worker go and either get lost in the plant or use the washroom facilities for at least 30 minutes. Upon his return, the worker discovered that the group had informed management that he was not feeling well enough to work. Also, many times during the summer, if the majority of the group did not feel like working they would leave and shut down the entire line. Management complained a lot but did not do much for fear of union reprisal.

Communication upward in the firm is very poor, if not almost nonexistent. Employees consistently keep as much information from the supervisor as possible. Even if a special order is being searched for and an employee knows where it is, it is left up to the supervisor to find it.

Many problems have gradually come to the surface and lately the following have become major concerns for Columbia's management:

- Poor quality of goods with a high number of rejects in tonnage per year.
- Low employee turnover in jobs due to the high wages and overtime but employees still talk a lot about planning to quit.
- The rate of grievances is high.
- Absenteeism and slowdowns occur frequently.
- Employee morale is low.

In this company, fear and threats are used and employee morale is thought to be a function of regular pay, overtime pay, fringe benefits, and social functions. The firm does have social committees, which organize both social outings and weekly draws. However, turnout for the outings is always very poor and considered a big joke among most employees. Because of the monotony of the work, absenteeism is high even on overtime shifts paying time and a half. After five days the employees have had just about enough and want to spend the weekend with family or friends. This is considered to be more important than the work.

Slowdowns also occur frequently. They take two forms. First, employees on the whole are either upset at management or else do not feel like working, which causes an overall fall in productivity. Secondly, sabotage of equipment sometimes takes place. Employees know ways in which to deliberately jam moving tables or other parts of the machinery, which causes "downtime" to happen. This downtime is recorded on production sheets, which are handed in to management daily. There is hardly a day without some downtime being listed on the production sheets.

In general, the Columbia Paper Company is in difficulty since it has problems in all the key areas. The firm must seek solutions in order to increase productivity and reduce costs. It is rumoured that the Ontario plant is not cost-efficient enough to warrant the expansion program which the Quebec plant underwent. The company must make extra efforts and strive toward a new model of organizational behaviour.

Discussion Questions

1. List the outward manifestations, in terms of organizational performance and/or employee behaviour, that indicate that Columbia Paper Co. is in trouble
2. Under the OB concepts and the topic headings of communications, team dynamics, sources of power and influence, leadership styles, and organizational structure, diagnose the major causes of ineffective organizational behaviour at Columbia Paper.
3. What are your recommendations, based on your diagnosis, for improving the effectiveness of the organization?

SOURCE: S. Anwar Rashid, Maurice Archer, and Randy Hoffman, *Canadian Cases in Organizational Behaviour*, 3rd ed.

integrative case 4

Fox Business Equipment

The company that we look at in this case is a supplier of various types of business document solutions and information-processing software. Within the company, the division that we are concerned with is sales. Recently, top management decided for purposes of company prestige (and the fact that they could now afford it) to move into a brand new office building in the downtown area of a major Canadian city. However, the new office space that was leased was located on two different floors: the fifth and sixth floors of the new building. This meant that the sales division had to be divided into two groups, one on each floor.

The first group, which we call Group "A," consisted of one manager, two administrative assistants, and eight salespeople. They moved to the fifth floor, along with top management and the managers of the other departments of the firm. The second group (Group "B"), consisting of nine salespeople and one administrative assistant, moved to the sixth floor, on their own, without a sales manager. Here they shared the floor with another major tenant.

Before long, this division of the sales department into two groups, physically separated in the building, began to create friction—especially as neither group had been informed as to why they had been separated. Soon, a minor competition arose between the two groups as each fought to prove itself better than the other. Each group believed, incidentally, that the other had the better office setup: the grass always being greener ... At the same time, a strong camaraderie developed in Group B—whereas before the move, the salespeople had had very little to do with each other—each being intent on obtaining more clients and sales. Now they became strongly reliant on each other, particularly in the physical absence on their floor of a sales manager.

The second disruptive factor, from the viewpoint of Group "B" (the first being the splitting of the sales department), was the appointment of a full-time manager for their group—at a time when the sales reps in that group, who had become more and more self-reliant, were beginning to feel that they did not need one. The person appointed as manager for the group, Tony Rice, was both relatively young (28 years old) and inexperienced in the field. In fact, surprising as it may seem (and this is a true story), this was his third career, each in a different and unrelated field. As a result, several of the salespeople began to make remarks about the nature (or the absence) of an effective staff selection process. Some were also indignant about the fact that no one had even mentioned the job opening or the possibility that one of them might have qualified for the opening.

Within one year, Tony Rice, the new manager, had managed to go through five administrative assistants, four original salespeople, and two new ones (whom he had himself hired but declared unsuitable after a few weeks). Although he did not get involved in direct sales himself, he did collect a referral fee for leads that he obtained—usually because of his position as manager. As this referral fee came out of the salespeople's commissions, he was in fact taking some of their money. Also, the salespeople claimed that he was not doing much in the way of managing, and what he did left much to be desired. From the moment he arrived, he started to reorganize the offices—from filing cabinets and desks to the people themselves. He also revised most of the office and sales procedures—from proper placement of advertisements, correct form of letters to clients, and even etiquette, to the best way to make a sale.

He was also paranoid about keeping original contracts—instead of leaving them in their customary filing cabinets, he had them all transferred to his office where they were kept under lock and key. Unfortunately, whenever he was out, he took the key with him and thereby made the job of the salespeople much more difficult, even holding up some deals for several days. Because he was afraid of what some of the salespeople were saying about him, he asked one or two of them to start spying on the others—which accomplished nothing except to cause hostility and fear to permeate the office, ending in closed doors everywhere, for fear of being overheard.

One of the salespeople, fed up with the situation, tried to alert top management to the situation—but without much success. He then tried to get a transfer to another department. But, although the other department was willing to have him, his present boss, the new manager, held up the transfer, arguing that he needed time to find a replacement. Eventually, two months later, the salesperson left the firm in disgust. Gradually, other salespeople left or were fired for no apparent reason. Those that remained were suspicious of each other and refused to share deals.

Discussion Questions

1. Identify and list the outward manifestations in company performance and/or employee behaviour that suggest that Fox is a less effective organization than it could be.
2. Using theories and concepts from the leadership, motivation, and team dynamics chapters, diagnose the main causes of ineffective organizational behaviour (1) after the sales division was split into two groups and (2) after the introduction of Tony Rice.
3. If the situation had been brought to your attention just prior to the hiring of Tony Rice, what measures would you have taken to maintain or enhance the effectiveness of the group as well as the organization?
4. Given the current indications of ineffective organizational behaviour, what would you recommend be done to improve the company's performance?

SOURCE: S. Anwar Rashid, Maurice Archer, and Randy Hoffman, *Canadian Cases in Organizational Behaviour,* 3rd ed.

integrative case 5

The Case of the Amalgamated Laboratory

Claude quickly walked into his office and locked the door behind him. He closed the blinds, lunged into his chair, put his head in his hands, and started shaking uncontrollably. He had just met with his supervisor, who ordered him to "get the situation in the lab under control by the end of the year 'or else.'" Claude was expected to improve productivity twofold, stop the haemorrhaging of employee resignations, and bring a "calm, friendly disposition" to his work unit within six months—all without any increase in budget allocation. "I feel betrayed," Claude thought to himself as he cried in despair. He has been the manager of the Amalgamated Laboratory for only four months. Prior to this assignment, Claude had been the successful manager of a similar operation in another city. He has 20 years of experience working in a laboratory, moving his way up the career ladder from being a laboratory technologist, a supervisor, and, finally a lab manager for the past 5 years. During the employment interviews, Claude's supervisor described his prospective work situation as "an exciting and challenging opportunity to work with a team of motivated professionals in building a world class laboratory in a progressive health district." "It's challenging all right," Claude muttered to himself. "But it's also a war zone with heavy casualties, and I'm going to be the next casualty if I don't figure out what to do."

Background

One year prior to Claude's arrival at the Amalgamated Laboratory, the medical laboratories of three acute care hospitals, one rehabilitation centre, and numerous private facilities were amalgamated into a single laboratory. This centralization effort was one of several initiatives undertaken by an urban health district as a means of reducing health care costs and in direct response to decreased provincial and federal funding to the district. The implementation of the amalgamated laboratory was phased in over a three-year period. The centralized laboratory was designed as a multi-site laboratory and was situated primarily at two of the acute care facilities due to the shortage of space at any one site and the lack of funding to develop a separate site. The centralized laboratory was expected to provide an efficient, high-volume centre for the entire health district, meeting both its day-to-day and specialized laboratory requirements.

This restructuring was planned by the health district's senior management team in a series of planning meetings. They frequently dispatched representatives to "talk to the staff" as a means of providing the laboratory staff with a certain level of involvement. During these staff meetings, the management representative would describe management's plan and then solicit comments and ideas from the staff. Although the staff members were pleased with the opportunity to voice their concerns and opinions, when the final restructuring plan was announced, it became evident that their input was discarded.

The Plan

It was determined that the multi-site laboratory would consist of a high-volume core lab and small stat labs at two acute care facilities. These latter facilities required stat labs in order to respond to urgent requests for lab work. Also, 13 collection centres with minimal testing capability would be provided to the community (as a replacement for privately operated laboratories). The laboratory at the rehabilitation centre, which had previously provided a "full-service menu" to the centre, would be providing only collection services and, therefore, the layoff of one full-time medical laboratory technologist would result. Of the three acute care facilities, one was slated for closure one and one-half years following the completion of the project. Because this facility provides trauma care, which requires laboratory service, a stat lab was to be maintained until the trauma service is relocated to another centre.

The Amalgamated Laboratory required the development of three new specialities: (1) the laboratory information system (LIS); (2) the accessioning or order entry area; and (3) the call centre, which would handle inquiries. Within each section of a laboratory were supervisory personnel who acted independently under the general guidance of the institution's laboratory manager. Prior to the amalgamation, there were four laboratory managers, each of whom was allocated a position as an assistant manager in the new centralized laboratory, with one to be selected as the overall laboratory manager. In addition to supervisors, each lab section also had two other levels of medical laboratory technologists. In the amalgamated laboratory, 19 separate sections were to be combined to form 7 sections. However, during the restructuring, these seven sections were further combined to form four units. Thus, the 19 supervisory positions were replaced by 4 unit manager positions. Unit managers were responsible for all of the existing supervisory duties and also for the unit budget. Only two of the four unit managers who were hired were past supervisors. The other two unit managers were a biochemist whose job had been discontinued and a level one laboratory technologist (the lowest level of the medical laboratory technologist job classification). Another biochemist whose job was discontinued became the LIS manager.

The supervisors who were not hired into the new unit manager positions became "working level senior technologists"—a step down in the hierarchy. These staff members were "grandfathered"—retained at their current salary rate. Many had excellent performance records and had continuously improved their educational level. In addition to performing routine bench work, these senior technologists were given responsibilities associated with the laboratory information system for their areas. They were also required to perform relief supervisory functions in the event of unit manager absence. Former level two technologists became level one technologists (grandfathered at their current wage rate) and were no longer required to perform any supervisory activities, but were expected to work all the shifts that were previously level one duties.

All laboratory staff belong to different locals of the same union, and union permission is required in order to shuffle staff to various facilities throughout the district. Negotiations with the union are currently underway that would see the laboratory staff become members of a single local. Staff employed at the acute care centre scheduled to close would not lose their jobs, but would be retained by seniority. However, the junior staff members at the remaining facilities were threatened with the possibility of being "bumped" from their jobs. Management assured the staff that the overall number of staff would not be reduced to any great extent past the normal level of attrition for the laboratory, including normal and early staff retirement. The total number of technical, office, and support staff within the hospital laboratories prior to the amalgamation was 237 and would be reduced to 195. The majority of the job loss would be at the privately owned labs, which would be reduced to collection centres only (i.e., no testing performed). The development of the new areas would result in fewer medical laboratory technologist positions and more "non-medical" staff in the overall projected numbers for staffing the new centralized laboratory.

The Implementation

Each unit met to standardize procedures and formulate plans for their implementation. Training for the implementation of the LIS and for movement of staff between sections was initiated. The amalgamation was to proceed in steps over a three-year period, with sections moved as soon as the renovation of their area was complete. However, in some cases, some sections were moved "just to test the waters" even though their area was fully renovated. Some sections were shuffled before the LIS was in place and operational, but the bulk of the movement of staff occurred when the LIS became functional. Within two years, the new sections were implemented and the core lab came into existence. As planned, the laboratories at the other two acute care centres became stat labs. One entire "unit" was located at the acute care facility, which would not be closed, and the remaining three "units" were located at the facility with the "high-volume" core lab. The staff worked hard and within a few months they were ready to take on the increased work load from the community.

One Year Post-Amalgamation

When Claude arrived at the laboratory, the amalgamation had already been in place for a year. He found that, although the restructuring appeared to be successful "on the surface," many troubles were brewing within the laboratories. Staff morale was exceedingly low. The technical staff (the laboratory technologists) within the units were accusing the other units of having too many staff members, having staff who do nothing or don't do what they were hired to do, not working shift work, or, more generally, having better working conditions. Intra- and inter-unit conflict within the laboratory erupted on a continual basis.

This conflict was fuelled by the existence of distinct cultures in the laboratories prior to the restructuring. The laboratory at Institution 1 was the only CAP-accredited facility. CAP is a prestigious designation which certifies that a laboratory adheres to extremely high standards of quality. In order to qualify for and maintain this certification, the staff were required to put in many extra hours of work to write and adhere to stringent procedures of quality assurance. In contrast, the laboratory at Institution 3 maintained a very relaxed and casual atmosphere. This congenial atmosphere facilitated the development of a very close working relationship with the other specialties within the institution and served to ease a potentially highly stressful work situation. The culture at Institution 2 fell somewhere between that of Institutions 1 and 3.

In one particular unit, the antagonism between members who were previously employed by two different laboratories undermined the well-being of the unit. The unit existed as three cultures within one. Each subculture retained its own methodology and techniques and each refused to cooperate with the other or adopt the "standardized procedures." The subcultures used different specimen logging (numbering) practices and refused to cover for each other at break time. Also, one subculture would discard another's reagents and stains because "they were not labelled correctly." As a result of this year of ongoing discord, the frustrated and berated unit manager resigned.

Claude also had to contend with the issue of annual and sick leave benefit usage. Employees were making full use of their sick leave benefits to the extent that, on any given day, every unit had one or more staff members away on sick leave. Also, the laboratory staff were some of the most senior staff within the health district and had accumulated four to six weeks of annual leave. Many had carried over their annual leave in the previous year as a means of boosting staffing levels during the amalgamation process. Now that the restructuring was completed, many employees began applying for annual leave.

A higher-than-normal level of attrition has occurred throughout the laboratory as staff have chosen to move into other jobs within the district, or into positions in different organizations. Unfortunately, those individuals who have departed from the laboratory were among its most talented and qualified. Although staffing shortages are being experienced throughout the Amalgamated Laboratory, staffing levels in one particular unit have plunged to a critically low level.

In response to this urgent problem and as a means of ensuring that minimal staffing levels were maintained, Claude reallocated staff from other sections and hired casual staff as needed. These measures, however, required that existing staff (who are already burdened by an excessive workload) train and closely supervise the new, inexperienced, and generally underqualified staff members. In addressing the issue of the heavy workload, Claude decided to streamline the frequency and availability of testing services. Whereas in the past some tests were performed on several samples, they were now limited to being performed on only one sample. Also, testing now became available "at regular hours only" rather than at all times as needed by other specialities within the health care system. Unfortunately, this measure seems to have backfired. Staff seem to have a reduced level of pride in their work and the service provided to clients. Also, the removal of some laboratory services from several institutions has made it difficult for the medical and nursing staff from these institutions to obtain information on testing and specimen collection from laboratory staff. This situation stands in stark contrast to previous service levels where laboratory staff provided services in person and with pride, so that overall quality of patient care was improved. Laboratory staff no longer view themselves as members of a team working toward improving the health of a patient. Rather, they feel like they are part of a bureaucracy, just trying to get as much work done as possible.

Since his arrival four months ago, Claude has been attempting to familiarize himself with his new work situation and has been responding to situations and incidents on a continual basis. He has met with staff members as a group and individually (where possible) to discuss options for improving the performance and the morale of the laboratory. These meetings seem futile, however. They consist of a great deal of talk, blaming, and demands for higher staffing levels. The staff appear to be drowning in a sea of confusion—unable to look beyond their more immediate needs. But another important issue looms on the horizon. In the next two months, an acute care facility will close and its laboratory staff will need to be absorbed within the Amalgamated Laboratory. Claude was determined to resolve the problems of the Amalgamated Laboratory. "After all," he thought to himself as he adjusted his tie in the mirror, "I'm a winner, and winners never quit."

Discussion Questions

1. List all the symptoms (outward manifestations) in terms of organizational performance and/or employee behaviour that indicate that the Amalgamated Lab is in trouble.
2. Under the topic headings of organizational change and development, job design, conflict management and organizational culture, use OB concepts to diagnose the major causes of ineffective management at Amalgamated.
3. What constraints might influence the selection of alternative courses of action?
4. What alternative courses of action should the manager of the Amalgamated Laboratory pursue? Discuss the appropriateness, advantages, and disadvantages of these alternatives.
5. What course of action do you recommend given the available alternatives? Identify and justify the selected alternative(s) and some suggestions for implementation.

integrative case 6

Metropolitan General Insurance

This case involves the Oshawa branch of a large international insurance company, Metropolitan General Insurance Co., one of the top 15 general insurance companies in Canada, with annual premium income of almost $200 million. Although its head office is located in Toronto, the company transacts business through independent insurance agents and brokers right across Canada, through 20 branches located from coast to coast.

Metropolitan General is committed to a decentralized operating structure with the various branches having autonomy for their daily operations, including types of business written, agents to deal with, selection and utilization of staff, and a full branch operating budget. Head office is used as a resource centre in the financial area (investment planning and control), and also with respect to technical expertise (e.g., the various product line managers provide guidance and knowledge to the branch staff). The company has outperformed the industry over the past five years in the areas of underwriting profit and premium income growth. Unfortunately, such is not the case with the Oshawa branch.

The Oshawa Branch

The Oshawa branch employs 30 people, including the branch manager and the various department managers (see Exhibit IC6.1 for the organizational chart). The branch was opened seven years ago to take advantage of the growth opportunities that were developing east of Toronto in the areas of personal insurance (i.e., homes and cars) and commercial insurance (i.e., fire, liability, and casualty insurance for commercial enterprises).

The staff complement of 30 is made up as follows:

- branch manager
- 3 department managers
- 1 human resources supervisor
- 3 senior underwriters/examiners
- 7 intermediate underwriters/examiners
- 5 junior underwriters/examiners
- 10 clerical staff

The staff are divided into four departments in order to facilitate the overall branch operation. These departments, and the applicable staff complement, are as follows:

- Management/administration: 7 staff
- Commercial lines department: 9 staff
- Personal lines department: 7 staff
- Claims department: 7 staff

The various departments operate almost independently of each other. Liaison between them is the responsibility of the branch manager. The branch transacts business through an independent agency network consisting of 152 brokers located throughout its five territories (running east of Toronto to Kingston, as well as the recently acquired territory north of Toronto to Barrie). The branch had premium income, at the end of last year, of $8.5 million and an underwriting loss (i.e., excess of claims paid out over premiums paid in) of $1.1 million. Its projected premium income for this year is $7.6 million and it hopes to break even with respect to underwriting profit/loss.

EXHIBIT IC6.1

Organizational Chart of the Oshawa Branch of Metropolitan General Insurance

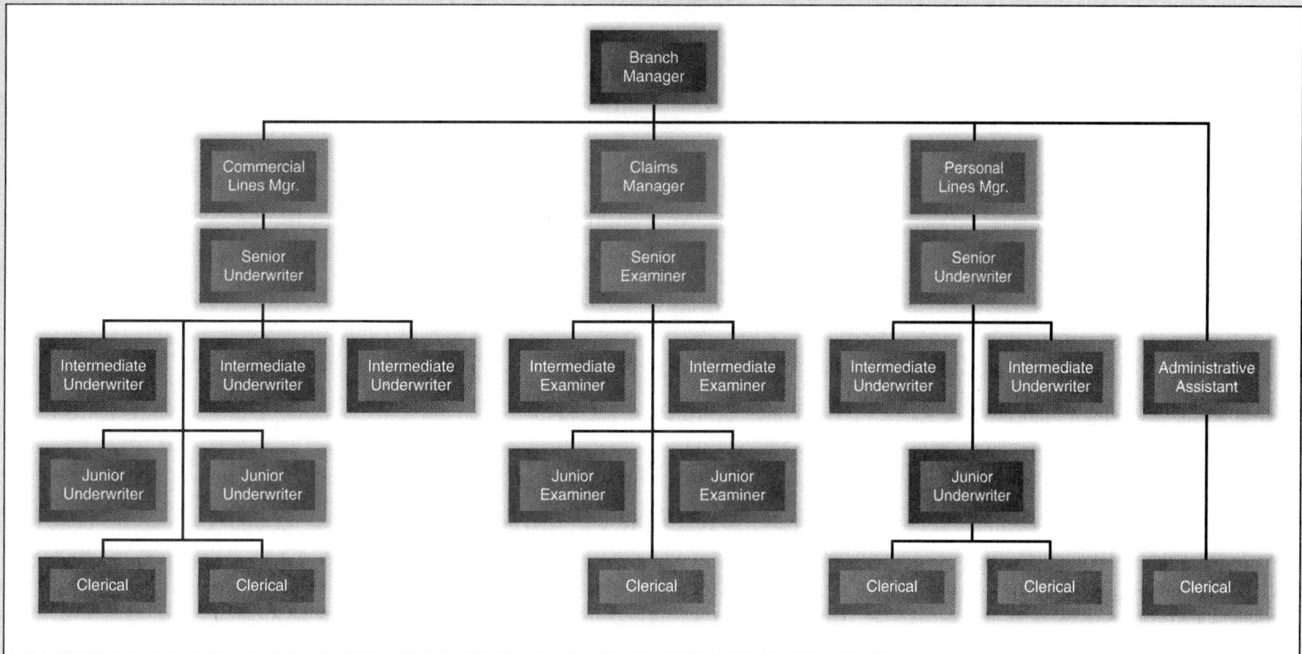

The following is a brief description of the managers and other key staff members within the Oshawa branch.

Branch Manager—Larry Gelbart

Larry is 43 years old and has been a branch manager for 10 years. Larry is a college graduate, has been with Metropolitan General for over 25 years, and worked his way up through the ranks to the branch manager position. Gelbart was given the Oshawa branch to open (he had previously been manager of a smaller branch in another province) on the understanding that significant growth and profit would enable him to progress further up the corporate ladder to the executive level at head office. He is considered to be a close friend of the company president, having worked with him as a department manager. However, he is not well liked by many of the other senior executives in the firm, as they consider him pushy. Branch employees, on the other hand, feel that they hardly know him.

Commercial Lines Manager—Sadie Tompkins

Sadie is 29 years old and has held this position for approximately one year. Prior to being appointed commercial lines manager in the Oshawa branch, she had been an assistant to one of the head office line managers for two years. There she dealt very effectively with the paper flow, but rarely with people. Sadie has been with Metropolitan General for almost eight years and had worked, prior to her most recent appointment, purely in a technical, underwriting capacity. Her employees perceive her to be quite demanding—sometimes unreasonable.

Claims Manager—Harry Higman

Harry is 55 years old and has been in the insurance business for over 35 years (the last 11 with Metropolitan General). Prior to becoming claims manager in Oshawa, Harry had been a senior examiner in a larger branch in Ontario. His appointment as a department manager was somewhat of a surprise to the others. He had not previously exhibited any management ambitions. Higman is considered to be technically competent by the line managers he deals with in head office. However, he considers that head office is interfering in his department whenever they query anything. Problems among his staff make him feel uncomfortable.

Personal Lines Manager—Connie Burns

Connie is 27 years old and has held her present position for only two months. She was appointed from within Oshawa branch to replace an incumbent who had been demoted to the position of senior underwriter within the branch. Previously, she had spent one year in the Oshawa branch as a commercial lines underwriter and five years in other branches, in the personal lines area. She is well regarded in head office, particularly for her "people skills," and her appointment as a manager in Oshawa was looked upon very favourably by the rest of the staff.

Administrative Assistant—Ruth Burkholtz

Ruth is 34 years old and has held her present position since the opening of the Oshawa branch. She is a close confidant of the branch manager, Larry Gelbart, and he relies on her input in his decision making. She has tended to be jealously protective of Gelbart, to the extent that she occasionally restricts input and access to him by other staff, including managers. She screens all his phone calls and e-mails and anytime Larry needs information, he goes to her to get it.

Senior Underwriter, Personal Lines—Helen Whiteface

Helen is 54 years old and has been with Metropolitan General for 28 years (7 years in her present position with Oshawa Branch, and 21 years in a similar position in another branch). She is considered to be technically very sound and enjoys the confidence of Gelbart, who had worked with her previously in another branch and specifically requested her for Oshawa. She is seen by some of the junior staff as a benign matriarch. That is a perception that pleases her and she does nothing to discourage it. She views herself as the expert in personal lines and the anchor for the department over the past seven years. She is often the focal point of small groups of staff during lunch time and coffee breaks.

Senior Underwriter, Commercial Lines—Bob Hood

Bob is 41 years old and has been in the insurance business for 17 years. He was hired by Metropolitan General three years ago to fill his present position in Oshawa branch. Bob is considered technically expert in his line, but is seen as somewhat reluctant to make decisions and disorganized. He had been promoted briefly by Gelbart to commercial lines manager. However, he was quickly and quietly demoted when he encountered problems and complaints from some brokers. Bob has become somewhat resentful of both Gelbart and the company.

The Problem

The branch has been losing premium income, consistently, for the past five years. Exhibit IC6.2 shows the breakdown of such annual premium income.

The projected volume for the end of this year is $7.5 million, including the new territories, and this projection may be difficult to achieve in the current competitive market. The staff turnover in the branch has been in excess of 20 percent each year for the past three years. Recently, one intermediate underwriter and one junior examiner resigned. Another junior underwriter was fired after 16 months in the branch. In addition, the recent changes in the personal lines manager's position (with the incumbent being demoted to a senior underwriter's position within the branch) has created some resentment among the staff in general.

EXHIBIT IC6.2

Annual Premium Income

Year	Premium Income
Year 1	$7.6 million
Year 2	$7.2 million
Year 3	$6.3 million
Year 4	$5.1 million
Last year	$8.3 million*

* Growth last year is the result of the transfer of the territories north of Toronto to the Oshawa branch. The total volume transferred with these territories was $3.5 million.

Productivity levels have dropped significantly, which has adversely affected the level of service to, and the attitude of, the branch's independent brokers. When Larry Gelbart held a marketing meeting recently for his senior staff, his response to the question of broker alienation was, "They are going to regret treating us this way. If they don't want to do things our way—then to hell with them!" The quality of underwriting in the branch has also deteriorated over the past few years, resulting in the acceptance of substandard risks. Because of this, the branch has lost money in each of the past three years. Low profitability has been of great concern to the corporate head office. In light of the loss in premium income as well, the viability of maintaining this branch in operation has been under examination.

At a recent meeting of the branch management and senior staff, held to discuss the branch problems, the following series of exchanges took place:

Larry Gelbart: "I know why we keep losing business. The territories we service are the most competitive in Canada and head office won't give us competitive prices on our products."

Connie Burns: "But our brokers say that we're competitive at least in some products. It's a case of us not providing the service and backup that they need. They tell me that when they phone in for a quotation, the staff doesn't really seem interested in handling their requests."

Helen Whiteface: "You haven't been here long enough, dear, to realize that we've done everything we can for these brokers. You can't expect us to work 24 hours a day just to satisfy them! I'm sure that our people are doing their best. And I should know by now."

Larry Gelbart: "That's right; we run this branch, not those brokers. If we could give them better service with the staff we have, we would. We sure pay them enough. And didn't we just move you into your job in an effort to improve things, Connie? Anyway, I'm not aware of anyone acting like that."

Harry Higman: "Besides, there's only so much that we can do. We have to satisfy head office all the time and they're more difficult to deal with than the brokers. If we try to change too many things, head office will be on our backs again looking for information and asking questions. I say: Let sleeping dogs lie!"

Sadie Tompkins: "I'd have no problem giving these brokers the service they want, if only I had some time to do some underwriting. Every time I sit down to move some paper my staff keep interrupting me with their problems! How am I supposed to get anything done in that situation?"

Ruth Burkholtz: "I know what you mean, Sadie; Larry faces the same problem every day. Fortunately I've been able to filter the interruptions somewhat and this allows him to get on with the work."

Larry Gelbart: "Yes, I appreciate your efforts, Ruth. The problem for you, Sadie, may be solved if you had someone to run interference for you in your department. Perhaps Bob here could act as your screening person to give you time to get some real work done."

Bob Hood: "I could do that if you want. Of course I'd need a little help in determining which items or people should be passed on to Sadie and which items should be passed elsewhere. And I assume that this would mean some relief from my more routine work—not just more work added on. You know, the usual policy of loading it all on 'old Bob.' Anyway, I could check this out with you later and we can decide something then!"

Sadie Tompkins: "Fine, Bob, then maybe I can give some of these brokers the service that Connie was talking about!"

Larry Gelbart: "Well, I'm not too sure that we can do much in that area, not with the pricing structure head office has saddled us with. However, see what you can do, and let me know. I appreciate that feedback, Connie. But I also think Helen and Harry may be right. Don't hesitate to keep me informed if you hear anything else. Well, I guess that does it for now. Keep trying your best and we'll just have to see what happens."

During the next few months there was a half-hearted implementation of some of these ideas. Larry Gelbart seemed not to be overly concerned with changing the traditional way the office operated. Then he received word from head office that the continuing poor performance of the Oshawa branch had made its closure a distinct possibility for the near future. In a final attempt to turn the situation around, head office has decided to send an OD consultant to assess the present operations, and make recommendations either to change existing practices or to close the office. The entire staff awaits the arrival of this person with mixed feelings, but in a universal mood of desperation.

Discussion Questions

1. Under the headings of motivation, communication, organization structure, power, and leadership, discuss the performance of the Oshawa office.
2. To what do you attribute the accelerating trend toward poorer results?
3. If you were the OD consultant hired by head office, what recommendations would you make to: (a) the branch manager (assuming the branch remains open), and (b) the head office of Metropolitan General?

SOURCE: S. Anwar Rashid, Maurice Archer, and Randy Hoffman, *Canadian Cases in Organizational Behaviour*, 3rd ed.

integrative case 7

Ridgway Furniture Limited

Ridgway Furniture Limited started manufacturing on a small scale about 20 years ago but now employs over 700 people, producing a wide range of wood and metal home and office furniture. The firm enjoys a good reputation in the furniture industry, and its products, sold in the medium to high price range, are considered good quality products by the general public. The firm is also recognized for its own special furniture styles. To produce its furniture, the firm uses the latest in modern technology. The firm's most rapid expansion took place in its first 10 years of operation. However, although the firm has kept on growing since then, the rate of growth is now much slower.

Connie Carson, who has been with the company since its start, is the head of the Furniture Design Department. Dick Prindles, who also joined the firm at that time, is now the company president and Connie's boss. Both are good friends and have together witnessed the company's growth to its present size. Carson is regarded as one of the pillars of this organization because of the many contributions she has made toward the growth of the enterprise. She is well recognized for her creative abilities, which have led to the firm's unique furniture designs, one of the hallmarks of the company.

Until five years ago, Carson had a small staff of eight employees engaged in the task of creating new furniture designs, five of them male and three female. They were all hand-picked, bright young individuals. They were all highly creative, and most of them had received formal training in the art of furniture design at various community colleges. Carson rated them as "high performers."

By last year, Carson's department had expanded considerably and the number of employees in designing had jumped from 8 to 19, which included two clerical employees and an administrative assistant to the head of the department. In addition to these 19 employees, Carson had hired John Gilbert as her assistant. His title was somewhat vague but it is believed that Carson created this position so that the new man could assist her in running the department. Carson's workload had become unusually heavy and John Gilbert's appointment came in response to this problem. It was expected that Gilbert would relieve Carson of much of the supervisory work and also take care of many administrative details, thus releasing Carson to perform developmental work, relate to customers, and plan for the future. John Gilbert was hired from outside the firm, and was regarded as particularly suitable for the position because of his supervisory experience as well as his knowledge of furniture design. He shared a large office with the other artists and designers.

The relationships in the department were very informal and people felt free to approach Carson any time they wanted. In fact, Carson's office door was always open. The employees liked Carson as a boss because she was always willing to listen to their ideas as well as their problems. Three years ago Carson decided to hire another supervisor who would look after the specialized work being done by a group of six designers involved in the development of "modular furniture." A young and dynamic person by the name of Martin Starke was chosen for the newly created position. Starke was well respected in the industry for his designing ability and had come to the company with excellent credentials. It was believed that he would bring new vitality to the group and would be responsible for the training of his workers. It was also expected that his work group would gradually increase in size as there appeared to be a strong demand for the kind of furniture they were designing. In the new organizational structure, Starke was responsible to Gilbert for his work but as usual he would have free access to Carson, the head of the department. It was assumed that the other employees would report directly to Gilbert and also receive their instructions from him.

During the next two years, some interesting practices and patterns of relationships developed in this organization. While it was understood that some of the employees would report to Gilbert and some would report to Starke, it did not seem to work that way in practice. The designers had acquired the habit of keeping in touch with Carson for almost everything they did and they looked to her for all sorts of decisions. They even approached Carson with relatively insignificant work-related problems that could have been handled by Gilbert or Starke. The six designers working under Starke kept on going to Carson for every little detail. With the best of intentions, or perhaps for expediency, Carson went along with this by resolving their problems. Carson never turned the designers away or referred them to the supervisors concerned. Perhaps because he had been hired by Carson or, more likely, because he was easier to talk to, Starke also frequently approached Carson directly with his problems, rather than going to Gilbert.

As time passed, Gilbert began to show strong signs of resentment toward Carson's policy of discussing work with the designers, but he never lodged a formal protest or confronted Carson with his "beefs." Since Starke was still fairly new to the company, he preferred to lie low and adopt a do-nothing approach. In fact, he had never seriously tried to assert his position as a supervisor, except recently when he had a showdown with his group, who were now openly defying his authority. As a result of this incident, Carson arranged a meeting attended by the six designers, Starke, Gilbert, and herself. During the meeting Starke was accused by the designers of "not being around" when help was needed! They also complained that Starke had made very little effort to train them in design techniques. Two of them complained of not getting straight answers from him to any of the questions they had raised in the past. Starke responded by saying that he was involved with a lot of other work, which caused him to overlook some of the immediate, routine activities. He apologized to the team and promised to develop a "think-tank" type of training program for his designers. Starke took a defensive approach during this confrontation meeting. Strangely enough, Gilbert never said a word. Carson pointed out to the designers that, in accordance with the organizational structure, they were responsible to Starke and they should go to him with their problems. It was also suggested by Carson that another meeting should be arranged to be attended by the remaining employees, Gilbert, and Carson, so that the departmental policies could be clarified with them.

In the meantime, another development had taken place. The president, Dick Prindles, had informed Carson that the company would soon undertake a major expansion program, creating an additional position for a vice president. The president had made it clear that he would like Carson to take over the new position. But Carson realized that if she were to move into the vice president's office, a gap would be created in the design department because, in her estimation, Gilbert was not ready to assume the responsibility of department head. Carson felt that Gilbert had lately become quite uninvolved and uninterested in the affairs of the department. It was Carson herself who was dealing with all the administrative work as well as carrying out the necessary supervision of the employees. The only things that Gilbert attended to were those of a semi-clerical nature and, on occasions, answering simple questions raised by some of the customers. It seemed to Carson that, because of Gilbert's apathetic attitude, the employees preferred to come directly to her. Also, they seemed to be satisfied with the answers she gave them.

However, Carson was now spending too much time supervising the tasks being performed by various people in the design department. In fact, some of them should have been dealt with by Gilbert and some by Starke. Together, these two should have run most of the departmental activities, leaving Carson free to attend to other developmental work. Carson realized that there was something wrong with the organization of this department and some action had to be taken to rectify the situation. She decided to have a quiet chat with Gilbert as well as with Starke to remind them of their main responsibilities and of the fact that the morale of the entire department was being affected. She told them over coffee to assert the necessary authority over their subordinates and insist that they come to *them* for instructions and decisions and not to her. Both the supervisors gave certain reasons for their present dilemma or predicament and promised to put things right for the future.

Over the next few months, Carson failed to perceive any change in the prevailing practice followed by the design employees, nor did she notice any change in the attitudes of Gilbert and Starke. Employees continued to come directly to Carson, and when she tried to discourage them, they explained that they had come to her after failing to get a satisfactory answer from the supervisor. Motivation and morale had gone down considerably in the past few weeks. It was virtually impossible for Carson to deal with her own departmental work, which had been increasing all the time, and to relate to market developments and at the same time be involved in organizational changes.

She had to make her choice now and set priorities that would be acceptable to her as well as to the others. She had to encourage Gilbert to use discretion and take control. She must also ensure that Starke, a brilliant man in many ways, would come up to his expectations as well as to the expectations of his subordinates. Both these men must perform as supervisors or team leaders by taking the initiative, demonstrating ambition, and making decisions. Carson knew well that there was no lack of technical knowledge on the part of these two. They had the ability, but did they have the willpower? If things remained unchanged, it would not be possible for Carson to move up to the new position likely to be open soon.

Discussion Questions

1. Draw the organizational chart of the company. Indicate the problems of authority, roles, and relationships. Point out the main problems and the reasons for their occurrence.
2. How do you view the role of Carson as the head of the department?
3. What do you see as the problems of Gilbert and Starke?
4. What recommendations would you make in order to rectify the situation?

SOURCE: S. Anwar Rashid, Maurice Archer, and Randy Hoffman, *Canadian Cases in Organizational Behaviour,* 3rd ed.

integrative case 8

Structuring Work at the Living Skies Long-Term Care Home

Raymond wondered how he should handle his newest challenge. In his relatively new position as regional facilities manager, Raymond was responsible for providing operational maintenance services for the 20 or so facilities that his health region owned in the northeast region of the province. Each of the facilities (hospitals, nursing homes, health centres, etc.) was managed by a program manager who was Raymond's peer (i.e., Raymond and these 20 program managers all reported directly to the CEO of the health region. The transition had gone smoothly, primarily as a result of Raymond's exceptional interpersonal flair, tremendous client orientation, and well-developed property management expertise. He met with the program manager for each facility (his functional peers in the organization) who told him that his employees were doing a good job of providing maintenance services for the facilities. There was one problem, however. Claudette, the Living Skies program manager, was growing tired of meeting with resistance every time that she approached Kelly, the Living Skies maintenance manager, regarding repairs that needed to be done.

Raymond decided to work with Claudette to develop a five-year maintenance plan for Living Skies. Unfortunately, when Raymond met with Kelly to discuss the completed plan, Kelly would have nothing to do with it. In the six months since Raymond began his new position, not only has Kelly consistently blocked any suggestions for improvement that Raymond has made, but he also spoke in vague generalities every time that Raymond made inquiries regarding the functioning of the operation. Raymond and Claudette were concerned about the maintenance operation's apparent lack of planning, deteriorating client relationship, and general absence of control over the functioning of the individual trades shops.

Having been assigned the role of mentoring Judy as part of a management development program, Raymond decided that he would get Judy to "find out what was going on" at Living Skies and to report back to him. Judy was glad to work on this special project, and she soon settled into her new office at the desk in the machine shop. Claudette had offered Judy an office in the executive suite but Judy wanted to be situated in the maintenance offices themselves. She thought that this would allow her to have a closer relationship with the maintenance workers, and it might take away some of the fear that comes with having someone from the regional office assessing the local operations.

Judy spent two months acquiring data by job shadowing each trades shop head for one day. Jean-Luc, the journeyman electrician, had provided an extensive tour of the operations, including shadowy hallways, a large dimly lit room that was full of residents but that was eerily quiet, and chambers whose contents gave Judy nightmares for an entire month. Judy interviewed all the maintenance staff and reviewed written maintenance records, including (a) current maintenance policies (breakdown maintenance; assigned versus centralized maintenance); (b) current maintenance organization/planning and scheduling (who's doing what and the time required, who performs inspections and analyzes maintenance cost information, weekly and daily forecasts, long-term planning for use of resources); (c) current preventative maintenance routines and practices; (d) work order system (written work order procedures, standard request form, number of orders versus past-due work orders); (e) inventory control (inventory records, permanent record of maintenance work performed, materials control: establishing maximum and minimum stock levels); and (f) management information (monthly and annual budget, actual versus budgeted costs, reporting mechanisms in place). To engender staff cooperation, Judy decided to use the nonconfrontational, disarming, and unassuming approach used by a classic television character, Detective Colombo.

Raymond now had Judy's report in front of him, and he knew that he had some major decisions to make. "I guess that's why they pay me the big bucks," Raymond said to himself as he looked in his desktop mirror and tousled his hair.

Background

The Living Skies Long-Term Care Home, home to over 450 residents who needed special care, was staffed by 600 health care workers. Historically, maintenance reported to the program manager, but reporting was transferred to the facilities manager five years ago as part of a regional reorganization. Its operating expenses for the previous year totalled $2.7 million, including $1.2 million for salaries and benefits. Approximately 30 employees and 5 full-time contractors worked in Living Skies' maintenance operation. Of the employees, 14 were employed in the power plant. All of the employees were members of a union except for two out-of-scope employees: the maintenance manager, Kelly, and Mitch, the power plant's chief engineer. Although the organizational chart in Exhibit IC8.1 depicts seven shops, the machine shop and sheet metal shop had no assigned employees or full-time contractors, so they were not included in the chart. A summary of current shop operations, as described by shop heads, is provided in Appendix A.

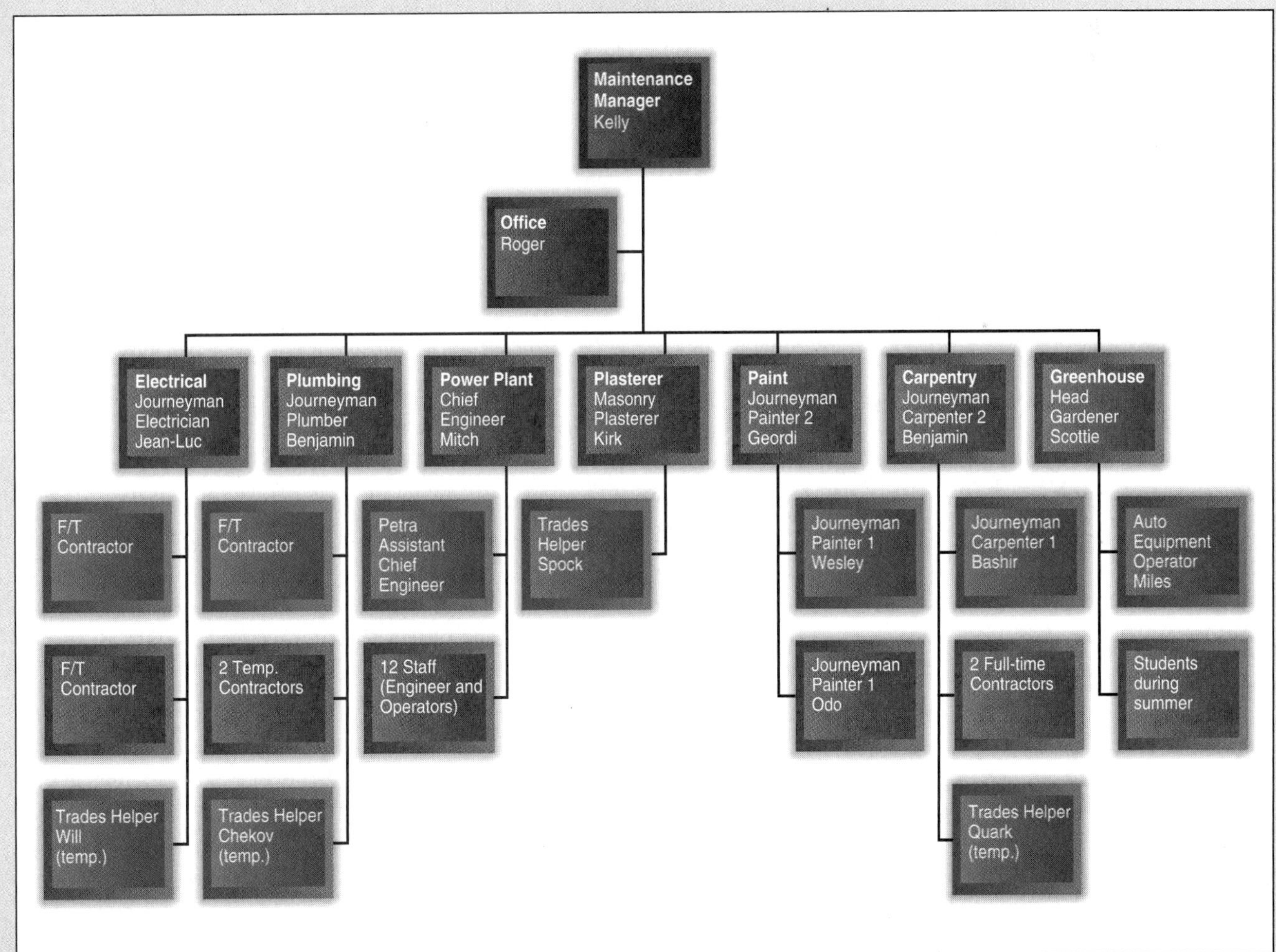

Except for power plant shift employees, the employees enjoyed the benefit of flex-time. They worked from 7:30 to 4:30 with half an hour for lunch, and earned half an hour off for each day worked. They tracked the total number of hours that they worked through the use of a punch clock. When Judy informally suggested that the punch clock be put out of commission (given that punch clocks were, in Judy's words, "an antiquated means of controlling employees"), she found strong opposition from the employees. Apparently, the employees used the punch clock as protection against potential accusations of time theft. "It's the only way that we can prove that we're working," they argued.

Office Management

Kelly and Roger (a journeyman carpenter) represented the office staff of the maintenance operation. Two years ago, Kelly conducted informal interviews for a maintenance superintendent with the goal of finding someone to lighten his load and replace him, as he was expecting a promotion in the near future. Roger was subsequently transferred from his duties as a carpenter with the expectation that he would become the building manager within a few months.

Roger described his daily job responsibilities as follows:

1. *Coding and sorting job requisitions:* Roger receives 25 new requisitions per day from Claudette's program office and 10 per day from the shops. He also receives 20 requisitions back from the shops each day indicating that the jobs have been completed. Each requisition requires one minute to process, with a total of approximately 55 minutes per day.
2. *Obtaining estimates from contractors:* An average of one estimate per month requires half an hour of his time. This totals approximately 1.5 minutes per day.
3. *Supervising trades:* Particularly the paint, carpentry, plasterer and machine shops, which requires three hours per day.

Thus, according to Roger, he is occupied four hours per day. The shop heads told Judy that not only did they not receive supervision from Roger, but that it was neither desired nor necessary. Also, as noted earlier, the machine shop was not staffed. In Judy's view, Roger appeared to be doing the work of a junior clerk who would normally earn half of what he was earning.

Kelly, the maintenance manager, described his job responsibilities as follows:

1. Making rounds of Living Skies Long-Term Care Home and shops, requiring anywhere from half an hour to three hours per day.
2. Doing paperwork and other assorted duties for five hours per day as follows:
   a. Picking up mail from the downtown office of the health region.
   b. Approving purchase orders, job requisitions, and work authorizations.
   c. Writing memos and reviewing the budget.
   d. Hiring all contractors. (At a subsequent meeting, Kelly indicated that the shop heads hire and supervise all contractors, whether for job-specific projects or ongoing maintenance requirements. He also stated that contractors do 40 percent of all the work at Living Skies.)
   d. Managing all major projects. (At a subsequent meeting, Kelly said that the shop heads manage all major projects.)
   e. Holding informational staff meetings once per month. (According to the staff, these meetings were not taking place.)
   f. Holding shop head meetings once per month to review old work and discuss job load/completion dates. (Again, these meetings were not being held.)

Judy found that getting a straight answer from Kelly was a challenging task. For example, when asked for a list of approved maintenance projects, he provided a list of 15 when there were actually only 4 projects. The shop heads later indicated to Judy that they also experienced similar difficulties in getting Kelly to answer their questions.

Supervision Given to Shops

All of the shops reported that they received little or no supervision from the maintenance manager. No formal oral or written reporting relationship existed. There were no shop head meetings; no one-on-one meetings to report project progress or review ongoing workload; no interactions dealing with objectives, budgeting, responsibilities, and authority levels; and no communication regarding new staff, the transfer of trades helpers, and the contracting of work. This absence of a two-way information flow left both parties, Kelly and the shop heads, with insufficient information upon which to base decisions. As a result, potentially inappropriate decisions were being made. For example, due to his lack of knowledge regarding current shop workloads, Kelly could not effectively make decisions regarding the hiring of contractors. Kelly's off-the-cuff management style meant that decisions were not made on the basis of a business case. Since, as indicated in the research literature, employees generally tend to model the management style of their supervisor, the shop heads were having difficulty being good managers themselves. They were not sure what their responsibility and authority levels were. They did not hold themselves accountable for the performance of their individual shops. They did not take any initiative to ensure that projects were completed on time or were properly staffed. They did not feel a need to communicate with the client.

Plans and Work Prioritization

Even since Living Skies began operations until approximately five years ago, the shops had annual operating plans listing approximately 200 projects to be undertaken by one or several shops. Although the plans did not specify the estimated completion date and project costs, they did provide some direction to the shop heads. Raymond and Claudette's five-year plan for Living Skies outlined required expenditures in the areas of maintenance, operations management, program improvements, and capital upgrades. Had these plans been translated into one-year operating plans, they would have been particularly useful in the annual budgeting and planning cycle. Unfortunately, Kelly did not take the five-year plans this extra step. Nor did he communicate the contents of the five-year plans to the shops. As a result, the plans were not as effective as they could be in directing operations.

The shops did not operate according to an annual maintenance plan. The paint shop had developed a six-year paint schedule but was informed by Kelly that they should follow the plan only if they ran out of work. With Judy's prodding, the shop heads prepared some brief plans reflecting projects they hoped to complete by the end of the year. They greatly resisted this "waste of time," since they would probably not be allowed to follow the plans. A review of the plans indicates some inconsistencies between them and the priority projects. Many priority projects were either not listed or were scheduled for varying completion dates. Judy was beginning to wonder if any amount of structure would be accepted by the shop heads. In an experiment, Judy worked with the shop heads to develop summer student plans. These plans proved to be very effective in guiding the work of the summer students that Judy hired.

Judy found that the shops were operating on a day-to-day basis with little or no prioritization of work. Decisions were made on impulse with no thought to their consequences. Each carpenter, for example, chose the requisitions that they felt like working on that day. The less desirable requisitions (i.e., the more time-consuming ones) were not chosen. The carpentry shop's priority was repairing locks. The paint shop's priority was glass repairs. The electrical shop's priority was phone calls. The other shops did not prioritize their work. As such, the head gardener may spend a month or two transplanting flowers instead of ensuring that the irrigation system and his equipment (tillers, mowers, etc.) were working properly or that a seeding and tree planting plan was in place. Another example is a project listed in the carpentry shop's work program to rebuild part of the maintenance door ramp this summer using contractors at $8000. This unapproved project was usurping funds that might be better spent on the client's priority projects. A summary of current shop operations, as described by shop heads, is provided in Appendix A.

Kelly did not encourage the development of work plans because he felt that the program-based renovation projects would render them useless. As a result, he did not assist in prioritizing the shop workload. The shops were basically left on their own to determine their priorities. In the cases where Claudette communicated (on an ongoing basis) that she wanted a certain high-priority project completed, Kelly would normally initiate the project. However, initiating a project and doing everything in your capacity to ensure that it was completed immediately are two different things. The renovation to the front entrance of the program office was initiated over three months ago and was still not completed. The carpeting wasn't even on order.

Project Coordination

Project coordination was not a strength of the maintenance operation. Several factors may have contributed to this:

- Lack of initiative on the part of the building manager and the shop heads. The shop heads would not take the initiative to determine or communicate what urgent projects need to be carried out.
- Lack of communication within all the shops. The shop heads may inadvertently hear about a renovation project but feared that they would be reprimanded if they met to set a plan. Shortly before project initiation, Kelly would inform the shop involved in the first stage of the project. He would not develop schedules or requirements with the shops involved in any of the subsequent stages.
- Lack of scheduling. Decisions appear to be made on an ad hoc basis without any thought to their consequences.
- Ineffective communication with the client regarding their needs and expectations and the maintenance operation's ability to meet these expectations.

Budgeting

Budgets were developed by extrapolating the costs of the previous year to the current year. Because a plan outlining anticipated expenditures did not exist, the budget was not developed with Living Skies' needs in mind. Generally, the budget was spent until the money ran out. No attempt was made to acquire approval and funding for additional projects. As such, the interests of Living Skies may not be adequately represented and communicated to those individuals in the health region who allocate funds.

Furthermore, the shop heads did not know what their costs were. They did not maintain any records and were not given any information that would assist them in making decisions relating to the purchase or use of materials. The shop heads indicated that that they just kept ordering materials and spending money until, near the end of the year, Kelly would say they had run out of money. At one point, Kelly told Judy that he intended to give each shop their own budget to manage. However, he later suggested that they have too much paperwork as it is, and he would not give each shop their own budget. Subsequent to this, he suggested that the shops would be given their own budgets in the near future.

Client Liaison

The maintenance operation's average requisition turnaround times were as follows:

- Average turnaround time for a base requisition: 45.9 days
- Average turnaround time for a program requisition: 10.1 days
- Average turnaround time for all requisitions: 28 days

In sum, approximately a month will pass before a requisition is completed. The average age of the overdue job requisitions was 6.6 months and ranged from 5 months (Paint Shop) to 10 months (Electrical Shop). For example, the requisitions in the Electrical Shop in-basket were on average 10 months old. Therefore, of the outstanding requisitions, a job requisition from the North Wing, for example, would still be outstanding 8.2 months down the road. In other words, if a requisition were sent to maintenance in November of one year, it would still be incomplete in May of the following year. The maintenance operation's poor relationship with the program folks had several causes:

- Kelly's definitions of program and maintenance repairs were not always consistent with those of the client. Even within the maintenance operation, repairs of settees, for example, were classed as a program repair on one day and maintenance work on the next day. No consistent communicated policy existed that outlined the responsibilities of both parties in relation to definitions of repairs, expenditure processing, and written reporting requirements. The latter may include, for example, client renovation plans, maintenance plans, or monthly reporting on costs of repairs to program equipment.
- Kelly's approach to client requests was to indicate that shops were too busy and the request could not be met. Although at times this statement was likely to be true, the client still required some indication of the activities that would be displaced if the client's project was undertaken. The client needed to be told the level of activity that the shops could manage. In cases where the project is undertaken with no impact on other activities, the client may develop a lack of trust in Kelly and the entire maintenance operation.
- Kelly's lack of diplomacy skills resulted in an adversarial relationship with Claudette, who believed that projects (mis)managed by the maintenance operation were best characterized by delays, "jacked-up" costs, and frustration.

Inventory Control

A significant problem existed regarding the size of the maintenance operation's inventory, pegged at approximately $400 000 not including the value of obsolete inventory (i.e., inventory not used in the past five years). In determining inventory turns, Judy divided the cost of goods sold (materials billed out minus the surcharge, if any) by the average value of the inventory (beginning inventory plus ending inventory divided by 2). Although Judy could not calculate the exact inventory turns due to the lack of information regarding the cost of goods sold, her impression was that the inventory probably did not turn even once per year. The shops ordered materials when they saw fit without any system of checks and balances being imposed. Since no additional inventory records were available, Judy could not determine the presence of a downward trend. If the inventory turns for each shop could be calculated, they could be compared with the relevant industry averages. This would provide a more accurate picture of the size that the inventory should be.

For example, there were over 10 washing machines in storage. A review of the requisitions for the last three months revealed that, during this time, no washing machines had been replaced and several had been serviced. This level of activity does not justify the 10 washing machines in stock. At most, a shop should have about one month's inventory in stock. An effective supplier relationship is essential in maintaining an appropriate inventory level. If Living Skies is one of the largest operations in the community, and if the construction economy is as depressed as Judy has been told, then the shops should be able to use their suppliers to their advantage. Accurate record keeping would help to determine the appropriate inventory levels. Also, the ratio of hours billed out to materials used could be calculated and compared to industry averages to determine appropriate staffing levels. (These industry averages may be somewhat more difficult to find than inventory turns, but Judy thought that they were available.) The excessive inventory results in high stock counting costs totalling, for example, $16 000 in the last year.

Shop Errands

All of the shop heads spent a minimum of three hours per week picking up supplies and making deliveries in the community. Their justification for this was one or more of the following reasons:

1. They did not have the authority to request a courier and did not want to get involved in the additional paperwork that this might require.
2. No one else was around to pick up supplies or deliver program equipment to repair depots. They did not trust trades helper Quark to run errands within a reasonable time or to pick up the right supplies.
3. They wanted to make sure that the supplier sent them the right supplies and did not substitute inferior quality goods.

Kelly approved of this practice since "the shop heads deserved to get away from this place." Judy calculated that this "travel opportunity" resulted in an average monthly cost of $1800. These costs exclude the frequent deliveries and errands made by Kelly and Quark.

Trades Helpers

There were four trades helpers in total. Kelly tended to transfer the trades helpers from shop to shop on an ad hoc basis. For example, a trades helper may be employed in an urgent tree planting project, but, without consulting the head gardener, Kelly would reassign the trades helper to a two-day "travel opportunity" in a major centre to pick up cleaning and office supplies.

The trades helpers were generally not productively employed. Their activities varied greatly and included guarding materials wagons, running back to the shop to get parts that the journeymen forgot to bring with them, accompanying journeyman carpenters in case their assistance is required, and changing light bulbs. They were primarily employed as "go-fers" rather than learning and practising a trade. For example, instead of filling a crack in a wall, a trades helper would accompany the journeyman and guard the wagon so that the journeyman could fill the crack. It was obvious to Judy that the journeymen would be more productively employed in projects requiring their level of skill, and that the trades helpers could perform many of the minor maintenance tasks currently being performed by journeymen.

Raymond's Problem

At first, Raymond thought that he would solve this problem by giving one of his motivational speeches; the employees would see that he cares about them, and they would work extra hard to iron out the problems. "After all, isn't good supervision the art of getting average people to do good work?" Raymond asked himself. "Or maybe this is one of those times when heads should roll. Or maybe I could just organize things for them. I don't know...." Raymond and Judy agreed that the Living Skies maintenance people were genuinely concerned about helping others and had a positive attitude toward life. Also, no one could fault the quality of the work that was being performed by the trades staff at Living Skies, given the challenging work situation. Residents would sometimes steal and eat materials that the trades people were using to make repairs. Judy reported that a resident put his hands around her neck but was pushed away by the wheelchair repair person, who said that this was not such an unusual occurrence and that she shouldn't be alone in the hallway. At other times, as Judy walked the hallways (by herself), she would often find a hand being clasped tightly around her own and would continue to hold hands for 20 or more minutes (when she would excuse herself to go to the washroom). She would turn her head and she would see a big smile on the resident's face. More than anything, this made Judy and Raymond realize that Living Skies was about creating a comfortable and welcoming home for these individuals who had no other home. "I have to do something," Raymond thought, "but what?"

Discussion Questions

1. What are the key problems and their causes?
2. What potential solutions would you recommend? Be as specific as possible.

APPENDIX A: Current Shop Operations

Electrical Shop

Organization

- Journeyman Electrician 2: Jean-Luc (10 years at Living Skies, 2 years as Shop Head)
- 2 full-time contractors for the past three years

Shop Responsibilities

To ensure that anything that has an electrical power source (car batteries, flashlights, kitchen equipment, heating equipment, air conditioning and refrigeration, lights, plugs and switches, transformers, high-voltage equipment, all motors—large or small, televisions and other electronic appliances, laundry equipment, cleaning equipment, etc.) are replaced or repaired as required in a safe working manner. Jean-Luc feels that electrical repairs should be given top priority along with heating and mechanical. He stated that every room has electrical equipment, whereas the other shops, such as plumbing, may have a smaller workload because they don't have equipment in every room.

Priorities

Phone calls

Job Activities

Job requisitions received: 50 percent program equipment, 50 percent base work

Jean-Luc's Job Activities

- 70 percent non-electrical work:
- 20 percent supervising contractors, assigning them work every morning on a day-to-day basis;
- 50 percent office work: job requisition screening, ordering parts and materials, pricing out materials used on jobs completed, work authorizations, time sheets, answering phone, advising machine shop contractor on ordering parts, and actually making machine shop–related repairs.
- 30 percent actual electrical work (in the shop) as per job requisitions.

Contractors' Job Activities

- 50 percent repairing program equipment and investigating equipment to be sent to private shops for repair work.
- 20 percent in crawl spaces doing base repair work (one day per week).
- 30 percent on-site repair work; i.e., air changers, kitchen equipment, ventilation, motors and controls, lighting problems, and renewals and upgrades.

- Kitchen—three days per week.
- Laundry—one day per week.

Average Length of Projects

0.5–1.5 hours	45 percent
1.5–3 hours	30 percent
3–8 hours	15 percent
8–40 hours	10 percent

Therefore, 10 percent of the electrical shop's work is major projects.

The electrical shop currently has enough job requisitions in the in-basket to keep the shop busy for six months if no further requisitions come in.

Ideal Staffing Levels as Described by Shop Head

- Shop head (journeyman electrician 2)
- Three permanent journeymen electrician 1; one doing only servicing and installations.
- One trades helper (2nd- or 3rd-year apprentice)
- Total of five staff

Issues

Jean-Luc spends an inordinate amount of time "doing paperwork" rather than doing electrical work. Many of the other shops resent that he is able to "get away with sitting around." The contractors should have some knowledge of the materials they used on a job and their cost. They don't need to have this activity performed by the shop head. This extra time that Jean-Luc spends in the office isn't reflected in any greater degree of organization than shops where the shop head may spend only two hours per week in his shop. A preventative maintenance program has never existed in the electrical shop, yet the nature of the work is such that a preventative maintenance program is essential to prolong the life of both old and new equipment. Living Skies is around 35 years old and 85 percent of the original electrical equipment still exists. Jean-Luc has indicated that their heavy workload allows them only to "put out fires" instead of trying to prevent them.

Plumbing Shop

Organization

- Journeyman plumber 2: Sulu
- One full-time contractor plus two contractors currently working on irrigation project

Job Activities

Workload:

- 33 percent job requisitions
- 67 percent maintenance-related functions not on job requisitions
- 90 percent base work especially unplugging sewers, toilets, sinks, etc.
- 10 percent program equipment repairs and installation
- 55 percent emergencies, 45 percent nonemergencies

Shop Head's Work Time Allocation

- 60 percent paperwork—pricing materials, ordering supplies, processing requisitions
- 40 percent actual plumbing-related work

Ideal Staffing Levels as Described by Shop Head

- Three journeymen
- Three helpers (working in pairs with journeymen)
- Six employees total

Power Plant

Organization

Total: 14 staff

- Chief engineer: Mitch (employed as chief engineer for approximately two years)
- Assistant chief engineer: Petra (employed as assistant chief engineer for approximately one year)

As a result of early retirement, approximately 30 percent of the staff are new and are in the process of being trained.

Most employees (five engineer 1 and five engineer 2) work on 12-hour shifts (2 days, 2 nights, then 4 days off) in pairs: an operator (engineer 2), who cannot leave the plant, and a helper (engineer 1), who is assigned responsibilities as described below throughout the complex.

Job Activities

Operators are responsible for general plant functioning during their shift. They monitor readings and perform tests. Helpers are assigned a group of service rooms and one boiler on their shifts.

Night shift duties:

- Put salt in water softeners and run tests.
- Check the pump house twice per shift.
- Check all heating systems twice per shift.
- Check the sump pump behind the hydraulic elevator.
- Clean both filters for the condensate tank on Sunday night.
- Oil all circulating pumps within the institution on Wednesday night.
- Replace burnt-out light bulbs in assigned service rooms, power house, and pump house.
- Clean power house floors and service rooms.
- Paint, dust assigned boiler.
- Feed phosphate to tanks—takes half an hour every two days.
- Follow greasing schedules for boilers, pumps, and pump house equipment once per month.

Day shift duties:

- Are given maintenance assignments on a daily basis.

Mitch and Petra (were unable to distinguish who performs which duties or how much time is required):

- Order parts, chemicals, salt, supplies, etc.
- Discuss major projects with Kelly.

- Prepare documentation required to obtain contracts (e.g., Bailey Board equipment).
- Scheduling/vacation authorization.
- Coordinate any major projects that may be taking place.
- Prioritize activities on a day-to-day basis.
- Paperwork: prepare monthly plant efficiency report; update major equipment records.

Ideal Staffing Levels

As is plus another full-time day person. Total: 15 employees.

Issues

Operators: Because the operators don't do any maintenance work, they appear to be, and in fact are, sitting around most of the time. It is felt that their complete attention is required to monitor alarms and boiler readings. Thus, whether they're sitting outside or in an office doing a crossword puzzle and eating popcorn, power plant management feels that the operators are being productive. Also, according to occupational health and safety regulations (as described by power plant management), when the temperature reaches 32 degrees or above in the power plant, the employees are allowed to spend half of every hour outside resting.

Helpers: A junior helper (two years' experience) has indicated that once helpers understand the job, they can find at least 4 hours on every 12-hour shift to do as they please. (This information has been substantiated by other sources.) Based on a starting salary of $1800 a month for a helper, not including benefits, this represents a $40 loss on every shift, a $600 loss per helper per month, or a total loss of $3000 per month to the power plant.

The electrical shop and power plant both urgently require a preventative maintenance program. They have suggested that they can't start a program without additional staff. The electrical shop, in particular, has no written records of servicing received or required by program and base equipment. "It's all in my head," Jean-Luc says.

Plasterers' Shop

Organization

- Masonry plasterer, Kirk
- Trades helper, Spock (permanently assigned to this shop)

Priorities

Holes in walls and floors

Job Activities

- Bricklaying
- Plastering (majority of the work)
- Tile setting
- Drywalling
- Concrete

Preparation time (mixing, gathering materials and travelling) is half the time required.

Kirk spends two hours per week on paperwork.

Ideal Staffing Levels

- Two journeymen
- Two helpers
- Four employees total

Issues

The shop head and the trades helper insist that they must work in pairs, with the trades helper guarding the materials wagon from the residents. This is a complete waste of the trades helper's time, which is worth approximately $2060 per month.

Paint Shop

Organization

- Journeyman painter 2, Geordi (employed for 25 years)
- Journeyman painter 1, Wesley (long-time employee)
- Journeyman painter 1, Odo (long-time employee)

Priorities

1. Glass
2. Follow-up of plasterer
3. Paint schedule
4. Calls from Kelly

Job Activities

Shop head:

- 30 percent of time: glasswork; done 70 percent of time by shop head, 30 percent by Wesley
- 20 percent of time: paperwork
- 50 percent of time: shop work, requisitions

Most of the work is major projects. It would take five days to catch up to requisitions.

Ideal Staffing Levels

As is.

Carpentry Shop

Organization

- Journeyman carpenter 2, Benjamin
- Journeyman carpenter 1, Bashir
- Two full-time contractors: operate in an identical fashion to employees with full responsibility for paperwork, etc.

Priorities

- Lock repairs
- Doors
- "Safety" jobs
- Phone calls

Job Activities

On a day-to-day basis, journeymen simply select the requisitions that they prefer to do. This has led to problems of some guys always taking the easy ones.

It would take one month to catch up to current requisitions.

Benjamin:

- 40 percent locks
- 10 percent program equipment (w/c trays)
- 20 percent supervising
- 30 percent paperwork (mostly ordering), deliveries

Bashir:

- 5 percent locks
- 95 percent requisitions

Job Requisitions

- 50 percent program equipment construction repair; 50 percent base work
- 95 percent general maintenance; 5 percent renovation

Ideal Staffing Levels

- Three journeymen
- Two trades helpers
- Five employees total

Issues

The shop head spends an inordinate amount of time on locks (40 percent) and other non-carpentry work (supervising and paperwork total 50 percent).

Greenhouse

Organization

- Head gardener, Scottie
- Automotive equipment operator, Miles

The greenhouse relies heavily on student help (six students) during the summer months.

Job Activities

Scottie:

- One hour per day supervising
- The rest of the time "working"

Ideal Staffing Levels

Need extra person to scrape snow, etc.
3 employees total

Issues

The greenhouse shop head would rather transplant flowers for one month than develop a plan outlining the grounds' needs. That month represents a cost of $2016 (excluding benefits). The greenhouse is used solely for bedding plants.

Machine Shop

Organization

The machine shop is staffed on an intermittent basis by a plumbing company employee apprenticing as a plumber. The power plant and the electrical shop have been performing some of the functions of the machine shop.

Ideal Staffing Levels as Described by Power Plant

Two journeymen industrial mechanics

Sheet Metal Shop

Trades staff members have been using the equipment in this shop as required. Occasionally, a plumbing company employee is hired for particular projects. The sheet metal shop does not require any employees.

integrative case 9

Mark Prentice

After my graduation from high school, I decided to work for a year before finally making a decision as to whether to continue working or to go back to school. And I found my first job in the shipping area of the catalogue operation of a large mail-order organization.

In all, I worked one year on the shipping dock, where I was responsible for loading trailers with catalogue merchandise bound for various parts of Canada. The catalogue building in which I worked was quite old, but it is where the merchandise is still collected, packaged, and shipped out. Once the merchandise reaches the firm's many retail outlets across Canada, the merchandise is either picked up by the customer or delivered to the customer's home. The headquarters building is located right beside the catalogue building. It is a central operation, responsible for buying, controlling, and operating all the retail outlets across Canada.

The department that I worked in was just a small part of the total operation, but performed a very important function. Our shipping department consisted of seven workers (Howie, Paul, Lorne, Wally, Jeff, Pete, and myself, plus the foreman, Tom, and our supervisor, Rick). This shipping department was part of the responsibility of the manager, Chris, who was also responsible for managing the listing room, the receiving dock, and the sorting floor. The shipping floor is separate from the receiving area and has a small office where our supervisor spends his time. Outside this office is a desk where our foreman does his paperwork. On the shipping dock, which has eight bays, there are five conveyor lines leading to each worker. On a floor above the shipping area is a round table where Howie is responsible for sorting the boxes and sending them down to each worker, who loads them onto a trailer. Paul and I were responsible for loading the trailers for certain destinations, and the loading of trailers for the other destinations was allocated among the other five workers.

Leadership on the Shipping Dock

Both the supervisor, Rick, and the foreman, Tom, were responsible for this function. Rick had been working for the company for over 20 years and was quite knowledgeable about the shipping functions and how to handle problems. He had worked his way up to being the supervisor and was quite well liked by the workers. Several times during my time there a problem would arise, such as a conveyor line breakdown, and Rick would immediately handle the situation and have the problem resolved by the maintenance workers. Rick also had some influence with the department manager, Chris, and would have frequent discussions and meetings with him. Rick was the first contact I had when I started working, besides the manager, and he introduced me to all the workers on the dock and had Paul train me on the work that I was supposed to do. After I had been working for a while, Rick would occasionally talk to me, having a few jokes to tell and giving me orders to do certain jobs. He did not do any physical work himself. Sometimes conflicts occurred on the dock and Rick would try to resolve them. For example, Pete and Jeff who worked on one side of the dock would be friendly toward each other and help each other in their work, but Pete had a very short temper and if he felt you were not helping him when he needed help, he would get angry and refuse to talk to you. Several times, Jeff and Pete could be heard yelling at each other and threatening to fight. Eventually, Tom had to quiet them down, and as a result they would not talk to or help each other.

This situation continued on and off throughout my term of work with very little done by Rick or Tom to resolve the conflict. The way Tom handled the problem was to have me help Jeff or Pete when they needed help. But I found that after a while I was working much harder than anyone else. Also, I realized that Pete was expecting too much help from me and that he would never help me when I was busy working and loading trailers. I realized then and there that Pete was the type of worker who helps his co-workers very little but expects others to help him a lot. Conflict then developed between Pete and myself and from then on he never spoke to me and I never helped him with his work unless absolutely necessary. Pete was very much a loner and did not communicate with Jeff or myself and would only occasionally talk to Lorne or Paul, the other dock workers. After I returned to school, I went back to see what the dock was like. I noticed that Jeff and Pete were now separated, with a buffer worker placed between them. Rick and Tom probably had to do this because Jeff and Pete couldn't get along with each other.

Tom, the dock foreman, was not a great favourite. Many of the workers disliked him and the way he ordered them around. He showed favouritism toward Paul and would allow Paul to do his paperwork and other foreman duties. This meant that I had to work harder on the centre line, which required two workers to handle the line, load flat trucks, and then load the trailers. Also, Tom had the habit of having me work on other lines to help the other workers when the work was heavy. Being in the middle of the dock I was the most readily available and easiest to order to help someone else on another line. I very much disliked this habit and was beginning to find ways to avoid being ordered to help someone else when no other worker ever came to help me when I was busy.

Tom was also a very weak boss because there were many times when one of the other workers would tell him "where to go" and he would go running to Rick for help. He was not very effective in maintaining morale, team work, or in the handling of grievances. Being a weak boss, he was very much disliked by the workers, who did not respect him and his authority. The only one on the dock who liked him was Paul, whom he favoured and helped develop to become a foreman for the future. Paul was also a worker who was not liked by some workers, such as Lorne and Pete, who despised him and were constantly refusing to talk with him. The only reason I disliked Paul was because he was not always there to help me load the trailers, but was somewhere else running errands for Tom or helping him do his paperwork.

Because of these conflicts the dock was not a tight, uniform group, but in fact individuals working on their own to earn a paycheque. This was the fault of Tom and Rick because they were not able to resolve the conflict that existed between the dock workers. But, since I left the job, the workers have changed: Paul now works for the night-shift foreman, Rick has been transferred to another building, and Lorne works for another department on another floor, so that the only workers left from the original group are Pete and Jeff, who now have a buffer worker between them.

Although there was conflict when I was working, it did not affect our productivity, for even though we worked as individuals, we did all our work and were quite efficient. Paul and Pete were the only ones who were not particularly liked by the other workers, but the rest of us would socialize and play cards in the lunch room during our breaks.

Motivation on the dock was a problem because the job was not very enriching and did not provide us with any meaningfulness. It involved very little responsibility, challenge, self-control, or chance to apply our knowledge. Much of the work, day in and day out, was the physical loading of trailers. The pay was not too bad, but the working conditions were very cold in the winter and very hot and humid in the summer. Doing the same work every day led to boredom. Also, the fact that promotion did not occur unless you had been there for a long time and continually requested to be transferred, gave me little choice but to continue my education to obtain a more challenging career. Not only was there little motivation, but the working area was dirty and our lunch room beside the dock was filthy and unfit to eat in. Much of the equipment, such as rollers to help push merchandise into the trailers, was broken and never repaired. This led to unnecessary exertion in dragging boxes into the trailers and stacking them.

Working hours were good (eight hours) with a half-hour lunch break and two 15-minute coffee breaks. Also, most days we were allowed to leave 10 to 15 minutes early. Other good features were the profit-sharing plan and suggestion schemes, which allowed the workers to earn extra money. However, I could not enter the profit-sharing plan as it required a minimum of one year of work service. Holidays were fairly good. So also was the vacation period, for after only three years of service an employee was entitled to three weeks of holidays. Economic security included group insurance plans, disability compensation, and retirement pensions provided by the firm.

Since working conditions were poor, and the work lacked challenge, morale was poor among the workers on the docks and many of them would spend their money and time drinking at the pubs, trying to forget the type of work they were doing. Many of these workers were in fact in a cycle from which they could not escape, living only from paycheque to paycheque.

Many memos and notices were posted to keep employees informed about happenings around the organization. The workers could join baseball or hockey teams during the year to make them feel as if they were one big happy family. Brochures and booklets were given to the new workers and a brief classroom talk was given to inform each new employee about the organization and its procedures before each worker was taken to his or her area of work.

Even though Rick or Tom would inform us of situations occurring within the organization, including meetings that would be taking place, communication on the shipping dock was for the most part vertical. For example, when I consulted Rick about trying to transfer to another job position in the office part of the firm, he informed Chris, the manager, and I was given tests in the Human Resources Department. However, I was never contacted later about these tests or told how well I had done.

There were some forms of oral communication—for example, formal meetings to deal with profit-sharing and safety improvement schemes and suggestions. These were all designed to meet the security needs of the employees. Eventually, heaters were installed on the dock to keep us warm during the winter. However, nothing was done to improve the meaningfulness of the job. It was probably because not much could be done to enrich it. Perhaps the environmental and security features were improved to help compensate for this problem.

This is the brief story of my experiences at my first full time job, one that I will never forget.

Discussion Questions

1. Discuss the role of the supervisor or manager in providing a conducive climate for high performance by employees. Relate your discussion to the facts presented in this case, with particular reference to Rick and Tom.
2. Analyze the causes of conflict or breakdown in the relationships, indicating the way in which it was handled in this case.
3. Comment on the problem of employee motivation in this case. If you were Rick, what steps would you have taken to improve the situation?
4. Discuss the factors that appear to be contributing to Rick's effectiveness as a supervisor.

SOURCE: S. Anwar Rashid, Maurice Archer, and Randy Hoffman, *Canadian Cases in Organizational Behaviour,* 3rd ed.

integrative case 10

Khoshaba Rugs

Khoshaba Rugs was started many years ago by Salem Khoshaba, who is the sole owner and driving force behind this rather successful business. Mr. Khoshaba is engaged in selling both very expensive rugs as well as cheaper lines. The company has 1860 square metres (20 000 square feet) of commercial space, spread over three floors. On the main floor showroom are displayed all the expensive Persian rugs. In the basement, all the cheaper broadloom; and on the upper floor, an extremely wide variety of Indian rugs, a repair facility, and a customized carpet cleaning service.

Before Mr. Khoshaba established his own business, he worked for his father, who was an expert in Persian rugs. At that time, these rugs were strictly luxury items and, consequently, their price was very high. Even today the really good rugs are regarded as an "investment" because they may cost well over $25 000 each. Some years ago, Mr. Khoshaba's business was really in a slump, so much so that he was almost bankrupt. However, economic events made many people realize the benefits from investing in quality rugs. In particular, the fall in the value of the Canadian dollar encouraged people to invest in objects of art, diamonds, and Persian rugs as a hedge against inflation.

As Mr. Khoshaba's sales began to pick up, he enlarged his stock and began a newspaper advertising program. In recent years, the sales volume has risen considerably and the rug business has once more become profitable. Last year, the value of Mr. Khoshaba's sales reached $2 000 000, and he hopes for an even higher figure this year. As his staff, excluding himself, has increased to 40 people (compared with 15 three years ago) he is faced with staff problems.

Of the 40 people employed by Khoshaba Rugs, 11 are full-time employees and the other 29 are part-time staff. The full-time staff consists of the store manager, a bookkeeper, seven salespeople, a handyperson, and a rug repairer. The part-time staff comprises 24 salespeople, three part-time rug repairers, and two assistant bookkeepers. There are no written policies at the present time. However, there are unwritten policies and practices, which vary from time to time.

The organizational structure appears to be simple and somewhat flat, with few levels of hierarchy In fact, Mr. Khoshaba is accessible to all his employees and they maintain a direct line of communication. Mr. Khoshaba is the owner as well as the president of the company.

Basic Job Responsibilities

- *President:* Mr. Khoshaba is fully responsible for running the business, as well as buying merchandise and hiring new personnel. He travels frequently to Iran as well as to India and the Far East, where he has established important contacts with producers of expensive rugs.
- *Manager:* The manager is fully responsible for the running of the business only when the owner is away on buying trips. Otherwise, he is responsible for the repair and cleaning operations. He does not travel on company business and is not authorized to conclude any deals with foreign manufacturers. He also works as a salesperson.

- *Full-time and part-time salespeople:* Usually, their only responsibility is selling to and assisting customers.
- *Factory workers:* Their job is to clean and repair carpets.
- *Bookkeeper:* Responsible for bookkeeping and other business paperwork.
- *Handyman:* Responsible for cleaning the premises and moving stock from one place to another within the store.

Working Conditions

Mr. Khoshaba motivates his sales staff by working hard himself, usually 60 hours per week, and by giving the employees numerous benefits.

Employee's working hours can be flexible with notice ahead of time, and there is no fixed break or lunch time. This means employees can take their breaks any time, so long as they are not involved with customers. All employees are on straight salary, and their hourly wage is relatively high. There is also an annual Christmas party for the staff at a prominent hotel.

The Owner

The owner, Salem Khoshaba, is a very dynamic person. He practically runs the store by himself—doing all the buying for the store, hiring and managing the staff, and making all the other business decisions. He does not like delegating authority to members of his sales staff. Salem received his practical training in the rug business from his father, who owned a carpet shop. However, due to a family dispute, Salem left his father's company and started his own business.

Salem's hiring philosophy is that more sales staff working in the shop will result in more sales. This is because each salesperson develops his or her own list of clients. The problem with this approach is that when there are no customers in the store, the sales staff have nothing to do, even though they are being paid by the hour.

Mr. Khoshaba, perhaps unconsciously, hires people who have very few aspirations of "getting ahead" in the company. He feels that if he hires people who have no career ambitions, they will be content with their present positions and remain in his employ for a long time. His philosophy concerning his employees is to keep them happy and content with their present job. This policy, together with good wages, has worked well for the company as there has always been a very low staff turnover.

Mr. Khoshaba insists that his employees use low-pressure selling techniques; however, there are still some people who use high-pressure techniques. The reason he favours low-pressure selling is that he wishes to satisfy potential and actual customers, not just to make immediate sales. The salespeople who sell in the store have different areas of specialization. Some sell only the high-priced merchandise, whereas others sell only low-priced goods. Salem feels that his staff, as a whole, use a good mixture of selling techniques, reflecting the different personalities involved. However, there have been some problems caused by this mix. For example, customers coming into the store may be ignored by the high-priced merchandise salespeople if they are not buying these items, and vice versa. Also, some customers may be over-pressured and others under-pressured.

The Manager

The manager, Michael Enders, was hired by Salem Khoshaba even though he had no formal training and little experience, either in the rug business or in management. Michael's previous job was in fact delivering rugs. The manager is responsible for running the store only when Salem, the owner, is away. When Salem is in charge, Michael's responsibilities are limited to selling and to managing the repair and cleaning facilities.

Usually, the staff go to Salem with their problems, bypassing Michael. The manager does not seem to mind this arrangement, as he was made aware of it at the time of his hiring.

The manager has no formal training, but would like to take a management course in the near future. This may be a problem, as he works a 60-hour week that leaves little time for any outside training. Also, the owner would not reimburse Michael for any education fees, since he feels that formal education is a waste of time.

Another problem with Michael's position as manager of Khoshaba Rugs is lack of job security—he may lose his job to the owner's son in the next few years. Salem Khoshaba's son will be finishing high school in the next two years and it is presumed that he will assist his father in running the business.

The Staff

The staff at Khoshaba Rugs were all hired personally by Salem Khoshaba. Also, everyone has some connection with Salem Khoshaba personally, either through social contact or blood tie. In his hiring, Salem relies solely on the personal references of a prospective employee. He feels that he can rely on his staff to work well together and help one another as required. Informal work groups have been established, and rarely does any one worker feel alienated.

Staff members receive no formal training. Some have had sales experience in other areas; however, the staff learns "on the job," aided by the more experienced staff. Their only duties are to sell and to maintain security against theft. The problem inherent in this system is that the staff can sell only when there are customers in the store. When there are no customers, the staff must sit and wait. They play a waiting game. All the employees have been told to remain at the front of the store and keep an eye on the door. However, when a potential customer does enter the store in a slack period, he or she may be confronted with five or more people sitting around the front door.

The seven full-time sales staff work five days a week; the 24 part-time sales staff work one to four times per week. Salem schedules 5 or 6 people to staff the store on week nights and 20 on Saturday.

Unfortunately, the staff does not always follow the schedule. They come and leave early or late, and sometimes do not come on their scheduled days. However, they make up the lost time at their convenience. The part-time salespeople are all female, and generally students who do not intend making a long-term career in the store. The full-time saleswoman is there because she needs the money. The ages of the employees range from 16 to 36. The manager feels the women subordinate themselves to the men; however, the women do not feel this way.

Salem keeps his employees happy by paying relatively high wages and by giving merit raises. He also keeps a refrigerator stocked with food so that his employees do not need to leave the store to eat. Nightly, he buys the dinners for his staff. Unfortunately, when everyone is eating, there is no one on the sales floor.

Salem does not expect too much from his staff. So long as they sell reasonably well, he is content. The exception to this is Ruth. She is 18 years old, a Grade 10 dropout, and has been with the company for two years. Because of her excellent ability, she has now taken over the bookkeeping and as a result she is paid top wages. Salem is encouraging her to improve her bookkeeping, skills through a night school course. Because Ruth is "in good" with Salem, as one employee remarked, she seems to think and act as if she is "better" than the other women in his employ. She often tells the staff what to do, and Salem backs her up. There is great employee resentment of Ruth for this reason.

There are no hard and fast rules for the staff, and no dress code other than that the men must wear jackets and ties. The staff has so far presented little problem in the overall operation of Khoshaba Rugs. There have been only three firings in seven years, and these were due either to theft or personality conflicts with the owner.

Discussion Questions

1. Draw an organization chart for this firm.
2. Discuss the type of leadership displayed by the owner of this firm.
3. How does the owner motivate his employees?
4. Highlight the problems of this small family-owned business.
5. What changes would you recommend in the way this firm is run?

SOURCE: S. Anwar Rashid, Maurice Archer, and Randy Hoffman, *Canadian Cases in Organizational Behaviour,* 3rd ed.

part six

1. STRESS AND WELL-BEING AT WORK
2. EMOTIONAL INTELLIGENCE
3. BEHAVIOUR MODIFICATION
4. SELF-MANAGED WORK TEAMS (SMWTs)
5. MANAGING IN A VIRTUAL WORLD

Stress and Well-Being at Work

Did you know that ...

- Stress costs an estimated $8 billion annually in Canada?[1]
- The main causes of stress are the job and financial issues?
- The afternoon hours have been cited as the most stressful time of day?[2]
- Employees who reported high levels of work-life conflict missed an average of 13.2 days versus 5.9 days for those with low conflict levels?[3]
- Sleep and health are most negatively affected by stress?
- Exercise relieves stress?[4]
- In 2020, serious depression and heart disease are projected to be the leading causes of work days lost in the global economy?[5]
- A leading source of stress at work is managers changing priorities without notice or reason?[6]

WORKPLACE STRESS

SARS, mad cow disease, corporate mergers, downsizing, or a new job. Which one of these has affected you?

The reality is that today we are faced with a plethora of everyday stresses that affect our lives. Recently the world experienced a major health threat that impacted all of us in some way. This stress presented itself in the form of a health epidemic called severe acute respiratory syndrome—SARS. SARS was an epidemic of vast proportions that the world has not seen since the major flu epidemic of 1918. Public health departments across Canada placed travel bans on some countries, resulting in a significant decrease in international travel. Fearful of contamination, people became afraid to eat in restaurants or go to any public places. Anxiety, fear, and paranoia were common responses to the fear of SARS. As a result, commerce virtually came to a standstill, consumers stopped spending, businesses stopped producing, and the health care industry became obsessed with trying to gain control of a disease that they did not understand.

The retail, hotel, and construction industries were hit the hardest. Due the lack of work, employees were laid off, which added to the already overwhelming stress the country was facing. People cancelled their regular appointments, preferring to remain at home in fear of contamination, resulting in loss of work for many professionals. The threat of being contaminated became so great that businesses had to develop policies and procedures to ensure SARS did not enter their workplace, further decimating their productivity. Visitors who entered facilities were asked to review company policies and sign a form saying that they had not been exposed to this devastating disease.

Public health departments across the country mandated certain protocols be followed; these protocols required anyone who thought they may have been exposed to or infected by SARS to voluntarily place themselves into quarantine. The economy lost billions in revenues and the stress levels of a nation reached critical levels.

While collectively SARS created an environment filled with fear, each person reacted in a different way to this threat. Some people continued to follow their normal daily routines while others became so debilitated that they virtually could not function, frozen with anxiety. The most significant effect was on the frontline health care worker, who experienced isolation, frustration, depression, anxiety, and fear working around the clock to help our nation manage this crisis.[7]

Workplace stress is the number one issue affecting the bottom line directly. It costs an estimated $8 billion annually in Canada and globally costs employers $200 billion annually.[8] The most common causes cited for Canadians are work-related (43 percent) and financial stress (39 percent) reasons. According to an Ipsos-Reid survey, the top two contributors to absenteeism and/or heath costs in the workplace are stress and other mental health disorders.[9]

Business leaders today recognize that they have a moral and corporate obligation to address health issues in the workplace and that creating a healthy work environment is a true win-win approach for employers and employees. At CIBC, CEO John Hunkin is acutely aware of the impact of stress. In a recent speech as chairman of the Round Table of Workplace Stress he indicated that job stress is the number one issue facing businesses today.[10] Among the most common concerns: excessive work demands and changing priorities!

Learning more about the causes of stress, how we respond to stress, and the various ways to reduce stress will enable us to achieve greater work-life balance and optimize our contributions both to the organization and in our personal lives.

WHAT IS STRESS?

Stress, or the stress response, is the unconscious preparation to fight or flee that a person experiences when faced with any demand.[11] It is any action or situation that upsets the body's normal equilibrium. A *stressor,* or demand, can be precipitated by a person or event which triggers a stress response. Stress occurs when an event is perceived to challenge one's resources or capabilities.

The experience of stress is *individual, variable,* and *cumulative.* The experience is *individual* because what stresses one person doesn't necessarily stress another person. Stress is largely perceptual and is a function of how important the situation is perceived to be in personal terms and the extent to which individuals are not bothered by situations that are unimportant to them.[12] The same stressful events may lead to distress and strain for one person and to excitement and healthy results for another. Ever encounter someone who is really stressed but you can't understand why? To you the situation seems so straightforward and manageable. Think about your friends and their stress reaction when a paper is due. How is their response different from yours? Did you know that your personality can be a major determinant in your reaction to stress? Take the mini test on page 515 to find out more.

Stress is *variable* in that the more experience one has with a particular situation the less stressed one is. Remember the first time you attended a new school? Remember how stressed you felt? Now compare that feeling to how you felt after being at the school after several months.

Stress can be *cumulative.* Prolonged periods of stress can produce overloading or a decreased capacity to resist and tolerate future stress of any kind. Think about the end of term at school. Every project is due and exams are imminent. How would you compare your level of stress at the beginning of the term to the end of term? How many times have you thought that you needed a "very long vacation" after final exams?

Take a Mini Test to Find out More about You

Take this test to find out whether you exhibit type A or B personality characteristics and about your personality and how you react to stress.

Our personality can be a key component in how we react to stress. Consider the following characteristics that describe a type A and type B personality. Then take the "A index" test to ascertain your behavioural orientation.

Type A Behaviour Pattern

A little impatient? Can't wait for someone to make their point and move on? Individuals who are type A tend to be tense, hyper alert, and impatient and energize themselves through competitiveness, exploits, and a significant focus on obtaining a goal. Some of the personality and behavioural characteristics include competitiveness, time urgency, social status insecurity, aggression, hostility, and a quest for achievements. These individuals can be so charged and hyper that they are more prone to stress and are candidates for coronary disease.

Type B Behaviour Pattern

Take the time to smell the roses and enjoy the day? Individuals who are type Bs tend to be more relaxed and easygoing, take time to enjoy the things in life besides work, are not easily irritated, seldom impatient, and work steadily.

Test 1. The A Index

The questions in this test attempt to define your behavioural orientation. There are no right answers. The more honest you are, the more valid will be the results of this questionnaire. It is *important* that you respond to *all* statements. For each statement, place a number from 1 to 4 on the line to the left of the item. The numbers mean:

1 = Very untrue 2 = Somewhat untrue 3 = Somewhat true 4 = Very true

____ 1. Whenever I undertake a task, I try to work as quickly as I can to complete it.

____ 2. I seem to never have time to enjoy some of the things that I have accomplished.

____ 3. Even though I may not show it, I like to win.

____ 4. I tend to undertake a number of tasks or assignments at the same time.

____ 5. I get impatient whenever I listen to a conversation or speech that does not interest me. I get the feeling that I am wasting my time.

____ 6. I often compare myself with others in terms of my accomplishments, income, performance, achievements, or value of property.

____ 7. I enjoy competition.

____ 8. I sometimes do other work (for example, write letters or notes or make mental plans) when I am in a meeting, working on the computer, answering the telephone, or listening to others.

____ 9. I feel impatient when other people do not carry out their tasks quickly.

____ 10. I often find myself analyzing how I could have done a task better.

____ 11. I become irritated when others show no interest in working hard to achieve things.

____ 12. I rush into tasks or make decisions quickly. Sometimes, I feel like I have been too hasty in making decisions.

____ 13. I feel that I could never complete the many tasks I have to do.

____ 14. My standards for success are extremely high. I find that my expectations are getting increasingly higher.

____ 15. When I meet aggressive people, I usually feel compelled to compete with them.

____ 16. I rarely find myself sitting around doing nothing. I often do many related tasks (for example, write letters or notes or make mental plans) at the same time.

____ 17. Time is quite important to me. I do not like wasting time when I could be doing something productive.

____ 18. I sometimes review my day and ask myself how I could have accomplished things more effectively.

____ 19. I enjoy being in good arguments or debates.

____ 20. I often find myself in situations where people say "You are just doing too much."

Scoring Test 1. Your Type A Personality

The test on type A characteristics is made up of four subscales representing hyperaggression, time urgency, overachievement, and polyphasic behaviour. The questions representing each subscale are listed below. Add up the items for each subscale. This will give you an indication of the range of Type A behaviours you exhibit.

	Hyperaggression	Time Urgency	Overachievement	Polyphasic Impulsive
	3. ________	1. ________	2. ________	4. ________
	7. ________	5. ________	6. ________	8. ________
	11. ________	9. ________	10. ________	12. ________
	15. ________	13. ________	14. ________	16. ________
	19. ________	17. ________	18. ________	20. ________
Totals:	________	________	________	________

B1	B2	A2	A1
0–25	26–50	51–75	76–100

B1: strong Type B behaviours
B2: moderate Type B behaviours
A2: moderate Type A behaviours
A1: strong Type A behaviours

SOURCE: J. Barton Cunningham, *The Stress Management Sourcebook, Everything You Need to Know,* 2nd ed. (New York: Lowell House, 2000). Reprinted with permission.

The Consequences of Stress

Stress can be good or bad. Some managers and executives thrive under pressure because they practise what world-class athletes already know:[13] to bring mind, body, and spirit to peak condition requires recovering energy, which is just as important as expending energy. Hence, world-class athletes and managers who practise what they know get high marks on any "stress test" because they use stress-induced energy in positive, healthy, and productive ways.

The consequence of healthy, normal stress is called *eustress,* meaning "eu-phoria + stress."[14] Healthy amounts of eustress are desirable because they improve performance by arousing a person to action. The Yerkes-Dodson law, shown in Exhibit OBX1.1, indicates that stress can lead to improved performance up to an optimum point.[15] Beyond the optimum point, further stress and arousal can have a detrimental effect on performance. It is in the mid-range of the curve that the greatest performance benefits from stress are achieved, with performance declining beyond the midpoint because of the increasing difficulty of the task to be performed.[16] In a recent Canadian survey on stress, three in ten employed Canadians say the stress in their lives has had a positive impact on the quality of work they do at work.

What are the consequences of stress? We can view distress or strain from a psychological, physical, and behavioural perspective.

Physiological Response

How does your body tell you that you are stressed? What is your physical response to stress? Is it in your back, neck, or head? Are you the type of person who needs to close the door and be in a dark room to calm down? Perhaps a visit to your chiropractor helps you manage stress more effectively.

In a recent Ipsos-Reid survey, sleep patterns (48 percent) and personal health (41 percent) were the areas that Canadians said were the most negatively affected by the stress in their lives.[17] Some people have difficulty sleeping, others experience muscle pain, others get tension headaches, others get backaches, and still others come down with

EXHIBIT OBX1.1

Yerkes-Dodson Law

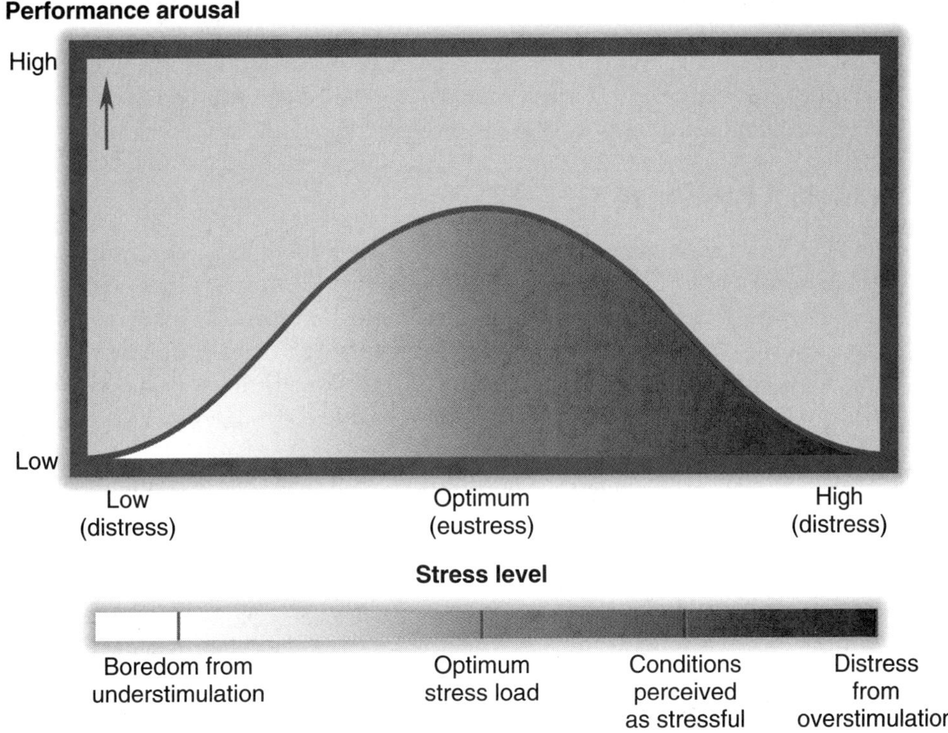

a cold. The most significant medical illnesses are heart disease and strokes, backaches, peptic ulcers, and headaches.

The stress response begins with the release of chemical messengers, primarily adrenaline, into the bloodstream. These messengers activate the sympathetic nervous system and the endocrine (hormone) system. These two systems work together and trigger four mind–body changes to prepare the person for fight or flight: (1) The redirection of the blood to the brain and large-muscle groups and away from the skin, internal organs, and extremities; (2) increased alertness by way of improved vision, hearing, and other sensory processes through the activation of the brainstem; (3) the release of glucose (blood sugar) and fatty acids into the bloodstream to sustain the body during the stressful event; and (4) depression of the immune system, as well as restorative and emergent processes (such as digestion). This set of four changes shifts the person from a neutral or naturally defensive posture to an offensive posture. This physiological response can explain the tension we feel in our bodies and why some of us get sick.

On a positive note, this response can be very functional in preparing a person to deal with legitimate emergencies and to achieve peak performance. The stress response does provide momentary strength and physical force for brief periods of exertion, thus providing a basis for peak performance in athletic competition or other events.

Specific stressful activities, including aerobic exercise, weight training, and flexibility training, improve health and enhance a person's ability to manage stressful demands or situations. W.B. Cannon argues that the stress response better prepares soldiers for combat.[18] In survival or combat situations, stress provides one with the necessary energy boost to manage the situation successfully. Did you ever read the Superman or Hulk comic book series? The stress response fuelled these characters and provided them with superhuman powers.

Behavioural Response

Ever feel like staying home from work when you feel really stressed? Stress can manifest itself in absenteeism, lowered job performance, and increased workplace aggression and workplace accidents. In a recent Ipsos-Reid survey, 31 percent of human resource professionals indicated that stress was the most serious organizational issue with respect to causing absenteeism.[19] Some employees may become aggressive when stressed. The recent case of a B.C. government worker who killed two co-workers and turned the gun on himself because he was overworked and very stressed and had been asked to fire his staff is a chilling reminder of what workplace stress can do in its most extreme form.[20]

Psychological Response

Stress can affect an individual's mental health. Depression, job burnout, and psychosomatic disorders can be consequences of high stress. In the early stages, depression and burnout result in a decline in efficiency; diminished interest in work; fatigue; and an exhausted, run-down feeling. It can also exacerbate psychosomatic disorders, which are physical disorders with a psychological origin. Interestingly, mental illness claims, primarily relating to depression, are rising at the fastest rate among major categories of disability insurance.[21]

Job burnout is emotional exhaustion. This exhaustion is due to continual and excessive demands made on a person to the point at which the person's capacity to resist or cope is highly compromised. It is cumulative and excessive. Consider what your level of stress would be if all your assignments are due the same week and a close family member gets sick and was in hospital. How do you cope with these excessive demands?

How Does Stress Affect You? Take a Stress Test and Find Out!

Go to the Canadian Mental Health Association website and take a stress test at **http://www.cmha.ca/english/info_centre/stresstest.htm.**

Sources of Stress—Work and Nonwork Situations

So where does stress come from? What are the sources of stress?

Your boss has just told you that a project deadline has been moved up and your work needs to be delivered several weeks in advance of the original date. Your thoughts automatically move to your commitments at home. You have just moved into a new house, you have a baby on the way, and your wife/husband is the type that values family time and expects you to be home on weekends and evenings. There is pressure from work and pressure from home! Where do you turn? How do you juggle these responsibilities?

There can be several sources of stress. Some of these sources originate from the work environment while others stem from nonwork situations. The main sources of stress according to a recent Ipsos survey are shown in Exhibit OBX1.2.

Work-Related Stresses (Demands)

We can organize these sources of stress into four general categories: (1) task demands, (2) role demands, (3) interpersonal demands, and (4) physical demands.

Task Demands

Globalization, technological changes, and organizational consolidations all necessitate that organizations find new ways to manage effectively and efficiently in today's business environment. In order to compete, organizations are looking for the most cost-effective

EXHIBIT OBX1.2

Main Causes of Stress—Canadian Population, 2004

Job	43%
Finances	39%
Children	10%
Health	7%
School	5%
Too much to do/too little time	4%
Personal relationships	3%
Spouse or partner	3%
Pace of life	2%

Note: 67 percent indicate that they put too much pressure on themselves, and four in ten (40 percent) say they feel stressed because the world around them changes too quickly.

SOURCE: Ipsos, "Canadians and Stress: A Special Report," September 19, 2002, accessed August 18, 2004, from http://www.ipsos-na.com/news/pressrelease.cfm?id=1620.

way to get their product or service to the customers in the shortest period of time while not compromising the quality of the service or product. This can mean frequent changes to the way employees do their work, what work needs to be done, and when the work needs to be completed. Tight deadlines are common, which can result in work overload and, for some, create extreme stress. Additionally, thinning of the management ranks and the adoption of participative management practices has influenced the volume of work and the level of responsibility expected of employees.

Intended to make life and work easier and more convenient, information technology creates its own challenges. With the continual use of cell phones and e-mails, individuals are finding themselves working longer and longer hours.[22] Learning new technologies also creates both career stress and "technostress" for people at work who wonder if they will be replaced by "smart" machines.[23]

Role Demands

Have you ever had a job where you were unclear as to what your responsibilities were? Or worse, you discovered that a colleague was responsible for the same work that you were responsible to deliver? The social–psychological demands of the work environment may be every bit as stressful as task demands at work. People encounter two major categories of role stress at work: role conflict and role ambiguity.[24] *Role conflict* results from inconsistent or incompatible expectations communicated to a person. The conflict may be an interrole, intrarole, or person–role conflict. Interrole conflict is caused by conflicting expectations related to two separate roles, such as employee and parent. For example, the employee with a major sales presentation on Monday and a sick child at home Sunday night is likely to experience interrole conflict. Intrarole conflict is caused by conflicting expectations related to a single role, such as employee. For example, the manager who presses employees for both very fast work *and* high-quality work may be viewed at some point as creating a conflict for employees.

The second major cause of role stress is *role ambiguity.* Role ambiguity is the confusion a person experiences related to the expectations of others. Role ambiguity may be caused by not understanding what is expected, not knowing how to do it, or not knowing the result of failure to do it. For example, a new magazine employee asked to copy edit a manuscript for the next issue may experience confusion because of lack of familiarity with copy editing procedures and conventions for the specific magazine.

Interpersonal Demands

Abrasive personalities, sexual harassment, and the *leadership style* in the organization are some of the interpersonal demands people face at work. The abrasive person may be an able and talented employee, but one who creates emotional waves that others at work must accommodate. Organizations are increasingly less tolerant of sexual harassment, a gender-related interpersonal demand that creates a stressful working environment both for the person being harassed and for others. Leadership styles in organizations, whether authoritarian or participative, create stress for different personality types. Employees who feel secure with firm, directive leadership may be anxious with an open, participative style. Those comfortable with participative leadership may feel restrained by a directive style.

Physical Demands

Extreme environments, strenuous activities, hazardous substances, and *global travel* create physical demands for people at work. Work environments that are very hot or very cold place differing physical demands on people and create unique risks. One cross-cultural study that examined the effects of national culture and ambient temperature on role stress concluded that ambient temperature does affect human well-being, leading to the term *sweat shop* for inhumane working conditions.[25] The strenuous job of a steelworker and the hazards associated with bomb disposal work are physically demanding in different ways. The unique physical demands of work are often occupation specific, such as the risk of gravitationally induced loss of consciousness for military pilots flying high-performance fighters or jet lag and loss of sleep for globe-trotting CEOs like Sir Richard Branson of Virgin Group Ltd.[26] The demands of business travel are increasingly recognized as sources of stress.[27] Office work has its physical hazards as well. Noisy, crowded offices can prove stressful for work. Working with a computer terminal can also be stressful, especially if the ergonomic fit between the person and machine is not correct. Eyestrain, neck stiffness, and arm and wrist problems can occur. Office designs that use partitions (cubicles) rather than full walls can create stress. These systems offer little privacy for the occupant and little protection from interruptions.

What is your level of stress at work? Diagnose your level and find out!

The following exercise gives you an opportunity to work within a group to compare the work demands and job stressors found in different work settings. Intervention for preventive stress management should always be based on a good diagnosis. This exercise gives you a start in this direction.

Step 1.

Rate the degree to which each of the following work demands is a source of stress for you and your co-workers at work. Use a 7-point rating scale for assigning the stressfulness of the work demand, with 7 = very high source of stress, 4 = moderate source of stress, and 1 = very little source of stress.

___ Uncertainty about various aspects of the work environment

___ Lack of control over people, events, or other aspects of work

___ Lack of career opportunities and progress

___ The implementation of new technologies

___ Work overload; that is, too much to do and not enough time

___ Conflicting expectations from one or more people at work

___ Confusing expectations from one or more people at work

___ Dangerous working conditions and/or hazardous substances

___ Sexual harassment by supervisors, co-workers, or others

___ Abrasive personalities and/or political conflicts

___ Rigid, insensitive, unresponsive supervisors or managers

Step 2.
Write a brief description of the most stressful event that has occurred in your work environment during the past 12-month period.

Step 3.
The class will form into groups of approximately six members each. Each group elects a spokesperson and then compares the information developed by each person in Steps 1 and 2 above. In the process of this comparison, answer the following questions:

a. What are the similarities between work environments in terms of their most stressful work demands?

b. What are the differences between work environments in terms of their most stressful work demands?

c. Are there similarities in the descriptions of the most stressful events? If so, what are they?

Step 4.
Each group will share the results of its answers to the questions in Step 3. Cross-team questions and discussion follow.

Step 5 (Optional).
Your instructor may ask you to choose one or another of the work environments in which to develop some preventive stress management strategies. Complete parts (a) and (b) below in your group.

a. Identify one to three preventive stress management strategies that you think are the best to use in the work environment. Why have you chosen them?

b. How should the effectiveness of these strategies be evaluated?

Nonwork Demands

Which one of these nonwork stresses has impacted you lately: moving, illness, new baby on the way, purchase of a new house, sick parent, day care, or financial issues? Nonwork demands create stress for people, which may carry over into the work environment, or vice versa.[28]

STRESS MANAGEMENT—A HOLISTIC OR TOXIC APPROACH?

Stress is an inevitable feature of work and personal life. It is neither inherently bad nor destructive. Stress can be managed but it takes both the employer and the employee to work together. Creating and sustaining a healthy work environment that minimizes stress takes work and dedication and a persuasive desire to continually explore those factors that contribute to workplace stress. Success will mean adopting a balanced approach to workplace wellness. Preventive stress management is an organizational philosophy about people and organizations taking joint responsibility for promoting health and preventing distress and strain. This philosophy approaches stress holistically, taking into account employee and employer factors. For example, three Canadian organizations that have been highly successful at adopting this approach are Decoma International, Canada Post, and MDS Nordion.

Decoma International designs, engineers, and manufactures automatic exterior components and systems for the global market. It is headquartered in Concord, Ontario, and has several plants across Canada. This organization has developed health-related programs that help employees manage stress in the workplace. Its goal is to create and sustain a healthy, stress-free environment. The driving force for these initiatives is the company's CEO, Alan Power, who believes that paying attention to employee health concerns contributes to the bottom line. Each plant has a health program designed according to employee needs. Employees receive a newsletter called "Good for You." This bimonthly health and wellness publication is filled with tips and stories about "employee heroes." Health education and awareness are developed through short monthly seminars offered on paid time on a variety of topics, such as nutrition, back care, and repetitive strain. There are screening clinics such as healthy heart seminars, blood pressure clinics, and discounts to a local gym, smoking cessation programs, and stretch breaks.[29]

At MDS Nordion, a health care organization that employees about 1000 workers from machinists to radio pharmacists, managing stress is about understanding all the components in the workplace that can contribute to stress. It is a comprehensive approach that has gained this company a reputation for having one of the most progressive health and wellness programs in the country. In addition to providing several heath-related and educational programs, MDS first and foremost works at understanding the things in the workplace or even in peoples' homes that cause stress in the workplace, and provides the support needed for its employees.[30]

At Canada Post, proactively managing stress is considered a major part of this company's workplace strategy. This organization defines a healthy workplace as "the quality of the working environment—one that fosters respect, support and dignity and they build this concept into their everyday management practices." Canada Post offers flexible benefits and employee assistance programs and surveys employees looking for input as to how the company can sustain a healthy workplace.[31]

An additional benefit that many of these organizations offer is in the form of work-life solutions. Typically organizations outsource these services to an employee assistance provider (EAP) that offers programs such as healthy lifestyles and lifecycle, and personal services such as nutritional counselling, smoking cessation, helping select a doctor or child care provider, psychological counselling, dealing with loss, illness, budgeting, and money management, career counselling, and legal advisory support. There are several different providers in Canada. To learn more about EAPs and the services they can provide, go to www.fgiworld.com or http://www.warrenshepell.com.

Not all organizations subscribe to this balanced approach. What are some of the toxic practices that companies engage in? In a recent speech by Bill Wilkerson, the Global Business and Economic Roundtable on Addiction and Mental Health co-founder and CEO indicated several practices in organizations that contribute significantly to stress, as shown in Exhibit OBX1.3.

EXHIBIT OBX1.3

Leading Sources of Problem Stress at Work

- Managers rejecting employee workload and deadline concerns
- Managers creating a treadmill effect in the allocation of work priorities
- Managers pushing unnecessary deadlines as force-feeding management techniques
- A general atmosphere whereby e-mail is the primary method of communication
- Managers changing priorities without notice or reason
- Managers tolerating a culture of ambiguity or confusion where job expectations are not understood, job definitions are constantly changing, and job outcomes are unclear

SOURCE: Bill Wilkerson (co-founder and CEO, Global Business and Economic Roundtable on Addiction and Mental Health), text of speech to the Canadian Pensions and Benefits Institute National Conference, May 31, 2004, Victoria, B.C. Reprinted with permission.

Factors That Organizations Must Consider When Managing Stress

The National Quality Institute, in conjunction with Health Canada, has identified several factors that organizations can subscribe to, so that they can proactively manage stress:[32]

- Leadership must demonstrate commitment to and reinforcement of a healthy workplace. This means creating and sustaining a culture that values employee well-being.
- Organizations must ensure that employees have opportunities to make healthy lifestyle choices, providing an array of programs and benefits that will be targeted to the specific needs of the workforce.
- Organizations must recognize that workplace health is both an employer and employee responsibility, fostering an environment where employees can get involved in healthy workplace activities.
- Organizations must recognize the impact that work processes can have on employees and provide employees with support to help them manage change and enhance skill development.

To learn more, go to www.nqi.ca.

Want to know more about what business leaders are doing to manage stress?

Formed in 1998, the Global Business and Economic Roundtable on Addiction and Mental Health consists of business, health, and education leaders who have undersigned the proposition that mental health is a business and economic issue. The Roundtable was inspired by the findings of the Harvard School of Public Health in its 1996 landmark study, "Global Burden of Disease," in which the growth of psychiatric illness as the leading source of human disability was vividly chronicled.

Learn more about what businesses are doing today to manage stress in the workplace. Go to www.mentalhealthroundtable.ca/.

THE IMPACT OF STRESS ON ORGANIZATIONAL EFFECTIVENESS

At the organizational level the cost of stress can fall into two categories: direct costs, such as loss of staff through absenteeism, tardiness, turnover, or stress-related illnesses and accidents; and indirect costs, such as low productivity, accidents resulting from lost concentration, low morale, and reduced motivation. In a recent "StressPulse" survey by ComPsych Corporation, results indicated that employee stress levels experienced an 18-point spike within the second half of 2004. Some outcomes of these stress levels are shown in Exhibit OBX1.4.

EXHIBIT OBX1.4

Costs of Stress

- *Decreased productivity:* Looking at the impact of stress upon daily productivity, 44 percent said they lose one hour or more per day in productivity due to stress, up 9 percent. Thirty-seven percent said they lose 15–30 minutes per day.
- *Increased benefit costs:* More that a third of disability insurance claims being recorded by Canada's largest insurers relate to mental health problems.
- *Increased absenteeism:* Forty-eight percent said they missed one to two days per year due to stress, and 33 percent said they missed three to six days per year due to stress.
- *Dissatisfied workforce:* To cope with stress, 59 percent said they take frequent stress breaks at work to talk to others.

SOURCES: M. Cox, "Employee Stress Levels Spiking Up," Human Resources Professional Association of Ontario, accessed October 27, 2004, from http://www.hrpao.org/HRPAO/KnowledgeCentre/newscluster2/Employee+Stress+Levels+Spike.htm; Bill Wilkerson (co-founder and CEO, Global Business and Economic Roundtable on Addiction and Mental Health), speech to the Royal Ottawa Hospital Business Luncheon, May 6, 2004, Ottawa, Ontario. Reprinted with permission.

A FINAL NOTE ABOUT STRESS

Living with stress is inevitable. As we have seen, stress can have a significant impact on organizational effectiveness and on our own personal lives. So what can we as employees do to personally manage stress? The Canadian Mental Health Association, a nationwide, voluntary organization that promotes the mental health of all, has listed several things you can consider.

The Top 12 Things You Can Do to Manage Life Stress

- Recognize symptoms of stress—consider how you exhibit stress and recognize that there are some things you can control and others you cannot.
- Look at your lifestyle and see what can be changed. What habits do you have that contribute to greater stress levels?
- Use relaxation techniques such as yoga, massage, deep breathing, meditation.
- Exercise—consider the type of exercise that helps prevent stress versus promotes stress.
- Manage your time.
- Get enough rest and sleep.
- Talk with others.
- Help others—consider volunteering, becoming a peer tutor, a coach. Revisit Organizational Reality 2.2 to see what volunteering can do for you.
- Get away for a while.
- Work off your anger.
- Don't try to be perfect.
- Have some fun.

SOURCE: Canadian Mental Health Association, *Coping with Stress,* http://www.cmha.ca/english/coping%5 Fwith%5Fstress/.

Emotional Intelligence

Did you know that ...

- Emotional intelligence (EI) is our ability to recognize and understand the impact that our emotions have on ourselves and on our relationships with others?[1]
- EI is not the same as intellectual intelligence (IQ)?
- EI can be measured? There is a significant correlation between a high EI score and job performance.[2]
- The older we get, the more emotionally intelligent we can become?[3]
- An individual's personality contributes to EI?
- We can learn how to become more emotionally intelligent?
- EI can significantly influence individual and organizational effectiveness?

THE ROLE OF EMOTIONS IN THE WORKPLACE

Have you ever had an experience where someone inappropriately expressed their emotions toward you because they had a hard day? Why is it that some individuals can control their emotions and others can't? Being able to recognize and understand our emotions and use this knowledge to manage ourselves and our relationships more effectively is called emotional intelligence (EI). Although there has been considerable discussion of the origins of the term EI, there is a consensus among researchers that the seminal publication was an article published by Peter Salovey and Jack Mayer in 1990. They described emotional intelligence as a form of social interaction that involves the ability to monitor one's own and others' feelings and emotions and to use this information to guide one's thinking and actions.[4]

Emotional intelligence has to do with knowing when and how to express emotions as well as understanding how to control them. It has to do with our abilities to deal with social and political environments, understand these environments, and grasp how best to handle situations in them. Emotional intelligence, referred to as emotional quotient or EQ especially in more recent works, enables us to grasp the needs and wants of others and respond accordingly.[5] For the purpose of simplicity and clarity of this text, emotional intelligence will be referred to as EI.

We all bring emotions into the workplace and we express these emotions in the workplace. But it is how we manage these emotions to work effectively with others that makes the difference as to whether our responses are appropriate or not.

Consider how you might react to this situation:

You enter a store and encounter a problem with the customer service. You ask to speak to the manager. After waiting for several minutes, the manager finally comes to greet you. He is very matter-of-fact in dealing with your concern and you get the feeling that you are an annoyance at best. When you try to tell the manager about your concern, to your surprise the manager shifts the conversation to himself and proceeds to tell you about his frustrating day: his inventories are not matching, there had been an incident with an employee and a customer, and he is stressed because of a daycare issue. You think to yourself that this behaviour is highly inappropriate, but you want to be polite. However, none of your concerns are being heard and you are not getting any satisfaction from this interchange! How do you respond? How do you deal with this manager? Do you show exasperation? Do you mask your feelings? How do you control your emotions?

Emotional Intelligence Skills

EI is made up of four unique skills: self-awareness, self-management, social awareness, and relationship management,[6] as illustrated in Exhibit OBX2.1.

Self-Awareness

Do you know how you will respond when faced with a certain situation? Ever think to yourself that your reaction was completely predicable and wished this wasn't so? Self-awareness refers to our ability to accurately perceive our emotions and to recognize a feeling as it happens. It is this ability to self-monitor that is important to understanding ourselves and gaining valuable insights into our emotions. This means keeping on top of how you tend to respond to specific situations and people.

EXHIBIT OBX2.1

Emotional Intelligence Skills

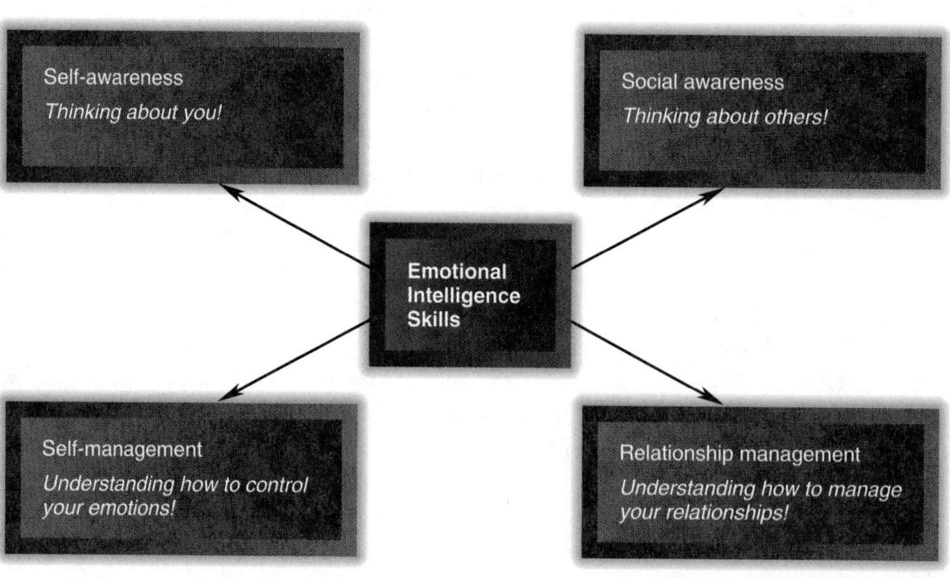

SOURCE: S. J. Stein and H. E. Book, *The EQ Edge: Emotional Intelligence and Your Success* (Toronto: Stoddart, 2000).

Self-Management

Can you control your emotions once you recognize how you are going to respond to a particular situation? Self-management refers to our ability to use awareness of our emotions to stay flexible and positively direct behaviour. This means managing how we react emotionally to all situations and people. It is about self-control and delaying gratification. Consider how you calm yourself down and reduce your own level of anxiety. What stops you from "letting go" and telling the people you work with what you really think? Or think about how you manage your response to stress. Think about the first time you made a presentation to your class or to your colleagues at work. Were you nervous? Was your heart beating and knees knocking? How did you manage this response? Were your colleagues able to see your emotions or were you effective at masking your reactions?

Social Awareness and Empathy

Ever walked into a store and, when you indicate that you are "just looking," the sales person continues to "hound" you? Social awareness refers to our ability to recognize emotions in others and understand what the other person is thinking and feeling. This means having empathy for others and showing concern. Teaching is an example of a profession where social awareness and empathy are important. Do you agree?

Relationship Management

Once you are aware of others' needs and emotions, how do you relate to these individuals? Relationship management refers to our ability to use this awareness to manage interactions in a positive way, for example, collaborating as opposed to demonstrating aggressiveness.[7]

Take a Mini Test of EI

There are many tools developed to assess EI and competence. Try this one.

When it comes to Emotional Intelligence, how savvy are you?

1. You are on an airplane that suddenly hits extremely bad turbulence and begins rocking from side to side. What do you do?

   ___ Continue to read your book or magazine, or watch the movie, trying to pay little attention to the turbulence.
   ___ Become vigilant for an emergency, carefully monitoring the stewardesses and reading the emergency instructions card.
   ___ A little of both a and b.
   ___ Not sure—never noticed.

2. You are in a meeting when a colleague takes credit for work that you have done. What do you do?

   ___ Immediately and publicly confront the colleague over the ownership of your work.
   ___ After the meeting, take the colleague aside and tell her that you would appreciate in the future that she credits you when speaking about your work.
   ___ Nothing; it's not a good idea to embarrass colleagues in public.
   ___ After the colleague speaks, publicly thank her for referencing your work and give the group more specific detail about what you were trying to accomplish.

3. You are a customer service representative and have just gotten an extremely angry client on the phone. What do you do?

   ___ Hang up. It doesn't pay to take abuse from anyone.
   ___ Listen to the client and rephrase what you gather he is feeling
   ___ Explain to the client that he is being unfair, that you are only trying to do your job, and you would appreciate it if he wouldn't get in the way of this.

___ Tell the client you understand how frustrating this must be for him, and offer a specific thing you can do to help him get his problem resolved.

4. You are a college student who had hoped to get an A in a course that was important for your future career aspirations. You have just found out you got a C– on the midterm. What do you do?

   ___ Sketch out a specific plan for ways to improve your grade and resolve to follow through.
   ___ Decide you do not have what it takes to make it in that career.
   ___ Tell yourself it really doesn't matter how much you do in the course; concentrate instead on other classes where your grades are higher.
   ___ Go see the professor and try to talk her into giving you a better grade.

5. You are a manager in an organization that is trying to encourage respect for racial and ethnic diversity. You overhear someone telling a racist joke. What do you do?

   ___ Ignore it—the best way to deal with these things is not to react.
   ___ Call the person into your office and explain that their behaviour is inappropriate and is grounds for disciplinary action if repeated.
   ___ Speak up on the spot, saying that such jokes are inappropriate and will not be tolerated in your organization.
   ___ Suggest to the person telling the joke that he or she go through a diversity training program.

6. You are an insurance salesman calling on prospective clients. You have left the last 15 clients empty-handed. What do you do?

   ___ Call it a day and go home early to miss rush-hour traffic.
   ___ Try something new in the next call, and keep plugging away.
   ___ List your strengths and weaknesses to identify what may be undermining your ability to sell.
   ___ Sharpen up your resume.

7. You are trying to calm down a colleague who has worked herself into a fury because the driver of another car has cut dangerously close in front of her. What do you do?

   ___ Tell her to forget about it—she's OK now and it is no big deal.
   ___ Put on one of her favourite tapes and try to distract her.
   ___ Join her in criticizing the other driver.
   ___ Tell her about a time something like this happened to you, and how angry you felt, until you saw the other driver was on the way to the hospital.

8. A discussion between you and your partner has escalated into a shouting match. You are both upset and in the heat of the argument start making personal attacks which neither of you really mean. What is the best thing to do?

   ___ Agree to take a 20-minute break before continuing the discussion.
   ___ Go silent, regardless of what your partner says.
   ___ Say you are sorry, and ask your partner to apologize too.
   ___ Stop for a moment, collect your thoughts, then restate your side of the case as precisely as possible.

9. You have been given the task of managing a team that has been unable to come up with a creative solution to a work problem. What is the first thing that you do?

   ___ Draw up an agenda, call a meeting, and allot a specific period of time to discuss each item.
   ___ Organize an off-site meeting aimed specifically at encouraging the team to get to know each other better.
   ___ Begin by asking each person individually for ideas about how to solve the problem.
   ___ Start out with a brainstorming session, encouraging each person to say whatever comes to mind, no matter how wild.

10. You have recently been assigned a young manager in your team and have noticed that he appears to be unable to make the simplest of decisions without seeking advice from you. What do you do?

   ___ Accept that he "does not have what it take to succeed around here" and find others in your team to take on his tasks.

___ Get an HR manager to talk to him about where he sees his future in the organization.
___ Purposely give him lots of complex decisions to make so that he will become more confident in the role.
___ Engineer an ongoing series of challenging but manageable experiences for him, and make yourself available to act as his mentor.

To score this test, go to http://ei.haygroup.com/resources/content_ieitest.html.

Note: The purpose of the above quiz is to provide you with an introduction to emotional intelligence. The results you get from this quiz are NOT a comprehensive picture of your EI and the quiz is NOT representative of Hay Group surveys. If you are interested in testing and developing your EI, you should contact us at 617-425-4500 for information on our Emotional Competence Inventory, a tool designed to be administered by accredited users only.

SOURCE: Emotional Intelligence Services. Reprinted with permission.

THE RELATIONSHIP OF EI TO IQ, EI TO PERSONALITY, EI TO AGE, EI TO EMPLOYEE PERFORMANCE, AND EI TO ORGANIZATIONAL EFFECTIVENESS

Over the past several years, the research conducted on EI has focused on five main areas: the relationship of emotional intelligence to intellectual intelligence (IQ), the relationship of EI to personality traits, the relationship of EI to age, the relationship of EI to employee performance in the workplace, and the relationship of EI to organizational effectiveness.

The Relationship of EI to Intelligence

Surprisingly, research has found little or no connection between EI and IQ. IQ is a measure of an individual's intellectual, analytical, logical, and rational abilities, whereas EI is more about how we manage in our interpersonal relationships. Think about how many people you know whom you would consider intellectually smart but who cannot deal effectively with others; they rub people the wrong way and act inappropriately around others. IQ scores tend to mildly decline in life, whereas EQ increases.[8] According to Daniel Goleman in his 1995 book *Emotional Intelligence: Why It Can Matter More Than IQ*, he states that "at best IQ contributes about 20% to the factors that determine life's success, which leaves 80% to other forces.... No one can yet say exactly how much of the variability from person to person in life's course it accounts for. What data does exist suggests it can be as powerful and at times more powerful than IQ."[9]

The Relationship of EI to Age

A study on EI conducted by Multi Health Systems Inc. on 3831 individuals in Canada and the U.S. found that the older one gets, the more emotionally intelligent one can become. All participants took a test called the Bar-On Emotional Quotient Inventory (BarON EQ-i). Results indicated that the total EQ score increased significantly with age, peaking in the late 40s and early 50s.[10] "People with high EQ scores enjoy success at work regardless of gender and ethnicity," note the authors.

The Relationship of EI to Personality

Personality can influence how EI takes form in any one person, but the connection is remote. Personality traits are fixed, whereas EI is made up of short-term, tactical, dynamic skills that can be brought into play as the situation warrants.[11] A recent incident regarding the behaviour of a Liberal MP serves to illustrate this point. A very outspoken MP inappropriately expressed her emotions to a group of people who were protesting against the U.S. missile defence program, calling the U.S. a "coalition of idiots," and, when asked by her boss, Prime Minister Paul Martin, to withdraw these controversial comments, the MP refused to retract her statement.[12] Do you think this is an appropriate emotional response from a Liberal MP? What types of personality traits do you think an MP should possess? Perhaps empathy and sensitivity to public issues come to mind.

The Relationship of EI to Employee Performance

There has been considerable evidence which suggests a strong link between emotional intelligence and job performance. People who understand their own emotions and know how to manage their emotions are more effective in their jobs.[13] Just think about how effective the customer service manager would have been had he managed his emotions differently in the scenario discussed earlier. Daniel Goleman in his research found that EI is the foundation upon which certain competencies and skills can be built. Individuals with higher EI tend to have higher performance than their low EI counterparts and those who work to improve their EI outperform colleagues of similar EI levels who do not make the same effort.[14] A study by Joseph Hee-Woo Jae at Ateneo de Manila University evaluated 100 bank employees using a popular EQ test called the BarOn EQ-I test, developed by Dr. Reuven Bar-On. The study found that EQ scores were far more related to actual on-the-job performance than IQ.[15]

The Relationship of EI to Organizational Effectiveness

A core trait of an effective leader is high emotional intelligence. In a study of CEOs in U.S. insurance companies, companies whose CEOs exhibited more EI competencies showed better financial results as measured by both profit and growth.[16] McClelland's 1998 study, which focused on the division heads of a global food and beverage company, indicated that the divisions of the leaders who demonstrated a critical mass of strengths in EI competencies outperformed yearly revenue targets by a margin of 15 to 20 percent. The divisions of the leaders weak in EI competencies underperformed by about the same margin.[17]

On an individual level, a key determinant of how successful individuals are in an organization is how well they can develop their social and personal competencies. The more well developed these competencies are, the greater the employee satisfaction and productivity at work.[18] The greater the satisfaction and productivity, the greater the contribution to the organization.

Next, let's turn our attention to how individuals can improve their EI.

HOW TO IMPROVE EMOTIONAL INTELLIGENCE—'DEVELOPING EMOTIONAL LITERACY'

According to Daniel Goleman, our emotional intelligence determines our potential for learning the practical skills that underlie the four EI clusters. Our emotional competence shows how much of that potential we have realized by learning and mastering skills and translating intelligence into on-the-job capabilities.[19] For example, your teacher may be highly empathic yet have poor skills in terms of handling student concerns. What can this teacher do to become more self-aware? How can we develop our "emotional literacy" to increase our social and emotional competence?[20] Consider adopting some of the suggestions below.

Self-Awareness

Think about a time you or a friend was faced with a panic situation? What was the response? Some people may react hysterically, others withdraw, while others may become assertive and take charge of the situation. To increase self-awareness, practise watching your own emotions. We are all different in terms of how we respond to emotionally charged situations. What happens to you? Do you feel numb, or does your mind go blank, or perhaps your thoughts speed up, or does your heart pump? Now that you know how you respond, think about how you can control your negative reactions. Individuals who are effective at being able to exercise greater control typically are aware of their strengths and weaknesses, realize the link between feeling, thinking, and action, and are highly reflective with respect to their experience.

Self-Management

Ever heard the saying "take a deep breath and count to 10"? To increase self-management, take some time each day to problem-solve and, when things get tough, pause, take a breath, and step back for a little while to gain perspective. Individuals who are more effective at managing their impulses exhibit a greater ability to be adaptable and flexible. How do you manage when the situation is not always straightforward?

Social Awareness and Empathy

Ever walk in another person's shoes? Visualize what this would feel like. To increase social awareness, take some extra time when you are around others to watch, ask and listen to others. Understanding where someone is coming from requires that we seek understanding by asking questions when we are not sure, by reflecting back what another person is feeling. To improve the accuracy of your perceptions check in with others to see if you are in sync. Go to Chapter 7 to learn about some communication techniques you can use.

Relationship Management

Getting along well with others is not always easy. When was the last time you felt that you were successful in this regard? To increase your skills in this area, think about the role emotions play when you are relating to others. Think about what worked well in the past and what didn't and use this knowledge to enrich your interactions. Developing skills in mediation, conflict resolution, and problem solving are some examples of important skills to develop, as illustrated in Exhibit OBX2.2.

EXHIBIT OBX2.2

Five Steps toward Emotional Literacy

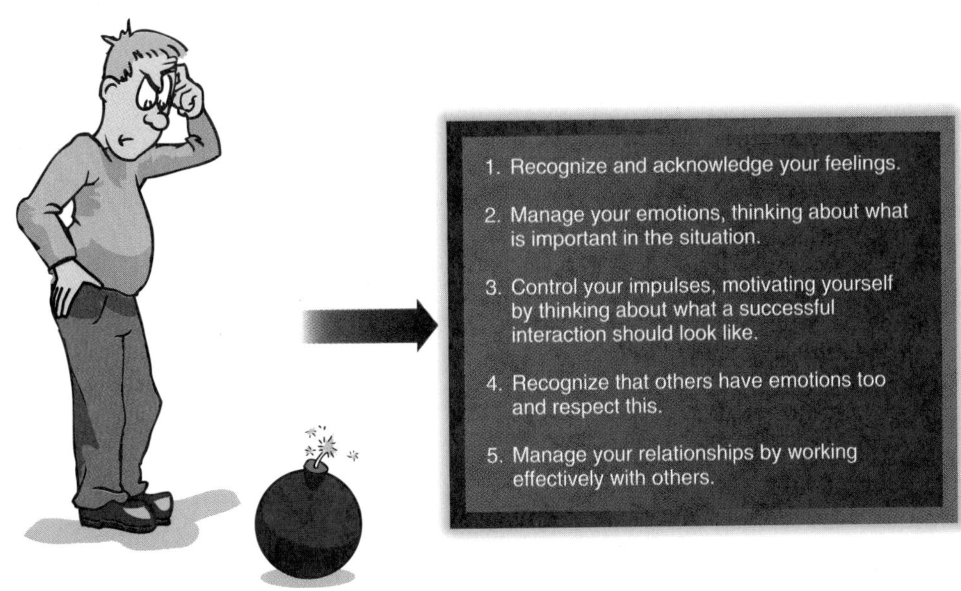

A FINAL NOTE ON EMOTIONAL INTELLIGENCE

We are all unique and we differ in our abilities to express ourselves from an emotional perspective. But if you work on these skills and competencies you will no doubt experience better interpersonal relationships, be more effective at working with others, and significantly enhance your contribution to your organization.

Want to learn more about emotional intelligence?

- The Consortium for Research on Emotional Intelligence in Organizations is an association dedicated to aiding the advancement of research and practice related to emotional intelligence in organizations. Go to www.eiconsortium.org to learn more.
- Visit the EQ directory. Go www.eq.org.
- The HAY Consulting Group has partnered with Daniel Goleman, author of the bestselling book *Emotional Intelligence: Why It Can Matter More Than IQ,* to provide world-class information, resources, and tools to enable individuals to improve personal effectiveness and organizational performance. Go to http://ei.haygroup.com/default.asp to learn more.

Behaviour Modification

Did you know that ...

- When the reinforcers of money, feedback, and social recognition are combined, performance improves by as much as 45 percent?[1]
- When 6000 adults were asked the question, "Can you think of a situation when it's OK for a husband to slap a wife in the face," almost half of those who had grown up being spanked three or more times a week said yes?[2]
- In one U.S. study of children's TV viewing behaviour, researchers were able to reduce average TV viewing time from 7.5 hours a day to 3.7 hours per day by using a simple token exchange system whereby TV-watching tokens were earned by engaging in a variety of school, play, or housework-related activities?[3]
- Cognitive behavioural therapy (CBT), which involves changing negative thought patterns into positive ones, has been used successfully to break cycles of sleeplessness? When an individual is trying to sleep and thinks "I won't be able to function tomorrow," he or she is taught to practise thinking instead, "I'm probably getting more sleep than I think."[4]

REINFORCEMENT STRATEGIES

B.F. Skinner's ground-breaking research in the early and mid-twentieth century is based on the principle that behaviour is largely a function of its consequences, which may be either positive or negative.[5] Skinner's work has come to be known as behaviour modification or reinforcement theory.

Behaviour modification has been used successfully in a variety of organizations to shape behaviour, and it is also considered to be a theory of motivation or learning, which is defined as any change in behaviour that is acquired through experience.[6] A major review of the research on the influence of behaviour modification in organizations found that it had significant and positive influences on task performance in both manufacturing and service organizations, but that the effects were most powerful in manufacturing organizations.[7] Other research has shown that incentive-based reinforcement improved performance more than routine pay, social recognition, or performance feedback.[8]

All reinforcement strategies rely on the use of positive and negative consequences following a specific behaviour that either reinforce or punish that behaviour.[9] Positive consequences are those that the person finds attractive or pleasurable. Negative consequences are those that the person finds unattractive or aversive. Thorndike's law of effect states that behaviours followed by positive consequences are more likely to recur and behaviours followed by negative consequences are less likely to recur.[10] Positive and negative consequences must be defined for the person receiving them, so individual, gender, and cultural differences are important to consider when selecting consequences or rewards.

There are four behaviour modification strategies that are used to influence or shape behaviour. These four strategies are positive reinforcement, negative reinforcement, punishment, and extinction, as shown in Exhibit OBX3.1.

Positive Reinforcement

Positive reinforcement is an attempt to increase or maintain the frequency of a desirable behaviour by following it with positive consequences. Awards given to students for contributions to student life are examples of positive reinforcement. The recognition letters sent out by WestJet mentioned in Chapter 4 are also examples of positive reinforcement. Positive reinforcement can take the form of money, feedback, and social recognition. Research indicates that when these positive reinforcers are combined, performance improved by as much as 45 percent.[11] Positive reinforcement is often used to modify undesirable behaviour in children, and research indicates that it is more effective and with fewer unintended results than the use of punishment.

Negative Reinforcement

Negative reinforcement is an attempt to increase or maintain the frequency of desirable behaviour by withholding expected negative consequences when a desirable behaviour occurs. For example, a teacher who criticizes a student (negative consequences) for arriving late to class (undesirable behaviour) and refrains from doing so when the employee is on time (desirable behaviour) has negatively reinforced the employee's on-time behaviour. The employee avoids the negative consequence (a critical remark) by exhibiting the desirable behaviour (being on time for class).

Punishment

Punishment is the attempt to eliminate or decrease the frequency of undesirable behaviour by either introducing negative consequences or withholding positive consequences. An example of punishing by introducing a negative consequence would be when a professional athlete who is excessively offensive to an official (undesirable behaviour) may be ejected from a game (negative consequence). Another way to punish a person is to withhold a positive consequence following an undesirable behaviour. For example, a teenager who breaks his or

EXHIBIT OBX3.1

Behaviour Modification Strategies

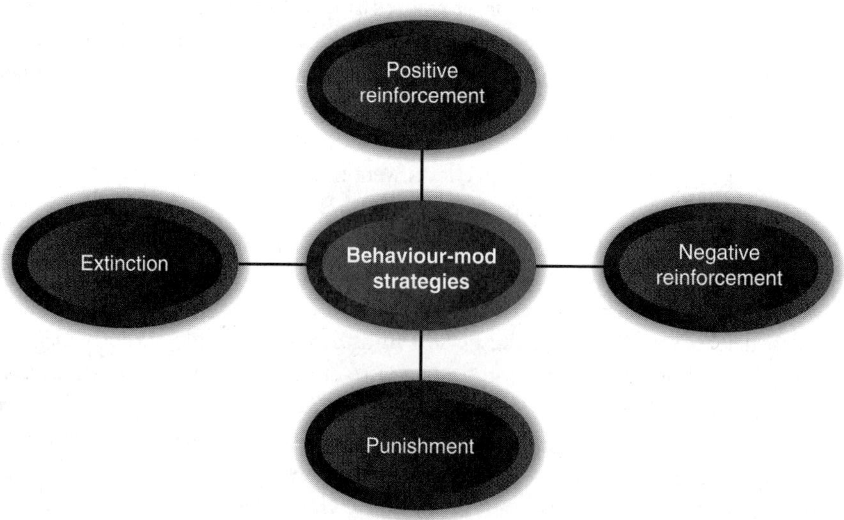

her curfew one week (undesirable behaviour) might be punished by having his or her access to the family car taken away (withhold positive consequence).

One problem with punishment is that it often has unintended results. Because punishment is discomfiting to the individual being punished, the experience of punishment, especially corporal punishment, may result in negative psychological, emotional, performance, or behavioural consequences. For example, the person being punished may become angry, hostile, depressed, or despondent. From an organizational standpoint, this result becomes important when the punished person translates negative emotional and psychological responses into negative actions. An extreme example of this is the following: In 1999 an OC Transport employee in Ottawa who had for years been the victim of harassment, finally responded by slapping one of his tormentors. He was reprimanded, suspended, threatened with dismissal, and sent to anger management class. All these were attempts at modifying his behaviour through punishment without getting at the real cause of the undesirable behaviour. Tragically, this employee reacted to the punishments by returning and killing four co-workers before taking his own life.[12]

In other examples, a General Motors employee who had been disciplined pulled an emergency cord and shut down an entire assembly line. A hardware store owner was killed by a man he had fired for poor performance. Work slowdowns, sabotage, and subversive behaviour are all unintended negative consequences of punishment.

Outside of work, studies have also demonstrated the negative effects of punishment, especially spanking children, in terms of the later development of conscience as well as attitudes to violence and conflict resolution. In a 2002 U.S. study in which 6000 adults were asked the question "Can you think of a situation when it's OK for a husband to slap a wife in the face," almost half of those who had grown up being spanked three or more times a week said "Yes."[13]

Is Spanking an Effective Punishment?

According to researchers at the University of Manitoba and Brock University, between 70 and 75 percent of parents use corporal punishment (spanking) to try to modify the behaviour of their children. Is it effective? When a group of 807 mothers of children aged six to nine were observed and the relationship between use of spanking as a punishment and resulting antisocial behaviour was measured, it was found that 44 percent of mothers reported spanking their children the previous week, an average of 2.1 times. On average, the more they spanked, the higher the level of antisocial behaviour in their children two years later. In other studies, findings suggested that children who were spanked were often more likely to become aggressive and delinquent teenagers and to commit more crimes as adults. They were more likely to hit their spouses, they had higher rates of depression, and their marriages were characterized by high levels of conflict.

While the negative emotional and psychological responses to punishment and especially corporal punishment are well documented, researchers also suggest that if spanking is used judiciously by parents who provide their reasons and are warm and highly involved with their children, it can work. Jalal Shamsie, a child psychiatrist who founded the Toronto-based Institute for the Study of Anti-Social Behaviour in Youth, argues that the key is to reward the good behaviour and punish the bad. "We know from research that rewards work much better than punishment." He suggests attention as the first reward and argues that the most effective type of punishment is to withhold a positive consequence like taking away TV time. When parents bring their children to see Shamsie, he insists on assessing the parents, too. "I'm a child psychiatrist but I work with adults. Every time I fail it's because I was unable to modify the behaviour of the parents."

SOURCE: S. Fine, "Is Corporal Punishment Effective?" Canadian Press Newswire, Toronto, January 13, 1999. Reprinted by permission of The Canadian Press.

Extinction

Extinction is an alternative to punishing undesirable behaviour. It is the attempt to eliminate or decrease the frequency of a behaviour by attaching *no* consequences to it, that is, by ignoring the behaviour. This strategy often requires a great amount of patience to be successful. The rationale for using extinction is that a behaviour not followed by any consequence is weakened. Extinction may be practised, for example, by not responding (no consequence) to the sarcasm (behaviour) of a colleague. Extinction may be most effective when used in conjunction with the positive reinforcement of desirable behaviours. Therefore, the best approach with the sarcastic colleague might be to compliment the colleague's constructive comments (reinforcing desirable behaviour) while ignoring sarcastic comments (extinguishing undesirable behaviour).

Extinction is not always the best strategy, however. In cases of dangerous behaviour, punishment might be preferable to deliver a swift, clear lesson. It might also be preferable in cases of seriously undesirable behaviour, such as employee embezzlement and other illegal or unethical behaviour.

REINFORCEMENT SCHEDULES

Reinforcement strategies can be applied according to a variety of schedules. Reinforcement can be applied after every response (continuous schedule) or intermittently and not after every response. Reward systems are chosen and designed according to one of the five possible schedules as shown in Exhibit OBX3.2. An example of continuous reinforcement would be giving a dog a cookie every time it sits on command. An example of a fixed ratio schedule would be giving an extra $25 in commission for every 10 suits sold. An example of a variable ratio would be a salesperson earning a big commission sometimes after 10 calls per day, sometimes after 25, and other times after only two. An example of a fixed interval schedule is a regular biweekly paycheque. Finally, an example of a variable interval schedule is a friend calling sometimes three times a day, sometime once a week, and at other times less than once a month. Which of these schedules creates the most motivation and the performance? Take a look at Exhibit OBX3.2 to find out.

POSITIVE SELF-TALK

Behaviour modification has also been applied to changing thought patterns. Albert Bandura pioneered the concept of *self-efficacy,* which refers to "an individual's conviction (or confidence) about his or her abilities to mobilize the motivation, cognitive resources, and courses of action needed to successfully execute a specific task within a given context."[14] Self-efficacy was initially part of Bandura's social learning theory, which was an alternative and complement to the behaviouristic approaches just discussed.[15] Bandura saw the power of social reinforcement, recognizing that financial and material rewards often occur following or in conjunction with the approval of others, whereas undesirable experiences often follow social disapproval. As Bandura said,

> Unless people believe that they can produce desired effects and forestall undesired ones by their actions, they have little incentive to act. Whatever other factors may operate as motivators, they are rooted in the core belief that one has the power to produce desired results.[16]

Individuals with high self-efficacy believe that they have the ability to get things done, that they are capable of putting forth the effort to accomplish the task, and that they can overcome any obstacles to their success. Employees with low task-specific self-efficacy quit trying prematurely and may even fail at a task. There is strong evidence that self-efficacy leads to high performance on a wide variety of physical and mental tasks.[17]

EXHIBIT OBX3.2

Schedules of Reinforcement

Schedule	Description	Effects on Responding
Continuous	Reinforcer follows every response	1. Steady high rate of performance as long as reinforcement follows every response 2. High frequency of reinforcement may lead to early satiation 3. Behaviour weakens rapidly (undergoes extinction) when reinforcers are withheld 4. Appropriate for newly emitted, unstable, low-frequency responses
Intermittent	Reinforcer does not follow every response	1. Capable of producing high frequencies of responding 2. Low frequency of reinforcement precludes early satiation 3. Appropriate for stable or high-frequency responses
Fixed Ratio	A fixed number of responses must be emitted before reinforcement occurs	1. A fixed ratio of 1:1 (reinforcement occurs after every response) is the same as a continuous schedule 2. Tends to produce a high rate of response that is vigorous and steady
Variable Ratio	A varying or random number of responses must be emitted before reinforcement occurs	Capable of producing a high rate of response that is vigorous, steady, and resistant to extinction
Fixed Interval	The first response after a specific period of time has elapsed is reinforced	Produces an uneven response pattern varying from a very slow, unenergetic response immediately following reinforcement to a very fast, vigorous response immediately preceding reinforcement
Variable Interval	The first response after varying or random periods of time have elapsed is reinforced	Tends to produce a high rate of response that is vigorous, steady, and resistant to extinction

SOURCE: Table from *Organizational Behavior Modification* by Fred Luthans and Robert Kreitner. Copyright © 1985, p. 58, by Scott Foresman and Company and the authors. Reprinted by permission of the authors.

Thus, self-efficacy and social reinforcement can be powerful influences over behaviour and performance at work. A comprehensive review of 114 studies found that self-efficacy is positively and strongly related to work performance, especially for tasks that are not too complex.[18] High self-efficacy has also led to success in breaking addictions, increasing pain tolerance, and recovering from illnesses. Conversely, success can enhance one's self-efficacy. For example, women who trained in physical self-defence increased their self-efficacy, both for specific defence skills and for coping in new situations.[19] There are four sources of task-specific self-efficacy according to Bandura: prior experiences, behaviour models (witnessing the success of others), persuasion from other people, and assessment of current physical and emotional capabilities.[20] As discussed in OBXtra4, managers can help employees to develop self-efficacy and self-esteem by providing job challenges, coaching and rewarding them for achievements, and by empowering them.[21]

A FINAL NOTE ON BEHAVIOUR MODIFICATION

Cognitive behavioural therapy, a relatively recent development that involves changing negative thought patterns into positive ones, has been used successfully to build self-efficacy as the first step in behaviour modification.[22] For example, in order to break the cycle of insomnia, individuals have learned to change the way they think about the situation so as to have more self-efficacy. Instead of thinking "I won't be able to function tomorrow," they are taught to practise thinking instead, "I'm probably getting more sleep than I think."[23]

Self-Managed Work Teams (SMWTs)

Did you know that ...

- At the Harley-Davidson Kansas City plant, there are no team leaders? Instead, consensus decisions are made by SMWTs known in the plant as "natural work groups," or NWGs. All financial and operations information is available to all team members, which allows them to monitor budgets and production quotas.[1]
- Nine out of 13 quasi-experimental studies found that people reported higher levels of job satisfaction in SMWTs than in more traditional work environments?[2]
- At Four Seasons Hotels and Resorts, guest services employees are empowered to do whatever is necessary to make guests happy—without consulting their superiors?[3]
- SMWTs at the Alcoa-Lauralco aluminum smelter plant in Deschambault, Quebec, helped reduce the frequency rate for work injuries by 50 percent in one year?[4]

WHAT ARE SMWTs?

Self-managed work teams (SMWTs), also called *self-directed teams* or *autonomous work groups,* are a unique kind of permanent team defined as a group of interdependent individuals that can self-regulate on relatively whole tasks.[5] Members of SMWTs have autonomy to carry out tasks and make decisions that were once reserved for managers. These decisions include work scheduling, job assignments, and staffing. The decision-making activities of self-managed work teams are more broadly focused than those of quality circles, discussed in Chapter 7, which usually emphasize quality and production problems. Self-managed teams are increasingly used by North American corporations. Many companies, such as Ford, GM, Harley-Davidson, Proctor & Gamble, Federal Express, Levi Strauss, Westinghouse, and Four Seasons Hotels and Resorts, have implemented them.[6] See Exhibit OBX4.1 for examples of responsibilities in a self-managed work team.

At Four Seasons, for example, guest services employees are empowered to do whatever is necessary to make guests happy—without consulting their superiors.[7] WestJet Airlines reported use of a SMWT to order and deliver the company's first direct-buy aircraft from the new Boeing 737-700 series. The SMWT was handpicked by team leader Steve Ogle, who explained that he chose the 13-member team "based on finding people who represented either their respective departments or related fields of expertise; ... a motley crew, to be sure, but a great one." The team created a detailed specification binder

EXHIBIT OBX4.1

Examples of an SMWT's Responsibilities

1. Safety of the workplace's layout
2. Accident and incident records
3. Monitoring work station modifications
4. Informing and training new team members
5. Training team members to safely carry out tasks
6. Training team members in the use of controlled products and the identification of dangerous and toxic materials

SOURCE: Adapted from S. Hirshorn, "Team-Work-Team," *OH & S Canada,* Don Mills ON, January/February 2005 (vol. 21, no. 1), 33.

of all the preferred options for the new aircraft, reviewed all the vendor proposals for parts that had to be purchased and sent to Boeing for installation, inspected the aircraft during the building process, and accepted the new aircraft and delivery documents.[8]

DO SMWTS WORK?

There have been contradictory findings in the OB research literature regarding whether SMWTs actually improve organizational effectiveness. Many evaluations of self-managed teams have been positive. For example, Alcan Company's aluminum smelter at Laterrière in the Saguenay region of Quebec divided their employees into 52 work teams of six workers each. The teams alternated between consecutive 12-hour day and night shifts. There were no supervisors and managers at night and on weekends. Throughout the plant it was up to workers to make decisions and find solutions to production problems that arose during those periods, which constituted more than 70 percent of production time. Only 6 percent of the workers indicated that the absence of supervision resulted in problems in the organization of their work. In general, the workers derived a great deal of satisfaction from the fact that their high degree of autonomy allowed them to make a significant contribution to the efficient production process. They were proud of their self-managed work teams and of their considerable autonomy from supervisors and managers. As one worker put it, "They have the plant for 8 hours; we've got it for 16."[9]

Southwest Industries, a high-technology aerospace manufacturing firm, embarked on a major internal reorganization in the early 1990s that included the creation of self-managed work teams to fit its high-technology production process. Southwest's approach resulted in a 30 percent increase in shipments, a 30 percent decrease in lead time, a 40 percent decrease in total inventory, a decrease in machinery downtime, and almost a one-third decrease in production costs.[10] Self-managed teams were also the foundation for the miraculous resurrection of the former Chrysler (now DaimlerChrysler) Corporation's oldest plant in New Castle, Indiana, as the United Auto Workers' union and company management forged a partnership for success.[11] An analysis of 70 studies concluded that self-managed teams positively affected productivity and attitudes toward self-management. However, the analysis indicated no significant effects of self-managed teams on job satisfaction, absenteeism, or turnover.[12]

In addition, the implementation of teams does not guarantee improved performance. One evaluation of SMWTs and TQM programs found that companies associated with these popular management techniques did *not* have higher economic performance.[13] A comprehensive Australian study that examined the benefits of quality circles (QCs) and SMWTs had the following findings: (1) Firms that used only QCs had higher levels of productivity than firms with no teams. (2) Firms with only SMWTs and those with SMWTs and QCs benefited from increased productivity, a reduced management hierarchy, and reduced employee turnover. (3) Apart from higher levels of productivity that occurred only within the first two years of implementing self-managing work teams, firms with these structures continued to improve upon the initial benefits of reduced employee turnover and a flatter hierarchy as their experience with the new structure increased. However, one disadvantages that was found was that (4) firms with either or both team structures were found to have less industrial harmony than firms with no teams at all, and there was no support for the hypothesized benefits of reduced absenteeism, improvements in product or service quality, and profitability.[14] The following description of a four-country study discusses the role of employee resistance behaviour in self-managed work teams, showing how resistance is influenced by cultural values and how it affects employee attitudes.

Resistance to Self-Managed Work Teams: A Four-Country Study

As international business competition has increased, multinational companies have used various practices to improve their competitiveness. One popular practice is self-managed work teams, which are used internationally. Employees differ in their responses to teams, teamwork, and especially self-managing teams. While some employees very much like such work arrangements, other employees resist self-managed work teams. One study examined the relationships among national culture, resistance to self-managed teams, and the employee attitudes of job satisfaction and organizational commitment. Two United States-based multinational companies with operations in four different countries (the U.S., Belgium, Finland, and the Philippines) participated in the study. Hofstede's framework for examining cultural differences (see Chapter 2) was used in the study along with two measures of resistance and the two measures of employee attitudes. The investigators found the same pattern of cultural value differences in North American, European, and Asian countries that have been found in other studies. They also found the same pattern of differences in employee attitudes of job satisfaction and organizational commitment found in other studies. What is new in this study is the finding that resistance behaviour accounts for some but not all of these differences in employee attitudes. Finally, they discovered that cultural values do influence employee resistance to self-managed work teams.

SOURCE: B. L. Kirkman and D. L. Shapiro, "The Impact of Cultural Values on Job Satisfaction and Organizational Commitment in Self-Managing Work Teams: The Mediating Role of Employee Resistance," *Academy of Management Journal* 44 (2001): 557–69.

WHAT DOES SMWT EFFECTIVENESS DEPEND ON?

A number of factors have been found to influence the degree to which self-managed work teams are effective. Successful SMWTs have the proper resources within their control, a wide range of skills and expertise among their members, and access to all the information they need to make good decisions on their own. At Harley-Davidson, all financial and operations information is made available to all team members. This allows them to monitor budgets and production quotas.[15]

Self-managed work teams are more likely to be successful in decentralized organizational structures and in organizations with established cultures of participative decision making. Also, the more formalized the organization's structure, the less likely that an SMWT will be effective.[16]

The effectiveness of an SMWT depends in large part upon the size of the team and the stability of membership. Also, the members' goal orientations, expertise, norms, and degree of self-efficacy have been found to influence effectiveness.[17] For example, individuals with learning-goal and performance-proving orientations are predicted to be more productive in SMWTs. Take the following quiz to assess your own goal orientation.

Would you do well in an SMWT? Take this quiz.

	Strongly Disagree						Strongly Agree
1. I am willing to select a challenging work assignment that I can learn a lot from.	1	2	3	4	5	6	7
2. I often look for opportunities to develop new skills and knowledge.	1	2	3	4	5	6	7
3. I enjoy challenging and difficult tasks at work where I'll learn new skills.	1	2	3	4	5	6	7
4. For me, development of my work ability is important enough to take risks.	1	2	3	4	5	6	7
5. I prefer to work in situations that require a high level of ability and talent.	1	2	3	4	5	6	7
6. I like to show that I can perform better than my co-workers.	1	2	3	4	5	6	7
7. I try to figure out what it takes to prove my ability to others at work.	1	2	3	4	5	6	7
8. I enjoy it when others at work are aware of how well I am doing.	1	2	3	4	5	6	7
9. I prefer to work on projects where I can prove my abilities to others.	1	2	3	4	5	6	7
10. I would avoid taking on a new task if there was a chance that I would appear rather incompetent to others.	1	2	3	4	5	6	7
11. Avoiding a show of low ability is more important to me than learning a new skill.	1	2	3	4	5	6	7
12. I'm concerned about taking on a task at work if my performance would reveal that I had low ability.	1	2	3	4	5	6	7
13. I prefer to avoid situations at work where I might perform poorly.	1	2	3	4	5	6	7

Interpretation:

- Items 1–5 measure your **learning goal orientation.** This is the degree to which you focus on developing your competence by acquiring new skills, mastering new situations, and learning from experience.
- Items 6–9 measure **performance (proving) goal orientation.** This is the degree to which you focus on demonstrating your competence and on gaining favourable judgments from others.
- Items 10–13 measure **performance (avoiding) goal orientation.** This is the degree to which you focus on avoiding negation of your competence and avoid negative judgments of others.

SOURCE: C. M. Carson, D. C. Mosley, and S. L. Boyer, "Goal Orientation and Supervisory Behaviors: Impacting SMWT Effectiveness," *Team Performance Management* 10, no. 7 (2004): 156, 162.

Employees who work in self-managed work teams "are only capable of being fully self-reliant when they feel securely attached to trusted others."[18] This has been called the paradox of self-reliance: managers face the paradox of how to support others who must rely mostly on themselves, without becoming controlling. Supervisors or managers who tend to be most effective in these roles exhibit a number of key characteristics and behaviours: They help the SMWTs address issues outside of their teams (boundary issues) and they focus more on the team processes rather than on the content of the work. In addition, because membership in an SMWT tends to be stressful and burnout is a common concern, effective supervisors help team members deal with anxiety.[19] Effective SMWT supervisors have also been found to encourage self-observation, self–goal setting, self-reinforcement, self-criticism, and task rehearsal.[20]

A FINAL NOTE ON SMWTs

While cohesion in self-managed work teams tends to lead to higher performance, SMWTs, like any cohesive group, can also fall victim to groupthink, which was discussed in Chapter 8.[21]

Managing in a Virtual World

Did you know that ...

- At IBM Canada, four-fifths of employees have the option of teleworking some of the time and a quarter are official teleworkers who spend 80 percent of their working hours outside the office?[1]
- "Swift trust" can emerge among virtual team members but such trust is fragile and may be hard to maintain, making it difficult for members to develop a real understanding of one another and to develop the third stage of trust, called identification-based trust?[2]
- Since 1991, AT&T has gained $550 million in cash flow from eliminating office space and reducing overhead costs?[3]
- Unethical leaders with limited resources can now impact more people in a negative way?[4]

Close your eyes and imagine this picture on the cover of a popular business magazine: An empty freeway leading to a deserted metropolis. The caption reads: "It's 8:45 a.m.—do you know where your employees are?"[5]

For many employers the virtual workplace, in which employees operate remotely from each other and from managers, is a reality now, and all indications are that it will become even more prevalent in the future. The Internet has radically changed the way organizations communicate and perform work anytime, anywhere, and with anyone. The concept involves work being where people are, rather than people moving to where the work is. Information technologies make connectivity, collaboration, and communication easy. Managing OB in a virtual world involves managing individual employees, teams, and whole organizations.

For example, BP has been employing this technique as far back as 1994. In 1995 the work on a North Sea drilling ship ground to a halt because of equipment failure. The workers on board could not ascertain the cause of the problem and were faced with the prospect of taking the ship back to port. This was not an appealing option because the leasing cost was $150 000 a day. Fortunately for the crew, they were participating in a BP pilot project called "virtual teamwork." All they had to do was show the faulty machinery to an onshore team expert through a video satellite link-up that had recently been installed on the ship. The expert was then able to diagnose the problem, enabling work to continue in a relatively short time and saving BP thousands of dollars.[6]

At IBM Canada, four-fifths of employees have the option of teleworking some of the time and a quarter are official teleworkers who spend 80 percent of their working hours outside the office.[7] IBM's effort in "follow-the-sun" development provides a vivid example of different ranges of "virtualness." Carmel describes the project, the purpose of which was to develop software components in locations that spanned five nations: The teams were a mix of IBM employees, joint venture firms, and other developers. The teams were first structured in a traditional centralized fashion, with a "hub and spoke" design that gave headquarters the responsibility for initiating, reviewing, and allocating tasks. But that structure created bottlenecks, and a decentralized network ultimately evolved, with each site doing its own initiation. Collaborative technologies such as a central repository, structured communication tools, and Lotus Notes provided the connections within and among these virtual teams. The example reminds us that people often work in traditional teams within their local sites at the same time that they work virtually through team membership at other levels and locations, adding to the complexity of working on both types of teams.[8]

MANAGING THE VIRTUAL EMPLOYEE

Telecommuting, also called "telework," is when an individual employee works from the home, a satellite office, or mobile office with a computer connection to the main office. According to the Canadian Telework Association (CTA), over 50 companies, including Xerox, IBM, the Alberta Government, HP Canada, and Sony Music Canada, permit telework.[9] While many individual teleworkers work from their homes, increasingly, companies are setting up satellite offices and hotelling arrangements at head offices, as described in Exhibit OBX5.1.

MANAGING THE VIRTUAL TEAM

The concept of virtual teaming has been around for more than 20 years, but with the upsurge of globalization and continuous technological developments, it has taken on a new impetus. A *virtual team* is a collection of individuals who are geographically and/or organizationally or otherwise dispersed, and who collaborate via communication and information technologies in order to accomplish a specific goal.[10] For example, a software development team may have members in Canada, the United States, India, Taiwan, and Brazil, and their only communication may be through the Internet, telephone, and video-conferencing technologies. Creating virtual teams is not simply about connecting a number of employees by e-mail and asking them to perform a task.

There are, in fact, a number of different types of virtual team arrangements, as shown in Exhibit OBX5.2. Teleworkers could be single managers of a team at one location, single managers of a team distributed across multiple locations, multiple managers of a team at one location, or multiple managers across multiple locations.

EXHIBIT OBX5.1

Alternative Work Arrangements

Hotelling	A shared-office arrangement. Employees have mobile file cabinets and lockers for personal storage, and "hotel" work spaces. These spaces must be reserved instead of being permanently assigned. The computer system routes phone calls and e-mail as necessary. Personal photos and memorabilia are stored electronically and "placed" on occupants' computer desktops upon arrival.
Satellite Offices	Large facilities are broken into a network of smaller workplaces that are located close to employees' homes. Satellites are often located in comparatively inexpensive cities and suburban areas. They usually have simpler and less costly furnishings and fixtures and can save a company as much as 50 percent in real estate costs.

SOURCE: M. Apgar, IV, "The Alternative Workplace: Changing Where and How People Work," *Harvard Business Review* (May–June 1998): 123–24. Reprinted by permission.

EXHIBIT OBX5.2

Virtual Team Arrangements

		Managers: One	Managers: Multiple
Locations	One	Teleworkers	Matrixed teleworkers
	Multiple	Remote team	Matrixed remote teams

SOURCE: W. Cascio and S. Shurygailo, "E-Leadership and Virtual Teams," *Organizational Dynamics* 31, no. 4 (January 2003): 362–76. Copyright © 2003, with permission from Elsevier.

The Canadian Telework Association provides national leadership for the promotion and development of telework, and telecommuting programs and initiatives across all of Canada. Visit http://www.ivc.ca/cta/index.htm.

Decision Making in the Virtual Workplace

Virtual teams seldom meet face to face, and membership often shifts according to the project at hand, so how are decisions made in virtual teams? These teams require advanced technologies for communication and decision making. Three basic technologies currently aid virtual teams in decision making: desktop videoconferencing systems (DVCS), group decision support systems (GDSS), and Internet/intranet systems.[11] Desktop videoconferencing systems are the major technologies that form the basis for other virtual team technologies.

DVCS re-create the face-to-face interactions of teams and go one step beyond by supporting more complex levels of communication among virtual team members. Small cameras on top of computer monitors provide video feeds, and voice transmissions are made possible through earpieces and microphones. High-speed data connections are used for communication. All team members can be connected, and outside experts can even be added. A local group can connect with up to 15 different individuals or groups. Users can simultaneously work on documents, analyze data, or map out ideas.

GDSS make real-time decision making possible in the virtual team. They are ideal systems for brainstorming, focus groups, and group decisions. By using support tools within the GDSS, users can turn off their individual identities and interact with anonymity, and can poll participants and assemble statistical information relevant to the decision being made. GDSS are thus the sophisticated software that makes collaboration possible in virtual teams.

Internal internets, or intranets, are adaptations of Internet technologies for use within a company. For virtual teams, the Internet and intranets can be rich communication and decision-making resources. These tools allow virtual teams to archive text, visual, audio, and data files for use in decision making. They permit virtual teams to inform other organization members about the team's progress and enable the team to monitor other projects within the organization.

By using DVCS, GDSS, and Internet/intranet technologies, virtual teams can capitalize on a rich communications environment for decision making. It is difficult, however, to duplicate the face-to-face environment. The effectiveness of a virtual team's decision making depends on its members' ability to use the tools that are available. Collaborative systems can enhance virtual teams' decision quality if they are used well.[12]

Andy Esparza, vice president of Human Resources/Operations at Dell Computer, says that using shared information between his virtual team members saves enormous amounts of time. His global team uses software called HR Direct, an intranet-based tool that allows him to stay connected with other managers on his team. Using shared data on compensation programs for Dell's 40 000 employees worldwide, the team is now able to create reports in 30 days for the senior executive team on tools and compensation program design such as base pay, stock options, bonuses, and profit sharing. The process used to take two months.[13]

Group Roles in Virtual Teams

In Chapter 7 you learned about the various task-oriented and maintenance-oriented roles that team members need to play. One research team in the early 1990s studied these *roles* in the new virtual environment. Ten virtual teams using TeamFocus software were studied. The software included such features as electronic brainstorming, topic commenting, voting, and ranking, with both private and group feedback and display screens. The teams in this study used the software for such varied activities as strategic planning, quality assessment, and vision development. A surprising result from this study was that over half the participants from all 10 teams felt that the software had filled the role of "recorder," and almost 40 percent viewed it as filling a "proceduralist" role. These roles are not surprising, given that the system kept a record of every comment, kept the agenda visible, and helped to structure the process. But beyond these obvious roles, the software was also perceived by many as a "gatekeeper" and by some as an "information/opinion seeker" and a "motivator." Team members also felt that the software had taken over some of the roles they expected to fill, at the same time that the sessions were rated very positively overall. This research suggests that the software itself substituted for leadership in these teams, at least to some extent.[14]

Building Trust in the Virtual Workplace

Trust building in virtual organizations presents unique challenges for managers and employees. So-called *swift* trust can emerge among virtual team members and can help facilitate sharing essential ideas and perspectives early on in the team's development. However, such trust is fragile and may be hard to maintain due to the primacy effect discussed in Chapter 3, making it difficult for members to develop a real understanding of one another and develop to the third stage of trust, called identification-based trust.[15] The different types of trust between team members is shown in Exhibit OBX5.3.

Researchers have discovered that there are three key ingredients to communicating trustworthiness and building trust in virtual organizations: First, the information and communication technology used in the virtual organization must have standardization, bandwidth, and reliability as well as features that communicate emotion. Second, there must be a common business understanding for those involved in the virtual organization, which is achieved through the sharing of values, vision, and organizational identity. Third, the development of trust is contingent on the establishment and recognition of high standards of business ethics.[16]

An empirical analysis of the development of trust in 29 global virtual teams that communicated strictly by e-mail over a six-week period found that teams with the

EXHIBIT OBX5.3

Types of Trust between Team Members

Calculus-based trust	Team members must trust fellow workers to behave consistently across different team situations.
Knowledge-based trust	Team members get to know each other well enough so that they can anticipate how they will behave. Develops from repeated interaction over a variety of situations.
Identification-based trust	Team members understand and share each others' values.

SOURCE: S. J. Zaccaro and P. Bader, "E-Leadership and the Challenges of Leading E-Teams: Minimizing the Bad and Maximizing the Good," *Organizational Dynamics* 31, no. 4 (January 2003): 377–87, with permission from Elsevier.

highest levels of trust tended to share three characteristics. First, they began their interactions with a series of social messages—introducing themselves and providing some personal background—before focusing on the work at hand. Second, they set clear roles for each team member, thus enabling all team members to identify with one another. Third, all team members demonstrated positive attitudes. Team members consistently displayed eagerness, enthusiasm, and an intense action orientation in all of their messages. There are two lessons for e-leaders from this research: first impressions are critical, and, especially in virtual work environments, initial messages need to be handled well. Just one pessimist in the group has the potential to undermine trust in the entire virtual team, and lack of trust affects overall group productivity. Not surprisingly, low-trust teams were less productive than high-trust ones.[17]

Guidelines for Managing Virtual Teams

- Employees must be available during certain core hours.
- Participating in phone meetings should be an acceptable norm.
- Each employee is accountable for regular communications.
- If employees are time-shifted, try to match them effectively to jobs that need attention when they are in the workplace. For example, the early bird is a good candidate for checking that an all-night process has been completed correctly, while the night owl might be a good candidate to start that process. It might not work out to match early bird and night owl on the same tasks.
- Team-building meetings and exercises are now more important; those occasions may be the only times some employees see each other.

SOURCE: Adapted from W. Cascio and S. Shurygailo, "E-Leadership and Virtual Teams," *Organizational Dynamics* 31, no. 4 (January 2003): 362–76. Copyright © 2003, with permission from Elsevier.

CHALLENGES OF MANAGING IN A VIRTUAL WORLD

Telecommuting has disadvantages and challenges. Misunderstandings can result from missing nonverbal cues that are so very important to effective communication. Teleworkers do not socialize with other workers, or interact face to face as much with their supervisors. Not everyone can handle the isolation from work colleagues.[18] Working with a computer can be stressful, both physically and psychologically, especially if employees are being monitored electronically.[19] Team members often find themselves overloaded with work because the technology makes them accessible 24 hours a day and the increased emphasis on speed creates added pressure. In addition, virtual teams face constant threats to security posed by hackers in the online environment. Familiar practices are still preferred by individual team members, creating a potential barrier to creativity from both technology and human perspectives. Technology barriers also exist, as team members in different parts of the globe experience different levels and consistency of access.[20]

ADVANTAGES OF MANAGING IN A VIRTUAL WORLD

By telecommuting, employees gain flexibility, save the commute to work, and enjoy the comforts of being at home. Studies show that telecommuters often report higher job satisfaction.[21] Companies encourage telecommuting because cost reductions are an obvious motivator. Since 1991, AT&T has gained $550 million in cash flow from eliminating office space and reducing overhead costs. Another reason is to increase productivity. At IBM, a survey of telecommuters indicated that 87 percent believed they were more productive in the alternative work arrangement. First, e-teams are less limited by geographic constraints placed on face-to-face teams, and therefore have greater potential to acquire the necessary "human capital" or skills, knowledge, and capacities to complete complicated projects. Once formed, e-teams can also be more flexible in how they respond to changing events, as team members can be rotated out of projects when demands and contingencies alter the team mission. Another unique feature of e-teams is their greater potential for generating "social capital," which refers to the quality of relationships and networks that leaders and team members form in their operating environment.[22]

A FINAL NOTE ON MANAGING IN A VIRTUAL WORLD: E-LEADERSHIP

E-leadership refers to conducting many of the processes of leadership largely though electronic channels.[23] Major issues that are having an impact on the trend toward e-leadership are as follows:

1. Leaders and followers have more access to information and to each other, which changes the nature of their interactions.
2. Leadership is migrating to lower levels as well as out through the traditional boundaries of the organization to customers, suppliers, and networks.
3. Followers may know more, earlier, which may affect the credibility of leaders.
4. Unethical leaders with limited resources can now impact more people in a negative way.
5. The amount of time and contact that a leader can have with followers is increased, even though it may not be face to face.[24]

Endnotes

Preface

1. Adapted from B. S. Bloom, ed., *Taxonomy of Educational Objectives: The Classification of Educational Goals: Handbook I, Cognitive Domain* (New York, Toronto: Longmans, Green, 1956).

Chapter 1

1. C. Heath and S. B. Sitkin, "Big-B versus Big-O: What Is Organizational about Organizational Behaviour?" *Journal of Organizational Behaviour* 22, no. 1 (February 2001): 9.
2. N. Schmitt, ed., "Industrial/Organizational," *Encyclopedia of Psychology* (Washington, D.C.: American Psychological Association, and New York: Oxford University Press, 2000); M. Warner, "Organizational Behaviour Revisited," *Human Relations* 47, no. 10 (1994): 1152.
3. Warner, "Organizational Behaviour Revisited," 1152.
4. N. Gross, W. Mason, and A. McEachen, *Explorations in Role Analysis: Studies of the School Superintendency Role* (New York: Wiley, 1958); J. S. Adams, A. Tashchian, and T. H. Stone. "Codes of Ethics as Signals for Ethical Behavior," *Journal of Business Ethics* 29 (2001): 199–211.
5. F. W. Taylor, *The Principles of Scientific Management* (New York: Norton, 1911).
6. E. A. Locke and G. P. Latham, *A Theory of Goal Setting and Task Performance* (Englewood Cliffs, N.J.: Prentice-Hall, 1990).
7. A. L. Wilkins and W. G. Ouchi, "Efficient Cultures: Exploring the Relationship between Culture and Organizational Performance," *Administrative Science Quarterly* 28 (1983): 468–81.
8. M. F. R. Kets de Vries and D. Miller, "Personality, Culture, and Organization," *Academy of Management Review* 11 (1986): 266–79; H. Schwartz, *Narcissistic Process and Corporate Decay: The Theory of the Organizational Ideal* (New York: NYU Press, 1990).
9. J. G. March and H. A. Simon, *Organizations* (New York: Wiley, 1958).
10. J. R. Schemerhorn Jr., *Management,* 7th ed. (New York, Wiley, 2000).
11. L. Karakowsky, *The Nature of Management and Organization* (Concord, ON: Captus Press, 2002), 43.
12. R. F. Stolz, "The Capital Idea," *Human Resource Executive* (February 2005): 28.
13. H. Mintzberg, *The Nature of Managerial Work* (New York: Harper & Row, 1973).
14. C. A. L. Pearson and S. R. Chatterjee, "Managerial Work Roles in Asia: An Empirical Study of Mintzberg's Role Formulation in Four Asian Countries," *Journal of Management Development* 22, no. 8 (2003): 694–707; C. A. L. Pearson, S. R. Chatterjee, and K. Okachi, "Managerial Role Perceptions in Japanese Organizations: An Empirical Study," *International Journal of Management* 20 (March 2003): 101–08.
15. J. P. Kotter, "What Effective General Managers Really Do," *Harvard Business Review* (March–April 1999): 148.
16. P.-L. Chang and W. Chen, "The Effect of Human Resource Management Practices on Firm Performance: Empirical Evidence from High-tech Firms in Taiwan," *International Journal of Management* 19 (December 2002): 622–31.
17. A. Charette, "Stop the Human Resources Leak: It's Costing You Money!" *Dental Practice Management* (Winter 2002): 18; Hewitt Associates, "Positive Perception of Leadership Key Ingredient to Being a Best Company, Says Hewitt Associates," Canada Newswire, December 27, 2002, 1.
18. J. Pfeffer and J. F. Veiga, "Putting People First for Organizational Success," *The Academy of Management Executive* 13, no. 2 (May 1999): 39; S. London, "No Time for Small Minds," *National Post,* October 6, 2003, FE08.
19. Watson Wyatt Worldwide, *Linking Human Capital Management to Business Value—A Worldwide View,* www.watsonwyatt.com/multinational/render2.asp?ID=11741; D. Dearlove, "Profits through People," *The Times* (London), October 28, 1999, 5.
20. J. Pfeffer, "Producing Sustainable Competitive Advantage through the Effective Management of People," *The Academy of Management Executive* 9 (February 1995): 56; J. Pfeffer, "Seven Practices of Successful Organizations," *California Management Review* 40 (Winter 1998): 96–125.
21. R. L. A. Sterba, "The Organization and Management of the Temple Corporations in Ancient Mesopotamia," *Academy of Management Review* 1 (1976): 16–26; S. P. Dorsey, *Early English Churches in America* (New York: Oxford University Press, 1952).
22. Sir I. Moncreiffe of That Ilk, *The Highland Clans: The Dynastic Origins, Chiefs, and Background of the Clans and of Some Other Families Connected to Highland History,* rev. ed. (New York: C.N. Potter, 1982); D. Shambaugh, "The Soldier and the State in China: The Political Work System in the People's Liberation Army," *Chinese Quarterly* 127 (1991): 527–68.
23. M. G. Trefry, "The Carrier Truck: An Exercise Exploring Organizations as opEn Systems," *Journal of Management Education* 26 (2002): 462.
24. R. L. Daft, *Organization Theory and Design,* 8th ed. (Mason, OH; South-Western, 2004), 136.
25. Ibid., 145.
26. T. G. Cummings and C. G. Worley, *Essentials of Organization Development and Change* (Mason, OH: South-Western, 2001), 52.
27. Harold Leavitt, "Applied Organizational Change in Industry: Structural, Technological, and Humanistic Approaches," in *Handbook of Organizations,* ed. J. G. March (Chicago: Rand McNally, 1965), 1145. Reprinted by permission of James G. March.
28. Cummings and Worley, *Essentials of Organization Development and Change,* 56.
29. F. J. Roethlisberger and W. J. Dickson, *Management and the Worker* (Cambridge, Mass.: Harvard University Press, 1939).
30. S. R. Maheshwari, "Formal Organisation and Informal Organization," *Employment News* (New Delhi), February 13–19, 1993, 1–2.
31. C. Wang and P. K. Ahmed, "Structure and Structural Dimensions for Knowledge-based Organizations," *Measuring Business Excellence* 7, no. 1 (2003): 51–62.
32. J. A. Oxman and B. D. Smith, "The Limits of Structural Change: Although Most Companies Obsess about It, the Structure of an Organization Is Increasingly Irrelevant to How Work Is Actually Done," *MIT Sloan Management Review* 45 (Fall 2003): 78.
33. M. Wheatley, *Leadership and the New Science* (San

Francisco: Berrett-Koehler, 1994), 52.
34. Ibid., 68.
35. Ibid., 56.
36. E. E. Olson and G. H. Eoyang, *Facilitating Organization Change: Lessons from Complexity Science* (San Francisco: Jossey Bass, 2001); S. Johnson, *Emergence: The Connected Lives of Ants, Brains, Cities, and Software* (New York: Touchstone, 2001).
37. H. H. Owen, *The Practice of Peace* (New York: Open Space Institute, 2003), 51.
38. D. P. Ashmos, D. Duchon, R. R. McDaniel, Jr., and J. W. Huonker, "What a Mess! Participation as a Simple Managerial Rule to 'Complexify' Organizations," *Journal of Management Studies* 39 (March 2002): 191.
39. Olson and Eoyang, *Facilitating Organization Change*, 11–14.
40. R. S. Fosler, W. Alonso, J. A. Meyer, and R. Kern, *Demographic Change and the American Future* (Pittsburgh, Pa.: University of Pittsburgh Press, 1990).
41. M. Choquette and Z. Ezekiel, *Is Canada Pulling up SOX? New Regulatory Proposals and Their Impact on Corporate Ethics Management in Canada,* The Conference Board of Canada, publication 618-04.
42. J. R. Schermerhorn, Jr., *Management,* 7th ed. (New York: Wiley, 2002), 221.
43. M. Schacter, "2003 National Governance Conference-Observations," *Executive Summary* (April 2003), Publication 421-03.
44. S. Stewart, "BMO to Split CEO, Chairman Roles," *The Globe and Mail,* February 25, 2004, B1.
45. U. Vu, "Top Firms See Advantage in Employee Satisfaction," *Canadian HR Reporter* 16 (January 2003): 1–3.
46. J. Snider, R. P. Hill, and D. Martin, "Corporate Social Responsibility in the 21st Century: A View from the World's Most Successful Firms," *Journal of Business Ethics* 48 (December 2003): 176.
47. Ibid.
48. "Corporate Social Responsibility: Why Now?" *Report on Business, The Globe and Mail,* March 2004, 45.
49. Ibid., 45, 46.
50. "Corporate Social Responsibility," *Management Today* (London), December 2003, 18.
51. J. S. Mill, *Utilitarianism, Liberty, and Representative Government* (London: Dent, 1910).
52. C. Fried, *Right and Wrong* (Cambridge, Mass.: Harvard University Press, 1978).
53. I. Kant, *Groundwork of the Metaphysics of Morals,* trans. H. J. Paton (New York: Harper & Row, 1964).
54. R. C. Solomon, "Corporate Roles, Personal Virtues: Aristotelean Approach to Business Ethics," *Business Ethics Quarterly* 2 (1992): 317–39; R.C. Solomon, *A Better Way to Think about Business: How Personal Integrity Leads to Corporate Success* (New York: Oxford University Press, 1999).
55. M. A. Hitt, R. E. Hoskisson, and J.S. Harrison, "Strategic Competitiveness in the 1990s: Challenges and Opportunities for U.S. Executives," *Academy of Management Executive* 5 (1991): 7–22.
56. M. K. Gowing, J. D. Kraft, and J. C. Quick, *The New Organizational Reality: Downsizing, Restructuring and Revitalization* (Washington, DC: American Psychological Association, 1998); T. Tang and R.M. Fuller, "Corporate Downsizing: What Managers Can Do to Lessen the Negative Effects of Layoffs," *SAM Advanced Management Journal,* 60 (1995): 12–15, 31.
57. B. Spindle, "Sinking in Sync—The Global Slowdown Surprises Economists and Many Companies," *The Wall Street Journal* (December 21, 2000): A1–10.
58. K. Sera, "Corporate Globalization: A New Trend," *Academy of Management Executive* 6 (1992): 89–96.
59. K. Ohmae, *Borderless World: Power and Strategies in the Interlinked Economy* (New York: Harper & Row, 1990).
60. C. A. Bartlett and S. Ghoshal, *Managing across Borders: The Transnational Solution* (Boston: Harvard Business School Press, 1989).
61. "Bombardier Inc.—SWOT Aalysis," Dow Jones and Reuters, February 2, 2004.
62. G. S. Day, "Creating a Superior Customer-Relating Capability," *MIT Sloan Management Review* 44 (Spring 2003): 77–83.
63. D. Ciampa, *Total Quality* (Reading, Mass.: Addison-Wesley, 1992).
64. T. J. Douglas and W. Q. Judge, Jr., "Total Quality Management Implementation and Competitive Advantage: The Role of Structural Control and Exploration," *Academy of Management Journal* 44 (2001): 158–69.
65. American Management Association, *Blueprints for Service Quality: The Federal Express Approach* (New York: American Management Association, 1991); P. R. Thomas, L. J. Gallace, and K. R. Martin, *Quality Alone Is Not Enough* (New York: American Management Association, 1992).
66. Xiaoyun Wang, "Harmony in Our Diverse Workplace," *National Post,* October 20, 2003, FE10.
67. T. Belford, "Canada's Lawyers Stake out Global Turf; Cultural Sensitivity and Relative Inexpensiveness Make Them Popular Internationally," *The Globe and Mail,* September 22, 2003, B16.
68. R. Loo, "A Structured Exercise for Stimulating Cross-Cultural Sensitivity," *Career Development International* 4 (1999): 321.
69. E. Brandt, "Global HR," *Personnel Journal* 70 (1991): 38–44.
70. M. Legault, "Caution: Mixed Generations at Work," *Canadian HR Reporter* 16 (December 1, 2003): 23.
71. K. Reynolds-Lewis, "Managers Face Generation Gap at Work: How They Handle It Will Determine a Company's Success," *National Post,* November 5, 2003, FP16.
72. Legault, "Caution: Mixed Generations at Work," 23.
73. D. Foot, "Canadian Education: Demographic Change and Future Challenge," *Education Canada* 41 (Spring 2001): 24; D. Foot and D. Stoffman, "The Toronto That Will Be," *Toronto Life,* January 2000, 84.
74. "Graying Canada Welcomes Immigrants," *Population Today* 30 (August/September 2002): 7–8.
75. Statistics Canada, "Labour Force Characteristics by Age and Sex, 2004," http://www.statcan.ca/english/Pgdb/labor20a.htm; Statistics Canada, *Women in Canada: Work Chapter Updates,* 2003, Catalogue no. 89F0133XIE, http://www.statcan.ca/english/freepub/89F0133XIE/89F0133XIE02001.pdf; Statistics Canada, "People Employed by Educational Attainment, 2004," http://www.statcan.ca/english/Pgdb/labor62.htm.
76. Statistics Canada, *Education in Canada, 2000,* 14.
77. Statistics Canada, "Average Earnings by Sex and Work Pattern," 2003, http://www.statcan.ca/english/Pgdb/labor01a.htm; Catalyst, *2003 Catalyst Census of Women Board of Directors of Canada,* February 19, 2004, www.catalystwomen.org/2004can_wbd.htm; E. Church, "Women Still Shut Out of Boardroom," *The Globe and Mail,* February 20, 2004, B3.
78. Statistics Canada, "Average Earnings by Sex and Work Pattern," 2003, 13; Statistics Canada, "A Profile of Disability in Canada," 2001, http://www.statcan.ca/english/freepub/89-577-XIE/pdf/89-577-XIE01001.pdf.
79. B. Wilkerson, "Business Case for Accessibility" (Queen's Printer of Ontario, 2001), 18, 21.
80. M. Ramsey, "Nearly Half of Vancouverites Born Outside Canada," *CanWest News,* September 29, 2003, 1; E. McIsaac, "Immigrants in Canadian Cities: Census 2001—What Do the Data Tell Us?" *Policy Options* (May 2003): 58–63; R. Mofina, "Immigrants Mostly Asian: Canada in Demographic Revolution," *The Gazette* (Montreal), July 3, 2003, A9.
81. J. Hobel, "Embrace Diversity or Be Left Behind," *Canadian HR Reporter* 16 (March 10, 2003): 4; Government of Canada,

Focus on Workplace Equity: 2003 Employment Equity Merit Awards, 6–7, http://www.hrsdc.gc.ca/en/lp/lo/lswe/we/merit_awards/2003/merit_awards_ENG_2003.pdf.

82. D. Yourk, "Census Gives First Count of Same-Sex Couples," *The Globe and Mail,* October 22, 2002, www.globeandmail.com; Statistics Canada, "2001 Census: Marital Status, Common-Law Status, Families, Dwellings and Households," *The Daily,* October 22, 2002, http://www.statcan.ca/Daily/English/021022/td021022.htm.
83. N. E. Day and P. Schoenrade, "Staying in the Closet versus Coming Out: Relationships between Communication about Sexual Orientation and Work Attitudes," *Personnel Psychology* 50 (1997): 147–63.
84. J. Hobel, "Embrace Diversity or Be Left Behind," *Canadian HR Reporter* 16 (March 10, 2003): 4; "Bank of Montreal Counters Myth with Fact," *Human Resource Management International Digest* 9, no. 7 (2001): 4–7; A. Eyring and B. A. Stead, "Shattering the Glass Ceiling: Some Successful Corporate Practices," *Journal of Business Ethics* 17 (1998): 245–51.
85. J. Ganz, *A Business Case for Diversity,* Ontario Ministry of Citizenship, www.equalopportunity.on.ca/eng_g/subject/index.asp?action=search_7&page_id=785&file_id=5859.
86. "Recognizing Commitment to Diversity," *Canadian HR Reporter* 16 (November 3, 2003): 12.
87. Government of Canada, *Employment Equity Merit Awards, 2001,* http://www.hrsdc.gc.ca/en/lp/lo/lswe/we/merit_awards/2001/index-we.shtml.
88. B. Marr, O. Gupta, S. Pike, and G. Roos, "Intellectual Capital and Knowledge Management Effectiveness," *Management Decision* 41 (2003): 771–81; K. Bell DeTienne, G. Dyer, C. Hoopes, and S. Harris, "Toward a Model of Effective Knowledge Management and Directions for Future Research," *Journal of Leadership and Organizational Studies* 10 (Spring 2004): 26.
89. K. Bell DeTienne, G. Dyer, C. Hoopes, and S. Harris, "Toward a Model of Effective Knowledge Management and Directions for Future Research," *Journal of Leadership and Organizational Studies* 10 (Spring 2004): 28.
90. H. Lin and G. Lee, "Perceptions of Senior Managers toward Knowledge-Sharing Behaviour," *Management Decision* 42 (2004): 110.
91. M. Hammer, D. Leonard, and T. Davenport, "Why Don't We Know More about Knowledge?" *MIT Sloan Management Review* 45 (Summer 2004): 13–18.
92. K. Bell DeTienne, G. Dyer, C. Hoopes, and S. Harris, "Toward a Model of Effective Knowledge Management and Directions for Future Research," 31.
93. G. M. Steyn, "Harnessing the Power of Knowledge in Higher Education," *Education* 24 (Summer 2004): 615.
94. M. H. Zack, "Rethinking the Knowledge-Based Organization," *MIT Sloan Management Review* 44, no. 4 (Summer 2003): 69.
95. E. C. Wenger and W. M. Snyder, "Communities of Practice: The Organizational Frontier," *Harvard Business Review* (January–February 2000): 139.
96. E. L. Lesser and J. Storck, "Communities of Practice and Organizational Performance," *IBM Systems Journal* 40 (2001): 831.
97. N. Eagle, "Can Serendipity Be Planned?" *MIT Sloan Management Review* 46 (Fall 2004): 9–14.

Chapter 2

1. J. Izzo and P. Withers, "Balance and Synergy: The Greatest Benefit? How Companies Are Responding to Changing Employee Values," *Compensation & Benefits Management* 17 (Summer 2001): 23–29.
2. Ibid.
3. Towers Perrin, "New Realities in Today's Workforce," *Towers Perrin Talent Report* (2002).
4. K. Macklem, "Top 100 Employers," *Maclean's,* October 20, 2003, 28.
5. Vital Enterprises, http://www.vitalentusa.com/services/services_main.php, accessed July 17, 2004.
6. R. Kanter, "Getting the Best from the Best," *Best Practice* (New York: Perseus Publishing, 2003); Vital Enterprises, "Services: Consulting," www.vitalentusa.com/services/services_main.php, accessed July 17, 2004.
7. T. Nolan, L. Goodstein, and J. W. Pfeiffer, *Plan or Die* (San Francisco: Pfeiffer and Company, 1993).
8. L. Gratton and S. Ghoshal, "Beyond Best Practice," *MIT Sloan Management Review* 46, no. 3 (Spring 2005): 49–57.
9. A. Bartel, R. Freeman, C. Ichniowski, and M. M. Kleiner, "Can a Work Organization Have an Attitude Problem? The Impact of Workplaces on Employee Attitudes and Economic Outcomes," National Bureau of Economic Research Working Paper No. 9987 (September 2003), http://www.nber.org/papers/W9987, accessed August 19, 2004.
10. "CEO's Talk," *Canadian HR Reporter* 15 (December 2002): 21–24.
11. A. Bartel et al., "Can a Work Organization Have an Attitude Problem?" NBER, http://www.nber.org/papers/W9987, accessed August 19, 2004.
12. R. H. Fazio and M. P. Zanna, "On the Predictive Validity of Attitudes: The Roles of Direct Experience and Confidence," *Journal of Personality* 46 (1978): 228–43.
13. A. Tversky and D. Kahneman, "Judgment under Uncertainty: Heuristics and Biases," in D. Kahneman, P. Slovic, and A. Tversky, eds., *Judgment under Uncertainty* (New York: Cambridge University Press, 1982), 3–20.
14. D. Rajecki, *Attitudes,* 2nd ed. (Sunderland, Mass.: Sinauer Associates, 1989).
15. B. T. Johnson and A. H. Eagly, "Effects of Involvement on Persuasion: A Meta-Analysis," *Psychological Bulletin* 106 (1989): 290–314.
16. K. G. DeBono and M. Snyder, "Acting on One's Attitudes: The Role of History of Choosing Situations," *Personality and Social Psychology Bulletin* 21 (1995): 629–36.
17. D. W. Organ and L. Andreas, "Personality, Satisfaction, and Organizational Citizenship Behaviour," *Journal of Social Behaviour* 135 (1995): 339.
18. Four Seasons Hotels and Resorts, "About Us," http://www.fourseasons.com/about_us/company_information/about_us_10.html, accessed August 24, 2004.
19. E. A. Locke, "The Nature and Causes of Job Satisfaction," in *Handbook of Industrial and Organizational Psychology,* M. Dunnette, ed., (Chicago: Rand McNally, 1976).
20. P. C. Smith, L. M. Kendall, and C. L. Hulin, *The Measurement of Satisfaction in Work and Retirement* (Skokie, Ill.: Rand McNally, 1969).
21. S. W. Lester, "Psychological Contracts in the 21st Century: What Employees Value Most and How Well Organizations Are Responding to These Expectations," *Human Resources Planning* 24, no. 1 (2001):10–21.
22. D. M. Rousseau, "Psychological Contracts in the Workplace: Understanding the Ties That Motivate," *Academy of Management Journal* 18, no. 1 (2004).
23. Ipsos, "What Makes Employees Stay and What Drives Them Away?" 2001, http://www.ipsos-na.com/news/pressrelease.cfm?id=1193, accessed August 20, 2004.
24. X. Huang and E. Van De Vliert, "Where Intrinsic Job Satisfaction Fails to Work: National Moderators of Intrinsic Motivation," *Journal of Organizational Behaviour* 24 (2003): 159.
25. A. Krishnan and R. Krishnan, "Organizational Variables and Job Satisfaction," *Psychological*

Research Journal 8 (1984): 1–11.

26. Galt Global Review, "World at Work," 2001, http://www.galtglobalreview.com/world/satisfied_workers.html, accessed August 21, 2004.
27. M. R. Testa, "Organizational Commitment, Job Satisfaction, and Effort in the Service Environment," *Journal of Psychology* 135, no. 2 (2001): 226–37.
28. R. T. Mowday, L. W. Porter, and R. M. Steers, *Employee–Organization Linkages: The Psychology of Commitment* (New York: Academic Press, 1982).
29. H. S. Becker, "Notes on the Concept of Commitment," *American Journal of Sociology* 66 (1960): 32–40.
30. J. P. Meyer, N. J. Allen, and C. A. Smith, "Commitment to Organizations and Occupations: Extension and Test of a Three-Component Model," *Journal of Applied Psychology* 78 (1993): 538–51.
31. J. P. Curry, D. S. Wakefield, J. L. Price, and C. W. Mueller, "On the Causal Ordering of Job Satisfaction and Organizational Commitment," *Academy of Management Journal* 29 (1986): 847–58.
32. S. E. Martin, "Staff Stay at Companies with Heart," *National Post* (August 16, 2004): FP10.
33. A. al-Meer, "Organizational Commitment: A Comparison of Westerners, Asians, and Saudis," *International Studies of Management and Organization* 19 (1989): 74–84.
34. F. Luthans, H. S. McCaul, and N. C. Dodd, "Organizational Commitment: A Comparison of American, Japanese, and Korean Employees," *Academy of Management Journal* 28 (1985): 213–19.
35. R. Eisenberger et al., "Reciprocation of Perceived Organizational Support," *Journal of Applied Psychology* 86 (2001): 42–51; J. E. Finegan, "The Impact of Person and Organizational Values on Organizational Commitment," *Journal of Occupational and Organizational Psychology* 73 (2000): 149–69.
36. W. H. Bommer, E. W. Miles, and S. L. Grover, "Does One Good Turn Deserve Another? Coworker Influences on Employee Citizenship," *Journal of Organizational Behavior* 24 (2003): 181.
37. Dofasco, "Dofasco in the Community," http://www.dofasco.ca/bins/content_page.asp?cid=339-410, accessed July 17, 2004.
38. J. Harris, "Employee Engagement: An Easy Investment with Large Returns," *Public Relations Tactics* 11 (2004): 13.
39. C. Howe, "Best Companies: Can You Make the Grade?" *HR Professional* (April/May 2003): 24–29.
40. Ibid.
41. L. A. Bettencourt, K. P. Gwinner, and M. L. Meuter, "A Comparison of Attitude, Personality, and Knowledge Predictors of Service-Oriented Organizational Citizenship Behaviors," *Journal of Applied Psychology* 86 (2001): 29–41.
42. D. W. Organ, *Organizational Citizenship Behavior: The Good Soldier Syndrome* (Lexington, Mass.: Lexington Books, 1988).
43. B. Macdonald, "After the Money, Show Me the Love," *The Canadian Manager* 28 (2003): 17.
44. T. Watson, "People Make Profit," *Advertising Age,* April 28, 2003, 24.
45. M. T. Iaffaldano and P. M. Muchinsky, "Job Satisfaction and Job Performance: A Meta-Analysis," *Psychological Bulletin* 97 (1985): 251–73.
46. E. Mellina, "Happy Doesn't Always Mean Productive," *Canadian HR Reporter* 16 (November 2003): 15.
47. W. H. Turnley and D. C. Feldman, "The Impact of Psychological Contract Violations on Exit, Voice, Loyalty and Neglect," *Human Relations* 52 (July 1999): 52–59.
48. J. Teresko, "Driving Employee Engagement," *Industry Week* 253 (September 2004): 74.
49. C. Garvey, "Connecting the Organization Pulse to the Bottom Line," *HR Magazine* 49 (June 2004): 70.
50. U. Vu, "Top Firms See Advantage in Employee Satisfaction," *Canadian HR Reporter* 16 (January 2003): 1–3.
51. D. J. Weiss, R. V. Davis, G. W. England, and L. H. Lofquist, *Manual for the Minnesota Satisfaction Questionnaire* (Minneapolis: Industrial Relations Center, University of Minnesota, 1967).
52. M. Rokeach, *The Nature of Human Values* (New York: Free Press, 1973).
53. J. M. George and G. R. Jones, "Experiencing Work: Values, Attitudes and Moods," *Human Relations* 50 (April 1997): 393–417.
54. M. Rokeach, *The Nature of Human Values.*
55. R. Konopaske and J. M. Ivancevich, *Global Management and Organizational Behavior* (New York: McGraw-Hill, 2004).
56. Statistics Canada, "Labour Force Characteristics by Age and Sex, 2004," http://www.statcan.ca/english/Pgdb/labor20a.htm; Statistics Canada, *Women in Canada: Work Chapter Updates,* Catalogue no. 89F0133XIE, http://www.statcan.ca/english/freepub/89F0133XIE/89F0133XIE02001.pdf.
57. Statistics Canada, "People Employed by Educational Attainment, 2004," http://www.statcan.ca/english/Pgdb/labor62.htm.
58. Statistics Canada, *Education in Canada, 2000,* 14.
59. Catalyst, *2003 Catalyst Census of Women Board of Directors of Canada* (February 19, 2004), www.catalyst-women.org/2004can_wbd.htm.
60. E. Church, "Women Still Shut Out of Boardroom," *Globe and Mail,* February 20, 2004, B3.
61. Statistics Canada, "Average Earnings by Sex and Work Pattern (All Earners)," 2005, http://www.statcan.ca/english/Pgdb/labor01a.htm, accessed May 20, 2005.
62. "Bank of Montreal Counters Myth with Fact," *Human Resource Management International Digest* 9, no. 7 (2001): 4–7.
63. G. Hofstede, "Cultural Constraints in Management Theories," *The Executive* 7 (February 1993): 81–95.
64. M. Javidan and R. J. House, "Cultural Acumen for the Global Manager: Lessons from Project GLOBE," *Organizational Dynamics* 29 (2001): 289–305; R. J. House, Paul J. Hanges, M. Javidan, P. W. Dorfman, and V. Gupta, *Culture, Leadership, and Organizations* (Thousand Oaks, CA: Sage Publications, 2004).
65. House et al., *Culture, Leadership, and Organizations.*
66. K. Hodgson, "Adapting Ethical Decisions to a Global Marketplace," *Management Review* 81 (1992): 53–57.
67. A. Dawson, "Stewart Unapologetic over Irving Trip," *Ottawa Citizen,* October 30, 2003, final edition, A3.
68. F. Navran, "Your Role in Shaping Ethics," *Executive Excellence* 9 (1992): 11–12.
69. K. Labich, "The New Crisis in Business Ethics," *Fortune,* April 20, 1992, 167–76.
70. E. A. Lind, J. Greenberg, K. S. Scott, and T. D. Welchans, "The Winding Road from Employee to Complainant: Situational and Psychological Determinants of Wrongful-Termination Claims," *Administrative Science Quarterly* 45 (2000): 557–90.
71. C. McLean, Nortel Comes Clean: Five Leave Board, a Review Fingers Dunn, *The Globe and Mail Report on Business,* January 12, 2005.
72. G. Flynn, "Make Employee Ethics Your Business," *Personnel Journal* (June 1995): 30–40.
73. J. O. Cherrington and D. J. Cherrington, "A Menu of Moral Issues: One Week in the Life of The Wall Street Journal," *Journal of Business Ethics* 11 (1992): 255–65.
74. K. R. Andrews, "Ethics in Practice," *Harvard Business Review* (September–October 1989): 99–104.
75. J. B. Rotter, "Generalized Expectancies for Internal versus External Control of Reinforcement," *Psychological Monographs* 80 (1966): 1–28.

76. N. Machiavelli, *The Prince,* trans. George Bull (Middlesex, England: Penguin Books, 1961).
77. L. Kohlberg, "Stage and Sequence: The Cognitive Developmental Approach to Socialization," in *Handbook of Socialization Theory and Research,* ed. D. A. Goslin (Chicago: Rand McNally, 1969), 347–480.
78. C. I. Malinowski and C. P. Smith, "Moral Reasoning and Moral Conduct: An Investigation Prompted by Kohlberg's Theory," *Journal of Personality and Social Psychology* 49 (1985): 1016–27.
79. M. Brabeck, "Ethical Characteristics of Whistleblowers," *Journal of Research in Personality* 18 (1984): 41–53.
80. W. Y. Penn and B. D. Collier, "Current Research in Moral Development as a Decision Support System," *Journal of Business Ethics* 4 (1985): 131–36.
81. A. Bhide and H. H. Stevens, "Why Be Honest if Honesty Doesn't Pay?" *Harvard Business Review* (September–October 1990): 121–29.
82. S. A. Goldman and J. Arbuthnot, "Teaching Medical Ethics: The Cognitive-Developmental Approach," *Journal of Medical Ethics* 5 (1979): 171–81.
83. R. Levering and M. Moskowitz, "The 100 Best Companies to Work For," *Fortune,* January 12, 2004, 56–78.
84. T. Watson, "People Make Profit," *Advertising Age,* April 28, 2003, 24.
85. Galt Global Review, "Engaging Your Employees Is a Must for Shareholder Value," Watson Wyatt, http://www.galtglobalreview.com/business/engage_employee.html, accessed August 21, 2004.

Chapter 3

1. M. E. P. Seligman, *Learned Optimism: How to Change Your Mind and Your Life* (New York: Pocket Books, 1998).
2. C. Cherniss, "Emotional Intelligence: What It Is and Why It Matters," eiconsortium.org, http://www.eiconsortium.org/research/what_is_emotional_intelligence.htm, accessed July 28, 2004.
3. Consulting Psychologists Press.
4. N. Adler, *International Dimensions of Organizational Behavior,* 2nd ed. (Boston: PWS-Kent, 1991).
5. L. R. Offerman and M. K. Gowing, "Personnel Selection in the Future: The Impact of Changing Demographics and the Nature of Work," in *Personnel Selection in Organizations,* ed. Schmitt, Borman & Associates (San Francisco: Jossey-Bass, 1993).
6. J. Park and M. R. Banaji, "Mood and Heuristics: The Influence of Happy and Sad States on Sensitivity and Bias in Stereotyping," *Journal of Personality and Social Psychology* 78 (2000): 1005–23.
7. M. W. Levine and J. M. Shefner, *Fundamentals of Sensation and Perception* (Reading, Mass.: Addison-Wesley, 1981).
8. J. E. Rehfeld, "What Working for a Japanese Company Taught Me," *Harvard Business Review* (November–December 1990): 167–76.
9. M. W. Morris and R.P. Larrick, "When One Cause Casts Doubt on Another: A Normative Analysis of Discounting in Causal Attribution," *Psychological Review* 102 (1995): 331–55.
10. G. B. Sechrist and C. Stangor, "Perceived Consensus Influences Intergroup Behavior and Stereotype Accessibility," *Journal of Personality and Psychology* 80 (2001): 645–54.
11. L. Copeland, "Learning to Manage a Multicultural Workforce," *Training* (May 1988): 48–56.
12. R. Konopaske and J. M. Ivancevich, *Global Management and Organizational Behavior* (New York: McGraw Irwin, 2004), 133.
13. E. Burnstein and Y. Schul, "The Information Basis of Social Judgments: Operations in Forming an Impression of Another Person," *Journal of Experimental Social Psychology* 18 (1982): 217–34.
14. R. L. Gross and S. E. Brodt, "How Assumptions of Consensus Undermine Decision Making," *MIT Sloan Management Review* 42 (Winter 2001): 86–94.
15. R. Rosenthal and L. Jacobson, *Pygmalion in the Classroom: Teacher Expectations and Pupils' Intellectual Development* (New York: Holt, Rinehart & Winston, 1968).
16. N. M. Kierein and M. A. Gold, "Pygmalion in Work Organizations: A Meta-Analysis," *Journal of Organizational Behavior* 21 (2000): 913–28.
17. D. Eden, "Pygmalion without Interpretation Contrast Effects: Whole Groups Gain from Raising Manager Expectations," *Journal of Applied Psychology* 75 (1990): 394–98.
18. F. Heider, *The Psychology of Interpersonal Relations* (New York: Wiley, 1958).
19. B. Weiner, "An Attributional Theory of Achievement Motivation and Emotion," *Psychological Review* (October 1985): 548–73.
20. P. D. Sweeney, K. Anderson, and S. Bailey, "Attributional Style in Depression: A Meta-Analytic Review," *Journal of Personality and Social Psychology* 51 (1986): 974–91.
21. P. Rosenthal, D. Guest, and R. Peccei, "Gender Differences in Managers' Causal Explanations for Their Work Performance," *Journal of Occupational and Organizational Psychology* 69 (1996): 145–51.
22. L. Ross, "The Intuitive Psychologist and His Shortcomings: Distortions in the Attribution Process," in *Advances in Experimental Social Psychology,* ed. L. Berkowitz (New York: Academic Press, 1977).
23. D. T. Miller and M. Ross, "Self-Serving Biases in the Attribution of Causality: Fact or Fiction?" *Psychological Bulletin* 82 (1975): 313–25.
24. J. R. Schermerhorn, Jr., "Team Development for High-Performance Management," *Training and Development Journal* 40 (1986): 38–41.
25. J. G. Miller, "Culture and the Development of Everyday Causal Explanation," *Journal of Personality and Social Psychology* 46 (1984): 961–78.
26. G. Si, S. Rethorst, and K. Willimczik, "Causal Attribution Perception in Sports Achievement: A Cross-Cultural Study on Attrigutional Concepts in Germany and China," *Journal of Cross-Cultural Psychology* 26 (1995): 537–53.
27. J. Silvester, "Spoken Attributions and Candidate Success in Graduate Recruitment Interviews," *Journal of Occupational and Organizational Psychology* 70 (1997): 61–71.
28. R. A. Giacolone and P. Rosenfeld, eds., *Impression Management in Organizations* (Hillside, N.J.: Erlbaum, 1990); J. Tedeschi and V. Melburg, "Impression Management and Influence in the Organization," in *Research in the Sociology of Organizations,* ed. S. Bacharach and E. Lawler (Greenwich, Conn.: JAI Press, 1984), 31–58.
29. A. Colella and A. Varma, "The Impact of Subordinate Disability on Leader-Member Exchange Relationships," *Academy of Management Journal* 44 (2001): 304–15.
30. D. C. Gilmore and G. R. Ferris, "The Effects of Applicant Impression Management Tactics on Interviewer Judgments," *Journal of Management* (December 1989): 557–64.
31. S. J. Wayne and R. C. Liden, "Effects of Impression Management on Performance Ratings: A Longitudinal Study," *Academy of Management Journal* 38 (1995): 232–60.
32. R. A. Baron, "Impression Management by Applicants during Employment Interviews: The 'Too Much of a Good Thing' Effect," in *The Employment Interview: Theory, Research, and Practice,* ed. R. W. Eder and G. R. Ferris (Newbury Park, Calif.: Sage Publications, 1989).
33. J. Fitzgerald, "Power Freaks are Few, but Not Too Far Away," *Chicago Tribune,* September 25, 2002, 2.

34. D. C. Funder, *The Personality Puzzle*, 2nd ed. (New York: Norton, 2001); M. R. Barrick and A. M. Ryan, *Personality and Work* (San Francisco: Jossey-Bass, 2003).
35. Barrick and Ryan, *Personality and Work*.
36. T. J. Bouchard, Jr., "Twins Reared Together and Apart: What They Tell Us about Human Diversity," in *Individuality and Determinism*, ed. S. W. Fox (New York: Plenum Press, 1984).
37. R. D. Arvey, T. J. Bouchard, Jr., N. L. Segal, and L. M. Abraham, "Job Satisfaction: Environmental and Genetic Components," *Journal of Applied Psychology* 74 (1989): 235–48.
38. Y. T. Lee, C. R. McCauley, and J. G. Draguns, *Personality and Person Perception across Cultures* (Mahwah, N.J.: Lawrence Erlbaum Associates, 1999).
39. Ibid.
40. G. Allport, *Pattern and Growth in Personality* (New York: Holt, 1961).
41. J. M. Digman, "Personality Structure: Emergence of a Five-Factor Model," *Annual Review of Psychology* 41 (1990): 417–40.
42. T. A. Judge, J. J. Martocchio, and C. J. Thoresen, "Five-Factor Model of Personality and Employee Absence," *Journal of Applied Psychology* 82 (1997): 745–55.
43. H. J. Bernardin, D. K. Cooke, and P. Villanova, "Conscientiousness and Agreeableness as Predictors of Rating Leniency," *Journal of Applied Psychology* 85 (2000): 232–34.
44. S. E. Seibert and M. L. Kraimer, "The Five-Factor Model of Personality and Career Success," *Journal of Vocational Behavior* 58 (2001): 1–21.
45. G. M. Hurtz and J. J. Donovan, "Personality and Job Performance: The Big Five Revisited," *Journal of Applied Psychology* 85 (2000): 869–79.
46. Lee et al., *Personality and Person Perception across Cultures.*
47. S. Freud, *An Outline of Psychoanalysis* (New York: Norton, 1949).
48. C. Rogers, *On Becoming a Person: A Therapist's View of Psychotherapy*, 2nd ed. (Boston: Houghton Mifflin, 1970).
49. D. D. Clark and R. Hoyle, "A Theoretical Solution to the Problem of Personality-Situation Interaction," *Personality and Individual Differences* 9 (1988): 133–38.
50. D. Byrne and L. J. Schulte, "Personality Dimensions as Predictors of Sexual Behavior," in *Annual Review of Sexual Research*, vol. 1, ed. J. Bancroft (Philadelphia: Society for the Scientific Study of Sex, 1990).
51. J. B. Rotter, "Generalized Expectancies for Internal vs. External Control of Reinforcement," *Psychological Monographs* 80, whole no. 609 (1966).
52. T. A. Judge and J. E. Bono, "Relationship of Core Self-Evaluations Traits—Self-Esteem, Generalized Self-Efficacy, Locus of Control, and Emotional Stability—with Job Satisfaction and Job Performance: A Meta-Analysis," *Journal of Applied Psychology* 86 (2001): 80–92.
53. S. S. K. Lam and J. Shaubroeck, "The Role of Locus of Control in Reactions to Being Promoted and to Being Passed Over: A Quasi Experiment," *Academy of Management Journal* 43 (2000): 66–78.
54. A. Bandura, *Self-Efficacy: The Exercise of Control* (San Francisco: Freeman, 1997).
55. J. Shaubroeck, J. R. Jones, and J. L. Xie, "Individual Differences in Utilizing Control to Cope with Job Demands: Effects on Susceptibility to Infectious Diseases," *Journal of Applied Psychology* 86 (2001): 265–78.
56. B. W. Pelham and W. B. Swann, Jr., "From Self-Conceptions to Self-Worth: On the Sources and Structures of Global Self-Esteem," *Journal of Personality and Social Psychology* 57 (1989): 672–80.
57. A. H. Baumgardner, C. M. Kaufman, and P. E. Levy, "Regulating Affect Interpersonally: When Low Esteem Leads to Greater Enhancement," *Journal of Personality and Social Psychology* 56 (1989): 907–21.
58. J. Schmiel, T. Pyszcznski, J. Arndt, and J. Greenberg, "Being Accepted for Who We Are: Evidence that Social Validation of the Intrinsic Self Reduces General Defensiveness," *Journal of Personality and Social Psychology* 80 (2001): 35–52.
59. P. Tharenou and P. Harker, "Moderating Influences of Self-Esteem on Relationships between Job Complexity, Performance, and Satisfaction," *Journal of Applied Psychology* 69 (1984): 623–32.
60. R. A. Ellis and M. S. Taylor, "Role of Self-Esteem within the Job Search Process," *Journal of Applied Psychology* 68 (1983): 632–40.
61. J. Brockner and T. Hess, "Self-Esteem and Task Performance in Quality Circles," *Academy of Management Journal* 29 (1986): 617–23.
62. B. R. Schlenker, M. F. Weingold, and J. R. Hallam, "Self-Serving Attributions in Social Context: Effects of Self-Esteem and Social Pressure," *Journal of Personality and Social Psychology* 57 (1990): 855–63.
63. M. K. Duffy, J. D. Shaw, and E. M. Stark, "Performance and Satisfaction in Conflicted Interdependent Groups: When and How Does Self-Esteem Make a Difference?" *Academy of Management Journal* 43 (2000): 772–82.
64. T. Mussweiler, S. Gabriel, and G. V. Bodenhausen, "Shifting Social Identities as a Strategy for Deflecting Threatening Social Comparisons," *Journal of Personality and Social Psychology* 79 (2000): 398–409.
65. M. Snyder and S. Gangestad, "On the Nature of Self-Monitoring: Matters of Assessment, Matters of Validity," *Journal of Personality and Social Psychology* 51 (1986): 123–39.
66. A. Mehra, M. Kilduff, and D. J. Brass, "The Social Networks of High and Low Self-Monitors: Implications for Workplace Performance," *Administrative Science Quarterly* 46 (2001): 121–46.
67. W. H. Turnley and M. C. Bolino, "Achieving Desired Images While Avoiding Undesired Images: Exploring the Role of Self-Monitoring in Impression Management," *Journal of Applied Psychology* 86 (2001): 351–60.
68. M. Kilduff and D. V. Day, "Do Chameleons Get Ahead? The Effects of Self-Monitoring on Managerial Careers," *Academy of Management Journal* 37 (1994): 1047–60.
69. A. H. Church, "Managerial Self-Awareness in High-Performing Individuals in Organizations," *Journal of Applied Psychology* 82 (1997): 281–92.
70. A. M. Isen and R. A. Baron, "Positive Affect and Organizational Behavior," in *Research in Organizational Behavior*, vol. 12, ed. B. M. Staw and L. L. Cummings (Greenwich, Conn.: JAI Press, 1990).
71. D. Watson and L. A. Clark, "Negative Affectivity: The Disposition to Experience Aversive Emotional States," *Psychological Bulletin* 96 (1984): 465–90.
72. R. A. Baron, "Interviewer's Moods and Reactions to Job Applicants: The Influence of Affective States on Applied Social Judgements," *Journal of Applied Social Psychology* 16 (1987): 16–28.
73. J. M. George, "Mood and Absence," *Journal of Applied Psychology* 74 (1989): 287–324.
74. M. J. Burke, A. P. Brief, and J. M. George, "The Role of Negative Affectivity in Understanding Relations between Self-Reports of Stressors and Strains: A Comment on the Applied Psychology Literature," *Journal of Applied Psychology* 78 (1993): 402–12.
75. S. Barsade, A. Ward, J. Turner, and J. Sonnenfeld, "To Your Heart's Content: A Model of Affective Diversity in Top Management Teams," *Administrative Science Quarterly* 45 (2000): 802–36.
76. H. Rorschach, *Psychodiagnostics* (Bern: Hans Huber, 1921).
77. C. G. Jung, *Psychological Types* (New York: Harcourt & Brace, 1923).

78. Consulting Psychologists Press.
79. R. Benfari and J. Knox, *Understanding Your Management Style* (Lexington, Mass.: Lexington Books, 1991).
80. O. Kroeger and J.M. Thuesen, *Type Talk* (New York: Delacorte Press, 1988).
81. S. Hirsch and J. Kummerow, *Life Types* (New York: Warner Books, 1989).
82. I. B. Myers and M.H. McCaulley, *Manual: A Guide to the Development and Use of the Myers-Briggs Type Indicator* (Palo Alto, Calif.: Consulting Psychologists Press, 1990).
83. C. Walck, "Training for Participative Management: Implications for Psychological Type," *Journal of Psychological Type* 21 (1991): 3–12.
84. C. O. Longenecker, J. L. Simonetti, and T. W. Sharkey, "Why Organizations Fail: The View from the Front-Line," *Management Decision* (1999): 503.
85. C. Cherniss, "Emotional Intelligence: What It Is and Why It Matters" (paper presented at the Annual Meeting of the Society for Industrial and Organizational Psychology, New Orleans, LA, April 15, 2000), eiconsortium.org, http://www.eiconsortium.org/research/what_is_emotional_intelligence.htm.

Chapter 4

1. M. Troy, "Motivating Your Workforce: A Home Depot Case Study," *Discount Store News,* June 10, 2002, 30.
2. Ibid.
3. Home Depot, "Living Our Values," www.recruitingsite.com/corpfiles/homedepot/livingourvalues.htm.
4. G. Crone, "Home Schooling: Before They Sell Their First Can of Paint, Home Depot Wants Its 'Associates' to Spend a Lot of Time at Its Harvard of Hardware," *Financial Post,* January 31, 2000, C01.
5. C. C. Pinder, *Work Motivation in Organizational Behaviour* (Upper Saddle River, N.J.: Prentice Hall, 1998).
6. K.W. Thomas, "Intrinsic Motivation and How It Works," *Training* 99 (October 2000): 130–35.
7. V. Galt, "Poll Finds Low Staff Morale," *The Globe and Mail,* November 12, 2001, M1.
8. P. Wilson, "The Human Investment: What's Your ROI on People?" *CMA Management* 75 (October 1, 2001): 27–29.
9. "The 50 Best Companies to Work for in Canada," *The Globe and Mail Report on Business,* January 2003.
10. A. William and S. Lankford, "Evaluating Esprit de Corps," *Parks and Recreation* 38 (January 2003): 20–27.
11. Manitoba Lotteries Corporation, Performance and Development Program, 2003
12. J. P. Campbell and R. D. Pritchard, "Motivation Theory in Industrial and Organizational Psychology," in *Handbook of Industrial and Organizational Psychology,* ed. M. D. Dunnette, (Chicago: Rand McNally, 1976), 63–130.
13. A. H. Maslow, "A Theory of Human Motivation," *Psychological Review* 50 (1943): 370–96.
14. E. E. Lawler, III, and J. L. Suttle, "A Causal Correlational Test of the Need Hierarchy Concept," *Organizational Behavior and Human Performance* 7 (1973): 265–87.
15. W. Immen, "Part-Timers Need Support," *The Globe and Mail,* October 17, 2003, C1.
16. "For the First Time, IT Professionals Rate Job Security More Important Than Pay," *Canada Newswire,* April 2, 2003.
17. J. Katzenbach, "Pride Gets the Job Done Right," *The Globe and Mail,* April 2, 2003, C1.
18. K. Harding, "Firms Offer a Hand Up the Ladder," *The Globe and Mail,* February 5, 2003, C3.
19. J. F. Tanner, "Motivations of Salespeople Differ by Country," *Asia Pulse,* September 8, 2003.
20. C. Lachnit, "Brave Old World," *Workforce* 82 (March 2003): 8–11.
21. M. Skapinker, "I'll Have to Keep This Short, the Boss Is Watching," *Financial Times,* London (UK), June 25, 2003, 12.
22. D. M. McGregor, *The Human Side of Enterprise* (New York: McGraw-Hill, 1960).
23. D. E. Petersen and J. Hillkirk, *A Better Idea: Redefining the Way Americans Work* (Boston: Houghton Mifflin, 1991).
24. C. P. Alderfer, *Human Needs in Organizational Settings* (New York: Free Press, 1972).
25. D. C. McClelland, "Achievement Motivation Can Be Learned," *Harvard Business Review* 43 (1965): 6–24.
26. "An Entrepreneur Can Be Made as Well as Born," *Irish Times,* July 6, 2001, 53.
27. D. C. McClelland and D. Burnham, "Power Is the Great Motivator," *Harvard Business Review* 54 (1976): 100–111; J. Hall and J. Hawker, *Power Management Inventory* (The Woodlands, Tex.: Teleometrics International, 1988).
28. McClelland and Burnham, "Power Is the Great Motivator."
29. F. Luthans, "Successful versus Effective Real Managers," *Academy of Management Executive* 2 (1988): 127–31.
30. S. Schachter, *The Psychology of Affiliation* (Stanford, Calif.: Stanford University Press, 1959).
31. T. Goulet, "Born Leader Inspires the Best from Staff," *StarPhoenix,* Saskatoon, February 3, 2001, F20.
32. F. Herzberg, B. Mausner, and B. Snyderman, *The Motivation to Work* (New York: Wiley, 1959).
33. F. Herzberg, *Work and the Nature of Man* (Cleveland: World, 1966).
34. "CEO's Talk," *Canadian HR Reporter* 15 (December 16, 2002): 21.
35. V. H. Vroom, *Work and Motivation* (New York: Wiley, 1964/1970).
36. W. Van Eerde and H. Thierry, "Vroom's Expectancy Models and Work-Related Criteria: A Meta Analysis," *Journal of Applied Psychology* 81 (1996): 576.
37. S. B. Schepman and L. Richmond, "Employee Expectations and Motivation: An Application from the 'Learned Helplessness' Paradigm," *Journal of American Academy of Business* 3 (September 2003): 405.
38. D. R. Hancock, "Effects of Test Anxiety and Evaluative Threat on Students Achievement and Motivation," *Journal of Educational Research* 94 (May/June 2001): 284–91; R. J. Sanchez, D. M. Truxillo, and T. N. Bauer, "Development and Examination of an Expectancy-Based Measure of Test-Taking Motivation," *Journal of Applied Psychology* 85 (2000): 739–50.
39. "Keeping Top Talent Motivated in a Tough Year," *Canada Newswire,* January 23, 2002.
40. M. C. Kernan and R. G. Lord, "Effects of Valence, Expectancies, and Goal-Performance Discrepancies in Single and Multiple Goal Environments," *Journal of Applied Psychology* 75 (1990): 194–203.
41. R. Cropanzano, Z. S. Byrne, D. R. Bobocel, and D. E. Rupp, "Moral Virtues, Fairness Heuristics, Social Entities, and Other Denizens of Organizational Justice," *Journal of Vocational Behaviour* 58 (2001): 164–209.
42. L. Y. Fok, S. J. Hartman, A. L. Patti, and J. R. Razak, "Human Factors Affecting the Acceptance of TQM," *International Journal of Quality & Reliability Management* 17 (2000): 714.
43. Ibid.
44. D. S. Conner, "Social Comparison in Virtual Work Environments: An Examination of Contemporary Referent Selection," *Journal of Occupational and Organizational Psychology* 76 (March 2003): 133–48; J. Greenberg, "Setting the Justice Agenda: Seven Unanswered Questions about "What, Why and How," *Journal of Vocational Behaviour* 58 (2001): 210–19.
45. R. A. Cosier and D. R. Dalton, "Equity Theory and Time: A Reformulation," *Academy of Management Review* 8 (1983): 311–19.
46. R. Cropanzano et al., "Moral Virtues, Fairness Heuristics, Social Entities, and Other Denizens of Organizational

Justice," in J. Greenberg and R. Cropanzano, *Advances in Organizational Justice* (Palo Alto: Stanford University Press, 2001).

47. R. Cropanzano et al., "Moral Virtues, Fairness Heuristics, Social Entities, and Other Denizens of Organizational Justice," 166.
48. Ibid., 172.
49. B. Erdogan, M. L. Kraimer, and R. C. Liden, "Procedural Justice as a Two-Dimensional Construct: An Examination in the Performance Appraisal Account," *Journal of Applied Behavioral Science* 37 (2001): 205–22.
50. J. S. Jordan, J. A. Gillentine, and B. P. Hunt, "The Influence of Fairness: The Application of Organizational Justice in a Team Sport Setting," *International Sports Journal* 8 (Winter 2004): 142.
51. E. A. Locke and G. P. Latham, *A Theory of Goal Setting and Task Performance* (Englewood Cliffs, N.J.: Prentice-Hall, 1990).
52. G. P. Latham, "The Reciprocal Effects of Science on Practice: Insights from the Practice and Science of Goal Setting," *Canadian Psychology* 42 (February 2001): 1–11.
53. G. H. Seijts, G. P. Latham, K. Tasa, and B. W. Latham, "Goal-Setting and Goal Orientation: An Integration of Two Different Yet Related Literatures," *Academy of Management Journal* 47 (2004): 227–39.
54. E. A. Locke and G. P. Latham, "Building a Practically Useful Theory of Goal Setting and Task Motivation," *American Psychologist* 57 (September 2002): 706–07.
55. G. H. Seijts, "Setting Goals: When Performance Doesn't Matter," *Ivey Business Journal* 64, no. 3 (January/February 2001): 40–44.
56. Ibid.
57. M. E. Schweitzer, L. Ordonez, and B. Douma, "Goal-Setting as a Motivator of Unethical Behaviour," *Academy of Management Journal* 47 (2004): 422–32.
58. Locke and Latham, "Building a Practically Useful Theory of Goal Setting and Task Motivation."
59. G. P. Latham, "Goal Setting: A Five-Step Approach to Behaviour Change," *Organizational Dynamics* 32 (2003): 309–18.
60. T. O. Murray, *Management by Objectives: A Systems Approach to Management* (Fort Worth, Tex.: Western Company, n.d.).
61. G. P. Latham and G. A. Yukl, "A Review of Research on the Application of Goal Setting in Organizations," *Academy of Management Journal* 18 (1975): 824–845.
62. P. F. Drucker, *The Practice of Management* (New York: Harper & Bros., 1954).
63. C. L. Hughes, *Goal Setting: Key to Individual and Organizational Effectiveness* (New York: American Management Association, 1965).
64. F. Price, "HR Leaders Talk," *Canadian HR Reporter* 16 (February 2003): 15.
65. H. Levinson, "Management by Whose Objectives?" *Harvard Business Review,* January 2003, 107–16.
66. N. J. Adler, *International Dimensions of Organizational Behavior* (Boston: PWS-Kent, 1991).
67. G. Hofstede, "Motivation, Leadership, and Organization: Do American Theories Apply Abroad?" *Organizational Dynamics* 9 (1980): 42–63.
68. R. W. Brislin, B. McNab, R. Worthley, F. Kabigting, Jr., and B. Zukis, "Evolving Perceptions of Japanese Workplace Motivation: An Employee–Manager Comparison," *International Journal of Cross Cultural Management* 5 (2005): 87–104.
69. G. H. Hines, "Cross-Cultural Differences in Two-Factor Theory," *Journal of Applied Psychology* 58 (1981): 313–17.
70. L. Laroche, "Hiring Abroad," *CMA Management,* March 2002, 58.

Chapter 5

1. F. W. Taylor, *The Principles of Scientific Management* (New York: Norton, 1911).
2. R. R. Hirshfeld and H. S. Field, "Work Centrality and Work Alienation: Distinct Aspects of General Commitment to Work," *Journal of Organizational Behaviour* 21 (2000): 789–800.
3. P. Cappelli, "A Market-Driven Approach to Retaining Talent," *Harvard Business Review* 78 (2000): 103–11.
4. J. O'Brien, "Manufacturing: Toyota Members Stop at Nothing for Build Quality," *Birmingham Post* (Birmingham, U.K.), February 20, 2003, 26.
5. G. A. Gull and J. Doh, "The 'Transmutation' of the Organization: Toward a More Spiritual Workplace," *Journal of Management Inquiry* 13 (June 2004): 128–39.
6. D. R. May, R. L. Gilson, and L. M. Harter, "The Psychological Conditions of Meaningfulness, Safety and Availability and the Engagement of the Human Spirit at Work," *Journal of Occupational and Organizational Psychology* 77 (2004): 11–37.
7. V. E. Frankl, *Man's Search for Meaning* (New York: Simon and Schuster, 1963).
8. J. Whitmore, "Something Really Has to Change; Change Management as an Imperative Rather Than a Topic," *Journal of Change Management* 4 (March 2004): 5–14.
9. D. R. May et al., "The Psychological Conditions of Meaningfulness, Safety and Availability and the Engagement of the Human Spirit at Work."
10. V. M. Kinjerski and B. J. Skrypnek, "Defining Spirit at Work: Finding Common Ground," *Journal of Organizational Change Management* 17 (2004): 26–42; G. A. Gull and J. Doh, "The Transmutation of the Organization: Toward a More Spiritual Workplace," *Journal of Management Inquiry* 13 (June 2004): 128–39.
11. C. L. Jurkiewicz and R. A. Giacalone, "A Values Framework for Measuring the Impact of Workplace Spirituality on Organizational Performance," *Journal of Business Ethics* 49, no. 2 (January 2004): 129–42; G.A. Gull and J. Doh, "The Transmutation of the Organization: Toward a More Spiritual Workplace."
12. I. Harpaz and X. Fu, "The Structure of the Meaning of Work: A Relative Stability amidst Change," *Human Relations* 55 (2002): 641.
13. G. W. England and I. Harpaz, "How Working Is Defined: National Contexts and Demographic and Organizational Role Influences," *Journal of Organizational Behavior* 11 (1990): 253–66.
14. A. Wrzesniewski and J. E. Dutton, "Crafting a Job: Revisioning Employees as Active Crafters of Their Work," *Academy of Management Review* 26 (2001): 179–201.
15. N. D. Warren, "Job Simplification versus Job Enlargement," *Journal of Industrial Engineering* 9 (1958): 435–39.
16. C. R. Walker, "The Problem of the Repetitive Job," *Harvard Business Review* 28 (1950): 54–58.
17. M. A. Campion, L. Cheraskin, and M. J. Stevens, "Career-Related Antecedents and Outcomes of Job Rotation," *Academy of Management Journal* 37 (1994): 1518–42.
18. Department of Foreign Affairs and International Trade, *Recruitment Campaign.* www.dfait-maeci.gc.ca/department/service/career-en.asp, accessed June 4, 2003; Canadianretail.com, *Welcome to Gap Inc!,* http://profile.canadianretail.com/gap, accessed June 2, 2003; Ford Canada, *Human Resources,* www.ford.ca/english/learnabout/career-centre/HR.asp, accessed June 4, 2003; Bank of Canada, "Our Offer: Important Work; Challenging Work," www.bankofcanada.ca/en/hr/our_offer/work_e.html, accessed June 4, 2003.
19. M. Turner and G. Welbourn, "Turn a Cost Centre into a Profit Centre," *Communications News* 35 (October 1998): 10.
20. F. Herzberg, "One More Time: How Do You Motivate Employees?" *Harvard Business Review* 46 (1968): 53–62.

21. R. N. Ford, "Job Enrichment Lessons from AT&T," *Harvard Business Review* 51 (1973): 96–106.
22. R. J. House and L. A. Wigdor, "Herzberg's Dual-Factor Theory of Job Satisfaction and Motivation: A Review of the Evidence and a Criticism," *Personnel Psychology* 20 (1967): 369–89.
23. J. R. Hackman and G. R. Oldham, "Development of the Job Diagnostic Survey," *Journal of Applied Psychology* 60 (1975): 159–70.
24. A. N. Turner and P. R. Lawrence, *Industrial Jobs and the Worker* (Cambridge, Mass.: Harvard University Press, 1965).
25. J. R. Hackman and G. R. Oldham, "The Job Diagnostic Survey: An Instrument for the Diagnosis of Jobs and the Evaluation of Job Redesign Projects," *Technical Report No. 4* (New Haven, Conn.: Department of Administrative Sciences, Yale University, 1974).
26. R. J. Torraco, "Work Design Theory: A Review and Critique with Implications for Human Resource Development," *Human Resource Development Quarterly* 16 (Spring 2005): 89.
27. S. Ramlall, "A Review of Motivation Theories and Their Implications for Employee Retention within Organizations," *Journal of American Academy of Business, Cambridge* 5 (September 2004): 52–63.
28. P. H. Birnbaum, J.-L. Farh, and G. Y. Y. Wong, "The Job Characteristics Model in Hong Kong," *Journal of Applied Psychology* 71 (1986): 598–605.
29. J. R. Hackman and G. R. Oldham, *Work Design* (Reading, Mass.: Addison-Wesley, 1980).
30. S. Lin and A. Hsieh, "Constraints of Task Identity on Organizational Commitment," *International Journal of Manpower* 23 (2002): 151.
31. E. Sadler-Smith, G. El-Kot, and M. Leat, "Differentiating Work Autonomy Facets in a Non-Western Context," *Journal of Organizational Behaviour* 24 (2003): 711.
32. G. R. Salancik and J. Pfeffer, "A Social Information Processing Approach to Job Attitudes and Task Design," *Administrative Science Quarterly* 23 (1978): 224–53.
33. J. Pfeffer, "Management as Symbolic Action: The Creation and Maintenance of Organizational Paradigms," in *Research in Organizational Behavior*, vol. 3, ed. L. L. Cummings and B. M. Staw, 1–52 (Greenwich, Conn.: JAI Press, 1981).
34. J. Thomas and R. Griffin, "The Social Information Processing Model of Task Design: A Review of the Literature," *Academy of Management Review* 8 (1983): 672–82.
35. D. J. Campbell, "Task Complexity: A Review and Analysis," *Academy of Management Review* 13 (1988): 40–52.
36. M. A. Campion and P. W. Thayer, "Job Design: Approaches, Outcomes, and Trade-offs," *Organizational Dynamics* 16 (1987): 66–79.
37. M. A. Campion and C. L. McClelland, "Interdisciplinary Examination of the Costs and Benefits of Enlarged Jobs: A Job Design Quasi-Experiment," *Journal of Applied Psychology* 76 (1991): 186–99.
38. G. Farias and A. Varma, "Integrating Job Characteristics, Socio-technical Systems and Reengineering: Presenting a Unified Approach to Work and Organization Design," *Organization Development Journal* 18, no. 3 (Fall 2000): 13.
39. H. Hummels and J. de Leede, "Teamwork and Morality: Comparing Lean Production and Sociotechnology," *Journal of Business Ethics* 26 (2000): 75–88.
40. B. Kogut, *Country Competitiveness: Organizing of Work* (New York: Oxford University Press, 1993).
41. L. R. Gomez-Mejia, "The Cross-Cultural Structure of Task-Related and Contextual Constructs," *Journal of Psychology* 120 (1986): 5–19.
42. A. Wrzesniewski and J. E. Dutton, "Crafting a Job: Revisioning Employees as Active Crafters of Their Work," *Academy of Management Review* 26 (2001): 179–201.
43. J. C. Quick and L. E. Tetrick, eds., *Handbook of Occupational Health Psychology* (Washington, D.C.: American Psychological Association, 2002).
44. W. E. Deming, *Out of the Crisis* (Cambridge, Mass.: MIT Press, 1986).
45. L. Thurow, *Head to Head: The Coming Economic Battle among Japan, Europe, and America* (New York: Morrow, 1992).
46. M. A. Fruin, *The Japanese Enterprise System—Competitive Strategies and Cooperative Structures* (New York: Oxford University Press, 1992).
47. W. Niepce and E. Molleman, "Work Design Issue in Lean Production from a Sociotechnical System Perspective: Neo-Taylorism or the Next Step in Sociotechnical Design?" *Human Relations* 51 (1998): 259–87.
48. E. Furubotn, "Codetermination and the Modern Theory of the Firm: A Property-Rights Analysis," *Journal of Business* 61 (1988): 165–81.
49. B. Gardell, "Scandinavian Research on Stress in Working Life" (paper presented at the IRRA Symposium on Stress in Working Life, Denver, September 1980).
50. J. de Leede and J. K. Looise, "The Mini-Company: A Specification of Socio-technical Business Systems," *Personnel Review* 31 (2002): 341.
51. L. Levi, "Psychosocial, Occupational, Environmental, and Health Concepts; Research Results; and Applications," in *Work and Well-Being: An Agenda for the 1990s*, ed. G. P. Keita and S. L. Sauter, (Washington, D.C.: American Psychological Association, 1992) 199–211.
52. L. R. Murphy and C. L. Cooper, eds., *Healthy and Productive Work: An International Perspective* (London and New York: Taylor & Francis, 2000).
53. M. D. Lee, S. M. MacDermid, M. L. Williams, M. L. Buck, and S. Leiba-O'Sullivan, "Contextual Factors in the Success of Reduced-Load Work Arrangements among Managers and Professionals," *Human Resources Management* 41 (2002): 209–23.
54. Ibid.
55. T. O'Neill, "Crunch Time for Families," *Citizen Centre Report* 30, no. 4 (2003): 36–40.

Chapter 6

1. S. Brearton and J. Daly, "The 50 Best Companies to Work for in Canada," *The Globe and Mail Report on Business Magazine,* December 27, 2002, 60.
2. Johnson & Johnson, *Johnson & Johnson Global Standards of Leadership Reference Guide,* Johnson & Johnson Management Education Department, 2003.
3. D. A. Kolb, J. S. Osland, and I. M. Rubin, *Organizational Behaviour: An Experiential Approach,* 6th ed. (Upper Saddle River, N.J.: Prentice Hall, 1995), 170.
4. J. J. Lynch, *A Cry Unheard: New Insights into the Medical Consequences of Loneliness* (Baltimore, Md.: Bancroft Press, 2000).
5. Brearton & Daly, "The 50 Best Companies to Work for in Canada," 60–61.
6. M. E. Boon, *Managing Interactively: Executing Business Strategy, Improving Communication, and Creating a Knowledge-Sharing Culture* (New York: McGraw-Hill, 2002), 90.
7. F. Luthans, "Successful versus Effective Real Managers," *Academy of Management Executive* 2 (1988): 127–32.
8. L. E. Penley, E. R. Alexander, I. E. Jernigan, and C. I. Henwood, "Communication Abilities of Managers: The Relationship of Performance," *Journal of Management* 17 (1991): 57–76.
9. A. Furhham and P. Stringfield, "Congruence in Job-Performance Ratings: A Study of 360 Degree Feedback Examining Self, Manager, Peers, and Consultant Ratings," *Human Relations* 51 (1998): 517–30.

10. D. Kelly, "Using Vision to Improve Organizational Communication," *Leadership and Organization Development Journal* 21 (2000): 92–101.
11. R. B. Adler, N. Towne, and J. A. Rolls, *Looking Out/ Looking In: Interpersonal Communication,* 1st Can. ed. (Toronto: Harcourt, 2001), 13.
12. M. L. Knapp, *Nonverbal Communication in Human Interaction* (New York: Holt, Rinehart & Winston, 1978); J. McCroskey and L. Wheeless, *Introduction to Human Communication* (New York: Allyn & Bacon, 1976).
13. R. L. Birdwhistell, *Kinesics and Context* (Philadelphia: University of Pennsylvania Press, 1970).
14. D. Morand, "Language and Power: An Empirical Analysis of Linguistic Strategies Used in Superior–Subordinate Communication," *Journal of Organizational Behaviour* 21 (2000): 235.
15. C. Barnum and N. Wolniansky, "Taking Cues from Body Language," *Management Review* 78 (1989): 59.
16. A. M. Katz and V. T. Katz, eds., *Foundations of Nonverbal Communication* (Carbondale, Ill.: Southern Illinois University Press, 1983), 181.
17. E. Dorsa, "Space: The First Frontier," *Technology and Children* 7, no. 4 (2003): 8.
18. R. T. Barker and C. G. Pearce, "The Importance of Proxemics at Work," *Supervisory Management* 35 (1990): 10–11.
19. B. Evenson, "Could You Run That by Me Again, Doctor?" *National Post,* October 2, 2000.
20. E. A. Gerloff and J. C. Quick, "Task Role Ambiguity and Conflict in Supervision–Subordinate Relationships," *Journal of Applied Communication Research* 12 (1984): 90–102.
21. D. Morand, "Language and Power," 235.
22. D. Tannen, "The Power of Talk," *Harvard Business Review,* September–October, 1995, 138–48.
23. E. H. Schein, "Reassessing the 'Divine Rights' of Managers," *Sloan Management Review* 30 (1989): 63–68.
24. M. Crawford, *Talking Difference: On Gender and Language* (Thousand Oaks, Calif.: Sage, 1995).
25. D. Tannen, "The Power of Talk," 140.
26. J. Gray, *Men Are from Mars and Women Are from Venus: The Classic Guide to Understanding the Opposite Sex* (New York: Harper Collins, 2003); D. Tannen, *That's Not What I Mean! How Conversational Style Makes or Breaks Your Relations with Others* (New York: Morrow, 1986); D. Tannen, *You Just Don't Understand* (New York: Ballentine, 1990).
27. D. Tannen, "The Power of Talk," 146.
28. S. P. Ferris and S. Roper, "Same and Mixed Gender Intimacy in a Virtual Environment," *Qualitative Research Reports in Communication* (Summer 2002): 47–55.
29. J. Campbell, "Female Managers Discover Secret Weapon at Carleton: Program Builds Self-Confidence, Communications Skills, Jennifer Campbell Reports," *Ottawa Citizen,* June 8, 2002, H3.
30. D. Morand, "Politeness and the Clash of Interaction Orders in Cross-Cultural Communication," *Thunderbird International Business Review* 45 (2003): 521.
31. D. Morand, "The Emotional Intelligence of Managers: Assessing the Construct Validity of a Nonverbal Measure of 'People Skills,'" *Journal of Business and Psychology* 16 (2001): 21–33.
32. G. Hofstede, *Culture's Consequences: International Differences in Work-Related Values* (Beverly Hills, Calif.: Sage Publications, 1980).
33. G. Hofstede, "Motivation, Leadership, and Organization: Do American Theories Apply Abroad?" *Organizational Dynamics* 9 (1980): 42–63.
34. P. Benimadhu, "Adding Value through Diversity: An Interview with Bernard F. Isautier," *Canadian Business Review* 22 (1995): 6–11, http://www.cbc.ca/stories/2002/03/hurricane020315.
35. A. Kaminsky, "Understanding the Dance," *Canadian HR Reporter* 14, no. 22 (2001): 10–11.
36. R. B. Adler and N. Towne, *Looking Out/Looking In,* 9th ed. (New York: Harcourt Brace, 1999), 221.
37. J. R. Gibb, "Defensive Communication," *Journal of Communication* 11 (1961): 141–48.
38. R. D. Laing, *The Politics of the Family and Other Essays* (New York: Pantheon, 1971).
39. R. B. Adler, N. Towne, and J. A. Rolls, *Looking Out/Looking In,* 1st Can. ed., (Toronto: Harcourt, 2001), 276.
40. H. Wilkie, "Are You in Breach of the Communication Contract?" *The Canadian Manager* 27 (Summer 2002): 14.
41. R. Reik, *Listen with the Third Ear* (New York: Pyramid, 1972).
42. M. M. Helms and P. J. Haynes, "Are You Really Listening? The Benefit of Effective Intra-organizational Listening," *Journal of Managerial Psychology* 7, no. 6 (1992): 17–21.
43. "CEO's Talk," *Canadian HR Reporter* 15 (October 7, 2002): 18.
44. A. G. Athos and J. J. Gabarro, *Interpersonal Behavior: Communication and Understanding in Relationships* (Englewood Cliffs, N.J.: Prentice-Hall, 1978).
45. J. Newman and D. Grigg, "Ego Management Solves Serious Clashes," *Ottawa Citizen,* September 13, 2003, H12.
46. R. B. Adler, N. Towne, and J. A. Rolls, *Looking Out/ Looking In,* 290.
47. D. Tannen, "I Only Say This Because I Love You," *Good Housekeeping,* May 2001, 115.
48. D. A. Whetten and K. S. Cameron, *Developing Management Skills,* 6th ed. (Upper Saddle River, N.J.: Prentice Hall, 2005), 215.
49. W. R. Forrester and M. F. Maute, "The Impact of Relationship Satisfaction on Attribution, Emotions, and Behaviors Following Service Failure," *Journal of Applied Business Research* (2000): 1–45.
50. D. L. Christain, "From Conflict to Connection: The Fine Art of Giving and Receiving Feedback," *Communities,* Winter 2001, 53–57.
51. Newman and Grigg, "Ego Management Solves Serious Clashes."
52. Whetten and Cameron, *Developing Management Skills,* 225–26.
53. Ibid., 227–28.
54. Ibid., 219–20.
55. Ibid., 227.
56. M. W. Kramer and J. A. Hess, "Communication Rules for the Display of Emotions in Organizational Settings," *Management Communications Quarterly* 16 (2002): 66–80.
57. I. M. Jawahar and C. R. Williams, "Where All the Children Are Above Average: The Performance Appraisal Purpose Effect," *Personnel Psychology* 50 (1997): 905–25; P. Young, "Review in Progress: Employee Reviews Have Evolved into a Useful Tool for Worker and Boss Alike," *The Globe and Mail,* July 9, 2003, C1.
58. J. W. Gilsdorf, "Organizational Rules on Communicating: How Employees Are—and Are Not—Learning the Ropes," *Journal of Business Communication* 35 (1998): 173–201.
60. "Effective Communication Linked to Greater Shareholder Returns, Watson Wyatt Study Finds," *PR Newswire,* New York, November 3, 2003, 1.
61. Ibid.
62. IABC, "Global Perspectives: Tell Us about a Recent Best Practice That Got Results for Your Organization," *Communication World,* June 1, 2003, 8.
63. B. Bowes, "People Power Saves Day: Remarkable Turnaround for Manitoba Lotteries," *Winnipeg Free Press,* April 12, 2003, Metro, F1.
64. Manitoba Lotteries Corporation Training Catalog, 2002, 6-4.
65. A. Tomlinson, "Employees Should Be Buying What HR Is Selling," *Canadian HR Reporter,* December 3, 2001, 1–2.

66. "Canfor goes iDirect to the Heart of Employee Communications," *Canada Newswire,* June 18, 2003, 1.
67. M. Goulding and T. Pendlebury, "Corporate 'News Show' Introduces Bottom Line to Staff," *Canadian HR Reporter,* June 17, 2002, 16.
68. T. White, "Supporting Change," *Communication World,* April/May 2002, 22–23; J. Gast, "Management Opens Up in New Program: Better Communications Resulting from Sessions," *Sudbury Star,* October 24, 2000, A1.
69. D. R. Holtzhausen, "The Effects of Workplace Democracy on Employee Communication Behaviour: Implications for Competitive Advantage," *Competitiveness Review,* 12, no. 2 (2002): 30–48.
70. P. Sniderman, *Organizational Behaviour Course,* CMHR405, Module 6, 2002, Organizational Communication, Distance Education, Ryerson University.
71. T. White, "Supporting Change: How Communicators at Scotiabank Turned Ideas into Action," *Communication World,* April 1, 2002, 22.
72. B. Bowes, "People Power Saves Day: Remarkable Turnaround for Manitoba Lotteries."
73. A. Tomlinson, "Employees Should Be Buying What HR Is Selling."
74. P. Kamen, "The Way That You Use It," *CMA Management,* April 2003, 10–12; Young, "Review in Progress: Employee Reviews Have Evolved into a Useful Tool for Worker and Boss Alike."
75. *Richness* is a term originally coined by W.D. Bodensteiner, "Information Channel Utilization under Varying Research and Development Project Conditions" (Ph.D. Dissertation, University of Texas at Austin, 1970).
76. N. Frohlich and J. Oppenheimer, "Some Consequences of E-Mail vs. Face-to-Face Communication in Experiment," *Journal of Economic Behavior & Organization* 35 (1998): 389–403.
77. E. Spragins, "Sending the Wrong Message," *Fortune Small Business,* July/August 2003, 32.
78. S. Kiesler, J. Siegel, and T. W. McGuire, "Social Psychological Aspects of Computer-mediated Communication," *American Psychologist* 39 (1984): 1123–34.
79. "Mercer Human Resources Consulting Deploys Polycom Video Communications Solution across the UK Supplied by BT Conferencing," *BT Presswire,* October 14, 2003, 1.
80. S. Wilson, "Forming Virtual Teams," *Quality Progress* 6 (June 2003): 36.

Chapter 7

1. P. Booth, *Challenge and Change: Embracing the Team Concept,* Conference Board of Canada, Report no. 123-94, 1994.
2. WestJet, "That 'New Plane' Smell: How WestJet Goes about the Purchase and Outfitting of the New 700-Series Jets," *2002 WestJet Annual Report,* 14–15.
3. J. R. Katzenbach and D. K. Smith, "The Discipline of Teams," *Harvard Business Review* 71 (1993): 111–20; M. Plovnick, R. Fry, and I. Rubin, "New Developments in OD Technology: Programmed Team Development," *Training and Development Journal,* April 1975, 19–25.
4. "A Group Is Not a Team: Key Factors That Determine Team Forming and Team Performance," *Human Resource Management International Digest,* 2003, 3.
5. D. Francis, "MDS Has a Science All Its Own," *National Post,* September 6, 2003, FP1.
6. R. C. Liden, S. J. Wayne, R. A. Jaworski, and N. Bennett, "Social Loafing: A Field Investigation," *Journal of Management* 30 (2004): 285–304.
7. S. London, "A Most Harmonious Collaboration (How the Conductorless Orpheus Chamber Orchestra Manages Itself)," *Financial Times* (U.K.), January 2002, 13.
8. Ironlink, *Featured Case Study: Oil Sands Refinery Construction Project.* http://www.ironlink.ca/services/casestudy_index.html, accessed November 3, 2003.
9. "Trillium Health Centre Wins National Award for Quality and Innovation," *Canada Newswire,* June 6, 2002.
10. W. L. Mohr and H. Mohr, *Quality Circles: Changing Images of People at Work* (Reading, Mass.: Addison-Wesley, 1983).
11. R. W. Griffin, "A Longitudinal Assessment of the Consequences of Quality Circles in an Industrial Setting," *Academy of Management Journal* 31 (1988): 338–58.
12. W. Bennis and H. Shepard, "A Theory of Group Development," *Human Relations* 9 (1956): 415–37; B. W. Tuckman, "Developmental Sequence in Small Groups," *Psychological Bulletin* 63 (1965): 384–99; B. W. Tuckman and M. A. C Jensen, "Stages in Small Group Development Revisited," *Group and Organizational Studies* 2 (1977): 419–27; S. A. Wheelan and J. M. Hochberger, "Validation Studies of the Group Development Questionnaire," *Small Group Research* 27 (1996): 143–70; S. A. Wheelan, *Group Processes: A Developmental Perspective* (Boston: Allyn & Bacon, 1994); S. A. Wheelan and R. McKeage, "Development Patterns in Small and Large Groups," *Small Group Research* 24 (1993): 60–83; D. L. Miller, "The Stages of Group Development: A Retrospective Study of Dynamic Team Processes," *Canadian Journal of Administrative Sciences* 20, no. 2 (2003): 121.
13. D. C. Lau and J. K. Murnighan, "Demographic Diversity and Faultlines: The Compositional Dynamics of Organizational Groups," *Academy of Management Review* 23 (1998): 325–40.
14. S. A. Wheelan, B. Davidson, and F. Tilin, "Group Development across Time: Reality or Illusion?" *Small Group Research* 34 (2003): 223–45.
15. D. A. Whetten and K. S, Cameron, *Developing Management Skills,* 6th ed. (Upper Saddle River, N.J.: Prentice Hall, 2005), 462.
16. Ibid., 465.
17. Ibid., 463.
18. Ibid., 467.
19. A. Chang, P. Bordia, and J. Duck, "Punctuated Equilibrium and Linear Progression: Toward a New Understanding of Group Development," *Academy of Management Journal* 46 (2003): 106.
20. A. Seers and Steve Woodruff, "Temporal Pacing in Task Forces: Group Development or Deadline Pressure?" *Journal of Management* 23 (1997): 184.
21. C. J. C. Gersick, "Time and Transition in Work Teams: Toward a New Model of Group Development," *Academy of Management Journal* 31 (March 1988): 9–41.
22. Chang et al., "Punctuated Equilibrium and Linear Progression."
23. L. Hirschhorn, *Managing in the New Team Environment,* (Upper Saddle River, N.J.: Prentice-Hall, 1991), 521A.
24. R. Hackman, interviewed by P. Sniderman for Ryerson University Distance Learning OB Course, Cambridge, Mass., August 29, 1995.
25. M. Hardaker and B. K. Ward, "How to Make a Team Work," *Harvard Business Review* 65 (1987): 112–20.
26. Katzenbach and Smith, "The Discipline of Teams."
27. J. R. Hackman, *Leading Teams: Setting the Stage for Great Performances* (Boston: Harvard Business School Press, 2002).
28. D. Ancona, H. Bresman, and K. Kaeufer, "The Comparative Advantage of X-Teams," *MIT Sloan Management Review* 43 (Spring 2002): 33–39.
29. T. J. B. Kline and J. McGrath, "Development and Validation of Five Criteria for Evaluating Team Performance," *Organization Development Journal* 16, no. 3 (1998): 19–27.
30. Katzenbach and Smith, "The Discipline of Teams."

31. J. R. Rentsch and R. J. Klimoski, "Why Do 'Great Minds' Think Alike? Antecedents of Team Member Schema Arrangement," *Journal of Organizational Behavior* 22 (2001): 107; Katzenbach and Smith, "The Discipline of Teams."
32. E. J. Thomas and C. F. Fink, "Effects of Group Size," in *Readings in Organizational Behavior and Human Performance,* ed. L. L. Cummings and W. E. Scott (Chicago: Irwin, 1969), 394–408.
33. Katzenbach and Smith, "The Discipline of Teams."
34. Rentsch and Klimoski, "Why Do 'Great Minds' Think Alike? Antecedents of Team Member Schema Arrangement."
35. R. Hackman, interviewed by P. Sniderman for Ryerson University Distance Learning OB Course, Cambridge, Mass., August 29, 1995; N. Gorla and Y. W. Lam, "Who Should Work with Whom? Building Effective Software Teams," *Communications of the ACM* 47 (June 2004): 79–82.
36. J. R. Hollenbeck, D. Scott DeRue, and R. Guzzo, "Bridging the Gap between I/O Research and HR Practice: Improving Team Composition, Team Training, and Team Task Design," *Human Resource Management* 43 (2004): 356.
37. S. B. F. Paletz, K. Peng, M. Erez, and C. Maslach, "Ethnic Composition and Its Differential Impact on Group Processes in Diverse Teams," *Small Group Research* 35 (2004): 128–57.
38. K. W. Phillips et al., "Diverse Groups and Information Sharing: The Effects of Congruent Ties," *Journal of Experimental Social Psychology* 40 (2004): 497–510.
39. Hollenbeck et al., "Bridging the Gap between I/O Research and HR Practice"; L. Karakowsky, K. McBey, and Y. Chuang, "Perceptions of Team Performance: The Impact of Group Composition and Task-Based Cues," *Journal of Managerial Psychology* 19 (2004): 506–25.
40. Plovnick et al., "New Developments in OD Technology: Programmed Team Development," 41; C. R. Gowen, "Managing Work Group Performance by Individual Goals and Group Goals for an Interdependent Group Task," *Journal of Organizational Behavior Management* 7 (1986): 5–27.
42. Katzenbach and Smith, "The Discipline of Teams," 113.
43. E. McFadzean and A. O'Loughlin, "Five Strategies for Improving Group Effectiveness," *Strategic Change* 9, no. 2 (2000): 103–14.
44. Plovnick et al., "New Developments in OD Technology: Programmed Team Development."
45. Ibid.
46. G. Parker, *Team Players and Teamwork* (San Francisco: Jossey-Bass, 1990).
47. T. A. Stewart, "The Search for the Organization of Tomorrow," *Fortune* (May 18, 1992): 92–98.
48. J. D. Quick, G. Moorhead, J. C. Quick, E. A. Gerloff, K. L. Mattox, and C. Mullins, "Decision Making among Emergency Room Residents: Preliminary Observations and a Decision Model," *Journal of Medical Education* 58 (1983): 117–25.
49. W. J. Duncan and J. P. Feisal, "No Laughing Matter: Patterns of Humor in the Workplace," *Organizational Dynamics* 17 (1989): 18–30.
50. WestJet Airlines Ltd., "Plane Talk," *2002 Annual Report,* 6–7.
51. N. Steckler and N. Fondas, "Building Team Leader Effectiveness: A Diagnostic Tool," *Organizational Dynamics* 23 (1995): 20–35.
52. K. L. Bettenhausen and J. K. Murnighan, "The Emergence of Norms in Competitive Decision-Making Groups," *Administrative Science Quarterly* 30 (1985): 350–372; K. L. Bettenhausen, "Five Years of Groups Research: What We Have Learned and What Needs to Be Addressed," *Journal of Management* 17 (1991): 345–81.
53. K. L. Bettenhausen and J. K. Murnighan, "The Development and Stability of Norms in Groups Facing Interpersonal and Structural Challenge," *Administrative Science Quarterly* 36 (1991): 20–35.
54. V. U. Druskat and S. B. Wolff, "Building the Emotional Intelligence of Groups," *Harvard Business Review* 79 (2001): 80–90.
55. J. E. McGrath, *Groups: Interaction and Performance* (Englewood Cliffs, N.J.: Prentice-Hall, 1984).
56. K. L. Gammage, A. V. Carron, and P. A. Estabrooks, "Team Cohesion and Individual Productivity," *Small Group Research* 32 (2001): 3–18.
57. I. Summers, T. Coffelt, and R. E. Horton, "Work-Group Cohesion," *Psychological Reports* 63 (1988): 627–36; A. Chang and P. Bordia, "A Multidimensional Approach to the Group Cohesion–Group Performance Relationship," *Small Group Research* 32 (2001): 379–405; B. A. Wech, K. W. Mossholder, R. P. Steel, and N. Bennett, "Does Work Group Cohesiveness Affect Individuals' Performance and Organizational Commitment? A Cross-Level Examination," *Small Group Research* 29 (1998): 472–94; P. A. Chansler, P. M. Swamidass, and C. Cammann, "Self-Managing Work Teams: An Empirical Study of Group Cohesiveness in 'Natural Work Groups' at a Harley-Davidson Motor Company Plant," *Small Group Research* 34 (2003): 101–20.
58. S. E. Seashore, *Group Cohesiveness in the Industrial Work Group* (Ann Arbor, Mich.: University of Michigan, 1954).
59. Plovnick et al., "New Developments in OD Technology: Programmed Team Development."
60. K. H. Price, "Working Hard to Get People to Loaf," *Basic and Applied Social Psychology* 14 (1993): 329–44.
61. R. Albanese and D. D. Van Fleet, "Rational Behavior in Groups: The Free-Riding Tendency," *Academy of Management Review* 10 (1985): 244–55.
62. R. C. Liden, S. J. Wayne, R. A. Jaworski, and N. Bennett, "Social Loafing: A Field Investigation," *Journal of Management* 30 (2004): 286.
63. Ibid.
64. E. Pfaff and P. Huddleston, "Does It Matter if I Hate Teamwork? What Impacts Student Attitudes toward Teamwork," *Journal of Marketing Education* 25 (2003): 37.
65. C. M. Brooks and J. L. Ammons, "Free Riding in Group Projects and the Effects of Timing, Frequency, and Specificity of Criteria in Peer Assessments," *Journal of Education for Business* 78 (2003): 268–73.
66. E. Diener, "Deindividuation, Self-Awareness, and Disinhibition," *Journal of Personality and Social Psychology* 37 (1979): 1160–71.
67. "Police Report on Stanley Cup Riot: Blames Communication, Equipment," *Canadian Press Newswire,* February 3, 1995.
68. "No One Scored Like Dark-Eyed Rocket Richard: Eclipsed TV Stars: Goal Scoring Was 'the Most Important Thing in My Life,'" *National Post,* May 29, 2000, A15.
69. R. A. Cook and J. L. Goff, "Coming of Age with Self-Managed Teams: Dealing with a Problem Employee," *Journal of Business and Psychology* 16 (2002): 485–96.
70. Whetten and Cameron, *Developing Management Skills,* 459–60.
71. N. J. Adler, *International Dimensions of Organizational Behavior* (Mason, Ohio: South-Western, 2001).
72. W. A. Randolph and M. Sashkin, "Can Organizational Empowerment Work in Multinational Settings?" *Academy of Management Executive* 16 (2002): 102.
73. P. C. Earley and E. Mosakowski, "Creating Hybrid Team Cultures: An Empirical Test of Transnational Team Functioning," *Academy of Management Journal* 43 (2000): 26–49.
74. T. Cox, Jr., and S. Blake, "Managing Cultural

Diversity: Implications for Organizational Competitiveness," *Academy of Management Executive* 5, no. 3 (1991), 45–56; C. L. Taylor, "Dimensions of Diversity in Canadian Business: Building a Business Case for Valuing Ethnocultural Diversity," The Conference Board of Canada Report no. 143-95, 1995; T. Cox, "The Multicultural Organization," *Academy of Management Executive* 5 (1991); E. J. Mighty, "Valuing Workforce Diversity: A Model of Organizational Change," *Canadian Journal of Administrative Sciences* 8, no. 2 (1991): 64–71; Taylor D. Cox, Jr., *Cultural Diversity in Organizations: Theory, Research & Practice* (San Francisco: Berrett-Koehler Publishers, 1993); Trevor Wilson, *Diversity at Work: The Business Case for Equity* (Mississauga: John Wiley & Sons Canada, 1996).

75. D. Thomas, E. Ravlin, and D. Barry, "Creating Effective Multicultural Teams," *University of Auckland Business Review* 2 (2000).
76. D. L. Fields and T. C. Bloom, "Employee Satisfaction in Work Groups with Different Gender Composition," *Journal of Organizational Behavior* 18 (1997): 181–96.
77. L. Karakowsky and D. Miller, "Teams That Listen and Teams That Do Not: Exploring the Role of Gender in Group Responsiveness to Negative Feedback," *Team Performance Management* 8, no. 7/8 (2002): 146–56.
78. G. Morse, "The Emancipated Organization: A Conversation with Kim Campbell," *Harvard Business Review* 90 (September 2002).
79. J. R. Goktepe and C. E. Schneier, "Role of Sex, Gender Roles, and Attraction in Predicting Emergent Leaders," *Journal of Applied Psychology* 74 (1989): 165–67.
80. D. Harvey and D. R. Brown, *An Experiential Approach to Organization Development*, 6th ed. (Upper Saddle River, N.J.: Prentice Hall, 2001), 284.
81. T. G. Cummings and C. G. Worley, *Essentials of Organization Development and Change* (Mason, Ohio: South-Western, 2001), 133.
82. K. Simmons, "Financial Advisors Aim for the Top: Climbing Together for a Better Team," *Hamilton Spectator,* December 21, 2002, N01.
83. R. Hough, "One, Two, Three … Rock. The Latest Motivational Exercise Involves Learning to Play 'La Bamba' with Your Co-workers. Fun, Isn't It?" *The Globe and Mail,* September 27, 2002, Metro, 37.
84. K. Harding, "From the Play Room to the Boardroom: Lego, Storytelling and Jazz Are New Training Tools Being Used to Help Build Managers," *The Globe and Mail,* October 16, 2002, Metro, C3; P. Jalsevac, "Teamwork in the Kitchen: Stratford 'Trattoria' Switches Focus to Offer Lessons in Italian Cooking—and in Corporate Teambuilding," *Kitchener-Waterloo Record,* January 15, 2003, F1.
85. Cummings and Worley, *Essentials of Organization Development and Change,* 287.
86. S. Cohen and G. E. Ledford, "The Effectiveness of Self-Managing Teams: A Quasi-Experiment," *Human Relations* 47 (1994): 13–43; J. L. Cordery, W. S. Mueller, and L. M. Smith, "Attitudinal and Behavioral Effects of Autonomous Group Working: A Longitudinal Field Study," *Academy of Management Journal* 34 (1991): 464–76; E. E. Lawler, S. A. Morham, and G. E. Ledford, *Employment Involvement and Total Quality Management: Practices and Results in Fortune 1000 Companies* (San Francisco: Jossey-Bass, 1992); J. A. Pearce, II, and E. C. Ravlin, "The Design and Activation of Self-Regulating Work Groups," *Human Relations* 40 (1987): 751–82; E. Trist and H. Murray, eds., *The Social Engagement of Social Science: The Socio-Technical Perspective,* Vol. II (Philadelphia: University of Pennsylvania Press, 1993); P. M. Podsakoff, M. Ahearne, and S. B. MacKenzie, "Organizational Citizenship Behavior and the Quantity and Quality of Work Group Performance," *Journal of Applied Psychology* 82 (1997): 262–70.

Chapter 8

1. L. Livingstone, "Person–Environment Fit on the Dimension of Creativity: Relationships with Strain, Job Satisfaction, and Performance" (Ph.D. diss., Oklahoma State University, 1992).
2. G. Morgan, *Riding the Waves of Change* (San Francisco: Jossey-Bass, 1988); M. A. West and J. L. Farr, "Innovation at Work," in *Innovation and Creativity at Work: Psychological and Organizational Strategies,* ed. M. A. West and J. L. Farr, 3–13 (New York: Wiley, 1990).
3. C. S. Wong and W. L. Pang, "Barriers to Creativity in the Hotel Industry—Perspectives of Managers and Supervisors," *International Journal of Contemporary Hospitality Management* 15 (2003): 29–37.
4. J. Mauzy, "Should You Be a Chief Creativity Officer? An Interview with Creativity Consultant Jeff Mauzy," *Optimize,* August 2003, www.optimizemag.com/issue/022/briefing.htm.
5. Ibid.
6. G. Wallas, *The Art of Thought* (New York: Harcourt Brace, 1926).
7. R. G. Kalischuk and K. Thorpe, "Thinking Creatively: From Nursing Education to Practice," *Journal of Continuing Education in Nursing* 33 (2002): 155–63.
8. M. Cernetig, "Trivia: It's Who We Are," *Toronto Star,* September 26, 2004, D1.
9. M. D. Mumford and S. B. Gustafson, "Creativity Syndrome: Integration, Application, and Innovation," *Psychological Bulletin* 103 (1988): 27–43.
10. T. Poze, "Analogical Connections—The Essence of Creativity," *Journal of Creative Behavior* 17 (1983): 240–41.
11. I. Sladeczek and G. Domino, "Creativity, Sleep, and Primary Process Thinking in Dreams," *Journal of Creative Behavior* 19 (1985): 38–46.
12. F. Barron and D. M. Harrington, "Creativity, Intelligence, and Personality," *Annual Review of Psychology* 32 (1981): 439–76.
13. R. J. Sternberg, "A Three-Faced Model of Creativity," in *The Nature of Creativity,* ed. R. J. Sternberg (Cambridge, England: Cambridge University Press, 1988), 125–47.
14. A. M. Isen, "Positive Affect and Decision Making," in *Research on Judgment and Decision Making,* ed. W. M. Goldstein and R. M. Hogarth (Cambridge, England: Cambridge University Press, 1997).
15. R. Von Oech, *A Whack on the Side of the Head* (New York: Warner, 1983).
16. D. F. Caldwell and C. O'Reilly, "The Determinants of Team-Based Innovation in Organizations: The Role of Social Influence," *Small Group Research* 34 (2003): 497–517.
17. M. F. R. Kets de Vries, R. Branson, and P. Barnevik, "Charisma in Action: The Transformational Abilities of Virgin's Richard Branson and ABBS's Percy Barnevik," *Organizational Dynamics* 26 (1998): 7–21.
18. "3M Develops Its Own Solution to the Challenge of the New," *Human Resources Management International Digest* 9, no. 2 (March/April 2001): 4–6.
19. N. Nohria, W. Joyce, and B. Roberson, "What Really Works," *Harvard Business Review,* July 2003, 50.
20. M. P. Rice, G. C. O'Connor, R. Leifer, C. M. Mcdermott, and T. Standish-Kuon, "Corporate Venture Capital Models for Promoting Radical Innovation," *Journal of Marketing Theory and Practice* 8 (2000): 1.
21. Mauzy, "Should You Be a Chief Creativity Officer?" 3.
22. T. Tetenbaum and H. Tetenbaum, "Office 2000: Tear Down the Wall," *Training* (February 2000): 58–64.

23. Ibid.
24. J. Mauzy and R. A. Harriman, "Three Climates for Creativity," *Research Technology Management* 46, no. 3 (May/June 2003): 29.
25. D. M. Harrington, "Creativity, Analogical Thinking, and Muscular Metaphors," *Journal of Mental Imagery* 6 (1981): 121–26; R. M. Kanter, *The Change Masters* (New York: Simon & Schuster, 1983).
26. K. H. Hammonds, "Growth Search," *Fast Company,* April 2003, 74.
27. "Connecting Personal KM to Innovation," *Knowledge Aforethought,* February 8, 2004, www.knowledgeaforethought.blogs.com/knowledge_aforethought/2004/02.
28. T. Raphael, "At Google, the Proof Is in the People," *Workforce* 82 (March 2003): 50.
29. A. G. Robinson and S. Stern, *How Innovation and Improvement Actually Happen* (San Francisco: Berrett Koehler, 1997).
30. T. M. Amabile, R. Conti, H. Coon, J. Lazenby, and M. Herron, "Assessing the Work Environment for Creativity," *Academy of Management Journal* 39 (1996): 1154–84.
31. C. S. Wong and W. L. Pang, "Barriers to Creativity in the Hotel Industry—Perspectives of Managers and Supervisors," *International Journal of Contemporary Hospitality Management* 15 (2003): 29–37.
32. M. Kostera, M. Proppe, and M. Szatkowski, "Staging the New Romantic Hero in the Old Cynical Theatre: On Managers, Roles, and Change in Poland," *Journal of Organizational Behavior* 16 (1995): 631–46.
33. Livingstone, "Person-Environment Fit."
34. M. M. Clapham, "Employee Creativity: The Role of Leadership," *The Academy of Management Executive* 14 (2000): 138.
35. R. L. Firestein, "Effects of Creative Problem-Solving Training on Communication Behaviors in Small Groups," *Small Group Research* (November 1989): 507–21.
36. H. A. Simon, *Administrative Behavior* (New York: Macmillan, 1957).
37. G. Huber, *Managerial Decision Making* (Glenview, Ill.: Scott, Foresman, 1980).
38. G. Colvin, "The Most Valuable Quality in a Manager," *Fortune* (December 29, 1997): 279–80.
39. K. Blanchard and N. V. Peale, *The Power of Ethical Management* (New York: Fawcett Crest, 1988).
40. H. A. Simon, *Administrative Behavior* (New York: Macmillan, 1957).
41. E. F. Harrison, *The Managerial Decision-Making Process* (Boston: Houghton Mifflin, 1981).
42. R. L. Ackoff, "The Art and Science of Mess Management," *Interfaces* (February 1981): 20–26.
43. M. Augier and K. Kreiner, "Rationality, Imagination and Intelligence: Some Boundaries in Human Decision Making," *Industrial and Corporate Change* 9 (2000): 659.
44. R. M. Cyert and J. G. March, eds., *A Behavioral Theory of the Firm* (Englewood Cliffs, N.J.: Prentice-Hall, 1963).
45. M. D. Cohen, J. G. March, and J. P. Olsen, "A Garbage Can Model of Organizational Choice," *Administrative Science Quarterly* 17 (1972): 1–25.
46. Larsen, B. "The Garbage Can Life Cycle Model of Quality Management," *The TQM Magazine* 13 (2001): 95; J. G. March and J. P. Olsen, "Garbage Can Models of Decision Making in Organizations," in *Ambiguity and Command,* ed. J. G. March and R. Weissinger-Baylon (Marshfield, Mass.: Pitman, 1986), 11–53.
47. H. Mintzberg, "Planning on the Left Side and Managing on the Right," *Harvard Business Review* 54 (1976): 51–63.
48. A. M. Hayashi, "When to Trust Your Gut," *Harvard Business Review At Large,* February 2001, 60.
49. D. J. Isenberg, "How Senior Managers Think," *Harvard Business Review* 62 (1984): 81–90.
50. M. Novicevic, T. J. Hench, and D. A. Wren, "'Playing by Ear'... 'in an Incessant Din of Reasons': Chester Barnard and the History of Intuition in Management Thought," *Management Decision* 40 (2002): 992–1003.
51. N. Khatri and H. A. Ng, "The Role of Intuition in Strategic Decision Making," *Human Relations* 53 (2000): 57–86.
52. C. I. Barnard, *The Functions of the Executive* (Cambridge, Mass.: Harvard University Press, 1938).
53. R. Rowan, *The Intuitive Manager* (New York: Little, Brown, 1986).
54. Novicevic et al., "'Playing by Ear'... 'in an Incessant Din of Reasons.'"
55. Khatri and Ng, "The Role of Intuition in Strategic Decision Making," 59.
56. Ibid.
57. W. H. Agor, *Intuition in Organizations* (Newbury Park, Calif.: Sage, 1989).
58. Khatri and Ng, "The Role of Intuition in Strategic Decision Making," 60.
59. J. Sutherland, "It Takes a Village," *The Globe and Mail ROB Magazine,* April 2005, 32.
60. Ibid.
61. J. L. Redford, R. H. McPhierson, R. G. Frankiewicz, and J. Gaa, "Intuition and Moral Development," *Journal of Psychology* 129 (1994): 91–101.
62. Hayashi, "When to Trust Your Gut," 64.
63. Ibid., 65.
64. D. van Knippenberg, B. van Knippenberg, and E. van Dijk, "Who Takes the Lead in Risky Decision Making? Effects of Group Members' Risk Preferences and Prototypicality," *Organizational Behavior and Human Decision Processes* 83 (2000): 213–34.
65. T. S. Perry, "How Small Firms Innovate: Designing a Culture for Creativity," *Research Technology Management* 28 (1995): 14–17.
66. B. M. Staw, "Knee-Deep in the Big Muddy: A Study of Escalating Commitment to a Chosen Course of Action," *Organizational Behavior and Human Performance* 16 (1976): 27–44; B. M. Staw, "The Escalation of Commitment to a Course of Action," *Academy of Management Review* 6 (1981): 577–87.
67. G. Whyte, A. M. Saks, and S. Hook, "When Success Breeds Failure: The Role of Self-Efficacy in Escalating Commitment to a Losing Course of Action," *Journal of Organizational Behaviour* 18 (1997): 415–32.
68. B. M. Staw and J. Ross, "Understanding Behavior in Escalation Situations," *Science* 246 (1989): 216–20.
69. S. Finkelstein and S. H. Sanford, "Learning from Corporate Mistakes: The Rise and Fall of Iridium," *Organizational Dynamics* 29 (2000): 138–48.
70. Whyte et al., "When Success Breeds Failure," 415.
71. Ibid., 423.
72. H. Drummond, "Take Off Optional, Landing Compulsory: Risk and Escalation in Decision Making," *Business Strategy Review* 14 (2003): 42.
73. B. M. Staw, "The Escalation of Commitment: An Update and Appraisal," in *Organizational Decision Making,* ed. Z. Shapira (Cambridge, England: Cambridge University Press, 1997).
74. L. Festinger, *A Theory of Cognitive Dissonance* (Evanston, Ill.: Row, Peterson, 1957).
75. G. Whyte, "Diffusion of Responsibility: Effects on the Escalation Tendency," *Journal of Applied Psychology* 76 (1991): 408–15.
76. H. Drummond, "Take Off Optional, Landing Compulsory," 43–44.
77. C. G. Jung, *Psychological Types* (London: Routledge & Kegan Paul, 1923).
78. I. I. Mitroff and R. H. Kilmann, "On Organization Stories: An Approach to the Design and Analysis of Organization through Myths and Stories," in *The Management of Organization Design,* ed. R. H. Killman, L. R. Pondy, and D. P. Slevin (New York: Elsevier–North Holland, 1976); B. K. Blaylock and L. P. Rees, "Cognitive Style and the Usefulness of Information," *Decision Sciences* 15 (1984): 74–91; D. L. Davis, S. J. Grove, and P. A. Knowles,

"An Experimental Application of Personality Type as an Analogue for Decision-Making Style," *Psychological Reports* 66 (1990): 167–75.

79. C. R. Leana, E. A. Locke, and D. M. Schweiger, "Fact and Fiction in Analyzing Research on Participative Decision Making: A Critique of Cotton, Vollrath, Froggatt, Lengnick-Hall, and Jennings," *Academy of Management Review* 15 (1990): 137–46; J. L. Cotton, D. A. Vollrath, M. L. Lengnick-Hall, and K. L. Froggatt, "Fact: The Form of Participation Does Matter—A Rebuttal to Leana, Locke, and Schweiger," *Academy of Management Review* 15 (1990): 147–53.
80. L. A. Witt, M. C. Andrews, and K. M. Kacmar, "The Role of Participation in Decision Making in the Organizational Politics–Job Satisfaction Relationship," *Human Relations* 53 (2000): 341–58.
81. G. Hamel, "Reinvent Your Company," *Fortune* 141 (June 12, 2000): 98–118.
82. V. H. Vroom and P. W. Yetton, *Leadership and Decision Making* (Pittsburgh: University of Pittsburgh, 1973).
83. V. H. Vroom, "Leadership and the Decision-Making Process," *Organizational Dynamics* 28 (2000): 82–94.
84. J. S. Black and H. B. Gregersen, "Participative Decision Making: An Integration of Multiple Dimensions," *Human Relations* 50 (1997): 859–78.
85. V.H. Vroom, "Leadership and the Decision-Making Process."
86. W. J. Duncan, K. G. LaFrance, and P. M. Ginter, "Leadership and Decision Making: A Retrospective Application and Assessment," *Journal of Leadership and Organizational Studies* 9, no. 4 (Spring 2003): 1; Vroom and Yetton, *Leadership and Decision Making.*
87. M. E. Shaw, *Group Dynamics: The Psychology of Small Group Behavior*, 3rd ed. (New York: McGraw-Hill, 1981).
88. P. W. Yetton and P. C. Bottger, "Individual versus Group Problem Solving: An Empirical Test of a Best Member Strategy," *Organizational Behavior and Human Performance* 29 (1982): 307–21.
89. W. Watson, L. Michaelson, and W. Sharp, "Member Compentence, Group Interaction, and Group Decision Making: A Longitudinal Study," *Journal of Applied Psychology* 76 (1991): 803–09.
90. R. F. Maier, "Assets and Liabilities in Group Problem Solving," *Psychological Review* 74 (1967): 239–49.
91. I. Janis, *Victims of Groupthink* (Boston: Houghton Mifflin, 1972).
92. M. A. Hogg and S. C. Hains, "Friendship and Group Identification: A New Look at the Role of Cohesiveness in Groupthink," *European Journal of Social Psychology* 28 (1998): 323–41.
93. P. E. Jones and H. M. P. Roelofsma, "The Potential for Social Contextual and Group Biases in Team Decision-Making: Biases, Conditions, and Psychological Mechanisms," *Ergonomics* 43 (2000): 1129–52; J. M. Levine, E. T. Higgins and H. Choi, "Development of Strategic Norms in Groups," *Organizational Behavior and Human Decision Processes* 82 (2000): 88–101.
94. C. P. Neck and G. Moorhead, "Groupthink Remodeled: The Importance of Leadership, Time Pressure, and Methodical Decision Making Procedures," *Human Relations* 48 (1995): 537–57.
95. J. K. Esser and J. S. Lindoerfer, "Groupthink and the Space Shuttle *Challenger* Accident: Toward a Quantitative Case Analysis," *Journal of Behavioral Decision Making* 2 (1989): 167–77.
96. R. R. Sims, "Linking Groupthink to Unethical Behavior in Organizations," *Journal of Business Ethics* 11 (1992): 651–62.
97. G. Moorhead, R. Ference, and C. P. Neck, "Group Decision Fiascoes Continue: Space Shuttle *Challenger* and a Revised Groupthink Framework," *Human Relations* 44 (1991): 539–50.
98. J. A. F. Stoner, "Risky and Cautious Shifts in Group Decisions: The Influence of Widely Held Values," *Journal of Experimental Social Psychology* 4 (1968): 442–59.
99. S. Moscovici and M. Zavalloni, "The Group as a Polarizer of Attitudes," *Journal of Personality and Social Psychology* 12 (1969): 125–35.
100. G. R. Goethals and M. P. Zanna, "The Role of Social Comparison in Choice of Shifts," *Journal of Personality and Social Psychology* 37 (1979): 1469–76.
101. A. Vinokur and E. Burnstein, "Effects of Partially Shared Persuasive Arguments on Group-Induced Shifts: A Problem-Solving Approach," *Journal of Personality and Social Psychology* 29 (1974): 305–15.
102. C. J. Nemeth, "Managing Innovation: When Less Is More," *California Management Review* 40 (1997): 59–68.
103. K. Dugosh, P. Paulus, E. Roland, and H. Yang, "Cognitive Stimulation in Brainstorming," *Journal of Personality and Social Psychology* 79 (2000): 722–35.
104. W. H. Cooper, R. B. Gallupe, S. Pollard, and J. Cadsby, "Some Liberating Effects of Anonymous Electronic Brainstorming," *Small Group Research* 29 (1998): 147–78; S. S. K. Lam and J. Schaubroeck, "Improving Group Decisions by Better Pooling Information: A Comparative Advantage of Groups Decision Support Systems," *Journal of Applied Psychology* 85 (2000): 565–73.
105. A. Van de Ven and A. Delbecq, "The Effectiveness of Nominal, Delphi and Interacting Group Decision-Making Processes," *Academy of Management Journal* 17 (1974): 605–21.
106. A. L. Delbecq, A. H. Van de Ven, and D. H. Gustafson, *Group Techniques for Program Planning: A Guide to Nominal, Group, and Delphi Processes* (Glenview, Ill.: Scott, Foresman, 1975).
107. R. A. Cosier and C. R. Schwenk, "Agreement and Thinking Alike: Ingredients for Poor Decisions," *Academy of Management Executive* 4 (1990): 69–74.

Chapter 9

1. P. Drinnan, "A New Lifeline for the Field," *Transmission and Distribution World* 55, (July 1, 2003): 34.
2. D. O'Byrne and B. Leavy, "Horizontal Power Differences: An Exploratory Study," *IBAR* (Dublin) 18 (1997): 178–91.
3. M. A. Rahim, D. Antonioni, and C. Psenicka, "A Structural Equations Model of Leader Power, Subordinates' Styles of Handling Conflict, and Job Performance," *International Journal of Conflict Management* 12 (2001): 191.
4. A. Zanzi and R. N. O'Neill, "Sanctioned and Non-sanctioned Political Tactics," *Journal of Managerial Issues* 13 (Summer 2001): 246.
5. S. Applebaum, J. A. Asmar, R. Chehayeb, N. Konidas, et al., "Organizational Citizenship: A Case Study of MedLink Ltd.," *Team Performance Management* 9 (2003): 140.
6. R. M. Kanter, "Power Failure in Management Circuits," *Harvard Business Review* (July–August 1979): 31–54.
7. R. M. Kanter, "Power Failure in Management Circuits," *The HealthCare Forum Journal* 41, no. 2 (March/April 1998): 44–46.
8. J. R. P. French and B. Raven, "The Bases of Social Power," in *Group Dynamics: Research and Theory*, ed. D. Cartwright (Evanston, Ill.: Row, Peterson, 1962); T. R. Hinkin and C. A. Schriesheim, "Development and Application of New Scales to Measure the French and Raven (1959) Bases of Social Power," *Journal of Applied Psychology* 74 (1989): 561–67.
9. W. Burmeister, "Leadership Simplified: Abandoning the Einsteinian 'Unified Field Theory' Approach," *Journal of American Academy of Business* 3 (2003): 152.
10. P. P. Carson, K. D. Carson, and P. L. Pence, "Supervisory Power and Its Influence on Staff Members and Their

Customers," *Hospital Topics* 80, no. 3 (Summer 2002): 11–16.

11. Burmeister, "Leadership Simplified."
12. A. R. Elangovan and J. L. Xie, "Effects of Perceived Power of Supervisor on Subordinate Work Attitudes," *Leadership and Organization Development Journal* 21 (2000): 319–28.
13. Carson et al., "Supervisory Power and Its Influence on Staff Members and Their Customers."
14. "Bully Bosses Destroy Their Companies," *The Citizen,* April 3, 2002.
15. Elangovan and Xie, "Effects of Perceived Power of Supervisor on Subordinate Work Attitudes."
16. Ibid.
17. Ibid.; Rahim et al., "A Structural Equations Model of Leader Power, Subordinates' Styles of Handling Conflict, and Job Performance."
18. Elangovan and Xie, "Effects of Perceived Power of Supervisor on Subordinate Work Attitudes."
19. K. D. Elsbach and G. Elofson, "How the Packaging of Decision Explanations Affects Perceptions of Trustworthiness," *Academy of Management Journal* 43, no. 1 (2000): 80–89.
20. P. Scontrino, "The Infinite Organization: Celebrating the Positive Use of Power in Organizations," *Personnel Psychology* 56 (Autumn 2003): 767.
21. J. Conger and R. Kanungo, *Charismatic Leadership: The Elusive Factor in Organizational Effectiveness* (New York: Jossey-Bass, 1988).
22. J. Berdhal, "In Search of Power Equilibrium," *The Globe and Mail,* September 9, 2003, B11.
23. A. Papmehl, "For Most Knowledge Workers, It's a Question of Culture," *CMA Management* 75, no. 10 (February 2002): I2; L. Holdsworth and S. Cartwright, "Empowerment, Stress and Satisfaction: An Exploratory Study of a Call Centre," *Leadership and Organization Development* 24, no. 3 (2003): 131–40.
24. G. M. Spreitzer, M. A. Kizilos, and S. W. Nason, "A Dimensional Analysis of the Relationship between Psychological Empowerment and Effectiveness, Satisfaction, and Strain," *Journal of Management* 23 (1997): 679–704; A. K. Mishra, "Organizational Responses to Crisis: The Centrality of Trust," in *Trust in Organizations: Frontiers of Theory and Research,* ed. R. M. Kramer and T. R. Tyler (Thousand Oaks, Calif.: Sage, 1996), 261–87.
25. G. M. Spreitzer and A. K. Mishra, "To Stay or to Go: Voluntary Survivor Turnover Following an Organizational Downsizing," *Journal of Organizational Behaviour* 23 (September 2002): 707; "Transcending Academia: Rosabeth Moss Kanter," *Ivey Business Journal* 66 (May 1, 2002): 56.
26. J. Gleick, *Chaos: Making a New Science* (New York: Penguin, 1987), 136.
27. H. S. Laschinger and J. A. Sabiston, "Staff Nurse Empowerment and Workplace Behaviours," *The Canadian Nurse* 96, no. 2 (February 2000): 18.
28. Holdsworth and Cartwright, "Empowerment, Stress and Satisfaction: An Exploratory Study of a Call Centre."
29. D. A. Whetten and K. S. Cameron, *Developing Management Skills,* 5th ed. (Upper Saddle River, N.J.: Prentice Hall, 2002), 416.
30. Ibid., 90.
31. Ibid., 4–5; R. M. Kanter, "The New Managerial Work," *Harvard Business Review* 67, no. 6 (November/December 1989): 87.
32. W. R. Forrester and M. F. Maute, "The Impact of Relationship Satisfaction on Attribution, Emotions, and Behaviors Following Service Failure," *Journal of Applied Business Research* (2000): 4.
33. Ibid., 3.
34. J. J. Gabarro and J. P. Kotter, "Managing Your Boss," *Harvard Business Review* (January–February 1980): 92–100.
35. L. Whitney, "It's Best to Manage the Boss as Well as Your Job: Career Mail," *Daily Mail,* August 13, 2003, 1st, 66.
36. C. R. Hinings, D. J. Hickson, J. M. Pennings, and R. E. Schneck, "Structural Conditions of Intra-organizational Power," *Administrative Science Quarterly* 19 (1974): 22–44; P. J. Hickson et al., "A Strategic Contingencies Theory of Interorganization Power," *Administrative Science Quarterly* 16 (1971): 216.
37. C. S. Saunders, "The Strategic Contingencies Theory of Power: Multiple Perspectives," *The Journal of Management Studies* 27, no. 1 (1990): 1–18.
38. J. Pfeffer and G. Salancik, *The External Control of Organizations* (New York: Harper & Row, 1978).
39. T. M. Welbourne and C. O. Trevor, "The Roles of Departmental and Position Power in Job Evaluation," *Academy of Management Journal* 43, no. 4 (2000): 761–71.
40. R. H. Miles, *Macro Organizational Behavior* (Glenview, Ill.: Scott, Foresman, 1980).
41. D. Hickson, C. Hinings, C. Lee, R. E. Schneck, and J. M. Pennings, "A Strategic Contingencies Theory of Intra-organizational Power," *Administrative Science Quarterly* 14 (1971): 219–20.
42. I. Cohen and R. Lachman, "The Generality of the Strategic Contingencies Approach to Sub-unit Power," *Organization Studies* 9, no. 3 (1988): 371.
43. J. E. Barbuto, "Power and the Changing Environment," *Journal of Management Education* 24 (2000): 288–96.
44. S. Prashad, "Fill Your Power Gap," *The Globe and Mail,"* July 23, 2003, C3.
45. D. Kipnis, S. M. Schmidt, and I. Wilkinson, "Intra-organizational Influence Tactics: Explorations in Getting One's Way," *Journal of Applied Psychology* 65 (1980): 440–52; D. Kipnis, S. Schmidt, C. Swaffin-Smith, and I. Wilkinson, "Patterns of Managerial Influence: Shotgun Managers, Tacticians, and Bystanders," *Organizational Dynamics* (Winter 1984): 60–67; G. Yukl and C. M. Falbe, "Influence Tactics and Objectives in Upward, Downward, and Lateral Influence Attempts," *Journal of Applied Psychology* 75 (1990): 132–40.
46. Elangovan & Xie, "Effects of Perceived Power of Supervisor on Subordinate Work Attitudes."
47. L. A. Witt, M. C. Andrews, and K. M. Kacmar, "The Role of Participation in Decision-Making in the Organizational Politics–Job Satisfaction Relationship," *Human Relations* 53 (2000): 341–58.
48. P. M. Podsakoff and C. A. Schriesheim, "Field Studies of French and Raven's Bases of Power: Critique, Reanalysis, and Suggestions for Future Research," *Psychological Bulletin* 97 (1985): 387–411.
49. M. A. Rahim, D. Antonioni, and C. Psenicka, "A Structural Equations Model of Leader Power, Subordinates' Styles of Handling Conflict, and Job Performance," *The International Journal of Conflict Management* 12 (2001): 194; M. A. Rahim, "Relationships of Leader Power to Compliance and Satisfaction with Supervision: Evidence from a National Sample of Managers," *Journal of Management* 15 (1989): 545–56.
50. P. P. Carson, K. D. Carson, E. L. Knight, and C. W. Roe, "Power in Organizations: A Look through the TQM Lens," *Quality Progress* (November 1995): 73–78.
51. C. Argyris, "Management Information Systems: The Challenge to Rationality and Emotionality," *Management Science* 17 (1971): 275–92; J. Naisbitt and P. Aburdene, *Megatrends 2000* (New York: Morrow, 1990).
52. G. Yukl, P. J. Guinan, and D. Sottolano, "Influence Tactics Used for Different Objectives with Subordinates, Peers, and Superiors," *Groups & Organization Management* 20 (1995): 272–96.
53. P. David, M. A. Hitt, and J. Gimeno, "The Influence of Activism by Institutional Investors on R&D," *Academy of Management Journal* 44, no. 1 (2001): 144–57.

54. L. M. Andersson and T. S. Bateman, "Individual Environmental Initiative: Championing Natural Environmental Issues in U.S. Business Organizations," *Academy of Management Journal* 43 (2000): 548–70.
55. R. A. Thacker and S. J. Wayne, "An Examination of the Relationship between Upward Influence Tactics and Assessments of Promotability," *Journal of Management* 21 (1995): 739–56.
56. K. K. Eastman, "In the Eyes of the Beholder: An Attributional Approach to Ingratiation and Organizational Citizenship Behavior," *Academy of Management Journal* 37 (1994): 1379–91.
57. S. H. Appelbaum and B. Hughes, "Ingratiation as a Political Tactic: Effects within the Organization," *Management Decision* 36, no. 2 (1998): 85; R. A. Gordon, "Impact of Ingratiation on Judgments and Evaluations: A Meta-Analytic Investigation," *Journal of Personality and Social Psychology* 71 (1996): 54–70.
58. G. R. Ferris and T. A. Judge, "Personnel/Human Resources Management: A Political Influence Perspective," *Journal of Management* 17 (1991): 447–88.
59. B. T. Mayes and R. T. Allen, "Toward a Definition of Organizational Politics," *Academy of Management Review* 2 (1977): 672–78.
60. Appelbaum and Hughes, "Ingratiation as a Political Tactic," 85.
61. Whetten and Cameron, *Developing Management Skills*, 277.
62. Zanzi and O'Neill, "Sanctioned and Non-sanctioned Political Tactics."
63. E. Vigoda, "Reactions to Organizational Politics: A Cross-Cultural Examination in Israel and Britain," *Human Relations* 54, no. 11 (2001): 1483–1518.
64. D. Murphy, "In One Era and Out the Other: Management Using Industrial Age Model in Knowledge Age World, Author Says," *San Francisco Chronicle*, June 2, 2002, J1.
65. S. Applebaum, J. A. Asmar, R. Chehayeb, N. Konidas, V. Maksymiw-Duszara, and I. Duminica, "Organizational Citizenship: A Case Study of MedLink Ltd.," *Team Performance Management* 9, no. 5/6 (2003): 142; M. Valle and P. L. Perrewe, "Do Politics Perceptions Relate to Political Behaviors? Tests of an Implicit Assumption and Expanded Model," *Human Relations* 53, no. 3 (2000): 359–86.
66. M. L. Seidal, J. T. Polzer, and K. J. Stewart, "Friends in High Places: The Effects of Social Networks on Discrimination in Salary Negotiations," *Administrative Science Quarterly* 45 (2000): 1–24.
67. "Politics at Work: Backstabbing, Stolen Ideas, Scapegoats," *Director* 56, no. 4 (November 2002): 79.
68. Zanzi and O'Neill, "Sanctioned and Non-sanctioned Political Tactics," 247, 252.
69. D. A. Ralston, "Employee Ingratiation: The Role of Management," *Academy of Management Review* 10 (1985): 477–87; D. R. Beeman and T. W. Sharkey, "The Use and Abuse of Corporate Politics," *Business Horizons* (March–April 1987): 25–35.
70. W. E. O'Conner and T. B. Morrison, "A Comparison of Situational and Dispositional Predictors of Perceptions of Organizational Politics," *The Journal of Psychology* 135, no. 3 (May 2001): 301–12.
71. K. Kumar and M. S. Thibodeaux, "Organizational Politics and Planned Organizational Change," *Group and Organization Studies* 15 (1990): 354–65.
72. K. M. Kacmar and D. S. Carlson, "Further Validation of the Perceptions of Politics Scale (POPS): A Multiple Sample Investigation," *Journal of Management* 23 (1997): 627–58.
73. Ibid.
74. Beeman and Sharkey, "Use and Abuse of Corporate Politics," 37.
75. S. J. Ashford, N. P. Rothbard, S. K. Piderit, and J. E. Dutton, "Out on a Limb: The Role of Context and Impression Management in Selling Gender-Equity Issues," *Administrative Science Quarterly* 43 (1998): 23–57.

Chapter 10

1. R. J. House, P. J. Hanges, M. Javidan, P. W. Dorfman, and V. Gupta, *Culture, Leadership, and Organizations: The GLOBE Study of 62 Societies* (Thousand Oaks, Calif.: Sage Publications, 2004).
2. W. Burmeister, "Leadership Simplified: Abandoning the Einsteinian 'Unified Field Theory,'" *Journal of American Academy of Business* 3 (September 2003): 152.
3. Ibid.
4. S. Huhtala, "Celebrating Excellence—Northern Ontario Business Awards 2002: Good Leaders Are Effective Managers—MacKenzie," *Northern Ontario Business* 23 (November 2002): 15.
5. R. M. Stogdill, "Personal Factors Associated with Leadership: A Survey of the Literature," *Journal of Psychology* 25 (1948): 35–71.
6. S. A. Kirkpatrick and E. A. Locke, "Leadership: Do Traits Matter?" *Academy of Management Executive* (May 1991): 48–60.
7. J. P. Kotter, "Leadership Engine," *Executive Excellence* 17, no. 4 (April 2000): 7.
8. A. Walmsley, "Introducing Linda Cook," *The Globe and Mail*, June 27, 2003.
9. A. W. Halpin and J. Winer, "A Factorial Study of the Leader Behavior Description Questionnaire," in *Leader Behavior: Its Description and Measurement*, ed. R. M. Stogdill and A. E. Coons, research monograph no. 88, (Columbus, Ohio: Bureau of Business Research, The Ohio State University, 1957), 39–51.
10. P. Brethour, "Queen of the Machine, Brenda Hoffman, Was Brought in to Replace the TSE's Crash-Prone Trading Engine. Tough Job. Good Thing She's Pushy," *The Globe and Mail*, August 31, 2001, Metro, 23.
11. E. A. Fleishman, "Leadership Climate, Human Relations Training, and Supervisory Behavior," *Personnel Psychology* 6 (1953): 205–22.
12. CEO's Talk," *Canadian HR Reporter* 15 (July 2002): 17–20.
13. Ibid.
14. A. Davidson, "New Boss Poised to Take Care of Sick Kids," *The Globe and Mail*, November 19, 2004.
15. R. Tannenbaum and W. H. Schmidt, "How to Choose a Leadership Pattern," *Harvard Business Review* (March/April 1958).
16. R. J. House, "A Path–Goal Theory of Leader Effectiveness," *Administrative Science Quarterly* 16 (1971): 321–38; R. J. House and T. R. Mitchell, "Path–Goal Theory of Leadership," *Journal of Contemporary Business* 3 (1974): 81–97.
17. M. G. Evans, "Extensions of a Path–Goal Theory of Motivation," *Journal of Applied Psychology* 59, no. 2 (1974): 172.
18. C. A. Schriescheim and V. M. Von Glinow, "The Path–Goal Theory of Leadership: A Theoretical and Empirical Analysis," *Academy of Management Journal* 20 (1977): 398–405; E. Valenzi and G. Dessler, "Relationships of Leader Behavior, Subordinate Role Ambiguity, and Subordinate Job Satisfaction," *Academy of Management Journal* 21 (1978): 671–78; N. R. F. Maier, *Leadership Methods and Skills* (New York: McGraw-Hill, 1963).
19. C. Silverthorne, "A Test of Path–Goal Theory in Taiwan," *Leadership and Organization Development Journal* 22, no. 4 (2001): 151–59.
20. F. E. Fiedler, *Personality, Motivational Systems, and Behavior of High and Low LPC Persons*, tech. rep. no. 70-12 (Seattle: University of Washington, 1970); J. T. McMahon, "The Contingency Theory: Logic and Method Revisited," *Personnel Psychology* 25 (1972): 697–710; L. H. Peters, D. D. Hartke, and J. T. Pohlman, "Fiedler's Contingency Theory of Leadership: An Application of the Meta-analysis Procedures of Schmidt and Hunter," *Psychological Bulletin* 97 (1985): 224–85.
21. F. E. Fiedler, "The Contingency Model and the Dynamics of the Leadership

Process," in *Advances in Experimental and Social Psychology*, vol. 11, ed L. Berkowitz (New York: Academic Press, 1978).

22. F. E. Fiedler, "When IQ + Experience = Performance," *Leadership and Organization Development Journal* 22 (2001): 132; F. E. Fiedler, "Engineering the Job to Fit the Manager," *Harvard Business Review* 43 (1965): 115–22.
23. J. Hampton, "CEO Steps Down in Clash of Personalities," *Canadian HR Reporter* (October 23, 2003).
24. S. Kerr and J.M. Jermier, "Substitutes for Leadership: Their Meaning and Measurement," *Organizational Behavior and Human Performance* 22 (1978): 375–403.
25. P. M. Podsakoff, S. B. MacKenzie, and W. H. Bommer, "Meta-Analysis of the Relationships between Kerr and Jermier's Substitutes for Leadership and Employee Job Attitudes, Role Perceptions, and Performance," *Journal of Applied Psychology* 81 (1996): 380–99.
26. B. N. Smith, R. V. Montagno, and T. N. Kuzmenko, "Transformational and Servant Leadership: Content and Contextual Comparisons," *Journal of Leadership and Organizational Studies* 10 (Spring 2004): 80; B. M. Bass, "Power to Change: A Conversation with Bernard M. Bass," *Leadership In Action* 23, no. 2 (May/June 2003): 9.
27. B. N. Smith, R. V. Montagno, and T. N. Kuzmenko, "Transformational and Servant Leadership: Content and Contextual Comparisons"; B. M. Bass, "Theory of Transformational Leadership Redux," *Leadership Quarterly* 6 (1995): 469.
28. R. J. House and M. L. Baetz, "Leadership: Some Empirical Generalizations and New Research Directions," in *Research in Organizational Behavior*, vol. 1, ed. B. M. Staw (Greenwood, Conn.: JAI Press, 1979), 399–401; K. Toole, "Gzowski's Life Showed Us the Power of Charisma," *Winnipeg Free Press*, Metro, February 2, 2002, E10.
29. D. Waldman, G. G. Ramirez, R. J. House, and P. Puranam, "Does Leadership Matter? CEO Leadership Attributes and Profitability under Conditions of Perceived Environmental Uncertainty," *Academy of Management Journal* 44 (2001): 134–43.
30. J. M. Howell, "Two Faces of Charisma: Socialized and Personalized Leadership in Organizations," in *Charismatic Leadership: Behind the Mystique of Exceptional Leadership*, ed. J. A. Conger (San Francisco: Jossey-Bass, 1988).
31. R. Khurana, "Cult of Charisma: False Prophets, Lost Profits: Investors Have Thronged to Charismatic CEO's Promises of Financial Paradise. Now It's Judgement Day," *The Globe and Mail*, July 3, 2002, B1.
32. F. J. Yammarino, F. Dansereau, and C. J. Kennedy, "A Multiple-Level Multidimensional Approach to Leadership: Viewing Leadership through an Elephant's Eye," *Organizational Dynamics* 29 (2001): 149–63.
33. D. Sankowsky, "The Charismatic Leader as Narcissist: Understanding the Abuse of Power," *Organizational Dynamics* 23 (1995): 57–71.
34. D. McMurdy, "Yorkton's Anti-Scott Keeps an Even Keel: Bill Fulton Opposite Side of the Coin to Fiery Predecessor," *National Post*, February 25, 2002, FP1, FP12.
35. R. Kanungo, "Leadership in Organizations: Looking Ahead to the 21st Century," *Canadian Psychology* 39, no. 1–2 (1998): 78.
36. J. P. Kotter, *Leading Change* (Boston: HBS Press, 1996), 68–69.
37. G. Wheelwright, "The Martha Effect: Martha Piper Has the Intellect to Go Head-to-Head with the Academics at UBC and the Strategic Vision to Have Engineered a Quite Stunning Turnaround in UBC's Fortunes," *BC Business*, April 2003, 45.
38. C. Daniels, "Housley Rules: After Making His Mark at Zellers, Where He Garnered a Reputation as a Visionary Change Artist, Peter Housley Is Now Tackling the Burgeoning Business of High-Tech Personals," *Marketing Magazine*, April 24, 2000, 11–13.
39. A. E. Rafferty and M. A. Griffin, "Dimensions of Transformational Leadership: Conceptual and Empirical Extensions," *The Leadership Quarterly* 15 (2004): 329–54.
40. B. Z. Posner, "A Leadership Development Instrument for Students: Updated," *Journal of College Students Development* (July/August 2004): 444.
41. B. M. Bass, "From Transactional to Transformational Leadership: Learning to Share the Vision," *Organizational Dynamics* 19 (1990): 19–31; B. M. Bass, *Leadership and Performance beyond Expectations* (New York: Free Press, 1985).
42. W. Bennis, "Managing the Dream: Leadership in the 21st Century," *Training* 27 (1990): 43–48.
43. P. M. Podsakoff, S. B. MacKenzie, R. H. Moorman, and R. Fetter, "Transformational Leader Behaviors and Their Effects on Followers' Trust in Leader, Satisfaction, and Organizational Citizenship Behaviors," *Leadership Quarterly* 1 (1990): 107–42.
44. Bass, "Power to Change," 10.
45. T. A. Judge and J. E. Bono, "Five-Factor Model of Personality and Transformational Leadership," *Journal of Applied Psychology* 85 (2001): 751–65.
46. G. B. Graen and M. Uhl-Bien, "Relationship-Based Approach to Leadership: Development of Leader–Member Exchange (LMX) Theory of Leadership over 25 Years," *Leadership Quarterly* 6 (1995): 219–47; C. R. Gerstner and D. V. Day, "Meta-Analytic Review of Leader–Member Exchange Theory: Correlates and Construct Issues," *Journal of Applied Psychology* 82 (1997): 827–44; R. C. Liden, S. J. Wayne, and R. T. Sparrowe, "An Examination of the Mediating Role of Psychological Empowerment on the Relations between the Job, Interpersonal Relationships, and Work Outcomes," *Journal of Applied Psychology* 85 (2001): 407–16.
47. J. Townsend, J. S. Phillips, and T. J. Elkins, "Employee Retaliation: The Neglected Consequence of Poor Leader–Member Exchange Relations," *Journal of Occupational Health Psychology* 5 (2000): 457–63.
48. D. Nelson, R. Basu, and R. Purdie, "An Examination of Exchange Quality and Work Stressors in Leader–Follower Dyads," *International Journal of Stress Management* 5 (1998): 103–12.
49. S. J. Zaccaro and P. Bader, "E-Leadership and the Challenges of Leading E-teams," *Organization Dynamics* 31 (2003): 377.
50. W. Cascio and S. Shurygailo, "E-Leadership and Virtual Teams," *Organizational Dynamics* 31 (2003): 362–76.
51. Ibid., 372, 374.
52. A. Malhotra, A. Majchrzak, R. Carman, and V. Lott, "Radical Innovation without Collocation: A Case Study at Boeing-Rocketdyne," *MIS Quarterly* 25 (2001): 229–49.
53. G. N. Powell, A. A. Butterfield, and J. D. Parent, "Gender and Managerial Stereotypes: Have the Times Changed?" *Journal of Management* 28 (2002): 177–93; M. E. Heilman, C. J. Block, R. F. Martell, and M. C. Simon, "Has Anything Changed? Current Characteristics of Men, Women, and Managers," *Journal of Applied Psychology* 74 (1989): 935–42.
54. A. H. Eagly and M. C. Johannesen-Schmidt, "The Leadership Styles of Women and Men," *Journal of Social Issues* 57 (2001): 781–97; A. H. Eagly, S. J. Darau, and M. Makhijani, "Gender and the Effectiveness of Leaders: A Meta-Analysis," *Psychological Bulletin* 117 (1995): 125–45; S. H. Appelbaum, L. Audet, and J. D. Miller, "Gender and Leadership? Leadership and Gender? A Journey through the Landscape of

Theories," *Leadership and Organization Development Journal* 24 (2003): 43–51.
55. A. H. Eagly and L. L. Carli, "The Female Advantage: An Evaluation of the Evidence," *The Leadership Quarterly* 14 (2003): 807–34.
56. Ibid., 825.
57. G. Pitts, "Men and Women Don't Manage Differently After All, Study Finds," *The Globe and Mail,* May 27, 2002, Metro, B1; S. Burke and K. M. Collins, "Gender Differences in Leadership Styles and Management Skills," *Women in Management Review* 16 (2001): 244–57.
58. N. J. Adler, *International Dimensions in Organizational Behavior* (Mason, Ohio: South-Western, 2001).
59. D. Carl, "Project GLOBE," Presentation at Ryerson University, February 15, 2005; R. J. House, P. J. Hanges, M. Javidan, P. W. Dorfman, and V. Gupta, *Culture, Leadership and Organizations, The GLOBE Study of Societies* (Thousand Oaks, Calif.: Sage Publications, 2004).
60. M. Javidan and R. J. House, "Cultural Acumen for the Global Manager, *Organizational Dynamics* 29 (2001): 289–305.
61. F. C. Brodback et al., "Cultural Variation of Leadership Prototypes across 22 European Countries," *Journal of Occupational and Organizational Psychology* 73 (2000): 1–29.
62. M. Smith-Carsley, "Look Out Future Shop," *Canadian Business,* July 9–23, 2001, 46–50.
63. R. K. Greenleaf, L. C. Spears, and D. T. Frick, eds., *On Becoming a Servant-Leader* (San Francisco: Jossey-Bass, 1996).
64. J. Walker, "A New Call to Stewardship and Servant Leadership," *Nonprofit World* 21, no. 4 (July/August 2003): 25; S. Sendjaya and J. C. Sarros, "Servant Leadership: Its Origin, Development, and Application in Organizations," *Journal of Leadership & Organization Studies* 9, no. 2 (Fall 2002): 57–65; R. F. Russell, "The Role of Values in Servant Leadership," *Leadership & Organization Development Journal* 22, no. 2 (2001): 76–84.
65. A. G. Stone, R. F. Russell, and K. Patterson, "Transformational versus Servant Leadership: A Difference in Leader Focus," *Leadership and Organization Development Journal* 25 (2004): 349–61.
66. B. Alimo-Metcalfe and R.J. Alban-Metcalfe, "The Development of a New Transformational Leadership Questionnaire," *Journal of Occupational and Organizational Psychology* 74 (2001): 1–27.
67. P. B. Murphy and G. Enderle, "Managerial Ethical Leadership: Examples Do Matter," *Business Ethics Quarterly* 5 (1995): 117–28.
68. R. Kanungo, "Ethical Values of Transactional and Transformational Leaders," *Revue Canadienne de Science de l'Administration* 18 (2001): 257–66; B. M. Bass and P. Steidlmeir, "Ethics, Character, and Authentic Transformational Behaviour," *Leadership Quarterly* 10 (1999): 181–217.
69. R. A. Mang, "Corporate Social Responsibility," *The Globe and Mail,* September 10, 2003, N1.
70. "The 2004 Best 50 Corporate Citizens," Corporate Knights.ca, 2004, http://www.corporateknights.ca/best50/2004best50.asp.

Chapter 11

1. D. Tjosvold, *The Conflict-Positive Organization* (Reading, Mass.: Addison-Wesley, 1991).
2. C. Bendersky, "Organizational Dispute Resolution Systems: A Complementarities Model," *Academy Management Review* 28 (2003): 643–55.
3. "Workplace Tiffs Boosting Demand for Mediators: Settling Conflicts Quickly Can Be an Aid to Bottom Line," *National Post,* March 17, 2003, FP8.
4. J. K. Jameson, "Toward a Comprehensive Model for the Assessment and Management of Intra-organizational Conflict: Developing the Framework," *International Journal of Conflict Management* 10 (1999): 269.
5. J. P. Meyer, J. M. Gemmell, and P. G. Irving, "Evaluating the Management of Interpersonal Conflict in Organizations: A Factor-Analytic Study of Outcome Criteria," *Canadian Journal of Administrative Science* 14 (1997): 1–13.
6. B. Bowes, "Conflict Resolution Solution: Mediation Services Offer Courses to Deal with Discord in the Workplace," *Winnipeg Free Press,* August 23, 2003, F1.
7. M. Fitzgerald, "We Can Work It Out," *The Globe and Mail,* March 10, 2004, C1.
8. K. Jehn and E. A. Mannix, "The Dynamic Nature of Conflict: A Longitudinal Study of Intra-group Conflict and Group Performance," *Academy of Management Journal* 44 (2001): 238; A. M. Bodtker and J. K. Jameson, "Emotion in Conflict Formation and Its Transformation: Application to Organizational Conflict Management," *International Journal of Conflict Management* 12 (2001): 259–76.
9. Bodtker and Jameson, "Emotion in Conflict Formation and Its Transformation," 259.
10. Ibid.
11. Ibid., 261.
12. Ibid., 261; H. Schacter, "Healthy Organizations Must Handle Pain," *The Globe and Mail,* April 16, 2003, Metro, C2.
13. A. W. Pearson, M. D. Ensley, and A. C. Amason, "An Assessment and Refinement of Jehn's Intragroup Conflict Scale," *The International Journal of Conflict Management* 13 (2002): 110–26.
14. Jehn and Mannix, "The Dynamic Nature of Conflict."
15. Jameson, "Toward a Comprehensive Model for the Assessment and Management of Intra-organizational Conflict," 272.
16. Pearson et al., "An Assessment and Refinement of Jehn's Intragroup Conflict Scale."
17. G. Fjetland, "Irreconcilable Differences," *BC Business,* October 2003, 73.
18. Jehn and Mannix, "The Dynamic Nature of Conflict," 239.
19. Ibid.
20. D. E. Lewis, "Company Culture Role Seen in Internal Strife," *Boston Globe,* July 13, 2003, Third, G2.
21. C. A. Schopler, J. Insko, J. Wieselquist, et al., "When Groups Are More Competitive Than Individuals: The Domain of the Discontinuity Effect," *Journal of Personality and Social Psychology* 80 (2001): 632–44.
22. Ibid.
23. J. D. Thompson, *Organizations in Action* (New York: McGraw-Hill, 1967).
24. G. Walker and L. Poppo, "Profit Centers, Single-Source Suppliers, and Transaction Costs," *Administrative Science Quarterly* 36 (1991): 66–87.
25. R. Miles, *Macro Organizational Behavior* (Glenview, Ill.: Scott, Foresman, 1980).
26. H. Levinson, "The Abrasive Personality," *Harvard Business Review* 56 (1978): 86–94.
27. B. Dyck, N. S. Bruning, and L. Driedger, "Potential Conflict, Conflict Stimulus, and Organizational Performance," *International Journal of Conflict Management* 7 (1996): 296.
28. R. A. Cosier and D. R. Dalton, "Positive Effects of Conflict: A Field Experiment," *International Journal of Conflict Management* 1 (1990): 81–92.
29. Tjosvold, *The Conflict-Positive Organization,* 4.
30. R. Sutton, "Why Innovation Happens When Happy People Fight," *Ivey Business Journal* 67, no. 2 (2002): 1–6.
31. J. R. Darling and W. E. Walker, "Effective Conflict Management: Use of the Behavioural Style Model," *Leadership and Organization Development Journal* 22 (2001): 230–42.
32. D. Tjosvold, "Making Conflict Productive," *Personnel Administrator* 29 (1984): 121–30; D. Schley, "Managing Conflict in Organizations," *International Journal of Conflict Management* 12 (2001): 88–90.

33. I. Janis, *Groupthink*, 2nd ed. (Boston: Houghton Mifflin, 1982).
34. A. C. Amason, W. A. Hochwarter, K. R. Thompson, and A. W. Harrison, "Conflict: An Important Dimension in Successful Management Teams," *Organizational Dynamics* 24 (1995): 25–35.
35. Tjosvold, "Making Conflict Productive."
36. Ibid.
37. R. Taylor, "Workplace Tiffs Boosting Demand for Mediators: Settling Conflicts Quickly Can Be an Aid to the Bottom Line," *National Post,* March 17, 2003, FP8.
38. Ibid.
39. R. Blake and J. Mouton, "Overcoming Group Warfare," *Harvard Business Review* 64 (1984): 98–108.
40. D. G. Ancona and D. Caldwell, "Improving the Performance of New Product Teams," *Research Technology Management* 33 (1990): 25–29.
41. D. K. Sobek, II, J. K. Liker, and A. C. Ward, "Another Look at How Toyota Integrates Product Development," *Harvard Business Review,* July–August 1998, 44.
42. Ibid., 42.
43. M. Rajim, "A Measure of Styles of Handling Interpersonal Conflict," *Academy of Management Journal* 26 (1983): 368–76.
44. H. Schachter, "Companies Don't Profit When the CEO Gets Sacked," *The Globe and Mail,* December 13, 2002, C1.
45. R. J. Lewicki, D. M. Saunders, and J. W. Minton, *Negotiation,* 3rd ed. (New York: Irwin, McGraw-Hill, 1999), 16.
46. K. W. Thomas, "Conflict and Conflict Management," in *Handbook of Industrial and Organizational Psychology,* ed. M. D. Dunnette (Chicago: Rand McNally, 1976), 900.
47. C. W. Lee, "Referent Role and Styles of Handling Interpersonal Conflict: Evidence from a National Sample of Korean Local Government Employees," *The International Journal of Conflict Management* 13 (2002): 128.
48. A. M. Rahim, D. Antonioni, and C. Psenicka, "A Structural Equations Model of Leader Power, Subordinates' Styles of Handling Conflict, and Job Performance," *International Journal of Conflict Management* 12 (2001): 192.
49. R. A. Baron, S. P. Fortin, R. L. Frei, L. A. Hauver, and M. L. Shack, "Reducing Organizational Conflict: The Role of Socially Induced Positive Affect," *International Journal of Conflict Management* 1 (1990): 133–52.
50. Lee, "Referent Role and Styles of Handling Interpersonal Conflict," 128.
51. Rahim, Antonioni, and Psenicka, "A Structural Equations Model of Leader Power, Subordinates' Styles of Handling Conflict, and Job Performance."
52. M. A. Rahim, N. R. Magner, and D. L. Shapiro, "Do Justice Perceptions Influence Styles of Handling Conflict with Supervisors? *International Journal of Conflict Management* 11, no. 1 (2000): 11.
53. S. L. Phillips and R. L. Elledge, *The Team Building Source Book* (San Diego: University Associates, 1989).
54. Lee, "Referent Role and Styles of Handling Interpersonal Conflict," 128.
55. Rahim, Antonioni, and Psenicka, "A Structural Equations Model of Leader Power, Subordinates' Styles of Handling Conflict, and Job Performance."
56. M. A. Gross and L. K. Guerrero, "Managing Conflict Appropriately and Effectively: An Application of the Competence Model to Rahim's Organizational Conflict Styles," *International Journal of Conflict Management* 11 (2000): 203.
57. Lee, "Referent Role and Styles of Handling Interpersonal Conflict"; P. J. Moberg, "Linking Conflict Strategy to the Five-Factor Model: Theoretical and Empirical Foundations," *The International Journal of Conflict Management* 12, no. 1 (2001): 49.
58. Rahim, Antonioni, and Psenicka, "A Structural Equations Model of Leader Power, Subordinates' Styles of Handling Conflict, and Job Performance."
59. S. Alper, D. Tjosvold, and K. S. Law, "Conflict Management, Efficacy, and Performance in Organizational Teams," *Personnel Psychology* 53 (2000): 625–42.
60. Gross and Guerrero, "Managing Conflict Appropriately and Effectively," 200; Rahim, Magner, and Shapiro, "Do Justice Perceptions Influence Styles of Handling Conflict with Supervisors?" 11.
61. K. W. Thomas, "Toward Multidimensional Values in Teaching: The Example of Conflict Behaviors," *Academy of Management Review* 2 (1977): 484–90.
62. W. King and E. Miles, "What We Know and Don't Know about Measuring Conflict," *Management Communication Quarterly* 4 (1990): 222–43.
63. J. Barker, D. Tjosvold, and I. R. Andrews, "Conflict Approaches of Effective and Ineffective Project Managers: A Field Study in a Matrix Organization," *Journal of Management Studies* 25 (1988): 167–78.
64. M. Chan, "Intergroup Conflict and Conflict Management in the R&D Divisions of Four Aerospace Companies," *IEEE Transactions on Engineering Management* 36 (1989): 95–104.
65. H. M. Guttman, "The Art of Managing Conflict: It Does No Good to Run Away from Disagreement and Discord," *USA Today* 132, January 2004, 62.
66. G. P. Latham, "A Five-Step Approach to Behaviour Change," *Organizational Dynamics* 32 (2003): 309; A. Tyerman and C. Spencer, "A Critical Text of the Sheriff's Robber's Cave Experiments: Intergroup Competition and Cooperation between Groups of Well-Acquainted Individuals," *Small Group Behavior* 14 (1983): 515–31; R. M. Kramer, "Intergroup Relations and Organizational Dilemmas: The Role of Categorization Processes," in *Research in Organizational Behavior* 13, ed. B. Staw and L. Cummings (Greenwich, Conn.: JAI Press, 1991), 191–228.
67. M. Chupp, "Reaching for Higher Ground in Conflict Resolution: Tools for Powerful Groups and Communities," *International Journal of Conflict Resolution* 13 (2002): 196.
68. ADR Institute of Canada, "FAQs," *News and Information,* http://www.adr-canada.ca/news/faq.html.
69. D. Mose and B. H. Kleiner, "The Emergence of Alternative Dispute Resolution in Business Today," *Equal Opportunities International* 18, no. 5/6 (1999): 54.
70. C. K. W. De Dreu, S. L. Koole, and W. Steinel, "Unfixing the Fixed Pie: A Motivated Information-Processing Approach to Integrative Negotiation," *Journal of Personality and Social Psychology* 79 (2000): 975–87.
71. Jameson, "Toward a Comprehensive Model for the Assessment and Management of Intra-organizational Conflict," 270, 271.
72. J. E. Lynch, "Beyond ADR: A Systems Approach to Conflict Management," *Negotiation Journal* 17 (2001): 213.
73. L. Tracy, "Sticks and Stones," *Today's Parent,* February 2004, B25.
74. "Healthy Interactions: Resolving Interpersonal Conflicts," *ATA News,* Edmonton, September 10, 2002.
75. K. Bickmore, "Education for Peacebuilding Citizenship: A Proposal for Teaching and Learning in the Context of Fragile Peace," *Canadian Issues,* September 2002, 19.
76. S. Cote and M. Pistorio, "Resolving Disputes," *CMA Management* 75, no. 7 (2001): 18–19.
77. Mose and Kleiner, "The Emergence of Alternative Dispute Resolution in Business Today," 57.
78. I. Sakinofsy, personal communication, April 2005.
79. R. J. Lewicki, D. M. Saunders, and J. W. Minton, *Negotiation,* 3rd ed. (New York: Irwin, McGraw-Hill, 1999), 1.

80. Ibid.; T. A. Kochan and D. B. Lipsky, *Negotiations and Change* (Ithaca, NY: ILR Press, 2003), 15–19.
81. D. M. Kolb, "Staying in the Game or Changing It: An Analysis of Moves and Turns in Negotiation," *Negotiation Journal* 20 (2004): 253–68.
82. Kochan and Lipsky, *Negotiations and Change,* 16.
83. P. H. Kim and A. R. Fragale, "Choosing the Path to Bargaining Power: An Empirical Comparison of BATNAs and Contributions in Negotiation," *Journal of Applied Psychology* 90 (2005): 373–81.
84. Kolb, "Staying in the Game or Changing It," 253.
85. C. K. W. De Dreu, S. L. Koole, and W. Steinel, "Unfixing the Fixed Pie: A Motivated Information-Processing Approach to Integrative Negotiation," *Journal of Personality and Social Psychology* 79 (2000): 975–87.
86. I. Sakinofsy, personal communication, April 2005.
87. M. H. Bazerman, J. R. Curhan, D. A. Moore, and K. L. Valley, "Negotiation," *Annual Review of Psychology* 51 (2000): 279.

Chapter 12

1. C. O'Reilly, "Achieve Extraordinary Results with Ordinary People," zfu.com (2003), accessed July 10, 2004, from http://www.zfu.ch/service/fartikel/fartikel_01_cor.htm.
2. J. Boorstin, "J. M. Smucker," *Fortune* (January 12, 2004): 58–59.
3. K. Macklem, "Top 100 Employers," *Maclean's* (October 20, 2003): 22.
4. D. S. Sundaram and C. Webster, "Exploring the Relationships among Organizational Culture, Customer Satisfaction, and Performance," byu.edu (1999), accessed July 10, 2004, http://marketing.byu.edu/htmlpages/ccrs/proceedings99/webster.htm.
5. J. Chatman and S. Cha, "Leading by Leverage Culture," *California Management Review* 45 (Summer 2003).
6. E. H. Schein, *Organizational Culture and Leadership,* 2nd ed. (San Francisco: Jossey-Bass, 1992).
7. J. Want, "When Worlds Collide: Culture Clash: Corporate Culture—Illuminating the Black Hole," *Journal of Business Strategy* 24 (July–August 2003): 14–22.
8. B. Schneider, "The People Make the Place," *Personnel Psychology* 40 (1987): 437–53.
9. S. Robbins, "Culture as Communication," *Harvard Management Communication Letter* (2001).
10. J. P. Kotter and J. L. Heskett, *Corporate Culture and Performance* (New York: The Free Press, 1992).
11. P. Pritchett, D. Robinson, and R. Clarkson, *After the Merger* (New York: McGraw-Hill, 1997).
12. "Most Organizations Mishandle the People Side of Mergers and Acquisitions, According to Study by Right Management Consultants," *Business Wire,* December 3 2003, http://www.findarticles.com/p/articles/mi_m0EIN/is_2003_Dec_3/ai_110820142.
13. "HP-Compaq Merger Completed," BBC News website, May 3, 2002, http://news.bbc.co.uk/1/hi/business/1960977.stm, accessed July 28, 2004.
14. S. Bekker, "Investors Hammer HP-Compaq after Merger Announcement," *ENT News,* September 4, 2001, http://www.entmag.com/news/article.asp?EditorialsID=4913, accessed July 28, 2004.
15. G. Morgan, *Images of Organization: The Executive Edition* (San Francisco: Berrett-Koehler Publishers, 1998).
16. Kotter and Heskett, *Corporate Culture and Performance;* Schein, *Organizational Culture and Leadership.*
17. J. Chatman and S. Cha, "Leading by Leverage Culture," *California Management Review* 45 (Summer 2003); Schein, *Organizational Culture and Leadership.*
18. Robbins, "Culture as Communication."
19. Indigo Books & Music, Inc., *Employee Handbook* (October 2001).
20. Canadian Imperial Bank of Commerce website, July 20, 2004, http://www.cibc.com.
21. C. D. Sutton and D. L. Nelson, "Elements of the Cultural Network: The Communicators of Corporate Values," *Leadership and Organization Development* 11 (1990): 3–10.
22. J. M. Beyer and H. M. Trice, "How an Organization's Rites Reveal Its Culture," *Organizational Dynamics* 16 (1987): 5–24.
23. Craig Bradshaw (Vice President, Human Resources, Bacardi Canada Inc.), interview with author, August 3, 2004, Toronto, Ont.
24. H. M. Trice and J. M. Beyer, "Studying Organizational Cultures through Rites and Ceremonials," *Academy of Management Review* 9 (1984): 653–69.
25. H. Levinson and S. Rosenthal, *CEO: Corporate Leadership in Action* (New York: Basic Books, 1984).
26. V. Sathe, "Implications of Corporate Culture: A Manager's Guide to Action," *Organizational Dynamics* 12 (1987): 5–23.
27. "Apple to Post $45 Million Profit," Cnet News.com, January 6, 1998, http://news.com.com/2100-1001-206820.html?legacy=cnet, accessed July 27, 2004.
28. "The Steve Jobs Way," Cnn.com, April 23, 2004, http://www.cnn.com/2004/WORLD/americas/04/16/jobs/, accessed July 27, 2004.
29. J. Martin, M. S. Feldman, M. J. Hatch, and S. B. Sitkin, "The Uniqueness Paradox in Organizational Stories," *Adminstrative Science Quarterly* 28 (1983): 438–53.
30. R. Goffee and G. Jones, "What Holds the Modern Company Together?" *Harvard Business Review* (November–December 1996): 133–43.
31. Craig Bradshaw (Vice President, Human Resources, Bacardi Canada Inc.), interview with author, August 3, 2004.
32. Indigo Books & Music, Inc., *Employee Handbook* (October 2001).
33. C. Argyris and D. A. Schon, *Organizational Learning* (Reading, Mass.: Addison-Wesley, 1978).
34. A. Lindgren, "Tax Hike Is Biggest since NDP," *The National Post,* May 19, 2004; T. Blackwell, "Balanced Budget Act to be Repealed," *The National Post,* May 19, 2004.
35. C. Edwards, M. Ihlwan, and P. Engardio, "The Samsung Way," *Business Week* (June 16, 2003): 56–64; Samsung website, http://www.samsung.com, accessed July 28, 2004.
36. Heather Reisman (CEO, Indigo Books Inc.), interview with author, July 29, 2004, Toronto, Ont.
37. T. M. Nolan, L. D. Goodstein, and J. W. Pfeiffer, *Plan or Die!* (Amsterdam: Pfeiffer & Company, 1993).
38. Terrence E. Deal and Allen A. Kennedy, *Corporate Cultures: The Rites and Rituals of Corporate Life* (Reading, MA: Addison Wesley, 1982).
39. R. Harrison and H. Stokes. *Diagnosing Organizational Culture* (San Francisco: Pfeiffer, 1992).
40. J. Want, "When Worlds Collide: Culture Clash: Corporate Culture—Illuminating the Black Hole," *Journal of Business Strategy* 24 (July–August 2003): 14–22.
41. T. E. Deal and A. A. Kennedy, "Corporate Tribes Identifying the Culture," *Modern Office Procedures* 28 (1983): 12–15.
42. T. Van Alphen and R. Westhead, "Gains Creditor Protection," *Toronto Star,* January 30, 2004, A1; D. Olive, "Culture Clash Underlines Woes," *Toronto Star,* January 30, 2004, A1.
43. Want, "When Worlds Collide."
44. Westjet Airlines website, from http://www.westjet.com, accessed July 25, 2004.
45. W. E. Schneider, "Why Good Management Ideas Fail: The Neglected Power of Organizational Culture," *Strategy & Leadership* 28 (January/February 2000): 24.
46. Schein, *Organizational Culture and Leadership.*
47. J. C. Collins and J. I. Porras, *Built to Last* (New York: HarperBusiness, 1994).
48. T. E. Deal and A. A. Kennedy, *Corporate Cultures* (Reading, Mass.: Addison-Wesley, 1982).

49. Chatman and Cha, "Leading by Leverage Culture."
50. D. McMurdy, "Reinventing the Bay: CEO George Heller Is Returning Canada's Oldest Corporation to Its Roots," *Calgary Herald*, May 9, 2004, E5.
51. T. Noda and D. J. Collis, "The Evolution of Intraindustry Firm Heterogeneity: Insights from a Process Study," *Academy of Management Journal* 44 (2001): 897–925.
52. D. Rynecki and L. Clifford, "Ten Stocks to Last the Decade," *Fortune* 142 (2000): 114–22; T. Harbert, "A Tale of Two Mobile Telephone Makers," *Company Business and Marketing* 26 (2000): 88.
53. R. H. Kilman, M. J. Saxton, and R. Serpa, eds., *Gaining Control of the Corporate Culture* (San Francisco: Jossey-Bass, 1986).
54. J. P. Kotter, *A Force for Change: How Leadership Differs from Management* (New York: Free Press, 1990); R. M. Kanter, *The Change Masters* (New York: Simon & Schuster, 1983).
55. T. Peters and N. Austin, *A Passion for Excellence: The Leadership Difference* (New York: Random House, 1985).
56. Kotter and Heskett, *Corporate Culture and Performance.*
57. Denison Consulting, *The Denison Model*, accessed June 23, 2004, from http://www.denisonculture.com.
58. Schein, *Organizational Culture and Leadership.*
59. Robbins, "Culture as Communication."
60. P. Selznick, *Leadership in Administration* (Row, Peterson, 1957). In T. J. Peters, *Harvard Business Review on Breakthrough Leadership: Leadership: Sad Facts and Silver Linings* (USA: Harvard Business School Publishing Corporation, 2001).
61. E. Heinrich, "RBC's 'Perfect Storm' Has Lessons for All," *Toronto Star*, July 19, 2004, D1.
62. D. C. Feldman, "The Multiple Socialization of Organization Members," *Academy of Management Review* 6 (1981): 309–18.
63. D. Stauffer, "Cultural Fit: Why Hiring Good People Is No Longer Good Enough," *Harvard Management Update* (1998).
64. Ibid.
65. D. Milmo, "Holling Scandal Deepens with SEC Subpoena," *The Guardian*, November 20, 2003.
66. C. Gillis, "The Nortel Shipwreck," *Maclean's* (May 10, 2004).
67. E. Mendes, "CEO of Major Canadian Brokerage Firm Fired over Conflict of Interest," Institute for Global Ethics, December 4, 2001, http://www.globalethics.org/newsline/members/issue.tmpl?articleid=12240111000436, accessed August 19, 2004.
68. "The End of Enron?" Cnn.com, 2002, http://www.cnn.com/SPECIALS/2002/enron/, accessed August 19, 2004.
69. S. W. Gellerman, "Why Good Managers Make Bad Ethical Choices," *Harvard Business Review* 64 (1986): 85–90.
70. J. Davidson, K. McLaughlin, and R. Benson-Armer, "Turn the Tide: What Companies Need to Do Today to Begin Regaining the Public's Trust," *Canadian Business* (February 16, 2004).
71. A. Bhide and H. H. Stevenson, "Why Be Honest if Honesty Doesn't Pay?" *Harvard Business Review* (September–October 1990): 121–29.
72. Johnson & Johnson, "Social Responsibility," accessed August 5, 2004, from http://www.jnj.com/community/index.htm.
73. B. Munck, "Changing a Culture of Face Time," *Harvard Business Review* (November 2001).
74. Ibid.
75. Ibid.
76. N. J. Adler, *International Dimensions of Organizational Behavior*, 2nd ed. (Boston: PWS Kent, 1991).
77. A. Laurent, "The Cultural Diversity of Western Conceptions of Management," *International Studies of Management and Organization* 13 (1983): 75–96.
78. P. C. Earley and E. Mosakowski, "Creating Hybrid Team Cultures: An Empirical Test of Transnational Team Functioning," *Academy of Management Journal* 43 (2000): 26–49.
79. P. Bate, "Using the Cultural Concept in an Organization Development Setting," *Journal of Applied Behavior Science* 26 (1990): 83–106.
80. K. R. Thompson and F. Luthans, "Organizational Culture: A Behavioural Perspective," in *Organizational Climate and Culture*, ed. B. Schneider (San Francisco: Jossey-Bass, 1990).
81. V. Sathe, "How to Decipher and Change Corporate Culture," *Managing Corporate Cultures*, ed. R. H. Kilman et al. (San Francisco: Jossey-Bass, 1985).
82. D. Lei, J. W. Slocum, Jr., and R. W. Slater, "Global Strategy and Reward Systems: The Key Role of Management Development and Corporate Culture," *Organizational Dynamics* 19 (1990): 27–41.
83. R. Konopaske and J. M. Ivancevich, *Global Management and Organizational Behavior* (New York: McGraw Hill Irwin, 2004).
84. S. H. Rhinesmith, "Going Global from the Inside Out," *Training and Development Journal* 45 (1991): 42–47.

Chapter 13

1. B. A. Spector, "From Bogged Down to Fired Up: Inspiring Organizational Change," in *Managing Change: Cases and Concepts*, 2nd ed., eds. T. D. Jick and M. A. Peiperl (New York: McGraw-Hill, 2003), 113.
2. L. Kehoe, "Traveling at the Speed of Cheese: Keep Pace, Best Seller Warns," *Financial Post*, April 19, 2001, C7.
3. L. Cranston, "Rehabilitating Canada's Blood," *Canadian Speeches* 13, no. 5 (November–December 1999): 53–58.
4. L. Ackerman, "Development, Transition, or Transformation: The Question of Change in Organizations," *OD Practitioner* 4 (December 1986): 1–8.
5. L. Sugden, "Building for Tomorrow," *CMA Management*, November 2001, 40–42.
6. C. MacKay, "Tactical Talk: Successful Company Transition," *Manitoba Business*, July/August 1999, 8.
7. Jick and Peiperl, *Managing Change*, xvi.
8. Ackerman, "Development, Transition, or Transformation."
9. Jick and Peiperl, *Managing Change*, xviii.
10. H. Schachter, "Masters of Their Own Destruction," *The Globe and Mail*, August 22, 2001, M1.
11. T. D. Jick, *Managing Change* (Homewood, Ill.: Irwin, 1993), 3.
12. J. A. Chapman, "A Framework for Transformational Change in Organizations," *Leadership and Organization Development* 23 (2002): 16–25.
13. A. Budros, "The Mean and Lean Firm and Downsizing: Causes of Involuntary and Voluntary Downsizing Strategies," *Sociological Forum* 17 (June 2002): 307–42.
14. M. Armstrong-Stassen and T. H. Wagar, "Sustaining a Service Quality Initiative in the Midst of Downsizing," *Journal of Quality Management* 6, no. 2 (2001): 211–33.
15. C. Zehir and F. Z. Savi, "A Field Research about Implications of Organizational Downsizing on Employees Working for Turkish Public Banks, *The Journal of American Academy of Business* 5 (September 2004): 343–49; R. J. Burke, "Nursing Staff Survivor Responses to Hospital Restructuring and Downsizing," *Stress and Health* 17 (2001): 195–205.
16. B. Wright and J. Barling, "The Executioners' Song: Listening to Downsizers Reflect on Their Experiences," *Canadian Journal of Administrative Sciences* 15 (1998): 339–55.
17. R. Karambayya, "Caught in the Crossfire," *Canadian Journal of Administrative Sciences* 15 (1998): 337.
18. K. Devine, T. Reay, L. Stainton, and R. Collins-Nakai, "Downsizing Outcomes: Better a Victim Than a Survivor?" *Human Resource Management* 42, no. 2 (Summer 2003): 109–24.

19. K. S. Cameron, S. J. Freeman, and A. K. Mishra, "Best Practices in White Collar Downsizing: Managing Contradictions," *Academy of Management Executive* 5, no. 3 (1991): 57–73.
20. P. Tellier, "Turning CN Around," *Canadian Business Review,* Spring 1995, 31–32.
21. "BCE Reorganizes Bell Canada for a 'Competitive Future,'" *The Globe and Mail,* May 8, 2003, B1.
22. B. Gowigati, "The Winds of Change: Change Management Takes Off at Bombardier," *CMA Management,* November 2001, 34–38.
23. MacKay, "Tactical Talk: Successful Company Transition."
24. D. Brown and A. Tomlinson, "First Time Atlantic Canada Awards Celebrate HR," *Canadian HR Reporter,* August 12, 2002, 2–3.
25. F. Cheyunski and J. Millard, "Accelerated Business Transformation and the Role of the Organizational Architect," *Journal of Applied Behavioral Science* 34 (1998): 268–85.
26. N. A. M. Worren, K. Ruddle, and K. Moore, "From Organizational Development to Change Management: The Emergence of a New Profession," *Journal of Applied Behavioral Science* 35 (1999): 273–86.
27. D. Miller, "Successful Change Leaders: What Makes Them? What Do They Do That Is Different?" *Journal of Change Management* 2 (June 2002): 359–68.
28. P. G. Audia, E. A. Locke, and K. G. Smith, "The Paradox of Success: An Archival and a Laboratory Study of Strategic Persistence Following Radical Environmental Change," *Academy of Management Journal* 43 (2000): 837–53.
29. "Resistance to Change: Enemy or Ally?" *Strategic Direction,* June 2002.
30. J. W. Brehm, *A Theory of Psychological Reactance* (New York: Academic Press, 1966).
31. M. Johne, "Wanted: A Few Good Egocentric, Self-Serving Risk-Takers," *The Globe and Mail,* May 27, 2002, C1.
32. J. A. Klein, "Why Supervisors Resist Employee Involvement," *Harvard Business Review* 62 (1984): 87–95.
33. B. L. Kirkman, R. G. Jones, and G. L. Shapiro, "Why Do Employees Resist Teams? Examining the 'Resistance Barrier' to Work Team Effectiveness," *International Journal of Conflict Management* 11 (2000): 74–92.
34. D. L. Nelson and D. A. White, "Management of Technological Innovation: Individual Attitudes, Stress, and Work Group Attributes," *Journal of High Technology Management Research* 1 (1990): 137–48.
35. D. Sull, "Belay That Idea," *The Globe and Mail,* May 28, 2003, C1.
36. A. Reichers, "Understanding and Managing Cynicism about Organizational Change," *The Academy of Management Executive* 11 (1997): 48–59.
37. J. Thomas and R. Griffin, "The Social Information Processing Model of Task Design: A Review of the Literature," *Academy of Management Review* 8 (1983): 672–82.
38. D. Carter, "HR Must Engage Middle Managers," *Canadian HR Reporter,* July 14, 2003, 4.
39. Deloitte & Touche, *CIO Survey,* 1998.
40. B. Daigle, "Moving toward a Competency-Based HR Process," *Education Canada* 40, no. 4 (Winter 2001): 14–15.
41. K. Lewin, "Frontiers in Group Dynamics," *Human Relations* 1 (1947): 5–41.
42. W. McWhinney, "Meta-Praxis: A Framework for Making Complex Changes," in *Large-Scale Organizational Change,* ed. A. M. Mohrman, Jr., et al. (San Francisco: Jossey-Bass, 1989), 154–99.
43. Jick and Peiperl, *Managing Change,* 301.
44. M. Beer and E. Walton, "Developing the Competitive Organization: Interventions and Strategies," *American Psychologist* 45 (1990): 154–61.
45. K. Trader-Leigh, "Case Study: Identifying Resistance in Managing Change," *Journal of Organizational Change Management* 15, no. 2 (2002): 138–55.
46. Ibid.
47. J. P. Kotter, *Leading Change* (Boston: HBS Press, 1996).
48. "CEO's Talk," *Canadian HR Reporter,* December 16, 2002, 21–23.
49. D. St. Amour, "Successful Organizational Change: Effective Management of People and Cultural Issues," *Canadian Manager,* Summer 2001, 20–22.
50. "People Power Saves Day Remarkable Turnaround for Manitoba Lotteries," *Winnipeg Free Press,* April 12, 2003, F1.
51. "Young Entrepreneurs Take on the Market with Simulations Software," *The Training Report,* July 1998.
52. "Voices of Experience: Vita Health's Employee Initiative Committee as Invigorating Exercise in Making Changes," *Winnipeg Free Press,* June 15, 2002, Metro, F1.
53. P. Frost, "Toxic Shock," *The Globe and Mail,* February 5, 2003, C1.
54. E. Church, "Benefits of Being Worker and Boss, Employee Ownership Carries Much Potential, Prof. Carol Beatty Tells Elizabeth Church," *The Globe and Mail,* February 22, 2002, Metro, C1.
55. R. A. Dean, K. R. Ferris, and C. Konstans, "Reality Shock: Reducing the Organizational Commitment of Professionals," *Personnel Administrator* 30 (1985): 139–48.
56. J. P. Kotter and D. S. Cohen, *The Heart of Change* (Boston: HBR Press, 2002).
57. Jick and Peiperl, *Managing Change,* 115–20.
58. Ibid., 91.
59. "Understanding Needed to Overcome Resistance to Change," *Canadian HR Reporter,* May 6, 2002, 4.
60. M. Joffe and S. Glynn, "Facilitating Change and Empowering Employees," *Journal of Change Management* 2, no. 4 (June 2002): 369.
61. M. Pettapiece, "A Team Leader Steps Down; John Mayberry, Who Led a Revival at Dofasco, Is Passing the Torch," *Hamilton Spectator,* April 26, 2003, A01.
62. T. G. Cummings and C. G. Worley, *Organization Development and Change,* 7th ed. (Stamford, CT: Thomson, 2001), 1; D. Harvey and D. R. Brown, *An Experiential Approach to Organization Development,* 6th ed. (Upper Saddle River, NJ: Prentice Hall, 2001), 5.
63. A. Huczynski, *Encyclopedia of Organizational Change Methods* (Brookfield, VT: Gower, 1987).
64. Cummings and Worley, *Organization Development and Change,* 24.
65. T. Belford, "Engineers Seen Posing Challenges to Change Consultant Must Try to Convert 'Blockers,'" *The Globe and Mail,* April 21, 2003, B10.
66. W. L. French, C. H. Bell, Jr., and R. A. Zawacki, *Organization Development and Transformation: Managing Effective Change,* 6th ed. (New York: McGraw-Hill Irwin, 2005), 153.
67. "BMW Selects WebSurveyor for Online Survey Solutions," *PR Newswire,* May 6, 2003; C. Cammann, M. Fichman, G. D. Jenkins, and J. Klesh, "Assessing the Attitudes and Perceptions of Organization Members," in *Assessing Organizational Change: A Guide to Methods, Measures, and Practices,* ed. S. Seashore, E. Lawler, III, P. Mirvis, and C. Cammann (New York: Wiley, 1983), 71–138.
68. T. G. Cummings and C. G. Worley, *Essentials of Organization Development and Change* (Mason, OH: South-Western, 2001), 133.
69. W. Dyer, *Team Building,* 3rd. ed. (Boston: Addison-Wesley, 1995); A. Edmondson, "Psychological Safety and Learning Behavior in Work Teams," *Administrative Science Quarterly* 44 (1999): 350–83.
70. E. Schein, *Process Consultation: Its Role in Organization Development,* Vol. 1 (Reading, Mass.: Addison-Wesley, 1988).
71. H. Hornstein, "Organizational Development and Change Management: Don't Throw the Baby Out with the Bath Water," *Journal of Applied Behavioral Science* 37 (2001): 223–26.

72. J. Magruder Watkins and D. Cooperrider, "Appreciative Inquiry: A Transformative Paradigm," *OD Practitioner* 32, no. 1 (2000): 6–12.
73. M. J. Mantel and J. D. Ludema, "From Local Conversations to Global Change: Experiencing the Worldwide Web Effect of Appreciative Inquiry," *Organization Development Journal* 18, no. 2 (Summer 2000): 42; "Accentuating the Positive," *The Globe and Mail*, April 23, 2003, C2.
74. J. M. Watkins and B. Mohr, "Appreciative Inquiry: Change at the Speed of Imagination," *Organization Development Journal* 19, no. 3 (Fall 2001): 92–94.
75. B. H. Chen, "A National Survey of Student Investment Clubs in Taiwan: The Use of Appreciative Inquiry Approach," *Journal of American Academy of Business* 3 (2003): 256; G. Johnson and W. Leavitt, "Building on Success: Transforming Organizations through Appreciative Inquiry," *Public Personnel Management* 30 (Spring 2001): 129–37; L. Yballe and D. O'Conner, "Appreciative Pedagogy: Constructing Positive Models for Learning," *Journal of Management Education* 24 (2000): 474.
76. Mantel and Ludema, "From Local Conversations to Global Change," 44.
77. H. H. Owen, *Open Space Technology: A User's Guide*, 2nd ed. (San Francisco: Berrett-Koehler, 1997).
78. Ibid., 95.
79. H. H. Owen, *The Practice of Peace* (San Francisco: Berrett-Koehler, 2003).

Chapter 14

1. J. W. Rivkin and N. Siggelkow, "Balancing Search and Stability: Interdependencies among Elements of organizational Design," *Management Science* 49, no. 3 (2003): 292.
2. P. Lawrence and J. Lorsch, "Differentiation and Integration in Complex Organizations," *Administrative Science Quarterly* 12 (1967): 1–47.
3. R. Dewar and J. Hage, "Size, Technology, Complexity, and Structural Differentiation: Toward a Theoretical Synthesis," *Administrative Science Quarterly* 23 (1978): 111–36.
4. J. Child, *Organization* (New York: Harper & Row, 1984).
5. C. R. Littler, R. Weisner, and R. Dunford, "The Dynamics of Delayering: Changing Management Structures in Three Countries," *Journal of Management Studies* 40, no. 2 (2003): 225–56.
6. J. Hunter, "Improving Organizational Performance through the Use of Effective Elements of Organizational Structure," *International Journal of Health Care Quality Assurance* 15, no. 4/5 (2002): 12–21,
7. "Leave Your Ego at the Door," *Maclean's*, November 5, 2001, 50.
8. R. Daft, *Organization Theory and Design*, 7th ed. (Mason, OH: South-Western/Thomson Learning, 2000), 18.
9. Ibid., 96.
10. M. Hammer, "Processed Change: Michael Hammer Sees Process as 'The Clark Kent of Business Ideas,'" *Journal of Business Strategy* 22, no. 6 (2001): 11–16.
11. S. Stewart, "RBC's Nixon Overhauls Bank, Poaches Stymiest from TSX," *The Globe and Mail*, September 10, 2004, B13.
12. Sierra Systems Group Inc., *Annual Report 2002*, 15.
13. Daft, *Organization Theory and Design*, 112.
14. M. H. Overholt, "Flexible Organizations," *Human Resource Planning* 20, no. 2 (1997): 30.
15. http://www.magellanaero space.com/; organizational chart provided by J. Ball (Senior VP Human Resources).
16. D. Pugh, D. Hickson, C. Hinnings, and C. Turner, "Dimensions of Organization Structure," *Administrative Science Quarterly* 13 (1968): 65–91; B. Reimann, "Dimensions of Structure in Effective Organizations: Some Empirical Evidence," *Academy of Management Journal* 17 (1974): 693–708; S. Robbins, *Organization Theory: The Structure and Design of Organizations*, 3rd ed. (Englewood Cliffs, N.J.: Prentice-Hall, 1990).
17. C. A. Clarke, "Between a Rock and a Hard Place: RCMP Organizational Change," *Policing* 25, no. 1 (2002): 14.
18. Lawrence and Lorsch, "Differentiation and Integration," 1–47.
19. J. R. R. Galbraith, *Designing Complex Organizations,* (Reading, Mass.: Addison-Wesley-Longman, 1973).
20. W. Altier, "Task Forces: An Effective Management Tool," *Management Review* 76 (1987): 26–32.
21. P. Lawrence and J. Lorsch, "New Managerial Job: The Integrator," *Harvard Business Review* 45 (1967): 142–51.
22. V. Borg, "Barrick Gold Corp—Barrick to Make Major Changes in 2004," *Canada Stockwatch,* September 23, 2003.
23. J. Lorsch and P. Lawrence, "Organizing for Product Innovation," *Harvard Business Review* 43 (1965): 110–11.
24. E. Lawler, "Rethinking Organization Size," *Organizational Dynamics* 26, no. 2 (1997): 24–35.
25. D. F. Twomey, "Organizational Competitiveness: Building Performance and Learning," *Competitiveness Review* 12, no. 2 (2002): 1.
26. Daft, *Organization Theory and Design,* 103.
27. T. Burns and G. Stalker, *The Management of Innovation* (London: Tavistock, 1961); Mintzberg, *The Structuring of Organizations* (Englewood Cliffs, N.J.: Prentice-Hall, 1979).
28. C. Wang and P. K. Ahmed, "Structure and Structural Dimensions for Knowledge-Based Organizations," *Measuring Business Excellence* 7 (2003): 53.
29. H. Kolodny, M. Liu, B. Stymne, and H. Denis, "New Technology and the Emerging Organizational Paradigm," *Human Relations* 49 (1996): 1476.
30. J. Hunter, "Improving Organizational Performance through the Use of Effective Elements of Organizational Structure," *International Journal of Health Care Quality Assurance* 15, no. 4/5 (2002): 19.
31. J. Courtright, G. Fairhurst, and L. Rogers, "Interaction Patterns in Organic and Mechanistic Systems," *Academy of Management Journal* 32 (1989): 773–802.
32. P. Stahle and J. Hong, "Dynamic Intellectual Capital in Globally Rapidly Changing Industries," *Journal of Knowledge Management* 6, no. 2 (2002): 179.
33. Ibid.
34. Lawler, "Rethinking Organization Size."
35. M. Goulding and T. Pendlebury, "Corporate 'News Show' Introduces the Bottom Line to Staff," *Canadian HR Reporter,* June 17, 2002, 16.
36. Daft, *Organization Theory and Design.*
37. E. Lawler, "Managing Change," *Executive Excellence* 19 (February 2002): 18.
38. R. L. Heneman, M. M. Fisher, and K. E. Dixon, "Reward and Organizational Systems Alignment: An Expert System," *Compensation and Benefits Review* 33, no. 6 (2001): 18–29.
39. D. Miller, "The Structural and Environmental Correlates of Business Strategy," *Strategic Management Journal* 8 (1987): 55–76.
40. G. Verona and D. Ravasi, "Unbundling Dynamic Capabilities: An Exploratory Study of Continuous Product Innovation," *Industrial and Corporate Change* 12 (2003): 579.
41. Ibid., 595.
42. "Growing a Business by Chopping It to Bits," *Management Decision* 34 (1996): 5.
43. Lawler, E., *Rethinking Organization Size.*
44. R. Eisenstat, N. Foote, J. Galbraith, and D. Miller, "Beyond the Business Unit," *The McKinsey Quarterly* 1 (2001): 56–57.
45. Ibid., 54.
46. J. Woodward, *Industrial Organization: Theory and Practices* (London: Oxford University Press, 1965).
47. C. Perrow, "A Framework for the Comparative Analysis of Organizations," *American Sociological Review* 32 (1967):

194–208; D. Rosseau, "Assessment of Technology in Organizations: Closed versus Open Systems Approaches," *Academy of Management Review* 4 (1979): 531–42.
48. Perrow, "A Framework for the Comparative Analysis of Organizations."
49. H. Kolodny, "New Technology and the Emerging Organizational Paradigm," 1457.
50. P. Nemetz and L. Fry, "Flexible Manufacturing Organizations: Implication for Strategy Formulation and Organization Design," *Academy of Management Review* 13 (1988): 627–38; G. Huber, "The Nature and Design of Post-Industrial Organizations," *Management Science* 30 (1984): 934; E. Feitzinger and H. L. Lee, "Mass Customization at Hewlett-Packard: The Power of Postponement," *Harvard Business Review* 75 (1997): 116–21.
51. M. E. Raynor and J. L. Bower, "Lead from the Center: How to Manage Divisions Dynamically," *Harvard Business Review,* May 2001, 93.
52. T. C. Lawton and K. P. Michaels, "Advancing the Virtual Value Chain: Learning from the Dell Model," *Irish Journal of Management* 22 (2001): 91; S. Wang, "Impact of Information Technology on Organizations," *Human Systems Management* 16, no. 2 (1997): 83; C. C. Dibrell and T. R. Miller, "Organization Design: The Continuing Influence of Information Technology," *Management Decision* 40 (2002): 620–27.
53. Wang and Ahmed, "Structure and Structural Dimensions for Knowledge-Based Organizations," 51.
54. F. Twomey, "Leadership, Organization Design, and Competitiveness for the 21st Century," *Global Competitiveness* 10 (Annual 2002): S31.
55. Daft, *Organization Theory and Design,* 106; B. A. Spector, review of "The Horizontal Organization: What the Organization of the Future Looks Like and How It Delivers Value to the Customer," *The Academy of Management Executive* 13, no. 2 (1999): 97.
56. Spector, review of "The Horizontal Organization," 109.
57. H. H. Larsen, "Oticon: Unorthodox Project-Based Management and Career in a Spaghetti Organization," *Human Resource Planning* 25, no. 4 (2002): 30–37.
58. Eisenstat et al., "Beyond the Business Unit," 56–57.
59. J. Galbraith, *Tomorrow's Organization: Crafting Winning Capabilities in a Dynamic World* (San Francisco: Jossey-Bass, 1998), 52–53.
60. Lawler, "Rethinking Organization Size," 30.
61. J. Galbraith, "Building Organizations around the Global Customer," *Ivey Business Journal* 66 (2001): 17.
62. Ibid., 51.
63. P. Burrows, "Why a Bold Management Plan Didn't Work," *Business Week,* April 1, 2002, 36.
64. D. Lei and J. W. Slocum, Jr., "Organization Designs to Renew Competitive Advantage," *Organizational Dynamics* 31, no. 1 (August 2002): 1–18; J. Fulk, "Global Network Organizations: Emergence and Future Prospects," *Human Relations* 54 (2001): 91–100.
65. A. J. Daboub and J. M. Calton, "Stakeholder Learning Dialogues: How to Preserve Ethical Responsibility in Networks," *Journal of Business Ethics* 41 (2002): 85.
66. The use of the theatrical troupe as an analogy for virtual organizations was first used by David Mack circa 1995.
67. S. Ariss and A. A. Col-Laramore, "Trust and Technology in the Virtual Organization," *S.A.M. Advanced Management Journal* 67, no. 4 (Autumn 2002): 22.

Chapter 15

Website only:
www.sniderman.nelson.com

OBXtra 1

1. "Employee Satisfaction Relieves Stress," *Galt Global Review* (2001), http://www.galtglobalreview.com/business/satisfaction_stress.html, accessed August 21, 2004.
2. Ibid.
3. "Health Workplace Checkup: On the Road to Excellence, *NQI,* February 17, 2003, http://www.nqi.ca/articles/article_details.aspx?print=yes&ID=256 (accessed August 21, 2004).
4. Ipsos, "Canadians and Stress: A Special Report," September 19, 2002, accessed August 18, 2004, from http://www.ipsos-na.com/news/pressrelease.cfm?id=1620.
5. Bill Wilkerson (Roundtable co-founder and CEO), text of speech to the Canadian Pensions and Benefits Institute National Conference, May 31, 2004, Victoria, B.C.
6. Ibid.
7. National Union of Public and General Employees, "Intolerable Stress for Toronto Health Care Workers," May 30, 2003, http://www.nupge.ca/news_2003/n30my03b.htm, accessed September 14, 2004.
8. "Employee Satisfaction Relieves Stress."
9. Ipsos, "Canadians and Stress."
10. Bill Wilkerson, speech to the Canadian Pensions and Benefits Institute National Conference.
11. J. C. Quick, J. D. Quick, D. L. Nelson, and J. J. Hurrell, Jr., *Preventive Stress Management in Organizations* (Washington, D.C.: American Psychological Association, 1997).
12. J. B. Cunningham, *The Stress Management Sourcebook* (New York: Lowell House, 2000).
13. J. Loehr and T. Schwartz, "The Making of a Corporate Athlete," *Harvard Business Review* 79 (2001): 120–29.
14. J. D. Quick, R. S. Horn, and J. C. Quick, "Health Consequences of Stress," *Journal of Organizational Behavior Management* 8 (1986): 19–36.
15. R. M. Yerkes and J. D. Dodson, "The Relation of Strength of Stimulus to Rapidity of Habit-Formation," *Journal of Comparative Neurology and Psychology* 18 (1908): 459–82.
16. J. E. McGrath, "Stress and Behavior in Organizations," in *Handbook of Industrial and Organizational Psychology,* ed. M. D. Dunnettex (Chicago: Rand McNally, 1976), 1351–95.
17. Ibid.
18. W. B. Cannon, *Bodily Changes in Pain, Hunger, Fear, and Rage* (New York: Appleton, 1915).
19. Ipsos-Reid, "Contributors to Workplace Absenteeism and Healthcare Benefits Costs," March 18, 2004, http://www.ipsos-na.com/news/pressrelease.cfm?id=2089&content=full, accessed August 14, 2004.
20. M. Smyth, "Being Fired Was Last Straw for Gunman," *Providence,* May 10, 2003.
21. H. Henderson, "Healthy Employees Good for Business," *Toronto Star,* November 2, 2002, from Mental Health Roundtable, http://www.mentalhealthroundtable.ca/torstarnov3.html., accessed September 11, 2004.
22. GPC Research, "CEO Survey on Mental Health," commissioned by the Global Business and Economic Roundtable on Addiction and Mental Health, March 23, 2004.
23. S. Zuboff, *In the Age of the Smart Machine: The Future of Work and Power* (New York: Basic Books, 1988).
24. R. L. Kahn, D. M. Wolfe, R. P. Quinn, J. D. Snoek, and R. A. Rosenthal, *Organizational Stress: Studies in Role Conflict and Ambiguity* (New York: Wiley, 1964).
25. M. F. Peterson and P. B. Smith, "Does National Culture or Ambient Temperature Explain Cross-National Differences in Role Stress? No Sweat!" *Academy of Management Journal 40* (1997): 930–46.
26. K. K. Gillingham, "High-G Stress and Orientational Stress: Physiologic Effects of Aerial Maneuvering," *Aviation, Space, and Environmental Medicine* 59 (1988): A10–20.
27. R. S. DeFrank, "Executive Travel Stress: Perils of the Road Warrior," *Academy of Management Executive* 14 (2000): 58–72.

28. R. S. Bhagat, S. J. McQuaid, S. Lindholm, and J. Segovis, "Total Life Stress: A Multimethod Validation of the Construct and Its Effect on Organizationally Valued Outcomes and Withdrawal Behaviors," *Journal of Applied Psychology* 70 (1985): 202–14.
29. G. McKeown, "Case Study: Decoma International Inc: Commitment to a Healthy Workplace," National Quality Institute, July 28, 2001, http://www.nqi.ca/articles/article_details.aspx?print=yes&ID=55.
30. W. Immen, "Tackling a Hidden Health Menace," *The Globe and Mail,* July 14, 2004.
31. NQI, "Healthy Workplace Check-Up: On the Road to Excellence," February 17, 2003, http://www.nqi.ca/articles/article_details.aspx?print=yes&ID=256.
32. NQI, *Canadian Healthy Workplace Criteria—Overview,* http://www.nqi.ca/nqistore/Product_details.aspx?ID=63, accessed August 21, 2004.

OBXtra 2

1. T. Bradberry and J. Greaves, *The Emotional Intelligence Quickbook* (San Diego: Talentsmart, 2003), 18.
2. "Emotional Intelligence (EQ) More Important Than IQ for Work Success," Irish Management Institute, http://gwimi.imi.ie/eqhtml/articles_eq_iq_work_success.shtml, accessed January 17, 2005.
3. "Emotional Intelligence (EQ) Gets Better with Age," Irish Management Institute, http://gwimi.imi.ie/eqhtml/articles_eq_and_age.shtml, accessed January 17, 2005.
4. "Emotional What? Definitions and History of Emotional Intelligence," EQ Today, http://www.eqtoday.com/02/emotional.php, accessed January 17, 2005.
5. S. J. Stein and H. E. Book, *The EQ Edge: Emotional Intelligence and Your Success* (Toronto: Stoddart, 2000).
6. Bradberry and Greaves, *The Emotional Intelligence Quickbook.*
7. Bradberry and Greaves, *The Emotional Intelligence Quickbook,* 22–23.
8. "Emotional Intelligence (EQ) Gets Better with Age."
9. J. Kierstead, "Human Resource Management Trends and Issues: Emotional Intelligence (EI) in the Workplace," Research Directorate, Public Service Commission of Canada, http://www.hrma-agrh.ca/research/personnel/ei_e.asp, accessed January 17, 2005.
10. "Emotional Intelligence (EQ) Gets Better with Age."
11. Bradberry and Greaves, *The Emotional Intelligence Quickbook,* 22–23.
12. J. Taber, "PM Rebukes Parrish for New Insult to U.S.," *The Globe and Mail,* August 26, 2004.
13. Bradberry and Greaves, *The Emotional Intelligence Quickbook.*
14. D. Goleman, *Emotional Intelligence* (New York: Bantam Books, 1995).
15. "Emotional Intelligence (EQ) More Important Than IQ for Work Success."
16. D. Williams, *Leadership for the 21st Century: Life Insurance Leadership Study* (Boston: HayGroup, 1994).
17. D. Goleman, "An E-I Based Theory of Performance," in *The Emotionally Intelligent Workplace,* ed. C. Cherniss and D. Goleman (San Francisco: Jossey-Bass, 2001), available at http://www.eiconsortium.org/reaseach/ei_theory_performance.htm, accessed January 17, 2005.
18. C. Cherniss, "Emotional Intelligence: What It Is and Why It Matters," paper presented at the Annual Meeting of the Society for Industrial and Organizational Psychology, New Orleans, La., April 15, 2000, available at http://www.eiconsortium.org/research/what_is_emotional_intelligence.htm, accessed July 28, 2004.
19. D. Goleman, "An E-I Based Theory of Performance."
20. D. Goldman, *Emotional Intelligence: Why It Can Matter More Than IQ* (New York: Bantam Books, 1995).

OBXtra 3

1. A. D. Stajkovic and F. Luthans, "Behavioral Management and Task Performance in Organizations: Conceptual Background, Meta-analysis, and Test of Alternative Models," *Personnel Psychology* 56 (Spring 2003): 155.
2. B. F. Meltz, "Spanking May Have Lifelong Consequences, Study Says," *Boston Globe,* July 25, 2002, H7.
3. L. A. Jason and M. Fries, "Helping Parents Reduce Children's Television Viewing," *Research on Social Work Practice* 14, no. 2 (2004): 126.
4. J. C. Dooren, "Talking Yourself to Sleep: Behavioral Therapies to Teach Insomniacs to Snooze without Relying on Drugs," *Wall Street Journal,* March 29, 2005, D1.
5. B. F. Skinner, *Science and Human Behavior* (New York: Free Press, 1953).
6. F. Luthans and R. Kreitner, *Organizational Behavior Modification and Beyond* (Glenview, Ill.: Scott, Foresman, 1985).
7. A. D. Stajkovic and F. Luthans, "A Meta-analysis of the Effects of Organizational Behavior Modification on Task Performance, 1975–95," *Academy of Management Journal* 40 (1997): 1122–49.
8. A. D. Stajkovic and F. Luthans, "Differential Effects of Incentive Motivators on Work," *Academy of Management Journal* 44 (2001): 580–91.
9. B. F. Skinner, *Contingencies of Reinforcement: A Theoretical Analysis* (New York: Appleton-Century-Crofts, 1969).
10. J. P. Chaplin and T. S. Krawiec, *Systems and Theories of Psychology* (New York: Holt, Rinehart & Winston, 1960).
11. Stajkovic and Luthans, "Differential Effects of Incentive Motivators on Work."
12. W. M. Glenn, "An Employee's Survival Guide," *OH & S Canada* 18, no. 3 (April/May 2002): 26–31.
13. Meltz, "Spanking May Have Lifelong Consequences, Study Says."
14. F. Luthans, "Positive Organizational Behaviour: Developing and Managing Psychological Strengths," *Academy of Management Executive* 27 (2002): 60.
15. A. Bandura, *Social Learning Theory* (Englewood Cliffs, N.J.: Prentice-Hall, 1977); A. Bandura, "Self-Efficacy: Toward a Unifying Theory of Behavioral Change," *Psychological Review* 84 (1977): 191–215; G. Latham and P. A. Heslin, "Training the Trainee as Well as the Trainer: Lessons to Be Learned from Clinical Psychology," *Canadian Psychology* 44 (2003): 218–31.
16. A. Bandura, "Cultivate Self-Efficacy for Personal and Organizational Effectiveness," in *The Blackwell Handbook of Principles of Organizational Behavior,* ed. E. A. Locke (Oxford: Blackwell, 2000), 120.
17. J. M. Phillips and S. M. Gully, "Role of Goal Orientation, Ability, Need for Achievement, and Locus of Control in the Self-Efficacy and Goal-Setting Process," *Journal of Applied Psychology* 82 (1997): 792–802.
18. A. D. Stajkovic and F. Luthans, "Self-Efficacy and Work-Related Performance: A Meta-analysis," *Psychological Bulletin* 124 (1998): 240–61.
19. J. C. Weitlauf, R. E. Smith, and D. Cervone, "Generalization Effects of Coping-Skills Training: Influence of Self-Defense Training on Women's Efficacy Beliefs, Assertiveness, and Aggression," *Journal of Applied Psychology* 85 (2000): 625–33; A. D. Stajkovic and F. Luthans, "Social Cognitive Theory and Self-Efficacy: Going Beyond Traditional Motivational and Behavioral Approaches," *Organizational Dynamics* (Spring 1998): 62–74.
20. A. Bandura, "Regulation of Cognitive Processes through Perceived Self-Efficacy," *Developmental Psychology* (September 1989): 729–35.
21. V. Gecas, "The Social Psychology of Self-Efficacy," *Annual Review of Sociology* 15 (1989): 291–316.
22. F. Luthans, "The Need for and Meaning of Positive Organizational Behavior," *Journal of Organizational Behavior* 34 (2002): 695.

23. Dooren, "Talking Yourself to Sleep."

OBXtra 4

1. P. A. Chansler, P. M. Swamidass, and C. Cammann, "Self-Managing Work Teams: An Empirical Study of Group Cohesiveness in 'Natural Work Groups' at a Harley-Davidson Motor Company Plant," *Small Group Research* 34, no.1 (2003): 101–20.
2. H. V. Mierlo, C. G. Rutte, M. A. J. Kompier, and H. A. C. M. Doorewaard, "Self-Managing Teamwork and Psychological Well-Being: A Review of a Multilevel Research Domain," *Group and Organizational Management* 30 (2005): 211–35.
3. Four Seasons Hotels and Resorts, www.fourseasons.com.
4. S. Hirshorn, "Team-Work-Team," *OH & S Canada,* January/February 2005, 32.
5. C. W. Langfred, "Too Much of a Good Thing? Negative Effects of High Trust and Individual Autonomy in Self-Managing Teams," *Academy of Management Journal* 47 (2004): 385–99.
6. J. Tata and S. Prasad, "Team Self-Management, Organizational Structure, and Judgments of Team Effectiveness," *Journal of Management Issues* 16 (Summer 2004): 248.
7. Four Seasons Hotels and Resorts, www.fourseasons.com.
8. "That 'New Plane' Smell: How WestJet Goes about the Purchase and Outfitting of the New 700-Series Jets," *2002 WestJet Annual Report,* 14–15.
9. J. Belanger, P. K. Edwards, and M. Wright, "Commitment at Work and Independence from Management," *Work and Occupation* 30, no. 2 (2003): 234–52.
10. R. M. Robinson, S. L. Oswald, K. S. Swinehart, and J. Thomas, "Southwest Industries: Creating High-Performance Teams for High-Technology Production," *Planning Review* 19, published by the Planning Forum (November–December 1991): 10–47.
11. A. Lienert, "Forging a New Partnership," *Management Review* 83 (1994): 39–43.
12. P. S. Goodman, R. Devadas, and T. L. Griffith-Hughson, "Groups and Productivity: Analyzing the Effectiveness of Self-Managed Teams," in *Productivity in Organizations,* ed. J.P. Campbell, R.J. Campbell, and Associates (San Francisco: Jossey-Bass, 1988), 295–327.
    J. L. Cordery, W. S. Mueller, and L. M. Smith, "Attitudinal and Behavioral Effects of Autonomous Group Working: A Longitudinal Field Study," *Academy of Management Journal* 34 (1991): 464–76.
13. B. M. Staw and L. D. Epstein, "What Bandwagons Bring: Effects of Popular Management Techniques on Corporate Performance, Reputation, and CEO Pay," *Administrative Science Quarterly* 45 (2000): 523–56.
14. L. I. Glassop, "The Organizational Benefits of Teams," *Human Relations* 55, no. 2 (2002): 225–49.
15. Chansler, Swamidass, and Cammann, "Self-Managing Work Teams."
16. Tata and Prasad, "Team Self-Management, Organizational Structure, and Judgments of Team Effectiveness," 248–65.
17. C. M. Carson, D. C. Mosley, and S. L. Boyer, "Goal Orientation and Supervisory Behaviors: Impacting SMWT Effectiveness," *Team Performance Management* 10, no. 7 (2004): 152–62.
18. W. A. Kahn, "Managing the Paradox of Self-Reliance," *Organizational Dynamics* 30, no. 3 (2002): 240.
19. Ibid., 239–56; Hirshorn, "Team-Work-Team," 34.
20. D. F. Elloy, "The Influence of Superleader Behaviors on Organizational Commitment, Job Satisfaction and Organization Self-Esteem in a Self-Managed Work Team," *Leadership and Organizational Development* 26, no. 2 (2005): 120–27.
21. G. Moorhead, C. P. Neck, and M. S. West, "The Tendency toward Defective Decision Making within Self-Managing Teams: The Relevance of Groupthink for the 21st Century," *Organizational Behavior & Human Decision Processes* 73 (1998): 327–51.

OBXtra 5

1. G. Buckler, "Teleworking Helps Attract Far-Flung Staff," *The Globe and Mail,* March 18, 2004.
2. I. Zigurs, "Leadership in Virtual Teams: Oxymoron or Opportunity?" *Organizational Dynamics,* January 2003, 350.
3. S. J. Zaccaro and P. Bader, "E-Leadership and the Challenges of Leading E-Teams: Minimizing the Bad and Maximizing the Good," *Organizational Dynamics* 31 (2003): 377–87.
4. B. Avolio and S. S. Kahai, "Adding the 'E' to E-Leadership: How It May Impact Your Leadership," *Organizational Dynamics* 31 (2003): 333.
5. W. Cascio and S. Shurygailo, "E-Leadership and Virtual Teams," *Organizational Dynamics* 31 (2003): 362–76.
6. Adapted from *Human Resource Management International Digest* 11, no. 3 (2003): 8–11.
7. Buckler, "Teleworking Helps Attract Far-Flung Staff."
8. Zigurs, "Leadership in Virtual Teams."
9. Canadian Telework Association, "About the Canadian Telework Association," http://www.ivc.ca/cta/index.htm.
10. A. M. Towsend, S. M. DeMarie, and A. R. Hendrickson, "Virtual Teams: Technology and the Workplace of the Future," *Academy of Management Executive* 12 (1998): 17–29; Zigurs, "Leadership in Virtual Teams."
11. Townsend, DeMarie, and Hendrickson, "Virtual Teams."
12. L. M. Jessup and J. F. George, "Theoretical and Methodological Issues in Group Support Systems," *Small Group Research* 28 (1997): 394–413.
13. C. M. Solomon, "Managing Virtual Teams," *Workforce,* June 1, 2001, 60–65.
14. Zigurs, "Leadership in Virtual Teams."
15. Ibid.
16. E. Kasper-Fuehrer and N. M. Ashkanasy, "Communicating Trustworthiness and Building Trust in Interorganizational Virtual Organizations," *Journal of Management* 27 (2001): 235–54.
17. Cascio and Shurygailo, "E-Leadership and Virtual Teams."
18. D. Burger, "No Need to Fight the Traffic," *Computing Canada,* March 17, 1997, 37; G. Downey, "Home Work," *Computing Canada,* August 8, 2003, 20.
19. B. L. Hawkins, "Finding the Right Alternative," *Facilities Design & Management,* December 1999, 17.
20. Zigurs, "Leadership in Virtual Teams."
21. M. Apgar, IV, "The Alternative Workplace: Changing Where and How People Work," *Harvard Business Review,* May–June 1998: 121–36; Royal Bank of Canada Survey, 2002.
22. Zaccaro and Bader, "E-Leadership and the Challenges of Leading E-Teams."
23. Ibid.
24. Avolio and Kahai, "Adding the 'E' to E-Leadership."

Glossary

A

accommodating
The style of conflict management (also known as obliging) that involves giving in to the other's wishes without attending to one's own. It indicates low concern for self and high concern for others.

action research
An approach to change management in which initial research about an organization provides information to guide subsequent action.

active inertia
A tendency to respond to the most disruptive changes by accelerating activities that succeeded in the past.

active listening
A process that goes beyond passively absorbing a speaker's words. It consists of hearing, attending, understanding, responding and remembering

adaptive culture
An organizational culture that encourages confidence and risk taking among employees, has leadership that produces change, and focuses on the changing needs of customers.

adjourning
The final stage of team development for temporary teams, characterized by concern with wrapping up.

affective commitment
The type of organizational commitment that is based on an individual's desire to remain in an organization.

alternative dispute resolution (ADR)
Informal methods used to resolve disputes, such as simple negotiation and mediation, which are outside the formal grievance and discipline process.

anthropocentric
Placing human considerations at the centre of job design decisions.

anthropology
The science of the *learned* behaviour of human beings.

appreciative Inquiry (AI)
A tool for connecting organizations to their positive change core by opening every strength, innovation, achievement, imaginative story, hope, positive tradition, passion, and dream to systematic inquiry

arbitration
A formal process in which a third party, who has been chosen by the disputing parties, after hearing evidence and oral argument, renders a decision that is binding on all parties.

artifacts
Symbols of culture in the physical and social work environment.

assertiveness
The extent to which a society encourages people to be confrontational and assertive with respect to their views.

assumptions
Deeply held beliefs that guide behaviour and tell members of an organization how to perceive and think about things.

attitude
A psychological tendency expressed by evaluating an entity with some degree of favour or disfavour. It is the basis of an evaluative response to a particular situation, event, or issue.

attribution theory
A theory that explains how individuals pinpoint the causes of the behavior of themselves and others.

autocratic leadership style
A style of leadership in which the leader spells out duties and specific tasks, tells people what to do and how to do it, ensures employees follow rules, and encourages employees to reach peak performance. Also referred to in early studies as *initiating structure.*

autonomy
The degree to which the job provides the employee with substantial freedom, independence, and discretion in scheduling the work and in determining the procedures to be used in carrying it out.

avoiding
Style of conflict management that is a deliberate decision to take no action on a conflict or to stay out of a conflict situation. It indicates low concern for self and low concern for others.

B

bargaining zone
The area identified by the bargaining limits (resistance points) of each side, in which compromise is possible, as is the attainment of a settlement satisfactory to both parties.

barriers to communication
Factors that block or significantly distort successful communication.

BATNA
The best alternative to a negotiated agreement and also the resistance point.

behavioural component of emotion
The verbal and nonverbal messages we express when we communicate.

behavioural measures
Personality assessments that involve observing an individual's behaviour in a controlled situation.

behavioural perspective of leadership
A perspective that proposes that effective leaders behave in certain desirable ways.

behavioural science
Research that improves one's ability to understand, predict, and influence the behaviour of others.

best practice methods
The processes, practices, and systems that an organization does particularly well and that are widely recognized as improving the organization's performance and efficiency in specific areas.

blocking roles
Roles that inhibit the team or its members from achieving what they could have achieved and destroy morale and cohesion.

boundary-spanning roles
Jobs that link and coordinate an organization with key elements in the task environment.

bounded rationality
A theory that suggests that there are limits upon how rational a decision maker can actually be.

brainstorming
A technique for generating as many ideas as possible on a given subject, while suspending evaluation until all the ideas have been generated.

C

centralization
The degree to which decisions are made at the top of the organization.

change agent
An individual who is assigned to guide and facilitate a change effort and who is able to influence organizational members while at the same time teaching them how to solve their own problems in the future.

charisma
A personal trait that gives the leader referent power over followers.

co-dependency
When one person tries to control another and to be responsible for the consequences of the behaviour of that other person.

coercive power
Power that is based on a person's ability to punish. Others comply because they fear punishment or some negative consequence.

cognitive component of emotion
The way our mind appraises or interprets emotion.

cognitive dissonance
A state of tension that is produced when an individual experiences conflict between attitudes and behaviour.

cognitive moral development
The process of moving through stages of maturity in terms of making ethical decisions.

cognitive style
An individual's preference for

gathering information and evaluating alternatives.

collaborating
The style of conflict management (also known as integrating or problem solving) in which an attempt is made to fully satisfy the wishes of both parties. It indicates high concern for self and high concern for others.

collectivism
A cultural orientation in which individuals belong to tightly knit social frameworks and depend strongly on large extended families or clans.

communication
The process by which information is exchanged between a sender and a receiver with the goal of reaching mutual understanding.

communication champions
Employees who take on communication responsibilities in addition to their regular responsibilities.

communities of practice (CoP)
Groups of people informally bound together by shared expertise and passion for joint enterprise.

competencies
Learned behaviours such as skills, abilities, and values.

competing
The style of conflict management in which the individual pursues his or her wishes at the other's expense (also known as dominating and forcing). It indicates high concern for self and low concern for others.

complexity
The number of elements and amount of knowledge needed to understand the various stakeholders.

compromising
The style of conflict management that involves seeking an outcome midway between the preferred outcomes of both parties. It indicates intermediate concern for self and others.

conflict
The perception, in an interdependent relationship, of incompatible wishes, goals, attitudes, emotions, or behaviours.

conflict management strategy
Any action taken by a disputant or a third party to try to manage or resolve a conflict.

congruent communication
Communicating verbally and nonverbally exactly what a person is thinking and feeling.

consideration
A style of leadership in which the leader shows mutual trust and respect, engages in two-way communication, listens, encourages, gives recognition, and provides socio-emotional support.

contextual variables
The set of internal and external elements that influence the organization's design processes.

contingency perspective of leadership
A perspective that proposes that effective leadership depends upon the degree of fit between the leader's style and various factors in the particular situation.

continuance commitment
The type of organizational commitment that is based on the fact that an individual cannot afford to leave.

conversion
A withdrawal mechanism in which emotional conflicts are expressed in physical symptoms.

core or dominant culture
The primary values that are accepted throughout the organization.

corporate governance
The system of control and performance monitoring of top management.

corporate social responsibility (CSR)
The obligation of a firm to use its economic, legal, ethical, and philanthropic resources in ways to benefit the society at large and to improve the welfare of society at large, independent of direct gains of the company.

counterfeit questions
Disguised attempts to send a message, not receive one.

creativity
A process influenced by individual and organizational factors that results in the production of novel and useful ideas, products, or both.

cross-training
A variation of job enlargement in which workers are trained in different specialized tasks or activities.

cynicism
A loss of faith in the leaders of the change based on a history of change attempts that have not been entirely successful.

D

decentralization
The extent to which decision-making authority has been delegated to lower levels of an organization.

decision making
A conscious process of making choices among one or more alternatives and developing a commitment to a course of action.

defensive communication
Communication that can be aggressive, attacking and angry, or passive and withdrawing.

degree of routineness
The extent of repetitiveness and routine required in an organization's technology to transform inputs into outputs.

de-layering
The planned vertical compression of managerial levels of the hierarchy.

Delphi technique
A structured approach to decision making that gathers the judgments of experts.

democratic leadership style
A style of leadership in which the leader shows mutual trust and respect, engages in two-way communication, listens, encourages, gives recognition, and provides socio-emotional support.

departmental grouping
The way that differentiated jobs are grouped together into departments. Also called *departmentation.*

developmental change
The improvement of a skill, method, or condition that for some reason does not measure up.

devil's advocacy
A technique for preventing groupthink in which a group or individual is given the role of critic during decision making.

differentiation
The process of deciding how to divide the work in an organization.

disability
An activity limitation or a participation restriction associated with a physical or mental condition or a health problem.

discounting principle
The assumption that an individual's behaviour is accounted for by the situation.

distress
The adverse psychological, physical, behavioural, and organizational consequences that may arise as a result of stressful events.

distributive bargaining
A win-lose negotiating strategy, such that one party gains at the expense of the other.

distributive justice
The term given to judgments regarding the fairness of outcomes or allocations, as discussed in equity theory.

divergent thinking
The individual's ability to generate several potential solutions to a problem.

diversity
All forms of individual differences, including race, ethnicity, culture, gender, age, marital status, religious beliefs, educational background, stage in one's career, physical and mental ability, personality, social status, and sexual orientation.

divisional grouping
Departmentation that groups together employees based upon the organization's main outputs or geography.

dominating
The conflict management style in which the individual pursues his or her wishes at the other's expense. It indicates high concern for self and low concern for others.

downsizing
Intended reductions in the number of employees.

downward communication
Communication that flows from one level of a group or organization to a lower level.

dysfunctional conflict
An unhealthy, destructive disagreement between two or more people. Its danger is that it takes the focus away from the work to be done and places the focus on the conflict itself and the parties involved.

E

effective decision
A timely decision that meets a desired objective and is acceptable to the individuals affected by it.

e-leadership
Leadership processes conducted largely through electronic channels.

emotional intelligence (EQ)
The ability to recognize and manage emotion in oneself and in others.

empathy
Understanding and being sensitive to someone else's feelings and thoughts.

employee engagement
A state of emotional and intellectual involvement that employees have in their organization.

employee, people-oriented, or democratic leadership style
A style of leadership in which the leader shows trust and respect, engages in two-way communication, listens, encourages, gives recognition and provides socio-emotional support. Also referred to as *consideration*.

empowerment
Creating conditions for heightened motivation through the development of a strong sense of personal self-efficacy.

enacted values
Values reflected in the way individuals actually behave.

engineering
The applied science of energy and matter.

environmental uncertainty
The amount of stability and complexity in the organization's task environment.

equity theory
A motivation theory that states that people determine whether they have been treated fairly by first examining the ratio of their inputs relevant to their outcomes, and then comparing this ratio to the input-to-outcome ratio of a comparison other.

ERG theory
Alderfer's theory that people are motivated by three sets of needs and that as a lower need is gratified, the person becomes motivated by the next need in the hierarchy but when unable to fulfill a higher need, they will regress to a lower one.

escalation of commitment to a losing course of action
The tendency to continue to support a failing course of action.

espoused values
What members of an organization say they value.

ethical behaviour
Acting in ways consistent with one's personal values and the commonly held values of the organization and society.

ethical decision
A decision that is made having explored alternatives and their consequences so that actions are consistent with one's personal values and commonly held values of the organization and society.

eustress
Healthy, normal stress.

expectancy
The belief that effort leads to performance (E–P).

expectancy theory
Theory that people exert effort if they expect that their effort will result in good performance, and that this performance will be instrumental in getting them valued outcomes.

expert power
Power based on a person's expertise, competence, and information in a certain area. Others comply because they believe in the power holder's knowledge and competence.

external task environment
Sectors with which the organization interacts directly and that have a direct impact on the organization's ability to achieve its goals.

extinction
The attempt to eliminate or decrease the frequency of a behaviour by attaching *no* consequences to it, that is, by ignoring the behaviour. An alternative to punishing undesirable behaviour.

extraversion
A preference indicating that an individual is energized by interaction with other people.

extrinsic motivation
Motivation that comes from outside the person such as pay, tangible rewards. or a promotion.

F

feedback
Any information that people or organizations receive about their behaviour or performance, its effect on others, or comparison to a standard or expectation.

feedback from the job itself
The degree to which carrying out the work activities results in the employee's obtaining direct and clear information about the effectiveness of his or her performance.

feeling
Making decisions in a personal, value-oriented way.

filtering
Deleting, delaying, or softening negative information as it moves up the hierarchy, so that it sounds more favourable.

first-impression error
The tendency to form lasting opinions about an individual based on initial perceptions.

flat organizational structure
A structure with few layers of management and wide spans of control.

flextime
An alternative work pattern that enables employees to set their own daily work schedules.

forcing
Conflict management style in which the individual pursues is or her wishes at the other's expense. It indicates high concern for self and low concern for others.

formalization
The degree to which an employee's role is defined by formal documentation (procedures, job descriptions, manuals, and regulations).

formal organization
The official, legitimate, and most visible part of the system.

forming
The first stage in team development, characterized by politeness, superficiality, and uncertainty.

front-back structure
An organization structure that consists of front-end units focused on customer segments and back-end units focused on products and technologies. All units are profit-measurable.

frustration regression hypothesis
Theory that when people are frustrated in their ability to satisfy a higher order need they regress to the next lower category of needs and intensify their desire to gratify these needs.

functional conflict
A healthy, constructive disagreement between two or more people. Functional conflict can produce new ideas, learning, and growth among individuals.

functional grouping
Departmentation that groups together those employees who perform similar functions or who have similar expertise.

fundamental attribution error
The tendency to make attributions to internal causes when focusing on someone else's behaviour.

G

garbage can model of decision making
A theory that contends that decisions in organizations are random and unsystematic.

gender differentiation
The extent to which a society views gender roles as different.

generalized self-efficacy
An individual's beliefs and expectancies about his or her ability to accomplish a specific task effectively.

glass ceiling
A transparent barrier that keeps women from rising above a certain level in organizations.

goals (G)
Those action strategies that leaders create and follow to accomplish the organization's purpose and vision.

goal setting
The process of establishing desired results that guide and direct behaviour.

group
Two or more people with common interests, objectives, and continuing interaction.

group polarization
The tendency for group discussion to produce shifts toward more extreme attitudes among members.

groupthink
A deterioration of mental efficiency, reality testing, and moral judgment resulting from pressures within the group.

growth-need strength
The desire to grow and fully develop one's abilities.

H

Hawthorne studies
Studies conducted at the Hawthorne plant of Western Electric in the 1920s and 1930s and demonstrated the impact of psychological processes and peer pressure on individual behaviour and performance.

heuristics
Shortcuts in decision making that save mental activity.

hierarchy of authority
The degree of vertical differentiation through reporting relationships and the span of control

within the structure of the organization.

high context cultures
Cultures that value language as a way to maintain social harmony

high-performing organizations
Organizations that produce extraordinary results and sustain this performance over time and over changing market conditions. These organizations adapt industry best practices while preserving their unique processes. They view failures as opportunities for continuous learning.

horizontal differentiation
The degree of differentiation between organizational subunits, based on employees' specialized knowledge, education, or training.

horizontal structure
An organizational structure based on core processes where work focuses on the customer and on the entire sequence of activities (end-to-end) rather than on one activity.

human capital
The knowledge that employees possess and generate, including their skills, experience, and creativity.

human resources (H)
The employees and managers in the organization including the nature of their relationships, their values, and the impact of the reward system on their behaviour.

humane orientation
The degree to which a society encourages and rewards individuals for being altruistic, caring and generous.

humanistic theory
The personality theory that emphasizes individual growth and improvement.

hybrid grouping
Departmentation that combines characteristics of each of the other types of grouping, tailored to specific strategic needs.

hygiene factors
Extrinsic factors surrounding the job that lead to dissatisfaction, such as company policies and pay.

I

impression management
The process by which individuals try to control the impression others have of them.

individualism
A cultural orientation in which people belong to loose social frameworks, and their primary concern is for themselves and their families.

individualism versus collectivism
The degree to which individuals are expected to be part of a group in their organization or in their society.

influence
The process of affecting the thoughts, behaviour, and feelings of others.

informal organization
The unofficial and less visible part of the system.

information power
Power based on a person's access to important information. Others comply because they want the information the power holder has.

in-group collectivism
The extent to which members of a society take pride in membership in their immediate social group.

initiating structure
A style of leadership in which the leader spells out duties and specific tasks, tells people what to do and how to do it, ensures employees follow rules, and encourages employees to reach peak performance.

instrumentality
The belief that performance is related to rewards/outcomes (P–O).

instrumental values
Values that represent the acceptable behaviours to be used in achieving some end state.

integrating conflict management style
Style of conflict management that represents a desire to fully satisfy the wishes of both parties. It indicates high concern for self and high concern for others.

integration
The process of coordinating the different parts of an organization.

integrative approach
The broad theory that describes personality as a composite of an individual's psychological processes.

integrative bargaining
A negotiating strategy in which there is acknowledgement that achieving a win-win outcome will depend on mutual trust and problem solving.

interactional justice
The term given to judgments regarding the fairness of interpersonal interactions.

intergroup conflict
Conflict that occurs between different groups or teams within an organization.

interorganizational conflict
Conflict that occurs between two or more organizations.

interpersonal communication
Communication between two or more people in an organization.

interpersonal conflict
Conflict that occurs between two or more individuals.

intragroup conflict
Conflict that occurs within a single group or team.

intrinsic motivation
A person's internal drive to do something because of such things as interest, challenge, and personal satisfaction.

introversion
A preference indicating that an individual is energized by time alone.

intuiting
Gathering information through "sixth sense" and focusing on what could be rather than what actually exists.

intuition
The internal reservoir of cumulative experience, from which one distills, at a level below consciousness, a direction, or an urge to do or not do something.

J

Job Characteristics Model
States that workers who perform jobs that contain five core job characteristics will be more likely to achieve favourable work outcomes. In addition, workers who have high growth need strengths (GNS) are more likely to achieve these outcomes than those with low growth need strengths.

job design
The process of assigning tasks to a job, including the interdependency of those tasks with other jobs.

Job Diagnostic Survey (JDS)
The survey instrument designed to measure the elements in the Job Characteristics Model.

job enlargement
A method of job design that increases the number of activities in a job to overcome the boredom of overspecialized work.

job enrichment
A method of job design that increases the degree to which workers control the planning, execution, and evaluation of their work.

job rotation
A variation of job enlargement in which workers are exposed to a variety of specialized jobs over time through rotation.

job satisfaction
A pleasurable or positive emotional state resulting from the appraisal of one's job or job experiences.

job sharing
An alternative work pattern in which there is more than one person occupying a single job.

judging preference
Preferring closure and completion in making decisions.

jurisdictional ambiguity
The presence of unclear lines of responsibility within an organization.

K

kinesics
The study of body movements, including posture.

knowledge management (KM)
A conscious strategy of getting the right knowledge to the right people ate the right time and helping people share and put information into action in ways that strive to improve organizational performance.

L

laissez faire leadership style (uninvolved)
An employee-centred leadership style in which the manager permits his or her employees to function within prescribed limits.

large group interventions
OD interventions that bring all the key members of an organization together in one room for an extended period of time to diagnose and plan organizational change.

leader-member relations
The quality of interpersonal relationships between a leader and the group members.

leadership
The ability of an individual to influence, motivate, and enable others to contribute toward the effectiveness and success of organizations of which they are members.

Leadership (Managerial) Grid
A model that proposes that the best way to lead is to show high concern for results (task) and high concern for people.

leadership substitutes theory
The theory that in some situations leaders can reduce the amount of leadership they exercise because it becomes unnecessary due to existing substitutes or "neutralizers."

lean production
Using committed employees with ever-expanding responsibilities to achieve zero waste, 100 percent quality product, delivered on time, every time.

learning goals
Goals that provide clear markers of progress and reduce the risk of self-demoralization that can occur when current accomplishments are gauged against an outcome goal.

learning map
A communication tool that uses pictures and other visuals to deliver key messages in a consistent manner while at the same time engaging employees.

least preferred co-worker (LPC)
The person a leader has least preferred to work with over his or her career.

legitimate power
Power that is based on a person holding a formal position. Others comply because they accept the legitimacy of the position of the power holder.

locus of control
An individual's generalized belief about internal control (self-control) versus external control (control by the situation or by others).

loss of individuality
A social process in which individual group members lose self-awareness and its accompanying sense of accountability, inhibition, and responsibility for individual behaviour.

low context cultures
Cultures that use language primarily to express thoughts, feelings, and ideas as clearly and logically as possible.

M

Machiavellianism
A personality characteristic indicating one's willingness to do whatever it takes to get one's own way.

maintenance-oriented roles
Activities essential to effective, satisfying interpersonal relationships within a team.

management
The study of overseeing activities and supervising people in organizations.

management by objectives (MBO)
A participative goal-setting process in which organizational objectives are cascaded down the organization and integrated with unit and individual goals and objectives.

managers
People in organizations who perform jobs that involve the direct supervision of other people.

Managerial (Leadership) Grid
A model that proposes that the best way to lead is to show high concern for results (task) and high concern for people.

masculinity
The cultural orientation in which assertiveness and materialism are valued.

matrix structure
Structures in which individuals simultaneously report to both a functional and a product or project manager.

meaningfulness
The value of a work goal or purpose, judged in relation to an individual's own ideals or standards.

mechanistic structure
An organizational design that emphasizes structured activities, specialized tasks, and centralized decision making.

media richness
The amount and variety of information that a communication medium can carry.

mediation
A formal process in which a neutral third party, with no decision-making power, helps the disputing parties voluntarily settle the dispute by establishing ground rules for negotiation, opening channels of communication, articulating the needs of each, identifying the issues, and, if requested, making recommendations on disputed issues.

message
The thoughts and feelings that the communicator is attempting to elicit in the receiver.

mission
The overall purpose of a team.

motivation
The set of forces, internal (individual needs and motives) and external (environmental forces) that initiate work-related behaviour and determine its form, direction, intensity, and duration.

motivators
Intrinsic factors in the job that lead to satisfaction, such as achievement and the work itself.

moving
The second step in Lewin's change model, in which new attitudes, values, and behaviours are substituted for old ones.

multi-source (360-degree) feedback
Structured feedback received from supervisor, subordinates, peers, and customers.

Myers-Briggs Type Indicator (MBTI)
An instrument developed to measure Carl Jung's theory of individual differences.

N

need for achievement
A learned need that concerns individuals' issues of excellence, competition, challenging goals, persistence, and overcoming difficulties.

need for affiliation
A learned need that concerns an individual's need to establish and maintain warm, close, intimate relationships with other people.

need for power
A learned need that concerns an individual's need to make an impact on others, influence others, change people or events, and make a difference in life.

need hierarchy
Maslow's theory that people are motivated by five sets of needs, and that as a lower need is gratified, the person becomes motivated by the next need in the hierarchy.

negative affect
An individual's tendency to accentuate the negative aspects of himself or herself, other people, and the world in general.

negative reinforcement
An attempt to increase or maintain the frequency of desirable behaviour by withholding expected negative consequences when a desirable behaviour occurs.

negotiation (bargaining)
Any interaction between two or more parties aimed at reaching an agreement based on both common and dividing interests.

network structure
An organizational structure in which the organization subcontracts most of its functions to separate companies and coordinates their activities from a small headquarters.

nominal group technique (NGT)
A structured approach to group decision making that focuses on generating alternatives and choosing one.

nonprogrammed decision
A new, complex decision that requires a creative solution.

nonsanctioned influence tactics
Those influence attempts that are for personal gain and are not officially sanctioned by an organization. They are also referred to as *political tactics.*

nonsubstitutability
The extent to which a group performs a function that is indispensable to an organization and for which there is no alternative provider.

nonverbal communication
All elements of communication that do not involve words.

normative commitment
The type of organizational commitment that is based on an individual's perceived obligation to remain with an organization.

norming
The third stage of team development, characterized by cohesion, trust, and clarification of group roles and norms.

norms of behaviour
The standards that a work group uses to evaluate the behavior of its members.

O

obliging conflict management style
The conflict management style that means giving in to the other's wishes without attending to one's own. It indicates low concern for

self and high concern for others.

OD intervention
Any diagnostic or problem-solving activity that members of an organization participate in during an OD program that is designed to help them change.

open space technology (OST)
A way to catalyze effective working conversations and problem solving in groups of up to 2000 people. Open space technology encourages individuals to self-organize and take responsibility for their own learning and actions.

organic structure
An organizational design that emphasizes teamwork, open communication, and decentralized decision making.

organizational behaviour
A field of study that seeks to understand, explain, predict, and change human behaviour, both individual and collective, in the organizational context.

organization development (OD)
A system-wide application of behavioural science knowledge to the planned development and reinforcement of the strategies, structures, and processes that lead to organizational effectiveness and adaptability.

organizational citizenship behaviour
Behaviour that is above and beyond the call of duty.

organizational commitment
The strength of an individual's identification with an organization.

organizational (corporate) culture
A pattern of basic assumptions that are considered valid and that are taught to new members as the way to perceive, think, and feel in the organization.

organizational design
The process of constructing and adjusting an organization's structure to match its environment and achieve its goals.

organizational inputs
All the human, informational, material, and financial resources taken from the external task environment and used by the organization.

organizational outputs
The products and services, as well as the more intangible outputs such as reputation, image, and ideas.

organizational structure (OS)
The manner in which an organization's work is designed, as well as how departments, divisions, and the overall organization are designed.

organizations
Groups of people who work interdependently toward some common purpose.

outcome goals
Goals that provide clear direction as to a desired end or outcome in the long term.

owning communication
Communication in which one takes responsibility for one's statements and acknowledges that the source of the ideas is oneself and not the other person or group.

P

participative decision making
Decision making in which individuals who are affected by decisions influence those decisions.

people-oriented leadership style
A style of leadership in which the leader shows mutual trust and respect, engages in two-way communication, listens, encourages, gives recognition, and provides socio-emotional support.

perceiving preference
Preferring to explore many alternatives and flexibility.

perceptual screens
The windows through which we interact with people in the world.

performance orientation
The degree to which a society values initiative, continuous improvement, and exceptional performance.

performing
The fourth stage in team development, when the team has achieved synergy and is reaching its full potential.

personality
A relatively stable set of characteristics that influence an individual's behaviour.

physiological component of emotion
The bodily experience of emotion.

planned change
Change that is an intentional and goal-oriented activity.

political behaviour
Influence attempts that are for personal gain and are not officially sanctioned by an organization.

position power
The authority associated with the leader's formal position in the organization.

positive affect
An individual's tendency to accentuate the positive aspects of himself or herself, other people, and the world in general.

positive reinforcement
An attempt to increase or maintain the frequency of a desirable behaviour by following it with positive consequences.

power
The ability of one party to change or control the behaviour, attitudes, opinions, objectives, needs, or values of another party

power distance
The degree of inequality among people that a culture considers normal.

powerlessness
A lack of power.

problem-solving conflict management style
Style of conflict management that represents a desire to fully satisfy the wishes of both parties. It indicates high concern for self and high concern for others.

procedural justice
The term given to judgments regarding the fairness of elements in organizational processes.

process conflict
Controversies about aspects of *how* task accomplishment will proceed.

process consultation and facilitation
An OD intervention that helps a group focus on its internal processes, such as norms, communication, and group roles. It has a more specific focus than team building and involves a process facilitator/consultant.

production-oriented leadership style
A style of leadership in which the leader spells out duties and specific tasks, tells people what to do and how to do it, ensures employees follow rules, and encourages employees to reach peak performance. Also referred to in early studies as *initiating structure.*

programmed decision
A simple, routine matter for which a manager has an established decision rule.

progression hypothesis
States that the lowest level of ungratified need motivates behaviour.

projection
Overestimating the number of people who share our own beliefs, values, and behaviours.

projective test
A personality test that elicits an individual's response to abstract stimuli.

psychodynamic theory
The personality theory that emphasizes the unconscious determinants of behaviour.

psychology
The science of human behaviour.

punishment
The attempt to eliminate or decrease the frequency of undesirable behaviour by either introducing negative consequences or withholding positive consequences.

Q

quality circle
A small group of employees who work voluntarily on company time, typically one hour per week, to address work-related problems such as quality control, cost reduction, production planning and techniques, and even product design.

R

rationality
A logical, step-by-step approach to decision making, with a thorough analysis of alternatives and their consequences.

referent power
A power that is based on a person's attractiveness to and friendship with others. Others comply because they respect and like the power holder.

reflective listening
A skill intended to help the receiver and communicator clearly and fully understand the message sent.

refreezing
The final step in Lewin's change model, in which new attitudes, values, and behaviours are established as the new status quo.

relationship (affective) conflict
Interpersonal incompatibilities, typically including feelings of tension and friction.

reward power
Power based on a person's access to rewards. Others comply because they want the rewards the power holder can offer.

risk aversion
The tendency to choose options that entail fewer risks and less uncertainty.

role
A set of behaviours that are expected of a person occupying a particular position in a social unit.

S

sanctioned influence tactics
Those tactics that are approved of and that people consider acceptable because they are part of the organization's norms.

satisfice
To select the first alternative that is "good enough," because the costs in time and effort are too great to optimize.

scientific management
Frederick Taylor's system for using research to determine the optimum degree of specialization and standardization for a job task.

selective perception
The process of selecting information that supports our individual viewpoints while discounting information that threatens our viewpoints.

self-efficacy,
An individual's beliefs and expectancies about his or her ability to perform a specific task effectively.

self-esteem
An individual's general feeling of self-worth.

self-fulfilling prophecy
The situation in which our expectations about people affect our interaction with them in such a way that our expectations are fulfilled.

self-managed work team (SMWT)
A team whose members have autonomy to carry out interdependent tasks and make decisions that were once reserved for managers.

self-monitoring
The extent to which people base their behaviour on cues from other people and situations.

self-serving bias
The tendency to attribute one's own successes to internal causes and one's failures to external causes.

sensing
Gathering information through the five senses.

servant leadership
The view that the leader is the servant of his or her followers. It places the interest of the followers before the self-interest of the leader and emphasizes personal development and empowerment of followers.

skill variety
The degree to which a job includes different activities and involves the use of multiple skills and talents of the employee.

social information-processing (SIP) model
A model that suggests that the important job factors depend in part on what others tell a person about the job.

social loafing
The failure of a group member to contribute personal time, effort, thoughts, or other resources to the team.

social perception
The process of interpreting information about another person.

sociology
The science of society.

socio-technical systems (STS) theory
Theory proposing that work design should jointly optimize the social and technical systems of an organization.

span of control
The number of people directly reporting to a manager.

specialization
The degree to which jobs are narrowly defined and depend on unique expertise.

stability
The extent to which *unpredictable changes* affect the organization's work and make it uncertain.

standardization
The extent to which work activities are described and performed routinely in the same way.

stereotype
A generalization about a group of people.

storming
The second stage of team development, characterized by conflict, confusion, power struggles, and the emergence of cliques.

strategically appropriate culture
The perspective that a culture is good only if it fits its context. The context can refer to the objective conditions of the industry or perhaps the firm's strategy.

stress
The unconscious preparation to fight or flee that a person experiences when faced with any demand.

stressor
The person or event that triggers the stress response.

strong culture
An organizational culture with a consensus on the values that drive the company and with an intensity that is recognizable even to outsiders.

subculture
Mini-cultures within an organization, typically defined by specific departments, teams, or divisions.

superordinate goal
An organizational goal that captures the imagination, and hence galvanizes people to take action that is more important to both parties in a conflict than their individual or group goals.

supportive communication
Communication that addresses the problem at hand while seeking to preserve a positive relationship between the communicators.

survey feedback
A process of collecting data from an organization or department through the use of a questionnaire or survey and feeding the data back.

synergy
A positive force that occurs in groups when group members stimulate new or better solutions through the process of mutual influence and encouragement.

T

tacit knowledge
Knowledge that resides within an individual.

tall organizational structure
A structure with many layers of management and narrow spans of control.

task (cognitive) conflict
Differences in viewpoints and opinions pertaining to group task.

task environment
The elements of an organization's environment that are related to its goal attainment.

task identity
The degree to which the job requires completion of a whole and identifiable piece of work—that is, doing a job from beginning to end—or being able to see how one's work fits in.

task interdependence
The degree of task-driven interaction among work team members.

task-oriented leadership style
A style of leadership in which the leader spells out duties and specific tasks, tells people what to do and how to do it, ensures employees follow rules and encourages employees to reach peak performance. Also called production or autocratic style, and referred to in early studies as *initiating structure*.

task-oriented roles
Activities directly related to the effective completion of a team's work.

task significance
The degree to which the job has a substantial impact on the lives or work of other people, whether in the immediate organization or in the external environment.

task-specific self-efficacy
An individual's beliefs and expectancies about his or her ability to perform a specific task effectively.

task structure
The degree of clarity, or ambiguity, in the work activity assigned to the group.

team
Two or more people with a common objective who are interdependent upon each other to achieve a particular task and who hold themselves accountable to each other.

team building
A broad range of planned activities that help teams improve the way they accomplish tasks and help team members enhance their interpersonal and problem-solving skills.

team cohesion
The interpersonal attraction binding team members together.

team composition
The collection of the team members' characteristics.

team development
An educational process (and OD intervention) of continually reviewing and evaluating team

functioning and identifying and establishing new and more effective ways of operating.

team effectiveness
Achieved when the team survives, meets its objectives, and the needs of its members are satisfied to the extent that they would be willing to work together again.

technocentric
Placing technology and engineering at the centre of job design decisions.

technology (T)
The wide range of tools, knowledge, and/or techniques used to transform the inputs into outputs.

technostress
The stress caused by new and advancing technologies in the workplace.

telecommuting
When an employee works from the home, a satellite office, or mobile office with a computer connection to the main office.

terminal values
Values that represent the goals to be achieved, or the end states of existence.

Theory X
A set of assumptions of how to manage individuals who are motivated by lower-order needs.

Theory Y
A set of assumptions of how to manage individuals who are motivated by higher-order needs.

thinking
Making decisions in a logical, objective fashion.

third party
Any individual who is not part of the initial conflict, but becomes involved in order to help manage or resolve it.

time orientation
The orientation of a culture's values toward the future (long-term orientation) or toward the past and present (short-term orientation).

total quality management (TQM)
The total dedication to continuous improvement and to customers so that the customers' needs are met and their expectations exceeded.

trait perspective of leadership
A perspective that proposes that leaders are more likely to have certain personality, social, physical, or intellectual traits, than nonleaders.

trait theory
The personality theory that states that in order to understand individuals, we must break down behaviour patterns into a series of observable traits.

transactional leadership
A process of social exchange between followers and leaders that involves a number of reward-based transactions. The transactional leader clarifies performance expectations, goals, and a path that will link achievement of the goals to rewards.

transformational change
Change in which the organization moves to a radically different, and sometimes unknown, future state.

transformational leadership
Leadership that inspires followers to share a vision, empowers them to achieve the vision, and provides the resources necessary for developing their personal potential. Transformational leaders serve as role models, support optimism, and mobilize commitment as well as focus on the followers' needs for growth.

transitional change
Change that is introduced to have an organization evolve slowly: current ways of doing things are replaced by something new.

transnational organization
An organization in which the global viewpoint supersedes national issues.

triple bottom line
A company's ability to generate economic, environmental, and social benefits.

Type A behaviour pattern
A complex of personality and behavioural characteristics, including competitiveness, time urgency, social status insecurity, aggression, hostility, and a quest for achievements.

U

uncertainty avoidance
The degree to which people in a country prefer structured over unstructured situations.

unfreezing
The first step in Lewin's change model, in which individuals are encouraged to discard old behaviours by shaking up the equilibrium state that maintains the status quo.

upward communication
Communication that flows to a higher level in the group or organization.

V

valence
The importance, attractiveness, desirability, or anticipated satisfaction one places on a particular outcome.

values
Enduring beliefs that a specific mode of conduct or end state of existence is personally or socially preferable to an opposite or converse mode of conduct or end state of existence.

vertical differentiation
The difference in authority and responsibility in the organizational hierarchy.

virtual organizations
Temporary network organizations consisting of independent enterprises.

virtual team
A collection of individuals who are geographically and/or organizationally or otherwise dispersed, and who collaborate via communication and information technologies in order to accomplish a specific goal.

vision
A picture of the future with some implicit or explicit commentary on why people should strive to create that future.

W

work alienation
The extent to which a person is disengaged from the world of work and holds a generalized unenthusiastic outlook toward it.

work centrality
A person's beliefs regarding the degree of importance that work plays in his or her life.

workplace spirituality
That which grounds people through the meaningfulness of their work, enabling them to transcend the tedious aspects of their work and to connect to others.

work simplification
Standardization and the narrow, explicit specification of task activities for workers.

Copyright Acknowledgments

Grateful acknowledgment is made to the copyright holders who granted permission to use material under copyright.

PHOTOS

Front cover: Nick Daly/Getty Images (students in lecture theatre); Holly Harris/Getty Images (students in meeting room); Stockbyte Gold/Alamy (student presentation).

Part openers: The front-cover photos appear also on each part opener: pages 1, 75, 165, 363, 465, and 511.

Chapter 1: Chapter opener, page 3: Bob Thomas/Getty Images.

Page 4: © 2005 JupiterImages and its licensors. All rights reserved.

Page 11: Courtesy of Josie Gullusci/Home Depot.

Page 12: © Kristiina Paul.

Page 16: © 2005 JupiterImages and its licensors. All rights reserved.

Page 20: NASA Glenn Research Center C-1995-02395.

Chapter 2: Chapter opener, page 35: Courtesy of Dofasco.

Page 41: Four Seasons logo courtesy of Four Seasons.

Page 46: Courtesy of Blake, Cassels & Graydon LLP.

Page 50: CP Photo/Peterborough Examiner – Clifford Skarstedt.

Page 59: Norm Betts/Bloomberg News/Landov.

Chapter 3: Chapter opener, page 77: © Universal/courtesy Everett Strevt/CP Archive.

Page 79: Photodisc/Getty Images.

Page 82: © Jose Luis Pelaez, Inc./Corbis.

Page 88: Courtesy of The Second City.

Chapter 4: Chapter opener, page 107: Courtesy of Home Depot.

Page 110: CP Photo.

Page 114: © Wide World Photos.

Page 119: Photo courtesy of Human Genome Sciences, Inc.

Page 124: CP Photo.

Chapter 5: Chapter opener, page 135: Norm Betts/Bloomberg News/Landov.

Page 138: CP Photo/Toronto Star – Dick Loek.

Page 140: Norm Betts/Bloomberg News/Landov.

Page 146: © Francisco Cruz/SuperStock/PictureQuest.

Page 152: Corel.

Page 153: © 2005 JupiterImages and its licensors. All rights reserved.

Chapter 6: Chapter opener, page 167: Courtesy of Janssen-Ortho, Inc.

Page 171: © Warren Morgan/Corbis.

Page 174: © 2005 JupiterImages and its licensors. All rights reserved.

Page 177: © Ariel Skelley/Corbis.

Page 181: Tony Latham/Getty Images.

Page 185: © Clara/Shutterstock.

Chapter 7: Chapter opener, page 197: Photodisc/Getty Images.

Page 198: Courtesy of WestJet.

Page 202: Neal Hamberg/Bloomberg News/Landov.

Page 204: © Bill Varie/Corbis.

Page 212: Wendy Ashton/Getty Images.

Chapter 8: Chapter opener, page 233: CP Photo/John Ulan.

Page 234: © Reuters NewMedia, Inc./Corbis.

Page 240: © Bob Rowan, Progressive Image/Corbis.

Page 254: © Bettmann/Corbis.

Page 257: Ron Chapple/Getty Images.

Chapter 9: Chapter opener, page 271: © Tad Denson – MyShotz.com/Shutterstock

Page 275: Ghislain and Marie David de Lossy/Getty Images.

Page 276: CP Picture Archive/Globe and Mail/Fred Lum.

Page 278: © Kristiina Paul.

Page 287: © Archivo Iconografico, S.A./Corbis.

Chapter 10: Chapter opener, page 299: Courtesy of Manitoba Lotteries Corporation.

Page 301: CP Photo/Fred Chartrand.

Page 304: CP Photo/Hamilton Spectator – Kaz Novak.

Page 307: Courtesy of Kingston Technology.

Page 313: © Kristiina Paul.

Chapter 11: Chapter opener, page 331: © Paul A. Souders/Corbis.

Page 334: © Reuters/Corbis.

Page 339: Gerd George/Getty Images.

Page 349: © 2005 JupiterImages and its licensors. All rights reserved.

Chapter 12: Chapter opener, page 365: © Bettmann/Corbis.

Page 368: Photo courtesy of Elke Price.

Page 369: Munshi Ahmed/Bloomberg News/Landov.

Page 370: Courtesy of Roots.

Page 379: Courtesy of Research In Motion.

Page 384: Peter Jones/Reuters/Landov.

Page 386: Courtesy of Nestlé.

Chapter 13: Chapter opener, page 397: © Kristiina Paul.

Page 402: Photo courtesy of Newfoundland Power Inc.

Page 413: Courtesy of John Kotter.

Page 417: © Andrew Taylor/Shutterstock.

Page 419: Courtesy of Pat R. Sniderman.

Chapter 14: Chapter opener, page 427: Courtesy of Amy Marcus.

Page 432: Shawn Thew/EPA/Landov.

Page 436: Courtesy of Magellan Aerospace.

Page 442: Bloomberg News/Landov.

Page 447: Photo courtesy of Oticon A/S.

Page 453: These materials have been reproduced by Nelson, a division of Thomson Canada Limited, with the permission of Cisco Systems Inc. Copyright © 2005 Cisco Systems, Inc. All rights reserved.

Chapter 15: Chapter opener, page W-3: © Kristiina Paul.

Page W-7: Photodisc Green/Getty Images.

Page W-10: Susan Goldman/Bloomberg News/Landov.

Page W-14: Photodisc/Getty Images.

Page W-15: Comstock/Getty Images.

Index Company Names

Subject Index

D

E

J

K

L

M

N

O

U

V

W

Y

Z